WOMEN MEDIEVALISTS

and the Academy

WOMEN MEDIEVALISTS

and the Academy

Edited by Jane Chance

THE UNIVERSITY OF WISCONSIN PRESS

This book was published with the support of
the Office of the Dean of Humanities at Rice University

The University of Wisconsin Press
1930 Monroe Street
Madison, Wisconsin 53711

www.wisc.edu/wisconsinpress/

3 Henrietta Street
London WC2E 8LU, England

Copyright © 2005
The Board of Regents of the University of Wisconsin System
All rights reserved

5   4   3   2   1

Printed in the United States of America

Library of Congress Cataloging-in-Publication Data

Women medievalists and the academy / edited by Jane Chance.
   p. cm.
   Includes bibliographical references and index.
   ISBN 0-299-20750-1 (hardcover : alk. paper)
1. Women medievalists—Biography. 2. Middle Ages—Bio-bibliography.
I. Chance, Jane, 1945–

D116.5.W66 2005
940.1′092′2—dc22
                     2004025225

For "Betty's Church," from whose community and support the idea for this book sprang

Contents

List of Portraits and Photographs	xiii
Preface and Acknowledgments	xvii
Introduction: "What has a Woman to do with Learning?" JANE CHANCE	xxiii
Women Medievalists Profiled (listed alphabetically)	xxxix
Chronology of Women Medievalists Profiled, with Fields and Institutional Affiliations	xliii
1. Elizabeth Elstob (1683–1756) and the Limits of Women's Agency in Early-Eighteenth-Century England SHAUN F. D. HUGHES	3
2. Anna Jameson (1794–1860): "Primitive" Art and Iconography CORDELIA WARR	25
3. By Her Works Shall Ye Know Her: The Quest for Jessie L. Weston (1850–1928) ANGELA JANE WEISL	37
4. Lina Eckenstein (1857–1931): Seeking Scope for Women PENELOPE D. JOHNSON	55
5. Mary Bateson (1865–1906): Scholar and Suffragist MARY DOCKRAY-MILLER	67

Contents

6. Elise Richter (1865–1943): First Austrian *Privatdozentin*
   ELIZABETH SHIPLEY, with Excerpts from a Memoir on "Education and Development" by ELISE RICHTER, translated by ELIZABETH SHIPLEY   79

7. Eleanor Prescott Hammond (1866–1933): Pioneer Scholar of Middle English Manuscript Study   A. S. G. EDWARDS   91

8. Caroline F. E. Spurgeon (1869–1942): First Woman Professor of English in England   RENATE HAAS   99

9. "Hark the Herald Angels Sing": Here's to Georgiana Goddard King (1871–1939)   JANICE MANN   111

10. "Miss Rickert of Vassar" and Edith Rickert at the University of Chicago (1871–1938)   ELIZABETH SCALA   127

11. Mildred K. Pope (1872–1956): Anglo-Norman Scholar
    ELSPETH KENNEDY   147

12. The Justices' Chronicler: Bertha Haven Putnam (1872–1960)
    DAVID DAY   157

13. Nellie Neilson (1873–1947): A Historian of "Wit, Whimsy, and Sheer Poetry"   ANNE REIBER DEWINDT   167

14. Evelyn Underhill (1875–1941): The Practical Mystic
    MICHELLE M. SAUER   183

15. Kindred, College, and Scholarship in the Lifework of Bertha Surtees Phillpotts (1877–1932)   RUSSELL POOLE   201

16. Eleanor Shipley Duckett (1880–1976): Historian of the Latin Middle Ages   SUSAN MOSHER STUARD   213

17. Hope Emily Allen (1883–1960): An Independent Scholar
    JOHN C. HIRSH   227

18. Laura Hibbard Loomis (1883–1960): "Mrs Arthur"
    KATHRYN L. LYNCH   239

19. Helen Cam (1885–1968): Charting the Evolution of Medieval Institutions   EUAN TAYLOR and GINA WEAVER   255

20. Grace Frank (1886–1978) and Medieval French Drama
    DEBORAH NELSON-CAMPBELL   273

21. Margaret Rickert (1888–1973): Art Historian
    ANNE RUDLOFF STANTON   285

22. Charlotte D'Evelyn (1889–1977): An Instinct to Explore
    CAROLYN P. COLLETTE   295

23. Eileen Edna Le Poer Power (1889–1940)
    MARJORIE MCCALLUM CHIBNALL   311

24. Helen Waddell (1889–1965): The Scholar-Poet
    JENNIFER FITZGERALD   323

25. "Aimer la musique ancienne": Yvonne Rihouët Rokseth (1890–1948)
    CATHERINE PARSONEAULT   339

26. The German Historian Elisabeth Busse-Wilson (1890–1974):
    Academic Feminism and Medieval Hagiography, 1914–1931
    ULRIKE WIETHAUS   353

27. "An Extraordinary Sense of Powerful Restlessness": Nora Kershaw
    Chadwick (1891–1972)   SANDRA BALLIF STRAUBHAAR   367

28. "Persephone Come Back from the Dead": Maude Violet Clarke
    (1892–1935)   JENNIFER FITZGERALD   381

29. Joan Evans (1893–1977): Art Historian and Antiquary
    NICOLA COLDSTREAM   399

30. Dorothy L. Sayers (1893–1957): Medieval Mystery Maker
    MITZI M. BRUNSDALE   423

31. Doris Mary Stenton (1894–1971): The Legal Records and the Historian
    PATRICIA R. ORR   441

32. Helen M. Roe (1895–1988): Champion of Medieval Irish Art and
    Iconography   RORY O'FARRELL and CHRISTINE BROMWICH   459

33. Suzanne Solente (1895–1978): A Life in the Manuscript
    Department of the Bibliothèque Nationale
    MARIE-HÉLÈNE TESNIÈRE, translated by ROBYN FRÉCHET   471

34. Sirarpie Der Nersessian (1896–1989): Pioneer of Armenian Art History
    DICKRAN KOUYMJIAN   483

35. Women and Medieval Scholarship in Bulgaria: Vera Ivanova-Mavrodinova
    (1896–1987) and Vasilka Tapkova-Zaimova (1924–)
    LILIANA V. SIMEONOVA, with a Memoir by VASILKA TAPKOVA-ZAIMOVA   495

36. Margaret Schlauch (1898–1986): "Professor Prefers Iron Curtain Land"
    CHRISTINE M. ROSE   523

37. Pearl Kibre (1900–1985): Manuscript Hunter and Historian of
    Medieval Science and the Universities
    Elspeth Whitney and Irving A. Kelter   541

38. An Anglo-Saxonist at Oxford and Cambridge: Dorothy Whitelock
    (1901–1982)   Jana K. Schulman   553

39. Ruth J. Dean (1902–2003): "Dean" of Anglo-Norman Studies
    Kevin J. Harty   565

40. James Bruce Ross (1902–1995) and the Sources for Medieval and
    Renaissance History   Constance Hoffman Berman   575

41. Marie-Thérèse d'Alverny (1903–1991): The History of Ideas in the
    Middle Ages in the Mediterranean Basin   Charles S. F. Burnett   585

42. Christine A. E. M. Mohrmann (1903–1988) and the Study of
    Christian Latin   Carmela Vircillo Franklin   599

43. Mary Dominica Legge (1905–1986): Anglo-Norman Scholar
    Harriet Spiegel   613

44. Daughter of Her Time: Anneliese Maier (1905–1971) and the
    Study of Fourteenth-Century Philosophy
    Alfonso Maierù and Edith Sylla   625

45. A Woman Historian in Oxford (1905–2003)
    Marjorie Ethel Reeves   647

46. Beryl Smalley (1905–1984): The Medieval Bible in the Modern Academy
    Henrietta Leyser and Deeana Copeland Klepper   657

47. Cora Elizabeth Lutz (1906–1985): Magistra Egregii
    Deanna Delmar Evans   671

48. Voicing Silenced Rituals: The Unearthing of the Life Story of
    Arthurian Legend by Helaine Newstead (1906–1981)   Gale Sigal   683

49. Articulating the Middle English Lexicon: Margaret Ogden (1909–1988),
    Medieval Medical Texts, and the *Middle English Dictionary*
    Michael Adams   697

50. Debunking the Myths, Transmitting Knowledge in Clear Language:
    Régine Pernoud (1909–1998)   Josette A. Wisman   711

51. María Rosa Lida de Malkiel (1910–1962) and Medieval Spanish
    Literary Historiography   Ana M. Gómez-Bravo   723

52. "To Open a Door upon the Past of Scotland": Helena Mennie Shire (1912–1991)   JANET HADLEY WILLIAMS — 733

53. Memoir (1914–)
    MARJORIE MCCALLUM CHIBNALL — 747

54. A Singular Career: College Professor and Army Wife (1914–)
    CHARITY CANNON WILLARD — 759

55. A Scholar of Early Britain: Rachel Bromwich (1915–)
    GERALD MORGAN — 769

56. Jane Hayward (1918–1994): "Radiance and Reflection"
    MARILYN J. STOKSTAD — 781

57. Getting It All Together (1923–)
    MARIE BORROFF — 789

58. "Magistra Studentorum per Armeniam et Byzantium":
    Nina G. Garsoïan (1923–)   LEVON AVDOYAN — 803

59. Elizabeth Salter (1925–1980): Teacher and Scholar of Middle
    English Literature   JULIA BOFFEY — 815

60. Rosemary Estelle Woolf (1925–1978): A Serious Scholar
    JOYCE BORO — 825

61. Historian of Art (1928–)
    ILENE H. FORSYTH — 839

62. Elisabeth Gössmann (1928–): Overcoming Obstacles
    REBECCA L. R. GARBER — 857

63. My Way with Misericords (1929–)
    ELAINE C. BLOCK — 873

64. Professor Rosemary Cramp (1929–): The Hild of Durham
    PHYLLIS R. BROWN — 885

65. The Networked Life (1931–)   JO ANN MCNAMARA — 901

66. Another Perspective on Alterity and the Grotesque (1932–)
    ELIZABETH A. R. BROWN — 915

67. Ars Longa, Vita Brevis (1932–)
    MEREDITH PARSONS LILLICH — 933

68. Benedicta Ward, S.L.G. (1933–): The Love of Learning and the
    Love of God   DEBRA L. STOUDT — 945

69. Latent Feminist Loosed on Medieval History (1935–)
    SUSAN MOSHER STUARD   955

70. Joan M. Ferrante (1936–): Going the Distance in Life and Literature
    JULIE CROSBY   969

71. Marcia L. Colish (1937–): Intellectual Historian   E. ANN MATTER   981

72. My Life and Works (1941–)   CAROLINE WALKER BYNUM   995

    List of Contributors   1007

    Photograph and Citation Credits   1019

    Index   1023

Portraits and Photographs

1. Portrait of Elizabeth Elstob (1683–1756) from her *Rudiments of Grammar for the English-Saxon Tongue* (1715) — 4
2. Portrait of Anna Brownell Jameson (1794–1860), ca. 1843–48, by artist David Octavius Hill (and Robert Adamson) — 26
3. Lina Eckenstein (1857–1931) — 56
4. Mary Bateson (1865–1906), ca. 1900–1906 — 68
5. Elise Richter (1865–1943), taken from *Führende Frauen Europas: Elga Kerns Standardwerk von 1928/1930,* new and revised edition by Bettina Conrad and Ulrike Leuschner (Munich and Basel: Ernst Reinhardt, 1999) — 80
6. Caroline F. E. Spurgeon (1869–1942), taken from *Führende Frauen Europas: Elga Kerns Standardwerk von 1928/1930* — 100
7. Georgiana Goddard King (1871–1939), by an unknown photographer — 110
8. Edith Rickert (1871–1938) — 126
9. Mildred K. Pope (1872–1956) — 146
10. Bertha Haven Putnam (1872–1960) — 158
11. Nellie Neilson (1873–1947) — 168
12. Evelyn Underhill (1875–1941) — 182
13. Bertha Surtees Phillpotts (1877–1932) — 200
14. Eleanor Shipley Duckett (1880–1976) in 1942, photographer unknown — 214
15. Hope Emily Allen (1883–1960) and Marietta Pallis (with the cat) in summer, late 1920s, at Long Gores, near Hickling, Norfolk — 228
16. Laura Hibbard Loomis (1883–1960) — 240
17. Helen Cam (1885–1968) in 1948 — 256
18. Margaret Rickert (1888–1973) — 284

19. Charlotte D'Evelyn (1889–1977) 296
20. Eileen Edna Le Poer Power (1889–1940), photographed for the BBC in February 1933 310
21. Helen Waddell (1889–1965) in 1920 322
22. Yvonne Rihouët Rokseth (1890–1948) 340
23. Elisabeth Busse-Wilson (1890–1974) 352
24. Nora Kershaw Chadwick. C.B.E. (1891–1972), photograph by Elliott & Frye 366
25. Maude Violet Clarke (1892–1935) in 1934 380
26. Dame Joan Evans (1893–1977) 400
27. Dorothy L. Sayers (1893–1957) 424
28. Doris Mary Stenton (1894–1971) 440
29. Helen M. Roe (1895–1988), in 1966, as president of the Royal Society of Antiquaries of Ireland 460
30. Suzanne Solente (1895–1978), seated, with her colleagues in the manuscript department at the Bibliothèque nationale de France at her retirement celebration in November 1960; Marie-Thérèse d'Alverny stands to her left 472
31. Sirarpie Der Nersessian (1896–1989) at the 1948 Dumbarton Oaks symposium. Rear row, L-R: Milton Anastos, Glanville Downey, Albert M. Friend, Francis Dvornik, Paul Underwood 482
32. Vera Ivanova-Mavrodinova (1896–1987) 494
33. Vasilka Tapkova-Zaimova (1924–) at the reunion of the Association internationale des études du Sud-Est Européennes-Athènes 1974 (with Professor Berza, director of the Institut des études du Sud-Est Européennes, Bucarest). Tapkova-Zaimova is the woman with the black hair, in the middle 494
34. Margaret Schlauch (1898–1986) 522
35. Pearl Kibre (1900–1985) in her office at the Graduate School and University Center of City University of New York 540
36. Dorothy Whitelock (1901–1982), photograph by Bertl Gaye, copied by Nigel Cassidy 552
37. Ruth J. Dean (1902–2003) 564
38. James Bruce Ross (1902–1995) in March 1960, photographed by Mary Martin McLaughlin 576
39. Marie-Thérèse d'Alverny (1903–1991) 586
40. Christine A. E. M. Mohrmann (1903–1988), from the memorial issue published in *Sacris Erudiri* 32, no. 1 (1991): 6 598
41. Mary Dominica Legge (1905–1986), from the *Proceedings of the British Academy* 74 (1989) 614
42. Anneliese Maier (1905–1971), from *Studi sul XIV secolo in memoria di Anneliese Maier* 626

43. Marjorie Ethel Reeves (1905–2003) 646
44. Beryl Smalley (1905–1984) 658
45. Cora Elizabeth Lutz (1906–1985) 670
46. Helaine Newstead (1906–1981) 684
47. Margaret Ogden (1909–1988), with H. V. S "Harry" Ogden in 1954, selecting illustrations for their book on seventeenth-century landscape in the English imagination (a book that appeared in 1955) 698
48. Régine Pernoud (1909–1998) 712
49. María Rosa Lida de Malkiel (1910–1962), from the memorial issue published in *Romance Philology* 17 (1963): between pp. 6 and 7 724
50. Helena Mennie Shire (1912–1991), photographed by Alisoun Gardner-Medwin on 19 January 1989, at Shire's sister's house in Newcastle upon Tyne, England, on the occasion of the eightieth birthday of their brother, Professor Duncan Mennie 734
51. Marjorie McCallum Chibnall (1914–), photographed by Edward Leigh for Clare Hall in 1975 748
52. Charity Cannon Willard (1914–) with her cat 760
53. Rachel Bromwich (1915–), taken from J. E. Caerwyn Williams, *Ysgrifau Beirniadol* 13 (Denbigh, N. Wales: Gwasg Gee, 1985) 768
54. Jane Hayward (1918–1994), photographed by Peter Barnet 782
55. Marie Borroff (1923–) 790
56. Nina G. Garsoïan (1923–), photographed by Jack Vartoogian in the 1980s 802
57. Elizabeth Salter (1925–1980) 814
58. Rosemary Estelle Woolf (1925–1978) 826
59. Ilene H. Forsyth (1928–), ca. 1985, photographed by Bob Kalmbach, University of Michigan Photo Services 840
60. The Morgan Madonna, New York, Metropolitan Museum of Art 844
61. The Samson Monolith, from the Abbey of Saint Martin, Savigny: Samson Destroys the Temple of the Philistines, Durham, Duke University Museum of Art 851
62. Elisabeth Gössmann (1928–) 858
63. Elaine C. Block (1929–) 874
64. Rosemary Cramp (1929–), photographed by Trevor Woods, Department of Archaeology, Durham University 886
65. Jo Ann McNamara (1931–) 902
66. Elizabeth A. R. Brown (1932–), photographed by her husband, Ralph S. Brown Jr. 916
67. Meredith Parsons Lillich (1932–) in mid-seminar, Syracuse University, 7 February 1995, photographed by Stephen Sartori, Syracuse University Photo and Imaging Center 932
68. Sister Benedicta Ward, S.L.G. (1933–) 946

69. Susan Mosher Stuard (1935–) at graduation at Haverford College, Haverford, Pennsylvania, in May 1988 — 956
70. Joan M. Ferrante (1936–), speaking at Columbia's School of General Studies Reunion (June 2001) — 968
71. Marcia L. Colish (1937–) — 980
72. Caroline Walker Bynum (1941–), photographed by Elaine Barrasco — 996

Preface and Acknowledgments

This collection of biographical essays and memoirs tracing the history of the woman medievalist began life in response to a telephone request from Anne Clark Bartlett in fall of 1998 to participate in a session titled "Autobiographical Criticism" that she and Linda McMillan were organizing at Kalamazoo for May 1999. These two former participants in my 1997 National Endowment for the Humanities Summer Institute for College Teachers, "The Literary Tradition of Medieval Women," had just received an abstract from Norman Cantor, who wished to talk about his book *Inventing the Middle Ages;* Anne thought it would be wonderful to couple his talk with an edgy one by a woman medievalist. Because I knew Anne and had read Norman's book, which contains an essay on only one woman medievalist, Eileen Power, I understood immediately what Anne was up to and thought the idea of the session and the coupling of a male historian and a female literary critic would be provocative and timely. Jane Tompkins had changed her teaching style to a more personalized, nonauthoritarian approach, Nancy K. Miller was calling for the interjection of the personal in criticism, and it seemed time to do something similar for the Middle Ages.

The writing of my essay took place the same year the Society for Medieval Feminist Scholarship had scheduled "The Reception of Feminist Scholarship in Medieval Literary Study," a session organized by Regina Psaki at the annual Modern Language Association convention, on 27 December 1998, in which I participated as a respondent and talked about the gender composition of the Medieval Academy; my essay on autobiographical criticism was finally delivered in May 1999. That was also the year I organized a petition to be sent to Carolyn Walker Bynum, president of the Medieval Academy, and then to her successor, Ted Andersson, on the participation of women in the Medieval Academy and the need to change the demographics of such participation at every level and every way, in terms of geography, gender, field, and institution. From that standpoint it was easy to look at our predecessors in the Medieval Academy who had served as presidents and fellows and ask, Who were they? And why did women seem to be having such a difficult time? If we in this seemingly enlightened age had such hurdles to overcome, what did the early women encounter, and how did they accomplish so much? What astounded me was the low number of women among the Medieval Academy Fellows: in 1998, only twenty of the ninety-nine were women, around 20 percent who have earned that distinction, the same percentage as for 1993, although the fellows still living in 1998 who were inducted in 1983 number thirty-eight, with the female fellows six—86 percent men to 14 percent women.

After I had followed up Anne's request by asking for two sessions on "Women Medievalists in the Academy: An Oral History" for Kalamazoo in May 2000, six women medievalists agreed to participate: Charity Cannon Willard, Mary Martin McLaughlin, Joan M. Ferrante, Constance Hoffman Berman, Sheila Delany, and Jo Ann McNamara. The Medieval Institute, through the kindness of Paul Szarmach and Timothy Graham, videotaped the occasion for the archives, and Bonnie Wheeler moderated at one of the sessions. At the same time Bonnie was organizing a memorial volume to honor Maureen Fries, who had recently passed away. The moment seemed right to collect these essays in a volume, adding to them others about those women medievalists who had come before. What I wanted was a real history of our female predecessors.

Women of my generation who chose the Middle Ages as a subject were still—by the late sixties—unusual, even as graduate students at a state university; certainly the Middle Ages were rarely taught by women medievalists, or by women in any field of the academy (by which I mean any higher education initiative, not necessarily the Medieval Academy). Today that has changed—the demographics mark a singular increase in numbers in all fields, even medieval fields. What may not have changed, even yet, is the treatment of women within the male-dominated halls of academe, and therefore the institutional insistence on their silence, or voicelessness, may make it seem as if they do not in fact exist (note the article by Ellen Ostrow, "Don't Go It Alone," that recently appeared in the *Chronicle of Higher Education* [Monday, 12 August 2002], about the isolation and discrimination that still shadow the new woman assistant professor in many departments). If not voicelessness, then strangely bizarre behavior or patterns often mark a woman's entry into the profession. In this regard the situation does not appear to differ in other countries, no matter what the field or the time period.

This collection of *Women Medievalists and the Academy* is intended to illuminate the lives and careers of women who have helped build a field or a discipline or an area or a specific subject in medieval studies, women who were born predominantly before 1935 (a select few born after 1935 have been added in response to their nominations by scholars and to suggest new directions in the careers of women medievalists). The focus falls primarily on scholars from the earlier twentieth century in a variety of fields and countries, but also on those younger distinguished women whose careers have already demonstrated a major contribution to scholarship and a kind of closure and who might either contribute an essay about themselves or perhaps participate in an interview by a former student. The intention is to provide some variety in terms of fields, that is, include contributions in literature and history but also in art history, philosophy, and philology, among other possibilities. Each essay sketches the woman's life and her intellectual contribution to medieval studies and supplies a bibliography of major works by the woman subject along with a list of works cited, but it might also discuss particular problems confronted by the woman working in a predominantly masculine field and how she circumvented those problems. My hope is that this venture will function as a corrective history of the founding of the academy (that is, higher education in general) and the role of women medievalists in its development.

In several senses this collection is incomplete. First, we've had to limit the length of essays, which by necessity means omitting much of interest about the woman medievalist (personally or academically) and reducing the select bibliographies that appear at the end of their essays to the most important works. It is hoped, however, that these biographies will point readers to other published works, festschriften, biographies, and full-length biographies. For some women such as Dorothy Sayers, Eileen Power, and Helen Maud Cam, full-length biographies already exist. The task, then, in such cases is one of reduction or identification rather than of amplification. Second, for many other cases there is limited archival documentation. Margaret Schlauch's papers in Poland were apparently discarded at the time of her death. Jessie Weston's personal papers and photographs seem also to have been destroyed. Third, what is lacking altogether may be worse: occasionally women who were invited to contribute a memoir (or a biographical essay, once the most appropriate knowledgeable possibility had been identified) either were not able or chose not to take advantage of the opportunity, for a variety of reasons, including previous commitments. I would have liked to have included—and in some cases planned to include essays by or about—Dorothy Bethurum Loomis, Katharine Drew, Margaret Gibson, Anne Hudson, Valerie Legorio, Gertrud Jaron Lewis, Ruth Mellinkof, Mary Martin McLaughlin, Vivian Lillian Randall, Lucy Sandler, Claire Richter Sherman, Lucy Toulmin Smith, and Sylvia Thrupp, among others. We hope that whoever is not included in this volume will be included in subsequent, similar collections and studies. I apologize if a distinguished woman who should have been profiled (given the general parameters of selection) is absent—there comes a moment when time and space considerations rule out further additions or changes.

But in several other senses the collection represents a triumph of collaboration and good will. In the sense of historiographical research truly original work has emerged in the creation of the woman medievalist's portrait. The constant refrain from biographers has been, "Where can I find sources of information about this woman medievalist?" Obituaries in home newspapers, the *Medieval Academy Newsletter*, or *Speculum*; archives at colleges; and high school and college newspapers and yearbooks and the like have netted rich results. In addition biographical facts only exist for some of these women in the *National Biographical Dictionary* or *Who's Who*. The archives of significant institutions where women last taught or worked—whether Girton or Newnham College, Cambridge, Smith College, Mount Holyoke, Harvard, University of Chicago, or Yale—do contain marvelous sources of information. In other cases relatives and former associates or colleagues have provided helpful details and information in interviews, e-mails, letters, or anecdotes (these sources are usually cited in notes or the bibliographies).

My debt to other colleagues and scholars who have generously offered the names of women medievalists who deserve to be included and the names of possible biographers is great. I am thankful for assistance by the *Medieval Academy Newsletter*, the *Modern Language Association Newsletter*, *Publications of the Modern Language Association Forum*, the *American Historical Association Newsletter*, websites associated with each of the societies, the *Medieval Feminist Forum* (formerly *Medieval Feminist Newsletter*), and Medfem-list and their readers in circulating requests for information and recommendations for biographers and biographees. Most of the contributors to this volume have made recommendations of one sort at some point or another, met with other contributors to provide information about women medievalists, or read other essays by contributors or by me, most especially, Christine Bromwich, Elizabeth A. R. Brown, Caroline Walker Bynum, Marjorie McCallum Chibnall, Charles Burnett Renate Haas, Irving Kelter, Alisoun Medwin-Gardner (in many ways), Gerald Morgan, Elizabeth Scala, Harriet Spiegel, Susan Mosher Stuard, Ulrike Wiethaus, and Josette A. Wisman. Others who did not actively participate by writing an essay contributed above and beyond by tracking down biographers and suggesting names to be included: Susan Groag Bell, Institute for Research on Women and Gender, Stanford; Judith Bennett, history, North Carolina; Joan Cadden, history, University of California–Davis; Joyce Coleman, English, University of South Dakota; Natalie Zemon Davis, history, Princeton; Sheila Delany, English, Simon Fraser University; Liliane DuLac, French, Université Paul-Valéry, Montpellier; Laura Finkel and Nanci Young, archivists at Smith College; Monica Green, history, Duke University; Barbara Hanawalt, history, Ohio State; Ann Haskell; Jacquelyn Jenkins; Helen Lemay, philosophy, SUNY–Stonybrook; Katharine Park, history, Harvard; Kate Perry, archivist at Girton College, Cambridge; Mary Shepard; Linda Voigts, history, University of Missouri–Columbia; Claire Richter Sherman; Gabrielle M. Spiegel, history, Johns Hopkins University; Nancy Siraisi, history, Hunter College, City University of New York; and Anne Thomson, Newnham College Archives. Others who have helped specific contributors to this volume have been named in the individual essays. There may have been others still who helped in countless other ways, with permissions and photographs, with suggestions and recommendations, whom I have inadvertently omitted or about whom I do not know: thanks to you, this volume got finished.

My gratitude to Paul Szarmach and the Medieval Institute at Western Michigan University is great: he and his program committee authorized the initial sessions that have brought women together, provided rooms and videotaping, and added a reception I had requested for the "Oral History of Women Medievalists in the Academy" sessions in 2000 at the International Congress on Medieval Studies at Kalamazoo. The Medieval Institute also approved two sessions relating specifically to this project for the 2000 International Congress, at which six women presented their memoirs: Constance Hoffman Berman, Sheila Delany, Joan M. Ferrante, Mary Martin McLaughlin, Charity Cannon Willard, and Jo Ann McNamara. My thanks go to the audio-visual department at Western Michigan University for generously supplying excellent video copy of these "Oral Histories of Women Medievalists." Helena Michie, graduate chair in the English department at Rice at the time, and Jordan Konisky, dean of the Rice University Graduate School, provided funds for the festive reception after the two sessions. Bonnie Wheeler, medieval studies, Southern Methodist University, organized an evening's repast for those who had participated in the sessions and for other colleagues to share their stories. Again at the 2002 International Congress on Medieval Studies two sessions on women medievalists in the academy were approved, and shorter versions of five of these essays were delivered as papers, on Mary Bateson, by Mary Dockray-Miller; Nellie Neilson, by Anne R. DeWindt; Elisabeth Busse-Wilson, by Ulrike Wiethaus; Anneliese Maier, by Edith Sylla; and Cora Lutz, by Deanna Delmar Evans.

At Rice, Theresa Munisteri, editorial assistant in the English department, rechecked almost all of these essays against our model for house style and suggested corrections—a monumental labor, for which I express here my deepest appreciation. Steve Iltis and Carolynne White, both computer technicians in humanities, helped translate disks for some papers into a modern word-processing program and along the way assisted when some one or another computer problem interfered with the completion of this project (to a large extent this project is a result of the opportunities offered by e-mail, especially post-9/11). Early in the project Jamie Cook and other English department staff helped with reformatting, photocopying, and printing out (as well as mailing and labels), for which I am also grateful.

To Gale Stokes, dean of humanities at Rice during the period of the writing of this collection, and to his successor Gary Wihl, I am deeply indebted for the publication subsidy to enable this book to reach the widest possible audience by means of a hardbound and paperbound copy and for funds for typing and secretarial assistance and an index. To this latter end I had the aid initially of English dissertation student Andrew Yerkes, and later, and most helpfully, during much of the editing of the volume, English graduate student Gina Weaver, to both of whom I am grateful. Emily Jones, a Rice Century Scholar during the 2001–2 academic year, helped edit the early drafts of several essays. The Electronic Resource Center at Rice University and in particular Lisa Spiro scanned and cropped various problem photographs and electronic images to fit the press requirements and therefore speeded delivery of the final manuscript, for which I am also grateful. To the checking of editorial queries when the manuscript was in production, English graduate student Joy Pasini focused her attention as my spring 2004 research assistant, as did Jill Designe to proofs, in Fall 2004.

At the Press, editor Susanne Breckenridge and copyeditor Barb Wojhoski were gracious, more than competent, and truly helpful in bringing this book into existence. To Press director Robert A. Mandel I am also grateful for believing in this project and facilitating its publication. Thanks go as well to indexer Blythe Woolston. The cost of the index was met by means of the Annual Research Grant awarded to me by Dean of Humanities Gale Stokes for the years 2003-2005 and an additional special grant in 2004 by Dean.

Most especially, my thanks to the countless women worldwide who supported the creation of this book in some way, small or large. Their zeal and enthusiasm fostered the completion of this book: now, as I look back on its history, a labor of love, a work of scholarship and historiography that I hope will fill in gaps in our understanding of the formation of our profession, and last but not least, a tribute to those women medievalists who have come before us.

Houston, Texas
September 2004

Introduction
"What has a Woman to do with Learning?"

JANE CHANCE

> Language as a whole gives everyone the same power of becoming an absolute subject through its exercise. But gender, an element of language, works upon this ontological fact to annul it, to strip them of the most precious thing for a human being—subjectivity. The result of the imposition of gender, acting as a denial at the very moment when one speaks, is to deprive women of the authority of speech, and to force them to make their entrance in a crablike way, particularizing themselves and apologizing profusely. The result is to deny them any claim to the abstract, philosophical, political discourses that give shape to the social body.
>
> Monique Wittig, The Mark of Gender

THE HISTORY OF academic medievalists, although neglected as a subject of research, has begun to attract attention from contemporary scholars. Eighteen years ago, for example, Lee Patterson, in *Negotiating the Past: The Historical Understanding of Medieval Literature* (1987), traced the history of medieval academics politically, but primarily by focusing only on the men involved.[1] Patterson distinguished the powerful conservative school of nineteenth-century scholars (who subscribed to the view of the Middle Ages as universalist and hierarchical because of its faith in a common church and authority that dominated society) from the less powerful "pluralist, primitivist, and above all else, individualist" school of the Pre-Raphaelites (10). He argued that modern and postmodern approaches to the Middle Ages derive from these two Victorian schools. Note his similarly Victorian emphasis on the masculine pronoun in the poem "England's Trust" (1841) by "the leading Young Englander" Sir John Manners to characterize the conservative strain of medievalism:

> Each knew *his* place—king, peasant, peer or priest—
> The greatest owned connexion with least;
> From rank to rank the generous feeling ran,
> And linked society as *man to man*.²

Equally evident in Patterson's description of the liberal sentimental strain of medievalism is his privileging, again, of that which is gendered male:³ "Ruskin's enormously popular 'The Nature of Gothic' argued that the medieval cathedral represented not a corporate Christian consciousness but the 'outspeaking of the strong spirit' of the *men of the north*. . . . Morris celebrated a voluntary 'Fellowship of Men' that characterized medieval life at its best."⁴ The omission of almost any reference in *Negotiating the Past* to the existence of women, either in Patterson's glance back at the Middle Ages in Morris or Ruskin or in the present gaze of Patterson himself, however, appears odd (at least to a woman reader). Were there—are there—no women medievalists in the ivory tower? And if not, why not?

The reaction of shame by the (woman) reader over the apparent absence of women in the history of medieval criticism would echo the reaction of Virginia Woolf in her famous polemical essay *A Room of One's Own* (1929) when she observes that she cannot attend Cambridge or Oxford, nor use their libraries, nor walk on their grass, nor, at the commons—in thinly disguised versions of the women's colleges Girton or Newnham—enjoy the same kind of food as do male students in their colleges. So she scolds women for being "disgracefully ignorant": "You have never made a discovery of any sort of importance. You have never shaken an empire or led an army into battle. The plays of Shakespeare are not by you, and you have never introduced a barbarous race to the blessings of civilization. What is your excuse?"⁵ Although she does not discuss the paucity of women professors in particular, she does assume the professor (especially one who does research on women) must be male, because she compares the domed ceiling of the Reading Room in the British Library with the bald head of a professor.

Woolf also answers her own charge when she acknowledges, with scathing irony, that in England at least two colleges for women existed from 1866; that legally a married woman could own property beginning in 1880; and that a woman could vote in elections and choose a profession after 1919 (112). The "excuse" women might offer for this ignorance—according to Woolf or, further back in time, to women writers such as Mary Wollstonecraft and Mary Astell before her—is the lack of education of women and, accordingly, the lack of the disciplined cast of mind that only emerges with education. At the British Library Woolf employs a masculine pastoral metaphor to characterize the thinking of the educated: "The student who has been trained in research at Oxbridge has no doubt some method of *shepherding his question* past all distractions till it runs into its answer as a *sheep runs into its pen*" (28; my emphasis). What happens when (uneducated) women do think? Woolf responds with a feminine metaphor of sheeplike disorder, stupidity, and fear for survival: "[I]f, unfortunately, one has no training in a university, the question far from being shepherded to its pen flies like *a frightened flock hither and thither, helter-skelter, pursued by a whole pack of hounds*" (28). But what about when women speak, and speak with authority—as subjects, but as professing subjects, professing the most difficult and inaccessible (because the earliest) of literatures in English? Can women speak without making crablike gestures and movements either personal or eccentric? Can women research and profess their subjects in the same ways as men?

In other words, when women are trained in research at a university, can women speak with authority about a subject that has long been claimed by men? Even a response to this question has to be negative—or, to pick up Monique Wittig's concept, from the epigraph at the beginning of this essay, of the crablike way women enter into conversation as indicative of female difference—women's speaking with authority must be marked by eccentricity. For example, about Beryl Smalley, Henrietta Leyser and Deeana Klepper, writing in this volume, note that "in 1935 Smalley became research fellow at Girton College, Cambridge, although *she had not been Girton's first choice*. She had published four articles (in addition to her work with Georges Lacombe), but her work was so *unusual* as to be considered *eccentric*" (my emphasis).[6] What this important perception conveys is that even a woman's research may be so marked by the personal and individualistic that it fits no predictable pattern—original, yes, but rarely conventional in the sense used when speaking about the (masculine and authoritative) norm. So Elizabeth Elstob, the earliest woman scholar profiled in this collection, interweaves the "personal and the professional, the private and the public," according to Shaun Hughes, by including on the title page of her work on Old English the towns of "Elstob" and "Foxton" (associated with the Elstob patrimony).[7] But conscious of how unusual it is for a woman to be writing scholarship at all, Elstob starts off in her preface to her translation of Ælfric's homily on the birthday of Saint Gregory—the church father who argued in *Pastoral Care* for the preaching of clergy in their native language—with the question, "What has a Woman to do with Learning?" She then rephrases the question to ask in a more pointed way, "Where is the Fault in Women's seeking after Learning?"[8] In a similar acknowledgment both of the rarity of such a venture and how those rare women were perceived, Liliana V. Simeonova, writing in this collection on Bulgarian women medievalists and archaeologists, remarks that archaeology in Bulgaria was, early in the century, like medieval history, not a field upon which women embarked or were allowed to embark. And therefore, she concludes, "Women like the American Garrett, who paid a visit to prehistoric sites in Bulgaria in the mid-1930s, were regarded as *eccentric*" (my italics).[9]

In this sense the gender difference among modern women scholars seeking to enter the profession is no different from that experienced by medieval women writers. As Estelle Jelinek has argued in *The Tradition of Women's Autobiography: From Antiquity to the Present* (1986) in her comparison of the autobiographies of Augustine and medieval religious women such as Julian of Norwich, Margery of Kempe, and Teresa de Cartagena, it is clear that the first wrote from a confident position as church leader, not—like the others—from an insecure position as marginal members of an institution that did not want them.

> When Augustine wrote his *Confessions* (ca. 400), he was an accepted leader and scholar in the new church. From his secure position he could detail with intellectual equanimity the excesses and sins he committed before his conversion to Christianity. He had no need to justify himself or prove his authenticity. As with later spiritual writers, he envisioned himself dueling with contrary but abstract forces that were eventually resolved in God. But these women [Julian, Margery, and Teresa] lived at a time when women had no status in the Catholic hierarchy, and therefore any eccentric behavior, any "excesses," on their part was suspect. They accepted their otherness and humbly sought acceptance. They thus took greater risks than Augustine in presenting their experiences.[10]

In general the presentation of an autobiography is always a risk, for it entails the comparison of the Self with the Other, in the pitting of an individual experience against an implied norm.

It is no accident that the modern as well as the medieval autobiography is often described as a confession, in that both genres involve what Michel Foucault, in *The History of Sexuality*, calls a ritual of penance and liberation:

> The confession is a ritual of discourse in which the speaking subject is also the subject of the statement; it is also a ritual that unfolds within a power relationship, for one does not confess without the presence (or virtual presence) of a partner who is not simply the interlocutor but the authority who requires the confession, prescribes and appreciates it, and intervenes in order to judge, punish, forgive, console, and reconcile; a ritual in which the truth is corroborated by the obstacles and resistances it has had to surmount in order to be formulated; and finally, a ritual in which the expression alone, independently of its external consequences, produces intrinsic modifications in the person who articulates it: it exonerates, redeems, and purifies him; it unburdens him of his wrongs, liberates him, and promises him salvation.[11]

One hopes such autobiography exonerates, redeems, and purifies her as well as him.

With women of today or yesterday consciousness of gender difference in being a woman is magnified by the usual autobiographical contrast of Self and Other. There exists, in short, a double gender-difference for women writing autobiography; this gender-difference may be expressed by a redefinition of the Other itself as personal. Maya Bivoet-Williamson, in her translation of the memoirs of the fifteenth-century Austrian chambermaid Helenne Kottaner, explains: "As Freud and Lacan observed and as is illustrated by most autobiographical texts, the self only becomes a meaningful concept when viewed through the provision of an 'Other' or others. While male autobiography may be seen as using a mostly implied, imagined 'Other,' namely

Woman, to define and confirm the male subject, female autobiography more often than not emphasizes an explicit, genuinely experienced relation or relations of self to a significant other or others, often a man, a lover, husband, or father, but also frequently women, a mother, an aunt, or other female role models."[12] When the autobiography involves a modern woman scholar, even the definition of the "Other" begins to change, so that the role models or "family" under discussion take on the context of the schools of history and criticism that dominate the universities of today. Of course, when the form is a biography of the role model herself rather than an autobiography, as in this collection, the invisible relation of Self to Other is frequently marked by the genealogy of the mentoring relationships between the woman professor and her disciples or admirers within the same university.

This collection of *Women Medievalists and the Academy* is intended to illuminate the lives and careers of women who have helped build a field or a discipline or an area or a specific subject in medieval studies, along the lines of Helen Damico's monumental three-volume series *Medieval Scholarship* (1995–2000), which, however, includes (presumably for reasons of length) only seven women among the seventy-five or so medieval scholars surveyed therein (Elizabeth Elstob, Eileen Power, Edith Rickert, Rosemary Estelle Woolf, Dorothy Whitelock, Beryl Smalley, and Sirarpie Der Nersessian—all of whom are also included in this volume). This book of essays about distinguished women medievalists mostly from the last century thus also contrasts in nature rather dramatically with Norman Cantor's nearly womanless book *Inventing the Middle Ages: The Lives, Works, and Ideas of the Great Medievalists of the Twentieth Century* (1991), a National Book Critics Circle Award nominee (Cantor includes only Eileen Power). *Women Medievalists and the Academy* has garnered enthusiastic endorsement among the medievalists who have participated in its shaping thus far, and many contributors and nominators have responded to published and electronically circulated calls for essays and nominations.[13]

Women Medievalists and the Academy appears at a time when other fields throughout the profession are professionalizing and feminizing their histories. Personal essays similar to those included in this volume have been published in the two issues of the 2000–2001 *Medieval Feminist Forum*, under the heading *Feminist Legacies: Female Medieval Scholars and the Academy*, both edited by general editor Sarah Stanbury, in reflection of increased theoretical and literary interest in what is known as personal criticism.[14] Specific historical interest in how early women have shaped specific fields throughout the United States is rising: a recently published volume (1999) on southeastern U.S. women archaeologists traces their lives and work between 1920 and 1960.[15] Also representative of current historiography are books that track the relationship between the personal and the professional—including the memoirs of feminist women historians who have participated in the Coordinating Council for Women in History (CCWH) (1999)—and, more theoretically, the impact of the issue of gender in writing history (1998).[16] In relation to art history and its women academics, published recently are several different kinds of biographical dictionaries (1996) and works exposing the feminist theorization of the field (1999).[17] Even Arthurian scholars have honored women academics: close in intent to this collection is the memorial volume for Maureen Fries edited by Bonnie Wheeler and Fiona Tolhurst (2001), which also includes various lives of women Arthurian scholars that are also excluded, for the most part, from this study.[18]

The split between the professional and the private in the biography or the memoir may take a more analytic or a more lyrical form, depending on the individual subject, the author, and the time period in which the author developed as a writer. That the academy tags the private, the personal, and the emotional as embarrassing and inappropriate—and therefore, like the female, other or different in itself—also reflects gender difference in the writing of autobiography and historiography. Summing this difference up, although without explicit reference to gender, of course, is this comparison of the two kinds of writing one detects in Julian of Norwich and her contemporary Margery Kempe by Robert Stone in *Middle English Prose Style: Margery Kempe and Julian of Norwich* (1970): "The work of Julian is strikingly intellectual. She is an analytical mystic, carefully examining her visions, her conclusions, and her questions about the conclusions.... The work of Margery Kempe, on the other hand, is basically nonintellectual. There is little or no examination of philosophical causes, effects, or questions. Instead, we find a primarily emotional reaction, personalized, focusing on Margery herself: her feelings, reassurances from God about her own worth, her involvements with the most sacred personages of Christian theology.... What we get from her, therefore, is mainly emotional autobiography."[19] "Emotional autobiography" like Margery's personalizes her experiences in an unintellectual, gendered way that is unacceptable to this male reviewer.

How do analytic scholars present the Self—or how is it perceived by the Other—when the Other is female? Nancy K. Miller has argued that "representativity is a problem within feminism itself: a matter of self-representation."[20] She calls autobiographical criticism "narrative criticism" and defines it: "[I]t entails an explicitly autobiographical performance within the act of criticism. Indeed, getting personal in criticism typically involves a deliberate move toward self-figuration, although the degree and form of self-disclosure of course vary widely" (1). Elsewhere she notes that personal criticism marks individuality of the subject: "Personal criticism, as we will see, is often located in a specified body (or voice) marked by gender, color, and national origin: a little like a passport" (4).

The problem for academics is the pronoun "I," nearly always expunged from academic formal writing. What does it mean when a scholar, particularly a woman scholar, deliberately uses the first-person pronoun—and how difficult is that to do? Apparently very difficult, according to some of the most distinguished women writing memoirs in this volume. Eve Kosofsky Sedgwick, in *Tendencies* (1993), analyzes the moment of its usage as revelatory:"I'd find it mutilating and disingenuous to disallow a grammatical form that marks the site of such dense, accessible effects of knowledge, history, revulsion, authority, and pleasure. Perhaps it would be useful to say that the first person throughout represents neither the sense of a simple, settled congratulatory 'I,' on the one hand, nor on the other a fragmented postmodernist postindividual—never mind an unreliable Narrator. No, 'I' is a heuristic; maybe a powerful one."[21] The use of the first person does characterize the unimportant (academically speaking) genre of occasional writing, for example, that found in MLA sessions sponsored by the Commission on Women, "the kind of writing that was polemical, overtly political, often anecdotal, and shaped by the intensity of personal voice."[22] Indeed, perhaps the real question, as Miller phrases it, is this: "Is it personal only if it's embarrassing?" (19). Miller concludes,

> By the risks of its writing, personal criticism embodies a pact, like the autobiographical pact" binding writer to reader in the fabulation of self-truth, that what is at stake matters also to others: somewhere in the self-fiction of the personal voice is a belief that the writing is worth the risk. In this sense, by turning its authorial voice into spectacle, personal writing theorizes the stakes of its own performance: a personal materialism. Personal writing opens an inquiry on the cost of writing—critical writing or Theory—and its effects. The embarrassment produced in readers is a sign that it is working. At the same time the embarrassment blows the cover of the impersonal as a masquerade of self-effacement—at least by indirection—and points to the narcissistic fantasy that inheres in the poses of self-sufficiency we identify with Theory; notably, those of abstraction. (24)

In contrast to the memoir the biographical essay represents a kind of preface to a book, or "postcard," that implies a given audience to which it is directed specifically. Jacques Derrida, writing in *The Post Card: From Socrates to Freud and Beyond* (1980), remarks on the envoi as a preface to an unwritten book, as if to ask, "Who is writing? To whom? And to send, to destine, to dispatch what? To what address? Without any desire to surprise, and thereby to grab attention by means of obscurity, I owe it to whatever remains of my honesty to say finally that I do not know."[23] The envoi, or the postcard, marks a very specific lack of boundaries between or among associates: "To tell the truth, it is not only disagreeable, it places you in relation, without discretion, to tragedy. It forbids that you regulate distances, keeping them or losing them" (5).

The audience for whom these essays have been shaped has obviously been educated in feminist criticism dating from the seventies. Miller notes that

> [f]eminist theory has always built out from the personal: the witnessing "I" of subjective experience. The notion of the "authority of experience" founded a central current in feminist theory in the 1970s and continues—dismantled and renovated—to shape a variety of personal and less personal discourses at an oppositional angle to dominant critical positionings. . . . In literary studies, the works of pioneering feminist literary scholars . . . were clearly fueled by a profound understanding of the consequences of taking the personal as a category of thought and gender as a category of analysis. But

as academic feminists... they on the whole wrote like everyone else who belongs to the third sex of "Ph.Ds" Carolyn Heilbrun has added to the categories of male and female readers ("Millett's Sexual Politics," 39). This self-conscious depersonalization was increased in the mid-eighties with a certain level of institutionalization, by which I mean the construction and recognition of feminist theory as a body of knowledge, as well as by the "theory" frenzy that affected most academic writing—at least on the level of the signifier. At the same time, however, the experiments in autobiographical or personal criticism that I have been describing were also going on and constituted a contrapuntal effect, breaking into the monolithic and monologizing authorized discourse.[24]

It is the voice of the woman medievalist that we long to capture. Hence my decision to include memoirs as well as biographical essays and interview essays. These rare glimpses of the woman scholar herself offer unusual insights into her own perceptions of her life and career. Through its selection of subjects this collection seeks to provide some variety in terms of fields, that is, contributors not just in literature, philology, and history but also in archaeology, art history, philosophy, and so forth. Although such women scholars come from the earlier twentieth century, others still living whose careers have already demonstrated a major contribution and a kind of closure (in most cases these women were born before 1935) are also included, by way of an essay by those women themselves or essays based on interviews with them. The essays involve as subjects women scholars from many countries—Argentina, Armenia, Australia, Austria, Bulgaria, Canada, England, France, Germany, Holland, Ireland, Japan, the United States, and Wales, among others. Each essayist sketches the woman's life and her intellectual contribution to medieval studies and discusses particular problems confronted by the woman working in a predominantly masculine field and how she circumvented those problems. All names recommended for inclusion by specialists in specific fields have been cross-checked by means of library volumes (generally at least three books published, but usually many more) and lists of Medieval Academy fellows and presidents (including foreign fellows) and Kalamazoo plenary lecturers (this list is only twenty-plus years long). All biographers were asked to submit short biographies or curriculum vitae and have been selected by a variety of means: most especially, recommendations and nominations by senior researchers in the field, specialty in the same field, familiarity with the biographee because of her mentorship, or archival or university proximity (for example, Eleanor Shipley Duckett's papers are held at Smith College; Helen Cam's papers are held at Girton College, Cambridge).

This extraordinary record of female achievement in the nineteenth and, chiefly, twentieth centuries tells repeatedly the story of the academy's resistance to female excellence and achievement and the complementary triumph of female perseverance and continuing achievement in its despite. Whether the obstacles are cultural, scholastic, economic, social, or political, women have gone about their business and masked (for the most part) their disappointment over their lack of recognition by their male colleagues and their superiors. When women were barred from the halls of academe, they sought other means to write about the Middle Ages. Dorothy Sayers, the best-known example of such women, translated (and glossed) Dante in her beautiful translation, just as she worked medieval materials (and materials about Oxford University) into her detective fiction. Jessie Laidlay Weston and Evelyn Underhill, both of whom circumvented academic structures, were pilloried (in the case of Weston) or vaunted (in the case of Underhill) for their independent, often speculative and unfounded ventures. Archaeologist Helen Roe, fighting political divisiveness and segregation in Ireland, forged an original course on her own, without academic backing, by describing and cataloging (as it were) so many Celtic monuments—and she went on to serve as president of the Irish archaeological society. Without any academic grants, art historian Elaine C. Block quietly spends her retirement traveling around the world to amass her collection of photographs of misericords—and thereby create an entire field.

Other women did persevere in their attempts to be educated as men were, or recognized as men were, even if it meant drastic relocation, or they worked as scholars side by side without complaint with men who received much more renown for the equivalent work. If Cambridge or Oxford did not offer a Ph.D., then women who sought the degree obtained it at other schools that did offer it: for example, Caroline F. E. Spurgeon at the Sorbonne or Edith Rickert at the University of Chicago. If Elisabeth Gössmann could not receive recognition in her own country of Germany for her first published book—to earn her *Habilitation*—then she moved to Japan, where she was welcomed. If women have needed men to succeed—whether male mentors, publishers, editors, colleagues, or bosses—they have therefore depended on the largesse of extraordinary men to recognize them. And there have been some men who did foster their students' success, as is the case with Marjorie Chibnall and Elizabeth Brown. So also have the men who studied under the mentorship or scholarship of significant women supported their mentors by writing biographical essays or books about them (as is the case with Kevin Harty writing about Ruth J. Dean or with men who have today recognized the contribution of previous women pioneers in their own fields, such as Charles Burnett writing about Marie-Thérèse d'Alverny or David Day writing about Bertha Haven Putnam or Russell Poole writing about Bertha Phillpotts).

A third group of women often succeeded despite their acquiescence to social pressures that silently demanded they subordinate their careers to their husbands'. Some women scholars followed husbands and flourished in spite of this subordination of self and work. Art historian Meredith Lillich followed hers to Syracuse as an adjunct but was later recognized in her own right as a distinguished professor and teacher. Christine de Pizan scholar Charity Cannon Willard and her husband, both graduate students, she at Radcliffe and he at Harvard, had to pursue separate careers that nevertheless blended inexorably—he at West Point (which barred women) and she nearby at the appropriately named Ladycliffe College. Yet at the end of their careers she found herself mentoring some of his students.

A fourth group often suffered professional rejection, isolation, elimination in competitions, and verbal abuse, but they soldiered on quietly. Cora Lutz, who was unfairly and offensively criticized by a single (male) critic for her Latin editing in her edition of the ninth-century cleric Remigius of Auxerre, silently endured, going on to finish her teaching and publishing career at the Yale Beinecke Library, where she catalogued manuscripts in a monumental effort. Art historian Joan Evans had to endure years of being ignored (although men inferior to her were recognized) until she was granted the title of "Dame." Nellie Neilson, who also served as president of the American Historical Association, was nevertheless paid less than she should have been while she chaired the history department at Mount Holyoke. Joan Ferrante, also chair of her department, spoke out on behalf of women and others at Columbia, which may have been responsible for her smaller salary raises and lack of other perks—and yet she also served as president of the Medieval Academy. Whatever international or national acclaim women have received, they often seem to suffer reproach and even indignity within their home institutions.

It is perhaps appropriate to end the collection with a memoir by a woman medievalist, Caroline Walker Bynum, who wrote what seemed a curious, eccentric book, *Jesus as Mother,* that signified the beginning of a whole field of study of women mystics and the representation of the female body. This work has earned her a permanent berth at the Institute for Advanced Study in Princeton. Like the best, most distinguished women, she has been selected to serve the one-year term as president of the Medieval Academy. While the many men who have served as president of the Medieval Academy have been fine scholars and teachers, they did not always match the distinction of the handful of extraordinarily distinguished women who have done so. Even at the top, there is inequity.

The fields in which women have worked most successfully and originally on their own have been art history and archaeology and women's history and literature. Jane Hayward almost single-handedly created the study of stained glass, although she did not live to complete her catalogues. Helen Roe created Irish archaeology as a field, as did Elaine Block the study of misericords. Library work—paleography and codicology—have allowed room for the many excellent paleographical specialists, including Anneliese Maier (who never served in a university post) at the Vatican Library. Women have also been allowed (indeed, encouraged) to edit and translate works by women and to write about women, a kind of double occlusion, or to put it another way, Victorian parlor politics—Suzanne Solente for Christine de Pizan, Hope Emily Allen for Margery Kempe, and Benedicta Ward, Mary Dominica Legge, Eileen Power, and Caroline Walker Bynum for medieval women more generally.

Women who have chosen difficult or unusual paths in their personal and political lives have been treated differently, sometimes because of the age and culture in which they lived, which often treated men in the same circumstances similarly, and sometimes dependent on their individual circumstances and contexts. Maude Violet Clarke faced college antifeminism and homophobia at Somerville College, Oxford, about women living together who might be (or become) "inverts." Yet Eleanor Shipley Duckett, who wrote on the early Latin Middle Ages at Smith College and who lived most of her life with another woman, Mary Chase Smith, the novelist, was memorialized at Smith by means of the adjacent residence colleges named one for each. But Margaret Schlauch, an avowed Communist, had to flee the United States as the result of a rampant, repressive McCarthyism and right-wing persecution in the thirties. In Poland she finished her career and died alone. Her Polish doctoral student Jacek Fisiak, former rector of Adam Mickiewicz University and minister of education for Poland, recently rectified the general neglect of the importance of his mentor by honoring her memory with a symposium at the university on 12–15 May 2002 and collecting papers delivered there for a volume. Germany and Austria have not been collegial to the women profiled in this collection, whether Elisabeth Busse-Wilson, Anneliese Maier, or Elisabeth Gössmann. The women of Bulgaria have also suffered political pressure—as medievalists they had to choose the old-fashioned path of studying classical or Slavic philology in order to achieve some acclaim. In France Suzanne Solente and Marie-Thérèse d'Alverny, despite their many gifts as paleographers, met with indifference by the Bibliothèque nationale. Having admitted all this, we have to add that England itself was not very open to the presence of women in its colleges and universities, or their earning of degrees in the twenties and thirties, and treated even women in single-sex colleges with a certain paranoia and homophobia about their sexuality or possible lesbianism; therefore, those women who did achieve during this period—in spite of this period—are remarkable for their tenacity and their perseverance.

The memoirs herein provide the voices of women who (left to write whatever they wish about their careers and lives as women medievalists) often choose to tell us why they became medievalists (such a daunting, unenviable choice, given the misogyny of the period, which has been circumvented in part by the support of male mentors and colleagues). Ilene H. Forsyth, like Mary McCarthy, talks about the old stones of Florence; Marjorie Chibnall chose Orderic Vitalis as her life's work; Elizabeth Brown emphasized French intellectual history; and Charity Cannon Willard read manuscripts of Christine de Pizan alone at most of the world's major libraries with only an occasional archivist to share her joy. Elaine Block came to her monumental study of misericords (the little carved figures, often grotesque, that are concealed under seats in choir stalls and exhibit their creators' playfulness) in the long period of her retirement, when she had time and money to collect the worldwide illustrations for the many volumes that Brepols began publishing in 2002. Single-handedly creating a new discipline, Block has started her own journal for such study (*The Sacred and the Profane*) and annual conferences at significant sites where misericords are found (that is, at monasteries and cathedrals). Ruth J. Dean and Mary Martin McLaughlin, among others, have also published their lifeworks in the sunset of their careers, well into retirement.

Propinquity may have been responsible for some of the successes of women—someone who finished at Harvard or Cambridge or Yale and who continued to live nearby or who yearned to return to recapture an exhilarating graduate-school experience—might have been tapped for a significant position or work experience, as were so many male professors of the earlier generations. But propinquity may also have been responsible for the work of some women who have collaborated with men—like Edith Rickert—having had their work swallowed up by their collaborators' reputations because they lacked an endowed or professorial position.

Although women from non-English-speaking countries are indeed a minority in this volume, they are represented by the German and Austrian, Spanish, Armenian, and French scholars who do appear here. Of the German and Austrian scholars, Elisabeth Gössmann, Elise Richter, and Elisabeth Busse-Wilson were isolated and silenced by the Nazis during their rise to power because they were either women or Jewish. The Austrian specialist in natural philosophy and science Anneliese Maier spent most of her life working in an unauthorized position at the Vatican Library. Some foreign-born medievalists, such as María Rosa Lida de Malkiel from Spain, came to the United States to take up a position or, like Nina Garsoïan from Armenia, retired to high acclaim in their field. The French scholars Suzanne Solente and Marie-Thérèse d'Alverny both specialized in French periods, one in the late and one in the high Middle Ages (twelfth century) in medieval Latin, flourishing in their fields in France.

The general tone in these autobiographical essays is one of pleasure and contentment, whatever the nature of the career (and it must be said that this tone may be a result of the very acceptance of the task, for others who declined to write may have been in some cases less sanguine about their lack of recognition by the academy—if that has been the case). Where women have attested to a rich matrix of support for their teaching and scholarship, it is almost exclusively at institutions where women have predominated, as at a formerly single-sex college (Smith, Mount Holyoke), or where women faculty have created a network of intercommunication and mediation (New York University, City University of New York–Graduate Center, and the Berkshire Conferences organized by Jo Ann McNamara). Women medievalists knowing other women medievalists have helped build a network of support based on family ties, mutual respect, and a shared discipline, in many cases—among them, the two Rickert sisters, Eileen Power and her students, presumably the Loomis wives, Laura Hibbard Loomis and Dorothy Berthurum Loomis, friends Helen Waddell and Maude Violet Clarke, Hope Emily Allen and Margaret Ogden, Beryl Smalley and Marie-Thérèse d'Alverny, Mildred K. Pope and Mary Dominica Legge, Dorothy Whitelock and Marjorie Ethel Reeves, Dorothy Whitelock and Doris Mary Stenton, Marjorie Chibnall and Constance Hoffman Berman, and Nina G. Garsoïan and Sirarpie Der Nersessian. Alternatively, women medievalists have had mentors (often male) who fully supported and encouraged their work (or married them, as in the case of Doris and Frank Stenton), or they have had some source of independent income, as from an inheritance, or (as in the case of Elaine Block, whose development began in earnest after her retirement) time. Truly, as Virginia Woolf noted so sagely seventy-five years ago, five hundred pounds and a room of one's own (that is, control over income and privacy), as well as nurturing mentors, colleagues, and institutions, have contributed to the success of these women (for example, Elizabeth Scala applied for a fellowship specifically to use the archives of Edith Rickert at the University of Chicago, which has led to the publication of many articles and will culminate in a book). In some cases (an Anneliese Maier or a Nellie Neilson), women have decided not to marry or pursue some other full-time personal relationship, which has allowed them to focus fully on their careers, and in other cases (for example, Helen Roe) an alternate career (nursing and postmistress) has had to supplement the desire to write scholarly materials. Other women, such as Doris Stenton, married their professors (in her case, Sir Frank Stenton) or, in the case of Margaret Ogden and Charity Cannon Willard, their colleagues, and devoted their time equally to their careers and their husbands. Still others, such as Joan Ferrante, waited until the sunsets of their careers to marry. Not all women in this volume earned Ph.D.s—in an era when higher degrees were difficult for women to come by. Nor have all women had access to funding that would permit travel to the great European libraries so necessary for scholarship of the Middle Ages.

But those who have published scholarship in medieval studies have ultimately overcome whatever barriers that have prevented their advancement—whether a higher degree, travel funding, time, political forces, cultural and social stereotypes, or academic misogyny—and triumphantly earned distinction within their universities and the academy as a whole. To these academic grandmothers and great-grandmothers the women and men medievalists of today owe a debt of gratitude for having paved the way(s) to success and achievement. May this collection serve as one small recognition of their triumph and one token reflection of our immense admiration.

Notes

1. Lee Patterson despises "Exegetics"—the so-called Robertsonian (Princetonian) form of historical (patristic) criticism that assumes a monolithic church—and embraces the (Yalesque) New Criticism of E. Talbot Donaldson and the humanistic historical stylistics of Charles Muscatine. What both the original schools he describes share—and indeed, what circles and recycles endlessly through Patterson's polemic—is a near-complete omission of women as agents in the history of medievalism. See Patterson, *Negotiating the Past*.

2. This poem is in Patterson, *Negotiating the Past*, 9 n. 11, quoted from Girouard, *Return to Camelot*, 83, and Chandler, *Dream of Order*, 161 (my emphasis).

3. Mentioned in Patterson's footnotes are Sheila Delany and Margaret Schlauch as Marxists.

4. Patterson, *Negotiating the Past*, 10, my emphasis.

5. Woolf, *Room of One's Own*, 112. Subsequent citations from this work are documented with page numbers in the text.

6. See Henriette Leyser and Deeann Copeland Klepper, "Beryl Smalley (1905–1984): The Medieval Bible in the Modern Academy," chapter 46 of this volume.

7. See Shaun F. D. Hughes, "Elizabeth Elstob (1683–1756) and the Limits of Women's Agency in Early Eighteenth-Century England," chapter 1 of this volume.

8. Elizabeth Elstob, ed., *An English-Saxon Homily on the Birthday of Saint Gregory, Anciently*

used in the English-Saxon Church, giving an Account of the Conversion of the English from Paganism to Christianity (London: W. Bowyer, 1709), ii.

9. See Liliana V. Simeonova, "Women and Medieval Scholarship in Bulgaria: Vera Ivanova-Mavrodinova (1896–1987) and Vasilka Tapkova-Zaimova (1924–)," chapter 35 of this volume.

10. Jelinek, *Tradition of Women's Autobiography*, 21.

11. Foucault, *History of Sexuality*, 1:61–62.

12. Williamson, *Memoirs of Helene Kottanner*, 55.

13. These calls for nominations and contributions appeared in the March 2001 "Professional Forum" of *PMLA*, the 2001 (spring) issue of *Medieval Feminist Forum*, and the September 2001 issue of the *Medieval Academy Newsletter*.

14. See, for example, in *Medieval Feminist Forum*, no. 30 (fall 2000), 9–37, autobiographical essays by Sheila Delany, Jane Chance, and Madeline Caviness and a biographical essay about Edith Rickert by Elizabeth Scala; and in no. 31 (spring 2001), autobiographical essays by Mary Carruthers and biographical essays about Hope Emily Allen by John C. Hirsh and by Marva Mitchell, about Eleanor Prescott Hammond by Derek Pearsall, and about Margaret Schlauch by Laura Mestayer Rogers.

15. White et al., *Grit-Tempered*.

16. Boris and Chaudhuri, *Voices of Women Historians*; Gillespie and Clinton, *Taking Off the White Gloves*; and Smith, *Gender of History*.

17. Scanlon and Cosner, *American Women Historians, 1700s–1900s*; and Pollock, *Differencing the Canon*.

18. See Wheeler and Tolhurst, *On Arthurian Women*. Included in this volume are essays about Lady Charlotte Guest (1812–95), Gertrude Schoepperle Loomis (1882–1921), Dorothy Berthurum Loomis (1897–1987), Vida Dutton Scudder (1861–1954), Elspeth Kennedy (1923–), Fanni Bogdanow (1927–), and, of course, Maureen Fries (1941?–99). Included in both *On Arthurian Women* and *Women Medievalists and the Academy* are Jessie Laidlay Weston (1850–1928), Laura Hibbard Loomis (1897–1987), Rachel Bromwich (1915–), and Helaine Newstead (1906–81).

19. Stone, *Middle English Prose Style*.

20. Nancy K. Miller, "Getting Personal: Autobiography as Cultural Criticism," in *Getting Personal*, x. Subsequent citations from this work are documented with page numbers in the text.

21. Sedgwick, *Tendencies*, xiv. Sedgwick, made a target because of her 1989 MLA paper, "Jane Austen and the Masturbating Girl," at the opening of the published version of her paper acknowledges as an example of one of her accusers "Roger Kimball in his treatise on educational 'corruption,' *Tenured Radicals*, [who] cites the title 'Jane Austen and the Masturbating Girl' from an MLA convention program quite as if he were Perry Mason, the six words a smoking gun" (109).

22. Miller, "Getting Personal," 15.

23. Derrida, *Post Card*; 5. The subsequent citation from this work is documented with the page number in the text.

24. Miller, "Getting Personal," 14–15.

Works Cited

Boris, Eileen, and Nupur Chaudhuri, eds. *Voices of Women Historians: The Personal, the Political, the Professional*. Bloomington: University of Indiana Press, 1999.

Cantor, Norman. *Inventing the Middle Ages: The Lives, Works, and Ideas of the Great Medievalists of the Twentieth Century*. New York: William Morrow, 1991.

Chandler, Alice. *A Dream of Order: The Medieval Ideal in Nineteenth-Century English Literature.* Lincoln: University of Nebraska Press, 1970.

Damico, Helen, and Joseph B. Zavadil (vol. 1 only), with Donald Fennema and Karmen Lenz (vols. 2 and 3 only), eds. *Medieval Scholarship: Biographical Studies on the Formation of a Discipline.* Vol. 1, *History;* vol. 2, *Literature and Philology;* vol. 3, *Philosophy and the Arts.* New York: Garland, 1995–2000.

Derrida, Jacques. *The Post Card: From Socrates to Freud and Beyond.* Translated by Alan Bass. Chicago: University of Chicago Press, 1987.

Foucault, Michel. *The History of Sexuality.* Vol. 1, *An Introduction.* Translated by Robert Hurley. New York: Random House, 1978.

Gillespie, Michele, and Catherine Clinton, eds. *Taking Off the White Gloves: Southern Women and Women Historians.* Columbia: University of Missouri Press, 1998.

Girouard, Mark. *The Return to Camelot: Chivalry and the English Gentleman.* New Haven, Conn.: Yale University Press, 1981.

Jelinek, Estelle. *The Tradition of Women's Autobiography: From Antiquity to the Present.* Boston: Twayne Publishers, 1986.

Miller, Nancy K. *Getting Personal: Feminist Occasions and Other Autobiographical Acts.* New York: Routledge, 1991.

Patterson, Lee. *Negotiating the Past: The Historical Understanding of Medieval Literature.* Madison: University of Wisconsin Press, 1987.

Pollock, Griselda. *Differencing the Canon: Feminist Desire and the Writing of Art's Histories.* London: Routledge, 1999.

Scanlon, Jennifer, and Sharon Cosner, eds. *American Women Historians, 1700s–1990s: A Biographical Dictionary.* Westport, Conn.: Greenwood Press, 1996.

Sedgwick, Eve Kosofsky. *Tendencies.* Durham, N.C.: Duke, 1993.

Smith, Bonnie G., ed. *The Gender of History: Men, Women, and Historical Practice.* Cambridge: Harvard University Press, 1998.

Sherman, Claire Richter, with Adele M. Holcomb, eds. *Women as Interpreters of the Visual Arts, 1820–1979.* Westport, Conn.: Greenwood Press, 1981.

Stanbury, Sarah, guest ed. *Feminist Legacies: Female Medieval Scholars and the Academy. Medieval Feminist Forum,* nos. 30–31 (2001).

Stone, Robert Karl. *Middle English Prose Style: Margery Kempe and Julian of Norwich.* Studies in English Literature, vol. 36. The Hague: Mouton, 1970.

Tompkins, Jane. *A Life in School: What the Teacher Learned.* Reading, Mass.: Addison-Wesley Publication, 1996.

Wheeler, Bonnie, and Fiona Tolhurst. *On Arthurian Women: Essays in Memory of Maureen Fries.* Dallas: Scriptorium Press, 2001.

White, Nancy Marie, et al. *Grit-Tempered: Early Women Archaeologists in the Southeastern United States.* Gainesville: University Press of Florida, 1999.

Williamson, Maya Bijvoet, trans. *The Memoirs of Helene Kottanner (1439–1440).* With Introduction, Interpretative Essay, and Notes by Maya Bijvoet Williamson. Cambridge: D. S. Brewer, 1998.

Woolf, Virginia. *A Room of One's Own.* London: Harcourt Brace and Co., 1929.

Women Medievalists Profiled (Alphabetically)

1. Hope Emily Allen (1883–1960)
2. Mary Bateson (1865–1906)
3. Elaine C. Block (1929–)
4. Marie Borroff (1923–)
5. Rachel Bromwich (1915–)
6. Elizabeth A. R. Brown (1932–)
7. Elisabeth Busse-Wilson (1890–1974)
8. Caroline Walker Bynum (1941–)
9. Helen Maud Cam (1885–1968)
10. Nora Kershaw Chadwick (1891–1972)
11. Marjorie McCallum Chibnall (1914–)
12. Maude Violet Clarke (1892 1935)
13. Marcia L. Colish (1937–)
14. Rosemary Cramp (1929–)
15. Marie-Thérèse D'Alverny (1903–1991)
16. Ruth J. Dean (1902–2003)
17. Sirarpie Der Nersessian (1896–1989)
18. Charlotte D'Evelyn (1889–1977)
19. Eleanor Shipley Duckett (1880–1976)
20. Lina Eckenstein (1857–1931),
21. Elizabeth Elstob (1683–1756)
22. Dame Joan Evans (1893–1977)
23. Joan M. Ferrante (1936–)

24. Ilene H. Forsyth (1928–)
25. Grace Frank (1886–1978)
26. Nina G. Garsoïan (1923–)
27. Elisabeth Gössmann (1928–)
28. Eleanor Prescott Hammond (1866–1933)
29. Jane Hayward (1918–1994)
30. Vera Ivanova-Mavrodinova (1896–1987)
31. Anna Jameson (1794–1860)
32. Pearl Kibre (1900–1985)
33. Georgiana Goddard King (1871–1939)
34. Mary Dominica Legge (1905–1986)
35. María Rosa Lida de Malkiel (1910–1962)
36. Meredith Parsons Lillich (1932–)
37. Laura Hibbard Loomis (1883–1960)
38. Cora Elizabeth Lutz (1906–1985)
39. Jo Ann McNamara (1931–)
40. Anneliese Maier (1905–1971)
41. Christine A. E. M. Mohrmann (1903–1988)
42. Nellie Neilson (1873–1947)
43. Helaine Newstead (1906–1981)
44. Margaret Ogden (1909–1988)
45. Bertha Surtees Phillpotts (1877–1932)
46. Mildred K. Pope (1872–1956)
47. Bertha Haven Putnam (1872–1960)
48. Régine Pernoud (1909–1998)
49. Eileen Edna Le Poer Power (1889–1940)
50. Marjorie Ethel Reeves (1905–2003)
51. Elise Richter (1865–1943)
52. Edith Rickert (1871–1938)
53. Margaret Rickert (1888–1973)
54. Helen M. Roe (1895–1988)
55. Yvonne Rihouët Rokseth (1890–1948)
56. James Bruce Ross (1902–1995)
57. Elizabeth Salter (1925–1980)
58. Dorothy L. Sayers (1893–1957)
59. Margaret Schlauch (1898–1986)
60. Helena Mennie Shire (1912–1991)
61. Beryl Smalley (1905–1984)
62. Suzanne Solente (1895–1978)
63. Caroline F. E. Spurgeon (1869–1942)
64. Doris Mary Stenton (1894–1971)
65. Susan Mosher Stuard (1935–)

66. Vasilka Tapkova-Zaimova (1924–)
67. Evelyn Underhill (1875–1941)
68. Helen Waddell (1889–1965)
69. Sister Benedicta Ward, S.L.G. (1933–)
70. Jessie Laidlay Weston (1850–1928)
71. Dorothy Whitelock (1901–1982)
72. Charity Cannon Willard (1914–)
73. Rosemary Estelle Woolf (1925–1978)

Chronology of Women Medievalists Profiled, with Fields and Institutional Affiliations

Listed below are the major field(s) and institutional affiliation(s) (if any) of the women medievalists profiled in this collection, in chronological order by date of birth. Although the list does not pretend to be comprehensive, it provides the beginnings of an institutional genealogy of medieval studies and women medievalists in the history of the academy.

1. Elizabeth Elstob (1683–1756); Old English; Independent Scholar
2. Anna Jameson (1794–1860); Art History; Independent Scholar
3. Jessie Laidlay Weston (1850–1928); Arthurian Romance; Independent Scholar and Translator
4. Lina Eckenstein (1857–1931); Medieval Monastic Women; Independent Scholar
5. Mary Bateson (1865–1906); Medieval History; Newnham College, Cambridge
6. Elise Richter (1865–1943); Romance Linguistics, Vulgar Latin, French, Provençal, Italian, Portuguese, and Spanish Language and Literature; University of Vienna
7. Eleanor Prescott Hammond (1866–1933); Middle English Literature, Textual Criticism; University of Chicago and Wellesley College
8. Caroline F. E. Spurgeon (1869–1942); Medieval English Literature; Bedford College, University of London
9. Georgiana Goddard King (1871–1939); Medieval Iberian Art; Chair of History of Art; Bryn Mawr College
10. Edith Rickert (1871–1938); Chaucer; University of Chicago
11. Mildred K. Pope (1872–1956); Anglo-Norman; Chair of French Language and Romance Philology, University of Manchester

12. Bertha Haven Putnam (1872–1960); Medieval English Judicial History; Mount Holyoke College
13. Nellie Neilson (1873–1947); Medieval History; Mount Holyoke College,; first woman President of the American Historical Association
14. Evelyn Underhill (1875–1941); Medieval Mysticism; Independent Scholar
15. Bertha Surtees Phillpotts (1877–1932); Old Icelandic Studies; Mistress, Girton College, Cambridge University
16. Eleanor Shipley Duckett (1880–1976); Medieval Latin Literature; Smith College
17. Hope Emily Allen (1883–1960); Middle English Literature; Independent Scholar
18. Laura Hibbard Loomis (1883–1960); Arthurian Romance and Middle English Literature; Wellesley College
19. Helen Maud Cam (1885–1968); Medieval History; Harvard University and Girton College, Cambridge University
20. Grace Frank (1886–1978); Medieval French Literature; Bryn Mawr College
21. Margaret Rickert (1888–1973); Medieval Art History; University of Chicago
22. Charlotte D'Evelyn (1889–1977); Middle English Literature; Mount Holyoke College
23. Eileen Edna Le Poer Power (1889–1940); Medieval Economic History; London School of Economics
24. Helen Waddell (1889–1965); Medieval Latin Poetry and Prose; Independent Scholar and Translator
25. Yvonne Rihouët Rokseth (1890–1948); Medieval Music; University of Strasbourg
26. Elisabeth Busse-Wilson (1890–1974); Medieval Cultural History (Saint Elizabeth of Thuringia); Independent Scholar
27. Nora Kershaw Chadwick (1891–1972); Nordic and Celtic Studies; Newnham and Girton Colleges, Cambridge University
28. Maude Violet Clarke (1892–1935); Medieval English and Irish Constitutional History; Fellow and Vice-Principal, Somerville College, Oxford
29. Joan Evans (1893–1977); Medieval French Art History; Independent Scholar; and President of the Society of Antiquaries
30. Dorothy L. Sayers (1893–1957); Dante Studies; Independent Scholar, Translator, and Novelist
31. Doris Mary Stenton (1894–1971); Medieval Legal History; Oxford University
32. Helen M. Roe (1895–1988); Medieval Irish Art and Archaeology; Independent Scholar, Librarian, and President of the Royal Society of Antiquaries of Ireland
33. Suzanne Solente (1895–1978); Medieval French Literature (Christine de Pizan); Archivist
34. Sirarpie Der Nersessian (1896–1989); Armenian Art History and Byzantine Studies; Harvard University and Dumbarton Oaks (Senior Fellow), last woman
35. Vera Ivanova-Mavrodinova (1896–1987); Medieval Archaeology and Medieval Slavic Epigraphy and Paleography; Bulgarian Academy of Sciences

36. Margaret Schlauch (1898–1986); Old Norse, Middle English Literature, and Philology; New York University; University of Warsaw
37. Pearl Kibre (1900–1985); Medieval History of Science; Hunter College and Graduate Center of City University of New York
38. Dorothy Whitelock (1901–1982); Old English Studies; Elrington and Bosworth Professor of Anglo-Saxon, Cambridge University
39. Ruth J. Dean (1902–2003); Anglo-Norman and French Language and Literature; Mount Holyoke College and Medieval English and French Studies, University of Pennsylvania; first woman president of the Medieval Academy
40. James Bruce Ross (1902–1995); Medieval and Renaissance Italian History; Vassar College
41. Marie-Thérèse d'Alverny (1903–1991); Intellectual History of the Middle Ages and Arabic Influence on Latin Literature; École des Chartres, Department of Western Manuscripts (Cabinet des manuscrits), Bibliothèque nationale de France, Centre d'études supérieures de civilisation médiévale at Poitiers, editor of *Archives d'histoire doctrinale et littéraire du Moyen Âge*, foreign fellow of the Medieval Academy of America
42. Christine A. E. M. Mohrmann (1903–1988); Christian and Medieval Latin; Independent Scholar
43. Mary Dominica Legge (1905–1986); Anglo-Norman Studies; University of Edinburgh; and Somerville College, Oxford (Honorary Fellow)
44. Anneliese Maier (1905–1971); Fourteenth-Century Philosophy; Biblioteca Apostolica Vaticana
45. Marjorie Ethel Reeves (1905–2003); Medieval History; Saint Anne's College, Oxford University and Medieval Academy of America (Corresponding Member)
46. Beryl Smalley (1905–1984); Medieval Latin Literature; Saint Hilda's College, Oxford University
47. Cora Elizabeth Lutz (1906–1985); Medieval Latin Literature; Wilson College and Beinecke Library, Yale University
48. Helaine Newstead (1906–1981); Arthurian Romance; Graduate Center of the City University of New York
49. Margaret Ogden (1909–1988); Middle English Lexicography; University of Michigan
50. Régine Pernoud (1909–1998); Medieval French History (Joan of Arc); Curator, Museum of French History
51. María Rosa Lida de Malkiel (1910–1962); Medieval Spanish Literary Historiography; University of California–Berkeley
52. Helena Mennie Shire (1912–1991); Medieval Scottish Literature and Music; Aberdeen University and Cambridge University
53. Marjorie McCallum Chibnall (1914–); Medieval Church History; Girton College, Cambridge University

54. Charity Cannon Willard (1914–); Medieval French Literature (Christine de Pizan); Ladycliffe College
55. Rachel Bromwich (1915–); Celtic Studies; Cambridge University and University of Wales
56. Hayward (1918–1994); Medieval Art History (Stained Glass); Cloisters, Metropolitan Museum of Art
57. Marie Borroff (1923–); Middle English Language and Literature; Yale University
58. Nina G. Garsoïan (1923–); Armenian History and Civilization and Byzantine History; Columbia University
59. Vasilka Tapkova-Zaimova (1924–); Byzantine Studies; University of Sofia
60. Elizabeth Salter (1925–1980); Middle English Literature; York University
61. Rosemary Estelle Woolf (1925–1978); Old and Middle English Literature; Somerville College, Oxford University
62. Ilene H. Forsyth (1928–); Medieval Art History (Romanesque, Byzantine), History of Art; University of Michigan (Arthur F. Thurnau Professor)
63. Elisabeth Gössmann (1928–); Medieval Philosophy and Theology (Women and the Study of Gender); University of Tokyo and Ludwig-Maximilians-Universität-Munich
64. Elaine C. Block (1929–); Medieval Art History (Misericords); Hunter College–City University of New York; and Independent Scholar
65. Rosemary Cramp (1929–); Archaeology; University of Durham
66. Jo Ann McNamara (1931–); Medieval History (Feminist Studies); Hunter College–City University of New York
67. Elizabeth A. R. Brown (1932–); Medieval History; City University of New York
68. Meredith Parsons Lillich (1932–); Medieval Art History; Syracuse University
69. Sister Benedicta Ward, S.L.G. (1933–); History of Christian Spirituality (Medieval Religious History); Oxford, Royal Historical Society (Fellow); and Harris-Manchester College (Honorary Lecturer)
70. Susan Mosher Stuard (1935–); Medieval Women's History; Haverford College
71. Joan M. Ferrante (1936–); Medieval Literature; Columbia University and President of the Medieval Academy of America
72. Marcia L. Colish (1937–); Medieval Philosophy; Oberlin College and President of the Medieval Academy of America
73. Caroline Walker Bynum (1941–); Medieval Religious and Intellectual History; Columbia University; Institute for Advanced Study-Princeton; President of the Medieval Academy of Americaand the American Historical Association

WOMEN MEDIEVALISTS

and the Academy

CHAPTER I

Elizabeth Elstob (1683–1756) and the Limits of Women's Agency in Early-Eighteenth-Century England

Shaun F. D. Hughes

Elizabeth Elstob (1683–1756) was the first person to publish a grammar of Old English in the vernacular. Her *Rudiments of Grammar for the English-Saxon Tongue* (1715) remains after nearly three hundred years one of the very few such works to be published by a woman.[1] She had previously published *An English-Saxon Homily on the Birth-Day of St. Gregory* (1709) and had under way an edition and translation of Ælfric's *Catholic Homilies* at the point when her scholarly career was cut short.[2] That she was able to do so much at this time in history says a great deal about the changes that were rippling through English society at the beginning of the long eighteenth century. That she accomplished so little (there would be no complete edition of Ælfric's homilies until Benjamin Thorpe published the two volumes of his *Homilies of Ælfric* [1844–46]) is a reminder of how superficial some of these changes were, especially as far as women were concerned.[3]

Elizabeth Elstob was born in Newcastle-upon-Tyne in 1683.[4] Her father was a merchant and well connected in the community. Although he died in 1688, when Elizabeth Elstob was only five years old, when she published her *Homily* twenty-one years later, the twenty-four subscribers identified as being from Newcastle included the mayor, four city aldermen, and four described as merchants.[5] Her mother died in 1691, but Elizabeth Elstob remembers her as a great lover of books who encouraged the desire for learning in her as well as in her elder brother, William (1673–1715). At her mother's death William was still a minor, so Elizabeth Elstob became the ward of her father's brother, Charles Elstob, prebendary of Canterbury, recently married, and a man with decidedly conservative views about women's education. Charles Elstob has often been harshly treated in the literature on Elizabeth Elstob; in reality, perhaps,

G

the severest criticism that ought to be made of him was that he meant well in his handling of the affairs of his niece and nephew. In later years Elizabeth Elstob's opinion of him seems to have hardened, and she recalls somewhat bitterly his (probably frequently repeated) firm conviction that "one tongue is enough for a woman."[6] He was certainly supportive enough to be listed as a subscriber to the *Homily*. And while he did not countenance her continuing her Latin studies, in which she had already made considerable progress, she did eventually receive permission to study French. In this she received the support of her aunt, Matilda Elstob, who was herself fluent in the language. This aunt seems to have had sympathies toward women's education similar to those of Elizabeth Elstob's mother, although presumably she would have needed to be somewhat more discreet in expressing them.

Elizabeth Elstob lived with Charles and Matilda Elstob first at Canterbury and then from 1697 in the town of Tillington in Sussex, although contact with the cathedral city was still maintained. In the meantime her brother William completed his education at Eton in 1691 and at the end of that year matriculated at Queen's College, Oxford, from which he received an A.B. in 1694. He then moved to University College, where he received his M.A. in 1697. At this time Queen's and University Colleges were the main centers in Great Britain for both Saxon and septentrional studies. The university press had just published the *Institutiones Grammaticae Anglo-Saxonicae et Mœso-Gothicae* (Principles of Old English and Gothic grammar) (Oxford, 1689), prepared by George Hickes (1642–1715), the controversial nonjuror.[7] The volume also included the Icelandic grammar of Runólfur Jónsson, first published in 1651, and a catalog of Old English manuscripts.[8] Hickes had been suspended from his position as dean of Worchester the same year the volume appeared, and by the time William Elstob arrived at Oxford, Hickes was a fugitive. But Hickes was not the only person interested in Saxon studies. Among the more prominent were Edward Gibson (1669–1748), who received his M.A. from Queen's in 1694 and had published an edition of the *Anglo-Saxon Chronicle* (*Chronicon Saxonicum* [Oxford, 1692]); Edward Thwaites (1677–1711), who entered Queen's in 1689, was college preceptor in 1698, taught a class in 1699 in Old English with fifteen students and only one dictionary, and published his edition of the Old English *Heptateuch* (Oxford, 1698); Christopher Rawlinson (1677–1733), who published his edition of Alfred's translation of Boethius's *Consolation* (Oxford, 1698); Arthur Charette (ca. 1655–1722), master of University College from 1692, who was an enthusiastic supporter of Saxon studies although he himself published nothing in the field; and Humphrey Wanley (1672–1726), assistant keeper to the Bodleian Library, who was an expert paleographer and major contributor to the second edition of Hickes's *Institutiones,* which appeared as *Linguarum Vett. Septentrionalium Thesaurus Grammatico-Criticus et Archæologicus* (An archaeological and grammatico-critical storehouse of the ancient northern languages) (Oxford, 1703–5).[9]

It is not surprising, therefore, that when William Elstob arrived at Queen's in late 1691 he soon wanted to associate himself with the Saxon circle. He not only demonstrated an interest in Old English studies, but he soon showed a flair for them and became a valuable member of the circle, although he never lost sight of his primary vocation, which was his calling to the clergy. He worked for some time on an edition of Alfred's Old English translation of Orosius's history, but only the title page and two leaves were published in 1699.[10] (William Elstob's materials for his edition eventually came into the hands of Joseph Barrington [1727–1800], who, after tampering with the text—to its great disadvantage—published them under his own name as *The Anglo-Saxon Version from Orosius* [1773].) Among William Elstob's numerous other publications, not all connected with Saxon studies, was his edition of the *Sermo Lupi ad Anglos* (Wulfstan's sermon to the English) (Oxford, 1701), which was reprinted in Hickes's *Thesaurus* (1:98–106). In 1703 William Elstob moved to London and took up his appointment as rector of the joint parishes of Saint Swithin's and Saint Mary Bothow. Since this position was governed by Canterbury, Charles Elstob may have been influential in seeing that it went to William. Although it cannot be proved for certain, it is likely that at this time Elizabeth Elstob, now almost at the age of majority, moved to London to live with her brother.

An eighteenth-century tradition holds that Elizabeth Elstob moved to Oxford to be with William. The arguments against this seem strong, however, given the conservative disposition of her guardian and the fact that the facilities at Oxford would have been inappropriate for Elizabeth Elstob to have lived at University College, although she may very well have visited him there. In the preface to the *Homily*, Elizabeth Elstob describes how she became interested in Old English. She says that she "accidentally encountered" a copy of the specimen pages William Elstob had printed of his proposed Orosius edition.[11] Responding perhaps to his sister's frustrations at being linguistically confined to the polite boundaries of English and French, he responded positively to her requests to learn more about the language by teaching her and encouraging her studies. But this may have occurred just as easily in London as at Oxford. Had she begun her studies as early as 1699, it is a little difficult to explain why ten years elapsed before any of her work came into print, whereas the preface to the *Homily* and her subsequent work patterns suggest a much tighter time frame. From the elementary grammar she moved to a study of the familiar texts in Thwaites's edition of the *Heptateuch* and then to copying passages from manuscripts, among them the version of the Athanasian Creed in the Cambridge Psalter. This last work in particular won the approval of the now rehabilitated Hickes, who arranged its inclusion in the abridgement (*Conspectus Brevis* [Short overview] [London, 1708]) of the *Thesaurus* prepared by William Wotton (1666–1727), but under Hickes's supervision and with some new material added.[12] Her first Old English publication appeared in the same year as her first solo authored piece, published anonymously. As part of her training in French, her aunt must have set her the task of translating works of a suitably edifying nature, such as texts on topics such as glory, including a text by Madeleine de Scudéry (1607–1701).[13] Elizabeth Elstob was subsequently to publish anonymously a translation of this work in 1708: a slight work of only sixteen pages of text virtually overwhelmed by the two dedications that take up almost as much space.[14] The first dedication is to Matilda Elstob ("Mrs. Elstob, at Canterbury"), and it praises her for encouraging and nourishing Elizabeth Elstob's intellectual ambitions. There is here no hint of any obstacles that her uncle, Charles Elstob, might have placed in her way. The second dedication is to a woman friend from Canterbury, Mary Randolph, who was her companion in study. Here she reveals how the two of them translated sections of Cicero on glory (presumably extracts from works such as his "First Philippic against Marcus Antonius" and arguably not from the Latin). This work of Elizabeth Elstob does not seem to have attracted much attention (the printer and bookseller specialized in plays and works for a genteel audience and were the publishers of *The Tatler*), but it does suggest that she was ambitious and eager to see her work in print and that she must have received encouragement to do so from various quarters, as this was a work far from her current interests. The work that had actually been the focus of her attention was to see the light of day the following year, her edition of Ælfric's *Homily on the Nativity of St. Gregory*.

Through her brother Elizabeth Elstob had become acquainted with the Oxford Saxonists. Although some of these introductions may have occurred during earlier visits to Oxford, the contacts seem to have increased after she settled in London, where the Elstob house became something of a gathering place for those interested in Saxon studies. William Elstob was also one of the founding members of a group that began to meet monthly in 1707 and that evolved into the Antiquarian Society, receiving its charter in 1717. The Elstobs clearly moved in genteel circles, and Elizabeth Elstob's circle of acquaintances must have been considerable. Among them was the celebrated Mary Astell (1666–1739), like Elizabeth Elstob a native of Newcastle, a tireless supporter of women's rights and women's education, and one whose publications and activities had provoked a reaction disproportionate to her actual proposals.[15] There is evidence that Elizabeth Elstob was acquainted with Mary Astell's circle. In 1709 the *Tatler* published two attacks on Mary Astell, to whom it referred as "Madonella." The second of these, almost certainly written by Richard Steele, is dated 3 September (no. 63). The opening remarks from White's Chocolate-House (a section reserved for accounts of "*Gallantry, Pleasure,* and *Entertainment*") begin sympathetically enough with a discussion of how late-Roman glory diminished itself.[16] Subsequently follows a letter from "Tobiah Greenhat" mocking "Madonella"'s plans to educate women in Greek, Latin, and Hebrew, instead of in "Scissors, Needles, and Samplers," clearly a reference to Mary Astell's Chelsea Charity School, which finally opened in June 1709.[17] Among the professors of the institution "is to be a certain Lady, who is newly publishing two of the choicest *Saxon* Novels, which are said to have been in great Repute with the Ladies of Queen *Emma*'s court."[18] Almost certainly this is a reference to Elizabeth Elstob and the "two *Saxon* novels" are her two publications: the *Essay upon Glory* from the previous year and the *Homily*, which was in the process of appearing.[19]

These first years in London must have been a period of intense intellectual activity for Elizabeth Elstob as she tried to make up for the time lost under the genteel restrictions of her uncle's household. Under William Elstob's tutelage she increased her fluency in Latin and was introduced to Greek, for he was well versed in both. And she studied Old English assiduously. William Elstob was still working on his Orosius edition and preparing a project for a new edition of the Old English legal codes. He continued to publish in Old English, producing a separately paginated appendix, "A Publick Office of Daily and Nightly Devotion," for Hickes's *Several Letters which Passed between Dr. Hickes and a Popish Priest* (London, 1705; redone with a newly edited text for the second edition of 1715). This was apparently taken from MS Junius 121. Elizabeth Elstob, too, had access to the manuscript; while she uses Abraham Wheloc's edition of Bede's *Ecclesiastical History* (Cambridge, 1643) for the base text of the Old English versions of the Pater Noster and Creeds in the *Homily*, she footnotes variants from a Junius manuscript (*Homily*, xxxii–xxxv).[20]

Ælfric's homily on Saint Gregory, the ninth sermon in his second series of *Catholic Homilies* according to the numbering in Godden's edition, is an original work composed during the last decade of the tenth century. The most recent editors use as their base text the almost contemporaneous Cambridge University Library MS Gg.3.28.[21] Elizabeth Elstob believed that she was basing her edition on a transcript of Cotton MS, Vitellius D.17 (subsequently damaged in the Cottonian Library fire of 1731). However, Malcolm Godden's collation of all the manuscripts has revealed that she was using a transcript of Bodleian MS, Hatton 114, itself so defective that Elizabeth Elstob quotes textual "variants" from the Hatton manuscript in her footnotes.[22]

Elizabeth Elstob's edition of the *Homily* is a complex volume. She lavished considerable expense on the edition and was determined that it should be "as beautiful as possible."[23] The printer, Bowyer, generally published a better class of books than did her previous one; in the same year that the *Homily* appeared, Bowyer also published the first volume of Alexander Pope's translation of the *Iliad*. In addition to various relatively standard ornaments and engraved initials throughout the volume, Elizabeth Elstob was able to engage the well-known engraver Simon Gribelin (1661–1733) to do the frontispiece, the quarter-page engravings on the title page and heading of each separately paginated section of the book, the dedication, the text of the homily, William Elstob's Latin translation, and the appendix (all signed or initialed, except the last).[24] Gribelin also executed the elaborate pictorial initials introducing the dedication, the text of the homily (two), the Latin translation, and the appendix (although only the last two bear his initials).

The *Homily* begins with an eight-page dedication to Queen Anne, headed by a quarter-page engraving of a medallion seemingly struck for the completion of Saint Paul's Cathedral in 1709 (old style) and bearing the queen's profile on one side and the cathedral on the other. It is not clear if this plate was engraved expressly for the *Homily* or for some other publication during this period of celebration, but it is certainly appropriate where it is placed, linking the dedication to the queen and the theme of church and state that is prominent throughout. The preface is next, occupying sixty pages and followed by the forty-five pages of the homily itself—with Old English text, translation, and notes (many of them extensive). William Elstob contributed an eleven-page translation of the homily into Latin prefaced by a two-page dedication to "his most dear sister." The volume concludes with an appendix containing ten letters by Saint Gregory, all except the first translated into English, and then, on pages 23–49, additional discursive notes to the homily.

Elizabeth Elstob's edition has a double agenda: to promote women's rights to education and the fruits of scholarship and to engage in polemics over the Church of England's roots in the perceived "purity" of the doctrine and governance of the Anglo-Saxon Church.[25] It was coincidently appropriate for her purposes that England was ruled by a queen. The dedication to Anne opens with an initial *I* in which there are five female figures. On the left is (surprisingly) the Virgin Mary, recognizable by her pose and her nimbus. Looking at her is Saint Helena, identified by the cross she is carrying. On the right-hand side is a crowned figure facing the viewer, who by costume and crown is clearly Elizabeth I. To her right gazing left is a figure carrying the scepter and orb, who is clearly Queen Anne. The third figure, who is gazing at Anne, wears modern dress but with no distinguishing symbols about her person and is thus not so easy to identify. In terms of the women mentioned in the preface and in terms of relative dating of the figures moving from left to right, this could be a depiction of Bertha, the wife of Æthelbert, king of Kent, but one can also make a case for it being a representation of Elizabeth Elstob herself.[26]

In her dedication in the *Homily,* Elizabeth Elstob positions Old English as the language of the queen's forbears and the tongue in which they "received that Orthodox Faith, of which You are the undoubted Defender" (A2ᵛ). The spiritual genealogy that she then posits is a female one, stretching back to Saint Helena and Bertha. Helena, too, has an English connection of which Elizabeth Elstob may have been aware, although she does not mention it, for according to Geoffrey of Monmouth, Helena is the daughter of King Coel.[27] In Elizabeth Elstob's narrative it is women who promote the faith: Helena, Bertha, and Queen Elizabeth. Anne, too, is encouraged to stand firm in protecting faith from corruption. In the dedication, therefore, politics and religion are clearly linked together, and there is much more of the same in the rest of the volume.

The preface almost immediately takes up the question, "What has a Woman to do with Learning" (ii). To this is given a most spirited response, with references to other women scholars such as Anna Maria van Schurmann (1607–78). And by learning Elstob means study and scholarship, not the polite learning of the drawing room. She follows this with her own account—mentioned earlier in this discussion—of how she became interested in Old English. She refers warmly to Hickes without naming him (vii) in appreciation for his help in getting her transcript of the creed published and in encouraging her "that by publishing somewhat in *Saxon,* I wou'd invite the Ladies to be acquainted with the Language of their Predecessors" (vii).[28] With this goal in mind, she published the *Homily,* and she notes a number of patristic writers who have encouraged learning in women. In turning to her presentation of the homily, she regards her translation as literal, more a guide to understanding the Old English than one to elegant modern English. She is aware that not everyone will be pleased with her notes "and that things will either please or displease, according to the different Humour and Relish of the Several Readers" (ix). In her praise of Gregory, who purchased Anglian slaves and then set them up in the monasteries he had established, she turns to a matter that was becoming a very real concern in some quarters: "A Zeal [converting slaves "for the future Service of their Country"] fit to be consider'd and imitated by those who are concern' in the Plantations, who have doubtless a Power of turning many souls to God, and of rescuing them from that Slavery, under which they are held by the Prince of Darkness; to which I wish the remembrance of our own Conversion to Christianity, may prove an early incitement" (xii–xiii). These are some of the first stirrings of the antislavery movement, which would gain momentum as the century progressed and be bitterly opposed by the planters and their powerful lobby.[29]

For Elizabeth Elstob, Gregory is not just the pope who sent a mission to the English, important though that is for her. She considers him a church leader without imperial ambitions and a guardian of the virtues of the primitive church by virtue of what she posits as his own austere and humble lifestyle: "It is true, we received the Christian Faith from the *Roman* Church, but when that Church was a sound and uncorrupt Branch of the Catholick Church" (xiii). It was this "Primitive Purity" that was "revived and restored by the Reformation" (xiii). She argues that Augustine and Gregory should be regarded as the instigators of Christianity in England, even though it existed there much earlier, before the mission arrived, and she gives the letter of Gregory to Augustine found in Bede, which she sees as guaranteeing the "Liberties" of the English church from Rome.[30] She discusses the issues that were at the center of the controversy at the Synod of Whitby (A.D. 664) and disposes of those who would argue that Augustine was involved in the slaughter of the monks of Bangor.[31] As an example of the faith and prayers of the Anglo-Saxon Church, she gives the Old English versions of the Pater Noster and the Athanasian and Nicene Creeds taken from Wheloc's edition of Bede with her own translations (xxxii–xxxv). She presents extracts from the Laws of Canute on the Lord's Prayer and the Creeds (xxxv–xxxvii) and from selections from the homilies of Ælfric and elsewhere to deny the claims of papal supremacy (xxxvii–xlv), to oppose the devotion to saints and images (xlv–xlix), and to deny transubstantiation (xlix–li).[32] She then offers a consideration of the Roman Catholicism of her own time (liv–lv). Only then can she turn to the text itself.

Her text is based on a copy of the homily made by a close friend of Hickes, William Hopkins (1647–1700), who presumably gave it to her. She believed it to be a copy of Cotton MS, Vitellius D.17, and she checked it against the Hatton manuscript in the Bodleian, to which she was granted access by John Hudson (1662–1719), the Bodleian librarian since 1701, a man who usually zealously guarded his treasures and to whom Elizabeth Elstob is very genuine in her expression of thanks (lvii). She concludes by affirming that the work is her own, at the same time acknowledging the support and assistance of her brother. She then expresses thanks; in particular, she says,

"I am very glad to find so many of the Ladies, and those, several of them of the best Rank: favouring these Endeavours of a Beginner, and one of their Sex" (lviii).[33] She links the accomplishments of women to their role in the Conversion, such as that of Bertha; her daughter Edelburga (Æthelburgh), wife of Edwin, king of Northumbria; and various Frankish and Lombard women who contributed "to the advancement of Religion in their several Ages." She concludes again with the example of Elizabeth I (lix–lx).

The text of the homily is prefaced by a quarter-page plate depicting the scene from Bede where Gregory and a companion encounter the Anglian slaves and their master.[34] Both the Old English and the English translation have ornamented initials, the Old English a portrait of Gregory modeled on either Hickes or Thwaites, and the English with a portrait of Elizabeth Elstob herself.[35] The homily occupies forty pages, but most of them are taken up with often extensive notes (there is only one page of text without a footnote) in which Elizabeth Elstob demonstrates her command of Greek, Latin, Old English, and French. The notes continue to reinforce her interpretation of the contentious issues she raised in the preface, such as a note demonstrating that *Papa* (Pope) does not mean "Universal Bishop" (3). There are a series of footnotes on pages 13–17 on Deira, the part of the kingdom of Northumbria ruled by king Ælla and the homeland of the slave boys who had attracted Gregory's attention and compassion. This region Elizabeth Elstob claims as her own, and these notes now explain the illustration on the title page: a man in Roman armor identified as "Ælla" and the place as "Deira," flanked by two towns, one identified as "Ellanstowe" and the other as "Foxesdæn." The notes explain that towns in the region beginning with "El-" can be traced back to Ælla, including "Ellanstowe," which, by sleight of hand rather than sound linguistic principles, she makes into "Elstobbe" (16). The inclusion on the title page and in the notes of the towns of Elstob and the nearby town of Foxton, the site of the Elstob patrimony, both southwest of Sedgefield in County Durham, is an example of the intertwining of the personal and the professional, the private and the public, that is one of the defining characteristics of Elizabeth Elstob's Old English work.

William Elstob's Latin translation of the homily follows, and the volume concludes with an appendix of Gregory's letters and the supplemental notes, which include passages from the Old English calendar poem the "Menologium." As might be expected, while Elizabeth Elstob's translations of Old English prose are competent, her translation of the poetry leaves much to be desired.[36] Sometimes her turn of phrase is startling to modern sensibilities, as, for example, her translation of "Bryten ricu" (*Menologium*, line 230) as "*British* Empire" (28).[37] The bulk of these notes involves discussion of matters affecting the calendar and feast days, with an antiquarian excursus on the word "Yule." The notes close with a fragment of a homily by Ælfric and other text dealing with matters surrounding the mission, all commented on at length and ending with Gregory's epitaph as recorded by Bede (2.1) in Latin and Old and modern English.

It was the preface in particular that annoyed Thomas Hearne (1678–1735), as he noted in his diary for 20 October 1709.[38] In principle he should have been sympathetic to Elizabeth Elstob's political position, but he seems to have had a conservative position on behavior appropriate for a woman that did not extend to approving of their involvement in issues of politics and religion. To him the volume is a "Ferrago of Vanities."[39] He also claims that the work is not hers but that of William Elstob.[40]

With her edition of the *Homily* completed, what was Elizabeth Elstob to do next? On 10 October 1709 she wrote to Ralph Thoresby, "Having nothing else to do, I have some thought of publishing a set of Saxon homilies."[41] This is the first hint of her ambitious plan to prepare an edition and translation of Ælfric's complete *Catholic Homilies,* a project that was to occupy her for nearly ten years.

During the period 1710–15 the Elstobs were busy on their various projects. William Elstob was working on a new edition of the Old English law codes, and Elizabeth Elstob on her edition of the *Homilies.* She was able to finish a version of the Old English text of the first series in fair copy with some translations ready by February 1711 (old style); her transcription of the second series was complete by November 1712.[42] Sometime in 1712 Bowyer printed a "Set of Proposals and a Specimen of the Projected Edition," although no copy appears to have survived. Hickes was also doing his best to get Charette and the Oxford Press interested in publishing the work. The problem was to get a sufficient number of subscribers to underwrite the cost; since this work was a more substantial project than the *Homily,* the subscription price of thirty shillings made this a more daunting prospect. In 1713 Elizabeth Elstob published a pamphlet in the form of a letter to her uncle, Charles Elstob, in which she records her gratitude to him for his support and defends the right of a woman to undertake such a task.[43] But finances were the problem, and through her connections Elizabeth Elstob sought financial help from the queen. The queen granted assistance in 1714, but it came to naught because she died in August of that year, before the grant could be executed. Her death meant that the prospects of those who favored the Stuart cause took a turn for the worse.

In terms of publication 1715 was a busy year for Elizabeth Elstob. The University Press at Oxford published a prospectus for her edition of the *Homilies,* in which it stated that the book would be ready by autumn.[44] The press must have begun to prepare for this goal in earnest, because a set of proofs exist for Ælfric's prefaces and first five homilies in Old English with translations. In May 1715 her *Rudiments of Grammar* appeared, printed by Bowyer, who had a new Old English font cut especially for the edition. While not as elaborately produced as the *Homily,* the volume is not without its touches.[45] Elizabeth Elstob had intended to dedicate the volume to Sophia (1630–1714), electress and dowager duchess of Hanover, the granddaughter of James I, and a learned woman in her own right, but unfortunately she had died in July 1714 before the book was ready for distribution. The dedication is therefore made to Wilhelmina Carolina of Brandenburg-Ansbach (1683–1737), the wife of the Prince of Wales, the future George II. The quarter-page plate portrays a giant medallion depicting the princess in profile and is flanked by two seated women, the one on the left reading, and the one on the right wearing a casque, having put her book to one side.[46] The dedication begins with an elaborate initial *T* depicting a large warship coming into port and apparently having nothing to do with the dedication or the main body of the text—this time there was no extra money to commission new engravings. Elizabeth Elstob makes the most of the connection between her Saxon studies and the origins of the princess's family in Saxony and somewhat optimistically hopes that she will be "diverted" by the "*German, Francick,* and *Gothick* Words" with which she has enlivened her grammatical discourse (A3ᵛ). But as a whole the dedication is perfunctory, revisiting briefly themes expressed much more effectively in the dedication to Queen Anne in the *Homily.*

The preface to the *Grammar* is in the form of a letter to Hickes and is a spirited defense of Saxon studies against its detractors, in this case principally Jonathan Swift and Charles Gildon (1665–1724). It opens with the account of a visit Elizabeth Elstob made to Canterbury soon after the publication of the *Homily.* During this visit she encountered "a young Lady, whose Ingenuity and Love of Learning, is well known and esteem'd, not only in that Place but by your self" (ii). This young woman wanted to learn Old English and to become Elizabeth Elstob's student, which started her thinking about preparing a grammar of the language. In one of the surviving copies of the *Rudiments of Grammar,* in an eighteenth-century hand, maybe even that of Elizabeth Elstob herself, the young woman in question is identified in the margin as "Miss Stanhope, filia Decani Stanhope," that is, Mary Stanhope, daughter of George Stanhope (1660–1728), dean of Canterbury.[47] In 1712 Mary Stanhope had married the eldest son of Gilbert Burnet (1643–1715), bishop of Salisbury, William (1688–1729), the future governor of New York and later of Massachusetts and New Hampshire.[48] As a result, nothing came of Mary Stanhope's desire to learn Old English, yet the idea of a grammar of Old English had remained.

Elizabeth Elstob bases her grammar on that of Hickes in the *Thesaurus* and the abridgment of it made by Thwaites.[49] But she also consulted the Latin–Old English grammar of Ælfric printed by William Somner at the end of his dictionary.[50] From Ælfric she borrowed in particular his grammatical terms, in order "to shew the *polite* Men of our Age, that the Language of their Forefathers is neither so barren nor barbarous as they affirm, with equal Ignorance and Boldneß" (iii). Elizabeth Elstob is at the top of her form in the preface, witty, erudite, and merciless in her scorn for the half-baked arguments of her opponents. In attacking the preface to the *Grammar* of Charles Gildon and John Brightland (d. 1717) for slighting the work of Hickes,[51] Elizabeth Elstob demonstrates that her commitment to Saxon studies (let alone her loyalty to her most important mentor and supporter) far outweighs her commitment to the education of women, for she should have been allied with Gildon and Brightland as they state in the preface to the first edition of their *Grammar:* "What we propos'd to our selves first, was to make our selves perfect Masters of what he [Brightland] design'd, which we found was to have a *Grammar* of our own Mother Tongue, by which Children and Women, and others, who were ignorant of those call'd the

Learned Tongues, might learn to Read and Write *English* with as great Justness and Exactness as the Learned may be suppos'd to do" (A5ʳ). But they were insisting on a synchronic approach to the learning of grammar, and in this they were far in advance of their time and eventually no more successful in pushing through their agenda than Elizabeth Elstob was to be with her insistence on the necessity of a diachronic approach to language understanding.[52] Also, even though Gildon and Brightland's work had appeared anonymously, Elizabeth Elstob may have been well aware of Gildon's role in its preparation and furthermore, had in mind the statement that a character had made in another work long attributed to him: "Sir, I tell you we are abus'd: I hate these Petticoat-Authors: 'tis false Grammar, there is no Feminine for the *Latin* Word, 'tis entirely of the Masculine Gender, and the Language won't bear such a thing as a She-Author."[53] In this preface Elizabeth Elstob does not need to defend women's learning; her every paragraph is sufficient demonstration of her erudition and her confidence in expressing it.[54]

The "English-Saxon Grammar" is prefaced by the same half-page plate that had adorned the first page of the *Homily*, although in this context the appearance of Saint Gregory and the Anglian slaves is a little incongruous. But the capital *G* with her portrait is an appropriate piece of ornamentation. The grammar itself follows closely the arrangement of the parts of speech and their analysis that was found in Hickes, but she has appropriated additional passages from Ælfric.[55] Since she is committed to using Ælfric's grammatical terminology, she runs into a problem in her discussion of the moods, because the grammatical theory to which she was heir had identified a mood, the "potential," that was unknown to Ælfric. Rather than make a fuss about it, she quietly invents a word, *mægenlic,* to make up the deficiency (31). In general, the grammar is clear and well laid out. Its chief drawback is in the handling of the verbs, but that is not her fault; in her time the verbal system of the Germanic languages was still inadequately understood, and the practice of assuming that it followed the same conjugational structure as did Latin was a severe handicap obscuring more than it illuminated. Despite this flaw, one can grasp the principles of Old English grammar from her work. The attractiveness and elegance of the work as well as the fact that it was written by a woman continue to draw attention to it.[56] It is ironical that her *Grammar* was eventually ignored, and other works cluttered with all sorts of extraneous material came to be the norm for more than a century until the *Grammar* of Rasmus Rask made all that preceded it obsolete.[57]

If 1715 had been a good year for Elizabeth Elstob in that it saw the publication of her *Grammar* and the prospectus for her edition of the *Homilies,* it was a disaster in every other respect. In March 1715 William Elstob died intestate, and the administration both of his estate and his debts (added to her own considerable liabilities connected with the publication of the homilies) became her responsibility. Her situation became increasingly desperate over the next several years, and one must wonder how she was able to hold out as long as she did. During the time of a Tory ascendancy under Queen Anne, she had mixed politics and scholarship to her advantage. Under

George I the Whigs for the first time had a monopoly on the ministries of government, and once they were firmly in control, doors began to close to supporters of the party previously in power. Whereas it had been fashionable to be seen as a subscriber to the *Homily,* now it was equally fashionable to have nothing to do with Elizabeth Elstob's current project. The rebellion raised by the Earl of Mar in September 1715 against the Hanoverian succession made those in the south who were known to have Stuart or nonjuror sympathies guilty by association. It is significant that during this time there is no indication of any support from the Elstobs of Foxton or from the Elstobs of Tillington. Even though Elizabeth Elstob had an audience with the Princess of Wales in June 1715, nothing in the way of support came from it. And then in December died her staunchest and best-connected supporter, George Hickes. Worse, it is clear that not only did subscriptions to the *Homilies* continue to be well below expectations, but the monies already collected had been spent and the production work stalled. Now that William Elstob was dead, his sister was faced with the harsh economic realities of having to make a living, something for which her education had not prepared her. According to tradition the only person to offer her financial support was George Smallridge (d. 1719), bishop of Bristol.

In 1718 she made one last desperate attempt to salvage matters. She appears to have moved to Chelsea around 1716, and sometime early in 1718 she opened a school for young ladies. However, the venture was undercapitalized, and within six months it collapsed.[58] Whereupon, Elizabeth Elstob vanished.

In 1735 the antiquarian George Ballard discovered her living in the Worcestershire market town of Evesham, where she was in charge of a small private school under the name of Frances Smith.[59] While some of her closest friends, such as Humphrey Wanley, may have known of her whereabouts before this time, it was Ballard who "found her out" and eventually set in motion the efforts that were to bring some comfort to her final years. From her he was able to obtain hints as to what had happened during the intervening years. She wrote for him a brief biography (see note 4) in 1738, and in 1748 in response to Ballard's enquiry about her brother's manuscripts, she stated, "I entrusted my manuscripts and books with several other things in the hands of a person, with whom I believed they wou'd be very safe, but to my great surprize and grief I heard soon after she was gone to the West Indies to a daughter that was settled there."[60] She was not aware that her papers (and presumably her books and other possessions) were probably sent to Charles Elstob—to be sold upon his death in 1721. This suggests a serious estrangement from her family, for she never indicated that she was aware of—or cared to know of—her uncle's death or the death of Matilda Elstob in 1739. While it seems she was pleased to have the opportunity to correspond with Ballard, she still insisted that her whereabouts be kept secret. She had found a way to survive, exhausting though her teaching duties were, and had a measure of respect from the local townspeople. She was never again to tackle any Saxon project, rejecting such an offer that Ballard made in his first letter. That Elizabeth Elstob, that intellectual endeavor, were irrevocably buried in the past. Ballard visited her for the first time in October 1735. In the following months her situation came to the attention of numerous friends and admirers, and eventually a small subscription was collected on her behalf. In 1738 Ballard was able to inform her that he had tracked down a considerable quantity of her papers, although he did not give her a list until more than a year later. During the winter of 1738–39 she was so ill that she was unable to teach, but her friends were still working behind the scenes on her behalf. William Bentinck (1709–62), second duke of Portland, and his wife, Lady Margaret Cavendish Harley (1715–85), were looking for a governess, having just celebrated the birth of their third child, William Cavendish Bentinck (1738–1809), the future third duke and Whig prime minister. Elizabeth Elstob was offered the post in 1738 and assumed her duties in November 1739, a position she held until her death seventeen years later. Although her final years were made difficult by repeated illnesses, she devoted all her energies to her responsibilities in the household and kept up a considerable correspondence, especially with Ballard.[61] An object of curiosity to some, she kept her own counsel and died on 30 May 1756. If mourned by no one else, her passing was surely an occasion of sorrow to the children she had raised into young adulthood.

Elizabeth Elstob's life and career demonstrated two important matters. The first was that women could be just as accomplished scholars as men, that gender was no essential impediment to intellectual achievement. The second was that in Elizabeth Elstob's times and for many, many years to follow, unless a woman was of independent means (which usually meant she had no interest in scholarship), there were no opportunities for her in the scholarly world without the support and forbearance of male patrons and supporters. Elizabeth Elstob was well connected with the Oxford Saxonists, but she could never really be one of them. She could never be a member of a college, and despite her flair for theological argument she could never receive the calling to the cloth that supported the scholarly endeavors of her brother (and her own, as it turns out). There was no place for a woman in the world of politics, and while it might be possible for a woman to earn a living as a writer, this was not the same as being a scholar. Looking back over her dedications and prefaces, one gets the sense that she was not fully cognizant of just how anomalous (and fragile) her situation was. She was intoxicated with learning and vigorously pursued her version of the truth. And when the consequences of her position caught up with her, she could not go underground like Hickes and win eventual reinstatement to favor without any break in scholarly activity. She had to vanish. But when her reinstatement came and she returned to the light of public scrutiny, there was to be no more world of scholarship for her, only the faded genteel role of a governess. This role was an insult perhaps to her intellect, but it was seen as socially appropriate, for it was only then, when she had been thoroughly subdued and domesticated, that her "friends" rallied to her aid.

Notes

1. E. Elstob, *Rudiments of Grammar for the English-Saxon Tongue*, subsequently cited as *Grammar*. Page references are given parenthetically in the text.

2. E. Elstob, *English-Saxon Homily on the Birth-Day of St. Gregory*, subsequently cited as *Homily*. Page references are given parenthetically in the text.

3. Thorpe, *Homilies of the Anglo-Saxon Church*.

4. Unfortunately, the best biography of Elizabeth Elstob, Sarah Huff Collins's "Elizabeth Elstob: A Biography," remains unpublished. I am heavily indebted to her research and note only direct quotations in order to save space. See also Ashdown, "Elizabeth Elstob, the Learned Saxonist"; Beauchamp, "Pioneer Linguist"; Ferguson, "Elizabeth Elstob," 239–46; Green, "Elizabeth Elstob," 137–60; Reynolds, *Learned Lady in England,* 169–85; Shaw, "Anglo-Saxon Attitudes of the 'Ingenious and Learned Mrs. Elstob,'" 327–49; Sutherland, "Elizabeth Elstob," 59–73; and Wallas, *Before the Bluestockings,* 133–89. Elizabeth Elstob wrote a brief biographical sketch in 1738 at the behest of the antiquarian George Ballard (1706–55). It can be found in a not completely reliable transcript in Reynolds, *Learned Lady,* 170–71.

5. The totals are taken from the edition I consulted in the library of Western Michigan University. It has three names "Omitted by Mistake" added to the list of subscribers at the end of the volume, for a total of 268. Yumi Hanashima reports that in some copies an extra leaf had been added to the subscriber list, which itself exists in a number of states. Her final count of subscribers is 281, although the number of Newcastle subscribers remains the same. See Hanashima, "Encouragers Sought and Gain'd for Elstob's *English-Saxon Homily* (1709)," 93.

6. Reynolds, *Learned Lady,* 170.

7. Hickes, *Instutiones Grammaticæ Anglo-Saxonicæ*. On Hickes, see the biographical introduction to Harris, *Chorus of Grammars,* 3–125.

8. Runólfur Jónsson, *Recentissima Antiqvissimæ Linguæ Septentrionalis incunabula*.

9. Gibson, *Chronicon Saxonicum*; Thwaites, ed., *Heptateuchus*; Rawlinson, *An. Manl. Sever. Boethi Consolationis Philosophiæ Libri V. Anglo-Saxonice Redditi ab Alfredo;* Hickes, *Linguarum Vett. Septentrionalium Thesaurus Grammatico-Criticus et Archæologicus*.

10. W. Elstob, *Hormesta Pauli Orosii Quam Olim Patrio Sermone Donavit Ælfredus Magnus*.

11. Elizabeth Elstob's exact words are "[h]aving accidentally met with a Specimen of K. *Alfred's Version* of *Orosius* into *Saxon*, design'd to be publish'd by a near Relation and Friend" (*Homily*, vi). I take "specimen" to refer to a copy of the three leaves William Elstob had had printed, which, including a title page with his name on it, seems a more likely candidate to have aroused her curiosity than his working papers.

12. E. Elstob, "Transcript of the Old English Athanasian Creed from the Salisbury Psalter," 77–84.

13. Scudéry, *Discovrs de la Gloire*.

14. [E. Elstob], *Essay upon Glory*.

15. Wallas, *Before the Bluestockings,* 111–30; Reynolds, *Learned Lady,* 297–311. On the links between Elizabeth Elstob and Mary Astell, see Perry, *Celebrated Mary Astell,* 25, 109–11, 269, 366.

16. [Addison and Steele], *Tatler,* 1:16.

17. Addison and Steele, *Tatler,* 1:439. The first attack on "Madonella" is found in no. 32, 23 June 1709 (1:238–41). The school received extensive financial support from Lady Elizabeth Hastings (1682–1739), the daughter of Theophilus Hastings (1650–1701), the seventh earl of Huntingdon, (Reynolds, *Learned Lady,* 120–24), and Lady Katherine Jones (1672–1739), second daughter (twin), of Richard Jones (1641–1712), earl of Ranelagh. Both women subscribed to the *Homily,* and although Mary Astell did not subscribe, she received a copy from Lady Elizabeth Hastings, 18 February 1709 (old style) (Hanashima, "Encouragers," 96).

18. Addison and Steele, *Tatler*, 1:440. "Emma" is unidentified but might possibly be a substitute for "Anna." The "Ladies of the Court" might then be women like Elizabeth Hastings and Katherine Jones.

19. The exact publication date of the *Homily* is not known, but the variant forms of the subscription list suggest that binding and distribution might have been somewhat leisurely by modern standards. The first copies may have already appeared in September; the volume's appearance was certainly announced by then. Thomas Hearne in Oxford received his copy, 20 October 1709 (see note 41), and Elizabeth Elstob's aunt, Matilda, dated her copy 12 November 1709 (Hanashima, "Encouragers," 105), while Elizabeth Elstob's friend, Ralph Thoresby (1658–1725), the Leeds topographer, did not receive his until 3 January 1709 (old style) (Hanashima, "Encouragers," 91). All three are on the original subscription list.

20. Wheloc (1593–1653), *Venerabilis Bedæ Historia Ecclesiastica*. Each volume has a slightly different title page because each contains more than Bede's work. That for volume 1 reads: *Historiæ Ecclesiasticæ Gentis Anglorum Libri V. A Venerabili Beda Presbytero scripti,... Ab Augustissimo veterum Anglo-Saxonum Rege Aluredo (sive Alfredo) examinati, ejúsque paraphrasi Saxonicâ eleganter explicati... Vnà cum annationibus & analectis è publicis Veteris Ecclesiæ Anglicanæ Homiliis,... hinc indè excerptis,... Quibus in calce operis Saxonicam Chronologiam,... contexuimus*; and for volume 2: *Historiæ Ecclesiasticæ Gentis Anglorum Libri V.... Quibus accesserunt Anglo-Saxonicæ Leges: Et ultimò, Leges Henrici I. nunc primùm editæ*.

21. *Ælfric's "Catholic Homilies": The First Series*; *Ælfric's "Catholic Homilies": The Second Series*; Godden and Clemoes, *Ælfric's "Catholic Homilies."*

22. Godden, "Old English," 21, 32.

23. Elizabeth Elstob, letter to Ralph Thoresby, 22 March 1708 (old style), in Thoresby, *Letters of Eminent Men*, 2:148, cited from Collins, "Elizabeth Elstob," 107. See also Hanashima, "Encouragers," 91.

24. This plate shows Jesus surrounded by the apostles. Under the engraving stands "Qui Præest Sit Perinde ac qui Ministrat. Luc 22" [Who is in control, let be accordingly, but who serves? Luke 22]. This refers to but does not quote Luke 22:27. I suspect this plate was originally cut for another of William Bowyer's publications and used here because of its appropriateness.

25. On the politics of Saxon studies, see Frantzen, *Desire for Origins*, 45–54.

26. See Sutherland, "Editing for a New Century," 231. For this construal to work, the figure with the nimbus must be Helena, and the one with the cross, the missionary queen, Bertha. However, the iconography of the figures seems not to permit such an interpretation. Gribelin, on the other hand, was French and presumably a Catholic. He may have inserted the figure of the Virgin into this work with its pronounced anti-Catholic bias as a protest, whatever his original instructions for the piece may have been.

27. "[I]nsigniat se constantius regni diademante. duxitque filiam coel. cui nomen erat helena" [Constantius crowned himself with the insignia of the kingdom and married the daughter of Coel whose name was Helena]. Other manuscripts add the comment that there was not anywhere a woman who was reputed to be more learned on musical instruments or in the liberal arts than this Helena (Geoffrey of Monmouth, *Historia Regnum Britannia of Geoffrey of Monmouth*, bk. 5, sec. 6, 338).

28. Hickes was an enthusiastic supporter of women's education, and he had published a combined translation of Mothe-Fénelon (1651–1715), *Education des Filles*, and Chétardie (d. 1703), *Instruction pour une jeune princesse*, as *Instructions for the Education of a Daughter: to which is added*,

A small Tract of Instructions for the conduct of young ladies of the Highest Rank, with Suitable Devotions Annexed. Elizabeth Elstob uses a quote from this work on the title page of the *Essay upon Glory*.

29. On women and the antislavery movement, see Ferguson, *Subject to Others;* and Midgley, *Women against Slavery*. What is of interest here is that Elizabeth Elstob was not a Quaker, as were most of the women in the early antislavery movement (Ferguson, *Subject to Others,* 73–76).

30. See the complete text of this letter in Latin with English translation in Bede, *Bede's Ecclesiastical History of the English People,* bk. 1, chap. 27, 78–103.

31. See Bede, *Ecclesiastical History,* bk. 2, chap. 2, 140–43.

32. On the use of Ælfric in this controversy, see Leinbaugh, "Ælfric's *Sermo de Sacrificio in Die Pascae*," 51–68.

33. Hanashima counts 159 men and 122 women among the subscribers for a ratio of 4:3 ("Encouragers," 96).

34. See Bede, *Ecclesiastical History,* bk. 2, chap. 1, 132–35.

35. For Hickes, see Collins, "Elizabeth Elstob," 111; for Thwaites, see Sutherland, "Editing for a New Century," 231 n. 32, quoting a source from 1778.

36. On the accuracy of Elizabeth Elstob's translations from Old English, see Mechthild Gretsch, "Elizabeth Elstob," 163–200, 494–502.

37. Although "geond Brytenricu / Sexna kynges" may mean no more than "throughout the spacious realm of the king of the Saxons."

38. It was Hearne who in the second decade of the eighteenth century became the leader of the Oxford Saxonists, although he himself had little facility in Old English. He was appointed assistant keeper of the Bodleian Library in 1701 following Humphrey Wanley and became second keeper in 1712, a position he held until he was dismissed in 1715 as a nonjuror.

39. Hearne, *Remains of Thomas Hearne,* 79. It may be a coincidence, but this phrase echoes the epitaph (frequently used by Addison) to the *Tatler,* no. 63, based on Juvenal, *Satire* 1.85–86: "Quicquid agunt Homines nostri Farrago Libelli [est]" [Whatever humanity does (is) the hodgepodge of our little book].

40. To judge by her comments in the preface (lvii–lviii), Elizabeth Elstob had to answer such a charge more than once. It is a common tactic of men attempting to denigrate the intellectual achievements of women to claim that the work is not theirs but that of some male relative or acquaintance. Examples can be cited from Aphra Behn (1640–89) (see Fraser, *Weaker Vessel,* 335) to the Kenyan writers Rebeka Njau (b. 1930) and Asenath Odaga (b. ca. 1950) (see James, *In Their Own Voices,* 107, 124).

41. Thoresby, *Letters of Eminent Men,* 2:198–99, cited from Collins, "Elizabeth Elstob," 102. See also Sutherland, "Editing for a New Century," 219 n. 18.

42. Collins, "Elizabeth Elstob," 138–42; and Collins, "Elstobs and the End of the Saxon Revival."

43. E. Elstob, *Some Testimonies of Learned Men in Favour of the Intended Edition of the Saxon Homilies, concerning the Learning of the Author of Those Homilies; and the Advantages to Be Hoped for from an Edition of Them. In a Letter from the Publishers to a Doctor in Divinity*. The "Doctor in Divinity" mentioned here is Elizabeth Elstob's uncle, Charles Elstob.

44. E. Elstob, *English Saxon Homilies of Ælfric, Arch-Bishop of Canterbury*.

45. On the *Rudiments of Grammar* and in particular for an explanation of the allusions in the preface and the intellectual climate in which the debate in it took place, see Hughes, "Mrs.

Elstob's Defense of Antiquarian Learning," 172–91; Morton, "Elizabeth Elstob's *Rudiments of Grammar* (1715)," 267–87.

46. Morton ("*Rudiments,*" 270) identifies the figure on the left as Saint Catherine of Alexandria, the patron of philosophers and librarians, and the figure on the right as either Britannia or Minerva.

47. Hanashima, "Encouragers," 88. Mary Stanhope was a subscriber to the *Homily*. Hanashima also credits Burnet with being a subscriber, but his name must be one of the late additions (see note 5).

48. "[A]n imprudent love-match with the beautiful and charming daughter of Dean Stanhope" as his younger brother Gilbert (1690–1726) put it. (T. E. S. Clarke et al., *Life of Gilbert Burnet, Bishop of Salisbury,* 455). Her husband, however, was "unable to efface the memory of a previous attachment; and she died of a broken heart within three years" (Clarke, *Life,* 455). This would place Mary Stanhope's death around the time the *Rudiments of Grammar* appeared in print.

49. Thwaites, *Grammatica Anglo-Saxonica ex Hickesiano Linguarum Septentrionalium Thesauro exerpta.*

50. Somner (1598–1669), *Dictionarivm Saxonico-Latino-Anglicum.* Ælfric's grammar, printed from an edition prepared by Francis Junius (1591–1677), appears on sigs. Xx3^r–Sss1^v.

51. [Gildon and Brightland], *Grammar of the English Tongue.* Actually she is attacking the form of their preface (itself based on an earlier work of Brightland's), that was first inserted into the second edition, second state, which also appeared in 1712. There the slight on Hickes was introduced on A4^{r-v}. For the printing complexities associated with this work, see Hughes, "Mrs. Elstob's Defense," 178–80.

52. On the failure of Gildon and Brightland to affect a "paradigm shift," see Hughes, "Salutary Lessons from the History of Linguistics," 306–22.

53. [Gildon], *Comparison between the Two Stages,* 26–27. Cf. Fraser, *Weaker Vessel,* 334. The modern consensus is that the work is not by Gildon.

54. Mechthild Gretsch tries to downplay the importance and relevance of Elizabeth Elstob's achievements to feminist history: "Elizabeth Elstob's most urgent preoccupation was not with the promotion of women's rights and female education, nor with the re-writing of history from a female point of view; her primary concern was with Anglo-Saxon studies" ("Elizabeth Elstob," 190). Strictly speaking, this may be so, but the very fact that Elizabeth Elstob, a woman, dared to undertake such an enterprise, to promote the scientific study of Old English grammar and to argue doctrine and politics in public, was itself an enormously transgressive act (and therefore revolutionary and feminist). In a sense her very failure to recognize the radical and threatening nature of her intellectual endeavors contributed to the desperate situation in which she found herself by the middle of 1718: "[T]he Language won't bear such a thing as a She-Author" (Gildon, *Comparison,* 27).

55. On the relationship of Elizabeth Elstob's grammar to those of Hickes and Ælfric, see Hughes, "Anglo-Saxon Grammars of George Hickes and Elizabeth Elstob," 119–47.

56. See, for example, Smol, "Pleasure, Progress, and the Profession."

57. Rask (1787–1832), *Angelsaksisk sproglære tilligemed en kort Læsebog.*

58. Perry, *Mary Astell,* 289, 525, 528.

59. Perry, *Mary Astell,* 325. What was she teaching? Collins suggests the curriculum included "grammar, reading composition and penmanship" ("Elizabeth Elstob," 201). At a groat (fourpence)

a week per pupil there was no place here for "*Greek, Latin,* and *Hebrew*" or even "English-Saxon" but certainly time for "Scissors, Needles, and Samplers" (see note 17).

60. Collins, "Elizabeth Elstob," 193.

61. A small selection of this correspondence to some of her female acquaintances and benefactors can be found in Robinson, "Eight Letters from Elizabeth Elstob," 241–52. Seven of these letters are from the period 1739–40 and the eighth is from 1753. In them there is no sign of the independent spirit that is such an engaging feature of her published writings.

Select Bibliography of Works by Elizabeth Elstob

An Essay upon Glory. Written Originally in French by the Celebrated Mademoiselle de Scudery. Done into English by a Person of the Same Sex. London: J. Morphew, 1708.

"Transcript of the Old English Athanasian Creed from the Salisbury Psalter." In *Linguarum Vett. Septentrionalium Thesauri Grammatico-Critici, & Archaeologici, Auctore Georgio Hickesio, Conspectus Brevis.... Cui, ab Antiquae Literaturae Septentrionalis Cultore Adjectae Aliquot Notae Accedunt,* ed. William Wotton with the assistance of George Hickes. 78–84. London: R. Sare, 1708.

An English-Saxon Homily on the Birth-Day of St. Gregory, Anciently Used in the English-Saxon Church. Giving an Account of the Conversion of the English from Paganism to Christianity. London: W. Bowyer, 1709.

Some Testimonies of Learned Men in Favour of the Intended Edition of the Saxon Homilies, Concerning the Learning of the Author of Those Homilies; and the Advantages to Be Hoped for from an Edition of Them. In a Letter from the Publisher to a Doctor in Divinity. London: W. Bowyer, 1713.

The English Saxon Homilies of Ælfric, Arch-Bishop of Canterbury ... Now First Printed and Translated. Oxford: At the Theatre, 1715.

The Rudiments of Grammar for the English-Saxon Tongue, First Given in English: With an Apology for the Study of Northern Antiquities. Being Very Useful towards the Understanding of Our Ancient English Poets, and Other Writers. London: W. Bowyer, 1715.

Works Cited

[Addison, Joseph, and Richard Steele]. *The Tatler.* Edited by Donald Frederick Bond. 3 vols. Oxford: Clarendon Press, 1987.

Ælfric's Catholic Homilies: The First Series. Edited by Peter Clemoes. EETS, supplementary series 17. Oxford: Oxford University Press, 1997.

Ælfric's Catholic Homilies: The Second Series. Edited by Malcolm Godden. EETS, supplementary series 5. Oxford: Oxford University Press, 1979.

Ashdown, Margaret. "Elizabeth Elstob, the Learned Saxonist." *Modern Language Review* 20 (1925): 125–46.

Barrington, Daines, ed. *The Anglo-Saxon Version from the Historian Orosius. By Ælfred the Great. Together with an English Translation from the Anglo-Saxon.* London: W. Bowyer, 1773.

Beauchamp, Virginia Walcott. "Pioneer Linguist: Elizabeth Elstob (1683–1756)." *University of Michigan: Papers in Women's Studies* 1, no. 3 (1974): 9–43.

Bede. *Bede's Ecclesiastical History of the English People.* Edited by Bertram Colgrave and R. A. B. Mynors. 1969. Reprint, Oxford: Clarendon Press, 1992.

Chétardie, Trotti de la. *Instruction pour une jeune princesse, ou, L'idée d'une honneste femme.* Paris: Théodore Girard, 1684.

Clarke, T. E. S., et al. *A Life of Gilbert Burnet, Bishop of Salisbury.* Cambridge: University Press, 1907.

Collins, Sarah Huff. "Elizabeth Elstob: A Biography." Ph.D. diss., Indiana University, 1970.

——. "The Elstobs and the End of the Saxon Revival." In *Anglo-Saxon Scholarship: The First Three Centuries,* edited by Carl T. Berkhout and Milton McC. Gatch, 107–18. Boston: G. K. Hall, 1982.

Elstob, William, ed. *Hormesta Pauli Orosii Quam Olim Patrio Sermone Donavit Ælfredus Magnus.* Oxford: E Theatro Sheldoniano, 1699.

——, ed. *Sermo Lupi Episcopi, Saxonice. Latinam Interpretationem Notasque Adjecit.* Oxford: E Theatro Sheldoniano, 1701.

Ferguson, Moira. "Elizabeth Elstob, 1683–1756." In her *First Feminists: British Women Writers 1578–1799.* 239–46. Bloomington: Indiana University Press, 1985.

——. *Subject to Others: British Women Writers and Colonial Slavery, 1670–1834.* New York: Routledge, 1992.

Frantzen, Allen J. *Desire for Origins: New Language, Old English, and Teaching the Tradition.* New Brunswick, N.J.: Rutgers University Press, 1990.

Fraser, Antonia. *The Weaker Vessel.* New York: Knopf, 1984.

Geoffrey of Monmouth. *The Historia Regnum Britannia of Geoffrey of Monmouth.* Edited by Acton Griscom and Robert Ellis Jones. London: Longmans Green, 1929.

Gibson, Edmund, ed. *Chronicon Saxonicum, Seu Annales Rerum in Anglia Præcipue Gestarum, A Christo nato ad Annum usque MCLIV. deducti, ac jam demum Latinitate donati. Cum Indice Rerum Chronologico. Accedunt Regulæ ad Investigandas Nominum Locorum Origines. Et Nominum Locorum ac Virorum In Chronico Memoratorum Explicatio.* Oxford: E Theatro Sheldoniano, 1692.

[Gildon, Charles]. *A Comparison between the Two Stages.* London: n.p., 1702.

[Gildon, Charles, and John Brightland]. *A Grammar of the English Tongue.* London: Printed for John Brightland, 1712; 2d ed., 2d state.

Godden, Malcolm. "Old English." In *Editing Medieval Texts English, French, and Latin Written in England,* edited by A. G. Rigg. 9–33. 1977. Reprint, New York: AMS Press, 1988.

Godden, Malcolm, and Peter Clemoes. *Ælfric's "Catholic Homilies": Introduction, Commentary, and Glossary.* EETS, supplementary series 18. Oxford: Oxford University Press, 2000.

Green, Mary Elizabeth. "Elizabeth Elstob: 'The Saxon Nymph' (1683–1756)." In *Female Scholars: A Tradition of Learned Women before 1800,* edited by J. R. Brink, 137–60. Montreal: Eden Press, 1980.

Gretsch, Mechthild. "Elizabeth Elstob: A Scholar's Fight for Anglo-Saxon Studies." Pts. 1 and 2. *Anglia* 117 (1999): 163–200, 481–524.

Hanashima, Yumi. "Encouragers Sought and Gain'd for Elstob's English-Saxon Homily (1709): A Preliminary Study of the Subscription List and Female Subscribers." *Colloquia* [Keio University, Tokyo] 21 (2000): 87–106.

Harris, Richard L. *A Chorus of Grammars: The Correspondence of George Hickes, and His Collaborators on the Thesaurus Linguarum Septentrionalium.* Publications of the Dictionary of Old English, 4. Toronto: Pontifical Institute of Mediaeval Studies, 1992.

Hearne, Thomas. *The Remains of Thomas Hearne: Reliquiae Hearnianae. Being extracts from his MS diaries.* Compiled by John Bliss. Revised by John Buchanan-Brown. Carbondale: Southern Illinois University Press, 1966.

Hickes, George. *Instutiones Grammaticæ Anglo-Saxonicæ, et Mœso-Gothicæ; . . . Grammatica*

Islandica Runolphi Jonæ, Catalogus Librorum Septentrionalium. Oxford: E Theatro Sheldoniano, 1689.

———. *Several letters which Passed between Dr. George Hickes, and a Popish Priest, upon Occasion of a Young Gentlewoman's Departing from the Church of England to that of Rome.... With an Appendix Containing Several Remarkable Papers.* London: R. Sare, 1705; 2d ed. London: R. Sare, 1715.

———, ed. *Linguarum Vett. Septentrionalium Thesaurus Grammatico-Criticus et Archæologicus.* 2 vols. Oxford: E Theatro Sheldoniano, 1703–5.

———, trans. *Instructions for the Education of a Daughter: to which is added, A small Tract of Instructions for the conduct of young ladies of the Highest Rank, with Suitable Devotions Annexed.* London: J. Bowyer, 1707.

Hughes, Shaun F. D. "The Anglo-Saxon Grammars of George Hickes and Elizabeth Elstob." In *Anglo-Saxon Scholarship: The First Three Centuries,* edited by Carl T. Berkhout and Milton McC. Gatch. 119–47. Boston: G. K. Hall, 1982.

———. "Mrs. Elstob's Defense of Antiquarian Learning in Her *Rudiments of Grammar for the English-Saxon Tongue* (1715)." *Harvard Library Bulletin* 27 (1979): 172–91.

———. "Salutary Lessons from the History of Linguistics." In *The Real-World Linguist: Linguistic Applications in the 1980s,* edited by Peter C. Bjarkman and Victor Raskin. 172–91. Norwood, N.J.: Ablex, 1986.

James, Adeola. *In Their Own Voices: African Women Writers Talk.* London: James Currey; Portsmouth, N.H.: Heinemann, 1990.

Leinbaugh, Theodore H. "Ælfric's *Sermo de Sacrificio in Die Pascae*: Anglican Polemic in the Sixteenth and Seventeenth Centuries." In *Anglo-Saxon Scholarship: The First Three Centuries,* edited by Carl T. Berkhout and Milton McC. Gatch. 51–68. Boston: G. K. Hall, 1982.

Midgley, Claire. *Women against Slavery: The British Campaigns, 1780–1870.* London: Routledge, 1992.

Morton, Richard. "Elizabeth Elstob's *Rudiments of Grammar* (1715): Germanic Philology for Women." *Studies in Eighteenth Century Culture* 20 (1990): 267–87.

Mothe-Fénelon, François de Salignac de la. *Education des Filles.* Paris: Pierre Aubouin et al., 1687.

Perry, Ruth. *The Celebrated Mary Astell: An Early English Feminist.* Chicago: University of Chicago Press, 1986.

Rask, Rasmus. *Angelsaksisk sproglære tilligemed en kort Læsebog.* Stockholm: M. Wiborg, 1817. Translated by Benjamin Thorpe under the title *A Grammar of the Anglo-Saxon Tongue, with a Praxis,* new edition, enlarged and revised (Copenhagen: S. L. Möller, 1830).

Rawlinson, Christopher, ed. *An. Manl. Sever. Boethi Consolationis Philosophiæ Libri V. Anglo-Saxonice Redditi ab Alfredo, Inclyto Anglo-Saxonum Rege.* Oxford: E Theatro Sheldoniano, 1698.

Reynolds, Myra. *The Learned Lady in England, 1650–1760.* Vassar Semi-Centennial Series. 1920. Reprint, Gloucester, Mass.: Peter Smith, 1964.

Robinson, Fred C. "Eight Letters from Elizabeth Elstob." In *The Endless Knot: Essays on Old and Middle English in Honor of Marie Borroff,* edited by M. Teresa Tavormina and R. F. Yeager, 241–52. Cambridge: Brewer, 1995.

Runólfur Jónsson. *Recentissima Antiqvissimæ Linguæ Septentrionalis incunabula[:] Id est Grammaticæ Islandicæ Rudimenta.* Copenhagen: Petrus Hakius, 1651.

Scudéry, Madeleine de. *Discovrs de la Gloire.* Paris: Pierre le Petit, 1671.

Shaw, Patricia. "The Anglo-Saxon Attitudes of the 'Ingenious and Learned Mrs. Elstob.'" In *Papers from the VII International Conference of the Spanish Society for Medieval English Language and Literature,* edited by B. Santano Moreno et al. 327–49. Cáceres, Spain: Servicio Publicaciones, Universidad de Extramadura, 1994.

Smol, Anna. "Pleasure, Progress, and the Profession: Elizabeth Elstob and Contemporary Anglo-Saxon Studies." *Studies in Medievalism* 9 (1997): 80–97.

Somner, William. *Dictionarivm Saxonico-Latino-Anglicum . . . Accesserunt Ælfrici Abbatis Grammatica Latino-Saxonica, Cum Glossario Suo Ejusdem Generis.* Oxford: Guliel[mus] Hall, 1659.

Sutherland, Kathryn. "Editing for a New Century: Elizabeth Elstob's Anglo-Saxon Manifesto and Ælfric's St. Gregory Homily." In *The Editing of Old English: Papers from the 1990 Manchester Conference,* edited by D. G. Scragg and Paul Szarmach. 213–37. Cambridge: Brewer, 1994.

———. "Elizabeth Elstob." In *Literature and Philosophy,* vol. 2 of *Medieval Scholarship: Biographical Studies on the Formation of a Discipline,* edited by Helen Damico et al. 3 vols. 59–73. New York: Garland, 1995–2000.

Thoresby, Ralph. *Letters of Eminent Men, Addressed to Ralph Thoresby, F.R.S.* 2 vols. in 1. London: H. Colburn and R. Bentley, 1832.

Thorpe, Benjamin, ed. and trans. *The Homilies of the Anglo-Saxon Church. The First Part, Containing The Sermones Catholici, or Homilies of Ælfric.* 2 vols. Ælfric Society, nos. [1]–4, 6–7, 9–12. London: Ælfric Society, 1844–46.

Thwaites, Edward, ed. *Grammatica Anglo-Saxonica ex Hickesiano Linguarum Septentrionalium Thesauro exerpta.* Oxford: E Theatro Sheldoniano, 1711.

———, ed. *Heptateuchus, Liber Job, et Evangelium Nicodemi; Anglo-Saxonice. Historiæ Judith Fragmentum; Dano-Saxonice.* Oxford: E Theatro Sheldoniano, 1698.

Wallas, Ada. *Before the Bluestockings.* London: Allen and Unwin, 1929.

Wheloc, Abraham, ed. *Venerabilis Bedæ Historia Ecclesiastica.* 2 vols. Cambridge: Rogerus Daniel, 1643–44.

CHAPTER 2

Anna Jameson (1794–1860)
"Primitive" Art and Iconography

CORDELIA WARR

ANNA JAMESON'S reputation as a medievalist and art historian rests today on a series of books, now known as *Sacred and Legendary Art,* which she wrote toward the end of her life, the first volumes being published in 1848.[1] The series has been characterized by Adele M. Holcomb, who has worked extensively on Jameson's art-historical publications, as "the first substantial study of Christian iconography in the English language." Furthermore, one of the books in the series—*Legends of the Madonna*—"would seem to be the first book on the imagery of the Virgin in art to appear in any literature."[2] *Sacred and Legendary Art* is still referred to today. James Hall used it in compiling his *Dictionary of Subjects and Symbols in Art* (1974) as well as his *History of Ideas and Images in Italian Art* (1983). Marina Warner cited *Legends of the Madonna* in *Alone of All Her Sex: The Myth and the Cult of the Virgin Mary* (1976). More recently Roelof van Straten, in his *Introduction to Iconography,* has commented that the books contain "some of the best explanations in English of Christian themes depicted in the fine arts" despite being the earliest publications cited in his section on "Christian Iconography."[3] The provision of such rich iconographical material represented the culmination of Anna Jameson's career as a professional writer. In thirty-five years of continuous publishing, her works made a sizeable contribution to art criticism and the knowledge of art.

Jameson's writing career developed out of necessity. For much of her life she relied on her own endeavors to make a living and to support dependent members of her family. Her father, Denis Murphy, was an Irish miniature painter who moved to England in 1798. Although he found work, his income was precarious and not always sufficient to support his family. As the eldest child—two younger sisters, Eliza and

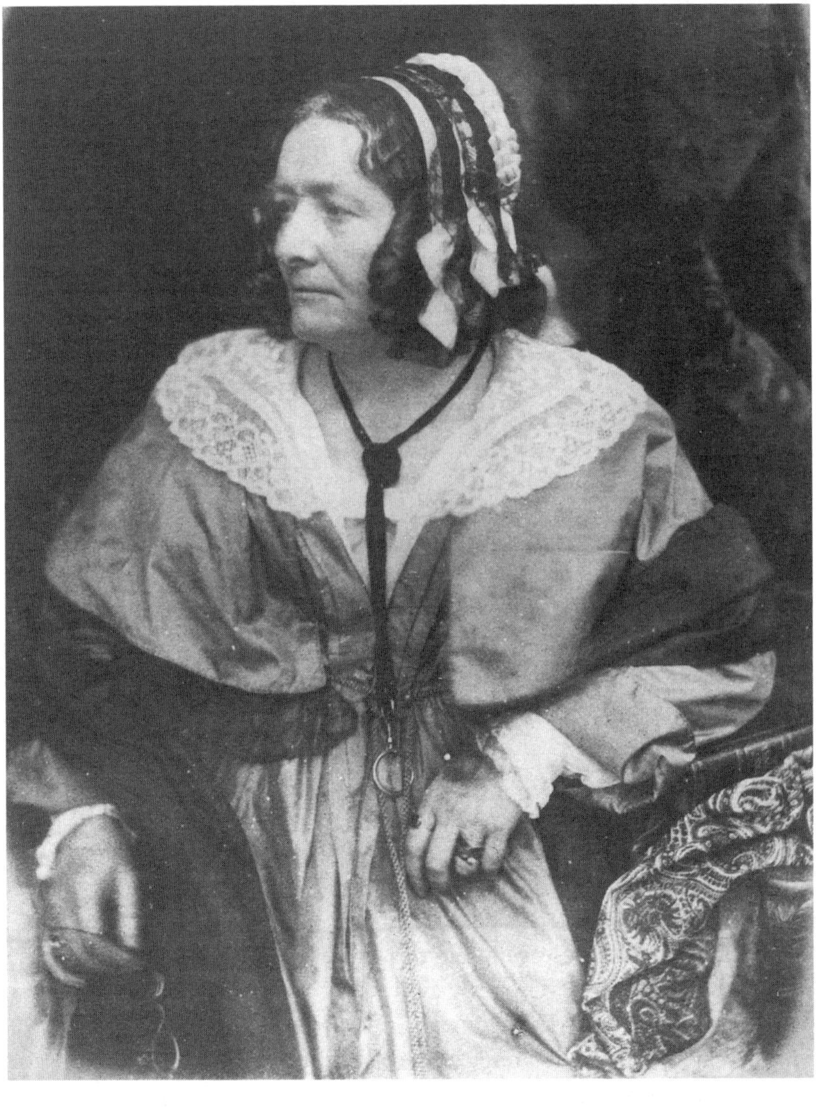

Charlotte, neither married nor were able to support themselves—Anna took on the responsibility of contributing to family income.[4] She began her working life in 1810 as governess to the family of the marquis of Winchester and continued in this profession, with some breaks, until her marriage to Robert Jameson in 1825.[5] The marriage was not a success. In 1829 Robert Jameson went to Dominica, where he was a puisne judge, and Anna chose not to accompany him.[6] Although she later went to Canada (Robert was appointed attorney general of Upper Canada in 1833), 1829 effectively marks the end of her marriage. Financial arrangements made between the couple meant that Anna Jameson was to receive three hundred pounds per annum from her husband.[7] However, after 1850 these payments stopped, and she was thrown back on the earnings from her writing until friends ensured her a stable income by securing a civil list pension granted by the queen.[8] The pension ameliorated the situation, but worse was to come. When Robert Jameson died in 1854, his wife found she had been cut out of his will, and once again her friends came to her aid by buying her an annuity.[9]

One of the most striking aspects of Anna Jameson's subject matter is its breadth. She wrote books and articles on travel and the theater as well as on art.[10] From circa 1840 onward, her published works focus almost exclusively on art, and Holcomb has convincingly characterized her as the "first professional English art historian."[11] Jameson's output during these years ranges from contemporary art, as shown in her introduction to *The Decorations in the Garden-Pavilion in the Grounds of Buckingham Palace* (1846) and her *Handbook to the Courts of Modern Sculpture* (1854), to Italian art, such as her *Memoirs of Early Italian Painters, and of the Progress of Painting in Italy* (1845).

Within the sphere of medieval or "primitive" art, Jameson was a vociferous proponent of the need to widen the examples available to the English public. She particularly championed the early Italian masters in several of her publications in the 1840s. In the general introduction to her *Companion to the Most Celebrated Private Galleries of Art in London,* Jameson gives a brief résumé of the history of collecting in England. Referring to the dispersal of the Orléans Collection at the end of the eighteenth century, she comments, "If at this time the taste or fashion had run in favour of the earlier Florentine, Umbrian and Venetian schools, we might have amassed precious things: but we knew not their value."[12] Her *Companion* covered the Gallery of Her Majesty the Queen, the Bridgewater and Sutherland Galleries, and the collections of the marquis of Lansdowne, the Right Honorable Robert Peel, and Samuel Rogers. In only one of these collections was there any painting from the fourteenth century, in that of Samuel Rogers. Jameson calls the reader's attention to works by Giotto, Fra Angelico, Jan van Eyck, and Hans Memling as "most valuable, as illustrating the progress of art."[13]

The level of knowledge of the early schools of art at this time was such that some of the attributions given to the paintings in Samuel Rogers's collection are inaccurate although based on the best available material at the time. The *Saint John and Saint Paul* ascribed to Giotto is now in the National Gallery, London, and has been attributed to Spinello Aretino (active 1373–died 1410/1411).[14] Jameson based her attribution on information provided by Giorgio Vasari, who had ascribed the frescoes in the Manetti Chapel in Santa Maria del Carmine, Florence, to Giotto and thus dated them about 1295.[15]

Jameson also strongly supported moves to ensure that the National Gallery in London, founded in 1824, made more wide-ranging acquisitions, especially those of the earlier European schools. She used her introduction to *A Handbook to the Public Galleries of Art in and near London* (1842) to argue just this point, that a national gallery "is not merely for the pleasure and civilization of our people, but also for their instruction in the value and significance of art. How far the history of the progress of painting is connected with the history of manners, morals, and government, and, above all, with this history of our religion, might be exemplified visibly by a collection of specimens in painting, from the earliest times of its revival, tracing the pictorial representations of sacred subjects from the ancient Byzantine types."[16] As such, she was among a number of women in the first half of the nineteenth century who championed late-medieval and early-Renaissance art, especially that of northern Europe and Italy.[17] These included Lady Maria Callcott, wife of the "most successful marine painter in England," who had herself planned a book on Italian painting, which she was unable to undertake due to ill health, and Elizabeth Eastlake, wife of the director of the National Gallery.[18] The Eastlakes formed part of Jameson's social circle, and it was under Charles Eastlake's directorship of the National Gallery (1855–1865) that the first major acquisitions of "primitive art," both northern European and Italian, were made.[19]

However, as Francis Haskell has pointed out, "No one ... relying on what he could see in any English museum could possibly have developed a taste for early Italian ... art before 1850 at the earliest."[20] This being the case, it was left to writers to form public taste.[21] Anna Jameson was one of the most successful of these writers. *Memoirs of Early Italian Painters* in its periodical form—it was published in the *Penny Magazine* in 1843, 1844, and 1845 as "Essays on the Lives of Remarkable Painters"—had a wide circulation, around fifty thousand copies per week at the time Jameson's articles were published.[22] Although this was a drop from the magazine's circulation at the height of its popularity—two hundred thousand copies per week—it still represented a far greater audience than could be reached by periodicals such as the *Art Journal*.[23] The publication of the collected articles in book form in 1845 further emphasizes their popular success. By 1891 at least six editions of the book had been published. This success was repeated by *Sacred and Legendary Art*. Published in two volumes in 1848, it had previously appeared in seventeen installments in the *Athenaeum* between 11 January 1845 and 21 February 1846 as "Sacred and Legendary Art."[24] In 1850 this publication was followed by *Legends of the Monastic Orders as Represented in the Fine Arts*, and in 1852 another volume appeared under the title of *Legends of the Madonna as Represented in the Fine Arts*. At her death in 1860 Jameson left incomplete *The History of Our Lord as Exemplified in Works of Art: With That of His Types; Saint John the Baptist; and Other Persons of the Old and New Testament*. She had been working on the book in the

Print Room of the British Museum and, early in March, had returned to her rooms in Conduit Street in a snowstorm. She caught pneumonia and died on 17 March.[25] *The History of Our Lord* was finished by Elizabeth Eastlake, thus completing the series, which took its title from that of the installments first published in the *Athenaeum*.[26]

By the time Jameson came to write *Sacred and Legendary Art,* the impetus for recognition of the Italian "primitives" had been growing for some time.[27] As John Steegman has pointed out, "The 'primitivism' was in fact medievalism, which at that time was often considered as synonymous with the primitive."[28] In describing the first section of *Sacred and Legendary Art* to the publishers Longmans in 1846, Jameson wrote that it contained "an account of the lives, legends, habits, and attributes of the sacred personages whose stories have been illustrated in the pictures and sculptures of the Middle Ages."[29] Longmans accepted the book despite the fact that the value of medieval art was still questioned, indeed actively opposed, in many quarters. One of Jameson's major achievements in the series was her success in interpreting that art for a wide public. The first section, published in two volumes, sold six hundred copies, according to a report Jameson sent to Ottilie von Goethe.[30] It remained highly successful to the end of the century, by far outselling Lord Lindsay's *Sketches of the History of Christian Art,* published in 1847, which only succeeded in reaching two editions (1847 and 1885) while *Sacred and Legendary Art* reached ten editions and remained profitable until at least 1863.[31]

The success of *Sacred and Legendary Art* depended on Jameson's ability to negotiate an English readership's frequent inability to separate religious beliefs from artistic styles. Maria Edgeworth, in a letter to Jameson of 17 November 1848, refers to this tendency by identifying adherents to the High Church as potential buyers: "The Puseyites will be delighted with the Legenda and Saints and Antiquarian lore and they are a vast class of purchasers."[32] Jameson employed various strategies to ensure that her work was acceptable to as wide a range of readers as possible, despite its subject matter being mainly medieval, and therefore Catholic, religious art and as such subject to English anti-Catholic prejudices.[33] The ability to capture a heterogeneous readership is in direct contrast to Lord Lindsay's *Sketches*. Lindsay initially addressed his book to a highly individualized reader: "a young, amateur artist, presumed to have started recently for Italy."[34] Jameson, on the other hand, believed that her focus on iconography allowed "even the most uninstructed in the technicalities of art" to understand some of its power.[35] She also consistently maintained her Protestant credentials, thus removing any suspicion that she was preaching Catholicism.[36]

Jameson's artistic focus was also wider than her profession that she would deal with the art of the Middle Ages indicates. In *Legends of the Madonna,* for instance, she cites works from an ancient Egyptian representation of Isis nursing Horus to Duccio di Buoninsegna's *Rucellai Madonna* (still attributed by Jameson to Cimabue) and even to an annunciation by Flaxman.[37] In part this was because many Victorians viewed the Middle Ages as a much longer period than is now generally accepted. Rather than perceiving the works of Giotto and Fra Angelico as marking the beginning of the

Renaissance, the Victorians saw them as medieval artists, mainly because of the religious nature of their art.[38] Based on this criterion, early Italian painting—and therefore medieval painting—could, in some instances, be extended to the end of the fifteenth century. This conformed to the change from medieval to modern, usually placed at the end of the fifteenth century, and a common distinction in periodization before the rise of the Renaissance as a historical, literary, and artistic concept. Thus, Anna Jameson's claim to her publisher that *Sacred and Legendary Art* dealt with the Middle Ages was no exaggeration. In part, however, the increased range of examples was chosen to enable Jameson—who because of her earlier publications on the public and private galleries in London had an almost encyclopedic knowledge of what was available to the viewing public in London—to cite artists whose works could be seen by the reader or whose name was familiar. Guido Reni (1575–1642) is a case in point. Reni's works were at the height of their popularity in mid-nineteenth-century England, and the National Gallery owned a number of examples.[39] The enormous time period covered in the examples also reflects, to some extent, the lack of clear equivalence between medieval art and Christian art.[40] Finally, by focusing on iconography, Jameson began to move away from questions of "taste." In her preface to *Legends of the Monastic Orders,* she states her purpose as "to interpret . . . those works of Art which the churches and galleries of the Continent, and our own rich collections, have rendered familiar to us as objects of taste, while they have remained unappreciated as subjects of thought."[41] She goes on to explain that by appreciating and judging "sacred pictures" only in relation to their artist and their style the viewer may miss a vital part of their importance. Despite this, she was scrupulous in her attempts to be as accurate as possible, remarking in the preface to the third edition of *Sacred and Legendary Art* (1857) that "the whole has been carefully revised" and that "references to the pictures and other works of art [have been] corrected from the latest authorities."[42]

By means of these strategies, Jameson was able to integrate her understanding of medieval art, particularly that of Italy, into a popular series. The scholarship contained in *Sacred and Legendary Art* cannot be said to be revolutionary. Her work on early Italian art followed in the well-worn footsteps of Italian historians and art historians such as Giovanni Rosini and Luigi Lanzi, who had been among the first to rediscover this area.[43] Jameson was also familiar with French writers on the subject, including Seroux d'Agincourt and Adolphe Napoléon Didron, both of whom she cites in *Sacred and Legendary Art.*[44] She had also met Alexis-François Rio (1806–74), the author of *De la poèsie Chrétiènne* (The poetry of Christian art) published in 1836, while she was in Paris in the autumn of 1841 researching for *Handbook to the Public Galleries,* and she was strongly influenced by his approach.[45] In her earlier *Memoirs of the Early Italian Painters,* Jameson demonstrates her familiarity with contemporary German scholarship, especially that of Franz Kugler and Carl Friedrich von Rumohr.[46] In fact, her work has been described as "essentially a summary of the author's reading."[47]

Throughout her work Jameson's evolution as a historian of art and as an iconographer is clear. Her firsthand knowledge of Italian painting made her well suited for this type of writing. Between 1821 and 1822, during her employment as a governess with the Rowles family of Bradbourne Park, Kent, she had toured the Continent and had, while in Italy, made good use of her spare time by visiting the art galleries.[48] Her interest in art is clear from letters sent to her family during this period. She visited Naples, Rome, and Florence as well as a number of other sites of art-historical interest. Writing from Florence, she says, "We have not been to the gallery yet, but I have on the sly: my impatience would not wait."[49] The Italian tour was to be used to good account in her first published book, *The Diary of an Ennuyée* (1826).[50] Structured as the account of the travels of a broken-hearted young lady and therefore, at least in part, as a guidebook, it is also concerned to a great extent with Italian art, one of the major attractions of a tour of Italy. The writing of guidebooks in the early nineteenth century "was an important step towards interpreting the visual arts. Travel, like knowledge of foreign languages, was an essential prerequisite for the study of art."[51] Anna Jameson had both. Not only had she traveled the length of Italy; she had also spent two years in Germany between 1834 and 1836, where she mastered the language, and she was to return a number of times during her life to visit friends and to undertake research for *Sacred and Legendary Art*.[52] Jameson's visits to Germany allowed her to view a number of "primitive" northern European paintings, which she later used to good effect in the *Sacred and Legendary Art* series. However, her main focus of attention remained Italian art, and the majority of examples she chose to illustrate in the series have an Italian provenance.

Although at the time she wrote the *Diary of an Ennuyée* Jameson clearly had no appreciation of medieval art, the beginnings of the idea that would later become *Sacred and Legendary Art* can be traced here. She comments on the subject of the Virgin and the Holy Family that "if a gallery could be formed of this subject alone, selecting one specimen from among the works of every painter, it would form not only a comparative index to their different styles, but we should find . . . that each has stamped some peculiarity of his own disposition on his Virgins."[53] At this point Jameson is looking to distinguish between artists, something she was later to dismiss as allowing only a very partial understanding of Christian art. Nevertheless, most of her first major writings on art in the 1840s accepted the primacy of the artist. This can be seen, for example, from a brief perusal of the contents of *Memoirs of Early Italian Painters,* a book that was indebted for its structure to Vasari's mid-sixteenth-century *Le vite de' più eccellenti pittori, scultori, e architettori* (The lives of the most excellent painters, sculptors, and architects).[54] Vasari was, of course, still the major source for the history of Italian art from the thirteenth to the sixteenth centuries, and all authors used him to a great extent.[55] While necessarily dependent on Vasari for much of her information, Jameson used recent scholarship to inform a critical reading of his work, and it is here that her knowledge of languages served her well. She is quick to point out that Vasari's decision to portray Cimabue as the artist who revived the art of painting is an "error or gross exaggeration."[56] In doing this Jameson was following the work of Lanzi, who had begun his *Storia pittorica dell'Italia* (1795–96) with a specific refutation of Vasari's argument that painting had been "altogether lost" in the period before Cimabue.[57] She was also encouraged in her criticism of Vasari by her reading of *Italienische Forschungen* (1827–31), in which Rumohr used his extensive archive research to assess Vasari's accuracy.[58]

The idea of comparing paintings of similar subjects and of arranging works of art by subject, first mentioned in the *Diary of an Ennuyée,* was to come to fruition in the *Sacred and Legendary Art* series. In order for Jameson to conceive the project, it was first necessary for her to view art in what she perceived to be its original context. This end was partially achieved as a result of her first trip to Italy, when Jameson acquired a measure of sympathy for Catholicism and an understanding of some of the ways in which devotional art was utilized in its intended context. A visit to a miraculous Madonna and her observation of the way in which the local population interacted with the image gave Jameson an insight into the importance of contextualization when dealing with art that initially did not seem aesthetically pleasing.[59] She was later at pains to explain her approach in the prefaces and introductions to her works on art of the 1840s and 1850s. In the introduction to volume 1 of *Sacred and Legendary Art,* she makes an argument for an "inquiry into the true spirit and significance of works of Art, as connected with the history of Religion and Civilisation," while in her introduction to *Memoirs of Early Italian Painters,* first published in the 1859 edition, she states, "Our first question, when we stand before a picture, should not be, 'Who painted it?' but 'What does it mean?' 'What is it about?' . . . We should be able to read a picture as we read a book."[60] Jameson thus seeks to bring new editions of this work into line with the *Sacred and Legendary Art* books and to break away from the Vasarian emphasis on biography and "stress on the primacy of the individual."[61]

John Steegman has described Anna Jameson as "rather a compiler than a thinker."[62] However, it is perhaps just because of this that her work is still used today. Jameson sought to elucidate aspects of medieval iconography and to place them in historical context. She avoided using her understanding of "primitive" art to preach about the direction contemporary English art should take, for example—a temptation many of her contemporaries could not resist. Her study of Christian iconography in *Sacred and Legendary Art* was something new in nineteenth-century English writings on art, and its continuing use as a reference work attests to its thoroughness.[63] Jameson's break from the contemporary concentration on style and attribution is possibly her greatest contribution to the study of medieval art. Jameson sidestepped the perceived need for attribution and recognized that the worth and interest of certain paintings and sculptures did not lie as much in their style as in their subject matter and religious, social, and historical context. In doing this she facilitated the study of a period that had previously been neglected because of its perceived artistic deficiencies and paved the way for the diversity and multidisciplinary character of the art-historical scholarship of the twentieth and twenty-first centuries.[64]

Notes

1. Two major monographs have been published on Jameson's life and works: Clara Thomas, *Love and Work Enough;* and Judith Johnston, *Anna Jameson*. In addition, Adele M. Holcomb has published on Anna Jameson as an art historian. See "Anna Jameson: The First Professional English Art Historian"; and "Anna Jameson (1794–1860): Sacred Art and Social Vision," 94–107.

2. Holcomb, "First Professional English Art Historian," 180.

3. Van Straten, *Introduction to Iconography*, 110.

4. Johnston, *Anna Jameson*, 2. In all there were five Murphy sisters: Anna, Eliza, Louisa, Camilla, and Charlotte. See Erskine, *Anna Jameson: Letters and Friendships*, 17.

5. Holcomb, "Sacred Art and Social Vision," 96.

6. Ibid., 97.

7. Needler, *Letters of Anna Jameson to Ottilie von Goethe*, xix.

8. Thomas, *Love and Work Enough*, 189–93.

9. Ibid., 194–97.

10. Holcomb, "Sacred Art and Social Vision," 93.

11. Holcomb, "First Professional English Art Historian."

12. Jameson, *Companion to the Most Celebrated Private Galleries of Art in London*, xxxi. For the Orleans Collection, see Haskell, *Rediscoveries in Art*, 39–44; Steegman, *Consort of Taste*, 56–59.

13. Jameson, *Most Celebrated Private Galleries of Art*, 390.

14. Davies, *Early Italian Schools before 1400*, 92–96.

15. Vasari, *Lives of the Artists*, 60.

16. Jameson, *Handbook to the Public Galleries of Art in and near London*, 13–14.

17. Richter Sherman with Holcomb, "Precursors and Pioneers (1820–1890)," 8.

18. Haskell, *Rediscoveries in Art*, 92–93.

19. Robertson, *Sir Charles Eastlake*, 298–323—an overview of the acquisitions of the National Gallery between 1855 and 1865.

20. Ibid., 157. See also Steegman, *Consort of Taste*, 66.

21. Haskell, *Rediscoveries in Art*, 166.

22. Johnston, *Anna Jameson*, 157.

23. Adele M. Holcomb gives the circulation figures for the *Art Journal* as fifteen thousand in 1849. See Holcomb, "First Professional English Art Historian," 181.

24. Thomas, *Love and Work Enough*, 177–78.

25. Ibid., 215.

26. For discussion of the *Sacred and Legendary Art* series, see Thomas, *Love and Work Enough*, 176–82, 215–17; Johnston, *Anna Jameson*, 180–207; Holcomb, "First Professional English Art Historian," 179–82; Holcomb, "Sacred Art and Social Vision," 107–15.

27. Haskell, *Rediscoveries in Art*, 87–91.

28. Steegman, *Consort of Taste*, 28–29.

29. Thomas, *Love and Work Enough*, 178.

30. Ibid., 181. The letter is published in Needler, *Letters of Anna Jameson to Ottilie von Goethe*, 163–64.

31. Johnston, *Anna Jameson*, 181.

32. Erskine, *Letters and Friendships*, 254–55.
33. Bullen, *Myth of the Renaissance*, 109–22.
34. Lord Lindsay, earl of Crawford, *Sketches of the History of Christian Art*, 1:vii, quoted in Johnston, *Anna Jameson*, 200.
35. Jameson, *Legends of the Monastic Orders as Represented in the Fine Arts*, xiii.
36. Jameson, *Sacred and Legendary Art* (London: Longmans, 1874), 1:6–7.
37. Jameson, *Legends of the Madonna*, xxii, 65, 183. The attribution of the *Rucellai Madonna* to Duccio was not widely accepted until the first half of the twentieth century. See Maginnis, *Painting in the Age of Giotto*, 65–68.
38. Bullen, *Myth of the Renaissance*, 14–15.
39. See Steegman, *Consort of Taste*, 57, for Guido Reni's popularity. Also see Robertson, *Sir Charles Eastlake*, 292–323, for an overview of the acquisitions of the National Gallery between 1824 and 1865, including a number of works attributed to Guido Reni.
40. This is discussed by Adele M. Ernstrom, "'Why Should We Be Always Looking Back?'" 421–35.
41. Jameson, *Legends of the Monastic Orders*, xiii.
42. Reprinted in the seventh edition of *Sacred and Legendary Art*.
43. Haskell, *Rediscoveries in Art*, 71–72, 151.
44. A.-N. Didron's *Iconographie Chrétiènne* (Christian iconography) had been published in 1843, and Jameson referred to it in later editions of *Sacred and Legendary Art*. On Seroux d'Agincourt, see Bullen, *Myth of the Renaissance*, 27–37.
45. Erskine, *Letters and Friendships*, 203–4.
46. Luigi Lanzi's *Storia pittorica dell'Italia* was first published in 1795–96, and an extended edition appeared in 1809. An English version appeared in 1828. See Maginnis, *Painting in the Age of Giotto*, 47–49. Franz Kugler's *Handbuch der Geschichte der Malerei* was published in 1837; an expanded version (prepared by Jacob Burckhardt) was published in 1847; this version, annotated by Charles Eastlake, was published in English in 1851. Karl Friedrich von Rumohr's *Italienische Forschungen* was published between 1827 and 1831. See Richter Sherman with Holcomb, "Precursors and Pioneers," 4–5.
47. Maginnis, *Painting in the Age of Giotto*, 83.
48. Thomas, *Love and Work Enough*, 14–17.
49. Quoted in Thomas, *Love and Work Enough*, 16. See also Erskine, *Letters and Friendships*, 45.
50. This was first published anonymously as *A Lady's Diary* (London: R. Thomas, 1826). The second edition, also published in 1826, was retitled *The Diary of an Ennuyée*.
51. See Richter Sherman with Holcomb, "Precursors and Pioneers," 10.
52. Johnston, *Anna Jameson*, xi–xiv.
53. Jameson, *Diary of an Ennuyée*, 314.
54. Johnston, *Anna Jameson*, 158.
55. Ibid.
56. Jameson, *Memoirs of Early Italian Painters*, 1.
57. Maginnis, *Painting in the Age of Giotto*, 47.
58. Richter Sherman with Holcomb, "Precursors and Pioneers," 4–5.
59. Gilley, "Victorian Feminism and Catholic Art," 386–87.
60. Jameson, *Sacred and Legendary Art*, 1:7–8; Jameson, *Memoirs of Early Italian Painters*, xi. See also Johnston, *Anna Jameson*, 157.

61. Fernie, *Art History and Its Methods*, 22–23.
62. Steegman, *Consort of Taste*, 186.
63. Richter Sherman and Holcomb describe Jameson as a "pioneer in the study of religious iconography." See Richter Sherman with Holcomb, "Precursors and Pioneers," 12.
64. See, for example, Rees and Borzello, introduction to *New Art History*, 2–10.

Select Bibliography of Works by Anna Jameson.

The Diary of an Ennuyée. London: Henry Colburn, 1826.
A Handbook to the Public Galleries of Art in and near London. London: John Murray, 1842.
Companion to the Most Celebrated Private Galleries of Art in London . . . with a Prefatory Essay on Art, Artists, Collectors and Connoisseurs. London: Saunders and Otley, 1844.
Memoirs of Early Italian Painters and the Progress of Painting in Italy. London: Charles Knight, 1845; rev. ed., London: John Murray, 1891.
Sacred and Legendary Art. 2 vols. London: Longmans, 1848.
Legends of the Monastic Orders as Represented in the Fine Arts. London: Longmans, 1850; 5th ed., London: Longmans, 1872.
Legends of the Madonna. London: Longmans, 1852; 5th ed., London: Longmans, 1872.
The History of Our Lord as Exemplified in Works of Art; with That of His Types; Saint John the Baptist; and Other Persons of the Old and New Testament. Completed by Elizabeth Eastlake. London: Longmans, 1864.

Works Cited

Bullen, J. B. *The Myth of the Renaissance in Nineteenth-Century Writing.* Oxford: Clarendon Press, 1994.
Crawford, Alexander, earl of Crawford. *Sketches of the History of Christian Art.* 3 vols. London: John Murray, 1847.
Davies, Martin. *The Early Italian Schools before 1400.* Revised by Dillian Gordon. London: National Gallery Publications, 1988.
Erksine, Beatrice (Mrs. Steuart), ed. *Anna Jameson: Letters and Friendships.* London: Fisher Unwin, 1915.
Ernstrom, Adele M. "'Why Should We Be Always Looking Back?' 'Christian Art' in Nineteenth-Century Historiography in Britain," *Art History* 22 (1999): 421–35.
Fernie, Eric. *Art History and Its Methods.* London: Phaidon, 1995.
Gilley, Sheridan. "Victorian Feminism and Catholic Art: The Case of Mrs Jameson." In *The Church and the Arts,* edited by Diana Wood. Oxford: Blackwell, 1992.
Haskell, Francis. *Rediscoveries in Art: Some Aspects of Taste, Fashion, and Collecting in England and France.* Oxford: Phaidon, 1976.
Holcomb, Adele M. "Anna Jameson: The First Professional English Art Historian." *Art History* 6 (1983): 171–87.
———. "Anna Jameson (1794–1860): Sacred Art and Social Vision." In *Women as Interpreters of the Visual Arts, 1820–1979,* edited by Claire Richter Sherman with Adele M. Holcomb. Westport, Conn.: Greenwood Press, 1981.
Jameson, Anna. *The Poetry of Sacred and Legendary Art.* 3 vols. 7th ed. London: Longmans, 1874.
Johnston, Judith. *Anna Jameson: Victorian, Feminist, Woman of Letters.* Aldershot, Hants., England: Scolar Press, 1997.

Maginnis, Hayden B. J. *Painting in the Age of Giotto: A Historical Reevaluation.* University Park: Pennsylvania State University Press, 1997.

Needler, G. H., ed. *Letters of Anna Jameson to Ottilie von Goethe.* London: Oxford University Press, 1939.

Rees, A. L., and Frances Borzello, eds. *The New Art History.* London: Camden Press, 1986.

Richter Sherman, Claire, with the assistance of Adele M. Holcomb. "Precursors and Pioneers (1820–1890)." In *Women as Interpreters of the Visual Arts, 1820–1979,* edited by Claire Richter Sherman with Adele M. Holcomb. 3–26. Westport, Conn.: Greenwood Press, 1981.

Rio, Alexis François. *De la poèsie Chrétiènne dans son principe, dans sa matière et dans ses formes.* Paris: Debecourt, 1836.

Robertson, David. *Sir Charles Eastlake and the Victorian Art World.* Princeton, N.J.: Princeton University Press, 1978.

Steegman, John. *Consort of Taste, 1830–1870.* London: Sidgwick and Jackson, 1950.

Thomas, Clara. *Love and Work Enough: The Life of Anna Jameson.* London: Macdonald, 1967.

van Straten, Roelof. *An Introduction to Iconography.* Translated by Patricia de Man. New York: Gordon and Breach, 1994. Originally published as *Een inleiding in de iconografie.* Muiderberg: Dick Coutinho, 1985.

Vasari, Giorgio. *Lives of the Artists.* Harmondsworth, Eng.: Penguin, 1965.

CHAPTER 3

By Her Works Shall Ye Know Her
The Quest for Jessie L. Weston (1850–1928)

Angela Jane Weisl

Although Jessie L. Weston is hardly an unfamiliar name in medieval circles, finding factual information about her is rather like the Grail Quest about which she wrote so extensively—difficult and perilous. Despite her significant contributions to the availability of medieval texts in both England and America, as a member of the scholarly community she has faded into obscurity. In the most extensive bibliographic and biographical study of Weston available, Janet Grayson notes about her that "nothing was to be gleaned from the usual sources. The DNB never heard of her," and "papers she had left no longer existed."[1] Despite her significant contribution to Arthurian studies, of anything personal—letters, journals, private notes, papers—little remains. Her correspondence with the David Nutt Company, her London publisher, burned in a warehouse fire; some exchanges with Houghton Mifflin, in Boston, and Cambridge University Press are all that are left. However, Grayson notes that Weston "lived for her work; there was no reason to think ahead to a future time when her life apart from her scholarship might be of interest to others."[2] It is in that spirit that we must consider her.

Jessie L. Weston, named for her father's first wife, Jessica Laidlay, daughter of a Scottish laird, was born in Clapham, England, on 29 December 1850, the daughter of William Weston and his second wife, Sarah Burton; her father was a tea merchant and member of the Salters' Company. After giving birth to two other daughters, Sarah died when Jessie was about seven; her father then married Clara King, who gave birth to five more children. The Weston family later moved to Abbey Wood, Kent. Jessie Weston was first educated at Brighton, where her family had a home; she then went to study in Hildesheim and then Paris under Gaston Paris, her lifelong mentor. Weston also studied at the Crystal Palace School of Art. As Grayson notes, "[H]er continental training prepared her not only for the demands of the scholar's life, but also for independence of movement and judgement that were exceptional if not unique in her day."³ Although her obituary in the London *Times* claims that "at an early age she gave abundant proof of exceptional intellectual powers," her particular interest in Arthurian legends did not solidify into her lifework until 1890.⁴ After attending the Wagner festival in Bayreuth, she expressed great regret that the Wagner operas, especially *Parsifal*, were not better known in Britain. Alfred Nutt, the renowned folklorist, was her companion, and it was he who suggested that she "was the person most suited to supply that lack" and persuaded her to translate Wolfram von Eschenbach's Middle High German *Parzival* into English.

This project began Weston's career as an "indefatigable translator of Arthurian romances from Old French, Middle English, Middle High German, and Dutch."⁵ Her translation of *Parzival* in free verse was published in 1894, followed in 1896 by *Legends of the Wagner Drama*. Having introduced the British public to Wagner's inspirations and sources, she continued producing accessible translations of other works: *Sir Gawain and the Green Knight* (1897), *Tristan and Iseult* (1899), the *Legend of Lancelot du Lac* (1901), *Morien: A Metrical Romance Rendered into English Prose from the Mediæval Dutch* (1901), *Sir Cleges and Sir Libeaus Desconus* (1902), *Sir Gawain at the Grail Castle* (1904), *Guingamor; Lanval; Tyolet; Le Bisclaveret: Four Lais Rendered into English Prose from the French of Marie de France and Others* (1910), *The Quest of the Holy Grail* (1913), and *The Chief Middle English Poets: Selected Poems* (1914), among others. While neither her best known nor most widely circulated, her translation of the Middle Dutch *Morien* is significant for its uniqueness; Norris J. Lacy comments that she was "quite possibly the only [person] who was not a professional Netherlandist—who even *read* the Moriaen, and she was in any event the first person to undertake a translation. (Indeed, a new translation is only now being made, by David Johnson and Geert Claassens)."⁶ Of the process of translation, Weston said that she aimed "to give such a rendering of the works as shall enable them to make their appeal to the modern reader, not as curious specimens of writing in a dead past, but as, what they should indeed be, part of a living literature."⁷ Her translations, although they seem a bit dated now, are lucid and accessible, as she hoped; indeed, the *Harvard Chaucer Page* comments of her version of the Middle English "Sir Orfeo," "[I]t's a bit old fashioned but fun to read."⁸ Many of Weston's translations can currently be found on the Internet, continuing their availability to scholars and students alike, which she would clearly have enjoyed.⁹ The majority of her translations were published by David Nutt at the Sign of the Phoenix (London) and appeared in the Grimm Library series, an early set of works on folklore.

When not using her "indefatigable energy" to translate, Weston showed her "ripe scholarship, keen critical faculty, sound and independent judgment" and a "remarkable memory for detail" to produce monographs and articles for the *Cambridge History of English Literature, The Cambridge Medieval History,* and the renowned eleventh edition of the *Encyclopedia Britannica,* for which she wrote twelve articles and bibliographies dealing with Arthurian subjects.[10] She contributed articles to journals in England, France, and America, most notably *Athenaeum, Modern Philology,* the *Journal of the Folklore Society, Romania,* and the *Revue Celtique.* Her studies of her beloved Arthurian literature include *King Arthur and His Knights: A Survey of Arthurian Romance* (1899), *The Romance Cycle of Charlemagne and His Peers* (1901), *The Three Days' Tournament: A Study in Romance and Folk-lore, Being an Appendix to the Author's "Legend of Sir Lancelot"* (1902), *The Legend of Sir Perceval: Studies upon Its Origin, Development, and Position in the Arthurian Cycle* (1906–9), *From Ritual to Romance* (1920), and the privately published *The Apple Mystery in Arthurian Romance* (1925). It is *From Ritual to Romance* for which Weston is best known; while most contemporary readers are introduced to it and her through T. S. Eliot's notes to *The Waste Land,* the work received significant praise in its own time and was awarded the Rose Mary Crawshaw Prize for Women Writers, given by the British Academy to "women, regardless of nationality, who have published outstanding works on English Literature."[11] The British Academy Web site lists Weston among "the roll call of great scholars of literature over the last century," and as such it is one of the few places willing to give Weston her due.[12] She put her substantial prize of one hundred dollars toward necessary cataract surgery to aid her failing eyesight, which had become a significant burden in the completing of *From Ritual to Romance.*[13] At her death she had nearly completed the work that she believed would be her most significant contribution to scholarship, a study of the origins of the French romance *Perlesvaux.*

Weston's writing was not limited to translation and scholarship. Her two works of what her obituary calls "belles letters," *The Rose-Tree of Hildesheim, and Other Poems* (1896) and *The Soul of the Countess and Other Stories* (1900), were both published by David Nutt. In 1915 she also undertook to examine the relationship of Germany and France in both political and literary terms, producing *Germany's Literary Debt to France* and *Germany's Crime against France.* These two strongly anti-German pamphlets support the French cause and are written for groups at British universities that expressed pro-German and pacifist sentiments, which she "deplored."[14] Unfortunately, these works are unavailable in the United States and rarely appear in bibliographies of Weston's work; however, her ability as a translator suggests that her style, if not her content, would be fluid and graceful, even when she was writing polemics. Weston was in Bayreuth when World War II broke out and during her return to England lost all her luggage; that aside, her sentiments remained firmly anti-German, despite her interest in their literature and culture. Indeed, apart from attending the Bayreuth festival and despite her Hildesheim education, she rarely visited Germany in her extensive travels, even before the war.

In 1923 Weston received a D. Litt. from the University of Wales in recognition of her services to Celtic literature; she bore the title of Dr. Weston with "pride and some modesty, still sensitive to the academy's exclusiveness, but satisfied that formal recognition of her achievements was complete."[15] Mary Williams, professor of French literature, presented her to the university, and Weston delivered a talk on the major Arthurian romances, described by Grayson as "thorough and entertaining and everywhere radiated her great talent for bringing her subject to every kind of audience."[16] Williams, who made a twenty-two-page transcription of Weston's talk, introduced her, saying, "Our debt to her as Welshmen is greater than we yet realize, for she is the first to have suggested the role Wales played in the formation of the romantic aspect of the Grail story, and she has contributed more than any other towards the elucidation of the very baffling problems of the true significance of the Grail legend."[17]

She was also one of the founders of the Lyceum (in 1904) and Halcyon Clubs, of which she remained "a lifelong and active member."[18] She was a member of the Wagner-Verein, the Folklore Society, and the Quest Society, a small folklore group founded in London in 1909 by G. R. S. Mead, another translator with significant interest in the Gnostic and hermetic Greco-Egyptian texts. Mead had been a secretary to Madame Blavatsky, the leader of the theosophists, and it is primarily this association that gives Weston a reputation for occultism, as the Quest Society believed in a "'secret tradition' of wisdom, stemming from the classical mystery religions and the high magic of the early Christian world, and concerned with the means by which a man could become divine."[19] However, Weston's interest in folklore was not primarily mystical or occult; she saw herself deeply indebted to the Cambridge Ritualists, of whom she was a contemporary, and was a disciple of James Frazer. She was a friend of the folklorist Alfred Nutt, who encouraged her to begin her writing life, and Gaston Paris was her valued mentor until his death; also instrumental in prompting her translations were other scholars, such as Professor W. H. Schofield, the author of *English Literature from the Norman Conquest to Chaucer*, who saw her translations of several Middle English texts as a supplement to his own work. W. P. Ker also suggested additions to her translation of *The Chief Middle English Poets*. She was friendly with Roger Sherman Loomis early in his career, knew James Frazer himself, and was always connected to the classicist Jane Harrison and the French and Celtic scholar Mary Williams.

Weston's close connections to her scholarly colleagues did not prevent her from taking part in several controversies and feuds. An early dispute with the American James Douglas Bruce took place over the key role of Chrétien de Troyes, who Bruce believed originated the Arthurian romance tradition, while Weston strongly believed in an earlier origin and remained undaunted by Chrétien's esteemed reputation.[20] Highly regarded in her work by many French scholars, led by Gaston Paris and Joseph Bédier, she was nevertheless critiqued strongly by the German scholars of her day such as Foerster and Golther and most severely by Ernst Brugger, who called her reconstruction of the prose *Perceval* "idle child's play."[21] This conflict was both nationalist—she was English and working in German territory—and sexist; Grayson quotes Weston's response to Brugger's mean-spirited comments: "[H]as not the writer . . . been solemnly warned off ground sacred to scholars of another sex, and dare we say of another nation?"[22] This scuffle continued in various journals, despite the warnings of Weston's mentors; her zealous enthusiasm was unchecked in the defense of her own ideas. Further conflicts followed: Weston and Loomis, for instance, shared certain positions for some time; their separation is attributable both to Loomis's changing views and Weston's willingness to skewer him in rather harsh reviews in which she called his method "radically unsound" and faulted his interpretations.[23] Loomis understandably found this galling, as he had asked her to review his work in the first place, and another journal feud began. Another, centered around the Quest Society, led to an exchange of nasty reviews between Weston and A. E. Waite, a Rosicrucian, Kabbalist, and Freemason, about their opposing views on the worth of the *Grand Saint Graal,* which Weston disliked and Waite valued highly; his *Holy Grail* attacked Weston overtly, although he acknowledged her extensive knowledge of the literature. Waite clearly felt some resentment that Weston failed to acknowledge his work on the Tarot in *From Ritual to Romance.*[24] Their conflict continued for some time. As Grayson notes, "[S]he never stood aside from an argument, and when provoked let fly spirited barbs that sharpened as she grew older."[25]

Despite this series of conflicts, throughout her scholarly life Weston expressed great interest in young scholars, for whom she was always ready to provide advice, assistance, and helpful criticism. She was particularly noted for her suggestions that aided scholars in their research, and her *Times* obituary comments that "[m]any a student will remember her with respect and gratitude, as well as admiration for her rich store of knowledge, which was always at their command."[26] This is particularly interesting given her place outside the world of academia; without the official recognition that a university affiliation would have provided, Weston was still able to forge a significant reputation as both a scholar and a teacher. Her best-known student is the fictional Miss Sybil Maiden, of Girton College, Cambridge, in David Lodge's *Small World,* who pays her debts to her mentor, saying, "I suppose you would call me a folklorist. . . . I was a pupil of Jessie Weston's."[27] Miss Maiden goes on to discuss *From Ritual to Romance* with Persse McGarrigle, a student of T. S. Eliot, noting that "[i]f Mr. Eliot had taken her discoveries to heart, we might have been spared the maudlin religiosity of his later poetry."[28] Miss Maiden goes on to expound Weston's theories throughout the novel, and at the end bestows her greatest praise on Angelica Pabst at a Modern Language Association panel, saying, "[W]asn't that a brilliant performance? If only Jessie Weston could have heard it."[29] Miss Maiden, however, is not Jessie Weston's only fictional devotee; in the new "director's cut" of Francis Ford Coppola's *Apocalypse Now,* Marlon Brando, as Colonel Kurtz, is seen reading Frazer's *Golden Bough* and Weston's *From Ritual to Romance* in his lair.[30]

Jessie Weston remained unmarried; she was Miss Weston all her life and after her death (despite the honorary doctorate). In place of the standard Victorian expectation that young ladies would choose home and family, either as a wife and mother or as a devoted "spinster daughter caring for the widowed father and whatever younger sisters and brothers remained," Weston chose to make use of her gift for languages and talent for scholarship instead.[31] She supported herself primarily with her inheritance from her father and her royalties, about which she was apparently very exacting:

"[S]he kept close scrutiny of her earnings down to the penny, continually objecting to changes in final copy that might be charged against future royalties."[32] These funds allowed her to maintain a residence in Paris on the Rue de la Ville D'Evêque in the eighth arrondissement until 1923, when anti-English sentiment sent her back to London. She then lived at Biddulph Mansions in Maida Vale until her death. Her finances also allowed her significant travel on the Continent and frequent visits to family in Carshalton, Brighton, and Bournemouth. She was, for instance, with her father when he died at Sydenhall Hill in Kent, and she was very attached to her sisters and her nieces, to whom she later willed her entire estate.[33]

Jessie L. Weston died on 29 September 1928 of complications following surgery for cancer. She was "buried in a perishable coffin, as she had requested, in Carshalton, near London, where she had spent much time at the home of her sister Edith and her favorite niece Mabel."[34] After a discussion of her career, Weston's London *Times* obituary ends by saying that "her charming personality and her great sense of humour won her the enduring affection of a host of friends all over the world. . . . Her death will be keenly regretted both in Europe and in the United States, where some of her volumes are familiar text-books at the great universities."[35] Less forthcoming than its London counterpart, the *New York Times* merely comments that "Jessie Laidlay Weston, who devoted her life to the elucidation of truths of Arthurian romances, died yesterday in London, aged 77."[36] The *New York Times*'s terseness echoes its general reception of Weston's work; despite her prolific achievements, none of her books ever received a review in the *New York Times*. The *Times Literary Supplement*, in her native England, was only slightly more forthcoming; her translation of *Morien* was reviewed in 1902, *Perceval* received notice in 1906, and *From Ritual to Romance* was given significant attention in 1920.

The paucity of available biographical material on Jessie Weston is echoed in her comments on the Middle English authors whom she translated: "[B]iographical data concerning the poets of this period unfortunately are both rare and incomplete. Thus concerning Layamon, Orm, Robert of Brunne, we know just what they tell us in the passages given in the text and no more, i.e., we know their position in life, where they lived, and why they wrote, but beyond that, even their date has to be determined by internal evidence. . . . With regard to the authorship of the romances, we are in even worse case: we have one name, Thomas Chester; for the rest we know neither their names, their date, nor the sources upon which they drew. These are all questions of internal evidence and critical hypothesis."[37] This paradigm is necessary to gain a greater appreciation for Weston herself as well as for her works; although factual material about her may be scarce, her abundant and energetic introductions to the works, as well as her scholarship and translation, reveal the attitudes and qualities that allow us to know her. Although more information is available about Weston than about her medieval counterparts, it is from her works that the best sense of Weston can be determined.

Weston's preface to *Romance, Vision, Satire: English Alliterative Poems of the Fourteenth*

Century (1912) shows her to be eager for knowledge of new material; by 1912 she had certainly established herself as an expert in the field of Arthurian literature, particularly the Continental examples that she had both translated and analyzed. In beginning this new project, suggested to her by W. H. Schofield of Harvard, Weston commented, "Fine as our English Arthurian literature undoubtedly is, it forms but a small section of the *Matière de Bretagne,* and outside the Arthurian romances I knew but little of our mediæval literature. I felt that, by undertaking the work, I should myself be the gainer, but how much I did not realize, but as time went on, and item after item of the list prepared by Professor Schofield for my guidance was marked off, I became more and more interested in the work, and more and more impressed with the extraordinary richness and beauty of mediæval English poetry."[38]

It is interesting that Weston felt herself unversed in Middle English literature, having already completed her translation of *Sir Gawain and the Green Knight* in 1898; her work in German, French, and Dutch shows a great versatility and facility for languages that make surprising her sense of lack in her own native traditions. However, she was clearly not one to resist a challenge and, in response to Schofield's request, produced not only the translation of *Sir Gawain,* which, she noted, "had hopelessly outgrown the original scheme of publication," but also a second, *The Chief Middle English Poets: Selected Poems* (1914).[39] Although she suggests that both volumes were essentially commissioned, thanking Schofield and Ker for their guidance and suggestions, in this second one Weston makes a strong statement of her independence while employing the medieval trope of *humilitas* at the same time: "But if I have been guided by others in the choice of texts, for the manner in which they are presented I am myself responsible. It has seemed to me desirable to give the poems as much as possible in their entirety, or, that being impracticable, in complete and representative episodes. I am, and always have been, strongly of the opinion that to compile such a manual as the present on the lines of short abstracts only results in inflicting injustice alike on the student and on the author."[40] For all her willingness to give credit where it is due, Weston and Schofield had a minor but "very unpleasant falling-out" following the publication of these translations; Schofield apparently felt that "he had received too little credit for his share in her work," although Weston finally "brushed aside his claims as overrating the value of his initial suggestions."[41] Ironic as this may seem in light of her general compliments to her mentors, it reflects the same independent spirit as her previous comments.

In contrast to her strong statement about complete texts, Weston is more reticent about her abilities as a translator, despite her significant success in this field. Understanding the inherent dichotomy in translation between readability and accuracy, she claims that she has "tried throughout to give a literal translation, but where a slavish adherence to the letter of the text would have meant hampering the rhythm, and marring the effect, I have held myself free to express the poet's idea in somewhat different words."[42] Despite her clear ability to make these kinds of choices, Weston still felt herself, in certain ways, unequal to the task: "I am well aware that some of these texts demanded for their adequate rendering a talent beyond my scope: the translation of *Pearl* needs a poet, rather than a versifier; while working on this text I was haunted by regret that it had not been known to the late Christina Rossetti, for, surely, of all modern English writers, she could best have reproduced the glowing imagery and mystic fervor of the original."[43] Weston was a fan of the Pre-Raphaelites, particularly Christina Rossetti, and a Rossetti translation of *Pearl* is delightful to imagine. Weston's understanding of both this poet and the Middle English poem show her to be a passionate reader as well as a scholar, someone with a sensitivity to language and form beyond the merely historical interest of the works she made accessible to her audience.

Striking in her introductions is Weston's strong sense of responsibility, both to the works' long-dead authors and to her audience, a group she seems often to define primarily as students. In her preface to her edition of *Sir Gawain and the Green Knight*, she points out that while "[scholars] can read the poem for itself in all its intricate phraseology, . . . this little book is not for them, and if to those to whom the tale would otherwise be a sealed treasure these pages bring some new knowledge . . . if by that means they gain a keener appreciation of our national heroes, a wider knowledge of our national literature,—then the spirit of the long-dead poet will doubtless not be the slowest to pardon my handling of what was his masterpiece."[44] In her second volume of Middle English translations, in reference to both the works included and the scholars and publisher who made suggestions, she noted, "[T]his collection may thus claim to be fairly representative of the best American and English opinion, and as such will, it is hoped, meet the requirements of the majority of students of our common literature."[45] In the first collection she leaves the verdict of its success to that same audience: "[F]or good or for ill, the work is now done, and I can only commend it to the verdict of students of English literature, trusting that they who are best able to judge of the difficulties of the task will be the most lenient toward any shortcomings in its fulfillment."[46]

Weston's sense of her relationship to other scholars seems at once dutiful and complex. Certainly she expressed gratitude to those who urged her to undertake her series of translations, and she also very much saw herself as engaged in dialogue with others interested in Arthurian material. She dedicates her *Legend of Sir Perceval: Studies upon Its Origin, Development, and Position in the Arthurian Cycle* (1906) to "the memory of Gaston Paris, whose genius, reverence for truth in research, and generous appreciation of the labours of others, will be held in lasting remembrance, these studies are inscribed."[47] This acknowledgment sets up an interesting discourse in the introduction of that work, in which Weston engages in a kind of dialogue with Joseph Bédier. Responding to his study of the *Tristan* of Thomas of Brittany, she addresses his use of the term *terra incognita* for the Tristan material and then places her own work within that context. Bédier places "nos plus anciens poèmes de Tristan" in that unexplored territory, and Weston feels she can lead her readers into it, as she says,

> Now, if I mistake not, it is precisely with the *première floraison de poèmes Arthuriens* that we shall, before the close of these studies, find ourselves dealing; it is a few steps further into this *terra incognita* that I hope to penetrate; and I feel it an augury of happy import that a scholar at once so capable and so cautious as M. Bédier should in such unmistakable terms have avowed his belief in the existence of the first, and profit likely to be derived from a venture into the second. The *terra incognita* is, let us hope, no longer a Forbidden Land, but rather a Land of Promise, to be entered very cautiously no doubt, but still to be entered with every hope of bringing thence some fruit to reward our toil.[48]

The familiarity of the names that Weston references as her colleagues and commentators locates her within an active dialogue from which her part has been unjustly forgotten. Both as a reader and a writer, Jessie Weston was clearly on the cutting edge of medieval studies in her time, which makes her absence from works like Norman Cantor's *Inventing the Middle Ages* all the more surprising. Given her construction of her work as a part of the body of scholarship that encompassed medieval studies in several languages and countries, Weston's contribution must, in its time, have reached well beyond the one thing for which she is best remembered.

If Jessie Weston's name is a faint memory for many contemporary medievalists, relegated to a brief and slightly sarcastic entry in the *New Arthurian Encyclopedia,* it is more common among modernists who know her because of T. S. Eliot. Eliot's first note to the *Waste Land* reads: "Not only the title, but the plan and a good deal of the incidental symbolism of the poem were suggested by Miss Jessie L. Weston's book on the Grail legend: *From Ritual to Romance* (Cambridge). Indeed, so deeply am I indebted, Miss Weston's book will elucidate the difficulties of the poem much better than my notes can do; and I recommend it (apart from the great interest of the book itself) to any who think such elucidation of the poem worth the trouble."[49] It is for this acknowledgment that Weston is best known, and for this reason perhaps *From Ritual to Romance* remains in print when much of the rest of Weston's work has moved into the public domain. However, it is also for this work that Weston receives the most criticism and, unfortunately, the most dismissal from the world of serious scholarship.

From Ritual to Romance, Weston's most theoretical work of scholarship, considers the relationship of the Grail legend to ancient fertility rites. Drawing on the folklore traditions she had studied extensively and particularly on James Frazer's *The Golden Bough,* Weston saw the Grail quest as a literary outgrowth of ancient ritual. Weston's interest in Frazer began well before this project; in *The Legend of Sir Perceval* she already shows significant debt to his work and to ritual theory. In that work she both addresses folklore and separates her own work from historical studies of Arthur. Noting that "Arthur as *dux bellorum* may very well date from the fifth century; Arthur and his knights as first folk-lore, then romantic heroes, are survivals of the Celtic

Wonder-world; and that, in its essential elements, preceded the birth of history, and will endure till the need for history shall pass away."[50] In her conception of romance and its beginnings, history plays second fiddle to other kinds of origins; while there may well have been an historical Arthur, Weston seems to feel that the literary material is a development from other traditions that perhaps co-opt the historical figure as a part of their process. She writes, "Professor Forester is right when he claims that, as a matter of date, in their present form, the historic Arthurian tradition is older than the romantic, but he is wrong when he claims therefore that the romantic is younger. It is but a later expression of an earlier stage, which antedated the historic."[51] This perception reveals a complex sense of the relationship of narrative, culture, and history. She believed that because romance traced a direct line of inheritance from "forgotten Faiths" through folklore to its present state, it revealed a change in outward expression with the same inherent elements. She saw the Grail as a symbol that essentially had come full circle, as she states, "I do not think it matters in the least whether or not the Grail was originally Christian, if it was from the first the symbol of spiritual endeavor."[52] In relation to these assumptions, Weston views her scholarly task in quite elevated terms: "[O]n whatever plan the effort be made, the attempt to penetrate from the outer to the inner, to apprehend behind the sign the thing signified, to bring the lower, the temporary, life into contact with the higher and enduring is a task worthy of the highest energy of man."[53] Although few current scholars approach their studies with equal zeal, Weston's language resonates with a very contemporary understanding of the relationship between things and their meanings.

Given the frequent modern treatment of Weston's work as occultist lunacy, it is interesting to note how firmly she placed herself within a specific scholarly community in the preface to *From Ritual to Romance*. Her charming acknowledgment of Frazer is worth repeating: "Like many others, I owe to Sir J. G. Frazer the initial inspiration which set me, as I may truly say, on the road to the Grail castle. Without the guidance of *The Golden Bough* I should probably, as the late M. Gaston Paris happily expressed it, still be wandering in the forest of Broceliande!"[54] Perhaps more widely recalled is her statement "I avow myself an impenitent believer in Sir J. G. Frazer's main theory."[55] She also pays tribute to several other scholars, including Jane Harrison, Gilbert Murray, F. M. Cornford, and E. K. Chambers, the former three members of the Cambridge Ritualists, showing folklore studies in 1920 to be a rich and fertile world with numerous inhabitants. Weston's concern that "my co-workers in the field of Arthurian research will accept these studies as a permanent contribution to the elucidation of the Grail problem" is matched with "I would fain hope that those scholars who labour in a wider field, and to whose works I owe so much, may find in the results here set forth elements that may prove of real value in the study of the evolution of religious belief."[56] Certainly in her own time, apart from T. S. Eliot, Weston had a number of successors, including C. L. Barber and Herbert Weisinger, who applied similar principles to Shakespeare, and Francis Fergusson, who examined the mythic and ritualistic roots of tragedy.

Weston's work is comparative, examining the pervasiveness of the "nature cults" among both ancient, primitive peoples and contemporary peasants. She examines practices from the *Rig-Veda,* among other works, to explore the Grail's cultural development, as always showing herself to be exceptionally widely read. Robert A. Segal sums up her argument effectively in his introduction to the 1993 edition of *From Ritual to Romance:* "Among the specific Grail symbols for which Weston finds ancient parallels, the most salient are the Lance, the Cup, the dish—which is sometimes identical with the Cup—and the Sword. Of the four, the most important are the Lance and the Cup, which is the Grail. For Weston, the Lance and the Cup are conspicuous symbols of male and female genitals. Her Frazerian argument is comparativist: 'That the Lance and the Cup are, *outside* the Grail story, "Life" [i.e., reproductive] symbols, and have been such from time immemorial, is a fact; why, then, should they not retain that character *inside* the framework of that story?'"[57] Weston's sexualizing of the Grail story works to separate it from the Christian interpretation of the Grail's origins. She suggests that that interpretation is invalid; if the Lance is the spear that pierced Christ's side, then what is its association with the Cup? If the Fisher King is drawn from the various fishing metaphors in the New Testament, then why is the Fisher King fallen? If the Lance is a phallic symbol and the fish a "Life symbol of immemorial antiquity," then the whole scheme makes more sense.[58] When the Christian paradigm works, it simply draws on the cultic and ritualistic elements of the Lance and the Cup; essentially, in Weston's terms, it is unoriginal. She does, however, find useful parallels in Gnosticism and locates the Grail's specific origins in the Naassenes. Thus, Weston sees the development of the story in a trajectory that leads from a vegetation cult to a mystery cult to the Naassenes, to the Mithraic cult, which was brought to Celtic Britain, where the Grail legend then developed and ultimately became Christianized.

Certain aspects of Weston's thesis, such as the Celtic origins of the Grail story, have maintained some authority. However, as Segal notes, "Weston's overall thesis has endured the same fate as the myth-ritualist theory of which it is an application. Initially lauded by professionals for its capacity to make sense of the Grail material, it has since been rejected as unsubstantiated."[59] One of the most notable shifts in her assessment comes from Roger Sherman Loomis, who in his 1927 *Celtic Myth and Arthurian Romance* accepted Weston's central argument, saying, "[T]he evidence is so palpable that one need not be either initiate or a specialist in primitive religion to feel its force."[60] However, by 1963 in *The Grail,* Loomis had summarily withdrawn his support, saying, "I retracted in particular my adherence to Dr. Jessie Weston's ingenious hypothesis concerning the Grail and the Lance, for lack of valid and clearly pertinent evidence."[61] This kind of assessment has pushed Weston's work from serious consideration in the scholarly world, although it remains popular among nonspecialists. A recent reviewer on Amazon.com, for instance, cheerfully comments that "though Weston's style is British, academic, and the length of her immaculately grammatical sentences would put Faulkner to shame, the information is riveting (and makes one wonder how modern filmmakers of the Arthurian genre managed to research their stories and miss so much good stuff)."[62] Grayson notes as well that "for many, Jessie Weston had solved the riddle of the Grail."[63]

To return to the beginning of my discussion of Weston's scholarly writing, a good part of her continued place in the literary imagination is due to the ongoing debate over her influence on Eliot's *Waste Land*. Indeed, despite Eliot's quite direct attribution of influence to her, scholars since the poem's publication have expended a great deal of energy trying to discredit Weston's role in Eliot's work. For instance, Patricia Sloane holds to I. A Richards's dismissal of Weston's book as "a theosophical tract with astral trimmings."[64] She believes that one must read *From Ritual to Romance* "to notice that Madame Sosostris, the savant who names so many cards incorrectly, may borrow some of her shortcomings from Weston."[65] She joins Leon Surette in his assessment that Eliot draws on *From Ritual to Romance* "for satirical purposes."[66] She also points further to Surette's contention that "how he [Eliot] came upon Weston, how many of her books he read, and what he thought of them is unclear. Like Frazer, whose methodology Eliot criticized at Harvard, Weston may not have been a favorite," adding that some pages of Eliot's copy of Weston's book remain uncut.[67] Building on Surette, Sloane continues her criticism, suggesting that "Eliot is more likely to have noticed that Weston, though she characterizes herself as a disciple of Frazer, may have read *The Golden Bough* only in part, or with limited attention."[68] Casting aspersions on Weston's scholarship and rigor seems hardly necessary; any perusal of her works shows her a careful and thorough reader, yet it is typical of the unnecessary zeal with which Eliot scholars criticize Weston.

While some readers, such as Cleanth Brooks and F. O. Mathissen, have been willing to see the value in Weston as a source for Eliot, they have been distinctly in the minority. Examining Eliot's comments about the notes to *The Waste Land* and his feeling that the poem might well have done without them, Hugh Kenner includes Eliot's comment: "[I]t was just, no doubt, that I should pay my tribute to Miss Jessie Weston; but I regret having sent so many enquirers off on a wild goose chase after Tarot cards and the Holy Grail."[69] His own assessment, however, is that Wagner was the more prominent source for the poem's introduction than Weston or Frazer.[70] In his entire discussion of the poem he mentions Weston only these two times. Perhaps, however, it is better to ignore than to impale her, as critics like Sloane and Surette choose to do. Indeed, Surette finds it repeatedly necessary to ally Weston with occultists such as Madame Blavatsky (although Weston is never mentioned in Blavatsky's biography), suggesting that Blavatsky's "more bizarre theories had little currency, although they are reflected by Weston in *From Ritual to Romance*."[71] The theories of which Surette speaks here, he implies, tie both the theosophist and the scholar to Hitler and Aryanism, making Weston's work sinister and dangerous. Given Weston's anti-German pamphlets and her fierce critique of anti-Semitism, this charge seems particularly misguided.[72] The energy Surette spends on skewering Weston's work, labeling it occultist rather than folkloric and generally discrediting any other critics who found it a valuable resource for Eliot's poem, seems extraordinarily excessive, considering that the poet he reveres appears to take it seriously and credits it as his source.

Weston's work has found a home in some odd places, despite her excision from medieval and modernist scholarship. Martin Shichtman sees her influence on the films of Francis Ford Coppola and John Boorman. The overt tribute in *Apocalypse Now* has already been mentioned; however, Boorman's *Excalibur*, Shichtman believes, "strive[s] to return to those early rituals on which the medieval Grail stories were founded; they attempt to arrive at the essence of the Grail myth, thereby to capture its universality."[73] In doing so, he argues, these two directors find their inspiration in Weston's writings, relying on her "to uncover for them the basis of the Grail myth"; like Weston, he notes, "they too seek the truth of paradigms."[74] Other popular works on Arthurian literature find value in Weston's assumptions; the Myth and Legend series published by the Aquarian Press is full of references to her work, and many online Arthurian sites make reference to *From Ritual to Romance*. My own research on modern manifestations of medieval narrative has found much of value in Weston's understanding of the mythical origins of the Arthurian story. That most Arthurian of films, *Star Wars*, is called by its author a "myth for modern times," and if George Lucas does not reference Weston, instead favoring Joseph Campbell, his production still owes a great debt to her way of thinking about medieval romance.

Although Jessie Weston's translations seem a bit old-fashioned now, and *From Ritual to Romance* is so well known for its controversies that it is hard to read it for its value, she nonetheless remains an important example of a woman medievalist whose remarkable energy and enthusiasm were directed in the service of bringing the pleasures of our discipline to students and scholars alike. As Grayson comments, "Jessie Weston knew as well as anyone else that few ideas outlast one's own time."[75] However, in her own day she was doubtless one of the most knowledgeable and well read scholars of Arthurian romance. If her ideas are no longer particularly valuable to us as medievalists, and if she is somewhat concealed by the dearth of available biographical information about her, her works still paint a picture of a warm and generous woman whose life's work was spent in an enterprise we all find familiar. For all her nods to the male scholars of her day who influenced her, Weston's willingness to hold her own opinions and express them freely make her an early inspiration at the time when Arthurian studies were being founded. In her preface to *The Legend of Lancelot du Lac,* Weston best reveals her own position:

> Undertaken, in the first instance, with an absolutely open mind . . . it was only by slow degrees that the real bearing of the evidence became clear, and I felt I had at last grasped a guiding thread through the perplexing maze. The results, which perhaps to some readers may appear startlingly subversive of opinions formally expressed by certain distinguished scholars, were wholly unforeseen. They are the outcome of genuine study of original texts; whether in the long run they be, or be not generally accepted, I would at least plead that they be judged on *the evidence of those texts.* . . . They may, I

hope they will, be hereafter added to, and confirmed. As they stand they encourage us to hope that further study of the material already available may yield welcome, and perhaps unsuspected, results.[76]

If for nothing else, it is worth remembering Jessie Laidlay Weston for her vision of scholarship as a responsible quest able to produce surprising and enlightening results, results that will lead others on the same quest.

Notes

I am sincerely indebted to Kristina Dzwonczyk, my research assistant, for her unflagging help with this project; her determination has helped find obscure sources, valuable information, and useful bibliographic references. This work is as much hers as mine; I believe she is a student whose rich appreciation for both literature and research would have made Jessie Weston proud.

1. Grayson, "In Quest of Jessie Weston," 1.
2. Grayson, "In Quest of Jessie Weston," 2.
3. Grayson, "In Quest of Jessie Weston," 5.
4. "Jessie L. Weston," obituary, *Times* (London).
5. "Jessie L. Weston," in *New Arthurian Encyclopedia*, 510.
6. Lacy, "Jessie Laidlay Weston (1850–1928)," 337.
7. Weston, *Romance, Vision, and Satire*, xviii.
8. *Harvard Chaucer Page*, "Sir Orfeo," trans. Jessie L. Weston, *The Chief Middle English Poets: Selected Poems* (New York: Houghton Mifflin Company, 1914). New URL: http://www.courses.fas.harvard.edu/-chaucer/special/litsubs/breton/orfeo.html
9. Jessie L. Weston's translation of *Sir Gawain and the Green Knight* is available as part of the Camelot Project at the University of Rochester (http://www.lib.rochester.edu/camelot/sggk.htm); her translation of "Sir Orfeo" can be found on the *Harvard Chaucer Page* (http://www.courses.fas.harvard.edu/-chaucer/special/litsubs/breton/orfeo.html). *Morien,* one of the least well known of the romances she translated, is online at York University (www.yorku.ca/inpar/morien-weston.pdf).
10. Obituary, *Times* (London).
11. *British Academy Homepage.*
12. *British Academy Homepage.*
13. Grayson, "In Quest of Jessie Weston," 43.
14. Grayson, "In Quest of Jessie Weston," 9.
15. Grayson, "In Quest of Jessie Weston," 47.
16. Grayson, "In Quest of Jessie Weston," 43.
17. From Mary Williams's address to the congregation, 21 July 1923, quoted in Grayson, "In Quest of Jessie Weston," 43.
18. Obituary, *Times* (London).
19. Cavendish, *King Arthur and the Grail*, 209.
20. The feud is discussed in some detail in Grayson, "In Quest of Jessie Weston," 11–12. Bruce was apparently so obsessed by this conflict that he was accused of having a "Jessie Weston Complex" (Grayson, 12).

21. Brugger used the words "müssige Spielerei" in his 1901 review of *The Legend of Sir Lancelot in Folk-Lore* 12 (1901): 495, quoted in Grayson, "In Quest of Jessie Weston," 13.

22. Grayson, "In Quest of Jessie Weston," 12.

23. Review of Roger Sherman Loomis's *Celtic Myth and Arthurian Romance, Modern Language Review* 32 (1928), 243–48, quoted in Grayson, "In Quest of Jessie Weston," 18.

24. This feud is discussed at length in Grayson, "In Quest of Jessie Weston," 35–40. Waite was associated with the Order of the Golden Dawn, the Quest Society, and other occult groups; surprisingly, he has not received the same criticism for just those leanings that Jessie Weston has, despite her rather less involved relationship to those groups. That said, he has also not been credited with her influence either. His interpretation of the Grail story sought a Christian origin, however, rather than the cultic, ritualist origin that Weston proposed (Grayson, 39).

25. Grayson, "In Quest of Jessie Weston," 48.

26. Obituary, *Times* (London).

27. Lodge, *Small World*, 13.

28. Lodge, *Small World*, 13.

29. Lodge, *Small World*, 367.

30. Obituary, *Times* (London).

31. Grayson, "In Quest of Jessie Weston," 5.

32. Grayson, "In Quest of Jessie Weston," 2 n. 2.

33. Grayson, "In Quest of Jessie Weston," 5.

34. Grayson, "In Quest of Jessie Weston," 49.

35. Obituary, *Times* (London).

36. "Jessie L. Weston," obituary, *New York Times*.

37. Weston, *Chief Middle English Poets*, 382.

38. Weston, *Romance, Vision, Satire*, v–vi.

39. Weston, *Romance, Vision, Satire*, vi.

40. Weston, *Chief Middle English Poets*, v.

41. Grayson, "In Quest of Jessie Weston," 9.

42. Weston, *Romance, Vision, Satire*, viii.

43. Weston, *Romance, Vision, Satire*, viii.

44. Jessie L. Weston, preface to *Sir Gawain and the Green Knight*, available online from http://www.lib.rochester.edu/camelot/sggk.html.

45. Weston, *Romance, Vision, Satire*, v.

46. Weston, *Romance, Vision, Satire*, vi.

47. Weston, *Legend of Sir Perceval*, iii.

48. Weston, *Legend of Sir Perceval*, v–vi.

49. Eliot, "Notes on *The Waste Land*," 91.

50. Weston, *Legend of Sir Perceval*, 336.

51. Weston, *Legend of Sir Perceval*, 336.

52. Weston, *Legend of Sir Perceval*, 335.

53. Weston, *Legend of Sir Perceval*, 335.

54. Weston, preface to *From Ritual to Romance*, vii.

55. Weston, *From Ritual to Romance*, 10.

56. Weston, preface to *From Ritual to Romance*, ix.

57. Segal, introduction to *From Ritual to Romance*, xxx; his quotation from Weston herself is found in the work on p. 76.
58. Weston, *From Ritual to Romance*, 125.
59. Segal, introduction to *From Ritual to Romance*, xxxv.
60. Loomis, *Celtic Myth and Arthurian Romance*, 261. (Loomis's reaction is also quoted by Segal, introduction, xxxv.)
61. Loomis, *Grail*, ix.
62. Anonymous review of *From Ritual to Romance*.
63. Grayson, "In Quest of Jessie Weston," 32.
64. Surette, *Birth of Modernism*, 76.
65. Sloane, "Richard Wagner's Arthurian Sources," 31.
66. Sloane, "Richard Wagner's Arthurian Sources," 31.
67. Sloane, "Richard Wagner's Arthurian Sources," 32; here Sloane further paraphrases Surette.
68. Sloane, "Richard Wagner's Arthurian Sources," 33.
69. Kenner, *Invisible Poet*, 151.
70. Kenner, *Invisible Poet*, 170.
71. Surette, *Birth of Modernism*, 77.
72. Grayson notes that Weston deplored anti-Semitism and wrote frequently of the "debt Christians owed to Jews." Citing Catholicism as the cause of Continental anti-Semitism, she urged England not to follow in its footsteps; she noted that only in the Gospels (the only part of the Bible she felt the Catholics knew anything about) was the Jew the great villain; however, she wrote, "This anti-Semitism . . . is in hot blood and the manifestations, not always spectacular as in pogroms or the Dreyfus case, are sad and chronic" ("Quo Vadis: Some Reflections upon the Anglo-Catholic Movement," unpublished essay, quoted in Grayson, "In Quest of Jessie Weston," 45).
73. Shichtman, "Hollywood's New Weston," 35.
74. Shichtman, "Hollywood's New Weston," 36.
75. Grayson, "In Quest of Jessie Weston," 19.
76. Weston, preface to *The Legend of Lancelot du Lac*, v–vi)

Select Bibliography of Works by Jessie L. Weston

Translator. *Parzival: A Knightly Epic*, by Wolfram von Eschenbach. London: David Nutt, 1894.
Translator. *Lohengrin Fifty Years After.* [A poem.] In *By One of the Folk*. London: David Nutt, 1895.
The Rose-Tree of Hildesheim, and Other Poems. London: David Nutt, 1896.
The Legends of the Wagner Drama: Studies in Mythology and Romance. New York: Scribner, 1896.
The Legend of Sir Gawain: Studies upon Its Original Scope and Significance. London: David Nutt, 1897.
King Arthur and His Knights: A Survey of Arthurian Romance. London: David Nutt, 1899.
Translator. *The Story of Tristan and Iseult: Rendered into English from the German of Gottfried von Strassburg*. With designs by C. Watts. 2 vols. London: David Nutt, 1899.
The Soul of the Countess and Other Stories. London: David Nutt, 1900.
The Legend of Sir Lancelot du Lac: Studies upon Its Origin, Development, and Position in the Arthurian Romantic Cycle. London: David Nutt, 1901; reprint, New York: AMS Press, 1972.
Translator. *Morien: A Metrical Romance Rendered into English Prose from the Mediæval Dutch*. London: David Nutt, 1901.

The Romance Cycle of Charlemagne and His Peers. London: David Nutt, 1901.
The Three Days' Tournament: A Study in Romance and Folk-lore, Being an Appendix to the Author's "Legend of Sir Lancelot." London: David Nutt, 1902.
Translator. *Two Old English Metrical Romances Rendered into Prose Sir Cleges and Sir Libeaus Desconus.* With designs by Caroline M. Watts. London: David Nutt, 1902.
Translator. *Sir Gawain at the Grail Castle.* With designs by C. Watts. London: David Nutt, 1904.
Editor. *Sir Gawain and the Green Knight: A Middle-English Arthurian Romance Retold in Modern Prose, with Introduction and Notes.* New York: New Amsterdam Book Co., 1905.
The Legend of Sir Perceval: Studies upon Its Origin, Development, and Position in the Arthurian Cycle. London: David Nutt, 1906–9.
Supplementer. *The Volsunga Saga.* Translated from the Icelandic by Eirikr Magnusson and William Morris, with an introduction by H. Halliday Sparling. Hon. Rasmus B. Anderson, LL.D., editor in chief. J. W. Buel, managing editor. London: Norrœna Society, 1907.
Translator. *Sir Gawain and the Lady of Lys.* Illustrated by Morris M. Williams. London: David Nutt, 1907.
Translator. *Guingamor; Lanval; Tyolet; Le Bisclaveret: Four Lais Rendered into English Prose from the French of Marie de France and Others.* London: David Nutt, 1910.
Translator. *Old English Carols from the Hill Manuscript,* by Richard Hill. London: David Nutt, 1911.
Legendary Cycles of the Middle Ages. In vol. 6 of *The Cambridge Medieval History,* planned by J. B. Bury and edited by H. H. Gwatkin. Cambridge: Cambridge University Press, 1912.
Romance, Vision and Satire: English Alliterative Poems of the Fourteenth Century. New York: Houghton Mifflin Company, 1912.
Translator. *The Quest of the Holy Grail.* London: G. Bell, 1913.
Editor. *The Chief Middle English Poets: Selected Poems.* New York: Houghton Mifflin Company, 1914.
Germany's Literary Debt to France. London: David Nutt, 1915.
Germany's Crime against France. London: David Nutt, 1915.
From Ritual to Romance. Princeton, N.J.: Princeton University Press, 1920. Reprint, edited by Robert A. Segal, Princeton, N.J.: Princeton University Press, 1993.
The Apple Mystery in Arthurian Romance. Aberdeen: privately printed, 1925. Reprinted from the *Bulletin of the John Rylands Library* 9 (1925): 417–30.

Works Cited

Anonymous review of *From Ritual to Romance,* by Jessie L. Weston [online]. Submitted by mailto: mxd8964@utarlg.uta.edu [16 March 2002]. Available from http://www.amazon.com and http://camelot.celtic-twilight.com/weston/fr2r/index.htm
British Academy Homepage [online] [16 March 2002]. Available from www.britac.ac.uk/news/releases.
Cavendish, Richard. *King Arthur and the Grail: The Arthurian Legends and Their Meaning.* New York: Taplinger Publishing, 1978.
Eliot, T. S. "Notes on *The Waste Land.*" In *Collected Poems: 1909–1935.* New York: Harcourt, Brace, 1936.
Grayson, Janet. "In Quest of Jessie Weston." *Arthurian Literature* 11 (1992): 1–80.
"Jessie L. Weston." In *The New Arthurian Encyclopedia*, edited by Norris J. Lacy. New York: Garland Publishing, 1996.

"Jessie L. Weston." Obituary. *New York Times,* 1 October 1928.
"Jessie L. Weston." Obituary. *Times* (London), 1 October 1928.
Harvard Chaucer Page [online] [16 March 2002]. Available from http://www.courses.fas.harvard.edu/-chaucer/special/litsubs/breton/orfeo.html.
Kenner, Hugh. *The Invisible Poet: T. S. Eliot.* New York: McDowell, Oblenksy, 1957.
Lacy, Norris J. "Jessie Laidlay Weston (1850–1928)." In *On Arthurian Women: Essays in Memory of Maureen Fries,* edited by Bonnie Wheeler and Fiona Tolhurst. Dallas: Scriptorium Press, 2001.
Lodge, David. *Small World.* New York: Warner, 1984.
Loomis, Roger Sherman. *Celtic Myth and Arthurian Romance.* New York: Columbia University Press, 1927.
———. *The Grail.* Princeton, N.J.: Princeton University Press, 1963.
Segal, Robert A. Introduction to *From Ritual to Romance,* by Jessie L. Weston. 1920. Reprint, Princeton, N.J.: Princeton University Press, 1993.
Shichtman, Martin B. "Hollywood's New Weston: The Grail Myth in Francis Ford Coppola's *Apocalypse Now* and John Boorman's *Excalibur.*" *Postscript* 4, no. 1 (1984): 35–48.
Sloane, Patricia. "Richard Wagner's Arthurian Sources, Jessie L. Weston, and T. S. Eliot's *The Waste Land.*" *Arthuriana* 11, no. 1 (2001): 30–53.
Surette, Leon. *The Birth of Modernism: Ezra Pound, T. S. Eliot, W. B. Yeats and the Occult.* Montreal: McGill-Queen's University Press, 1993.

CHAPTER 4

Lina Eckenstein (1857–1931)
Seeking Scope for Women

PENELOPE D. JOHNSON

LINA ECKENSTEIN does not belong in this volume on two counts: she was neither a professional scholar in the academy nor purely a medievalist.[1] She was an autodidact possessed of a passion for research in whatever area piqued her interest who functioned on the fringes of academic circles. Yet here she is in this volume, cheek by jowl with scholars who hold advanced degrees, have written extensive and important works in medieval studies, and frequent colleges and universities. If she were alive, she would thoroughly enjoy this intellectual company without hesitation or self-consciousness, and the other scholars would find her worthy of their attention, despite her lack of credentials.

Lina Dorina Johanna Eckenstein (1857–1931) was a woman whose life was shaped by the nineteenth century but who lived to transcend many of its limitations. She had no formal education and seems never to have held a professional position. Her closest companion was her younger brother, Oscar, an intrepid but irascible mountaineer, and as an unmarried adult she may have lived at home with her mother.[2] Yet this woman, whose life at first glance seemed limited by Victorian expectations to the family and domestic sphere, published more than a dozen books and articles, a collection of publications that is quirkily diverse. Sometimes her intended audience was children, for whom she wrote a collection of stories, and other times scholars, when she published journal articles in *Ancient Egypt* and the *English Historical Review*. The genres in which she worked were also diverse, including a travel guide and a novel; her topics encompass the Sinai peninsula, Albrecht Dürer, eastern Tuscany, nursery rhymes, ancient Egypt, and the subject that qualifies her for this volume, medieval monastic women. This apparently unfocused life's work demonstrates that to be

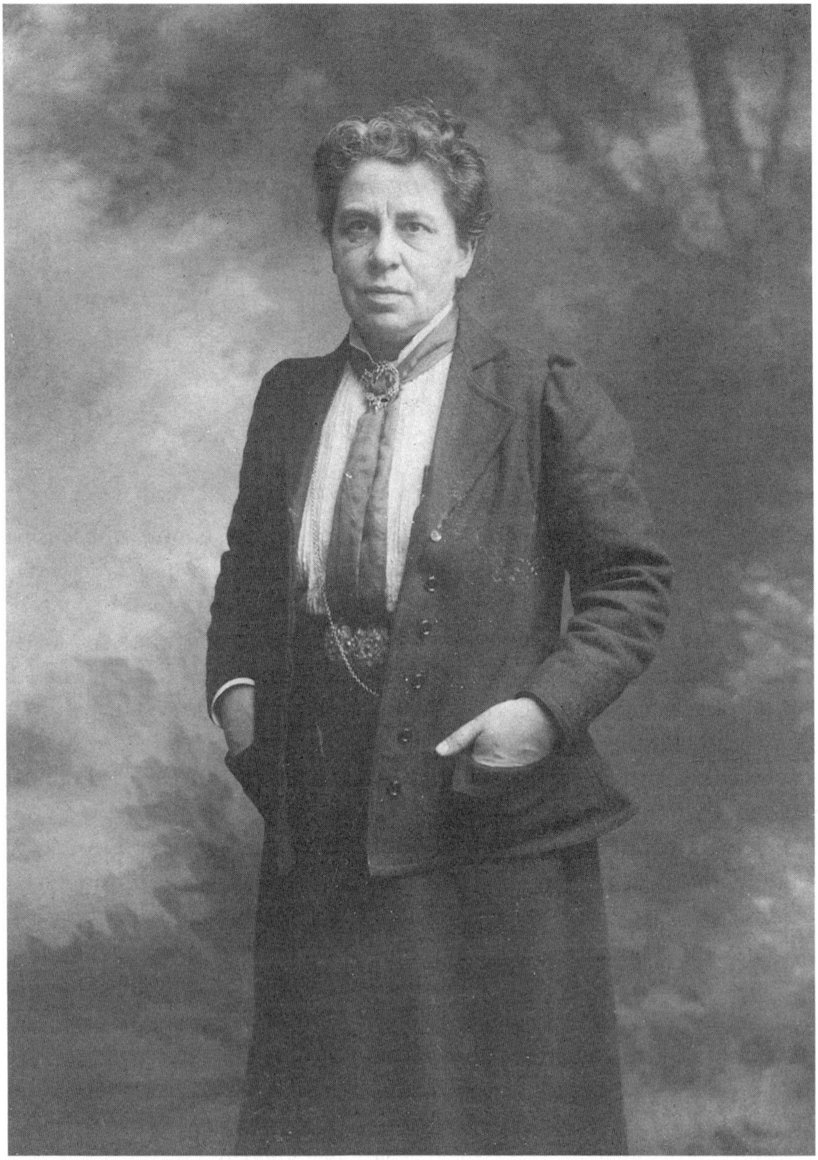

an able dilettante had its advantages. Eckenstein was free to follow her passions for the Renaissance and the Reformation, linguistics, travel, women and women's rights, and the study of religious beliefs. No constraints of professional training or departmental expectations limited her lively curiosity, and new friends and connections opened up areas ripe for her explorations.

Lina was born in Islington, England, on 23 September 1857, to a German immigrant, Frederick Gottlieb Eckenstein, and his wife, Julie Amalie Antonia Helmke, an English woman who may have been of German extraction. Frederick had fled in 1848 from Bonn to avoid prosecution for his revolutionary activities and ended up in England, where he supported his family as a merchant.[3] The family had three children in all: Lina, Oscar (two years younger than Lina), and Amelia.[4] The Eckensteins seem to have been a prosperous middle-class family, to judge by their life style.[5]

Lina never married or had children. She died 4 May 1931, having been born into a world of corsets and the cult of domesticity, adjusting in middle age to rucksacks and roughing it, and dying at seventy-four years old, still an active scholar in Little Hampden, Great Missenden, a respectable rural suburb of London.[6] When she died, she was hard at work on two projects that were published posthumously.[7] Lina was remembered by those who knew her as "a woman of very decided character and attainments. Like her brother Oscar, she seems to have been a natural rebel and she held a prominent place in Women's Freedom movements in England in the early part of [the] century."[8]

The important formative influences for Lina Eckenstein were traditional: her grandfather, her brother, and her friends were the personal contacts who opened areas of learning and travel unavailable to her as a woman on her own. There is no evidence that she attended a school of higher education, but rather she seems to have been taught at home, where there was a lively intellectual environment. She remembered the research of her grandfather that piqued her curiosity: "As a child I gazed with awe at those periodical publications of hieroglyph texts with their birds and little men, over which my grandfather pondered."[9] Her early fascination with the world of ancient Egypt would be later facilitated by friends whose contacts and expeditions would lead her to write on a variety of Egyptian topics.

Whoever were her teachers, Lina proved marvelously able at languages, and it was the ability to read widely in a rich variety of sources that undergirded her later research. She read Latin, Greek, Middle High German, and Middle English and was fluent in contemporary German, French, and Italian. She had an abiding interest in linguistics, probably fueled by her ability to read and speak various languages. A review of her publications reveals her catholic interests and how they grew out of personal contacts.

Eckenstein's bilingual background facilitated her first intellectual challenge—doing a transcription project in German. This was not simply the reading and translating of contemporary German; rather, she tackled the translation of Albrecht Dürer's notes, which were housed in the British Museum and written in his illegible hand and in early-sixteenth-century Franconian dialect. This project was undertaken to aid William Martin Conway, who was working on a book on Dürer and may well have found the hand and the dialect impossible to decipher. Conway was a mountaineer and explorer, a geographer, and later a museum director who began his research on Dürer about 1880. He knew Lina's brother, Oscar, and it may well have been through this connection that Conway discovered the gifted young woman who would become his transcriber and translator.[10] Although Conway may have been the first scholar outside her family to validate Lina's abilities, he proved to be rather offhand about her contributions. The work he published, *The Literary Remains of Albrecht Dürer; With Transcripts from the British Museum Manuscripts and Notes upon Them by Lina Eckenstein,* makes clear her contribution in its title, but she and her work are never even mentioned in his memoirs.[11] The personal connection with Conway also linked her to another intellectual, Karl Pearson, who shared his flat in London with Conway in the winter of 1880.[12] Pearson, together with his wife, Maria, and their children were to become important lifelong friends of Lina's.

Whether or not Conway was dismissive of Lina after her archival work for his project, she was not permanently deterred. Thirteen years after the publication by Conway of *The Literary Remains of Albrecht Dürer,* Lina published her own study of the painter in the Popular Library of Art series.[13] I like to think that whatever snubs she might have received as a young woman from Conway simply galvanized her to use her own hard-won expertise in the documents to popularize the painter she admired.

From the early work on Dürer, Eckenstein expanded her inquiries in two directions; one was to stay in the early modern period but shift to an Italian subject, and the other was to follow her fascination with language into research projects on linguistics. In 1906 she published a study of nursery rhymes, which has been republished and appears still today on reading lists and in college libraries as a useful source on the topic.[14] Another of her works, which was published posthumously and republished in 1969, attempts to study "words and customs side by side" by following six concepts across time and language as she builds a case for shared, Indo-European cultural roots.[15] This work, *A Spell of Words,* she dedicated to the three Pearson children, "worthy representatives of a new generation."[16]

Perhaps Eckenstein's single most scholarly work is a three-part article she published on the Italian Guidi family from Florence.[17] This carefully researched study of an important Tuscan family follows their fortunes from the tenth to the fourteenth century. It is exceedingly dry but thorough. While working on this project, Lina may have needed an occasional break from archival work; at least three years later she published a little guide book to the northern Tuscan area of the Casentino, which suggests that she had spent time exploring the hills of Tuscany, perhaps during the period of research on the Guidi.[18]

The guide is written as the travelogue of a walking tour Lina took through the area with a friend who was a "new-fledged M.D."[19] This format is lively and appealing, but it still allows the author to include material on the history and culture of the region. For example: "It was late one afternoon in April when we left the train at Bibbiena, and, shouldering our knapsacks, wended our way up from the station to the town. We were well in the land of the ancient Etruscans, that mysterious and visionary people whose fleet swept the Tyrrhenian Sea at a time when the greatness of Rome was not."[20] The guide is illustrated with charming little drawings by Lucy du Bois-Reymond, one of the four daughters of Emil du Bois-Reymond, a close childhood friend of Karl Pearson. Thus the personal ties of friendships intersect again with Lina's intellectual life.

The political climate in which she was raised her family may have laid the foundations for Lina's socialist beliefs, which were shared by her circle of friends. From at least 1890 to 1911 (and possibly longer), she was an active member of the Fabian Society and its discussion groups. George Bernard Shaw's diary notes that on 8 March 1890 he went to "Miss Brooke's in the evening to hear Miss Eckenstein read a paper on 'Parents and Children.'"[21] Lina was not content to talk to other like-minded adults about the need to educate children, particularly girls, in socialist ideals and the logic of women's rights; she took her concern directly to little girls by writing a collection of fairy tales for them that would educate as they entertained the audience.[22]

Lina's involvement in the Fabian group was shared by her friends the Pearsons. One evening in the winter of 1910–11, Lina and Maria Sharpe Pearson read papers together at a session.[23] Eckenstein, with her abiding interests in women and pre-modern history, presented "Types of Women before the Reformation," and Pearson read a paper titled "Laws and Regulations Relating to Prostitution, A.D. 800–1500."

Her concerns with women's status and rights generated Eckenstein's most important work, the one that qualifies her as a worthy entry in this volume, *Woman under Monasticism,* published by Cambridge University Press and dedicated to Karl and Maria Sharpe Pearson.[24] This study, as has been often noted, was the first modern scholarly contribution to the history of women's religious experience in the West and would hold pride of place for its coverage and generally even-handed treatment of the subject until recently, when Jo Ann McNamara published *Sisters in Arms* one hundred years after Eckenstein's monograph.[25]

My own discovery of Eckenstein's study came when, as an undergraduate looking for information about medieval nuns, I found *Woman under Monasticism* on the library shelf. It seemed to provide the overview I sought, although I had difficulties with the first chapter, which seemed unscholarly to me.[26] In this introductory chapter Eckenstein posits a golden-age theory of gender history to which scholars more modern than she have continued to succumb.[27] Her argument is that a primitive "mother-age, when women held positions of authority inside the tribal group and directly exercised influence on the doings of the tribe" was ousted by the "father-age. . . . [w]hen men as heads of families succeeded to much of the influence women had held in the tribe."[28]

All was not permanently lost for women, however, because the new religion, Christianity, created the institution of monasticism, which unwittingly provided new opportunities for women. It was in the convent that a woman would be able to find a place for her talents and interests during the Middle Ages, "[f]or the convent accepted the dislike women felt to domestic subjection and countenanced them in their refusal to undertake the duties of married life. It offered an escape from the tyranny of the family, but it did so on condition of such a sacrifice of personal independence, as in the outside world more and more involved the loss of good repute."[29] In other words, Eckenstein acknowledges the tensions in the choice by women of the celibate life, noting that the nun and the whore shared the active rejection of "married relations on the basis of the subjection imposed by the father-age."[30]

The medieval convent was rich with promise for women outside the home and the married state. Above all it offered an educational model for contemporary emulation: "Perhaps some of those who are interested in the educational movements of to-day may care to recall the history and arrangements of institutions, which favoured the intellectual development of women in the past."[31]

To make her argument for the importance of educating women, Eckenstein retells the history of monastic women, but she limits the story to the English and German orders and to individual abbesses and female saints from the northern regions. In so doing she writes an important compensatory history, rich with famous but forgotten women like Hildegard of Bingen, deploring that "no attempt has hitherto been made to submit the writings and influence of Hildegard to a detailed critical examination."[32] Eckenstein resurrected little-known holy women like Abbess Charitas Pirckheimer, translating paragraphs of her memoir and demonstrating the abbess's participation with the literati of her day.[33] Throughout the book Eckenstein translates medieval texts: for example, she introduces her readers to sections of Hroswitha of Gandersheim's plays and the *Ancren Riwle,* along with other works inaccessible to most English speakers.[34] By concentrating an entire chapter (chapter 7) on the conventual arts of monastic women, she privileges an entire field now recognized by scholars as significant.[35] Her admiration for her holy heroines is infectious, but Eckenstein transcends enthusiasm with scholarship, contextualizing women's monastic life within the broader sociopolitical developments of the times.

The concern she felt for mapping women's religious experience again found expression in her last published work, which dealt with the women of the early church.[36] This monograph was shepherded into print by her young friend Celia Roscoe, who had also played a role in the publication of *A Spell of Words*. Eckenstein continued to examine in this last study of early Christian women the ways in which Christianity offered options and opportunities to women who chose not to marry: "The preaching of no marriage by the Apostles directly influenced the lives of many individuals; witness the wife who left the intemperate husband, the bride who separated from the bridegroom, the daughter who refused marriage altogether,—and this with the direct approval of the ministers of religion. . . . The acceptance either of a married or an unmarried life had been made possible."[37] Gone is the mother-and-father age that intrigued her in her early writing as Eckenstein chronicles in the lives of the early Christians the "promise of better things to come" she anticipates in her own day.[38]

In addition to the areas of research and publication suggested to Eckenstein by her language training and her socialist ideals, the archeological digs of her great friends the Egyptologist Sir W. M. Flinders Petrie and his wife, Hilda, stimulated the next stage in her scholarly activities. Lina accompanied the Petries on four expeditions to Egypt, busying herself by taking "charge of the registration, mending, and storing of objects."[39] This exciting experience galvanized Eckenstein into writing a range of publications that included scholarly articles on the moon cult in Sinai and the Egyptian god Sopt, a monograph on the history of the Sinai, and then a novel based on a historical pharaoh's life.[40] The anthropologist Margaret Murray was together with Eckenstein in Petrie's camp on one expedition. Murray recorded that Lina "was an enterprising person, willing to travel anywhere. . . . In 1904–5 she and Mrs. Petrie went from Egypt to the camp in Sinai three days' journey by camel, alone without male escort except the camel men. This was . . . a most remarkable achievement, and at that period very risky."[41]

Lina Eckenstein exhibits interesting contrasts and contradictions in her work and her life. She was a rationalist yet highly romantic; she approached life with a pedantic literalism yet was not lacking a lively sense of humor. She had no children but cared for them strongly as individuals and as a group. She believed in women's rights yet does not seem to have been active in the suffragist movement. As an example of such contrasting impulses, in *A History of Sinai* Eckenstein carefully offers logical explanations for the burning bush and the pillar of fire; she notes contemporary Bedouin practice for finding water in the desert and suggests it as a rational explanation for how Moses obtained water by smiting a rock (Exod. 17:7).[42] Yet she is moved by the story from Exodus that she relates: "The passage of the Israelites through Sinai forms the most thrilling episode in the history of the peninsula."[43] Eckenstein can be painfully literal; she asks what was "the language and script that were used" for the Ten Commandments, and she posits that "[t]he 'writing of God' was possibly a Semitic script."[44] But this earnest scholar could describe a camel, tongue in cheek, as "to all purposes a huge goat" and mighty destructive at that![45] Although childless she concerned herself with advocating good education for girls and idealized Germany, where she believed "the modern movement for women's education [had] arisen."[46] She was remembered affectionately by one of the Pearson daughters to whom she had dedicated a book as "highly cultured but eccentric."[47]

Lina Eckenstein wrote in part to explore her own catholic interests, which encompassed art history, ancient Egyptian history and religion, linguistic-cultural theory, and the Italian Renaissance. But she also hoped to better the world she knew. She sought to improve women's position through a socialist political philosophy, speaking and writing about women's education and rights. She offered early Christian women and the nuns of the Middle Ages as models of the "wider scope for women's activities" she envisioned, seeing it as an improvement on the role of dutiful wife in her own day, which provided "insufficient scope for [women's] energies."[48] She did worry that a "perversion of instinct" might have lured lesbians into the cloister, but otherwise she depicts medieval convents as educational success stories, urging that "those who [were] interested in the educational movements of [the day might] care to recall the history and arrangements of institutions, which favoured the intellectual development of women in the past."[49]

But is her call for our attention still heard today? The answer, I am delighted to report, is yes. A computer search reveals that *Woman under Monasticism* crops up in numerous bibliographies and syllabi in institutions ranging from Georgia State University to Saint Mary's College in Twickenham, England. Sections of the text are published on-line in Yale Divinity School's "Adhoc Texts" and in the "Commentaria" section of Matrix. *Comparative Studies in Nursery Rhymes* also continues to be cited in bibliographies, and selections are published on-line. Overall, at least twenty-five colleges and universities cite one of these two works in their reading lists.

Does this bright, eccentric woman belong in the company of this group of women scholars? Despite her lack of academic credentials, I believe that she does. Not all her writing was intended to be scholarly, and even her most rigorous monograph, *Woman under Monasticism*, includes the rather silly quasi-mystical prehistory of the Germanic people. But the overall value of what Eckenstein produced is attested by its intellectual shelf life. The careful research on monastic women's history and the reasoned enthusiasm for the education of women are still worthy of our attention today, even if our interest in reading her work is partly to understand the late-nineteenth-century attitudes of a woman writer. Eckenstein's inquiring mind, language training, and socialist-feminist ideals were the tools for her research and writing. Her writing on monastic women stands as an early salvo in the struggle to create women's history, to unearth past female experience. *Woman under Monasticism* was encouragement to those women of her day and later times seeking greater opportunities for their self-realization and expression, or—in Eckenstein's words—"a wider scope" in which to flourish.[50]

Notes

1. Although, as Blakeney and Dangar assert , "she was a medievalist rather than an Egyptologist" (Dean, with Blakeney and Dangar, "Oscar Eckenstein, 1859–1921," 71), Lina's catholic intellectual interests in lieu of specialization would call into question her categorization as a medievalist in today's terms. The notation on her death certificate (U.K., General Register Office, Death Certificate for Lina Eckenstein, 5 May 1931) records her occupation as "writer," which seems closer to the mark to me. I am most grateful to Scott Christopher Wells and Katherine Smith for research assistance in this area.

2. Mrs. Eckenstein lived at 34 Greencroft Gardens in South Hampstead. Oscar lived there with her probably as late as his marriage in 1918. See Dean and Blakeney and Dangar supplement to Dean, "Oscar Eckenstein," 67 and 71. Since Oscar and Lina were constant companions, it is possible that they had chosen to reside together at their family home. When they were remembered, it was usually as a pair.

3. U.K., General Register Office, birth certificate for Lina Eckenstein, 4 April 1897. Blakeney and Dangar, supplement to Dean, "Oscar Eckenstein," 71.

4. Lina's sister, Amelia, married Dr. Cyriax and had children, one of whom, Hilda, was present at Lina's death in 1931. I have not been able to find Amelia's birth date. Their brother, Oscar Johannes Ludwig, was born in 1859 and married Margery Edwards on 6 February 1918; Oscar and Margery had no children. For Hilda's presence at Lina's deathbed, see the death certificate for Lina Eckenstein, 5 May 1931. For family details, see Blakeney and Dangar, supplement to Dean, "Oscar Eckenstein," 71–2; and Unsworth, *Because It Is There,* 78.

5. Lina Eckenstein's estate at death was valued at £9,499, which suggests that she probably had a comfortable income (*Times* [London], 22 July 1931, p. 15, col. 5). Margaret Schlegel felt herself to be well off enjoying an annual income of £600 (see Forster, *Howards End,* 180). However, one of Oscar Eckenstein's friends remembers him as being poor (Dean, "Oscar Eckenstein," 66). The difference may have everything to do with lifestyles.

6. The death certificate for Lina Eckenstein, 5 May 1931, states she died of coma and exhaustion due to chronic cystitis; she is categorized as a "spinster." The London *Times,* 22 July 1931, listed her will as that of "Miss" Eckenstein. Little Hampden is located about forty kilometers outside London.

7. Lina Eckenstein's *Spell of Words* and *Women of Early Christianity* were both prepared for press by Celia Roscoe after Lina Eckenstein's death.

8. Blakeney and Dangar, supplement to Dean, "Oscar Eckenstein," 71.

9. L. Eckenstein, *Tutankh-aten,* foreword.

10. "In the summer of 1891 I met Professor (now Sir) W. M. Conway at Zermatt, where we had often met before; and when he asked whether I was disposed to join him in an expedition to the Karakoram mountains to climb and to make geographical and other exact observations, I had no difficulty in realizing that, if the trip were practicable, I should very much like it" (O. Eckenstein, *Karakorams and Kashmir,* xi).

11. L. Eckenstein, with William Martin Conway, *Literary Remains of Albrecht Dürer.* Conway's memoir also pointedly fails to mention Oscar Eckenstein or Karl Pearson (see Conway, *Episodes in a Varied Life.* Thus, the lack of mention of Lina in Conway's memoirs may not be too surprising, given Conway's capacity to clash with friends. For the falling out with Oscar, see O. Eckenstein, *Karakorams and Kashmir,* 198; for the rupture with Pearson, see Evans, *Conways,* 207–8. Joan Evans, who inherited Conway's papers from her friend, Conway's daughter, and then wrote a history of the family, also leaves Lina unnoted in her work.

12. Evans, *Conways,* 67. Pearson was studying law and living at 2 Harcourt's Buildings, the Inner Temple, that winter.

13. L. Eckenstein, *Albrecht Dürer.*

14. L. Eckenstein, *Comparative Studies in Nursery Rhymes.* I located a copy in the Smith College library and was interested to note that it had been taken out quite often through the 1970s, 1980s, and 1990s, the last time before me by an Italian professor of educational theory.

15. L. Eckenstein, *Spell of Words,* 278.

16. Eckenstein, Dedication, *Spell of Words,* n.p.

17. L. Eckenstein, "Guidi and Their Relations with Florence," 235–49, 431–50, 656–75.

18. L. Eckenstein, *Through the Casentino.*

19. Eckenstein, *Through the Casentino,* 16.

20. Eckenstein, *Through the Casentino,* 2.

21. Weintraub, *Bernard Shaw: The Diaries, 1885–1897,* 1:596.

22. L. Eckenstein, *Little Princess and the Great Plot.* This was reviewed anonymously in the

Spectator 68 (1892): 57–8, and the author's name was spelled "Miss Ekenstein." The reviewer concluded disapprovingly that the author "means to satirize modern institutions more or less in her little stories."

23. Alexander, *Women's Fabian Tracts*, 159.

24. The full title is *Woman under Monasticism: Chapters on Saint-Lore and Convent Life between A.D. 500 and A.D. 1500*.

25. McNamara, *Sisters in Arms*. A session sponsored by *Magistra* was held at the International Medieval Studies Congress at Kalamazoo, Michigan, in May 1997 and was titled "From 'Woman under Monasticism' to 'Sisters in Arms': One Hundred Years of Nuns in Print." My paper in that session was published as "Two Women Scholars Look at Medieval Nuns: Lina Eckenstein and Jo Ann McNamara."

26. Reviewers had voiced this criticism long before me. See, for example, Bateson, review of *Woman under Monasticism* by Lina Eckenstein, *English Historical Review*, 140: "The introduction, which deals with pagan survivals, is the least powerful chapter in the book, and its relevance to the main purpose of the book is not clear." Also see Vincent, review of *Woman under Monasticism* by Lina Eckenstein, 120, which criticizes "the earlier pages' attempt to connect heathendom and Christianity through the tribal goddess and the woman saint by conjecture more than by evidence." Both reviewers were very positive about the work with the exception of their critique of the first chapter.

27. See Bennett, "Medieval Women, Modern Women," in which the "master narrative" of women's golden age is discussed and refuted.

28. L. Eckenstein, *Woman under Monasticism*, 2. To give the author her due, she notes that some of her model is hypothetical.

29. Eckenstein, *Woman under Monasticism*, 5.

30. Eckenstein, *Woman under Monasticism*.

31. Eckenstein, *Woman under Monasticism*, xi.

32. Eckenstein, *Woman under Monasticism*, 277. The lack of scholarship has been amply repaired in the last few decades, particularly in the case of Hildegard of Bingen. See the extension bibliography on this figure and her corpus, particularly the work of Newman, *Sister of Wisdom* and *Voice of the Living Light*.

33. L. Eckenstein, *Woman under Monasticism*, 467–76. She notes that Charitas had a correspondence with Dürer (465–66).

34. Eckenstein, *Woman under Monasticism*, 172–79, for translations of Hroswitha's plays, and 316–25, for the *Ancren Riwle*.

35. Entire conferences have been held in the last decade on female conventual arts. One such spawned the collection *Creative Women in Medieval and Early Modern Italy*, edited by E. Ann Matter and John Coakley. Another collection exploring the same theme is *The Crannied Wall*, edited by Craig A. Monson.

36. L. Eckenstein, *Women of Early Christianity*.

37. Eckenstein, *Women of Early Christianity*, xiv–xv.

38. Eckenstein, *Women of Early Christianity*, xv.

39. Drower, *Flinders Petrie*, 268. Eckenstein was part of the expeditions to Abydos in 1902–3, Ehnasya in 1903–4, Saqqara and Sinai in 1904–5, and Saqqara in 1905–6.

40. L. Eckenstein, "Moon-cult in Sinai on the Egyptian Monuments"; "God Sopt"; *History of Sinai;* and *Tutankh-aten*.

41. Blakeney and Dangar, supplement to Dean, "Oscar Eckenstein," 72, quoting Murray, *God of the Witches*. Murray maintains that from ancient times into the seventeenth century a pagan fertility cult existed in Europe. The believers worshipped the Horned God, were descended from Neolithic peoples, and were called fairies. After the bubonic plague of 1348, they intermarried with the Christian population.

42. L. Eckenstein, *History of Sinai*, 67–68, 70, 72.

43. Eckenstein, *History of Sinai*, 64.

44. Eckenstein, *History of Sinai*, 77.

45. Eckenstein, *History of Sinai*, 90.

46. L. Eckenstein, *Woman under Monasticism*, 484. These are the closing words for her book.

47. Blakeney and Dangar, supplement to Dean, "Oscar Eckenstein," 72.

48. L. Eckenstein, *Woman under Monasticism*, xi and ix.

49. Eckenstein, *Woman under Monasticism*, ix, Eckenstein, *Woman under Monasticism*, xi.

50. Eckenstein, *Woman under Monasticism*, xi.

Select Bibliography of Works by Lina Eckenstein

With William Martin Conway. *The Literary Remains of Albrecht Dürer: With Transcripts from the British Museum Manuscripts and Notes upon Them by Lina Eckenstein*. Cambridge: Cambridge University Press, 1889.

The Little Princess and the Great Plot. Children's Library. London: T. Fisher Unwin; New York: Cassell, 1892.

Woman under Monasticism: Chapters on Saint-Lore and Convent Life between A.D. 500 and A.D. 1500. 1896. Reprint, New York: Russell and Russell, 1963.

"The Guidi and Their Relations with Florence." *English Historical Review* 14 (1899): 235–49, 431–50, 656–75.

Albrecht Dürer. Popular Library of Art. London: Duckworth, 1902.

Through the Casentino: With Hints for the Traveller. Illustrated by Lucy du Bois-Reymond. London: J. M. Dent, 1902.

Comparative Studies in Nursery Rhymes. London: Duckworth, 1906. Reissued in Reader's Library, 1911. Reprint, Detroit: Singing Tree Press, 1968.

"Moon-Cult in Sinai on the Egyptian Monuments." *Ancient Egypt* 1 (1914): 9–13.

"The God Sopt." *Ancient Egypt* 4 (1917): 103–8.

A History of Sinai. 1921. Reprint, New York: AMS Press, 1980.

Tutankh-aten: A Story of the Past. London: J. Cape, 1924.

A Spell of Words: Studies in Language Bearing on Culture. 1932. [Prepared for press by Celia Roscoe.] Reprint, Detroit: Gale Research, 1969.

The Women of Early Christianity. Revised by Celia Roscoe. London: Faith Press; Milwaukee: Morehouse, 1935.

Works Cited

Alexander, Sally, ed. *Women's Fabian Tracts*. London: Routledge, 1988.

Bateson, Mary. Review of *Woman under Monasticism* by Lina Eckenstein. *English Historical Review* 12 (1897): 139–42.

Bennett, Judith. "Medieval Women, Modern Women: Across the Great Divide." In *Culture and History, 1350–1600, Essays on English Communities, Identities, and Writing*, edited by David Aers. Detroit: Wayne State University Press, 1992.

Conway, William Martin. *Episodes in a Varied Life, by Lord Conway of Allington.* London: Country Life, 1932.
Dean, David, with supplements by T. S. Blakeney and D. F. O. Dangar. "Oscar Eckenstein, 1859–1921." *Alpine Journal* 65 (1960): 62–79.
Drower, Margaret S. *Flinders Petrie: A Life in Archaeology.* London: Gollancz, 1985.
Eckenstein, Oscar. *The Karakorams and Kashmir: An Account of a Journey.* London: T. Fisher Unwin, 1896.
Evans, Joan. *The Conways. A History of Three Generations.* London: Museum Press, 1966.
Forster, E. M. *Howards End.* London: Edward Arnold, 1921.
Johnson, Penelope. "Two Women Scholars Look at Medieval Nuns: Lina Eckenstein and Jo Ann McNamara." *Magistra* 3 (1997): 30–47.
Matter, E. Ann, and John Coakley, eds. *Creative Women in Medieval and Early Modern Italy: A Religious and Artistic Renaissance.* Philadelphia: University of Pennsylvania Press, 1994.
McNamara, Jo Ann. *Sisters in Arms: Catholic Nuns through Two Millennia.* Cambridge, Mass.: Harvard University Press, 1996.
Monson, Craig, ed. *The Crannied Wall: Women, Religion, and the Arts in Early Modern Europe.* Ann Arbor: University of Michigan Press, 1992.
Murray, Margaret. *The God of the Witches.* 1931. Reprint, Oxford: Oxford University Press, 1952.
Newman, Barbara. *Sister of Wisdom: Saint Hildegard's Theology of the Feminine.* Berkeley: University of California Press, 1987.
———, ed. *Voice of the Living Light: Hildegard of Bingen and Her World.* Berkeley: University of California Press, 1998.
Unsworth, Walter. *Because It Is There: Famous Mountaineers; 1840–1940.* London: Gollancz, 1968.
Vincent, J. M. Review of *Woman under Monasticism* by Lina Eckenstein. *American Historical Review* 2 (1896): 120–22.
Weintraub, Stanley, ed. *Bernard Shaw: The Diaries, 1885–1897, with Early Autobiographical Notebooks and Diaries, and an Abortive 1917 Diary.* University Park: Pennsylvania State University Press, 1986.

CHAPTER 5

Mary Bateson (1865–1906)
Scholar and Suffragist

Mary Dockray-Miller

This volume, *Women Medievalists and the Academy,* celebrates the achievements and frustrations of the first generations of women to engage in professional medieval studies. The collection allows women working in the academy today to be aware of our foremothers and to learn from their examples, their successes, and their mistakes. Historian Mary Bateson, scholar and suffragist, lived one hundred years ago, on the cusp of the opportunity for academic professionalization for women. Her life illustrates an inspiring blend of serious scholarship, accessible publication, and devoted political activism. Her achievements can remind twenty-first-century women medievalists in the academy of the occasional necessity to move our work out of the enclosed enclaves of the university library and the professional conference and into the more immediate spheres of politics and popular publication.

Information about Mary Bateson's childhood must be inferred from the history of her family. Her father and mother married in 1857, the same year that William Henry Bateson became the Master of Saint John's College, Cambridge.[1] We can assume that Mary Bateson spent most of the first sixteen years of her life residing at the elegant and spacious Master's Lodge at Saint John's College, Cambridge. She attended the Misses Thornton's School in Cambridge in the mid-1870s before spending some time at the Institut Friedlaender in Baden, Germany.[2] Her command of German was substantial enough that she was engaged as the German teacher at the Perse School for Girls at the same time she was a student there.[3] Her father had been on the original board of the Perse School for Girls, which opened in January 1881, when Mary Bateson was fifteen. Her father, who is described in the *Dictionary of National Biography* as a "remarkably sweet and tender character," died in 1881; the family then moved

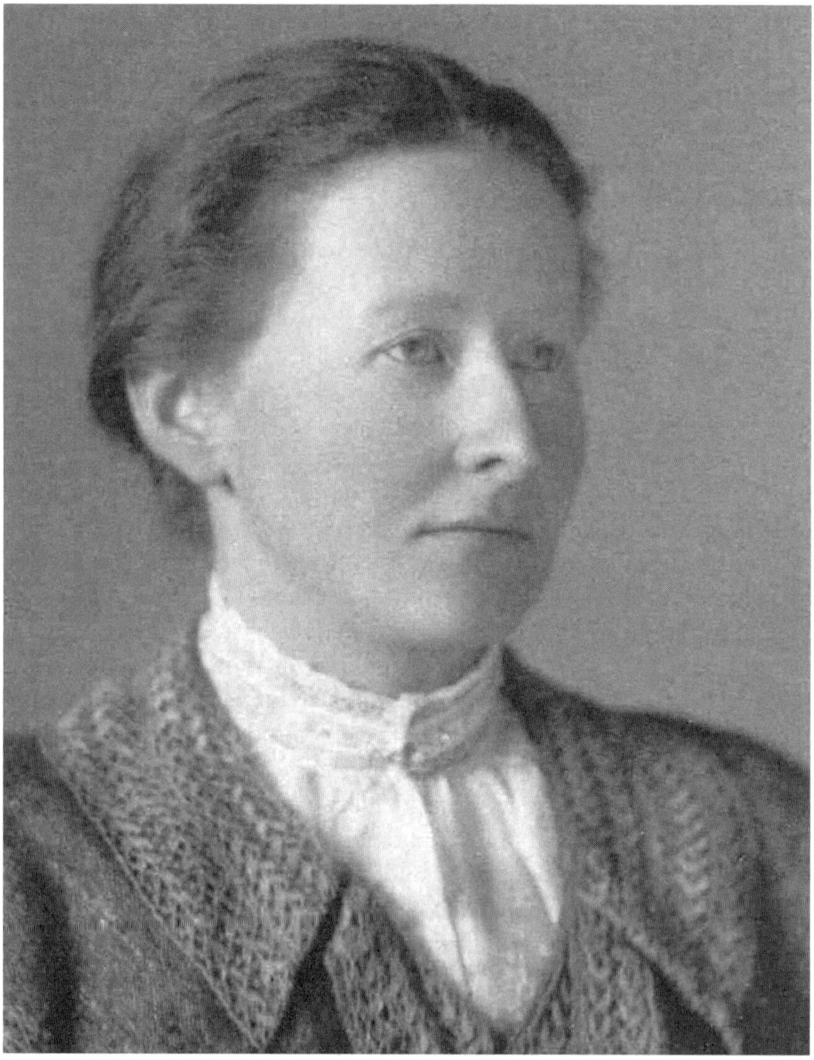

to a house on Harvey Road in Cambridge.[4] She studied at Perse from 1881 to 1884, presumably preparing to enter Newnham College, Cambridge, an institution with which her family was deeply involved.

When William Henry Bateson became master of Saint John's in 1857, there was no place for women in the world of Cambridge academics. By 1871 Newnham had formally opened, thanks to the efforts of a variety of proponents of women's higher education, including Mary Bateson's parents. Girton College opened for women during this period as well, but students at both colleges were not officially recognized members of Cambridge University. From 1871 to 1921 women at Newnham and Girton were issued "certificates" stating that they had passed the tripos rather than official degrees. Mary Bateson, for all her scholarly achievement, was not actually Mary Bateson, B.A. or M.A. or Ph.D.—she is always and only "Miss Mary Bateson." Newnham and Girton were not officially recognized as full member colleges of Cambridge University until 1948.[5]

Because of her parents' continuing involvement with the college's early history, Mary Bateson must have been intimately acquainted with the staff, the buildings, and many of the students at Newnham and in the university at large even before she entered the college in the fall of 1884. It was probably assumed throughout her childhood (she was six when Newnham opened) that she would attend.

The Newnham College that Bateson entered in 1884 was, then, full of her family's energy, goodwill, and money. Bateson lived at home during her first year as a Newnham student. There were forty-five students in her year, including Clara Skeat (daughter of noted medievalist W. W. Skeat) and Blanche Athena Clough (niece to the principal and a future lecturer and vice principal). Bateson's older sister, Anna, attended Newnham as well during these years, and Mary and Anna both lived in South Hall in the academic year 1885–86. Bateson returned to South Hall for the 1886–87 year, when she took a first class in the history tripos and was the secretary of the Newnham debating society.[6] Her undergraduate dissertation, "Monastic Civilisation in the Fens," won the Historical Essay Prize in 1887.[7] Bateson seems to have been involved with the debating society throughout her undergraduate career, and it was perhaps here that some of her initial engagement with the suffragette suffrage movement occurred. She met Dr. Mandell Creighton during these years, if she had not met him before; he became her academic mentor as she began to pursue serious historical scholarship.

Bateson's first-class history tripos did not end her academic affiliation with Newnham, an affiliation that would endure for the rest of her life. Traditionally, this would have been the time for Bateson, an upper-class educated woman, to marry; she did not. No historical documents (that I have been able to find) allude to any reason for Bateson's single status; whether she consciously chose not to marry or never had the opportunity to do so remains a mystery. Since she was a woman, there were no options for formal graduate study available; Bateson had to continue her education on her own, using her connections within the Cambridge University academic community to study manuscripts, write articles, edit texts, and produce both popular and scholarly publications.

From 1887 to 1893 she began to investigate medieval culture in earnest, with Creighton's informal guidance. His letters to her encourage specific topics of inquiry and praise her ongoing efforts.[8] Creighton, the Dixie Professor of Ecclesiastical History, envisioned that Bateson's career would be focused on monastic and ecclesiastical history (as his was). Creighton was also the founding editor of the *English Historical Review,* and in 1890 the *Review* published her first two, brief scholarly editions. Bateson's relationship with the *Review* endured for the rest of her life, and in it she published an article or short edited text almost every year from 1890 to 1906.

Bateson's relationship with the *Dictionary of National Biography* began in this period as well. To the original edition, published from 1885 to 1900, she contributed 108 biographical articles.[9] The subjects of all these are men; they include saints, monks, and noblemen. Some date to the Anglo-Saxon or early-modern periods; most cluster in the Anglo-Norman and High Middle Ages. Bateson wrote on no women for the *Dictionary;* she herself was included as a subject after her death.

During this period Bateson also refined her command of languages necessary for a serious medievalist. Newnham historian Alice Gardner's memorial to Bateson indicates that Bateson was a hard worker and dogged learner. Gardner remarks that Bateson's command of Latin was not strong when she entered Newnham; Bateson also worked hard on her own prose, refining her writing and laboring over each sentence to make it exactly right.[10] While Gardner's description provides a window into a late-nineteenth-century version of the writing process, it also shows that Bateson engaged in substantial foundational study. Her 1890 *English Historical Review* articles provide scholarly editions of early Modern English texts; within the following ten years Bateson would publish editions of Middle English, Old French, and Latin texts.

By 1892 her command of Latin was firm enough for her to produce the enormously important *editio princeps* of Ælfric's *Letter to the Monks of Eynsham;* it appeared as a rarely cataloged appendix in G. W. Kitchin's *Compotus Rolls*. Despite its obscurity, it remained the only available edition of this key Benedictine Reform document until 1984.

It is not clear whether Bateson taught at Newnham during these years, although she did remain an active member of the debating society (an 8 December 1889 letter from Newnham student Catherine Durning Holt to her mother mentions that Bateson spoke "exceedingly well" at a recent debate night).[11] The *Dictionary of National Biography* states that she began teaching immediately after her tripos. However, the *Newnham College Register* lists her as an "Associate and Fellow" of the college from 1893 to 1906, so perhaps her teaching career began as late as 1893. The early lecture lists for the college are organized by student and residence hall rather than by lecturer, but Bateson does not seem to be listed from 1887 to 1893. In the six years between her tripos exams and the documented beginning of her teaching career, Bateson may have done some teaching; she read widely, corresponded with professors and scholars in her community, worked on her languages, and produced her first scholarly publications—in short, she unofficially completed a graduate education.

Mary Bateson did not spend her life in a library. Much of her life, like that of any upper-class English woman, was spent in society. Bateson's social life revolved around the academic world of Cambridge, of course, and she is remembered in all her obituaries as a gracious, compassionate woman with a sense of humor and a keen intellect. Gardner even remarks that any party was sure to be successful if Mary Bateson was on the guest list, and she mentions Bateson's "unexpected sallies of wit" at college meetings.[12] Thomas Frederick Tout, a historian and administrator from the University of Manchester, states in an obituary that she "was popular socially in circles that cared little for her personal [academic] distinction" and refers to her "rare sense of humor . . . her deep, hearty laugh . . . [her] downright breezy good-fellowship."[13] Ellen A. McArthur recalls her as "absolutely honest, independent, and fearless, full of commonsense, and endowed with a sense of humor."[14]

Sometime between her tripos and her death, Bateson made the unusual step of moving out of her mother's house and into a home of her own. In her obituary in the *Manchester Guardian,* Tout notes that she "lived contentedly in her little house in the Huntington Road."[15] Since her mother's address at the time of Mary Bateson's death is at Oxford and Cambridge Mansions, it is clear that Bateson lived alone in the Huntington Road house. It seems Bateson valued her peace and quiet over the social convention of the adult, unmarried daughter living with her parents.

The years from 1893 to 1898 mark the beginning of her documented teaching career as well as the growth of her scholarly production. Her scholarly mentor Mandell Creighton had become bishop of Peterborough in 1891.[16] Bateson turned for guidance to F. W. Maitland, who was appointed Downing Professor of the Laws of England in 1888.[17] Founder of the Selden Society for the study of the history of English law, Maitland encouraged Bateson's turn from ecclesiastical to municipal subjects in the bulk of her work. By 1898 it was clear that Bateson's academic energies would be directed toward boroughs and towns, not monasteries and cathedrals.

Bateson never assumed the obligations of a full-time lecturer for the college. She did not live at Newnham after 1887 (most of the staff was in residence), and she only once gave more than one series of lectures in any term (in contrast Gardner gave two or three lecture series each term). Eleanor Balfour Sidgwick, in the Newnham principal's report for 1907, described Bateson's position not "as one of the regular teaching staff, but as a constant and valued teacher in her special field."[18] Sidgwick also celebrates Bateson's service on the college council during these years. Gardner remarks that Bateson's "great task in the college was to produce a noble discontent"—that Bateson never allowed Newnham's staff and students to "rest on [their] oars, to be satisfied if [they] produced good tripos results or merely came up to an ordinary college standard."[19] Bateson's quest for academic excellence in her individual work was considered an inspiration for the rest of the Newnham community.

During this period Bateson lectured on English constitutional history, but Tout remarks that "she could never interest herself very profoundly in the work of preparing pupils for examinations, especially for examinations over which she had no control."[20] This dissatisfaction Bateson felt at the college's second-class status is indicated as well by her leadership in Newnham's ultimately unsuccessful 1895 petition to the university to grant formal degrees (instead of "certificates") to women.

The years 1898–1905 mark the pinnacle of her prolific and brief career. She continued to teach her sole English constitutional history course at Newnham, sometimes for all three terms of an academic year, more often for just one or two. Bateson's scholarship flourished in this period, during which she was a vocal supporter of research fellowships for women. Since she was financially independent, she was not agitating for her own ends. She firmly believed, twenty-five years before Virginia Woolf addressed the faculty and students of Newnham College about the necessity of "a room of one's own," that women could not pursue serious scholarship without the financial and professional support of an academic institution.

Sidgwick, the second principal of Newnham, credits Bateson as the prime mover behind the foundation of the Newnham Research Fellowships.[21] Bateson was awarded one of the first of these in 1903 from a fund to which she had contributed £250. Upon the expiration of her fellowship, she gave the money back to the fund to be used by someone who needed it more.[22] Bateson, it seems, was interested more in the academic prestige and access associated with a research fellowship than in the financial assistance it provided. Many of the title pages of her later books term her "Associate and Fellow of Newnham College" rather than "Associate and Lecturer of Newnham College."

In this seven-year span she produced thirteen book-length scholarly textual editions (two in collaboration with other scholars), five short editions in the *English Historical Review,* three journal articles (two of which were enormously important in their fields), two annual bibliographies of English and Irish history, thirteen extensive encyclopedia articles, and one popular history book. Her reputation was such that she was asked to be the prestigious Warburton Lecturer at the University of Manchester in 1905; her two guest lectures were titled "Survivals of Ancient Customs in English Borough Law."[23]

Perhaps because it was somehow considered a more "feminine" scholarly occupation to edit texts than to produce monographs, the bulk of Bateson's work exists in the form of scholarly textual editions. Bateson had access to the extensive manuscript collections at the colleges of Cambridge University; the librarian at the central University Library also held manuscripts for her on loan from other libraries and depositories. Her final and probably most important editorial work was the mammoth two-volume *Borough Customs,* which brought together tenth- through seventeenth-century texts such as charters, law codes, custumals, letters patent, patent rolls, council orders, and ordinance rolls to "set out the rules which obtained in the borough-moots." One memorial to her notes that her "introductions are models of lucid and orderly statement."[24]

Two of Bateson's journal articles are still cited with frequency in their fields as seminal, originary analyses. Her 1899 essay, "Origin and History of Double Monasteries," is a foundational text in the history of women's religious communities, establishing a history and a precedent for "double monasteries," houses for monks and nuns ruled by an abbess, usually of royal birth. Her other important article, "The Laws of Breteuil," illustrates that the Norman town of Breteuil, not the English town of Bristol (as was previously believed), is the origin of many English borough laws and customs. Bateson adopts a wry tone in the beginning of the essay, noting that many of her English readers will not like to hear that some of their customs have a French origin.

During the same period that Bateson was producing traditional editions and bibliographies as well as revolutionary historical scholarship, she was also writing substantial amounts of popular history. The years 1903 and 1904 marked the publication of the bulk of Bateson's popular history contributions, in which she showed that she could present history in an engaging and informal manner that still retained her dedication to primary sources and nontraditional modes of analysis. Her contributions include the chapter titled "The French in America" in the 1903 edition of the *Cambridge Modern History; Mediaeval England*, which appeared in the popular Unwin history series *The Story of the Nations;* the chapter on "The Borough of Peterborough" for the *Victoria County History of Northampton;* and eleven essays titled "Social Life" throughout H. D. Traill's monumental five-volume historical encyclopedia, *Social England*. The most notable feature of her popular history writing is her constant use of primary-source quotations and anecdotes to bring the past directly in front of her reader. It is a testament to Bateson's skills as a writer for the general public that she was asked by Cambridge University Press to act as a general editor of the next edition of the *Cambridge Medieval History,* a post that she was unable to assume before her untimely death at the age of forty-one.[25]

Mary Bateson the historian was also Mary Bateson the suffragist and women's rights crusader, despite the disapproval of some of her Cambridge colleagues. On 4 August 1888 Creighton sent Bateson a letter discouraging her from suffragist and political activity.[26] Although some of Bateson's memorials indicate that she followed that advice, she actually remained an active suffragist throughout her life.[27]

Bateson's family was as involved in women's suffrage as it was in women's education. In 1884 her mother, Anne Bateson, was a founding member of the Cambridge Women's Suffrage Association (CWSA), of which all her daughters were to be members at one time or another; Mary's older sister, Anna, was a founding member of CWSA as well. Mary's sister Margaret Bateson Heitland seems to have been the most radical of the women in the family; after serving as assistant secretary of the CWSA in 1884, she quickly became interested in the economic imperatives of suffrage for working-class women and established herself as a journalist and political writer.[28]

Mary Bateson, then, lived in a world that was overtly political, activist, and liberal as well as traditionally academic. Her mother and sisters—the core of her family during her adult life—were all active in "the cause," providing time, money, and initiative to effecting social change. Mary Bateson herself served the CWSA in a variety of capacities throughout the 1880s and 1890s: in a paid position as meeting organizer (1888), and as an executive committee member (1889), secretary of the association (1892–98), secretary to the Special Appeal (1894), and national conference delegate (1896).[29] The association seems to have been moderate for a suffrage organization; the CWSA formally affiliated with the moderate National Union of Women's Suffrage Societies (NUWSS) rather than the radical Women's Political and Social Union (WPSU) in 1897.[30]

The pinnacle of Bateson's suffrage career was her speech during a deputation to the prime minister, Henry Campbell-Bannerman, on 19 May 1906. She represented women graduates of universities in a group of 350 representatives from twenty-five different NUWSS affiliates. Bateson spoke last (of the ten women who spoke), presenting to the prime minister a petition signed by 1,530 women university graduates. The NUWSS pamphlet commemorating the event records Bateson's speech on behalf of these university women, "who believe[d] the disenfranchisement of one sex to be injurious to both, and a national wrong in a country which pretend[ed] to be governed on a representative system."[31]

In the body of her speech Bateson refers to the accomplishments of women university graduates, women who are "professors or lecturers . . . [teachers] in secondary schools and primary schools . . . surgeons and physicians . . . who pursue scientific inquiry . . . who are in Civil Service . . . [who are] engaged in literary or political or social work."[32] She adroitly lists these accomplishments, augmented by the names of distinguished universities and respected professional societies, before pointing out the absurdity that these women cannot vote. This public declaration combined Bateson's academic and political lives; she argued for a relationship between academic inquiry and political activity that still makes sense one hundred years later.

Mary Bateson's death, after a nine-day illness at the age of forty-one, shocked all the communities of which she was a part. She left her library and all her financial resources (about twenty-five hundred pounds) to Newnham. Obituaries appeared in the *Times,* the *Queen,* the *Manchester Guardian,* the *Athenaeum,* and the *English Historical Review.*[33] She was included in the *DNB* and memorialized in a named research fellowship at her college.[34] All the memorials refer to her good nature, her firm work ethic, and her enormous scholarly production. Only the *Queen*'s obituary, written by her Girton colleague Ellen A. McArthur, provides any detail about or assigns any substantial worth to Bateson's suffrage activism (the *Queen* was "The Lady's Newspaper," and thus it makes unfortunate sense that this should be the only publication to valorize Bateson's political work).[35]

Bateson's life illustrates two important blends: that of academic and popular publication and that of historical research and political activism. It reminds us of the near impossibility of combining professional work with family life one hundred years ago. A bust of her, sculpted by her sister Edith Bateson, still stands at the old entrance to the Newnham College Library; it presents her, appropriately, reading a book.

Notes

1. Stephen et al., *Dictionary of National Biography on CD-ROM*, s.v. "William Henry Bateson." Hereafter this edition of the dictionary is cited as *DNB*.
2. *DNB*, s.v. "Mary Bateson."
3. Scott, *Perse School for Girls, Cambridge*.
4. *DNB*, s.v. "William Henry Bateson."
5. Tullberg, *Women of Cambridge*, 1.
6. Newnham College Club, *Newnham College Letter.*
7. *DNB*, s.v. "Mary Bateson."
8. Creighton, *Life and Letters*, 1:394–95, 408–9, 412–413; 2:406–7.
9. Fenwick, *Women and the Dictionary of National Biography*, 112–13.
10. Gardner, "In Memoriam," 37.
11. Holt, *Letters from Newnham College*, 22.
12. Gardner, "In Memoriam," 34.
13. Tout, "Mary Bateson."
14. McArthur, "In Memoriam."
15. Tout, "Mary Bateson," 6.
16. *DNB*, s.v. "Mandell Creighton."
17. *DNB*, s.v. "F. W. Maitland."
18. Sidgwick, "Report of the Principal," 24.
19. Gardner, *Short History*, 96.
20. Tout, "Mary Bateson," 6.
21. Sidgwick, "Report of the Principal," 24.
22. Ibid.
23. "Death of Mary Bateson," 33.
24. Poole, "Mary Bateson," 65; Poole is here quoting a personal communication to him from Professor James Tait.
25. Tout, "Mary Bateson," 6
26. Creighton, *Life and Letters*, 1:408.
27. *DNB*, s.v. "Mary Bateson" (this entry was written by Tout); Gardner, "In Memoriam," 37; Gardner, *Short History*, 97. Both of these authors state that Bateson followed Creighton's advice.
28. Information about the Batesons from Crawford, *Women's Suffrage Movement*, 38–39 and 282.
29. Ibid., 39.
30. Ibid., 91. "Suffragette" is used most commonly to describe the more radical WPSU members; hence, Bateson is more accurately termed a "suffragist."
31. National Union of Women's Suffrage Societies, *Women's Suffrage Deputation*, 11.
32. Ibid.
33. *Times* (London), 1 December 1906; *Queen*, 8 December 1906; *Manchester Guardian*, 3 December 1906; *English Historical Review* 22 (1907): 64–68; *Athenaeum*, 8 December 1906. Maitland's *Athenaeum* memorial was reprinted in *The Collected Papers of Frederick William Maitland*, ed. H. A. L. Fisher (Cambridge: Cambridge University Press, 1911), 3:541–43.
34. The Mary Bateson Memorial Research Fellowship was endowed with £794 in 1909 (*Record of the Benefactors*); the minutes of the meeting that led to the establishment of the fellowship are extant in the Newnham archives.
35. McArthur, "In Memoriam," 1033.

Select Bibliography of Works by Mary Bateson

"Aske's Examination." *English Historical Review* 5 (1890): 550–73.

"The Pilgrimage of Grace." *English Historical Review* 5 (1890): 330–45.

"Archbishop Wareham's Visitation of the Monasteries, 1511." *English Historical Review* 6 (1891): 18–35.

"Clerical Preferment under the Duke of Newcastle." *English Historical Review* 7 (1892): 685–97.

"Excerpta ex institutionibus monasticis Æthelwoldi episcopi Wintoniensis compilata in usum fratrum Egneshamnensium per Ælfricum abbatem." In *Compotus Rolls of the Odedientiaries of Saint Swithun's Priory, Winchester,* edited by G. W. Kitchin. London, Simpkin and Co. 1892.

"Rules for Monks and Secular Canons after the Revival under King Edgar." *English Historical Review* 8 (1894): 690–708.

"The Supposed Latin Penitential of Egbert and the Missing Work of Halitgar of Cambrai." *English Historical Review* 9 (1894): 320–26.

"A Collection of Original Letters from the Bishops to the Privy Council, 1564." *Camden Miscellany* 9 (1895): iii–84.

"A Worcester Cathedral Book of Ecclesiastical Collections, Made circa 1000 A.D." *English Historical Review* 10 (1895): 712–31.

Editor. *Catalogue of the Library of Syon Monastery.* Cambridge: Cambridge University Press, 1898.

Editor. *A Narrative of the Changes in the Ministry, 1765–1767, Told by the Duke of Newcastle in a Series of Letters to John White, M.P.* London: Longmans, 1898.

Editor. *George Ashby's Poems.* Early English Text Society, o.s., 76. London: Oxford University Press, 1899.

"Origin and History of Double Monasteries." *Transactions of the Royal Historical Society,* n.s., 13 (1899): 137–98.

Editor. *Records of the Borough of Leicester.* Vol. 1. London: C. J. Clay, 1899.

Editor. *Register of Crabhouse Nunnery.* Norwich, Eng.: Norfolk and Norwich Archaeological Society, 1899.

"Some Legal Texts in the *Leicester Vellum Book.*" *English Historical Review* 14 (1899): 502–6.

"The Laws of Breteuil." *English Historical Review* 15 (1900): 73–78, 302–18, 496–523, 754–57.

Various articles in *The Dictionary of National Biography.* Edited by Leslie Stephen and Sidney Lee. Oxford: Oxford University Press, 1900.

Editor with F. W. Maitland. *The Charters of the Borough of Cambridge.* Cambridge: Cambridge University Press, 1901.

"The Laws of Breteuil (cont.)." *English Historical Review* 16 (1901): 92–110, 332–45.

Editor. *Records of the Borough of Leicester.* Vol. 2. London: C. J. Clay, 1901.

"Social Life." In *Social England: A Record of the Progress of the People in Religion, Laws, Learning, Arts, Industry, Commerce, Science, Literature, and Manners, from the Earliest Times to the Present Day,* edited by H. D. Traill and J. S. Mann. 5 vols. London: Cassell and Co., 1901–4.

"The Creation of Boroughs." *English Historical Review* 17 (1902): 284–96.

Editor with Reginald Lane Poole. *Index Britanniae scriptorum.* Oxford: Clarendon Press, 1902.

"A London Municipal Collection of the Reign of John." *English Historical Review* 17 (1902): 480–511, 707–30.

Editor. *Cambridge Gild Records.* Cambridge: Cambridge Antiquarian Society, 1903.

"The French in America." In *The United States,* vol. 7 of *The Cambridge Modern History,* 70–113.

Edited by A. W. Ward, G. W. Prothero, and Stanley Leathes. Cambridge: Cambridge University Press, 1903.

Editor. *Grace Book B*. Cambridge: Cambridge University Press, 1903–5.

"The Huntington Song School and the School of Saint Gregory's, Canterbury." *English Historical Review* 18 (1903): 712–13.

"Irish Exchequer Memoranda and the Reign of Edward I." *English Historical Review* 18 (1903): 497–513.

Mediaeval England. London: Unwin, 1903.

Editor. *Borough Customs*. Vol. 18 of *Publications of the Selden Society*. London: B Quaritch, 1904.

"The English and Latin Versions of a Peterborough Court Text, 1461." *English Historical Review* 19 (1904): 526–28.

"Gross Britannien und Irland bis 1500." *Jahresberichte der Geschichtswissenschaft* 27 (1904): 186–234.

"The Scottish King's Household and Other Fragments: From a Fourteenth-Century Manuscript in the Library of Corpus Christi College Cambridge." *Scottish History Miscellany* 44 (1904): 1–43.

"Gross Britannien und Irland bis 1500." *Jahresberichte der Geschichtswissenschaft* 28 (1905): 79–107.

Editor. *Records of the Borough of Leicester*. Vol. 3. London: C. J. Clay, 1905.

Editor. *Borough Customs*. Vol. 21, *Publications of the Selden Society*. London: B. Quaritch, 1906.

"The Borough of Peterborough." In *Victoria History of the County of Northampton,* edited by W. Ryland and D. Adkins. London: Archibald Constable, 1906.

"The Burgesses of Domesday and the Malmesbury Wall." *English Historical Review* 21 (1906): 709–23.

Works Cited

Crawford, Elizabeth. *The Women's Suffrage Movement: A Reference Guide, 1866–1928*. London: University College London Press, 1999.

Creighton, Louise, ed. *Life and Letters of Mandell Creighton*. 3 vols. London: Longmans, 1904.

"Death of Mary Bateson." *Newnham College Letter* (1906): 32–33.

Fenwick, Gillian. *Women and the Dictionary of National Biography*. Aldershot, Eng.: Scolar Press, 1994.

Gardner, Alice. "In Memoriam—Mary Bateson." *Newnham College Letter* (1906): 34–39.

———. *A Short History of Newnham College*. Cambridge: Bowes and Bowes, 1921.

Holt, Catherine Durning. *Letters from Newnham College*. Edited by E. O. Cockburn. 3d ed. Cambridge: Newnham College, 1987.

McArthur, Ellen A. "In Memoriam. Mary Bateson, 1865–1906." *Queen: The Lady's Newspaper,* 8 December 1906, 1033.

National Union of Women's Suffrage Societies. *Women's Suffrage Deputation*. London: NUWSS, 1906.

Newnham College. *Record of the Benefactors Made in the Jubilee Year of the College, 1921*. Cambridge: Newnham College, 1921.

Newnham College Club. *Newnham College Letter*. Cambridge: Newnham College, 1884, 1885, 1886, 1887.

Newnham College Lecture Lists. 1893–1906. Newnham College Archives.

Poole, Reginald. "Mary Bateson." *English Historical Review* 22 (1907): 64–68.

Scott, M. A. *The Perse School for Girls, Cambridge*. Cambridge: Perse School, 1981.

Sidgwick, Eleanor Balfour. "Report of the Principal." *Records of Newnham College* (1907): 23–24.
Stephen, Leslie, et al., eds. *The Dictionary of National Biography on CD-ROM.* 1.0 ed. Oxford: Oxford University Press, 1995.
Tout, Thomas Frederick. "Mary Bateson." *Manchester Guardian,* 3 December 1906, 6.
Tullberg, Rita McWilliams. *Women of Cambridge.* 2d ed. Cambridge: Cambridge University Press, 1998.

CHAPTER 6

Elise Richter (1865–1943)
First Austrian Privatdozentin

ELIZABETH SHIPLEY

*With Excerpts from a Memoir on "Education and Development"
by Elise Richter, translated by Elizabeth Shipley*

Introduction
ELIZABETH SHIPLEY

ELISE RICHTER'S REPUTATION as a Romance medievalist and linguist is well established. The prize of the German Society for Romance Studies for doctoral and postdoctoral work of distinction in German Romance studies carries her name (the Elise Richter Research Prize), and over thirty years after her death, her most important shorter works were collected and republished with an introduction by Yakov Malkiel.[1]

Although Richter published on medieval literature (e.g., *La Vie de Saint Alexis* and Chrétien de Troyes's *Ivain*), her work as a Romance medievalist was primarily centered on philology. Her major work in this field, published in 1934 in still incomplete form as *Chronologische Phonetik des Französischen bis zum Ende des 8. Jahrhunderts* (Chronological phonetics of French up to the end of the eighth century), is described by Benjamin Woodbridge in his comprehensive annotated bibliography of Richter's works as a "trail-breaking attempt to establish the chronology of sound changes in the prehistory of French."[2] In addition to medieval studies, Richter is known for her innovative work in general linguistics. According to Malkiel, one of her greatest achievements was "having successfully mediated between general linguistics at its most provocative and Romance studies at their most sophisticated—in a time when most of her peers preferred to go one way or the other, without bothering to reconcile the two almost irrevocably diverging disciplines."[3]

Since her scholarly work is comprehensively represented elsewhere by specialists in the field, this introduction will concentrate on Richter's historical importance for women's place in the academy, which in recent years has gained renewed attention.[4]

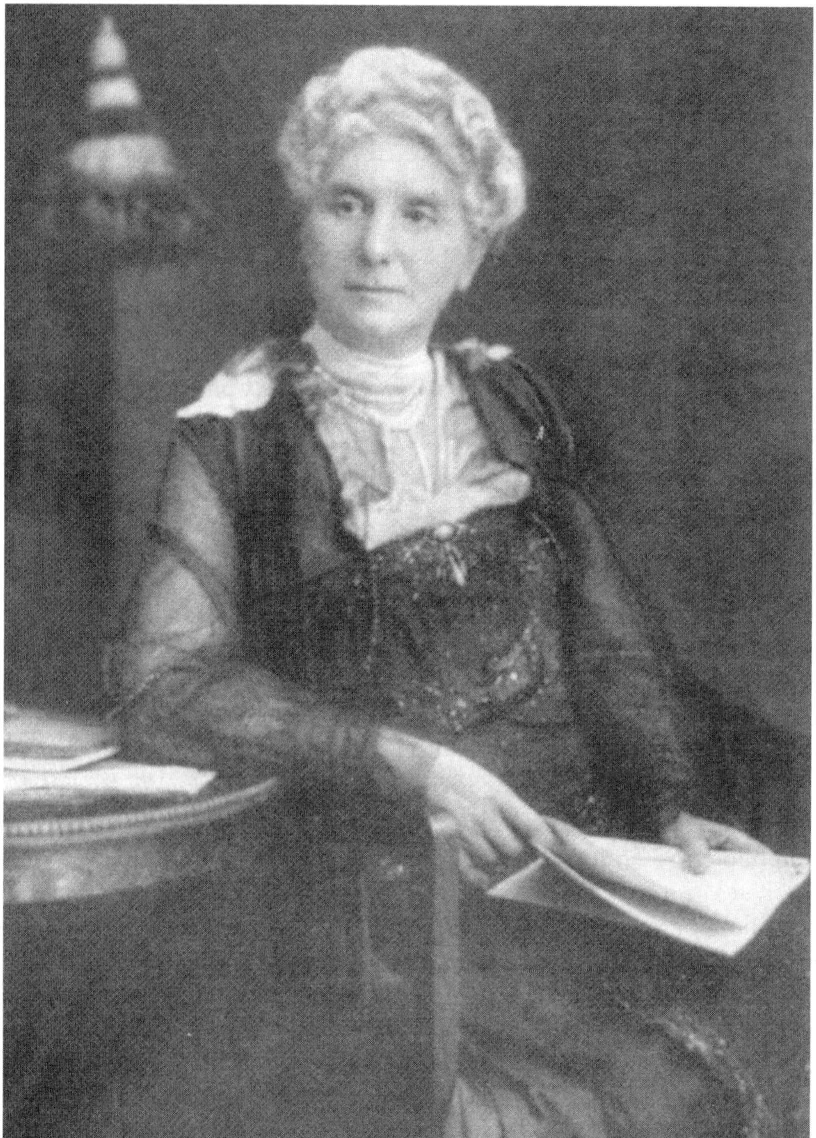

Elise Richter was born on 2 March 1865 into a cultivated but strict doctor's family of Jewish heritage in imperial Vienna.[5] According to the custom of the time in her social class, she and her older sister, Helene, were educated at home under the instruction of a governess. Afterward, envious of those educational opportunities open only to boys, Elise Richter continued to study on her own. To her disappointment, Latin was forbidden her as inappropriate for young women. However, in her twenties, while confined to bed for a year with very painful rheumatoid arthritis, she received a Greek grammar and an edition of Homer in the original as a Christmas present. After the early death of both parents within eighteen months of each other, Helene and Elise Richter struck out on their own, at first traveling extensively and then beginning, in 1891, to audit classes at the University of Vienna, the most to which academic-minded women at that time could aspire. In 1896 and 1897, however, Elise Richter was one of the first women in Austria to take advantage of two new ministerial decrees that allowed her to formally pursue the study to which she was already devoted, that of Romance philology. The 1896 decree allowed women to be admitted to the state *matura* examination (prerequisite for university studies) as "private pupils" (that is, those who had not attended the gymnasium, the upper state secondary school that prepared pupils for university studies). However, women were still excluded from entering universities as regular students. The 1897 decree then allowed women with the state *matura* diploma to enroll in certain faculties at a university as regular students.

After passing the *matura*, Richter immediately began her studies at the University of Vienna under the Romance philologist Adolph Mussafia and the man she later acknowledged most directly as her teacher, Wilhelm Meyer-Lübke. Meyer-Lübke, only four years her senior, was to influence her interests and the main direction of her work in linguistics. Her doctoral dissertation on the development of word order in Romance languages from Latin was to be the start of her life's work: the investigation of language change, particularly from Latin to French.

After completing her doctorate at the University of Vienna, she successfully fought for the right to continue her academic career beyond the doctorate and was the first woman in Austria to attain the postdoctoral qualification of the habilitation in 1907, twelve years before women in Germany were first allowed to do so.[6]

The *venia legendi* of the habilitation formally qualified Richter for a professorial appointment as well as for teaching at a university as a *Privatdozentin* (a university lecturer who has fulfilled the prerequisites for a professorship). For fourteen years Richter exercised the privilege conferred by her status as an (unpaid) *Privatdozentin* at the University of Vienna, teaching in a wide breadth of subject areas, including phonetics, general linguistics, pedagogy, Romance linguistics, Vulgar Latin, French language and literature, Provençal language and literature, Italian language and literature, Portuguese language and literature, Spanish language, and the history of poetic motifs in the Romance languages.[7] It was not until 1921 that Richter achieved the title of professor (again the first woman in Austria to do so), though only with the rank of *professor extraordinarius*. At first this position was also unpaid. She received payment for her teaching at the University of Vienna for the first time in 1923 as an adjunct for a weekly two-hour phonetics course. In 1935, because of the importance of the phonetics program she had built up at the university and within which she was irreplaceable, she was asked by the ministry to continue teaching past the age of retirement. At the same time the ministry rejected her appointment to the rank of an *ordinarius*. Not until 1956 was an Austrian woman to achieve this rank.[8]

Although Richter did not consider herself politically active on behalf of women's issues, she nevertheless founded the Austrian Federation of University Women in 1922 (at the request of the International Federation of University Women) and became its first president. Even after stepping down as president in 1930, she continued to remain active in the association until its dissolution under the Anschluss in 1938.

In 1938 Elise Richter and her sister suffered because of their Jewish heritage. Her teaching contract was withdrawn, and her application for a pension after thirty-one years of teaching service at the University of Vienna was rejected. She was refused entrance to the library and to other institutions that she needed for her work. In 1939 the Society of Friends brought an invitation to come to England from the International Federation of University Women, but she and her sister, Helene, herself a notable and widely published author in English studies, decided to remain in their beloved Vienna in the house that Elise had designed and where the two of them, both unmarried, had made a home together. Elise Richter continued to write, publishing in the Netherlands and Italy. In 1942 Elise and Helene Richter were transported to Theresienstadt, SS General Heydrich's "old-age ghetto" for Jewish people over sixty-five. Here, under conditions of extreme hardship, Helene Richter died on 8 November 1942, and Elise Richter on 21 June 1943.

In the late twenties Elise Richter was asked to contribute to Elga Kern's collection of self-portraits of leading European women. The result, "Erziehung und Entwicklung" (Education and development), is a rare authentic document of the history of early women medievalists. What follows is my translation of a central passage from this self-portrait.[9]

Education and Development
Elise Richter, translated by Elizabeth Shipley

My *matura* was an experience sui generis. Das Akademische Gymnasium in Vienna, at which the female "private pupils" would be examined, had the unchallenged reputation of being the best and strictest of schools. In contrast to the current way of conducting the *matura* examination, this was medieval torture. If there were strict regulations at that time for "private pupils" in general, I was informed from the beginning that as the first female "private pupil" to make use of the new law I would be examined more "comprehensively," though not more strictly, than the regular pupils. For all those subjects of the earlier grades—naturally without exception—in which the regular pupils would not be examined at all in the *matura*, I had to submit to a preexamination.

In other words, I had to keep all twelve subjects of the gymnasium in my head at once. The preexamination (in April) lasted two hours; the *matura* oral exams themselves four and a half (that of Greek and Latin alone an hour each, thus as long as a doctoral examination). The written exams took place on five days of the first week of May. I am generally of the opinion that there are fewer malicious examiners than unprepared examination candidates, and I found this also confirmed here. Only the chair, the province school inspector Sch., a classical philologist, was a declared opponent of allowing women to study. As I climbed the high stairs of the school on 15 July 1897 at 7:30 in the morning—an incredible physical achievement for me—I was greeted by young men who, as fellow examination candidates, had the right to look at the "novelty" somewhat more closely.[10] They brought me the message that the chair had commented that he would possibly fail me. Indeed, he did monopolize the exam, allowing none of the examiners from the gymnasium to ask any of the questions during the two hours in the Greek and Latin exams. When he failed to get a wrong answer from me to any of his questions, he still managed to lower my grade to a mere 4, the lowest of the passing grades, for those two subjects. I was really sick about those two 4s, but I made it through.

Now my studies lay before me, for in the midst of the examination preparations I was surprised by the ministry's decision that opened the way to the Faculty of Arts and Letters at the university for women with a state *matura*. Immediately following the *matura*, I was the first woman to enjoy the privilege of enrolling at the university as a regular student. At that time (1897) there were altogether three of us enrolled as regular students.

The university lectures and the seminars in particular were a source of indescribable pleasure for me. I filled out the Nietzsche phrase *Gaya scienzia [gaya scienza]* with a personal significance. It became my life's motto. I enjoyed university life and not only for myself alone but also, fully aware, for all those who in the past may have considered it a worthy goal but for whom the time had not yet arrived. [. . .][11]

Since I was the only female in all my subjects for two years, I had to set the rules of etiquette. I made a point of paying attention to exact equality with my fellow students, both in relations among ourselves and with the professor. I adamantly refused all privileges as a woman. However, I was not always successful in persuading the professors, even those who allowed themselves to be greeted first by a lady, to enter a room before me. It was amusing when, as a result of my presence, they stumbled over addressing their class with "Gentlemen" but did not manage to bring out a "Lady."

Mussafia said quite definitively, "Gentlemen." I spoiled his fun, however, by explaining to him that I understood this manner of address in the sense of the Old Provençal *midons* ("My Lord," address of the troubadour singing to his lady). The entire tone was naturally affected by the fact that I was not only significantly older than my fellow students but also older than some of my teachers. We were, incidentally, very friendly with one another. To the horror of the older generation that was barely able to tolerate a female attending lectures, I took part in student social events and outings, though not without some initial reservations that I might lower the level of pleasant conversation. "You could only raise it," declared a fellow student. I tried to break a new trail with the concept that there were male and female students and that was all. I practiced a sort of mimicry in which I appeared exclusively in dark, simple clothing, unadorned (with the strictest avoidance of either genius-like neglect or tasteless philistinism).

Every semester I wrote a paper. (The one from the fifth semester in 1899/1900 about the Rumanian third-person possessive pronoun, my first publishable work, appeared in Gröber's *Zeitschrift für romanische Philologie*, volume 25). [. . .] At the end of the sixth semester, the last chapter ("Word Order") of Meyer-Lübke's just published *Syntax* caught my interest with a strange intensity.[12] I threw myself into it as a topic for the doctoral dissertation, which at first was only to be an examination of Old Spanish word order but was soon extended to the other Romance languages with the question, "Where does Latin end, and where do the Romance languages begin?" Thus I arrived at the scholarly problem on which I have been working my entire life.

The preparation for the "most rigorous" exam, the doctoral *rigorosum*, was systematic and concentrated in contrast to the *matura* preparation, which had been unsettling and frantic, and the *matura* itself, which had been nerve-racking. I had only to concern myself with "my" subject, with affairs that were only my own, and my examiners had followed my work for years. In this way the exams were the complete opposite of the *matura*. As I put on my best clothing on a wonderful May morning in 1901, my soul swelling with gratitude that I was allowed to reach this goal, the 6/8 rhythm with the triangle tones of "Exulting as a knight in victory" from Beethoven's Ninth hummed within me. I found the *rigorosum* examination, like the colloquia in the past, an extremely stimulating conversation, an entertainment it was my task to provide. As I was the first woman examination candidate and this caused a great deal of interest among the other students, an unusual double examination of me and a gifted young male doctoral candidate was set up. Mussafia and Meyer-Lübke had agreed to ask each of us exactly the same questions. Since the exams took place at the same time, neither of us could hear the questions asked to the other, but the audience could compare our answers. We achieved the same results (as also in the *philosophicum* examination): summa cum laude. Though I was very calm during the examinations, I was overwhelmed by the ceremony of the awarding of the doctorate degree. I had asked the beadle to let me read through the words of the oath ahead of time so that I knew its contents. He explained, however, that no man had ever thought of doing that and that I could trust the contents. [. . .]

From the beginning the academic profession appeared to me in the light of brightest radiance. Once it happened that Meringer organized exercises at the end of the semester for his seminar students.[13] We were each to present a small lecture on the topic of the seminar, and he had us go to the podium to do so. Whereas, to my surprise, this situation left the others completely cold, it moved me immensely to sit on the podium, and I took it as highly significant that it fell precisely on my birthday.

However, I never dared to give any sort of expression to this thought. The decisive word first fell when my revised dissertation was in print (1903) and Meyer-Lübke told me that Gröber, a renowned Romance expert from Strasbourg, had written him that it was too bad that I did not live in America. There I would certainly have immediately received a professorship on the basis of the book. At that point I dared to ask whether I could apply for the position of lecturer at the University of Vienna, and Meyer-Lübke, without whose agreement and support nothing, of course, could be done, encouraged me. The battle plan was soon made. Since this required, above all, writing a habilitation thesis, a preparatory step had to be taken first: I applied to the Faculty of Arts and Letters with the formal inquiry as to whether they would be prepared in principle to admit me after fulfillment of all requirements. The shock was great. The secretary of the dean's office did not want to take responsibility for that piece of writing and attempted to get me to hand it over to the dean personally. The dean, the highly respected epigraph expert Eugen Bormann, who courteously kissed every lady's hand, became totally disconcerted. Did my professors know of this step? Did I know how completely impossible it would be for men to be taught by a woman? As his pleas did not soften me, he had to send my fatal piece of writing on to the faculty. "Is she good?" one of the gentlemen asked Meyer-Lübke. Receiving an affirmative answer, he went on to say, "Then by all means let her come. An intelligent woman is preferable to me than a stupid man." The others were not as large-hearted, giving me no answer. After a long period of time that I naturally used to work industriously on the new book, I learned that the faculty had found the way out, deciding that they were not a "question box." Until I fulfilled all the requirements for the habilitation, they had no reason to concern themselves with my inquiry. In the summer of 1904 the habilitation thesis was printed, and in the fall the storm began. "Oh, this is the lady for whose sake we have the long meetings!" said a member of the faculty to whom I was introduced in the course of the winter. They spared no time and pains to reject me. Horrible vistas into the future were opened to their eyes: once she is a lecturer, she will want to be a professor and then dean and president. It took immense powers of persuasion to convince them that the majority of them would certainly no longer be around to experience that. The habilitation *ad personam*, which, of course, would have been simpler for me, was rejected. It was hoped the entire matter could be quashed in principle. When in the end the general acceptance of admission for women passed against all expectations, the *ad personam* problem was naturally solved. In May 1905 I passed the habilitation oral examination before ten examiners, of whom, in addition to Meyer-Lübke, only two made use of the right to examine (Minor, of German studies, and Hauler, of Latin studies). Only a few days later I held the lecture about the Spanish Celestina tragicomedy, which, like almost all habilitation lectures that I have heard, was not as good as it should have been, read instead of spoken freely, and rather long. But I enjoyed one aspect: after they had made me wait so long, now it was their turn to just sit there for once.

The good atmosphere was destroyed through bad news from Florence, where

Mussafia had already spent the entire winter and where we traveled to his deathbed at the beginning of June. Mussafia had thought that when I managed to get the habilitation through in the Faculty of Arts and Letters, the ministry would not make any difficulties at all. That was an error. On the contrary, everything was thought up that might be turned into a stumbling block. At first all the other Vienna faculties were to make a statement on the matter, then all the Austrian universities, and then the additional question of whether women could become research assistants at university needed to be dealt with as well. As again and again positive answers came in and the decision remained in the ministry's hands, a clerical minister of education took office, who simply let the matter lie; then a liberal, who explained that in view of the difficulty of his position, Elise Richter could not demand that he run the risk of being forced into a debate in parliament just because she wanted to give a couple of lectures. And so I waited in nerve-racking excitement for two and a half years. Often I was so unnerved that I thought of emigrating. However, the love of our home, which filled Helene and me in the same way, made the thought unbearable. With all my heart I clung to Vienna, to the countryside, the architecture, the Burg Theater, the philharmonic concerts, to the immeasurable help of the scientific and museum collections that for the historian of words are absolutely necessary, to our not large but select circle of friends, to the Vienna air (in spite of all the hardships to be endured), to the small garden I had put in myself. I was too solidly rooted. And thus I continued to wait.

As unhappy lovers throw themselves into impossible relationships, so I threw myself in the summer of 1907 into a work of literary scholarship, a piece of textual criticism that was far away from my area of studies up to then and that I hoped would distract me from my obsession. It required a stay of several weeks in Paris and a trip into central France as far as Angoulême, a trip that normally would have had great appeal for me. Physically and mentally exhausted, and in a state of deep depression, I spent several weeks recovering in Saint-Malo. It was there that, after many false and thus doubly disappointing pieces of news, the official message reached me that my *venia legendi* was confirmed. Like one who has lain for weeks with a temperature and suddenly feels the illness begin to lessen, I awoke in the morning released from the long pressure. Although in the torment of the waiting period I had thought nothing could ever compensate for this torture, all difficulties were forgotten after the first lecture. As it happened, the first lecture did not go so smoothly. In order to avoid unwanted newspaper publicity and well-meant sympathy that could easily provoke a counterdemonstration, the day and time of the course were not announced until the evening before, and so the attempt to spare the "novelty" any ugly sensationalism and to put the first official "female" lecture on the same footing as the "male" one, albeit an unusually well attended one, was successful. A few hecklers appeared, but their laughter died. Out of fear that my listeners were expecting only chitchat in the lecture or were coming to hear me out of curiosity, I had chosen a completely abstract topic ("History of the Undeclinable Words in French") and demanded more of my listeners than ever afterward. However, they understood my intention, and right from the first semester, contact was good. When I gave the first colloquia, I was much more nervous than when I had taken them myself. [. . .]

Little contact developed with the other members of the Faculty of Arts and Letters, who were now colleagues, for the same reasons as previously with my fellow students. Here there was more resistance out of principle than before, which naturally did not prevent me from going everywhere that my position as lecturer entitled me to and forcing my unwelcome sight upon them. In 1915/16 I was a representative of the nonprofessorial lecturers at the faculty meetings. However, these lecturers had at that time practically no rights at all in the committees. Among both the professorial and nonprofessorial colleagues, there was no lack of teaching staff who not only did not forgive my presence but also did everything possible to put stumbling blocks in my way. Thus, only after fourteen years of service did I receive the title of *professor extraordinarius,* in 1921.

I was never intent on fighting for women's rights. I wanted with all my heart to go the way that my inner impulses led me, and I often would have loved to hand over to someone else the position for which I was often reproached, that of being the "novelty." To be "the first" is not an uninteresting position, but much of the energy necessary for this could have been used to better effect for academic work. In the final years the work was seriously inhibited by physical illness caused by the privations of the 1914–18 war years and the incomparable emotional shocks of these experiences. I was not one of those who believed they had to change horses in midstream. I was not ashamed of Romance studies; on the contrary, I believed I could grasp even more purely the sublimity of academic research over all daily events, particularly in my area. However, I certainly felt a citizen's duty as a woman to show herself worthy of that political emancipation that fell into her lap and, with a full sense of responsibility, to take part in the rescue work out of the destruction, in the necessary new structuring of all relations. For this reason I have been politically active since the collapse of the Habsburg Empire. I never went through the change of mood in which one wishes to have lived one's life completely differently; I always only wanted to be a linguist. However, I was not of the opinion that academics should live in an ivory tower. Perhaps it is precisely my academic field that sharpened my insight into reality, for linguistics, properly understood, is research of the world with everything that is in it, everything earthly and spiritual, and is the form and content of the human experience.

In May of this year the thirtieth anniversary of women's admission to university was commemorated. If one looks from a fixed point, such as an anniversary, back to what was aimed for and what was achieved, there is probably no one for whom these two things are identical. The best—fortunately—always remains to be done. Who could continue to live without the illusion that work gives us? My main work—the understanding of all language development out of the spiritual-rhythmic and the documentation of it via the history of the Romance elements in Latin from the fourth century B.C. up to the tenth century A.D.—is far from being written. It may be that several generations will have to do some digging before this work can be brought to a conclusion. When I began, I believed I possessed the power not only to envision new directions but also to blaze the trail and to follow it through to the end. However, she who starts the way fourteen years later than others will of necessity not arrive at the most beautiful vistas before dusk falls, and thus I will be happy in the end if I am conceded an *et voluisse sat est.*

Vienna, February 1927

Notes

I am grateful to Renate Haas for drawing my attention to Elise Richter and the importance of an English translation of her historic autobiographical essay for this volume as well as for references to seminal literature.

1. Richter, *Kleinere Schriften zur allgemeinen und romanischen Sprachwissenschaft* (Shorter works of general and romance linguistics). This volume includes an introduction and commentaries by Yakov Malkiel and an annotated bibliography by Benjamin Woodbridge.

2. This work is also titled *Beiträge zur Geschichte der Romanismen* 1 (Contributions to the history of Romance elements 1), as Richter intended further volumes to follow. See Woodbridge, "Bibliography of the Writings of Elise Richter," 347. In a footnote to his comprehensive bibliography of 230 entries, Woodbridge writes, "I am well aware that the bibliography is not complete" (342 n).

3. Woodbridge and Malkiel, "Elise Richter," 338.

4. This renewed attention is demonstrated by the publication of her 1940 autobiographical manuscript *Summe des Lebens* (Summation of life) in 1997. In addition Richter has been included in a number of important collections in the 1990s, such as Elisabeth Andraschko's sketch "Elise Richter—eine Skizze ihres Lebens" (Elise Richter—a sketch of her life), 221–31; and Brigitta Keintzel's portrayal in "Elise Richter (1865–1943)," 104–8.

5. This brief biographical sketch is strongly indebted to Christmann's excellent and comprehensive portrait of Elise Richter in *Frau und "Jüdin" an der Universität: Die Romanistin Elise Richter* (Woman and "Jew" at the university: The Romance philologist Elise Richter). Christmann bases his portrait on the earlier published biographical information on Richter as well as on unpublished correspondence, journals, and manuscripts from the archives of the Vienna City Library. One of the most important documents, the autobiographical manuscript *Summe des Lebens,* has since been published (1997).

6. A concise overview of the struggles of European women for admission to school education, higher education, doctoral and postdoctoral work, and subsequent academic careers, particularly in the field of English studies, can be found in Haas's "European Survey," 349–71.

7. Christmann, *Frau und "Jüdin" an der Universität,* 26–27.

8. That was the physicist Berta Karlik. See Plechl, "Das Frauenstudium an den philosophischen Fakultäten"(Women studying in the faculties of arts and letters), 23.

9. Ernst Reinhardt Verlag has given kind permission for me to translate Richter's "Erziehung and Entwicklung," pages 53–61 of the new edition of Elga Kern's collection of self-portraits, *Führende Frauen Europas.*

10. Climbing the stairs would have constituted a physical feat for Richter. At the age of twenty she was confined to bed with rheumatoid arthritis for about a year and continued to

suffer from it for many years afterward, never fully recovering. See Richter, "Erziehung und Entwicklung," 50–51.

11. All brackets with omissions are part of the 1999 edition of the text. Richter's original article was abridged for the new edition.

12. *Romanische Syntax* (Romance syntax), published in 1899, was the third volume of Meyer-Lübke's four-volume *Grammatik der romanischen Sprachen* (Grammar of the Romance languages).

13. This was Rudolf Meringer (1859–1931), the Indo-Germanic philologist, who soon afterward left Vienna to accept a professorship at the University of Graz.

Select Bibliography of Works by Elise Richter

Woodbridge considered his comprehensive 230-entry bibliography of Elise Richter's work to be incomplete. Thus the decision about which of her most important works should be chosen for inclusion here was difficult and will be of necessity somewhat subjective. Richter's papers are housed in the archives of the Vienna City Library. See http://www.stadtbibliothek.wien.at.

"Zur Syntax des rumänischen Possessiv-Pronomens 3. Person." *Zeitschrift für romanische Philologie* 25 (1901): 424–48.

Zur Entwicklung der romanischen Wortstellung aus der lateinischen. Halle: M. Niemeyer, 1903.

Ab im Romanischen. Halle: M. Niemeyer, 1904.

"Zur Geschichte der Indeklinabilien." *Zeitschrift für romanische Philologie* 32 (1908): 656–77.

"Die Rolle der Semantik in der historischen Grammatik." *Germanisch-romanische Monatsschrift* 2 (1910): 231–43.

"Der innere Zusammenhang in der Entwicklung der romanischen Sprachen." In *Prinzipienfragen der romanischen Sprachwissenschaft (Festschrift für Wilhelm Meyer-Lübke).* Vol. 2. Halle: M. Niemeyer, 1911.

Wie wir sprechen: Sechs volkstümliche Vorträge. Leipzig: B. G. Teubner, 1912.

"Die künstlerische Stoffgestaltung in Chrestien's *Ivain*." *Zeitschrift für romanische Philologie* 39 (1917–19): 385–97.

"Das Scheinsubjekt 'es' in den romanischen Sprachen." *Zeitschrift für romanische Philologie* 39 (1917–19): 738–43.

"Grundlinien der Wortstellungslehre." *Zeitschrift für romanische Philologie* 40 (1919–20): 9–61.

"Beiträge zur provenzalischen Grammatik." *Zeitschrift für romanische Philologie* 41 (1921–22): 83–95.

"Zur Klärung der Worstellungsfragen." *Zeitschrift für romanische Philologie* 42 (1922–23): 704–21.

"Die Aussprache des [u] im Altprovenzalischen." *Zeitschrift für romanische Philologie* 45 (1925–26): 385–401.

"Über Homonymie." In *Beiträge zur griechischen und lateinischen Sprachforschung: Festschrift für Paul Kretschmer.* Vienna: Deutscher Verlag für Jugend und Volk, 1926.

"Impressionismus, Expressionismus, und Grammatik." *Zeitschrift für romanische Philologie* 47 (1927): 349–71.

"Sprachwissenschaftliche Probleme." In *Dreißig Jahre Frauenstudium in Österreich, 1897–1927: Festschrift,* edited by the Festausschuss. Vienna: Kaltschmid, 1927.

"Erziehung und Entwicklung." In *Führende Frauen Europas in sechzehn Selbstschilderungen,* edited by Elga Kern. Munich: Ernst Reinhardt, 1928.

"Die Entwicklung der Phonologie." *Die neueren Sprachen* 38 (1930): 529–43.

"Über die Reihenfolge der Organeinstellungen beim Sprechen." *Volkstum und Kultur der Romanen* 3 (1930): 25–38.
With Helene Adolf and E. Winkler. "Studien zum altfranzösischen *Alexiuslied*." *Zeitschrift für französische Sprache und Literatur* 57 (1933): 80–95.
Chronologische Phonetik des Französischen bis zum Ende des 8. Jahrhunderts (= Beiträge zur Geschichte der Romanismen. Vol. 1). Halle, Ger.: M. Niemeyer, 1934.
"Grundsätzliche Erklärungen und Nachträge zur Chronologischen Phonetik." *Zeitschrift für romanische Philologie* 56 (1936): 604–8.
"Das psychische Geschehen und die Artikulation." *Archives néerlandaises de phonétique expérimentale* 13 (1937): 41–71.
"Zur Syntax der Inschriften und Aufschriften." *Vox Romanica* 2 (1937): 104–35.
"Länge und Kürze." *Archiv für vergleichende Phonetik* 2 (1938): 12–29.
"Unterbewußte Vorgänge im Sprachleben." In *Mélanges de linguistique offerts à Charles Bally*, under the auspices of the Faculty of Letters of the University of Geneva and with the collaboration of Albert Sechenaye. Geneva: Georg et Cie, 1939.
Kleinere Schriften zur allgemeinen und romanischen Sprachwissenschaft. Selection, introduction, and comments by Yakov Malkiel. Bibliography by Benjamin N. Woodbridge Jr. Edited by Wolfgang Meid. Innsbruck: Innsbrucker Beiträge zur Sprachwissenschaft, 1977.
Summe des Lebens. Edited by the Austrian Federation of University Women. Vienna: WUV-Universitätsverlag, 1997.
"Erziehung und Entwicklung." In *Führende Frauen Europas: Elga Kerns Standardwerk von 1928/1930*, edited by Bettina Conrad and Ulrike Leuschner. Munich/Basel: Ernst Reinhardt, 1999.

Works Cited

Andraschko, Elisabeth. "Elise Richter—eine Skizze ihres Lebens." In *"Durch Erkenntnis zu Freiheit und Glück . . .": Frauen an der Universität Wien (ab 1897)*, edited by Waltraud Heindl and Marina Tichy. Vienna: WUV-Universitätsverlag, 1990.
Christmann, Hans Helmut. *Frau und "Jüdin" an der Universität: Die Romanistin Elise Richter*. Mainz: Akademie der Wissenschaften und der Literatur, 1980.
Haas, Renate. "European Survey: Parameters and Patterns of Development." In *European English Studies: Contributions towards the History of a Discipline*, edited by Balz Engler and Renate Haas. Leicester: English Association, 2000.
Keintzel, Brigitta. "Elise Richter (1865–1943), Romanistin." In *Wir sind die Ersten, die es wagen*, edited by Ilse Korotin. Vienna: Bundesministerium für Unterricht und Kunst, 1993.
Meyer-Lübke, Wilhelm. *Grammatik der romanischen Sprachen*. Leipzig: Reisland, 1890–1902.
Plechl, Pia Maria. "Das Frauenstudium an den philosophischen Fakultäten." In *Frauenstudium und Akademische Frauenarbeit in Österreich*, edited by Martha Forkl and Elisabeth Koffmahn. Vienna: Wilhelm Braumüller, 1968.
Woodbridge, Benjamin M., Jr. "A Bibliography of the Writings of Elise Richter." *Romance Philology* 26 (1972): 342–60.
Woodbridge, Benjamin M., Jr., and Yakov Malkiel. "Elise Richter: Two Retrospective Essays." *Romance Philology* 26 (1972): 335–41.

CHAPTER 7

Eleanor Prescott Hammond (1866–1933)
Pioneer Scholar of Middle English Manuscript Study

A. S. G. EDWARDS

Eleanor Prescott Hammond was born in Worcester, Massachusetts, on 26 April 1866, the daughter of Andrew Hill and Rhoda Maria Hammond. She attended the University of Leipzig in 1891. The following year she went to Oxford as a member of the Society of Oxford Home Students (now Saint Anne's College). She obtained a first-class honors certificate in English there in 1894.[1] In 1895 she began work on a Ph.D. at the University of Chicago and completed her dissertation in 1898 on "Lydgate's Danse Macabre." She taught at the University of Chicago from 1898 until 1904, at which point she resigned. After 1904 she appears to have maintained some connection with the University of Chicago for several years (she uses it as an academic address until 1907). For a period she may have been associated with Northwestern University, although details of her time there have proved difficult to recover.[2] Although for much of her life she remained in Chicago, in her later years she moved to Boston and taught occasionally (1922–23, 1926–27, 1927–28) at Wellesley College; she left Wellesley a number of books. She died in Boston on 21 February 1933, aged sixty-six, after a long illness. She was unmarried.[3]

As this summary suggests, Hammond's career does not conform to a conventional academic pattern. For only about six years of her scholarly life, while at Chicago, did she have a full-time academic post. She seems to have had no students. Much of her scholarly activity was undertaken, therefore, outside the academy. There is no evidence to suggest that she was able to travel regularly to England to undertake research. She lived in Chicago and Boston and wrote steadily for nearly thirty years.

These circumstances make Eleanor Hammond's achievements all the more extraordinary, for she was among the foremost scholars of Middle English manuscripts and texts in the early twentieth century. Indeed, she was possibly the first American scholar to pay serious attention to fifteenth-century English manuscripts and to examine the circumstances of their production and circulation. A number of her early publications demonstrate a detailed knowledge of the poetical manuscripts of the poet John Lydgate (ca. 1375–1449) and their dissemination. This knowledge finds its most developed expression in two articles on Lydgate manuscripts she published in the German journal *Anglia* while still at the University of Chicago. These articles are of fundamental importance to Middle English manuscript studies in their accounts of the compilation and circulation of Lydgate's works. The first article establishes the relationship between two important manuscripts of Lydgate's shorter poems in the British Museum, MSS Harley 2251 and Additional 34360, copied by the same scribe, now often known as the "Hammond scribe," which are then set in the wider context of the circulation of these poems.[4] In the second article she examines the career of the famous fifteenth-century scribe John Shirley, identifying many of his manuscripts and assessing their importance.[5] Her study has provided the basis for all subsequent work on this complex figure. Both these articles are important for their pioneering research on the activities of particular scribes. Such questions of scribal activity remained recurrent interests in her work; she was to return to them later in her career in her article "A Scribe of Chaucer," an extended account of the corpus of manuscripts written by the "Hammond scribe."

This early work was a substantial achievement. But Eleanor Hammond suffered two serious handicaps, which may have led to her research being insufficiently acknowledged by her scholarly contemporaries. The first was her period of study. The fifteenth century was generally regarded with barely concealed scorn as a field of scholarly enquiry for literary historians, a state of affairs that has changed only in very recent times. Lydgate in particular still lay under the shadow of the contemptuous dismissal of Joseph Ritson a century earlier as "this voluminous, prosaick and driveling monk." And Hammond's concern with manuscript study was unlikely to find much sympathetic response in a country where manuscripts of the kind that concerned her were largely unavailable and where in consequence there was little impetus for, or interest in, such research.

But although Lydgate was to remain a constant interest in Hammond's scholarly life, her work on Middle English manuscripts quickly revealed far wider implications. In 1903 she returned to England, and various articles from around that time detail her researches in public and private libraries on particular manuscript collections of Chaucer's works.[6] Chaucer had clearly preoccupied her for some time. In an article in 1904 she reports herself at work on a study of "The Manuscripts of the Minor Poems of Chaucer."[7] She had published an important textual study of *The Parliament of Fowls* in 1902 and an article on Caxton's editions of the *Canterbury Tales* in 1905. And in 1906 she published an outline of a projected book-length Chaucer bibliography.[8] But these studies barely hint at what was soon to come. In 1908 she published *Chaucer: A Bibliographical Manual*, a volume that runs to 579 pages. The bulk of the book is devoted to careful accounts of Chaucer's life and canon, of all known manuscripts and printed editions, together with discussion of his versification (this last was another recurrent interest of Hammond's). The importance of this book cannot be overemphasized. The quality and accuracy of her researches have stood the test of time. It remains the best succinct but compendious and authoritative guide to the textual forms and history of Chaucer's works. It is still a standard reference work for any student of Chaucer's manuscripts. Indeed, while it can be supplemented through information that has come to light since it was published, it is hard to see how it could ever be surpassed. It appeared the year after Hammond had ceased any association with the University of Chicago.

One can only speculate on the reasons why she could not find, or chose not to find, regular academic employment elsewhere. Probably she had sufficient resources to make regular work unnecessary. But some of her early publications suggest interests sufficiently removed from her general scholarly ones as to seem directly related to her teaching experiences and to indicate some interest in pedagogy.[9] This makes her seeming disinclination to seek further employment as a university teacher all the more puzzling.

One possible clue to this question may lie in her other writings on nonmedieval subjects, particularly during the decade after she left the University of Chicago. From about 1910 her publications reveal an interest in the drama, particularly Shakespeare.[10] In 1914 her play *Susannah Shakespeare* was performed and subsequently published in a privately printed edition. And in 1919 she produced a translation of Cantos 1–7 of Dante's *Inferno* in terza rima, again in a privately printed edition, which one obituarist termed "a true tour de force."[11] It may be that she found some creative liberation outside academic life that left her disinclined to return to it on any regular basis.

Whatever the truth of the matter, she did continue with research in fifteenth-century manuscripts and verse texts. Some of the articles she published after the appearance of *Chaucer: A Bibliographical Manual* seem to be related to the unfolding design of what would be her second and last major scholarly book. But it was to be nearly twenty years before that volume was published. *English Verse between Chaucer and Surrey* appeared in 1927 from Duke University Press. This was the first—and remains the only—anthology of English verse devoted exclusively to the century or so after Chaucer's death.

The conception of the edition seems to have changed over this long period. As early as 1908 she had announced in a published letter an anthology called *Gower: Chaucer's Followers,* scheduled to appear in Heath's Belles Lettres series.[12] In 1921 she felt she could announce that her "volume, *From Gower to Surrey,* [was] now nearing completion."[13] But neither Gower nor Surrey were to have a place in the final volume.

Her 1908 announcement spells out the contents of the volume in terms that contrast clearly with the volume she finally published. The projected volume was to include substantial selections from Gower, Lydgate, Walton, Charles d'Orleans, and Thomas Hoccleve, as well as a number of anonymous poems, which she lists, from early fifteenth-century manuscripts. In addition to the absence of Gower, almost none of the anonymous poems appear in the published volume. Only Lydgate, Walton, Charles d'Orleans, and Hoccleve remain, with the first far outnumbering the others in the quantity of verse included. There are other curious omissions. Hammond herself notes the omission of *The Flower and the Leaf*, even though as late as 1925 she had reported that she was at work on an edition of it.[14] Several years earlier she had written an article on the Wyatt canon.[15] Thomas Wyatt does not appear in the published volume either.

There are some significant changes to the fifteenth-century contents: the inclusion of John Hardyng's *Chronicle* and George Ripley's *Compend of Alchemy* and such major anonymous works as *The Libelle of English Policy* and *The Court of Sapience*. But, most strikingly, what Hammond's initial announcement did not foresee was the very substantial commitment she was to make to works of the first half of the sixteenth century: Stephen Hawes, William Neville, Robert Copland, Alexander Barclay, John Skelton, George Cavendish, and Henry Parker, Lord Morley, are not mentioned in 1908. This increased historical range is one of the book's most remarkable features. It draws together a number of works that continue to demonstrate the potency of the "Lydgate tradition" long after the advent of print.

The work is not just remarkably ambitious in its scope; it is also unusual in its scale and form. It runs to nearly six hundred pages. All the texts are reproduced afresh, largely from manuscript but not in a critical form: for most poems "one text is printed verbatim et literatim, with mention of variants in the Notes" (x).[16] There is no modern punctuation, so that the student "is then given his proper share in the editorial problem of following the medieval mind" (ix). There are separate introductions to each work that give concise biographical and bibliographical information about each author and/or text, together with other relevant information, often about versification. Each text is very fully annotated. Not all this editorial work is always as accurate as one would wish. It has been demonstrated, for example, that there are over eighty errors in Hammond's transcription in her edition of the manuscript portion of Skelton's *Garland of Laurel*.[17]

The anthology of texts is prefaced by a general introduction setting out Hammond's views on the verse of this period. It represents the distillation of over thirty years' experience of studying manuscripts and texts of a neglected period of English literary history. She sees the period covered by her anthology as "the English Transition" (7; the term recurs), between Chaucer's death and the advent of the Elizabethan era. She analyzes the various factors she believes have inhibited any wider flowering of the seeds of Chaucer's genius: the Black Death, the weakness of Richard II; the emergence of what she terms "the bourgeoisie, in all its impulses antagonistic to the social order which had endeavored to hold it in check" (11). But the chief weight of her analysis falls again on the metrical changes she perceives between Chaucer and his major followers, Lydgate and Hoccleve. She concludes: "Chaucer attained his rhythmical and critical poise in an imperfectly developed and ill-adjusted age. He could not bequeath it. The power to control material can be received only by those mentally capable of receiving it; and the resettlement of the stereotype on English society just after his death, the increasing lack of educational opportunity of the early fifteenth century in England, smothered the growth of any such mentality" (27).

She talks more than once about the failure of verse in this period to "raise the pitch of life" (28, 30) and finds few figures capable of achieving this—although Robert Henryson and his fellow Scot poets receive some praise. She has more admiration for prose writers, particularly Thomas Malory, who is singled out for especial approval. But she is critical of what she perceives as the dominant modes of verse of "the Transition," allegory and romance, for their "formlessness and didacticism" (28). Indeed, throughout the book Hammond manifests a resolute disinclination to find a lot to praise in the poetry of the fifteenth and sixteenth centuries, a detached skepticism that refuses to see too much merit in the materials she had spent so long editing.

Her argument is buttressed not just by a wide range of reference to medieval writers, both English and European, but also by frequent parallels with works of later periods. Her introduction is studded with allusions to William Shakespeare, Anne Radcliffe, John Keats, Percy Shelley, Leigh Hunt, George Eliot, Thomas Carlyle, William Morris, Coventry Patmore, George Bernard Shaw, J. M. Barrie, Hilaire Belloc, and Edgar Lee Masters's *Spoon River Anthology,* among others, as well as to modern social and cultural theorists such as George Santayana and Walter Lippmann. She reveals a breadth of literary knowledge unconstrained by narrow periodicity. Indeed, her introduction suggests obliquely why she might have found the narrow specialization of an English department so uncongenial.

The overall importance of Hammond's achievement was recognized by her reviewers. These can represented by F. P. Magoun, who observed that "[w]e have for the first time in commonly accessible form a rich collection of material illustrating important, yet in the past somewhat neglected, literary genres of the later . . . Middle Ages . . . Miss Hammond's name on the title-page virtually guarantees the scholarship."[18] Her collection has yet to be superseded.

Hammond seems to have published little after *English Verse.* (She suffered a stroke two years before she died.) In her final article, which appeared in the year of her death, she reports herself as "engaged upon the revision and completion of [her] 1908 Bibliographical Manual of Chaucer."[19] This revision was never to appear. But her words are testimony to the resolution and singleness of vision that guided her throughout her scholarly life.

It is difficult to recover much sense of the personality behind the scholar. Vida Scudder, who knew her at Wellesley, writes of "her serious joy in a large range of pursuits, some of them far from scholarly: mountain climbing; solving Mystery-novel puzzles; translating Dante."[20] Another old friend, George L. Marsh, speaks of her "zest for living, her keen Yankee wit."[21] Unsurprisingly, her scholarly writings convey little sense of this human warmth. Rather, they reflect an austerity, an unremitting rigor consistent with the nature of her scholarly interests. Hers was a life devoted largely to the pursuit of forms of research that were never likely to bring her wide scholarly acclaim. Apart from her two great books, such research found its expression most frequently in the scholarly note, dealing with some aspect of bibliographical, paleographical, and editorial scholarship. Such forms of academic research are more likely to be gratefully used than fulsomely acknowledged. But there is some irony in the fact that such acknowledgment as they might have received would have come within the academy of which Hammond was not a part for most of her life.

Notes

1. Her first book, *Chaucer: A Bibliographical Manual*, is dedicated to "that sweet city with her dreaming spires" and her last, *English Verse between Chaucer and Surrey*, is dedicated to the late Merton Professor at Oxford, A. S. Napier, "Scholar. Master. Friend."

2. A note in the Register of Saint Anne's College, Oxford, describes her as "late N. Western Univ." I am indebted to Dr. Vincent Gillespie for help with Hammond's time in Oxford.

3. There were several obituaries: in the *New York Times* ("Eleanor P. Hammond"); by G. L. Marsh in *Modern Philology*; and by Vida Scudder in *Wellesley College News*; there is also a brief notice in *Who Was Who in America* (1940).

4. "Two British Museum Manuscripts (Harley 2251 and Adds. 34360)."

5. "Ashmole 59 and Other Shirley Manuscripts," "Scribe of Chaucer."

6. For example, "Ms Pepys 2006" and "Ms Longleat 258."

7. "Omissions from the Editions of Chaucer."

8. "The Need of Bibliographies in Literary History."

9. For example, her articles on "The Use of Episode in the Teaching of Fiction" and "The Tent Scene in Richard III."

10. For example, her articles on "A Pyramus-and-Thisbe Play of Shakespeare's Time"; "Shakespeare's Fools"; "Mob-Psychology in Le Bon and Lear"; and "Greek Theatre and Its Drama."

11. The characterization is Scudder's in her obituary.

12. "Texts of 'Chaucer's Followers.'"

13. "Lost Quire of a Shirley Codex," 184–85.

14. Regarding the omission of *The Flower and the Leaf*, Hammond noted, "It is accessible in a modern edition." (*English Verse between Chaucer and Surrey*, vii). She reports her work on an edition of it in "Grey and Green Wood."

15. "Poems Signed by Sir Thomas Wyatt.".

16. Page numbers for quotations from *English Verse between Chaucer and Surrey* are given in parentheses here and in the following discussion.

17. This is the calculation of Brownlow, *Book of the Laurel*, 39.

18. Magoun, review of *English Verse between Chaucer and Surrey*,

19. "Chaucer's 'Book of the Twenty-five Ladies'," 514–16.

20. Vida Scudder, *Wellesley College News*, 23 March, 1933, n.p.

21. G. L. Marsh, *Modern Philology*, 30 (1933): 449.

Select Bibliography of Works by Eleanor Prescott Hammond

"London Lickpenny." *Anglia* 20 (1898): 404–20.

"Lydgate's Mumming at Hertford." *Anglia* 22 (1899): 364–74.

"The Tent Scene in *Richard III*." *Modern Language Notes* 17 (1902): 257–62.
"On the Text of Chaucer's *Parlement of Foules*." *Decennial Publications of the University of Chicago* 7 (1902): 3–25.
"The Use of Episode in the Teaching of Fiction." *Modern Language Notes* 17 (1902): 65–71.
"The Departing of Chaucer." *Modern Philology* 1 (1903): 331–36.
"Lydgate and the Duchess of Gloucester." *Anglia* 27 (1904): 381–98.
"Ms Pepys 2006: A Chaucerian Codex." *Modern Language Notes* 19 (1904): 196–98.
"Omissions from the Editions of Chaucer." *Modern Language Notes* 19 (1904): 35–38.
"Ms Longleat 258: A Chaucerian Codex." *Modern Language Notes* 20 (1905): 77–79.
"On the Order of the *Canterbury Tales:* Caxton's Two Editions." *Modern Philology* 3 (1905): 159–70.
"Two British Museum Manuscripts (Harley 2251 and Adds. 34360): A Contribution to the Bibliography of John Lydgate." *Anglia* 28 (1905): 1–28.
"The Need of Bibliographies in Literary History." *Papers of the Bibliographical Society of America* 1 (1906): 65–70.
"Ashmole 59 and Other Shirley Manuscripts." *Anglia* 30 (1907): 320–48.
"The Lover's Mass." *Journal of English and Germanic Philology* 7 (1907): 95–104.
"A Parliament of Birds." *Journal of English and Germanic Philology* 7 (1907): 105–9.
"Two Chaucer Cruces." *Modern Language Notes* 22 (1907): 51–52.
Chaucer: A Bibliographical Manual. New York: Macmillan, 1908.
"On the Editing of Chaucer's Minor Poems." *Modern Language Notes* 23 (1908): 20–21.
"Texts of 'Chaucer's Followers.'" *Modern Language Notes* 23 (1908): 157.
"Danse Macabre." *Modern Language Notes* 24 (1909): 63.
"The Lament of a Prisoner against Fortune." *Anglia* 32 (1909): 481–90.
"Lydgate's New Year's Valentine." *Anglia* 32 (1909): 190–96.
Review of *The Harleian Manuscript 7334 and Revision of "The Canterbury Tales,"* by J. S. P. Tatlock. *Journal of English and Germanic Philology* 9 (1910): 564–65.
"Shakespeare's Fools." *Atlantic Monthly* 106 (July 1910): 90–100.
"Two Tapestry Poems by Lydgate: 'The Life of Saint George' and the 'Falls of Seven Princes.'" *Englische Studien* 43 (1910): 10–26.
"A Burgundian Copy of Chaucer's *Troilus*." *Modern Language Notes* 26 (1911): 32.
"The Eye and the Heart." *Anglia* 34 (1911): 235–65.
"Latin Texts of the Dance of Death." *Modern Philology* 8 (1911): 399–410.
"A Reproof to Lydgate." *Modern Language Notes* 26 (1911): 74–76.
Review of *The Ancestry of Chaucer*, by A. A. Kern. *Journal of English and Germanic Philology* 10 (1911): 147–49.
"Chaucer and Lydgate Notes." *Modern Language Notes* 27 (1912): 91–92.
"Lydgate's Prologue to the Story of Thebes." *Anglia* 36 (1912): 360–76.
"Lear and His Daughters." *Poet Lore* 24 (1913): 110–12.
"Poet and Patron in the Fall of Princes." *Anglia* 38 (1914): 121–36.
"A Pyramus-and-Thisbe Play of Shakespeare's Time." *The Drama: A Quarterly Review* 5, no. 17 (1915): 288–300.
"Chaucer, Dante and Their Scribes." *Modern Language Notes* 31 (1916): 121.
"The Lover's Mass in England and Spain." *Modern Philology* 14 (1916): 253–54.
"Mob-Psychology in Le Bon and Lear." *Unpopular Review* 5 (1916): 275–80.

Susanna Shakespeare: A Romantic Comedy. Chicago: privately printed, 1916.
"A Manuscript Perhaps Lost." *Modern Language Notes* 32 (1917): 187.
"Greek Theatre and Its Drama." *The Drama: A Quarterly Review* 8, no. 30 (1918): 280–83.
Dante in English: A Terza Rima Translation and Critique of Terza Rima Translations of the "Inferno" of Dante. Chicago: privately printed, 1919.
"The Lost Quire of a Shirley Codex." *Modern Language Notes* 36 (1921): 184–85.
"The Texts of Lydgate's Danse Macabre." *Modern Language Notes* 36 (1921): 250–51.
"Poems Signed by Sir Thomas Wyatt." *Modern Language Notes* 37 (1922): 505–6.
"Charles of Orleans and Anne Molyneux." *Modern Philology* 22 (1924): 215–16.
"How a Lover Praiseth His Lady." *Modern Philology* 21 (1924): 379–95.
"The Chance of the Dice." *Englische Studien* 59 (1925): 1–16.
"Grey and Green Wood." *Modern Language Notes* 40 (1925): 185.
"The Nine-Syllabled Pentameter Line in Some Post-Chaucerian Manuscripts." *Modern Philology* 23 (1925): 129–52.
"Boethius: Chaucer: Walton: Lydgate." *Modern Language Notes* 41 (1926): 534–35.
English Verse between Chaucer and Surrey. Durham, N.C.: Duke University Press, 1927.
"Lydgate and Coluccio Salutati." *Modern Philology* 25 (1927): 49–57.
Review of *The Book of Troilus and Criseyde,* edited by R. K. Root. *Anglia Beiblatt* 38 (1927): 315–18.
Review of *The Nun's Priest's Tale,* edited by K. Sisam. *Anglia Beiblatt* 38 (1927): 314–15.
Review of *Thomas Chaucer,* by M. R. Ruud. *Anglia Beiblatt* 38 (1927): 54–56.
Review of *Chaucer and the Medieval Sciences,* by W. C. Curry. *Anglia Beiblatt* 39 (1928): 185–87.
"A Scribe of Chaucer." *Modern Philology* 27 (1929): 27–33.
"Chaucer's 'Book of the Twenty-five Ladies.'" *Modern Language Notes* 48 (1933): 514–16.

Works Cited

Brownlow, F., ed. *The Book of the Laurel,* by John Skelton. Newark, N.J.: University of Delaware Press, 1990.
"Eleanor P. Hammond." *New York Times*, 24 February 1933, 20:2.
"Hammond, Eleanor Prescott." In *Who Was Who in America,* 513. Chicago: A. N. Marquis, 1940.
Magoun, F. P. Review of *English Verse between Chaucer and Surrey,* by E. P. Hammond. *Speculum* 3 (1928): 269–70.
Marsh, George L. Obituary of E. P. Hammond. *Modern Philology* 30 (1933): 449.
Scudder, Vida. "Dr. Hammond." *Wellesley College News,* 23 March 1933.

CHAPTER 8

Caroline F. E. Spurgeon (1869–1942)
First Woman Professor of English in England

Renate Haas

Caroline Frances Eleanor Spurgeon is best remembered in three fields: in English studies both for her monumental volumes *Five Hundred Years of Chaucer Criticism and Allusion* and for her fundamental book *Shakespeare's Imagery* and in the International Federation of University Women as a central founding figure. In her former university, the University of London, a prize, a scholarship, and a fellowship still carry her name. Nevertheless, there is hardly any recent literature about her to be found. Even the comprehensive *British Biographical Archive* offers only a single, meager entry. Fortunately, Spurgeon already enjoyed such international renown by the late 1920s that Elga Kern invited her to contribute to her pioneering collection of self-portraits of leading European women. To this fruit of the first women's movement, the following characterization owes various details that otherwise would have been lost.[1]

Spurgeon was born in 1869 and, in many respects, represents the European social type of the (upper-) middle-class daughter. More precisely, she may be called an (upper-) middle-class daughter of the British Empire, because she was born in India as the only child of a captain. The early years of her youth were spent in Germany and France. As was still common for girls, no great value was attached to her school education. According to Spurgeon's own description, it was limited almost completely to languages and music—not such a bad basis for specializing later in English. It was at quite an advanced age, twenty-four, that she began her studies at King's College and University College, London, out of the desire to "attain a thorough and healthy education."[2] Encouraged by a committed vice principal, Lilian Faithfull, she read for the Oxford Honors School in English Language and Literature and passed these examinations in 1899.[3]

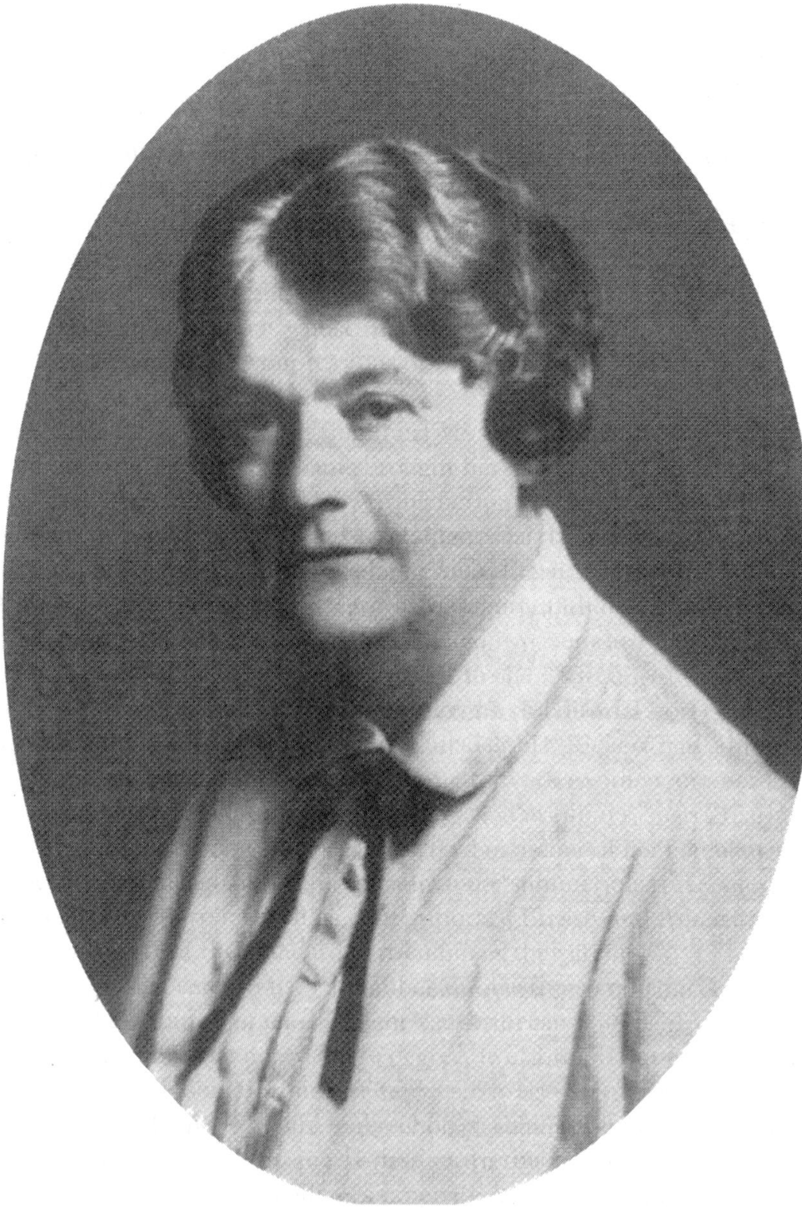

Although Spurgeon no longer belonged to the first generation of women students, the fulfillment of her wish "to accomplish something definitive" and an academic career were still extremely difficult to obtain.[4] As a woman she was not eligible for an Oxford degree, and one back door through which a number of others of her sex would soon be able to enter was not open to her: since she had not taken the full course in Oxford, she was not able to legitimate her success in the examinations by securing a degree *ad eundem* from Trinity College, Dublin.[5] At least she had the opportunity to join the teaching faculty of Bedford College. She had never intended to become involved in teaching, but this was a chance to get a foot in the door of academia, particularly since during the reorganization of the University of London it had been Bedford among the women's colleges that was immediately integrated and thus recognized as fully academic.[6]

The difficulties confronting Spurgeon with a view to a doctorate deserve closer scrutiny than is possible here. What is clear is that she worked ten years on her dissertation. One factor that hindered her progress was that the University of London (which had been among the first British universities to admit women to their degrees) still had to fight hard for its full recognition. As late as 1908 Sidney Webb observed that it was still difficult to persuade people that there was a University of London, although it was the biggest in the country and the fourth or fifth largest in the world.[7] Two years earlier an "intellectual *entente cordiale*" was established with the Sorbonne, one of the oldest universities outside Italy, with a view to increasing the respectability of the "newcomer."[8] At the Sorbonne, English studies was a field already well established, compared to other universities or countries on the Continent, and it was there that Spurgeon turned, for the formalities at any rate.[9] Of the two professors of English, Alexandre Beljame and Emile Legouis, Legouis in particular maintained close contact with England and had suitable research interests.[10] In 1911, at last, at the age of forty-two, Spurgeon attained a doctorate of literature on the basis of *Chaucer devant la critique en Angleterre et en France depuis son temps jusqu'à nos jours*.

That a formal qualification was important because of the manifold prejudices against women in academia can be seen from the example of Spurgeon's friend Edith Morley. Morley did not want to spend so much time, money, and energy on a few letters after her name; she built up English at Reading almost single-handedly, only to find that when the college was being elevated to a full university, she was to be the only lecturer in charge of a subject who would not be promoted to the professorial ranks. Morley ultimately managed to obtain the title of professor (in 1908, not for English literature but for English language). Nevertheless, she suffered intensely from discrimination throughout her further career, especially since the college authorities continued to regard it as unacceptable for men to be responsible to a woman.[11]

In comparison with Morley, Spurgeon had two great advantages: publications in the most prestigious field, medieval studies, and certain protective mechanisms of a women's college. Because the importance of official qualifications had been perfectly clear to a number of women networking for the promotion of female higher education, the British Federation of University Women, founded in 1907, soon created an annual prize fellowship, and Spurgeon was the first recipient. Thanks to her doctoral degree and further qualification, she was then able to succeed in open competition against other applicants for the new university chair in English literature, tenable at Bedford College in 1913. Thus Spurgeon attained her chair not merely by internal promotion, and accordingly she could consider herself the first proper and fully accepted woman professor of English English studies and the first fully accepted woman professor in England in general.[12] Within the University of London she remained the only exception for quite a while, and Oxford and Cambridge were even further from accepting women on an equal footing.

That the first fully recognized female professor of English English studies had to take a very important, perhaps even *the* decisive step of her academic career abroad, in a non-English-speaking country, comes as no surprise to someone familiar with the history of women's higher education. In order to counter the massive opposition, women depended heavily on the international exchange of information and mobility. No country was progressive in all areas concerning the improvement of their position. Even in the United States, in spite of its early establishment and recognition of women's colleges, and in spite of its early admission of women to diverse coeducational institutions, there had also been great difficulties at the higher levels—graduate study, doctoral work, and academic career—and often these difficulties continued. In the late 1870s, for instance, Martha Carey Thomas, after obtaining a Bachelor of Arts from Cornell, had been admitted not to the seminars at Johns Hopkins but only to individual instruction. She had moved on to Leipzig. There she was allowed to participate in the seminars and even to write a thesis, but she was not allowed to receive a degree and so had to content herself with the philological prestige study at Leipzig imparted. She then resorted to the liberal University of Zurich, a mecca for academic women, where, in 1882, she obtained a doctorate summa cum laude for a dissertation dealing with *Sir Gawain and the Green Knight*.

The example of Thomas (1857–1935), however, also illustrates how much further the academic establishment of women had already progressed in the United States by the first decade of the twentieth century. As early as 1884 Thomas had become professor of English and dean at the Quaker women's college Bryn Mawr, and since 1894 she had served as president there. Nevertheless, a decisive factor should not go unmentioned: Thomas's rich friend Mary Garrett, the daughter of a railway boss, gave Bryn Mawr ten thousand dollars each year that Thomas served as president. In the new century Thomas was an American celebrity and leading spokeswoman for women and higher education. Her criticism of Harvard president Charles W. Eliot's outdated notions of women's roles had been reported by newspapers throughout the States, and her monograph *Education of Women* had been published by the U.S. government for the Paris Exposition of 1900.[13] In Europe, in contrast, even for a doctorate Spurgeon still had to turn to a country where women were helped by the fact that the universities did not enjoy such high esteem as they did at home or in various other states.[14]

Spurgeon's academic establishment coincided with a period of reorientation in English studies, namely, the decisive phase for the establishment of English literature, which, after surmounting the initial obstacles, she was able to influence and use. The wider context was the expansion of the education system, the general broadening of teaching at school and university levels, whose corollary was a heightened demand for teachers and for teaching the national tongue. Of the three traditional domains of university English—language, literature, and preparation for teaching the subject in schools—the first had an overwhelmingly philological character. The third area was being greatly extended, which fact, however, was ignored by most in academia.[15] For the establishment of a proper discipline "English lit," study of the modern national literature first had to win full academic recognition, which above all meant recognition by Oxbridge, because postmedieval works had, of course, already been dealt with in higher education. But since this had been done primarily in courses for women, in the newer universities or working men's colleges, and in the colonies, full acceptance was still missing. It was only in 1904 that Oxford got its first really "literary" professor of English, Walter Raleigh, and as late as 1911 that a specifically literary chair was founded in Cambridge.[16]

While the model of classical philology still loomed large, scholars were groping for a paradigm of their own, and the close connection of literary criticism with culture in general harbored advantages as well as disadvantages. An important drawback arose from the fact that proof of academic dignity was much more difficult for literary criticism than for philology. On the other hand, the very proximity to life and school also meant that broad educated circles took a lively interest, with all kinds of motivations—religious, political, et cetera—and often tried to promote institutionalization. Consequently, entrance through the borderlands between strict scholarship and cultural life was somewhat easier for women than entrance into Oxbridge exclusivity. For instance, Spurgeon had the opportunity to write a foreword to the edition of a classic (Walpole's *Castle of Otranto*, 1907). But in spite of her prize-winning work on Samuel Johnson (Quain essay, 1898), the Johnson Club refused to admit her.[17] The man who opened for her a dissertation perspective was not an established professor but Frederick James Furnivall, whom she first met in 1901. Furnivall had been looking for someone to collect a body of opinion on Chaucer for quite a while, and Spurgeon's edition of *Richard Brathwait's Comments, in 1665, upon Chaucer's Tales of the Miller and the Wife of Bath* for the Chaucer Society, which he still presided over, formed the first steppingstone. The task proved much vaster than anticipated. After ten years the Sorbonne dissertation represented a first summa, and only from 1914 onward was Spurgeon able to publish the long-delayed installments of her *Five Hundred Years of Chaucer Criticism and Allusion*.[18] Because other things intervened, it was not until 1925, after a quarter century, that she concluded her big project with the definitive edition. Many people contributed to her collection, and the 1914 volume was published together with another woman, but until his death in 1910, the vital support came from Furnivall. His "encouragement, inspiration and generous and unsparing aid of every kind" were decisive for the first stage of Spurgeon's scholarly career, as the warmth of her thanks in the final foreword, thirteen years after his death, movingly demonstrates.[19]

At the beginning of the second decade of the twentieth century, the religious fervor of the time provided Spurgeon with additional opportunities. Evelyn Underhill, who had also studied at King's College, with her book of 1911 further boosted the fascination with mysticism, and Spurgeon was allowed to contribute an essay, "William Law and the Mystics," to the *Cambridge History of English Literature*. In 1913, the year of her professorial establishment, she was able to publish *Mysticism in English Literature* (for which the *Cambridge History* essay and an article in the *Quarterly Review* had formed the starting point) in the series of Cambridge Manuals. In this volume (which is available as a 1998 reprint), only 15 out of the 158 pages are devoted to the Middle English mystics, in the main Richard Rolle and Julian of Norwich, which is very little—less, for instance, than is given to Blake alone. But Middle English literature *is* dealt with as an integral part of the literary tradition and with methods of literary criticism. In other words, both the book on mysticism and her great Chaucer project represent a transitional stage between traditional philology and English literature: they deal with medieval works but from decidedly modern perspectives. On the basis of the encyclopedic record, Spurgeon was finally able to make the first comprehensive analysis of Chaucer reception and, in doing so, also achieved her large-scale aim of supplying "a humble but solid brick [for] the future building of a history of English poetics and poetical taste" as well as of literary criticism.[20]

World War I accelerated changes in society and academic paradigms. It was waged not merely on the actual battlefields but also on the much wider levels of culture and research. The latter fights were far vaster inasmuch as they prepared and continued concrete combat and involved countries free from military operations, such as the United States. In the "war of the professors" the disciplines concerned with the respective national language and literature, and national culture in general, played a prominent role on both sides. To women the total war brought unprecedented opportunities. Like others Spurgeon was able to extend her sphere of work, consolidate her position, and move into the public eye. Thus, her inaugural address to King's College of Women of October 1914 focused on "The Privilege of Living in War-Time." Soon, like Evelyn Underhill, she served on the executive committee of the Fight for Right Movement. This organization had been founded by Sir Francis Younghusband, the explorer of Manchuria and Tibet, and its twenty-one vice presidents were a corona of personalities of high society (e.g., the Duchess of Bedford), famous academics, and writers like Robert Bridges, Edmund Gosse, Thomas Hardy, and Henry Newbolt. In her 1916 speech, "The Training of the Combatant," Spurgeon employed full-blown propaganda rhetoric in the service of general moral armament and mobilization of all energies at home in order to forestall an "inconclusive peace" before the final victory. Quite typically she presented German intellectualism as subaltern and the fight against it as the fight for the future of civilization itself. In contrast she showed much more moderation in "Poetry in the Light of War," a speech presented to the English Association in January 1917. Early in 1918 she was able to give a lecture, "The Charm of Walpole's Letters," to the Royal Society of Literature.

At the end of the war educational reforms were energetically pursued. Even during the most critical period an education act had been passed, and before the fighting ended on all fronts, a universities mission was sent to the United States. On the instigation of the English Association, which, founded in 1906 by two schoolmasters, had acquired great influence, notably in cooperation with powerful circles, the board of education established a departmental committee to report on the teaching of English at all levels of the education system. Parallel reports were initiated for the classics, modern languages, natural science, and adult education. Commonly called after its chairman, the Newbolt report signaled the change of paradigm and expansion of the subject most emphatically. English, in particular English literature, was to become the keystone of national education, while philology was often defamed as German.

Spurgeon was a member both of the universities mission and of the Newbolt committee. In the first case this was only thanks to U.S. protests against the absence of women.[21] Evidently the greater say won in the total war would not simply last. Spurgeon's experience in the United States turned out to be of far-reaching consequences for her. She was almost overwhelmed by the country's "eager and thrilling vitality" and was particularly fascinated by the better opportunities for women.[22] She gained various new friends, especially among her own sex and the rich New York elite. The relationship to Virginia Gildersleeve, English scholar and dean of Barnard, soon became so close that they lived together much of the time, alternating between the Old World and the New. Such affection had not been promised by their first meeting. Spurgeon struck Gildersleeve as of medium height, stout, and with extraordinary bright brown eyes mustering her coldly. At the start Gildersleeve preferred Rose Sidgwick, the other woman on the universities mission, whom she found "less impetuous, more prudent and the better speaker of the two."[23] Through Gildersleeve and her manifold other contacts, Spurgeon was invited to lecture at a number of universities and to teach as a visiting professor at Columbia. In all likelihood she was the first Englishwoman accorded such a high honor by a renowned U.S. university.[24] The final foreword to her *Five Hundred Years of Chaucer Criticism and Allusion* was written in New York. After concluding this great project, Spurgeon scarcely devoted herself to medieval subjects again. One reason may also have been the demands of her chair, as the other professorship at Bedford covered both English language and medieval literature.

It was in the United States that Spurgeon received the impetus to pursue the two other commitments for which she is still remembered best. The first impulse was fortuitous, or perhaps not quite so fortuitous if one considers the appropriateness of the circumstances: an American woman, a friend of her new friends, drew her attention to the fact that Keats's Shakespeare edition slumbered in a private library at Princeton.[25] Spurgeon was enthralled and made a thorough analysis of it, which resulted in her first substantial Shakespeare publication (*Keats's Shakespeare: A Descriptive Study*, 1928).

Spurgeon was close to sixty when she began work in her second major field. Generous support from American friends allowed her to take repeated leaves of absence from Bedford College and finally to retire from active duties in 1929. She enjoyed being able to devote herself completely to research and was most grateful that Lucretia Perry Osborn—the wife of the famous paleontologist and director of the American Museum of Natural History, Henry Fairfield Osborn—put so much trust in her and organized financial aid at a time when she had as yet done very little work on Shakespeare.[26] Under such happy conditions she was able to assess the state of research quickly and to focus on an area that permitted an innovative approach and yielded novel insights: Shakespeare's imagery. Thanks to assistance and secretarial help, she managed to finish this extensive project in comparatively short time. After several lectures and articles she published her definitive book *Shakespeare's Imagery and What It Tells Us* in 1935.

The climactic conclusion of her acknowledgments in that book reads as follows: "What I owe to my friend Dean Virginia Gildersleeve, of Barnard College, New York, from the very inception of this book to the final reading of the proof sheets, it is not possible, within these formal limits adequately either to describe or to acknowledge." Whether the last clause was intended as ambiguous remains their secret.

Already during Spurgeon's first visit to the United States, in autumn 1918, the second great commitment of her later years had begun. She had been discussing the recent war with Sidgwick and Gildersleeve when she had a momentous idea: "We should have . . . an international federation of university women, so that we at least shall have done all we can to prevent another such catastrophe." Since her friends readily agreed, according to Gildersleeve, the International Federation of University Women (IFUW) was born.[27] The actual founding meeting took place in 1919, and in 1920 Spurgeon's college, Bedford, hosted the first conference.[28] She was elected first president and in 1922 was reelected for another period (contemporaneously serving as president of the British Federation of University Women). In this function she visited various universities in the southern states and gave preference to her U.S. duties over the Newbolt committee, most of whose meetings and final drafting of its report she missed. Thanks to existing official and unofficial networks and energetic campaigning, the IFUW grew rapidly. According to Gildersleeve, Spurgeon possessed a "dynamic ability not only to inspire people with a vision but to make them work for its fulfillment."[29] In 1925 the IFUW already boasted 28,114 members (today they number about 180,000).

In accordance with its pacifistic roots, the IFUW soon established contacts with the League of Nations. International fellowships were initiated, of which one for the humanities was to carry Spurgeon's name.[30] The conference concluding her presidency was called "The Place of University Women in the World's Work," and Spurgeon and the Viscountess Rhondda gave a report titled "Careers for Educated Women in the Higher Branches of Industry, Commerce, and Finance." In her endeavor to widen the scope of opportunities for her students, Spurgeon already realized the potential of advertising. Her insight that the education of fathers was fundamental deserves mention as well.[31] During World War II the IFUW fulfilled vital tasks. After its Polish president and Belgian second vice president were cut off from communication and the third vice president in Switzerland was absorbed by relief work, the running of the IFUW again rested squarely on the shoulders of its founders.[32] All in all, Spurgeon richly repaid the female solidarity that had been of great importance for her own academic establishment and in various other contexts afterward.

Spurgeon died in the United States in 1942.[33] She had attained great academic eminence. Not only her books but even several of her lectures have repeatedly been reprinted and thus become classics.

Notes

1. Spurgeon, "Mein Arbeitsweg," 88–92. I also want to thank my former assistant, Elizabeth Shipley, for her resourceful and indefatigable bibliographical help.

2. Spurgeon, "Mein Arbeitsweg," 88 (my translation).

3. Dyhouse, *No Distinction of Sex?* 157–58.

4. Spurgeon, "Mein Arbeitsweg," 88 (my translation).

5. Between 1904 and 1907 a considerable number of women used this not particularly dignified route (nearly seven hundred, according to a recent estimate, which, however, seems rather high). They became locally known as "the steamboat ladies," as most of them arrived in Dublin by ferry only the night before graduation (Dyhouse, *No Distinction,* 158 and 184).

6. Sutherland, "Plainest Principle of Justice," 46.

7. Harte, *University of London,* 180.

8. Harte, *University of London,* 180.

9. Regarding English studies on the Continent, see Haas, "European Survey," 359.

10. Legouis's theses about the chronology of the two prologues of the *Legend of Good Women* of 1900 had sparked a lively discussion in Chaucer research on both sides of the Atlantic, in England, and on the Continent.

11. Dyhouse, *No Distinction,* 160–61.

12. Spurgeon, "Mein Arbeitsweg," 90. Perhaps some female lobbying also helped (Dyhouse, *No Distinction,* 140–42).

13. *American National Biography* (1999) 21·519–22.

14. It was also only in 1908 that the prestigious École nationale supérieure admitted women to its entrance examinations.

15. Dyhouse, *No Distinction,* 18–21.

16. Baldick, *Social Mission of English Criticism,* 76–80.

17. Dyhouse, *No Distinction,* 169.

18. Regarding the delay, cf. Hammond, *Chaucer: A Bibliographical Manual,* 541.

19. Spurgeon, *Five Hundred Years,* vi.

20. Spurgeon, *Five Hundred Years,* vi–ix.

21. Batho, *Lamp of Friendship,* 3.

22. Spurgeon, "Refashioning of English Education," 67.

23. Batho, *Lamp of Friendship,* 3.

24. Spurgeon, "Mein Arbeitsweg," 91.

25. Gildersleeve's dissertation had been titled *Government Regulation of Elizabethan Drama*.
26. Spurgeon, *Shakespeare's Imagery*, vii.
27. Batho, *Lamp of Friendship*, 3.
28. Among the U.S. delegates to the founding meeting was the previously mentioned M. Carey Thomas, then sixty-two years of age.
29. Batho, *Lamp of Friendship*, 3.
30. Spurgeon, "Mein Arbeitsweg," 91.
31. Spurgeon, "Careers for Educated Women in the Higher Branches of Industry, Commerce, and Finance," 9.
32. Batho, *Lamp of Friendship*, 18–19.
33. Batho, *Lamp of Friendship*, 19.

Select Bibliography of Works by Caroline Spurgeon

Spurgeon's papers, which upon her death were presented to the Bedford College Archives, are now housed at Royal Holloway, University of London. They comprise thirty-two boxes and cover the years 1896–1928. See http://jsp.genesis.ac.uk/archive.jsp?typeofsearch=q&term=notimpl&highlight=1&pk=49.

Richard Brathwait's Comments, in 1665, upon Chaucer's Tales of the Miller and the Wife of Bath. Chaucer Society Publications, 2d ser., 33. London: K. Paul, Trench, & Trübner, 1901.

Chaucer devant la critique en Angleterre et en France depuis son temps jusqu'à nos jours. Paris: Hachette, 1911.

"William Law and the Mystics." In *The Cambridge History of English Literature*, edited by Adolphus Ward and A. R. Waller, vol. 9. Cambridge: Cambridge University Press, 1912.

Mysticism in English Literature. Cambridge: Cambridge University Press, 1913.

The Privilege of Living in War-Time: An Inaugural Address to King's College for Women. London: University of London Press, 1914.

The Training of the Combatant: An Address Delivered for the Fight for Right Movement. London: Dent, 1916.

Poetry in the Light of War. London: English Association, 1917. Reprinted in *Perspectives of Poetry: The English Association Pamphlets,* edited by the English Association (London: Dawsons, 1968).

"The Refashioning of English Education: A Lesson of the Great War." *Atlantic Monthly* (January 1922): 55–67.

"Careers for Educated Women in the Higher Branches of Industry, Commerce, and Finance." In *The Place of University Women in the World's Work*, edited by the International Federation of University Women, Occasional Paper 4. London: John Roberts Press for IFUW, 1925.

Five Hundred Years of Chaucer Criticism and Allusion. 3 vols. Cambridge: Cambridge University Press, 1925.

Keats's Shakespeare: A Descriptive Study. London: Oxford University Press, 1928.

"Mein Arbeitsweg." In *Führende Frauen Europas: Elga Kerns Standardwerk von 1928/1930,* new and revised edition by Bettina Conrad and Ulrike Leuschner. Munich: Ernst Reinhardt, 1999.

Leading Motives in the Imagery of Shakespeare's Tragedies. London: Oxford University Press, 1930.

Shakespeare's Iterative Imagery. London: Milford, 1931.

Shakespeare's Imagery, and What It Tells Us. Cambridge: Cambridge University Press, 1935.

Works Cited

Baldick, Chris. *The Social Mission of English Criticism: 1848–1932.* Oxford: Oxford University Press, 1987.

Batho, Edith C. *A Lamp of Friendship: A Short History of the International Federation of University Women.* N.p.: International Federation of University Women, 1968.

Dyhouse, Carol. *No Distinction of Sex? Women in British Universities, 1870–1939.* London: University College London Press, 1995.

Eagleton, Terry. *Literary Theory.* Oxford: Blackwell, 1983.

Haas, Renate. "European Survey: Parameters and Patterns of Development." In *European English Studies: Towards the History of a Discipline,* edited by Balz Engler and Renate Haas. Leicester: English Association, 2000.

Hammond, Eleanor Prescott. *Chaucer: A Bibliographical Manual.* New York: Macmillan, 1908.

Harte, Negley. *The University of London, 1836–1986: An Illustrated History.* London: Athlone Press, 1986.

International Federation of University Women. "IFUW 1918–2000" [online]. Available from www.ifuw.org/timeline/ifuw80-timeline.htm (7 August 2002).

Matthews, David. *The Making of Middle English: 1765–1910.* Minneapolis: University of Minnesota Press, 1999.

Stanzel, Franz Karl, and Martin Löschnigg, eds. *Intimate Enemies: English and German Literary Reactions to the Great War, 1914–1918.* Heidelberg: Winter, 1993.

Sutherland, Gillian. "The Plainest Principle of Justice: The University of London and the Higher Education of Women." In *The University of London and the World of Learning: 1836–1986,* edited by F. M. L. Thompson. London: Hambledon Press, 1990.

Tuke, Margaret J. *A History of Bedford College for Women: 1849–1937.* London: Oxford University Press, 1939.

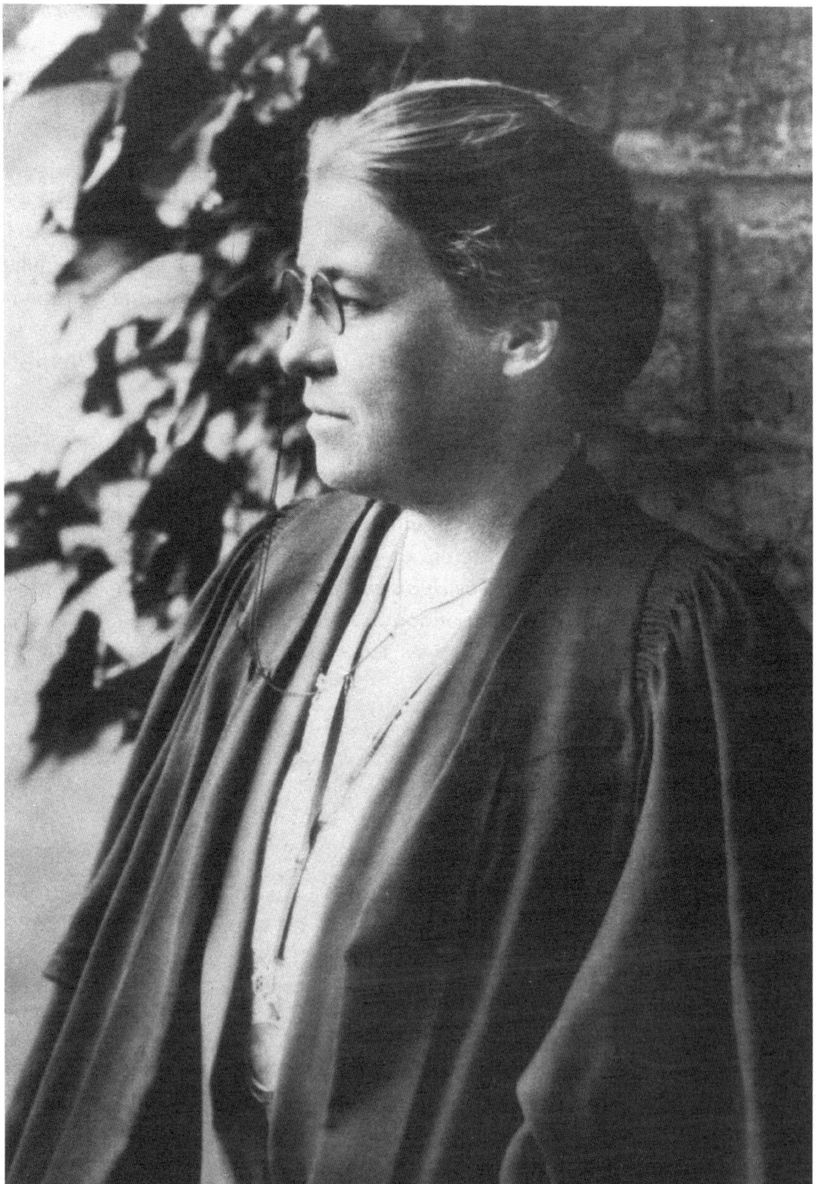

CHAPTER 9

"Hark the Herald Angels Sing"
Here's to Georgiana Goddard King (1871–1939)

JANICE MANN

IN ALL LIKELIHOOD unless you have studied at Bryn Mawr College or unless your field of expertise is the art and architecture of the medieval Iberian Peninsula, you have probably never heard of Georgiana Goddard King (1871–1939). Although she founded the Department of Art History at Bryn Mawr College in 1914, wrote nine books and thirty-six articles, seven of which appeared in the prestigious *Art Bulletin,* and trained at least twelve women who followed her into art history, King and her work have all but vanished from current scholarly memory.

I first heard about Georgiana Goddard King in a lecture on Spanish Romanesque architecture when I was a graduate student in the 1980s. She was mentioned in passing along with her more prominent male contemporaries, such as Kingsley Porter, who were the first Americans to overlook the more celebrated art of modern Paris, Renaissance Italy, or the ancient Mediterranean in favor of the unexplored territory of medieval Spain. My professor created a romantic picture of King as a female Indiana Jones, dressed in culottes, wearing a pith helmet, and brandishing an umbrella. I learned she had traveled alone through early-twentieth-century rural Spain, facing every challenge undaunted. However, my heroic image of King deflated when my professor added, albeit rather apologetically, that her work had not really been very good. Unlike my former professor, however, I have developed a deep appreciation for King's scholarship, not so much for her learned views on medieval Spanish monuments, but because it reveals so much about the study of medieval architecture in the early twentieth century and the position of female scholars in the field.

Georgiana Goddard King spearheaded American interest in the art and architecture of medieval Christian Spain. She was the first of a generation of scholars employed at prestigious East Coast universities who left the better traveled art historical roads to strike off into the virtually uncharted territory of Spanish medieval art. In the first decades of the twentieth century, when art history was just beginning to become a systemized discipline, King, followed quickly by Kingsley Porter (1883–1933) of Yale and Harvard Universities, his colleague at Harvard, Chandler Post (1881–1959), and Walter Cook (1888–1962) of New York University's newly inaugurated fine arts department, left her comfortable office and sought out obscure sites in remote areas of rural Spain. No less an art historian than Erwin Panofsky typifies this moment of American art history as animated by "the spirit of discovery and experimentation" and "a spirit of youthful adventurousness."[1] The art of medieval Spain was a field barely known to serious scholars in Europe, much less America, and it was frequently maligned as unoriginal by the authors of guide books. It provided, nevertheless, a wide-open field of study in which King and the other pioneers of art history in America could discover unpublished works of art and formulate the principles of their new discipline with little or no competition.

King was born into an affluent family in Columbia, West Virginia, in 1871. Perhaps because her mother was a woman with intellectual tastes, King was given a serious education.[2] Education for girls and young women was a new and exciting venture in King's day. First, she attended Leache-Wood Seminary for girls, founded in 1872, and upon graduation, she moved on to the even more recently established Bryn Mawr College to study classics. Founded in 1885, Bryn Mawr offered young women an unprecedented combination of a university with serious academic study and the sheltered atmosphere of a women's college. M. Carey Thomas, initially as dean (1885–94) and then as president (1894–1922), was the first feminist to gain authority over an institution of higher learning.[3] She insisted that the college provide a rigorous intellectual environment for its young women by adopting the standards for curriculum and scholarship from the Johns Hopkins University in Baltimore, which, in turn, followed the model of German research universities. Outspoken and charismatic, Thomas consciously endeavored to create an intellectual community at Bryn Mawr where women's influence and high academic standards prevailed. Georgiana Goddard King was very much a part of this formative period of Bryn Mawr's history, first as a student and then as a professor.

King graduated with a B.A. in 1896, winning the George W. Child Essayist Award, but she stayed on to pursue graduate work in political science, German philosophy, and English. No art history was taught at Bryn Mawr when King was a student so it was probably not until she traveled abroad that she became seriously interested in the profession. In 1898 she left Bryn Mawr for a semester of study at the Collège de France in Paris. That summer she made an intense study of Renaissance painting in the libraries and galleries of Italy.[4] Her friendship with Bernard Berenson, the eminent expatriate American connoisseur, and his wife, Mary, fostered her interest in painting and architecture.

If it was European travel and Bernard Berenson that familiarized King with historical art, it was Gertrude and Leo Stein, the foremost American patrons of avant-garde European art, who introduced her to modern painting.[5] According to King, mutual friends introduced her to Gertrude Stein in New York, although Stein claimed in *The Autobiography of Alice B. Toklas* that they had met in Baltimore. Later in life King described how she "enjoyed sitting in the [Stein's Paris] studio staring at a picture and presently moving around to the other side of the table and staring some more." It was Stein, too, who introduced King to Picasso's dealer Richard Kahnweiler. King made a habit of visiting him when she was in Paris to look at his new pictures.[6]

After a seven-year hiatus in New York teaching at a private girl's school and publishing the occasional work of fiction, Georgiana Goddard King returned to Bryn Mawr College in 1906. She was first employed as a reader in English at the salary of seven hundred dollars a year, but she was soon to devote her energies to the history of art. King, with her tongue in her cheek, explained the shift in her teaching, claiming, "In 1910, four years after returning to Bryn Mawr, I grew weary of explaining sentence structure to young women and asked Miss Thomas if I might give elective lectures in art."[7] The 1909 Bryn Mawr College calendar names King as a reader in English, but it also lists her as teaching a course on Italian Renaissance painting from the mid-thirteenth to the mid-fourteenth century.[8] In 1912 an art history major was begun at the college thanks to the popularity of King's courses, and by 1914 an independent Department of Art History was founded with her as its chair.[9] Against the advice of her male peers at Harvard and Princeton, King insisted that Asian art be included in the curriculum.[10] Her own courses covered material ranging from "the cave paintings of Altamira to Picasso, from the Lady of Elche to Brancusi, from the most desolate little Spanish church to the Cathedral of Chartres, but also from Plato to Schopenhauer, from Chaucer to Browning, from Saint Jerome to Saint Bernadette of Lourdes."[11]

Unfortunately, none of King's personal accounts reveals directly what motivated her preoccupation with the sculpture and architecture of medieval Spain, which in her day had not yet, to use her own words, "become a part of the general scheme of things as Sienna."[12] On the most prosaic level the combination of her tenuous finances and her friendship with Archer Huntington, the millionaire founder of the Hispanic Society of America, did much to further her interest in medieval Iberia. King literally "mortgaged her ink-pot" to the Hispanic Society, which financed several of her trips.[13] She reimbursed the society, at the rate of a penny a word, through writing works on Spanish topics, such as her *Brief Account of the Military Orders in Spain,* published by the society as part of its Hispanic Notes and Monographs in 1921.[14]

King, however, left clues between the lines of her scholarship that hint at the underlying reasons for her attraction to the art of medieval Spain. For example, in her preface to *Heart of Spain,* finished in 1926 but published posthumously in 1941, she asserts her preference for the "significant" over the "celebrated" and her love for "the rare and strange."[15] In her day both Spain and its monuments were "less familiar to the gentle reader than the immortal ambiance of the Lombard plain and the hill-towns of Tuscany."[16] But King was drawn rather than daunted by the prospect of doing the spadework in the field, and her love of opening up new territory persisted throughout her career. Her only doctoral student, Delphine Fitz Darby, remarked that "in her sixties, [King was] impaired by a stroke yet hoping for one last trip—this time to Portugal, then a nation less attractive to travelers than was neighboring Spain. But G. G. loved to pioneer."[17]

Although King was at the forefront of Spanish medieval architectural studies in the United States, her first venture into the field followed a trail blazed by another. In 1914 she published an annotated edition of the earliest book in English on Spanish medieval architecture, George E. Street's *Some Account of Gothic Architecture in Spain*, originally issued in 1865. Archer Huntington, one of the most ardent promoters of Spanish culture at the time in the United States, suggested this project to King.[18] Although not made clear by its title, *Some Account of Gothic Architecture in Spain* includes accounts of both Romanesque and Gothic architecture. Street, a British architect, was better known for his Gothic revival buildings than for his writing. He intended his book to be a vade mecum for the traveler interested in Spanish medieval architecture, which in his day had not yet been studied in a comprehensive and systematic manner by either Spaniard or foreigner.

King's goal was to update Street and to "widen his range a little." She saw her business as editor as "helping out" the author "with as little ostentation as may be."[19] She fulfilled her task by adding lengthy annotations at the end of each of Street's chapters. These summarize the current scholarship, augment Street's descriptions, mention buildings not included in the original text, or update information on transportation and lodgings. Sometimes she describes the difference in the environment between her own visit and Street's. She corrects minor details only, for she felt that disagreement in fundamentals would be presumptuous.

If modest in its outcome by today's standards, King's first project was an ambitious undertaking in terms of research. She was no armchair art historian. Her annotations were the result of three trips to Spain, following Street's "tracks with an exact piety all the way."[20] From the beginning of her career, she lived up to her dictum that "[t]he only way to know anything is to go and look. . . . [N]othing else will serve. The opinion of one's master, the description of one's companion, the best of photographs, will not yield the secrets that personal study on the spot can solve."[21]

The process of annotating Street—the repeated reading of his text and her three research trips—provided a kind of apprenticeship for King in which she taught herself the art historical method. Through Street's work King came to understand the desire generated by the distant monument, the importance of firsthand knowledge of "the stones," the tenacity required of the traveling scholar, and the appeal of combining personal commentary with archaeological observation. Bernard Berenson supplemented what she had learned from Street.[22] From Berenson she learned the importance of developing a connoisseur's eye, trained to see and compare the essence of works in order to distinguish the qualitative difference between master and apprentice or between a refined tradition and the awkward or the provincial.[23]

With the lessons she had learned from Street and Berenson, King mixed what she had garnered from her more formalized philosophical and literary training to create her own brand of art history. She combined an archaeologist's concern for fabric and dates with an art historian's interest in iconography and style. To this she added an aesthete's attention to beauty and poetry and an anthropologist's awareness of cultural customs and legend. Travelogue is interspersed among these other concerns. Often her works incorporate lengthy personal observations. All are written in an emotive poetic prose that holds more in common with romantic nineteenth-century travel writing than it does with most twentieth-century art history.

King moved quickly away from the scholarly timidity of annotation to the publication of original material. Her most ambitious work, *The Way of Saint James,* is also the most revealing in terms of her attitudes toward Spain, art history, and the Middle Ages.[24] She began work on *The Way* in 1911, and by 1914 she was entirely devoted to it.[25] Huntington encouraged King's work by having the Hispanic Society fund two of her research trips and by publishing the work in 1920.[26]

In *The Way of Saint James,* King examines the medieval monuments lining the road that pilgrims followed from Toulouse in southern France to Saint James's shrine at Santiago de Compostela in northwestern Spain.[27] The book gives an account of King's trip with a fictitious female companion named Jehane along the road from Toulouse, across the Somport Pass, and through northern Spain to Santiago. In this work the results of King's rigorous art historical investigations are woven together with the more personal account of her trip. Her journey provides more than just a framing device for the history and analysis of the architecture and sculpture encountered along the route. King's observations of her own times serve to link the present to the past, revitalizing all that lay inanimate there.[28] Throughout the book she weaves together the present and the past, the legendary and the historical, and her personal experiences with a more objective scholarly account.

King was the first art historian to examine the idea that the pilgrimage to Santiago stimulated artistic creation and cultural exchange. However, it was not until her male colleagues Kingsley Porter, Émile Mâle, and Paul Deschamps adopted and deployed this conceptual framework in their heated quarrel over the national origins of Romanesque sculpture that it became a standard art historical paradigm.[29] The ultimate source of inspiration for this approach to medieval creativity was French philologist Joseph Bédier, who claimed that the free movement of jongleurs and pilgrims along the pilgrimage routes generated and disseminated the chansons de geste.[30] Unlike Bédier, who could formulate his ideas from written texts in any locale, King had to move physically along the route followed by the pilgrims in order to gather the material for *The Way*. This gave rise to a different kind of understanding of the Middle Ages and their relationship to the present. For King the road traveled both across geography and back through time.[31] It became both the means to and the repository of history.

King's fictitious travel companion, Jehane, might be a veiled reference to King's real-life travel companion, photographer, collaborator, and intimate friend E. (Edith) H. Lowber. It is not clear how Edith and Georgiana met, although they seem to have been part of the same circle at Bryn Mawr. In 1919 the Hispanic Society paid Lowber a thousand dollars to accompany King to Spain in order to take photographs for *The Way*.[32] King dedicated her 1923 *Sardinian Painting* to Lowber, suggesting that their relationship went beyond merely the professional. In addition to *The Way*, the two women collaborated on several articles and on *Heart of Spain*, published after their deaths.

King wrote *The Way of Saint James* at a time before art history was subject to a set of regulatory regimes that prescribed a problem-solving teleology; hence, it is more descriptive than analytical. Occasionally King makes deductions about dates and sources of style or motifs, but her main task is to reveal unknown and obscure buildings and to make them familiar to the reader through her words. For early-twenty-first century scholars King's prolix descriptions of monuments might seem at best tedious and at worst pointless. Her prose does not yield "the facts" or conclusions in the efficient, orderly way we have come to expect. It demands a reader with both leisure and an active visual imagination not dulled by the postmodern proliferation of visual images. *The Way of Saint James* is not lavishly illustrated. As often as not, the photographs represent a picturesque scene such as a narrow unpaved street in a mountain village or a beggar at Santiago rather than a monument.[33] King placed more faith in the mimetic preciseness of words than she did in photographs. She claimed that "Spain is a long way off, and pictures are not always explicit."[34] She was willing to trust the photograph to establish context but not to depict the buildings she wrote about.

King's text never focuses on an art historical monument in isolation. The process of getting to the site; the setting, not simply the geography of the site, but the surrounding people, aromas, and sounds; and the present social and historical contexts of the buildings are all parts of the discussion. For instance, in her treatment of the Romanesque church of Santa María in Santa Cruz de la Serós, King describes "the purple starlight" of the early morning, the flowers by the riverside, loggers at their work, and the sound of water rushing through an irrigation system and into the fields. Against this backdrop of the present King describes the medieval convent church in prolonged detail, concluding only that its tympanum, copied from that of Jaca, is "Benedictine, twelfth century, regional."[35] Next she gives an account of the foundation of the convent and its subsequent history. Then she returns to the present, describing the village, its few art treasures, and her departure. By situating her comments about the medieval church and its history in the anecdotal immediacy of the present, King erases the distance between the Middle Ages and her own day. Santa María and the other medieval churches she treats live in the present rather than in the cool detachment of the past.

For King nowhere are the Middle Ages more alive in the present than at Santiago de Compostela. It is "the bourne, the end of heart's desire . . . like places you have come to in a dream and remember that you have known them long ago."[36] She substitutes the medieval for the modern by focusing on its legacy in the present, the ringing bells, candlelit churches, religious rituals, relics, legends, and the vestments of the clergy. She tends to ignore the middle class and focuses instead on the upper and the lower reaches of society, the archbishop surrounded by cardinals or royalty accompanied by soldiers and the canons in the order of Santiago, or peasants and beggars "tricked out in calico capes sewn over with scallop shells, and staffs on which the gourd is reduced to a symbolic knob."[37] Cars, trains, cameras, and other clear signifiers of modernity, while mentioned elsewhere in her account, all but disappear from her discussion of Santiago. King intersperses her text with the observations made by pilgrims from other eras, which harmonize with her own, creating an intertextuality that reinforces the notion of the timelessness of Santiago and the universality of pilgrimage experience.[38]

King's understanding of the pilgrimage to Santiago surpassed the tangible. She wrote that it predated Christianity and was in fact as old as the human race.[39] This parallels her understanding of Spain itself as timeless.[40] The road's magnetic draw is rooted in the very forces of nature that summoned the pilgrim: "Along that way the winds impel, the waters guide, earth draws the feet. The very sky allures and insists."[41] The pilgrimage cannot really be rationally comprehended but only accounted for by mystics, who "can tell how journeys to such shrines are made: *The way is opened before you, and closed behind you.* Simple, that: believe it or not, it happens. So with Compostella [*sic*] . . . it draws you."[42] Even King was probably not enough of a romantic to have believed her own words literally. Yet, she intended their poetry to mobilize the imagination rather than the intellect of the reader and thereby to communicate a kind of knowledge not wholly dependent on fact.

King does not expunge her deeply felt religious sentiments from her text. For her, as for Ruskin, the aesthetic and the spiritual were joined. In the foreword to *The Way of Saint James,* she pays gratitude first to Saint James himself and last to "the glory of religion and of Spain."[43] Throughout the book she refers to prayer, saints, and the liturgy without irony or cynicism. Both religious and romantic by nature and not yet bound by a scientifically objective art history that devalued the subjective response, King believed that the way art, architecture, or ritual expressed the sacred and inspired the sublime was of the utmost importance. She understood that the authority of medieval architecture lay in its power to evoke religious exaltation across the centuries. This was for King as significant a part of art historical knowledge as construction campaigns, iconographic identification, or the historical context of a monument.

King found cause for exaltation in the prosaic as well as in the profound. She frequently stops the flow of her scholarly account to relate a personal encounter with "the picturesque." For example, she diverges from a description of Santiago de Compostela to say how she saw a peasant, in pilgrim's dress, "with an ecstatic face, who looked a little like S. Francis. His head was the same shape, and his brown frock helped the illusion. For a long time I watched him praying, and when he got up and went out I ran after and asked leave to photograph, readily yielded: then he asked an alms. Why not? Give and take is fair."[44] She includes a photograph of the pilgrim as if to add weight to her testimony or in hopes of allowing the reader an actual glimpse of local color, albeit two-dimensional. Her evocative prose imbues these vignettes of Spanish daily life with a sense of dignity. King's representations of Spanish culture are nevertheless generated by her understanding of Spain as "still unspoiled and romantic."[45] Yet, they are more than just a romanticized anthropology; they serve to foreground the medieval architecture King discusses in the present, making it and its history relevant to the early twentieth century and creating a putative continuity between the past and the present.

King's scholarship is marked by the amalgam of the personal with the scholarly and the past with the present. By this means she makes evident that her narrative is a construct. Her very personal style confused at least one reader of *The Way of Saint James*. An anonymous reviewer in the *Times Literary Supplement* chided King for being unable to "make up her mind whether to write a series of rather romantic travel sketches or a serious work of research, and she confused the two."[46] Rather than stemming from indecision or conflict, King's dialogistic method simply exposes the private experiences in which her scholarly observations were formulated. For an author writing before postmodern critical theory, King shows a remarkable awareness of the fictional contingencies of scholarship and the importance of personal positioning. In the foreword of *The Way* she unreservedly acknowledges that she has made "one straight story out of three years' wanderings, and places visited and revisited."[47] Much of her commentary is openly grounded in the subjective. Frequently King's personality, especially in terms of her gender, breaks through the formality of her scholarly text. It should come as no surprise, considering that she lived in a female scholarly community and that her closest emotional ties were with women, that King's account pays close attention to women. Her text expresses keen interest in Spanish women in both the present and the past. Medieval Spanish queens, such as Doña Mayor of Navarre, Queen Sancha of Leon, Doña Elvira, her daughter, and Queen Urraca, and their accomplishments find a revered a place in King's account.

King's eye is likewise often engaged by contemporary Spanish women, and she often notes them and their concerns and habits. For instance,

> Every little town has these little churches, that stay open after dark for a few veiled, whispering women. They have a special feeling, like the scent of dried leaves, like the taste of night air, like the hushed Friday evening of the return from Calvary in Ribalta's painting. To Spanish women they are very comfortable. The subdued glow of light, the warm smell, the rustling human figures, offer something of the attraction of the hearth, without the *ennui* of home. The great point is that in church one is never bored; that prayers lull, like the nursery rocking-chair. . . . It will be hard to break the women of the habit, at winter nightfall, while men are in the cafés, of going to church.[48]

Frequently, without reserve, King describes her experience as a woman researcher in the field. She makes clear how gender stereotypes can complicate relationships with men and threaten to impede research in an account of a trip on horseback with a young male guide to remote sites around Villafranca: "Three days out, he mentioned that his friends all said a woman who would go off that way was not worth . . . I never quite made out the phrase, though I have heard it, first and last, three times or four, but spoken always rapidly, and under the breath. The idea is, that she could not be worth much. In fine, he was fatally compromised by coming. Then I turned in the saddle and laughed. 'Boy,' said I, 'I am forty-two, old enough to be your mother. I can't compromise you, nor you me.'"[49]

In an account of her stay in Pamplona she points out to the reader how socially prescribed gender roles make life unpleasant for the female traveler, especially on long winter evenings: "For a woman alone, they are hard. She has been out seeing things while the daylight lasted and is honestly tired. . . . She cannot walk up and down the pavement, in the light of shop windows, as men are doing. She goes back to her room at the hotel. There she cannot go to bed to keep warm, for dinner is still three hours away; she makes her tea, then fills a rubber hot-water-bottle, and wrapping it and herself in a rug lies down under a faint electric bulb to read and shiver and not dare to doze."[50]

Although she makes plain the disadvantages for women in a world where social customs restrict their behavior, King does not see herself as a victim of such circumstances. To the contrary, she tends to present herself as more intrepid than, and morally superior to, men. For instance, she ridicules the English travel writer Richard Ford for his slack pace of travel and his snobbery while flattering herself: "It would be absurd to assert that a woman alone, unused to the saddle, should be a stouter traveller than the great Englishman, but I may perhaps say modestly that with light saddle-bags I have often outrun his estimate by virtue of much resolution and urgent haste, and I have never yet been compelled to market for myself, or in his phrase, *attend to the provend,* simply because I was content to share what those about me ate."[51]

The expression of her entitlement to the same activities and locales as men was no mere literary conceit for King. A former student reported that King frequently told her all-female classes, "I have done everything known to man."[52] She clearly believed that she was entitled to occupy the public sphere of erudition so often associated with the masculine and to extend her research into any uncharted area of the discipline. The extent to which some of her students were made uncomfortable by King's bold character and challenge to women's traditional social roles lurks beneath the humorous mockery of the following poem, which circulated among the students at Bryn Mawr:

Hark the herald angels sing,
Here's to Georgiana Goddard King.
Who is this who knows each thing

> Yet she wears no wedding ring?
> Peace on earth and mercy mild
> Has she ever had a child?[53]

Nevertheless, *The Way of Saint James,* written at a time when social roles for women in the United States were shifting because of improvements in women's education and the success of the suffrage movement, provided a sense of legitimacy for adventurous female readers, for it presents an unglamorized picture of a woman successfully pursuing her desire to perform a challenging task and overcoming the difficulties involved.

King's work provided a sense of legitimacy for female scholars, and her classes proved an inspiration to at least twelve of her students who followed her into the field of art history. Among the most well established of her students were Marion Lawrence, an expert in early Christian sarcophagi, who taught in the Department of Art History at Barnard College for thirty-seven years; Marianna Jenkins, who taught at Duke; Leila Barber, who taught at Vassar; and Katharine Neilson, who held many jobs in the profession including teaching posts at Wheaton and Hartford Colleges and museum work at the Wadsworth Atheneum and the Yale University Art Gallery. Preeminent among King's students was longtime curator of drawings and director of Harvard's Fogg Art Museum, Agnes Mongan.[54]

According to Delphine Fitz Darby, King used the Socratic method in her classes, and thus by "subtle query" she was able "to draw the truth out of the pupil, while less gifted teachers merely drive it into him."[55] She seldom lectured from notes. Instead, she actively engaged her students with her questioning while holding them spellbound with her ability to re-create the spirit of a time past and its art. She had the ability to make a student feel the joy of having discovered a painting by herself.[56] She demanded hard work and was intolerant of smugness or stupidity, yet she was compassionate and kind. So forceful was King's presence in the lecture hall that undergraduates did not refer to themselves as studying art history but as "taking G. G.," as they affectionately referred to King.[57]

Although entranced by the Middle Ages of the Iberian Peninsula, King also embraced modernity. She wrote some of the earliest reviews of Stein's *Three Lives,* published in 1909.[58] After learning about modern art firsthand from Stein in Paris, King taught cubism to her students at Bryn Mawr the year before the Armory Show introduced Americans to European avant-garde art in 1913.[59] When she had difficulty finding reproductions of modern art for her students, she wrote directly to Alfred Stieglitz and asked him if she could borrow the photographs of modern paintings he had reproduced in *Camera Work.*[60] Unlike her contemporary, Kingsley Porter of Harvard's fine arts department, King expressed no regrets about the arrival in Spain of modern conveniences such as the railroad. She was delighted by the forward-looking Republican government in Spain.[61]

In the fall of 1935, at age sixty-four, King went on sabbatical to Portugal to research a book on Portuguese Romanesque. She fell ill while there and had to return home. Her poor health forced her into retirement, and she lived with her sister Margaret in Hollywood until she died in 1939. Bryn Mawr College satisfied King's request to be buried in the cloister of the college, where a small, discrete stone, inscribed with "GGK," is still present.

By the 1930s the personal grounding of much of King's scholarship caused it to lose credibility with the next generation of art historians, whose art historical methods were more regimented and scientific. Under the influence of the German émigré scholars, who began to come to America after the Nuremberg Decrees in 1933 forced Jewish academics from their posts in Germany and Austria, art history in the United States acquired more standardized methods and more restricted epistemologies that left no room for scholarship like King's. Art history today, however, with its increased emphasis on the personal, the interdisciplinary, and the fluidity of history, allows for a more generous appraisal of King's remarkable legacy.

NOTES

1. Panofsky, "Three Decades of Art History in the United States," 327, 329.
2. King's mother was so keenly devoted to cultural pursuits that she passed her domestic duties to her sister, Betty, who joined the family to take care of the children and run the household. For an excellent biography of King, see Saunders, "Georgiana Goddard King," 213.
3. Lefkowitz Horowitz, *Alma Mater,* 6.
4. "Miss King to Return to Live in Bryn Mawr," *College News,* 24 February 1937, 3.
5. Wethey, "American Pioneer in Hispanic Studies," 33.
6. King, "Gertrude Stein and French Painting," 2.
7. "Miss King to Return," 3.
8. Bryn Mawr College Calendar, 1909, p. 143.
9. Saunders, "Georgiana Goddard King," 216.
10. George Rowley taught the course ("Miss King to Return," 3).
11. Dorothea Shipley, unpublished tribute to King (delivered at the memorial service when King's ashes were placed in the Bryn Mawr cloister, October 1939), Bryn Mawr College Archives, Canaday Library, Bryn Mawr College.
12. Georgiana Goddard King, cited in "Miss King to Return," 3.
13. Georgiana Goddard King, letter to Archer Milton Huntington, 3 January 1923, Hispanic Society of America, New York.
14. Regarding the rate of reimbursement, see Georgiana Goddard King, letter to Archer Milton Huntington, 3 January 1923, Hispanic Society of America, New York.
15. King, author's preface to *Heart of Spain,* xi.
16. King, *Way of Saint James,* 1:vii.
17. Delphine Fitz Darby, letter to Suzanne Lindsay, 27 May 1989, Bryn Mawr College Archives, Canaday Library, Bryn Mawr College.
18. An unpublished letter (Hispanic Society of America, New York) from the librarian of the Hispanic Society of America to Georgiana Goddard King, 7 January 1912, mentions that Huntington suggested the idea to King.
19. King, introductory note to *Some Account of Gothic Architecture,* 1:xi, xiv.
20. King, essay in *Unpublished Notes and Reprinted Papers,* by George Edmund Street, 44.

21. Georgiana Goddard King, cited by Mitchell, "Mr. Cooper and Miss King," 6.

22. King depended heavily on Berenson in her teaching. According to Agnes Mongan, King's students virtually memorized Berenson ("Agnes Mongan Interviewed by Caroline Smith Rittenhouse, March 11, 1985," unpublished manuscript in Bryn Mawr College Archives, Canaday Library, Bryn Mawr College).

23. King, introductory note to *Some Account of Gothic Architecture*, by George Edmund Street, 1:xiii.

24. Harold Wethey said that "*The Way of Saint James* is the most complete expression of the author's mind and personality; it is a cloth woven of her numerous and varied interests, interests which she transformed into something peculiarly her own through the creative powers of her imagination" ("American Pioneer in Hispanic Studies," 33).

25. Georgiana Goddard King, letter to Isabel K. Macdermott, 21 November 1917, Hispanic Society of America, New York.

26. King reminds Huntington that he promised to fund her research on this project at seven hundred dollars a year for two consecutive summers in 1915 (Georgiana Goddard King, letter to Archer Milton Huntington, 1 March 1915, Hispanic Society of America, New York).

27. Five years earlier she had already begun to explore how the pilgrimage routes led French and Lombard masons and sculptors into Spain in search of employment. See King, "French Figure Sculpture on Some Early Spanish Churches," 250–67.

28. Rhys Carpenter described King's process of scholarship, saying that King "believed the scholar's function to be one of creative reinterpretation, a personal revitalization of all that had lapsed into the inanimateness of the past" ("Faculty Tribute to Miss King," 8).

29. See Mann, "Romantic Identity, Nationalism, and the Understanding of the Advent of Romanesque Art in Christian Spain," 156–65.

30. Bediér first presented his ideas in lectures in 1904 and 1905 and subsequently in the four volumes of *Les Légendes épiques*, published between 1908 and 1914. King quotes a long passage from volume 3 of this work that discusses how the *Chanson de Roland* indicates knowledge of the pilgrimage to Santiago de Compostela (*Way of Saint James*, 1:30–31).

31. In an article published during the years King was working of on *The Way of Saint James*, she wrote, "Where the Romans marched, ran the roads of the Middle Age, and there, today, the railways lay down their lines of steel. That, for instance, which runs from Salamanca to Astorga, keeps yet, for the traveler, a curious frontier feeling. To the right lies all of known Spain; to the left, mountains and then something vaguely imaged as Portuguese. Just so the road, which it scarcely supersedes, will have felt to Ferdinand the Great, and his ill-fated son, King Sancho, and his ill-used daughters Doña Urraca and Doña Elvira" (King, "Early Churches in Spain, Part III, Toro and Zamora," *Journal of the American Institute of Architects* 6 [1918]: 559).

32. From 1919 to 1920 King and Lowber traveled in Spain at the expense of the Hispanic Society. King was paid thirty-five hundred dollars for her research and writing, and Lowber was paid one thousand dollars for her photographs (Georgiana Goddard King, letter to Archer Milton Huntington, 16 April 1919, Hispanic Society of America, New York).

33. See King, "A Mountain Town," in *Way of Saint James*, 1:409, and "A Beggar by the Puerta Santa," in *Way of Saint James*, 3:109.

34. King, *Way of Saint James*, 1:iii–iv.

35. King, *Way of Saint James*, 1:165, 169.

36. King, *Way of Saint James*, 3:17–18.

37. See especially King's description of a mass in the cathedral (*Way of Saint James*, 3:27–33).
38. See King, *Way of Saint James*, 3:143–44, 152–54, 169–71, 172, 181, 182, 184, 207, 209–10, 211.
39. King states, "Paleolithic man had moved along it, and the stations of the living devotion today he had frequented." (*Way of Saint James*, 1:22).
40. King describes Spain in *Heart of Spain* as a place where "time has no power upon her beauty, which was ordained before time was" (67).
41. King, *Way of Saint James*, 1:22.
42. King, *Way of Saint James*, 1:24–25.
43. King, *Way of Saint James*, 1:vii, ix.
44. King, *Way of Saint James*, 3:23.
45. King, *Way of Saint James*, 1:407.
46. "Pilgrims of Saint James," *London Times Literary Supplement*," 30 December 1920, 89.
47. King, *Way of Saint James*, 1:iii.
48. King, *Way of Saint James*, 2:66–67.
49. King, *Way of Saint James*, 2:380.
50. King, *Way of Saint James*, 1:261.
51. King, *Way of Saint James*, 2:169.
52. Saunders, "Georgiana Goddard King," 232.
53. Saunders, "Georgiana Goddard King," 237 n. 86.
54. Other King students included Roberta Fansler, Elizabeth Conger, Delphine Fitz Darby, Dorothy Shipley, Margaretta Salinger, Margaret Veeder, and Jean Leonard.
55. Delphine Fitz Darby, letter to Susanna Saunders, 9 November 1975, Bryn Mawr College Archives, Canaday Library, Bryn Mawr College.
56. Dorothea C. Shipley, "Georgiana Goddard King as a Teacher," unpublished paper in Bryn Mawr College Archives, Canaday Library, Bryn Mawr College.
57. Carpenter, "Faculty Tribute to Miss King," 7.
58. Stein, *Autobiography of Alice B. Toklas*, 142.
59. Mitchell, "Mr. Cooper and Miss King," 5.
60. This is made clear in written correspondence between King and Stieglitz in 1915, which is located in the Beineke Rare Book and Manuscript Library, Yale University.
61. King makes this clear in an unpublished letter to Archer Huntington, saying, "Were you glad of a Republican Spain? . . . I am full of hope and delight" (Georgiana Goddard King, letter to Archer Milton Huntington, 30 May 1931, Hispanic Society of America).

SELECT BIBLIOGRAPHY OF WORKS BY GEORGIANA GODDARD KING

Editor. *Some Account of Gothic Architecture in Spain,* by George Edmund Street. 1865. Reprint, London: J. M. Dent & Sons, 1914.
"French Figure Sculpture on Some Early Spanish Churches." *American Journal of Archaeology* 19 (1915): 250–67.
"A Change in León Cathedral, Spain." *Art and Archaeology* 4 (October 1916): 243.
"Early Churches of Spain." *Journal of the American Institute of Architects* 6 (1916): 395–402, 435–42, 559–66.
"A Note on the So-Called Horse-Shoe Architecture of Spain." *American Journal of Archaeology* 20 (1916): 407–16.

"Some Famous Paintings in Barcelona." *Art and Archaeology* 4 (July 1916): 55–56.
"Three Notes on Capitals." *American Journal of Archaeology* 20 (1916): 417–25.
Essay in *Unpublished Notes and Reprinted Papers,* by George Edmund Street. New York, Hispanic Society of America, 1916.
"Saint Mary of Melón." *American Journal of Archaeology* 21 (1917): 387–96.
"Fiona Macleod." *Modern Language Notes* 33 (1918): 352–56.
"Three Unknown Churches in Spain." *American Journal of Archaeology* 22 (1918): 154–65.
"Granada of the Moors." *Journal of the American Institute of Architects* 7 (1919): 71–77.
"Notes on the Portals of Santiago de Compostella [sic]." *American Journal of Archaeology* 23 (1919): 73.
"Soria, Osma, and Cuenca." *Journal of the American Institute of Architects* 7 (1919): 103–11.
"Spanish Abbeys." *Journal of the American Institute of Architects* 7 (1919): 399–405.
"Spanish Cloisters." *Journal of the American Institute of Architects* 7 (1919): 481–88.
"Saint James of Compostella and The Vision of Thurkill . . . [sic]." *Romanic Review* 10 (1919): 38–47.
The Way of Saint James. 3 vols. Hispanic Notes and Monographs. New York: G. P. Putnam's Sons, 1920.
A Brief Account of the Military Orders in Spain. Hispanic Notes and Monographs. New York: Hispanic Society of America, 1921.
"Bryn Mawr Notes and Monographs." *Bryn Mawr Alumnae Bulletin* (April 1921): 13–14.
"Castles in Spain." *Journal of the American Institute of Architects,* part 1, 9 (1921): 271–74; part 2, 9 (1921): 294–301; part 3, 10 (1922): 377–82.
A Citizen of the Twilight: José Asunción Silva. Bryn Mawr Notes and Monographs, 4. New York: Longmans, Green & Co., 1921.
"The Importance of Sometimes Looking at Things, as Exemplified in the Cardona Tomb at Bellpuig and the Retables of Barbastro and S. Domingo de la Calzada." *American Journal of Archaeology* 35 (1921): 81.
The Play of the Sibyl Cassandra. Bryn Mawr Notes and Monographs, 2. New York: Longmans, Green & Co., 1921.
"The Shepherds and the Kings." *Art and Archaeology* 12 (December 1921): 265–72.
"Towered Cities." *Journal of the American Institute of Architects,* part 1, 9 (1921): 349–58; part 2, 10 (1922): 346–52; part 3, 12 (1924): 103–9.
"Algunos elementos ingleses en las fundaciones de Alfonso VIII." *Arquitectura* 4 (1922): 453–58.
"Prettiness and Discomfort, with Some Sociological Implications." *Journal of the American Institute of Architects* 10 (1922): 43–44.
"The Rider on the White Horse." *Art Bulletin* 5 (1922): 3–9.
"Some Oriental Elements in Medieval Spanish Architecture." *American Journal of Archaeology* 26 (1922): 79–80.
"Algunos rasgos de influjo oriental en la arquitectura española de la edad media." *Arquitectura* 5 (1923): 85–193.
Sardinian Painting. Bryn Mawr Notes and Monographs, 5. New York: Longmans, Green & Co., 1923.
"Some Churches in Galicia." *Art Studies* 1 (1923): 55–64.
"Little Churches in Greece." *Journal of the American Institute of Architects,* part 1, 12 (1924): 13–16, 23–24; part 2, 14 (1926): 434–41.

Pre-Romanesque Churches of Spain. Bryn Mawr Notes and Monographs, 7. New York: Longmans, Green & Co., 1924.

"The Problem of the Duero." *Art Studies* 3 (1925): 3–11.

"Fact and Inference in the Matter of Jamb Sculpture." *Art Studies* 4 (1926): 113–46.

"Claude Monet." *Bryn Mawr Alumnae Bulletin* (February 1927): 20–21.

Mudéjar. Bryn Mawr Notes and Monographs, 8. New York: Longmans, Green & Co., 1927.

"The Triumph of the Cross." *Art Bulletin* 11 (1929): 316–26.

"Divagations on the *Beatus.*" *Art Studies* 8 (1930): 1–58.

"Some Reliefs at Budapest." *American Journal of Archaeology* 37 (January 1933): 64–76.

"Gertrude Stein and French Painting." *Bryn Mawr Alumnae Bulletin* (May 1934): 2–5.

"Iconographical Notes on the Passion." *Art Bulletin* 16 (1934): 291–303.

"The Journey of Ferrer Bassa." *Art Bulletin* 16 (June 1934): 116–22.

"The Virgin of Humility." *Art Bulletin* 17 (December 1935): 474–91.

"Mattia Preti." *Art Bulletin* 18 (September 1936): 371–86.

"Little Romanesque Churches in Portugal." In vol. 1 of *Medieval Studies in Memory of A. Kingsley Porter.* Edited by Wilhelm R. W. Koehler, ed. Cambridge, Mass.: Harvard University Press, 1939.

Heart of Spain. Edited by Agnes Mongan. Cambridge, Mass.: Harvard University Press, 1941.

Works Cited

Carpenter, Rhys. "Faculty Tribute to Miss King." *Bryn Mawr Alumnae Bulletin* (June 1939): 8.

Lefkowitz Horowitz, Helen. *Alma Mater: Design and Experience in the Women's Colleges from Their Nineteenth-Century Beginnings to the 1930s.* 2d ed. Amherst: University of Massachusetts Press, 1993.

Mann, Janice. "Romantic Identity, Nationalism, and the Understanding of the Advent of Romanesque Art in Christian Spain." *Gesta* 36 (1997): 156–65.

Mitchell, Charles. "Mr. Cooper and Miss King." *Bryn Mawr College Alumnae Bulletin* (spring 1961): 5–7.

Panofsky, Erwin. "Three Decades of Art History in the United States." In *Meaning in the Visual Arts.* 1955. Reprint, Chicago: University of Chicago Press, 1982.

Saunders, Susanna Terrell. "Georgiana Goddard King (1871–1939): Educator and Pioneer in Medieval Spanish Art." In *Women as Interpreters of the Visual Arts, 1820–1979,* edited by Claire Richter Sherman with Adele M. Holcomb, 209–38. Westport, Conn.: Greenwood Press, 1981.

Stein, Gertrude. *The Autobiography of Alice B. Toklas.* New York: Literary Guild, 1933.

Wethey, Harold E. "An American Pioneer in Hispanic Studies: Georgiana Goddard King." *Parnassus* 11 (1939): 33–35.

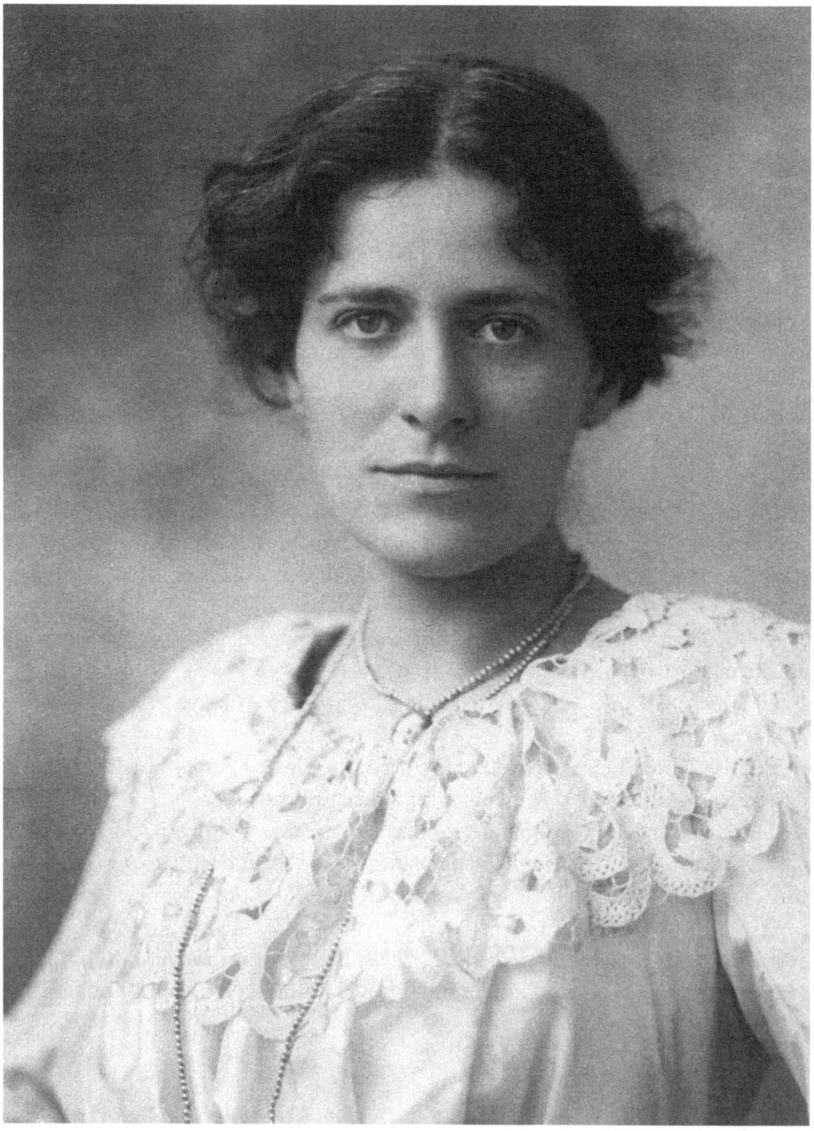

CHAPTER 10

"Miss Rickert of Vassar" and Edith Rickert at the University of Chicago (1871–1938)

Elizabeth Scala

One of the more vivid memories of my undergraduate introduction to medieval literary scholarship concerns the latter's formal inscription of gender. By this I refer not to the female characters or even female authors that comprised the subjects of such scholarship. Instead, I was curious about the mode of address toward women scholars themselves. Reading these critical materials, I noticed how often female scholars tended to be addressed by their marital rather than institutional status, most often as "Miss." Where male scholars were called "Doctor" or "Professor," female scholars were always marked by their gender. Such labels led me initially to question whether these women had graduate degrees or university positions as the men's titles clearly attested. Finding that most of them did hold the Ph.D. and even held a teaching post, I remained perplexed by the fact that they continued to be addressed by titles that called attention to their sex rather than their accomplishments. Among the much larger constituency of male academics, "Miss Hammond," "Miss Hibbard," and "Miss Rickert" were all clearly foregrounded as female before they were evaluated as scholars.[1] The requisite "Miss" not only marked them by marital status; it also appeared to diminish them as well. Next to the learned "Professor" or the lettered "Doctor," "Miss" seemed remarkably belittling, no matter how politely tendered.[2] As an undergraduate at a women's college in Massachusetts, I was infuriated at the disrespect I assumed these women endured in the academy. I was even further shocked to learn that the conventional practice had persisted as late as the 1960s.[3] When, I wondered, did sex cease to matter in scholarly circles? For how long had this practice continued?

One response to these polite yet Neanderthal practices might be to ignore gender: our attention, after all, should be paid to such scholarship *despite* the biological sex of its writer. But as progressive as it might seem, that practice would also fail to restore proper attention to this body of critical and editorial work. Gender was so enmeshed in the work that these women did, and that they were allowed to do, that ignoring it sets no record straight. For example, the division in scholarship between masculine and feminine subjects—a division between, on the one hand, important canonical poets like Langland and Chaucer and, on the other, peripheral and "popular" subjects, such as the mystics or romance—genders this work from its inception. Women were typically given "appropriate" research tasks and set to work on particularly feminine subjects by their dissertation advisors. In an academic culture that worked far more like an apprenticeship system than it does today, directed research was in itself gendered. Such a statement in no way excludes men from the effect of this gendered system; male students were also assigned their research topics. In fact, Edith Rickert herself used to collect short lists of potential thesis topics for masters and doctoral students. Some of these lists, for which she used pocket address books, have her students' names penciled in. "Giving" a thesis topic to a student appears as a common academic practice; part of a thesis director's work was to instruct students about what work needed doing. Yet gender assumptions cannot help but figure into this regular academic practice, as Rickert's own deliberations about her thesis topic may finally attest.[4]

I forgot about this issue of academic titles and the gendered academic system they entailed until, while on fellowship at the University of Chicago, I began researching Rickert's career. Reading through the boxes of personal and professional materials on deposit in the university archives, I was confronted with "Miss Rickert" everywhere and began to realize in what contexts the practice worked. It was certainly not in terms of the feminism of the latter 1980s, when descriptions according to marital status would have been forbidden. Rickert's title refers instead to a social standard of politeness and decorum lost to the postmodern world. Where I had been reading with particular assumptions about what such inappropriate attention to her gender indicated, the generation in which Rickert lived would have seen disrespect and perhaps felt fury at a *lack* of recognition for her gender. I do not want to suggest that a simple kind of historicism could rectify the problem I thought I had detected. No special context would explain—indeed, explain away—the slight toward these women I thought I had detected. But if neither modern feminism nor a simple historical shift in assumptions could offer an appropriate reaction to her official title, the issue still had the power to evoke a complex, little understood set of circumstances. I raise the matter now, after writing three biographical pieces about Rickert, in order to engage further the academic culture in which she lived and worked. Where my previous work has sought to address Rickert's accomplishments as a fiction writer and medievalist literary scholar as well as her relationship with her eminent colleague John Matthews Manly, my efforts here will be to outline a cultural context in which we might better understand some of the facts of Rickert's official and unofficial academic career at the University of Chicago.[5] To do so, I will offer a biographical account of

Rickert's career that also tries to relate the early history of women in the academy. I hope to offer a picture of what "Miss Rickert's" academy might have looked like. In the account that follows, my particular attention will be turned to contextualizing her career from 1914 to 1924, the years between her first unofficial and then official appointment at Chicago, a period from which little material survives in her papers. I will also attend to the span of her official appointment at the University of Chicago, 1924–34, the years in which she was promoted from associate to full professor and then retired once reaching the maximum allowable age.

Born on 11 July 1871, Martha Edith Rickert was the eldest child of Francis and Josephine Newburg Rickert of Canal Dover, Ohio. Rickert spent most of her childhood living in La Grange, Illinois, with her parents and her three sisters who had survived childhood. Her good Protestant family was of modest means, and her acceptance to Vassar College was a momentous occasion for everyone in the Rickert clan. Once graduated from Vassar, Rickert began a career of writing, research, and scholarship that would earn her a doctorate from the University of Chicago, a nine-year sojourn living as a writer in England, and eventually a full professorship at her graduate institution. A prolific fiction writer, Rickert is best known as one of the coeditors of the monumental *Text of the Canterbury Tales, Studied on the Basis of All Known Manuscripts*. This brief sketch of her career might suggest a conventional progress through academic ranks, but Rickert trod an indirect and somewhat unusual path between the various high points of her career.

When Rickert headed off to college at Vassar in 1887, the present University of Chicago was yet to be founded. In fact, when Rickert began graduate study in 1894, that university was only two years old.[6] These facts illuminate the "frontier" nature of Chicago and the "Middle West" during Rickert's lifetime. In 1890 Chicago was still dominated by the stockyards; the university was located out in the middle of nowhere, well beyond the city and its rail station. The East Coast, and Boston in particular, was the intellectual seat of the nation, "the Athens of America."[7] Vassar was clearly a conservative and prestigious choice for her education. She attended the Chicago public schools and won her place at Vassar (and the vexed prestige of a woman's college) through scholarship. Passing her Vassar entrance examinations handily, she would excel in her four years of undergraduate study.[8] Rickert's journals and letters do not debate the decision to attend Vassar; the archive of materials deposited in the University of Chicago library effectively begins with her arrival.[9] The earliest surviving letter written by Rickert was composed that night and recorded for her parents her very first impressions of Vassar College and the life she was to begin there. One might try to surmise the basis upon which Rickert chose Vassar in light of the history and function of the women's colleges at the time. While coeducation was a great experiment for many institutions in the late nineteenth century, and particularly for the less conventional "western" universities, Vassar was part of a historic tradition of educating women. Rickert's scholarship award made her attendance at

Vassar possible—the venerable eastern women's colleges were much more expensive than the public "land grant" universities of the West—but such financial support cannot determine fully her enrollment there. Rickert certainly had the grades and the determination to attend one of these coeducational institutions, like the University of Michigan, some of which were tuition-free. Instead, it may have been the status of Vassar that attracted Rickert. As one of the oldest women's colleges, educating women since 1865, Vassar would have a prestige in Rickert's lower-middle class community, whose daughters were being educated for the first time.

In the period between the Civil War and World War I, the most important factor leading to a woman's decision to attend college, according to Barbara Solomon, was familial support. In this respect Rickert appears typical in that she had the emotional backing of her parents if not the financial help others had. Fortunately for Rickert, her parents valued education and spared this eldest sister of four from her home.[10] Always attentive to their bright and studious daughter, they must have realized the seriousness of her intent. Rickert's fit at Vassar seems to have been a good one, despite the fact that her father worried about the finery other families afforded their daughters that he could not.[11] While the women's colleges were the more expensive choice for one's daughter, they were not filled with the *most* socially elite women. Even when wealth was on display at the women's colleges, the very richest Americans educated their daughters elsewhere. Solomon writes, "New rich millionaires obsessed with making good marriages for their daughters imitated the patterns of the older families [private education in the home and through travel], dismissing college as preparation for women who had no option but to be schoolteachers."[12] As the daughter of a struggling father who worked in downtown Chicago at a chemist's shop, Rickert was certainly such a woman. These remarks illustrate the tension between elitist and vocational aspects of the women's colleges, and Rickert seems to have attended a Vassar that partook of both. While Vassar trained her and even employed her for two years as a teacher, giving Rickert the means of helping her family and having an independent future, it also lent a prestige to her "pedigree."

She left Vassar after her graduation in 1891 and kept house for her father and younger sisters: her mother died sometime after her Vassar graduation and certainly before 1893. Rickert began teaching at Lyons Township High School near Chicago shortly after her Vassar graduation. With her undergraduate degree she was always guaranteed some income, though teaching clearly was not her first choice of occupation.

While many women headed to college, and to the women's colleges particularly, to begin a teaching career, Rickert's lifelong fascination was scholarship. This excerpt from a letter to her parents, dated February 1890, about the allure of old books and musty libraries is indicative of her attraction to research and scholarly activity:

> I am perfectly delighted with some old books which I found in the library to-day, Bibles, Latin authors and long harangues and discourses (in Latin also) of people long forgotten, Brentius, Arnobius and others. They date way back in the sixteenth century,

1565, 1542, 1524. . . . In many cases they have the owner's name on the title-page and his notes in the margin just as he wrote them three hundred and fifty years ago. . . . Such things as these make me perfectly happy. Wouldn't I like to be loose to pasture in a library like that of Oxford or Cambridge. I am afraid I would be as gray and musty as the books themselves before I came out.[13]

This letter clearly presages the doctorate in English, specializing in medieval literature, Rickert would eventually earn at the University of Chicago. But it would also lead her further away from American institutions of higher learning, whether as a graduate student at Chicago or as an instructor at Vassar. Her attraction to scholarship and to writing—fiction writing, newspaper reporting, and essay writing—led Rickert to make one of the most dramatic changes in her life. Having attained her Ph.D. while teaching at Vassar (1896–1900), and after a number of years of high-school teaching (1894–96), she decided to abandon her Vassar position when the opportunity arose to live in England. Where many academic women between 1899 (the year she earned her doctorate) and 1914 (the year she returned to teaching as an "assistant" in the Department of English at the University of Chicago) took various kinds of teaching and administrative posts, Rickert left the United States and the strictures of its university bureaucracy. We will explore in more detail some of the features that made this kind of work unattractive to Rickert.

One gets to know Rickert through the many reminiscences and sketches recorded in her journals, particularly of her travels abroad. Among the stunning landscapes and architectures that impressed her, we also see her responses to things that held a more personal significance. For instance, she mentions a striking image from her first trip to Europe that relates to the female domesticity Rickert emphatically renounced and to hardships her mother endured caring for her financially troubled family, hardships that Rickert chronicled in her Vassar journals and letters. On her first day in London, Rickert notices "the sharp contrast in classes—many extremely poor." One image in particular is worth noting. Rickert writes, "[S]aw poor woman with baby and with her eyes all bruised and discolored with hard blows—made my *blood boil.*"[14] This description of urban poverty and marital abuse stands out sharply in these writings, most of which note the formalities of British culture, the intellectual milieu of Frederick J. Furnivall's "societies," and the almost girlish behavior of her boarding-house companions. Her expression of anger and resentment here is aimed not only at the class divisions she witnessed in London but also at the gender inequality that she saw written on the face of this young mother. Rickert saw similar—if entirely symbolic—"blows" to her own mother's health up until her death. Though she was extremely affectionate toward her parents and her younger siblings, even "maternal" toward her little sisters, Rickert expresses no desires for a conventional family life. Any wish for a husband is put into a future beyond her college and independent years.[15] Her discussions with other female residents of her London boardinghouse, recorded in her journals, indicate an expectation to marry eventually. But her immediate focus was always on intellectual, literary, and socially reformist pursuits. She was much more mentally engaged with the meetings of the Ethical or Philological Societies that she attended at Furnivall's invitation.

Smitten with England from her first visit in 1896, Rickert became a true Anglophile. It is therefore no surprise that she chose to leave the security of a teaching appointment at Vassar for what would be a nine-year sojourn in England. Writing in 1897 to a Hyde Park High School friend and colleague, Mary Herrick, Rickert recounts much of her stay in Germany and the beginning of her visit to England, which she "does not merely like" but loves—despite its awful "blood-boiling" poverty.[16] Similarly, when she returns to Chicago in December of the same year, she says that it "doesn't seem a bit like home—oh not a bit. Wish I hadn't come—except for the girlies' sake."[17] Clearly, she refers here to her younger sisters, Ethel, Edna (or "Eddie"), and Margaret, about whose birthdays and letters she makes note throughout her journals. These early impressions of England clearly had a lasting effect. Four years later Rickert would move to Britain.

Rickert left for England, "burning [her] Vassar ships behind her," in 1900.[18] She remained there until a financial panic brought her back to the United States in 1909. She supported herself in England by writing fiction and newspaper stories (for which she took her own photographs) and by doing research on medieval manuscripts in the British Library for American academics like Eleanor Prescott Hammond, who was also a graduate student at Chicago with Rickert, and John Matthews Manly, her "mentor" and later eminent colleague at Chicago.[19] When the financial trouble made supporting herself difficult, Rickert returned to the United States to work in publishing. Beginning in New York and then moving to editorial posts at D. C. Heath in Boston and the *Ladies' Home Journal* in Philadelphia, Rickert had a more practical and less academic education. Returning home to work for the Commercial Club of Chicago in pursuit of a bill for vocational education in Illinois, "particularly from the girls' end of it," Rickert eventually began teaching part-time at her graduate institution, the University of Chicago, in 1914, typically in the summer quarter.[20] Her specialties were the Chaucer course as well as contemporary British and American literature, which were not part of the standard curriculum as they are now.

Rickert's unusual career raises a number of questions and concerns. Clearly not interested in the vocation of teaching, she taught because it enabled her to do other things: assist her family, gain a graduate degree, live abroad. But looking at Rickert's career as a completely self-affirming, feminist story also casts shadows too important to ignore.[21] If her choice to abjure high-school teaching is understandable, her "academic" work between 1914 and 1924 is less so. In this period Rickert held a kind of adjunct position at Chicago. While her expertise was once coveted by some at Vassar and Wellesley, she had a more vexed relation to the faculty of the University of Chicago, which she would eventually join.[22]

Part of the situation must be understood in terms of the difference between the women's colleges (and their largely female faculties) and the coeducational institutions.

In her history of women and higher education, Solomon writes, "[C]onsistently one generalization holds: coeducational schools made plain both directly and indirectly what could be denied at women's colleges, that society attached greater importance to men's achievements."[23] This was evident at both the student and the faculty level. The privileges—often of teaching itself—at the women's colleges were not afforded the female faculty of the coeducational institutions. Women scholars dominated, sometimes entirely, the faculty of the women's colleges.[24] Except for courses in biology and hygiene, which were thought (because of their physiological content and the problems of decorum it raised) in special need of female faculty, the women professoriat was largely a social and administrative body. For women Ph.D.s, whose faculty appointment (usually as an assistant professor) was often nominal, the post of dean of women put them on a faculty where they had few teaching responsibilities. For instance, when Alice Freeman Palmer, formerly president of Wellesley College, was asked to join the University of Chicago faculty at its inception, she was given the title dean of women and professor of history. The dean of women was "responsible for the good name of the women of the University."[25] Her appointment was advertised as a great coup for Chicago, which was proud of the nine women included in its initial faculty of 120.[26] However, Palmer did no teaching in the history department. Instead, such women administrators were to make sure that the female students, graduate and undergraduate alike, behaved properly and were adequately sheltered. In fact, Palmer's affiliation with Chicago was largely in name only. From Wellesley she brought with her Marion Talbot as her assistant dean of women (Talbot was then also assigned as an assistant professor of sanitary science), and it was Talbot who performed the administrative duties of Palmer's post and who stayed on at the university (after Palmer's departure in 1895) until 1925 as dean of women. While her husband remained a prominent member of its classics faculty, Palmer canceled her association with Chicago within a year (from the beginning she had been contracted to spend a mere twelve weeks out of the year in residence at Chicago). Her appearance on the initial faculty list looks more like a promotional gesture than any significant commitment to an integrated faculty.

Rickert herself notes the neglect of women, as well as the division between the women's colleges and the coeducational university sketched here, in some of the commentary in her journal. Writing in December 1897 and January 1898 about her recent return to Chicago after her first trip abroad, she notes the following about both her professors at the university and some colleagues at Hyde Park High School: "It amuses me vastly to observe the consideration paid to 'Miss Rickert of Vassar,' denied to the same person, graduate student at the U of C and teacher at HPHS." Shortly thereafter she would write, "After all, I suppose I must come to look upon college as my real home."[27] Rickert does not elaborate on the meaning of this "home," but some of the historical and sociological accounts of life at these women's colleges do. The women's colleges provided a residential and intellectual environment for their female faculty. These institutions "were the only reliable source of employment for female scholars and academics. Male and coeducational institutions rarely appointed women to the faculty; when women were given faculty rank, it virtually always carried an adjunct or inferior status."[28]

If Rickert found herself slighted as a graduate student at Chicago, for others it comprised a great experiment in women's education. Solomon writes, "The opening in October 1892 of the Baptist- and Rockefeller-sponsored University of Chicago was a landmark in the history of coeducation." This "landmark" was materialized in the forward vision of its first president, William Rainey Harper, who welcomed female undergraduates, graduate students, and faculty when the University of Chicago opened its doors.[29] The success of coeducation produced unexpected results. The university, "initially so proud of its commitment to women, fell into significant controversy in 1902 when the percentage of women students (and Phi Beta Kappa awards) rose above that of the men. In response, Harper tried to segregate the women.[30] For five years women in Chicago's Junior College (i.e., freshmen and sophomores) were separately educated from the men. The policy ended because of financial and bureaucratic strain. But where segregation sounds like reprimand to the female student body, these "objections to women in higher education attested to their success as students."[31] Rickert would have been part of this wave of sometimes troubling, successful female students, eventually earning her Ph.D. magna cum laude (only the second individual to be granted such an honor at Chicago by 1899).

Where Rickert abjured what we might think of as her proscribed role as a primary- or secondary-school teacher by removing herself from the United States shortly after receiving her Ph.D., she finally (re)turned to teaching and, more importantly, to research. Rickert continually published academic and nonacademic writing; there is no clear separation in her work. But if the period 1901–9, the time she lived in England, represents her most prolific novel- and story-writing period, then the period from 1910 to 1926 reflects a marked turn toward the scholarly in her writing. Within this period we see Rickert's return to the university in 1914, when she began teaching as an assistant, usually in the summer sessions, and her eventual promotion to associate professor in 1924. Between these two appointments we have only a sketch of Rickert's professional activities and little direct knowledge of her institutional role.

In 1918 Manly invited Rickert to join in the code-breaking efforts at the War Department in Washington. They returned to the university in 1919 and resumed their normal duties, which for Rickert was only part-time work. While Manly's genius for code breaking, his "cipher-brains," is detailed in Herbert Yardley's *The American Black Chamber* (1931), others on his team, like Rickert, go unmentioned. Rickert herself left little to augment Yardley's account in this respect. While the retrospective temporal lists of events in her career that are scattered in her journals and writings—her informal, self-authored vitae—include "busting the German code," there is little material from this period of her life with which a biographer may work.

Filling in these gaps may be dangerous or imaginative but in some sense narratively necessary. We can see that her published research and collaborative plans with

Manly surely had to influence her official appointment as associate professor in 1924. Although there is no evidence as to why Rickert was given rank at this particular time, we may surmise that her published scholarship and research plans had some causal relation to her promotion.[32] At the age of fifty-three Rickert finally received something like the official post that she deserved, even if it was not the one she would have held had she continued at Vassar or gone to Wellesley at the turn of the century. But appointments can tell only so much of her story, and clearly Rickert worked for reasons other than university "position." For instance, although appointed in 1924, her editorial and paleographical work had begun earlier. In that year she was already involved with Manly on the Chaucer project that was to consume the rest of their lives. Rickert was appointed in September and by December was headed for the libraries of England to begin photostating manuscripts. Since permissions would have had to be secured in advance, the project must have been started before her appointment date. The relationships she maintained with her graduate students also suggest that she was already advising them in a higher capacity than her academic rank might indicate.

The connections to be drawn between the various periods of Rickert's life, as well as the various forms of her experience, are indirect and sometimes elusive. For instance, her impressions of English life and of the world such travel opened up to her would effect her relations with her students many years later. On Rickert's first trip abroad in the summer of 1896, she had occasion to change rooming houses in London. Her journal records the excitement of the initial trip and the thirst with which she drank in all the details of her surroundings, as she notes in some detail the furnishings and accommodations available to her. The "study" she finds "absolutely charming—furnished in dull artistic colors, with old-fashioned windows, books, couch, easy and working chairs. A grate fire is burning all the time. In [the] center of [the] room is a round table with a lamp and writing materials—so we shall be the 'Ladies of the Round Table.'"[33] The description is not merely quaint with its overly indulged detail. The experience of this boardinghouse would also provide the exemplar for the way she addressed her female graduate students more than thirty years later in Chicago.[34] Among her papers a number of letters survive addressed to "the Round Table" and clearly refer to a group of her *female* students.[35] This address to the "Ladies of the Round Table" hints that she thought seriously about her role in the community of women scholars of her day, a stronger community of whom she might have appreciated.[36] How she was addressed by others, however, asks us to think about that community from a different angle. And here I would like to return to the "Miss" in "Miss Rickert."

In telling us something about the social gestures of the day and age in which she lived, Rickert's title of address succeeds brilliantly, but it fails miserably in telling us about her scholarly qualifications. Much information comes with that failure. In a complex fashion it potentially dispatches the anxieties surrounding real women in the academy when the academy itself can be said to have been gendered feminine by a larger world. Claude Charleton Bowman's curious study of the college professor in 1938 provides interesting sociological information about the popular perception of academics during the period in which Rickert worked.[37] Drawing evidence from general magazines, Bowman chronicles the assumptions about university professors during the period 1890 to 1938, the year of Rickert's death. Neither Bowman's study nor the "general magazines" from which he culls his information offers evidence of a female professoriat in America. If Bowman's work were to suggest to future generations the complexion of the American professor in this period, it would be overwhelmingly male.[38]

Not only were some of America's professoriat female (despite the characterizations Bowman offered), but that femininity, as we have seen in Rickert's own case, was always clearly foregrounded. Published materials, in which one's body is always separated from one's words in some way, take pains to ensure that a lady's gender is never in question. While this display of femininity appears unnecessary and somewhat condescending today, we must try to account for this cultural difference and explain it beyond the assumptions of current feminist thought. These questions are difficult to answer because we lack specific discussion of them from the period in question. Perhaps because such practices seemed so "natural," they are not addressed in the record. No one, for instance, comments about being called "Miss" rather than "Professor." Rickert's reaction to the lack of respect for the Chicago graduate student (in contrast to the respect afforded the Vassar woman) appears to take no issue with such a title. It simply appears taken for granted. Why might this society, indeed the women themselves, insist on the markings of gender in professional circles?

Marion Talbot's memoir, *More Than Lore,* might offer an appropriate context. She tells of women's participation in convocation ceremonies at the University of Chicago at the turn of the century. Student assistance was eventually needed at these formal occasions to aid the faculty, "and the appointments [of student marshals and assistants] made a mark of great distinction."[39] When "it was soon pointed out that the distinction might well be bestowed on women also"—a seemingly modern recognition—the 2 April 1900 convocation program included the names of two women students in its list of newly appointed marshals.[40] Shortly thereafter one of them declined reappointment. Talbot writes, "No small incident could show more vividly the social changes which were soon to take place in the position of women than the reason given, which was that the public appearances required were not in accord with the modesty and refinement which marked a well-bred lady!"[41]

The incident appears to be directly related to the concerns with title raised earlier: "Following this experience, only men marshals were appointed until the system was adopted which differentiated the women from the men."[42] When finally a number of women "aides" were designated to complement an equal number of male marshals at such ceremonies, we see the desire for equal *but separate* positions that respected the divisions of gender and gendered behavior. By its analogy this story potentially illuminates the desire of women academics for a title that foregrounds gender. Clearly there was felt a kind of threat at being masculinized in such situations, a fear that some woman might be mistaken for a man. While such a fear seems unusual (and expresses a condition even a bit desirable to us now), we must be careful to acknowledge the desires of the women for whom we pretend to speak. Part of our feminist historical work is to give voice to their desires—however culturally and historically constructed—and not to confuse them with our own.

While I have taken issue with the failure of Rickert's title to designate her educational degree or her institutional status, that failure itself is illuminating and meaningful. Miss Rickert's title tells us something important about the academic women who carried it, something beyond the mark of femininity it was meant *not* to efface: these women scholars were largely unmarried. Family life would entail a cost to a female academic's career not incurred by her male colleagues. In the 1920s "3/4 of the women [academics] were unmarried, a figure attesting to the commitment required by a scholarly lifesyle."[43] Marriage made a woman, many assumed, unsuitable for professional life. Indeed, Geraldine Jonçich Clifford writes, "It was expected that a woman who married would naturally give up her position."[44] Such assumptions were clearly in place at Brown University in 1905, when its beloved dean of women left to marry a classics professor. Alice Freeman left the presidency of Wellesley under these same circumstances. Lyde Cullen Sizer explains, "Married women by custom, if not explicitly by policy, did not teach at Brown. Marriage was considered—for women—to be its own career."[45] Another way to make the distinction would be to say that while for men scholarship in the university comprised a "profession," for women it entailed a "lifestyle." In an entirely odd and ironic way the gendered title marking their unmarried status thus also suggests women's commitment to scholarly work. While Miss Rickert's name did not inform her readers of her doctor's degree or her university post, it did suggest her devotion to her profession—the lifestyle she was willing to adopt for it—after a manner. That her male colleagues were not forced to make similar choices—nor were they labeled for having made them—makes for a frustrating comparison. It also makes clear the layered significance of Miss Rickert's name, reminding us that no single explanation can satisfy the array of cultural and historical questions it generates.

While she left little evidence of her experiences at the University of Chicago between 1914 and 1924, the period in which she served as an "assistant," Rickert probably felt the same frustrations as did other female academics stuck in low-ranking, subordinate positions. In Linda Eisenmann's words, "The scatter-shot nature of women's employment outside the women's colleges provided female academics little chance to shape departments by applying the press of numbers. In addition, because the diffusion of women's employment was coupled with the notable lack of promotion for women, their chance of exerting leadership in their fields was sorely weakened."[46] According to the historians Penina Migdal Glazer and Miriam Slater, who contextualize the rise of the "professions"—college teaching, medicine, scientific research, and psychological social work—out of group occupations in the nineteenth century, these women were "systematically . . . paid less, advanced more slowly, and regarded with less esteem."[47] Rickert worked, like many at the time, where "no special policy excluded women from professional possibilities. Decisions to offer most appointments to men and to pay women less, promote them more slowly, and exclude them from eligibility for grants or from editorial boards of important journals were as a rule neither deliberate nor articulated policies. But they occurred with persistent regularity, and their exclusions had profound consequences for professional women."[48] Such observations as these, which index the inequality of remuneration and promotion in the academy, must also be seen alongside the gendering of various kinds of academic work. Because Rickert was a teacher of English, her area of expertise was in some ways an already gendered one. But in the field of medieval scholarship, and the even further particularized field of textual scholarship, we might look to the implicit gendering of her contributions.

If Rickert's title always gendered her scholarship for her readers, we might look to the ways her role in the university and her work as a medievalist was gendered more subtly. From the reminiscences of Virginia Leland, a former student who focused on Rickert in the Chaucer laboratory at Chicago, we learn that "[i]t was she who supervised our training, saw that we studied palaeography and medieval Latin with Charles H. Beeson, greatest of the pupils of E. A. Lowe; and Old French with the formidable William A. Nitze; and that we did not neglect Italian, medieval history, and a broad range of Old and Middle English, including *Pearl* with Sir William Craigie."[49] Leland's essay is meant to restore Rickert's reputation and to secure her place in the Chicago Chaucer project (and its students' education). But reading Leland's reminiscences from the present, with modern expectations for such a restoration and recovery, sometimes suggests otherwise. The lineage of great male professors that Rickert brought to her students, for instance, places her in something of a maternal rather than a scholarly role. Her scholarly role appears perhaps maternal in distinction to the masculine disciplinary expertise on offer here. But if removing Rickert one degree from the pedagogical and scholarly effect on these students does not gender her relation to them fully, we might see a more clearly "feminine" role sketched for Rickert in another of Leland's anecdotes. Rickert also appears as the intermediary handmaiden of real scholarship in the following story of the discovery of a Canterbury fragment. Neither heroic nor scholarly in her direct actions (yet ultimately both), Rickert unearths the clues to the whereabouts of the oldest fragments of the *Tales* known. Leland recalls the story of discovery: "During World War I Sir John Ballinger of the National Library of Wales had been offered a book with [a] fragment of the *Canterbury Tales* pasted inside. He could not afford it and later as the result of a stroke could not remember the details. But one summer evening, sitting with him in a garden, Edith Rickert gently brought the clues back to his memory, 'Merthyr' and 'a Latin dictionary.'"[50] Leland's personal and often endearing memories of Rickert are moving, but they are also gendered in subtle and invidious ways. Rickert appears in neither of these reminiscences laboring over Chaucer or her students. Rather, she plays a subtle, advisory role that we might characterize as stereotypically "feminine." It is Rickert's careful patience with her students and with Ballinger's ailing memory, rather than her intellectual or codicological rigor, that Leland invokes. Upon such subtle and gendered divisions of labor various assumptions about her work have been laid.

Where Leland's stories are of a distinctly personal and familiar nature, others are written on public record. Take, for example, J. R. Hulbert's biographical entry on Rickert for *The Dictionary of American Biography,* which makes shifting claims about Rickert's scholarly labors in both explicit and implicit ways. Complementing "her very extensive published output" as the product of a singularly "tireless worker" and clearly stating that she and Manly "were complete collaborators" ("each kept in touch with all phases of the work"), Hulbert subtly indicates whose project the Chaucer edition really was when he writes, "During the last dozen years of her life she gave much of her time to assisting Professor Manly in *his* project of a critical edition of Chaucer's *Canterbury Tales,* to be based on a detailed study of all the existing manuscripts."[51] Hulbert also tries to distinguish their different areas of expertise: "Manly concerned himself with the problems of manuscript relationship and the establishment of the critical text; Miss Rickert was responsible for the historical ownership of the mss and for the search for new information on Chaucer's life."[52] Such information will be helpful to a revaluation of Rickert's participation in the *Canterbury Tales* project, but it also poses a particular interpretive problem itself. Although many of Rickert's students mark manuscript study and paleography as her particular area of expertise, the topic of a popular graduate course that she taught, Hulbert would make Rickert's contribution to the edition ancillary.[53] Her focus, according to this entry, was on the peripheral materials to the Chaucer edition. Here one sees in this individualizing of expertise a subtle hierarchizing of labor. While Rickert concerned herself with the material that provided some introductory chapters and eventually two volumes of biographical and cultural background materials, Manly focused on the central and "real" work of editing.[54] Though Manly railed against such characterizations of Rickert's role as his "assistant," one can see that it was hard to avoid, even when one looks to friends and admirers for contemporary assessments of their partnership.

Where such subtle characterizations of her involvement may remove her from the textual work of the Chicago project, we might remember that Rickert literally died working on the Chaucer edition. In 1936 she suffered a heart attack from which she never fully recovered. She eventually succumbed to a stroke on 21 May 1938 and died two days later. Rickert's papers in the University of Chicago archives record Manly's grief, documented in a number of personal letters, at losing his close colleague and companion.[55] He recalls her working on the Chaucer materials in her sickbed only days before her death. His elegy to Rickert was published in the prefatory material to the Chaucer edition she did not live to see in print. Rickert's sister Margaret, an art historian specializing in the Middle Ages, wrote a similar piece for Rickert's posthumously published book, *Chaucer's World.* One regrets that, while Manly dedicates the work to her memory and so clearly recalls her partnership at the time of its publication, her collaboration was not more publicly acknowledged, particularly in the scholarly awards given to Manly for the Chaucer work.[56] Clearly more feminist and historical studies are needed to set the record in some order.

NOTES

1. The triumvirate of women medievalists mentioned here bear a curious relation to one another. Both Eleanor Prescott Hammond and Laura Hibbard were each at the University of Chicago at the same time Edith Rickert was there (though Hammond and Hibbard were not there simultaneously). Hammond and Rickert were graduate students in the same period. Some years later Hibbard seems to have taken her courses as a graduate student at Chicago during the summer session, when Rickert was teaching. (Hibbard may also have crossed paths with Rickert at Hyde Park High School.) Curiously, Rickert never mentions Hibbard (and only mentions Hammond in passing) in the documents that survive. Here lies the material for a further investigation of women medievalists and female academic culture. I owe these provocative questions to Kathryn L. Lynch, whose chapter on Hibbard appears elsewhere in this volume. Though I had initially chosen these female scholars at random (or so I thought), Lynch pointed out the latent Chicago connection between Rickert and Hibbard. The topic of influence and female academic culture is an interesting one for the writers of these essays as well. Lynch was, coincidentally, my undergraduate teacher at Wellesley College, 1985–88.

2. Alongside the clear marking of gender with such titles, a related phenomenon must have been the tendency to publish under one's initials instead of one's first name. Many women must have made the decision to use their initials instead of their proper names in order to experience a scholarly authority similar to men. We may see it as an effort to disguise their gender, to have their work assessed for itself. Even if such were not their specific goals, they were following a male-dictated convention and thus effectively styling their authorship in masculine terms. Such terms are masculine precisely because they were considered "ungendered," which was what the politely feminine "Miss" was clearly meant to mark.

3. Let me offer here the most random example at hand to show the ubiquity of the tendency. While teaching from the Norton Critical edition of *Robinson Crusoe* this fall (2001) as I was writing this essay, I happened across an excerpt from a critical work written in 1966. Discussing scholarship on *Crusoe,* J. Paul Hunter defends the work of "Professor [George A.] Aitkins" while also referencing in his notes the relevant work of "Miss [Charlotte E.] Morgan." See Hunter's excerpt from *The Reluctant Pilgrim* (Baltimore: Johns Hopkins University Press, 1966), in Defoe, *Robinson Crusoe,* 267 and 267 n. 3.

4. The choice of her dissertation topic is written loosely, even allusively, across her private papers. The edition of the romance *Emaré* that she eventually produced for the Ph.D. in September 1899 was not decided on until 1898, when she wondered if she could get the approval of her examiners ("Decided to edit *Emaré* if the powers will let me, for my thesis" [letter dated 1 April 1898; Edith Rickert Papers, box 2, folder 3]). It is unclear what kind of hardship she had in finding a topic that would gain approval. Earlier, while living in London in 1896, Rickert talked to Frederick James Furnivall and N. R. Ker about possible dissertation research on the romances (journal entry, Edith Rickert Papers, box 1, folder 5). She also conjectures at one point about an edition of the (then) little read *Morte Arthur* as the subject of some future work.

5. My biographical publications on Rickert include the entry on her in Schultz and Hast, *Women Building Chicago, 1790–1990,* 747–49. I wrote a longer biographical essay on Rickert and

Manly that can be found in Damico, *Literature and Philology,* 297–311. A lengthy bibliography of Rickert's scholarly, pedagogical, and literary output can be found there. Most recently I published an essay addressing Rickert's relationship with Manly; see "Scandalous Assumptions."

6. The University of Chicago was founded in 1890 with an endowment from John D. Rockefeller. It superseded a first University of Chicago at Cottage Grove and 35th Street (located north of the present site), which closed in 1886. Opening as an undergraduate institution in 1890, it became a "real" university when it absorbed the Chicago Theological Seminary in 1892 and could then offer the doctor's degree in divinity. For a full history, see Goodspeed, *History of the University of Chicago,* as well as his *Story of the University of Chicago.*

7. Such a description of Chicago can be found in Marion Talbot's memoir, *More Than Lore* as she chronicles her move from Wellesley College to the new frontier university in 1892, 5–10. The quotation about Boston is on p. 7.

8. Because many women were not educated in secondary schools for entrance into college, most took an initial semester or year in the "preparatory department" before beginning their college course.

9. The first letter in the Rickert papers is a letter from her grandmother. After that point her letters begin with her arrival at Vassar.

10. The Rickerts clearly valued education. Edith Rickert worked at Vassar while her younger sister Ethel was a student there and seems to have helped pay for Ethel's education in this way. Margaret Rickert, her youngest sister, attended Grinnell College and the University of Chicago for her M.A. and Ph.D. Margaret eventually became an associate professor of art history at the University of Chicago; see chapter 21 in this volume.

11. Letter from her father dated 26 December 1887 (Edith Rickert Papers, box 1, folder 1). Yet in another letter written 24 October 1897 from Vassar (after Rickert's graduation) she remarks, "The college has changed very greatly since my day. It has doubled its students and almost doubled its faculty. . . . The girl who goes to college for fun, or because her brother does or because her father sends her is much less in evidence now than in '91" (Edith Rickert Papers, box 1, folder 6).

12. Solomon, *In the Company of Educated Women,* 64.

13. Edith Rickert Papers, box 1, folder 4. Cited by Phyllis Franklin, "Edith Rickert at Vassar and the University of Chicago," paper delivered before the MLA meeting, Washington, D.C., 29 December 1984, from a copy deposited in Rickert's biographical file in the University of Chicago archives.

14. Journal entry dated 30 September 1896, Edith Rickert Papers, box 1, folder 13

15. For a discussion of Rickert's romantic interests, see Scala, "Scandalous Assumptions," 30–31.

16. Edith Rickert Papers, box 1, folder 6.

17. Edith Rickert Papers, box 2, folder 3.

18. These are Rickert's own terms for the decision from a letter written by Katherine Lee Bates, dated 13 October 1908 (Edith Rickert Papers, box 1, folder 7).

19. I have discussed Rickert's status as Manly's "student" in "Scandalous Assumptions," 31.

20. This quotation comes from a letter to Robert S. Yard, editor of the *Century Magazine,* dated 27 June 1914 (Edith Rickert Papers, box 1, folder 8).

21. It would be too simplistic to attribute Rickert's status to her Vassar pedigree, as some historians of the women's colleges might. Such feminist narratives are far too interested

in promoting and valorizing the project of women's education, which blinds them to the limitations of the project itself.

22. Rickert's work at Vassar has been detailed earlier in this essay. One gets a clear sense that a future career may have lain in wait for her there had she not left in 1900. Though she never received anything like a formal offer from Wellesley College, Bates did invite her to Wellesley to meet her "Phi Sigma girls" in a note dated 21 November [1929], in which she inquires: "You have abjured teaching? You wouldn't consider a position with us?" (Edith Rickert Papers, box 1, folder 10).

23. Solomon, *In the Company of Educated Women*, xix.

24. Until 1916 Wellesley College employed an entirely female faculty. See Palmieri, *In Adamless Eden*, 261.

25. Talbot, *More Than Lore*, 67.

26. Goodspeed, *Story of the University of Chicago*, 85. This gave Chicago "more female faculty than any other contemporary coeducational institution." See Gordon, *Gender and Higher Education in the Progressive Era*, 87.

27. Edith Rickert Papers, box 3, folder 3. These entries are dated 23 December 1897 and 3 January 1898, respectively.

28. Glazer and Slater, *Unequal Colleagues*, 26.

29. Solomon, *In the Company of Educated Women*, 57. A secret narrative of Harper's reluctant admission of women is chronicled in Gordon, *Gender and Higher Education*, 87.

30. Gordon gives an excellent account of the many forces at the University of Chicago behind this action, largely supported by the mostly male faculty. She notes that "faculty discomfort with women students may have stemmed from their attraction to them. Male faculty educated in single-sex institutions, and accustomed to teaching men, had difficulty seeing women as students rather than as simply objects of romance" (*Gender and Higher Education*, 113). She points out how Robert Herrick, in his roman à clef about life at the University of Chicago, *Chimes,* dramatized such faculty attitudes toward female students through a failed romance between the fictional Professor Clavercin and the brilliant scholar Jessica Stowe. "According to Clavercin, intellectual women unsexed themselves" (113). This is a cultural assumption of "Miss Rickert's" day, as we shall see, that some women may have shared.

31. Solomon, *In the Company of Educated Women*, 60.

32. The archives at the University of Chicago (beyond the confines of Rickert's papers) must certainly contain the clues to this missing story. In 1924, for instance, Talbot joined other Chicago faculty women, Elizabeth Wallace and Edith Foster Flint, in petitioning the university's president concerning their dissatisfaction with women's limitations at the university, which included, among other things, the fact that "women did not sit on the Board of Trustees, were inadequately represented on the faculties of arts, literature, and science, and did not get promotions or salary increases at the same rate as men" (Gordon, *Gender and Higher Education*, 119). Gordon notes that other than the promotion of Sophonisba Breckinridge to full professor, these women got no response. Rickert's promotion to a regular faculty position this same year, however, might be another, unaccounted response.

33. Edith Rickert Papers, box 1, folder 13.

34. She addresses them as such in letters written from England, particularly one dated 13 April 1930 reporting on the Chaucer work she and Manly sent back to the Chaucer Laboratory from abroad (Edith Rickert Papers, box 1, folder 9).

35. Rickert would address a mixed group of her students working in Chicago in the Chaucer laboratory as her "Chaucer family" (Edith Rickert Papers, box 1, folder 9).

36. See also Rickert's "The Fraternity Idea among College Women," *Century Magazine*, 97–106, in Edith Rickert Papers, box 7, folder 10.

37. Bowman, "College Professor in America."

38. A number of the critical and historical studies cited in my essay testify to the existence and struggle of a female professoriat in the period. Such struggle and the isolation from which it ensued were responsible for the formation of the AAUP, formerly the American Association of Collegiate Women. See Talbot and Rosenberry, *History of the American Association of University Women*.

39. Talbot, *More Than Lore*, 49.

40. Talbot, *More Than Lore*, 49.

41. Talbot, *More Than Lore*, 50.

42. Talbot, *More Than Lore*, 50.

43. Eisenmann, "Costs of Partial Support," 162.

44. Introduction to Clifford, *Lone Voyagers*, 31.

45. Sizer, "'Place for a Good Woman,'" 187.

46. Eisenmann, "Costs of Partial Support," 156.

47. Glazer and Slater, *Unequal Colleagues*, 11.

48. Glazer and Slater, *Unequal Colleagues*, 11–12.

49. Leland, "Miss Rickert, Mr. Manly, and the Chaucer Laboratory," 6–8.

50. Leland, "Miss Rickert, Mr. Manly, and the Chaucer Laboratory," 7.

51. Hulbert, "Martha Edith Rickert," 558, emphasis added.

52. Hulbert, "Martha Edith Rickert," 558.

53. For such information about Rickert's manuscript expertise, see Millet, *Edith Rickert*.

54. The biographical and cultural background volumes were posthumously published by Rickert's students Martin M. Crow and Clair C. Olson as *Chaucer's World* and *The Chaucer Life-Records*.

55. For his letter to Karl Young, see Scala, "Scandalous Assumptions," 35.

56. In a piece of personal correspondence Virginia Leland wrote of her regret at not finding "any memorial articles [for Rickert] in the learned journals in the years after her death" (Letter to me dated 23 May 1996).

Select Bibliography of Works by Edith Rickert

A full bibliography of Rickert's work, including her translations, pedagogical publications, and children's books, can be found in my essay "John Matthews Manly (1865–1940) and Edith Rickert (1871–1938)." Rickert also published more than fifty short stories in various magazines and annuals.

Out of the Cypress Swamp. London: Methuen, 1902.
The Reaper. Boston: Houghton and Mifflin, 1904. Reprint, New York: Grosset and Dunlap, 1925.
"The Old English Offa Saga." *Modern Philology* 3 (5) (1905): 29–76, 321–77.
Emaré. Early English Text Society. London: Kegan Paul, Trench and Trübner, 1906; issued, 1908.
Folly. New York: Baker and Taylor, 1906.
The Golden Hawk. New York: Baker and Taylor, 1907.

The Beggar in the Heart. New York: Moffat, Yard and Co., 1909.
"John But, Messenger and Maker." *Modern Philology* 10 (1913): 107–16.
"A New Interpretation of *The Parlement of Foules.*" *Modern Philology* 18 (1920): 1–29.
"Political Propaganda and Satire in *A Midsummer Night's Dream.*" *Modern Philology* 21(1923): 53–87, 136–54.
New Methods for the Study of Literature. Chicago: University of Chicago Press, 1927. Second imprint, 1928.
Severn Woods. New York: Harcourt, Brace and Co., 1930. Published in Great Britain as *Olwen Growing* (London: Chapman and Hall, 1930).
"Some English Personal Letters of 1402." *Review of English Studies* 8 (31) (1932): 257–63.
"Chaucer at School." *Modern Philology* 29 (1932): 257–75.
"King Richard II's Books." *The Library* 4 (13) (1933): 144–47.
With John Matthews Manly. *The Text of the Canterbury Tales, Studied on the Basis of All Known Manuscripts.* 8 Vols. Chicago: University of Chicago Press, 1940.
Editor. *Chaucer's World.* New York: Columbia University Press, 1942.

Works Cited

Bowman, Claude Charleton. "The College Professor in America: An Analysis of Articles Published in the General Magazines, 1890–1938." Ph.D. diss., University of Pennsylvania, 1938.
Clifford, Geraldine Jonçich, ed. *Lone Voyagers: Academic Women in Coeducational Universities, 1870–1937.* New York: Feminist Press, CUNY, 1989.
Crow, Martin M., and Clair C. Olson, eds. *The Chaucer Life-Records.* New York: Oxford University Press, 1966.
Damico, Helen, ed. *Literature and Philology.* Vol. 2 of *Medieval Scholarship: Biographical Studies on the Formation of a Discipline.* New York: Garland, 1998.
Defoe, Daniel. *Robinson Crusoe.* Edited by Michael Shinagel. New York: Norton, 1975.
Eisenmann, Linda. "The Costs of Partial Support: One Hundred Years of Brown Graduate Women." In *The Search for Equity: Women at Brown University, 1891–1991,* edited by Polly Welts Kaufman, 155–82. Providence, R.I.: Brown University Press, 1991; distributed by the University Press of New England..
Glazer, Penina Migdal, and Miriam Slater, eds. *Unequal Colleagues: The Entrance of Women into the Professions, 1890–1940.* New Brunswick, N.J.: Rutgers University Press, 1987.
Goodspeed, Thomas. *The History of the University of Chicago.* Chicago: University of Chicago Press, 1916.
———. *The Story of the University of Chicago.* Chicago. University of Chicago Press, 1925.
Gordon, Lynn D. *Gender and Higher Education in the Progressive Era.* New Haven, Conn.: Yale University Press, 1990.
Herrick, Robert. *Chimes.* New York: Macmillan, 1926.
Hulbert, J. R. "Martha Edith Rickert." In *The Dictionary of American Biography* (New York: Scribner, 1964), 557–58.
Kaufman, Polly Welts, ed. *The Search for Equity: Women at Brown University, 1891–1991.* Providence, R.I.: Brown University Press, 1991; distributed by University Press of New England.
Leland, Virginia. "Miss Rickert, Mr. Manly, and the Chaucer Laboratory." *Chaucer Newsletter* 9 (2) (fall 1987): 6–8.
Millet, Fred. *Edith Rickert: A Memoir.* Boston: Kinnekat Press, 1940.

Palmieri, Patricia Ann. *In Adamless Eden: The Community of Women Faculty at Wellesley.* New Haven, Conn.: Yale University Press, 1995.

Scala, Elizabeth. "Edith Rickert." In *Women Building Chicago, 1790–1990: A Biographical Dictionary,* edited by Rima Lunin Schultz and Adele Hast, 747–49. Bloomington: Indiana University Press, 2001.

———. "John Matthews Manly (1865–1940) and Edith Rickert (1871–1938)." In *Literature and Philology,* edited by Helen Damico, vol. 2 of *Medieval Scholarship: Biographical Studies on the Formation of a Discipline,* 297–311. New York: Garland, 1998.

———. "Scandalous Assumptions: Edith Rickert and the Chicago Chaucer Project." *Medieval Feminist Forum* 30 (fall 2000): 27–37.

Schultz, Rima Lunin, and Adele Hast, eds. *Women Building Chicago, 1790–1990: A Biographical Dictionary.* Bloomington: Indiana University Press, 2001.

Sizer, Lyde Cullen. "'A Place for a Good Woman': The Development of Women Faculty at Brown." In *The Search for Equity: Women at Brown University, 1891–1991,* edited by Polly Welts Kaufman, 183–218. Providence, R.I.: Brown University Press, 1991; distributed by University Press of New England.

Solomon, Barbara Miller. *In the Company of Educated Women: A History of Women and Higher Education in America.* New Haven, Conn.: Yale University Press, 1985.

Talbot, Marion. *More Than Lore.* Chicago: University of Chicago Press, 1936.

Talbot, Marion, and Lois Kimball Mathews Rosenberry. *The History of the American Association of University Women.* Boston: Houghton Mifflin, 1931.

Yardley, Herbert O. *The American Black Chamber.* Indianapolis: Bobbs-Merrill, 1931.

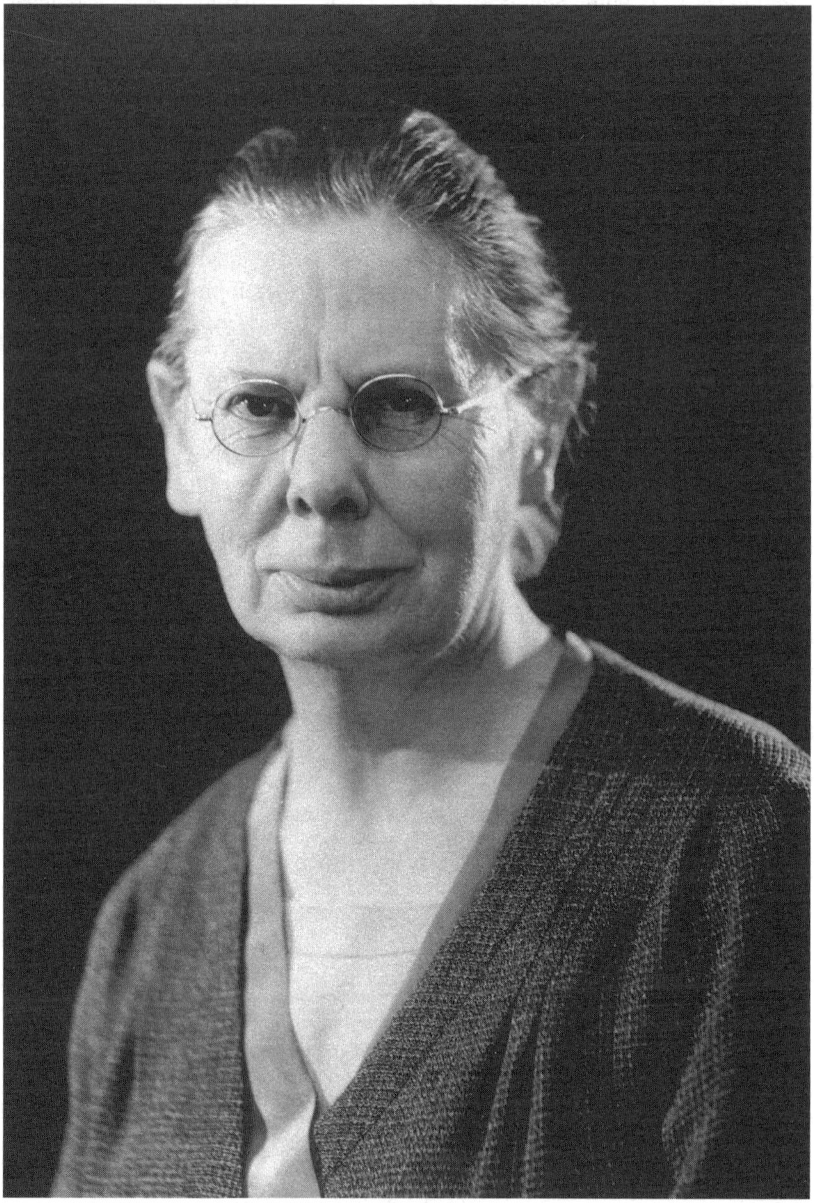

CHAPTER 11

Mildred K. Pope (1872–1956)
Anglo-Norman Scholar

ELSPETH KENNEDY

"To MILDRED KATHERINE POPE in recognition of her services as a teacher and of her contribution to learning this book is presented in gratitude, affection and homage." This dedication on the opening page of the volume of studies presented to Miss Pope would seem to express accurately the affectionate admiration in which this great scholar and teacher was held by the contributors to the book, from distinguished professors in Britain (including professors in Romance languages such as Eugène Vinaver and John Orr and the medieval historians A. J. Carlyle and E. F. Jacob) and in France (including Alfred Jeanroy, Mario Roques, and E. Hoepffner) to junior medievalists at an early stage in their careers.[1] Many of the contributors, including Eugène Vinaver and Ruth Dean (who has recently published an extremely important work on Anglo-Norman manuscripts), were her pupils.[2]

Miss Pope, daughter of the Reverend Edwin Pope, was born in 1872 at the vicarage of Paddock Wood in Kent. At the age of nine she was sent to Edgbaston High School and remained there until she was sixteen. After spending nine months in Leipzig, she taught at the Maidstone Grammar School, then at her old school at Edgbaston. In 1891 she went up to Somerville College, Oxford, as an exhibitioner and read French and German for her first year and then read French as her sole subject. In the university as a whole the Modern Language Honours School was not founded until 1903; there was at that time little teaching in Old French and French philology, but Miss Pope did get some help from Paget Toynbee of Cambridge through correspondence. In 1893 she took the honors examination in modern languages (Oxford University Examination for Women) and was placed in the first class. She remained at Somerville the following year as librarian and secretary, but in the long vacation she pursued her linguistic studies under Fritz Neumann at Heidelberg and returned to the college as modern language tutor while still keeping the position of librarian, which she held until 1899. In 1902 the college granted her a sabbatical year, which she spent in Paris working under Gaston Paris and Paul Meyer. In 1904 she was awarded the degree of doctor from the University of Paris for her thesis on Frère Angier. She held the post of modern language tutor at Somerville from 1894 to 1934, but as the only teacher of Old French for the early part of that period she taught widely across the Oxford colleges. Indeed, her learning, enthusiasm, and sympathy for beginners in research exercised an important influence on a wide circle of pupils and on the Modern Language School in general. When the First World War came in 1914, Miss Pope remained at her post but spent three of her vacations working in the war-damaged areas of France with the Anglo-American Mission of the Society of Friends.

After the First World War women were admitted as members of Oxford University; Miss Pope was given the degree of master of arts by decree and was appointed Taylorian Lecturer in French. She became university reader in French philology in 1928 and vice principal of her college in 1929. She had worked on her book *From Latin to Modern French* for a number of years before it finally appeared in 1934. Dorothy Sayers based her meticulously scholarly but gentle and caring Miss Lydgate, whose proofs of her great work on English prosody were damaged in *Gaudy Night* (first published in 1935), on her own old tutor, Miss Pope, whose complicated proofs, revised and corrected over a long period, were famous in Oxford. In the same year, 1934, Miss Pope was invited by the University of Manchester to become a visiting professor, a post which she was able to combine with her Oxford teaching. The following year, however, she left Oxford to fill the position of chair of French language and Romance philology, and for five years she was a much appreciated colleague of Eugène Vinaver. When I spent twelve years teaching in Manchester after the Second World War, I heard a great deal about her contribution to the French department in particular and to the university in general. She was the first woman professor in the university. Her teaching was much appreciated, and she achieved acceptance and respect from a wide range of colleagues. I was told that she enlivened her lectures on the *Chanson de Roland* by demonstrating with the long pole for opening and closing the windows how to use a lance. She also set up a society for the wives of members of the staff, who up until then had had little contact with the university (female members of the staff were also invited to join); she organized excursions to places like the Staffordshire potteries that were much enjoyed. She was made an honorary fellow of Somerville College in 1935, and in 1939 the University of Bordeaux conferred on her the degree of doctor honoris causa, an honor that a French university had not previously given a woman.

Before Miss Pope retired in 1939 to live with her sisters in the village of Garford, not far from Oxford, she had already played a large part in the founding of the Anglo-Norman Text Society (A.N.T.S.) and had started work on her edition of the *Romance of Horn by Thomas,* which was to represent numbers 9–10 and 12–13 in the series. However, she interrupted her work on the edition during the Second World War to work for the Red Cross Books Service for Prisoners of War and to help students in her own subject while the Oxford teaching system was under pressure during the war. The first volume of the edition came out in 1955; it consisted of an introduction with a full study of the manuscripts including a, for me, particularly interesting analysis of scribal corrections in the two main ones and an illuminating section on the classification of the manuscripts and the reasons for her choice of Cambridge University Library manuscript, Ff.6.17 as the base for her edition, with variants from the other version to be found in the Oxford manuscript (Bodleian, Douce 132). This fifty-nine-page introduction was followed by an edition of the text itself (over five thousand lines) and critical notes on the text. She did much of the work for the second volume (which appeared in 1964); it contains a descriptive introduction, explicative notes, and a glossary and was revised and completed by T. B. W. Reid, to whom Miss Pope had entrusted the completion of the work, as her failing eyesight made it difficult for her to achieve the necessary accuracy. Indeed, her deteriorating vision had caused her problems even in the first volume, published a year before her death, and Reid incorporated into the explicative notes a number of corrections to the edited text, to the variants and critical notes, and to passages in the critical introduction, referred to in the notes to let the reader know at every point exactly what stands in the base manuscript. However, Reid writes that the contents of the volume remain exactly as planned by Miss Pope and for the most part as drafted by her, and that the index of proper names, with its detailed analysis of the content of the poem, is entirely her own work. Miss Pope has provided an even more detailed study of the work edited than is usually found even in this excellent series. The Anglo-Norman poem is a particularly interesting work in its own right, quite apart from the problem of its precise relationship with the rather different Middle English versions of the story. It is part of a trilogy of which it is the only branch to survive. It relates the adventures of Horn; he is son of Aaluf, who himself eventually discovers that he is son of the emperor of Germany. Horn as a child, after the death of his father, is put into a rudderless boat that drifts to Brittany. There the king's daughter, Rigmel, falls in love with him. As a result he is banished by her father, takes refuge in Ireland, but returns to save Rigmel from marriage to a man she dislikes. While he is attempting to recover his kingdom and find his mother, Rigmel is abducted, and he has to return again to save her. Miss Pope brings out clearly the combination of elements from epic and romance. She suggests that the work retains the form of the chanson de geste, modified by innovations introduced in the later twelfth century (the use of the twelve-syllable line, of rhyme, and of enjambment) and by an individual treatment of the caesura. However, the epic themes are interwoven with those of romance. The emphasis is still very much on the love of the woman for the man, but there are signs of the influence of Ovid, typical of romance from the *roman d'antiquité* onward. The allusions in the poem are to epics, not to romance, but Miss Pope puts forward the interesting idea that the emphasis in *Horn* on the defense of chastity and fidelity may be partly a reaction against the emphasis on adulterous love in a romance such as the *Tristan* of another Thomas, also Anglo-Norman, of which a recent edition and translation by Stewart Gregory was published by Garland in 1991 as *Tristran / Thomas of Britain*. Miss Pope tended to support a date of about 1170 for the *Romance of Horn*. The opening and closing lines would indicate a poem composed at the end of the author's professional career; lines 5231–33 suggest that his son was already a proficient poet. She presumed that the formative period for the author fell in the last years of Henry I and in the turmoil of Stephen's reign. Reid suggests that the two volumes will prove a valuable contribution to the study not only of the *Romance of Horn* but of Anglo-Norman and Western French in general.

However, this last work of Miss Pope to be published, important as it was in terms of worldwide influence, was surpassed by her seminal book *From Latin to Modern French with a Special Study of Anglo-Norman*. First published in 1934, it is still an indispensable book of reference for French phonology and morphology from Vulgar Latin to Early Modern French. It sets the development of French from Latin through the centuries, within the historical context, but above all studies it in relation to the physical and psychological processes involved. I propose to analyze the book in some detail because it is Miss Pope's insistence on examining the development of French in all its detailed complexity that makes it such a fundamental contribution to medieval scholarship.

In part 1 ("The External History of the Language"), chapter 1 gives a general account of how the difference between the very conservative language of law and letters (classical Latin) and that of the everyday life of the people (Vulgar Latin) came to diverge so markedly throughout the Roman Empire. The possible local influences are also examined. Chapter 2 deals with the formation of French from the end of the fifth century up to and including the sixteenth century; it divides this into periods somewhat different from the traditional ones of earlier scholars. Period I extends roughly from the end of the fifth century to the end of the eleventh (from the Germanic invasions to the First Crusade). Miss Pope subdivided it into two: Gallo-Roman, from the end of the fifth century up to the appearance of the Strasbourg Oaths of 842, in which, for the first time, the difference between Latin and a separate vernacular derived from it was recognized in written form; and Early Old French, from the Strasbourg Oaths to the First Crusade. Period II extends from the end of the eleventh century to the beginning of the seventeenth and can also be subdivided: Later Old French (Old French ii) from the end of the eleventh century to the end of the thirteenth century; and Middle French comprising roughly the fourteenth, fifteenth, and sixteenth centuries. In Period I the effect of Frankish invasion and of the marked breath stress associated with it on the development of the sounds of Latin as spoken in the northern half of Gaul led to changes greater in accented and unaccented vowels and in the development of consonants than in the other Romance languages and in the language of the southern part of Gaul where langue d'oc was spoken. In Period II the rhythm of the language changed to a smoother flow: the diphthongs were gradually leveled, a strong stress within the individual word weakened, stress on the final syllable of a group of words became more important, and words were run together with a consequent effect on final consonants. These changes are set within a social and historical context in part 1, chapters 2 and 3, and also within the framework of the expansion of French abroad.

Part 2 deals at length and in great detail with phonology. The first chapter provides a phonetic introduction, examining the formation of those sounds that are or have been employed in French and Latin and the main processes and predisposing conditions of sound change. It classifies the sounds and examines the role of stress (prominence given to a syllable) and the difference between word stress and sentence stress. The influence of speech on sounds is explored, and the different characteristics of sound change and sound substitution are explained. The last section deals with the various causes of sound changes. The second chapter provides a survey of sound changes in Late Latin, Period I and Period II, with a final section on modern French, where sound changes slowed down under the influence of education and printing. Chapter 3 deals with isolative changes. The vowel system was affected strongly in the early period of the language, and isolative change induced a more forward pronunciation of vowels. Miss Pope suggests that Celtic influence may have played a part in this movement. In chapter 4 she shows how the position of consonants within a word could also exercise considerable influence on their development. Chapter 5 examines the influence of the expiratory word stress, whose intensity under Frankish influence considerably increased, but its position was unchanged. It remained strong in Period I but diminished steadily in Period II until, by the end of the seventeenth century, French had become a language of almost level word stress. Chapter 6 surveys the palatalization of consonants. Chapter 7 examines the voicing and opening of consonants, chapter 8 the reduction of consonantal groups, chapter 9 the development of *l* sounds and *r* sounds, chapter 10 the influence of palatal sounds on vowels, chapter 11 the influence exercised by nasal consonants on vowels, chapter 12 the influence of labial sounds on vowels, chapter 13 the influence exercised by *l* sounds and *r* sounds on vowels, chapter 14 the leveling of oral diphthongs and triphthongs, chapter 15 vowel lengthening in Middle French, and chapter 16 the quality of vowels in Later Old and Middle French. Chapter 17 moves to a different area, syntactical phonetics, that is, the influence exercised on the pronunciation of words by their position and use in the sentence. Chapter 18 examines the treatment of loan words from Greek, Frankish, Latin, and Italian. These may be borrowed from a spoken source, where the pronunciation current at the time of the borrowing and the accentuation and sound system of both the languages concerned must be taken into account. If the word is borrowed from a written source, the starting point is the pronunciation accorded to that word in the language of the people borrowing it. The final chapter in part 2 consists of sound tables that show how vowels and consonants developed from Gallo-Roman to modern French according to their context and degree of stress, with clear references to the section in which this is discussed. As an undergraduate I already found these tables with their references very useful when I was trying to work out the probable pronunciation of an Old or Middle French text and when I was trying to link up with the physical processes involved.

Part 3 deals with orthography and its varying relationship with pronunciation from Gallo-Roman up to modern French. Some splendid quotations from the sixteenth- and seventeenth-century grammarians are included, and reference is made to the influence of the early dictionaries on the development of orthography.

Part 4 deals with morphology, the modification that flexional systems undergo. An introductory chapter examines the role of contamination, the associative process that modifies words or forms in isolation—for example, blending two partially remembered words—and analogy, the associative process that affects forms arranged in grammatical systems and is a creative process. Chapter 2 deals with the declension system in relation to substantives and adjectives and shows how the remodeling of the Latin system was the result not only of sound change but of psychological factors such as the desire for greater intelligibility, manifested, for example, in the increased use of prepositions and the growing inability to handle a complicated and subtle flexional system. The various parts of speech are handled in turn. The chapter on verbs, where the changes in the conjugation system throughout the centuries are studied in all their complexity, is long and detailed and ends with very useful tables of the conjugation of verbs in Old French.

Part 5 provides an extensive and detailed study of Anglo-Norman, an area of research that formed a very significant part of Miss Pope's general contribution to medieval scholarship. The introductory chapter opens with a section on the external history of Anglo-Norman, on the areas in which it was most used, and on its continuing importance as the legal language up to the sixteenth century. The period of development in the use of a dialect of French, a living local form of speech in England, extends up to about the middle of the thirteenth century. In this first period, for fifty or sixty years after the Norman Conquest, early Anglo-Norman differed little from Western French or neighboring dialects (William did not draw all his men from Normandy; some came from further north). However, in the later twelfth and early thirteenth century, when Anglo-Norman was used by a wider range of people not necessarily of Western French descent, it began to be modified quite rapidly under the influence of English speech habits and relative isolation from France. Nevertheless, there are often interesting parallels with Continental dialects or even with Francien, the speech of the Isle de France that gradually gained a dominant position. By the thirteenth century Anglo-Norman was sometimes a subject for jest, but so were some of the northern dialects (see pp. 23–24). Even quite early, Anglo-Norman began to show the combination of conservatism and neologism that is usually characteristic of a language no longer in continuous close contact with its parent stock. Anglo-Norman was based on the *speech* of western France, as French as a written language was still comparatively unimportant, and there was no strong orthographic tradition. Nevertheless, people from England might well study in Paris and so be influenced by the speech of that region. The development of spoken French in England, therefore, is complicated to analyze; the difficulty is increased, Miss Pope emphasizes, by the instability of Anglo-Norman spelling, so that neglect to distinguish between spelling and pronunciation has vitiated much of the early work done on the subject, as has the unsatisfactory nature of many of the early editions of texts. Chapter 2 deals with phonology. It starts with a characterization of the French introduced: Western with a Northern element. It places Anglo-Norman within the context of sound changes in process in Old French. The characteristics of Anglo-Norman that may be ascribed to conservatism in pronunciation through the relative isolation of insular speech are listed. However, English speech habits were the most important factor in the growing instability of Anglo-Norman pronunciation, and this element is studied in detail in a comparison of Old French and Middle English sound systems. Chapter 3 deals with the "unstable and motley" character of Anglo-Norman orthography, which includes archaisms and varying scribal tradition; it examines the often "semi-phonetic" attempts to represent the influence of sound change on the value of symbols. Chapter 4 is concerned with declension in Anglo-Norman. It points out that the declension system of substantives and adjectives, already threatened in Western French in the twelfth century, was early shaken by contact with the English system, and its disintegration in relation to substantives and adjectives was completed in the thirteenth century by the sound changes of the time, in particular by the frequent effacement of final *s* and mute *e*. Among the pronouns English influence was relatively slight. Chapter 5 deals with the conjugation system. In earlier Anglo-Norman there is a great variety of forms, which leads to an instability of tradition. In later Anglo-Norman the outstanding characteristics are a wealth of analogical forms, simplifying tendencies, and an ever-growing lack of discrimination in the use of variant forms. Middle English tended to accelerate disintegration and exercised little positive influence here. Useful tables demonstrate the evolution of declension and conjugation systems in Anglo-Norman, with lists of texts and manuscripts cited. This is still, and will probably for some time remain, an essential guide to Anglo-Norman, although important new research is being carried out in this area.

This groundbreaking survey of Anglo-Norman is followed by an appendix: "Conspectus of Dialectal Traits Mainly of the Later Old French Period." More work has been done on this subject in France and elsewhere since the appearance of Miss Pope's book; indeed, her survey pointed toward the need for such research. However, as a World War II undergraduate from 1945 to 1947 and in my postgraduate work on an edition of a text to be found in a wide range of manuscripts, I found Miss Pope's survey of dialects extraordinarily useful, and I think that I was typical of many. The book is completed by an excellent series of indexes that enable an editor like myself to relate the particular form to be found in a manuscript to the general development of the language at that particular date. The tables of sound change are very useful, but Miss Pope always makes clear that they need to be linked to the effect on the evolution of a language such as French of the ways that the human mouth and mind works, of the complex processes of analogy, and of various factors that can affect the presentation of the spoken language in written form.

If, or indeed perhaps because, *From Latin to Modern French* was many years in the making, its importance was early recognized, as the number of editions, the distinguished list of contributors to Miss Pope's festschrift, and the wording of its dedication to her reveal. When I went to Paris for my first year's work on my doctoral thesis in 1947 and was sent by Mario Roques to the distinguished medievalist Lucien Foulet for advice, *From Latin to Modern French* was out of print. Lucien Foulet did not own a copy and told me that he had had to read it in a library straight through like a novel. Fortunately, I was able to bring him a battered secondhand copy, and I will never forget his delight in receiving it. Over seventy-five years after its publication, it is still being used by scholars working on Old and Middle French.

Miss Pope had the humility of a truly great scholar, as I discovered when I was still only an undergraduate at Somerville. I was supposed to be promising, and as an honorary fellow of the college, she expressed a desire to talk to me. I had come up after four and a half years war service and was in my final year in the very cold winter of 1947. I had been skating on the Cherwell to keep fit while working very hard for "Schools," the Oxford final examinations. I had managed to hitch a lift from a lorry driver (an old "Desert Rat" who had fought under Montgomery in North Africa) and was very conscious of a wet seat and a missing button. Miss Pope asked me about my particular interests in philology. I said that I enjoyed studying syntax, and she replied that she knew a little about phonology and morphology but almost nothing about syntax. It was evident to me that this was not false modesty and that she really meant it, but her "little" knowledge was greater than that of anyone else. She then said that she hoped I had been having some skating. I confessed that I had just come back from skating up the Cherwell. She said, "I do hope I didn't interrupt," and then she gave a graphic account of skating on the Thames (or rather the Isis) in 1898. The second and last time that I saw her must have been in 1955, the year before her death in September 1956, when I drove Eugène Vinaver down from Manchester to visit her. It was an unforgettable occasion to see those two great medieval scholars together, so different in their areas of excellence but sharing so many memories as close colleagues in Oxford and Manchester. Vinaver's respect and affection for Miss Pope were shared by all those who contributed to her festschrift, but as an "academic grandchild" of hers, I would like to end with a tribute to her by one of her old pupils, printed by the college in one of the annual reports sent to Old Somervillians. Mrs. Phillips (Margaret Mann, undergraduate at Somerville, 1924–27) wrote the following:

> For many of us "M. K. P." was the most powerful influence of our Oxford years; and how lucky for us that was! She stood for the true spirit of scholarship with its integrity, its search for truth, its pride and its humility. It was what we had come to Oxford to find, and in her, our tutor, our dreams of a world of scholarship were more than realised.

But it was not only in intellectual things that she had that profound influence upon us; what was startling was the combination of that austere singleness of purpose with the warmest, cheerfullest, most human understanding of our needs, our characters, our minds and hearts.

M. K. P. had the faculty of making you feel two things: first, that she was more interested in *you,* the visitor of the moment, than in anyone else in the world; secondly, that you were capable of much greater things than you had imagined possible. Her selflessness was such that all the powers of a keen mind and a gay spirit were free to inspire and encourage the young. So it was no wonder that generations of Somervillians thought of her with such gratitude, or that the University of Manchester, after debating solemnly over the doubtful experiment of appointing a woman Professor found itself only too anxious to prolong as far as possible her tenure of the Chair. I think we all felt the same about her: "the Pope" was so genuinely herself that everything she touched seemed to turn more real and yet more manageable, whether it were Old French syntax or the everyday problems of our lives.[3]

Notes

1. See *Studies Presented to M. K. Pope*. I will from now on refer to the great scholar and subject of this chapter as "Miss Pope," as that was what my generation used for both her and her major work, *From Latin to Modern French with Especial Consideration of Anglo-Norman.*
2. Dean with Boulton, *Anglo-Norman Literature.*
3. Mann, *Somerville College Report and Supplement.*

Select Bibliography of Works by Mildred K. Pope

Etude sur la langue du frère Angier suivie d'un glossaire de ses poèmes. (Thèse présentée à la Faculté des lettres de Paris pour le doctorat de l'université.) Paris, 1903.

With Eleanor C. Lodge. *Life of the Black Prince by the Herald of Sir John Chandos: Edited from the Manuscript in Worcester College with Linguistic and Historical Notes.* Oxford: Oxford University Press, 1910.

"The *Tractatus Orthographiae* of T. H., Parisii Studentis." *Modern Language Review* 5 (1910): 185–93.

"Four Chansons de Geste. A Study in Old French Epic Versification." *Modern Language Review* 8 (1913): 352–67; 9 (1914): 41–52; 10 (1915): 310–19

"A Note on the Dialect of Beroul's *Tristan* and a Conjecture." *Modern Language Review* 8 (1913): 189–92.

"The Dialect of *Gormont and Isembart.*" *Modern Language Review* 13 (1918): 335–38.

"The So-Called 'Irrational' Negative in Anglo-Norman Concessive Sentences." *Modern Language Review* 15 (1920).

"A Clue to the Dialect of the *Chanson de Roland?*" In *Mélanges de linguistique et de littérature offerts à M. Alfred Jeanroy par ses élèves et ses amis.* Paris: E. Droz, 1928. 411–13.

From Latin to Modern French with Especial Consideration of Anglo-Norman. Manchester: Manchester University Press, 1934.

"Notes on Some Ambiguous Passages in the *Chanson de Roland.*" *Medium Aevum* 5 (1936): 1–10.

Editor with T. A. Jenkins, J.-M. Manly, and J. G. Wright. *La Sainte Resurrection, from the Paris and Canterbury Manuscripts.* Oxford: Basil Blackwell for the Anglo-Norman Text Society, 1943.

"Notes on the Vocabulary of the Romances of *Horn* and *Rimel.*" In *Mélanges Hoepffner.* Paris: Les Belles Lettres, 1949.

Variant Readings in Three Anglo-Norman Poems." In *Studies Presented in French Languages, Literature, and History,* edited by R. L. Graeme Ritchie. Cambridge: Cambridge University Press: 1949.

Editor. *The Romance of Horn by Thomas.* Vol. 1. Oxford: Basil Blackwell for the Anglo-Norman Text Society, 1955.

Editor. *The Romance of Horn by Thomas.* Vol. 2. Revised and completed by T. B. W. Reid. Oxford: Basil Blackwell for the Anglo-Norman Text Society, 1964.

Pope also regularly published reviews in *Modern Language Review.*

Works Cited

Dean, Ruth J., with Maureen B. M. Boulton. *Anglo-Norman Literature: A Guide to Texts and Manuscripts.* London: Anglo-Norman Text Society, 1999.

Mann, Margaret (Mrs. Phillips). *Somerville College Report and Supplement* (1956): 23.

Studies Presented to M. K. Pope. Manchester: University of Manchester Press, 1939.

CHAPTER 12

The Justices' Chronicler
Bertha Haven Putnam (1872–1960)

DAVID DAY

BERTHA HAVEN PUTNAM was in her own time and remains today one of the foremost historians of local English judicial administration in the later Middle Ages. Her status in medieval English legal history is especially remarkable because it was a field dominated prior to World War II by some of the greatest names of legal historiography—Frederic Maitland, Theodore Plucknett, Paul Vinogradoff—all of them male. And yet Putnam knew many of these men, worked with some of them, and gained their enthusiastic treatment as a colleague and an equal, all at a time when both academia and the law itself were overwhelmingly dominated by men. Looking at her scholarly work, one is impressed by her achievements in this field but not surprised at her success—all of her work is meticulously and painstakingly supported by the original sources for medieval English legal history, which she knew as well or better than any scholar who had worked with them before or has since. In her years as a teacher at Mount Holyoke, she also built up a reputation as a rigorous and yet well regarded teacher of medieval history, while participating in that school's transition from a women's seminary to a respected college and scholarly institution. Her professional achievements as both a scholar and an educator importantly contributed to the successful integration of women into medieval studies in the first half of the twentieth century.

Putnam was born in New York City in 1872, the daughter of George Haven Putnam and Rebecca Kettel (Shepard) Putnam. Her father was the son of George Palmer Putnam, founder of the publishing firm that would eventually be known as G. P. Putnam's Sons. George Haven Putnam served in the Union army during the Civil War, and after G. P. Putnam's death became president of the company. Her

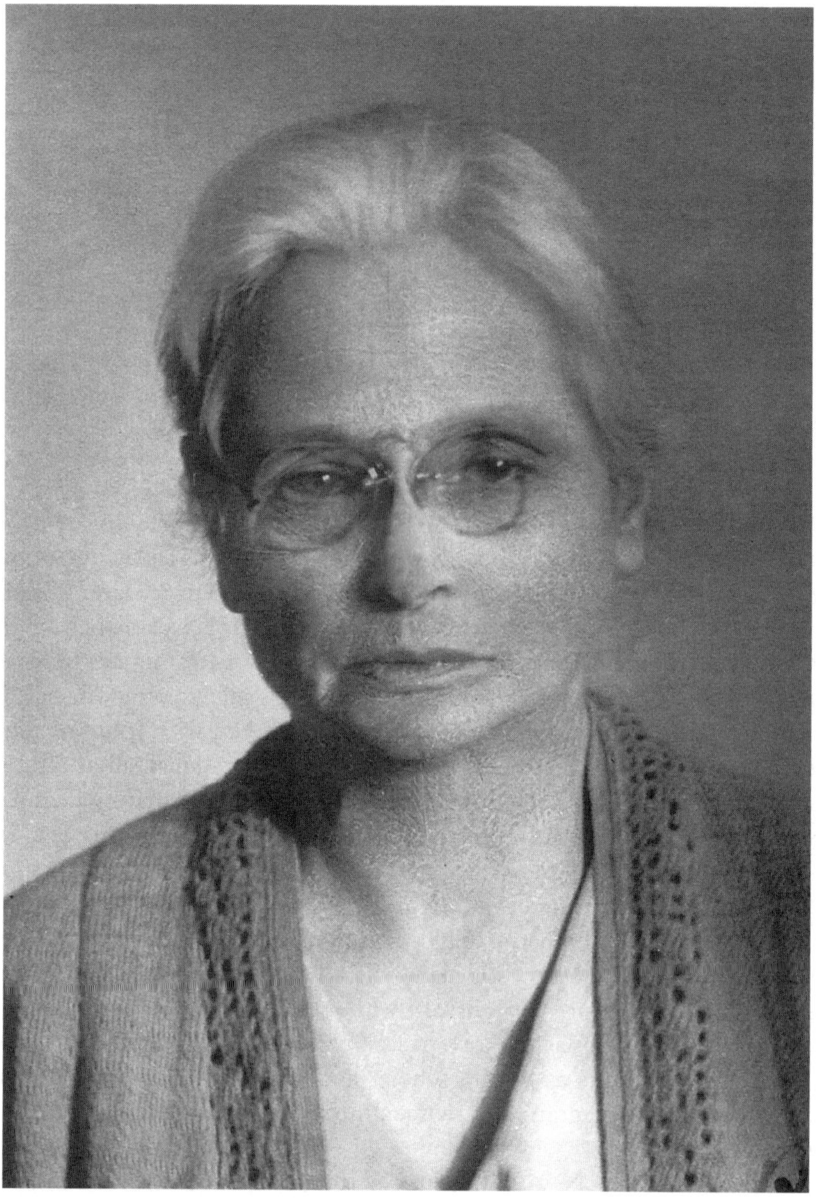

mother attended Antioch College but left to serve as a nurse in a military hospital. Before her marriage she taught Greek and Latin at Worcester High School in Massachusetts. Both Putnam's mother and father were active socially and philanthropically in New York City in the later nineteenth century, her father backing various reform movements and her mother working to have kindergartens placed into city schools and to improve women's working conditions. Putnam attended private girls' schools in New York and eventually went on to Bryn Mawr, receiving an A.B. degree in 1893. She then taught Latin at the Bryn Mawr School in Baltimore before returning home to live with her father after her mother's death in 1895. While back in New York, she taught for several years at the Brearley School and also attended graduate school at Columbia, taking her doctorate there in 1908.

Putnam's dissertation, published in 1908 as *The Enforcement of the Statutes of Laborers during the First Decade after the Black Death,* was an in-depth consideration of the enforcement and effectiveness of the labor regulations passed by Edward III's government following the initial outbreak of the plague in England in 1348. She chose her topic initially less because of its potential significance as legal history than for its social and economic interest as an attempt to legally regulate the mobility and freedom of labor.[1] However, the research required her to work extensively with manuscript court and assize rolls in the Public Records Office in London, and it was here that Putnam began the series of scholarly labors that were to make her so well known in her field. While working in London, she identified among assize and indictment manuscripts session records of proceedings before the justices of laborers, the magistrates specially created to enforce the plague-related labor legislation of Edward III.[2] These documents form the basis of much of Putnam's argument in her dissertation, and her basic method here—a meticulous attention and devotion to the actual records of legal administration, which often led to the discovery of archival discrepancies that alone would be enough to assure her stature among medieval historians—would be deployed repeatedly in her research over the next forty years.

Putnam's argument in her dissertation is interesting and worth considering in some detail not only for its intrinsic interest but for what it tells us about her scholarly attitudes and approach. She answers two questions about the Statutes of Laborers that scholars still have not fully settled: Was the legislation a reactionary attempt to "freeze" feudal labor practices when they were being decimated by the phenomenal death rate? And was it effective? Putnam examines the enforcement of the statutes both by the specially established justices of laborers' commissions and the old local courts (hundred, seigniorial, municipal, etc.) and by the central courts (King's Bench and Common Pleas), as well as the role of the King's Council in enacting the original Ordinance of Laborers in 1349. She relies primarily on court rolls and other documents detailing legal cases but also considers statutory evidence to answer very detailed questions about the personnel enforcing the statutes, their organization and salaries, and also the disposition of fines levied. Putnam notes that those criticizing the statutes as reactionary usually point to the way they set wage rates that were too low and discount the attempts of the statute also to regulate prices.[3] She responds to these criticisms with a considerable degree of insight and sympathy for the situation actually facing the legislators: it was essentially an emergency in which both wages and price rates had become completely dislocated by the crisis of the plague (*The Enforcement of the Statutes of Laborers during the First Decade after the Black Death*, 219). She also notes that the laissez-faire economic ideas prevalent in her own day (and interestingly enough, here at the start of the twenty-first century as well) simply did not exist in the mid-fourteenth century: "In an age when the idea of a competitive price had not yet been evolved and when for normal conditions regulation by local authorities of both wages and prices was the accepted custom, it was natural and equitable that in an emergency the central government should exert itself to the utmost to check the evil" (220). Here Putnam displays what would become a notable feature of her scholarly work's interpretive side: an admirable effort to avoid judging medieval legislation and legal practices according to twentieth-century views of the role government ought (or ought not) to play in regulating social functions and practices. She was essentially a modest and cautious scholar who rarely if ever sought to judge the Middle Ages on the terms of her own day and time.

After taking her doctorate Putnam became an instructor in history at Mount Holyoke and was promoted to assistant professor in 1912 and full professor in 1924. She continued at Mount Holyoke until her retirement in 1937. Putnam came to Mount Holyoke during the tenure of Mary Emma Woolley as president (1901–37), and she participated in Woolley's efforts to raise the academic stature of Mount Holyoke in particular and women's higher education generally. Woolley sought to turn Mount Holyoke "into a scholarly institution comparable to men's colleges. She expanded the faculty and sought the best scholars to replace teachers who retired. Whenever possible she chose women."[4] Putnam's colleagues remembered her as part of a coterie of formidable women scholars who dominated faculty life at Mount Holyoke during the first four decades of the last century—Ada Snell, Ellen Ellis, Nellie Neilson, and others. One remembered Putnam and other Bryn Mawr graduates sitting together in the front row at faculty meetings and dominating the discussion throughout by right of age and scholarly prestige: "They always sat together down in front; they made a solid phalanx down there, just like a wall. And in a way we felt it was a wall, the younger ones as we sat in back."[5] Another faculty member recalled the way that Putnam dominated the dining arrangements at the Mount Holyoke Faculty House: "I know that the Putnam-Snell table in particular was often hilarious and noisily argumentative, too noisy, I sometimes felt," even though Putnam was always "most generous in sharing with lesser lights the various well-known medieval scholars who visited her."[6] While at Mount Holyoke, Putnam was esteemed as one of the top scholars working there.[7]

At Mount Holyoke, Putnam was predominantly responsible for teaching medieval history, a job she shared with Nellie Neilson, another noted woman medieval scholar. As she did in her scholarly work, Putnam approached her lectures methodically and logically, valuing background and context to understand the complexities of medieval social and economic history.[8] However, she was not in any sense dull, illustrating her lectures with interesting anecdotes and, outside the classroom, talking enthusiastically about her research and telling "vivid historical anecdotes gathered in her summers abroad."[9] She was also quite innovative in her methods of examination; one former student recalled how she dismayed her class by turning "Mount Holyoke College into a feudal society for an examination question—and just ruined [them]!"[10] Another recalled how Putnam's class on fourteenth-century economic history brought out parallels between medieval labor relations and those in the twentieth century.[11]

All through her teaching career and after it, Putnam continued to research local medieval English judicial and legislative administration, mostly at the Public Records Office in London on her summers off from Mount Holyoke. While working there on her dissertation, she had delved deeply into the records dealing with the administration of the Statute of Laborers and so become interested in the origins and functions of the justices of the peace, who held first partial and then eventually most of the responsibility for enforcing that law. She returned to the justices of the peace in her subsequent scholarship, and almost all of her work after her dissertation related to that subject in some way. It is difficult to overstate the importance of Putnam's work on the documentary evidence concerning the justices of the peace. When she began work in the Public Records Office in the first decade of the twentieth century, most of the materials dealing with the justices of the peace were in manuscript form, some of it miscataloged. In the course of more than thirty years of intensive research there, she identified misclassified assize and indictment rolls concerning both the justices of laborers and the keepers and justices of the peace, edited many of them, and brought them out in a series of scholarly editions and compilations.[12] These works have value not just because they made these records accessible for subsequent generations of legal scholars but also for Putnam's extensive and authoritative historical introductions to the documents themselves.

In 1924 Putnam published her earliest book-length contribution to this work, *Early Treatises on the Practice of the Justices of the Peace in the Fifteenth and Sixteenth Centuries*. Here she expressed her conviction about the necessity of cataloging and classifying documentary evidence on the justices of the peace: "Until the abundant material, most of it in manuscript, has been thoroughly examined, it is useless to attempt a complete account of their [the justices of the peace's] powers and their activities before 1500" (1). As the title suggests, this early volume enumerates, describes, and discusses the various documentary sources from the fifteenth and sixteenth centuries for studying the justices of the peace, by which time the first printed treatises dealing with justice of the peace qualifications, practices, and procedures were starting to appear. Putnam's later work in the 1930s would present and critique the documentary evidence for the development of the justices of the peace at various points in their history prior to 1500, an area of study that she largely made her own personal scholarly domain prior to the Second World War. *Kent Keepers of the Peace, 1316–1317* (1933) presented two assize roles covering keeper of the peace activities in Kent following the Great Eyre of Kent of 1313 to 1314. *Yorkshire Sessions of the Peace, 1361–1364* (1939) is a similar detailed study of specific assize rolls for northern England compiled during the height of Edward III's reign.

As their titles suggest, both these works represent Putnam's efforts to edit and publish detailed local evidence of justice of the peace activities. Her greatest work in this area, though, was undoubtedly *Proceedings before the Justices of the Peace in the Fourteenth and Fifteenth Centuries, Edward III to Richard III* (1938). Here Putnam notes that to effectively study the development of justice of the peace practice and power prior to 1500, there must be a detailed consideration of the role justices of the peace played in superceding earlier forms of local legal administration (e.g., manorial and hundred courts) and also in applying a uniform standard of statutory justice throughout the realm (xv). She notes that to do this some comparative method considering similarities and differences in justice of the peace practice over the fourteenth and fifteenth centuries is needed, and that her edition partly fulfills this need, drawing as it does from court rolls detailing justice of the peace procedure and jurisdiction that come from twelve counties, distributed in time over the subject period (xv). Again Putnam uses her close consideration of the manuscript sources to rectify misapprehensions about actual justice of the peace court practice, staffing, and jurisdiction. She notes that the justices of the peace have often been seen as steadily acquiring more and more power over the centuries, until they emerged as the predominant means of local judicial and governmental administration from the sixteenth century on. Contrary to this view, her study of the sources led her to conclude that "there is plenty of evidence to show that their competitors were numerous and formidable, and that there was nothing inevitable about the continuous existence of the office of the justice of the peace" (cxxx). She also notes that their powers shifted variously in the fourteenth and fifteenth centuries: they gradually acquired powers as justices over the reign of Edward III, until by the time of Richard II they had become criminal judges and administrators of economic legislation (among them the Statute of Laborers) (cxxx). She notes that they did not always figure as allies of the crown against the feudal nobility, instead being favored by "the commons, at any rate by the country gentry, from whose ranks many of them were drawn" (cxxx). They lost ground as criminal judges in the political turmoil of the fifteenth century but gained power as local administrators of various statutory enactments so that by the time of Henry VII they were starting to take on the roles in local government with which they are characteristically associated from the sixteenth through the early twentieth centuries.

Proceedings before the Justices of the Peace was in many ways Putnam's crowning scholarly achievement. The Medieval Academy of America awarded her their first Haskins Medal for it.[13] From the 1930s on, this volume and her other editorial efforts on the justice of the peace rolls generated a certain scholarly momentum in which other historians, many of them former students of Putnam, continued her work on these neglected documents.[14] As a result of her truly pioneering efforts in this area, the amount of material available to legal scholars for study has been tremendously increased; it is difficult to imagine what the field would be like had it not been for Putnam's work. The importance of that work was recognized by her contemporaries: in addition to receiving the Haskins Medal for her *Proceedings* volume, Putnam was elected a fellow of the Medieval Academy in 1949. Legal scholars and institutions also recognized and valued her contributions to their field and honored her for it. In 1938 she became the first woman nonlawyer to be awarded a research grant by Harvard Law School, and in 1945 Smith College awarded her an honorary LL.D.

By the late 1930s Putnam's scholarly and teaching career was drawing to a close. She retired from Mount Holyoke in 1937 but lectured for another year at Bryn Mawr before finally withdrawing from teaching in 1938. In 1940 she suffered an attack of shingles that left her partly blind. Despite her disability, she continued her scholarly work throughout the 1940s. Her final book, *The Place in Legal History of Sir William Shareshull, Chief Justice of the King's Bench, 1350–1361,* came out in 1950. It considers the life, career, and reputation of Sir William Shareshull, probably the most important jurist of Edward III's reign. Putnam explains that her interest in Shareshull grew from the repeated references to him in documents she found while researching the justices of the peace. As she did in her dissertation, Putnam acts as something of a righter of historical wrongs here, ending up championing Shareshull against a local tradition of prejudice against him as a venal judge. Shareshull is probably best known to students of English literature from a rare, specific reference to him by Wastoure in "Wynnere and Wastoure":

> And thies beryns on the bynches with [bonets] one lofte
> That bene knowen and kydde for clerkes of the beste,
> Als gude als Arestotle or Austyn the wyse,
> That alle shent were those schalkes, and Scharshull itwiste,
> Þat saide I prikkede with powere his pese to distourbe![15]

Wastoure's hostile alignment of Shareshull with the forces of Wynnere interestingly fits in well with Putnam's analysis of the documentation of his life, which shows him "on the side of law and order, of right doing, of economic and social stability" (148). She dismisses the charges of Staffordshire writers that he was venal or dishonest, noting all they have shown is that he came from rather humble origins and that he did very well for himself as a lawyer; no dishonesty is necessary to explain his success (148). She defends him against charges that stipends such as he received from the Knights Hospitalers for representing them might be unethical according to modern standards; she explains that they were quite acceptable, given fourteenth-century practices of legal remuneration (148). Putnam thus again shows a tendency to judge historical actions and personalities as much as possible according to the standards and practices of their own day.

The bulk of Putnam's final book, though, is concerned less with Shareshull's personal biography and reputation than with an assessment of his importance to legal developments in the mid-fourteenth century. She finds that he was basically a social conservative and, from his enforcement of contemporary legislation, including the Statute of Laborers, "that he wished to keep laborers in their place, that he favoured a strong central government, that he meant by all possible methods to discourage corruption of officials and to check violence, whether committed by members of the upper or lower classes" (103). With characteristic caution Putnam resists the temptation to formulate the expressions of Shareshull and his legal contemporaries into a general support of fourteenth-century ideas that the common law was somehow aligned with "natural" or "divine" law (104). She does, though, find Shareshull refusing to enforce law rigidly according to its letter, preferring to support positions that not only had legal backing but also accorded to "reason" (105). She notes his extension of the appellate and original jurisdiction (especially over economic legislation such as the Statute of Laborers) of the King's Bench during his tenure as chief justice from 1350 to 1361 (110–11). Finally, she finds that, because of his place on the king's council, first as a sergeant and then later as a justice, he was responsible for helping to frame some of the important economic legislation of the mid-fourteenth century, especially the Statute of Laborers (68–72).

Putnam died of arteriosclerosis in 1960, and she was widely recognized and eulogized at the time in publications as diverse as the London *Times* and *Speculum*. There is little evidence in the record of her life that she ever thought deeply about her position as a woman working in a field that was, when she started her career, overwhelmingly dominated by men. But it is difficult to imagine that she had no appreciation of how her contributions to legal and medieval history helped to open up that field for women, simply by the force of their quality and success. Certainly her male colleagues in medieval English legal history appreciated the impressive nature of her scholarship, acknowledging many times in their prefaces and commentaries to her work the debt that historians owed her. In his "Commentary on the Indictments" to her *Proceedings before the Justices of the Peace,* Theodore Plucknett noted that "Professor Putnam has placed historians under immense obligations in opening up an entirely new field of study, in discovering and listing a large quantity of material whose existence was hitherto unknown, in devising a technique of editing it, and in settling the main lines of the history of the mediaeval justice of the peace" (clx–clxi). In training at Mount Holyoke a generation of female medieval historians who would follow her and continue her work, she again helped integrate women firmly into the field of medieval legal historiography. Both as a scholar and as a teacher she was without a doubt one of the most important woman medievalists working in the first half of the twentieth century.

Notes

1. Hastings and Kimball, "Two Distinguished Medievalists," 145.
2. Hastings and Kimball, "Two Distinguished Medievalists," 145.

3. Putnam, *Enforcement of the Statutes of Laborers during the First Decade after the Black Death*, 219.
4. Hastings and Kimball, "Two Distinguished Medievalists," 146.
5. Viola F. Barnes, interview by Elizabeth Green.
6. Anna J. Mill, interview by Elizabeth Green.
7. Ellen Deborah Ellis, interview by Elizabeth Green.
8. Hastings and Kimball, "Two Distinguished Medievalists," 158.
9. Hastings and Kimball, "Two Distinguished Medievalists," 158.
10. Christianna Smith, interview by Elizabeth Green.
11. Sydney Robertson McLean, interview by Elizabeth Green.
12. Hastings and Kimball, "Two Distinguished Medievalists," 145.
13. Hastings and Kimball, "Two Distinguished Medievalists," 154.
14. Hastings and Kimball, "Two Distinguished Medievalists," 155.
15. Trigg, *Wynnere and Wastoure*, lines 314–18.

Select Bibliography of Works by Bertha Haven Putnam

The Enforcement of the Statutes of Laborers during the First Decade after the Black Death. Studies in History, Economics and Public Law 32. New York: Columbia University Press, 1908.

Early Treatises on the Practice of the Justices of the Peace in the Fifteenth and Sixteenth Centuries. Oxford Studies in Social and Legal History 7. Edited by Paul Vinogradoff. 1924. Reprint, New York: Octagon Books, 1974.

"The Transformation of the Keepers of the Peace into the Justices of the Peace, 1327–1380." *Transactions of the Royal Historical Society*, 4th ser., 12 (1929): 19–48.

Kent Keepers of the Peace, 1316–1317. Kent Records, vol. 13. Kent Archaeological Society. Ashford: Printed for the Kent Archaeology Society Records Branch by Headley brothers, 1933.

Proceedings before the Justices of the Peace in the Fourteenth and Fifteenth Centuries, Edward III to Richard III. Edited by Theodore F. T. Plucknett. Publications of the Ames Foundation. London: Spottiswoode, Ballantyne & Co., 1938.

Yorkshire Sessions of the Peace, 1361–1364. Records Series. Vol. C. Yorkshire Archaeological Society, 1939.

"Shire Officials: Keepers of the Peace and Justices of the Peace." In *The English Government at Work, 1327–1336*, edited by James F. Willard and William A. Morris, vol. 2. Cambridge: Mediaeval Academy of America, 1940.

"Chief Justice Shareshull and the Economic and Legal Codes of 1351–1352." *University of Toronto Law Journal* 5 (1944): 251–81.

"Sixteenth Century Treatises for Justices of the Peace." *University of Toronto Law Journal* 7 (1947): 137–61.

The Place in Legal History of Sir William Shareshull, Chief Justice of the King's Bench. 1950. Reprint, Holmes Beach, Fla: Wm. W. Gaunt & Sons, 1986.

Works Cited

Barnes, Viola F. Interview by Elizabeth Green, 9, 10 March 1972. Transcript in "Mount Holyoke in the Twentieth Century," Mount Holyoke Archives, Mount Holyoke College, South Hadley, Mass.

Ellis, Ellen Deborah. Interview by Elizabeth Green, November 1971–March 1972. Transcript in "Mount Holyoke in the Twentieth Century," Mount Holyoke Archives, Mount Holyoke College, South Hadley, Mass.

Hastings, Margaret, and Elisabeth Kimball. "Two Distinguished Medievalists: Nellie Neilson and Bertha Haven Putnam." *Journal of British Studies* 18 (1979): 142–59.

McLean, Sydney Robertson. Interview by Elizabeth Green, 23 February 1972. Transcript in "Mount Holyoke in the Twentieth Century," Mount Holyoke Archives, Mount Holyoke College, South Hadley, Mass.

Mill, Anna J. Interview by Elizabeth Green, 16–18 June 1971. Transcript in "Mount Holyoke in the Twentieth Century," Mount Holyoke Archives, Mount Holyoke College, South Hadley, Mass.

"Putnam, Bertha Haven." In *American Women Historians, 1700s–1990s*. Ed. Jennifer Scanlon and Sharon Cosner. Westport, Conn.: Greenwood Press, 1996.

"Putnam, Bertha Haven." In *National Cyclopaedia of American Biography*, vol. 43. New York: James T. White, 1961.

"Putnam, Bertha Haven." In *Notable American Women, the Modern Period*. Ed. Barbara Sicherman and Carol Hurd Green. Cambridge: Harvard University Press, 1980.

Smith, Christianna. Interview by Elizabeth Green, 23 February 1972. Transcript in "Mount Holyoke in the Twentieth Century," Mount Holyoke Archives, Mount Holyoke College, South Hadley, Mass.

Trigg, Stephanie, ed. *Wynnere and Wastoure*. Early English Text Society, no. 297. Oxford: Oxford University Press, 1990.

CHAPTER 13

Nellie Neilson (1873–1947)
A Historian of "Wit, Whimsy, and Sheer Poetry"

ANNE REIBER DEWINDT

WHEN HUGH LLOYD-JONES wrote his essay on Jane Ellen Harrison, the Cambridge classicist, he raised a question well worth considering.[1] To what extent should a biographical tribute to a scholar concern itself with her personal life? Do we need to know that Nellie Neilson could cut a perfect figure eight with her skates on an ice-covered Lower lake at the Mount Holyoke campus, or that she loved hiking in the Adirondack Mountains so much that she once described her cabin there as "the only place that seems like home to me"?[2] Does it help our understanding to realize that Neilson's strong blue eyes and prematurely white hair attracted the notice of students as well as colleagues? Or that her exaggerated fondness for small pet dogs also inspired affection as well as ridicule?

In the end I have found that my attempts to breathe life into a tribute to this hardworking medieval historian have inevitably evoked an intriguing personality as well as an industrious scholar and enthusiastic teacher who became the first woman to be president of the American Historical Association (AHA). My colleagues who have joined the subsequent generations of scholars interested in unearthing—Neilson called it spade work, in fact—details of the day-to-day life of the medieval villager will, I believe, also want to learn about her personality as well as about her professional achievements and accompanying struggles.

The Green and Pleasant Land

England was to Neilson the "green and pleasant land" that she loved.[3] Her commitment to English history is unsurprising given her apprenticeship at Bryn Mawr and

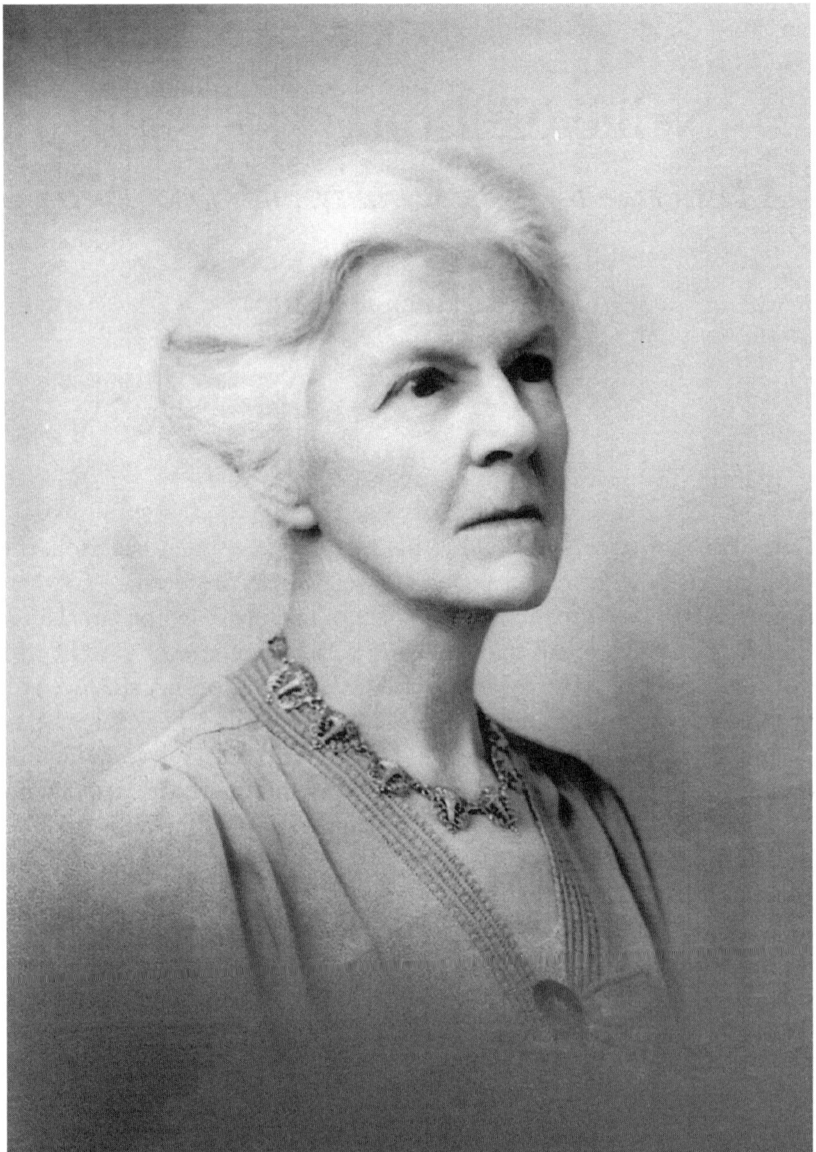

the late-nineteenth-century fascination with English constitutional history. Late in life, when Neilson wrote a tribute to her mentor, Charles Andrews, she remembered the seminar room at Bryn Mawr where she "found a great love for early English history which [had] never lessened."[4]

Beginning with her participation in seminars at Oxford, Neilson also developed strong ties with English colleagues. The English medievalist Helen Cam wrote a tribute to Neilson on the occasion of her death, pointing out that "her researches and her friendships spanned the Atlantic" and that "few can have embodied our personal and academic alliance [between England and the United States] more completely or more subtly than Nellie Neilson."[5]

But there were personal reasons as well for Neilson's interest in English history. Raised in Philadelphia and the product of Quaker schools, Neilson was a devout Episcopalian with a great love for the Book of Common Prayer, "which she had known as a girl and always loved."[6] Nellie was the oldest of six children. Her father was a mining engineer described as "comfortably affluent, but not wealthy."[7] The family apparently could afford to maintain close contacts with English relatives, and later in life her brother William kept a flat in Piccadilly.[8]

The Atlantic was therefore both a bridge and a barrier. Over the years Neilson made more than fifteen trips to England to pursue her research, not allowing even World War I to interfere with her voyages to the "promised land."[9] Indeed, she worked the night shift as a volunteer during that war, helping to run a buffet at Victoria Station for the "convenience of the troops."[10] Her last trip to England was interrupted by the outbreak of World War II, and Neilson left that country for the last time most reluctantly in the fall of 1939. Referring to her niece and nephew who were living in England and working in munitions factories, Neilson wrote, "It all seems incredible, but since it has to be, anyone who loves England is lucky to be in the thick of it."[11]

The Manor as the Vill of South Hadley

Neilson's career at Mount Holyoke College began in 1902 shortly after the president, Mary Woolley, had written a letter to the president of the American Historical Association seeking a woman "of scholarship, of teaching power, of attractive personality and of Christian character!"[12] In October 2001 Norma Adams, a former student of Nellie Neilson, and her successor as head of the history department, was still living across the street from the Mount Holyoke campus. Adams remembers Neilson primarily for her love of research and her personal charm. There is no doubt that Dr. Neilson's long tenure as professor and history department head made a lasting impression on Mount Holyoke College.

Among the documents in the college archives, the rave reviews of her teaching abilities so outnumbered the criticisms that one former colleague expected a shocked reaction when she mockingly depicted Neilson as an "actress manqué."[13] Students' letters reflect the power of Neilson's personality and the impact of her whimsical sense of humor. Very early in Neilson's Mount Holyoke career one student wrote about an incident with a "weegee" board when students conspired to tease Neilson by shaking the dinner table while presumably consulting spirits: "We wouldn't dare do such things if Miss Neilson didn't seem more like a girl than a Ph.D."[14] Norma Adams also remembered Neilson's "power to make the thing concrete . . . the manor as the vill of South Hadley or the manor of Lord Skinner. Prospect was always the wooded hill where pigs fed on acorns and faculty house was 'the barn where the better cows were kept.'"[15]

Her popularity must also have been due, in part, to her willingness to spend time outside the classroom with students. She founded the Outing Club in 1921 to promote student involvement in outdoor sports and even taught some of the students to waltz.[16] Once, in the spring of 1929, Neilson invited a group of history majors to her house in the evening to meet Charles Andrews, the scholar who had directed her own Ph.D. work. She wrote to Andrews of her students, "I am fond of them, and I like to have them have their chance at the best in history and historians."[17]

Perhaps the most memorable tribute, however, comes from Margaret Hastings, a student of Neilson who also became an important medieval scholar. Hastings described Neilson's lectures as lucid "works of art based on sound scholarship and full of wit, whimsy and sheer poetry. Students found themselves compelled to become scholars whether they would or no."[18]

After her student career at Bryn Mawr, where she received her B.A., M.A., and Ph.D., Neilson could not move directly into teaching history at the college level because of the lack of job opportunities for women. Instead, she reluctantly accepted an offer from the president of Bryn Mawr for a job in the "essay department" for a salary of seven hundred dollars and the requirement that she live on campus. Neilson was hesitant about the offer, noting in a letter, "I might find the duties of the position interfering too seriously with my own work in history . . . having made historical research a definite object."[19] Ever loyal to her vocation, Neilson resigned the Bryn Mawr post by 1902 and planned to return to England and "her historical investigations" if she did not find another job.[20]

Three years into her career at Mount Holyoke College Neilson was promoted to professor and became chair of the Department of History and Political Science in 1905, earning a salary by 1910 of sixteen hundred dollars.[21] She exercised a great deal of curricular power and had strong feelings about the direction the department should take. Neilson explained that she wanted to bring the "scientific treatment of history" to her students and that she hoped to inspire a "love of history for its own sake." Rather than seeing the study of history as a pragmatic enterprise, she even disapproved of attempts to use history in the quest for explanations of later events. She wrote that "our subject is primarily to be studied for itself and for no pragmatic object." So, while supporting the need for courses in modern political history and political science because of the global politics of the 1920s, her history department remained committed to heavy concentration on medieval courses and required a full year's work in either English or American constitutional history.[22]

The history department grew quickly under Neilson's leadership. By 1911 there were six members of the department, and eighteen courses were offered to a student body grown by that time to 754.[23] It was a rather homogeneous group; only one man was hired (in 1932), and only one of the women on the faculty was married (in 1931)—and she taught part time.[24]

Always interested in research herself, Neilson was eager to have the opportunity to guide her students into the adventure of more sophisticated historical endeavors than are usually possible at the undergraduate level. As a result she encouraged the development of a master's program and an honor's program for the history department, and most master's students did their theses with her. Margaret Hastings observed that Neilson turned students loose on a set of documents, only to criticize their work after it was done. In Hastings's estimation, "For most of us the method worked well."[25] A total of eighteen Mount Holyoke students had received doctorates in history or political science by 1937.[26]

In 1939 Neilson was forced to retire before she was ready to do so. In a letter written during the summer of her last visit to England, Neilson revealed her feelings about the sudden change of college policy. "Having reached the fatal age of sixty-five I have been retired from my teaching post. The funeral services are now over, but it is a trying time."[27] Elsewhere she wrote, "I went out then to my great regret and inconvenience, financially considered."[28] It must have been painful as well to see reaction against her leadership taking the form of a reduction in the term of office for chairs of the history department to three years and to see the political science department split off from the history department.

Later, after Neilson's election to the presidency of the American Historical Association, the department held a dinner in her honor. Guests included not only family and colleagues from Mount Holyoke but also the history department chairs of nearby colleges and universities.[29] During the fall after this college celebration of her distinguished career, Neilson was persuaded, either through financial exigency or for the simple pleasure of teaching once again, to give a series of lectures on nursing practice in ancient and medieval times at the Columbia Medical Center in New York. This she did in spite of her failing health.[30] The last reference to Neilson in the Mount Holyoke history department records reveals a determined scholar, ignoring her health problems as best she could. "Miss Neilson, with some understandable groaning, is in the midst of the difficult labors of proofreading her forthcoming book."[31]

Research—A Definite Object

The roots of Neilson's academic achievements reach deep into the nineteenth century. Having been trained in philology, she was nourished by Charles Andrews on a profound respect for the German tradition of scientific history.[32] By the end of her career she was raising issues that foreshadowed the work of scholars three and four generations younger than she. Just as her love for English history and her dedication to archival work inspired her to cross the Atlantic regularly, so her intellectual achievements bridged the historiographical traditions of two centuries. In her later work she contributed to the new social history by concentrating on the living conditions of the lower orders, attributing to villagers a degree of agency not usually afforded "mere" serfs. In a laudatory review of H. S. Bennett's *Life on the English Manor,* she wrote that the historian's goal is a "presentation which makes the medieval peasant a real part of humanity and kin to ourselves."[33] Perhaps her affinity for discovering the details of day-to-day existence explains in part Helen Cam's observation that Neilson's career illustrated "the special aptitude that the woman historian has for economic history."[34]

In her compact little book *Medieval Agrarian Economy,* designed for use by undergraduates, Neilson recognized the power of local custom and suggested that the manor court might be the "expression of local society rather than of the lord's arbitrary will."[35] Indeed, Cam praised her work by citing her 1928 paper delivered at the AHA annual conference as representing the "first frontal attack on the standardized conception of 'The Manor'."[36]

Her main goal, however, was to present students with a meticulous "slice of life" image of a peasant lifestyle and mind-set. Detailed descriptions of smoke-filled cottages shared with pigs and fowl; depictions of the peasants' tunics, caps, and long hose; portrayals of week-work on the lord's demesne relieved periodically by cock fighting and church ales—these all culminate in her insistence that "there is an essential unity in all humanity, and we should be wrong in ascribing to the medieval peasant inevitable stupidity and stolidness."[37] Her own love of the countryside inspired an idealized vision of a peasant lifestyle "close to nature." The result was a very romantic vision as can be seen by her decision to seal the final chapter with a quotation from G. G. Coulton's *The Medieval Village.* "The sights, the sounds, the scents of English country life in the Middle Ages were all that they are pictured in William Morris's romances, and a hundred times sweeter than prose or verse will ever tell."

Neilson's careful study of manorial accounts, extents, and cartularies covered the English landscape from the East Midlands and Lincolnshire to Warwickshire, North Wales, and Kent, giving her an intimate acquaintance with the great variety of local customs. Her first publication was her Bryn Mawr dissertation, "Economic Conditions on the Manors of Ramsey Abbey," in which she revealed, for the benefit of later scholars who mined the same lode, the wealth of information available in the Ramsey cartulary, extents, and accounts. E. P. Cheyney's review of Neilson's next publication, "Customary Rents," (based largely on her Ramsey research) praised her "tireless industry" and "insight and power of comparison."[38]

Into the 1920s Neilson continued to provide her colleagues with editions of manuscripts valuable for the study of peasant life and began as well to make suggestions as to the significance of these sources to a study of the relationship between local custom and the development of a national system of common law. In 1920 she published her edition of the *Terrier of Fleet* for the British Academy in which she shed light on a complex system of intercommoning in the fenland where village-level management of marsh resources was overseen by local jurors articulating and continually reshaping local custom to meet the needs of a pastoral economy.

Work on the *Cartulary and Terrier of the Priory of Bilsington,* where she focused on customs peculiar to the weald and marshland of Kent, led to her submission to the *Harvard Law Review* of the first article it published by a woman: "Custom and Common Law in Kent." Later, at the end of the decade, when she published her article "English Manorial Forms," she made a plea for the recognition of variety and used her work as an opportunity to raise questions rather than offer generalizations about life on the English medieval manor. The questions she raised are fascinating to read with the advantage of a modern scholar's hindsight. For example, she appreciated the value of aerial photographs to the study of medieval settlement patterns. She raised questions about the differences between lay lordship and the management practices of large ecclesiastical estates and noted the importance of hired labor on the manor. She also called attention to manorial courts and wondered about the nature of those meetings of villagers and to what extent they were capable of independent action. Her interests thus combined what we would today classify as historical geography and legal history as well as economic and social history.

During the 1930s she edited another text of interest to economic and social historians, what she described as a "beautiful manuscript" in the cathedral library of Canterbury, "The Domesday Monachorum." But she also began to enter the domain of the legal historian in what she called a "venture into the unknown ... undertaken with trepidation."[39] For the Selden Society she edited some contemporary attempts to record the legal arguments and opinions of judges and sergeants speaking in the court of Common Pleas—yearbooks from the reigns of Edward IV and Henry VI. This project was her least successful, and she was criticized at length for her choice of manuscripts and for some of her translations, though praised for her industry and for her identification of many of the cases referred to in those yearbooks.[40] H. G. Richardson's review stung Neilson, and she was unable to forget it.[41]

It was during the last decade of her life that Neilson reached her largest audience and made her greatest impact on the profession. She contributed chapters to Willard and Morris's volume *The English Government at Work* and to Clapham and Powers's *The Cambridge Economic History of Europe.* She delivered her presidential address to the American Historical Association, "The Early Pattern of the Common Law," and completed her edition of the *Stoneleigh Leger Book.* In this final collection she had the opportunity to summarize the achievements of a life's work, and in that process she identified herself more closely with the fields of social and constitutional history than with what today might qualify more specifically as economic history.

Indeed, her contribution to the *Cambridge Economic History of Europe,* a project undertaken by an admired friend, Eileen Power, revels in the physical description of village buildings and furnishings, field systems, crops, farming methods, the products of village craftsmen, and most importantly to her, the vast variety of regional variations in rural customs. She was much more interested in providing a "slice of life" montage than in wrestling with statistics. Definitions, institutions, and landlord-tenant relations interested her much more than impersonal economic forces; unfortunately, she died before there was a sophisticated interest in demography. Yet her awareness of economic factors never left her, and while claiming that the thirteenth century was hard on the peasant in some ways, she also questioned the relevance of legal status to peasant well-being, pointing out that standard of living would have seemed more relevant. She rejected the old fashioned image of a "static, self-contained medieval village" as she acknowledged the important role played by markets in the lives of villagers.[42]

Nowhere was Nellie Neilson more passionate, however, than in her defense of the study of medieval English legal history, which she expressed during her AHA presidential address. That passion arose partly, of course, from its historical context of wartime struggle. But it also arose from a firm conviction that English common law had provided the English-speaking world—indeed, the world at large—with a model for the peaceful evolution of a political system that protects civil liberties and promotes self government. Inspired by what she and many others saw as the wartime struggle for Americans "pledged against . . . tyranny," Neilson insisted that "one can still read legal records with profit to see how the free governments of the English-speaking peoples have come into being."[43]

Even among the Men

Nellie Neilson had acquired this opportunity to plead on behalf of English legal history only after a ten-year-long campaign succeeded in getting a woman elected president of the American Historical Association. She was not an ambitious woman, and this was not an office she coveted. In a letter to Andrews she confided, "The AHA business is an honour, of course, and I appreciate it deeply, but it has a terrifying side."[44]

In fact, she had been invited by Charles Homer Haskins to participate in an AHA program as early as 1912, when she was thirty-nine years old, and she refused. She wrote, "I don't speak well at all."[45] But Neilson certainly attended AHA meetings. She appeared in 1920, for example, at the Washington, D.C., conference along with her Mount Holyoke colleague Bertha Putnam.[46] By 1922 Mary Williams of Goucher College was on the AHA Council and suggested Nellie Neilson, among several women, be a candidate to succeed her. Neilson was elected, at the age of forty-nine; Jacqueline Goggin implies that her candidacy was perhaps more attractive to many male voters than that of a younger woman, who was more likely to be an active feminist.[47]

The decade of the 1920s was Neilson's most productive in terms of scholarly publications and also her most active period as a participant in professional organizations. She was elected to the Royal Historical Society in 1923, the same year she finally agreed to speak at an AHA session and delivered her paper "Customs and Common Law in Kent."[48] In the summer of 1925, during one of her research trips to

London, she served as member of the Anglo-American Historical Committee at the Institute of Historical Research at the University of London.[49] The next year she was elected the only female fellow of the Medieval Academy and won a place on the AHA executive council as well.

Neilson was no longer reluctant to participate in AHA programs by this time and delivered her paper "English Manorial Forms" at the AHA annual conference the following winter. She later chaired a session, "Feudalism and Serfdom," in 1930 at Boston and delivered a paper in Toronto on English plea rolls at the AHA conference.

Neilson was first suggested as a possible candidate for president of the AHA in 1932, and the following year Mary Williams began active lobbying by organizing a letter-writing campaign among women historians.[50] Williams wrote to the female member of the nominating committee, suggesting that there had been more than one AHA president who "has been far less of a scholar than Nellie Neilson."[51] In another letter to a male colleague sympathetic to the cause, Williams wrote, "I take it that you are working too, especially with the brethren, who are more in need of salvation in this matter than the sisters; for the sisters are not likely to think that the sky will fall if a woman presides over the AHA."[52] Meanwhile there was considerable opposition to the female candidates, attributed to "anti-feminine bias."[53]

By 1934 the chair of the nominating committee was a woman, and she was now willing to promote Neilson's candidacy, even as Neilson's own colleague at Mount Holyoke, Viola Barnes, was not supportive. But as opposition to her presidency persisted, respect for her scholarship grew, and Neilson was appointed to the editorial board of the *American Historical Review,* a position she occupied until 1940. Perhaps because of her influence, nine women subsequently published articles in the *Review* between 1935 and 1940.[54]

By the end of the 1930s Neilson was on the ballot for first vice president of the AHA and was third vice president of the Medieval Academy. (She served on the advisory board of *Speculum* and was president of the Council of Fellows of the Medieval Academy when she died in 1947.)[55] When she won the AHA election, however, her reaction was mixed. Concerned about her health and distressed that she had been forced to retire earlier than her finances permitted, Neilson was hardly in a celebratory mood by the time the election results came in. In a letter to Charles Andrews, Neilson wrote, "Thank you for your kind words about the latter: I shall dread it horribly but a woman could not possibly refuse it,—and anyway perhaps I shall be dead first."[56]

For reasons such as this, her student Margaret Hastings later wrote that Neilson's election as president of the AHA in 1942 came "too late for full enjoyment of the honor."[57] With her customary humility Neilson was concerned about her presidential address and was feeling the burdens of ill health. She wrote to Andrews: "It seems to me that my mental processes, such as they are, just go out of commission when I think of that address!"[58]

Neilson invited her brother and a friend to the AHA dinner, where she gave her address, "The Early Pattern of the Common Law."[59] There was not to be another woman president of the AHA until 1985.

Somehow Neilson learned to function in the male world of professional historians. She was the only woman among thirty-three fellows of the Medieval Academy in 1926 and one of only two women elected to the AHA executive council that same year. She coped, I think, by developing two rather different personalities. She was able to play a "male" role at Mount Holyoke College, much like the undergraduates during her days at Bryn Mawr who would give the leading male roles in their theatrical productions to the juniors and seniors.[60] As head of the history department she was a firm defender of strongly held beliefs about the direction that department should take. Out in the broader world she maintained working relationships with her male colleagues by playing a different role. While serving on the editorial board of the *American Historical Review,* she wrote to that journal's managing editor, "Please give me criticism and advice. I feel very inadequate!"[61]

Charles Andrews saw both sides to this complex personality. She wrote to him about her first meeting with the English scholar T. F. Tout, describing him as "terrifying to a shy person like me. . . . People laugh when I say I am shy, but you know better!"[62] It is not easy to reconcile the image created by these letters to her male colleagues with her local Mount Holyoke reputation revealed by the following anecdote. A fellow researcher at the Mount Holyoke College archives told me a story about Nellie Neilson's confrontation with a bear while she was hiking in the Adirondack Mountains. It was the bear who took flight.

Describing Neilson and others of her generation, Margaret Hastings wrote that while they were "not feminists in the meaning of the current women's rights movement, they believed that women as scholars should be judged by the same standards as men and accorded recognition only if they earned it."[63] Such judgment was, indeed, passed down by her Bryn Mawr mentor. "She has fully lived up to the expectations of that training, becoming a distinguished scholar—perhaps the most distinguished *even among the men in this country* in the field of English economic history."[64] In any case, we do know that Neilson was very conscious of her role as a female historian and that she was a member of "a group of pioneers who were gaining recognition for women in scholarship."[65]

NOTES

I want to thank Edwin DeWindt and my colleagues Carol Chadwick and Sarah Stever for reading drafts of this essay and providing many helpful comments and suggestions. I also want to thank Patricia Albright, Archives Librarian at Mount Holyoke College, for her very generous assistance and Judith M. Bennett, a Mount Holyoke alumna, for her help and support.

1. Lloyd-Jones, "Jane Ellen Harrison," 29.
2. N. Neilson, letter to Blakely, 12 August 1927, Bertha E. Blakely Papers, Archives and Special Collections, Mount Holyoke College, South Hadley, Mass. (hereafter: MHA).
3. Adams, "Nellie Neilson," 153.

4. Quoted in Vaugn, "Enigma," 187. This article is particularly useful for its analysis of the scholarly debt Nelson owed Andrews.

5. Cam, "Nellie Neilson, Scholar," 155.

6. Ibid.

7. Hastings and Kimball, "Two Distinguished Medievalists," 144.

8. Neilson, letter to Evangeline Andrews, 27 April 1923, Charles M. Andrews Papers, Manuscripts and Archives, Yale University Library [hereafter: YU].

9. Judson, *Breaking the Barrier,* 82, 84.

10. Dorothy Foster, letter to her father, 25 July 1915, Dorothy Foster papers, MHA.

11. N. Neilson, letter to H. Stuart Moore, 6 February 1940, Nellie Neilson Correspondence, Selden Society Papers, Manuscripts Department, Cambridge University Library [hereafter: CU].

12. Mary E. Woolley Correspondence, 21 March 1902, J. F. Jameson Papers, file 1786, box 136, Manuscripts Division, Library of Congress [hereafter: LC].

13. "Mount Holyoke in the Twentieth Century," vol. 2, transcript of interview of Sydney Robertson McLean, 1972, p. 8, MHA.

14. Edna Ferry, letter to her mother, 18 January 1903, Edna Ferry papers, MHA.

15. Adams, "Nellie Neilson, Scholar," 154.

16. Judson, *Breaking the Barrier,* 20, 27.

17. N. Neilson, letter to Andrews, 13 May 1929, Charles M. Andrews papers, box 27, folder 324, YU.

18. Hastings and Kimball, "Two Distinguished Medievalists," 158.

19. N. Neilson, letter to M. Carey Thomas, 19 March 1900, and M. Carey Thomas to N. Neilson, April 1900, M. Carey Thomas Papers, Bryn Mawr College Library [hereafter: BM].

20. M. Carey Thomas, letter to Presidents Seeley, Taylor, and Woolley, 2 May 1902, M. Carey Thomas Papers, BM.

21. Horowitz, *Alma Mater,* 234.

22. Neilson, "History and the Aims of the Department," 2.

23. MHA, Record Group RG 18.19: http://www.mtholyoke.edu/lits/library/arch/col/rg18si.htm.

24. History Department Records, 1931, MHA.

25. Hastings and Kimball, "Two Distinguished Medievalists," 158.

26. History Department Records, series A, file 1, MHA.

27. N. Neilson, letter to H. Stuart Moore, 17 June 1939, Nellie Neilson Correspondence, Selden Society Papers, CU.

28. N. Neilson, letter to Charles Andrews, 15 January 1941, Charles M. Andrews papers, box 42, folder 456, YU.

29. Department report by Norma Adams, 1 June 1943, History Department Records, series B, MHA.

30. N. Neilson, faculty biographical file, press release, 28 December 1943, MHA.

31. Department report by chairman, Frederick H. Cramer, 1946, History Department Records, series B, MHA.

32. Vaugn, "Enigma," 189–91.

33. N. Neilson, review of *Life on the English Manor,* by H. S. Bennett, *American Historical Review* 43 (1938): 838.

34. Cam, "Nellie Neilson, Scholar," 156.

35. Neilson, *Medieval Agrarian Economy*, 36.

36. Cam, "Nellie Neilson, Scholar," 155.

37. Neilson, *Medieval Agrarian Economy*, 92–93.

38. E. P. Cheyney, review of *Customary Rents*, by N. Neilson, *American Historical Review* 16 (1911): 803.

39. Neilson, introduction to "Domesday Monarchum."

40. H. G. Richardson, review of *Year Books of Edward IV; 10 Edward IV and 49 Henry VI, A.D. 1470, The Law Quarterly Review* 48 (1932): 111–16.

41. Referring to her unfinished edition of another yearbook: "Please do anything that is convenient with my beginnings. I am sorry that it happened this way. I had not the heart to take it up again for some time after Mr. Richardson's demolition of me and then the war came and it seemed better to come home" (N. Neilson to H. Stuart Moore, 4 March 1947, Neilson Correspondence, Selden Society Papers, CU).

42. Neilson, "Medieval Agrarian Society in Its Prime: England," 1, 465.

43. Neilson, "Early Pattern of the Common Law," 212.

44. N. Neilson, letter to Charles Andrews, 10 February 1943, Charles M. Andrews Papers, box 43, folder 471, YU.

45. N. Neilson, letter to Charles H. Haskins, 20 October 1912, Papers of the American Historical Association, box 245, file "Conference on Mediaeval History, 1912," LC.

46. Register of Attendance, Papers of the American Historical Association, box 466, LC. Judith Williams of Wellesley and Mary W. Williams of Goucher were also present.

47. Goggin, "Challenging," 793.

48. N. Neilson, letter to Secretary of the Royal Historical Society, 4 March 1923, Royal Historical Society Library, University of London.

49. Minutes of the Anglo-American Historical Conference, 7 July 1925, J. F. Jameson papers, box 17, LC.

50. Goggin, "Challenging," 770, 797.

51. Goggin, "Challenging," 798.

52. Mary W. Williams, letter to Conyers Read, 5 April 1933, Papers of the American Historical Association, box 88, LC.

53. Goggin, "Challenging," 798.

54. Goggin, "Challenging," 800 n.

55. Gras, Lunt, and Strayer, "Nellie Neilson," 417–18.

56. N. Neilson, letter to Charles Andrews, 15 January 1941, Charles M. Andrews papers, box 42, folder 456, YU.

57. Hastings and Kimball, "Two Distinguished Medievalists," 151.

58. N. Neilson, letter to Charles Andrews, 10 February 1943. And yet her address is still appreciated. Bennett's "Medievalism and Feminism" ends with a quotation therefrom.

59. N. Neilson, letter to Guy Stanton Ford, 5 November 1943, box 132, Papers of the American Historical Association, LC.

60. Horowitz, *Alma Mater*, 162; Glazer and Slater, *Unequal Colleagues*, 46. Glazer and Slater describe Neilson and Putnam as "superperformers in a separatist institution," and point out that men were often ignored when they attempted to speak at faculty meetings (6).

61. N. Neilson, letter to H. E. Bourne, 1 February 1935, Papers of the American Historical Association, box 324, LC.

62. N. Neilson, letter to Charles Andrews, 6 September 1927, Charles M. Andrews Papers, box 26, folder 307, YU. Neilson referred to the Andrews family as her "second family" (N. Neilson, letter to Evangeline Andrews, 5 June 1945, Charles M. Andrews Papers, box 44, folder 483, YU).

63. Hastings and Kimball, "Two Distinguished Medievalists," 159.

64. Charles M. Andrews, "Bryn Mawr and the Past," *Bryn Mawr Alumnae Bulletin* (July 1943): 11, cited by Vaugn, "Enigma," 212; emphasis is mine.

65. Adams, "Nellie Neilson, 1873–1947," 154. Neilson's term of office at the AHA was hardly a major turning point for women in the profession. Mount Holyoke College's new male president preferred to hire young male faculty after 1938, and women made no major gains throughout the 1940s and 1950s. By 1939 only half of the female history Ph.D.s had found academic employment. During the 1930s only 16 percent of women historians were full professors, and in 1970 there were none (Judson, *Breaking the Barrier*, 75–77; Goggin, "Challenging," 777, 802.

Select Bibliography of Works by Nellie Neilson

"Boon-Services on the Estates of Ramsey Abbey." *American Historical Review* 2 (1897): 213–24.

Economic Conditions on the Manors of Ramsey Abbey. Philadelphia: Sherman and Co., 1899.

Customary Rents. Oxford Studies in Social and Legal History 2, ed. Paul Vinogradoff. Oxford: Oxford University Press, 1910.

"Rents and Services." In *Survey of the Honour of Denbigh, 1334.* British Academy Records of the Social and Economic History of England and Wales, 1, ed. Paul Vinogradoff and F. Morgan. London: Oxford University Press, 1914.

"History and the Aims of the Department." *Mount Holyoke Alumnae Quarterly* 4:1 (April 1920): 1–3.

A Terrier of Fleet, Lincolnshire. British Academy Records of the Social and Economic History of England and Wales, 4, ed. N. Neilson. London: Oxford University Press, 1920.

"Custom and the Common Law in Kent." *Harvard Law Review* 38 (1925): 482–98.

Editor. *The Cartulary and Terrier of the Priory of Bilsington, Kent.* British Academy Records of the Social and Economic History of England and Wales, 7. London: Oxford University Press, 1928.

"English Manorial Forms." *American Historical Review* 34 (1929): 725–39.

Editor. *Year Books of Edward IV; 10 Edward IV and 49 Henry VI, A.D. 1470.* Selden Society, 47. London: Quaritch Press, 1931.

"Domesday Monachorum" and "Domesday." *Victoria County History, Kent* 3. London (1932). 177–269.

"The Manor." In *Collier's Encyclopedia.* New York: P. F. Collier and Son, 1935.

Medieval Agrarian Economy. Berkshire Studies in European History. New York: Henry Holt, 1936.

"The Forests." In *The English Government at Work, 1327–1336,* vol. 1, edited by J. F. Willard and W. A. Morris. Cambridge, Mass.: Mediaeval Academy of America, 1940.

"Medieval Agrarian Society in Its Prime: England." In *The Cambridge Economic History of Europe from the Decline of the Roman Empire*, vol. 1, edited by J. H. Clapham and Eileen Power. Cambridge: Cambridge University Press, 1941.

"Early English Woodland and Waste." *Journal of Economic History* 2 (May 1942): 54–62.

"The Early Pattern of the Common Law." *American Historical Review* 49 (1944): 199–212.

"Court of Common Pleas." In *The English Government at Work, 1327–1336,* vol. 3, edited by J. F. Willard, W. A. Morris, and W. H. Dunham Jr. Cambridge, Mass.: Mediaeval Academy of America, 1950.

The Stoneleigh Leger Book. Edited by R. H. Hilton for the Dugdale Society based on a transcription by N. Neilson. Oxford: Oxford University Press, 1960.

Reviews of over forty books for the *American Historical Review* and many more for *Speculum* and other journals.

Works Cited

Adams, Norma. "Nellie Neilson, 1873–1947." *Mount Holyoke Alumnae Quarterly* 31 (February 1948): 153–54.

Bennett, Judith M. "Medievalism and Feminism." *Speculum* 68 (1993): 309–31.

Cam, Helen. "Nellie Neilson, Scholar." *Mount Holyoke Alumnae Quarterly* 31 (February 1948): 155–56.

Glazer, Penina Migdal, and Miriam Slater. *Unequal Colleagues: The Entrance of Women into the Professions, 1890–1940.* New Brunswick, N.J.: Rutgers University Press, 1987.

Goggin, Jacqueline. "Challenging Sexual Discrimination in the Historical Profession: Women Historians and the American Historical Association, 1890–1940." *American Historical Review* 97 (June 1992): 769–802.

Gras, N. S. B., William E. Lunt, and J. R. Strayer. "Nellie Neilson." *Speculum* 25 (1950): 417–18.

Hastings, Margaret, and Elisabeth G. Kimball. "Two Distinguished Medievalists: Nellie Neilson and Bertha Putnam." *Journal of British Studies* (spring 1979): 143–59.

Horowitz, Helen Lefkowitz. *Alma Mater: Design and Experience in the Women's Colleges from Their Nineteenth-Century Beginnings to the 1930s.* New York: Alfred A. Knopf, 1984.

Judson, Margaret A. *Breaking the Barrier: A Professional Autobiography by a Woman Educator and Historian before the Women's Movement.* New Brunswick, N.J.: Rutgers University Press, 1984.

Lloyd-Jones, Hugh. "Jane Ellen Harrison, 1850–1928." In *Cambridge Women: Twelve Portraits,* edited by Edward Shils and Carmen Blacker. Cambridge: Cambridge University Press, 1993.

Vaugn, Gerald. "The Enigma of Mount Holyoke's Nellie Neilson." *Historical Journal of Massachusetts* 28 (summer 2000): 187–212.

Unpublished Works Cited

From Archives and Special Collections, Mount Holyoke College, South Hadley, Mass.:

Bertha E. Blakely Papers

History Department Records. Series A and B

"Mount Holyoke in the Twentieth Century." Vol. 5, Transcript of Interview of Sydney Robertson McLean, 1972

Neilson, Nellie. Faculty biographical file, press releases

From Bryn Mawr College Library:

M. Carey Thomas Papers

From Manuscripts and Archives, Yale University Library:

Charles M. Andrews Papers

From the Manuscripts Department, Cambridge University Library, U.K.:

Nellie Neilson correspondence. Selden Society Papers

From the Manuscripts Division, Library of Congress:
Papers of the American Historical Association

Nellie Neilson correspondence with H. E. Bourne
Nellie Neilson correspondence with Charles H. Haskins, Conference on Mediaeval History, 1912
Nellie Neilson correspondence with Guy Stanton Ford
Mary W. Williams correspondence with Conyers Read
Register of attendance, box 466
List of members present, 1889, box 125

J. F. Jameson Papers

Mary E. Woolley correspondence
Minutes of the Anglo-American Historical Conference, 1925

From the Royal Historical Society Library, University of London:
Nellie Neilson Correspondence

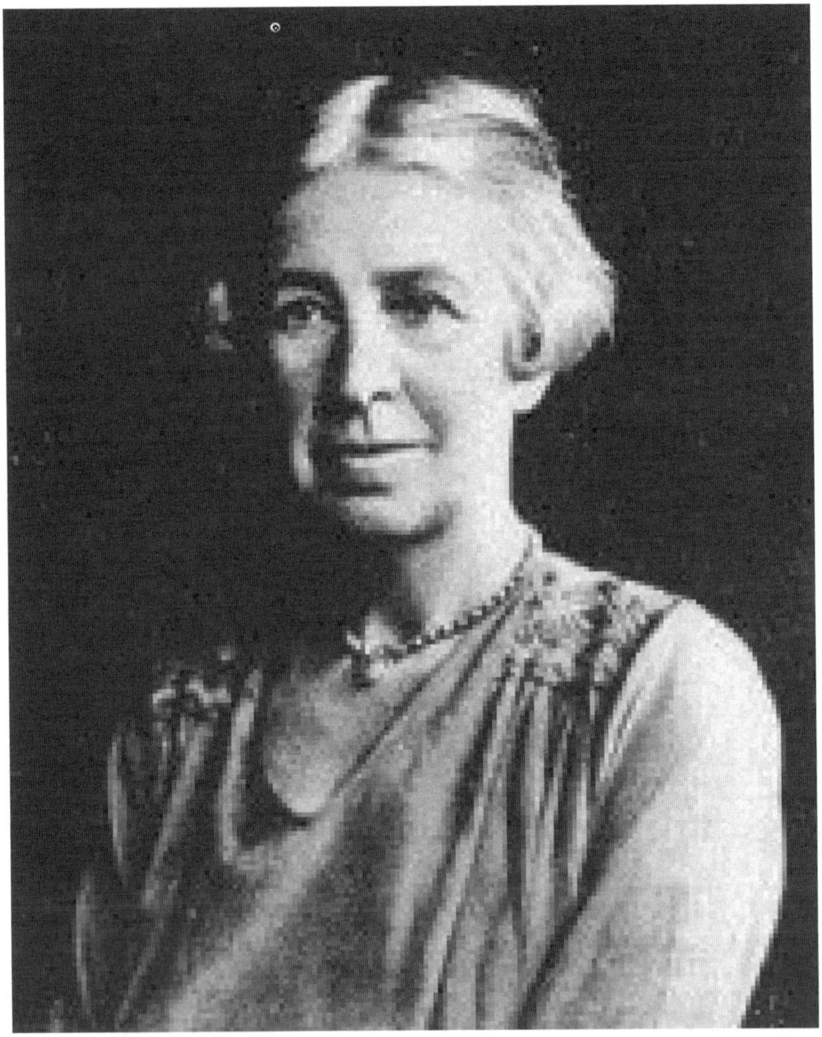

CHAPTER 14

Evelyn Underhill (1875–1941)
The Practical Mystic

MICHELLE M. SAUER

EVELYN UNDERHILL lived a life of paradoxes. Though she had little formal education, never held an official position, and certainly never considered herself a medievalist, Underhill became a celebrated scholar who produced numerous books, articles, poems, essays, and letters. Though she never desired to become a spiritual guide, she inspired a multitude. Though Underhill did not set out to redefine mysticism, she did so. These accomplishments merit her a place in this collection, as do her original works and translations that continue to be important to today's medieval scholars. Nevertheless, despite her worldwide reputation and her prominence in the theological world, Underhill was reluctant to promote a singular view of mysticism other than practicality.

Evelyn Underhill's complex nature can be traced back to her formative years. She was born on 6 December 1875 at Wolverhampton, in the North Midlands area of England, into an upper-middle-class Tory family. Shortly after her birth the family moved to London. Her father, Arthur Underhill, who was knighted in 1922, was an accomplished barrister.[1] Her mother, Lucy Ironmonger, seems to have faded in the presence of her outgoing husband, preferring the role of hostess and companion.[2] Religion was not a central part of family life. Though nominally Anglican, neither of her parents practiced their religion, and Underhill herself would later write, "I was not brought up to religion."[3] Yet, religion was not unheard of in her family, as her father's brother, Ernest, was an Anglican priest.[4] She was the only child of parents who were not openly affectionate, though she became known for her friendly affection. She was also the only one who attended church services.[5]

Despite the lack of a religious element in her family life, the young Evelyn assiduously prepared for her confirmation, an event that transpired on 11 March 1891. It was also during these teenage years that she met her future husband, Hubert Stuart Moore. The Moores lived around the corner from the Underhills, and the motherless boys were taken under Lucy Underhill's wing. Also at this time Evelyn was sent to a small boarding school called Sandgate House, which was in the village of Sandgate near Folkestone. Despite her apparent lack of parental affection, Evelyn's letters home during her tenure at Sandgate indicate a certain plaintive loneliness: "*Please* darling Mummie fetch me on the 25 or 26, the former if possible because we should not do many lessons and it is *not* nice to be last left" (13 July 1888, original emphases).[6]

As she fought loneliness and prepared for confirmation, Evelyn Underhill kept a small black notebook in which she recorded private thoughts, prayers, and hymns.[7] This notebook sustained her while she was away at school and provided a place for her to reflect on her personal spiritual development. In it a portrait of the teenage Evelyn Underhill, and of the beginning of the practical mystic, emerges.[8] Certainly this history of self-reflection aided her mystic journey. It is in this black notebook that she first indicated her fascination with mystic saints, citing Joan of Arc as one of her personal heroines.[9] At the same time, however, she expressed doubt that religious writings, including the Bible, were inspired.

This same notebook also outlined Underhill's persistent practicality, even in matters of the spirit. In its confines she firmly established her intent to be a writer: "When I grow up I should like to be an author because you can influence people more widely by books than by pictures."[10] Obviously attracted to a literary career, Underhill also saw the practical value of the pursuit of letters.[11] Similarly, she took a practical approach to God: "I don't believe in worrying God with prayers for things we want. If he is omnipotent he knows we want them, and if he isn't, He can't give them to us."[12] Besides illustrating Underhill's pragmatic approach to God, this statement also shows her ambivalence. Though she practiced her faith, her journal entries reflect the skepticism she was experiencing: "As to religion, I don't quite know, except that I believe in a God, and think it is better to love and help the poor people round me than to go on saying that I love an abstract Spirit whom I have never seen. If I can do both, all the better, but it is best to begin with the nearest. I do not think anything is gained by being orthodox" (5 December 1892).[13] Most of her biographers and admirers believe that these uncertainties enhanced Underhill's work. For instance, Dana Greene notes that Underhill's inclusivity, her willingness to put aside social, political, and religious differences, "naturally put her at odds with institutional religion that she found narrow and constricting."[14] Had she been a rote follower of orthodoxy, Underhill would perhaps not have been the pioneer she was; also the tendency to explore the limits of her faith served Underhill well in later years. It is somewhat ironic to see the champion of mysticism and a staunch defender of faith begin life so diametrically opposed to her eventual position. However, it is equally easy to see the seeds of Underhill's ecumenical approach in this early refusal to adhere to a doctrine.

Though Underhill would later become a champion of established religion, she never lost her sensible attitude toward other beliefs. Also this history of self-reflection aided Underhill's own mystical development.

In 1893, after Underhill left Sandgate House, she returned to London and registered at King's College, London, where a Ladies' Department had recently been established. There she studied botany, history, art, and languages.[15] Though theology was offered there, Underhill did not avail herself of the opportunity.[16] Studies alone, however, did not occupy her time. One of her favorite occupations was bookbinding. This allowed her to combine her love of books and learning with her desire for order, precision, and beauty, and as Greene notes, "her intellectual studies were supplemented by practical ones."[17] These practical pursuits led to a deepening relationship with Hubert Stuart Moore. He was the one who kept her binding knives sharp, and when she took up bicycling, it was he who assisted her with routes and listened to her tales.[18] Though she never did graduate from King's, the experiences there and during that time influenced Underhill's sense of practicality.

When Underhill was twenty-three years old, her parents decided to holiday in Switzerland and Italy, and the prospect of seeing the Alps excited her. She looked forward to seeing mountains, fields, and churches, hoping to draw closer to her "Spirit." The trip started out rough—bad weather caused some traveling difficulties—but Underhill and her family were soon comfortably exploring. Though Switzerland intrigued her, Underhill's real inspiration came while in Italy: "Italy, the holy land of Europe, the only place left, I suppose, that is really medicinal to the soul."[19] This trip also brought about two new experiences for the young woman—her first long separation from Moore and her first opportunity to travel by herself. The separation from Moore she resolved through long letters. Traveling alone to Florence allowed her to seek enlightenment among the many churches and galleries of the city and to revel in solitude, a state she rarely experienced. Practically she turned these experiences to her advantage: "The place [Florence] has taught me more than I can tell you: a sort of gradual unconscious growing into an understanding of things."[20] Through such missives Underhill both unraveled her own growing sense of spirit and tightened her bond with Moore.

Several years later, in 1902, Evelyn Underhill and Hubert Moore became officially engaged, though they still did not marry for another five years. As with everything else, practical concerns overshadowed her heart. Ostensibly the marriage was repeatedly postponed because Moore was settling into the practice of law.[21] In this same year Underhill also published her first book. A small collection of satirical poems about the law, *The Bar-Lamb's Ballad Book,* was dedicated to the family cat and was heralded by several law journals. Two years later she published her first novel, *The Grey World,* which received generally favorable reviews. Superficially a novel, *The Grey World* reads more like a psychological study than a standard work of fiction. In fact, the novel can be considered Underhill's first foray into the mystic world. The hero of the novel, Willie Hopkinson, begins life as a child of the slums, is reincarnated as a suburbanite, and works his way toward spiritual fulfillment. Though *The Grey World* was not exactly a "good" novel, it did serve as an effective introduction to Underhill's outlook: "[H]er ability to integrate the practical and spiritual and even to view the practical as spiritual, was evident in her first novel, *The Grey World*."[22] Moreover, because of this novel, she had her first experience as a spiritual director. Margaret Robinson, a Scottish Presbyterian, sent an effusive letter, thanking Underhill for allowing her to see "Reality." Underhill's response, which is preserved in her collected letters, discusses her perception of reality and encourages the woman to pursue her own vision and offers to continue correspondence. It is clear that Underhill was not yet comfortable in the role thrust upon her. Her letter is full of hesitation and apology, yet it is infused with her ever-present practicality: "[T]he finding of reality is the one thing that matters, and that always mattered, though it has been called by many different names."[23] Reality is all that counts.

Soon after the publication of *The Grey World,* Underhill began experimenting with religious opportunities. She first joined the Hermetic Society of the Golden Dawn, which was "dedicated to a communal search for the world of spirits through ritual."[24] She joined a branch of the society founded by Arthur Waite in 1903, which, unlike the main fellowship, "focused exclusively on Christian mysticism and ritual" instead of on the occult.[25] Golden Dawn, however, was merely feeding Underhill's search for Spirit. Her search for meaningful authorship continued as well. Shortly after the publication of *The Grey World,* she had the opportunity to complete her first scholarly work, *The Miracles of Our Lady, Saint Mary.* This work consists of translations of twenty-five medieval legends about the Virgin.

Underhill had been introduced to these legends by their keeper, J. A. Herbert, a Roman Catholic. At this time, too, she struck up a friendship with Ethel Ross Barker, who felt drawn toward Roman Catholicism. The pressure increased, for "the lure of Roman Catholicism through literature and friendship had become powerful for [Underhill]."[26] Her attraction to ritual and her practical approach to mysticism both called her to the Roman Catholic Church. Her predilection is illustrated in her early novels. Willie Hopkinson, for instance, has a fondness for Roman Catholic churches: "He had been, of course, in Protestant churches, but they had left no mark on his spirit, and gave him no clue to this experience—to the hush, the awe, the weight of a new form of life."[27] Hopkinson found mysticism and holiness in Roman Catholic churches. Similarly Paul Valéry, the protagonist of *The Lost World,* upholds the beauty of Catholicism: "And in the long run, Catholic forms are the loveliest and the rightest; all the better because they are so incredible."[28] Both the mystery and the practicality of ritual called to Underhill. In February 1907 Ethel Barker and she made a retreat, an event that propelled Underhill toward Catholicism.[29] It also thrust her into her first relationship with a spiritual director. Robert Hugh Benson, a priest, a convert, and a son of the Archbishop of Canterbury, became her guide. A letter to him reveals Underhill's reluctance to confuse admiration with desire to convert: "I have got halfway from agnosticism to Catholicism, and seem unable to get any farther. . . . As I understand the matter, before one can become a Catholic, and for me Catholicism is the only possible organized faith, one must get into the state of mind which ignores all the results of the study of Comparative religions, and accepts, for instance the Ascension, in as literal and concrete a spirit as the Spanish Armada. Is this really so?"[30] This letter reflects her practical concerns about belief. Benson responded warmly, urging her to visit another convent and reminding her to keep her own "incredible smallness" in the face of God in mind.[31] Practical advice for a practical woman.

Though she was steadfast in her belief in the rightness of Catholicism, Underhill was hesitant to commit herself fully without discussing her position with her fiancé. When she approached him, Moore was furious, and fell into a deep depression, fueled by the idea that "all hope of [our] happiness [was] at an end."[32] He particularly objected to the sacrament of confession, fearing that marital secrets would be revealed, and demanded that Underhill delay her conversion at least another year. Moore insisted that he could "never again trust [her]."[33] Though spiritually heartbroken, Underhill acceded to his demand in anticipation of finally realizing their marriage. On 3 July 1907 Hubert Moore and Evelyn Underhill were married in an Anglican service and moved to a home in London.

After marriage life settled into a comfortable routine for Underhill. She spent her mornings doing research for her planned book on mysticism, had lunch with her mother, and spent the evenings with friends. As Greene notes, "[T]he quiet support of Hubert, the regularity of leisure, her social commitments, the cats and garden, were all essential to keep her romantic spirit on course."[34] Practical issues kept her on track. Within the first few years after her marriage, Underhill not only worked on her large project; she also published her third, and last, novel, *The Column of Dust,* and her first purely theological work, *The Path of the Eternal Wisdom,* which was published under the pseudonym John Cordelier. Though Underhill later came to dislike this work, her own interpretation of the *Way of the Cross,* it signifies her first attempt to be a spiritual guide. She also spent time traveling on the Continent, sometimes with her husband and sometimes with her mother. These trips were profoundly spiritual, as they afforded Underhill the opportunity to connect with religion in a physical way. For instance, she haunted cathedrals and museums, she wandered Rome, and she met Pope Pius X. As she settled into her spiritual fulfillment, Underhill pushed herself to complete her "big book."

The "big book," as Underhill called *Mysticism,* came out in 1911 and is the work for which she is probably best known. Reviews were overwhelmingly favorable, and this text, labeled a classic almost immediately, made Underhill a major name in theological writing. What appealed to the public was the accessibility of her text. Underhill wrote in a clear, precise manner yet did not neglect research. A letter to J. A. Herbert illustrates her thoroughness: "I wonder if you can give me a bit of information I rather badly want? Is there in the Museum—or elsewhere in London—a copy, printed or MS., of Richard Rolle's *Incendium Amoris:* the Latin not the English? . . . I am using him a lot for the book on mystics which I am writing just now."[35] This combination of careful scholarship and readability, of practicality with spirituality, engaged readers. A contemporary review upholds this view: "[T]he most striking characteristic of this book is found in the fact that the writer has one eye constantly fixed on the most concrete matters and incidents, while the other is as constantly engaged in exploring the spiritual depths."[36] Integration resulted in popularity.

The form of the book illustrates this common sense connection. The work is divided into two parts. The first portion serves as an introduction to the subject of mysticism, though it goes beyond a mere definition of the mystic phenomenon. Underhill sought to establish mysticism as a topic that could be studied scientifically—through psychology, symbology, and theology—instead of a tradition that should be shrouded in mystery and magic. The second part of the text, called "The Mystic Way," outlines the path to mystic understanding. Underhill's map contains five sections (as opposed to the traditional Victorine threefold path): "The Awakening of Self," "The Purgation of Self," "The Illumination," "The Dark Night," and "The Unitive Life." Though not differing excessively with the traditional view, Underhill asserts that the final union resulted in an awesome creativity for the mystic, so that he or she became the most agile agent of heaven. Finally the work includes a concluding chapter that provides a link between the wonder of mystic union and the lives of ordinary Christians. Ultimately Underhill suggests that mystics are important to everyone because they belong to society at large. Mystics, or the "pioneers" of humanity, "follow the same path as all others but with greater intensity."[37] Furthermore, Underhill insisted that mysticism was a dynamic activity, not a passive undertaking. Practically speaking, mysticism was achievable by anyone: "[T]he Absolute of the mystics is lovable, attainable, alive."[38] As Thomas Kepler says, Underhill's philosophy was "an *ethical mysticism*" (original emphasis).[39] The book concludes with an appendix that lists famous mystics and their times.

The aftermath of her publication left Underhill somewhat breathless. Though she was now considered a major theological force, she was uncomfortable with the role of prophet that was thrust upon her. She combatted this problem by resuming her travels and her studies. In 1913 she published a shorter version of the big book, *The Mystic Way*. Though based on the second section of *Mysticism*, *The Mystic Way* was a more concise exposition written for the mystic seeker that was intended to provide the testimony of experience. Though it sold well, several reviewers charged Underhill with being a modernist, an accusation against which she vigorously defended herself.[40] However, it is obvious that she did indeed have "modernist leanings," for her disappointment with Pope Pius X's encyclical *Pascendi Dominici Gregis*, in which the Roman Catholic Church officially condemned modernism, was profound; as Michael Ramsey points out: "Drawn towards Rome for its spirituality rather than its dogma, Evelyn recoiled before Rome's determination to suppress Biblical scholarship."[41] Ramsey's view is a bit pro-Anglican, for despite Underhill's reunion with Anglicanism, she maintained Catholic "sympathies"; nevertheless, the encyclical signaled the end of her open affiliation.[42] This same year offered a unique ecumenical opportunity as well. Underhill met with the Indian mystic Rabindranath Tagore, who was recuperating in London, and the result of this meeting was a collaborative effort. Together Underhill and Rabindranath, as he was commonly known, translated a series of the Indian mystic Kabir's poems, for which Underhill wrote the introduction. Her letters reveal the intensity of her connection with her fellow mystic. She calls Rabindranath her "beloved Indian prophet" and describes their project as "fascinating work and a real joy and education to be with him."[43] The publication of *Mysticism* also brought Underhill to the attention of other scholars and theologians, most notably Baron Friedrich von Hügel, who would later become her spiritual director.

War erupted for England in 1914, and Underhill had another volume ready to go to press in 1914, shortly before England became involved in World War I. This work, *Practical Mysticism,* subtitled *A Little Book for Normal People,* was written specifically for readers who held no allegiance to a particular church. However, the onset of war brought about a conflict of conscience within Underhill. She was troubled by the idea that her book, which included guides for contemplation, called for a quietness that could not be achieved within a war-torn environment. However, Underhill eventually came to believe that the need for spiritual nourishment outweighed her concerns, and in her introduction, she even described her decision as a patriotic one. Annice Callahan notes, "[P]ractical mysticism increased efficiency, wisdom, and perseverance, helping us enter into the life of the group to which we belonged, teaching us to see the world in relationship to the eternal."[44] Also during the war years Underhill composed the majority of the essays that were later collected and published as *The Essentials of Mysticism*. As always she also remained active publishing reviews, articles, essays, and translations in various journals. As the war progressed, she began translating guidebooks for the admiralty and published her second book of poems *(Theophanies)*. This was her last foray into poetry, as she felt that particular expression to be "too easy."[45] Only in her theological expositions could her desire for purgation and exploration of her deepest self be fulfilled.

The end of the war brought not relief but sorrow, as Underhill suffered the loss of her best friend, Ethel Barker. After Barker's death she felt adrift and finally turned to the Anglican Church for comfort. Her choice seemed providentially reaffirmed. By 1921 Underhill was an acknowledged expert on mysticism and the theological toast of London. She was invited to deliver the initial lectures on religion at Manchester College of Oxford. These lectures were later collected and published in the volume *The Life of the Spirit and the Life of Today.* The text of these lectures indicates that Underhill had come to hold that membership in an established church was an essential key to achieving spiritual fulfillment as a Christian, a position quite different from her original one. And though she remained committed to Anglicanism after her reinvestment with that church, during these postwar years Underhill came to rely on von Hügel, a strong Catholic, and by 1921 he was firmly established as her advisor. Though he knew of Underhill's struggles with established churches, he never pressed her to convert to Catholicism; instead, he provided a touchstone in her own search for spiritual direction. In turn this search led to a deeper understanding of mysticism, a view that would color Underhill's later works, namely, "the ability to appreciate the fact that the finite was the way to the infinite, that history and matter were in fact the way to God. This was a direct counter to her 'exclusive' or 'pure' mysticism."[46] Von Hügel worried that Underhill desired to de-intellectualize mysticism in favor of personal experience, in essence over-practicalizing. He determined to direct her toward a more christocentric philosophy. E. I. Watkins points out that "the Baron influenced his disciple in two allied directions. He gave her a greater appreciation of the social, institutional and sacramental aspects of religion and directed her devotion, hitherto exclusively theocentric, to the person of Christ the Incarnate Son."[47] It is mainly because of von Hügel's influence that she continued to combine careful research with practical application; as Greene notes, "under the guidance of von Hügel Underhill [came] to a deeper sense of her vocation as a spiritual guide."[48] The settling of the question of a spiritual director also eased Underhill's mind and allowed her to concentrate more fully on her work.

Soon after she found redirection, Underhill completed two new editions of medieval mystical texts. In 1922–23 she produced her translations of *The Cloud of Unknowing* and Walter Hilton's *Scale of Perfection*. Underhill felt a particular personal connection with these two works, and her introductions were pointedly about the echoing of mystic sentiment throughout the centuries. But she continued moving toward the fulfillment of practical theology. In 1924 Underhill was selected to be a part of the Conference on Politics, Economics, and Christianity (COPEC) as a member of the committee that created the "Report on the Nature and Purpose of God." Though she had also been scheduled to speak at the conference's opening, her mother's death prevented that engagement.[49] That same year she was invited to conduct her first retreat, which she held at Pleshey, an Anglican center in the country. This experience was a great joy to Underhill, who was one of the first women to be so prominently favored by the Anglican Church. Again success was overshadowed by tragedy—von Hügel died early in 1925. She faced this loss with sadness and joy: "[I]t *has* been a bit hard now it has come, in spite of one's rejoicing for him" (original emphasis).[50] Otherwise, her busy schedule of lectures, essay writing, and traveling continued unabated.

By 1926 Underhill was considered such an expert in Christian mysticism and religious psychology that she was invited to speak at the Conference of Clergy from the Liverpool diocese, the first laywoman to do so. These talks primarily centered on the need for prayer and for personal spiritual direction. Moreover, she continued to grow more and more comfortable with her role as spiritual guide, dispensing advice with a surer tone and passing on her sense of the practical.[51] Underhill also found herself addressing Wesleyan, Quaker, Baptist, and Free Church ministers and congregations. Moreover, she was working on the new edition of *Mysticism*. Though the "big book" did not change in format, she took the opportunity to clarify and refine several points. In 1929 Underhill was appointed the religious editor of the *Spectator*. She began her new position by arranging for a series of articles by famous theologians. She introduced the series herself and also contributed an article. This same year Underhill published *The House of the Soul,* a collection of retreat addresses. This initial book met with such success that she later published other collections of this sort, most of which grew out of retreat experiences and had their bases in a particular ritual: *The Golden Sequence, Abba, The Mystery of Sacrifice,* and *The School of Charity.* Each volume had a theme. For instance, *The Golden Sequence* was a series of reflections based on the Latin hymn "Veni, Sancte Spiritus," which was quite popular in the Middle Ages; *Abba* was centered on the Lord's Prayer; and *The Mystery of Sacrifice* was a collection of Eucharistic prayers she had gleaned from older texts, along with her commentaries. In these shorter works Underhill proved herself to be not only a student of medieval mysticism but also a creator of mystic expression. For example, she described the House of the Soul as consisting of two floors: the ground floor of biological conditions and the upper floor of supernatural elements. These shorter works, which combined the culmination of Underhill's mystic explorations and her experiences as a spiritual director, paved the way for her next major project.

By the last decade of her life Underhill was consumed mostly with directing retreats, and her publications came out of her experiences with them. After many struggles she had also found a new spiritual director. In 1932 Underhill's friend Margaret Cropper introduced her to Reginald Somerset Ward, a man Greene refers to as an "Anglican 'soul specialist.'"[52] Ward provided the firm, practical base Underhill needed. She described him as "brimming over with common sense."[53] New stability and purpose fueled the publication of her final major work, *Worship,* in 1936. *Worship* is best described as a book on personal religion. Like *Mysticism* this book is divided into two parts, which correspond to the theory and practice of worship. The theoretical portion contains notes on ritual and symbol, sacrament and sacrifice, and liturgical elements and principle rites. However, Underhill does not neglect the connections between these components and the personal relationship each Christian should cultivate with God. The second part of *Worship* is a historical tracing of ritual. It opens with Jewish worship, as the precursor of Christianity, moves to the rites of early Christianity, then continues with Catholic rites before examining various Protestant rituals. The Protestant denominations she explored included the Reformed Churches, the Free Church, the Religious Society of Friends, and Anglicanism. The scholarship required for *Worship* was as extensive as that necessary for *Mysticism,* and overall the book was as well received. Even though many of Underhill's younger readers were disappointed in its style since it dwelled so much on a personal relationship and little on the reality she attempted to impose on the mystic world in her earlier book, her clerical admirers were vastly impressed. The invitations to speak at clergy conventions remained as numerous as ever.

Underhill's international reputation was secure as well. In the spring of 1937 *Worship* was chosen Religious Book of the Month in the United States. The biggest honor was yet to come, however. In 1938 Aberdeen University created her a doctor of divinity. Unfortunately, she was not well enough to attend the ceremony, despite its having been delayed for a year. Asthma, a condition that had plagued Underhill her whole life, was making traveling difficult. Still, she remained as active as she could in correspondence, charitable works, and prayer groups. The beginning of 1939 brought even more troubles. Arthur Underhill passed away in January. Despite their awkward relationship Underhill felt the loss of her remaining parent. Now she had only her husband, who was also sick, and her own poor health. Only the cheer of good friends and her cats, as well as a short period of recovery, kept her motivated.[54] As Underhill grew weaker, she remained in good spirits, declaring that her suffering was part of God's plan. Her suffering was one thing, but the onset of World War II was another. Though not a social reformer, Underhill spoke out against the war as a pacifist. Greene believes that "her pacifism was not some ancillary aspect of her life and work; it was rather its culmination and followed logically from the redirection of her life."[55] Underhill had spent her life examining the personal relationships possible between human beings and their God. During World War I her essays and poems supported the war effort, even linking mysticism to patriotism, arguing that real mystics did not divorce themselves from conflict. This war was different. Her own spiritual journey led her toward acceptance of a conflicted life yet instilled in her the idea that mystics must necessarily support pacifism, since it is their duty to provide a small pool of quietness. Underhill kept up with her writing on pacifism until the end of her life. Eventually the weakness became too much to bear, and Evelyn Underhill passed away on 15 June 1941.

Without doubt looking back at what Underhill, herself an interesting combination of scholar and practicing mystic, accomplished is inspirational. She was a prolific author who wrote in clear, unencumbered prose. Many of her pieces were originally composed for radio or magazines, widening their appeal. She was a laywoman who was never formally educated in any of the subjects—theology, spiritual psychology, and mysticism—in which she is now considered to have been an expert. Still the question remains, Why was Underhill so important? Her life was an example of practical mysticism. She was "the most prolific English female religious writer of her time."[56] She was a boundary breaker—the first laywoman to write extensively on theology, the first woman to lecture at Oxford, and the first woman to lead retreats. She was firmly committed to the vocation of spiritual direction. She believed in ecumenism: "Long before it was fashionable, her ecumenical approach [in *Worship*] provided a new methodology for exploration of religious phenomena."[57] Her ecumenism extended beyond *Worship,* however. Her joint projects with Rabindranath and her consultation with theologians of various faiths proved her commitment to a multicultural approach. Likely her unusual situation aided her ecumenism, since "as a laywoman, who in mid-life made a new and public commitment to the church of her baptism, and with the widest possible Christian sympathies ... she could not be accused of belonging to any clerical or theological clique."[58] Indeed, Underhill herself, near the end of her life, taught that "it [Christianity] must, in fact, have the courage to apply its own inherent sacramentalism, without limitation, to the whole mixed experience of humanity."[59] To the Anglican community, she is "one of the Anglicans . . . who most deeply influenced [their] earlier years" since she is the person who did the most to nurture and keep alive the spiritual life in Anglicanism.[60] To the world she will forever be associated with the study of mysticism.

Indeed, the text that Underhill is best known for, *Mysticism,* is also the one for which she is most important to medieval scholarship. Overall, it is an examination of the affective spirituality that seized the medieval world. It is primarily a historical study, complete with quotations from source materials, and still serves as a valuable introduction to the phenomenon. Moreover, when it appeared in 1911, *Mysticism* served as an introduction to some mystics, such as Richard Rolle and Walter Hilton, who had resided in semiobscurity before then; as Greene suggests, *Mysticism* was "the rediscovery and recovery of the mystical tradition."[61] Greene goes on to point out that the book filed a niche in early-twentieth-century society. By looking at a tradition that did not rely on dogma and doctrine, Underhill ushered in an ecumenism that had previously been stilted. Though William Inge (*Christian Mysticism*), William James (*Varieties of Religious Experience*), and von Hügel (*The Mystical Element*) had all examined mysticism in their own books, Underhill clarified it in a way that appealed to a lay audience. Moreover, "the power and authenticity of *Mysticism* are linked to the fact that this book was not a detached, objective study of mystic texts, but a highly interpretive and personal examination born of an intellectual crisis in her own life."[62] Medieval studies benefited from this personal twist. Since mysticism was never a coldly detached or easily definable concept, Underhill's attempt to connect it to individuals, the first of its kind, made the entire discipline more accessible. Kepler believes that the difficulty of "relating the subjective experience of the Christian mystic to the historical facts of the Christian faith seemed a harassing problem for Evelyn Underhill."[63] In facing this difficulty Underhill approached and surmounted the difficulty that modern medievalists encounter when working with mystic works and practitioners. At what point does one separate the sometimes fantastic experiences recorded by the mystics from the culture in which that person lived? Underhill partially answered this question by concentrating on definition and presentation. Greene writes that "she never principally associates mysticism with extraordinary phenomena—visions, voices, etc., but with the quiet movement of the heart."[64] Underhill viewed mysticism as an act of love that led her to hold that "she should treat all apparently mystical experiences as in principle equally relevant . . . the unique common denominator of all mystical experience: men and women in love with God."[65] In turning mystic expression inward Underhill was able to forge clearer connections between cultural context and religious expression. Moreover, her assertions about mysticism—that it was an active lifestyle, not a passive one, and that mystics did not flee the world but labored within it—would influence medieval scholarship and reshape understanding of early Christianity.[66]

Underhill's scholarship is also significant in terms of recovery and presentation of source materials. She was instrumental in establishing the priority of original texts, as she "quotes her sources verbatim far more often than do most writers."[67] She also looked at traditional works in new ways. For example, Henry Bodgener notes that she "makes more references to St. Augustine, and particularly to the *Confessions,* than to any other mystic or book."[68] Though Augustine was not a mystic, he craved the unity with God that mystic contemplation sought, and Underhill carefully explored the connections between his public theology and the mystics' private expressions. Underhill provided interesting and unique hagiographic portraits of well-known saints and mystics such as Angela of Foligno, Saint Teresa of Avila, Julian of Norwich, and Saint John of the Cross. She also investigated lesser-known figures. For instance, "her two most important biographical studies were those of Ruysbroeck, her favorite mystic, and Jacopone da Todi."[69] Both Ruysbroeck, a fourteenth-century mystic, and da Todi, a thirteenth-century mystic, not only illustrated her ideas of reconciling vision and action but also reintroduced them to modern scholars. But even more significant pieces were to come. In fact, the two projects dovetailed nicely: "These biographical studies were augmented by her editing of original texts."[70] Of most value to medieval scholars are probably her extracts of *The Mirror of Simple Souls* and her editions of *The Cloud of Unknowing* and Hilton's *Scale of Perfection.* These translations and critical editions, in which she provides carefully researched theories on authorship, translations, and manuscript history, are very useful. Moreover, she played a role in text recovery with pieces such as her editions of Ruysbroeck's works. In each of these projects, though, Underhill ultimately maintained her focus on spiritual guidance. Her introductions usually included comments on how a modern practitioner of mysticism could utilize the older work.

As a woman writing on a traditionally male subject, Underhill broke many barriers and established a place for female theologians in the twentieth century. Greene believes that Underhill has "particular appeal for us because she is a modern woman.... by that [Greene means] not only that she lived in our century, but that she was well aware of the forces which shape our contemporary world and appreciated the power and achievement of modern science and technology."[71] Though her work surmounted gender hurdles, Underhill herself was not a suffragette. In fact, many biographers believe that she "had a view of the ministry of women which did not threaten male clergy."[72] Indeed, she remained firmly opposed to women's ordination, a position she expressed publicly at the 1932 Central Council for Women's Church work.[73] Still, her work had a positive influence on many women. However, history has not necessarily focused on her contributions to the feminist cause. As biographers have noted, she repeatedly submitted to her husband's will. Many writers refer to her as "childless," even before describing her as an author. And as Greene comments, she is listed as the "daughter of Sir Arthur Underhill" on her tombstone: "The defining of this prominent female writer in terms of the men in her life, while historically appropriate, is ironic for those of us who follow her."[74] Even when gender does not seem to be an issue, it remains one: "John MacQuarrie in his *Twentieth Century Religious Thought* claims that Underhill is one of three women in the early part of this century who made a significant contribution to religious scholarship."[75] Yet, this praise is faintly condemning. According to MacQuarrie, the two other "significantly contributing" women, Simone Weil and Georgia Harkness, were also interested in mysticism. Greene believes that this list implies a connection between gender and expertise, and I agree. In fact, this view persists even today, as inquiry into medieval mysticism is often considered the realm of women scholars. Still, without Underhill's work, our current view of mysticism would not be what it is, an engaging, objective, and *practical* area of study.

NOTES

1. He was considered an expert on torts and private trusts. Some of Arthur Underhill's more famous works include *A Summary of the Law of Torts, or, Wrongs Independent of Contract* (1911); *A Practical and Concise Manual of the Procedure of the Chancery Division of the High Court of Justice both in Actions and Matters* (1881); *The Line of Least Resistance: An Easy but Effective Method of Simplifying the Law of Real Property* (1919); *A Concise Guide to Modern Equity Being a Course of Nine Lectures* [revised and enlarged] (1885), all published by Butterworth in London. He also produced an autobiography, *Change and Decay: The Recollections and Reflections of an Octogenarian Bencher* (London: Butterworth, 1938).

2. This seems to be the generally accepted view of the Underhill family life. Little is actually known, and as Greene notes, "she was unwilling to talk about it [her early life] publicly or privately with friends." See her *Evelyn Underhill*, 8. What little is known has been gleaned from Lucy Menzies's Biography of Evelyn Underhill, TS [typescript] unfinished, Saint Andrews University Archives, Saint Andrews, Scotland, and from the Evelyn Underhill Collection (EUC) Archives, King's College, London. Arthur Underhill's memoirs provide equally little knowledge about the family's inner workings. One is simply left with a vague sense of the rather cool relationship between Underhill and her father.

3. Though every biographer faithfully reproduces this quotation, no source can be readily identified.

4. Most biographies note this familial affiliation with the Church of England. Greene attributes this knowledge to the Menzies biography and the EUC Archives.

5. Though these details may seem intimate, they are standards of all her biographies.

6. Armstrong, *Evelyn Underhill*, 7.

7. Of this notebook there remains no trace. Only transcriptions, primarily in Cropper's *Evelyn Underhill*, exist.

8. Greene notes that "what dominates in her twenties and thirties is a desire for intimacy that she found neither with her parents nor with Hubert. In the mystic's relationship with God, however, she saw both intimacy and freedom from self" (*Artist*, 107).

9. Entry dated 5 December 1892, in Cropper, *Evelyn Underhill*, 6.

10. Ibid.

11. Interestingly, though Underhill clearly demonstrates her desire to influence the world, she later described a woman's role as being observant, interested, and a pleasant and sociable companion. See Evelyn Underhill, "How Should a Girl Prepare Herself for a Worthy Womanhood," *Hearth and Home* 27 (July 1893); archived EUC, folder 57.

12. Cropper, *Evelyn Underhill*, 6.

13. Cropper, *Evelyn Underhill*, 5.
14. Greene, *Artist*, 9.
15. Greene, *Artist*, 11.
16. Greene, *Artist*, 12. From "Speech by Evelyn Underhill at King's College, London, 1927," EUC Archives, folder 57.
17. Greene, *Artist*, 12.
18. Greene, *Artist*, 12; Cropper, *Evelyn Underhill*, 9–10.
19. Cropper, *Evelyn Underhill*, 13.
20. Letter to Hubert Stuart Moore, in Greene, *Artist*, 12, from Menzies, *Collected Papers*, 11.
21. Hubert Moore specialized in marine law.
22. Callahan, *Spirituality*, 12.
23. 29 November 1904, in Williams, *Letters*, 51.
24. Callahan, *Spirituality*, 2.
25. Greene, *Artist*, 17.
26. Greene, *Artist*, 21.
27. Underhill, *Grey World*, 194.
28. Underhill, *Lost World*, 88.
29. The retreat was held at Saint Mary's of the Angels, a Franciscan convent in Southampton.
30. Cropper, *Evelyn Underhill*, 29. Original not extant.
31. Martindale, *Life of Monsignor Robert Hugh Benson*, 1:260.
32. Cropper, *Evelyn Underhill*, 30.
33. Ibid.
34. Greene, *Artist*, 47.
35. 8 March 1909, in Williams, *Letters*, 94.
36. Quoted in Callahan, *Spirituality*, 13, from Menzies, *Collected Papers*, 3:4.
37. Greene, "Adhering to God," 22–38.
38. Underhill, *Mysticism*, 28.
39. Kepler, introduction, 17.
40. See Cropper, *Evelyn Underhill*, 31.
41. Ramsey, "Evelyn Underhill," 273–79.
42. Indeed, the book and her response to charges damaged her relationship with some Catholic friends, particularly J. A. Herbert. A series of letters, dating from early 1913, indicate the depth of their spat. See 30 March 1913, April 1913, and ? 1913 in Williams, *Letters*, 141–44.
43. Letter to J. A. Herbert, ? 1913, in Williams, *Letters*, 144.
44. Callahan, *Spirituality*, 22, based on Underhill, *Practical Mysticism*, vii–xi.
45. Cropper, *Evelyn Underhill*, 59. Cropper believes this statement indicates Underhill's fear of her inability to express herself fully within the confines of poetry.
46. Greene, *Artist*, 81.
47. Watkins, "Evelyn Underhill," 45–50.
48. Greene, *Artist*, 89.
49. In *Artist* Greene questions the nature of Underhill's relationship with her mother: "Although she experienced sadness at her [mother's] death, she felt ambivalence toward her" (94). Similarly Cropper reports that "it is difficult to know how much sympathy there was between Evelyn and her mother" (*Evelyn Underhill*, 120).

50. Letter to Lucy Menzies, 1 February 1925, in Williams, *Letters,* 162.

51. See the letter dated 20 June 1924, to W. Y., a student: "I think your 'practical' difficulty is really a mental and spiritual difficulty. That is to say it arises out of the inadequacy of your present religious and philosophic outlook.... What you are really short of is the conviction of *personal* responsibility to a *personal* God" (original emphasis) (Williams, *Letters,* 154–55).

52. Greene, *Artist,* 104.

53. Letter to Margaret Cropper, 8 December 1932, in Armstrong, *Evelyn Underhill,* 251. Only partial transcript extant.

54. Evelyn's Easter Confession of 1933, which would be forwarded to Reginald Somerset Ward, though written several years before these incidents, outlines her relationships with the men in her life: "I feel there is a horrible streak of hardness and bitterness somewhere in me.... As towards my husband, I often fail to show interest in his affairs and amusements, not rousing myself to respond when I'm tired or concerned with other things.... In my relations with my father which are difficult and where I'm often met by coolness and indifferent in my turn" (from the *Flowered Notebook,* collected in Greene's *Fragments from an Inner Life,* 94).

55. Greene, "Response to War," 127–35.

56. Greene, "Response to War," 127.

57. Greene, "Adhering to God," 33.

58. Loades, *Evelyn Underhill,* 10.

59. Evelyn Underhill, "Education and the Spirit of Worship," the Winifred Mercier Memorial Lecture, delivered at Whitelands College, Putney, November 1937, reprinted in Menzies, *Collected Papers,* 229.

60. This influence on the Anglican community was noted by Michael Ramsey, former Archbishop of Canterbury; see foreword to Armstrong's *Evelyn Underhill,* ix–x. Quotation from Allchin, "Evelyn Underhill," 146–55.

61. Greene, "Toward an Evaluation," 549–62.

62. Greene, "Toward an Evaluation," 552.

63. Kepler, introduction, 19.

64. Greene, "Adhering to God," 24.

65. Armstrong, *Evelyn Underhill,* 114–15.

66. For instance, Geoffrey Galt Harpham, in his book *The Ascetic Imperative in Culture and Criticism* (Chicago: University of Chicago Press, 1987), posits a similar theory about asceticism.

67. Bodgener, "Spiritual Director," 45–50.

68. Bodgener, "Spiritual Director," 47.

69. Greene, *Artist,* 62.

70. Greene, *Artist,* 63.

71. Greene, "Adhering to God," 23.

72. Loades, *Evelyn Underhill,* 10.

73. Evelyn Underhill, "The Ideals of Ministry of Women," *Theology* 26 (151) (January 1933): 37–42. In fairness Underhill's position on women's ordination most likely had more to do with its potential to deepen the chasm between the Anglican Church and the Roman Catholic Church than with women's position in organized religion.

74. Greene, "Adhering to God," 25.

75. Greene, citing MacQuarrie, in "Toward an Evaluation," 549.

Select Bibliography of Works by Evelyn Underhill

The Grey World. London: William Heinemann, 1904.
The Miracles of Our Lady Saint Mary Brought Out of Divers Tongues and Newly Set Forth. London: William Heinemann, 1905.
The Lost World. London: William Heinemann, 1907.
Introduction to *The Mirror of Simple Souls* [extracts]. *Porch* 1 (1910): 2–4.
Mysticism: A Study of the Nature and Development of Man's Spiritual Consciousness. London: Methuen, 1911.
Editor. *Cloud of Unknowing.* London: John M. Watkins, 1912.
"A Franciscan Mystic of the Thirteenth Century: The Blessed Angela of Foligno in Franciscan Studies." In *Franciscan Studies*, edited by Paul Sabatier et al., 88–107. Aberdeen: Aberdeen University Press, 1912.
The Mystic Way: A Psychological Study in Christian Origins. London: J. M. Dent, 1913.
Practical Mysticism. London: J. M. Dent; New York: E. P. Dutton, 1914.
Ruysbroeck. London: G. Bell, 1914.
Translator with Rabindranath Tagore. *One Hundred Poems of Kabir.* London: Macmillan, 1915.
Editor. *John Ruysbroeck: The Adornment of the Spiritual Marriage. The Sparkling Stone. The Book of Supreme Truth.* Translated by C. A. Wynschenck. London: J. M. Dent, 1916.
Jacopone da Todi: Poet and Mystic, 1228–1306: A Spiritual Biography. London: J. M. Dent, 1919.
The Essentials of Mysticism and Other Essays. London: J. M. Dent, 1920.
Editor. *The Scale of Perfection,* by Walter Hilton. London: John M. Watkins, 1923.
Introduction to *Nicholas of Cusa: The Vision of God.* Translated by Emma Gurney Salter. London: J. M. Dent, 1928.
Worship. London: Nisbet, 1936.

Works Cited

Allchin, A. M. "Evelyn Underhill, and Unity in the Love of God." *Institute of Christian Studies* 3 (1975–76): 146–55.
Armstrong, Christopher. *Evelyn Underhill: An Introduction to Her Life and Writing.* Grand Rapids, Mich.: William B. Eerdmans, 1975.
Bodgener, Henry. "Evelyn Underhill: A Spiritual Director to Her Generation." *London Quarterly and Holborn Review* (January 1958): 45–50.
Callahan, Annice. *Evelyn Underhill: Spirituality for Daily Living.* Lanham, Md.: University Press of America, 1997.
Cropper, Margaret. *Evelyn Underhill.* London: Longmans, Green, 1958.
Greene, Dana. "Adhering to God: The Message of Evelyn Underhill for Our Times." *Spirituality Today* (spring 1987): 22–38.
———. *Evelyn Underhill: Artist of the Infinite Life.* New York: Crossroad, 1990.
———. "Evelyn Underhill and Her Response to War." *Historical Magazine of the Protestant Episcopal Church* 15 (1986): 127–35.
———. *Fragments from an Inner Life: The Notebooks of Evelyn Underhill.* Harrisburg, Penn.: Morehouse Publishing, 1993.
———. "Toward an Evaluation of the Thought of Evelyn Underhill." *History of European Ideas* 8 (1987): 549–62.
Kepler, Thomas. Introduction to *The Evelyn Underhill Reader.* Nashville: Abingdon, 1962.

———, ed. *The Evelyn Underhill Reader,* by Evelyn Underhill. Nashville: Abingdon, 1962.
Loades, Ann. *Evelyn Underhill.* Fount Christian Thinkers Series. London: Fount, 1997.
Martindale, C. C. *The Life of Monsignor Robert Hugh Benson.* London: Longmans, Green, 1916.
Menzies, Lucy, ed. *Collected Papers of Evelyn Underhill.* New York: Longmans, Green, 1946.
Ramsey, Michael. "Evelyn Underhill." *Religious Studies* 12 (1976): 273–79.
Watkins, E. I. "Evelyn Underhill." *Month* 22 (July 1959): 45–50.
Williams, Charles, ed. *The Letters of Evelyn Underhill.* London: Longmans, Green, 1945.

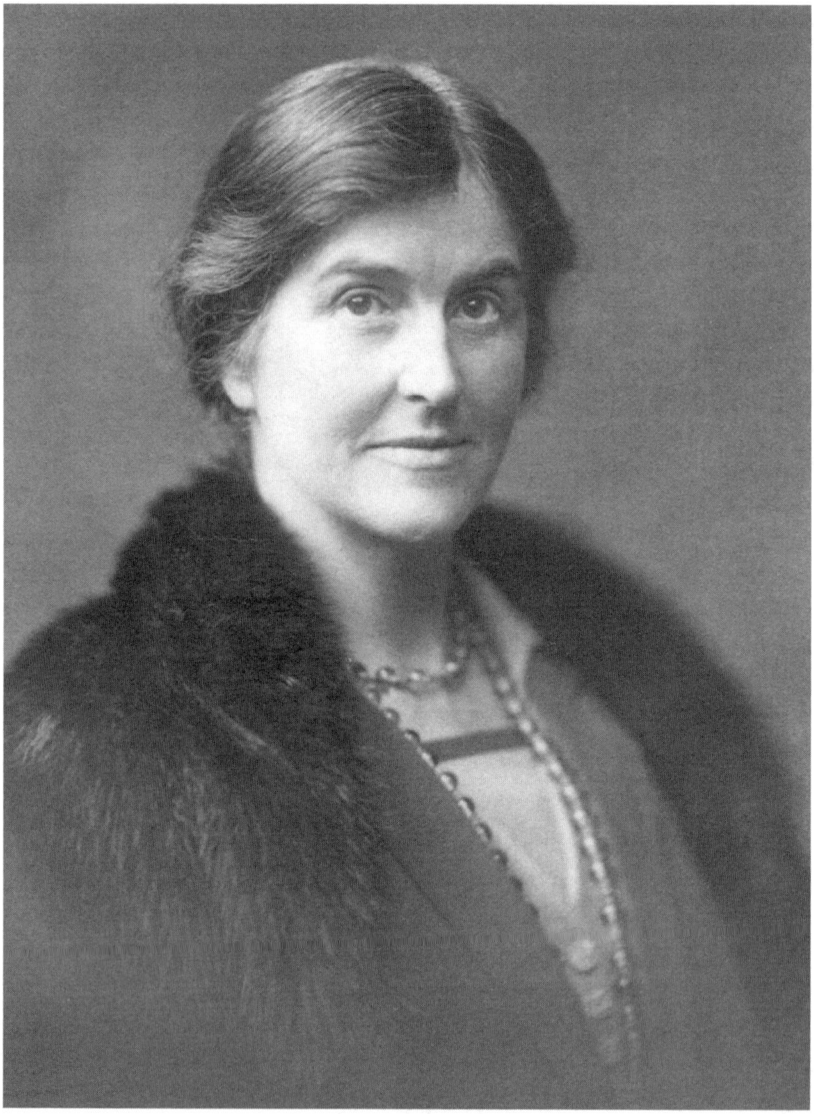

CHAPTER 15

Kindred, College, and Scholarship in the Lifework of Bertha Surtees Phillpotts (1877–1932)

Russell Poole

> Róa nam ríki, rifu kjöl hálfan,
> hömlur slitnuðu, háir brotnuðu
> [They began to row mightily, tore half the keel apart, the oar thongs snapped, the rowlocks broke]
>
> *Atlamál*, v. 37, in the *Poetic Edda*

How might a Cambridge undergraduate know of Bertha Phillpotts nowadays? An answer for the more ambitious might be the Dame Bertha Phillpotts Memorial Fund, which provides travel grants to promote Old Icelandic studies. Were Phillpotts a student today, she would be avidly applying, despite the modest basic stipend of fifty pounds. Travel and application and honors were central elements in a life so unremittingly active that to encapsulate it into a brief essay forces one's very prose style into a kind of hyperactivity.

Born on 25 October 1877 in Bedford, Bertha Phillpotts was the daughter of James Surtees Phillpotts (1839–1930) and Marian Hadfield nee Cordery (1843–1925) and the fifth of six children. Her kindred led enterprising lives. On leaving school at seventeen, her mother announced her disdain of novels, learned Greek, translated European literature, and enjoyed walking, cycling, and sketching. Phillpotts's maternal aunt Henrietta married Thomas Jex-Blake (1832–1915), the brother of Sophia Jex-Blake (1840–1912), who opened careers in medicine to women. Phillpotts's two female cousins on the Jex-Blake side served as principals of women's colleges. Phillpotts's father, as an exceptionally effective headmaster of Bedford Grammar (1874–1903), enriched the school's literary, science, crafts, and sports activities. This family played as hard and as closely outdoors as it worked indoors, with the father, famed among Old Boys as a hardy son of the West Country, setting the pace. His children built and sailed a boat named *The Phantom,* from its translucent oiled calico, and on several adventures narrowly escaped drowning.

Surprisingly in an education-conscious family but not abnormally for Victorian girls, Phillpotts received virtually no formal schooling other than a term at a private establishment, which was curtailed by diphtheria. Her mother supplied some tutoring, helped by colleagues of her father, but otherwise Phillpotts learned independently. Inspired by her father's gift of a William Morris saga translation, she acquired some knowledge of Old English and possibly Old Icelandic. Visitors at the school, including Fridtjof Nansen (1861–1930) and Eiríkr Magnússon (1833–1913), provided further stimulus. At nineteen Phillpotts won the Gold Medal of the Société nationale de professeurs de Français en Angleterre and the following year a scholarship to Girton. Her parents had not intended to send her to college, because they were counting on her help as an unofficial school secretary, but the scholarship (reducing her fees to £21.13.4 per term) and her father's impending retirement no doubt cleared the way.

Between 1898 and 1901 Phillpotts studied French and German. At two years older than most new entrants, she felt disappointed not to be doing more rarified subjects but welcomed the innovative thinking of university lecturers like Hector Munro Chadwick (1870–1947), Francis Cornford (1874–1943), and William Ridgeway (1853–1926), who held classes at Girton in support of women's education. Students could also cycle into Cambridge to attend lectures, a commuting exercise that Phillpotts facilitated by rigging her bicycle with a sail. No bluestocking, she starred as a valuable center forward in the hockey eleven and gained first-class honors in the medieval and modern languages tripos. Marriage or teaching were not on the horizon—though in 1905 she was to follow the example of many ex-Girtonians in the professions by taking up her entitlement to a B.A. and an M.A. at Trinity College, Dublin. Instead of a definite career she embarked on further study in medieval English and Icelandic with H. M. Chadwick and Eiríkr Magnússon. But for an onset of ill health, characterized by headaches and loss of appetite, she could have taken a second tripos in 1902. Her decision to pursue research after her four student years would have had the endorsement of fellows at Girton, who wished to demonstrate that their graduates could excel in scholarship as well as in teaching and other professions.

Byrði betri berrat maðr brautu at,
enn sé manvit mikit.
[No better burden does a man carry on the road than plenty of mother wit.]
Hávamál, v. 10, from the *Poetic Edda*

Phillpotts had no funding for 1902–3 and worked on Snorri Sturluson at home under Eiríkr's supervision. Her promising draft paper proposing Icelandic authorship of the *Völuspá* moved him to join her up with the Viking Club and place her article with the Swedish journal *Arkiv för nordisk filologi*. This immediately gained Phillpotts, its youngest contributor, status as a serious scholar, in a context of nationalistically driven philology. Meanwhile, again through Eiríkr, she was accepted by the family of the High Court judge in Reykjavík as a live-in English teacher for the summer of 1903. On the first of what would be six visits to Iceland, she spent a few days mute, not knowing the modern pronunciation, but soon was advocating women's education and keenly debating politics in this hotbed of Home Rule controversy. Yet, to her hosts' wonderment, she adhered to her parents' strict standards of chaperonage when traveling to photograph saga locales. She impressed such scholars as Geir Tómasson Zöega (1857–1928) and Finnur Jónsson (1858–1934). Björn Magnússon Ólsen (1850–1919), rector of the Latin School and an eminent literary historian, heard of her article from Eiríkr Magnússon and visited with generous praise, avoiding reference to a publication of his own that had anticipated her arguments. Reciprocally she admired his scholarship, though—noting that he lacked control over the boys at the school—not his headmastership.

Modest funding of fifty pounds toward study in Copenhagen during 1903–4 came from the Pfeiffer Research Studentship. Determined not to burden the family budget, Phillpotts scrimped and saved to the further detriment of her health. She found a congenial colleague in the librarian Sigfús Blöndal (1874–1950), who was engaged in editing an Icelandic-Danish dictionary and the diaries of the seventeenth-century navigator Jón Ólafsson. But Phillpotts chafed at the Copenhagen style of minutely detailed philology, which Eiríkr to some extent partook of. Though unsure of her abilities, she yearned for more expansive scholarship and more readerly expression. Here she had models in England in W. P. Ker (1855–1923) and H. M. Chadwick, both distinguished comparativists. While Eiríkr strove to maintain her morale, she coaxed him into acknowledging the importance of a broader perspective.

The summer of 1904 saw a return visit to Iceland, with her brother Brian, to do the first of five tours. Experience in 1903 had proved cycling impracticable and horseback riding too expensive, so, then as later, she compromised by buying a pony to carry a tent and other gear, while she and her companion walked, to the amazement of the Icelanders. An itinerary almost exhaustively covering Snorri's various haunts served as useful reconnaissance toward her research. But despite Phillpotts's skills as a water diviner and her brother's as an angler, the two hikers were inadequately equipped and ended up relying on country folk, who themselves—even Síra Þorvaldur Bjarnason, the erudite dean of Melstaðir—sometimes had little else to eat than sour milk and dried fish.

In 1904–5 Phillpotts was once again without funding and continued independent study, relying—perhaps to excess—on Eiríkr's generosity with advice and books. In 1905–6, however, came better fortune, with a second award of the Pfeiffer Studentship, suggesting Girton's confidence in this emerging scholar. Commissions from the *Encyclopedia of Religion and Ethics* and the *Encyclopedia Britannica* prompted a research trip to Sweden, where the eminent archaeologist Oscar Montelius (1843–1921) devoted several days to guiding her round the National Museum. Then Phillpotts and her two women companions, equipped with a scrubbing brush and rubber bathtub, engaged in fieldwork, cleaning moss off rock carvings at Fossum and elsewhere. As she rubbed chalk into the carvings, so as to obtain clear photographs, Phillpotts experienced an "epiphany" concerning the extraordinary activity of the society that produced these dramatic scenes.

From September 1906 Phillpotts held the position of librarian at Girton, with occasional teaching in French and German. She found, much like Eiríkr and Sigfús Blöndal, that librarianship combined well with research, but she was keenly aware that her resources did not match theirs. The college, though helped by bequests, could not support an ambitious acquisitions program. Phillpotts later told the story of finding a sick sheep inside an Icelandic homestead with its head on the new *Larousse Dictionary*, a title that she had unsuccessfully recommended for the library that year. Her extensive tours continued in 1909 in the west of Iceland and won Phillpotts and her companion, Mary Beatrice Thomas, a chemistry lecturer at Girton, praise as role models for Icelandic youth. After wearing out three pairs of shoes, Phillpotts tried the slippers worn locally. Eiríkr urged her to publish about her insights into the endurance of the country folk, but she never did so. Few writers other than Halldór Laxness have found a style commensurate to the task.

After resigning the librarianship, Phillpotts took up a secretarial position in January 1910 with Baron Anatole von Hügel (1854–1928), curator of the Museum of General and Local Archaeology at Cambridge University. This placed her strategically for ethnological research toward her first book project, while also allowing her to do some Icelandic teaching. This year's trek, in company with her third cousin and lifelong friend, Mary Clover, started in the east of Iceland, traversed the highlands to Akureyri, and from there followed the inland route to Þingvellir and Reykjavík. The following year saw a double boost to her career as a researcher—the Gamble Prize, adjudicated by W. P. Ker, and (her first honor from an institution other than Girton) a fellowship in the Society of Northern Antiquities in Copenhagen. In the winter she completed the archival component of her book project with a round of European libraries, a major feat for an unaccompanied woman scholar. Then Phillpotts sallied forth on yet another strenuous Icelandic excursion, during the unseasonal heavy snows of August and September 1912. She repaid Eiríkr, now in his last illness, for his many kindnesses by doing a round of his relatives in the east of the country, thus witnessing the solidarity of an Icelandic kindred firsthand.

Nineteen thirteen was a year of huge achievement. Phillpotts successfully applied for the first Lady Carlisle Research Fellowship at Somerville College, Oxford, proposing, with Chadwick's recommendation, a comparative project on the history of the Icelandic commonwealth. She had also received a commission to translate the Jón Ólafsson diaries for the Hakluyt Society, probably on the instance of Sigfús Blöndal. Meanwhile, Cambridge University Press promptly accepted her book, with a grant from the Maitland Fund, and on 28 October *Kindred and Clan in the Middle Ages and After* appeared. As an essay in medieval sociology, with nods to the modern sociology of trade unions, it represents an interdisciplinary effort of heroic proportions. It traces the survival of the kindred as a social force in the various Germanic countries, making firsthand use of judicial records. Though simplistic on Icelandic law and betraying a tendency to determinism throughout, her work remains significant. Trinity College, Dublin, conferred a doctorate on Phillpotts on the strength of it in 1919, and the reviews were strongly favorable. At the end of the year she read a noteworthy paper, "Temple-Administration and Chieftainship in Pre-Christian Norway and Iceland," to the Viking Society.

Entry to a new college meant an exciting new milieu. She was befriended by its vice president, the classicist Gilbert Murray (1866–1957), who shared with his mother-in-law, Lady Carlisle, an admiration for women "who had entered at universities."[1] Phillpotts naturally warmed to his enthusiasm for ethnological and comparative approaches. She also found kindred spirits in Mildred Pope (1872–1956) and Janet Spens (1876–1963), who were investigating, respectively, ballads and folk drama as progeners of more sophisticated genres. Phillpotts was stimulated into devising an entirely new project on the precursors of the *Poetic Edda,* sidelining the originally envisaged historical project. Chadwick read a draft during 1915, and only two chapters remained unwritten by March 1916. She dedicated the book, as finally published in 1920, with these typically gracious words: "This book is my gift to Somerville College. In a more fundamental sense it is the gift of Somerville College to me."[2]

The outbreak of war caught Phillpotts in Iceland, and she nearly missed the last boat back to Britain. Soon she had a war assignment of her own. In November 1914 her brother Owen had been appointed to the British legation in Stockholm, where he played a vital role in maintaining the blockade of supplies to Germany and, conversely, safe transit of supplies to Britain and Russia. Although he was as capable and dedicated as his sister, his occasional carelessness afforded opportunities to enemy agents and risked alienating the Swedes, many of whom were partisan toward Germany.[3] Called on to act as a sisterly "minder," Phillpotts arrived in Stockholm early in 1916, accompanied by the Murrays on the dangerous journey. In a small flat with her brother, she diligently maintained heating levels, cooked economical but appetizing dishes, and enticed him into sailing and other healthy outdoor activities.

From March 1916 this work evolved into voluntary assistance at the legation proper. She found that research had prepared her well for office work, a point she later made in public discussions of careers for women graduates. Moreover, with her knowledge of the language, she was the ideal person to monitor reports and opinion pieces in the Swedish press. Accordingly, she resigned her fellowship and accepted a salaried appointment with the legation on 20 March 1917. This appointment in turn burgeoned into a private secretaryship to the minister, Sir Esme Howard, with responsibility for drafting numerous telegrams. The German agents detailed a spy to watch her movements, but Phillpotts, ever keen for exercise, watched him in turn, taking him on cruelly extended Sunday walks. In such tense times friendship was still forthcoming from some Swedish families, especially in the commercial sector, and Phillpotts recognized, with her characteristic fair-mindedness, that Sweden could be more enlightened, at least in industrial welfare, than Britain. Gratified to be doing war work, perhaps not least because her brother Brian had been killed in Belgium, she worked to excess until her right hand seized up with writer's cramp. She then taught herself to write left-handed, injuring that hand as well. Only in 1919, with a visit to a Dublin hypnotist, did she receive what she regarded as effective treatment, and even then the associated insomnia continued to trouble her. In recognition of these efforts Phillpotts received the civil honor of an OBE (Order of the British Empire) in 1918.

> Enn orðstírr deyr aldregi,
> hveim er sér góðan getr.
> [But reputation never dies, for someone who gains a good one.]
> *Hávamál*, v. 76, from the *Poetic Edda*

Meanwhile Westfield College, a residential institution founded in 1882 within the University of London and attractively located in Hampstead, was advertising for a principal. Qualified faculty for women's colleges were difficult to find (not least because of the uncompetitive salaries), so Phillpotts's application was the sole viable one to be received. She was induced to apply out of a combination of family persuasion, worry about her health, and hopes of contributing to Scandinavian studies at the University of London. Phillpotts's health was indeed far from robust—her medical adviser instructed her to sleep out on her verandah, regardless of the weather, and not to rise before 10 A.M.—but that in no way prevented her from initiating substantial improvements in conditions at Westfield immediately upon assuming the position in May 1919.

The end of the war saw a surge in applications for admission to women's colleges, as the natural sequel to secondary school for the brighter student. For this Westfield, though academically well regarded, found itself ill prepared, with shortfalls in funding for salaries, pensions, scholarships, research, laboratories, library, and sports fields. Access to public funding, channeled through the University Grants Committee and the London County Council, was urgently required. As a master of diplomacy (Howard himself had endorsed her exceptional abilities), Phillpotts secured the funding by enlisting support from her male counterparts at the other London colleges. She played one principal or provost off against another in carefully drafted memoranda, showed her reliability and integrity at meetings by speaking sparingly and to telling effect, and charmed her male colleagues on less formal occasions with anecdotes that reduced them to helpless laughter. She employed the same tactics in rationalizing teacher training. The principal at the London Day Training College was insisting that students in teacher training spend long hours doing needlework and other practical subjects, on top of their studies at Westfield. Phillpotts campaigned against him successfully on the basis that this drudgery bore no relevance to the secondary school curriculum, put students off teaching, and compromised their health. Her status as a member of the Consultative Committee of the Board of Education also served Westfield well, helping to gain the college equivalent status to the larger colleges within the London University constitution. But in spite of this considerable public profile, her manner was a disarming mixture of charm and shyness, and she thrived most on informal occasions.

Pastoral care was expected of the principal, and Phillpotts used the Sunday evening assembly, called the "Function," not to monitor attendance but rather to foster rapport with students by discussing political issues or recounting her adventures. Noting a pattern of overwork, she devised an examination about Hampstead Heath, with the offer of a prize for the best result. This lured students out of the library and into healthy fieldwork activity, for instance, to find sources of drinking water. To diversify the college and in the hope of improving postwar relations, as a supporter of the League of Nations she encouraged applications from foreign students. Among those for whom she found a bursary was Anna Bjarnadóttir, an Icelander who had assisted Sigfús Blöndal with his dictionary.

In the midst of these administrative responsibilities, using research that she had fitted into her time in Sweden, Phillpotts added two final chapters to *The Elder Edda and Ancient Scandinavian Drama,* which then appeared on 15 October 1920. In developing her central argument, she started from the familiar observation that poems in the *Poetic Edda* have a strong element of direct speech. The speech format, she contended, was ancient, originating in Norway rather than Iceland, and constituted a core around which later redactors had built narrative poems. Impatient as ever with conventional philology, she backed up this literary-historical reconstruction by appealing to an analogy with archaeology. Oscar Montelius had posited typological sequences, with which it is possible to trace one technology gradually giving way to another.[4] Thus the design of a bronze ax may betray traces of an older flint technology. Analogously Phillpotts postulated that the speeches in the *Poetic Edda* represented traces of primitive drama. Building on previous scholarship but also with a basis in her ethnological reading, she singled out the poem *Skírnismál* as bearing all the hallmarks of a miniature ritual play, designed to promote fertility through the enactment of a courtship myth. From there she took a further large step by asserting that this hypothesized Scandinavian tradition of cult drama was of a more primitive type than that of ancient Greek drama and held valuable clues as to the evolution of drama in general. Most ambitious of all was her claim that primitive Scandinavian drama was the source of folk and liturgical drama in France and England.

These striking hypotheses met a mixed reception. W. P. Ker wrote a cordial review but was uncomfortable, predictably, with her rather mechanistic typological modeling and lack of allowance for poetic flexibility in the handling of traditional material. The eminent Eddaic scholar Andreas Heusler (1865–1940) dismissed her theories outright, emphasizing the lack of concrete evidence for enactments. Research in the next decade moved in other directions, and in her later teaching Phillpotts herself manifested a certain detachment from her book.[5] Icelandic textuality, as something quintessentially sui generis, tends to resist comparative or influence-tracing approaches, and perhaps the book has its greatest value nowadays as an exploration of the methodological limits. Still, some present-day scholars have sought to build on its theories.[6]

Phillpotts's next move, to an appointment as mistress of Girton College, was not one she personally sought. To her embarrassment the mere possibility of her moving became the subject of fevered journalistic speculation—an implied tribute, however undesirable in itself, to the keenness of public interest in women's education. And indeed, women's education in Cambridge had reached a crisis. Other English universities had long since given women equal academic rights, including conferment of degrees, and in 1920 the University of Oxford had fallen into line, leaving Cambridge isolated in its conservatism. Phillpotts's supporters at Girton believed that she, if anyone, as a distinguished scholar and able diplomat, could redress this situation. Phillpotts, for her part, felt obliged out of loyalty to accept the invitation.[7] At Westfield sorrow prevailed, only partially allayed by ceremonies such as the unveiling of her portrait by Gilbert Murray.

Before entering into her new duties, Phillpotts ensured herself some sorely needed personal space by taking a few months of leisure to visit friends and relatives in Europe. A subsequent stay in Copenhagen enabled her to consult Sigfús Blöndal's dictionary, now close to final printing. With its assistance on obscure nautical vocabulary, a subject after her own heart, Phillpotts was able to finish off the long-delayed Jón Ólafsson translation. The first volume appeared in 1923, and the second posthumously in 1932.

Then, in October 1922, Phillpotts started her reign as ninth mistress of Girton. This was England's senior women's college; to be its mistress was the highest position open to an English woman scholar. So as now to make Girton a college by law as well as by custom, Phillpotts completed the draft constitution and statutes prepared by Katharine Jex-Blake and her colleagues on the college council and obtained a Royal Charter in 1924.

Meanwhile, in 1923 Phillpotts was appointed, as the sole female member, to a statutory commission for the University of Cambridge. When, in 1927, it completed its reorganization of teaching, eleven fellows of women's colleges gained university lectureships. Phillpotts had once again succeeded in gaining the confidence of her male colleagues through tact, goodwill, and a nonpartisan attitude. Her gradualist approach also involved persuading Girton students, whom she had liberated from various constraints, to show discretion so that male conservatives could not discredit the college.

Preparing Girton for a full place in the university involved soliciting benefactions. The library, always a concern of hers, needed to be brought closer to parity with the men's colleges, and this physically isolated college needed to be placed more prominently on the social map. To help her pay visits and undertake diplomatic missions, Sir Alfred Yarrow (1842–1932), the shipbuilding magnate and philanthropist, defrayed half the cost of a Morris Cowley car—known, in allusion to his name, as "Freda." A photograph (Girton College Archives) shows Phillpotts standing in the Girton gateway beside Freda, with her secretary in the passenger seat. After a few driving lessons she was negotiating narrow Cambridge streets with admirable aplomb. Complementarily, so as reciprocate hospitality, she saw to the setting up of a Fellows' Dining Room, which was later paneled in oak in her memory.

As at Westfield she had a strong concern for the welfare of her approximately two hundred students. After the strict though well-meaning reign of her cousin, Phillpotts imparted a more relaxed ethos to Girton while still maintaining control. She was admired for her willingness to accept that students would not necessarily conform to a type and for her imaginative consideration of their personal situations. At examination times she would take any particularly harassed candidates for a relaxing drive between sessions. She conducted her one-to-one tutorials in a similarly low-key manner, sometimes at Mary Clover's house, with the student and herself sitting on the kitchen table drinking cocoa. At other times poor health obliged her to recline on the sofa in her mistress's study when seeing students. When three students started a geographical society, she not only found an explorer to address them but also gave a dinner party so that they could meet him beforehand. She researched careers for female graduates, pointing, for example, to the potential of industrial relations for women who were willing to familiarize themselves with factory work. She found some personal space by going sailing in the Norfolk Broads during the vacations, usually with Mary Clover as crew but sometimes with senior faculty. She handled a heavily canvased dinghy unerringly, and despite her failing health she achieved notable successes in the Blakeney Regatta. Meanwhile she discreetly campaigned against the University Sailing Club's exclusion of women, eventually carrying her point.

In March 1925 the inevitable disruption to this lifestyle occurred, with the unexpected death of her mother in an accident. Phillpotts's father was by now in advanced old age and growing deaf. Some associates wondered at her decision to resign from Girton, so forfeiting her pension, and move to Tunbridge Wells to take care of him as in keeping more with a dutiful unmarried daughter of Victoria's day than with a proponent of modern intellectual womanhood. Phillpotts, for her part, would have been mindful of her dependence on her parents during a decade of private research. Also, residing at Tunbridge Wells did not exclude writing. The college immediately elected her to a research fellowship, and presently, finding that her father did not need constant care, she commuted to Cambridge each week in Freda, regardless of the weather, herself attending to maintenance of the car. Fittingly, when he died in 1930, her father acknowledged her self-sacrifice by making her a special bequest of one thousand pounds.

Meanwhile her teaching activities within the university increased. From 1924 she lectured unofficially in Old Norse, later also in Old English. She had already attracted Icelandic students to Girton, and when a Swedish group presented ten thousand pounds to foster Scandinavian studies at Cambridge, it was Phillpotts who set up the program of study. In due course the reformed statutes gave her official lecturer status as well as the title of director of Scandinavian studies. Senior appointments followed, as examiner for the archaeology and anthropology tripos and head of the Department of Other Languages (meaning languages other than French, German, Italian, or Spanish). She also sat on three boards of studies—archaeology and anthropology, English, and modern languages—a heavy cross-disciplinary workload, which the university with some sophistry justified (and she accepted) as necessary to instruct the new women colleagues in its practices.

Her teaching load amounted to two to four lectures a week, most of it material that had to be newly prepared, besides supervision of a few research students. The excellence of her lectures was remarkable for somebody who, though close to some outstanding teachers, had not received teacher training herself and for many associates represented the archetypal scholar-administrator. Though clear that lectures should first and foremost communicate knowledge and firsthand research, Phillpotts strove to be lively and diverting—a standard she had set herself at Girton twenty years before. Now facing a mixed male-female audience, she effectively related medieval institutions such as the law to her students' experience, often with sly humor. In a lecture from 1926 she explains one of her own specialist legal topics as follows: "Well, supposing we were under Anglo-Saxon law, the only way of bringing me to justice would be for you to bring a case against me with an oath. It would make a great deal of difference to me whether this was this year or last, when I was Mistress of Girton. I admit that the status of heads of women's colleges is questionable, but I think perhaps they might count like abbesses as *gesithcund,* or in the earliest Kentish laws *eorlcund.* . . . In that case, last year my oath that I hadn't left my car in K[ing's] P[arade] would need fewer oath-helpers than I should need this year, belonging no doubt to the *ceorlic* class."[8] The reference is to a characteristic misadventure: Phillpotts walked home after shopping in Cambridge and departed on overseas travel the next day, forgetting that her car was still parked in town. In lecturing on the sagas she showed slides to illustrate lines of communication and so explain tactics used by the characters. As a supervisor she urged students, just as Eiríkr Magnússon had urged her, to develop scholarly contacts outside the university.

In 1926 she was appointed a member of the Statutory Commission for the University of London and served until 1928, work that she found interesting because it enabled her to see the university through the eyes of almost all its constituent institutions. Amid these time-consuming duties, which led to the award of Dame of the British Empire in 1929 for services to education, she somehow managed to sustain and increase her research activities. In a series of papers for the Cambridge Philological Society, she explored such topics as Danish borrowings in the "The Battle of Maldon" and the relation between Wyrd and Providence in Anglo-Saxon thought. She received a commission for her future book *Edda and Saga* from the popularizing Home University Library series, for which Gilbert Murray was a general editor. Toward this project she spent a summer in Sweden following up new work on possible early datings of texts in the *Poetic Edda.*

In June 1931 she married her friend Hugh Frank Newall (1857–1944), emeritus professor of astrophysics and twenty years her senior, as his second wife. Newall shared most of her wide-ranging interests, with the enthusiasm of a Victorian gentleman amateur, but loathed motor vehicles, preferring the old-fashioned horse and carriage. Ostensibly the hope was that a holiday in the Italian Alps would restore Phillpotts's health, but perhaps neither of them really expected a long marriage. She was already partially bedridden and had made Newall, along with others, some small bequests. She died on 20 January 1932, reportedly of cancer, and was buried beside her parents at Tunbridge Wells.

Edda and Saga, published the previous autumn and well received, appeals to the "general reader" while also allowing itself some personal allusions to the "astronomers and physicists of today."[9] We sense the presence of the zealous scholar, keen for us to learn the language and disabuse ourselves of misleading impressions conveyed by previous popularizations. *Snorra Edda* and the sagas receive compact treatment, pointing to a waning of energy in the concluding chapters but also to Phillpotts's view that the sagas, even at their best, fall short of Eddaic poetry. Far from idealizing them as an authentic record, she limits herself to the modest claim that much of their content turns out, upon investigation, to be historically based. By contrast it is the poems that she privileges, in a characteristic fusion of literary appreciation and "archaeological" reconstruction, as very ancient primary evidence for the mentality of early Scandinavia. One statement on this theme encapsulates her thinking, evoking her "epiphany" at Fossum as she viewed the rock carvings: "Nowhere else in Europe—perhaps nowhere in the world—do we find a literature approaching this in the impression it gives of incessant activity."[10]

Another statement from the book will serve as a coda: "Fame is a challenge flung down by man to the powers ordering the world. Fate can destroy the most valiant hero, but in Fate's despite men and women can give him a life after death."[11]

Notes

Thanks are due to Kate Perry, archivist at Girton College, Cambridge, and her staff; also to Guðmundur Hálfdanarson, Terry Gunnell, Robin Gwynn, Roger Gwynn, Geoffrey and Heather Harlow, Julie McKenzie, Richard and Ingegerd Perkins, Debbie Rayner, and Phil Weinstein.

1. Murray, *Unfinished Autobiography,* 100.
2. Phillpotts, *Elder Edda and Ancient Scandinavian Drama,* vii–viii.
3. Regarding Owen Phillpotts's carelessness, see Howard, *Life Seen from the Stalls,* 236. Swedish sympathy for Germany is documented in Murray, *Impressions of Scandinavia in War Time,* 3, 28.
4. Klindt-Jensen, *History of Scandinavian Archaeology,* 90–91.
5. Regarding the shift in her research efforts, see Lloyd Thomas, "Dame Bertha Surtees Newall," 650.
6. Gunnell, "Dame Bertha Phillpotts and the Search for Scandinavian Drama."
7. Sondheimer, *Castle Adamant in Hampstead,* 92.
8. Girton College Archives, Phillpotts I.29–31.
9. Phillpotts, *Edda and Saga,* 146.

10. Phillpotts, *Edda and Saga*, 29.
11. Phillpotts, *Edda and Saga*, 128.

SELECT BIBLIOGRAPHY OF WORKS BY BERTHA PHILLPOTTS

"Surt." *Arkiv för nordisk Philologi* 21 (1905): 14–30.

Kindred and Clan in the Middle Ages and After: A Study in the Sociology of the Teutonic Races. Cambridge Archaeological and Ethnological Series. Cambridge: Cambridge University Press, 1913.

"Temple-Administration and Chieftainship in Pre-Christian Norway and Iceland." *Saga-Book* 8, no. 2 (1914): 264–84.

The Elder Edda and Ancient Scandinavian Drama. Cambridge: Cambridge University Press, 1920.

Translator. *The Life of the Icelander Jón Ólafsson, Traveller to India, written by himself and completed about 1661 A.D. with a continuation, by another hand, up to his death in 1679.* Translated from the Icelandic edition of Sigfús Blöndal. Hakluyt Society, 2d ser., 53 and 68. London: Hakluyt Society, 1923–32.

"Wyrd and Providence in Anglo-Saxon Thought." *Essays and Studies* 13 (1928): 7–27.

Edda and Saga. Home University Library, 150. London: Butterworth, 1931.

WORKS CITED

Gunnell, Terry. "Dame Bertha Phillpotts and the Search for Scandinavian Drama." In *Anglo-Scandinavian Cross-Currents, 1850–1914,* edited by Inga-Stina Ewbank. Norwich: Norvik Press, 1999.

Heusler, Andreas. Review of *Elder Edda,* by Bertha Phillpotts. *Arkiv för nordisk Filologi* 38 (1922): 347–53.

Howard, Esme. *Life Seen from the Stalls, 1905–1936.* Vol. 2 of *Theatre of Life.* London: Hodder and Stoughton, 1936.

Ker, W. P. Review of *Kindred and Clan,* by Bertha Phillpotts. *Modern Language Review* 17 (1922): 201–2.

Klindt-Jensen, Ole. *A History of Scandinavian Archaeology.* Translated by Russell Poole. London: Thames and Hudson, 1975.

Lloyd Thomas, M. G. "Dame Bertha Surtees Newall." In *Dictionary of National Biography, 1931–1940,* edited by L. G. Wickman Legg. London: Oxford University Press, 1949.

Murray, Gilbert. *Impressions of Scandinavia in War Time.* London: Unwin, 1917.

———. *An Unfinished Autobiography.* London: Allen and Unwin, 1960.

Sondheimer, Janet. *Castle Adamant in Hampstead: A History of Westfield College, 1882–1982.* London: Westfield College, 1983.

CHAPTER 16

Eleanor Shipley Duckett (1880–1976)
Historian of the Latin Middle Ages

SUSAN MOSHER STUARD

Eyes so pale that the blue of the irises fairly disappeared into the white that rimmed them. This was nature's doing, certainly, but by her seventy-fifth year it owed something as well to Eleanor Shipley Duckett's startled response as she negotiated a return to the present from her preferred world of the early Middle Ages. Stepping out of room 408 in Neilson Library at Smith College broke in on Duckett's absorption with her beloved early texts, and honors students in carrels nearby caught a brief glimpse of how the life of the mind displaces all other considerations. Students gained insight into how a fine mind flourishes even into old age, and how the life of the mind may become an all-encompassing concern.

Eleanor Shipley Duckett was already legendary when, as a student, I first met her in 1955. She had been born in Highbridge, Somerset, England, in 1880, so this was her seventy-fifth year. On her retirement in 1949, Smith College had awarded Duckett an honorary degree, encouraged her to keep her precious office as Sophia Smith Scholar, and urged her to more scholarly effort that would add luster to the college's name. She became an honorary member of Smith's chapter of Phi Beta Kappa in 1954. By the 1960s Duckett would be pointed out to visitors proudly, as a pioneer among women in the academy. By the 1970s she would receive standing ovations when she processed in her bright University of London academic robes. She had endured to become a heroine for aspiring young women; her life was celebrated and honors proliferated into very old age.

Through these sweet late years of life, and after retiring from the John M. Greene Chair in Classics, Duckett pursued a remarkably productive second career as a published, and read, historian of the early Middle Ages; this was evidently the most

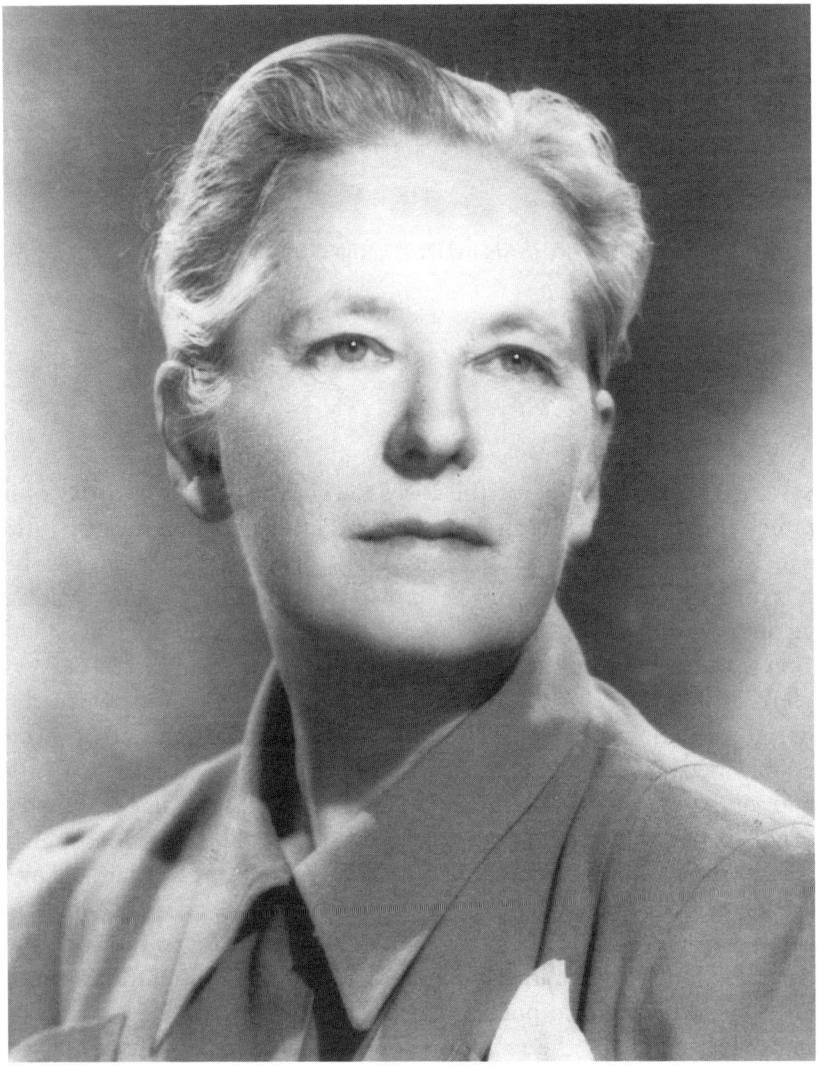

satisfying stage of her long life. Her early publications in classics had been brief philological studies with the exception of *Latin Writers of the Fifth Century,* published in 1930. This transitional study, on an age Duckett called the first Christian century, along with her popular *Gateway to the Middle Ages,* published in 1938, pointed the direction to her future successes. In retirement Duckett became an expert text-grounded historian who lived with her early medieval saints and scholars on intimate terms. She found an assured voice, a more eloquent style, and an enthusiastic audience for her work; in time she gained the scholarly recognition that had eluded her in early years. Duckett journeyed far in her life, geographically to America and academically to independent institutions of higher learning devoted to educating women. Over the years her career took on the character of a philosophical journey as well. Duckett changed her discipline to history: she learned to imagine a remote and little-known age through the eyes of its authors and to convey what those authors saw and understood in their own time to modern readers.

Espousing history and withdrawing from her original discipline of classics meant a rupture with schooling, with mentors and early aspirations, with her home in England, and with the recognition from her peers that a career in classics bestowed, but there were sound reasons for the choice. In Duckett's own words, from 1965: "Many years ago I sat in the University Library of Cambridge, England, looking at my first-born book.... There it was, dull as ditch water, without doubt, but my own and I was filled with a nicely balanced mixture of pride and diffidence. A god-parent, I decided, might help to catch a publisher, and since I was not wise enough to know better, I carried my manuscript to an eminent scholar of the University. Would he of his charity read it? With courteous voice and complete British sincerity he replied: 'Do you want me to judge it on its own merits or as the work of a woman?'"[1]

At that juncture Duckett was pursuing a fellowship at Cambridge that had been won on the merits of her University of London credentials (bachelor and master's degrees in classics, a further degree in pedagogy). At Cambridge she became a member of Girton College and received a high second when she stood for the classical tripos (Latin, Greek, and Hebrew). Apparently women scholars did not qualify for firsts. Nonetheless, her publications over the next quarter century, including those in a series she founded, Smith College Classical Studies, played by the strict rules of philological analysis advocated by her Cambridge mentors. Her offerings to the scholarly world were never very well received; in all likelihood they were judged as the work of a woman. A brief anonymous comment in *Notes and Queries [of the Oxford University Press?],* from Wycombe, Bucks County, United Kingdom, on Duckett's *Catullus in English Poetry,* was curt and dismissive of both Duckett's project and interpretation: "Dr. Duckett is very liberal in interpretation of her task, including several things, which, in the writer's mind, can have had no reference to Catullus. The translations and paraphrases are interesting, but rather stimulate criticism than satisfy. Catullus, we would be ready to maintain, is more difficult to translate than Virgil."[2] Duckett was judged by the magisterial, and anonymous, "we" voice of the high tradition of

English letters and found wanting. The dismissive tone taken here was echoed elsewhere, suggesting that Duckett's rising prestige at a women's college in America was not reinforced in the greater world of classical learning still dominated by the two great universities of England.

But Duckett reacted to rebuffs with enterprise. In 1912 she responded to her courteous dismissal as a serious scholar at Cambridge by obtaining another fellowship, this time to Bryn Mawr College across the Atlantic Ocean. She resubmitted her monograph "Studies in Ennius" as a dissertation toward the requirements for the Ph.D.[3] By 1914, armed at last with the highest degree awarded in academia, she taught briefly as an instructor at Western College for Women in Oxford, Ohio. In 1916 Duckett became an instructor in Latin at Smith College and began her academic ascent. In 1928 she was made a full professor; somewhat later she became John M. Greene Professor of Classical Languages and Literature. She held that chair until she retired in 1949.

New World institutions that educated women did not alone remake Duckett into the confident scholar of her later years. Her lifelong partner, Mary Ellen Chase, preformed the miracle of coaxing Duckett out of her diffidence in large part. Duckett was already a faculty member at Smith College when Mary Ellen Chase arrived in 1926 to teach on the English faculty and offer courses on the English novel and the King James's version of the Bible. Chase was articulate, opinionated, confident, and determined; that is, she possessed all the brash qualities that Eleanor Duckett lacked. By 1930 the two women had set up housekeeping and lived together happily, only to be parted by Chase's death in 1973. Their small white house with its view of Paradise Pond, sandwiched between the president's imposing quarters and the new quadrangle of residences that allowed Smith to become the largest women's college in the United States, was a haven for Duckett, a genuine source of strength. It was Duckett's "unflagging routine" to leave that house each morning for her office, return to a good lunch prepared by a capable Chase, and then repeat the program for the afternoon.[4] The two scholars attended dinner parties together and traveled widely between terms and on sabbaticals. They walked to Saint John's Episcopal Church three blocks away each Sunday and sat in the front of the church but in separate pews. In "Mary Ellen Chase, A Portrait: 1962" for the *Colby College Library Quarterly,* Duckett praised Chase and made clear her debt to her great friend and supporter.[5] It is quite clear that a deep bond of love united these two women. In this nurturing partnership Duckett would gain the confidence to throw off her timidity, evolve in her interests, and learn to write with verve, all under the influence of Mary Ellen Chase. If hers was a career that reflected triumph over early critics, it was so because Duckett found in Chase deep appreciation for her talents and no-nonsense support for plotting a new course.

The contrast between a vivid Mary Ellen Chase and a pale Eleanor Shipley Duckett struck everyone who knew them. Chase wore bright red whenever she could; Duckett preferred pale blue or sedate gray. Chase wore makeup and fixed others with a piercing eye—indeed, her eyes practically snapped. Duckett wore no makeup, and her eyes tended to slide away when meeting others'. Chase gloried in her classroom popularity; Duckett became an excellent teacher through intense effort. She rued her 8:30 Latin 28 class, where on a Monday morning she had to engage the minds of "bored, tired students" still focused on their weekend dates.[6] But as her colleague Charles Henderson noted when writing her obituary, Duckett could dazzle a class by translating into good Latin any current phrase, saying, or news headline (she expected this of her students as well). She would throw back her head and narrow her eyes and perfect Latin would pour forth.[7] For Duckett students tried their best. They were not in advanced Latin to be entertained but to learn appreciation of an ancient language by both translating Latin into English and writing simple English phrases in Latin. They were not being "trained" into a profession but introduced to the liberal arts and "in a special way to the meaning of words."[8]

Had her career as a faculty member continued in the discipline of classics, Duckett would be remembered as an excellent teacher and a careful scholar who produced a small body of scholarly work. Duckett might have continued to emulate her instructors by writing as they did, using the magisterial "we" in a somewhat heavy-handed prose. She might have remained true to her early Ciceronian sentence structure interwoven with many subordinate (dependent) clauses. In matter of fact, in early writings Duckett could produce paragraphs with a lead sentence followed by two subsequent ones, ten lines and eleven lines respectively, both bristling with semicolons and studded with parenthetical phrases.[9] Clearly she aspired to models set for her in early life.

Sometime in the late 1920s Duckett changed the focus of her study, exchanged classical philology for history, and began to write for a wider audience, eschewing Cicero and other classical models for the most part. She began to explore the late-antique world and the Latin texts of Christian authors, so she figures among those scholars who helped to reestablish the first centuries of the Common Era as a period worth scholarly attention rather than as a wasteland to be skipped over. This led in very short order to engagement with early medieval Christian authors whose Latin differed substantially in tone and content from the Golden Age and Silver Age authors of antiquity (these were Duckett's preferred descriptors).[10] Duckett recognized that the early Middle Ages were understudied in contrast to the classical age, and she realized that the medieval age required interpretive skills that were not present in the discipline of classics as practiced early in the twentieth century.

Little evidence survives on Duckett's thoroughgoing reorientation, but the model of Mary Ellen Chase's own success and coaching for her appreciated and diffident friend should not be discounted. Letters exchanged by Duckett and Chase have not been preserved; the women were seldom apart, so letters would not provide help in any case. Still, the example of Chase looms over Duckett's transformation. Chase wrote for an audience of educated persons—particularly educated women. Chase wrote in brief sentences with active verbs; she avoided the passive voice as far as possible. She enjoyed popular success and wrote with rising confidence, stemming in large part from best-selling works, both fiction and nonfiction: her *Bible for the Common Reader* was perhaps her most enduring work; *Windswept,* her most popular.[11]

Under Chase's tutelage Duckett managed to keep her own voice but adapted her writing to a more general audience. She began to write in shorter sentences with considerable wit and sympathetic insight into character. Her writing reflected the same respect for the educated that underlay Mary Ellen Chase's success. Beyond this Duckett began the challenging task of educating herself in the discipline of history. Whereas her former classicism was a product of the schools, Duckett's history would be the interpretation of a self-educated scholar. It owed very little to current concerns in the academy on either side of the Atlantic Ocean, as her reviews make more than clear. In a sense Duckett's history was a departure and an adoption of a novel sympathetic voice for a little known age and its Christian believers. Old stories brought to life were treated as novel histories holding surprises for contemporary readers. Duckett marveled that such lives could be lived and such thoughts articulated in early times. Her creativity as a scholar and writer, so evident in her later works, had its origins in midcareer efforts to reform her writing style while thoroughly reeducating herself.

Among her new concerns chronology figured importantly. There was to be no mixing of texts as the works of Golden or Silver Age authors might be mingled in classical philology: in Duckett's history the fifth century received attention and then, systematically, she moved forward into the sixth century (*The Gateway to the Middle Ages,* 1938). Marching onward, Duckett produced *Anglo-Saxon Saints and Scholars* on England's age of conversion. She then wrote *Alcuin, Friend of Charlemagne: His World and History,* bringing her concerns into the eighth and ninth centuries, followed soon by *Saint Dunstan of Canterbury: A Study of Monastic Reform in the Tenth Century.* Duckett's *Alfred the Great,* about a king from the same century, appeared in 1956; her *Wandering Saints of the Early Middle Ages* (1959) encompassed lives from all the early Christian centuries. Her subsequent works—*Carolingian Portraits: A Study in the Ninth Century, Women and Their Letters in the Early Middle Ages, Death and Life in the Tenth Century,* and *Medieval Portraits from the East and West*—cast attention on the entire early-medieval era or focused on the Carolingian Renaissance and the tenth century. Linearity in narrative voice characteristic of her fifth-century Christian models, Saint Augustine and the somewhat later Isidore of Seville in particular, became her trusted historical method, and they served her well.

Next Duckett, a woman of deep faith and devotion to the Episcopal Church, trusted the spirit and truthfulness of her Christian authors. The classics were parent to many civilizations; the early Middle Ages by contrast were witness to the birth of Europe and an age of conversion. She saw the struggle toward orthodoxy as a moving drama and the formation of the church as a holy task. Her trust in early Christian texts was deep and perhaps somewhat unquestioning: for example, she accepted without challenge the opinion of Caesarius of Arles, who blamed Jews for the fall of his besieged city in 507. Her trust could be uncritical—at least her reviewers were sometimes of that opinion. Evaluating *Gateway to the Middle Ages* in the *Cambridge Review,* Philip Grierson noted that Duckett's history was, in the main, selective, in part because of its trust in Christian authors. For example, he criticized her acceptance of Bishop Gregory's account of the baptism of Clovis, noting that Duckett ignored recent scholarship in which a Belgian scholar contended the baptism did not occur in 496 but later in 506.[12] Still, Grierson affirmed, such lapses did not detract from the excellence of the book. Mario A. Pei said of her *Alcuin* in the *Romanic Review* that he appreciated Duckett's history but believed she was not up on recent linguistic scholarship, which might, of course, have sharpened her critical sensibilities.[13] Richard Sullivan, reviewing Duckett's *Alfred,* noted that the technique of writing on Alfred's world made Wessex appear to be "the hub of the universe, which it was not."[14] Duckett's presentation of the learned and Christian King Alfred took on immediacy that endowed his time and place with great consequence, perhaps more than it warranted. But Alfred's struggles were those of a learned Christian ruler in an age of settlement, so Duckett regarded his life as momentous, as a devout Christian woman born in the West Country of England might well see it.

If strong allegiance to her Anglican beliefs informed Duckett's work, so did her feminism. Duckett's only essay devoted exclusively to women, *Women and Their Letters in the Early Middle Ages,* did not appear until 1965 and then only in response to a request that she consider medieval women for the Katharine Asher Engel Lecture Series. But in a sense Duckett had been writing on women all along. She noted in 1965 that "scribes who then copied texts were busy in recording for the future epistles of Pope and Emperors, of bishops and abbots. They had no time for the problems and perplexities, the aims and ambitions of mere women."[15] Still, her earlier works were studded with references to women and what they wrote. When she discussed Saint Benedict in *Gateway to the Middle Ages,* she wrote about his sister Saint Scholastica as well. The correspondence of Boniface and Leoba had appeared in earlier work; indeed, the paired saints, whenever they appeared, were of special interest to her. Single Christian women came into her narratives as well. In *Wandering Saints* the fourth-century's Etheria [Egeria], who traveled over Europe and Asia Minor, figured prominently, with full credit given for her writing and gift of liturgy to the West. As a classicist Duckett had encountered few texts by or about women, the accidents of redaction or preservation being the cause, as she stated. The Christian centuries by no means brought parity of women to men, but for Duckett early Christianity afforded at least some women a place, if small, in the world of letters. Some had learned Latin and possessed the temerity to address Christian men with their concerns and opinions. If Duckett tended to identify herself with early Christian authors generally, she identified herself wholeheartedly with those among them who were women. She understood women had received little attention because of the concerns of traditional scholarship. Women may not have been, as she noted in 1965, abbots, bishops, emperors, or popes, but for an audience of educated women early women authors were significant, whatever their concerns. Duckett wrote about them with sympathy.

More surprising perhaps was her treatment of notorious women of the early-medieval world. Brunhild, for example, received positive treatment at her hands, at least during her early years as queen to Sigebert, king of Austrasia. The true hero of her narrative was, of course, Gregory, bishop of Tours, whose history she regarded as "an unvarnished story of humanity" and a "very plain record."[16] In taking up Gregory's perspective Duckett viewed Brunhild as energetic, a queen capable of holding her own even against the nobles of Austrasia. Brunhild had the great advantage of conversion to orthodox Christianity from Arianism when she first became a queen of the Franks. Brunhild was literate and wrote to the powers of the day—such as the emperor Maurice and the empress Anastasia. Duckett was even sympathetic in the face of Brunhild's vengeance against Fredegund, up to a point. Brunhild, as the power behind the throne in her later years, was presented as highly enterprising and every inch a ruler, even when beset by strong enemies. Women of the medieval world matched men in their ambitions as Duckett portrayed them.

Judith, daughter of Charles the Bald and stepmother (later also sister-in-law) to Alfred the Great, was treated even more sympathetically. Duckett recognized that Judith assumed the office of crowned queen rather than live under the title of king's wife in Wessex. Duckett emphasized the importance of the rite that endowed Judith with her crown and quoted it at length. This invention of queenship as medieval office has received subsequent treatment by Pauline Stafford that goes far beyond what Duckett presented in her pages.[17] However, as a discerning historian Duckett recognized the importance of the precedent established by Judith as queen and brought it to light.[18]

But that was the early medieval world that might on occasion champion women's cause, and now was now. Duckett never overtly espoused feminism, and for her the authorial voice of the scholar was always masculine, as she had been instructed to speak and write in her early years. Well into her retirement, in 1954 when she addressed the Smith chapter of Phi Beta Kappa, Duckett still spoke as "he" when she spoke as a scholar. This is worth, perhaps, quoting at length.

> The second way of scholarship is no road proper. It is but a trail, has many windings, is frequently lost in fog, is beset by muddy tracks, by slippery places on which men weary be broken, by pits from which they sometimes fail to rise. It is a way of fear and hesitations, or groping and struggle; the way of the scholar who walks alone to find knowledge, to search after learning for its own sake; the path of the man who is bold to walk hand and hand with the Lady Philosophy perhaps to greet undismayed her sister, the Lady Poverty.
>
> Yet hard though it is, this solitary climbing of the hill of knowledge brings its own pleasure, its own immediate reward. Every one—child, youth and mature man—enjoys finding out things by himself and for himself. There comes at last to our scholar a moment when he has long stumbled alone upon his path absorbed purely in his tubes or compass or telescope or text, when at last he has climbed high enough by his toil to

gain a wide view from his intellectual hill of difficulty. Now as he revels in this view, the necessity seizes him to pass it on to others, those in the valley below, something of that which he, the student and scholar, is gazing upon. They too, shall learn and understand and enjoy this view, through his words, his power of communicating.[19]

Duckett never entirely forsook the complex sentence and extended metaphor that struck her as appropriate to the requirements of formal oration. Here the cadence of classicism was placed at the service of lauding scholarship, in a very real sense Duckett's own values. But the scholar is masculine, a man who seeks the hand of Lady Philosophy and perhaps of Lady Poverty. The edifying example of the scholarly life that Duckett presented to young women at Smith College was unwaveringly masculine. If women were to become scholars like her, they were enjoined to leave behind a feminine persona and adopt a masculine voice. It was not particularly unusual for a woman academic of Duckett's generation to adopt the generic "he" for commonality of experience, but in this context, when Duckett presented a passionate call to the scholarly life to women undergraduates, it seems misplaced to contemporary ears.

Throughout her career Duckett wrote and taught about the enduring influence of the classics. "Some English Echoes of Catullus," composed in 1922 and disparaged by her anonymous critic as an inappropriate subject, found echoes of Catullus in Ben Jonson, Thomas Campion, John Donne, and others.[20] Duckett sought out the spirit of the ancients in modern works, and her careful textual analysis remained attuned to echoes of classical voices. When she turned her attention to early-medieval literature, that sure eye for classical influence—in spirit, stylistic elements, or subject matter—served Duckett very well. A running commentary on classical antecedents marked her historical writing, most aptly one might add, given her strong self-identification as a text-based historian. Medieval scholars recognized an acute literary sensibility when they read her work, which in no small part accounts for the greater frequency with which her books were reviewed as serious works of history. If, as Duckett claimed, she had taken an "over-dose of Classical authors" in her early years, she knew how to put that overdose to good use in her medieval history.[21] Richard Sullivan recognized her erudition and applauded it in his review for *Manuscripta*. In the *New York Times Book Review* Kenneth Setton called *Carolingian Portraits* the best kind of popular history because it treated medieval texts to thoroughgoing analysis. A. L. Rowse said of Duckett's *Alfred* that it was "the kind of history I like," in the *New York Times Book Review* in 1956. In the *London Times Literary Supplement,* 22 February 1968, the anonymous reviewer of *Death and Life in the Tenth Century* noted, "Miss Duckett carries her learning so lightly that there is a danger of underrating the wide erudition which pervades these chapters."[22]

This was gratifying praise for a writer whose early works had been greeted with little respect. But Duckett had learned how to cultivate scholarly recognition as well. She obtained positions as a reviewer herself, most notably for the *New York Times Book Review;* this helped to assure that her own works were given attention when they appeared. She corresponded with her reviewers and thanked them for their notice and comments. The young Michael Wallace-Hadrill wrote back to her from his post in the Department of History at the University of Manchester, 6 January 1955, that his was but a "piffling review" and thus not worthy of mention. However, he appreciated her letter once received. David Knowles acknowledged the gift of a copy of her *Anglo-Saxon Saints and Scholars,* but apparently this did not win Duckett a review from him.[23] Knowles did have nice things to say about her *Carolingian Portraits* in *Notes and Queries of the Oxford University Press* after its publication; some contacts took a long time to cultivate. Of the later work Knowles noted its good qualities and warned, "[B]ut [it was] not meant for a scholarly audience." Over the years historians came to greater realization of the service Duckett performed for their discipline. She wrote works that were accessible to general readers, thus raising awareness of a little-known age. After reading Duckett readers might attempt more formidable scholarly works on the subject. Her books could be assigned to undergraduates as well. On college and university library shelves their worn condition suggests that they were taken up and read for college courses while other nearby tomes languished. Duckett had found a place in the world of letters and a growing recognition of her importance to that world.

In her years as a faculty member and later in her retirement, Duckett revisited Cambridge frequently, composed her monographs using the excellent resources of its libraries, and while there she cultivated a circle of friends. Mary Ellen Chase frequently accompanied Duckett on her trips back to Cambridge and appears to have been as borne up and stimulated by these visits as Duckett. Among their friends Eric Milner-White, dean of King's College, Cambridge, proved to be a particularly close and valuable link with the English academic establishment. He produced the cover blurb for her *Gateway to the Middle Ages* in 1938, lending the work the prestige of his Cambridge office. That very year Milner-White and Duckett collaborated on her only foray into fictional writing, *The Book of Hugh and Nancy.* Mary Ellen Chase contributed the forward to the book. It is the story of orphaned twins separated: Nancy to live with her aunt in Northampton, Massachusetts, and Hugh to remain in England. During their separation the children keep precocious journals and share them by mail. Although ostensibly a children's book, it was also a comparative study of grade-school education in England and the United States. Hugh, first at a council school, finally gains entrance to a choir school, and his fortunes look up. Nancy seems better pleased with school in America, and ultimately the twins are happily reunited in America through the kind intercession of their aunt.

This is about as far as Duckett's feelings for a maternal role in life appear to have taken her. Her imaginings of a family do reveal something about her own Atlantic crossing and adoption of a new land. Duckett came to appreciate the less restrictive environment in American education, even while she remained powerfully in the grip of England and the values of traditional schooling there. She kept a foot in both worlds and thoughtfully combined what she found best both in her own career and in her writing. When, in 1942, it was necessary for Duckett to register as a resident alien in the basement of the post office in Northampton, Massachusetts, she underwent fingerprinting as well as a thoroughgoing interview. She sent a letter to the *Daily Hampshire Gazette,* 4 September 1942, on the encounter. Duckett claimed she had approached it with distaste, but the ceremony was full of goodwill and comfort due to the good offices of officials.[24]

Once she discovered her strength in writing about the early Middle Ages, Duckett never wavered. As her retirement years lengthened, her publications brought honors and invitations that reconfirmed the wisdom of this decision. Smith awarded Duckett an honorary degree in 1949. According to the *Biographical Dictionary of North American Classicists,* the University of London had also awarded her an honorary degree many years earlier, in 1920.[25] Her popularity as an author was acknowledged when the Pen and Brush Club awarded her a prize for *Anglo-Saxon Saints and Scholars* as the most distinguished work of nonfiction for 1947. With the publication of *Saint Dunstan,* Saint Dunstan's University in Charlottetown, Prince Edward's Island, Canada, awarded Duckett an honorary degree. Duckett traveled far and wide on the academic lecture circuit, buoyed up by her newfound eminence in retirement.

It would be valuable to know if requests to lecture at Cambridge held special meaning for Duckett over and above the other invitations to speak or be honored at institutions of higher learning. When at Cambridge Duckett did give lectures and was introduced as a product of its classics training with the requisite tripos that crowned that course of study. Duckett saved a letter from an M. L. Cartwright, 2 March, 1957, inviting her to give the Founder's Day Lectures at Girton College the following February, to which she assented promptly. Some biographical accounts of Duckett's life state that by 1957 she had already been awarded an honorary degree from Girton College, in 1952.[26] But on Duckett's own insistence that degree was in no way honorary but earned. In her retirement years Duckett received a doctorate from Girton College by sending in four of her published works for examination. They were *Latin Writers of the Fifth Century, Anglo-Saxon Saints and Scholars, Gateway to the Middle Ages,* and *Alcuin, Friend of Charlemagne,* in other words, the four volumes of early-medieval history that she had completed to date. These four published works were submitted for examination to the Old Schools [Committee] and the Board of Research Studies of Cambridge University. On their strength Duckett was approved and at last earned her final degree at Cambridge. It was perhaps a moment of vindication for a woman scholar. Only beginning in 1948 was Girton College authorized to award a doctor of letters degree, so Duckett figures among the college's earliest doctors, despite the fact that her years as a student there had been completed before World War I broke out.

One wonders at the tenacity of this woman scholar who finally wrung recognition from the university that inspired and educated her but also treated her to painful rebuffs in her student years. Her career concluded with great satisfaction but with some sorrow at the end. After the death of Mary Ellen Chase in 1973, Duckett lost the house on Paradise Pond, perhaps the result of a straitened financial condition.[27] She entered a nursing home and was not sufficiently coherent to be interviewed in the last year of her life. Her books, her most prized personal possessions, were auctioned off in Easthampton, Massachusetts, in June 1978. A final scholarly project, a précis of the earliest church councils, was of no interest to the University of Chicago Press. These were sad events, but none could compare to the loss of her companion, Mary Ellen Chase. When Duckett in turn died in 1976, she was buried next to Chase near that well-loved Maine summer home, Windswept, as she had requested. Smith College named two neighboring student residences Chase and Duckett in 1968. "Eleanor Duckett, Smith College Legend, Dies" the *New York Times* proclaimed, 30 November 1976. Honors and eminence had been Duckett's portion in retirement. She was blessed with the long years necessary to at last fulfill her dream to be a recognized, indeed an honored, scholar in her own right.

Notes

1. Duckett, *Women and Their Letters*.

2. Eleanor Shipley Duckett Papers, box 2, Smith College Archives. The review was clipped and preserved among Duckett's papers without full citation. Only the first four words of the journal title were penciled in; the assumption about the rest is the author's.

3. Eleanor Shipley Duckett, "Studies in Ennius" (Ph.D. diss., Bryn Mawr College, 1914).

4. Henderson, "Obituary."

5. Duckett, "Mary Ellen Chase."

6. Eleanor Shipley Duckett Papers, box 1, Smith College Archives.

7. Henderson, "Obituary," 58.

8. Duckett, "'Latin Prose' and Modern Learning," 436.

9. See Duckett, "Classics," 75.

10. Duckett, "Classics," 70.

11. See Mary Ellen Chase Papers, box 1, Smith College Archives, for numerous reviews of this book, published by Macmillan in 1944, and revised in 1952. Duckett favored Chase's publishers for her manuscripts as well.

12. Grierson, review of *Gateway to the Middle Ages*.

13. Mario A. Pei, review of *Alcuin*.

14. Sullivan, review of *Alfred the Great*.

15. Duckett, *Women and Their Letters*, 3.

16. Duckett, *Gateway to the Middle Ages*, 227.

17. Stafford, *Queens, Concubines, and Dowagers*.

18. Duckett, *Alfred the Great*, 34–40.

19. Eleanor Shipley Duckett, unpublished manuscript, Phi Beta Kappa address, April 1954, Eleanor Shipley Duckett Papers, box 1, Smith College Archives.

20. Review of "Some English Echoes of Catullus," by Eleanor Shipley Duckett, *Classical Weekly*, 177–80.

21. Henderson, "Obituary," 58.

22. Eleanor Shipley Duckett Papers, box 2, Smith College Archives. Duckett preserved most of her reviews.

23. Eleanor Shipley Duckett Papers, box 2, Smith College Archives.
24. Eleanor Shipley Duckett Papers, box 1, Smith College Archives.
25. Briggs, *Biographical Dictionary of North American Classicists*, s.v. "Eleanor Shipley Duckett." The entry may have confused her degree in pedagogy for an honorary degree.
26. Briggs, *Biographical Dictionary of North American Classicists*, s.v. "Eleanor Shipley Duckett."
27. Financial statements were not preserved with Duckett's other private papers. It is clear that Duckett earned royalties from some of her books in retirement. Commercial houses would have paid more than university presses. She would not have earned anything like the royalties that came to Mary Ellen Chase, and this stream of income may have left her with Chase's death, since Chase's heirs were relatives. Duckett would have had a small pension from Smith and, possibly, Social Security in her last three years of life.

Select Bibliography of Works by Eleanor Shipley Duckett

"The Influence of Alexandrian Poetry upon the Aeneid." *Classical Journal* 11 (1915/16): 333–48.
Hellenistic Influence on the "Aeneid." Smith College Classical Studies, 1. Northampton, Mass.: Smith College, 1920.
"Latin Prose and Modern Learning." *Classical Journal* 17 (1921/22): 430–37.
"Some English Echoes of Catullus." *Classical Weekly* 15 (October 1921–May 1922): 177–80.
"Special Honors System as Carried on in Smith College." *Education* 46 (March 1926): 420–22.
Latin Writers of the Fifth Century. New York: H. Holt, 1930.
"The Classics." In *Roads to Knowledge*, edited by William Allen Neilson, 66–92. New York: W. W. Norton, 1933.
With Eric Milner-White. *The Book of Hugh and Nancy.* New York: Macmillan, 1938.
The Gateway to the Middle Ages. New York: Macmillan, 1938.
Anglo-Saxon Saints and Scholars. New York: Macmillan, 1947.
Alcuin, Friend of Charlemagne, His World and His Work. New York: Macmillan, 1951.
Saint Dunstan of Canterbury: A Study of Monastic Reform in the Tenth Century. London: Collins; New York: Norton, 1955.
Alfred the Great. Chicago: University of Chicago Press, 1956. Published in 1957 under the title *Alfred the Great and His England* (London: Collins).
The Wandering Saints of the Early Middle Ages. New York: Norton; London: Collins, 1959.
Carolingian Portraits. A Study in the Ninth Century. Ann Arbor: University of Michigan Press, 1962.
"Mary Ellen Chase, A Portrait: 1962," *Colby College Library Quarterly* 6 (1) (1962): 2.
Women and Their Letters in the Early Middle Ages. Margaret Asher Engel Lecture, 1965. Northampton, Mass: Smith College, 1965.
Death and Life in the Tenth Century. Ann Arbor: University of Michigan Press, 1967; London: Sidgwick & Jackson, 1972.
Papers. Smith College Archives. Smith College. Northampton, Mass.

Works Cited

Briggs, Ward W. Jr., ed. *Biographical Dictionary of North American Classicists.* Westport, Conn.: Greenwood Press, 1994.
Chase, Mary Ellen. *Windswept.* New York: Macmillan, 1941.

Grierson, Philip. Review of *Gateway to the Middle Ages*. *Cambridge Review* (11 November 1938): 88
Henderson, Charles. "Obituary: Eleanor Shipley Duckett." *Smith Alumnae Quarterly* 68 (2) (1977): 58–59
Pei, Mario A. Review of *Alcuin, Friend of Charlemagne*. *The Romanic Review* 43 (1952): 54–55.
Stafford, Pauline. *Queens, Concubines, and Dowagers*. Athens: University of Georgia Press, 1983.
Sullivan, Richard. Review of *Alfred the Great*. *Manuscripta* 2 (1) (1958): 51–52.

CHAPTER 17

Hope Emily Allen (1883–1960)
An Independent Scholar

JOHN C. HIRSH

HOPE EMILY ALLEN, one of the foremost students of medieval history, literature, and religion of her generation, was born in Oneida, in upstate New York, originally the perfectionist "holy community" that the radical reformer John Humphrey Noyes had founded in 1848 to test his biblically based teachings concerning sexual and other relationships. Noyes' teachings held, among other things, that marriage became over time an encumbrance to love, so that at Oneida sexual relationships were overseen by a committee that allowed, and sometimes disallowed, their formation and continuation. Thanks to the skills that some of its members brought with them, the community became proficient in the manufacture of metal products (these included animal traps and table ware), so that it was able to incorporate itself and flourish. The factories and the social experiment that gave birth to them continued until 1879, when, somewhat abruptly, Noyes deserted his foundation, which was by then coming under pressure from authorities outside the community and from dissension within, for the legal safety of Canada. In September 1880, following a vote by members of the community, the Oneida community was officially and legally broken up, to be replaced by Oneida Community, Ltd., a joint-stock company, in which all members of the original community and their descendants held stock. It was these stock holdings that largely funded Hope Allen's medieval research over the course of her career.[1]

Hope Allen's parents had met in the community and parented their first child, Grosvenor Noyes Allen, in January 1873. The birth of the child increased their love, so much so that it was deemed by the community elders to have become a "special attachment," and the two were ordered to separate. True to their commitment they

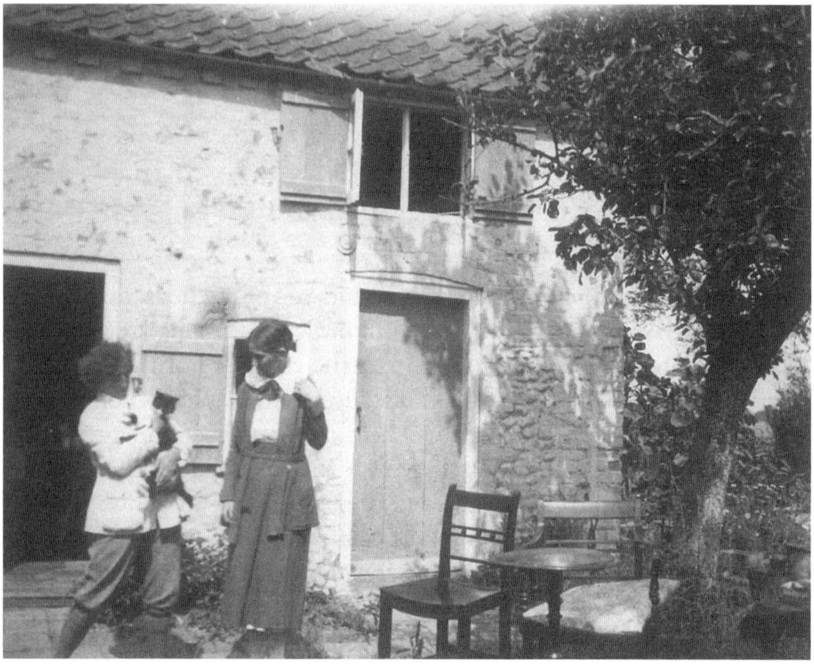

did so, and later in life Hope Allen would ascribe that commitment to a strong desire to escape the religious legalisms of their childhood. But whatever its source their love remained with their commitment, and after the 1880 breakup of the community they married. In November 1883 they announced the birth of their second (and last) child, whom they named Hope Emily Allen.

Precocious though sickly in childhood (she was thought to be "tubercular"), Hope Allen distinguished herself at school, and her early interests in religious history (in adolescence she was much interested in the Puritans) and in objects that had historical or cultural associations, which were then called "relics," remained with her throughout life.[2] Her family confidently intended that she would attend college, and the choice fell, for unknown reasons, on Bryn Mawr. For a short while the young woman resisted, wanting to become a writer instead, but in the end she acquiesced and entered Bryn Mawr. At the time its president was the formidable M. Carey Thomas, whose forthright and energetic feminism motivated generations of Bryn Mawr students. "I have forgotten everything I learned at Bryn Mawr," one student (not Allen) wrote to Dr. Thomas in later years, "but I can still remember you standing in chapel telling us to believe in women."[3] But Allen's Bryn Mawr was also that of Carleton Brown, who would soon distinguish himself in Middle English studies, a field to which he introduced Allen. In her last two years in college she was particularly engaged by two visiting speakers, the great novelist Henry James, now on an American tour, who addressed the students in her senior year, and more importantly Mary Berenson, who a year earlier lectured on the methods that she and her husband, Bernard Berenson, employed to fix the authenticity of the Renaissance paintings they studied. She emphasized their attention to revelatory detail in a way that attracted Allen, who recorded both addresses in campus publications; Berenson's may have awakened an interest that years later found expression in Allen's studies of the authenticity of works attributed to the fourteenth-century English mystic Richard Rolle.

In 1905 Allen graduated from Bryn Mawr as one of "The Ten," the ten graduates with the highest academic averages. She stayed on for another year to take an M.A. (which proved to be her last degree), and it was during this period that she developed her reading of the thirteenth-century English work she (and her contemporaries) called "Ancren Riwle" and began her studies of Richard Rolle. At the completion of the year she moved to Radcliffe College, at that time attached to, but not a part of, Harvard University, in Cambridge, Massachusetts, there to study for a Ph.D.

Her time in Cambridge was useful and served to introduce her into a wider world of academic accomplishment and ambition, but it is difficult to believe that she was altogether happy there. At Bryn Mawr she had become accustomed to being treated as a mature scholar and an adult, but at Radcliffe women were both regarded and treated as second-class citizens of Harvard. As at many American universities, women were forbidden to attend lectures with men, and since Radcliffe had no faculty of its own, the lectures of senior Harvard scholars were repeated to Radcliffe students, sometimes on the same day, usually by graduate students and by younger colleagues of the great men, though in such cases Radcliffe graduate students were mixed with undergraduates and the lectures were reworked so as to appeal to all present. The practice constituted an almost gratuitous insult to the Radcliffe graduate students, one of several slights that Allen (and her fellow students) had to endure. Her academic work, however, continued apace, and in 1910 she published a fifty-five-page article, "The Authorship of the *Prick of Conscience*," which appeared in *Studies in English and Comparative Literature Presented to Agnes Irwin, Litt.D. Dean of Radcliffe College 1894–1909*. Her year at Radcliffe had deepened her studies and even begun her scholarly reputation, but when she left it for Newnham College at Cambridge University, she did so willingly and never looked back.

It was Hope Allen's Radcliffe connection that led her to Cambridge, however, and it was to it that she first appealed. Arriving in Cambridge in 1911, she presented herself as a Ph.D. student at Radcliffe, working under William Henry Schofield on a dissertation tentatively titled "A Study of the Canon of Richard Rolle of Hampole," an extension of her work on the *Prick of Conscience*. This was not her first trip to England (she had visited with her mother the previous year), but it was the first time she could set up independently, in her own room, with privacy and an income. Not long after she arrived, however, she made a life-altering choice and turned down an offer from Dr. M. Carey Thomas of a readership in English at Bryn Mawr ("$800 the first year, $900 the second, $1000 the third"). Rather she cast her lot with Cambridge and research, both of which she had come to love. But in this visit she extended herself too far, working with such industry that in February 1912 she suffered a breakdown, which, for an unknown period, curtailed all work. Evidence for this important event is limited, and some of it may well have been destroyed. A letter from Allen to Radcliffe postponing the date on which she was to submit for her degree gives a physical breakdown as the reason; another from Dean Coes of Radcliffe to her supervisor is more candid and suggests that she may have to abandon her work on Rolle for a less arduous project on *Ancrene Riwle*. Later in the year she returned to Oneida, where she both recovered and took up academic work again in earnest. But in September 1913 her mother died, and the care of her aging father fell to her. Not long thereafter Europe was at war. Throughout the war Allen remained in Oneida, publishing article after article, note after note. She did not doubt that after the war was over she would return to England and to Richard Rolle, though not this time to Cambridge. The war ended in November 1918, but family bonds held her still. Then on 7 July 1920 her father died, and the last tie to hold her back was cut. By the end of the year she was again in London, having secured lodging at 116 Cheyne Row with a former and still close Cambridge friend and painter named Marietta Pallis.

During the next twenty years, from 1920 until the beginning of the Second World War in 1939, Hope Allen produced her most important and lasting work and distinguished herself as a medievalist of the first order, focusing on medieval English religion, especially mysticism, and the role of medieval women in the development of religious expression in the fourteenth and fifteenth centuries. These interests were reflected in the three major intellectual projects that occupied Allen from 1920 to 1939: her studies in the *Ancrene Riwle,* an early thirteenth-century (she mistakenly thought early-twelfth-century) rule for three anchoresses that she studied extensively and whose audience and author she sought to identify; her identification of the works inscribed by the fourteenth-century English mystic Richard Rolle and her construction of the probable course of his life; and finally her 1934 identification, naming, and subsequent annotation of the *Book of Margery Kempe,* a fifteenth-century work detailing the religious and (some) other preoccupations of Margery Kempe, whose social position, determined religiousness, and devout practices caused Allen to rethink her understanding of the development of English religious life at the close of the medieval period. During this period she also pursued other interests: Anglo-Norman and medieval Latin literature; the Vernon manuscript, a huge codex containing numerous items written in Middle English, whose early history she meticulously explored; the local history of Oneida, particularly where it connected with Native American history; and the writing of fiction. But these were all finally subordinate to the larger projects in which she became deeply invested.

The first of these projects had its origins while she was a student at Bryn Mawr, and no doubt owed its inception to work in a class or seminar with Carleton Brown, though possibly her own special circumstances—having been born into a religious community and now settled into an academic environment—may have played a part as well. But she would not have found *Ancrene Riwle* easily accessible. Probably she first encountered it in the Camden Society edition of 1853, edited and translated by James Morton (even today, many editions later, it remains a difficult text to read accurately). Only with some difficulty can scholars today appreciate the difficulties that faced students and scholars at the beginning of the twentieth century, a time that lacked not only many of the handbooks, facsimiles, and editions that are now available, but also most of the means of photographic reproduction that are today everywhere at hand. This relative isolation may have increased the interest, at least away from Britain, in some of the more recondite texts, and *Ancrene Riwle,* a work known today in academic circles as *Ancrene Wisse* from its title in MS. Corpus Christi College Cambridge 402, seems to have benefited from this circumstance. Certainly when Hope Allen began to study the text she was drawn to its reception and in particular to the three consanguineous young sisters who had asked that it be drawn up for their use. She began not by asking who its author was (though she would come to that in time) but who these women were and how the work itself figured in the intellectual environment that gave it birth.

A 1918 article in the journal *PMLA,* "The Origin of the *Ancrene Riwle,*" at once advanced her case and added to her reputation, even among those who, whether immediately or in the end, dissented from her conclusions. Hope Allen came to believe that the work was associated with Kilburn Priory, a twelfth-century foundation that she identified as an Augustinian house attached to the Benedictine community of

Westminster. It had been located in what is now North London, on a site that may possibly now be covered by Saint Mary's Church, Priory Road, Hampstead, and the names of its original community members are known: Christine, Emma, and Gunhilda. These Allen identified with the three young women who caused *Ancrene Riwle* to be inscribed. Her important *PMLA* article was followed by other notes and articles, which added to our knowledge of the text and had the effect of supporting her identification, which still required, however, an early twelfth-century date for the text.

Scholars now understand that the date she proposed was almost certainly too early and that as a result the identification with Kilburn was very probably mistaken. In spite of this circumstance, however, her studies on the text and its environment contributed markedly to the developing understanding of medieval English religious practices and attitudes that took place in the first part of the twentieth century. In January 1925 R. W. Chambers published an article in the *Review of English Studies*, "Recent Research on the *Ancrene Riwle*," in the course of which he treated Hope Allen's work. He did not disguise the difficulties he found with it, for example, the fact that the text of the *Ancrene Riwle* contained embedded references to works of Saint Aelred of Riveaux, canonized in 1191, too late for the date Allen was proposing, and thirteen citations from Saint Bernard of Clairvaux, which he thought particularly indicative, since they appear most often in the literature following the saint's death in 1153. He acknowledged that scribal contamination could account for some of what troubled him, but he thought the allusions to Saint Bernard in particular required a later date. He insisted too that, even if the early date was finally rejected, as it has been, Allen's work was of lasting value. "Miss Allen has linked the *Ancrene Riwle* with the religious movements of the twelfth century," he wrote, "and shown it as the work of a man living at a time of many strong religious influences, sensitive to all, but not giving the zeal of a partisan to any."[4] With some changes, he could have been writing about Hope Allen herself.

Allen never gave up her interest in *Ancrene Riwle*, and she never withdrew the early date she had proposed for its composition, though in the 1950s she sometimes indicated to friends that she would be inclined to posit such an early date more tentatively. But during the time she was working on *Ancrene Riwle* she was also developing an interest in Richard Rolle and becoming aware of the difficulties inherent in his canon. Editions of Rolle were widely available, and it is possible that she first encountered him in Carl Horstman's edition *Yorkshire Writers: Richard Rolle of Hampole, an English Father of the Church and His Followers*, published in two volumes in London in 1895 and 1896. As we have seen, she began her studies in a graduate seminar with Carleton Brown at Bryn Mawr and proposed a study of Rolle's canon as the topic for her Radcliffe Ph.D. dissertation. When she returned to England in 1920, it was to undertake this project, adding to it what she came to call "materials for his biography." The addition was important: throughout her life (probably since Bryn Mawr, possibly earlier) Allen was a consistent though unassertive agnostic, a circumstance that informed her academic work. What initially attracted her both to *Ancrene Riwle* and to Richard

Rolle was the narrative implicit in each: with *Ancrene Riwle* that narrative also involved her nascent interest in woman's history, and both were no doubt informed by her years in Oneida and her understanding of its background. The advantage of her agnosticism was that it inclined her to stay well away from the religious or theological implications of whatever text she was considering and to focus on matters of fact and cultural connection (it was thus that she dealt with such religious matters as were inescapable); the limitation was that she would sometimes treat the concept of mysticism somewhat uncritically and was disinclined to explore how far it extended, whether in the mind or in the text she had under review.[5]

But in matters of fact she excelled. Whether informed by Mary Berenson's example, her own interest since childhood in genealogy, or the Oneida community's past, she took easily to working with manuscripts, with which she had had only limited experience. Here she was greatly assisted by an excellent student of manuscripts and a British Museum assistant, J. A. Herbert, whose experience was considerable and whom she paid for consultation and for actual work; indeed, it is not too much to say that he acted virtually as a paid collaborator in the writing, editing, and proofreading of *Writings Ascribed to Richard Rolle, Hermit of Hampole, and Materials for His Biography*, the five-hundred-page great (in both senses) work that Allen produced at the beginning of 1928 (the book itself is dated 1927), which dealt with questions of authorship in virtually all works written by or ascribed to Richard Rolle. Seventy years later it is still consulted by scholars.

Throughout her research Hope Allen employed four criteria in identifying any work as Rolle's: dialect, attribution in at least one manuscript, style, and theme. The last two were particularly problematic: Rolle's style was imitated by countless followers, and his themes informed English spirituality for the next two centuries. There was thus considerable latitude for debate and disagreement. For example, Allen examined with a critical eye three short tracts, "Grace," "Prayer," and "Our Daily Work," which Horstman had confidently printed as Rolle's work in *Yorkshire Writers*. None of the works was ascribed to Rolle in any manuscript, she pointed out, and she was disinclined to believe that they were separate works: she estimated that there was a larger textual contamination at work too. In fact, we know now that she was not mistaken: the tracts are derived from a twelfth-century Latin work by Guido II, prior of Grand-Chartreuse, which incorporated passages from Hugo of Strasbourg's *Compendium theologicae veritatis;* it was there that the so-called Rolle tracts first appeared, thereafter to be translated in two Middle English works, *A Ladder of Foure Ronges by which Men Mowe Wele Clyme to Heuen,* and subsequently in *The Holy Book Gratia Dei.* It was from this second work that the tracts had been extracted and had Rolle's name attached as author, though in fact he was not. This was but one of the problems Allen encountered, but it is illustrative of the difficulties she faced.

Other problems concerned Rolle's biography: Had he, or had he not, been a priest? Allen was inclined to think not, but that complicated a well-known incident in his early life as a hermit, when, reportedly at the age of eighteen, he was called upon to preach in church. Had he been ordained (probably in Paris, said those who advanced this notion), there was nothing very remarkable in the account; but it contradicted the view Hope Allen had taken of her subject, whom she believed young and ardent, attached to his calling, and quite innocent of the charms of Paris. This view embroiled her in controversies that she found trying, and indeed the issue as to whether Rolle actually studied in Paris is still moot, though everyone who writes on it thinks he or she has said the last word. The complications she had to confront were considerable, and even with Herbert's expert help many of the hard choices were finally hers alone. But when completed the book was a triumph, and in 1929 Hope Allen was awarded the Rose Mary Crashay Prize from the British Academy, which included a check for one hundred pounds, almost five hundred 1929 U.S. dollars. A notice of the award appeared, among other places, in the *New York Times,* and almost every scholar Allen knew sent congratulations. In every sense of the phrase, she had arrived.

The year 1929 was a good one in which to receive a cash prize, but it soon became clear to Allen that her Oneida stocks would not be enough to sustain her through the Depression and that she would have to find paid employment. This she did in 1931 as assistant editor of the *Early Modern English Dictionary,* which then was being edited at the University of Michigan. In this capacity Allen advised on a variety of issues and also became a close friend of Margaret Ogden, about whom Michael Adams, who is undertaking a study that will include an examination of Hope Allen's work on the dictionary, writes elsewhere in this volume. It was in 1931 too that Oxford University Press issued a small book she had edited, *The English Writings of Richard Rolle, Hermit of Hampole.* Together the two events seemed to presage well for the future: the Oxford edition suggested that another edition of Middle English texts might be well received in spite of the financial climate, and the money she received for her services with the dictionary would enable her to return for an extended period to London.

During this period Allen also decided what her next project was to be. R. W. Chambers's *Continuity of English Prose,* which, drawing on Allen's published work, identified *Ancrene Riwle* as one of the main connecting links between Old English and Middle English literature, influenced her decision in 1932 to publish an anthology that would treat both the importance and the continuity of women's religious writing in the late medieval period. She successfully approached the American Council of Learned Societies (ACLS) for support, remarking in her application that "there was a general feminist movement in the twelfth century" and she meant to explore it, using the *Ancrene Riwle* (to which she continued to assign an early date) as a starting point but quoting extensively from many other texts she had examined in manuscript as well. Her work would make explicit her continuing interest in the writing of medieval religious woman, a topic that had engaged her from her days at Bryn Mawr but which she had been reluctant to press forward in the past. To advance this study and edition she returned to Britain in the summer of 1934 for a prolonged stay; a most important discovery awaited her there.

Summer is not always a good time to consult with British scholars, even in London, and when Colonel William E. I. Butler-Bowdon, a Lancashire landowner, brought an unidentified fifteenth-century manuscript to the Victoria and Albert Museum for identification, the curators were unsure where to turn. Their usual experts proved to be unavailable, and when they turned to Evelyn Underhill, she directed them to her visiting American cousin. Thus, in late July 1934, Hope Allen came to the V&A and identified the manuscript as the now-famous *Book of Margery Kempe,* a late Middle English account of a powerfully religious, Allen thought "mystical," woman from Lynn. With no interest in transcribing the manuscript or undertaking a philological assessment of its language, Allen suggested to the board of the Early English Text Society (EETS) that the job of editing the work be entrusted to a younger American colleague working on the *Dictionary,* Sanford B. Meech. She herself would collaborate with Meech, write the introduction, and comment on any matters associated with Margery Kempe's mysticism. It sounded so reasonable. If only it had been.

Thus far in her career Hope Allen had indeed been an independent scholar and, financially secure, had been able to work as she wished and with whom she chose. Her relationship with Sanford Meech, however, quickly deteriorated to such a degree that she came to believe, quite correctly, that he was seeking, possibly with the support of the manuscript's owner, to force her off the project (at one point he sought to change the name of the work to "The Journal of Margery Kempe," the name that survives on the frontispiece of the EETS edition). Only the timely and formal intervention of the EETS board, together subsequently with the efforts of the senior editors of the *Dictionary* projects in Michigan, served to deflect Meech from his purpose. Gender bias is sometimes hard to prove, and Hope Allen was not always easy to work with, but it is difficult to believe that Meech would have treated a senior male colleague with the irritation, anger, and contempt he showed, over many months, to Allen.[6] Finally, however, an accommodation was reached with the EETS board, in which Meech would edit the text, and Allen would contribute notes connected to mystical practices and also write a second volume, dealing with matters relevant to the *Book* and incorporating selections from other texts as well, to show where it fit into the development of late-medieval English spirituality. This was, of course, the book that she had proposed to the ACLS, and it was not at all inconvenient that Oxford University Press, through the EETS, would put it into print. The accommodation, from her point of view, could hardly have been better.

Thus in 1940, with England at war, volume 1 of the EETS edition appeared; it had been preceded in London by a popular edition in 1936, the text modernized by the manuscript's owner with Stanford Meech's assistance, though Meech reported that he had made only a very few changes. But the *Book of Margery Kempe* was so unusual, so unlike any other text known from the period, that students of literature and history apprehended it only guardedly and sought to fit it into attitudes that had become fixed and debates that were already underway.[7] Evelyn Underhill, writing in the *Spectator* of 16 October 1936, found the book "almost equally important to students of medieval manners, and disconcerting to students of medieval mysticism." She thought also that Margery Kempe's "hysterical" tendencies "poured themselves into a religious mould;" there was "very little in Margery's *Book* which can properly be defined as mystical," she insisted.[8] Writing in the academic journal *History* for 1937–38, D. L. Douie compared Margery Kempe to "women preachers of the Methodist revival," but suspected as well "a somewhat unbalanced temperament which may have been nurtured too exclusively on the mystical writings of the period."[9] It was against this background and particularly against the charge of "hysteria" that Hope Allen began to prepare her second volume.

Following discussions with the EETS board and in particular with her friend and colleague Robin Flower, Allen set out to produce long excerpts from related and illustrative texts (the microfilms she expected to draw on are today in the University of Pennsylvania Library) that would show the direction of late-medieval English spirituality and also to comment on the *Book of Margery Kempe* itself in greater detail than she had been able to do thus far. Allen had come to believe that the *Book* represented a new development in late medieval religiousness, a "mystical" development that originated in Rhineland spirituality, in particular in the writings of John Tauler (ca.1300–61), Gertrude (1232–91) and her younger sister Mechthild (1241–99) of Magdeburg, and above all in Henry Suso (ca. 1295-1366), a Dominican student of Meister Eckhart (ca. 1260–ca.1328), whose writings presented a powerfully "mystical" spirituality that came to influence (sometimes through merchants with Danzig connections, she believed) a native English tradition reaching back to the Old English period and rooted in less affective texts, of which *Ancrene Riwle* was only the best known. The hallmarks of this new tradition, which she associated with Syon Abbey, included warnings against too quick a reliance on mystical feeling, cautioned against in texts such as *The Chastising of God's Children,* and a deeply engaged spirituality, found in texts such as *The Orchard of Syon* and even in the Middle English translation of Marguerite Pourete's *The Mirror of Simple Souls.* This new tradition at once contextualizes and illuminates the *Book of Margery Kempe,* countering the charge of hysteria with a historically based explanation of some of its more discordant elements and putting its protagonist in the company of some very great mystics, such as Saint Bridget of Sweden, who influenced Margery Kempe herself. Throughout, Allen was concerned to show how far women were responsible for this new movement, particularly in England. No Englishwoman had been canonized since 1066, Allen once noted, but in devout religion silencing had failed, and they had found their voice. In July 1939 the Oxford scholar Helen Gardner had made a short memorandum of a conversation with Allen in which she noted: "Margery Kempe's inspiration was probably German movement, which was feminist, hysterical and visionary. German women mystics were connected with Dominicans; who were very strong in Norwich."[10] The word "hysterical" may have been Gardner's addition, though Allen was aware that certain of Margery Kempe's religious practices appeared outré, and the word may have its roots in that. In any event, the Norwich tradition to which the memorandum alludes refers to Julian of Norwich, with whom Margery Kempe is reported to have talked at length, and no doubt that connection too would have been explored in some detail had Allen lived to complete her work.

Alas, she did not. I have discussed the reasons elsewhere, though ill health was first among them.[11] But her final years were far from static.[12] As long as she was physically able to do so, she attended MLA meetings in New York and continued to work on the second volume of the *Book of Margery Kempe*. She received numerous visitors and maintained a widely ranging correspondence, regularly advising the council of the EETS on academic matters. As her position in the history of medieval scholarship began to be recognized, she received important academic honors from Bryn Mawr, from Smith College, and from the Medieval Academy of America. In her last years she was well attended to, and she spent them housebound in Oneida, visited intermittently by academic colleagues and surrounded by family and old friends.

NOTES

Throughout I have drawn upon and quoted verbatim sentences and phrases of my own composition from my biography *Hope Emily Allen: Medieval Scholarship and Feminism* and my articles, cited elsewhere.

1. Literature on the Oneida Community is extensive. See in particular Lawrence Foster, *Religion and Sexuality: The Shakers, the Mormons, and the Oneida Community* (London: Oxford University Press, 1981; Urbana: University of Illinois Press, 1984); and Spencer Klaw, *Without Sin: The Life and Death of the Oneida Community* (New York: Allen Lane/Penguin Press, 1993). The community members and their descendants are listed in John B. Teeple, *The Oneida Family: Genealogy of a Nineteenth-Century Perfectionist Commune* (Oneida, N.Y.: Oneida Community Historical Committee, 1985). Hope Allen's family roots are listed on p. 140.

2. Hirsh, "Past and Present in Hope Emily Allen's Essay 'Relics,'" 49.

3. Hirsh, *Hope Emily Allen: Medieval Scholarship and Feminism*, 8.

4. Chambers, "Recent Research upon the *Ancren Riwle*," 22.

5. Hirsh, "Hope Emily Allen and the Limitations of Academic Discourse," 94.

6. At least he would not have done so face-to-face and repeatedly as he did with Hope Allen. Michael Adams has pointed out that he did attack, in what he believed to be a confidential letter, a senior colleague whom he thought incompetent (Adams agrees). See Michael Adams, "Sanford Brown at the Middle English Dictionary," *Dictionaries: Journal of the Dictionary Society of America* 16 (1995): 151–85; see especially 164–76.

7. Hirsh, "Margery Kempe," 109–19.

8. Underhill, review of *The Book of Margery Kempe*, 642.

9. Douie, review of *The Book of Margery Kempe*, 70.

10. Hirsh, *Hope Emily Allen: Medieval Scholarship and Feminism*, 149.

11. Hirsh, "Hope Emily Allen, the Second Volume of the *Book of Margery Kempe*, and an Adversary," 11.

12. Mitchell, "'Ever-Growing Army of Serious Girl Students,'" 17.

SELECT BIBLIOGRAPHY OF WORKS BY HOPE EMILY ALLEN

"The Authorship of the *Prick of Conscience*." In *Studies in English and Comparative Literature Presented to Agnes Irwin, Litt.D., Dean of Radcliffe College, 1894–1909*. Radcliffe College Monograph Series, no. 15. Boston, Mass.: Ginn, 1910.

"The Mystical Lyrics of the *Manuel des Pechiez*." *Romanic Review* 9 (1918): 154–93.
"The Origin of the *Ancren Riwle*." *PMLA* 33 (1918): 474–546.
"The '*Ancren Riwle*' and Kilburn Priory." *Modern Language Review* 16 (1921): 316–22.
"Ancient Grief" [short story]. *Atlantic Monthly* 131 (February 1923): 177–87.
"A Glut of Fruit" [short story]. *Atlantic Monthly* 131 (September 1923): 343–52.
"Some Fourteenth-Century Borrowings from *Ancren Riwle*." *Modern Language Review* 19 (1923): 1–8.
"The Fanciful Countryman" [short story]. *Dial* 83 (December 1927): 477–500.
Writings Ascribed to Richard Rolle, Hermit of Hampole, and Materials for His Biography. MLA Monograph Series, vol. 3. New York: D. C. Heath; London: Oxford University Press, 1927.
"Further Borrowings from *Ancren Riwle*." *Modern Language Review* 24 (1929): 1–15.
"On the Author of the *Ancren Riwle*." *PMLA* 44 (1929): 635–80.
"A Medieval Work: Margery Kempe of Lynn" [letter to the editor]. *The Times* (London) 17 December 1934, 15.
"The Three Daughters of Deorman." *PMLA* 50 (1935): 899–902.
"Wynkyn de Worde and a Second French Compilation from the *Ancren Riwle* with a Description of the First." In *Essays and Studies in Honor of Carleton Brown,* edited by Percy W. Long. New York: New York University Press; London: Oxford University Press, 1940.
The Book of Margery Kempe. Edited with introduction, appendices and glossary by Sanford B. Meech, and notes and appendices by Hope Emily Allen. Vol. 1. EETS, o.s., 212. London: Oxford University Press, 1940.

Works Cited

Chambers, R. W. "On the Continuity of English Prose from Alfred to More and His School." In the introduction to *Nicholas Harpsfield's Life of Sir Thomas More,* edited by Elsie V. Hitchcock, xlv–clxxiv. Oxford: EETS 186 (1932). Reprinted as a separate work, EETS 191A (Oxford: Oxford University Press, 1957).
———. "Recent Research upon the *Ancren Riwle*." *Review of English Studies* 1 (1925): 4–23.
Douie, D. L. Review of *The Book of Margery Kempe, 1436.* In *History* 22 (1937–38): 70–72.
Hirsh, John C. "Hope Emily Allen and the Limitations of Academic Discourse." *Mystics Quarterly* 18 (1992): 94–102.
———. *Hope Emily Allen: Medieval Scholarship and Feminism.* Norman, Okla.: Pilgrim Books, 1988.
———. "Hope Emily Allen, the Second Volume of the *Book of Margery Kempe,* and an Adversary." *Medieval Feminist Forum* no. 31 (spring 2001): 11–17.
———. "Margery Kempe." In *Middle English Prose, A Critical Guide to Major Authors and Genres,* edited by A. S. G. Edwards, 109–19. New Brunswick, N.J.: Rutgers University Press, 1984.
———. "Past and Present in Hope Emily Allen's Essay 'Relics.'" *Syracuse University Library Associates Courier* 24 (1989): 49–61.
Mitchell, Marea. "'The Ever-Growing Army of Serious Girl Students': The Legacy of Hope Emily Allen." *Medieval Feminist Forum* no. 31 (spring 2001): 17–29.
Underhill, Evelyn. Review of *The Book of Margery Kempe, 1436.* In *Spectator* 157 (16 October 1936): 642.

CHAPTER 18

Laura Hibbard Loomis (1883–1960)
"Mrs Arthur"

KATHRYN L. LYNCH

WITHIN THE CONSTRAINTS of her day Laura Hibbard Loomis appears to have been an enviable early example of "having it all." At a time when very few women even attempted to combine college teaching, scholarship, and marriage, she kept all three balls in the air with a grace that amounted to legerdemain: she published widely and seriously; influenced generations of students at her alma mater, Wellesley College, where she taught for twenty-seven years; and enjoyed a long and happy marriage with Roger Sherman Loomis, the famous Arthurian scholar who shared her intellectual interests and her love of travel. Possessed of beauty, charm, and grace ("tall and lithe, with blowing gold hair, and arrows of the mind sharp and keen," as she was described by a member of her class of 1905 at Wellesley), she also maintained long and meaningful friendships with her colleagues at Wellesley and elsewhere.[1] At the same time it is worth noting how her success was both enabled and shadowed by the presence of her famous and remarkable spouse. She reports her students having called her "Mrs. Arthur," ostensibly because of her courses on Arthurian romance but surely also because of her marriage (she was also called "Mrs. Eastman Professor" when Roger held that prestigious post at Oxford).[2] Even today she is often remembered as Roger Sherman Loomis's wife (or as one of his three medievalist wives), despite the fact that her work, though less prolific, has arguably been as influential in the field as her husband's.[3]

Born in Chicago on 18 June 1883 Laura Alandis Hibbard was the second of two children and the only daughter of Frederick Alan and Anna (McMullen) Hibbard.[4] She prepared for college at Hyde Park High School in Chicago and went on to attend Wellesley College, where she was a member of the class of 1905. She received an M.A.

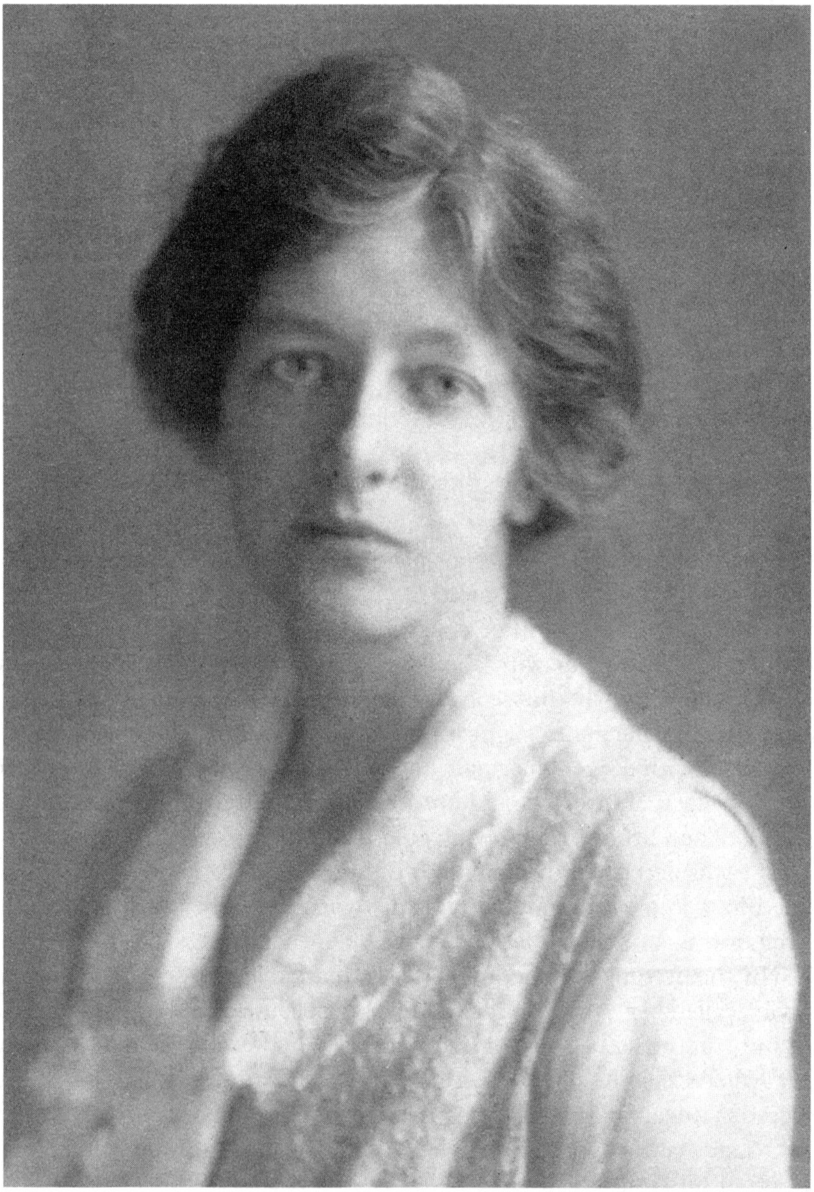

from Wellesley in 1908 for course work completed in 1907. During the academic year 1907–8 she took her first teaching job at Kemper Hall in Kenosha, Wisconsin. Between 1908 and 1916 she was an instructor at Mount Holyoke College, with a leave of absence to study at Oxford and the University of Chicago in 1910–11 on the Alice Freeman Palmer Fellowship. In 1916 she received the Ph.D. from the University of Chicago, where she studied with John Manly, and in the same year was appointed an instructor at her alma mater. She became an associate professor at Wellesley a year later when she officially resigned her position at Mount Holyoke, a full professor in 1929, and the first holder of the Katharine Lee Bates Chair in English Composition and Literature. In 1926 she served as vice president of the Modern Language Association, only the fourth woman to hold this office. After marrying Roger Sherman Loomis in 1925, Hibbard Loomis limited her teaching at Wellesley to one semester a year so that she could spend most of her time in New York City, where Roger was a professor at Columbia University. The strain of their yearly separations, however, led to her permanent retirement from Wellesley in 1943. Laura Hibbard Loomis died on 25 August 1960, at the age of seventy-seven.

The English department of Hibbard Loomis's Wellesley years was quite simply an extraordinary place. Wellesley was unusual, even among women's colleges, in having a faculty almost exclusively made up of women, and the English department was one of the most capable and collegial departments at the college as well as the one with the largest enrollments during the years 1890–1910.[5] A more severe or more elevating crucible for a young woman scholar can hardly be imagined. Led by the quietly charismatic Katharine Lee Bates (the poet-scholar most famous for writing "America the Beautiful"), the department included such other inspiring scholar/teachers as Sophie Chantal Hart, Vida Dutton Scudder, and Martha Hale Shackford, to mention just a few of the best known.[6] Laura Hibbard took courses from all of these professors, but the teacher with whom she developed the closest relationship seems to have been the poet and translator Sophie Jewett, who first introduced her to fourteenth-century English literature, and whom she addressed as "mia Maestra" in the dedication to her first book.[7] Even as an undergraduate, Hibbard's interest in medieval literature was immediately evident, sustained, and intense. She began with Anglo-Saxon literature as a first-year student, and in addition to the standard survey and period courses, her undergraduate study included fourteenth-century literature, studies in Arthurian romance, and the history of the English language—as well as course work in such related subjects as French, European history, biblical history, and philosophy (which she studied with the prominent philosopher Mary Whiton Calkins).[8] Indeed, with the exception of a single course in mathematics and another in hygiene, both required of freshmen, her course work formed a coherent preparation for the future medievalist.

Laura Hibbard was not the only product of the Wellesley English department in these early years to make a successful career as a writer and scholar. Indeed, one of that department's most distinctive achievements was its creation of an environment that encouraged serious intellectual and artistic accomplishment in its graduates:

another remarkable student was Florence Converse, medievalist, novelist, and teacher, who graduated in 1892 and, like Hibbard, returned to teach in the Wellesley department. And another was Gertrude Schoepperle, the future Vassar professor and scholar of medieval French, German, and Celtic literature, who became one of Laura's first and closest friends at Wellesley; in a poignant irony, Gertrude was also her husband's first wife.[9] We cannot be sure how Laura and Gertrude met, but they must have come to know each other well in a small year-long history of the English language course, taught by Alice Vinton Waite, which they took together when Laura was a sophomore and Gertrude a senior.[10] As the only sophomore in this class of seven students, which included five seniors and a graduate student, Laura may have been taken under the wing of the older girl, or perhaps Laura simply admired the energetic disregard for convention with which Gertrude Schoepperle embraced life. One of the most moving pieces Laura ever wrote was her valediction to Gertrude, after her untimely death in 1921 of peritonitis. Here she describes her friend as "ardent," "restive," "heedless," "audacious," "fearless," "as impatient of timidity or mediocrity in scholarship as she was of mere convention as a rule of life." "Gertrude," writes Laura, "was one of the few who carry their enthusiasm from the abstract, where alone it has been respectable for most women to have theirs, into the realm of life itself, of living men and women." The consummation of her passionate engagement with life, as Laura observes, "was a marriage so radiantly happy that its best analogue can only be found in the tales of old romance."[11]

That marriage lasted barely two years. Laura's sympathetic regard for his first wife must have been a comfort to Roger, as his loving appreciation of her friend must have consoled Laura as well. The circumstances of their mourning and of their courtship are impossible to reconstruct. In 1924 Laura Hibbard dedicated her second book, *Mediaeval Romance in England,* to Gertrude Schoepperle's memory, with the cryptic epigraph "Truth lies hid in the trappings of a tale." A year later and four years after Gertrude's death, Laura Hibbard would become Roger Sherman Loomis's second medievalist wife. Their marriage would endure for thirty-five years, and to all appearances it was a happy and stable union, if one that required some professional sacrifice on Laura's part. But it would not be Roger's final marriage. Three years after Laura's death in 1960, Roger would wed for the third time, again to an accomplished woman medievalist, Dorothy Bethurum.[12] Roger died three years later at the age of seventy-eight.

It is hard to know exactly how to present or interpret Roger Sherman Loomis's three marriages, or even if they require interpretation. In retrospect, of course, they constitute something of a spectacle; the temptation to characterize Gertrude, Laura, and Dorothy as "the three wives of Roger Sherman Loomis" or even, as one scholar has done recently, as "the Loomis Ladies" ("Just as King Arthur had questing knights, Roger Sherman Loomis had scholarly wives") is strong.[13] To do so, however, gives a patriarchal frame to the distinct and admirable careers of these three accomplished women. It also diminishes the network of female friendship and scholarship that entangled and complicated at least Laura's union with Roger. Laura's relationship with her husband began in a friendship with her college classmate, just as Laura's intellectual life had its origins in her close relationships with other brilliant women, colleagues, and teachers, and these were relationships she struggled to maintain long after she began her married life. She was forty-one at the time of that marriage, already an established scholar and no blushing schoolgirl; indeed, Roger was four years her junior.

At the same time there is a sense in which Laura's career *was* absorbed in Roger's after their marriage, as she was drawn further and further away from the community of women scholars that had given her a start. Similarly, it must be acknowledged that the fact that Roger had multiple wives gives him the appearance of having a surprising and fatal desirability to women; this appearance is reinforced by the story told in "The Loomis Ladies" of "the disappointment suffered by scholars whom Loomis didn't marry": "Loomis, who wrote so dryly of the romances, more than made up for it by his romantic nature."[14] When Roger's wives chose marriage over the life of an independent woman scholar, were they succumbing to the allure of a heterosexist romantic fantasy? Were they electing to subordinate their own intellectual individualities in the career of a powerful man? Alternatively, is Roger at fault for the imperious way in which he took over and subsumed the careers and intellectual lives of the women he married? Are such questions even fair ones? Was Roger's desirability, perhaps, a feature of his genuine respect for, interest in, and support of strong intellectual women, a character trait in high demand among women but not in strong supply among men? Was there even a rare synergy in the marriage of Laura Hibbard and Roger Loomis that made them *both* more effective scholars? Even if much more were known about their circumstances, there could be no final or simple answers to such questions, but—especially for Laura, who spent so much of her life in this marriage and who gave up so much to it—questions like these remain important, for they illuminate the hard choices for women, especially at that time. In retrospect it is the woman's involvement that is commonly erased from a scholarly collaboration with a man, as Elizabeth Scala has shown in her work on Edith Rickert, and Laura Hibbard is largely remembered today for the Loomis at the end of her name rather than for the quality of her own work.[15] Even in a contemporary review of her *Mediaeval Romance in England,* John Manly, who had supervised her graduate work at the University of Chicago, could not resist the parenthesis when he wrote of the "worthy addition [to scholarship of] Professor Laura A. Hibbard (now Mrs. Roger Loomis)."[16] That such a postscript was conventional in no way lessens its impact.

By the time of her marriage Laura Hibbard was well launched on a thriving career as a teacher, scholar, translator, and author of occasional pieces in the tradition of an academic department that included poets, novelists, memoirists, and essayists, as well as scholars. At Wellesley College, where she was known as a lively and engaging instructor, her teaching interests focused chiefly on medieval topics. She taught courses in Chaucer and Arthurian romance every year while at Wellesley and frequently also medieval survey courses, including several on fourteenth-century literature, though she branched out as well into the Renaissance and general surveys of English literature. Hibbard Loomis brought to her classroom the same combination of rigor and enthusiasm that also characterized her scholarship; as a colleague wrote at the time of her retirement from teaching, she conveyed to her students "both the austerities and the exhilaration" of research.[17] A similar report is offered by her niece, Mary, who studied Chaucer at Wellesley in the early 1930s with her aunt: "She was strict, but the students loved her. She had a precious, understanding way with people."[18] Such was her skill and popularity as a teacher that, after her departure from the college in 1943, enrollments in non-Chaucerian Middle English began to decline, causing the alarmed English department to invite Hibbard Loomis back to lecture in the fall of 1945 in order to stimulate interest.[19]

She was just sixty when she left Wellesley and clearly not ready to be done with teaching altogether. During her retirement she taught Chaucer in evening classes at Hunter College (perhaps these were the courses described in her Wellesley class notes in 1944 as those delivered to "educated refugees").[20] In 1955 she took over Roger Loomis's summer courses with evident relish: "[L]ike an old fire-engine horse hearing the fire-bell ring again, I found myself enjoying the experience."[21] Laura Hibbard Loomis was a popular lecturer, both during her years at Wellesley and afterward. She presented her work on Arthurian topics, on the Auchinleck manuscript, and, as time passed and her areas of expertise developed and expanded, on medieval art. Even after she had fully retired from teaching, she spoke at such diverse venues as the Pierpont Morgan Library, the Columbia University Celtic Society, the New York Engineering Women's Club, meetings of the MLA, and the Oxford University Medieval Society.[22] Although the abbreviation of her teaching career was a loss to her students and colleagues, Hibbard Loomis's light teaching load and relatively short career as a teacher were partly responsible for her impressive scholarly output.

Laura Hibbard Loomis was the author of four books and coauthor or coeditor of two others; the first published in 1911 was a retelling of three Middle English romances. Her second book, based on her University of Chicago thesis, *Mediaeval Romance in England: A Study of the Sources and Analogues of the Non-cyclic Metrical Romances,* was the first comprehensive treatment of noncyclic romances. More than a bibliographical manual (though that, too), this book surveys sources, analogues, and the state of scholarship and offers useful local observations on the meaning and literary quality of each of the thirty-nine romances that it covers. First published in 1924 by Oxford University Press, it was enthusiastically received and widely cited. "[A] product," as Kemp Malone put it, "in every way worthy of the ripe, broad scholarship which we have learned to associate with its author," *Mediaeval Romance in England* was republished in 1960 with a supplementary bibliographical index.[23] Although Hibbard Loomis's scholarly career was firmly grounded in her lifelong interest in English metrical romance, her contribution was not limited to this area. Her work in Chaucer studies was similarly influential, and both she and her husband developed over the years a serious interest and expertise in art history. Her third book, *Medieval Vista,* was an album-style descriptive study of twenty-four miniatures at the Pierpont Morgan Library in New York, which she published in 1953. She also coauthored the magisterial *Arthurian Legends in Medieval Art* with her husband, a book that appeared in 1938 but that still dominates the field. Laura and Roger also collaborated on a Modern Library edition of eight romances in modern translations titled *Medieval Romances,* published in 1957; Laura edited five of the eight, concentrating chiefly on the non-cyclic romances in English.

Laura Hibbard Loomis is probably best known for her more than thirty scholarly articles, especially the three that argue for Chaucer's knowledge of the Auchinleck manuscript, and her last book, *Adventures in the Middle Ages* (published posthumously), was appropriately a collection of many of her essays.[24] The title of this collection is apt, as Hibbard Loomis had herself applied the adjective "auntrous," with its connotations of rash daring, to the critical methods she refined.[25] Her essays on the Auchinleck manuscript reveal both her independent cast of mind and her specific virtues as a literary critic. Far from timid, Hibbard Loomis took pleasure in being something of a maverick in criticism, pushing her claims far beyond those made by previous scholars. Before Hibbard Loomis, only one scholar, Eugen Köbling, had even mentioned Chaucer in connection with this manuscript, and Köbling's conclusion was that Chaucer did not know it.[26] Not content to offer Chaucer's use of this manuscript merely as a "pleasant possibility" or even as a probability—or to take the more common course of suggesting that, if not this specific manuscript, another compilation similar to the Auchinleck manuscript had influenced Chaucer—Hibbard Loomis had the ambitious goal of proving that Chaucer's use of the Auchinleck was virtually certain, that it was "demonstrable," even that any other explanation of the parallels was "inconceivable."[27] Moreover, she was concerned not only to establish the specific case but to develop a general methodology that would permit scholars to make such arguments, as she did, on the basis of the best internal evidence.[28]

As this methodology suggests, Hibbard Loomis worked closely and patiently from the text. To demonstrate Chaucer's knowledge of the manuscript, she offers a comprehensive line-by-line analysis of the Auchinleck romances in comparison with "The Tale of Sir Thopas" (whose sources and analogues Hibbard Loomis knew well from work done for Bryan and Dempster's *Sources and Analogues*) and with "The Franklin's Tale."[29] In the third of the Auchinleck essays, Hibbard Loomis again presses new and unexpected claims and shows the value of her method of close reading to the traditional tasks of philology, while anticipating the kind of work done recently by the so-called New Philologists on the sociology of literary production. By narrowly comparing the texts of four romances in their Auchinleck versions, Hibbard Loomis was able to demonstrate several surprising conclusions, which, as she put it, "are at odds with a good many previous theories," including the collaboration of a group of scribes under the direction of an editor working together in London in a lay scriptorium, or bookshop, fifty years earlier than had previously been thought.[30] The seventy-fifth anniversary issue of *PMLA* cited this article as one of the two most significant contributions to the field of Middle English ever published in the journal.[31]

As her writing career progressed, her "adventures" were not limited to Chaucer's use of the Auchinleck manuscript. Her work with this famous manuscript led to new theories about the relationship between English and French literature. She argued, for example, that the tradition giving Charlemagne possession of the Passion Lance, reflected in the *Song of Roland,* had an English origin in stories of a gift to King Athelstan in the tenth century.[32] Even more daring, perhaps, was her salvo correcting the famous French scholar and editor Joseph Bédier on his interpretation of Charlemagne's war cry "Monjoie," which, on the basis of a highly detailed argument rehearsing the dates and provenance of the manuscripts, Hibbard Loomis identified as signifying "my joy" rather than "Mount Joy."[33] Such was the influence of this article that it was translated into French and republished with minor revisions four years later.[34] These two were surely among the essays she described in her contribution to her Wellesley class notes in 1951, when she reported working on "a crop of articles about tenth and twelfth century affairs. They will probably lead to some lively controversies. Didn't I use to be a rather mild person? Now I don't mind a row at all — at least if it's literary and on paper!"[35]

Beneath this self-effacing veneer of gentility, Laura Hibbard Loomis hid a sharp, combative, and tenacious mind.[36] Her gift was to combine the instincts of a sensitive reader, the learning of a life-long scholar, and the skepticism of one unimpressed by established pieties. At the same time she nurtured an abiding, almost mystical respect for the age and literature she devoted her life to studying, an age that never lost its romance for her. Her manuscript studies, for example, were clearly prompted by real excitement at the thought that she might see and touch what the poets she studied touched also, as she approached the question "whether Chaucer ever had this manuscript [the Auchinleck], to us so famous and so venerable, in his hands." Although she applied the most rigorous standards of scholarship, she plainly loved proving what to other scholars might seem "too good to be true" and sharing with others "the pleasure of believing that what he once handled we too can touch."[37] Descriptions of her frequent European travels with Roger take on the same romantic aura. Indeed, her entire marriage with Roger and their mutual scholarly pursuits seem, as she narrates them, inspired by a spirit of rare adventure. She wrote to her Wellesley classmates that the first five years of their marriage had been "the best of life for me," continuing with this characterization of their union and life together: "Husband and I are, I believe, supposed to be a very modernistic pair because for one semester of each year we teach in different places, Roger in Columbia, I for the first semester here in Wellesley. In reality we are as old-fashioned and romantic a pair as could be found. How could it be otherwise when we are both professors of medieval romance? To an exceptional extent, I suppose, we share each other's work and play and next year hope to bring out a new book together [this was almost certainly *Arthurian Legends in Medieval Art*]. We have had two glorious trips abroad when we went to places haunted by old legends, to the Forest of Broceliande in Brittany, to Cornwall and Wales for Arthurian lore, to Ireland for still more beautiful and ancient things."[38]

To be sure, we must be careful not to fall into the trap of taking such fanciful flights too seriously. At the same time nothing suggests that Laura and Roger were not well suited to each other both intellectually and emotionally throughout their thirty-five-year marriage. As one of R. S. Loomis's graduate students from the 1950s remembers, "Roger always spoke of her to us as if she were the greatest scholar in academe."[39] Not only were they partners in many scholarly interests — Arthurian literature, medieval romance, the visual arts — they also seem to have shared the same independent and somewhat iconoclastic spirit. Just as Laura Hibbard Loomis steadfastly championed new theories that might have raised some scholarly hackles, indeed took pleasure in the battle, so also was Roger's scholarly career built on an unorthodox claim, consistently maintained, that the Arthurian legend had a Celtic origin and was later disseminated on the Continent.[40] Was it Laura's defiance of orthodoxy that influenced her husband or the reverse? Or was some more complicated blend of the two the potion that unlocked their mutual scholarly ardor? It is impossible to be sure, but their collaborations were fruitful, and it is more than likely that her marriage to Roger Sherman Loomis did more than free up time for her to write. Certainly, it opened doors for Laura, introduced her into scholarly circles where she might not otherwise have been welcomed, and gave her access to library collections and parts of the world she might not have traveled to were she not the great Arthurian scholar's wife. But none of these advantages really makes up for the fact that, once married to Roger, Laura Hibbard Loomis never received the attention or support that was her due or that came to her husband, and she clearly had to make the compromises so often demanded of women. For example, when she took his summer courses off his hands in 1955, it was "in order that [Roger] might finish a book," though Laura herself was hard at work at a series of some of the trickiest and most controversial articles she would write.[41] Indeed, Laura had only a couple of years earlier been involved in caring for her elderly mother, who died at the age of ninety-four, accounting for the reduction in her scholarly productivity in the mid-1940s, between the Auchinleck essays and the essays that grew out of her study of the Athelstan gift story. "In the last two years of her life," wrote Laura to her classmates, "I had a part-time companion for her, and so was able to return again to writing."[42]

Laura herself was hobbled with ill health as she entered her final years. "Stoically, uncomplainingly she endured pain," remembered one friend.[43] And at least one student during the late 1950s recalls seeing her maneuvering her wheelchair around the Columbia University Library.[44] "[N]ever robust in health," according to her Wellesley obituary, Laura endured in the last fifteen months of her life significant physical challenges. She underwent, as she characterized it, "a severe lung operation" in late spring 1959 but still managed to produce the new bibliographical information for the second edition of *Mediaeval Romance* later that year; "There was not much left of me after I finished that job," she commented with grim humor.[45] Happily Laura mustered the strength for one last trip abroad with her husband in early 1960, where she planned to stay through September: "[O]n to France," she wrote her classmates gaily, "and to England for May to September, and so home for good!"[46] Those words were only too prescient. Laura returned "home for good" earlier than planned, to spend three months in the Harkness Pavilion of the Columbia University Medical Center. Before September she was gone.

In her largely successful quest for a life that would combine the personal satisfactions of love and marriage with the joys and rigors of scholarship, Laura Hibbard Loomis had many assistants and made many quiet compromises. It is hard to exaggerate the esteem and pride in which she was held as a faculty member at Wellesley. She held what was, as far as I can tell, the first professorship ever endowed in the Wellesley English department, named after the department's most powerful and famous member.[47] Like many of her Wellesley mentors, her early writing career included work that was not purely academic, such as her first book (a translation and modernization of three romances), or the short reflections she wrote for the *Nation* between 1916 and 1920 that compared contemporary political conditions to the Middle Ages, or her occasional travel pieces.[48] But it was in her more traditional and ambitious scholarship that Laura Hibbard Loomis really shone. Her *Mediaeval Romance* was the first of a new series published under Wellesley's name, the Semi-Centennial series, "meant," as a college reviewer described it, "to represent to the world Wellesley's finest intellectual achievement."[49] The college entrusted this standard to Laura Hibbard, and it must surely then have been disappointed to lose half of her time to her scholar-husband. That she was permitted to continue in this unusual arrangement was no small matter. The strains sometimes subtly show through the English department's careful reserve. "Recent years," observed a colleague on the occasion of her retirement, have "gradually withdrawn Mrs. Loomis from our midst. There have been leaves of absence for a year or a semester in too close succession as she has yielded inevitably to the claims of her New York home."[50] For eighteen years, though, Laura Hibbard Loomis deftly balanced the roles of wife and scholar. Hers is clearly not the only model of a successful or integrated life, but it was nonetheless a remarkable kind of life for her day.

Even at Wellesley, where women professors were the norm rather than an anomaly, a married woman professor who continued to teach during her marriage was extremely rare.[51] With a single, somewhat problematic exception, I have not been able to find record of another. This exception is Mary Bowen Brainerd, who was Laura's teacher in Old English and in Spenser. Like Laura, Mary Bowen was a University of Chicago Ph.D. (1897), who taught as an instructor in the English department until 1906, when she married the architect William Brainerd. But that was essentially the end of her teaching and scholarly career, as Laura, then a masters student at Wellesley, must have observed. Mary returned to do some part-time teaching from 1918 until 1923, but for all intents and purposes she retired from the academic life to become a wife and town resident.[52] Like so much else in Laura Hibbard Loomis's life, what Mary Bowen might have meant to her or how Laura understood the sacrifices she must have seen her slightly older colleague making can never be known. But the silent lesson of Mary Bowen Brainerd reminds me of the slender and sometimes almost invisible threads that tie the lives of women and of women scholars together and that this volume is meant to commemorate and to celebrate. If her marriage to Roger Sherman Loomis brought Laura Hibbard into the larger world of male scholars, it was the generous and supportive embrace of her women teachers and colleagues that lifted her up to the larger world and made that intellectual life possible.

Notes

1. Thrall, "Laura Hibbard Loomis Collection of Medieval Literature." In her 1952 alumnae questionnaire (Wellesley College Archives) she ranked the friendships formed in college on a scale of importance above her academic training.

2. As reported by Katharine C. Balderston in her obituary for Hibbard Loomis, "Laura Hibbard Loomis."

3. Regarding Roger Loomis's wives, see the recent essay by Peyton, "Loomis Ladies" 143–47.

4. "Laura Hibbard Loomis," in *Who's Who of American Women*, 779. To supplement the basic information provided by such sources as *Who's Who* and the obituaries, I conducted an interview with Laura Hibbard Loomis's niece, Mary Louise Hibbard, 4 December 2001, and reviewed the material in her biographical file in the Wellesley College Archives. My thanks to the archivists at Columbia University, Mount Holyoke College, and especially to Wilma Slaight and Jean Berry in the Wellesley College Archives for their assistance with this essay; special thanks also to my research assistant Emily See and to the friends, colleagues, and relatives of Laura Hibbard Loomis who shared their memories with me.

5. Regarding the preponderance of women professors at Wellesley, see Palmieri, *In Adamless Eden*, 57–58.

6. A vivid picture of this golden age in Wellesley's history is painted by Palmieri, *In Adamless Eden;* see especially the pages specifically on the English department, for example, 162–66.

7. Sophie Jewett, "Miss Jewett" as she was known to her students, died suddenly in 1909, but as Hibbard Loomis's colleague Katharine C. Balderston noted, Laura "never ceased to cherish" her memory; see Balderston, "Laura Hibbard Loomis." Laura Hibbard wrote a lyrical, appreciative review of Sophie Jewett's collected poems, published two years after her death (review of *The Poems of Sophie Jewett*), and later, after the death of her older sister Louise Rogers Jewett, a noted art historian, a celebration of her life and career ("Professor Louise Rogers Jewett"). For a discussion of Sophie Jewett's translation of *The Pearl,* see Palmieri, In *Adamless Eden,* 165. While it cannot be proven, it is within the realm of possibility that Laura Hibbard had encountered Edith Rickert as a high school student; some evidence suggests that Rickert was a teacher at Hyde Park High School during the period of time that Hibbard was a student there. Later Rickert was employed in an adjunct capacity by the University of Chicago when Hibbard Loomis was a graduate student. See Elizabeth Scala's essay "Miss Rickert's Academy," chapter 10 of this volume. Their association is not supported by any surviving records or correspondence. Hibbard's dedication to Jewett can be found in Hibbard, *Three Middle English Romances.* See also Balderston, "Laura Hibbard Loomis."

8. For more about Calkins, see Palmieri, *In Adamless Eden,* 172.

9. Gertrude Schoepperle was the author of fourteen essays, eight book reviews, and one

book and coeditor of another before her death in 1921. For a complete list of her publications, see *Medieval Studies in Memory of Gertrude Schoepperle Loomis* (New York: Columbia University Press, 1927), x–xi; Laura Hibbard Loomis's essay "Malory's Book of Balin" appears in this volume (175–95).

10. *President's Report of 1903*, appendix B, 25; Wellesley College Archives.

11. Hibbard, "Gertrude Schoepperle Loomis."

12. Dorothy Bethurum received her B.A. and M.A. from Vanderbilt University and her Ph.D. from Yale University. She taught at Southwestern University, Randolph-Macon College, Lawrence College (where she received an honorary doctorate in 1947), and Connecticut College and lectured after her retirement at Vanderbilt. Dorothy Bethurum was a Guggenheim fellow in 1937. With Randall Stewart she coedited several collections of English and American literature, and she was the author/editor of *The Homilies of Wulfstan* as well as numerous articles on topics ranging from Old English history and literature to Shakespeare, and the editor of *The Squire's Tale* and *Critical Approaches to Medieval Literature*.

13. Peyton, "Loomis Ladies," 343; this essay begins with an even more demeaning comparison of the three women scholars to "the tuneful trio, the Andrews sisters" (343).

14. Peyton, "Loomis Ladies," 345.

15. See especially Scala, "Scandalous Assumptions," and "John Matthews Manly (1865–1940) and Edith Rickert (1871–1938)," 297–322, especially 308.

16. Manly, review of *Medieval Romance in England*, 122.

17. Hughes, "Laura Hibbard Loomis."

18. Mary Louise Loomis, interview by the author, 4 December 2001.

19. English Department Annual Report (22 May 1945), Wellesley College Archives.

20. Hibbard Loomis, "Class Notes," *Wellesley Magazine* (February 1944): 167.

21. *The Record of the Class of 1905 of Wellesley College, 1949–55*, 38, Wellesley College Archives.

22. Biographical file of Laura Hibbard Loomis, Wellesley College Archives.

23. Malone, review of *Mediaeval Romance in England*, 406. Other reviews of this book consulted include an unsigned review in the *Saturday Review of Literature* and those by Patch, in the *Journal of English and Germanic Philology*, by Brett, in *Modern Language Review*, and by Manly, in *Modern Philology*, also cited earlier. All are strongly positive.

24. Hibbard Loomis, "Chaucer and the Auchinleck Manuscript," 111–28; "Chaucer and the Breton Lays of the Auchinleck Manuscript"; and "Auchinleck Manuscript and a Possible London Bookshop of 1330–1340."

25. Hibbard Loomis, "Chaucer and the Auchinleck Manuscript," 111. The title also seems to have been modeled on two of the chapter titles of Vida Dutton Scudder's memoir *On Journey*, "Adventures in Pedagogy" and "Adventures in Fellowship."

26. E. Köbling, *Beues of Hamtoun*, 219, l. 12n., cited in Hibbard Loomis, "Chaucer and the Auchinleck Manuscript," 114 n. 10.

27. "Pleasant possibility": Hibbard Loomis, "Chaucer and the Auchinleck Manuscript," 113; "demonstrable": Hibbard Loomis, "Chaucer and the Breton Lays," 33; "inconceivable": Hibbard Loomis, "Chaucer and the Auchinleck Manuscript," 117.

28. Hibbard Loomis, "Chaucer and the Auchinleck Manuscript," 115: The method requires "1. A unique combination of texts[;] 2. One or more unique texts[;] 3. Unique readings in one or more of its texts."

29. Hibbard Loomis, "Sir Thopas," 486–559.

30. Quotation from Hibbard Loomis, "Auchinleck Manuscript," 623. Additional evidence appears in her "Auchinleck *Roland and Vernagu* and the *Short Chronicle*." While he challenges many of her conclusions, the fact that Ralph Hanna cites and feels obliged to come to terms with Hibbard Loomis's model in his recent "Reconsidering the Auchinleck Manuscript" (91–102, especially 93, 101), shows how influential and methodologically advanced her work was.

31. Mack et al., "Mirror for the Lamp," 47. The other cited essay was Hope E. Allen's "The Origin of the *Ancren Riwle*," *PMLA* 33 (1918): 474–546. Mack additionally noted that one respondent to the survey on which the ratings were based "observed—a circumstance which the ratings amply confirm—that many of the best and most sensitive workers in the medieval field are of the feminine gender" (47).

32. Hibbard Loomis, "Athelstan Gift Story." In two other essays she prepared the way for this interpretation, first, by establishing the date of the tenth-century poem that was adapted by William of Malmesbury in his twelfth-century account of the gift and, second, by showing the influence of the gift narrative on Norse saga through the shift of Saint Mauricius (the original possessor of the banner given to Athelstan) to Saint Mercurius; see "Holy Relics of Charlemagne and King Athelstan"; and "Saint Mercurius Legend in Medieval England and in Norse Saga."

33. Hibbard Loomis, "Passion Lance Relic."

34. Hibbard Loomis, "Oriflamme of France," reprinted as "L'Oriflamme de France et le Cri 'Munjoie' au XIIe Siècle," *Moyen Âge* (1959): 469–99.

35. Hibbard Loomis, "Class Notes," *Wellesley Alumnae Magazine* (July 1951): 296.

36. Those who knew her frequently use the words "genteel" and "ladylike" to describe her.

37. Hibbard Loomis, "Chaucer and the Auchinleck Manuscript," 131–32.

38. *Record of the Class of 1905 of Wellesley College, 1925–1930,* 64.

39. Sigmund Eisner, letter to the author, 5 December 2001.

40. See Eisner, "Roger Sherman Loomis (1887–1966)," 381–93.

41. Hibbard Loomis, "Class Notes," *Wellesley Alumnae Magazine*, May 1956, 226.

42. Hibbard Loomis, "Class Notes," *Wellesley Alumnae Magazine*, July 1951, 296.

43. Helene Bullock, "Laura Hibbard Loomis: An Appreciation," foreword to Hibbard Loomis, *Adventures in the Middle Ages,* x.

44. Esther Quinn, interview by the author, 23 November 2001.

45. Balderston, "Laura Hibbard Loomis."

46. *Record of the Class of 1905 of Wellesley College, 1955–60,* 32–33.

47. This claim is made on the basis of my analysis of the *Record of the Trust Funds of Wellesley College,* held in the Wellesley College Archives.

48. Hibbard, "The War Raider," 710; "Mediaevalist Today"; and "Ancient Hunger Strike." For an example of her travel writing, see Hibbard Loomis, "Brassbound Holiday." The date of another such piece, "Gold of Palermo," printed in *Adventures in the Middle Ages,* 12–15, cannot be determined.

49. K. B., review of *Medieval Romance.*

50. Hughes, "Laura Hibbard Loomis."

51. See Palmieri, *In Adamless Eden,* 231; Palmieri mentions only Hibbard Loomis and Elisabeth Hodder, a history professor who was a widow when she was hired in 1905. These apparently are the two cited by Carey, in "Career or Maternity?" (It is not possible to identify precisely the time span to which Carey alludes here, but it certainly overlaps with Loomis's

years.) Although Carey's point of view is exceedingly biased, he seems to have made a fairly comprehensive survey of marriage patterns at women's colleges of the time; see also his "Sterilizing the Fittest." The fact that Hibbard Loomis would be used as a pawn in the argument (as Carey so uses her), a heated one in the press, over women's education and its effect on marriage and fertility, makes the college's flexibility and support of her arrangement to balance work and marriage, in my view, even more noteworthy.

52. See the obituary written by Scudder, "Mary Bowen Brainerd."

SELECT BIBLIOGRAPHY OF WORKS BY LAURA HIBBARD LOOMIS

"The Authorship and Date of the *Fayre Maide of the Exchange*." *Modern Philology* 7 (1910): 383–94.
Review of *The Poems of Sophie Jewett*. *The Wellesley Magazine* 19 (June 1911): 380–82.
Three Middle English Romances: "King Horn," "Havelok," "Beves of Hampton." London: David Nutt, 1911.
"The Sword Bridge of Chrétien de Troyes and Its Celtic Original." *Romanic Review* 4 (1913): 166–90.
"Professor Louise Rogers Jewett." *The Mount Holyoke*, March 1914, 417–24.
"*Guy of Warwick* and the Second *Mystère* of Jean Louvet." *Modern Philology* 13 (1915): 181–87.
"The Mediaevalist Today." *Nation*, 10 February 1916, supplement, 4.
"The War Raider," *Nation*, 15 June 1918.
"The Ancient Hunger Strike." *Nation*, 27 October 1920, 469.
"Erkenbald the Belgian: A Study in Medieval Exempla of Justice." *Modern Philology* 17 (1920): 669–78.
"Athelston, a Westminster Legend." *PMLA* 36 (1921): 223–44.
"Gertrude Schoepperle Loomis." *The Wellesley Alumnae Quarterly*, February 1922, 99–100.
"A Brassbound Holiday." *Atlantic Monthly*, June 1923, 766–71.
Medieval Romance in England: A Study of the Sources and Analogues of the Non-cyclic Metrical Romances. New York: Oxford University Press, 1924; 2d ed., New York: Burt Franklin, 1960.
"Arthur's Round Table." *PMLA* 41 (1926): 771–84.
"Malory's Book of Balin." In *Medieval Studies in Memory of Gertrude Schoepperle Loomis*. New York: Columbia University Press, 1927.
"The Table of the Last Supper in Religious and Secular Iconography." *Art Studies* 5 (1927): 71–88.
"Observations on the *Pèlerinage Charlemagne*." *Modern Philology* 25 (1928): 331–49.
"The Round Table Again." *Modern Language Notes* 44 (1929): 511–19.
"Geoffrey of Monmouth and Stonehenge." *PMLA* 45 (1930): 400–415.
"Arthurian Tombs and Megalith Monuments." *Modern Language Review* 26 (1931): 408–26.
With Roger Sherman Loomis. *Arthurian Legends in Medieval Art*. New York: Modern Language Association of America, 1938.
"Chaucer and the Auchinleck Manuscript: 'Thopas' and 'Guy of Warwick.'" In *Essays and Studies in Honor of Carleton Brown*. New York: New York University Press, 1940.
"Chaucer and the Breton Lays of the Auchinleck Manuscript." *Studies in Philology* 38 (1941): 14–33.
"Sir Thopas." In *Sources and Analogues of Chaucer's "Canterbury Tales,"* edited by W. F. Bryan and Germaine Dempster. Chicago: University of Chicago Press, 1941.
"The Auchinleck Manuscript and a Possible London Bookshop of 1330–1340." *PMLA* 57 (1942): 595–627.

Class Notes. *The Wellesley Magazine,* February 1944, 167.

"The Auchinleck *Roland and Vernagu* and the *Short Chronicle.*" *Modern Language Notes* 60 (1945): 94–97.

"The Saint Mercurius Legend in Medieval England and in Norse Saga." In *Philologica: Malone Anniversary Studies,* edited by T. A. Kirby and H. B. Woolf. Baltimore: Johns Hopkins Press, 1949.

"The Holy Relics of Charlemagne and King Athelstan: The Lances of Longinus and Saint Mauricius." *Speculum* 25 (1950): 437–56.

"The Passion Lance Relic and the War Cry 'Monjoie' in the *Chanson de Roland* and Related Texts." *Romanic Review* 41 (1950): 241–60.

Class Notes. *Wellesley Alumnae Magazine,* July 1951, 296.

"The Athelstan Gift Story: Its Influence on English Chronicles and Carolingian Romances." *PMLA* 67 (1952): 521–37.

"The Oriflamme of France and the War Cry 'Monjoie' in the Twelfth Century." In *Studies in Art and Literature for Belle Da Costa Greene,* edited by Dorothy Miner. Princeton, N.J.: Princeton University Press, 1954.

Class Notes. *The Wellesley Alumnae Magazine,* May 1956, 226.

"Secular Dramatics in the Royal Palace, Paris, 1378, 1389, and Chaucer's 'Tregetoures.'" *Speculum* 33 (1956): 242–55.

With Roger Sherman Loomis. *Medieval Romances.* New York: Random House, 1957.

"*Gawain and the Green Knight.*" In *Arthurian Literature in the Middle Ages,* edited by R. S. Loomis. Oxford: Clarendon Press, 1959.

Adventures in the Middle Ages: A Memorial Collection of Essays and Studies. New York: Burt Franklin, 1962.

Works Cited

Balderston, Katharine C. "Laura Hibbard Loomis." *The Wellesley Alumnae Magazine,* November 1960, 33.

Bethurum, Dorothy. *Critical Approaches to Medieval Literature.* New York: Columbia University Press, 1960.

———. *The Homilies of Wulfstan.* Oxford: Clarendon Press, 1957.

———. *The Squire's Tale.* Oxford: Clarendon Press, 1965.

Brett, Cyril. Review of *Mediaeval Romance in England. Modern Language Review* 20 (1925): 339–40.

Carey, Henry R. "Career or Maternity? The Dilemma of the College Girl." *The North American Review* 288, no. 6 (December 1929): 737–44.

———. "Sterilizing the Fittest," *The North American Review* 228, no. 5 (November 1929): 519–24.

Eisner, Sigmund. "Roger Sherman Loomis (1887–1966)." In *Medieval Scholarship: Biographical Studies on the Formation of a Discipline*, Vol. 2: *Literature and Philology,* edited by Helen Damico. New York: Garland, 1998.

English Department Annual Report. Wellesley College Archives. 22 May 1945.

Hanna, Ralph. "Reconsidering the Auchinleck Manuscript." In *New Directions in Later Medieval Manuscript Studies,* edited by Derek Pearsall. Woodbridge, Suffolk, Eng.: Boydell & Brewer, 2000.

Hughes, Helen Sard. "Laura Hibbard Loomis." *The Wellesley Magazine* 28, no. 1 (October 1943): 21.

K. B. Review of *Mediaeval Romance in England*. *The Wellesley Alumnae Magazine* 12, no. 5 (June 1928): 283.

Köbling, Eugen, ed. *Beues of Hamtoun*. EETS ES 46, 48, 65. London: Kegan, Paul, Trench, Trübner & Co., 1885, 1886, 1894.

"Laura Hibbard Loomis." In *Who's Who of American Women*. 1st ed., 1958–59. Chicago: Marquis Who's Who, 1958.

Mack, Maynard, et al. "A Mirror for the Lamp: Being the Nomination by Members of the Association of Outstanding and Influential Articles Published 1885–1958, and Questions concerning the Character of *PMLA* in the Future." *PMLA* 73 (1958): 46–71.

Malone, Kemp. Review of *Mediaeval Romance in England*. *Modern Language Notes* 51 (1926): 406–7.

Manly, John M. Review of *Mediaeval Romance in England*. *Modern Philology* 24 (1926–27): 122–24.

Medieval Studies in Memory of Gertrude Schoepperle Loomis. New York: Columbia University Press, 1927.

Palmieri, Patricia Ann. *In Adamless Eden: The Community of Women Faculty at Wellesley*. New Haven, Conn.: Yale University Press, 1995.

Patch, Howard R. Review of *Mediaeval Romance in England*. *The Journal of English and Germanic Philology* 25 (1926): 108–14.

Peyton, Henry Hall, III. "The Loomis Ladies: Gertrude Schoepperle Loomis (1882–1921), Laura Hibbard Loomis (1882–1960), Dorothy Bethurum Loomis (1897–1987)." In *On Arthurian Women: Essays in Memory of Maureen Fries,* edited by Bonnie Wheeler and Fiona Tolhurst. Dallas: Scriptorium Press, 2001.

President's Report of 1903. Appendix B. Wellesley: Wellesley College, 1903.

The Record of the Class of 1905 of Wellesley College, 1925–1930, 5 (1930).

The Record of the Class of 1905 of Wellesley College, 1949–55, 9 (1955).

The Record of the Class of 1905 of Wellesley College, 1955–60, 10 (1960).

The Record of the Trust Funds of Wellesley College. Wellesley: Wellesley College, 1940.

Review of *Mediaeval Romance in England*. *The Saturday Review of Literature,* 17 December 1924, 419.

Scala, Elizabeth D. "John Matthews Manly (1865–1940) and Edith Rickert (1871–1938)." In *Medieval Scholarship: Biographical Studies on the Formation of a Discipline*, Vol. 2, edited by Helen Damico and Joseph B. Zavadil. New York: Garland, 1996–98.

———. "Scandalous Assumptions: Edith Rickert and the Chicago Chaucer Project." *Medieval Feminist Forum* 30 (2000): 27–37.

Scudder, Vida Dutton. "Mary Bowen Brainerd." *The Wellesley Magazine* 29, no. 5 (June 1945), 287.

———. *On Journey*. New York: E. P. Dutton, 1937.

Thrall, Miriam. "The Laura Hibbard Loomis Collection of Medieval Literature." *Wellesley Magazine* 28, no. 5 (June 1944): 270.

CHAPTER 19

Helen Cam (1885–1968)
Charting the Evolution of Medieval Institutions

EUAN TAYLOR AND GINA WEAVER

HELEN CAM WAS A REMARKABLE HISTORIAN. Cam spent her academic career in the arcane business of charting the evolution of medieval institutions, an achievement that stands in importance to this day. Even more remarkable, however, is that Cam's life spanned an era of unprecedented social change—in the political, economic, and educational position of women; the apex and decline of British Imperialism; and continued European and world conflict. Despite these tumultuous times, for Cam the nature of humanity possessed a timeless quality, capable of bridging the chasm between the medieval plea roll and the modern broadsheet or poster.

Cam's ability to push for change in the present while exploring the past came from her own personal past; her roots in an academic family history ingrained in her a desire to push the limits of her social boundaries. William Herbert Cam, Helen's father, was born in 1854 at Dursley in Gloucestershire. During his attendance at New College, William Cam met Kate Scott in 1873 through her brothers, along with whom William was a member of the Oxford University Volunteers Contingent. The couple married after a protracted courtship during which William obtained a first-class degree in classics, studied at the Universities of Göttingen and Hannover, taught at Wellington College, and then went on six months' study leave to Paris. Hopes of a housemastership at Wellington were disappointed, and William took a post at Dudley Grammar School. Soon the couple had three children—Katherine (born 1880), William (1881), and Walter (1883). A lay preacher at both Wellington and Dudley, William took holy orders in 1879, before becoming headmaster, first, at Dudley and, then, at Roysse's Grammar School, Abingdon, in June 1883.[1]

Kate Scott was born at Clifton in 1858. The women members of the family demonstrated a high academic caliber; Helen Cam remembered, "My two grandmothers, my

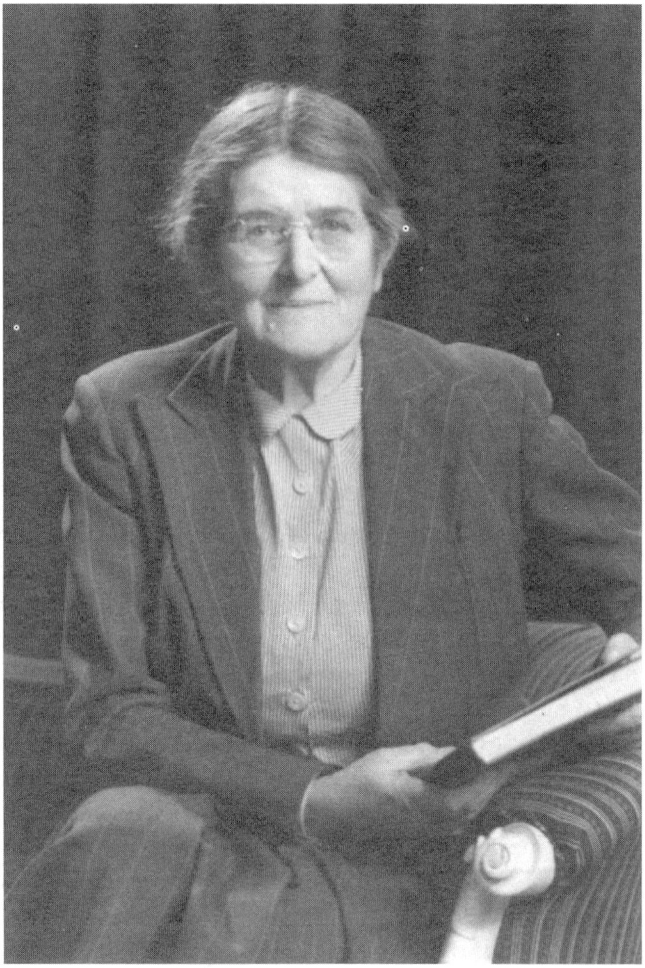

great-aunts and my aunts were all well read women, with artistic and musical tastes."[2] Her great-aunt Nelly had studied at Hannover, while her mother's sister Isie had sat the Cambridge Local Examinations and obtained a place at Newnham College, which in the event she could not afford to take up. Her maternal grandmother had opened a small private girls' school at Bridgwater in Somerset, where she taught her three daughters, just as in the next generation Kate was to teach four of her six daughters, including Helen. Thus, the Scott family women enjoyed scholarship as the norm in their daily lives, while university education, and particularly an Oxford education, was considered quite normal for Cams and Scotts alike.

Into this haven of female academia Kate bore her fourth child and second daughter, Helen Maud, on 22 August 1885. At this time William and his family lived in the modest headmaster's house, where they had been previously joined by his elderly and penniless parents in 1884. By 1891 three more daughters—Norah (1886), Edith (1888), and Avice (1891)—had been born. In 1893 William moved his family to Birchanger in Essex, taking up the ministry of Saint Mary. Another daughter, Marjorie, was born in 1898, completing the family at nine children. Despite the family's financial worries due to its large size, which, Helen recalled, "did not leave us room for pocket money, let alone boarding school fees for us [daughters]," the Birchanger days proved a happy and formative period in the children's lives—"[W]hat strikes one today is its combination of simplicity and security."[3]

The four middle sisters—Helen, Norah, Edith, and Avice—formed a clique; in "the little wood beyond the Rectory Garden . . . they planted primroses, climbed trees and acted out as plays books which their parents had read to them."[4] Helen, the eldest, was considered the organizer and devised rules for the "Good Child Society" and the "FSFF" (Floral Society for Finding Fun). These societies with their membership of four were sustained into adulthood, when each sister would contribute an article to the society's magazine. With Norah being considered more technically minded but equally as bright as Helen, the two sisters early on formed a pairing that would survive into retirement. Both won university scholarships, unlike Edith and Avice.

In the English counties the country parson was second only to the squire, and beyond a very few other middle-class residents, the congregation was made up of the agricultural laboring class. Though William and Kate were deeply committed to parish work, the children were not encouraged to mix with their social inferiors. Even though the family servants were treated well, they remained a species apart. The fourteen-year-old Helen recorded in her diary that "Nelly the maid went, for which let us be thankful. Her mother was drunk when she came for her—beastly!"[5] Such early childhood experiences helped to shape Helen Cam's brand of socialism: "People were not all alike and could not be treated as if they were. There was nothing wrong with privilege balanced by responsibility."[6]

The most significant aspect of the daughters' childhoods was their education. The four middle daughters were taught at home. William and Kate's efforts were born of economic necessity, and there was a clear division of responsibility. William taught the girls Latin, Euclid, algebra, and Scripture and encouraged them in other interests including his own—botany, astronomy, philately, and the recording of meteorological data. An interest in botany and astronomy remained with Helen for the rest of her life. Kate had a little teaching experience at her grandmother's school at Bridgwater. Helen remembered, "It was from my mother whom we learnt how to read and how to work."[7] Reading, writing, grammar, history, geography, and languages—besides Latin, French, and German—were taught via written exercises, readings aloud, tests, translations and double translations, arguments, and word games. Six days a week, two hours of formal "lessons" each morning were supplemented with several hours "preparation" before lunch and in the early evenings. The children then spent their afternoons with their father, whom they accompanied on parish visits.[8]

The sisters all studied for the Oxford Local Examinations, to which they were ferried periodically from age ten onward. These exams galvanized their minds to study and were approached in the spirit with which Cam claimed to approach all her later academic work—"fun": "My BA finals in 1907 was the first examination I did not wholeheartedly enjoy."[9] Helen and Norah did well in the preliminaries of 1899 and in the juniors list of 1901. Helen (aged sixteen) placed fourth in all England—prompting a characteristically measured response: "I worked hard, but I could have done more. And to be fourth girl at that."[10]

Besides examination success the children felt the deeper impact of their home education. Early in her career Cam wrote to her mother: "Talking of atmosphere dearest, I must tell you once again I have learnt all these things from you and Dad.... [T]he unconscious assumption at home always was respect for personality. 'Think for yourself' is what you said, and that took me everywhere at college and elsewhere."[11] As the children developed their own interests and opinions, so lessons turned into heated discussions: "By the time I was fifteen or sixteen lessons had grown very argumentative."[12] The family's religious, political, and social debates had the greatest impact on their later lives: "The assets which we carried from our home education to the next stage of college or other training were habits of independent working and thinking, standards of thoroughness and a demand for evidence, and above all an unspoilt appetite for learning."[13]

There was never any question that Cam would compete for a university scholarship. Since the family connections were with Oxford, she applied to Lady Margaret Hall and Somerville, and seeking a place to further her studies, her parents sent Helen to Oxford for a period to stay with her uncle, George Scott. Here for some months she embarked on a program of revision for the scholarship exams in March and April of that year. Averaging eight hours of study per day in the Bodleian and Radcliffe Libraries, she read Hallam, Ranke, Macaulay, Stubbs, Greer, and Freeman; in the evenings her uncle tutored her in Latin and ancient history.

Rejected first by Lady Margaret Hall and then by Somerville, Cam was forced to apply to London's Royal Holloway College. The Holloway examinations necessitated a specialization in two subjects; she chose history and English, supplementing her existing reading with a regime of Shakespeare, Milton, Pope, Chaucer, Hallam, Swift, and Dryden. Her extreme disappointment at failing to obtain an Oxford scholarship was ameliorated when she heard in July 1904 of her success at Royal Holloway. The scholarship exams were demanding, but Cam did outstandingly well, passing top in history and Latin and second in English.[14] Her performance earned her an award of fifty-five pounds per annum, one of eleven scholarships offered for 1904.

Royal Holloway College, founded in 1885 and housed in W. H. Crossland's grandiose chateau at Egham, had since 1897 been presided over by Emily Penrose, formerly principal of Bedford College.[15] Despising Holloway's reputation as a glorified girl's school, Penrose created a spirit of organized freedom to "free women from the imprisonment of domesticity and social triviality [to] prepare them for active citizenship and a life of service to society."[16] Considerably richer than most other women's colleges and trumpeting its royal connection, Holloway had also earned the reputation for opulence "in sharp contrast to other impoverished and comfortless women's colleges of the day."[17]

Cam's experience at Holloway, beginning with her arrival in 1904, allowed her much more freedom than she had had at home in the midst of her large family. On the other hand, she became part of an institution whose ethos rested on the notion of community living and of loyalty to friends and colleagues. This was most obviously demonstrated in the "college family" system, which formed an introductory friendship and support network. These families spent most leisure and social time together, and Cam took easily to such an ethos as a practical expression of her burgeoning personal, intellectual, and political interest in the idea of community.

Serious in demeanor and having little interest in petty jealousies or trivialities, Cam launched into the "Political" — "a shadow Parliament complete with parties, front and back benchers, Speaker and the forms and titles of the House of Commons. Conservatives and Liberals took office turn about."[18] Debates loosely mirrored those at Westminster—Ireland, suffragism, constitutional reform, and foreign affairs. For Cam its effects were magical, replicating the endless politicking at Birchanger, but in a grander and more plausible setting. Cam assumed several "ministerial" posts herself, and it was this experience of debate and argument that, more than any other single factor, shaped her emerging political and social views.[19] Arriving at Holloway an unconvinced Conservative, in her college years she undertook a process of political self-examination that converted her wholeheartedly to the Liberal cause, a foundation upon which was built her later conversion to socialism.

Besides her involvement in politics Cam also became chairman of Holloway's "Historical" society, debating historical theories, events, and movements. The college's strong religious ethos was strictly imposed on its students, and chapel attendance was compulsory. Cam devoted herself to religious societies, becoming president of the African Mission and Christian Union meetings and winning the Savory Divinity prize presented by the archbishop of Canterbury in 1905. In the company of her two closest friends, Fanny Street and Marguerite Tutin, Cam enjoyed other pursuits, including long walks in the surrounding countryside "botanising" as her father had taught her.[20]

The history honors degree course was taught by the principal, Miss Penrose, and the hugely popular Margaret Hayes-Robinson (who was to become an important mentor to Cam); it was under the nonresident direction of E. A. Carlyle of All Souls College, Oxford. Cam's decision to study history was an early indicator of her approach to academic work as something of intrinsic worth rather than merely for personal enjoyment.[21] Cam was considered very bright by her tutors. Thomas Seccombe found her "a thorough student in every way" and commended the "terseness, originality, pith and logical power of her writing."[22]

Toward the end of her undergraduate period, her interests broadened; indeed, Hayes-Robinson regarded her as "a most valuable member of the community . . . taking a leading part in college life in all its aspects, for she was interested in many subjects besides her special line of study."[23] A commitment to forging cross-curricular links, seeking a broader and more comprehensive picture—what Cam herself later described as "bridging the gap between abstract and concrete, theory and fact, printed page and flesh and blood"—was a central legacy of Cam's college experience.[24] Cam further demonstrated her academic prowess by winning a university exhibition in history, French, and German in 1905, a Driver Scholarship in history in 1906, and the Driver History Prize for 1906 and 1907. In the summer of 1907 she sat her finals and along with Fanny Street was awarded a first-class degree.

Her success at Holloway encouraged her ambitions toward higher research, and even her rejection for the two-year Shaw Scholarship at the London School of Economics in the early summer of 1907 did not blunt her enthusiasm for further study. She began research for her master's thesis, which was to become her first and only full-length comparative study, *Local Government in Francia and England*. Under the supervision of H. W. C. Davis of Balliol College, Cam resettled in Oxford for almost a year to be near her sources. Early in 1908 she applied for a resident fellowship in history at Bryn Mawr College, Pennsylvania (where her sister Norah was in the final year of her undergraduate studies), a fellowship that she won and decided to accept.

One of the "Seven Sisters" women's colleges, Bryn Mawr was marked by the radicalism of its principal, Martha Carey Thomas. Founded in 1885 by Joseph W. Taylor on Quaker principles, its ethos from the outset was to enable women to become "equal in taking part in the thoughts and discussions with the vital things with which Friends were constantly occupied."[25] After Thomas assumed the college's presidency in 1894, the emphasis changed toward furthering her distinctive conception of sexual equality. Thomas was a visionary in advocating the total abandonment of gender divisions between men and women. Marriage was to become "a kind of new union. . . . The college-educated couple would be working comrades."[26] Humanity would replace masculinity as the driving force of politics, morality, and personal relationships. For Thomas the standards of the social and the intellectual were at one, and in line with this philosophy, the college's social activities were relegated to weekends with the working week reserved for study. In the same interests excessive contact with homes and families was strongly discouraged.

For a year Cam continued work on her master's thesis, attending graduate classes in English and American history given by W. H. Allison, W. R. Smith, and Carleton F. Brown. During 1909 she met another lifelong friend, Lily Taylor, graduate of the University of Wisconsin and later professor of Latin at Vassar and Bryn Mawr. Much interaction between the East Coast women's colleges took place, and it is likely that Cam also met both Nellie Neilson and Bertha Haven Putnam, prominent women medievalists at Bryn Mawr College and now resident scholars at Mount Holyoke in neighboring Massachusetts. She saw in these women the embodiments of great women medievalists, and they became important role models. Cam's witnessing such possibilities for female scholarship in the United States could only serve to contrast unfavorably with the absence of their equivalent in England, save for the distant memory of Mary Bateson at Cambridge. As a consequence of her experience, U.S. scholarship became strongly associated in Cam's mind with opportunity as well as with freedom and liberal values.

By September 1909 Cam was back in England, where she had accepted a position as assistant mistress at Cheltenham Ladies' College. Founded in 1858, Cheltenham was a girl's boarding school whose principal, Lilian Faithfull, emphasized the domestic model of schooling: "It was felt that the boarding house should be as far as possible a home," and her staff were to be "taken as much as possible in one's confidence to let them feel that the school is a co-operative society. . . . Happiness in their professional life depends principally upon the friendliness of colleagues."[27] The school's cooperative, family-based philosophy stood in marked contrast to both the excessive sociability of Holloway and the brusque institutionalism of Bryn Mawr. The same home-style standards applied to both the younger members of the staff and the students. It was not a pleasurable experience for Cam. Rigid hierarchy, favoritism, and patronage rankled the young women, and there was a good deal of friction. She was unaccustomed to gossip and the formation of personal enmities, and Cheltenham soon became associated in her mind with division and unhappiness.

One fortunate outcome of this time was her meeting with Mary Gwaldys Jones, a graduate of Cambridge's Girton College, who was head of the training department at the college. Jones, a student contemporary of Eileen Power, took the unsure young academic under her wing, and the two began a deep friendship that was to develop later at Girton when Cam acted as Jones's deputy in the college's history department. It was Jones who encouraged Cam to maintain her academic contacts and continue independent research on her own time and who possibly later alerted her to the decisive opportunity of the Pfeiffer Scholarship at Girton. Another important acquaintance made during this time was with the learned Russian specialist of English manorial history and friend of Maitland, Paul Vinogradoff, whose sessions of seminars Cam attended at All Souls, Oxford. Vinogradoff became one of her professional heroes and encouraged her to turn her attention to the English medieval administrative unit—

the "hundred." Other students in the seminars included two future women professors, Nellie Neilson and Ada Elizabeth Levett, with whom she became good friends.

That Cam yearned to leave Cheltenham is demonstrated by testimonials dated 1910 and 1911 and written by Carlyle and Hayes-Robinson in support of Cam's repeated applications to return to Holloway as a history lecturer. Fanny Street, Cam's undergraduate friend, had replaced Hayes-Robinson as resident lecturer in 1911, though Carlyle remained in overall control. It was not until spring 1912 that Higgins and the Holloway governors appointed Cam resident assistant lecturer in history. For Cam the appointment was a godsend. It demanded no more than six hours of teaching a week, allowing ample time to put the finishing touches to the soon-to-be-published *Local Government in Francia and England* and simultaneously to begin work in earnest on an investigation of the medieval hundred, as suggested by Vinogradoff.

Fanny Street, Cam's senior by seven years, had been a close friend and mentor in her undergraduate days. Street became Cam's surrogate big sister in her college family and influenced her opinions on a number of issues, including matters political and religious. A year before Cam's return, Margaret Joyce Powell, a recent graduate of Newnham College, joined Holloway as an assistant lecturer in English and philology and soon formed a relationship with Fanny Street that was to last throughout their lives. With Cam's arrival and the addition of Miss Walters, a music lecturer, a new college family was created. However, her new college family's group dynamics were perhaps not as harmonious as they at first appeared; certainly Cam was the junior and submissive member of the circle. Emotions and an appeal to the aesthetic formed a large part of the women's relations, and personal jealousies centered on a competition for Street's affections caused much pain. Cam was deeply in love with Street, albeit platonically, and Street's apparent preference for Powell, to the partial exclusion of Cam, "gave [her] some of the greatest misery [she had] experienced—of which [her] life has had remarkably little."[28] The physical break came in October 1917 when, soon after having been elevated to senior staff lecturer, Street, soon followed by Powell, left the college to contribute to Britain's war effort at the Ministry of Food.

Having had no teaching responsibilities at Bryn Mawr and having been treated as little more than a pupil herself at Cheltenham, Cam was initiated into academic life through this second Holloway experience. The residential character of the appointment placed a number of strains on the fledgling researcher, not the least of which were the social and pastoral duties.[29] Modeling her teaching style on that of her now departed tutor, Margaret Hayes-Robinson, Cam rapidly formed an approach to students that was at once austere and kindly, a style that would mark the rest of her academic career. These years saw the emergence of "Auntie Cam," an unglamorous and spinsterish persona, who was, in some sense, intellectually inaccessible if not socially remote.[30]

After 1914 "the shadow of the war fell upon the College as it fell upon the whole of society."[31] A real worry for many was the fate of their male relatives at war on the European mainland or in the Near East. Cam had particular cause for concern, with her brothers Walter and Tom both called up for service; Walter was in the Royal Army Medical Corps in France and Tom in the Royal Engineers, successively stationed at Gallipoli and then in France. She took a keen interest in the progress of the war itself, though her views were at best naive and at worst insensitive: "Wasn't Zeebrugge gorgeous? Seafighting seems to me not so horrible, or so ugly as landfighting—cleaner somehow."[32] The family letters barely conceal a terrible anxiety for the safety of the brothers, and when Tom was shot dead on patrol near Ypres in August 1917, Kate Cam suffered a mental breakdown. There is no record of Helen Cam's reactions to her brother's death, and her feelings on the return, unopened, of her last letter to Tom at the front bearing the words "Killed in Action" can only be imagined.

Street's swift departure from Holloway opened the way for Cam's appointment as permanent resident lecturer in July 1917, though not without controversy. A Miss Strickland was appointed as her junior, and while Carlyle remained in overall charge, "the resident lecturer [had] considerable responsibility with regard to the organisation of the Department [and was] required to examine for the Entrance and Driver Scholarship examinations."[33] Cam's teaching duties, however, remained remarkably light at only eight hours per week, leaving time for her continued work for Paul Vinogradoff's Oxford Series *Studies in the Hundred Rolls,* which was due for completion in summer 1918.

Attending Hubert Hall's classes "Palaeography" and "Diplomatic" at the London School of Economics and giving similar classes herself back at Holloway, Cam continued to oscillate between teaching and research. By the early 1920s, with the Vinogradoff volume published to critical acclaim, her thoughts turned toward her future career and research possibilities. In March 1921 she sought and obtained permission from the Holloway governors to deliver a series of lectures on special aspects in European history at King's and University Colleges in London. For Cam this represented an important, if brief, exposure to an academic world beyond the confines of the isolated women's college.

Studies in the Hundred Rolls appeared in 1921—the product of nearly ten years of research. Previously the Hundred Rolls had been largely ignored for the historical purposes to which Cam enlisted them. Her approach signaled the importance of these documents in discovering the broader history of thirteenth-century administration. Critics acclaimed the study: "[T]he analysis of the Hundred Rolls in the second chapter contains useful warnings for those who use the printed edition for historical purposes." Also commended were "the elaborate tabular appendices to chapters I and II (which) must have cost much labour and [would] be of great service to those who have to work over the same ground."[34]

Following in the footsteps of Eileen Power, who had been the Pfeiffer Scholar for over three years from 1911, Cam received the Pfeiffer Fellowship at Girton, which opened up new opportunities for her. In the first place it afforded the chance for further and deeper research into the medieval hundred; in the second it gave access to a new academic world at the oldest women's higher-education college in the country, one associated with one of the most prestigious universities in the world. Oxford was the university at which Cam had yearned to study, London had afforded her the opportunity and the means of proving her academic caliber, and now at Cambridge the next stage of her development as an academic and a historian was to unfold. Though she regretted the loss of her established institutional roots, the fellowship was in every sense providential for her career.[35]

Cam's arrival at Girton provided a continuation of the residential college life she had known at Holloway and Cheltenham. Unlike the relatively liberal London, however, where women now sat on the faculty boards and other committees, where Hilda Johnstone had been appointed a professor of history at Holloway, and where Cam herself had been invited to lecture at the men's colleges—Girton stood in the shadow of Cambridge, and Cam, like all Cambridge women, suffered from the institutional gender bias of the university.[36] University attitudes toward Girton and Newnham ranged from irritated sufferance to condescension, and the central authorities and the men's colleges were overwhelmingly unwilling to accept the women's claims for equal status. Cam learned this lesson early, for Cambridge women suffered many mundane indignities, not least having to pay for the use of the university library.[37]

Cam's socialist ideals nurtured under Fanny Street's influence at Holloway now became important as a window to life outside Cambridge and college. Elected a member of the Girton Labour Party in 1924, Cam enjoyed her return to active political life and the social opportunities it brought. She was soon voted onto the General Committee of the Cambridgeshire Party. Attending a women's conference in Birmingham in 1925, she launched an appeal for the relief of miners in the depressed West Yorkshire coalfields and was elected to the Divisional Group's Executive in 1927.[38] The following year, supported by the Girton Party, Cam stood as Labour candidate for the Histon Division in the Cambridge County elections; she was beaten, however, by her sole opponent, the sitting Independent member. Although it was a respectable result, with Cam obtaining a third more votes than her nearest fellow Labour candidate, the campaign discouraged her from standing again or from any further active local political involvement.[39]

In 1929 Cam was voted onto the Cambridgeshire Education Committee's Juvenile Employment Subcommittee, and her continued interest in the career options open to her Girton students demonstrated her commitment to providing opportunities for the young, her concern with social questions, and her rejection of academic insularity.[40] Cam also began at this time a long association with Hillcroft College for Working Women at Surbiton. Supporting the ethos of bringing the benefits of residential-college life to women of the lower classes, for whom education was still regarded as superfluous, Cam was a member of the college council, raised money at Girton, and gave her own money and books to the project. She also founded the Girton College Bursary for Hillcroft in the 1930s and served as temporary college principal in the early 1960s.[41]

It would be inaccurate to suggest that Cam had entirely ignored the university in the first years of the 1920s. During her Pfeiffer research work for *The Hundred and the Hundred Rolls* (1930), she produced journal articles at an energetic rate and slowly formed friendships with several university men, particularly the American medievalist Gaillard Lapsley of Trinity College and Harold Temperley of Peterhouse. In *The Hundred and the Hundred Rolls,* the work for which she is most remembered, Cam "tried to do two things: to provide a guide to the study of the three great volumes of the Rotuli Hundredorum and Placita Quo Warranto, printed early in the nineteenth century, and to give a sketch of the local governmental system at work in the reign of Edward I."[42] The work cemented Cam's reputation, with reviewers acknowledging her as "the best authority we have on the Sheriff in the thirteenth century, the county court, the hundred court and the hundred bailiff."[43] However, reviewers differed on the level at which the book might best be read; while C. Stephenson condescendingly described the book as "having no pretension of being more than it is—a somewhat popular work of description and illustration," C. Johnson felt that "its theme and treatment might be described as more historical than antiquarian."[44] Cam herself certainly regarded the work as a scholarly rather than a popular work.

The academic community at Cambridge of which Helen Cam gradually became part was made up of diverse formal and informal structures. The main organ of Cambridge history—the faculty board, together with its subsidiary committees—only grudgingly accepted Girton and Newnham's historians. M. G. Jones, who was coopted to the board in an act of undisguised tokenism in the late 1920s, remained the sole female voice until the Second World War necessitated the inclusion of other women. Indeed, Cam was not invited to join the board until 1941, while her involvement with its other committees was sporadic. Perhaps it is unsurprising that in a university that denied women degrees until 1948 its female academics should occupy a second-class role. Cam felt the indignity of the progression of a generation of young male academics, as some of her former male students took their places in Cambridge's history hierarchy. Until the mid-1940s Cam's views on current academic issues were invited rather than delivered as a right. By the mid-1930s she was the recognized world authority in her field, and it became increasingly anomalous in the eyes of the younger faculty members that her contributions should be restricted in this way. The informal structures within the community—common rooms, college dinners, and clubs—had long excluded women from their number, and her formation of an association of fellow medievalists, "The Medieval Circle," may be seen as her practical reaction to women's exclusion from the established intellectual social groupings and an attempt, through her own innovation, to make her mark on her history colleagues and in the university.

Helen Cam became accustomed to slights at Cambridge on account of her sex. Besides the imposition of library charges and the more significant message that exclusion from faculty committees sent, a succession of other decisions affected her view of the university. On applying for sabbatical leave in 1934, she was told that a male lecturer—her junior in age, experience, and length of service—had already secured leave for the same period and took precedence. Cam considered this a personal slight on account of her sex. Another rebuff was received the same month when her application for the university's Litt.D. was refused, ostensibly on the grounds that her undergraduate degree had not been awarded by Cambridge, though again she suspected institutional bias. Four years later the Litt.D. was awarded, to the embarrassed relief of many of her male colleagues.

In 1937 a chair of medieval history was founded at the university. Its first incumbent, C. W. Previte-Orton, retired in 1942, by which time Cam regarded herself the most suitable replacement; she also wanted the post badly. Her world reputation as a medievalist was well established, and furthermore, she was beginning to be recognized in the formal structures of the university and the faculty; nevertheless, the chair was awarded to a male colleague. Cam took the rebuff personally, and it came to symbolize very forcibly the general and pervasive lack of appreciation for her and for other women at Cambridge.

During the Michelmas term of 1936 through the Lent term of 1937, Cam obtained permission for absence from Girton and traveled to India, Burma, the Mediterranean, India, the Middle East, and the Holy Land. On her return Gaillard Lapsley's retirement left Cam in sole charge of the English constitutional history course at Cambridge; this was at a time when the onset of war in 1939 increased the strain on all women at Cambridge, with many teaching, examination, and faculty responsibilities having fallen to the Girton and Newnham dons, opportunities certainly born of exigency rather than egalitarianism.

With the evacuation of her primary sources and burdened by her additional university responsibilities, Cam had virtually ceased substantive research work during the war. Her free time was spent compiling her collection of papers published as *Liberties and Communities in Medieval England* in 1944. This was the first of Cam's two collections, and she was never again to present a full-length scholarly monograph, instead coming to believe "that medieval local government can only be understood through much short-range study of particular places and institutions."[45]

Peacetime brought some respite from her heavy workload, and after 1946 Cam passed the directorship of studies to a former pupil, Jean Lindsay, and reverted to part-time teaching. The offer in March 1948 of the Zemurray Professorship at Harvard presented both an opportunity and a release for Cam. When being canvassed for the professorship, Cam agreed to accept only on the condition that she take no part in Harvard's faculty committees. True to her word, she eschewed all faculty business to concentrate on her English history lectures, her "documents class" for young research students, the legal history seminars at Harvard's Law School, and her series of "grandmother's seminars" for mature women students at Radcliffe.

Not only did the professorship lighten her workload; it also offered a fresh opportunity to concentrate on research. Indeed, Cam had three projects in hand—correcting the proofs of *England before Elizabeth* and the Victoria County History *City of Cambridge,* both substantially written prior to her departure; the outline of a second collection of essays relating to legal studies, eventually published as *Law-Finders and Law-Makers in Medieval England* in 1962; and most especially preliminary work for what would become her final study, *The Eyre of London 1321*.[46] It also effectively extended her academic career by at least four years, Cambridge dons then being obliged to retire at sixty-five.

Two years after her arrival at Harvard, she was invited to become president of the reformed International Commission for the History of Representative and Parliamentary Institutions (ICHRPI). This was an apt appointment, for throughout Cam's working life a keen sense of internationalism had shaped her notion of academia, if not so obviously in her substantive historical study. From 1913 she had attended the Comité International des Sciences Historiques conferences held in various European cities and had become an active participant in a number of international historical organizations. In wartime Cambridge she had coordinated two Allied Historians' conferences attended by nearly thirty representatives of eight countries. The ICHRPI sought to study the origins and links between the "representative" or parliamentary histories of different countries. Serving as president for ten years, Cam oversaw the reintroduction of Blochian comparative history, balanced the nationalities of its sprawling membership, and coped with severe financial worries and the administrative ineptitude of some colleagues.

Helen and Norah Cam both retired in the summer of 1954 and settled in Mochras, a semidetached cottage in the outskirts of Sevenoaks, Kent. But retirement brought no relaxation of Cam's intellectual occupations. Translating and composing an introduction to the *Eyre of London, 1321;* continuing responsibility as president of ICHRPI until 1960; writing a lengthy introduction and editing a volume of F. W. Maitland's papers, published as *Selected Historical Essays, F. W. Maitland* (1957); collecting essays for publication as *Law-Finders and Law-Makers in Medieval England* (1962); honoring frequent requests for reviews, short papers, and school-speech-day and prize giving duties—all these activities meant that Cam was obliged to spend a significant proportion of each day in her paper-strewn lean-to at the back of the house.

While Cam's studies up to the interwar period had focused on the hundred and the relationship of local and central government, she turned to a new path in her later concentration on legal and judicial sources and the associated themes of representation, custom, and enforceability. Her concern with legal study after the war, at Harvard, and into retirement was not a break with her old interests but a subtle shift of emphasis. *Law-Finders and Law-Makers in Medieval England,* Cam's second collection of papers and speeches, demonstrates her continuing and growing preoccupation with the legal aspects of English constitutional history. For Cam law within history operated at two levels—law as an approach to history and the importance of law in history—and she took particular analytical pleasure in the clarity of law. James Holt considered *Law-Finders and Law-Makers* the work of "a true successor of Maitland," declaring some of the essays, including the Raleigh Lecture and the appreciation of Maitland, to be "masterpieces."[47] The *Eyre of London, 1321,* which Cam dubbed her magnum opus, was her last work and the culmination of twenty years' research. Her treatment of materials, her lengthy introduction, and the conclusions she drew on the 1321 proceedings form the best example of her technique of legal history.

Public recognition for Cam on both sides of the Atlantic finally arrived in retirement. Besides the honorary doctorates at Smith College, the University of North Carolina, and Mount Holyoke, Cam was successively appointed vice president of both the Selden Society and the Historical Society in 1962 and honorary fellow of Somerville College in 1964. Two further awards gave her particular satisfaction. In 1957 she was invested as a Commander of the British Empire by the queen at Buckingham Palace. Better still was the doctor of letters honoris causa from Oxford, which she received in June 1962.[48]

Cam aged physically but not mentally. Although admitted to the hospital twice, once in 1960 and then again in 1965, her hospital stays provided an unfettered academic opportunity to read and correct proofs of her *London Eyre*. Cam continued to work right up to the time of the stroke that incapacitated her. She died ten days later on 9 February 1968, never having regained consciousness. Cam wanted it no other way; she presciently cited the following lines of two poems from a 1965 anthology: "Lord, let me not live to be useless" and "Lord, give me work while my life shall last, and life till my work is done."[49]

Notes

1. "List of the Candidates for the Headmastership of Roysse's School, 1883," School Archive, Abingdon School. He faced stiff competition at Abingdon—there were sixty-eight applicants.

2. "The Education of Girls before the Foundation of Women's Colleges," 8, CAM IX, file 8, Helen Cam Papers, College Archive, Girton College, Cambridge.

3. First quotation: Helen Cam, "Eating and Drinking Greek," *Listener* (21 May 1964): 12; second quotation: John Harkness, "Cams at the Rectory," box 3, Helen Cam Papers, Department of Western Manuscripts (Modern Papers), Bodleian Library.

4. Harkness, "Cams at the Rectory."

5. John Harkness's notes of Cam's diaries, 11 February 1899, box 1, Department of Western Manuscripts (Modern Papers), Bodleian Library.

6. Ibid.

7. Cam, "Eating and Drinking Greek," 11.

8. Ibid., 11.

9. Ibid., 12.

10. Harkness's notes of Cam's diaries, 24 September 2001, box 1, Department of Western Manuscripts (Modern Papers), Bodleian Library.

11. Letter from Helen Cam to her mother (20 January 1918), box 1, Department of Western Manuscripts (Modern Papers), Bodleian Library.

12. "Miss Cam, Harvard Professor, Taught at Mother's Knee."

13. Cam, "Eating and Drinking Greek," 12.

14. "Entrance Scholarship Examination Mark Book (1904–17)," AR/225/3, College Archive, Royal Holloway College. Her mark for mathematics is unrecorded.

15. See Elliott, *Palaces, Patronage and Pills.*
16. Bingham, *History of Royal Holloway College,* 109.
17. Queen Victoria opened the college in 1886, and a member of the royal family nearly always attended the college's summer garden party up until the Second World War. Quotation from Spurling, *Ivy When Young,* 147.
18. Bingham, *History of Royal Holloway College,* 104.
19. Cam reported being president of the Board of Agriculture in an "Independent Democratic" cabinet.
20. Marguerite Tutin (Mrs. Neville Smith), otherwise known at college and for many years afterward as "Peter," remained a lifelong friend and holiday companion for Cam. Cam played some hockey as an undergraduate at Holloway, and later as a tutor at both Holloway and Cheltenham she occasionally umpired. Being a little overweight, she early developed an ambivalence to sports.
21. "Making Friends with One's Work," 3, CAM IX, file 5, ii, College Archive, Girton College, Cambridge. "In my first year at college I was having the most exciting and wonderful lectures on English Literature and was very strongly tempted to change my subject and read for English honours instead of History. I [explained this] to my mother, and she said, 'Can you tell me how you feel about it?' and I said, 'I feel as if English would be play and History work,' and she said 'Then you had better stick to History.' I can't tell you how glad I am that I did."
22. Testimonial from Thomas Seccombe (n.d.), CAM I, file 15, viii, College Archive, Girton College, Cambridge.
23. Testimonial from Margaret Hayes-Robinson (May 1909), CAM I, file 15, iv, College Archive, Girton College, Cambridge.
24. "The Relation of Scholarship to the Life of Women," (n.d.), CAM XIII, file 3, College Archive, Girton College, Cambridge.
25. Meigs, *What Makes a College?* 16.
26. Martha Carey Thomas, "The Purpose of the College: Commencement Address at Bryn Mawr" (1907), in *The Educated Woman in America: Selected Writings of Catharine Beecher, Margaret Fuller, and M. Carey Thomas,* ed. Barbara Cross (New York: Teachers College Press, 1956), 141.
27. Faithfull, *In the House,* 153, 203.
28. Letter from Helen Cam to Louisa Alger, 22 November 1962, series I/19, Alger Family Papers, College Archive, Radcliffe Institute for Advanced Study.
29. "Living under the constant scrutiny of dozens of young eyes must have been somewhat daunting even for the most self-possessed. Their lectures were judged to impossibly high standards.... [S]tudents wanted them to be intellectually superior but personally accessible, bringing together better than ordinary women the emotional and the intellectual" (Vicinus, *Independent Women,* 151).
30. Martha Vicinus grouped the female academic staff: "Lecturers fell into three familiar categories: the traditional schoolteacher, the emotional and motherly, or the intellectual and asexual" (*Independent Women,* 148).
31. Bingham, *History of Royal Holloway College,* 127.
32. Letter from Helen Cam to her mother, 28 April 1918, box 1, Department of Western Manuscripts (Modern Papers, Bodleian Library).
33. Flyer, AR/162/9, College Archive, Royal Holloway College.

34. Tait, review of *Studies in the Hundred Rolls*.

35. See Dyhouse, *No Distinction of Sex*, 141, for a discussion of the importance of scholarship opportunities for aspiring women academics.

36. "[After 1926 s]everal pinpricks remained. . . . [T]hough their influence had been greatly increased, they still had no voice in the government of the University and could not vote in the Senate House on matters concerning the teaching which they were undertaking. On a more trivial level, the heads of Girton and Newnham and the staffs of these colleges attended University functions and ceremonials by courtesy only and were counted as 'wives' at social gatherings" (McWilliams-Tullberg, *Women at Cambridge*, 208).

37. As nonmembers of the university Girton and Newnham dons were required to apply for admission on the same terms as other members of the general public: "Persons who are desirous of using the Library for the purpose of study and research are required to fill up a form of application and furnish letters from two members of the Senate, certifying from personal knowledge that the applicant is a student of some specified subject, and is a fit and proper person to be admitted to the Library for the said purpose. The fee for these tickets of admission is one guinea for a year, or half a guinea for a single quarter. Holders of these tickets will have full use of the Library in the same manner as members of the University, except that they cannot take books out of the Library, this privilege being confined to members of the Senate of the University" (Aldis, *University Library Cambridge*, 29–30). Also see McWilliams-Tullberg, *Women at Cambridge*, 156.

38. Girton Labour Party Papers (January 1924–April 1936), Council Archive, Cambridge County Council.

39. She maintained links with the party, acting as treasurer to the Romsey Town branch of the party, and was a regular donor and an occasional lecturer to the party faithful.

40. Juvenile Employment Subcommittee papers, 7th–13th Reports (1929–36), Annual Reports, Cambridgeshire Education Committee, Council Archive, Cambridge County Council.

41. See Cockerill, *Second Chance*.

42. Cam, *Hundred and the Hundred Rolls*, preface.

43. Salter, review of *The Hundred and the Hundred Rolls*.

44. Stephenson, review of *Studies in the Hundred Rolls*; Johnson, review of *Studies in the Hundred Rolls*.

45. Helen Cam, "In Defence of the Study of Local History," in *Liberties and Communities in Medieval England*, ix.

46. Some Eyre records are preserved at Harvard's Law School.

47. Holt, review of *Law-Finders and Law-Makers in Medieval England*.

48. Letter from Helen Cam to Louisa Alger, 22 November 1962, folder 19, Alger Family Papers, 1809–1969, A103, box 1, College Archive, Radcliffe Institute for Advanced Study.

49. Letter from Helen Cam to Louisa Alger, 17 July 1965, refers to B. Greene and V. Gollancz, *God of a Hundred Names* (London: Gollancz, 1962) (folder 19, Alger Family Papers, 1809–1969, A103, box 1, College Archive, Radcliffe Institute for Advanced Study.

Select Bibliography of Works by Helen Cam

This bibliography does not include articles later compiled in *Liberties and Communities in Medieval England* (1944) or in *Law-Finders and Law-Makers in Medieval England* (1962).

Local Government in Francia and England. London: University Press, 1912.

"The English Lands of the Abbey of Saint Riquier." *English Historical Review* 31 (1916): 443–47.
"The Legend of the Incendiary Birds." *English Historical Review* 31 (1916): 98–101.
A Guide for Novel Readers. London: YWCA, 1920.
"The Dramatic Method in the Teaching of History." *Encyclopaedia and Dictionary of Education* 2 (1921): 802–3.
Studies in the Hundred Rolls. Oxford: Clarendon Press, 1921.
"Visus de Bortreming." *English Historical Review* 23 (1923): 224–46.
"An East Anglian Shire Moot of Stephen's Reign, 1148–1153." *English Historical Review* 39 (1924): 568–71.
"The Marshalry of the Eyre: Postscript." *Cambridge Historical Journal* 1, no. 2 (1925): 333.
"On the Material Available in the Eyre Rolls." *Bulletin of the Institute of Historical Research* 3 (1925–26): 152–60.
"The Borough." In *Encyclopaedia Britannica.* 14th ed.
With E. F. Jacob. "Notes on an English Cluniac Chronicle." *English Historical Review* 44 (1929): 94–104.
With A. S. Turberville. "A Short Bibliography of English Constitutional History." *Historical Association* (1929): leaflet 75.
Borough of Northampton (Victoria County History). London: VCH, 1930.
The Hundred and the Hundred Rolls. London: Methuen, 1930.
"Parliamentary Writs 'de Expensis' of 1258." *English Historical Review* 46 (1931): 630–32.
"The Hundreds of Northamptonshire." *Journal of the Northants Natural History Society and Field Club* (1934).
"Recent Books in English on the Parliamentary Institutions of the British Isles in the Middle Ages." *Histoire des assemblés d'états* in *Bulletin of CISH* 9, no. 4 (1937): 413–18.
"After the Crisis." *Speculum* 16 (1938): 429.
Editor with M. Coate and L. S. Sutherland. *Studies in Manorial History,* by A. E. Levett. Oxford: Clarendon Press, 1938.
John Mortlock III. Master of the Town of Cambridge. Cambridge: Cambridge Antiquarian Society, 1939.
Liberties and Communities in Medieval England. Cambridge: University Press, 1944.
"Quo Warranto Proceedings in Cambridge, 1780–1790." *Cambridge Historical Journal* 8, no. 3 (1946): 145–65.
"Zachary Nugent Brooke, 1883–1946." *Proceedings of the British Academy* 32 (1946): 381–93.
"Nellie Neilson, 1873–1947." *Bryn Mawr Alumnae Quarterly* (April 1947): 14–15.
England before Elizabeth. London: Hutchison & Co., 1950.
"Lesser Officials of the Shire." In *English Government at Work, 1327–1336,* ed. J. F. Willard, W. A. Morris, and W. H. Dunham, 3:143–83 Medieval Academy of America, , no. 56,. Cambridge, Mass.: Medieval Academy of America, 1950.
Editor with Geoffrey Barraclough. *Crown, Community, and Parliament in the Later Middle Ages,* by Gaillard Lapsley. Oxford: Basil Blackwell, 1951.
"The International Commission for the History of Representative and Parliamentary Institutions: Its Work at the Ninth International Congress of Historical Sciences, and Its Past and Future Activities." In *IXe Congrés international des sciences historiques, Paris, 1950. Recueil de travaux d'histoire et de philologie,* vol. 3, no. 45. Louvain: Bureaux du Recueil, Bibliothèque de l'Université, 1952.

"The Bill of Rights after 163 Years." *Journal of American Association of University Women* 47, no. 4 (1954): 203–6.

Preface to *Medieval Representation in Theory and Practice: Essays by American Members of the International Commission for the History of Representative and Parliamentary Institutions*. Studies presented to the International Commission for the History of Representative and Parliamentary Institutions, 17. Cambridge: Medieval Academy of America, 1954. Preface reprinted in *Speculum* 29, no. 2, pt. 2 (1954): 347–55.

Law as It Looks to an Historian. Cambridge: Cambridge University Press, 1956.

Editor. *Selected Historical Essays,* by F. W. Maitland. Cambridge: Cambridge University Press, 1957.

City of Cambridge (Victoria County History). London: VCH, 1959.

Album Helen Maud Cam. 2 vols. Louvain: UNESCO, 1960 and 1961.

"What of the Middle Ages Is Alive in England Today?" John Coffin Memorial Lecture (1960).

Historical Novels. London: Historical Association, 1961.

Law-Finders and Law-Makers in Medieval England. London: Merlin Press, 1962.

"Frederick Maurice Powicke, 1879–1963." In *Liber Memoralis Sir Maurice Powicke, Dubline, 1963.* Études presentées à la Commission internationale pour l'histoire des assemblées d'états, 27. Louvain, Belgium: International Commission for the History of Representative and Parliamentary Institutions, 1965.

Magna Carta: Event or Document? London: Selden Society, 1965.

The Eyre of London, 1321. 2 vols. London: Selden Society, 1968–69.

Works Cited

Aldis, H. G. *The University Library, Cambridge.* London: SPCK, 1922.

Bingham, Caroline. *The History of Royal Holloway College.* London: Constable, 1987.

Cockerill, Janet. *Second Chance: The Story of Hillcroft.* Surbiton, Surrey, Eng.: Emberbrook, 1992.

Dyhouse, Carole. *No Distinction of Sex.* London: UCL Press, 1995.

Elliott, John. *Palaces, Patronage and Pills: Thomas Holloway: His Sanatorium, College and Picture Gallery.* Egham, Surrey, Eng.: Royal Holloway, University of London, 1996.

Faithfull, Lilian M. *In the House of My Pilgrimage.* London: Chatto & Windus, 1924.

Gollancz, Victor. *God of a Hundred Names.* London: Gollancz, 1962.

Holt, J. C. Review of *Law-Finders and Law-Makers in Medieval England,* by Helen Cam. *History* 48 (1963): 360–61.

Johnson, C. Review of *Studies in the Hundred Rolls,* by Helen Cam. *English Historical Review* 46 (April 1931): 289

McWilliams-Tullberg, Rita. *Women at Cambridge: A Men's University though of a Mixed Type.* London: Gollancz, 1975.

Meigs, Cornelia. *What Makes a College? A History of Bryn Mawr.* New York: Macmillan, 1956.

"Miss Cam, Harvard Professor, Taught at Mother's Knee." *Boston Sunday Globe* (10 October 1948).

Salter, H. E. Review of *The Hundred and the Hundred Rolls,* by Helen Cam. *History* 16 (1931): 250.

Spurling, Helen. *Ivy When Young: The Early Life of Ivy Compton-Burnett.* London: Gollancz, 1983.

Stephenson, C. Review of *Studies in the Hundred Rolls,* by Helen Cam. *American Historical Review* 36 (1930/31): 422.

Tait, James. Review of *Studies in the Hundred Rolls,* by Helen Cam. *English Historical Review* 37 (1922): 574.

Vicinus, Martha. *Independent Women.* London: Virago, 1985.

CHAPTER 20

Grace Frank (1886–1978) and Medieval French Drama

DEBORAH NELSON-CAMPBELL

BORN IN NEW HAVEN, Connecticut, on 28 June 1886 to Murray Charles and Frances Ullman Mayer, Grace Edith Mayer was raised in Chicago, where she graduated from the Drexel Institute in 1902. In the fall of the same year she matriculated at the University of Chicago. After her third year at the university she was elected to Phi Beta Kappa. On 18 December 1906 she graduated with the degree of bachelor of philosophy, conferred with "Honorable Mention for Excellence in Senior College Work." In the summer of 1908 she registered for graduate work as Mrs. Grace Edith Mayer Frank. Grace probably met Tenney Frank, a noted scholar of classical studies who was ten years her senior, at the University of Chicago, where he was an instructor in Latin from 1901 to 1904. Her transcript indicates that she took advanced courses in Latin literature during that time.[1]

In 1908 Grace and Tenney took up residence at Bryn Mawr, where he was professor of Latin from 1904 to 1919. Grace immediately entered the graduate program and took courses from 1908 to 1910. When Grace Frank arrived at Bryn Mawr College, the awesome Miss Carey Thomas was president. Frank wrote her memories of Thomas with candor and humor in an undated document preserved in the Bryn Mawr archives. A forceful proponent of women's rights, Thomas directed her charges on the "duty of the college woman to devote herself to intellectual, rather than domestic pursuits, to hire servants for menial tasks and to earn their salaries by taking jobs and demanding proper pay for services rendered." In addition she thought that college women should bear children only during vacations. Grace Frank claims to have been terrified of Thomas while being deeply impressed and full of admiration at the same time. Every year Thomas summarized the accomplishments of the women who had graduated from Bryn Mawr; she concluded with those she considered failures, the group who were "married with no paid occupation." Frank states that the first time she heard that assessment, she vowed to escape "the despised category" as soon as she could.[2]

When Tenney spent his sabbatical leave in 1910–11 doing research at the Universities of Göttingen and Berlin, Grace took advantage of the opportunity to continue her studies at these institutions. During this time she also did research in England, France, and Italy. Upon their return to Pennsylvania, Grace continued her graduate studies at Bryn Mawr from 1913 to 1916. The Franks went abroad for another year in 1916, when Tenney was appointed annual professor at the American School of Classical Studies in Rome. After the United States entered World War I, Grace served as a Red Cross nurse in an Italian army hospital. On the brief and incomplete vita in her file at Bryn Mawr College, she also lists under "Education" that she was at the University of Pennsylvania in 1918–19, with no further details.

In 1919 Tenney Frank accepted an offer as professor of Latin at Johns Hopkins University, where he taught until his death in 1939. The Franks moved to Baltimore, and for twenty-five years (except for 1934–36) Grace commuted weekly from Baltimore to Bryn Mawr so that she could continue her career as a professor there while sharing her husband's life. Tenney served as professor in charge of the American Academy in Rome in 1922–23 and again in 1924–25. He was a very productive scholar of philology and the history of ancient Rome, author of twelve books, 150 articles, and numerous reviews during his lifetime.[3]

In 1926 Grace Frank was appointed lecturer in Romance philology at Bryn Mawr College. The following year her title changed to associate professor in Old French philology, and in 1933 she became a nonresident professor of French, since she resided in Baltimore. From 1934 to 1936 she served as a visiting professor of Romance philology at Johns Hopkins University, perhaps seeking an appointment there in an attempt to avoid commuting. However, the fall of 1936 found her back at Bryn Mawr.

During her career Frank was very active in professional organizations. A founding member of the Mediaeval Academy, she served as vice president from 1948 to 1951 and was elected a fellow in 1950. She also served as vice president of the Modern Language Association in 1957. In her curriculum vitae, Frank lists under "Organizations and Professional Positions" "Reviewer, The Saturday Review of Literature, Civilian Defense and Office of Strategic Services, Phi Beta Kappa, Modern Language Association of America, Johns Hopkins Philological Society, Johns Hopkins History of Ideas Club, Johns Hopkins Faculty Club, Hamilton Street Club." In 1936 she was named advisory editor of *Modern Language Notes,* published by the Johns Hopkins Press. In addition to her scholarly works she published numerous reviews of modern fiction for the *Saturday Review of Literature.*

Grace Frank was appreciated both in Baltimore and in Rome as a charming, witty, and gracious hostess and a delightful conversationalist, portrayed by Louise B. Burroughs as "vivacious, witty, wise, and gay."[4] She was an accomplished pianist and encouraged her students to explore the importance of music in medieval culture.

She was also an avid mountain climber until late in life and greatly enjoyed birds and flowers.

In 1952 she retired from Bryn Mawr and was given the title of professor emerita. In the summer of 1952 a former student, Edith Armstrong Wright, wrote in the *Bryn Mawr Alumnae Bulletin* of Grace Frank's influence on her intellectual development. She admired Professor Frank both as a person and as a scholar, finding her rigorous in her expectations while encouraging her students and sharing with them her enthusiasm for her subject. Her students "appreciated Mrs. Frank's mastery of the whole field of Old French, its bibliography and its problems."[5] She was generous with her time as a thesis director, and she maintained a genuine interest in each of her students. Frank's interest in Bryn Mawr College as well as her devotion to her husband are demonstrated by her donation of the Tenney Frank Room to the Canady Library at Bryn Mawr after her retirement.

Grace Frank died on 22 March 1978, at the age of ninety-one, survived by no close relatives, but she continues to live through the legacy of her research and warm enthusiasm for her subject that she left to all medieval scholars. According to articles published about her after her death, she was very involved with her students at Bryn Mawr even though she resided in Baltimore. She directed numerous dissertations, particularly in the area of French medieval drama and at the same time participated in the intellectual community at Johns Hopkins.[6]

To all appearances Grace Frank was the dutiful faculty wife who followed her eminent, scholarly husband and entertained his colleagues as he changed jobs, spent leaves abroad, and took temporary positions. However, far from a passive observer of her husband's career and simply a gracious hostess, Grace seized each change of location as an opportunity to benefit intellectually and professionally from wherever they might be living and from interaction with Tenney and his colleagues. Despite her personal accomplishments, she reflects her era when she consistently signs her name as "Grace Frank (Mrs. Tenney Frank)." She was certainly as distinguished in her own right as was her husband but felt no need to defy social conventions by expressing her independence from her husband in her signature. She followed President Carey Thomas's advice through her personal and intellectual pursuits while conforming publicly to cultural norms.

Grace Frank published five books and at least forty-one articles. Her main focus is medieval theater, and it is in this area that she made an indelible mark on the study of medieval French literature. However, she also demonstrates an encyclopedic knowledge of all the genres of French medieval literature and culture as well as of critical works written on those subjects. Her writing style is smooth, accessible, informed, and informative.

About half of Grace Frank's publications are concerned with medieval French theater. During the Franks' first stay in Rome (1916–17) the recently discovered manuscript of a fourteenth-century French passion play, *La Passion du Palatinus,* was brought to her attention by the prefect of the Vatican Library, Achille Ratti, who later became

Pope Pius XI. This play was the subject of Grace Frank's first article, which appeared in *Modern Language Notes* (*MLN*) in May 1920 and in which she demonstrated convincingly that extensive passages in this play came from a narrative called *La Passion des jongleurs*, written at the end of the twelfth or at the beginning of the thirteenth century.[7] When Dr. Karl Christ published an edition of the play in 1920, Grace Frank immediately published in *MLN* an article that politely praises his work and then continues on with six pages of detailed notes that clarify or correct his text.[8] Two years later she published her own edition of the play in the series Classiques françaises du Moyen Âge. From the very beginning of her publishing career, her work displays the thorough learning, the precision, the complete grasp of bibliography, and the editorial competence that characterize all her publications.

In addition to the passion play Grace Frank also discovered other previously unknown manuscripts in the Vatican Library: the works of Mellin de Saint-Gelais; seventy-five poems that provide insight into the life and times of Charles Fontaine, a poet from the early years of the sixteenth century; and an unpublished letter from Voltaire to Mazzuchelli.[9]

Her second critical edition, Rutebeuf's *Miracle de Théophile* (1925), became the standard text of this popular and important medieval play. When this edition was revised and reissued in 1949, Grace Frank published an article, "Rutebeuf and Théophile," in *Romanic Review,* in which she points out similarities in the trials and tribulations of Théophile and the personal problems that Rutebeuf expresses in his poetry. Presenting parallel passages from the play and the poetry to prove her thesis, she demonstrates, as always, the total grasp of her texts and subject that makes a watertight argument.

Grace Frank published three additional critical editions. The year after the appearance of *Le Livre de la Passion,* a narrative poem of the fourteenth century (1930), she published descriptions of the illuminations that accompany this work in the manuscript in the Vatican Library.[10] These illuminations reflect theatrical staging and costuming at the end of the fourteenth or the beginning of the fifteenth century.

In 1934 she published two poems, "La Passion de Biard" and "La Passion de Roman," known collectively as *La Passion d'Autun* (1934). In 1937, in collaboration with her friend Dorothy Miner, she published *Proverbes en rimes* (1937), which gives the text of a collection of proverbs in rhyming form along with 182 illustrations preserved in a manuscript at the Walters Gallery plus four additional comparative illustrations. Miner was responsible for the illustrations, while Frank was responsible for literary, linguistic, and textual matters. In 1940 Grace Frank published an article that includes text from a longer manuscript of proverbs located in the British Museum, text that is not in the manuscript in the Walters Art Gallery, the source of the edition of proverbs.[11] In the introduction she presents a thorough description of the manuscript and an analysis of the contents with references to pertinent scholarship. In a more general article, "Proverbs in Medieval Literature," she demonstrates a broad knowledge of English literature, showing that the love of tradition exemplified by the use of proverbs is very important in medieval literature but that by the sixteenth and seventeenth centuries proverbs were no longer greatly appreciated.

Grace Frank's interest in proverbs was not limited to medieval French literature. In a letter that appeared in *MLN* in 1940, she refutes the assertion of two Chaucer scholars that the expression "As by the whelp chastised is the leon" referred to current practice and not to a common proverb. She cites the first instance of this proverb in the fourth century along with subsequent uses in Latin, French, and Old English. Succinctly and firmly, she demolishes the statements of C. S. Brown and R. H. West.[12]

The approach in her many articles on medieval theater is divided between identification of characters and clarification of text. In two English plays and one French play she identifies the young child placed before the disciples at the Last Supper as Saint Martial of Limoges, an example of humility and the future leader of the apostles.[13]

Elsewhere she proposes that the words *Or se cante* and *Or dient et content et fabloient* in *Aucassin et Nicolette* are cues addressed to each other by the singer and reciter who are performing the *chantefable*.[14] In *La Farce de Maître Pathelin* it is the word *pathelin* that interests her. Before the farce was written, the word meant simply "language." Afterward it acquired the additional connotation of "crafty language" or "gibberish."[15] In *Jeu de la Feuillée* Grace Frank focuses on the expression *biaus niés,* explaining that Charles-Victor Langlois's interpretation of the word *niés* as "nephew" is incorrect and that it means "fool."[16] In the *Jeu de Saint Nicolas* she explains the terms used for quantities of wine served in the tavern and also the amounts charged for the wine. The humor of the scene rests on the understanding that cheaters are being cheated in the transactions and is lost if these terms are misunderstood.[17]

Another article explores the authorship of *Le Mystère de Griseldis*. Grace Frank presents convincing historical evidence that this play was written by Philippe de Mézières in 1395, during the marriage negotiations of Richard II and Isabelle de France.[18]

In addition to her great love of words and cultural history, Grace Frank was extremely interested in the broad picture of medieval French theater. Her orientation toward details contributes to the accuracy and credibility of her presentations on more general subjects and serves to render her opinions convincing. For example, in a 1936 *Modern Language Review* article she explores the origin of comedy in France and proposes that medieval comedy emerged naturally from the desire to tell a humorous story *par personnages*.[19] Occasionally, her intellectual exchanges with her husband surface, as when she discusses the relationship of the medieval French theater to the classical theater.[20] She concludes that the classical theater had disappeared completely before the French theater emerged from the liturgy.[21]

In her one article on the important *Jeu d'Adam* Grace Frank praises the great skill and creative imagination of the anonymous author and asserts that he follows no apparent predecessors in composition or in staging.[22]

After her retirement in 1952 Grace Frank published the most important work of her career, presenting to the scholarly world the culmination of her research and reflections on the medieval French theater. *The Medieval French Drama* appeared in 1954, published by the Clarendon Press, with two additional printings. This book of 296 pages contains a comprehensive historical survey of the development of the French theater, both religious and secular, from the earliest liturgical plays to the elaborate Passion plays and *mystères* of the fifteenth century. She also discusses the staging, the performers, the directors, and the manuscripts and devotes special chapters to the development of comedy and the works of Rutebeuf and Adam de la Halle. She includes *Aucassin and Nicolette,* which stands alone on the edge of the theater genre. *The Medieval French Drama* remains today an authoritative reference work, admired and appreciated by all who use it. Grace Frank dedicated this book to "T.F.," her husband Tenney Frank, fifteen years after his death, testimony to her continuing devotion to him.

After medieval French theater Grace Frank's favorite subject was the poetry of François Villon. In at least seven articles she explores the relationship between his life and his work and often attempts to date his poems. In "Villon's *Lais* and His Journey to Angers" she presents reasons for the dating of the *Lais* after the robbery of the Collège de Navarre some time before Easter in April 1457 and suggests that Villon left for Angers with the plan of committing another robbery there. Frank dates Villon's ballades written at the court of Blois at the end of 1457 or at the beginning of the following year. The first ballade was written soon after the birth of Charles d'Orléans's daughter on 19 December 1457.[23] Frank's love for close readings of texts comes into play in her discussion of the expression *faire ravoir les gages* in Villon's famous ballade "Je meurs de seuf." She refutes the interpretation of Lucien Foulet and Gustave Charlier by finding the same expression in a passage in the *Roman de la Rose,* where the meaning is clear.[24] In another article on Villon, Frank suggests that Villon's animosity toward Perrenet Marchant, Bastard de la Barre, expressed in the *Lais* and *Testament,* resulted from Marchant's having successfully supplanted Villon in his lady's affections, thus wounding both his pride and his heart.[25] She also points out the remarkable skill that Villon displays in his use of proverbs and his ability to take expressions popular in the language and make them personal.[26]

In a ten-page article published in 1967 in *L'Esprit Créateur,* Grace Frank discussed openly the subject of the biographical approach that she had utilized for her entire career and that had then gone out of fashion.[27] She refused to argue in the abstract against the assertion that the life of a poet has no relevance in evaluating his poetry but proceeded to give evidence that an understanding of François Villon as a man is basic to an appreciation of his poetry. She gave a brief history of Villon scholarship, mentioning that early on the biographical approach worked against Villon because he was considered a criminal who composed indecent verses. Frank continued with a detailed biography, concluding with a quotation from Ferdinand Brunetière: "[L]a grande supériorité de son oeuvre tient à ce qu'il a vécu sa poésie." Even the epic does not escape her attention. For example, she asserts that the "AOI" that appears after some verses indicates a break or halt of some sort in the narrative, perhaps but not necessarily a musical notation.[28] Frank's interest in the role of historical events in medieval literature is evident in another article on the chansons de geste. She asserts that the authors of this genre sought to entertain their audiences, not to educate them with historical facts.[29]

In her one article on Marie de France, Grace Frank maintains that in the *lai* "Chievrefueil" Tristan wrote his whole message to Iseut on the stick in runes or in ogham, and she cites other instances of love messages being conveyed in the same fashion. She pointedly disagrees with several contemporary scholars (Léopold Sudre, Lucien Foulet, Leo Spitzer, and Edith Rickert) who have expressed the opinion that such a long message could not be inscribed on a stick as described in the text.[30]

Perhaps Grace Frank's personality shows through her critical work most vividly when she is engaged in polemic with other scholars. In November 1942 in *Modern Language Notes*, she convincingly identifies Jaufré Rudel's *amors de terra lonhdana* as "love for a faraway land," that is, the Holy Land, personified as a mistress.[31] She counters previous attempts to identify this love as a countess of Tripoli, Eleanor of Aquitaine, the Blessed Virgin, or even Helen of Troy. By citing the efforts being made in 1146 by Louis VII and his queen, Eleanor of Aquitaine, to arouse enthusiasm for the Second Crusade, she suggests Rudel could have been inspired to speak metaphorically of the Holy Land as a mistress for whom he longed. Two years later Frank feistily responded to Leo Spitzer's "attempts to refute" her thesis.[32] Her first footnote citing Spitzer's article includes the caustic comment "Misprints in this pamphlet are too numerous to list."[33] The second footnote comments on the scholarship of Mario Casella, frequently cited by Spitzer in his article, mentioning that Casella re-created in his own words "the poems of Guillaume IX and Jaufré Rudel, poems which some of us would prefer to read in the original" (526). It is the tone of this article that strikes the reader as much as her skillful defense of her argument: expressions such as "his rigid conceptions" (527) and statements such as "[s]omewhat naïvely and pedantically S. lectures his readers on universally recognized facts" (528) and "S., who prefers to interpret the poets of the Middle Ages in the light of generalizations derived from St. Augustine rather than from contemporary documents, seems to know little of the spiritual exaltation and mystical devotion of those who preached the crusades and of those who thought to gain everlasting life in Paradise by taking part in them" (529). And again, "What is left of the essence of Jaufré Rudel's gracile verses after they have been filtered through the alien personalities and elaborate learning of S. and Casella?" (529). In the long seventh footnote Frank gives numerous instances in Spitzer's article that indicate he had misread her argument, demonstrating that he did not approach the project with care (531).

Five years later Grace Frank and Leo Spitzer again sparred, this time over the interpretation of line 2 of *Aucassin et Nicolette*. Frank states that Spitzer had arrived at his interpretation published in an article in *Modern Philology* in 1947 "implausibly and prosaically" and continues to propose her own with her usual confidence and thorough documentation.[34] Spitzer's response to Frank borders on patronizing as he disagrees strongly with her position. Mentioning her name numerous times throughout his article, he exhibits an irritation with her disagreement that obviously goes beyond the intellectual domain into the personal.[35] Since Spitzer was at Johns Hopkins from 1936 to his death in 1960, he and Grace Frank must have encountered each other frequently. One has to wonder if they were indeed enemies on a personal level.

In 1945 Anna G. Hatcher politely disagreed with Grace Frank's interpretation of the word *bise* found in the *Chanson de Roland,* among other texts.[36] Frank had proposed that *bise* meant "hard"—not "gray," "brown," or "dark," as had been previously assumed.[37] In her response to Hatcher, Frank displays once again her tendency to defend her opinions with caustic comments: "Dr. Hatcher unjustly makes me seem to imply"; "When she says that 'we tend to see rocks as of a uniform color,' one can only ask her to speak for herself, not for any true poet or nature-lover."[38] It is evident that Frank arrived at conclusions only after thorough consideration of all the evidence at hand and did not appreciate comments less well considered.

Grace Frank's numerous book reviews illustrate the rigorous standards that she set for other scholars as well as for her students. She does not hesitate to be critical about content, bibliography, or emphasis in a work and speaks with precision and authority. For example, in a review of Emanuel Walberg's *Quelques aspects de la littérature anglo-normande* (Droz, 1936), she begins politely by describing the book as "a useful general summary, for the most part wise and sane," and then she proceeds to point out outdated bibliographical material and historical factual mistakes and calls the work "inadequate," when, in her opinion, Walberg was capable of doing a much better job.[39]

Grace Frank's influence on medieval studies was important in her nurturing of students and budding scholars. It is not unusual to find a footnote similar to the following in an article: "I am grateful to Professor Grace Frank for valuable suggestions in connection with this article." Nan Cooke Carpenter had presented the substance of the paper "Rabelais and the Greek Dances," which includes the footnote, at the Modern Language Association meeting in December 1948.[40] It can be surmised that Grace Frank was a member of the audience and, in her usual helpful way, suggested improvements. She was never the egocentric, ambitious scholar interested only in her own prestige. Her impatience and sarcasm were reserved for those who claimed to know their subject and were careless with details.

From the very beginning of her career Grace Frank's work has been cited more times than can be counted. It seems almost impossible to read an article or a book on the subject of medieval French drama without finding a reference to her scholarship. As recently as 1998 the twenty-two articles on the *mystères* in Graham A. Runnals's edition of *Etudes sur les mystères* (Champion) cite regularly her critical editions and her *Medieval French Drama (La Passion du Palatinus,* 26, 49, 459; *La Passion d'Autun,* 49, 487; *Medieval French Drama,* 213, 246, 309, 459). It is evident that over twenty years after her death, Grace Frank's breadth of knowledge, founded in precise details and expressed with authority and confidence, continues to influence present and future medieval scholars.

As I worked on this article, I realized that many assumptions that I make as a medievalist were first proposed by Grace Frank: for example, the belief that the text of Tristan's message was written on the stick; the conviction that the classical theater had died out long before French drama rose from the church liturgy; and the originality of the *Jeu d'Adam*. Grace Frank virtually created the entire field of medieval French theater. She belonged to the generation of medieval scholars who sought to familiarize their audience with the many medieval texts and to explain the content in terms of a cultural context and the entire corpus. Without this solid foundation it would not be possible to continue the modern studies often considered much more sophisticated. With her warmth, enthusiasm, humor, and encyclopedic knowledge, Grace Frank continues to provide a model for both teachers and students.

Notes

1. My thanks to Andrew Hannah, acting registrar at the University of Chicago, for his help in tracing details of Grace Mayer Frank's studies there.

2. My thanks to Lorette Treese for sending me material on Grace Frank from the archives in the Special Collections Department at the Bryn Mawr College Canaday Library.

3. *American National Biography,* (Oxford University Press, 1999), s.v. "Frank, Tenney."

4. Louise Burroughs, "Vignette XL," *PMLA* 67 (December 1957): ii–iii.

5. Edith Wright, *Bryn Mawr Alumnae Bulletin* (summer 1952): 4–5.

6. The file on Grace Frank in the Special Collections Department at the Bryn Mawr College Canaday Library includes a newspaper obituary and a lengthy obituary written by John W. Baldwin, Ruth J. Dean, Frederic C. Lane, and William Roach, chairman of the French department.

7. Frank, "Vernacular Sources and an Old French Passion Play."

8. Frank, "Critical Notes on the Palatine Passion."

9. Regarding the Mellin de Saint-Gelais manuscript, see Frank, "Manuscript of Mellin de Saint-Gelais' Works." For the seventy-five poems illuminating Fontaine's life, see Frank, "Early Work of Charles Fontaine." Regarding the Voltaire letter, see Frank, "Voltaire to Mazzuchelli."

10. Frank, "Popular Iconography of the Passion."

11. Frank, "Proverbes en rimes (B)."

12. Grace Frank, letter to editor, *MLN* 55 (June 1940): 481.

13. Frank, "Saint Martial of Limoges in the York Plays."

14. Frank, "Cues in *Aucassin et Nicolette*."

15. Frank, "Pathelin."

16. Frank, "Biaus Niés."

17. Frank, "Wine Reckonings in Bodel's 'Jeu de Saint Nicolas.'"

18. Frank, "Authorship of *Le Mystère de Griseldis*."

19. Frank, "Beginnings of Comedy in France."

20. Frank, "Introduction to a Study of the Mediaeval French Drama," 62–78. See 6 n. 30, 65 n. 10, 75 n. 27.

21. Ibid., 78.

22. Frank, "Genesis and Staging of the *Jeu d'Adam*."

23. Frank, "Villon at the Court of Charles d'Orléans."

24. Frank, "Faire ravoir les gages."

25. Frank, "Villon's Adversary."

26. Frank, "Proverbs in Medieval Literature."
27. Frank, "Villon's Poetry and the Biographical Approach."
28. Frank, "AOI in the *Chanson de Roland.*"
29. Frank, "Historical Elements in the Chansons de Geste,"
30. Frank, "Marie de France and the Tristram Legend."
31. Frank, "Distant Love of Jaufré Rudel."
32. Spitzer, "L'Amour lointain de Jaufré Rudel et le sens de la poésie des troubadours."
33. Frank, "Jaufré Rudel, Casella, and Spitzer." Page numbers of citations from this article are given in parentheses in the text.
34. Frank, "*Aucassin et Nicolette,* Line 2."
35. Spitzer, "*Aucassin et Nicolette,* Line 2, Again."
36. Hatcher, "Pierre Bise Again."
37. Frank, "Pierre Bise."
38. Frank, "Pierre Bise; Semantics and Poetics: A Reply," 273.
39. Frank, review of *Quelques aspects de la littérature anglo-normande.*
40. Nan Cooke Carpenter, "Rabelais and the Greek Dances," *MLN* 64 (April 1949): 251–55.

Select Bibliography of Works by Grace Frank

"Vernacular Sources and an Old French Passion Play." *MLN* 35 (May 1920): 257–69.
"Critical Notes on the *Palatine Passion.*" *MLN* 36 (April 1921): 193–204.
La Passion du Palatinus, Mystère du XIVe siècle. Paris: Champion, 1922.
Le Miracle de Théophile: Miracle du XIIIe siècle, by Rutebeuf. 1925. Reprint, Paris: Champion, 1949.
"A Manuscript of Mellin de Saint-Gelais' Works." *MLN* 40 (January 1925): 61.
"The Early Work of Charles Fontaine." *Modern Philology* 23 (1926): 47–60.
"Saint Martial of Limoges in the York Plays." *MLN* 44 (April 1929): 233–35.
Le Livre de la Passion: Poème narratif du XIVe siècle. Paris: Champion, 1930.
"Popular Iconography of the Passion." *PMLA* 46 (1931): 333–40.
"The Cues in *Aucassin et Nicolette.*" *MLN* 47 (January 1932): 14–16.
"Villon's *Lais* and His Journey to Angers." *MLN* 47 (March 1932): 154–59.
"Villon at the Court of Charles d'Orléans." *MLN* 47 (December 1932): 498–505.
"AOI in the *Chanson de Roland.*" *PMLA* 48 (1933): 629–35.
La Passion d'Autun. Paris: Société des Textes Français, 1934.
"Wine Reckonings in Bodel's 'Jeu de Saint Nicolas.'" *MLN* 50 (January 1935): 9–13.
"The Authorship of *Le Mystère de Griseldis.*" *MLN* 51 (April 1936): 217–22.
"The Beginnings of Comedy in France." *Modern Language Review* 31 (1936): 376–84.
With Dorothy Miner. *Proverbes en Rimes: Text and Illustrations of the Fifteenth Century from a French Manuscript in the Walters Art Gallery Baltimore.* Baltimore: Johns Hopkins Press, 1937.
Review of *Quelques aspects de la littérature anglo-normande,* by E. Walberg. *Speculum* 12 (January 1937): 137–38.
"Faire ravoir les gages." *MLN* 53 (December 1938): 603–4.
"*Le Roman de la Rose* ou de Guillaume de Dole." *Romanic Review* 29 (1938): 209–11.
"Historical Elements in the Chansons de Geste." *Speculum* 14 (April 1939): 209–14.
"As by the Whelp Chastised Is the Leon." *MLN* 55 (June 1940): 481.

"Introduction to a Study of the Mediaeval French Drama." In *Essays and Studies in Honor of Carleton Brown*. New York: New York University Press, 1940.

"Proverbes en rimes (B)." *Romanic Review* 31 (1940): 209–38.

"Pathelin." *MLN* 56 (January 1941): 42–47.

"Voltaire to Mazzuchelli." *MLN* 57 (May 1942): 355–56.

"The Distant Love of Jaufré Rudel." *MLN* 57 (November 1942): 528–34.

"Pierre bise." *Romanic Review* 34 (1943): 193–95.

"Proverbs in Medieval Literature." *MLN* 58 (November 1943): 508–15.

"Biaus Niés." *MLN* 59 (February 1944): 92–93. "The Genesis and Staging of the *Jeu d'Adam*." *PMLA* 59 (March 1944): 7–17.

"Jaufré Rudel, Casella and Spitzer." *MLN* 59 (December 1944): 526–31.

"Pierre Bise; Semantics and Poetics: A Reply." *Romanic Review* 36 (1945): 272–74.

"The Impenitence of François V." *Romanic Review* 37 (1946): 225–36.

"Villon's Adversary." *MLN* 61 (February 1946): 113–15.

"Marie de France and the Tristram Legend." *PMLA* 63 (June 1948): 405–11.

"*Aucassin et Nicolette*, Line 2." *Romanic Review* 40 (1949): 161–64.

"Rutebeuf and Théophile." *Romanic Review* 43 (1952): 161–65.

Medieval French Drama. Oxford: Clarendon Press, 1954.

"French Literature in the Fourteenth Century." In *The Forward Movement of the Fourteenth Century*, edited by Francis Utley. Columbus: Ohio State University Press, 1961.

"Villon's Poetry and the Biographical Approach." *L'Esprit Créateur* (1967): 159–69.

Works Cited

Hatcher, Anna Granville Hatcher. "Pierre Bise Again." *Romanic Review* 36 (1945): 266–71.

Spitzer, Leo. *L'Amour lointain de Jaufré Rudel et le sens de la poésie des troubadours*. University of North Carolina Studies in the Romance Languages and Literature 5. Chapel Hill: University of North Carolina Department of Romance Languages, 1944.

———. "*Aucassin et Nicolette*, Line 2, Again." *Modern Philology* 48 (1951): 154–56.

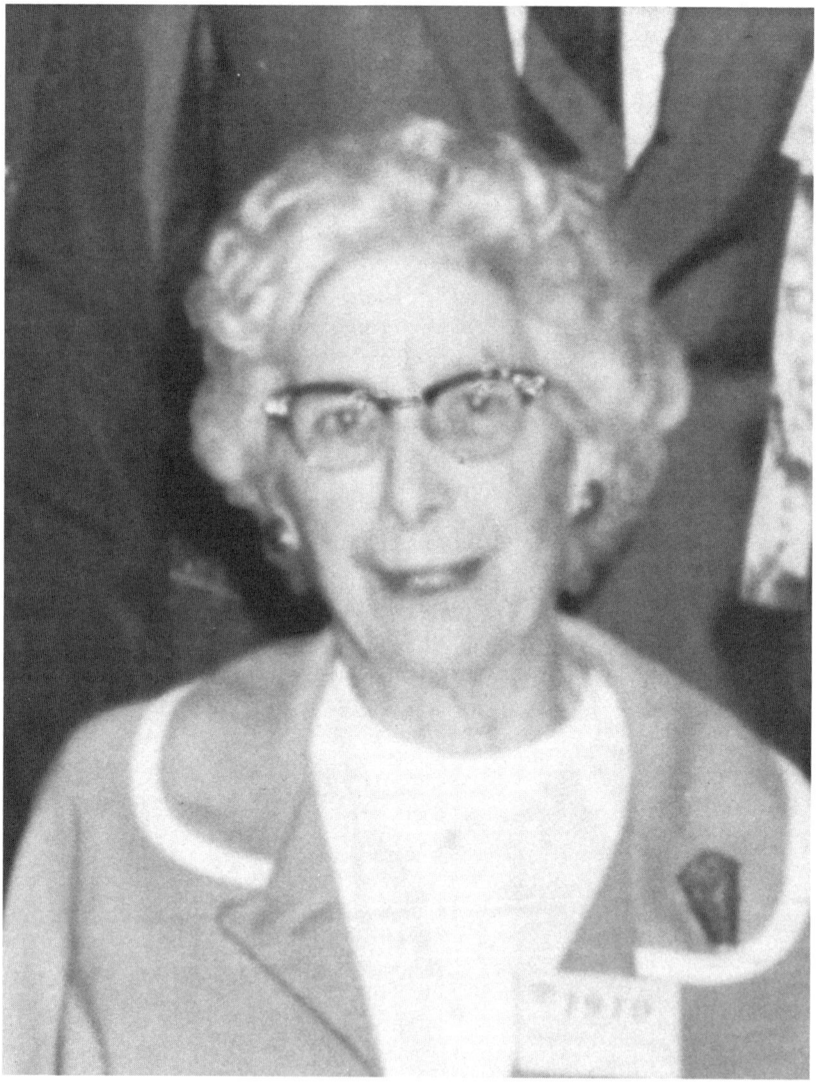

CHAPTER 21

Margaret Rickert (1888–1973)
Art Historian

Anne Rudloff Stanton

The Grinnell College 1910 yearbook memorialized the students of its graduating class with a photograph, a descriptive paragraph, and a suitable quotation. The entry for Margaret Rickert quoted an unidentified work by Shakespeare: "She'd baffle people to decipher her exactly" and described her as follows: "Margaret's jolly, yet serious face, and cordial, yet reserved manner, are a puzzle to many."[1] My search for biographical material to fuel this essay has led me to the same conclusion, although I have examined the papers Rickert archived at the University of Chicago Library and material from her last years in Grinnell, Iowa, as well as the richer resources documenting the life of her sister, Edith Rickert, who is the subject of another essay in this volume.[2] Nevertheless, the impact of Margaret Rickert's work on the study of medieval English art is clear, the more so because it can be seen in student papers as well as in scholarly books.

Margaret Rickert was born on 5 May 1888 to Francis E. Rickert and Josephine Newburgh Rickert, in La Grange, Illinois. After their mother died, the oldest daughter Martha Edith, better known as Edith, having graduated from Vassar in 1891, returned to the Chicago area to care for the three younger sisters, including the three-year-old Margaret.[3] The Rickerts had artistic leanings: their father was an amateur painter, and one of the sisters, Ethel, would become a designer and maker of jewelry.[4] While Margaret was attending elementary school, Edith taught high school and took graduate courses in the Department of English at the University of Chicago. Margaret was seven when Edith spent a year in England researching her dissertation and eleven when her sister completed a dissertation on the medieval romance *Emaré*, in 1899. By this time Margaret's sister Frances may have taken over her care, for two of the sisters were at Vassar: Ethel as a student and Edith as a member of the English department faculty.[5]

After Margaret earned her baccalaureate degree at Grinnell College in 1910, she taught high school as Edith had done. According to a biographical form she completed at the University of Chicago in 1940, she began her career as the principal of the high school in Greene, Iowa. In 1916 she left a high-school teaching position in Hillsboro, Oregon, and by 1922 she had returned to Chicago and was working in the photographic department of the Ryerson Library at the Art Institute. In 1923 she left to visit England with Edith, who was by now teaching at the University of Chicago and working on the Chaucer project that would consume the rest of her life. Margaret was drafted to help select illustrations and eventually wrote a chapter, "The Illuminations of the Chaucer Manuscripts," that was published in volume 1 of *The Text of the Canterbury Tales* after her sister's death in 1940.[6]

Margaret's activities continued to parallel those of her sister. In 1914 she had visited Europe, a trip she would later remember as a crucial event in the development of her interests. In 1923 she returned to Europe with Edith to gather illustrations for the Chaucer project and went on to a stay of four years in Italy, much of it at the I Tatti Institute helping in the revision of art historian Bernard Berenson's lists of Italian painters and their works. In a 1965 letter accepting an alumni award from Grinnell College, Rickert writes of those years: "I spent my whole time collaborating with Bernard Berenson in his first revision of his *Italian Painters*."[7]

Published biographies of Berenson, however, do not mention her as a collaborator on this project; instead she is only mentioned parenthetically, and incorrectly, in one source. Ernest Samuels's 1987 biography of Berenson notes only that in 1924 "a young lady from Chicago, Miss Richert [*sic*] was engaged to work on the Lists" as an assistant to Bernard's wife, Mary Berenson; furthermore, contemporary letters made it clear that Berenson did not look at the revised lists until he had completed other work.[8] Nevertheless, Rickert was in Berenson's orbit, if not in his constant presence, at the very time when he was becoming fascinated with medieval art. Just at the time she was engaged as an assistant, M. R. James had asked Berenson to write an essay for a facsimile edition of a luxurious Gothic manuscript of the *Speculum humanae salvationes*.[9] Certainly Rickert remembered that period of her life fondly, for she later wrote, "The years in Italy, I realize now, were the kind of training which any alert scholar would have given his eye teeth for."[10] Her own art-historical writing manifests a strong Berensonian influence in its commitment to formal analyses of styles and to the discernment of artistic personalities.

Rickert finished her time abroad by visiting her sister Frances Gazzard on her farm in Victoria, Australia, where she learned how to milk cows, an experience later recalled as "most interesting and unusual."[11] On returning to the Chicago area in 1928, Rickert continued to assist with the Chaucer project while earning a master's degree in art history, which she completed at the University of Chicago in 1933 with a thesis titled "A New Method of Analysis Applied to the Study of Manuscript Illumination." In this thesis she developed a quantitative method of analyzing the component parts of decorative motifs in a small group of five manuscripts of Chaucer's *Canterbury Tales,* supported by charts detailing numerical and statistical information about the appearance and frequence of motifs in these manuscripts. This methodology developed from the two large projects in which she had already been involved: the Chaucer project provided the five manuscripts, and Berensonian connoisseurship trained her to recognize the minute differences in motifs that supplied the data she quantified.

That same year a Margaret Rickert of the University of Chicago published an article on a Greek stele in the *American Journal of Archaeology.*[12] Our Margaret Rickert mentioned the article nowhere in her papers, and it is certainly out of her field, yet the coincidence of name and location makes a strong case that this was her work. The case is strengthened by the approach of the article, which is based on the observations of a well-cultivated eye. The author described the style of the piece in graceful language, discussing, for instance, "the curious flat, crescent-shaped ridges, curving and branching in opposite directions on the thigh of Krito," and she ended the article with a series of questions to be answered for further research.[13] This would be a frequent approach in Rickert's later work.

Rickert's experiences in working on two daunting projects, her sister's Chaucer study and the revision of Berenson's lists of painters, may have schooled her mind toward an exemplary retention of details and introduced her to important English medievalists such as Sydney Cockerell, M. R. James, and Francis Wormald. This mindset and these connections were invaluable in the study that earned Rickert her doctoral degree in 1938, the reconstruction of a late-fourteenth-century Carmelite missal. This remarkable project broke new ground in several areas of manuscript studies, from the careful consideration of textual models and iconographic guesswork to the analysis of styles and influences current in late-fourteenth- and early-fifteenth-century English manuscripts. Rickert's search for artistic connections and developments relating to her manuscript brought together material only recently published by M. R. James, Eric Millar, and others during her years in graduate school.[14] Furthermore, the manuscript represented a book type for which no extant comparison had been found, a missal for the Carmelite order that had been a relatively recent arrival in England. Thus, her work would be important in illuminating two understudied areas of English medieval manuscripts.

At the start of Rickert's project the "manuscript" in question consisted of over two thousand fragments pasted onto pink paper in a group of children's scrapbooks held in the British Museum. Between 1826 and 1833 its owner, collector Philip Hanrott, seems to have allowed his three children to cut out the decorative elements—historiated initials, decorated initials, some borders and line fillers, and a few bits of text—and paste them into scrapbooks.[15] In an article published in 1935, Rickert discussed the scope of her project: "From the meaningless confusion of a collection of cuttings arranged only according to their size and shape and firmly pasted down on delicately tinted pink, gilt-edged pages to a correctly ordered manuscript missal whose initials are beautifully inlaid on parchment-like paper in such a way as to expose the text on the backs, is a long step, involving a number of varied and difficult problems of the solution of which all sorts of evidence had to be used."[16]

Adding to the difficulty of the project, the British Museum originally refused to remove the fragments from the scrapbooks, so Rickert could not physically move the bits of parchment around; she could only imagine whether this initial and that border fragment were originally contiguous. Furthermore, she was working with only a portion of the available evidence since she could not see the fragments of text on the backs of the initials. Rickert later wrote, "Reconstructing the manuscript in imagination . . . was like trying to solve a jigsaw puzzle with the pieces scattered about in different places, and immovable."[17] After creating a partial reconstruction with photographs of the visible fragments, Rickert was able to convince the museum officials of the need to remove the fragments from their pink supports, and from 1936 to 1938 she effected a new presentation of the manuscript. With the additional data from the text on the backs of the decorative elements, Rickert was able to discern the overall dimensions of the pages, the approximate length of the original manuscript, and the distribution of the different "hands" of painters. The end product, as she wrote, was "a fragmentary copy of a unique Missal text, closely dated and localized, and illuminated in a manner which has not been surpassed in any other manuscript of the period, English or Continental."[18] Rickert's study received full publication only in 1952, when it was reviewed favorably by such luminaries as T. R. Boase and C. R. Dodwell. The book was also a strong entry in the relatively new field of codicological studies, in which the physical structure of manuscripts provided evidence that was as important as their texts, artistic style, iconography, or paleography.[19] *The Reconstructed Carmelite Missal* has held its place in subsequent decades, for even in the recent entry on the Carmelite missal in Kathleen Scott's *Later Gothic Manuscripts,* Rickert's analyses of the painting styles in the manuscript are only infrequently modified by later studies.[20]

By 1938, the year Rickert completed her dissertation, she had published a preliminary article on the reconstruction for the *Burlington Magazine* and another article on the identity of the illuminator Herman Scheerre, in whom she would remain interested for the rest of her working life.[21] Two other signal events occurred in that year: she joined the faculty of the art history department at the University of Chicago, and Edith Rickert died after a long illness. The surviving Rickert began to collaborate on a memorial volume for her sister, which because of the war and other events was published in a different form as *Chaucer's World* in 1948.[22] Rickert taught at the university, with few interludes, full-time until 1953 and was invited to teach again from 1958 to 1960.

One major interlude occurred from 1942 to 1944, when she moved to Washington, D.C., to work in the U.S. Signal Corps as a codebreaker.[23] Edith Rickert, along with other University of Chicago faculty, had worked with John Manly as a code breaker in the First World War; through them Margaret may have met William F. Friedman, with whom she worked in the 1940s.[24] I was able to discover little about Rickert's war work except that Friedman brought her and other scholars together in late 1944 to work on what he called an "'extra-curricular' piece of research" on a sixteenth-century cryptographic manuscript.[25] As Kahn noted with reference to the work of Edith Rickert, "The cast of mind that can thus sort out, retain, and then organize innumerable details into a cohesive whole was just what was needed for the Gothic complexity of the 424–letter Witzke cryptogram."[26]

When Rickert returned to Chicago after the war, she was asked to contribute a volume to the Pelican History of Art, edited by Nikolaus Pevsner. Rickert's connections with British medievalists like Cockerell and Wormald and her long years of toiling over the fragments of the missal in the British Library must have been influential in her selection, for her vita was not particularly distinguished at that time. Furthermore, she was the only American to contribute to the original series and the only woman author until a decade later. In the foreword to *Painting in Britain: The Middle Ages* (1954), Rickert thanks several British medievalists, particularly Francis Wormald, "to whom by his permission [she had] dedicated this book": "His initial encouragement to me to undertake a task for which he himself was eminently qualified and subsequently his unfailing generosity with information, suggestions, and criticism have contributed no small measure of whatever merit the book may possess."[27]

The book, in fact, possessed a great deal of merit and continues to be useful. Rickert adopted a much more comprehensive approach than had previously been attempted and dealt not only with manuscript painting but also with stained glass, mural painting, and textiles, particularly *opus anglicanum* embroideries. Reviewers noted the breadth of the book's coverage and illustration and the depth of detail Rickert provided about many objects, and they generally praised it as good value for the money.[20] Letters and notes archived at the University of Chicago Library suggest that this project consumed most of Rickert's research time until her retirement from the University of Chicago in 1953 and beyond, since work on a second edition seems to have begun soon after the first edition was published. The second edition appeared in 1965 with significant changes to the chapters that dealt with later fourteenth- and fifteenth-century artistic styles and with foreign artists working in England.

Rickert had long been interested in this aspect of artistic exchange, and her work on the Carmelite missal spurred research on Herman Scheerre and other artists that bore fruit in several publications.[29] Nevertheless, her focus on foreign-influenced styles, and indeed her focus on style in general, provided grist for one of the most consistent complaints about her book. C. R. Dodwell wrote in his *Burlington Magazine* review that "[t]here are times when the careful analysis of the styles of a sequence of paintings makes difficult reading.... To show little or no interest in iconography means also a lack of perspective."[30] Kathleen Scott, whose use of *The Reconstructed Carmelite Missal* was noted earlier, found Rickert's discussion of later Gothic painting styles "admirable" except for her "nearly exclusive interest in foreign painterly styles."[31]

While *Painting in Britain* has been largely superseded by later books on English manuscript illumination and other nonsculptural media, it is frequently referenced in those volumes. For instance, it is more frequently cited in Lucy Freeman Sandler's volume *Gothic Manuscripts, 1285–1385* than any other work.[32] For many reasons references remain common in student papers or in the works of scholars who are not art historians.[33] Rickert's one volume provides a broad sweep across many centuries and media, and because of its initial low price and its place in a well-known series it was obtained by nearly five hundred libraries as well as by countless private purchasers, making it more accessible for loan and also for purchase secondhand.[34] Each chapter begins with a brief historical summary that, although decried as "dry as mutton" by one contemporary reviewer, would serve as a particularly useful reminder for a student whose grasp of history is shaky.[35] Its focus on style does in fact make for difficult reading in some areas, but in others it allows Rickert's trained eye and sometimes lyrical writing to instruct her readers in seeing the works, rather than merely looking at them—an important aspect of the book for non-art historians as well as for undergraduate students. Quoting one of these descriptions in this essay without the accompanying illustration would not make the point, but the reader is invited to look, for example, at Rickert's chapter on what she called the East Anglian Period. While her terminology employs a misnomer that has now been supplanted in scholarly work, her descriptions of individual images can be poetic.[36] Because of these qualities, *Painting in Britain* may remain important in the early development of medieval art historians for years to come.

It is ironic that the bibliography appended to this chapter contains a relatively small yield for a scholarly career of some forty years: only seven journal articles, three book chapters, and four books, including the second edition of *Painting in Britain* and an Italian book on English manuscripts that was published while she was revising her first edition. Yet the books were big projects. The papers archived at the University of Chicago largely consist of notes for these books, often in visual form: photographs with comments on the back or meticulous drawings of line endings or corner bosses. Like many manuscript scholars Rickert used a specific format to standardize the basic information on each manuscript, which allowed her to ensure that when possible she always made note of things such as provenance and basic dimensions, although she did not include other kinds of codicological information.

Rickert's papers also provide traces of her life after her retirement from teaching in 1960. The archived correspondence includes several letters dealing with the Chaucer project and others revolving around the business of book publishing. She corresponded with doctoral students who had questions about her datings or attributions in *Painting in Britain* and with established scholars. She seemed to have a warm relationship with the manuscript scholar and codicologist L. M. J. Delaissé, who sent her an offprint of one of his articles inscribed "These very nice pictures might make you come to Belgium."[37] There are typescripts of articles that were never published and a very interesting proposal for a book on the art of illumination, conceived as a "suitable offering for the Christmas season."[38]

In September 1963 Rickert returned to Grinnell, Iowa, and moved into a retirement home to complete the revision of *Painting in Britain*. Like many scholars she remained active following her retirement; a few of the letters archived in Chicago date from after the move, as does an essay on manuscripts attributed to Herman Scheerre that was published in 1968.[39] She was also active in writing for the *Mayflower Log*, published by the residents of Mayflower Home, contributing, for instance, a thoughtful essay on retirement written just a few months after she moved in. This essay ends thus: "And what of the things one stored up to do in retirement? Unread library books pile up and become overdue; unfinished handwork projects multiply; unanswered letters accumulate; and nagging household tasks wait. Later on, perhaps, there will be an urge for these and other more active occupations. Just now it is good to sit quietly and watch the many little things all about that make up the pattern of life."[40]

In April 1967, three years after writing that essay, Rickert was on her way to Florence. At the time the *Mayflower Log* reported that she was going to Florence "because she wanted to go."[41] The *Log* obituary notice, however, stated that she had hoped to be of some help in restoring works of art damaged in the summer flooding. Certainly she had placed notices in the *Log* requesting donations for Italian flood victims and then thanking residents for their donations. According to her *Mayflower Log* obituary, however, she suffered a stroke and in June 1967 returned to Chicago and then to Grinnell.[42] In her last years she remained active, reading histories and mystery novels, corresponding with friends and scholars, and making fabric wall hangings. She died in October 1973 at the age of eighty-four, after having willed her body to the anatomy department of the University of Iowa's medical school.

Margaret Rickert's life paralleled that of her sister Edith in many ways. Neither sister married—both were most often referred to as "Miss" rather than as "Doctor" or "Professor"—and work seems to have been the driving force in each of their lives. Both began their teaching at the high-school level, became medieval scholars and then faculty at the University of Chicago, worked on projects that were either extremely wide-ranging or dauntingly complex, and also contributed their scholarly acuity to the war effort. Yet Edith's work on the Chaucer manuscripts was overshadowed by that of her collaborator John Manly, despite his efforts to highlight her contribution.[43] Margaret's two biggest projects were hers alone and continue to stand in testament to her own abilities. Her oeuvre demonstrates the workings of a scholarly mind of high quality: attentive to the tiniest of details, capable of keeping track of these details under daunting circumstances, and able to present them in a beautifully descriptive and yet orderly fashion. Although Rickert's personal life may, to echo the 1910 Grinnell College annual, remain a puzzle to many, her impact on scholarship in the last half of the twentieth century is clear.

NOTES

I am grateful to Marian Dunham and Elizabeth Ernst (Mayflower Home, Grinnell, Iowa), Karen K. Gould (independent scholar), Sealy Gilles (Long Island University), David Hatch

(Center for Cryptographic History), David Kahn (independent scholar), Daniel Meyer (University Archivist and Associate Director of the Special Research Center at the University of Chicago), Jim Reeds (Cryptography and Research Department, AT&T Labs), Lucy Freeman Sandler (New York University), Elizabeth Scala (University of Texas), and Sylvia Tomasch (Hunter College).

1. Catherine M. Rod, associate librarian and college archivist of Grinnell College, supplied the yearbook material and the photograph of Rickert that accompanies this essay.

2. See chapter 10, "'Miss Rickert of Vassar' and Edith Rickert," Elizabeth Scala's contribution to this volume; and Scala, "Manly and Rickert," 297–312.

3. Scala, "Manly and Rickert," 301.

4. Scala, "Manly and Rickert," 301; Schuyler and James, eds., *Dictionary of American Biography* (1958), vol. 11, s.v. "Rickert, Martha Edith," 22:557–58.

5. See Scala's essay in this volume, chapter 10, note 10.

6. Rickert, "Illuminations of the Chaucer Manuscripts," 561–605.

7. Margaret Rickert to Mrs. Edgar R. Mullins, 16 April 1965, Grinnell College Library.

8. Samuels, *Bernard Berenson*, 329–30. The preface to the posthumous publication of these lists in 1963 mentions the contribution of neither Mary nor her assistant; see Bernard Berenson, *Italian Pictures of the Renaissance: A List of the Principal Artists and Their Works with an Index of Places* (London: Phaidon Press, 1963).

9. Samuels, *Bernard Berenson*, 333.

10. Margaret Rickert to Mrs. Edgar Mullins, 16 April 1965, Grinnell College Library.

11. Margaret Rickert to Mrs. Edgar Mullins, 16 April 1965, Grinnell College Library. The name of Rickert's sister may have been Gozzard according to a biographical form Rickert filled out in 1940, which is now in the University of Chicago Special Collections Research Center.

12. Rickert, "Rhodian Stele."

13. Rickert, "Rhodian Stele," 408 and 411.

14. For example, see Millar's *English Illuminated Manuscripts of the Fourteenth and Fifteenth Centuries;* and James and Millar's *Bohun Manuscripts.*

15. Rickert, *Reconstructed Carmelite Missal,* 18–20.

16. Rickert, "Reconstruction" (1935), 100.

17. Rickert, "Reconstruction" (1941), 99.

18. Rickert, "Reconstruction" (1941), 102.

19. See Delaissé, "Towards a History of the Medieval Book," 75–83. Some of Rickert's warmest correspondences were with Delaissé; see Rickert's papers in the University of Chicago Special Collections Research Center, box 1, folder 1, and box 5, folder 5.

20. T. S. R. Boase, review of *The Reconstructed Carmelite Missal,* by Margaret Rickert, *English Historical Review* 68 (1953): 466–67; C. R. Dodwell, review of *The Reconstructed Carmelite Missal,* by Margaret Rickert, *Burlington Magazine* 95 (1953): 171; and Scott, *Later Gothic Manuscripts,* 2: 26–30.

21. Rickert, "Reconstruction" (1935); and Rickert, "Herman the Illuminator."

22. Rickert wrote the foreword and selected the illustrations for *Chaucer's World.*

23. "Margaret J. Rickert, '10,'" in *The 1965 Alumni and Senior Awards* (Grinnell, Iowa: Grinnell College Press, 1965), 2–3. She worked in the B-III subdivision of the Signal Security Agency.

24. Kahn, *Codebreakers,* 352. I am grateful to David Kahn and to David Hatch (Center for

Cryptographic History) for their advice in pursuing this topic. Further research could be undertaken by consulting the Military Records Branch at the National Archives in College Park, Md.

25. Jim Reeds (Cryptography and Research Department, AT&T Labs) supplied transcripts from some of these meetings and recalls letters between Rickert and Friedman that suggest she was interested in applying cryptographical methods to her manuscript work.

26. Kahn, *Codebreakers,* 352.

27. Rickert, *Painting in Britain,* xxiv.

28. See, for example, reviews of Margaret Rickert's *Painting in Britain* by Oakeshott in *Antiquaries Journal* and by Dodwell in *Burlington Magazine.*

29. Among these were the article on Herman Scheerre cited in note 21; "Illuminated Manuscripts of Meester Dirc van Delf's Tafel van den Kersten Ghelove"; "European Art about 1400"; "So-Called Beaufort Hours and York Psalter"; and "New Herman [*sic*] Attributions," 88–91.

30. Dodwell, review of *Painting in Britain,* 227.

31. Scott, *Later Gothic Manuscripts,* 1: 9.

32. Sandler, *Gothic Manuscripts,* Sandler herself notes the high visibility of Rickert's book in vol. 1, p. 8.

33. In a nonscientific search of the Internet in November 2001, I found twice as many research-paper citations of *Painting in Britain* than I found of Sandler's book; these appeared primarily in student papers and in papers posted by literature specialists.

34. This figure was obtained through the Library of Congress's First Search Web page, (cited 12 December 2001) available from http://firstsearch.oclc.org/.

35. Quotation from Oakeshott, review of *Painting in Britain,* 246.

36. For a useful discussion of "East Anglian" manuscripts, see Sandler, *Gothic Manuscripts,* 1:27. The continued application of the term "East Anglian" to now-dissociated manuscripts in studies such as Peter Brieger's essay "Manuscripts," in *Art and the Courts: England and France from 1259 to 1328,* ed. Philippe Verdier and Peter Brieger (Ottawa: National Gallery of Canada, 1972) shows the downside of Rickert's influence.

37. Rickert Papers, box 5, folder 5, University of Chicago Library.

38. Rickert Papers, box 1, folder 8, University of Chicago Library.

39. Rickert, "New Herman Attributions."

40. Margaret Rickert, "View from Buckley," *Mayflower Log* 6, no. 2 (May 1964) [no page number(s)]. I am grateful to Marian Dunham for sending me many items from the *Log* and for information about Rickert's reading habits and artistic interests.

41. [No author or title] *Mayflower Log* [no vol.] (May 1967) [no page number(s)].

42. For the obituary, see *Mayflower Log* (November 1973).

43. Scala, "Manly and Rickert," 308.

Select Bibliography of Works by Margaret Rickert

Rickert's letters and papers are archived in the University of Chicago Special Collections Research Center; letters and essays relating to her 1965 alumni award are at Grinnell College Library. Essays and notices from the *Mayflower Log* are held at the Mayflower Home in Grinnell, Iowa.

"A Rhodian Stele." *American Journal of Archaeology* 37 (1933): 407–11.

"Herman the Illuminator." *Burlington Magazine* 61 (1935): 39–40.

"The Reconstruction of an English Carmelite Missal." *Burlington Magazine* 67 (1935): 99–113.

"Illuminations of the Chaucer Manuscripts." In vol. 1 of *The Text of the Canterbury Tales, Studied on the Basis of All Known Manuscripts*, edited by John M. Manly and Edith Rickert. Chicago: University of Chicago Press, 1940.

"The Reconstruction of an English Carmelite Missal." *Speculum* 16 (1941): 92–102.

Foreword to *Chaucer's World*. Edited by Clair C. Olson and Martin M. Crow. New York: Columbia University Press, 1948.

"The Illuminated Manuscripts of Meester Dirc van Delf's Tafel van den Kersten Ghelove." *Journal of the Walters Art Gallery* 12 (1949): 78–108.

The Reconstructed Carmelite Missal: An English Manuscript of the Late Fourteenth Century in the British Museum (Additional 29704–5, 44892). Chicago: University of Chicago Press, 1952.

Painting in Britain: The Middle Ages. Pelican History of Art. Harmondsworth, Eng.: Penguin Books, 1954; 2d ed., 1965.

La miniatura inglese. 2 vols. Collana della storia della minatura, nos. 4, 5. Milan: Electa Editrice, 1959–61.

"European Art about 1400." *Burlington Magazine* 104 (1962): 367–72.

"The So-Called Beaufort Hours and York Psalter." *Burlington Magazine* 104 (1962): 238–46.

"New Herman Attributions." In vol. 1 of *Festschrift Ulrich Middeldorf*, edited by A. Kosegarten and P. Tigler. Berlin: De Gruyter, 1968.

Works Cited

Delaissé, L. M. J. "Towards a History of the Medieval Book." In *Codicologica*, edited by J. P. Gumbert, M. J. M. de Haan, and A. Grujis. Leiden: E. J. Brill, 1976.

Dictionary of American Biography. 1st edition. (1964 reprint). Vol. 11. Part 2, Supplement 2.

Dodwell, C. R. Review of *Painting in Britain: The Middle Ages*, by Margaret Rickert. *Burlington Magazine* 97 (1955): 227.

James, M. R., and Eric Millar. *The Bohun Manuscripts*. Oxford: Roxburghe Club, 1936.

Kahn, David. *The Codebreakers*. New York: Macmillan, 1967.

Millar, Eric. *English Illuminated Manuscripts of the Fourteenth and Fifteenth Centuries*. Paris: G. van Oest, 1928.

Oakeshott, Walter. Review of *Painting in Britain: The Middle Ages*, by Margaret Rickert. *Antiquaries Journal* 35 (1955): 245–46.

Samuels, Ernest. *Bernard Berenson: The Making of a Legend*. Cambridge: Belknap Press, 1987.

Sandler, Lucy Freeman. *Gothic Manuscripts, 1285–1385*. 2 vols. Survey of Manuscripts Illuminated in the British Isles, 5. London: Harvey Miller, 1985.

Scala, Elizabeth. "John Matthews Manly (1865–1940) and Edith Rickert (1871–1938)." In vol. 2 of *Medieval Scholarship: Biographical Studies on the Formation of a Discipline*, edited by Helen Damico. New York: Garland Publishing, 1998.

Schuyler, Robert Livingston, and Edward T. James, eds., *Dictionary of American Biography*. Vol. 22. Supplement 2. New York: Charles Scribner's Sons, 1958.

Scott, Kathleen. *Later Gothic Manuscripts, 1390–1490*. 2 vols. Survey of Manuscripts Illuminated in the British Isles, 6. London: Harvey Miller, 1996.

CHAPTER 22

Charlotte D'Evelyn (1889–1977)
An Instinct to Explore

CAROLYN P. COLLETTE

IN A EULOGY for one of her own teachers, Charlotte D'Evelyn touched on an essential difficulty all academic biographers encounter: how to recover and convey the passionate enthusiasm that sustains a life of scholarship. She expressed the problem this way: "The facts of the lives of scholars and teachers crystallize neatly into a familiar pattern:—degrees, academic positions, learned societies, publications.... Yet these are the lives of adventurers who, not content with one man's share of time and space, set out to explore all recorded experience."[1] The facts of Charlotte D'Evelyn's life are clear and available, but the essential spirit that informed her life of scholarship—what she would have regarded as the heart of her biography—is harder to convey. She left few personal letters, and although she was well remembered by her associates at Mount Holyoke, it was her idiosyncrasies that they tended to recall: her passion for striding for miles on the Holyoke range and for frigid classrooms, open to the winter air; her clinging to habit; and her resistance to change.[2] But her lifelong devotion to medieval English literature and culture makes it clear that, in her own quiet, self-disciplined fashion, Charlotte D'Evelyn was both an enthusiastic adventurer and a time-traveler. In an academic life that spanned forty-seven years, she shaped a career devoted to teaching, to contributions to learned journals, and to the meticulous editing of a series of major medieval texts—*Meditations of the Life and Passion of Christ* (1921), *Peter Idley's Instructions to His Son* (1935), the Latin text of the *Ancrene Riwle* (1944), and the *South English Legendary* (1956–59).

In large part her success and the comparatively untroubled course of her career stemmed from a strong and naturally sanguine personality, from early-twentieth-century American pragmatism, and from the support and opportunities she received in a life of scholarship spent entirely at women's colleges. She took her bachelor of

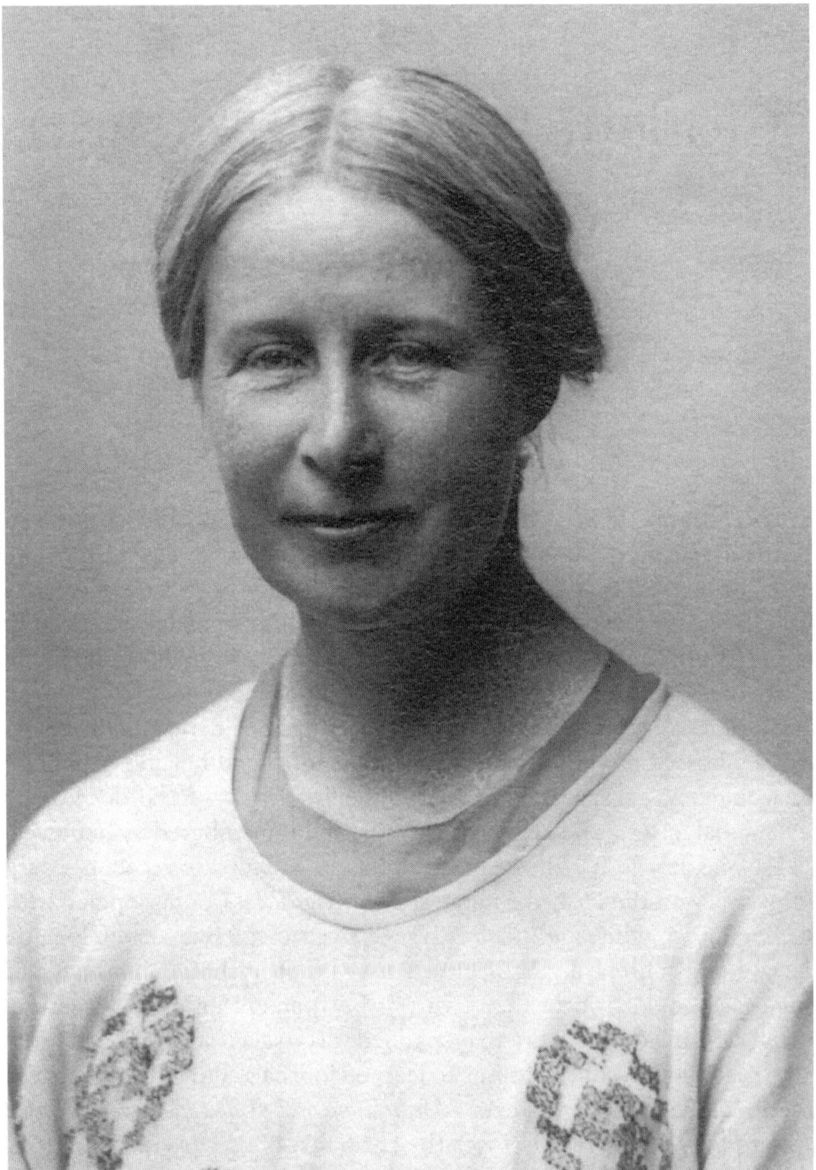

letters degree at Mills College in 1911 and her Ph.D. in English philology—with English literature and Old French as minors—from Bryn Mawr in 1917. That same year she was offered a job at Mount Holyoke College, where she stayed for her entire thirty-seven-year career until she retired in June 1954.

Unfortunately for a biographer, the record of her life—both of what she did and of what she thought—is spotty. Some parts, consisting largely of her career at Mount Holyoke, are only sporadically documented. Her name appears in various reports and records, but little about her thinking appears in such documents. Other parts, like the year she spent abroad researching while studying for her doctorate, are well recorded in a series of letters. Reading the letters she wrote as a young woman living abroad in 1915 offers the best insight into her personality and her relationship to her work. In them one detects an agreeable blend of realism, a lack of sentimentality; a delight in the odd, the humorous, or the ironic; and a sharply observant habit of mind. They also intimate, in their sketchy references to obstacles posed and overcome, that Mina, as she was called, was a force to be reckoned with. Like water on stone she worked carefully and thoroughly, through and by obstacles, moving forward inexorably at what she termed her own slow pace. This exacting, painstaking habit of mind appears in all her publications, particularly in her articles that record the fruit of careful reading, rereading, and researching a wide variety of manuscript material. Her colleague and fellow medievalist Anna Jean Mill, remembering her "absolute meticulousness," recalled that "[s]he was a real medievalist . . . her work was greatly admired by other medievalists. She took infinite pains. There was nothing ever shoddy or slapdash about it."[3]

Born on 23 May 1889 to a San Francisco family of comfortable circumstances, she grew up in a cultured household; her mother, Susan Taylor D'Evelyn, who died in 1892 when Charlotte was barely three, wrote as a correspondent for California and Irish newspapers and contributed regularly to women's journals, particularly those published by the Pacific Coast Woman's Press Association under the pseudonym Kate McBride.[4] Her father, Dr. Frederick D'Evelyn, was a learned and independent thinker, instrumental in establishing the San Francisco Society for Prevention of Cruelty to Animals. His second wife, Charlotte's stepmother, was also apparently a strong woman who helped create a pattern of loving, familial support that was to sustain Charlotte throughout her young adulthood. Correspondence written in affectionate terms to both her stepmother and her father shows an easy, comfortable relationship with them, one that thrived on news, humor, and intelligence. It also reveals her as an essentially private person who rarely shared deep emotion or firmly held opinion in such communications.

D'Evelyn first became seriously interested in medieval studies at Mills College. Working under Hope Traver, a graduate of Vassar and of Bryn Mawr's doctoral program, she explored medieval English and Old French. In 1913 she enrolled in a doctoral program at Bryn Mawr, where she studied French ("My ears ache when the day is over") and English.[5] At Bryn Mawr she met Carleton Brown, who became first her adviser and later a lifelong friend and colleague.[6] After two years of study she was awarded the prestigious Mary E. Garrett European Fellowship for a year's study at a European university. She chose to spend a year in England, researching at the British Museum and studying at Oxford. She arrived in England in June 1915, after an uneventful crossing; she wrote home joking that "[y]esterday we were handed our landing tickets, and I felt almost insulted to be given one marked 'alien'" (letter to her parents, 11 June 1915).

Letters home from this year of study focus on three topics: the war—about which she had much to say, but always in a distanced and unemotional tone—her work, and her social life. Having taken rooms at the Coogee House Residential Hotel on Montague Street in Russell Square, close to the British Museum, she applied to and received a reference from the American consulate to the British Museum. In these London letters she writes very little about her research; once she ventures a generalization that "[t]he British Museum still stands. Manuscripts are slow work especially when one is naturally slow" (letter to her parents, 4 July 1915). But she does take the time to tell the story of meeting an attendant at the British Museum, an "Irish lad" who had recently been paralyzed in the war and subsequently discharged. He shared with her his opinion that it was a "dirty war" in which German secret agents enlisted as British soldiers in order to sabotage British forces. Writing home in the same letter on 4 July 1915, she said, "One is continually struck by the waste of this war." On 11 July she went to the Guildhall to hear Lord Kitchener and the young Winston Churchill speak at a recruiting meeting. Her letter about the event reflects her characteristic ability to see events in present and past time. On the one hand, she writes of the Guildhall, "It is certainly rich and historic. One had patriotic thrills to be there on an historic occasion such as this meeting was"; on the other hand, she objected to the "false polish on every move" that she detected in the London press's war coverage as well as to their propensity to "make out that every defeat is twice as beneficial and strategic as a victory." Her sympathies undoubtedly lay with pacifism, as her opinion that "Bryan is on the right track, when he talks against the war," suggests (letter to her parents, 1 August 1915). Her letters hint at a natural sense of guilt as she describes a gathering of Americans celebrating Thanksgiving in England and eating turkey, "thinking of the less fortunate on their conscience; [they would] eat it with a pricke of conscience" (from an undated letter in a packet dated November–December 1915, Mount Holyoke College Archives).

Understandably, D'Evelyn's letters devoted more attention to her academic work, but even in them she sought to write for her audience, to select and describe what would be amusing to a reader, rather than to share her own private thoughts or specific information about her research. Her story of a trip to Cambridge for research purposes is typical:

> Yesterday I called at Magdalene College by appointment to see some of their mss. The librarian showed me first his Siamese cat and then took me to the library—or one of

them—which he opened with a huge silver (probably nickel) key. He asked me how long I'd be and then he went off and locked me in and came back again at the end of a stated time to let me out. I expected to be mildewed worse than the crops [in a previous letter she had commented on the wet summer and the mildewed crops in English fields]. The room—all richly carved (Grinling Gibbons, probably—all carving seems to have been done by him) and filled up to the ceiling with books, was simply musty and moldy from the old parchments. I wanted to spend my time looking around but I had to get through, so I didn't get a chance to see anything. (letter to her father, 22 August, 1915)

D'Evelyn's living arrangements in Oxford were also a matter of some concern, as she feared having to live "in one of the 'approved' boarding places—awful restriction on one's personal liberty: I think one also takes an oath not to go to dances during term. I suppose one can go to cricket matches" (letter to her sister, 28 September 1915). She did finally obtain lodging at 22 Park Crescent, chafing at "sitting around in the drawing room, having tea & wasting time being polite and social." Later in the same letter she praises this establishment in "the newer residence district which has spread to the north. There's a whole series of 'Parks,'" she writes, describing the section of Oxford off the Banbury Road. The location may have been agreeable, but she regretted the common meals at her residence—"I'd rather eat bread alone than cake in company—which isn't exactly a sociable attitude—but I suppose that would be too much like paradise." In closing she says, "The old Pricke of Conscience mss will seem like old friends when I get back to them, which I'll be glad to do" (letter to her father, 4 October 1915). She strained to get to her work and begrudged the time spent with comparative strangers: "Three afternoons in a row this week I have checked up on my calendar for 'teas.' I have to sandwich a few spare hours in at the Bodley just as best I can and spend the rest of the time drinking tea and washing my white gloves" (letter to her mother and sister, 28 October 1915).

D'Evelyn's letters convey a sense of impatience and skepticism about the world of Oxford. She writes that she is not taking classes "very seriously" (letter to her father, 31 October 1915) and that "some things are too easy and slow at present, so I'll drop them. When you pay according to the number of lectures you take there's no use taking ones that don't tell you anything new" (letter to her father, 21 November 1915). She complained that November meant that the Bodley closed an hour earlier, at three: "No artificial light allowed is the cause. Fortunately they do allow artificial heat, which is quite welcome in these chilly mornings" (letter to her father 31 October 1915). Her description of dinner at Lady Margaret Hall suggests that she fostered few romantic notions of life at Oxford:

It was interesting to see the inside of an Oxford woman's college, and to find that it wasn't very different from our own. I suppose there would be more different [sic] perhaps, inside the girls [sic] heads in the way of associations and general ideas of things and of what can be "done" and what can't. It was quite natural to eat in a room full of girls and noise, though I didn't feel a bit homesick to have all my meals under those conditions. The women's dining room is imitated after the men's with a "high" table—about 3 inches "high," where the dons and chosen victims sit. They have Latin grace also, but it is so short that by the time I was beginning to listen for it, during a bit of quiet, it was all over and every one was sitting down. For dinner we had soup, roast beef (or shepherd's pie) [*sic*] potatoes, cabbage and pudding & bread & butter—not as nice as Bryn Mawr—but I think Bryn Mawr has really an exceptionally good table. (letter to her father, 14 November 1915)

Even Oxford's venerable Saint Frideswide failed to impress: one day D'Evelyn explored the environs of the university, ending up in an "old Saxon church yard, where St. Margaret's Wishing Well stands. It is supposed to have been discovered by St. Frideswide, the patron saint of Oxford, and was a favorite resort of pilgrims probably in the early days,—as in 1915. There are a few little steps with ferns and mosses growing in them that lead down to the dark pool. We spent most of our energy picking out the Latin inscription which is of modern date, and I think we forgot to wish for anything except a little more intelligence in the matter of case endings" (letter to her father, 28 November 1915).

Part of D'Evelyn's impatience undoubtedly stemmed from the pressure of time she felt as she coped with what seemed like frivolous demands. She felt her own work took second place to other, less important, but nevertheless importunate demands. In a letter to her father on 21 November 1915, she expresses a sentiment familiar to all academics—"You'll be wondering where the business part of my time comes in. It certainly isn't getting full share, I'm afraid. I'm getting to depend, like the rest of the Oxfordians on the infinite possibilities for work in the 'vac.'" Nevertheless, she planned that month to send her work to her adviser, Carleton Brown: "It will soon come back with 'kindly rewrite' or 'you had better think about this a little more,' but at least I'll have it off my hands for a couple of weeks."

On her return to Bryn Mawr in 1916, D'Evelyn began her final year of graduate study, during which she completed her dissertation, which would become her first major publication, the edition of *Meditations on the Life and Passion of Christ*. She finished her Ph.D. at Bryn Mawr in 1917 and was offered a job at Mount Holyoke College as an instructor in the English department.[7] The offer of employment, a short note from Mount Holyoke's famous president Mary Woolley, also offered a relatively generous salary of eleven hundred dollars a year. No doubt the fact that Mount Holyoke was the mother college of Mills was a factor, however small, in her decision to accept.[8] A more important factor may have been the presence of the medieval historians Nellie Neilson and Bertha Putnam—both of whom held their doctorates from Bryn Mawr—on the Mount Holyoke faculty.[9] She joined a faculty with a distinguished cohort of medievalists and a college whose library was exceptionally strong in medieval materials.[10] Mount Holyoke recognized her strengths: she was promoted to assistant professor in 1920, associate professor in 1923, and full professor in 1932.

D'Evelyn's memories of these early days at Mount Holyoke formed the core of a talk she presented in honor of Mary Woolley's retirement, on "how it felt to be a newcomer at Mount Holyoke in Miss Woolley's middle years." The anecdotes that constitute this talk tell us about both D'Evelyn's sense of humor and the ethos and atmosphere of Mary Woolley's Mount Holyoke. She tells of the unannounced visit Miss Woolley paid to her Chaucer class:

> I forget the date but not the hour—second period, Tuesday morning, 2nd section of Chaucer in progress—at least in session. I'm not sure about the progress—there came a knock on the door and that was bad enough and when the door was opened there stood Miss W. & that was worse. And Miss W. came in & sat down in the front and stayed the rest of the period—and that was almost fatal. The students of course were no help at all. I had to do all the reciting and I explained all the Chaucer I knew & some that I didn't. Miss W. was most attentive but that only made me the more aware of pedagogical deficiencies & informational lacunae. It was a long long period.[11]

During her years as a professor at Mount Holyoke D'Evelyn became famous for her devotion to walking, striding the Holyoke range on Sunday afternoons. Apparently as she began one of these walks she was befriended by an unfamiliar dog who turned out to be Miss Woolley's collie, Arrow, who followed her for the rest of the day. As she came back into South Hadley, she was accosted by an "authoritative person ([she was] sure it was a detective)," who "stepped right up and said firmly, 'Where did you get that dog and where are you going with him?'" Then she learned that the dog was Miss Woolley's and that "the whole town had been looking for him all day." She concludes, "And off he marched with Arrow on a leash, leaving me to figure out the consequences. After that I was very careful not to associate too freely with dogs above my station."[12]

During Miss Woolley's tenure as president at Mount Holyoke an impressive and formidable array of women scholars joined the faculty. Anna Jean Mill, Charlotte D'Evelyn's colleague and coeditor of the *South English Legendary*, recalled the world she joined as one of passionate commitment and intensity, as an "atmosphere of anti-war, of passionate conviction for women's rights." She recalls, "it seemed I was carrying on in a familiar setting. And also my people were Congregationalists, and I just seemed to be living in the kind of world I knew."[13] Charlotte D'Evelyn's papers make no mention of her reaction to this atmosphere or, indeed, of her relation to Miss Woolley's inner circle of comrades—Miss Newhall and Miss Dietrich—who, along with Jeanette Marks, lived in the president's house with her. Nor does she mention the distress the board of trustees created when, on Mary Woolley's retirement in 1937, they disregarded her suggestion that Mary Ashby Cheek (Mount Holyoke Class of 1913) be named her successor and tapped Roswell Ham, an untenured professor from Yale, to be the next president of Mount Holyoke.[14] One of Ham's objectives was to create a faculty evenly divided between men and women, a goal not all faculty shared.

By the late 1930s Charlotte D'Evelyn had become a highly respected professor within the Mount Holyoke community. Ellen Deborah Ellis, professor emerita of history and politics, recalled that she was one of "those enjoying the highest prestige as scholars in the eyes of fellow scholars."[15] But as a teacher at Mount Holyoke she was unusual in her distance from her students and, perhaps not coincidentally, famous for her frigid classrooms open to the winter air, where students wore coats and gloves to read Chaucer.[16] She was famous, too, for the extensive collection of lantern slides she accumulated. These, the pictorial, visual dimension of Charlotte D'Evelyn's dedication to instruction in primary materials, illustrated both her Chaucer courses and the supplementary lectures that illustrated the survey course.[17] Mill, recalling D'Evelyn's dedicated pursuit of such material in manuscripts and early print sources, said, "I think that gave me my first impression of really some of the intellectual quality that one might expect at Mount Holyoke. You didn't shove post cards into a screen and that sort of thing. You tried to get original material."[18]

Years before it became fashionable, Charlotte D'Evelyn conceived of literature as a cultural study and taught her students that in order to understand a poem one had to understand the culture that created that poem. The series of supplemental lectures for the early British literature survey in 1931–32 included "Feudal England," "Social Background of the Middle English Period," "The Medieval Point of View," and "Literary Background of the Fourteenth Century."[19] In addition to teaching medieval romance and the Romantic tradition in English literature, she taught both an elementary and an advanced Chaucer course from 1930 on. In 1930 she also joined Jeanette Marks and Leslie Burgevin in a seminar called "Influence of Scientific Theory and Method," a year-long jointly taught English literature course.[20] In 1932 she also collaborated on a team-taught course titled "An Historical Outline of English Literature."[21] There were strains, however, among those who taught English, between the literature department, which, if Charlotte D'Evelyn's work is typical, focused on facts and information about literature, and the English division, devoted to expository and creative-writing instruction.[22]

Although highly respected, D'Evelyn was a comparatively quiet member of the Mount Holyoke community, one who "seldom intervened in any discussion" at faculty meetings. "She would always sit in the window seat in the New York Room, where she could better indulge her passion for fresh air . . . and where she could survey the scene; and you felt she was summing up things in her own way—not always favorably, and getting a certain kind of sardonic amusement from some of the contortions that some of us went through," recalled Mill.[23] But while she may have seemed distanced, she was apparently emotionally as well as intellectually involved in the world of the college. In the 1930s she drafted a defense of the liberal arts and of liberal education, arguing that the value of such an education is its "not immediate but ultimate usefulness to the individual and hence to society." She objected to the notion that the college campus was no longer a cloister but a marketplace: "We are in a sense at any given moment useless. I know only too well that if I give a cut to-morrow in Chaucer nobody will starve, nobody will die. On the contrary the immediate joy in living of 46 young ladies will be . . . increased. But I should hate to think that if all classes in Chaucer everywhere were permanently suspended there would be no ultimate loss to anybody."[24]

D'Evelyn became chair of the English department in 1939 and served in that capacity for six years. Her time as chair was marked by strains and challenges whose shadowy records appear in letters detailing her failed attempt to get the college to replace a worn rug and her contretemps with Jeanette Marks, whose speaking engagements would take her out of town for most of a semester when she was supposed to be teaching (D'Evelyn's recommendation that she take a leave of absence did not sit well with Marks). As chair of the department, she became privy to information about faculty salaries in the new world that President Ham had created. Mill remembered a conversation on the subject: "Miss D'Evelyn said to me during the Ham administration that if I could see the salary list for our own department—what the men were getting compared to the women—I would be thoroughly shocked."[25]

In fact the topic of money, particularly money for research, was a sore subject during the 1940s, when so much about the college seemed to be changing. In 1957 Natalie Biller interviewed members of the English department about research problems in English literature.[26] They spoke of a disparity between the amount of money dedicated to the humanities and that dedicated to the sciences to support research. The paper Biller wrote cites college statistics published in 1953 showing that 89.5 percent of grants that came to Mount Holyoke from 1947–53 went to the physical sciences, while only 6.4 percent went to the humanities. Scholars had to finance their own research and often had to defray the expense of publication.

When D'Evelyn and Mill collaborated on the edition of the *South English Legendary,* they encountered a whole other series of obstacles: their research was interrupted by the Second World War; using photostatic copies and microfilms could take them only so far before they had to consult the manuscripts, which, in turn, were often difficult to find. In the interview with Biller, D'Evelyn explained that once one had the appropriate manuscripts in hand, additional problems could still arise, for the scholar had to familiarize herself with scribal idiosyncrasies. These hurdles having been overcome, one then had to obtain permission to publish from owners, both museums and private collectors. Publishers, too, created problems because of the restrictions of length imposed on editors. Through all this the scholar constantly fought lack of time—no doubt a particular exasperation for D'Evelyn, who was both slow and meticulous in her work.

In spite of these obstacles Charlotte D'Evelyn was able to create a substantial body of work, well received as it appeared and well respected today. Her work recovered popular material that spoke to its original audience and to modern audiences as well, about ideal patterns of life and conduct. Even her first major publication, her dissertation, an edition of *The Meditations,* which she describes as "a compendium of the lyric themes of Middle English religions poetry," emerges from her introduction as a window on medieval interiority.[27] Following the philological orientation of medieval literary scholarship of that period, D'Evelyn explores the language, the influences, the borrowings, and the adaptations that appear in the text, in great and thorough detail. In an unusual gesture to the living reality of the past recorded in the text she edits, she concludes her lengthy introduction by envisioning the poet and engaging the reader's imagination in this moment as well: "[T]he poet, often with a curious mingling of artificiality and simplicity in thought and expression, draws from each incident of his narrative, subject matter for devout meditation and occasion for the expression of deep personal joy."[28] Her edition of the Latin text of the *Ancrene Riwle*, dedicated to Hope Emily Allen, appeared as her contribution to a larger scholarly project to publish all surviving manuscripts of the work.[29] A subsequent article in *PMLA*, "Notes on Some Interrelations between the Latin and English Texts of the *Ancrene Riwle*," argued for the English version as the original, in part because the Latin "omits most of the passages of personal reference and adds to the impersonality of its address."[30] She concludes, "Taking this textual evidence as a whole one may conclude with some confidence that Latin was not the original language of the *Ancrene Riwle*. The additions in the Latin text are insignificant; the omissions destroy the personal quality and disguise the primary purpose of the treatise."[31] Here, too, she saw the text both as an artifact and as an expression of personal devotion.

Like her earlier work her edition of *The South English Legendary* stands as a valuable means of understanding the intellectual landscape of later medieval England. Reviewing the edition, Dorothy Bethurum declared that the text "is important for the intellectual history of the thirteenth and fourteenth centuries. . . . Forming . . . the repertory of Franciscan friars . . . they [stories of saints' lives] undoubtedly purveyed to a large audience for several centuries ideals of conduct and models of sanctity that were widely used."[32] Bethurum takes the opportunity of the review to point out the ways in which such scholarship can be impeded by editors and presses; she chides the Early English Text Society for its failures to publish the volume with any critical apparatus: "This will come, we trust, in another volume; but we know how often in the history of the Early English Text Society the volume of notes has failed to follow the publication of the text. We want to know the editors' opinions on many matters connected with the *Legendary*."[33]

Of all her publications the one that seems to have been most widely reviewed, and the one in which the kind of critical apparatus Bethurum seeks appears in greatest detail, is her edition of *Peter Idley's Instructions to His Son*. Both Howard Rollins Patch, who reviewed it for *Speculum,* and Henry L. Savage, who reviewed it for *Modern Language Notes,* praise the scholarship and the fine achievement of the volume. Both, too, note the importance of the edition to modern understanding about the values and culture of what Savage terms "the squirearchy of the 15th century."[34] Patch praises the "masterly introduction" and the editor's erudition, observing that it is "one more study which has derived inspiration from the erudition and scholarship of Carleton Brown." (At the same time he laments that "such industry and skill were not applied to some far more significant document.")[35]

The Idley edition is the text on which D'Evelyn lavished her longest introduction, about which she wrote enthusiastic letters, and which seems to have engaged her imagination to the fullest—if we judge by the existing record. Why this should be so is not hard to guess, for the text is unusual in Middle English literature in having a known author, one whose personality actually appears in the selections and choices of the text. Two of the few letters in the Mount Holyoke archives about her work were written to Jeanette Marks about this text. On 12 January 1930 she wrote about her research for the Peter Idley edition, "[I] am working principally on an edition of *Peter Idle's [sic] Instructions to His Son*, a 15thc [sic] text in Chaucerian stanza. It is fairly interesting in spots & popular enough in its own day to be worth re-reading." In a letter of 5 August 1931 she expresses the highest degree of excitement about her work that is to be found in all her letters, for understandable reasons: "Peter Idle's [sic] outlines are getting clearer and clearer. I've been quite thrilled these last two days tracking down what I think will prove to be his authentic funeral brass in Dorchester Abbey Church, Oxfordshire." In the introduction she notes Idley appears in his work not just in the shadow of his borrowings from Albertanus of Brescia and Robert Mannyng: "He is not lost to sight. The same personality that scattered popular proverbs and pointed remarks throughout the serious subject-matter of Albertanus found in the material of the ten commandments and the seven sins even more outlet and invitation to comment" (52). Unlike the Stonors and Pastons, to whom he is often compared, Idley, says D'Evelyn, is "more ambitious than his contemporary letter-writers, had a glimmering sense of literary art, and for this he sought expression beyond the limitations of business correspondence by composing his metrical *Instructions* to his son" (56).

D'Evelyn's success as a scholar brought her concurrent prominence in a number of professional organizations, and particularly in the Modern Language Association (MLA), which during the 1930s actively supported the publication of medieval texts. She served as the chair of the Medieval English section of the MLA in 1932–33. She was a member of the American Association of University Professors (AAUP), the Medieval Academy of America, the Society for the Study of Medieval Language and Literature at Oxford, and the Modern Humanities Research Association. On her retirement a group of scholars, including Beatrice Brown, widow of Carleton, proposed her to the John Hay Whitney Foundation for the position of visiting professor in 1955. In 1966 Vernon Helming of the University of Massachusetts sponsored her inclusion in the graduate faculty of the University of Massachusetts. In 1961, at her Fiftieth Reunion at Mills College, she was awarded an honorary doctor of letters degree. The college described her as a "child of the West and teacher in the East, daughter of Mills long lent to our mother College, learned in literature and in life."[36]

Long after her retirement she continued to work in the Mount Holyoke library, a small, frail figure who appeared and disappeared in the stacks. Earlier in her career at Mount Holyoke she had been the object of some envy, for she had a private key that allowed her access to the library at all hours when it was closed to everyone else. She kept that key and the privilege it signaled all during her life at the college. Even in retirement it was her custom to work all day in the library, go home for dinner, and return in the evening to read her mail and the papers in her study, 6C, on the level of the stacks where the Medieval English literature books are shelved. In a very real and positive sense the library was her natural home. After she died, on 18 December 1977, a major memorial to her life became the Charlotte D'Evelyn Book Fund, whose plate marks a great many of the texts succeeding generations of students and professors at Mount Holyoke have read and relied upon.[37]

Charlotte D'Evelyn's academic life, represented by the events and letters cited here, was a quiet success, seemingly free of significant disappointment and strife. Every life so summarized raises the difficulties that began this essay: how can we recover the passions, the emotions, and the vitality of a complex life of which we know only a small, public part? Reading through her letters and her publications, we see two Charlotte D'Evelyns. We know the athletic, active woman who purposefully walked the Mount Holyoke range every Sunday morning for years. At the same time there was another Charlotte D'Evelyn, a woman who devoted her life to texts of a distant culture, an explorer whose imagination, fired by the thought she had discovered the brass of Peter Idley, was consumed by this adventure of reaching across time and recovering something of the reality of his life. Both her walking and her research sprang from an essentially adventurous spirit that roamed through time and space and that refused to accept limits. The two Charlotte D'Evelyns come into focus as one in her words at the beginning of a 1926 article for *The Mount Holyoke Alumnae Quarterly* on walks in and around South Hadley. There she shared, in passing, her own assumptions about the human spirit and its compelling desire for knowledge gained through adventurous exploration: "Eve was already exploring when the fall came. One of them must have found the fence at last, and with it the limits of paradaisical [sic] content. The instinct to explore would have carried them out of Paradise in the long run."[38]

Notes

I want to thank Patricia Albright of the Mount Holyoke College Archives and Yun Sadowski, Mount Holyoke '02, for help with the research for this brief biography. I am especially indebted to Professor Emerita Phyllis P. A. Smith, friend and colleague of Charlotte D'Evelyn, for information and guidance on this project.

1. D'Evelyn, eulogy for Hope Traver, who was her teacher. The discourse of scholarship as adventure that appears in this quotation echoes the same kind of language Kathryn Lynch cites in her biography of Laura Hibbard Loomis.

2. Anna Jean Mill, in "Mount Holyoke College in the Twentieth Century," 6:33, Mount Holyoke College Archives and Special Collections; except where noted, all quotations attributed to Anna Jean Mill are from this file.

3. Mill, recollections, 32.

4. I learned of Susan D'Evelyn's newspaper writing from a conversation with Phyllis Smith, 3 December 2001.

5. Quotation from a letter to her stepmother, 7 March 1915. All quotations from Charlotte D'Evelyn's letters in this biography are from letters now in the Charlotte D'Evelyn file in the Mount Holyoke College Archives. Subsequent citations from these letters will be identified parenthetically in the text with respect to date and recipient.

6. In a section titled "Life," which follows the introduction to her first book—an edition of her dissertation, *Meditations of the Life and Passion of Christ*—D'Evelyn outlines the events in her scholarly life with a special expression of gratitude to Carleton Brown, her dissertation adviser: "I gladly take this opportunity of recording my special indebtedness to Professor Brown for his guidance and criticism of my work, and of the very generous way in which he has put material for investigation at my disposal." She also thanks Professor Howard Rollins Patch "under whose supervision the dissertation was finished."

7. Laura Hibbard had taught in the same department but left in 1917; perhaps her leaving opened a position for Charlotte D'Evelyn.

8. Mills College had been founded in 1852 by Susan Tolman Mills, a Mount Holyoke alumna.

9. Nielson was at Mount Holyoke from 1902 to 1939 and Putnam from 1908 to 1939.

10. Mary Vance Young, a noted scholar of Romance languages, was at Mount Holyoke from 1901 to 1928, and Ruth Dean, the Anglo-Norman scholar, was on the faculty from 1934 to 1967.

11. D'Evelyn, handwritten draft of speech, dated 26 May 1937. The Charlotte D'Evelyn papers contain a letter from Miss Woolley thanking her for her "enjoyable" remarks.

12. D'Evelyn, speech draft, 26 May 1937 (date and place of speech are not known).

13. Mill, recollections, 11–12.

14. Consternation indeed ran high at the appointment of a man who was perceived, as Anna Jean Mill put it, to lack the sense of dedication to Mount Holyoke that characterized Miss Woolley's tenure; his fund-raising speeches, in which he compared Mount Holyoke students to various women in Shakespeare's plays, apparently did nothing to raise the level of faculty confidence. See Mill, recollections, 11.

15. Ellen Deborah Ellis, recollections, in "Mount Holyoke College in the Twentieth Century," 9:14, Mount Holyoke College Archives.

16. Regarding her distance from students, see Mill, recollections, 26. Reggie Ludwig recalled the frigid winter classrooms in her memories of being Charlotte D'Evelyn's student in an interview (Charlotte D'Evelyn Papers, Mount Holyoke College Archives).

17. Instruction in medieval literature and medieval English history at Mount Holyoke has always focused intensively on primary sources.

18. Mill, recollections, 1.

19. English department records, Mount Holyoke College Archives.

20. Jeanette Marks was Mary Woolley's partner and somewhat of a prima donna in the English department; a story that Marks fired Charlotte D'Evelyn but that D'Evelyn refused to leave circulates in Mount Holyoke culture. Perhaps this was the occasion on which Carleton Brown intervened to point out to the administration how fine a scholar D'Evelyn was. See Mill, recollections, 34.

21. English department records, Mount Holyoke College Archives.

22. See the letter in the English department records, Mount Holyoke Archives, dated 1 April 1942, from Charlotte D'Evelyn to President Ham: "It seems the Literature Division is

acquiring something of a nuisance value for the English division, in whatever campaign it is they have on hand. Perhaps we will finally acquire the sanctity of martyrs."

23. Mill, recollections, 33.

24. From a hand-written draft by Charlotte D'Evelyn, dated ca. 1930s, in the Mount Holyoke College Archives.

25. Mill, recollections, 16; President Ham, the first male president of the college, was opposed by a large contingent of alumnae and faculty who believed that the president of Mount Holyoke should be a woman.

26. English department records, Mount Holyoke College Archives.

27. *Meditations of the Life and Passion of Christ,* ix.

28. *Meditations of the Life and Passion of Christ,* xxxvi; she returned to this subject, as she did to many of her major research projects, in her contribution to the festschrift for Carleton Brown, "'Meditations on the Life and Passion of Christ.'"

29. The respect and admiration she apparently felt for Hope Emily Allen's work appear in the opening paragraph of her review of Allen's *Writings Ascribed to Richard Rolle, Hermit of Hampole, and Materials for His Biography,* Modern Language Association Monograph Series, 3, (New York: E. P. Dutton, 1928): "The book under review comes before the scholarly public doubly guaranteed, first by the fact that it has been approved for publication in the Monograph Series of the Modern Language Association of America, and second by the fact that its author is Miss Hope Emily Allen. The expectation of work thoroughly scholarly in method and significant in result which these two guarantees call forth is more than confirmed by a perusal of the work itself" (418).

30. D'Evelyn, "Notes on Some Interrelations between the Latin and English Texts of the *Ancrene Riwle,*" 1,176.

31. Ibid., 1,179.

32. Bethurum, review of *The South English Legendary,* 457. Bethurum's first paragraph suggests the dominant figure of Carleton Brown, both in D'Evelyn's life and in Middle English scholarship of the first half of the century: "The impetus given to the study of vernacular saints' legends and homilies by Carleton Brown at Bryn Mawr years ago continues to be felt. To his students we owe the already existing editions of the *Northern Passion* (by Frances Foster) and the *Southern Passion* (by Beatrice Daw Brown [Mrs. Carleton Brown]), and now comes the edition of the entire *South English Legendary* by Brown's former student, Charlotte D'Evelyn, and her colleague, Anna Mill. It is quite a harvest. More immediately, the present edition is the outcome of the plans made by a committee of the Modern Language Association on the editing of Middle English texts, of which Carleton Brown was a member" (457).

33. Bethurum, review of *The South English Legendary*, 458.

34. *Modern Language Notes* 54 (April 1939): 310.

35. Both quotations from Patch, review of *Peter Idley's Instructions to His Son,* 297.

36. From an obituary of Charlotte D'Evelyn, 19 December 1977, issued by Mount Holyoke College Office of Public Information, in Mount Holyoke College Archives.

37. Through Professor Emerita Phyllis Smith I have come into the possession of some of Charlotte D'Evelyn's books and papers and had the good fortune to use 6C in Williston Library for my study.

38. D'Evelyn, "For Pedestrians Only," 137.

Select Bibliography of Works by Charlotte D'Evelyn

"A Note on Bede's 'Death-Song.'" *Modern Language Notes* 30 (1915): 31.
"Sources of the Arthur Story in Chester's 'Love's Martyr.'" *Journal of English and Germanic Philology* 14 (1915): 1–14.
"The Gray's Inn Fragment of 'Sir Ysumbras.'" *English Studies* 52 (1918): 72–76.
"The Middle English Metrical Version of the *Revelations* of Methodius; With a Study of the Influence of Methodius in Middle-English Writings." *PMLA* 33 (1918): 135–203.
"*Piers Plowman* in Art." *Modern Language Notes* 34 (1918): 247–49.
Meditations of the Life and Passion of Christ. Early English Text Society, o.s., 158. Bungay, Suffolk, Eng.: R. Clay and Sons, 1921.
"For Pedestrians Only." *Mount Holyoke Alumnae Quarterly* 10 (1926): 137–42.
Review of *Writings Ascribed to Richard Rolle, Hermit of Hampole, and Materials for His Biography*, by Hope Emily Allen. *Englische Studien* 63 (1929): 418–22.
"An East Midland Recension of *The Pricke of Conscience*." *PMLA* 45 (1930): 180–200.
"A Lost Manuscript of *De Contemptu Mundi*." *Speculum* 6 (1931): 132–33.
Peter Idley's Instructions to His Son. MLA Monograph Series. Boston: D. C. Heath and Co., 1935.
"'Meditations on the Life and Passion of Christ': A Note on Its Literary Relationships." In *Essays and Studies in Honor of Carleton Brown*. New York: Modern Language Association, 1940.
The Latin Text of the "Ancrene Riwle." Early English Text Society, o.s., 216. London: Oxford University Press, 1944.
"Notes on Some Interrelations between the Latin and English Texts of the *Ancrene Riwle*." *PMLA* 64 (1949): 1,164–79.
South English Legendary: Edited from Corpus Christi College Cambridge MS. 145 and British Museum MS. Harley 2277. 3 vols. Early English Text Society, o.s., 235–36, 244. London: Oxford University Press, 1956–59.
Eulogy for Hope Traver. *Mills Quarterly* 20 (1957): 29–30.
"The Legend of the 'Seven Sleepers of Ephesus' in the *South English Legendary*." In *Studies in Language and Literature in Honour of Margaret Schlauch*. Warsaw: n.p., 1966.
Letters and papers. Mount Holyoke College Archives and Special Collections.

Works Cited

Bethurum, Dorothy. Review of *The South English Legendary: Edited from Corpus Christi College Cambridge MS. 145 and British Museum MS. Harley 2277*, edited by Charlotte D'Evelyn and Anna J. Mill. *Speculum* 34 (1959): 456–58.
Mount Holyoke College Department of English Archives. Mount Holyoke College Archives and Special Collections.
"Mount Holyoke College in the Twentieth Century." Mount Holyoke College Archives and Special Collections.
Patch, Howard Rollins. Review of *Peter Idley's Instructions to His Son*, by Charlotte D'Evelyn. *Speculum* 11 (1936): 295–97.
Savage, Henry L. Review of *Peter Idley's Instructions to His Son*, by Charlotte D'Evelyn. *Modern Language Notes* 54 (1939): 310–11.

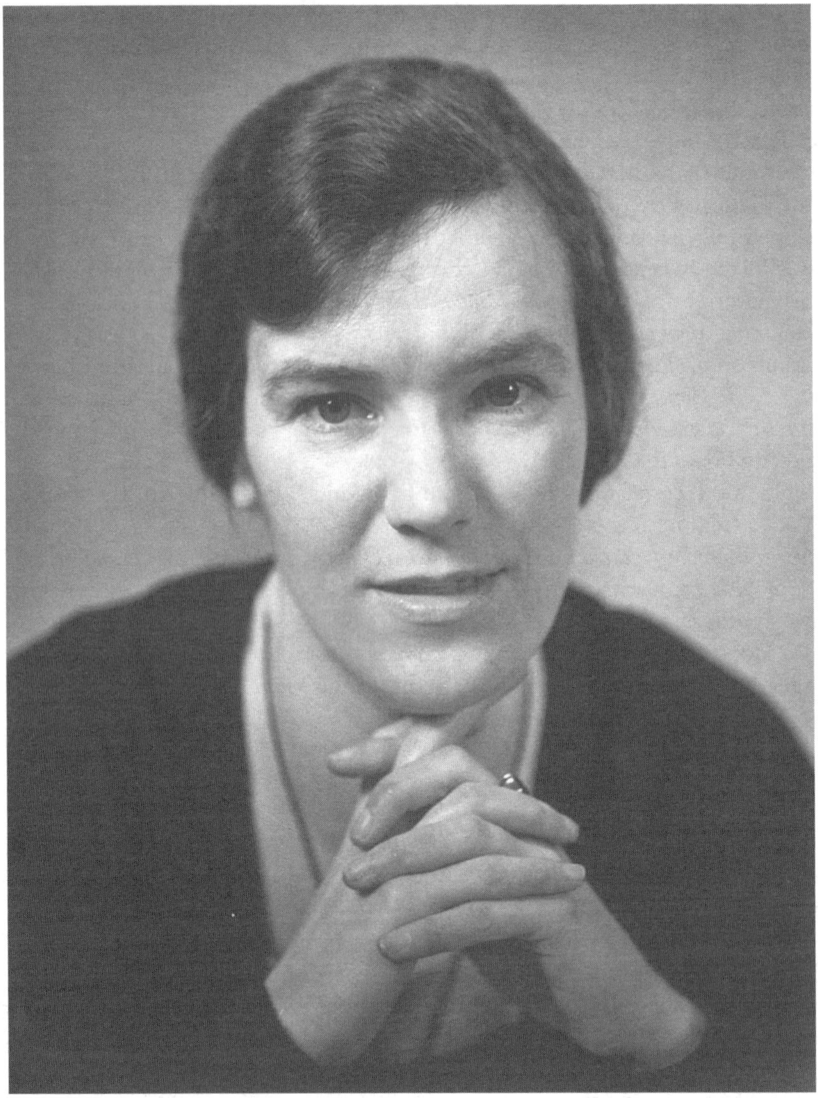

CHAPTER 23

Eileen Edna Le Poer Power
(1889–1940)

Marjorie McCallum Chibnall

WHEN EILEEN POWER DIED in August 1940 at the early age of fifty-one, she had already established a place for herself among the outstanding historians of the twentieth century. She held the chair of economic history at the London School of Economics (LSE), had given university lectures at Cambridge and been Ford Lecturer in Oxford, besides lecturing in academic institutions all over America and in China. Quite apart from her own publications, she had been actively involved in founding the Economic History Society and in the production of several historical series. She was also a popular radio broadcaster and had a continuing interest in historical teaching in schools. Even though she died at the height of her powers, with important work still to do, she had already had a decisive influence on the study, teaching, and enjoyment of economic and social history in England.

Eileen Edna Le Poer Power and her younger sisters, Beryl and Rhoda, were born into a prosperous middle-class family in the last years of the nineteenth century.[1] While they were still very young, the family fortunes collapsed through the disastrous enterprises undertaken by her father, a stockbroker; his imprisonment for fraud and the death of their mother meant that they were brought up by devoted aunts and knew from their school days that they would have to make their own way in the world. Fortunately their home, first in Bournemouth and then in Oxford, meant that, particularly in Oxford, they were able to attend some of the best girls' schools in the country, and in 1910 Eileen went up to Girton as the history scholar of her year.

So began a brilliant undergraduate career, with a first in both parts of the historical tripos and college graduate scholarships to launch her in a world where she had not yet decided on the career she wished to pursue. Eileen Power's success was grounded on very hard work, elegantly presented and leavened with wit. She had from the beginning a gift for friendship and a passionate interest in politics and social questions that led her into pacifism and the issue of women's suffrage. She read very widely in literature of all kinds. However, the need to earn her own living and the award of scholarship money for further study pointed the way to historical research; she readily took up the suggestion of spending a year in Paris at the École des chartes. Here she was plunged into the political and intellectual ferment of the city at a time of parliamentary instability, strikes, and cultural revival. There was plenty to excite and stimulate her outside her work, which included lectures and study in the Bibliothèque nationale. Charles Langlois, a somewhat traditional medieval professor, became her supervisor; after first advising her to study romance philology, paleography, and methods of research, he finally suggested as a thesis topic a biography of Isabella, the wife of Edward II, popularly regarded as the "she-wolf of France." Langlois was influenced in part by thinking that as a woman Power would want to study a woman; though this was not Power's view, she accepted the subject as good training. It was never more than this, and the thesis remained unfinished.

She returned to England knowing clearly that she wanted to write books; the award of a two-year Shaw studentship at the London School of Economics pointed to one way of doing this. Originally an open scholarship, new regulations had made the Shaw one for women only for research on women's social and economic history. This was not what Power, whose interests were not in economics, really wanted. However, she was able to choose as her topic a study of medieval English nunneries, which enabled her to include a good deal of general cultural history and at the same time to develop a deeper interest in social history. She also worked in Cambridge at Girton during the two summer vacations, and in 1913 she welcomed an invitation to return there as director of studies in history. Here she came under the influence of A. Hamilton Thompson and made effective use of the visitation records of religious houses that he was compiling. She also found the critical approach of G. G. Coulton to religious history stimulating, though she considered him too crude and confrontational. Her book made very slow progress, as she had to supplement her modest earnings at Girton with teaching at the London School of Economics in order to provide a home for her two younger sisters. Moreover her life, like that of all her contemporaries, was soon disrupted by the outbreak of war in 1914.

Power's influence at Girton extended far beyond her own history pupils. Mary Llewellyn Davies, a student first of classics and then of medicine, and her sister Theodora, a law student, who both became lifelong friends, have recorded their memories of her: "In the grey days of the war her vivid personality took hold of the imagination of her pupils.... She inspired respect not to say awe, and tolerated no slackness. She was felt to be very modern—her clothes were dashing, and she admired the poetry and art of the day and conducted Sunday poetry readings, which were eagerly attended. We realised that she belonged to a wider intellectual world than that of scholarship only. Our imaginations were caught by her brilliance, her beauty, and her goodness."[2]

Power's wider intellectual interests made her increasingly aware of the opportunities for friendship outside university circles that London provided, and her keen interest in contemporary politics and the possible contribution of academic study to world peace is brought out even in a preface that she wrote to a bibliography for teachers of history, published shortly after the war ended: "It seems clear that the history teacher who wishes her subject to foster that sense of world citizenship, without which a League of Nations will be like a machine lacking power to work it, will lay more stress than has hitherto been customary on the social side of history, and on the peaceful interdependence of nations, as well as upon the political and military side of the subject."[3]

Her wider interests in both politics and history found an outlet when, in 1920, she was awarded the Kahn Travelling Fellowship, which provided funds for a year's travel around the world. She was the first woman to hold it and had doubted after her interview whether it would be given to a woman, especially as Sir Cooper Perry had commented during the interview that she "might defeat the objects of the trust by subsequently committing matrimony." However, she was able to take such remarks in her stride, merely commenting to Coulton, "[H]e obviously can't help being made like that, so I possessed my soul in patience without argument."[4] The year of travel, described in the account she later wrote for the trustees of the Albert Kahn Travelling Fellowship, shows how the impact shaped her view of the way she wanted to write history. Her first impression of India was one of strangeness that soon gave way to a sense of familiarity; the particular political problems were new, but she felt that she knew intimately "the way of life of the great mass of the common people, the whole temper and habit of mind, the fundamental criteria upon which this civilisation was based.... India was the Middle Ages."[5] She described in detail the bazaars, the craftsmen, the silk merchants, each city famous for some particular product; these things reminded her of the *Livre des Métiers* of Étienne Boileau. The villages brought to mind the medieval court rolls and the illustrations in the Luttrell Psalter. She noted, too, the sudden susceptibility to famine and pestilence, the zest for pilgrimages, and the importance of itinerant entertainers. She had sat below the raised floor in a tiny Burman village and "watched the compilation of Domesday Book. It is true that it did not call itself Domesday Book: it called itself the assessment of land revenues for the village of Maingmaw," but the five village elders reminded her of the Saxon reeve and four men, and the questions asked were almost the same.[6]

China made a very different impression. Here she was struck by the intensity of cultivation that enabled the farmer of a few strips to support a family. "History has commonly shown that a social order founded upon a large peasant population is a static order.... So the civilization of China has stood unmoving, as solid as a beautiful pagoda, with its foundations firmly set in the soil." She was captured by the "all-pervading charm" of China, which remained in spite of the "Chinese faults of governmental inefficiency and corruption and extreme cruelty."[7]

On her return in the late summer of 1921, she was faced with a choice that was to prove decisive. Letters received during her travels contained the offer of a lectureship in history at the London School of Economics. Twice in her lifetime she had to choose between Cambridge and London; on both occasions, though for different reasons, she chose London. In 1921 she still felt a very strong attachment to Cambridge and Girton; she was still repelled by pure economics as the subject was then taught, and she had mixed feelings about the LSE. However, the London lectureship offered wider experience in a university setting, and she was beginning to feel the attraction of life in the city and the possibility of providing a home there for her sisters. Not until the following year did Cambridge vote once again to exclude women from full university degrees, so her choice was not influenced by that setback. Some years later, when as a professor at the LSE she decided not to apply for the Cambridge chair in economic history, her motives were more complicated; but once again London won.

The year 1922 saw the publication of her long-delayed book on *Medieval English Nunneries c.1275 to 1535*. It had been going through the Cambridge University Press, with help from Margaret Clapham, while she was still on her travels. The book contained the fruits of many years' hard study; although it never satisfied Power entirely and she hoped to the end of her life to prepare a second edition, it embodies much thought and useful research and shows how she was beginning to reshape social history. The bishops' visitation records were a mine of information about the difficulties experienced in the smaller houses of women religious, and they provided her with both statistics and vivid details of the lives of many individual nuns. Statistics showed her the relative poverty of the nunneries, with the exception of some half-dozen favored houses; they also showed that up to the fifteenth century recruitment was almost entirely from the nobility and gentry. These were the classes of women for whom almost the only alternative to matrimony was to take the veil. Poorer women might find employment in domestic service, in the fields, or in the family's trade. A few were taken into convents as lay sisters. For the gentry convents offered a refuge that required less financial outlay than marriage into a good family. Enough elementary education in singing and reading was necessary to enable novices to bear the burden of the choir, but after the Anglo-Saxon period nuns were not conspicuous for learning. Power noted the problems of estate management and the activities of convents as great employers and consumers in their districts. Her keen eye for social change picked out significant topics. In her concluding chapters she drew on her wide reading in medieval literature of all kinds—including songs, satires, and sermons—to show another side of women's monastic life. As yet, however, she had not quite learned to master a great mass of detailed information so as to present her conclusions forcefully; evidence is piled up indiscriminately, and her conclusions emerge slowly. These flaws in presentation were probably the reason for her dissatisfaction; ten years later she would have disciplined her evidence and presented it with the force and clarity shown in her more mature lectures and publications. Nevertheless, even this early volume showed both her deepening appreciation of the nature of social change and her ability to use every kind of source, from account rolls to poetry, to illustrate and explain it.

Two years later a publication of a different kind revealed the same qualities more selectively. *Medieval People* was published in 1924, and in the following three quarters of a century it has been studied and enjoyed by many thousands of readers. By choosing individuals from different walks of life and different periods, ranging from the Carolingian peasant through the Venetian traveler Marco Polo to a fourteenth-century Parisian housewife, Chaucer's pilgrim nun, and a prosperous wool-merchant, Power presented a vivid picture of daily life in town and country. The individuals were always shown in their social setting, whether it was a medieval manor, the great international trade routes, or the country town experiencing the impact of both local and European manufacture. Power's experience during her travels across Asia added a new dimension to her work, giving her insight into the way that trade, overflowing the bounds of geography and race, affected even the most local communities. This new perspective shaped her writing and teaching for the remainder of her life.

Teaching at all levels from the time she settled in London never exhausted her boundless energy. She plunged into new enterprises and found new friendships. With R. H. Tawney, a particular friend and colleague, she took a leading part in reshaping lecture courses and seminars in economic history at the LSE. Together they published a three-volume edition of *Tudor Economic Documents,* which was to prove a fundamental source book for students. Tawney believed in the importance of avoiding narrowness by lecturing on a long stretch of history, and in this Power was at one with him. Her work was not confined to reshaping and teaching university courses; she understood the need to enlarge the catchment area for future students. Her radio broadcasts and her advice on the history syllabus in schools helped to stimulate a deeper understanding outside the universities of both social and international history. When Ephraim Lipson first contemplated the production of a journal that was to be more concerned with history than economics, he had no difficulty in recruiting both Tawney and Power, who found it a project after their own hearts. Power was already secretary to the economic history section of the Anglo-American Conference, and when the *Economic History Review* was launched in 1926 at a meeting of the Anglo-American Historical Conference, she became its secretary. Since historians in Cambridge showed no interest, the new Economic History Society became centered in the LSE, and Power took a leading part in building it up and running the committee. Given the interests that she shared with Tawney, the *Economic History Review* soon attracted scholars from as far away as the United States, Russia, Belgium, and France. Up to the time of her death she was actively engaged in recruiting members and sponsors whenever the subscriptions flagged. She herself edited the first wartime number of the *Review,* insisting on the importance of keeping up scholarship in wartime.

Eileen Power also began to read widely in related subjects, particularly anthropology and sociology, which she realized had much to contribute to history. Her mind was always open to the work of French, German, and American scholars; she was one of the first in England to appreciate the work of Marc Bloch, who had been a slightly older research student during her year in Paris. She was also interested in economic changes in Asia and in international trade from the Middle Ages onward. Her publications, often in collaboration, show the range of her activities. A foreword to a translation of P. Boissonade's *Life and Work in Medieval Europe* and a translation of a medieval manual of conduct (*Le Ménagier de Paris*), which she called *The Goodman of Paris,* made some French sources more accessible, and she was involved in various series including the Broadway Travellers.[8] The seminar in fifteenth-century trade that she held led to the publication in 1933 (with M. M. Postan) of an important collection of papers titled *Studies in English Trade in the Fifteenth Century;* her own contribution was on the wool trade. By the time she was elected to the chair of economic history at the LSE, her views on the nature and value of economic history had been formed and were expressed in her inaugural lecture, delivered in January 1933.[9]

Power saw the subject as a companion study to economics and sociology. It must contribute historical analysis and synthesis to original research in sources and would also be concerned with surroundings and different periods. The Middle Ages were "far from being the subject of mere antiquarian or romantic interest."[10] Medieval, like modern, history "can provide the economist with empirical data for checking his deductions and the historian with material to the elucidation of which the formal deductive methods of the economist can properly be applied."[11] Medieval history provided a long period of time in which social change could be investigated. Power rejected the fallacious notion that it corresponded to a type of closed economy, unconcerned with the idea of profit; the "self-sufficing manor" was a myth. Moreover, the period provided material for comparative study of such topics as social control of the economic system and the problem of the industrialization of the East.

These views were enlarged in the chapter on "Peasant Life and Rural Conditions (c.1100–c.1599)," which Power wrote for the *Cambridge Medieval History.* It was a masterly survey of the variations in cultivation and social structure in rural communities across the whole of Europe, which showed the way in which geography and social custom were influenced by the steady growth in population, the rise of towns, the advance of clearance and colonization, the disintegration of the manor, and the later acquisition of estates by a new type of legally minded proprietor. Some of her views may have been hammered out in discussion with Marc Bloch, whose fundamental work on *Les Caractères originaux de l'histoire rurale française,* published in 1931, described the manorial reaction of the later Middle Ages on the great estates of Germany and France. Eileen showed how property came into the hands of a kind of *Gerichtsherrschaft,* who built up great estates worked by servile labor, in contrast to the medieval manors, whose smaller demesnes were cultivated partly by the customary labor of semi-independent peasants. The views she expressed on the effects of colonization on the frontiers of eastern Europe anticipated those of Robert Bartlett toward the end of the twentieth century. As always in her work, her knowledge of literature amplified the picture of peasant life as it was presented by legal historians, who considered the peasant primarily in relation to his land. *Piers Plowman* showed him as a new model of holiness, by exalting manual labor performed not by the monk but by the husbandman. Like Paul Vinogradoff, Power saw the importance of the village community, but she also enlivened her description of village life by drawing on sources ranging from French lais and fables to recently published parochial visitation records.

One of Power's most important enterprises was the seminar in economic history, in which she brought together and encouraged talented younger historians. Among them two or three were outstanding. Nora Carus-Wilson first became her pupil during part-time study in the intervals of school teaching; Power guided her into the history of the cloth trade, in which she made her name. Power also helped M. M. Postan, a man ten years her junior who had escaped from the politically unacceptable conditions in Russia; Postan worked for a time as her research assistant, after which Power assisted him into a lectureship at the LSE and later successfully prepared the way for his election to the Cambridge chair of economic history. He joined her in running the famous Power/Postan seminar, which attracted researchers from Oxford and Cambridge as well as London, and also from France and the United States. It was the live center of study and research in medieval economic history until the war changed everything. Presiding jointly, Power and Postan brought different and complementary talents to the group. Postan's contribution in stimulating ideas, in a grasp of abstract principles and in philosophical understanding, was an essential element in its success, yet Power always remained the senior partner. It was her deep knowledge of detailed sources, her light touch in indicating how to use them, and her ability to draw out the talents of her different pupils so that all contributed to the findings of the seminar that made it a major force in the study and teaching of economic history at a crucial stage in the establishment of the subject. Later, when Postan revived the seminar in Cambridge, it was a brilliant center of ideas, but it was more combative and more controversial.

As a teacher Power excelled. Her lectures were carefully structured, lively, and well illustrated; her students preserved and cherished the notes taken from them. The lectures were always perfectly attuned to the audience she was addressing and were delivered with poise and wit. Her work in the decade before she became a professor had made her a leading pioneer of a new conception of economic history; in the years that followed she was recognized as being one of its most brilliant exponents. On this achievement her reputation rests. There was time, fortunately, before her early death, for this to be appreciated both in England and abroad. To her delight the Medieval Academy of America made her a corresponding member, and she was warmly welcomed in the United States. In January 1939, at the invitation of Oxford University, she delivered the Ford Lectures—the first woman to do so.

Her Ford Lectures were the first fruits of many years' work on the records of the wool trade. The introduction opened with an apology for seeming to beat a dead horse by insisting on the weakness of the conventional view of the Middle Ages in western Europe as mainly a period of natural economy; the fact that twenty years previously, before Power began to promote a truer interpretation, most members of an academic audience would have found her viewpoint novel and even unacceptable showed the measure of her success. She was able to dwell in detail on the economy of the great estates that produced the fine wools, on widespread international trade and the social changes that came with the growing cities and the appearance of new types of merchants, and on taxation, credit, and government borrowing. It had never been her intention to publish the lectures, which were written to be delivered and should have been a foretaste of her great book, for which most of the notes had been collected. Tragically, her sudden death meant that the book never appeared. She died in the darkest days of the war, when no one could tell how long it would last or who would win. Her husband, Postan, was working in the Ministry of Economic Warfare in London, and the blitzkreig, then at its height, made it seem urgent to salvage immediately whatever could be saved. The lectures were published in 1941, almost as written, and with a minimum of notes.[12] Postan hoped then to be able to produce a fuller edition with all her notes, but it never appeared. War did not end until 1945, and by then he was submerged in other work. Posthumous publication always involves long, exacting, and self-sacrificing labor for successful completion, and probably Postan did not have the right temperament and qualities for the task. He was always impelled to reshape everything to fit his own interpretation; yet he was too devoted to the wife who had promoted his own successful career to hand over her notes to anyone else.

When R. H. Tawney delivered a memorial address at Golders Green Crematorium on 12 August 1940, he said of Eileen Power, "Her work was far from done, but she was her own greatest work. She seemed rounded and perfected and complete: crowned and mitred over herself."[13] Sixty years later it is possible to assess how much she had already accomplished and to see that even though the book that was never published would have rounded off her visible achievements, her work was carried on through her influence. She was never forgotten; sixty years later the face of a professor of science, too young to have ever seen her, could light up at the mention of her name. More substantially, her work lived on through her pupils, especially in London and Cambridge. In London, for example, Nora Carus-Wilson followed her into a chair of economic history at the LSE and carried on the work on the cloth trade and cloth manufacture first sponsored by Power. She also successfully revived the British Academy's series of Studies in Social and Economic History, which still continues to produce basic sources for the benefit of students and historians alike. In Cambridge Postan revived the former economic history seminar in a different form; this would have pleased her, as her wish was always to leave scholars to develop their own talents in different ways once she had helped them to take the first steps. Generous and imaginative, she was never possessive.

One aspect of her posthumous reputation has been a little strange. In 1975 Postan finally published a few of the studies of medieval people that Power had left very nearly complete, in a volume titled *Medieval Women*. At a time when a new type of feminism was gaining ground, Power was hailed as a historian of women, and this view has persisted. It would certainly have surprised her. Although she took up the cause of women's suffrage, felt passionately about the oppression of women in underdeveloped countries, and had been forced willy-nilly in her early career to study the history of some women, her interest was always in the whole of society. The suffragettes had fought for equal, not separate, rights for women, and Power's generation had the same desire for equal rights in a wider professional field. In common with the women of her day, she asked only for a level playing field. When, in 1920, the editor of a local Cambridge journal invited her to write a "provocative" weekly article to display to an attentive world the views of the women of Cambridge, she wrote: "I feel moved to provoke the Editor rather than the world, for I have a rooted objection to columns and articles which purport to contain the women's point of view." This she considered to be the Mrs. Harris of criticism:

> In art, in literature, in science, in learning "I don't believe there's no such person." I do not deny that there are certain sides of life and certain subjects . . . which affect women differently from men. There is, I admit, a vast mass of so-called feminist literature, but it arises out of social and political conditions in which women are specially handicapped, as contrasted with men; the feminism is a result of these artificial circumstances, and is a struggle for like treatment, not for different treatment. . . . There will be nothing specially feminine about the contents of this column. Being a woman is not a special profession, except in the eyes of the law (Name: Mary Jones; Profession: Spinster). . . . I do not believe that the research done by women and the books written by women are utterly different in their essence from those of men.[14]

J. H. Clapham recalled that when, at a learned gathering, her dress seemed to him more than usually glittering and he had said to her, "Eileen, you look like Semiramis," she had replied. "I thought I looked like a Professor of Economic History."[15]

In her personal life it would probably be true to say that she herself was able to secure equal treatment. This was because her brilliance, her charm and sincerity, and her invariable courtesy always carried the day, just as they had overcome the prejudices of some of the misogynists among the Albert Kahn Trustees. Normally she was able both to secure the appointments she sought and to place her students in good positions. She was aware of inequalities: J. H. Clapham recalled that "she resented fiercely the survivals in the older Universities of inequality between the sexes; and she was a little impatient of the single-sex life of a woman's college."[16] C. K. Webster wrote of her early experience in Cambridge, "If the Cambridge dons had known more of her they would have realised that they had a teacher of genius in their midst. But the History Faculty showed little interest in her."[17] Clapham wished her to apply for the Cambridge chair of economic history after his retirement from it in 1935 and believed that it would have been hers for the asking. This may have been wishful thinking, and the truth can never be known, as she decided to remain in the less purely academic world of London. She wished that Postan, whose application she furthered, should be elected and never regretted her choice. When, a few years later, she married him and the marriage brought her great happiness, they built a house in Cambridge, and she planned to retire there. Although tragedy cut short their plans soon afterward, I believe that if anyone had asked her whether there was anything in her past life that she would have wished to change, she would have replied that there was nothing. She had a remarkable record of achievement behind her, and she was indeed, in Dante's words (quoted by Tawney), "crowned and mitred over herself."

NOTES

1. For detailed information, see the excellent biography by Berg, *Woman in History*.
2. Mary Llewelyn Davies and Theodora Calvert, "Memories of Eileen Power at Girton," Power Papers, Girton College Archives.
3. Eileen Power, preface to *A Bibliography for Teachers of History* (London: Women's International League, 1919).
4. Eileen Power, letter to Coulton, 27 April 1920, Power Papers.
5. Eileen Power, *Report to the Trustees of the Albert Kahn Travelling Fellowship Sept. 1920–Sept. 1921* (London: University of London, 1921), passim.
6. Ibid.
7. Ibid.
8. P. Boissonade, *Life and Work in Medieval Europe: Fifth to Fifteenth Centuries*, with a foreword by Eileen Power (London: Kegan Paul, 1926).
9. Power, "On Medieval History as a Social Study," *Economica*, 22.
10. Ibid.
11. Ibid. Paraphrases from this same essay in the remainder of this paragraph come from p. 25.
12. Power, *Wool Trade in English Medieval History*.
13. R. H. Tawney, Memorial Address, 12 August 1940, Power Papers, Girton College Archives.
14. Eileen Power, "Women of Cambridge," *The Old Cambridge*, 14 February 1920.
15. Clapham, "Eileen Power," 355.
16. Ibid.
17. Webster, obituary of Eileen Power.

SELECT BIBLIOGRAPHY OF WORKS BY EILEEN EDNA LE POER POWER

A full bibliography appears in Berg, *Woman in History*, 266–68.
Eileen Power Papers. Girton College Archives.
The Paycocks of Coggeshall. London: Methuen, 1920.
Medieval English Nunneries c.1275–1535. Cambridge: Cambridge University Press, 1922.
Medieval People. 1924. 10th ed. with a new chapter compiled from her notes. London: Methuen: 1963.
Editor with R. H. Tawney. *Tudor Economic Documents*. 3 vols. London: Longmans, 1924.
"The English Wool Trade in the Reign of Edward III." *Cambridge Historical Journal* 2 (1926): 17–35.

Editor and translator. *The Goodman of Paris*. London: Routledge, 1928.
"Peasant Life and Rural Conditions (c.1100 to c.1500)." In *The Cambridge Medieval History*, vol. 7. Cambridge: Cambridge University Press, 1932.
"On the Need for a New Edition of Walter of Henley." *Transactions of the Royal Historical Society* 7 (1933): 101–16.
Editor with M. M. Postan. *Studies in English Trade in the Fifteenth Century*. London: Routledge, 1933.
"The Wool Trade in the Fifteenth Century." In *Studies in English Trade in the Fifteenth Century*, edited by M. M. Postan and Eileen Power. London: Routledge, 1933.
"On Medieval History as a Social Study." Inaugural lecture, London School of Economics, 1933. Reprinted in *Economica* 12 (1934): 13–29.
The Wool Trade in English Medieval History. Oxford: Oxford University Press, 1941.
Medieval Women. Edited by M. M. Postan. Cambridge: Cambridge University Press, 1975.

Works Cited

Berg, Maxine. *A Woman in History: Eileen Power 1889–1940*. Cambridge: Cambridge University Press, 1996.
Clapham, J. H. "Eileen Power." *Economica*, n.s., 7 (1940): 355
Webster, C. K. Obituary of Eileen Power. *Economic Journal* 50 (1940): 561–72.

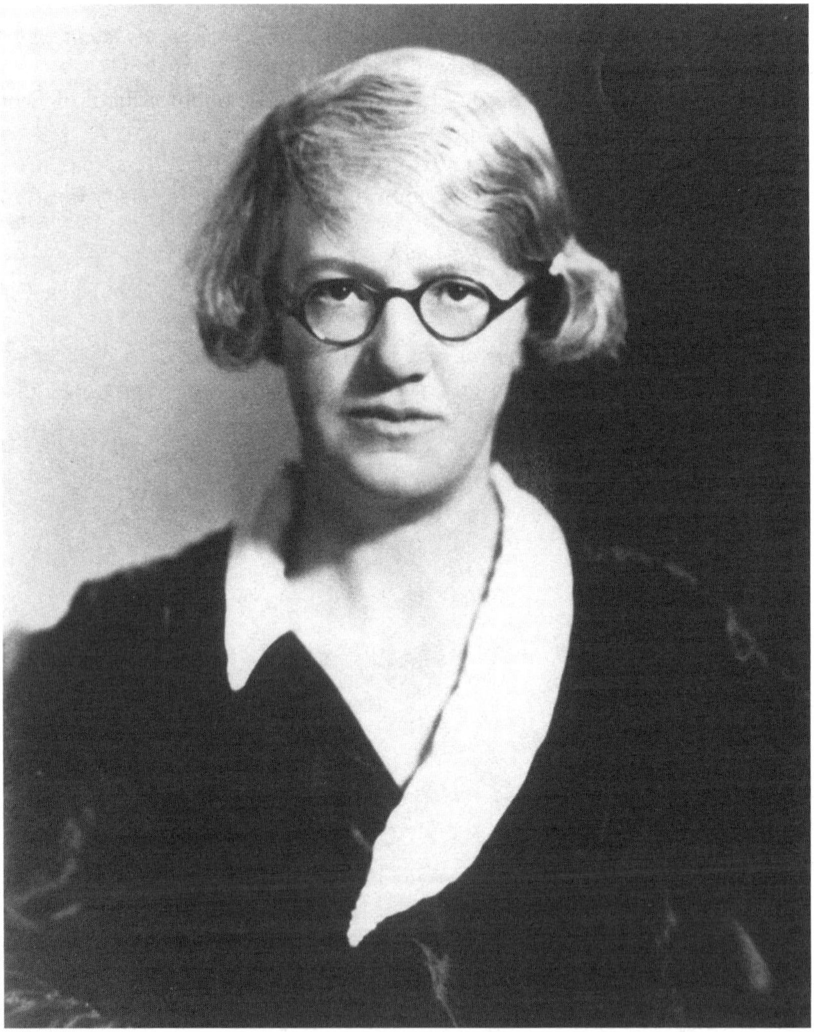

CHAPTER 24

Helen Waddell (1889–1965)
The Scholar-Poet

JENNIFER FITZGERALD

HELEN WADDELL was not a conventional medievalist. She never obtained full-time academic employment; her publications are anomalous, blurring the dividing line between scholarship and literature. Her best-known works are translations of medieval Latin poetry and prose, while her work on Peter Abelard, faithfully rooted in historical documents, was published as a novel.

Many a female would-be academic has been sidelined into a more acceptable career as a creative writer: in Waddell's case gender was certainly a factor, but so too was an inclination in both directions. Born in Tokyo, Japan, of an Irish missionary family, she graduated from Queen's University, Belfast, in 1911 with a first-class honors B.A. in English and in 1912 with an M.A. thesis on Milton. An ensuing scholarship should have permitted her to undertake manuscript research at Oxford, but, obedient to her stepmother's conviction that her youngest daughter's duty lay in Belfast as her companion, Waddell devised a topic she could research in Queen's University Library. Years later she reported on the reaction of the professor of English George Gregory Smith to her decision: "'Well, . . . it means your career will be literary—not academic. You've shut the gates on that.'"[1]

In the first instance, then, Waddell's "choice" in the interests of family duty was the first nail in the coffin of her academic career. There followed another: disaffection with some of the subject matter that the scholar was expected to treat objectively. Her topic seemed close to her interests: "'Woman as Dramatic Asset';—in other words, the evaluation of US—the Eternal Feminine, in fact, from Noah's wife in the Miracle Plays . . . down through Portia and Cleopatra and the naughtiness of the Restoration, to Bernard Shaw's Candida."[2] Smith's amused consent—"An excellent subject for *you*. . . . You have a good many of the qualifications"—referred no doubt to their "years of intermittent strife—in the matter of feminism in the University and other minor feuds."³ But to her disquiet, "Woman in the Drama before Shakespeare" led to a direct confrontation with misogyny. In 1913, having "sickened [her] very soul over Jean de Meung and yearn[ing] for anything, by way of dry disinfectant," she adapted the prose translations of James Legge's *Chinese Classics* into verse: *Lyrics from the Chinese* was published the same year.⁴ Even as a graduate student, then, the "inhuman" demands of "exact scholarship" stimulated an alternative immersion in literary creativity.⁵

During these years she received financial support for her research from George Taylor, a family friend and missionary in India, and she supplemented this by writing for children. Under Smith she learned to historicize in proper scholarly fashion and to deal with Rabelais's "astounding coarseness," "foulspoken" fifteenth-century plays, and the "sheer contempt in Restoration drama," while tracing the roots of misogyny.⁶ During the summer vacation of 1915, she collaborated with her best friend from undergraduate days, Maude Clarke, in writing a novel, "Discipline," a contemporary *Pride and Prejudice* whose heroine is the young wife of an antifeminist scholar, the latter explicitly based on Gregory Smith.⁷ The joke rather soured as she experienced academic sexism firsthand. During World War I many male faculty left Queen's for the war effort: Clarke returned from Oxford to substitute for the professor of history, F. M. Powicke. A few months later Waddell hoped that she, too, could be employed in the English department, but she fell foul of Gregory Smith's "prejudice."⁸

Waddell's stepmother died in June 1920; by October she had enrolled for the new Ph.D. degree in Somerville College, Oxford, where Maude Clarke had been appointed history tutor the year before. While her research interest had shifted to the Neoplatonic transfiguration of love, flesh, and, consequently, woman, she continued to focus on drama, giving a series of lectures on medieval mime in Oxford in 1921. After a year as a temporary lecturer at Bedford College, London, in June 1923 she was awarded the Susette Taylor Fellowship by Lady Margaret Hall, Oxford, worth £200 per annum for two years, with which she traveled to Paris.

She now transferred her attention to the love poems composed in Latin by twelfth- and thirteenth-century peripatetic university students known as goliards. (She seems to have come late to the gold mine of the *Carmina Burana*, available since 1847.) In Paris she immersed herself in "the literary furniture of their minds" by "reading only the things they would have read."⁹ She spent the last six months of the fellowship at the British Museum and lectured on her new subject at Oxford in 1926 during the Trinity term.¹⁰ Actively (but unsuccessfully) seeking academic employment, she approached the director of Constable and Co., Otto Kyllmann, who was enthusiastic and encouraging.¹¹ After a long gestation and significant shifts in focus, *The Wandering Scholars* was published in April 1927.

Waddell abandoned the Oxford degree, but her supervisor believed that, with a publisher's contract under her belt, there should be no obstacle to an academic career.[12] However, her age and lack of teaching experience—which could be laid at Gregory Smith's door—told against her in the competition for several jobs.[13] Kyllmann suggested part-time work for Constable's, which would leave her free to continue research.[14] Thus she gave up painfully chasing university lectureships and became an independent scholar resident in London, a vocation made even more feasible by royalties after the success of *Peter Abelard* in 1933.

The Wandering Scholars, both literary history and literary criticism, argues that romantic individualism survived from the classical era as an undercurrent to the theological asceticism of the Middle Ages, climaxing in the Latin lyrics of twelfth- and thirteenth-century university students. It complements analogous texts by Charles Homer Haskins, E. K. Rand, and Max Manitius, which were all about to be published.[15] Waddell's immersion in Migne's *Patrologia Latina* (as well as in the *Poetae Latini Aevi Carolini*) alerted her to traces of humanism and foretastes of Neoplatonism in theological and philosophical works, sermons, commentaries, letters, and literature: quotations and idiomatic paraphrases from these sources form the bedrock of the text.[16] Because her focus is on the human and the humane, the textual and historical arguments expand into biography: one reviewer complained, "She is so insistent that we shall see medieval scholars as men, she forgets that they are both scholars and medieval."[17] Nevertheless, her historical sense keeps her constantly aware of the difference of perspective. Her rhetoric practices "coevalness," making the past present, through the intimacy with which she describes the experience or feelings of individuals remote in time and in ideology, on the one hand, while, on the other, through verbatim translation and idiomatic paraphrase of medieval Latin, keeping the reader aware of the exotic difference of the past.[18]

The style of the work is academically unorthodox, featuring density of detail, lyrical metaphors, literary and cultural allusions, and analogies across centuries. It avoids pedantry, but such an impassioned interpretation runs the risk of partisanship. Waddell is evidently deeply committed to humanism, and not only in its medieval guise. She was disturbed by the Middle Ages' preoccupation with asceticism as an exclusive ideal—she had suffered as a child from a Presbyterian upbringing, "haunted" by the demands of a similar Calvinist "doctrine"—so the alternative offered by Neoplatonism attracted her personally.[19] It also had a specific impact on literature, since "every Platonist is at heart a poet."[20] But her critical assumptions were rooted in the nineteenth-century "myth of essential and universal Man," projected back to its seminal manifestation in Renaissance humanism.[21] She took it for granted that human feeling abided over time and place, finding in medieval Latin "something familiar in the landscape, some touch of almost contemporary desire or pain."[22] She also inherited the Arnoldian belief that the best literature is "criticism of life."[23] It is not surprising that her historical sense of the difference of the past should be complemented by a feeling for continuity and identity.

The Wandering Scholars is Waddell's most substantial scholarly work, but she is chiefly remembered for her lyric translations from medieval Latin, which continue to be anthologized, in *Medieval Latin Lyrics*. This volume received almost unanimous praise, with reviewers suggesting that "she might well claim poetry for her real vocation as a writer."[24] For others, however, her versions "are mere variations on the theme of the original, cast in the familiar moulds of English late-Romantic prosody, diction and sentiment."[25] Many felt that Waddell had achieved an emotional accuracy that surpassed linguistic precision: "I am not a scholar, but I have enough Latin, and understand poetry perhaps better than the critics. I cannot always see in the Latin what Miss Waddell sees; but directly I have read her version, I can see that it is there. Others read the poet's Latin as well as she; she reads the poet."[26] In fact, she treated translation as creative writing, explaining the omission of several lyrics thus: "I tried to translate them, but could not. . . . A man cannot say 'I will translate,' any more than he can say, 'I will compose poetry.' In this minor art also, the wind blows where it lists." She retained acknowledged "blunders . . . because the mould of the verse had set and I was too obstinate to break it."[27]

Waddell's scholarship was subsidized by her part-time work for Constable's: as she wrote her novel *Peter Abelard* (published in 1933, but seven years in the composition), she contributed to several publications, including a schoolbook on medieval Latin.[28] Her fascination with history as lived, intimate experience is evident in the long introductions that she wrote for two volumes of an eighteenth-century parson's diary: William Cole's *Journal of My Journey to Paris in the Year 1765* and his *Blechley Diary, 1765–67*, published in 1931.[29] She also translated the 1731 version of *Manon Lescaut*, the French classic by the Abbé Prévost more popularly known in an amplified, revised edition of 1753.[30] Captivated by documentary evidence that Prévost had repeated in his own life the tragedy of his hero two years *after* the first publication of his novel, she dramatized the events in a biographical play, *The Abbé Prévost*, published in 1931 and staged in 1935.[31]

It is not surprising, then, that Waddell's reputation as a scholar began to be overshadowed by that of translator and creative writer, a trend confirmed by her highly successful novel *Peter Abelard*. She had long been fascinated by the twelfth-century Socrates of Gaul and had planned a book since her undergraduate days.[32] Her early judgment of Abelard as "a prig and a cad," based on the *Letters* (comprising the *Historia calamitatum* [*Story of His Misfortunes*] and the personal letters between him and Heloise) changed over the years as she read the corpus of his work.[33] Then, in Paris in 1924 a strange experience concentrated her attention on the famous love affair. Recovering from an infected throat in the Institut Pasteur, after four sleepless nights,

> I passed, fully awake and not, I think, delirious, into some strange state of being. For suddenly I was Héloise, not as I ever imagined her, but an old woman, Abbess of the Paraclete, with Abelard twenty years dead: and I was sitting in a great chair lecturing to my nuns on his *Introductio ad Theologiam*. It was near the end of the lecture, and I pronounced the benediction, and sat watching them go out two by two. And one of them, the youngest and prettiest of my nuns for whom I felt some indulgence, glanced

at me sideways as she went out, and I heard her whisper to the older sister beside her, "*Elle parle toujours Abelard.*"

It stabbed me. And even when the first hurt of it was past, the realization that what once was a glory in men's minds had become an old woman's wearisome iteration, I began wondering if it were indeed true: if after all these years I were lecturing on his theology for the sake of now and then naming his name.... I began to wonder if I had perilled the souls in my charge by teaching them heretical doctrine for the sake of gratifying this ancient lust.[34]

This experience determined the form that her work on Abelard would take: "for in a biography one must abide by the existing [evidence] and be constantly saying, 'It is perhaps permissible to assume that'—But in a novel, I was free,... hang it all, *I had been there.*"[35]

Despite this vivid identification with the historical Heloise, Waddell was attracted by Abelard, "not so much the lover, oddly enough, but the heretic, truth's martyr, rather than Love's Martyr."[36] She believed that "most readers go wrong in judging Abelard only by the letters, written at a singularly cruel moment in his life."[37] As a result of Waddell's reading all his surviving works in preparation for *The Wandering Scholars,* her *Peter Abelard* is distinguished from so many previous versions of the famous love affair by a return to origins: on almost every page of the novel a phrase, an event, or an interchange can be traced back to documentary sources.[38] It reads entirely coherently as a twentieth-century novel, but its ethos is thoroughly medieval: prayer and liturgy are woven into the texture of everyday life, thought, and emotion; theological disputes provide the meat of canonical gossip; and twelfth-century humanism is in the air.

Waddell fictionalizes strong historical characters: Abelard, the most famous scholar and teacher of his day, champion of the individual conscience, of reason and understanding rather than of tradition and authority, intolerant, competitive and arrogant, twice on trial for heresy; Heloise (considered by contemporary critics to have been more learned than Abelard), glorying in public dishonor as his whore and determined to avoid marriage because of its repercussions on his reputation as a scholar.[39] Their personalities determine the course of their tragic love: the extremity of the historical Heloise's arguments are made more plausible by her representation as a tender, fervent young woman. Abelard's emotional conflicts are reflected in, and intertwined with, the arguments of his *Sic et Non* [*Yes and no*], *De Trinitate* [*On the Trinity*], and *Expositio in Epistolam ad Romanos* [*Commentary on Saint Paul's Epistle to the Romans*] (with echoes of his *Ethica* [*Ethics*] and different versions of his *Theologia* [*Theology*]).[40]

Waddell's accomplishment lies in making the extremes of feeling and belief that ricochet between the authors of the *Letters* not only emotionally but also theologically credible to the modern reader.[41] Abelard's insistence on the marriage that was their downfall is explained through a secular code of honor: "I have betrayed the man whose bread I have eaten.... I wounded his honor, but I wounded my own, nigh onto death."[42] But his response to Heloise's uncle is also motivated by compassion, the same empathy with the poor and suffering that emerges in the historical Abelard's evangelical theology.[43] Coming across a rabbit caught in a trap, Waddell's Abelard shares its anguish, as God suffers "all the pain in the world."[44] Empathy with the rabbit's agony, and with Christ's, completes Abelard's "conversion" from sin.

We know from the *Letters* that Heloise's passion for Abelard never wavered. Their contact was renewed nine years after his castration and their respective retreats into the religious life, when he assumed responsibility for the convent that he had founded and of which she was abbess. After vain attempts to engage him emotionally, Heloise "set the bridle of [his] injunction" on her "unbounded grief" while suggesting that this stifled, but did not eradicate, it.[45] The historical Heloise's continuing silence about her personal feelings has provoked centuries of conflicting interpretations.[46] Waddell intimates the possibility of a resolution to her character's pain through her emotional responsiveness to others. The novel closes when, four years after her profession as a nun, Heloise visits the fictional Gilles de Vannes, expecting a letter from Abelard. After she is cruelly disappointed, pity remains her strongest impulse. Responding to Gilles's distress on her own behalf, she assures him that her agony is momentary. The words are only meant to placate, but in speaking she makes them true. Heloise the sinner is thus in tune with the repentant Abelard. Both are training themselves to empathy, and in doing so they are imitating Christ: "*By whose grief our wound was healed: by whose pain our fall was stayed.*"[47]

"I have felt for so long now that once *Peter Abelard* was written the thing for which I was born would be done," Waddell remarked.[48] It was a tremendous success: reviews praised the frankness with which it addressed sexual passion and violence without crudity but also without attempting to smooth them over, and they marveled at Waddell's "saturation in the essential juices of the period."[49] Particularly significant was the approval of Etienne Gilson, who called it "penetrating and . . . faithful to reality."[50]

Her prose translations from Latin, *Beasts and Saints* (1934) and *The Desert Fathers* (1936), also drew acclaim. Given her initial resistance to medieval asceticism, at first sight it appears strange that she should have turned to these most extreme of Christian saints. But "the Desert," Waddell pointed out, "though it praised austerity, reckoned it among the rudiments of holy living, not as an end in itself." The texts highlight the saints' "humility, their gentleness, their heartbreaking courtesy . . . the seal of their sanctity to their contemporaries, far beyond abstinence or miracle or sign."[51] *Beasts and Saints* relates the tender, humorous, heartwarming "mutual charities" between these ascetics and the animals whose habitats they chose to share.[52]

The academy's response was more muted than that of the reading public. Waddell's gifts as a translator and poet were praised, but reservations were expressed about her accuracy as a scholar. Philip Schuyler Allen, one of the founders of the Medieval Academy of America, expostulated on *The Wandering Scholars* in its journal, *Speculum:* "Miss Waddell . . . must be reminded that the most delightful chatter, the most gorgeous guesswork, are not scholarship; that the very genius of her writing negates its appealing to a crowd of specialists. . . . [W]orst of all crimes to your scholarly person, she has jazzed the Middle Ages."[53] The editor, E. K. Rand (also a founding fellow), later wrote to Waddell, "saying that the review was unjust"; she noted that Allen then "swung to the other extreme of absurd adulation," including plagiarizing one of her paragraphs.[54] Allen's review also played a part in her prickly relationship with G. G. Coulton of Cambridge, who, in reviewing another book, went out of his way to draw attention to Allen's accusation.[55] Since her postgraduate days Waddell had bemoaned her deficiencies in "exact scholarship." One reads ambivalence in phrases such as "scholarship of the academic, indisuptable kind, exact, pedantic scholarship."[56] She admitted that she could not edit texts, since she was "congenitally incapable of that kind of exactness, grievous as it is to me to admit it," yet scholarly accuracy certainly mattered to her, as is clear from her correspondence with Coulton.[57] He sent Waddell a "charge sheet" of disputed references. (It obviously gave her pleasure to be able to point "out a howler in his own last book.") She responded with an apologia, which she repeated to her sister: "I am on your side in this controversy with reservations. I am no scholar: but am a tolerably industrious and, I hope, tolerably honest student of the Middle Ages. The WS was a first book, written with all the passion and most of the faults of the amateur, except one: respect for evidence, and preference for primary authorities: it was further marred by the fact that I am, I think, the worst proof-reader in the world. I could supply you, from my marginal notes and corrections for the last five years, with ammunition far more deadly than anything you have here." He replied by admitting that he had been motivated by jealousy: "I had my back to the wall. It was my own reputation that was challenged."[58]

Coulton's acknowledgment of unfairness could have been tinged with guilt: it is possible that he prevented Waddell from being elected a fellow of the British Academy, on a proposal from J. W. Mackail and George Saintsbury.[59] Her biographer notes that on the flyleaf of Coulton's copy of *The Wandering Scholars* one of his colleagues records the occasion and that G. G. Coulton provided effective counterarguments.[60] But Waddell offers another version: "They were, I am told[,] considering me for the British Academy in 1933 . . . but there was the fact that only one woman had ever been a member—then it was remembered that I was writing a novel, and I was subterraneously approached to hold up publication for a year as it would make my backers['] task more difficult. Well, to be a F.B.A. would have been very agreeable, but I felt that Abelard [sic] had been a book I was bound to do, and also I hated the strategic delay, so I went ahead and heard no more of the Academy. . . . I am . . . telling you this to show how deep is the prejudice of the academic mind against the novel."[61]

Clearly, Waddell straddled the scholarly-creative divide: the academy seemed readier to praise her poetry than her learning. (J. R. R. Tolkien and C. S. Lewis also problematically combined the personae of professional medievalist and creative writer: they nevertheless had the advantage of university employment.)[62] Howard Mumford Jones, who provided "English renderings" for Allen's *Romanesque Lyric,* understood the challenge of translation: "Fortunately Miss Waddell is not only thoroughly seen in the scholarship of medieval Latin . . . but she is also a true poet of insight, literary tact, and metrical mastery. . . . A lyrist of passion and power in the best tradition of English verse, she seeks to cram every rift with ore. . . . [T]hough I may quarrel with Miss Waddell at a hundred points, . . . I marvel and delight at her genius. . . . Miss Waddell is simply unsurpassable."[63] E. K. Rand, who used his own verse translations for *Founders of the Middle Ages,* also sympathized: he and Waddell became good friends. She confided in him why she would not review F. J. E. Raby's *Secular Latin Poetry:* "[H]e is . . . thoroughly decent and painstaking, and in himself, I think, gentle and generous. But of a dullness—This is piggy of me, but, with you, I do like a sense of humour and humanity in handling medieval stuff."[64] John Livingston Lowes began a warm correspondence when he wrote to compliment her on *The Wandering Scholars,* published at the same time as his work of equally idiosyncratic scholarship, *The Road to Xanadu.*[65] Among the British establishment she had the support of Professor C. H. Herford of Manchester and rather more ambivalent praise from F. M. Powicke, who had known her at Queen's University, Belfast, and who was about to be installed as Regius Professor of History at Oxford: "[*The Wandering Scholars*] deserves the utmost respect and demands a very precise use of terms from its reviewer. When I say that it is a remarkable, exciting, poignant, exasperating, and unbalanced book, I use these words deliberately and with no conventional desire to save myself trouble. . . . I dare to prophesy [Miss Waddell] will have many readers, and that, though some of them may often want to shake her, all of them will wish to thank her."[66]

However, despite scholarly unease with the emotional intensity of her writing, her success with the reading public, with reviewers, and with prominent opinion formers escalated. She was lionized by authors, aristocrats, diplomats, musicians, and the prime minister—and in demand as a lecturer everywhere.[67] The academy could not lag behind, especially after the fanfare that greeted *Peter Abelard:* the University of Durham had conferred an honorary D.Litt. on her in May 1931; in June 1934 Saint Andrews also honored her; and in July her alma mater, Queen's University, Belfast, followed suit; in June 1935 she crossed the Atlantic to receive the same from Columbia.[68] In 1932 she was made an associate member of the Irish Academy of Letters and in 1937 a corresponding fellow of the Medieval Academy of America.

The royalties on *Peter Abelard* increased her income, and in the spring of 1934 Waddell took out a thirty-year lease on a large house on Primrose Hill Road, with two sitting tenants and room for more. Thereafter she shared her accommodation with a painter friend, Rosamund Tweedy, with her niece, and with the chairman of Constable's, Otto Kyllmann, with whom she was in love. His status as married but separated made any sexual liaison between them impossible for her, no matter what gossips made of their living arrangements.[69] They holidayed together, annually returning to her sister's farm in Northern Ireland. As an independent scholar without a family, Waddell could have carved out personal space and freedom for her academic pursuits, but she also yearned for a home: inevitably the domestic burden of a large old house, plus its numerous inhabitants, took its toll of her time and peace of mind.

She was endlessly distracted: according to her niece, "there were two Helens, and while one was content to let day after day drift by, pottering in her house and garden, the other Helen was hag-ridden by the parable of the talents, and her talent lodged with her useless because she wasn't using it."[70] Many projects, such as a large-scale study of John of Salisbury, were begun but never completed.

During World War II her obligations at Constable's increased: she became assistant editor of *The Nineteenth Century and After* and fire-watched from the roof. She was enormously distressed by the German invasions; the deaths of two of her nephews in combat devastated her. As Europe was ravaged, just as Rome had been by the Goths and medieval Britain by the Danes, she found herself translating the very Latin poems—religious rather than secular—that had previously eluded her. She wrote to E. K. Rand: "I have a lot of medieval lyric—of the graver sort—collected, but somehow I can't get the last ounce of courage to get them into a book."[71] The translations, without indication of sources or authors, moldered for decades, some in a box under a leaky cistern.

Eileen Power described *The Wandering Scholars* as "the fruit of wide and solid learning, but it is the fruit of a poet's mind and scholars with poets' minds are rare enough in this wicked world."[72] Waddell's commitment to learning lay in its value for human living. The specialist expertise of the medievalist, meticulous and discriminating, was necessary, priceless, not as an end in itself but as the means to offer a vision of another world still similar, in essentials, to our own. In 1947 she delivered the W. P. Ker lecture, *Poetry in the Dark Ages,* based on the translations of the war years. As she addressed the survivors of war-torn Europe, delving backward through the depredations of Britain by the Danes and of Rome by the barbarians and, through Virgil, to the sack of Troy, she drew on "the obscure poets of an obscure age ... [who] kept the tradition of civilization alive" to show how light came out of darkness, hope out of fear and loss. Their poetry is mostly "sad stuff" and yet "suddenly a lark rises at your feet."[73] The verse she translates proves the point: humane feeling and, thus, poetry survived the sacking of the monasteries, as they did the collapse of Rome and as they would the devastation of Europe.

Waddell's achievement is founded on scholarship. It took an investment of months to plough through the fifty-five volumes of the *Analecta hymnica* to arrive at "a jewel which might otherwise have remained buried ... and has indeed been ignored by modern scholarship."[74] But her training and her inclination were old-fashioned: the point of study was not analysis but appreciation. Opening doors to the uninitiated, penetrating "ancient scroll" and finding there "not dust and bones but warm and breathing men and women," she distanced herself from the academy per se.[75]

She began her career late: it ended early. After the war she began to be troubled by short-term memory loss, which eventually degenerated into a form of dementia. *Stories from Holy Writ,* children's stories she had written years ago in Belfast, was published in 1949. In 1951 Barnard College offered her the first Virginia Greensleeve Fellowship, for six months' lecturing, but she had to decline.[76] At intervals she found the translations of Latin poems she had been working on, surprised at what had been done and forgotten. After her death her niece, Mary Martin, procured the help of Dame Felicitas Corrigan of Stanbrook Abbey, Worcester, who midwifed *More Latin Lyrics* into print in 1976.

For Waddell these poems "are like the inscriptions scratched on dungeon walls or prison windows, the defiance of the spirit of man against material circumstance."[77] Peter Dronke finds in her translations "a beautiful flexibility and sureness in the rhythms, and a keen imaginative penetration of the originals." However, the judgment of the academy remains: the "one real weakness . . . inseparable from Helen Waddell's poetic insight and sense of beauty" is "a certain lack of intellectual rigour."[78]

She died on 5 March 1965 and is buried in Magherally, County Down, Northern Ireland, beside the roofless church in which the grandparents of the Brontë sisters were married. She shares a grave with her mother, whom she lost at the age of two, and her great-grandmother. On her tomb is a line from a ninth-century epitaph, in her translation, in hopeful consolation for the darkness of her last years: "The light is on thy head."[79]

Notes

I should like to thank Mary Martin, Helen Waddell's niece, and Dames Felicitas Corrigan and Philippa Edwards of Stanbrook Abbey, Worcester, for their generosity and help and permission to quote from Helen Waddell's unpublished writings and letters, without which this essay could not have been written. These papers have not been catalogued, so I refer to them by title and/or by correspondent and date (some dates are established by internal evidence only: these are modified by square brackets, while uncertain dates are followed by a question mark). Unless otherwise stated, any reference to unpublished material is to the Helen Waddell Papers, Stanbrook Abbey, Worcester, England.

1. Helen Waddell to George Taylor, 23 March 1919.
2. Helen Waddell to Margaret Martin [1912?].
3. Waddell to Taylor [July/August 1915].
4. Waddell to Margaret Martin [autumn 1913]; Waddell, *Lyrics from the Chinese*.
5. Waddell to Taylor, 18 July, 15 September 1915, and 9 January 1916.
6. Waddell to Taylor [ca. January 1917] and 25 February 1918. Two chapters of this research, "The Thynge Itself" and "The Height of Seneca," survive: see also FitzGerald, "'Jazzing the Middle Ages,'" 11–12.
7. See the manuscript of "Discipline," Waddell Papers, Stanbrook Abbey.
8. Waddell to Taylor, 10 December 1916 (see also 8 June, 26 August, 2 September, and 26 October 1919). In the early 1930s she responded to a rumor that Queen's was about to award her a chair: "They wouldn't dream of giving it to a woman in a college like Queen's, and I can see their point: it's things like Faculty Meetings, Boards of Studies—all that. It cramps their style to have one woman round: they're so used to their half-monastic ways. I didn't realise it younger, but I do now. Maude did, in her brief tenure of the History Chair during the war" (Waddell to Margaret Martin [1933]). "Faculty Meetings" refers to formal meetings of the faculty of arts.
9. Helen Waddell, draft letter to G. G. Coulton [spring 1931]; Waddell to George Saintsbury, 24 October 1923.

10. These lectures were "a 'Owling success. . . . I'd a bigger crowd even that the Astronomer Royal who was giving one of the great fixed lectures last term" (Waddell to Margaret Martin [spring 1926]).

11. Although under financial stress, she would not accept a job involving residential responsibilities (Waddell to Margaret Martin [spring 1923?], [February 1926]). She also turned down the well-paid headship of her old school, Victoria College, Belfast (Waddell to Margaret Martin [spring 1923]), as she had refused £700 per annum (when a chair at Queen's was worth £600) as principal of another school in Belfast (Waddell to Taylor, 14 July, 21 July, and 18 August 1918). For Kyllman's response, see Waddell to Margaret Martin [February 1926].

12. Waddell to Margaret Martin [February 1926?].

13. Waddell to Margaret Martin [6 and 11 May 1926].

14. Waddell to Margaret Martin [May/June 1926?; 22–25 May 1927?].

15. Haskins, *Renaissance of the Twelfth Century* (published a week after *The Wandering Scholars*); Rand, *Founders of the Middle Ages;* and Manitius, *Geschichte der lateinischen Literatur des Mittelalters.*

16. Migne, *Patrologia Cursus Completus . . . Series Latina;* Dümmler et al., *Poetae Latini Aevi Carolini.* Waddell recounts the research she undertook for *The Wandering Scholars* in her draft letter to Coulton [spring 1931].

17. Jones, review of *The Wandering Scholars,* 497–98.

18. Catherine Brown argues the case for "coevalness" in her essay "In the Middle," 559.

19. Waddell to Taylor, 18 May 1918.

20. Waddell, *Wandering Scholars,* 52.

21. See Davies, *Humanism,* 24–25.

22. Waddell, preface to *Medieval Latin Lyrics,* vi.

23. Waddell, *Wandering Scholars,* 79, echoing Arnold, "Study of Poetry," 174.

24. W. J. W., review of *Medieval Latin Lyrics.*

25. Mirsky, review of *Wandering Scholars,* 416.

26. Roberts, review of *Medieval Latin Lyrics*

27. Waddell, preface to *Medieval Latin Lyrics,* vi–vii.

28. Waddell, *Book of Medieval Latin for Schools.*

29. Cole, *Journal of My Journey to Paris in the Year 1765; Blechley Diary of the Rev. William Cole, 1765–67.* In a review of the latter, Virginia Woolf referred to Waddell as "one of the finest scholars of her time" (165).

30. Prévost d'Exiles, *History of the Chevalier des Grieux and of Manon Lescaut.*

31. Waddell, *Abbé Prévost; The Abbé Prèvost* [sic], performed at Croydon Repertory Theatre, 13 May 1935 and Arts Theatre, London, 19–20 May 1935. This was not Waddell's first play, nor was it the first appearance on stage of one of her plays: *The Spoiled Buddha* was performed in the Grand Opera House, Belfast, from 30 January to 5 February 1915 and published by the Talbot Press.

32. Helen Waddell to William Rothenstein [1933?], reprinted in Rothenstein, *Fifty Years Since,* 119. In 1918 she and Maude Clarke were "thinking vaguely of a collaboration in the letters of Heloise and Abelard, translation and preface" (Waddell to Saintsbury, 15 March 1918). Waddell decided to translate "the Abelard letters . . . concurrently" with writing her novel (Waddell to Margaret Martin, 6 November 1931): see the three chapters of Abelard's *Historia calamitatum* [*Story of His Misfortunes*], translated from Migne, in the Waddell Papers, Queen's University

Belfast Library (MS 18/9). After the success of *Peter Abelard* the Greg-y-Nog Press asked her to translate the Heloise-Abelard correspondence for a parallel text limited edition: "I cannot yet make up my mind whether the text shall be Cousin's or whether I shall reproduce 1) the MS in Troyes which is the oldest or 2) the beautiful MS. that belonged to Petrarch" (Waddell to Arundell Esdaile, 6 January 1936). This edition was never prepared.

33. Waddell to Esdaile, 2 September 1936; Abelard and Heloise, *Letters*.

34. See her account of this experience: Blackett, *Mark of the Maker*, 220–21.

35. Waddell to Rothenstein [1933?], reprinted in Rothenstein, *Fifty Years Since*, 120. Rothenstein made errors of transcription ("ending" instead of "evidence"): she corrected these mistakes in her own hand in her copy of his book (photocopy in the possession of Mary Martin).

36. Rothenstein, *Fifty Years Since*, 119.

37. Waddell to Esdaile, 6 January 1936.

38. By the time Waddell wrote *Peter Abelard*, there had been six hundred versions in six hundred years: see Charrier, *Héloïse dans l'histoire et dans la légende*, v.

39. Regarding Heloise's scholarly reputation, see Dronke, *Women Writers of the Middle Ages*, 111–12; Clanchy, *Abelard*, 169–74; Abelard and Heloise, *Lost Love Letters*, 135–39. In medieval ideology even married sex was "conjugal voluptuousness," compromising the purity of the mind, so Abelard's marriage would have fatally undermined his professional and intellectual position (Clanchy, *Abelard*, 46).

40. The composition of these last three works postdate the chronology of Waddell's novel, but the perspective they develop has been traced to ideas that first surface in his correspondence with Heloise (McLaughlin, "Peter Abelard and the Dignity of Women," 331–33; Clanchy, *Abelard*, 278–87). The novel opens with Abelard working on his (now lost) commentary on Ezekiel (Clanchy, *Abelard*, 21).

41. Leclerq, "Modern Psychology and the Interpretation of Medieval Texts," 485 n. For a reading of the novel, see FitzGerald, "'Truth's Martyr or Love's Martyr.'"

42. Waddell, *Peter Abelard*, 152.

43. McLaughlin, "Peter Abelard," 331–33.

44. Waddell, *Peter Abelard*, 291.

45. Abelard and Heloise, *Letters*, 159.

46. See Newman, "Authority, Authenticity, and the Repression of Heloise."

47. Waddell, *Peter Abelard*, 304 (Waddell's italics).

48. Waddell to Margaret Martin [1932].

49. Gould, review of *Peter Abelard*; Pritchett, review of *Peter Abelard*.

50. Gilson, *Heloise and Abelard*, xii.

51. Waddell, *Desert Fathers*, 10, 22.

52. Waddell, *Beasts and Saints*, xi.

53. Allen, review of *The Wandering Scholars*, 109.

54. Waddell, draft letter to Coulton [spring 1931]; Waddell to Margaret Martin [March 1931].

55. Coulton, review of *A History of Late Latin Literature*.

56. Waddell, *Wandering Scholars*, 68.

57. She lamented this deficiency in a letter to Esdaile, 6 January 1936. Her letters to Coulton survive in the form of fragmentary drafts; she also quoted (or perhaps paraphrased) them in letters to her sister (and quoted from his responses).

58. Waddell to Margaret Martin [1931?].

59. Waddell to Margaret Martin [1933?].
60. Corrigan, *Helen Waddell*, 252.
61. Helen Waddell to Enid Starkie [1938?].
62. Note that Tolkien kept his creative writing hidden from his Oxford colleagues (Chance, *Tolkien's Art*, 7–8), while Lewis's fame as a proselytizing Christian writer as well as an author of children's books affected his academic advancement (Hannay, *C. S. Lewis*, 20).
63. Jones, review of *Medieval Latin Lyrics;* see Allen, *Romanesque Lyric.*
64. Helen Waddell to E. K. Rand, 18 November 1934, quoted in Corrigan, *Helen Waddell*, 288.
65. Lowes, *Road to Xanadu*. Lowes was also a fellow of the Medieval Academy. Its founder, Charles H. Haskins, reviewed *The Wandering Scholars,* recommending it "be judged as a literary essay rather than as a piece of historical research" (175).
66. Herford, review of *The Wandering Scholars;* Powicke, review of *The Wandering Scholars,* 298.
67. Corrigan, *Helen Waddell*, 277–78.
68. In 1993 Queen's named one of its visiting professorships, established to promote the participation of women in academic life, after Helen Waddell.
69. Corrigan, *Helen Waddell*, 263. Corrigan suggests that Kyllmann was not reciprocally in love with Waddell, although he stuck faithfully by her as she succumbed to dementia.
70. Quoted in Corrigan, *Helen Waddell*, 340.
71. Waddell to Rand, 4 May 1944, quoted in Waddell, *More Latin Lyrics from Virgil to Milton*, 25.
72. Power, review of *The Wandering Scholars*.
73. Waddell, *Poetry in the Dark Ages*, 3–4, 18–19.
74. Dronke, review of *More Latin Lyrics from Virgil to Milton*.
75. Shackleton, review of *Beasts and Saints*.
76. Corrigan, *Helen Waddell*, 349.
77. Waddell, translator's preface to *More Latin Lyrics*, 37.
78. Dronke, review of *More Latin Lyrics*.
79. Waddell, *Poetry in the Dark Ages*, 19.

SELECT BIBLIOGRAPHY OF WORKS BY HELEN WADDELL

Lyrics from the Chinese. London: Constable, 1913.
The Spoiled Buddha. Dublin: Talbot Press, 1919.
"Lady Mary Wortley Montagu." *Fortnightly Review*, n.s., 108 (1920): 503–14.
The Wandering Scholars. London: Constable, 1927.
"John of Salisbury." *Essays and Studies of the English Association* 13 (1928): 28–51.
Translator. *Medieval Latin Lyrics*. London: Constable, 1929.
The Abbé Prévost. Raven Miscellany. London: Constable, 1931.
A Book of Medieval Latin for Schools. Introduction by M. Dorothy Brock. London: Constable, 1931.
Translator. *The History of the Chevalier des Grieux and of Manon Lescaut,* by the Abbé Prévost d'Exiles. Translated from the original text of 1731 by Helen Waddell with an introduction by George Saintsbury. London: Constable, 1931.
Peter Abelard: A Novel. London: Constable, 1933.
Beasts and Saints: Translations by Helen Waddell. London: Constable, 1934.
The Desert Fathers: Translations from the Latin by Helen Waddell. London: Constable, 1936.

Poetry in the Dark Ages. The Eighth W. P. Ker Memorial Lecture Delivered in the University of Glasgow, 28th October 1947. London: Constable, 1948.
Stories from Holy Writ. London: Constable, 1949.
Translator. *More Latin Lyrics from Virgil to Milton.* Edited by D. Felicitas Corrigan. London: Victor Gollancz, 1976.
Papers of Helen Waddell (MS 18). Library, Queen's University, Belfast, Northern Ireland.
Helen Waddell Papers. Uncataloged letters and manuscripts of Helen Waddell. Stanbrook Abbey, Worcester, England.

Works Cited

Abelard and Heloise. *The Letters of Abelard and Heloise.* Translated by Betty Radice. London: Penguin, 1974.
———. *The Lost Love Letters of Heloise and Abelard: Perceptions of a Dialogue in Twelfth-Century France.* Translated by Neville Chiavaroli and Constant J. Mews. Basingstoke, Eng.: Macmillan, 1999.
Allen, P. S. Review of *The Wandering Scholars,* by Helen Waddell. *Speculum* 3, no. 1 (1928): 109–10.
———. *The Romanesque Lyric: Studies in Its Background and Development from Petronius to the Cambridge Songs, 50–1050,* with renderings into English verse by Howard Mumford Jones. Chapel Hill: University of North Carolina Press, 1928.
Arnold, Matthew. "The Study of Poetry" (1880). In *The Complete Prose Works of Matthew Arnold,* vol. 9, *English Literature and Irish Politics,* edited by R. H. Super. Ann Arbor: University of Michigan Press, 1972.
Blackett, Monica. *The Mark of the Maker: A Portrait of Helen Waddell.* London: Constable, 1973.
Brown, Catherine. "In the Middle." *Journal of Medieval and Early Modern Studies* 30, no. 3 (2000): 547–74.
Chance, Jane. *Tolkien's Art: A Mythology for England.* Rev. ed. Lexington: University of Kentucky Press, 2001.
Charrier, Charlotte. *Héloïse dans l'histoire et dans la légende.* Bibliothèque de la Revue de Littérature Comparée 102. Paris: Librairie Ancienne Honoré Champion, 1933.
Clanchy, M. T. *Abelard: A Medieval Life.* Oxford: Blackwell, 1997.
Cole, William. *The Blechley Diary of the Rev. William Cole, 1765–67.* Edited by Francis Griffin Stokes with an introduction by Helen Waddell. London: Constable, 1931.
———. *A Journal of My Journey to Paris in the Year 1765.* Edited by Francis Griffin Stokes with an introduction by Helen Waddell. London: Constable, 1931.
Corrigan, D. Felicitas. *Helen Waddell: A Biography.* London: Victor Gollancz, 1986.
Coulton, G. G. Review of *A History of Late Latin Literature,* by F. A. Wright and T. A. Sinclair. *The Observer* (London), 8 March 1931.
Davies, Tony. *Humanism.* New Critical Idiom. London: Routledge, 1997.
Dronke, Peter. Review of *More Latin Lyrics from Virgil to Milton,* by Helen Waddell. *Times Literary Supplement,* 17 June 1977, 727.
———. *Women Writers of the Middle Ages: A Critical Study of Texts from Perpetua to Marguerite Porete.* Cambridge: Cambridge University Press, 1984.
Dümmler, Ernst Ludwig, et al., eds. *Poetae Latini Aevi Carolini.* 4 vols. Berlin: Weidmann, 1881–84.

FitzGerald, Jennifer. "'Jazzing the Middle Ages': The Feminist Genesis of Helen Waddell's *The Wandering Scholars.*" *Irish Studies Review* 8, no. 1 (2000): 5–22.

———. "'Truth's Martyr or Love's Martyr': Helen Waddell's *Peter Abelard.*" *Colby Quarterly* 36, no. 2 (2000): 176–87.

Gilson, Etienne. *Heloise and Abelard.* Translated by L. K. Shook. 1938. London: Hollis and Carter, 1953.

Gould, Gerald. Review of *Peter Abelard,* by Helen Waddell. *The Observer* (London), 21 May 1933.

Hannay, Margaret Patterson. *C. S. Lewis.* New York: Frederick Ungar, 1981.

Haskins, Charles H. *The Renaissance of the Twelfth Century.* Cambridge: Harvard University Press, 1927.

———. Review of *The Wandering Scholars,* by Helen Waddell. *American Historical Review* 33 (1927–28): 175–76.

Herford, C. H. Review of *The Wandering Scholars,* by Helen Waddell. *Manchester Guardian,* 12 July 1927.

Jones, Howard Mumford. Review of *Medieval Latin Lyrics,* by Helen Waddell. *Speculum* 6 (1931) 165–67.

———. Review of *The Wandering Scholars,* by Helen Waddell. *Modern Philology* 25 (1928): 497–99.

Leclerq, Jean. "Modern Psychology and the Interpretation of Medieval Texts." *Speculum* 48 (1973): 476–90.

Lowes, John Livingston. *The Road to Xanadu: A Study in the Ways of the Imagination.* 1927. Boston: Houghton Mifflin, 1955.

Manitius, Max. *Geschichte der lateinischen Literatur des Mittelalters.* Vol. 3. Munich: Beck, 1931.

McLaughlin, Mary Martin. "Peter Abelard and the Dignity of Women: Twelfth Century 'Feminism' in Theory and Practice." In *Pierre Abélard, Pierre le Vénérable: Les Courants philosophiques littéraires et artistiques en occident au milieu du XIIe siècle,* edited by René Louis and Jean Jolivet, 287–333. Paris: Edition du Centre National de la Recherche Scientifique, 1975.

Migne, Jacques-Paul, ed. *Patrologia Cursus Completus . . . Series Latina.* 221 vols. Paris: Migne, 1844–66.

Mirsky, D. S. Review of *The Wandering Scholars,* by Helen Waddell. *London Mercury,* 16 August 1927: 409–16.

Newman, Barbara. "Authority, Authenticity, and the Repression of Heloise." *Journal of Medieval and Renaissance Studies* 22, no. 2 (1992): 121–57.

Power, Eileen. Review of *The Wandering Scholars,* by Helen Waddell. *Nation and Athenaeum* 41, no. 19 (13 August 1927): 639.

Powicke, F. M. Review of *The Wandering Scholars,* by Helen Waddell. *Scottish Historical Review* 24 (1927): 298–300.

Prévost d'Exiles, Abbé. *The History of the Chevalier des Grieux and of Manon Lescaut.* Translated from the original text of 1731 by Helen Waddell with an introduction by George Saintsbury. London: Constable, 1931.

Pritchett, V. S. Review of *Peter Abelard,* by Helen Waddell. *New Statesman and Nation,* 27 May 1933.

Rand, E. K. *The Founders of the Middle Ages.* Cambridge: Harvard University Press, 1928.

Roberts, R. Ellis. Review of *Medieval Latin Lyrics,* by Helen Waddell. *Bookman* 77 (February 1930): 298.

Rothenstein, William. *Fifty Years Since: Men and Memories, 1922–1938: Recollections of William Rothenstein.* London: Faber, 1939.

Shackleton, Edith. Review of *Beasts and Saints,* by Helen Waddell. *Time and Tide,* 10 November 1934: 1,427.

W., W. J. Review of *Medieval Latin Lyrics,* by Helen Waddell. *Studies: An Irish Quarterly Review of Letters, Philosophy and Science* 19 (1930): 517.

Woolf, Virginia. Review of *Blechley Diary,* by William Cole. *New Statesman and Nation,* 6 February 1932, 164–65.

CHAPTER 25

"Aimer la musique ancienne"
Yvonne Rihouët Rokseth (1890–1948)

CATHERINE PARSONEAULT

Yvonne Rihouët Rokseth was, according to Leo Schrade, "the first woman ever to teach musicology at a university."[1] A formidable scholar, performer, composer, and teacher, Rokseth was remembered in obituaries after her untimely death in 1948 with the deepest affection and respect by those who had worked with her. A scholar who had a deep commitment to sharing her pleasure in the music of the Middle Ages with everyone—including nonspecialists and children—she is best remembered in academic circles for her magisterial edition of thirteenth-century polyphonic music, *Polyphonies du XIIIe siècle: Le manuscrit H 196 de la faculté de médecine de Montpellier* (Thirteenth-century polyphony: Manuscript H196 from the Medical School of Montpellier) (Paris, 1935–39). Yet her interests encompassed a dauntingly broad array of topics, from Gregorian chant to Edvard Grieg, from musical iconography to Mendelssohn manuscripts. Her lasting influence on our understanding of thirteenth-century musical culture in France and on motet scholarship of the Ars Antiqua cannot be underestimated, even though it has frequently been underutilized.

Yvonne Rihouët was born on 17 July 1890 in Maisons-Lafitte, today a town of some twenty-three thousand, located a few kilometers northwest of Paris along the Seine. The daughter of a lawyer at the *cour d'appel* (appeals court) in Paris, Rihouët began her musical studies at the Paris Conservatory, where she earned her *baccalauréat* (secondary school certificate of completion and university admission) in 1907–8. Possessed of an avid curiosity and energy to match, she proceeded to study science and philosophy at the Sorbonne, earning the *license èssciences* (B.S.) and the *license ès letters* (B.A.) in 1915.[2] Simultaneously she supplemented her education by undertaking further music study at the Schola Cantorum, founded in 1895 by the composer Vincent d'Indy as an

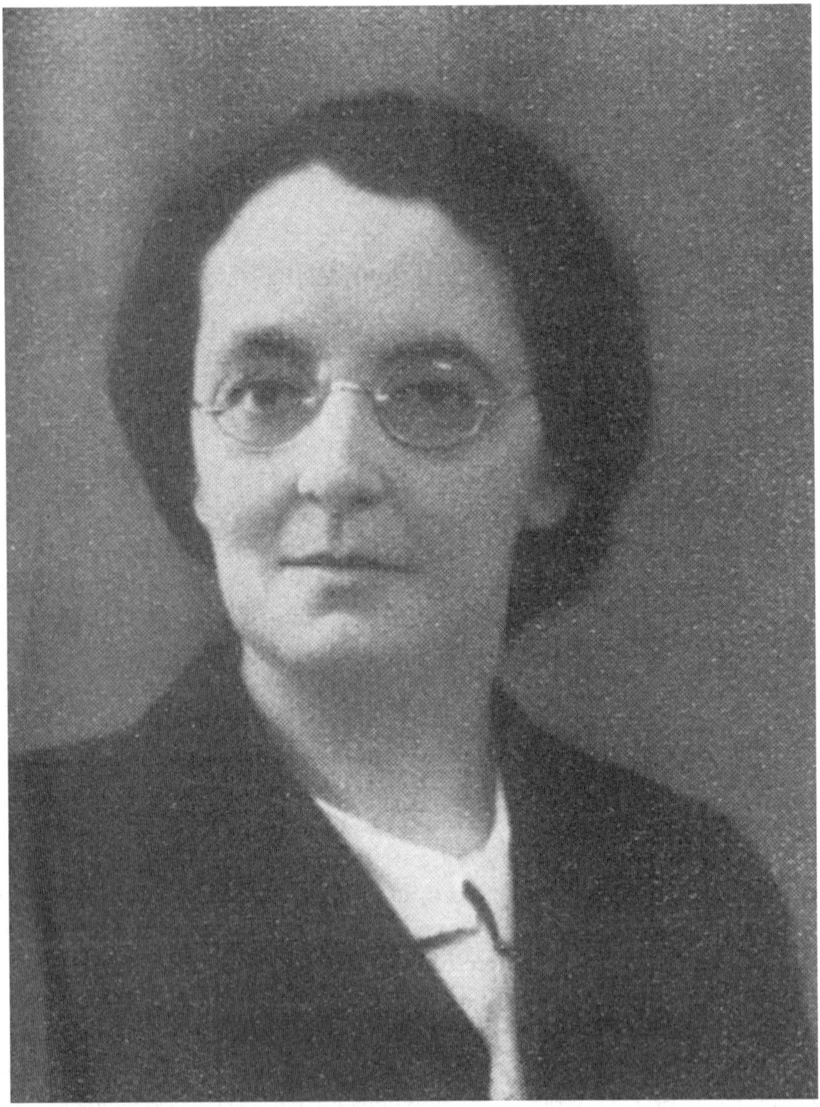

alternative to the more traditional Paris Conservatory. Rihouët studied composition with d'Indy and with Albert Roussel and organ with Abel Decaux.

By the time she completed her doctorate in June 1930, with a dissertation titled "La Musique d'orgue au XVe siècle et au début du XVIe" (Organ music of the fifteenth and early sixteenth centuries), she had established herself not only as a scholar but also as a composer and organist. It is from around the time she began her doctoral studies, back at the Sorbonne, that we find a witness who can give us a more personal idea of Yvonne Rihouët as a student, scholar, and colleague. Most of this information must be gleaned from a single source, the memorial obituary published by Yvonne Rihouët's younger colleague, fellow musicologist, and lifelong friend, Geneviève Thibault (also known as la comtesse de Chambure), in *Revue de musicologie* in 1948.[3]

Thibault recalls that she met Yvonne Rihouët in 1920 when they both enrolled in a seminar taught by André Pirro in the Bibliothèque Pierre Aubry, the music library of the Sorbonne. Every Wednesday afternoon the seminar students—including Geneviève Thibault, Dragan Plamenac, and Yvonne Rihouët—would gather.[4] The musicology students found a true mentor in Pirro, a teacher who encouraged them, challenged them, and evidently delighted them. Lacking photographs of the sixteenth-century incunabula or fifteenth-century manuscripts he wanted to use to teach his students how to decipher the arcane musical notation of the period, Pirro made copies of the sources himself for his students to transcribe, on the backs of the labels taken from bottles of mineral water, so that "it was on the little pink rectangles of Evian-Cachat or the white with blue borders of Source Hépar, that we came to know [the musical appearance of] Dufay, Ockeghem, and Busnois." Each Wednesday one hour was set aside to work over their transcriptions and correct their homework from the past week; another was spent on the writings of medieval music theorists (77).

Yvonne Rihouët had studied organ at the Schola Cantorum, and because Pirro encouraged his students to bring their own interests and lines of inquiry to their work, the selection of her dissertation topic seems to have grown naturally out of his seminar, a combination of her own interests and his focus on the music of the fifteenth and sixteenth centuries. With her topic accepted in 1921, she began her research, working in the archives and at the Bibliothèque nationale, but she found time for a plethora of other musical activities. Still studying composition with Roussel at the Schola Cantorum, she was awarded a prize in 1921 for her *Fantasie* for piano and orchestra.[5] She appears to have supported herself by accepting, at around the same time, the position of organist at the Lutheran Église de la Résurrection. And she began to publish, taking what she was learning in Pirro's seminar and through her dissertation research into the public arena. In 1924 her first short article appeared, followed in 1925 by two editions of sixteenth-century organ pieces and her French translation of Karl Nef's *Geschichte der Musik* (History of music), which she expanded through the addition of numerous musical examples.[6]

Thibault recalled Pirro's approval for Yvonne Rihouët's first publication, observing that "she managed, by felicitous juxtapositions and brilliant images, to make her readers comprehend the component elements and the deep structure of the pieces" (79). According to Thibault, Mlle. Rihouët manifested in these first publications a fundamental characteristic that she never abandoned: "[S]he wanted to be clear and to place everything she knew, everything she perceived, within the reach of everyone" (79).

In 1925, at about the same time that Rihouët published her edition of two organ books originally printed by Pierre Attaignant in 1531, Pirro offered his students a project that kept them very busy for several months. He was preparing an edition of the chansons from a manuscript in the Burgundian archives at Dijon and recruited his graduate students to work over his transcriptions. Almost twenty years later Yvonne Rokseth wrote that Pirro did not trust his own work and that his need for certainty was so great that he delayed publication of the edition, reluctant to take on the responsibility for an interpretation that risked calling for a later revision.[7] Joined by Eugenie Droz, who was entrusted with establishing a definitive critical edition of the chanson texts, Rihouët and Thibault labored at their task, which ultimately produced fifty chansons, only about a quarter of the oeuvre contained in the manuscript Dijon 517.

Rokseth's best-remembered achievement, her critical edition with commentary of the music in the Montpellier Codex (published a decade or more later), was surely possible only because of the careful training and experience she gained in Pirro's seminar projects, particularly the edition of the chansons from MS Dijon 517. Thibault relates that she went often to her friend's "charming little apartment" on the Boulevard Port-Royal, where the two musicologists tried to envision every possible solution to the problems presented by the considerable ambiguities in the musical notation of the chansons, arguing pros and cons of different interpretations, learning through experience the unyielding discipline and rigorous method that infused their final product. The only respite they permitted themselves from their "travail acharné" (fierce labor) was in midafternoon when Yvonne Rihouët's daughter, seven-year-old Odile Ledieu, arrived home from school. Thibault describes Odile as "a thoughtful child with a bright, curious mind" (79–80).

None of the biographical notices or obituaries explains the presence of this little girl in Yvonne Rihouët's life. Odile would have been born around 1918, after Rihouët had completed her undergraduate degrees in 1915, but before she began her doctoral studies in 1921—an almost completely silent part of her personal history (one can surmise that she continued her studies in composition during these years). She had probably not yet met Peter H. Rokseth, the Norwegian literary scholar she would encounter in Paris at the Bibliothèque nationale and whom she would marry in 1925. Thibault certainly does not shed much light on Yvonne Rihouët's earlier years, although she does remark in passing that her father and Yvonne's father had known each other in law school.

Despite previous family acquaintances, however, the two women had met only in Pirro's seminar, and Thibault writes of getting to know Yvonne's father and her sister, Simonne Rihouët-Coroze, while visiting Yvonne Rihouët's home during their collaboration on the edition of the chansons. Simonne was by then a devoted student and advocate of Rudolf Steiner, founder of the anthroposophy movement and the Waldorf School educational system. A year younger than Yvonne, Simonne published several books about Steiner, anthroposophy, and eurhythmics and served as the editor of *Triades: Revue trimestrielle de culture humaine,* a periodical devoted to anthroposophical matters. She lived until 1982 and seems to have continued corresponding and writing until the end of her life.[8]

One wonders whether Steiner's anthroposophic beliefs also affected Yvonne Rihouët. Thibault writes that during the times she spent visiting with her colleague she "realized how many religious and philosophical problems had weighed down upon the youth of Yvonne Rihouët: [I] . . . divined the difficulties of all kinds that [Yvonne] had been required to face, alone." But Thibault did not expand on these dark hints, except to comment that it was in 1925 that, with her marriage to Peter H. Rokseth, her friend finally found the happiness that had thus far eluded her (80).

Marriage certainly did not seem to distract Yvonne Rokseth from her work. On the contrary, she seemed to increase her scholarly activities during the next two years. She continued to work on her dissertation. She revised articles on Gregorian chant, polyphonic music of the Middle Ages and early Renaissance, and organ compositions for the new edition of *Dictionnaire de musique de Riemann.* She provided several reviews for *Revue de musicologie.* She prepared her edition of *Treize motets et un prélude pour orgue chez Pierre Attaignant en 1531* (published in 1930). She went with Thibault to Solesmes to correct the proofs of the long-awaited *Trois chansonniers français du XVe siècle* (80).

The only thing Yvonne Rokseth eventually gave up was her post as organist at the Église de la Résurrection, and that happened only in 1926 or 1927, at the birth of her second daughter, Anne-Cécile. Relinquishing the post of organist made sense because of Rokseth's personal plans—she evidently passed the years between 1927 and 1930 primarily in Norway. In 1927 Peter Rokseth accepted a professorship in the department of Romance languages at the University of Oslo. Fluent in at least five languages, he was a scholar of French in particular, having completed his doctoral studies in 1928 with a dissertation on the works of the French seventeenth-century dramatist Pierre Corneille. He published a Norwegian translation of *Madame Bovary* in 1930.

During this sojourn in Norway Yvonne Rokseth most likely completed work on her dissertation, balancing her work schedule with the needs of her family. She did not enjoy the cold weather, however, and after two winters in Oslo she decided not to endure the season there again but to return to France. After 1930 the marriage, like that of so many other academics, often took place primarily as a long-distance affair, although it seems to have continued as an affectionate one, with Peter Rokseth frequently dividing his time between his work in Oslo and his family in France.[9]

Yvonne Rokseth's own doctoral examinations took place on a hot day in June 1930, according to Thibault, who describes the scene. In the Amphitheater Edgar-Quinet, a committee—consisting of André Pirro from the musicology faculty; Charles Guignebert (1867–1939), history of Christianity; Francis Salet, French medieval art and architecture; Gustave Cohen (1879–1958), medieval literature and drama; and Étienne

Gilson (1884–1978), medieval philosophy—came together to hear the scholar's defense of her research. Rokseth's voice was low and soft, Thibault writes, and "in three quarters of an hour, she made a gripping summary of her work." The committee awarded Rokseth "mention très honorable" for her presentation, and Thibault wryly remarks that she believes Pirro was more pleased with the outcome than the recipient of the award was (80).

With her studies behind her, Rokseth turned her attention to the great century of French musical culture, the Ars Antiqua—the thirteenth century, whose music has been described as "the equivalent in sound of the French cathedral" (81). It was at this time, when she decided to devote herself to the study of the polyphony of the thirteenth century, that Rokseth chose to stop composing music herself. None of her compositions has been published, and in fact, many of them doubtless remain unmentioned and unidentified in the scant literature that exists about her. What little knowledge we do have comes primarily from Thibault's necrology. In addition to the previously mentioned pieces from 1920 and 1921, only one other composition of Rokseth's is known by name, and that one was much later in her life, a *Te Deum* brought about as a jubilant commemoration of the Allied liberation of France and the end of World War II. Of her work between 1921 and 1930, when she ostensibly stopped composing, nothing is known. If Rokseth's compositions do indeed survive in manuscript form, and if they could be located, their study might provide the subject of a graduate thesis or doctoral dissertation.

Thibault says that, above all else, Yvonne Rokseth wanted to teach medieval music. Between 1931 and 1936 she published a series of articles on organ music from the thirteenth through the fifteenth century, but her ambition to enter the classroom did not materialize for several years. Instead, she spent the years 1931 to 1933 traveling, accompanying her husband to Majorca three times and also to The Hague, for Peter Rokseth had been commissioned by the Norwegian government to diplomatic service, charged with the translation from Norwegian into French of documents that his government wanted to present at the International Court of Justice in The Hague. Mme Rokseth, who had mastered Norwegian by this time, worked alongside her husband. Thibault places her in the Hague in autumn of 1931 and back in Norway during the summer of 1932 (80).

In 1933 she published a study of the nationalist Norwegian composer Edvard Grieg, which Thibault says she researched and wrote during that previous summer spent at Hardanger Fjord in the heart of "Grieg country." Thibault puts a good face on a situation that may have played out a bit uneasily. She writes that Rokseth produced "a charming book, full of the Norse poetry about which she was so sensitive, but a brave book, for—having been a historian before she became Norwegian—Yvonne Rokseth had no fear to place Grieg in the position she regarded as his own, and which was not in the foreground [of musical achievement]. In the country of Peter Rokseth, there was great bitterness" (81).

In 1933 Yvonne Rokseth completed additional studies in librarianship. One wonders whether she chose this course because she had not been successful in her quest to secure a teaching position. She was promptly appointed librarian at the Paris Conservatory of Music, however, and immediately began work on a catalog of the autograph manuscripts in the collection. Having the position as librarian at the conservatory must have allowed Rokseth to immerse herself in research as well as in the work of cataloging and compiling bibliographic information about the collection there. She published two articles as a direct result of the project, one on the manuscript holdings of Franz Joseph Haydn (1933) and another on the manuscripts of Felix Mendelssohn (1934). Also in 1933 she published an article about two-part counterpoint "around 1248" (an early indication of her immersion in the sources of thirteenth-century polyphony that would shortly result in her most significant contribution to musical scholarship, her edition of the great Montpellier Codex); a study of Gothic ivory carvings as a source for musical iconography; and a brief survey of fifteenth-century musical instruments in the church.

Rokseth continued to occupy herself with musical matters at the Bibliothèque nationale, "where she laid the organizational basis of the future Department of Music" (82). She organized several concerts of medieval music. She traveled to Germany, visited collections in Munich, Berlin, and Leipzig, and returned to Paris full of resolve to create a national institute for musicology. At the same time, she must have been fully engaged in the enormous project of transcribing the 345 compositions, primarily motets, that filled the delicate vellum folios of the little book known to musicologists simply as the Montpellier Codex.

This deceptively small manuscript, not much larger than a modern paperback book, is the premier collection of the newest and most stylish music of the thirteenth century: the motet. A beautifully decorated little book, alive with gold-limned illuminations, luxuriously decorated letters, and lavishly pen-flourished initials, the Montpellier Codex was originally made in Paris but had found its way to Dijon by the seventeenth century, and it has been in the possession of the Bibliothèque Interuniversitaire of the University of Montpellier since Napoleonic times. It has been studied, since the mid-nineteenth century, by literary scholars, paleographers, art historians, and music historians, but when Rokseth undertook her project the music had not yet been transcribed or offered in a modern performing edition.

It is not clear just how Yvonne Rokseth got the idea for such an ambitious project, or how she went about the work of transcribing the compositions. The manuscript was housed in Montpellier. Did she spend time in that city to inspect the manuscript itself? Was it already at the publishing house of l'Oiseau-Lyre, perhaps to be photographed? Was it entrusted to Rokseth herself in Paris? We do not know. Among the people she thanked in her acknowledgments, not a single reference is to anyone in Montpellier appears.

However she gained access to the book, Rokseth performed a remarkable feat of research and scholarship. The first volume of *Polyphonies du XIIIe siècle* appeared in 1935 and consisted of a photographic sepia-tone facsimile of the entire manuscript.

The next two volumes appeared in 1936, and these included the transcriptions of every piece in the manuscript. The fourth volume of the set was ready for publication in 1939, but its appearance was delayed until 1948, one of the casualties of the Second World War. Volume 4 consisted of Rokseth's commentary on the manuscript, a brilliant piece of work in every regard—comprehensive, rigorous, innovative, and unquestionably musical in every respect. In June 1948 *Polyphonies du XIIIe siècle* was honored by the Institute of France with the first ever Médaille du Concours des Antiquités de la France.

Her studies in the thirteenth century were not limited to the Montpellier Codex nor to music manuscripts. In 1935, as the first volume of *Polyphonies du XIIIe siècle* was going to press, she published a groundbreaking article concerning female musicians of the twelfth through the fourteenth centuries. A comprehensive study of literary and historical sources, the article chronicled medieval women participating in the performance as well as the enjoyment of music.[10] The study seems to have been overlooked entirely by historians of music as well as by cultural historians and interdisciplinarians in women's studies. Yet Rokseth documented primary-source information about both noble and bourgeois women listening to and taking part in musical performances—information that is just now beginning to have an effect on research concerning the performance and reception of music by women in the French Gothic era.[11]

In 1936 Yvonne and Peter Rokseth welcomed another daughter, whom they named Eve-Marie. Rokseth carried on with her research, preparing several articles that would appear in 1937 on topics from the Middle Ages to the Baroque. And in 1937 she finally secured a faculty position at the University of Strasbourg. Perhaps her recent publication of the Montpellier Codex had brought her to the notice of the university, for the manuscript had been studied during the nineteenth century by the first chair of musicology there, the medievalist Gustav Jacobsthal. Rokseth was added to the music faculty with the title "maître de conferences," although she also served on the faculties of Protestant theology and of literature, teaching church music of the Reformation as well as the medieval topics that had become her specialty.

The Alsace was overrun early in the Second World War, and when Strasbourg fell to the Germans, the entire university moved itself to Clermont-Ferrand, the capital of Auvergne. From 1939 until 1943 Rokseth conducted her teaching and research as part of the university-in-exile. She contributed much energy to activities that doubtless helped re-create a sense of community among the faculty and students who had been recently uprooted. In 1939, while reestablishing her courses and adjusting to the new surroundings, she started a university chorale. Thibault writes that in a city that did not have much cultivated music Yvonne Rokseth prevailed upon all kinds of willing volunteers. By 1940 she had gathered together a group of some eighty choristers and instrumentalists, students, civilians, and military personnel alike (83). In the fall of 1942 she organized a series of chamber music concerts, the Cercle Musical Universitaire. Once a month an audience of around 150 heard performances of Mozart and Beethoven string quartets, songs by Henri Duparc, and works of César Franck.

Rokseth played viola and directed the performances herself, often lecturing about the compositions from the podium or accompanying the vocalists on the piano. She began new research on the music of the Reformation and undertook a study of the choral genre called the Passion (83).

As much as she cultivated a sense of community within the university, Rokseth also demonstrated her commitment to the clandestine community that was the wartime Resistance. She offered fugitive students, those "outlaws" (Jewish students? other members of the Resistance?) who were being hunted by the Nazis, sanctuary in her own apartment. She helped distribute secret leaflets and allowed a radio transmitting post to be stationed in her home—all, Thibault writes, with the calm tranquility that was so natural for her (83). She was eventually decorated by the French government for her efforts.

These activities must have come with an enormous personal risk to Rokseth and her children. Her husband had returned to Norway in 1939 and spent the duration of the war there, but her two younger daughters were with her in Clermont. Her eldest child, Odile, had married the musicologist Guillaume de Van and was with him in Paris. De Van, an American citizen born in Tennessee, had cultivated his French persona assiduously. During the war years he was in charge of the music department at the Bibliothèque nationale, a position that ostensibly was available only to French citizens. De Van was an enthusiastic collaborator with the Nazis in their efforts to confiscate musical instruments, materials, and manuscripts, as well as to identify Jewish musicians in Paris. So egregious was de Van's cooperation with the *Sonderstab Musik* that he was eventually arrested and taken into custody by the Vichy government, and he spent time during the latter months of the war, ironically, confined at Clermont-Ferrand. De Van's spectacular collusion has been chronicled as a case study in Willem de Vries's book on the subject of culture theft during the Third Reich.[12]

Rokseth had apparently gotten along well with her son-in-law before the war. In 1938 she referred the American musicologist Pauline Alderman to de Van to research French lute music and the *air du cour*. Alderman had met de Van previously in Paris, where he had advised her regarding the research topics she could pursue by using materials in the collections at the Bibliothèque nationale. Alderman registered for doctoral study at the University of Strasbourg, however, and studied French with Rokseth so she would be competent to take her examinations in that language. Even after she returned to Paris, Alderman reported to Rokseth once a month. By August 1939 Americans were directed to leave Paris. Alderman received an invitation to join Rokseth in Clermont, but the visit did not materialize, and she returned to New York in November.[13]

In addition to referring at least one student his way, Rokseth also took note of Guillaume de Van in her article titled "Musical Scholarship in France during the War," translated into English and published in 1946 in the *Journal of Renaissance and Baroque Music* (later *Musica Disciplina*). She reports that de Van organized a series of concerts in Paris, and she lists the composers of the music he selected for performance. Did she know of his collusion with the Nazis? How close could she have been to him during the war? And what of her daughter Odile?

Yvonne Rokseth's courage, Thibault reports, "never wavered" (83). Even as she assisted so many others, she also did what she could to see to it that her daughters, Anne-Cécile and Eve-Marie, did not suffer, and Thibault says that she "scoured the countryside" to provide for them. She wanted to create a secure home for the girls, so that they would, Thibault wrote, have good memories of their exile (83). Sadly, Odile died in August 1943 in Paris, leaving a six-year-old son.[14] How and when Yvonne Rokseth learned of her eldest child's death is not known.

On 25 November 1943 the Germans descended on the university in Clermont. Rokseth was able to avoid being taken and managed to get to Paris, where she lived in hiding until the liberation of Paris in late August 1944. She and her husband were finally reunited in July 1945, for the first time in almost six years. Yvonne Rokseth was back in Clermont by then, and it was there that she composed her celebratory *Te Deum* for choirs, soloists, organ, string orchestra, two trumpets, and tympani, dedicating the work to General Leclerc (84). The family returned to Strasbourg in August, and Peter Rokseth returned to Oslo shortly thereafter.

Yvonne Rokseth undertook the reconstruction of her life and career with characteristic energy and zest. Now a full professor, she worked hard at reestablishing the Institute for Musicology, and her library experience stood her in good stead as items packed away from the German incursions were restored to use. In November she received the news that her husband had died in Oslo. Thibault says that, despite her grief, Rokseth threw herself into her work (84). She occupied herself with her teaching and scholarly activity, continuing research on the history of Protestant music and on the Passion. She spoke at conferences and continued to organize musical performances.

Thibault went to visit Rokseth in June 1948 and found her characteristically overscheduled, full of enthusiasm for her teaching, her students, her research, and the concerts she was organizing, directing, and guiding. She was full of plans, and the two women agreed to meet again in the autumn. Then, on 23 August Yvonne Rokseth died suddenly. Pauline Alderman suggested that she may have died of a heart attack, "probably brought on by her problems during World War II."[15] She left behind her two young daughters and a body of incomplete research; Schrade voiced the hope, in his memorial article (1949), that one or more scholars would step forward to complete her unfinished work. Thibault, too, called for the students Rokseth had left behind to rally and dedicate themselves to realizing her dream of fine editions of the music of the thirteenth, fourteenth, and fifteenth centuries. "I believe that this would be the most beautiful monument that one could raise in memory of Yvonne Rokseth," she wrote, "the only one worthy of her" (85).

And yet Yvonne Rokseth offered her own memorial, one that spreads her legacy much farther than the academic circles Thibault and Schrade admonished. In an article published posthumously, titled "Aimer la musique ancienne" (Enjoying old music), Rokseth invites every person who has appreciated the architecture of the cathedral of Notre Dame, the paintings of Giotto, the tapestries of Jean de Bondol, the illuminated pages of manuscripts, to undertake the same exploration of the music of the medieval period. She concludes with a plea to bring this vanished art back to sound and life, not as an artifact, but for what listening to and appreciating early music could offer to the aesthetic development of the modern age: "The stiffness of routine is vanquished. The broadening [of awareness] proceeds best in two directions. A give-and-take between the present and the remote past is the most reliable agent of artistic feelings. The simple white ribbon of a route [through time] makes our heart pound when we dream about the traffic of the crowds that have flowed along that highway. That is the miracle of 'rediscovered times.' Let us not deprive ourselves of such lofty delights."[16]

Notes

1. Leo Schrade, "Yvonne Rokseth: In Memoriam," *Journal of the American Musicological Society (JAMS)* 2 (1949): 171–74.

2. Vladimir Fédorov says that Rokseth earned these degrees, plus the *diplôme d'études supérieures* (an advanced degree, sometimes defined as a master's degree), before completing her doctorate ("André Pirro [1869–1943] und Yvonne Rokseth [1890–1948]").

3. Thibault, "Yvonne Rokseth" (hereafter cited in text by page number). The article consists of Thibault's memoir and an extensive bibliography of Yvonne Rokseth's work that was compiled shortly after her death by the musicologist François Lesure. The bibliography was translated into German for inclusion in Fédorov's article in *Die Musikforschung* but has not yet been presented in English. Thibault's contribution, only nine pages long but packed with lively details that illuminate Yvonne Rokseth's personal history better than any other source, has led the present author to raise numerous additional questions about Rokseth's life and work. Its significance for shaping the present essay cannot be underestimated, and the debt owed to Thibault is enormous. Unless otherwise stated, the personal details of Yvonne Rokseth's life included in this essay are derived from information in Thibault's article. Direct quotations are cited in the text by the relevant page number. (N.B.: All translations of direct quotations from the original French of the article into English are this author's.)

4. Thibault mentions only one other young man in her account of the seminar students. She does not name him but says he soon left Paris to teach literature elsewhere (76).

5. Thibault identifies the prize as "*le prix de 'l'aide aux femmes de professions liberals*'" (78).

6. Rihouët's first article was "Un Motet de Moulu et ses diverses transcriptions pour orgue," 286–92. (N.B.: It was at about this time that Geneviève Thibault also began publishing. Her career as a musicologist was quite distinguished and would provide another interesting research topic.)

7. Rokseth, "André Pirro."

8. Georg Kühlewind, another notable anthroposophist, wrote in a letter published in *Stages of Consciousness* that he first corresponded with Mme Rihouët-Coroze in 1979, when she contacted him about translating his book, *Becoming Aware of the Logos*, into French. See http://www.anthropress.org/BooksPages/Kuhlewind.htm (as of 20 September 2002).

9. Tønnessen, "Peter H. Rokseth: Blinderns bannerfører." "I Frankrike traff han sin kommende kone, Yvonne Richouët, som var musikkhistoriker og senere professor i Strasbourg.

Med familie i Strasbourg og arbeid i Oslo, levde Rokseth på mange måter et splittet liv med mye reising mellom Norge og Frankrike."
10. Rokseth, "Les femmes musiciennes du XIIe au XIVe siècle."
11. Parsoneault, "Montpellier Codex."
12. de Vries, *Sonderstab Musik*.
13. Finger, "Pauline Alderman: Musicologist, Teacher, Composer: Part I."
14. de Vries, *Sonderstab Musik*, 203–5.
15. Alderman, "Four Generations of Women in Musicology."
16. Rokseth, "Aimer la musique ancienne."

Select Bibliography of Works by Yvonne Rihouët Rokseth

A bibliography of Yvonne Rokseth's publications was compiled by the French musicologist François Lesure shortly after Rokseth's death in 1948. It was published along with Geneviève Thibault's necrology and was translated into German for inclusion in Victor Fédorov's article about Pirro and Rokseth (1949). The bibliography has never been translated into English. The following list does not duplicate Lesure's work, for it is a selected bibliography, not as comprehensive as the earlier one. It also omits some forty reviews that appeared in various publications between 1925 and 1947.

"Note biographique sur Attaignant." *Revue de Musicologie* 10 (May 1924): 70–71.
"Un Motet de Moulu et ses diverses transcriptions pour orgue." In *Bericht über den musikwissenschaftlichen Kongress in Basel*, [no editor], Proceedings of the Musicological Congress in Basel, 26–29 September 1924. Leipzig: Breitkopf und Härtel, 1925.
Deux livres d'orgue parus chez Pierre Attaignant en 1531, transcripts et publiés avec une introduction. Publications de la Société française de musicologie, 1st ser., vol. 1. Paris: Droz, 1925.
Trois chansonniers français du XVe siècle. 1st fasc. Paris: Droz, 1927. Documents artistiques du XVe siècle, in collaboration with Eugenie Droz and Geneviève Thibault.
La Musique d'orgue au XVe siècle et au début du XVIe. Paris: Droz, 1930. (Ph.D. diss., University of Paris, 1930.)
Histoire de la musique: Edition française augmentée de nombreux exemples... Préface de M. André Pirro. Edited by Charles Nef. Paris: Payot, 1925;2d ed., with further augmentation, Paris: Payot, 1931.
Treize motets et un prelude pour orgue parus chez Pierre Attaignant en 1531, édités avec une introduction et les originaux des motets. Publications de la Société française de musicologie, 1st ser., 5. Paris: Droz, 1930.
"Une Source peu étudie d'iconographie musicale." *Revue de musicologie* 46 (May 1933): 74–85.
"Le Contrepoint double vers 1248." In *Mélanges de musicologie offerts à M. L. de la Laurentie*, Publications de la Société française de musicologie, 2d ser., vols. 3 and 4. Paris: Droz, 1933.
Grieg. Les maîtres de la musique, no. 13. Paris: Rieder, 1933.
Motets à jouer sur le pipeau: Six pieces inédites à deux parties recueillies et transcrites. Paris: l'Oiseau-Lyre, 1934.
"Les Femmes musiciennes du XIIe au XVe siècle." *Romania* 61 (1935): 464–80.
Polyphonies du XIIIe siècle: Le Manuscript H 196 de la Faculté médecine de Montpellier. 4 vols. Paris: l'Oiseau-Lyre, 1935–39.
Motets du XIIIe siècle. Paris: l'Oiseau-Lyre, 1936.
Lamentation de la Vierge au pied de la Croix: XIIIe siècle: Chant seul. Paris: l'Oiseau-Lyre, 1937.

"Antonio Bembo, Composer to Louis XIV." Translated from the French by Gustav Reese. *Musical Quarterly* 23, no. 2 (April 1937): 147–69.

"Les 'Laude' et leur édition par M. Liuzzi." *Romania* 65 (1939): 383–94.

"André Pirro." *Revue de musicologie* 23 (1944): 25–42.

"Musical Scholarship in France during the War." *Journal of Renaissance and Baroque Music* (later *Musica Disciplina*) 1, no. 1 (March 1946): 81–84.

"Un 'Magnificat' de Marc-Antoine Charpentier († 1704)." *Journal of Renaissance and Baroque Music* (later *Musica Disciplina*) 1, no. 3 (December 1946): 192–99.

"Réaction de la Réforme contre certains elements realists du culte." *Revue d'histoire et de philosophie religieuses* 2 (1946): 146–59.

"Dances cléricales du XIIIe siècle." *Études historiques,* fasc. 106 (1947). In *Mélanges* 1945, Publication of the Faculty of Literature at Strasbourg, fasc. 106. Paris: Belles Lettres, 1946–47.

"La Polyphonie parisienne du treizième siècle: Étude critique à propos d'une publication récente." *Les Cahiers techniques de l'art* (Strasbourg), 1, 2d fasc. (May–December 1947): 33–47.

"Aimer la musique ancienne." *Polyphonie* 3 (1949): 5–11 (posthumous).

Works Cited

Alderman, Pauline. "Four Generations of Women in Musicology." *Journal of the International Congress on Women in Music* 1 (June 1985): 1–13. Available at http://music.acu.edu/www/iawm/articles/csunpapers/alderman.html (as of 20 September 2002).

de Vries, Willem. *Sonderstab Musik: Music Confiscation by the Einsatzstab Reichsleiter Rosenberg under the Nazi Occupation of Western Europe.* Amsterdam: Amsterdam University Press, 1996.

Fédorov, Vladimir. "André Pirro (1869–1943) und Yvonne Rokseth (1890–1948)." *Die Musikforschung* 2 (1950): 106–19.

Finger, Susan. "Pauline Alderman: Musicologist, Teacher, Composer: Part I." *Journal of the International Congress on Women in Music* 1 (June 1985): 14–23. Available at http://music.acu.edu/www/iawm/articles/csunpapers/finger.html (as of 20 September 2002).

Kühlewind, Georg. *Stages of Consciousness.* Herndon, Va.: Lindisfarne Books, 1984.

Parsoneault, Catherine. "The Montpellier Codex: Royal Influence and Musical Taste in Late Thirteenth-Century Paris." Ph.D. dissertation, University of Texas at Austin, 2001.

Schrade, Leo. "Yvonne Rokseth: In Memoriam." *Journal of the American Musicological Society* (JAMS) 2 (1949): 171–74.

Thibault, Geneviève. "Yvonne Rokseth." *Revue de musicologie* 27 (1948): 76–90.

Tønnessen, Marianne. "Peter H. Rokseth: Blinderns bannerfører." *Apollon: Tidsskrift fra Universitetet i Oslo* (Apollon: Science and research magazine from the University of Oslo, Electronic Magazine) 8, no. 2 (1997), n.p. Available at http://www.apollon.uio.no/apollon02-97/rokseth.html (as of 7 October 2002).

Additional Sources about Yvonne Rihouët Rokseth

Davies, Hugh. "Rokseth [née Rihouët], Yvonne." In *The New Grove Dictionary of Music and Musicians,* 2d ed., edited by. Stanley Sadie and executive editor John Tyrrel. New York: Grove, 2001.

Fitzsimmons, Patricia Sue. "A Translation of Yvonne Rokseth's *La Musique d'Orgue au XVe Siècle et au Début du XVIe* Together with a Commentary." D.M.A. treatise, University of Rochester, 1978.

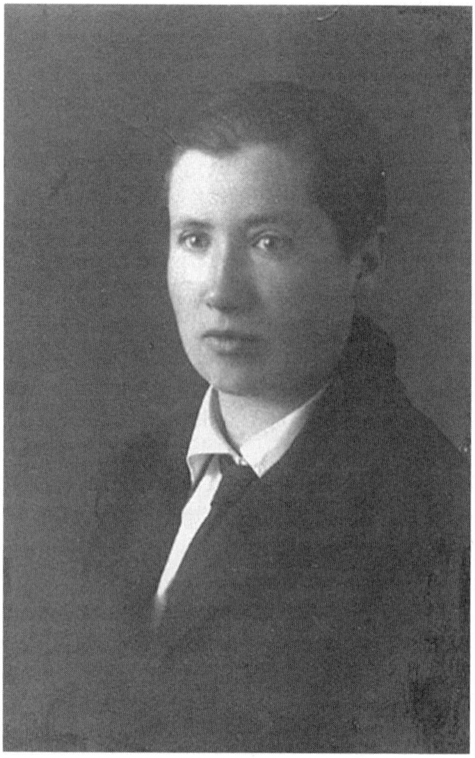

CHAPTER 26

The German Historian Elisabeth Busse-Wilson (1890–1974)
Academic Feminism and Medieval Hagiography, 1914–1931

ULRIKE WIETHAUS

Introduction

ELISABETH BUSSE-WILSON, born on 19 February 1890 in Sondershausen (Thuringia) as the daughter of a well-to-do legal administrator, belonged to the remarkable first generation of German women to pursue an academic education. Busse-Wilson studied history, art history, social sciences, and ethnography at several prominent German universities, and she received her doctorate in Leipzig in 1914. At the age of forty-one and with an impressive publication record to her name, yet without a secure university position, Busse-Wilson entered the stage of historiographical battles and feminist debates with a study of her namesake, Saint Elisabeth of Thuringia (1207–31).[1] Although her study won national acclaim both inside and outside the academy, the rise of the Nazi regime to power prohibited any prospect of an academic career. One year after her less-than-glamorous graduation, Elisabeth Wilson married Dr. Kurt Busse, like herself a social reformer and activist. She gave birth to her only child, Konrad, in 1929. She left her husband in 1938, but she did not remarry. In addition to her work as an independent scholar, Busse-Wilson worked as a teacher at the progressive Hermann-Lietz-Schule in Haubinda, Thuringia, and, during the war years, at a similar school in Gaienhofen, Bodensee. She also pursued a productive career as a journalist and feminist social activist. Most of her publications between 1914 and 1931 analyze contemporary feminist and social reform issues.[2] In 1933, two years after the publication of her study on Saint Elisabeth, intended in part also as a *Habilitationsschrift* (the entry requirement for a permanent academic post), Busse-Wilson applied for a position in the Department of History at the Pädagogische Akademie in Dortmund; as was to be expected in the increasingly repressive political climate, she was rejected because of her gender as much as because of her political views.

Despite her significant contributions to the women's movement and medieval studies, Busse-Wilson was unable to reenter academic life after the war. Franz-Josef Wehnes, a personal acquaintance of Busse-Wilson since his own years as a graduate student, noted her growing isolation after World War II. She lived in Überlingen, then in Bad Godesberg—near the postwar capital of Germany, Bonn—and died in Oberursel, Taunus, on 11 November 1974. Wehnes testified to her intellectual acumen and intense interest in culture, history, and politics, which she retained until her last days. Her unpublished papers contain a book-length biographical study of another remarkable German iconoclast, the religious poet and writer Annette von Droste-Hülshoff (1797–1848).[3]

The year 1931 marked the seven-hundred-year anniversary of the death of Saint Elisabeth of Thuringia, the most important female saint in Germany, associated especially with hospital care and nursing. To coincide with the nationwide celebrations, Busse-Wilson published a biography of Saint Elisabeth in the same year, *Das Leben der Heiligen Elisabeth von Thüringen: Das Abbild einer mittelalterlichen Seele.* The study came to be regarded, at least by some notable historians, as the most significant scholarly contribution to Saint Elisabeth studies in the twentieth century.[4]

Busse-Wilson could draw on the critically edited primary sources on Elisabeth's canonization process by the eminent expert on Saint Elisabeth, Albert Huyskens (1879–1956), published in 1908. Given the violent rejection of the study by several of her colleagues, it is important to note that Huyskens himself supported Busse-Wilson's interpretation in no uncertain terms. In his view Busse-Wilson set out to correct "naive" and "sentimental" Catholic and scholarly representations of Saint Elisabeth as a kind and loving healer and helper.[5] Busse-Wilson's stance was strongly and self-consciously feminist. She dismantled Saint Elisabeth's saintliness as an ideal formed by contemporary masculine concepts of female psychology, all too narrow and restrictive in its turn-of-the-century patriarchal deformity. As she put it with considerable criticism, "[T]he ideal female type must by all means be motherly and [elevated] on a pedestal."[6]

Underneath a sexist patina Busse-Wilson's feminist eye found instead the figure of an intensely self-destructive young woman. Rather than lauded as an expression of maternal nurture, Saint Elisabeth's religious commitments became redefined as the suicidal determination to seek out illness and early death. In such lethal devotional impulse the individual Saint Elisabeth manifested the collective ideological contribution of medieval Christian sainthood to Western civilization; in Busse-Wilson's view, "the Christian legend has only one standard for greatness: heroic suffering."[7] But her insubordinate rewriting of a popular devotional icon did not stop with the invocation of female self-annihilation. Perhaps German audiences would have forgiven Busse-Wilson's charges of saintly masochism if she had not pointed her finger at larger social and religious values and institutions that still existed in 1931, which she saw as having actively conspired in the demise of the young female saint, forces that thus stood accused of abuse if not murder.

Busse-Wilson proposed that Elisabeth's radical identification with the Christian ideal of self-immolation, consummated in her premature death, was shaped by a conservative social and religious system wary of female independence. Elisabeth's Franciscan ideals were shunned by her status-conscious and cynical aristocratic relatives; as a young and defenseless widow, she then had to submit to the brutal guardianship of her confessor, the inquisitor Konrad of Marburg.[8] In the hands of a feminist historian the icon of German Catholic femininity thus revealed a sinister class- and gender-driven dimension: that of a young woman struggling to move beyond the confines of class-specific expectations and norms, victimized and driven into suicide by church authorities and social convention, goaded on the path of self-destruction by a sadistic representative of ecclesial power and doctrinal rectitude, whose cruelty remained unchecked until he challenged a male member of the noble class.

Gender and the Academy in Germany, 1914–1931

No less a public figure than Nobel laureate Hermann Hesse (1877–1962) underscored the iconoclastic character of Busse-Wilson's bold perspective. His assessment, however, ultimately reinforced her marginal status as a female scholar in the German academy; although Busse-Wilson intended her study of one individual woman as paradigmatic of larger social patterns, Hesse read it as the description of an idiosyncratic chain of unfortunate events and personal chemistry, as an exceptional story that precisely because of its focus on gender and its female authorship lacked "universal," that is, "masculine," valence and relevance. In a mix of admiration and an *ad feminam* effort to contain the book's implications for indicting still present oppressive sexist structures in the construction of female sainthood, religious practice, and historiographical work, Hesse concluded, "[U]nfortunately, a not really beautiful biography has emerged, because the descriptive ability of the female author is weaker than the analytical. Yet an interesting, highly unusual book it became nonetheless: a very astute and yet lovingly observed history of a soul, with a special analytical focus on the relationship of the saint to her dreadful demon and confessor Konrad."[9] In contrast, the comments of another German-culture critic and member of the literati, Thomas Mann (1875–1955), like Hesse a recipient of the Nobel Prize in literature, welcomed Busse-Wilson's innovative approach in a less ambivalent vein. Unfortunately, his comments were not circulated publicly. Mann thus wrote in a personal letter to Busse-Wilson, "I admire the book. Uncannily and movingly, the Middle Ages become alive in its generously misled humanity, and the fate of the poor [and] pale dynastic children has probably never been perceived with greater forcefulness. Let me add that I find the pages on Konrad of Marburg exciting. And let me express to you my respect for the mental energy and courage with which you criticize with irony [*ironisieren*] snobbish notions of civilization."¹⁰

Not "really" beautiful then, this daring debut of a German feminist historiography of the medieval past, but still somehow beautiful nonetheless: despite academic marginalization, both the life and the work of Busse-Wilson were marked by the uncommon beauty of courage, the risk of interdisciplinary thinking, and the avant-garde aesthetics of feminist naming and analysis. By today's standards of a successful academic career, the impact of her magnum opus on the study of medieval women has been minimal, and Busse-Wilson's own effort to secure work and academic respectability within the German university system ended in failure. In the context of her times, however, such failure was the norm. Women who had completed their graduate work were not expected to break into the male ranks of academic luminaries and be able to compete or even flourish on an equal footing. Popular prejudice even feared that too much intellectual activity would spoil a woman's nurturing abilities as a mother and spouse—hence perhaps Hesse's indictment of Busse-Wilson's overly developed analytical perspective.¹¹ Busse-Wilson's social activism as a progressive teacher and writer and her social democratic politics provided additional nails for her academic coffin. In 1933, two years after the publication of her Saint Elisabeth study, Busse-Wilson was denied an academic position in the history department at the Dortmunder Pädagogische Akademie. Although she continued to write and engage in research after World War II, her life as a publicly active intellectual and productive historian of German women's *Kulturgeschichte* (the interdisciplinary historiography of world cultures) was over by the beginning of World War II.

From the onset of her graduate studies, Busse-Wilson fit Antonio Gramsci's notion of the "new" intellectual, who does not mediate hegemonic interests of the state but chooses "active participation in practical life, as constructor, organizer, 'permanent persuader.'"¹² Her experience of belonging to the first wave of female graduate students who could enter universities in tandem with their male peers radicalized Busse-Wilson's political views and academic philosophy.¹³ During her student years she became active in a progressive wing of the German youth movement, which stressed radical gender equality and promoted the full professional development of women.¹⁴ Academic work and social activism in the youth movement influenced and enriched each other. Both offered Busse-Wilson the conceptual tools to analyze her own status as a female scholar and, by extension, the status of women in a patriarchal society in general. As she reminisced much later in life, "[T]o have been an academic then meant a lot, to have been a woman nothing."¹⁵

Busse-Wilson's graduate studies in history, ethnography, social sciences, and art history were undertaken at universities in Jena, Bonn, Munich, and Leipzig. She received her doctorate in Leipzig five years before German women gained political suffrage.¹⁶ Busse-Wilson remarked that after she had passed her dissertation exams, "none [of the professors] congratulated [her]. [She] felt again that the leaders of the university only saw . . . academic women as an increase of their own workload. . . . They took very little personal interest in [them], not even curiosity."[17] This utter lack of personal mentoring and attention was especially detrimental to German students. As is still largely true today, the German university system fostered academic careers through intense attachments to a so-called *Doktorvater* (the academic mentor of a Ph.D. candidate), whose responsibility it was to place his favorite students in desirable academic positions.[18]

In terms of historiographical reflection and debate in Germany, Busse-Wilson was already used to controversy before the 1931 publication of her book on Saint Elisabeth. The University of Leipzig was at the center of heated debates about historical method. Since 1909 it had hosted the Royal Saxon Institut für Kultur- und Universalgeschichte, established by the brilliant but controversial cultural historian Karl Lamprecht.[19] Remarkably innovative, the institute set as its goal to study patterns of world history and culture and to integrate tenets of and research in progressive pedagogy.[20] Foreshadowing Busse-Wilson's own struggles, Lamprecht's pedagogical ideas and theoretical approaches to cultural historiography were furiously divisive and finally led to his isolation and vitriolic condemnation by colleagues. Busse-Wilson's work on Saint Elisabeth represents a self-conscious critical departure from an overemphasis in Lamprecht's Institut für Kultur- und Universalgeschichte on the achievements of (male) genius, whether in politics, the history of states, or the arts.[21]

Busse-Wilson approached the study of medieval hagiography from a position of a strongly developed feminist consciousness rooted in both social activism and intellectual reflection and nurtured by a sense of personal accomplishment and growth beyond gendered barriers, especially in her career as a freelance writer and leader in the youth movement. The provocative and innovative analysis of Saint Elisabeth's personality and cultural and religious context became possible because of Busse-Wilson's many years of experience as a public intellectual and activist. It provided her with the opportunity to reflect on and understand clearly the debilitating effects of female socialization into subservient roles and women's educational, political, and economic second-class status in a male-dominated contemporary Germany.

As she noted in her autobiographical sketch, Busse-Wilson's difficult experiences as a female graduate student led to an ethical commitment and sense of solidarity with "all human beings who had to work themselves out of any kind of ghetto into the light."[22] According to Magdalena Musial, her intellectual and personal elaboration of such an ethics of solidarity developed in three distinct stages in regard to feminism, beginning with her years as a university student: first, a critique and rejection of traditional female social roles and behavior as demeaning and alienated; second, the effort to articulate and emulate admirable masculine traits such as personal independence and self-confidence; and third, after 1925, the challenge to name and shape specifically feminine traits and attitudes from a position of strength, female self-confidence, and legal equality with men.[23]

The Study of Women in Nineteenth- and Early-Twentieth-Century German Historiography

Busse-Wilson's contributions to feminist historiography did not occur, of course, in a vacuum. Writing the biography of a striking female figure such as Saint Elisabeth of Thuringia was a common strategy female historians used to write women back into history. In a survey of mostly British historiography and its treatment of women's issues, Billie Melman noted that the proper historical subject for nineteenth-century historical scholarship was the male propertied citizen as he engaged in diplomacy and war.[24] Biographies of noteworthy women, especially noble women, represent early efforts to counteract such exclusionary historiographical practices; the biographical genre thus functioned to de-essentialize a femininity usually defined as outside the scope of history. Reclaiming individual women as historical agents simultaneously legitimized female scholars' growing presence in history departments, a presence strengthened by reforms in women's secondary education during the second half of the nineteenth century.[25] Female historians especially took advantage of the opportunities that the newly emerging fields of economic and social history granted them. Outside the walls of the academy women were increasingly defined as citizens, even though they still lacked suffrage. Female citizenship implied a public presence in social and civic terms, and to that end women's history provided a rationale and a vocabulary that could name and demarcate newly won extradomestic visibility.

Busse-Wilson, a contemporary of Eileen Power (1889–1940), thus was part of what Melman and others have named the period of "classical women's history," which extended from 1870 to 1940.[26] She was neither the first nor the only German medievalist of her generation to document, analyze, and problematize medieval women's roles in religion and society. In Martha Howell's survey of scholarly works on medieval women in Germany during the last two hundred years, she concludes that "women are a documented presence in the medieval histories produced by Germanic scholars, and we owe their presence to the craftsmanship that distinguishes these histories."[27]

Nineteenth-century German historians had gathered an impressive collection of primary sources by and about medieval German women, much of it about religious women. Although they deserve credit for the renewed attention to women's lives and contributions, their monographs and essays are frequently filled with partisan reflections on contemporary political, social, and cultural issues. Joseph von Görres, for example, who published his remarkably gender-inclusive multivolume study *Die christliche Mystik* in Munich in 1836, intended his encyclopedic oeuvre as a strong argument against secularism and the demythologization school of Protestant biblical scholarship, which he sarcastically compared to a "fatal stench of hell, fumes of sulphur, and arsenic smells of garlic."[28]

Wilhelm Preger's important *Geschichte der deutschen Mystik im Mittelalter* (History of German mysticism in the Middle Ages) appeared in Leipzig in 1874.[29] His monumental work was at least in part designed as a contribution to German nationalism and a celebration of a glorious national past. In his mind German women mystics of the Middle Ages extended a venerable lineage of strong Germanic women that reached deep into the pre-Christian past, reviving and invoking the awe-inspiring Germanic prophetesses described by the Roman historian Tacitus (ca. 56–ca. 120). Even more enthusiastically Preger claimed mysticism as such to be thoroughly German. He pronounced with patriotic gusto,

> Germany then is the proper basis for the history of mysticism in the Middle Ages. The sense of the unmediated sensation and preservation of the ideal, which we call disposition of the heart [*Gemüth*], is not the same among the different special characters of a people [*Volksnaturen*]. Nowhere does it reveal itself purer, deeper, and stronger than in the Germanic [national character]. In this meaning, however, does mysticism possess the natural basis of its life. The mysticism of a more ancient Christian time and the later [mysticism] of non-German countries occurred more sporadically, or they did not appear or they were not expressed in such diversity, or they did not rise to such equally high cognitive significance as German mysticism. In the German *Gemüth*'s might and its passion for freedom, it also found the protective defense, which it needed if it were not to be oppressed by hostile reactions.[30]

Apart from the monumental surveys by Görres, Preger, and others, German studies of individual religious women of the German Middle Ages focused especially on the playwright Hrotsvit of Gandersheim and the Benedictine abbess Hildegard of Bingen, but they also concentrated on the Dominican nuns of the fourteenth century, especially Margarete Ebner.[31] Even in these individual studies, however, medieval constructions of femininity and the contemporary awareness about modern women's move into the public sphere functioned as mirrors of each other. In a 1927 essay, for example, Hildegard was celebrated as "the first female German natural scientist and doctor"; also in 1927 the series *Quellenhefte zum Frauenleben in der Geschichte* (Sourcebooks of women's lives in history), by Emmy Beckmann and Irma Stoss, published primary sources on the public and private roles of German medieval women that highlighted women's ubiquitous presence in both domestic and public domains, as hausfrauen, as members of guilds, and as members of the noble class.[32]

Busse-Wilson's study of Saint Elisabeth was thus part of a larger, oftentimes nationalistic trend to recapture medieval women's economic and social status; it differs, though, in the bleak and highly critical assessment of a German past for women. Its tone contrasts dramatically with two other German landmark studies on medieval women that have influenced scholars to this day: Karl Bücher's seminal work *Die Frauenfrage im Mittelalter* (The question of women in the Middle Ages, 1910) and Herbert Grundmann's pathbreaking survey *Religiöse Bewegungen im Mittelalter* (*Religious Movements in the Middle Ages*, 1935). Bücher, a colleague of Lamprecht, endeavored to interpret medieval economic data within a set of questions about gender and social change; unlike Busse-Wilson, however, he did so with a clear ideological preference for a strict division of gender roles and the seclusion of German women in the home. Bücher suggested that a "surplus" of women in medieval cities led to women's intensive participation in all sectors of nondomestic labor; in his view, however, such female "intrusion" into public male spheres led to the neglect of home and family life. The lesson to be learned from the gendered nature of medieval urban-labor markets for women and men in 1910 was posed as a question: "Shouldn't we work with all our strength so that all classes of the population are assured the peace and the comfort of the domestic hearth, which strengthens family consciousness and which provides a woman the single sphere where she feels the happiest and in which she creates the value more precious to the nation than whatever increase in production she might achieve with her 'cheap labor'?"[33] Carefully and without Bücher's polemics, Grundmann delineated women's religious roles and contributions within the church, at its margins, and especially in heretical movements. It is to the credit of this eminent scholar of medieval Christianity and heresy that he joined Albert Huyskens and Thomas Mann in gracefully acknowledging Busse-Wilson's noteworthy achievements. In a book review of *Das Leben der Heiligen Elisabeth von Thüringen,* Grundmann concluded that "the biography deserves great attention as a highly individual, independent and very illuminating effort to penetrate the psychic structure and the fate of the saint."[34]

Apart from concerns about national identity, women's public roles in modern German society, and the impact of secularization on Catholicism, yet another controversial issue shaped German scholarship on medieval religious women: the Viennese export of psychoanalysis. It combined questions of gender and a critique of religion with a devastatingly forceful new vocabulary. Ironically, of all criticisms launched against Busse-Wilson's work, it was, at least at first glance, her use of psychological categories of analysis that provoked the most vituperative responses, including judgments of her book such as "a pseudo-scientific, tendentious work"; "the false book of a rational psychoanalyst"; "[H]ow else could one write about saints if one wishes that they would not exist?"; "Her dishonoring of the saint must hurt any sensitive religious feeling"; and "an unscrupulous concoction."[35] Despite such outrage Busse-Wilson ironically was not the first scholar to have employed psychological terminology in the study of history or even medieval mysticism; indeed, Germany could boast of some of the most innovative psychological research and theoretical contributions to a historical understanding of religious traditions thanks to the founder of experimental psychology, Wilhelm Wundt (1832–1920).[36]

As in the case of the methodology of *Kulturgeschichte* and of the study of medieval women, however, Busse-Wilson used the newly developed psychoanalytical categories with a decidedly feminist intention and as such differed strongly from other psychologically informed writers on medieval women. A case study in contrast is the work of one of Sigmund Freud's longtime friends, the Swiss Protestant pastor and psychoanalyst Oskar Pfister (1873–1956). In line with orthodox psychoanalytic views of female sexuality, Pfister asserted that the Dominican nun Margarete Ebner's (1291–1351) "inferior" mystical phenomena constituted a form of deplorable masochism. Whereas Busse-Wilson identified Saint Elisabeth's masochistic self-destruction as a hallmark of medieval Christianity and a response to male abuse, Pfister went no further than to identify Ebner's symptoms as "unhealthily" repressed sexuality. In her mystical fixation on Jesus, he claimed, the hysteric nun experienced religious orgasm, but not much else.[37]

This brief survey of themes and issues in Busse-Wilson's intellectual environment highlight her au courant affinity with new directions in the historiography of medieval women as well as her succinct personal contributions. She employed women historians' strategy of writing (noble) women back into history through the genre of biography, but she subverted this feminist strategy by depicting Saint Elisabeth as a victim, not a heroine. As a psychologically informed character study, Busse-Wilson's approach to Saint Elisabeth rejected the pathologization of medieval women's mystical experiences and sexuality and replaced it with descriptive categories of psychological self-abuse and of male violence against women. It is noteworthy that shortly before the publication of her study of Saint Elisabeth, Busse-Wilson published a critical study on the education of girls and moral issues, especially in regard to a healthy development of female sexuality.[38] Instead of expanding the nationalistic paradigm that informed Preger's work and the antisecularist multivolume studies by Görres, she radically demystified a national icon as much as its ecclesiastical and political creators, because, in her words, "the historiography of the nineteenth and twentieth century is indeed not less one-sided and bound by the spirit of an age as the glorification of a Christian hero in medieval literature, which seems naive to us. Both are naive in their own way."[39] Given that she worked in such close proximity to the German intellectual avant-garde of her times, this was no small charge.

Notes

1. See Irmgard Klönne for biographical information in the afterword for Busse-Wilson, *Die Frau und die Jugendbewegung*, 112–24. For the study of Saint Elisabeth, see Busse-Wilson, *Das Leben der Heiligen Elisabeth von Thüringen*. Hereafter, it will be abbreviated as *Das Leben*.

2. Busse-Wilson worked as a contributing author for the journals *Philosophie und Leben, Die Tat, Die Erziehung*, and *Zeitschrift für Völkerpsychologie und Soziologie*. See Musial, "Jugendbewegung und Emanzipation der Frau," 241.

3. Elisabeth Busse-Wilson, unpublished manuscript, Archiv der deutschen Jugendbewegung, Burg Ludwigstein.

4. Scholz, "Elisabethforscher," 152.

5. Scholz, "Elisabethforscher," 154, excerpts Huyskens's positive review in the *Zeitschrift des Vereins für thüringische Geschichte und Altertumskunde*.

6. Busse-Wilson, *Das Leben*, 4.

7. Busse-Wilson, *Das Leben*, 2.

8. Busse-Wilson's characterization of Konrad relied on Konrad's own writings about Busse-Wilson and their relationship, which were critically edited by Huyskens (1908). Busse-Wilson called the relationship a "spiritual marriage" (*Das Leben*, 111). On the issue of violence against

women and the construction of Busse-Wilson's and Konrad's relationship, see Wiethaus, "Naming and Un-naming Violence against Women"; and Wiethaus, "Feminist Historiography as Pornography."

9. "Leider ist dabei nicht eine wirklich schöne Biographie entstanden, denn das darstellende Vermögen der Autorin ist schwächer als das analytische. Aber ein interessantes, höchst merkwürdiges Buch ist es dennoch geworden, eine sehr scharf und dennoch liebevoll beobachtete Seelengeschichte, in welcher namentlich das Verhältnis der Heiligen zu ihrem schrecklichen Dämon und Beichtvater Konrad analysiert wird" (Hermann Hesse, in *Bücher warten auf Dich* [Berlin, 7 July 1931], cited in Wies, *Elisabeth von Thüringen*, 240; translation mine).

10. "Ich bewundere das Buch. Das Mittelalter wird unheimlich-rührend lebendig darin in seiner hochherzig verirrten Menschlichkeit, und das Schicksal der armen bleichen Dynastenkinder ist wohl nie eindringlicher gesehen worden. Lassen Sie mich hinzufügen, dass ich die Seiten über Konrad von Marburg aufregend finde. Und lassen Sie mich Ihnen meine Hochachtung ausdrücken für die geistige Energie und Tapferkeit, mit der Sie die snobistische Civilisationsauffassung ironisieren" (Thomas Mann, letter to Elisabeth Busse-Wilson, 14 September 1931, cited in Wies, *Elisabeth von Thüringen*, 240; translation mine).

11. Already in 1902, Ricarda Huch criticized the stereotype in her paper "Über den Einfluss von Studium und Beruf auf die Persönlichkeit der Frau," presented at the Verein für erweiterte Frauenbildung [Society for women's extended education], printed in Huch, *Gesammelte Werke*, 743–53. Smith discusses the charged issue of European and American women historians' "de-genderization" at the turn of the century in "Women Professionals: A Third Sex?" in *Gender of History*, 185–213.

12. Gramsci, *Selections from the Prison Notebooks*, 10.

13. Musial, "Jugendbewegung und Emanzipation der Frau," 238–44.

14. Musial, "Jugendbewegung und Emanzipation der Frau," 241.

15. Musial, "Jugendbewegung und Emanzipation der Frau," 241.

16. The title of Busse-Wilson's dissertation is "Das Ornament auf ethnologischer und prähistorischer Grundlage" (The ornament in ethnological and prehistorical perspective). See Scholz, "Elisabethforscher," 152.

17. "Keiner [der Professoren] gratulierte mir. Ich spürte wieder, die Führer der Universität sahen in uns akademischen Frauen nur eine Vergrößerung der Arbeitsanforderung an sie. . . . Aber persönliches Interesse nahm man wenig an uns, nicht einmal Neugierde" (quoted in Musial, "Jugendbewegung und Emanzipation der Frau," 238).

18. For Busse-Wilson's time period, see Caplan, "Historiography of National Socialism," especially pp. 555ff. In 1932 German universities employed seventy-four female professors and lecturers (*Privatdozentinnen*) vis-à-vis approximately seven thousand male professors and lecturers. See Thalmann, *Frausein im Dritten Reich*, 101. The proportion was the same for enrolled students at the Leipzig University in 1909, with forty-four female students out of a student body of more than forty-four hundred. See Chickering, *Karl Lamprecht*, 369, quoting Eulenburg, *Die Entwicklung der Universität Leipzig in den letzten hundert Jahren*, 194. I thank Robert Beachy for alerting me to Chickering's study.

19. See Chickering, *Karl Lamprecht*, 286–447.

20. For a contemporaneous American evaluation, see Show's highly critical essay "New Culture-History in Germany," 215–21.

21. See Busse-Wilson, *Das Leben*, 8.

22. "[A]llen Menschen, die sich aus irgendeinem Ghetto herauf ans Licht arbeiten mußten" (quoted in Wehnes, "Kritische Frau in der Männerwelt," 308).

23. Musial, "Jugendbewegung und Emanzipation der Frau," 239–42.

24. Melman, "Gender, History, and Memory," 5–39.

25. Melman, "Gender, History, and Memory," 12.

26. Melman, "Gender, History, and Memory," 19.

27. Howell, with Wemple and Kaiser, "Documented Presence," 101–31, 127. Howell does not cite Busse-Wilson.

28. Görres, *Die Christliche Mystik*. Quotation from vol. 1, preface, iii.

29. Preger, *Geschichte der deutschen Mystik im Mittelalter*. Preger discusses Saint Elisabeth of Thuringia's influence on German mysticism on pp. 88–91.

30. "Denn Deutschland ist der eigentliche Boden für die Geschichte der Mystik im Mittelalter. Der Sinn für die unmittelbare Empfindung und Bewahrung des Idealen, welchen wir Gemüth nennen, ist nicht der gleiche in den verschiedenen Volksnaturen. Er zeigt sich bei keiner reiner, tiefer und stärker als bei der germanischen. In diesem Sinne aber hat die Mystik den natürlichen Grund ihres Lebens. Die Mystik der älteren christlichen Zeit sowie die spätere der nicht deutschen Länder tritt veinzelter auf, oder sie ist nicht in so mannigfaltiger Weise zur Erscheinung oder zu Wort gekommen oder sie hat sich nicht zu gleich hoher Bedeutung für die Erkenntnis erhoben wie die deutsche Mystik. In der macht und dem Freiheitsbedürfnis des deutschen Gemüths fand sie zugleich die Schutzwehr, deren sie bedurfte, wenn sie durch die ihr feindlichen Richtungen nicht unterdrückt werden sollte" (Wilhelm Preger, *Geschichte der deutschen Mystik im Mittelalter*, 9; translation mine).

31. This focus represents a "second wave" of reviving interest in medieval religious women. In the fifteenth and sixteenth centuries German humanists reclaimed them as founding mothers of a Germanic humanistic "spirit," for example, Conrad Celtes, who published the first Hrotsvit edition in 1501.

32. Fischer, *Die heilige Hildegarde von Bingen*; Beckmann and Stoss, *Quellenhefte zum Frauenleben in der Geschichte*.

33. Bücher, *Die Frauenfrage*, 72. This translation and a short discussion of Bücher's views of women's roles are to be found in Howell, with Wemple and Kaiser, *Women in Medieval History*, 116–18.

34. "[V]erdient aber die Biographie als eigenwilliger, selbständiger und sehr aufschlussreicher Versuch, in die seelische Struktur und das Schicksal der Heiligen einzudringen, große Beachtung" (quoted in Scholz, "Elisabethforscher," 154; translation mine).

35. The comments are documented in Scholz, "Elisabethforscher," 154–56.

36. On Wundt's status at the University of Leipzig and his alliance with Lamprecht, see Chickering, *Karl Lamprecht*, 195ff.

37. Pfister, "Hysterie und Mystik bei Margarethe Ebner," 482. In the previous year Pfister had published the study "Zur Psychologie des hysterischen Madonnakultus" (On the psychology of the hysterical cult of the Madonna) in the *Zentralblatt;* his long involvement in the psychoanalytic movement culminated in his work on "religious hygiene," translated as *Christianity and Fear*.

38. Busse-Wilson, "Das moralische Dilemma der modernen Mädchen Erziehung," in *Die Kultur der Frau*, ed. Ada Schmidt-Beil (Berlin-Frohnau: n.p., 1930).

39. Busse-Wilson, *Das Leben*, 3.

SELECT BIBLIOGRAPHY OF WORKS BY ELISABETH BUSSE-WILSON

Die Frau und die Jugendbewegung: Ein Beitrag zur weiblichen Charakterologie und zur Kritik des Antifeminismus. Hamburg: Freideutscher Jugendverlag Saal, 1920. Reprint, Münster: Lit Verlag, 1989.
"Der Charakter des Antifeminismus: Beobachtungen an Hans Blüher." In *Freideutsche Jugend* 7, no. 5 (1921): 164–67.
"Freideutsche Jugend." *Die Tat* (1921): unpag.
"Liebe und Kameradschaft." *Stufen der Jugendbewegung* (Jena) (1925).
Die soziale Stellung der Frau in kulturgeschichtlicher Entwicklung. Bremen: Angestelltenkammer, 1925.
Stufen der Jugendbewegung: Ein Abschnitt aus der ungeschriebenen Geschichte Deutschlands. Jena: Eugen Diederichs, 1925.
"Der russische Mensch." *Zeitschrift für Volkspsychologie und Soziologie* (1927).
"Der moralische Schwachsinn beim weiblichen Geschlecht." Special reprint in *Zeitschrift für Menschenkunde* 2, no. 1 (1930): 71 ff.
"Die Frau im Proletariat." *Die Frau* 39 (1931/32): 557–60.
Das Leben der Heiligen Elisabeth von Thüringen: Das Abbild einer mittelalterlichen Seele. Munich: C. H. Beck, 1931.
"Mädchenerziehung und Frauenberufung." *Die Frau* 40 (1932/33): 753–56.
"Eine Franziskanerin des Nordens: Zur Heiligsprechung der Heiligen Elisabeth Pfingsten, 1235." *Die Wartburg* 34 (1935): 203–6.
"Die Wunder am Grabe der Heiligen Elisabeth in Marburg: Ein Beitrag zur Erhebung ihrer Gebeine im Jahre 1236." *Beiträge zur Hessischen Kirchengeschichte* 11 (1939): 184–209.
"Selbstdarstellung." Typescript in Archiv der deutschen Jugendbewegung, Burg Ludwigstein. 1969.

WORKS CITED

Beckmann, Emmy, and Irma Stoss. *Quellenhefte zum Frauenleben in der Geschichte.* Vol. 2. Berlin: F. A. Herbig Verlagsbuchhandlung, 1927.
Bücher, Karl. *Die Frauenfrage im Mittelalter.* 2d ed. Tübingen: F. A. Herbig, 1910.
Caplan, Jane. "The Historiography of National Socialism." In *Companion to Historiography,* edited by Michael Bentley. London: Routledge, 1997.
Chickering, Roger. *Karl Lamprecht: A German Academic Life (1856–1915).* Atlantic Highlands, N.J.: Humanities Press, 1993.
Eulenburg, Franz. *Die Entwicklung der Universität Leipzig in den letzten hundert Jahren: Statistische Untersuchungen.* Leipzig: S. Hirzel, 1909.
Fischer, Hermann. *Die heilige Hildegarde von Bingen, die erste deutsche Naturforscherin und Ärztin: Ihr Leben und Werk.* Munich: C. H. Beck, 1927.
Görres, Joseph von. *Die christliche Mystik.* 5 vols. Munich: Verlag G. J. Manz, 1836. Reprint, Graz: Akademische Druck- und Verlagsanstalt, 1960.
Gramsci, Antonio. *Selections from the Prison Notebooks of Antonio Gramsci.* Translated by Quintin Hoare and Geoffrey Nowell Smith. New York: International Publishers, 1971.
Grundmann, Herbert. *Religiöse Bewegungen im Mittelalter: Untersuchungen über die geschichtlichen Zusammenhänge zwischen der Ketzerei, den Bettelorden, und der religiösen Frauenbewegung im 12. und 13. Jahrhundert und über die geschichtlichen Grundlagen der deutschen Mystik.* Berlin: Verlag Dr. Emil Ebering, 1935.

Howell, Martha, with the collaboration of Suzanne Wemple and Denise Kaiser. "A Documented Presence: Medieval Women in Germanic Historiography." In *Women in Medieval History and Historiography,* edited by Susan Mosher Stuard, 101–31. Philadelphia: University of Pennsylvania Press, 1987.

Huch, Ricarda. *Gesammelte Werke.* Edited by Wilhelm Emrich. Vol. 5. Gütersloh, Ger.: Bertelsmann Verlag, n.d.

Huyskens, Albert. *Quellenstudien zur Geschichte der Heiligen Elisabeth, Landgräfin von Thüringen.* Marburg, Ger.: N. G. Elwert, 1908.

——. Review of *Das Leben der Heiligen Elisabeth von Thüringen,* by Elisabeth Busse-Wilson. *Zeitschrift des Vereins für thüringische Geschichte und Altertumskunde* 38, no. 30 (1933): 336–39.

——. *Die Schriften des Caesarius von Heisterbach über die heilige Elisabeth von Thüringen.* Publikationen der Gesellschaft für rheinische Geschichtskunde, 43. Bonn: Peter Hanstein, 1937.

——. *Der sogenannte Libellus de dictis ancillarum s. Elisabeth confectus.* Kempten, Ger.: Verlag der Josef Kösel'schen Buchhandlung, 1911.

Melman, Billie. "Gender, History, and Memory: The Invention of Women's Past in the Nineteenth and Early Twentieth Centuries." *History and Memory: Studies in Representation of the Past* 5, no. 1 (1993): 5–39.

Musial, Magdalena. "Jugendbewegung und Emanzipation der Frau: Ein Beitrag zur Rolle der weiblichen Jugend in der Jugendbewegung bis 1933." Ph.D. diss., University of Essen, 1982.

Pfister, Otto. *Christianity and Fear: A Study in History and in the Psychology and Hygiene of Religion.* London: George Allen and Unwin, 1948.

——. "Hysterie und Mystik bei Margarethe Ebner (1291–1351)." *Zentralblatt für Psychoanalyse* 19, no. 1 (1911): 468–85.

Preger, Wilhelm. *Geschichte der deutschen Mystik im Mittelalter.* Leipzig: Dörffling und Franke, 1874.

Scholz, Hans-Jürgen. "Elisabethforscher von Justi bis Busse-Wilson." In *St. Elisabeth: Kult, Kirche, Konfessionen,* edited by Brigitte Rechberg. Marburg, Ger.: J. A. Koch, 1983.

Show, Arley Barthlow. "The New Culture-History in Germany." *History Teacher's Magazine* 4 (1913): 215–21.

Smith, Bonnie. *The Gender of History: Men, Women, and Historical Practice.* Cambridge, Mass.: Harvard University Press, 1998.

Thalmann, Rita. *Frausein im Dritten Reich.* Munich: Carl Hanser Verlag, 1984.

Wehnes, Franz-Josef. "Kritische Frau in der Männerwelt: Elisabeth Busse-Wilson (1890–1974)." *Jahrbuch des Archivs der Deutschen Jugendbewegung* 9 (1977): 307–10.

Wies, Ernst W. *Elisabeth von Thüringen: Die Provokation der Heiligkeit.* Esslingen, Ger.: Bechtle Verlag, 1993.

Wiethaus, Ulrike. "Feminist Historiography as Pornography: Saint Elisabeth of Thuringia in Nazi Germany." *Medieval Feminist Newsletter* 24 (1997): 46–55.

——. "Naming and Un-naming Violence against Women: German Historiography and the Cult of Saint Elisabeth of Thuringia." *Studies in Medievalism* 1, no. 9 (1997): 187–202.

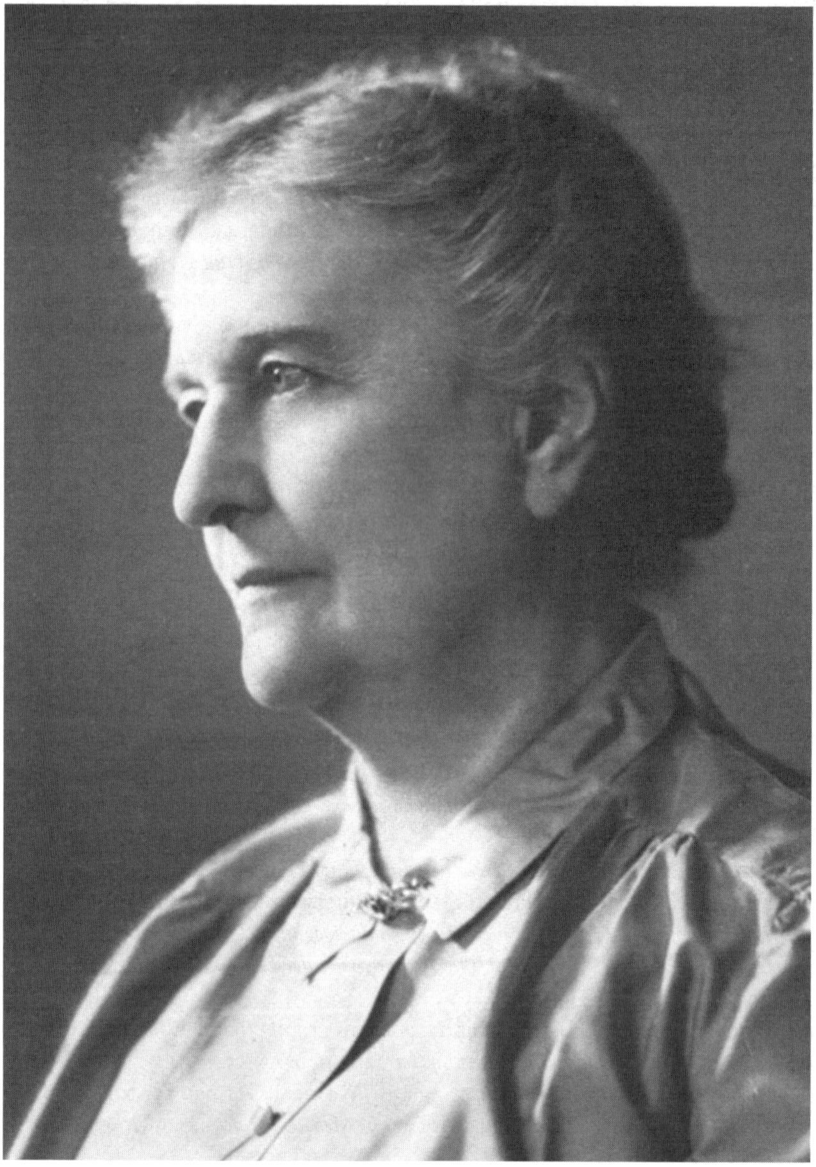

CHAPTER 27

"An Extraordinary Sense of Powerful Restlessness"
Nora Kershaw Chadwick (1891–1972)

SANDRA BALLIF STRAUBHAAR

Nora Kershaw Chadwick's interests in language, literature, history and archaeology were literally global, but she is largely remembered for her study of early northwestern Europe, specifically the British Isles from the Roman Conquest to the Norman Conquest. She was a prominent figure in Norse and Celtic studies at Cambridge University (in association with both Newnham College and Girton College) for fully half a century, both with her husband, Hector Munro Chadwick, and without him—after his death.

Today Chadwick is remembered in both the academic and the popular arena. Her collaboration with Hector Chadwick on *The Growth of Literature* is still seen as pathbreaking for its time, and her three Celtic books aimed at popular audiences—*The Druids*, *The Celtic Realms* (with Myles Dillon), and *The Celts*—are all still in print and selling.

Nora Kershaw was born on 28 January 1891 at Great Lever near Bolton, Lancashire, to James Kershaw, a manufacturer, and Emma Clara Booth Kershaw. There was one younger sister, Mabel, who later converted to Catholicism and became a Carmelite nun. Lifelong friend Enid Welsford remembered Nora's early passion for literature, citing an anecdote from former schoolmate Nan Ure at Stoneycroft School, near Southport, Lancashire: "I remember Nora's tussle with her mother over her clothes. Then one day she came to school in a state of great delight and excitement as she had been given a dress allowance and henceforward was to be responsible for her own clothes. That afternoon she went downtown and came back jubilant with a Chaucer, a Spenser and I don't know how many other books that she had bought with her dress allowance—no clothes of course."[1]

In 1910 Nora Kershaw entered Newnham College, one of only two women's colleges at Cambridge University at that time. She read for the English (section A) and Old English (section B) sections of the medieval and modern languages tripos, joining what Enid Welsford later recalled as a "small but keen group of young men and women" reading for section B and presided over by Professor Hector Munro Chadwick, whom Nora Kershaw eventually was to marry.[2]

H. M. Chadwick had read classics as an undergraduate but displayed wider interests even in his first publications, as *The Cult of Othin* (1899) and *Studies in Old English* (1899) both show. He was forty years old the year Nora Kershaw came up to Cambridge. Two years after that, his book *The Heroic Age* came out, a synthesizing work on Greek and Germanic heroic poetry, which anticipated the Chadwicks' later collaboration on *The Growth of Literature,* a three-volume work in which they explored oral poetry traditions from all parts of the globe.

All accounts of Hector Chadwick by his former pupils, male and female, stress his modesty, inclusivity, and gender blindness. Dorothy Whitelock recalled, "He behaved to us as though we were scholars on his level, and never showed irritation at our shortcomings."[3] José de Navarro wrote, "Even in the earlier days of his career, when the position of women in the University was not officially recognized, he treated them with the same consideration as his men students."[4] Alisoun Gardner-Medwin corroborates: "Nora Chadwick and her husband were both people who helped promote understanding. Even early last century . . . Hector Chadwick treated young ladies who were his students as equals with the young men, and later Professors of Anglo-Saxon in Cambridge followed his example. He and Nora promoted the scholarship of younger people, men and women, and when I knew her, just before she retired, Nora Chadwick was still eagerly helping younger scholars."[5]

In 1914 James Kershaw was accidentally killed while serving with a Y.M.C.A. canteen unit in France; Nora Kershaw completed her course at Newnham College that same year. Emma Booth Kershaw later remarried and settled in Houghton near Saint Ives, and Mabel Kershaw came to live at the Carmelite convent at Waterbeach. It was thus relatively easy for Nora to keep contact with family members while living in Cambridge, both before and after her marriage.

After taking this first degree, however, Nora Kershaw moved to Scotland, accepting a five-year post at the University of Saint Andrews as temporary lecturer in English language and assistant lecturer in English literature. While thus employed, she taught herself Russian. When the position came to an end, she returned to Cambridge with a small legacy she had meanwhile inherited and took rooms in Owlstone Road with Enid Welsford. There she studied Old English and Old Icelandic literature independently under the unofficial guidance of Hector Chadwick.

In 1921 *Stories and Ballads of the Far Past, Translated from the Norse (Icelandic and Faroese) with Introductions and Notes,* by N. Kershaw was published by Cambridge University Press. Kenneth Jackson has called this work her "first serious publication," and it still stands up very well.[6] The first half contains two sagas and two *þættir* from the *fornaldar sögur*. These include the full text of *Hervarar saga,* with its sword-wielding, cross-dressing Viking heroine, and an amusing rendering of *Sörla þáttr,* displaying two modest ellipses where the original text tells us exactly what the goddess Freyja offered to the four dwarf-smiths, on four consecutive nights, in exchange for the gold necklace she was later famous for owning. (Since Nora Kershaw, later Chadwick, seems to have otherwise flinched from nothing, I would like to think that these concessions to reader sensitivity were the suggestions of Cambridge University Press. Kershaw did select this *þáttr,* after all, when she could have chosen others.) After the prose texts there is a selection of late-medieval ballads, translated from Icelandic, Danish, Faroese, and Shetland Norn, all of them containing narratives connected with the prose texts in the first half of the book.

One of the few elements that dates *Stories and Ballads of the Far Past* for a modern reader is that the translated poetry from the sagas and *þættir* is anachronistically rendered in ballad stanzas with end-rhyme, presumably to show continuity with the ballad versions of the same narratives in the second half of the book. While no one would recommend this translation option now for Old Norse, the resulting verse is still edgy and energetic, as the two stanzas below indicate. In them, Hervör threatens her dead father and uncles with an uncomfortable afterlife, should they refuse to yield up the ancestral sword she has claimed from their graves:

> Hervarth, Hjörvarth, Angantyr
> And Hrani, great be your torment here
> If ye will not hear my words.
> Give me the blade that Dvalin made;
> It is ill becoming the ghostly dead
> To keep such costly swords!
>
> In your tortured ribs shall my curses bring
> A maddening itch and a frenzied sting,
> Till ye writhe in agonies,
> As if ye were laid to your final rest
> Where the ants are swarming in their nest
> And revelling in your thighs![17]

In 1921 Nora Kershaw took a trip to Italy with Hector Chadwick, chaperoned by Enid Welsford, and in 1922 the couple were married. Welsford recalled the occasion: "The wedding—or rather weddings—of Nora and Chadders took place in St. Benét's Church and the Cambridge Registry Office. St. Benét's Church was chosen on account of its Saxon tower, the Registry Office because Nora feared that her somewhat drastic expurgation of the Marriage Service might have rendered it illegal. Her mother and stepfather and myself were the only wedding guests. There was an hour's interval between the ceremonies, so the Professor took us to the museum of Archaeology and gave us an illustrated talk on funerary urns!"[8] The wedding party then adjourned to tea in Chadwick's rooms in Clare College.

Enid Welsford became a lodger at the Chadwicks' new home at the old Paper Mills, on Newmarket Road, adjoining the Norman "Leper Chapel" on the outskirts of Cambridge. The house was large, surrounded by gardens (gypsies camped in the back garden in the winter) and enclosed by a fortresslike wall with a locked postern gate. Callers who knew the couple well devised alternative entry methods, like Dame Bertha Phillpotts, who "was accustomed to stand on the saddle of her bicycle and throw stones into the mill-stream that flowed beneath their study window."[9]

Enid Welsford recalled how the host of the Globe Inn next door, a Mr. Leftley, enjoyed fulfilling the office of proxy host for the Chadwicks: "He soon became very discriminating. 'But I *want* to see Professor Chadwick,' wailed a caller. 'Ah,' said Leftley, 'but does he want to see *you*, that's the question.' On one occasion Nora was astonished to see the upper half of a bishop coming in through an open window on the first floor. Leftley had decided that a bishop from Central Africa who was also a former pupil of Professor Chadwick would be a welcome visitor, so when no-one answered the back door-bell he got a ladder and pushed him up through the window by his legs. It must not be thought, however, that Paper Mills was a dour, inhospitable place."[10]

Those who managed to come in by the gate in the wall had yet to pass the "plank bridge across the mill lade to the front door, and the succession of 'fierce' dogs with intimidating Germanic mythological names like Loki" before achieving their quest.[11] As Kenneth Jackson wrote in 1974: "I well remember, forty years since, the excitement of cycling the dark and windy miles down the Newmarket Road to the Paper Mills, penetrating the inner fortress, crossing the bridge, negotiating the 'savage' dogs, and listening entranced for an hour while 'Chadders' gave his evening lectures on early Britain and 'Mrs. Chadders' sat at the epidiascope projecting pictures of Bronze Age leaf swords or palstaves and Iron Age enameled horse harness on the screen, silent but radiating an extraordinary sense of powerful restlessness, if one may use such an oxymoron."[12]

Enid Welsford cited a corroborating impression from the Reverend Michael Dewar: "I cherish their first memory.... I was one of Chadders' very last pupils and I have a recollection of a strikingly beautiful woman with golden hair, in a long blue dress—rather Edwardian style—playing a harp at Paper Mills in December 1939, when I came up from Blundells to be interviewed by a Norfolk-jacketed knickerbockered Professor. They were my idols."[13]

Nineteen twenty-two saw the publication by Cambridge University Press of *Anglo-Saxon and Norse Poems*, edited by N. K. Chadwick. The volume included six Old English poems and six poems, both Eddic and skaldic, in Old Norse.

In 1923 Nora Kershaw Chadwick graduated with an M.A. from Cambridge University. In that year she became an associate of Newnham College, continuing until 1938; in 1953–65 she was again an associate of the college.

In 1927 Cambridge University Press published *An Early Irish Reader*, by N. K. Chadwick, which contained an edition of the "Tale of Mac Dathó's Pig" (Scéla mucce meic Dathó) for the use of the beginning student of Old Irish. The book soon became the standard undergraduate Old Irish text at Cambridge.[14]

An unrelenting desire to personally visit sites of historical and archaeological interest was one of Nora K. Chadwick's contributions to the Kershaw-Chadwick partnership. They bought a second house, the Old Rectory at Vowchurch in Herefordshire on the Welsh border, which became a vacation residence as well as a staging point for forays further out. Kenneth Jackson recalled "wide-ranging expeditions by car to visit historical and archaeological sites, which [Hector Chadwick] would never have done on his own ('Archaeologising, ye see, Master, archaeologising,' as the famous Chadwick story about their courting tells)."[15]

As mentioned earlier, the most celebrated product of the Chadwick team is *The Growth of Literature* (1932, 1936, and 1940). The motivation behind this work was entirely Nora's, as José de Navarro and Kenneth Jackson have both reported.[16] The book that Nora Chadwick had in mind would build upon Hector Chadwick's earlier conclusions about heroic poetry, extending them to cultures and literatures other than Greek and Germanic. De Navarro described the catalyst event behind Nora Chadwick's resolve. She had

> chanced upon a passage in Layard's *Early Adventures in Persia, Susiana and Babylonia* in which he vividly describes the effect of poetry upon Mehemet Taki Khan and his followers—"men who knew no pity and who were ready to take human life upon the smallest provocation." It tells of a scene in the Khan's camp: the minstrel seated by his chief, chanting in a loud voice from the *Shah Nameh* and how his listeners would shout and yell, draw their swords, and challenge imaginary foes, or weep as they listened to the moving tale of Khorsam and his mistress. "Such was probably the effect," wrote Layard, "of the Homeric ballads when recited or sung of old in the camps of the Greeks, or when they marched to combat." It was this passage which fired Mrs. Chadwick....
>
> [A]rchaeology was abandoned and a comparison of advanced oral traditions—"oral literature" was their term for it—was embarked upon.[17]

Hector Chadwick had no large blocks of time to devote to a project of this magnitude. His university work at the time that *The Growth of Literature* was being written was largely devoted to the updating of what Kenneth Jackson called "the famous Chadwickian Section B," then (narrowly) called the Anglo-Saxon tripos.[18] (Cambridge's current Anglo-Saxon, Norse, and Celtic tripos [ASNC tripos] still bears the strong stamp of Hector Chadwick's revisions.)

The organization of the three volumes of *The Growth of Literature*, which contains literary samples from a number of traditions, accordingly fell to Nora Chadwick. Contents of the volumes attributed to her include the Irish material in volume 1; the Russian material in volume 2; and the central Asiatic, Polynesian, and some of the

African material in volume 3. De Navarro, recounting the Chadwicks' work on this project, marveled at their "almost pentecostal knowledge of tongues.... [N]early all the languages of the many literatures studied in this book were known to one or other of its authors. If the term epoch-making may be applied to so large a synthesis and one which broke so much new ground, *The Growth of Literature* may well be so described."[19]

Kenneth Jackson recalled mixed reviews for the books, particularly of the Hebrew sections, which were H. M. Chadwick's; the Russian and Polynesian sections, on the other hand, were "highly praised by authorities on these subjects." He added: "However that may be, Vol. I, about which, unlike the other volumes, I have some claim to speak, was to me, as a young research student, one of the most exciting books I had ever read, and I still strongly recommend it to pupils as an illuminating comparative study of early Irish and Welsh literature."[20]

Nora Chadwick's work on the Central Asian sections of *The Growth of Literature* led to her publishing two additional articles on the Tatar shamans of Central Asia for the *Journal of the Royal Anthropological Institute* in the same year (1936). Later she expanded this material into a book, *Poetry and Prophecy*, published by Cambridge University Press in 1942.

Enid Welsford has described her friend Nora Kershaw Chadwick as an individual of "single-minded intensity," comparing her unflagging scholarly drive to her sister's vocation as a nun; she also cites Nora Chadwick's friend and former pupil Elsie Duncan-Jones's characterization of her as "a saint of scholarship."[21] Given that intensity on the academic front, it is astonishing to find what a charitable and generous hostess and landlady Nora Chadwick was through the years, as a number of independent accounts confirm.

The Harry Ransom Collection at the University of Texas at Austin retains a single letter from her to an unspecified admirer of *Stories and Ballads of the Far Past*, written with a chisel-point nib in a bold hand, rich in ligatures (a mark of haste or intensity?), dated "8 Jan. 1931." The printed stationery is captioned "Paper Mills, Newmarket Road, Cambridge." "Dear Sir," she writes, "I am very sorry that your letter has lain so long unanswered. I have been wholly preoccupied with sick nursing for some weeks past and have neglected my own affairs sadly."[22] This unnamed patient may well have been Hector Chadwick but could also have been a lodger or a visiting relative, of whom there were many.

With the advent of World War II in 1939, the Chadwicks moved into Cambridge proper, choosing a large house at 1 Adams Road in order to be closer to the university and its library. Hector Chadwick's sister came to live with them, and they also took in various students, scholars, and other tenants.[23]

From 1941 to 1944 Nora Chadwick was the Sarah Smithson Research Fellow at Newnham College, and from 1942 to 1946 she was an associate fellow. In the following year Hector Chadwick died. Enid Welsford recalled how this "was a terrible blow for Nora, which she met with characteristic fortitude and a positive determination to perpetuate his work."²⁴ One of her first projects in this vein was her finishing and editing of his book *Early Scotland,* which was issued by Cambridge University Press in 1949. Kenneth Jackson saw this as "her first real excursion into Celtic history," confirming the direction she would turn to for the rest of her academic life.²⁵

Nora Chadwick was appointed lecturer in early history and culture of the British Isles in Cambridge University from 1950 to 1958, and director of studies in Anglo-Saxon and Celtic studies in Newnham College from 1950 to 1959, when she was succeeded by Kathleen Hughes. She held the equivalent office in Girton College from 1950 to 1962.

Eventually the big house on Adams Road, which Nora Chadwick continued to share with women research students through the years, became too burdensome, and she moved to a flat at Causewayside in Sheeps' Green. To her friends the new flat hardly seemed like a change, for Nora Chadwick, "having crammed it with her books and old-fashioned furniture, lived in much the same way as before, writing at her huge desk or dispensing delightful hospitality."²⁶ In 1954 she edited and supplied three chapters for a collection called *Studies in Early British History,* published by Cambridge University Press.

In these last years preceding her retirement, Nora Chadwick's helpfulness to newly arrived scholars remained characteristic. Alisoun Gardner-Medwin recalls:

> I felt it myself—in my first year.... In the Easter vacation of 1957, Mrs Chadwick took Kathleen Hughes and myself, as her guests, on a week's tour of the north of England. She believed that it was important to see the actual sites where things happened. So we saw the Roman Wall, the site of the battle of Heavenfield, looked at the wastes of Stanemoor, and tried to find the church in Jarrow. At that time Jarrow was a mass of old houses, now swept away, and no church was visible from afar. We asked for "Bede's church," were confidently shown where it was, and walked in briskly—to discover half way up the aisle that we had entered a modern Catholic church, while mass was in process. We turned round smartly and walked out again! We did finally manage to find the Anglo-Saxon church, which contains lots of bits of Anglo-Saxon carved crosses in a little museum. Mrs Chadwick was a terror behind the wheel of a car. She drove up the A68, the Roman road (Dere Street) which goes, absolutely straight, due north across the Roman Wall into Scotland, as if leading the Roman troops against the Picts. As the road is so straight, and the land is hilly, there are many blind summits. She even turned off the engine occasionally at the top of a summit, and noted how far the impetus would take us up the next slope before she had to turn it on again. At Chollerford, the car wouldn't start, so she approached a small garage—still there—and asked for help. The man came out, listened, and then hit part of the engine with a hammer. It worked. At that time Nora Chadwick was in her mid-sixties.²⁷

Nora Chadwick continued to travel until the end of her life, not only to the north of England, but to Wales, Ireland, and Brittany. Kenneth Jackson has even reported that "at the age of 78 she tried unsuccessfully to persuade a colleague to journey across Russia by Trans-Siberian Railway, an ambition of hers from early days."[28]

As *The Growth of Literature* became known throughout the academic world, correspondence from all over the world poured in, and Nora Chadwick was awarded a number of academic honors. In 1956 she was made a Fellow of the British Academy. In 1958 she was given the degree of Hon. D.Litt. from the University of Wales. On the occasion of the awarding of this degree, Thomas Jones said:

> When the fair Rhiannon for the third time crossed the border from the Otherworld to Wales, Pwyll, Prince of Dyfed, prevailed upon her to stop and converse with him. She was as knowledgeable as she was gracious, she carried a magic satchel, and was attended by three birds whose song held listeners spellbound. Today, our University has halted on this, one of her frequent visits from across a nearer border, another lady, gracious and learned, with her own satchel and her own singing birds [i.e., former students], the lady I am privileged to present to you for the degree of *Doctor in Litteris, honoris causa*—Mrs Nora Kershaw Chadwick, *Magister in Artibus,* Director of Studies in Archæology and Anthropology, of Girton College, Cambridge.... Her satchel is heavy with treasures won in many fields: those of literature—Anglo-Saxon, Norse, Irish, Russian, and Gallo-Roman; those of history—Welsh, Irish and Romano-British; and that mysterious, unmapped field where poetry and prophecy meet.[29]

Also in 1958 Nora Chadwick was made an Honorary Life Fellow of Newnham College, a rare honor. In 1959 the National University of Ireland granted her the degree of Hon. D.Litt. Celt., and she was named O'Donnell Lecturer in Celtic Studies at the University of Edinburgh. In 1960 she was named O'Donnell Lecturer in Celtic Studies at the University of Wales and Riddell Memorial Lecturer at the University of Durham. In 1961 she was appointed C.B.E. (Commander of the Order of the British Empire) by the Queen as well as named as O'Donnell Lecturer in Celtic Studies at the University of Oxford. In 1963 the University of Saint Andrews awarded her the degree of Hon. D.Litt. On this occasion A. A. Matheson noted that "[s]uch is her stature as historian, anthropologist, polyglot, ecclesiologist, that she defies classification and confounds comparison."[30]

In 1965 Nora Chadwick was appointed the Sir John Rhys Memorial Lecturer by the British Academy. Her lecture was titled "The Colonization of Brittany from Celtic Britain."[31] She was also a fellow of the Society of Antiquaries, of the Royal Anthropological Institute, and of the Royal Asiatic Society.

In 1963 Nora Chadwick edited and supplied four chapters for *Celt and Saxon: Studies in the Early British Border,* published by Cambridge University Press. Also in 1963 she published *Celtic Britain,* number 34 in the series Ancient People and Places, edited by her former pupil Glyn Daniel and published by Thames and Hudson in London.

Nora Chadwick's last works include her three popular-audience books on Celtic topics: *The Druids* (1966), *The Celtic Realms* (with Myles Dillon, 1967; there was an immediate translation into German as well), and *The Celts* (1971). All three are currently in print. The Web site of U.K. Channel 4 sings the praises of *The Celts* to this day: "[This is] the original academic, rather than fanciful, book on the Celts in both Britain and Europe. Don't let the 'academic' description put you off, though. Now updated (with a new chapter by Barry Cunliffe) this remains one of the prime descriptions of the Celtic peoples."[32]

Kenneth Jackson, writing in 1972, could not restrain his embarrassment at what he saw as "remarkable lapses" in Nora Chadwick's popular books on the Celts.[33] It is hard to say whether he intended praise or condemnation when he stated that "[i]n fact the notable growth of public interest in Celtic of recent years must owe much to her," but I suspect the latter.[34] (Possibly he could see ahead to *Braveheart* and *Roar*, to Enya and Riverdance, to T-shirts, tattoos, and Celtic Wicca.) His concerns are doubtless genuine, but clearly in vain. As Ronald Hutton has recently pointed out, the parallel development of academic and popular culture, particularly on topics related to the imagined European tribal past, has been interlaced together for a good three centuries now and cannot be teased apart by wishing.[35] I suspect that Nora K. Chadwick knew this perfectly well.

Toward the end of 1968, as Enid Welsford recalled, Nora Chadwick's health took a turn for the worse. She had several bad falls. Two sisters, Vera Steven and Nelly Plumb, who had worked in her home for years, helped her to keep living there as long as possible. Chadwick stayed intermittently in the Hope Nursing Home in Cambridge after her falls; by 1971 she had to move there permanently. Visitors came daily, including Steven and Plumb. It was an unexpected bonus that the nuns and nurses on staff were great admirers of *The Celts*![36]

On 17 October 1970 a luncheon was held in the Combination Room of Saint John's College in honor of the centenary of Homer Chadwick's birth, with Nora Kershaw Chadwick as guest of honor. Glyn Daniel presided over the festivities, which were organized by a committee of former students including Isabel Henderson and Kenneth Jackson. Forty-five of the seventy-two guests had been pupils of either or both Chadwicks.[37]

In February 1971 the National Library of Scotland prepared a Chadwick exhibition. Nora Chadwick was by then not well enough to make the trip, so Isabel Henderson prepared a souvenir pamphlet of the exhibit to be presented to her later, also featuring Dorothy Whitelock's speech from the centenary's luncheon.

On 24 April 1972 Nora Kershaw Chadwick died. As she had requested, there was no funeral service. "Nora adhered to no definite creed," Enid Welsford recalled. She "never went to church unless the service was conducted in Welsh or Gaelic; [she] disliked all ritual and social ceremonial whether secular or sacred and yet seemed drawn sympathetically towards those who were addicted to all these things. She once startled her table-companions by murmuring as though thinking aloud:—'I never have been able to understand how anyone with a brain greater than that of a flea could be an atheist.'"[38] Hilda R. E. Davidson wrote of her: "I shall never cease to be grateful for the mixture of vision and good earthly common sense which she brought to her vision of the past."[39]

NOTES

The quotation in the title is from Jackson, "Nora Kershaw Chadwick," 548.

1. Welsford, *In Memoriam*, 1.
2. Welsford, *In Memoriam*, 1.
3. Henderson, *List of the Published Writings*, 26.
4. De Navarro, "Hector Munro Chadwick," 319.
5. Alisoun Gardner-Medwin, e-mail to Sandra Ballif Straubhaar, 19 September 2001.
6. Jackson, "Nora Kershaw Chadwick," 539.
7. Kershaw, *Stories and Ballads of the Far Past*, 96.
8. Welsford, *In Memoriam*, 3.
9. Welsford, *In Memoriam*, 4.
10. Welsford, *In Memoriam*, 3.
11. Jackson, "Nora Kershaw Chadwick," 538.
12. Jackson, "Nora Kershaw Chadwick," 547–48.
13. Welsford, *In Memoriam*, 2–3.
14. Jackson, "Nora Kershaw Chadwick," 540.
15. Jackson, "Nora Kershaw Chadwick," 538.
16. De Navarro, "Hector Munro Chadwick," 320; Jackson, "Nora Kershaw Chadwick," 540.
17. De Navarro, "Hector Munro Chadwick," 321.
18. Jackson, "Nora Kershaw Chadwick," 547.
19. De Navarro, "Hector Munro Chadwick," 323.
20. Jackson, "Nora Kershaw Chadwick," 540–41.
21. Welsford, *In Memoriam*, 1–2.
22. Letter from Nora Kershaw Chadwick to "Dear Sir."
23. Welsford, *In Memoriam*, 4–5.
24. Welsford, *In Memoriam*, 5.
25. Jackson, "Nora Kershaw Chadwick," 542.
26. Welsford, *In Memoriam*, 5–6.
27. Alisoun Gardner-Medwin, e-mail to Sandra Ballif Straubhaar, 25 August 2001 and 17 September 2001.
28. Jackson, "Nora Kershaw Chadwick," 538.
29. Henderson, *List of Published Writings*, 21.
30. Henderson, *List of Published Writings*, 23.
31. Jackson, "Nora Kershaw Chadwick," 544.
32. Http://www.btinternet.com/-johnandsandy.colby/ttbook/1999_series/kemerton.html, accessed 5/30/02.
33. Jackson, "Nora Kershaw Chadwick," 541.
24. Jackson, "Nora Kershaw Chadwick," 545.
35. Hutton, *Triumph of the Moon*.
36. Welsford, *In Memoriam*, 9.
37. Welsford, *In Memoriam*, 8.
38. Welsford, *In Memoriam*, 7.
39. Welsford, *In Memoriam*, 7.

Select Bibliography of Works by Nora Kershaw Chadwick

Stories and Ballads of the Far Past, Translated from the Norse (Icelandic and Faroese) with Introductions and Notes. Cambridge: Cambridge University Press, 1921.

Anglo-Saxon and Norse Poems. Cambridge: Cambridge University Press, 1922.

An Early Irish Reader. Cambridge: Cambridge University Press, 1927. An edition of *Scéla mucce maic Dathó*.

Letter to "Dear sir," 8 January 1931. Harry Ransom Center Manuscripts Collection. University of Texas at Austin Library.

With Hector Munro Chadwick. *The Growth of Literature.* Cambridge: Cambridge University Press, 1932, 1936, 1940.

Russian Heroic Poetry. Cambridge: Cambridge University Press, 1932.

"Gusfland Ferge: Scél mucce maic Dathó, ch. 15." *Scottish Gaelic Studies* 4, no. 1 (July 1934): 6–17.

"Lug Scéith Scál Find: Elegy on Labraid Loingsech." *Scottish Gaelic Studies* 4, no. 1 (July 1934): 1–5.

"Imbas Forosnai." *Scottish Gaelic Studies* 4, no. 2 (November 1935): 97–135.

"Shamanism among the Tatars of Central Asia." *Journal of the Royal Anthropological Institute* 66 (1936): 75–112.

"The Spiritual Ideas and Experiences of the Tatars of Central Asia." *Journal of the Royal Anthropological Institute* 66 (1936): 291–329.

"Geilt." *Scottish Gaelic Studies* 5 (September 1942): 106–53.

Poetry and Prophecy. Cambridge: Cambridge University Press, 1942.

"The Captive Lion: Translated from the Turkish of Sülleyman Nazif." *Cambridge Review* 64 (February 1943): 229.

"Early Russian Epic Poetry." *Man* 44 (1944): 49–50.

The Beginnings of Russian History: An Enquiry into Sources. Cambridge: Cambridge University Press, 1946.

"The Celtic Background of Anglo-Saxon England." *Yorkshire Celtic Studies* 3 (1946): 13–32.

"Norse Ghosts: A Study in the *Draugr* and the *Haugbúi*." *Folk-Lore* 57 (1946): 50–65, 106–27.

Editor. *Early Scotland*, by Hector Munro Chadwick. Cambridge: Cambridge University Press, 1949.

"The Story of Macbeth: A Study in Gaelic and Norse Tradition." *Scottish Gaelic Studies* 6, no. 2 (September 1949): 189–211.

"Sir Ninian: A Preliminary Study of Sources." *Transactions and Journal of Proceedings of the Dumfriesshire and Galloway Natural History and Antiquarian Society* 3, no. 27 (1950): 9–53.

"Thorgerthr Hölgabrúthr and the *Trolla Thing*: A Note on Sources." In *The Early Cultures of North-West Europe: H. M. Chadwick Memorial Studies,* edited by Sir Cyril Fox and Bruce Dickins, 395–417. Cambridge: Cambridge University Press, 1950.

"The Story of Macbeth (Continued)." *Scottish Gaelic Studies* 7, no. 1 (May 1951): 1–25.

"The Celtic West." In *The Heritage of Early Britain,* edited by M. P. Charlesworth and M. D. Knowles, 104–27. London: G. Bell and Sons, 1952.

"The Lost Literature of Celtic Scotland: Caw of Pritdin and Arthur of Britain." *Scottish Gaelic Studies* 7, no. 2 (August 1953): 115–83.

"Negro Literature." In *Cassell's Encyclopedia of Literature*, 1: 379. London: Cassell, 1953.

Editor. *Studies in Early British History.* Cambridge: Cambridge University Press, 1954.

"Literary Tradition in the Old Norse and Celtic World." *Saga-Book of the Viking Society for Northern Research* 14 (1955): 164–99.

"Pictish and Celtic Marriage in Early Literary Tradition." *Scottish Gaelic Studies* 8, no. 1 (December 1955): 56–115.

Poetry and Letters in Early Christian Gaul. London: Bowes and Bowes, 1955.

Reviser. *The Study of Anglo-Saxon,* by Hector Munro Chadwick. 2d ed. Cambridge: W. Heffer, 1955.

"The Name Pict." *Scottish Gaelic Studies* 8, no. 2 (December 1958): 130–45.

"Scéla Mucce Meic Dathó: The Story of Mac Dathó's Pig." *Scottish Gaelic Studies* 8 (December 1958): 130–45.

Editor. *Studies in the Early British Church.* Cambridge: Cambridge University Press, 1958.

"The Monsters and Beowulf." In *The Anglo-Saxons: Studies in Some Aspects of Their History and Culture Presented to Bruce Dickins,* edited by Peter Clemoes, 171–203. London: Bowes and Bowes, 1959.

"Scéla Muicce Meic Da Thó." In *Irish Sagas,* edited by Myles Dillon, 79–93. Dublin: Radio Éireann, 1959.

"The Welsh Dynasties in the Dark Ages." In *From the Earliest Times to 1485,* edited by A. J. Roderick, vol. 1 of *Wales Through the Ages.* Llandybie: Christopher Davies Publishers, 1959.

"Bretwalda, Gwledig, Vortigern." *Bulletin of the Board of Celtic Studies* 19 (1961): 225–30.

"The Vikings and The Western World." In *The Proceedings of the International Congress of Celtic Studies Held in Dublin, 6–10 July 1959,* 13–42. Dublin: University Press, 1962.

"The British or Celtic Part in the Population of England." In *Angles and Britons: O'Donnell Lectures,* 111–47. Cardiff: University of Wales Press, 1963.

Editor. *Celt and Saxon: Studies in the Early British Border.* Cambridge: Cambridge University Press, 1963.

Celtic Britain. Ancient People and Places, 34. London: Thames and Hudson, 1963.

"Saint Columba." In *Saint Columba: Fourteenth Cententary, 563–1963,* 3–17. Glasgow: Publishing Department for the Church of Scotland, 1963.

"Dalriada." In *Encyclopædia Britannica* (1964 and thereafter).

"The Russian Giant Svyatogor and the Norse Útgartha-Loki." *Folk-Lore* 75 (1964): 243–59.

"The Colonisation of Brittany from Celtic Britain." *Proceedings of the British Academy* 51 (1965): 235–99.

"England Is Celtic Too." *Irish Digest* 82 (1965): 77–80.

The Druids. Cardiff: University of Wales Press, 1966.

"The Borderland of the Spirit World in Early Literature." *Trivium* 2 (1967): 17–36.

With Myles Dillon. *The Celtic Realms.* London: Weidenfeld and Nicolson, 1967.

"Kenneth." In *Encyclopædia Britannica* (1967 and thereafter).

"Strathclyde." In *Encyclopædia Britannica* (1967 and thereafter).

"Sulpicius Severus." In *Encyclopædia Britannica* (1967 and thereafter).

"Dreams in Early European Literature." In *Celtic Studies: Essays in Memory of Angus Matheson, 1912–1962,* edited by James Garney and David Greene, 33–50. London: Routledge and Kegan Paul, 1968.

Early Brittany. Cardiff: University of Wales Press, 1969.

With Victor Zhirmunsky. *Oral Epics of Central Asia.* Cambridge: Cambridge University Press, 1969.

The Celts. With an introductory chapter by J. X. W. P. Corcoran. London: Penguin Books, 1971.

Wales and the Men of the North. Cardiff: University of Wales Press, 1971.

The Celts. With an introductory chapter by Barry Cunliffe. London: Penguin Books, 1997.

Works Cited

De Navarro, J. M. "Hector Munro Chadwick, 1870–1947." *Proceedings of the British Academy* 33 (1947): 307–30.

Henderson, Isabel. *A List of the Published Writings of Hector Munro Chadwick and of Nora Kershaw Chadwick.* Cambridge: Privately printed by Will and Sebastian Carter, 1971.

Hutton, Ronald. *The Triumph of the Moon: A History of Modern Pagan Witchcraft.* Oxford: Oxford University Press, 1999.

Jackson, Kenneth. "Nora Kershaw Chadwick, 1891–1972." *Proceedings of the British Academy* 58 (1973): 537–49.

Welsford, Enid. *In Memoriam: Nora K. Chadwick, 1891–1972.* Cambridge: Privately printed, 1973.

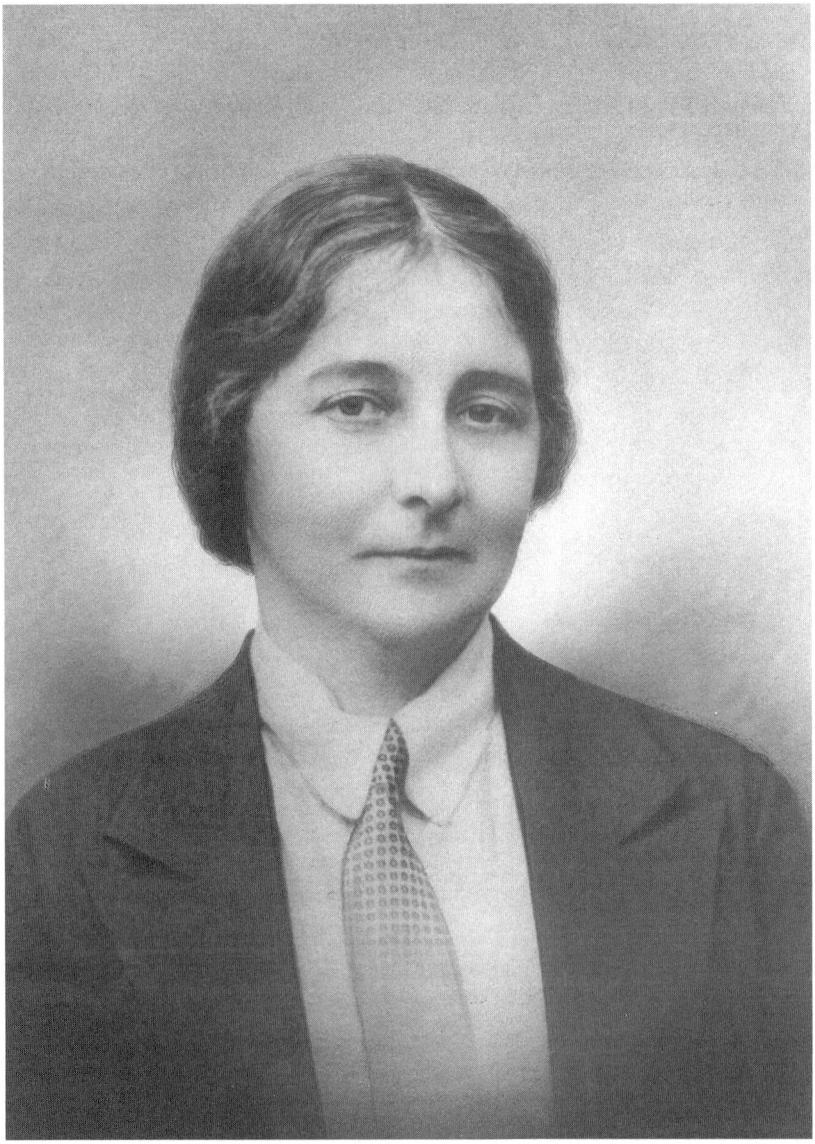

CHAPTER 28

"Persephone Come Back from the Dead"
Maude Violet Clarke (1892–1935)

JENNIFER FITZGERALD

Maude Violet Clarke was born on 7 May 1892 in Belfast and grew up in her father's rectory, Coole Glebe, at Carnmoney, County Antrim. During her childhood her mother was "never quite sane," the cause, Maude's friend Helen Waddell suggested, of "the faint air of tragedy that haunts her face."[1] Mrs. Clarke was hospitalized with mental illness in 1913 until her death in 1942. Her daughter was educated at Alexandra College, Dublin, and at Queen's University, Belfast, where she took a first-class honors degree in history in 1913, and proceeded to Lady Margaret Hall, Oxford, on the Jephson Scholarship. At Oxford, along with graduates from other "provincial" universities, she repeated an undergraduate degree in two years. During the vacations of 1915, she wrote, in collaboration with Waddell, a humorous novel about an antifeminist academic, his rebellious wife, and her friend, the independent scholar Anne Delahide, based explicitly on Maude.[2] After passing her history examinations (again with first-class honors) in 1915, she stayed on at Lady Margaret Hall for the academic year 1915–16, writing a thesis on Irish medieval history.[3]

In 1916 she returned to Queen's University, Belfast, as deputy professor of history, holding F. M. Powicke's chair after he moved to London for war work.[4] This gave her valuable teaching experience—she was described as "being an immense success . . . her classes are worshipping, but with awe."[5] But her experience at Queen's was not comfortable. While "anti-feminist" professors "dead against" the appointment of women might have been a minority, the presence of one woman "cramp[ed] their style, . . . their half-monastic ways."[6] She was also sickened by what she called "the selfish intrigues of a provincial University."[7]

In the spring of 1919 she was offered her choice of two posts at Somerville College, Oxford: the Carlisle Fellowship (which could be considered "the best fellowship in the country for women") and the history tutorship.[8] The fellowship would have given Clarke £120 per annum over five years, but she was strongly advised to take the academic post. The look on her face when she told Helen Waddell, "It's worth two years of *this,* to be going back," spoke volumes about what she felt for Queen's as well as for Oxford.[9] But a job in a residential college carried a heavy load: "eighteen hours coaching in the week, general supervision of about 32 history students, and endless small entertaining of Dons and students in her rooms."[10] It was not surprising that, a year into the post, Clarke suffered "a temporary collapse with overwork.... She had eight people to coach today... as [she] says, 'Eight hungry sheep look up and are not fed.'"[11] The tutoring burden remained heavy; in later years Clarke remembered "how fearfully tired [she] was all of the first three years or so [she] was in Somerville."[12]

Maude Clarke joined Somerville at a significant moment in its history: women's colleges in Oxford were on the verge of achieving their ultimate goal—degrees and admission to membership of the university. The injustice to female students of being deprived of the degrees for which they had proved themselves in the same examinations as their male counterparts was obvious. There were further "humiliating" disadvantages for women academics of being excluded from university membership: "[S]cholars who may have made contributions of value in their own subjects, not only are ineligible for any official position but... are not consulted and may not take part in any discussion formal or informal, with regard to the course of study to be followed by their pupils.... They have no prospect of ever having any influence in questions concerning the studies which are the occupation and interest of their lives, or of any further scope for their abilities."[13] One of the most vigorous campaigners for the dual prize of degrees for women and university membership was Emily Penrose, principal of Somerville. During the summer of 1919 the Sex Disqualification (Removal) Bill in Parliament and, in the fall, a University of Oxford statute indicated that its time had come.[14] The period immediately preceding its achievement was very stressful for Penrose, "prudent to a fault in discouraging any activity that might rebound unfavourably on the movement to secure degrees for women."[15] During May and June 1919, when hope was in the air but the momentous decisions had not yet been made, she had to confront two crises of a nature most likely to bring scandal to the college and to the cause.

The story of women's higher education was from the first haunted by the necessity for impregnable safeguards against sexual impropriety. A college in which young marriageable women resided, far from their families' protection, and which brought them into contact with unattached young men was under enormous pressure and constant threat. Elaborate rules, including chaperonage, were devised to ensure appropriate behavior.[16] During World War I Somerville's premises were taken over by the War Office for hospital purposes, the college renting the Saint Mary Hall Quadrangle of Oriel College for the duration. Massive brick walls were erected to separate the women's accommodation from the men's (of whom very few were left), for the explicit purpose of preserving the reputation of the women students.[17] On transferring to their temporary accommodation, Penrose emphasized the conduct demanded of Somerville's students: "She intimated that people were vaguely expecting us to do something unsuitable—she wasn't quite sure what, but anyhow she was sure we wouldn't do it."[18]

After the war undergraduates began to return to Oxford. Just before Somerville vacated Saint Mary's, on 19 June 1919, a group of inebriated Oriel undergraduates attacked the wall with a pickax: the female students who, because of the heat, were sleeping on the lawn, fled back to their rooms, and the Somerville dons were alerted. Penrose's question, "Do you think this will get into the papers?" obviously reflected her anxiety about negative publicity; in order to avoid any shred of scandal, she organized her colleagues to guard the hole all night long.[19]

Somerville's principal had been trying to negotiate safe passage through another sexual minefield during the previous month. In 1918 her attention had been drawn to a lesbian student; on 24 May 1919 twenty-three students formally wrote to Penrose declaring unease about this student's relationship with another and their sense "that it is unsafe and unfair" that she should enter a profession without notice of (in their opinion) "the nature of her influence on other women." Two of the signatories were sent to see Penrose in person. The latter seems to have dealt with the crisis discreetly and humanely: the couple were separated, encouraged to take a short break and to return to sit their final examinations, without resuming contact. However, the matter remained public in the college, the accused student "interviewing" the signatories of the letter and asking to read it. Penrose read her the letter out loud on 19 June—only to be woken up during the night with the news of male incursion in the pickax incident. The next day she was once again in correspondence on the lesbian issue.[20]

These incidents took place before Maude Clarke joined Somerville, but as we shall see, they had specific repercussions for her. They also point to the hidden history of lesbian students and faculty in women's colleges: women-only spaces, suspected of being able to dispense with men, were effectively policed by homophobia.[21] While personally baffled by lesbianism, Penrose followed advice that "no blame should be attached" to the student whose lesbian relationships from 1917 to 1919 were a matter of record. The student seems to have behaved in a resilient, perhaps defensive, manner; the college refused to supply letters of recommendation for a teaching post in a girls' school but does not seem otherwise to have impacted negatively on her career.[22] The crisis also highlights the conflict between the responsibilities of surveillance and confidentiality that weighed on women academics in residential posts. Among Penrose's records is a letter from the history tutor and vice principal of Saint Hilda's College, Oxford, A. Elizabeth Levett.[23] She enclosed a partial transcript of a letter from a recent graduate, which in turn revealed confidences received from a Somervillian "who was an invert." Levett obviously felt obliged to pass on information relating to the student under Penrose's care, while scrupulously preserving her anonymity and that of her own correspondent.[24]

With such burdens on the shoulders of women faculty, it would not be surprising if, in the crucial following months, Emily Penrose should have enjoined on her staff the necessity of avoiding any behavior that could be negatively interpreted. In a college where "[m]any of the tutors were scarcely—if at all—older than the students under their supervision," Maude Clarke may well have understood in September 1919 the need to keep her distance from her charges, to avoid any lingering lesbian suspicion.[25] At any rate, she gave this reason, many years later, for the coolness she showed to her oldest friend, Helen Waddell, when the latter came to Somerville as a research student in October 1920.[26] It may also go some way in explaining the negative portrait published by Vera Brittain, one of Clarke's first students.

Brittain originally came up to Somerville in 1914 to read English; during the war she lost her fiancé and brother and served as a nurse. On her return to Somerville at Easter 1919, she changed her degree to history and began her studies proper with Maude Clarke as her history tutor in the Michaelmas term. While Clarke was twenty-seven, Brittain was only eighteen months younger and obviously expected Clarke to treat her, given her years and experience, as an equal, or at least with sympathy: "[T]o Winifred [Holtby] and myself, with our still raw memories, [Maude Clarke's] elegant, dark-eyed youth lent an inhuman emphasis to the serene detachment with which she seemed to view the tragedy that had dislocated our lives.... With her smooth dark hair, attractive wedge-shaped face and soft Irish voice, she did not appear inhuman, but though her keen incisive mind could be moved to sympathy by intellectual struggles, the emotional conflicts of those whose work she directed seemed to leave her singularly unmoved."[27] Brittain does not mention the cautious, if not paranoid, atmosphere at Somerville in the fall of 1919, which might well have exacerbated Clarke's "serene detachment."[28] On the other hand, one recognizes a fundamental incompatibility between Brittain's emotional neediness and her tutor's "almost passionate reserve, which she treasured like a private possession."[29]

Brittain also portrayed Clarke as Patricia O'Neill, history tutor at "Drayton College, Oxford," in her novel *The Dark Tide*. One of the students, Daphne Letheridge, ends her Oxford career by marrying her male tutor. Daphne's marital failure and the voluntary spinsterhood of her friend, Virginia Dennison, are offset against the happy romance of Patricia O'Neill and her fellow academic, Alexis Stephanoff. Like the rest of Brittain's fiction, this is a roman à clef, in which "identifiable persons from real life are presented as thinly disguised fictional characters": readers had no difficulty in connecting the Polish Alexis Stephanoff with the Polish Lewis Namier or the Irish Patricia O'Neill with Maude Clarke.[30] Despite the sympathetic portrait oral tradition has it that Clarke was not well pleased at her appearance in fiction. Apparently, two Somerville students met her in an Oxford tea shop and told her that they had ceremonially burned *The Dark Tide,* page by page, in the yard; without a word Clarke walked around the table and shook them warmly by the hand. The story may be apocryphal: Brittain herself referred to "a ban by [her] own college upon circulation of the book," although there is no record of an official ban.[31]

However, one can speculate that Clarke did not like to be romantically connected in print with the recognizable alter ego of Lewis Namier, tutor at Balliol, where her own brother (in the novel, cousin) was an undergraduate. Patricia O'Neill's reluctance to marry is founded on her academic work, which she does not want to relinquish. Stephanoff suggests that marriage will not prevent her from coaching and research.[32] It was not against the rules for women academics to marry, but it was very rare.[33] In Oxford and Cambridge male dons had emerged from semimonastic seclusion to middle-class domesticity and family life in their own homes, but "[m]arriage and heterosexual partnership were virtually foreclosed to [women dons].... They knew that taking an academic job or even pursuing an academic degree meant renunciation of family life."[34] In the early twentieth century the married woman could not be guaranteed the independence of mind, not to mention career, essential to scholarship.[35] This, after all, had been the crux of Clarke and Waddell's 1915 novel: the heroine revolts against her husband in an attempt to assert her intellectual autonomy. The incompatibility of marriage and an academic career might well have been the decisive factor for Clarke, although Waddell believed "physical passion was left out in her."[36]

While Brittain's fictional version of Clarke is more compassionate than the biographical portrayal, according to Waddell, Clarke was reticent rather than unsympathetic.[37] Her academic standards were high—"like an acid when she isn't satisfied"—but "she had a rich and catholic delight in the whole business of living, and her mind continually feasted."[38] She was also capable of pranks: during Brittain's time, she engineered a hoax that threw Somerville into a turmoil.[39] She was a dedicated teacher, "exacting and, to the lazy, formidable." In the early years, she sacrificed her own research in order to master the whole undergraduate history curriculum.[40]

The teaching load in women's colleges was heavy: at one stage Clarke "hoped for a Readership ... [to] get free of the eternal tutoring"; in 1926 she applied unsuccessfully for the chair of history at Bedford College, University of London.[41] But as her Oxford career began to take shape, she became more involved in college and university matters, gaining considerable satisfaction along with new responsibilities. In 1921 Somerville's tutors were admitted to membership of its council; as a result, Clarke was elected one of the college's first fellows.[42] In 1930 she was appointed lecturer in modern history (a university position, as distinct from her position as a senior member of Somerville College), becoming "a force in both the undergraduate and postgraduate teaching of the University" as well as liaising with secondary schools.[43] At Queen's she had concluded "that good work was carried on only in spite of the obstruction of those who had their own ends to serve." At Somerville, on the contrary, she felt she "gained a moral education by serving on committees," especially through observing Emily Penrose's "unswerving justice, patience and complete obliteration of self."[44] By the 1930s Clarke and her friend Lucy Sutherland were the "really important people" among the Somerville faculty.[45] Her skills were particularly appreciated when a chapel was donated to Somerville—a divisive move for a college founded on nondenominational principles, and one that remains controversial to this day.[46] She became vice-principal in 1934; the consensus seems to be that if she had lived, she would have been an obvious choice as principal.[47]

She also traveled, particularly with her brother Stewart (nicknamed Chang), who shared her Oxford life, becoming a classical archaeologist and fellow of Exeter College in 1923. Chang was drowned during a research trip off a small boat in the Aegean in May 1924. In 1925 she went to Palestine with her father; in 1931 she visited her eldest brother, Harry, in Jamaica.[48] And of course, she returned to Ireland during the vacations, both to visit family and in pursuit of Irish historical material. Eventually she began to publish. Clarke's field—medieval constitutional history—permitted a double claim on professional, "scientific" history through its documentary sources and the specialist technical skills required.[49] Clarke advised her younger colleague Lucy Sutherland (later to become a formidable eighteenth-century historian) that "it would help establish you firmly on the historical side to publish something mediaeval."[50] Bonnie G. Smith notes, "From their entry into the academy, professional women followed the road to the same universally true scholarship that men valued." She identifies Clarke as one of a group of female historians "who made extensive use of records in monasteries and local archives. . . . publish[ing] philologically expert, densely referenced editions of institutional records and manuscripts, produced in an expository style congenial to experts."[51]

Clarke was passionate about research, from her postgraduate days making forays into libraries in the pursuit of manuscripts.[52] According to Waddell, Clarke's "flair for first hand documents" was remarkable. "Someone told her she should have gone into Science, instead of History: she has the same 'humility before the fact' that is rare in historians."[53] Her first published article, "Irish Parliaments in the Reign of Edward II," was tersely written, but almost immediately she got into her stride. *The Medieval City State: An Essay on Tyranny and Federation in the Later Middle Ages* (1926) is characterized by narrative ease and exemplary clarity. Drawing on published and well-known original documents (in Latin, German, Italian, and French as well as in English), this book is a lively synthesis of the history of the medieval city states, eliciting the political consequences of the dynamic, sometimes chaotic, constitutional arrangements that developed as the interests of three groups—capitalists, guilds, and workers—pulled in opposite directions. Clarke shows that, paradoxically, democracy evolved into oligarchy and hence into tyranny. It is "an admirably condensed and readable account . . . probably the best extant survey in English of the subject."[54] This work was followed in 1928 by the paper "The Lancastrian Faction and the Wonderful Parliament" (unpublished until 1937), in which a wealth of detail is bound into coherence by her flowing narrative.

Her next two publications were editions of unpublished manuscripts. This training ground of the serious academic involved not only the deciphering of medieval script but also the disinterring, layer by layer, of scribes, compilers, and multiple authors of the text, the history of the manuscript's transcription, and its ownership for the light these could throw on the author's perspective or knowledge of events recounted.

Exceptionally, this first attempt at the technicalities of scholarship led to an editorial in *The Times*.[55] The *Dieulacres Chronicle*, which she edited with expert paleographer Vivian Galbraith, shed new light on the deposition of Richard II, indicating the distortions and suppression of evidence that discredited the parliamentary roll's official version.[56] Since no less an authority than William Stubbs had based his interpretation of the constitutional implications on this flawed perspective, Galbraith and Clarke were breaking new ground. An edition of the *Kirkstall Chronicle* (with N. Denholm-Young) added documentary evidence supporting the conclusions derived from the *Dieulacres Chronicle*, while also illuminating Richard II's oppressive policies.[57]

She also began to train herself in iconography, as evidenced by her brilliant analysis of the Wilton Diptych, depicting the presentation of Richard II to the Virgin and Child. Reminding us that "Richard's subjects could read a coat more easily than they could read a letter," she adduces heraldic evidence to date the painting and to identify its function as propaganda for a new crusading order.[58] Furniture came next, as she examined the inventories of forfeitures during the crisis of 1388; this in turn uncovered valuable evidence about the law of treason.[59] An interest in Irish crosses, stimulated by research undertaken to help examine a thesis, involved fieldwork in Ireland.[60] A fellow of the Royal Historical Society since 1925, in 1934 she became a member of the Society of Antiquaries.

Clarke's reputation as a meticulous investigator of minute evidence—illuminated by a wide and detailed knowledge of historical events and in turn illuminating political concepts and institutions—was growing. Her clear, vivid writing style, which disentangled confused sequences of events and explained obscure points of evidence without losing sight of the main plot, helped her reader grasp clearly reasoned arguments. These were invaluable resources for a life of Richard II, which she had been planning to write since 1926. But as she researched into the immediate background of Richard's reign, she recognized features requiring detailed investigation: constitutional implications, in particular, were thrown into relief by Irish evidence.[61] This became her special contribution to fourteenth-century history.

These studies drew her attention to the *Modus Tenendi Parliamentum*, a short anonymous tract describing the composition and procedure of Parliament and its governing principles. *Medieval Representation and Consent* contextualizes this document historically, developing her theory of the English constitution based on the doctrines of representation and consent. A group of transcripts, with consistent textual variations, originate in Ireland: these she related to the history of the Irish Parliament in the later Middle Ages. This developed more slowly than its English counterpart; in particular, consent to parliamentary, as opposed to local, taxation took much longer to be accepted. Clarke suggested that the *Modus* was used specifically to shape the Irish Parliament according to English ideals and practices.

She proposed that the *Modus* was written in 1322 by a cleric anxious to emphasize the representative role of the proctors in the commons, echoing "the ideal of harmonious co-operation of all the estates" simultaneously expressed in the statute of

York, enacted in May 1322.[62] She pushed her conclusions too far for some reviewers, failing to convince them of the text's function as the working basis for constitutional practice. Later work by V. H. Galbraith confirmed her views.[63] Her book was deemed to have offered new insights—particularly on the ecclesiastical sources of representation and consent, which had been neglected by contemporary scholars in favor of legal origins—while also opening up Irish constitutional history.[64] And it did not escape notice that "[f]lashes of brilliance enliven[ed] the erudition of Miss Clarke's writing."[65]

Maude Clarke began *Medieval Representation and Consent* in 1930; most of it was written in 1933–35, when she was battling breast cancer. In a remarkably brief period she had built up a reputation as "the most distinguished of the women History dons in Oxford, and a brilliant and sympathetic exponent of the middle ages."[66] Through close and exact studies of texts she reinterpreted political and constitutional development in the fourteenth century: it comes as no surprise that in 1933 she was asked to synthesize this knowledge by writing the fourteenth-century volume of the *Oxford History of England*.

It is possible to view Clarke's attitude to the English constitution as idealistic, a Burkean harking after tradition.[67] She was not, however, naive: in the notes that rehearsed her ideas for the proposed *Fourteenth Century*, she recognizes that political history appears to be "largely pathological" because it involves a "close-up" perspective, like that of Swift's Gulliver in the land of Brobdingnag. The historian of church or Parliament "who has any standard of moral values is constantly threatened with nauseating attacks of Brobdingnagianism." This leads her to her "theme": that the "immediate intentions," however self-interested or base, of individuals are of less consequence to an institution than its own evolutionary "blind purpose."[68] The *Oxford History* volume—which should have cemented her reputation as a foremost historian—was eventually written by her student May McKisack.[69]

Before Clarke had published a word, Waddell had summed up her friend's brilliance: "She has an extraordinary mind: I think she forgets nothing, and yet she reads enormously: but it's not chaos. It's just as though the creative intelligence brooded over the mass. Do you remember—is it Shelley's phrase [?]—'the shaping spirit of imagination': that's mine, as much as it is good for anything. Maude is Matthew Arnold's phrase—'the imaginative reason.' Add to that ... an unerring gift for words.... I've never heard her use an adjective that wasn't the expression to the last nuance of her thoughts."[70] Clarke's oeuvre is notable not only for its "ruthlessly efficient scholarship" but also for its "great learning lightly borne."[71] In the face of obfuscation generated by layers of arcane data, she conferred clarity and reason. Her method of working from the known to the unknown imparts to her historiography "almost a detective story sequence, both unusual and welcome in such a learned work."[72] Indeed, as she began *Medieval Representation and Consent*, she devised a scheme of chapter headings appropriate for an alternative title, *The Mystery of the "Modus"*: "Chapter I: Experts Are Puzzled; Chapter II: The Scene of the Crime; Chapter III: False Clues; Chapter IV: A Clerical Suspect; Chapter V: Across the Channel; Chapter VI: Duped;

Chapter VII: Murder by Committee; Chapter VIII: The Wrong Letters; Chapter IX: On the Trail; Chapter X: Some Archdeacons in Council; Chapter XI: Money and Morals; Chapter XII: A Bundle of Papers; Chapter XIII: The Criminal; Chapter XIV: All's Well that Ends Well."[73] This is Clarke's "strong sense of mischief" at work, "the old freakish Maude," but also indicates her deep commitment to historiography.[74] She thought long and hard on how historical analysis could be synthesized without distortion and narrated in a way that engaged the reader in the historical experience. Her wide reading acted as a stimulus to reflection on issues close to her heart. Her notes delve into "the artistic problems that confront the historical writer," into "the special qualities required by the historian as thinker," into the role of fact, experience, and imagination in history.[75] W. P. Ker's *Epic and Romance* leads to an analysis of the art of narrative; G. M. Trevelyan's *England under Queen Anne* to the conclusion that "[t]o write well, at least to write history well, some emotion must be allowed to work on the heart"—followed immediately by the question, "Is this too much or too dangerous?"[76]

Even more interesting are the deliberations stimulated by a sentence in Virginia Woolf's *To the Lighthouse:* "And she thought, standing there with her book open, here one could let whatever one thought expand like a leaf in water; and if it did well here, among the old gentleman smoking and *The Times* crackling, then it was right."[77] Clarke muses: "To expand like a leaf in water. Something like this happens to facts in one's head when they have been soaked for a time by a subconscious process in the imagination. . . . Perhaps . . . everything should present itself first of all as appearance, before it becomes appearance with a meaning. The hard thing is to recognise the appearance before one has fumbled after the meaning . . . for it is thought, when the facts are dead, when it is an old thing known only from dry bones, that sets the imagination going. . . . Each fossilised phrase of a writer has had history beaten into it: to omit a gerund like *faciendum* may threaten a revolution or at least rob the king of the money that he needs to hold the Kingdom of Scotland."[78] She would have had direct knowledge of Woolf from Waddell and from her former student Winifred Holtby; nevertheless, this is a noteworthy application of *To the Lighthouse* to the process of historical thinking.[79] Her "humility before the fact" was shifting: by 1925 she "had grown sick of facts without an idea to make them luminous"; a few years later Waddell reported: "Maude used to make me academic and critical—now it's the romantic creative side she brings out. I think because she enjoys it so."[80] In notes titled "Stages of Mental Development necessary for historical study (or *better*) The equipment of a Historian," Clarke acknowledged, conventionally, that history is "*the science of ascertaining the facts of human affairs.*" But human sympathy and a sensitive, strong imagination are also required. Successful historiography "implies a projection of personality into the fact so complete that the events actually repeat themselves and become an experience of the mind."[81]

Despite the restrictions of college life, there were many advantages, not the least being strong friendships among colleagues.[82] During her vacations in Ireland Clarke was able to ask Lucy Sutherland, Dominica Legge, or others to send on notes or books left in her room or to order "rotographs" of medieval manuscripts from professional photographers in London.[83] These and her other friendships were of great importance to Clarke, but in the summer of 1935, when she knew that her illness was imminently terminal, she did not want her colleagues to know that she was leaving Oxford for good.[84] She left behind a letter of resignation from her Somerville fellowship and the other offices she held in the college; characteristically, she wrote again within a few days suggesting how she could be replaced at short notice. Equally characteristically, Somerville refused to accept her resignation, offering her instead two terms of sabbatical leave. Somerville was her home and (at least partly) her family: she could not express "strongly enough" what it meant to her to "remain a full member of the College."[85] Lucy Sutherland, May McKisack and Helen Waddell came to Ireland to visit her. A long-term agnostic (despite being the daughter of a minister), Clarke had recovered her faith a year before her illness was diagnosed.[86] Maude Clarke died at her father's rectory, Coole Glebe, on 17 November 1935 at the age of forty-three.

Many believed, with Vivian Galbraith, that, had she lived, "she would have been among the leading medievalists of her generation."[87] Fifty years after her death her ability to instill "the most rigorous scholarly standards" was still a matter of record, while her work on Richard II remains worth reading.[88] Somerville College established the Maude Violet Clarke Scholarship for the Promotion of Historical Research in 1936; in 1993 Queen's University, Belfast, named one of its visiting professorships, established to promote the participation of women in academic life, after her. In an obituary of her best friend, Helen Waddell used Gibbon's phrase, describing Maude as "Persephone come back from the dead, but with the knowledge of kingdoms of it in her face."[89] Clarke herself wrote: "Facts must not only be known but experienced or else they are not alive. . . . Only a great artist can do it for another."[90] It is her triumph that, as a historian bringing the past back to life, she too was an artist.

NOTES

I should like to thank Somerville College, Oxford, owners of Maude Clarke's copyright; Mary Martin, Helen Waddell's niece; Dames Felicitas Corrigan and Philippa Edwards of Stanbrook Abbey, Worcester, England, owners of Helen Waddell's copyright and Richard Clarke of Belfast and Bodleian Library, Oxford, for permission to quote from Maude Clarke's and Helen Waddell's unpublished writings and letters, without which this essay could not have been written. Many of these papers are not dated: when a date has been established by internal evidence, it is cited in square brackets; uncertain dates are followed by a question mark. I should also like to thank Somerville College for permission to quote from the Penrose: Correspondence File and the College Discipline File, and the Department of Women's Studies, San Diego State University, for giving me access to the university library. Special thanks to Somerville librarian Pauline Adams and to Richard Clarke, Maude Clarke's nephew, for generous help and information. I owe a debt of gratitude to Gianna Pomata, whose conversations on Helen Waddell and Maude Clarke have inspired me.

1. Helen Waddell to George Taylor [February 1919?], Waddell Papers, Stanbrook Abbey; Richard Clarke, letter to the author, 18 June 2001.

2. "Discipline" is still unpublished (Waddell Papers, Stanbrook Abbey).

3. Maude Clarke to R. J. Clarke [March 1916], courtesy of Richard Clarke. In 1918 she negotiated with a Dublin publisher for a book of lectures (never written) on medieval Ireland (Helen Waddell to George Taylor, ca. 13 October 1918, Waddell Papers, Stanbrook Abbey).

4. Helen Waddell to George Taylor, 21 June and 30 July 1916, Waddell Papers, Stanbrook Abbey. In 1919 F. M. Powicke (1879–1963) moved to the chair of history at Manchester; in 1928 he became Regius Professor of Modern History at Oxford (Southern, "Powicke, Sir [Frederick] Maurice.")

5. Helen Waddell to George Taylor, 5 November 1916, Waddell Papers, Stanbrook Abbey.

6. Helen Waddell to George Taylor, 21 June 1916; Waddell to Margaret Martin [1932], Waddell Papers, Stanbrook Abbey.

7. Maude Clarke to Emily Penrose, 24 November 1925, Penrose: Correspondence File, Somerville College.

8. Adams, *Somerville for Women,* 77–78; Helen Waddell to George Taylor, 23 March 1919, Waddell Papers, Stanbrook Abbey.

9. Helen Waddell to George Saintsbury, ca. 20 March 1919, Waddell Papers, Stanbrook Abbey.

10. Helen Waddell to George Taylor, 9 November 1919, Waddell Papers, Stanbrook Abbey.

11. Helen Waddell to Margaret Martin [winter 1920], Waddell Papers, Stanbrook Abbey.

12. Maude Clarke to Lucy Sutherland, 16 August 1929, Box 3, Sutherland Papers, Bodleian Library.

13. Emily Penrose and B. A. Clough, "Universities Commission: Report of Sub-Committee on Women's Colleges," quoted in Adams, *Somerville,* 56.

14. The first Somerville graduates received their Oxford degrees on 14 October 1920 (Adams, *Somerville,* 151); see also Howarth, "Women," 349. Clarke received her B.A. and M.A. on 13 November 1920 (Maude Clarke to R. J. Clarke, 20 November 1920, courtesy of Richard Clarke).

15. Adams, *Somerville,* 81. Vera Brittain acknowledged "the need for ultra-staid and exemplary behaviour demanded by authorities fearful of losing the battle at the last fence" ("Somerville School of Novelists," 124).

16. Adams, *Somerville,* 33, 115, 168; Howarth, "Women," 361–62.

17. Adams, *Somerville,* 89.

18. College meeting, 28 May 1915, quoted in Adams, *Somerville,* 91.

19. Verbatim account by one of the participants, Vera Fernall, quoted in Adams, *Somerville,* 100–102.

20. College Discipline File, 1919–1919, Somerville College.

21. Jeffreys, *Spinster and Her Enemies,* 112. Havelock Ellis made the association between women's access to equality (and higher education) and lesbianism:

> It has been stated by many observers who are able to speak with some authority—in America, in France, in Germany, and in England—that homosexuality is increasing among women. There are many influences in our civilisation to-day which encourage such manifestations. The modern

movement of emancipation—the movement to obtain the same rights and duties, the same freedom and responsibilities, the same education and the same work—must be regarded as, on the whole, a wholesome and inevitable movement. But it carries with it certain disadvantages. . . . [H]aving been taught independence of men and disdain for the old theory which placed women in the moated grange of the home to sigh for a man who never comes, the tendency develops for women to carry this independence still further and to find love where they find work. I do not say that these unquestionable influences of modern movements can directly cause sexual inversion . . . but they develop the germs of it, and they probably cause a spurious imitation. This spurious imitation is due to the fact that the congenital anomaly occurs with special frequency in women of high intelligence who, voluntarily or involuntarily, influence others. (Ellis, *Studies in the Psychology of Sex*, 2:147–48)

See also Sahli, "Smashing," 25–27; Leonardi, *Dangerous by Degrees*, 39–40.

22. College Discipline File, 1918–1919, Somerville College.

23. Levett provided Clarke with unpublished information on a medieval source (Clarke, *Medieval Representation and Consent*, 129 n. 3), while on Levett's sudden death Clarke undertook to edit her "Studies in the Manorial Organisation of Saint Alban's Abbey," a work interrupted by her own death. This was finally published by her colleagues: *Studies in Manorial History*, by Ada Elizabeth Levett, 74–368. Levett was a notable economic historian, moving from Oxford to the University of London, first as lecturer and then as reader at King's College and finally as professor of history at Westfield College (Jamison, "Ada Elizabeth Levett," ix; see also Berg, *Woman in History*, 63, 168).

24. College Discipline File, 1918–1919, Somerville College.

25. Adams, *Somerville*, 122.

26. The break in the friendship was very painful for Waddell, who did not understand the reason for Clarke's coolness for many years (Corrigan, *Helen Waddell*, 197).

27. Brittain, *Testament of Friendship*, 84–85. In later years Brittain herself drew attention to Clarke's position: "[A]t the early age of twenty-seven, she had to function as a don while several mature students who had served in the War were coming back to college, old in experience, impatient with scholastic seclusion, and only two or three years younger than herself. When tutor and student are too near in age a happy relationship is not easily achieved" (*Women at Oxford*, 143).

28. In May and June 1919 Vera Brittain was at Somerville; she does not refer to the lesbian scandal, although she is likely to have been aware of it, since one of her close friends was among Penrose's correspondents. However, some critics point to Brittain's accounts of Winifred Holtby's possible lesbian passion for her as a sign of protesting too much, a willing obtuseness about Holtby's feelings: see *Testament of Friendship*, 117–18, 328, and the discussion in Kennard, *Vera Brittain and Winifred Holtby*, 5–8. Brittain recounted the pickax incident but misremembered the date as 1915, just after the move to Saint Mary's Hall (*Testament of Youth*, 150; see also her *Women at Oxford*, 139).

29. Powicke, review of *Fourteenth Century Studies*. Powicke had taught Clarke as an undergraduate at Queen's University, Belfast.

30. Mark Bostridge, introduction to *The Dark Tide*, by Vera Brittain, x, xiv. Lewis Namier (Ludwik Bernstein Niemirowski) was educated in Europe, at the London School of Economics, and at Balliol College, Oxford. In 1920–22 he was a history tutor at Balliol. Following a career path similar to that of Brittain's Stephanoff, he initially left the academic world for that

of business and diplomacy. His historical interest focused, as did Clarke's, on the British Parliament, specializing in the eighteenth century, as did her friend Lucy Sutherland (Brooke, "Namier, Sir Lewis Bernstein").

31. Pauline Adams, letter to the author, 16 April 1998; Vera Brittain, 1935 preface to *Dark Tide,* xxiii; Pauline Adams, letter to the author, 2 July 2001.

32. Brittain, *Dark Tide,* 201.

33. The two most noted exceptions were Lilian Knowles and Eileen Power; both, however, taught at the London School of Economics and did not have residential responsibilities (Dyhouse, *No Distinction of Sex?* 162; Berg, *Woman in History,* 193–94).

34. Smith, *Gender of History,* 189.

35. Ibid., 190. Referring specifically to Helen Maud Cam, Beryl Smalley, Dorothy Whitelock, and Maude Clarke, Norman Cantor suggests that "[s]exual autonomy was perhaps a necessary defense for this generation of women medievalists making their way in a profession that was intrinsically hostile to them and accepted them begrudgingly and essentially required of them that they work within the prevailing ethos of a male-dominated medievalist world" (Cantor, *Inventing the Middle Ages,* 389).

36. Helen Waddell to unknown correspondent [October/November? 1935], Waddell Papers, Stanbrook Abbey.

37. "Maude *is* a goblin: but inside she is . . . the most exquisitely sympathetic person I know. If you are in a hole, she won't say very much: but you know that she will 'grieve' for you for days" (Helen Waddell to George Taylor, 11 March 1917 [Waddell Papers, Stanbrook Abbey]).

38. Helen Waddell to Margaret Martin [March 1925], Waddell Papers, Stanbrook Abbey; Waddell, "Miss N. V. Clark" [*sic*].

39. Adams, *Somerville,* 216–17.

40. Obituary, "Miss M. V. Clarke."

41. Helen Waddell to Margaret Martin [1925?] and [May 1926].

42. Adams, *Somerville,* 155.

43. Obituary, "Miss M. V. Clarke."

44. Maude Clarke to Emily Penrose, 24 November 1925, Penrose: Correspondence File, Somerville College.

45. Hilda Bryant, quoted in Adams, *Somerville,* 186.

46. Obituary, "Miss M. V. Clarke"; Adams, *Somerville,* 81–85, 354.

47. Woodward, "Memoir," xi.

48. Richard Clarke, letter to the author, 18 June 2001.

49. Smith, "Contribution of Women to Modern Historiography," 723.

50. Maude Clarke to Lucy Sutherland, 8 September 1932, Box 3, Sutherland Papers, Bodleian Library.

51. Smith, *Gender of History,* 197–98. The group includes A. Elizabeth Levett, Eileen Power, and Helen Cam. Like many of her female colleagues, Clarke published under the initials of her first name, leaving the question of gender ambiguous to those who did not read the code of her affiliation to Somerville College. One reviewer referred to her authorship in the masculine (Byrne, review of *The Medieval City State,* 103).

52. Helen Waddell to George Taylor, 16 January 1916 and [April 1917], Waddell Papers, Stanbrook Abbey.

53. Helen Waddell to George Taylor, ca. 13 October 1918, Waddell Papers, Stanbrook Abbey.

54. Byrne, review of *The Medieval City State*, 101.

55. Editorial, "The Deposition of Richard II."

56. Clarke with Galbraith, "Deposition of Richard II." As a result of the publicity generated by *The Times*, this was reprinted as a pamphlet.

57. Clarke with Denholm-Young, "Kirkstall Chronicle." Her other editions include "Henry Knighton and the Library Catalogue of Leicester Abbey"; and *Register of the Priory of the Blessed Virgin at Tristernagh*.

58. "Wilton Diptych," 283.

59. "Forfeitures and Treason in 1388."

60. Woodward, "Memoir," xii.

61. "William of Windsor in Ireland"; "Committees of Estates and the Deposition of Edward II"; "Origin of Impeachment."

62. Clarke, *Medieval Representation and Consent*, 173.

63. Haskins, review of *Medieval Representation and Consent*, 733; Cantor, *Inventing the Middle Ages*, 440.

64. However, one reviewer pointed to the "voluminous manuscript sources for mediaeval Irish history" that would have challenged Clarke's conclusions (Richardson, review of *Medieval Representation and Consent*, 67).

65. Russell, review of *Medieval Representation and Consent*, 118.

66. Myres, "May McKisack," xiii.

67. She seems to have brought these expectations into daily life: "She was concerned with the form, and not merely the spirit, of an institution. She insisted always upon the dignity, the permanent value of external observances and conventions as safe-guards against sentimentality or drift" (Woodward, "Memoir," xviii).

68. Clarke, "England C14," 26–27, Blue Exercise Book, Clarke Papers, Somerville College, referring to Tawney, "Introductory Memoir." (These notes can be dated between 1933, when she received the commission for *The Fourteenth Century*, and 1935, the date of her death.) See also her reflections on the value of corporate life versus the entirely individual experience of the lonely unit of consciousness proposed by Powys, in *In Defence of Sensuality* ("Historiography," 26–27, Blue Exercise Book, Clarke Papers, Somerville College. These notes can be dated between 1930, the date of publication of the texts she writes on, and 1935, the date of her death).

69. McKisack, *Fourteenth Century*. In the preface McKisack expresses gratitude "for the benefit of an incomparable tutor, Maude Clarke, whose book this should have been."

70. Helen Waddell to George Taylor, ca. 13 October 1918, Waddell Papers, Stanbrook Abbey.

71. Galbraith, "Thoughts about the Peasants' Revolt," 47; Galbraith, "Clarke, Maude Violet."

72. Russell, review of *Medieval Representation and Consent*, 118. Brittain's judgment that "as soon as [Clarke] attempted to put her knowledge into a book, the dry bones refused to live" is not sustained (*Testament of Friendship*, 85).

73. Maude Clarke to Lucy Sutherland, 4 August 1931, Box 3, Sutherland Papers, Bodleian Library.

74. Woodward, "Memoir," xix; Helen Waddell to Margaret Martin [March 1925], Waddell Papers, Stanbrook Abbey.

75. Notebook, 7–8; 10–11 (this notebook may have been written as she prepared for *The Fourteenth Century*, and hence between 1933 and 1935); "Stages of Mental Development necessary

for historical study (or *better*) The equipment of a Historian" (Clarke Papers, Somerville College). (There is no indication of when "Stages" was written.)

76. Clarke, "Historiography," 2–4; 12, Clarke Papers, Somerville College.

77. Woolf, *To the Lighthouse,* 282. In Clarke's edition, this quotation was on p. 291.

78. "Historiography," 7–9, Clarke Papers, Somerville College. Smith refers to Clarke's notes on "subliminal activities" (*Gender of History,* 235).

79. Woolf reviewed *The Blechley Diary of William Cole, 1765–67* with Waddell's introduction in the *New Statesman and Nation* and sent a holograph of the review to the latter in the form of a letter (Waddell Papers, Queen's University Library); Holtby, *Virginia Woolf.*

80. Helen Waddell to George Taylor, c. 13 October 1918; Helen Waddell to Margaret Martin [1925] and [November 1932], Waddell Papers, Stanbrook Abbey.

81. "Stages of Mental Development," Clarke Papers, Somerville College (emphasis is Clarke's). Clarke is echoing Dilthey's *Nacherleben,* or "reexperiencing" (Dilthey, "Understanding of Other Persons and Their Experience of Life," 132–35).

82. Vicinus, *Independent Women,* 7; Smith, *Gender of History,* 196.

83. See letters of Maude Clarke to Lucy Sutherland, Box 3, Sutherland Papers, Bodleian Library.

84. Helen Waddell to Margaret Martin [15 July 1935], Waddell Papers, Stanbrook Abbey.

85. Maude Clarke to Helen Darbishire, 23, 28 June, and 11 October 1935, Clarke Papers, Somerville College.

86. Helen Waddell to Margaret Martin [1932], Waddell Papers, Stanbrook Abbey.

87. Cited by Cantor, *Inventing the Middle Ages,* 389

88. Whiteman, "Sutherland, Lucy Stuart"; Cantor, *Inventing the Middle Ages,* 440.

89. Waddell, "Miss N. V. Clark [*sic*]."

90. "Stages of Mental Development," Clarke Papers, Somerville College.

Select Bibliography of Works of Maude Violet Clarke

The contents page of *Fourteenth Century Studies* indicates which of the following essays have been reprinted therein

"Irish Parliaments in the Reign of Edward II." *Transactions of the Royal Historical Society,* 4th ser., 9 (1926): 29–62.

The Medieval City State. An Essay on Tyranny and Federation in the Later Middle Ages. London: Methuen, 1926.

With V. H. Galbraith. "The Deposition of Richard II." *Bulletin of the John Rylands Library,* Manchester 14 (1930): 125–81; reprint, Manchester: Manchester University Press, 1930.

"Henry Knighton and the Library Catalogue of Leicester Abbey." *English Historical Review* 45, no. 177 (1930): 103–7.

"Forfeitures and Treason in 1388." *Transactions of the Royal Historical Society,* 4th ser., 14 (1931): 65–94.

With N. Denholm-Young. "The Kirkstall Chronicle, 1355–1400." *Bulletin of the John Rylands Library,* Manchester 15 (1931): 100–37.

"The Wilton Diptych." *Burlington Magazine* 58 (1931): 283–94.

"William of Windsor in Ireland, 1369–1376." *Proceedings of the Royal Irish Academy* 41C (1932): 55–130.

"Committees of Estates and the Deposition of Edward II." In *Historical Essays in Honour of*

James Tait, edited by J. G. Edwards, V. H. Galbraith, and E. F. Jacob, 27–45. Manchester: printed for the subscribers, 1933.

"The Manuscripts of the Irish 'Modus Tenendi Parliamentum.'" *English Historical Review* 48, no. 192 (1933): 576–600.

"The Origin of Impeachment." In *Oxford Essays in Medieval History Presented to Herbert Edward Salter,* 164–89. Oxford: Clarendon Press, 1934.

Medieval Representation and Consent: A Study of Early Parliaments in England and Ireland, with Special Reference to the "Modus Tenendi Parliamentum." London: Longmans, 1936.

Fourteenth Century Studies. Edited by L. S. Sutherland and M. McKisack. Oxford: Clarendon Press, 1937.

"The Lancastrian Faction and the Wonderful Parliament." In *Fourteenth Century Studies,* edited by L. S. Sutherland and M. McKisack, 36–52. Oxford: Clarendon Press, 1937.

Register of the Priory of the Blessed Virgin Mary at Tristernagh, Transcribed and Edited from the Manuscript at the Cathedral Library, Armagh. Dublin: Stationery Office, 1941.

With Helen Waddell. "Discipline: A Collaboration." Stanbrook Abbey, Worcester.

Letters to Lucy Sutherland. Box 3, Lucy Stuart Sutherland Uncatalogued Papers. Bodleian Library, Oxford.

Letters to R. J. Clarke. Courtesy of Richard Clarke.

Clarke Papers. Notes and Letters of Maude Violet Clarke. Somerville College, Oxford.

Works Cited

Adams, Pauline. *Somerville for Women: An Oxford College, 1879–1993.* Oxford: Oxford University Press, 1996.

Berg, Maxine. *A Woman in History: Eileen Power, 1889–1940.* Cambridge: Cambridge University Press, 1996.

Brittain, Vera. *The Dark Tide.* With a preface by Vera Brittain and introduction by Mark Bostridge. London: Virago, 1999.

———. "The Somerville School of Novelists." *Good Housekeeping,* April 1929, 52–53, 122–24.

———. *Testament of Friendship: The Story of Winifred Holtby.* London: Virago, 1997.

———. *Testament of Youth: An Autobiographical Study of the Years 1900–1925.* New York: Macmillan, 1934.

———. *The Women at Oxford: A Fragment of History.* New York: Macmillan, 1960.

Brooke, John. "Namier, Sir Lewis Bernstein." In *Dictionary of National Biography, 1951–1960.*

Byrne, Eugene H. Review of *The Medieval City State: An Essay on Tyranny and Federation in the Later Middle Ages,* by M. V. Clarke. *American Historical Review* 33, no. 1 (1927): 101–3.

Cantor, Norman F. *Inventing the Middle Ages: The Lives, Works and Ideas of the Great Medievalists of the Twentieth Century.* New York: William Morrow and Co., 1991.

College Discipline File, 1918–1919, Somerville College, Oxford.

Corrigan, D. Felicitas. *Helen Waddell: A Biography.* London: Gollancz, 1986.

Dilthey, Wilhelm. "The Understanding of Other Persons and Their Experience of Life." Translated by Kenneth L. Heiges. In *Descriptive Psychology and Historical Understanding, by Wilhelm Dilthey,* 121–44. The Hague: Martinus Nijhoff, 1977.

Dyhouse, Carol. *No Distinction of Sex? Women in British Universities, 1870–1939.* London: UCL Press, 1995.

Editorial. "The Deposition of Richard II." The *Times* (London), 29 January 1930.

Ellis, Havelock. *Studies in the Psychology of Sex.* Vol. 2, *Sexual Inversion.* Philadelphia: F. A. Davis, 1901.
Galbraith, V. H. "Clarke, Maude Violet." *Dictionary of National Biography, 1931–1940.*
——— "Thoughts about the Peasants' Revolt." In *The Reign of Richard II: Essays in Honour of May McKisack,* edited by F. R. H. du Boulay and Caroline M. Barron, 46–57. London: University of London, Athlone Press, 1971.
Haskins, George L. Review of *Medieval Representation and Consent: A Study of Early Parliaments in England and Ireland, with Special Reference to the "Modus Tenendi Parliamentum,"* by M. V. Clarke. *American Historical Review* 42, no. 4 (1937): 732–34.
Holtby, Winifred. *Virginia Woolf.* Folcroft, Penn.: Folcroft Press, 1969.
Howarth, Janet. "Women." In *The History of the University of Oxford,* vol. 8, *The Twentieth Century,* edited by Brian Harrison, 345–75. Oxford: Clarendon Press, 1994.
Jamison, E. M. "Ada Elizabeth Levett." In *Studies in Manorial History,* by Ada Elizabeth Levett, edited by H. M. Cam, M. Coate, and L. S. Sutherland, ix–xv. London: Merlin Press, 1963.
Jeffreys, Sheila. *The Spinster and Her Enemies: Feminism and Sexuality, 1880–1930.* London: Pandora, 1985.
Kennard, Jean E. *Vera Brittain and Winifred Holtby: A Working Partnership.* Hanover, N.H.: University Press of New England, 1989.
Ker, W. P. *Epic and Romance: Essays on Medieval Literature.* New York: Dover Publications, 1957.
Leonardi, Susan J. *Dangerous by Degrees: Women at Oxford and the Somerville College Novelists.* New Brunswick, N.J.: Rutgers University Press, 1989.
Levett, Ada Elizabeth. *Studies in Manorial History.* Edited by H. M. Cam, M. Coate, and L. S. Sutherland. London: Merlin Press, 1963.
McKisack, May. *The Fourteenth Century: 1307–1399.* Vol. 4 of *Oxford History of England.* Oxford: Clarendon Press, 1959.
Myres, J. N. L. "May McKisack." In *The Reign of Richard II: Essays in Honour of May McKisack,* edited by F. R. H. du Boulay and Caroline M. Barron, xiii–xvi. London: University of London, Athlone Press, 1971.
Obituary. "Miss M. V. Clarke." *Times* (London), 19 November 1935.
Penrose, Emily. Penrose: Correspondence File. Somerville College, Oxford.
Powicke, F. M. Review of *Fourteenth-Century Studies,* by M. V. Clarke, edited by L. S. Sutherland and M. McKisack. *Manchester Guardian,* 10 August 1937.
Powys, John Cowper. *In Defence of Sensuality.* New York: Simon and Schuster, 1930.
Richardson, H. G. Review of *Medieval Representation and Consent: A Study of Early Parliaments in England and Ireland, with Special Reference to the "Modus Tenendi Parliamentum,"* by M. V. Clarke. *History* 22 (June 1937): 66–69.
Russell, Josiah C. Review of *Medieval Representation and Consent: A Study of Early Parliaments in England and Ireland, with Special Reference to the "Modus Tenendi Parliamentum,"* by M. V. Clarke. *Speculum* 12, no. 1 (1937): 116–19.
Sahli, Nancy. "Smashing: Women and Relationships before the Fall." *Chrysalis* 8 (1979): 17–27.
Smith, Bonnie G. "The Contribution of Women to Modern Historiography in Great Britain, France and the United States, 1750–1940." *American Historical Review* 89 (1984): 709–32.
———. *The Gender of History: Men, Women, and Historical Practice.* Cambridge: Harvard University Press, 1998.
Southern, R. W. "Powicke, Sir (Frederick) Maurice." *Dictionary of National Biography, 1961–1970.*

Tawney, R. H. "Introductory Memoir." In *Studies in Economic History: The Collected Papers of George Unwin,* xi–lxxiv. New York: Augustus M. Kelley, 1966.

Trevelyan, George Macaulay. *England under Queen Anne.* Vol. 3, *Blenheim.* London: Longmans, Green and Co., 1930.

Vicinus, Martha. *Independent Women: Work and Community for Single Women, 1850–1920.* Chicago: University of Chicago Press, 1985.

Waddell, Helen. "Miss N. V. Clark [*sic*]." *The Times* (London), 25 November 1935.

——— Papers. Queen's University Library, Belfast.

——— Papers. Stanbrook Abbey, Worcester.

Whiteman, Anne. "Sutherland, Lucy Stuart." *Dictionary of National Biography, 1971–1980.*

Woodward, E. L. "Memoir." In *Fourteenth Century Studies,* by M. V. Clarke, edited by L .S. Sutherland and M. McKisack, ix–xxi. Oxford: Clarendon Press, 1937.

Woolf, Virginia. Review of *The Blechley Diary of William Cole, 1765–67,* edited by Francis Griffin Stokes, with an introduction by Helen Waddell. *New Statesman and Nation* (6 February 1932): 164–65.

———. *To the Lighthouse.* New York: Harcourt, Brace and Co., 1927.

CHAPTER 29

Joan Evans (1893–1977)
Art Historian and Antiquary

NICOLA COLDSTREAM

ALTHOUGH JOAN EVANS was only seven years old when Queen Victoria died in 1901, throughout her life she remained close to the liberal tradition of nineteenth-century England into which she had been born. Memory stretched back further: Joan was the last child of the antiquary Sir John Evans, who was seventy at the time of her birth and remembered seeing as a boy the fire that destroyed the Palace of Westminster in 1834; he had also met people who had lived through the great events of the late eighteenth century in America and France. Joan Evans herself collected pre-Revolutionary French jewelry, which she wore "with distinction."[1]

Joan Evans came from a noteworthy family. Its wealth based in the papermaking business of John Dickinson and Co. Ltd, it produced three generations of scholars: John Evans (1823–1908), who established a chronology for prehistory; his eldest son, Arthur (1851–1941), the excavator of Knossos in Crete, who defined the Minoan civilization; and Joan (1893–1977), forty-two years younger than her half-brother. All three were pioneers in their chosen areas of scholarship, and all three were elected president of the Society of Antiquaries of London, Joan Evans being the society's first woman president.[2] Joan's interests are easy to identify, but she herself fits no single category. Her background, unorthodox education, and the wealth that gave her independence and enabled her to be a prominent collector and connoisseur set her apart from scholars who can be defined through a professional position or writings on a consistent theme. Mindful of family tradition, to which she was "to some extent both hostage and guardian," Joan Evans thought of herself as an archaeologist.[3] The archaeology she studied at Oxford in 1914–15 did not concern itself with digging. It aimed to "educate the aesthetic faculty by the study of style in antique

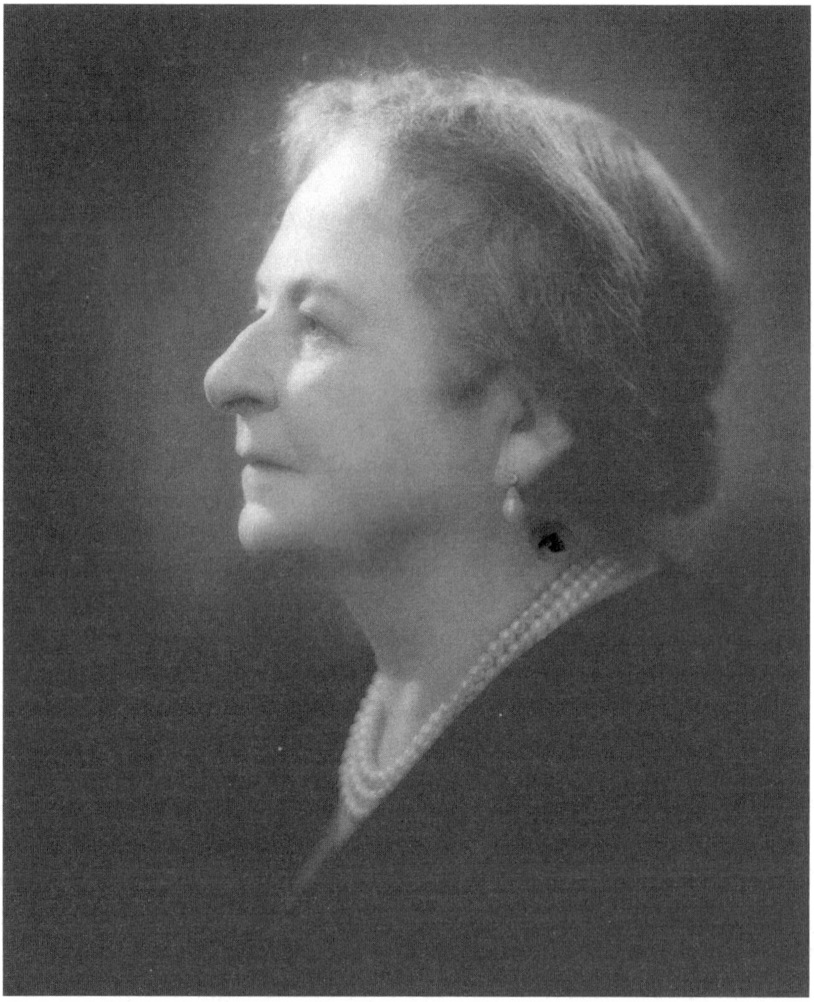

art."[4] As one of John Beazley's first pupils in sculpture and vase painting, she was subjected to his "Berensonian attributions" of vases to particular painters from the evidence "of no more than an ankle."[5] Lack of sympathy with Beazley's method encouraged her to develop her interests in a later period, but she still strongly believed that medieval archaeology should not solely concern digging. In the 1960s she deplored the absence of medieval archaeologists who were prepared to look beyond "plans and sherds" to "the study of greater architecture, of painting, of iconography. The methods of prehistory have . . . begun to take over historic and well-documented periods in which a more subtle, more aesthetic and more civilized method of approach should primarily be employed."[6] She wrote approvingly of Sir Alfred Clapham's remarks regretting the "scission between archaeology and art history."[7] Her vision of art history encompassed "the understanding of the environment that produced the work of art," including geographical contacts, economic conditions, and historical circumstances: in other words, art history and archaeology should be "the study of human civilization."[8] Nowadays her approach to the history of art is taken for granted, and it is difficult to appreciate her relative isolation as a scholar, but in the 1920s, when she began to publish her research, art history had not yet been established as an academic subject in British universities. The Courtauld Institute of Art in London was founded only in 1931, and even then it specialized in Italian postmedieval art, taught as a narrative of great painters. The proliferation of courses and pluralistic approaches occurred only from the 1960s, and Oxford, Joan Evans's own university, never taught art history to undergraduates in her lifetime. Joan Evans effectively created a subject for herself. As well as her work in the medieval period, which is the main subject of this essay, she published many studies of jewelry, French civilization down to 1789, aesthetics, and ornament. She wrote family history, biography, and autobiography; as a labor of love and respect, she compiled the index to Arthur Evans's four-volume *Palace of Minos,* when he had become too old to manage it himself. What drove all her intellectual activities was a deep love of beauty and an equally deep love of France. Together they unite her great range of material into a coherent scholarly universe; because she used her experience of each topic to enrich her thinking and illuminate the others, her medieval studies cannot wholly be separated from her other interests.

Joan Evans's world of the historical imagination was fully formed in her youth, assisted by visits to France, Italy, and Greece from a young age. Although it subsequently widened and deepened, it did not change. The breadth of her interests was in the family tradition inherited by both Arthur and Joan from their father; they shared with him the receptiveness and mental agility that can reveal fresh paths of knowledge. Joan's mother, the former Maria Lathbury, who did not attend Oxford University until she was thirty and married at thirty-six, never wanted a child. She was quite uninterested in nurturing the very young: she wanted to accompany her aging husband on his travels and also to be recognized as an intellectual personality in her own right.[9] Much younger than her three surviving half-siblings, Joan had a lonely childhood in the family home at Nash Mills in Hertfordshire, cared for by her nurse, Caroline Hancock (known as "Nannie"), who took the mother's place and may have been partly responsible for the difficult relationship that persisted between mother and daughter.[10] Joan's parents traveled every winter, only occasionally summoning their small daughter to join them, as in 1902 when Sir John Evans took Joan to see the quarries at Saint-Acheul, near Abbeville in northern France, where in 1859 he had first identified man-made flint implements.[11] John Evans also paid attention to Joan when he was at home, giving her an early training in archaeological method by teaching her about his collections of flint and bronze tools, coins, seals, and rings.[12] He introduced her to the leading scholars of the day, who were his friends, so that when she began to do her own research she already knew many of the museum curators, archaeologists, and other scholars who shared her interests. After John Evans's death in 1908, Joan's home life was more isolated than ever, since her mother, never very sociable, now invited even fewer people to the house.

Among Maria Lathbury's friends at Oxford in the 1880s had been Charlotte Jourdain, sister to Eleanor and Margaret Jourdain, both of whom were to make a significant and lasting impact on Joan's life. Eleanor ran a school, Corran, at Watford, not far from Nash Mills, to which the five-year-old Joan was sent before later going on to Berkhamsted Girls' School. Neither school provided the standard of education that she needed in order to realize her mother's plans for her to read Classics at Somerville College, Oxford, and when she was seventeen Joan had a nervous collapse, brought on by unresolved grief at her father's death and feelings of hopeless intellectual inadequacy. She "screwed up [her] courage to tell [her] mother with tears that [she] had rather not go to Oxford."[13] For some months she continued to work at home, using her parents' library, but the situation was transformed by a visit from Eleanor Jourdain's much younger sister, Margaret, who diagnosed Joan's woeful lack of self-confidence and commissioned her to write a book on English jewelry for a series that she was editing on the minor arts.[14] With John Evans's collection of rings to hand, Joan at once set to work. Margaret Jourdain had a habit of encouraging the young to build on their talents, but the significance of her rescue of Joan's nerve in 1911 cannot be overemphasized.[15] The commission for the book on jewelry, which was eventually published in 1921, started Joan Evans on her academic career. Yet Eleanor, unwittingly, and Margaret, wittingly, were to harm Joan as much as they benefited her, and in their dual role as supporters and destroyers their shadows hung over her long after both had died.

The Jourdains were daughters of an impecunious clergyman; as a family they were much given to feuds. Poverty forced them into early independence, hence Margaret's support for young people in similar straits.[16] Eleanor was romantic rather than intellectual. A pious High Anglican, she had tendencies to mysticism; it was she who, with C. A. Moberly, then principal of Saint Hugh's College, Oxford, thought they saw apparitions at Versailles in 1901, an experience that they later published as *An Adventure*.[17] Eleanor joined the Evanses in Rome during their visit to the city in 1912—the grandeur of Roman architecture helped to form Joan's tastes—and collaborated with Joan on the latter's first article, an inquiry into Roman topography.[18] Eleanor was by now the vice principal of Saint Hugh's and was able to offer Joan a place in the college to read for the diploma in classical archaeology, which she took up in 1914. Two years later Eleanor became principal of Saint Hugh's; Joan accepted the post of college librarian in 1917, and although Eleanor's eccentric temperament and habits of favoritism made her enemies in the college, Joan herself remained loyal to her despite misgivings, though she gave up the librarianship and left Saint Hugh's in 1922. When scandal broke in 1924 over Eleanor's unjustified dismissal of a young don whom she disliked, Joan was one of those who returned to Saint Hugh's to replace college tutors who had struck in sympathy with the victim. The university found against Eleanor Jourdain, who had to resign her post. Joan Evans gave her secret financial help. When Eleanor died of a heart attack six days later, it was discovered that she had made Joan her residuary legatee, leaving her young friend everything but her shares, including her jewelry.[19]

Margaret Jourdain was a tougher character than her sister. She was a realist and a skeptic, thinking nothing of Eleanor's mystical imaginings. By 1914 Margaret had turned herself into an expert on historic furniture and decoration, and for the rest of her life she made a living writing articles on those subjects for such periodicals as *Apollo,* the *Connoisseur,* and *Country Life.* Like Joan she loved beauty, but she deliberately suppressed any feelings she might have had toward the fanciful or romantic. With a passion for the truthful and the genuine, she even avoided drawing conclusions from original research, owing to their possible fallibility. Margaret cultivated an unadorned literary style that related the facts flatly and without flourishes. Highly disciplined, she trained Joan Evans in precision by making her translate French sonnets and present facts plainly. Like many other people, Joan came completely under Margaret's powerful spell. Margaret was a stern atheist, and she helped Joan "to shed crushing burdens of guilt and piety in adolescence," leaving Joan, who had "never encountered [religion] as a child in a form which [she] could accept," in a spiritual vacuum but with "a hankering after religion."[20] Joan believed that her scholarly achievements owed everything to Margaret. By 1919 Lady Evans had set up home in London; the Jourdain family home, which Margaret shared with her mother and dying sister Millie, broke up. Mrs. Jourdain and Millie went to live with Eleanor in Oxford, and Margaret was left homeless, bitterly resentful that Eleanor could not find room for her in her tiny house. Joan, the only person who managed to be friends with both Eleanor and Margaret, tried to give something back to her mentor by offering her a home in London, but Margaret eventually chose to live with Ivy Compton-Burnett. She disdained the whole concept of family and stayed aloof from Eleanor's difficulties at Saint Hugh's, but with her taste for jewelry, Margaret did not disdain what she saw as the family inheritance. When the contents of Eleanor's will became known, Margaret, encouraged by Ivy Compton-Burnett, chose to believe that Joan Evans had swindled her out of the jewels; that they were not valuable made no difference. Lady Evans sided with Margaret. The full situation—that Joan was meant to distribute some of the bequest—was never properly explained to either of them, and Joan was unable to tell the truth about her financial help to Eleanor because this had been in shares rather than cash, which Lady Evans regarded as the alienation of capital, something never to be undertaken. Margaret never spoke to Joan again.

Part of Joan Evans never recovered from the rupture with Margaret Jourdain. In her autobiography, *Prelude and Fugue,* she ignored the whole episode and elided over the events leading to it—one reason for this, however, is her belief that whatever may be said, some things are better left unwritten—and, holding "Poison Ivy" responsible, in old age she had to be persuaded to speak to Hilary Spurling when the latter was writing her biography of Compton-Burnett.[21] She saw Margaret only three more times after 1924, each an agonizing glimpse across a room or from a train. As late as 1949 the unforgiving Margaret went out of her way to write a scathing review of Joan Evans's *English Art, 1307–1461.*[22] This review is, however, very revealing of Margaret herself. It shows that, whatever Joan Evans may have believed, for posterity the break with Margaret Jourdain was not the tragedy it seemed. Margaret neither understood nor appreciated Joan's approach to the Middle Ages, and she disliked the book's lyrical tone. Had the two remained close, it is possible that, despite Joan's own strength of character, some essential qualities in her would have been denied. In the event, she was able to develop as a medievalist unhindered by Margaret's limitations and, most importantly, she was able to cultivate her gift for poetry. Joan began to write poetry in her youth, publishing "The Hamadryad" in 1917, and she continued all her life, though she destroyed her poems at the end.[23] Her lyricism and feeling for nature, both apparent in "The Hamadryad," could have been inhibited by prolonged exposure to Margaret Jourdain's increasing austerity. In their joint articles on early nineteenth-century jewelry, published in the *Connoisseur* in 1920 and 1921, Joan's contribution is impossible to detect. They are written in the dry, informative style cultivated by Margaret, a style inimical to Joan Evans. Joan's later writing, free of Margaret's strictures, has a lyric grace, its simple, elegant sentences leading the reader effortlessly onward. Joan made each of her books a journey of discovery for herself and her readers; she conveyed her own interest in the subject, and if her enthusiasm is tempered by good manners, it is never suppressed.

By the early 1920s Joan Evans was an established expert on jewelry and had had some training as a medievalist, although in truth she taught herself.[24] Already by about 1910 she had come across written sources, reading for the first time, in French, Jean de Joinville's *Histoire de Saint Louis,* which she was later to translate.[25] After gaining distinction in the Diploma of Classical Archaeology, she stayed on for another year to be tutored in medieval history and paleography. The distinction allowed her to go on to research; appointed librarian at Saint Hugh's, she wrote a thesis on magical jewels for the certificate of letters, which was all that women were awarded, owing to Oxford's refusal to admit them to degrees. She gained her certificate in 1919, just as the university finally succumbed to reality, and she was awarded the full degree of

Bachelor of Letters (B.Litt.) in 1920.[26] Joan had direct, practical knowledge of objects, since she started collecting while at Oxford and had access to the collections of John and Arthur Evans. *Magical Jewels of the Middle Ages and the Renaissance* was published in 1922, the year after *English Jewellery from the Fifth Century A.D. to 1800,* the book commissioned by Margaret Jourdain. They were followed in 1924 by *Anglo-Norman Lapidaries*. These books, with *English Posies and Posy Rings* (1932), elevated the study of jewels to a new plane. Joan demonstrated for the first time that magic jewels and posy rings were not simply a medieval phenomenon born of pre-Reformation superstition, as had been believed, but had continued down to the eighteenth century. She provided catalogs, sources, and texts. With these publications she set out the recurring pattern of her scholarship: the integration of the visual and literary arts, the insight into the small and the personal, and a chronological scope that ignored the traditional breaks between medieval and modern.

Joan Evans's first book on medieval culture was *Life in Medieval France,* published in 1925. It was dedicated to the memory of Eleanor Jourdain, with whom Joan had visited Paris in 1919, later that year traveling with her mother in Champagne.[27] This was the beginning of regular and frequent visits to France for pleasure and research. She was often accompanied by one or other of the friends—contemporaries—that she had finally been able to make at Oxford. She had a capacity for friendship with people of all ages, making many younger friends later in life. In *Prelude and Fugue* she hinted at a possibility of marriage, but the young man was killed in 1914, and Joan remained unmarried, one of the many women left single by the events of World War I.[28] Various friends did, however, find Joan's form of travel difficult to tolerate, and eventually Nannie became her preferred traveling companion. Joan worked in museums and libraries, examining objects, reading inventories, and acquiring a circle of like-minded French friends and colleagues, the most important of whom were J. J. Marquet de Vasselot, curator of jewelry at the Louvre, and his daughter, Claude Carnot. It was in these years that she went for the first time to Burgundy and saw the painted Romanesque chapel at Berzé-la-Ville, which she was to buy and present to the Académie of Mâcon in 1947. France now became her second country and the principal focus of her interests. Although she had some feeling for Spain, she did not engage at a deep level with Italian or German art.[29]

Life in Medieval France was written, it seems, partly with the aim of explaining to the English their own past: "[The men of medieval France] belong to the time when England held provinces in France. . . . In literature, in art, in learning, England is the daughter of France; if there had been no such French civilization in the Middle Ages there could have been no such English Renaissance."[30] *Life in Medieval France* is a book of cultural history, originally including a chapter on art, which was dropped from later editions after the publication of *Art in Medieval France*. Chapters on feudal society, town and monastic life, pilgrimage and crusade, learning, and education are sandwiched between "France in the Early Middle Ages" and "The End of the Middle Ages," introductory and concluding chapters that show that Joan, like her contemporaries in other branches of historical knowledge, saw the Middle Ages as tripartite, with biological phases of youth, maturity, and old age.[31] The Middle Ages were defined by feudalism and chivalry, which were at their height during the mature phase, when France was governed by wise rulers from Louis IX (1226–70) to Charles V (1364–80). The period after the Black Death and the Hundred Years' War constituted old age, with its connotations of decline and decadence, connotations to be found also in J. M. Huizinga's highly influential *The Waning of the Middle Ages*, which had been published in English in 1924, while Joan was writing her own book. The late period, when feudalism and chivalry had been abandoned, was no longer truly medieval, though not less interesting.

Joan Evans's study of jewelry and manuscripts, through inventories as well as the pieces themselves, had given her a unique insight into the relationship between public display and private life. She saw that they were not distinct but formed a double helix, two intertwined strands. This understanding led her to present medieval art in a new way. In those years it was interpreted as the architecture and sculpture of the church: grand, public art, with a message that, although powerful, was essentially impersonal. Joan brought in the private, personal world of individual ownership. Patronage was the key. As well as beauty, it gave art a sense of purpose. Later she was to write: "Nowadays we do not realize what art has lost from the lack of the direct patronage that it enjoyed in the Middle Ages: a patron who knew what he wanted and knew what he was going to do with it, and had the money to pay for it, and an artist infinitely skilled in his craft but also endowed with humility, could strike sparks from each other and create masterpieces. Art which is created to fulfil a direct function has an enormous advantage over the abstract doodlings of today."[32] Patronage stimulated creation. Joan wrote on three principal, mildly overlapping medieval themes—French art, the Cluniacs, and English art—all three primarily from the point of view of patronage. Like her work in jewelry, her study of patronage was an innovatory and lasting contribution to the historiography of art. Yet its originality is easy to overlook. Patronage is now one of the most popular topics in art history, but it owes its current preeminence to the impact made by such books as Francis Haskell's *Patrons and Painters*, which was published only in 1963. Rightly acclaimed, this book changed the way scholars looked at Italian seventeenth-century art. What they forgot, or had perhaps never realized, was that by then Joan Evans had been advocating such an approach to medieval art for forty years.

In *Life in Medieval France* the literary evidence is as important as the visual—extracts from contemporary poetry and chronicles, even prayers (rarely translated, although the book was for the general reader). In the 1920s and 1930s, however, she did publish several translations of medieval texts, including Joinville's *Histoire de Saint Louis*, on which she worked while in Jordan, Syria, and Palestine visiting her close friend Agnes Horsfield, the daughter of Martin Conway. Being in the land of the Crusades made Joan feel closer to the book, and the book brought her closer to the Crusades.[33] The long description of life in a fifteenth-century French country house in *The Unconquered Knight: A Chronicle of the Deeds of Don Pero Niño,* which she published in 1928, is directly related to her interest in the rituals of domestic life.[34] *Dress in Medieval France* (1952) was the direct outcome of this interest, and she again used literary and visual sources not only to illustrate changing fashion but also to elucidate the meaning of the vocabulary of costume. The book has been amplified and superseded by the more detailed research of later generations, but it was itself a radical reworking of some nineteenth-century studies and did much to clarify the subject as it then stood.[35]

Art in Medieval France (1948) is subtitled *A Study in Patronage.* As before, the first and last chapters respectively set the scene and close it out, the word "decline" being evident in the last pages.[36] But the body of the text concerns the art of different monastic orders, the secular clergy, the mendicants, and the aristocracy, townspeople, and peasants. Although Joan considered peasants more significant as guardians of the countryside than of the arts—anachronistically attributing to them the topography and orchards that she knew and loved in modern France—it was entirely characteristic of her to include them in a comprehensive survey. Royal and aristocratic display attracted her more, but no work of art was too modest to escape attention. As both a historian and a collector she reconciled two different attitudes, considering the function of objects while never ignoring their beauty. She aimed to show how the status and needs of a particular patron dictated the form of the work, that no work of art should be considered out of the context of its creation. Significantly, the reviewers who most fully appreciated her intentions were antiquaries. The architectural historian Nikolaus Pevsner, while praising the book, felt obliged to reiterate to his readers—in the *Architectural Review*—Joan's own statement that this was a book about "historical development, and not that of technique or style." Nevertheless, he seemed a little baffled by this; with his German-trained belief in *Stilkritik* he could be expected to remark on it, but his attitude was a warning of what would happen to Joan Evans's reputation in her later years.[37]

The main focus of Joan Evans's interest in France was, however, the monastery of Cluny. Cluny was among the many sites in Burgundy that she explored in the 1920s "with a feeling of discovery."[38] She wanted to excavate the remains of the abbey church but had to compete with Kenneth John Conant, who explored the site in 1927 and persuaded the Medieval Academy of America to support an excavation project. In the summer of 1928, partly in recognition of Conant's services to France in World War I, the French authorities awarded excavation rights to him.[39] Of Joan Evans's three books on Cluniac themes—*Monastic Life at Cluny* (1931), *Romanesque Architecture of the Order of Cluny* (1938), and *Cluniac Art of the Romanesque Period* (1950)—the last two in particular were the product of research in libraries and, more importantly, on the ground that had never been undertaken before. She described in *Prelude and Fugue* the work of identifying and listing all recorded Cluniac houses in western Europe and then visiting the sites, or what was left of them.[40] Her intention was to discover if there was a distinctive Cluniac style. She was satisfied that there was. Her belief in the existence of a specific Cluniac art may have been influenced by Arthur Kingsley Porter's *Romanesque Sculpture of the Pilgrimage Roads* (1923), a study that saw the decorated churches on the pilgrimage routes through France to Compostela as a discrete group, linked by a common purpose and the spread of influences along the routes. Joan Evans's theory has come up against two insurmountable objections: that there was no formal Order of Cluny at any stage in its history, and that what her collection of buildings shared was less a consistent style than a common tendency toward elaborate sculptural ornament. Monasteries designated as belonging to the order were reformed Benedictine houses with some Cluniac connections, but there were no common liturgies, customs, or any other trace of centralized government. A glance through her own illustrations demonstrates the varied approaches to decoration and styles from region to region. Yet Joan Evans's photographs of buildings that were then far less accessible and barely known and her lists of churches are, like much of her work, still a valuable resource.

In 1949 Joan Evans published *English Art, 1307–1461*. This was the fifth of a projected eleven-volume Oxford History of English Art from the early Middle Ages to the twentieth century, each volume to be written by a different author, the whole to be edited by T. S. R. Boase, formerly the director of the Courtauld Institute and from 1947 the president of Magdalen College, Oxford. No such history of English art for the general reader, or indeed for specialists, had been undertaken before, and it was badly needed. The instruction, to set art and architecture in their social and stylistic contexts, suited her perfectly, and although Joan could never suppress hints that English art was a paler relative of its French counterpart, she strongly believed that the English should value and study the art of their country.[41] She cared little for the ignorance of English people and wanted to rescue them from both their philistinism and what she recognized as cultural cringe. The periods allocated to the volumes of the Oxford History were arbitrary, some based on reigns of monarchs, others not. Volumes 3 to 6 were designed around regnal dates: that preceding Joan Evans's covered the reigns of Henry III and Edward I; hers was to begin with Edward II and end at the accession of Edward IV. Historically, this made little sense; artistically, none at all. The volume was meant to examine the Decorated and Perpendicular styles in architecture and the art that went with them, but Decorated, however it is defined, began before 1307, and the greatest Perpendicular architecture was built after 1461. Joan Evans dealt with this by starting the book in 1290, with the Eleanor Crosses built to commemorate the death of Eleanor of Castile, and by concentrating on houses, parish churches, and such smaller monumental works as tombs and crosses, with which she was able to represent the later period reasonably thoroughly. Joan Evans argued that Decorated, with its ogees, encrusted foliate ornament, and love of miniaturism, was essentially a style of decoration rather than architecture, which at that time offered no coherent statements. She saw that its motifs permeated all media and that the only way to understand the attitudes of the time was to study all its manifestations as one. The usual art historical method—of treating architecture, sculpture, painting, and the so-called minor arts separately—was misleading. So, although she was forced to categorize to some extent, her opening chapter barely mentions architecture but ranges over the Eleanor Crosses, tombs, psalters, and embroidery. Only after that are there chapters on architecture, contrasting the "graceful, flowing lines" of Decorated with the rectilinear purity of Perpendicular.[42] But her emphasis was on patronage and historical setting, with a bias toward display, similar in social range to *Art in Medieval France*. People generate art, from jewelry to buildings: half the book is devoted to domestic architecture, parish churches, villages, and tombs. *English Art* was and still is one of the few general books that pay proper attention to secular as well as ecclesiastical architecture.[43] Literary sources, including wills and inventories, amplify the evidence of surviving pieces and fill gaps.

Unlike Joan Evans's work on the Cluniacs, subsequent research has not invalidated her conclusions; it has reinforced them.[44] Yet *English Art* has almost disappeared from scholarly sight. The reasons are quite complex, both academic and personal. It was very much Joan Evans's book: no one else would have written it in this way, and, in fact, no one else could have written it, since at that time she was the only person with the necessary range and depth of knowledge. Most critics whose scholarly interests were deeper but narrower misunderstood her aims. Margaret Jourdain's review missed the point of the opening chapters, arguing that architecture—the "Mistress art"—had little in common with *opus anglicanum*.[45] J. C. Dickinson was unsympathetic to Joan Evans's belief in the indivisibility of life and art, complaining of unbalanced coverage and that woodwork and stained glass should have received more treatment, tournaments and guilds less; the gaps proved that the book should have been written by several authors, like the *Cambridge Medieval History*.[46] W. L. Hildburgh, collector of alabasters, even considered that architecture was too dominant.[47] Quaint though these opinions seem now, they did damage. The most interesting and rewarding review was written by Nikolaus Pevsner in the *Times Literary Supplement*.[48] It was the only one properly to engage with Joan Evans's ideas and to appreciate exactly what she was trying to do, but courteous and enthusiastic though he was, Pevsner radically disagreed with her interpretation of the architecture. He believed passionately that Decorated was a genuine style of architecture, its spatial explorations at Bristol, Wells, and Ely far in advance of anything in mainland Europe, and that Joan Evans's comparisons of English and French buildings were invalid.

Joan Evans was also strongly criticized for mistakes and errors, and this was to do her lasting harm, as such criticism appeared in reviews with increasing regularity.[49] Even now she is remembered for inaccuracy. The mistakes crept in partly from her working methods and partly from impatience. In 1939 Joan Evans had bought Thousand Acres, a house at Wotton-under-Edge in Gloucestershire set overlooking the green countryside of the Severn Vale and south Wales. Five years later, when her mother died, she sold the London house, bought an apartment, and from then on spent winters in London and summers at Wotton. In the winter she did research in libraries and museums, which she wrote up during the summer in the country, to be checked the following winter.[50] It was easy for errors to slip in. Yet most of them are editorial or inaccurate references rather than errors of fact. Joan Evans was clearly not naturally suited to the drudgery of checking references, and she liked to get on quickly with the next book. It is no surprise that hers was the first volume of the Oxford History of English Art to be completed. In his anniversary address to the Society of Antiquaries, Sir James Mann recalled that within a week of being invited to write the history of the society, Joan Evans had begun collecting material "and had even written the first page."[51] The errors can be irritating, but in the context of her achievement they scarcely matter. As Glyn Daniel wrote: "She worked quickly and did not always check back her reference cards: who does? It is often said that there are minor errors in her books: and in whose books do these not occur?"[52]

By the 1960s, as the present writer can testify from her own experience as a student at the time, *English Art* was being quietly denigrated, even though in the late 1960s there was talk of a new edition, which came to nothing.[53] The book had the misfortune to be published at just the wrong moment, when scholarly fashions were undergoing rapid change. Joan Evans's broad, unifying vision was being overtaken by a new generation of scholars who, often in pursuit of doctorates, studied much smaller topics at greater analytical depth. New controversies had arisen, particularly in architecture, where the origins of Perpendicular had just become a fashionable topic, owing to studies by Maurice Hastings and John Harvey, a controversy initially aired in the *Architectural Review*, of which Pevsner was then editor.[54] Joan Evans adroitly avoided the issue, but this was less significant than what the discussion itself portended: the emergence of architectural historians interested exclusively in architecture as form and space. But the scholarly wheel has turned once more: the rigorous pursuit of "pure" architecture that was fashionable in the 1950s and 1960s has yielded to the recognition that medieval art and architecture are indivisible, and that they can be best understood in their social, liturgical, and political setting.[55] Joan Evans's despised opening chapter is now seen as entirely justified. While she rarely analyzed any topic in depth, her text contains numerous insights with which later scholarship concurs, although, since decorum prevented her—on paper, at any rate— from vigorously enforcing her views, these can be missed. Almost in passing, she remarked that there was no Court style in early fourteenth-century art since the bishops were the significant patrons at the time; that the form of the aisle vaults of Saint Augustine's, Bristol, is related to woodwork; and that late fourteenth-century manuscript painting has no demonstrable links to Bohemia.[56]

Both *Art in Medieval France* and *English Art* are elegiac in tone, and they need to be read in the light of current events. Joan Evans began to write *Art in Medieval France* in 1944 and *English Art* in the years immediately after World War II. Throughout the war, unable to visit France, she had felt herself to be in exile and was deeply concerned with the suffering of both countries.[57] Joan Evans's feeling for poetry, the past, and nature is revealed in both books, perhaps especially in the closing paragraphs of *English Art:* "The most shining beauties of its architecture depend, as English beauties should, on fortuitous changes of light and shadow. English fourteenth-century buildings should be seen in the early morning or towards sunset, or at any time when passing clouds or driving rain give them a beauty that is no stronger than a flower."[58] Much of her writing concerned the natural world and its transformation into art. Three books were dedicated to the topic—*Pattern: A Study of Ornament in Western Europe from 1180 to 1900* (1931); *Nature in Design: A Study of Naturalism in Decoration from the Bronze Age to the Renaissance* (1934); and *Style in Ornament* (1950)—but she did not think deeply about it. To her naturalism was found in every motif based on nature, however stylized, so that distinctions were lost. Medievalists especially need more precise definitions.[59]

It was Joan Evans's interest in the transformation of nature into art that led to her work on John Ruskin. Nature is one of the unifying elements of her scholarship. Undistracted by domestic responsibilities or the need to earn her living, her output was prodigious and diverse: in 1950 alone she published books or articles on Cluniac art, the Wilton Diptych, John Everett Millais, ornament, and Arthur Evans. This list is a microcosm of the range of her interests, all of which she pursued simultaneously, so that each could inform her thinking about the others. Her tastes did not change: they are revealed, perhaps unwittingly, in all their immutability in *Taste and Temperament*, published in 1939, when she was forty-six. *Taste and Temperament: A Study of Psychological Types in Their Relation to the Visual Arts* is a curious book. She places artists and patrons into four categories: Quick and Slow Extraverts and Quick and Slow Introverts, ascribing particular aesthetic tastes to each type. It is rapidly apparent that the Quick Introvert—intuitive and with eclectic, elusive tastes—is the approved type. Among Quick Introverts are included herself, John and Arthur Evans, the Cluniacs, William Morris, Minoan pots, Greek gems, Gothic sculpture and illumination, Exeter Cathedral, and the Alhambra at Granada. The Cistercians, with their denial of beauty, are in the condemned category of Slow Extraverts.[60]

From the late 1940s, for the next thirty years, Joan Evans was an establishment figure. She presided over the Royal Archaeological Institute in London and her local Bristol and Gloucester Archaeological Society, and from 1948 to 1964 was closely involved with the Society of Antiquaries, receiving its Gold Medal in 1973. She had offered a paper to the Antiquaries in 1918, but since women were not then admitted, it had been read by Arthur Evans, who was president. Sir Martin Conway had tried unsuccessfully to have learned societies included in a parliamentary bill admitting women to the closed professions, but in 1920 he persuaded the Society of Antiquaries to agree that women should participate. The first woman elected fellow arrived in 1926, and Joan Evans was elected in 1933.[61] By 1948 she was an elected vice-president, and in 1954 became director for five years, when she did much good work sorting out uncataloged collections. The president at this time was Mortimer Wheeler, a talented, energetic archaeologist, who was doing much to popularize his subject and was a dedicated show-off and womanizer. He and Joan Evans did not get on. She, middle-aged and without good looks, never one to exploit her femininity in her negotiations with men, did not attract him, and although Arthur Evans had given Wheeler help as a young man, he resented Joan Evans's family pride. For her part Joan Evans thought his lectures and television programs trivialized archaeology and placed too much emphasis on digging at the expense of study. But at the Antiquaries they worked together as best they could until the question of the presidency arose. It was customary that the five-year post alternated between archaeologists and medievalists, and in 1959 it should have been the turn of a medievalist. Many of the fellows felt that Joan Evans, as director, was the obvious choice, particularly since both her father and brother had been president and she was the appropriate choice for the society's first woman to preside. Wheeler, however, was determined to put in his own candidate, the archaeologist Ian Richmond. The council was influenced to propose Richmond formally. But a group of fellows, led by the herald Anthony Wagner, was equally determined to elect Joan Evans. They conscripted three hundred fellows to write in her name on the ballot paper, and she was elected by a large majority. When the result was announced, the cheers and stamps could be heard on the floor above. All parties behaved with dignity; Wheeler recognized defeat, and Richmond succeeded Joan Evans as president in 1964. She, however, had been extremely upset by Wheeler's machinations and was unable to forgive him. Nonetheless, she presided over the Antiquaries with an enjoyment made all the keener by knowledge of their support.[62]

Wheeler's attempt to block Joan Evans's nomination was directed at her personally rather than at women in general. Since she never needed paid employment, Joan Evans was protected from discrimination against women in academic life: in 1947, when Boase left the Courtauld Institute for Oxford, she taught there for one year. (She had four undergraduate students, including Pamela Tudor-Craig and Donald King, and one postgraduate, Kathleen Morand.) Yet James Lees-Milne remarked, "I have often noticed how women who achieve success never cease rubbing it in to one.... [Joan Evans] is undoubtedly *very* clever, and highly respected as antiquarian, scholar and art historian. Yet all her stories redound to her credit."[63] She evidently felt that, despite her advantages, she had had to struggle. She was not a feminist and, except for practical help given to Saint Hugh's College, did not go out of her way to promote the interests of women scholars. The discrimination she suffered was that of being ignored, the perennial, careless kind of discrimination born of masculine lack of imagination and a desire to keep the status quo: an unthinking downgrading of women's attainments coupled with an unacknowledged contempt for single women, which was common until the 1960s, if not later. For example, it was then traditional to award the president of the Society of Antiquaries a knighthood under the British honors system. Ian Richmond, as Joan Evans wryly observed, was knighted within seven weeks of his election. Evans herself was not appointed Dame Commander of the British Empire (the female equivalent of a knighthood) until 1976, twelve years after her presidency ended, and even then it was given for services to charity.[64]

Joan Evans was elected a fellow of University College London (an honorific position) in 1950, and her achievements were recognized with honorary degrees from

Edinburgh in 1952 and Cambridge in 1956. She became a trustee of the British Museum and the Museum of London and was on the advisory council of the Victoria and Albert Museum. She was a fellow and member of council of Saint Hugh's. Rachel Trickett, newly arrived as a tutor in 1954, found her "imposing and formidable." Her figure certainly reflected her enjoyment of good living. Pamela Tudor-Craig remembers being taken out to lunch and advised always to eat à la carte in restaurants; Joan Evans's seventieth birthday was celebrated with a memorable lunch party at Cluny. Trickett described Evans as "dramatically hatted and befurred . . . the splendid rings on her small round fingers sparkled excitably."[65] Joan Evans had shared a love of hats and dressy feathers with the Jourdains; Tudor-Craig recalls her hats and also a large collection of beautiful, handmade shoes, which she bought in Paris. These she often gave away, along with rings and other pieces of jewelry, books, and pictures. Later in her life, visitors to Thousand Acres were urged to take books from her library. Joan Evans's generosity was legendary. It is remembered by both institutions and countless individuals who, as far back as Eleanor Jourdain in 1924, were quietly helped with substantial gifts of money or shares when they were in crisis.

These gifts were made privately, as were her donations to institutions. She was a benefactor to the Bristol and Gloucester Archaeological Society and to the British School at Athens. Although Arthur Evans had transferred ownership of the Palace of Minos at Knossos with his estate—including his house, the Villa Ariadne—to the British School in 1926, he kept up his links with frequent visits, and Joan Evans maintained them. She shared the resentment of working archaeologists when in 1949 Mortimer Wheeler, as secretary of the British Academy, argued that the school could no longer afford the upkeep on the villa and forced it to hand the house over to the Greek government.[66] This did not improve her relations with Wheeler; and she was a substantial donor to the costs of building the Stratigraphical Museum at Knossos as a proper store for Arthur Evans's finds. In 1966 she formally opened the museum and, with Marc Fitch, provided the champagne and raki for the celebratory feast.[67]

Joan Evans's main beneficiaries were, however, Saint Hugh's, the Victoria and Albert Museum, and the Society of Antiquaries. Already in 1924 she had bought, in the space of an afternoon, the house on Woodstock Road in Oxford that would enable Saint Hugh's eventually to acquire a whole island site. In 1945 she established an endowment fund for the college; and in 1953 an uncomfortable overnight stay provoked her into buying new mattresses for all the students' rooms.[68] To the Victoria and Albert Joan Evans donated her collection of jewelry. Arthur Evans had given her his collection of rings in recognition of her work compiling the *Index to the Palace of Minos;* he had originally paid her a hundred pounds, but when he realized what a huge labor it had been, he saw that the sum was quite inadequate.[69] She inherited the rest of his collection and that of her father; a friend from childhood of Charles Oman, the keeper of metalwork, she loaned the medieval rings and other jewels to the museum in the 1950s but insisted that they be displayed as a separate collection. In 1975 she made an outright gift of them, and in 1977 she at last allowed her collection to be integrated with the rest of the display. The display was redesigned and a new catalog prepared.[70] In 1962 Joan secured for the Society of Antiquaries the bequest of the fortune of her half-niece, Susan Minet, a fortune so large that it gave the society financial stability for the first time in its history. But she herself was a generous donor to the Antiquaries, not only giving two Gainsborough portraits but anonymously endowing the publications fund, a gift that was placed in jeopardy by Wheeler's plots against her, since she did not want the society to think she was buying office.[71]

Joan Evans had particularly wanted to become president of the Society of Antiquaries in 1959, since it was the centenary of her father's authentication of the Paleolithic discoveries at Saint-Acheul, and she felt that her election would be a neat tribute to the Evans family.[72] Wheeler so distrusted her pride in her family that he demanded to see the last three chapters of the *History of the Society of Antiquaries* in draft, for fear that she had included too much about them.[73] Her account is not only balanced and judicious but is notably generous to Wheeler. Arthur Evans died in 1941, leaving all the family papers for her to sort out. These went back three generations and provided her with material for *Time and Chance,* a family history and biography of Arthur Evans, and *The Endless Web,* the story of Dickinson's paper business. Agnes Horsfield was so impressed by Joan Evans as a family historian that she bequeathed her all the Conway family papers, with the implication that Joan should produce a similar book about them.[74] This she did, her great devotion to Agnes and perception of Martin Conway as a bad father and selfish husband perhaps leading her to underestimate his achievements as a scholar, although with her feeling for the natural world she appreciated his passion for high mountains.

In *Time and Chance* Joan Evans has been accused of romanticizing, and her biographical writing, including her autobiography, *Prelude and Fugue,* is often silent on unpleasant events.[75] But in this she was typical of her class and generation. Gossip was one thing—she loved to be kept informed—but in public and, above all, written accounts, discretion was the better part. She behaved similarly in her dealings over *An Adventure,* which continued almost to the year of her death. Joan Evans was concerned only with Eleanor Jourdain's integrity, in which she wholly believed; as Eleanor's literary executor Joan allowed the book to stay in print until she herself prepared its fifth edition in 1955. But two years later Lucille Iremonger published *The Ghosts of Versailles,* a fierce, intemperate attack on Moberly and Jourdain, which accused them of lies and invention and all but included Joan Evans in charges of dishonesty. Using the language of tabloid journalism, Iremonger wrote with relish of the need for "distasteful probing."[76] Joan Evans did not react publicly at the time, but in 1976 she was finally able, in an article in *Encounter,* to confirm the truth of what had happened. She accepted Philippe Jullian's suggestion that the women had seen not ghosts but rehearsals for a *tableau vivant* to be given at a party hosted by Robert de Montesquiou-Fezensac, a flamboyant homosexual famous for his love of wearing eighteenth-century costume. Moberly and Jourdain would never have heard of him, nor would their researches have produced a record of the event. Joan Evans was satisfied that the supernatural element of the story had been removed and, even more, that the women's integrity had been defended.

Prelude and Fugue, which she published in 1964, marked an end to much of her active scholarship. Her last appearance in print as a medievalist was the introduction to *The Flowering of the Middle Ages,* which she edited. She was over seventy then, and her powers were diminishing. *Monastic Architecture in France from the Renaissance to the Revolution,* which arose from lists she had made in 1944 to help the invading Allies avoid damaging important monuments, was much criticized for errors, though reviewers agreed that it was the starting point for anyone intending to take up research on the topic.[77] That her last publications should be devoted to France is wholly appropriate. A chevalier of the Légion d'honneur and in the eyes of her many French friends an honorary citizen, she loved France with a passion. She felt that her greatest achievement in life had been her rescue of the chapel of Berzé-la-Ville and its presentation to the Académie of Mâcon.[78] That this happened in 1947 may have been fortuitous, but it enabled Joan to express to the French people the sympathy and support that she had been prevented from giving during the war. As Peter Kidson put it, "Joan Evans called Bourges the most French of all cathedrals, which for her was the highest compliment, an oblique, Anglo-Saxon way of saying that it stands at a pinnacle of unapproachable excellence."[79] France was the standard by which she judged the art of other countries. As a medievalist she was not alone in this, since the use of France as a standard and model has bedeviled the study of Gothic architecture since it was first identified as a French invention.[80] Her books on the Cluniacs and post-Renaissance monastic architecture served French architecture in ways that no French scholar had yet done. It was wholly appropriate, as Glyn Daniel remarked, that she died on 14 July, Bastille Day, although she was essentially of the ancien régime.[81]

Reviewers were correct to see Joan Evans's work as the basis of future scholarship, if only because she tended to assemble accumulated facts, as if reproducing a card index, which are in themselves very useful.[82] She did not always go to the original documents, and reliance on printed inventories could lead her, as it led others, astray.[83] Her response was often sensuous rather than analytical. This is particularly true of her writing on architecture, which has faded from scholarly consideration since her preoccupations were with the appearance of the whole rather than building breaks and moldings. Yet her insights into architecture are illuminating and memorable. Her greatest gift to later generations was her comprehensive vision of medieval art and society, her insistence that the one cannot be understood without the other. In developing this vision she became a pioneer of many new branches of scholarship, of ways of looking at the Middle Ages, and of trying to understand people who were "of like passions with ourselves; they knew of pleasure and pain, freedom and limitation as we do; like us they were uncertain of the road they trod, yet ever went forward in hope."[84]

Notes

The preparation of this essay has been helped by many people. I particularly thank Deborah Quare, librarian of Saint Hugh's College, Oxford, and the Society of Antiquaries of London for permission to reproduce their photograph of Joan Evans and for allowing me access to unpublished papers in their possession. Among those who shared with me their memories of Joan Evans are John Hopkins, Charlotte Roueché, Diana Scarisbrick, Neil Stratford, Pamela Tudor-Craig, and George Zarnecki. Other assistance was given by Claude Blair, Marian Campbell, Peter Fergusson, and Amanda Simpson.

1. Leighton, "Memoir," 123.
2. The second, Rosemary Cramp, was elected 23 April 2001.
3. Quotation from Leighton, "Memoir," 124; Evans, "Anniversary Address," *Antiquaries Journal* 44.
4. Evans, *History of the Society of Antiquaries*, 381.
5. Evans, *Prelude and Fugue*, 74.
6. Evans, "Anniversary Address," *Antiquaries Journal* 41.
7. Evans, *History of the Society of Antiquaries*, 424.
8. First quotation: Evans, *Nature in Design*, 1; see also Evans, *Taste and Temperament*, 66–67. Second quotation: Evans, *History of the Society of Antiquaries*, 425.
9. Evans, *Prelude and Fugue*, 23.
10. Diana Scarisbrick, personal communication to author, October 2001. Nannie remained close to Joan until her death, aged ninety-seven, in 1961.
11. Evans, *Prelude and Fugue*, 52. This episode was important to Joan; she recalled it in conversation with Glyn Daniel, the editor of *Antiquity*, in the year of her death (*Antiquity* 51 [1977]: 179). John Evans also took Joan's mother to visit Saint-Acheul on their honeymoon.
12. Evans, *Prelude and Fugue*, 27–28.
13. Evans, *Prelude and Fugue*, 58.
14. Evans, *Prelude and Fugue*, 60.
15. Spurling, *Ivy*, 315–16.
16. The best account—a minibiography—of Margaret Jourdain is in Spurling, *Ivy*, 313–46. Much of my narrative of the relations between Joan Evans and Margaret Jourdain is based on this, though I have drawn my own conclusions.
17. See Moberly and Jourdain, *Adventure*. Lady Evans was among those to whom she told the story in the early 1900s, though Joan herself was considered too young for such ghostly tales.
18. Evans and Jourdain, "A Note on an Allusion to Rome in the *Divina Commedia*," 381.
19. Evans, *Prelude and Fugue*, 98–105, 114–18; Spurling, *Ivy*, 351–52.
20. First quotation: Joan Evans in conversation with Hilary Spurling (Spurling, *Ivy*, 316). Second quotation: Evans, *Prelude and Fugue*, 37.
21. Lees-Milne, *Mingled Measure*, 273–74.
22. The review, signed "J," is in *Apollo* 50 (1949): 178–79, giving the title of the book as *English Medieval Art*.
23. "The Hamadryad" appeared in Childe, *Oxford Poetry*, 21. The information about her destruction of her poems comes from Diana Scarisbrick, personal communication by telephone to author, in October 2001.
24. Brooke, "Dame Joan Evans."

25. *History of Saint Louis by Jean Sire de Joinville* (1938), vii.
26. Evans, *Prelude and Fugue,* 81–83, 114–17.
27. It was then that Eleanor Jourdain had another of her "psychic experiences," this time in Joan Evans's company, when they saw an old-fashioned carriage and pair. Evans later discovered that the contraption was real, having been pressed into service during World War I to carry stores.
28. Evans, *Prelude and Fugue,* 72.
29. She told Neil Stratford that her dislike of the political régimes in Germany, Italy, and Spain in the 1930s kept her away from the art. She did, however, possess at least one German work, a wooden Virgin and Child, seen by the present writer in 1977.
30. Evans, *Life in Medieval France,* 3d ed., vii.
31. Arthur Evans had reconstructed the Cretan Bronze Age along the same lines, as Early, Middle, and Late.
32. Evans, *Flowering of the Middle Ages,* 9.
33. Evans, *Conways,* 9; *History of Saint Louis* (1938), vii; *Prelude and Fugue,* 138–39.
34. Evans, *Unconquered Knight,* 134–39.
35. Viollet-le-Duc, *Dictionnaire raisonné du mobilier français de l'époque Carlovingienne à la Renaissance;* Quicherat, *Histoire du costume.*
36. Evans, *Art in Medieval France,* 275–79.
37. Compare reviews by Tonnochy in *Antiquaries Journal;* Granville Fell in *Connoisseur;* and Pevsner in *Architectural Review,* quoting Evans, *Art in Medieval France,* ix.
38. Evans, *Prelude and Fugue,* 160.
39. Peter Fergusson, conversation with author in August 2001; Conant, "Medieval Academy Excavations at Cluny."
40. Evans, *Prelude and Fugue,* 134–36.
41. Evans, "Anniversary Address," *Antiquaries Journal* 41.
42. Evans, *English Art,* 21 and 66.
43. Others include Platt, *Architecture of Medieval Britain;* and Coldstream, *Medieval Architecture.*
44. Coldstream, "Decorated Style."
45. Jourdain, review of *English Art.*
46. Dickinson, review of *English Art.*
47. Hildburgh, review of *English Art.*
48. Pevsner, review of *English Art.*
49. E.g., Blunt, review of *Monastic Architecture in France from the Renaissance to the Revolution,* 467; and Montague, review of *Monastic Iconography in France from the Renaissance to the Revolution.*
50. Pamela Tudor-Craig, conversation with author, September 2001.
51. Mann, "Anniversary Address."
52. Daniel, editorial.
53. Amanda Simpson, conversation with author, October 2001. She discussed with Joan Evans the possibility of helping with an updated version, but it was thought that the book would need to be entirely rewritten.
54. For full references, see Coldstream, "Le Decorated Style," especially nn. 21 and 22.
55. Alexander and Binski, *Age of Chivalry.*
56. Evans, *English Art,* 20–21, 67, and 84; for the problem of Court styles, see Coldstream,

Decorated Style, 186–92; for the vault at Bristol, see most recently Morris, "European Prodigy or Regional Eccentric?"; for Bohemia, see Simpson, *Connections between English and Bohemian Painting during the Second Half of the Fourteenth Century.*

57. Evans, *Prelude and Fugue,* 157.
58. Evans, *English Art,* 223. Margaret Jourdain thought this passage had no place in a work of serious scholarship (see n. 22).
59. Givens, "Leaves of Southwell Revisited."
60. Evans, *Taste and Temperament,* 47–50, 67–68, 80–84.
61. Evans, *History of the Society of Antiquaries,* 388–89; Evans, "Anniversary Address," *Antiquaries Journal* 44.
62. Pamela Tudor-Craig and John Hopkins, conversation with author, September 2001; Wagner, *Herald's World,* 168–69; Evans, "Memoir of an Antiquary." I am most grateful to the Society of Antiquaries of London for permission to see this document.
63. Lees-Milne, *Mingled Measure,* 100.
64. Evans, "Memoir of an Antiquary." It is generally believed that Mortimer Wheeler influenced the decision to delay the appointment (see Hawkes, *Mortimer Wheeler,* 331).
65. Trickett, "Dame Joan Evans."
66. Waterhouse, *British School,* 81, 86. The archaeological site had already been transferred into Greek care, but the school still owns the estate.
67. Waterhouse, *British School,* 88.
68. Trickett, "Dame Joan Evans," 33–34.
69. Diana Scarisbrick, telephone conversation with author, October 2001.
70. Bury, *Jewellery Gallery Summary Catalogue.*
71. Evans, "Memoir of an Antiquary."
72. Evans, "Memoir of an Antiquary"; Evans, *History of the Society of Antiquaries,* 284.
73. Evans, "Memoir of an Antiquary."
74. Evans, *Conways,* 8.
75. Regarding the accusations of romanticization, see MacGillivray, *Minotaur,* 5–7.
76. Iremonger, *Ghosts of Versailles,* 112.
77. Reviews by Blunt in *Burlington Magazine*; and Coope in *Antiquaries Journal.*
78. Diana Scarisbrick, telephone conversation with author, October 2001.
79. Kidson, "Bourges after Branner." The quote is from Evans, *Art in Medieval France,* 90. She ascribes it to "pure beauty of line and proportion."
80. Frankl, *Gothic;* Coldstream, *Medieval Architecture.*
81. Daniel, editorial.
82. See Dickinson, review of *English Art,* 90.
83. Staniland, "Extravagance or Regal Necessity?" 86.
84. Evans, *Life in Medieval France,* vii.

Select Bibliography of Works by Joan Evans

"Memoir of an Antiquary." Unpublished and unpaginated typescript in the possession of the Society of Antiquaries of London (n.d.).

With E. F. Jourdain. "A Note on an Allusion to Rome in the *Divina Commedia*." *Modern Language Review* 8 (1914): 381.

"Gilles Legaré and His Work." *Burlington Magazine* 30 (1917): 140.

"The Hamadryad." In *Oxford Poetry,* edited by V. R. Childe. Oxford: Oxford University Press, 1917.

"An Enamelled Lid at All Souls' College, Oxford." *Proceedings of the Society of Antiquaries*, 2d ser., 30 (1918): 192.

"The 'Lapidary' of Alfonso the Learned." *Modern Language Review* 14 (1919): 424.

With M. Jourdain. "Early Nineteenth-Century Jewellery." *Connoisseur* 57 (1920): 154.

With M. Jourdain. "Early Nineteenth-Century Jewellery." *Connoisseur* 60 (1921): 219.

English Jewellery from the Fifth Century A.D. to 1800. London: Methuen, 1921.

"Les emaux français du XVIIe siècle à décoration florale et leurs mutations." In *Compte-rendu analytique du Congrès de l'histoire de l'art à Paris, 1921.* Paris: n.p., 1921.

"Universities of To-morrow." *Times Educational Supplement* (October 1921).

Magical Jewels of the Middle Ages and the Renaissance, Particularly in England. Oxford: Oxford University Press, 1922.

With P. Studer. *Anglo-Norman Lapidaries.* Paris: Edouard Champion, 1924.

Life in Medieval France. Oxford: Oxford University Press, 1925. 2d ed., London: Phaidon, 1957; 3d ed., London: Phaidon, 1969.

"Un bijou magique dessiné par Hans Holbein." *Gazette des Beaux-Arts* 14 (1926): 357.

Editor. *Saint Joan of Orleans: Scenes from the Fifteenth-Century "Mystère du Siège d'Orleans."* Translated by P. Studer. Oxford: Clarendon Press, 1926.

"A Carved Mazer Cup at South Kensington." *Burlington Magazine* 53, no. 2 (1928): 32.

"English Influences on Scandinavian Furniture of the Seventeenth and Eighteenth Centuries." *Old Furniture* (September 1928): 15.

Translator and selector. *The Unconquered Knight: A Chronicle of the Deeds of Don Pero Niño Count of Buelna, by His Standard-Bearer, Gutierre Diaz de Gamez.* London: Routledge, 1928.

"Chaucer and Decorative Art." *Review of English Studies* 6 (1930): 408.

English Posies and Posy Rings: A Catalogue with an Introduction. London: Oxford University Press, 1931.

Monastic Life at Cluny, 910–1157. Oxford: Oxford University Press, 1931.

Pattern: A Study of Ornament in Western Europe from 1180 to 1900. 2 vols. Oxford: Clarendon Press, 1931.

"Die Adlervase des Sugerius." *Pantheon* 10 (1932): 221.

"The Origin of Morris." *Folk Lore* 43 (1932): 143.

With M. Serjeantson. *English Medieval Lapidaries.* Early English Text Society, o.s., 190. London: Oxford University Press, 1933.

"Huguenot Goldsmiths." *Proceedings of the Huguenot Society of London* 14 (1933): 496.

"Medieval Wheel-Shaped Brooches." *Art Bulletin* 15 (1933): 197.

Nature in Design: A Study of Naturalism in Decorative Art from the Bronze Age to the Renaissance. London: Oxford University Press, 1933.

Index to the Palace of Minos with Special Sections Classified in Detail and Chronologically Arranged by Sir Arthur Evans. London: Macmillan, 1936.

Translator. *The History of Saint Louis, by Jean Sire de Joinville.* Edited by N. de Wailly. Newtown, Wales: Gregynog Press, 1937.

With notes by Joan Evans. *The History of Saint Louis, by Jean Sire de Joinville.* Oxford: Oxford University Press, 1938.

The Romanesque Architecture of the Order of Cluny. Cambridge: Cambridge University Press, 1938.

Reprint, with foreword by K. J. Conant and additional bibliography by N. Stratford. Farnborough, Eng.: Gregg International, 1972.

Chateaubriand: A Biography. London: Macmillan, 1939.

Taste and Temperament: A Study of Psychological Types in Their Relation to the Visual Arts. London: Jonathan Cape, 1939.

"The First Restaurant in Paris." *Wine and Food* (1940): 145.

"The Duke of Orleans' Reliquary of the Holy Thorn." *Burlington Magazine* 78 (1941): 196.

With E. T. Leeds and A. Thompson. "A Hoard of Gold Rings and Silver Groats Found near Thame, Oxfordshire." *Antiquaries Journal* 21 (1941): 197.

"Noble Canonesses of France." *Archaeological Journal* 98 (1941): 62.

Time and Chance: The Story of Arthur Evans and His Forebears. London: Longmans, 1943.

"Shoehorns and a Powder Horn by Robert Mindum." *Burlington Magazine* 85 (1944): 283.

"An Inventory of Thomas Lord Wharton, 1568." *Antiquaries Journal* 102 (1945): 134.

The Pursuit of Happiness: The Story of Madame de Sérilly. 1946. Reprint, London: Longmans, 1947.

The Unselfish Egoist: A Life of Joseph Joubert. London: Longmans, 1947.

Art in Medieval France, 987–1498. 1948. Reprint, Oxford: Oxford University Press, 1952; New ed., with additional bibliography, 1969.

English Art, 1307–1461. Oxford History of English Art, 5. Oxford: Clarendon Press, 1949.

"A French Prototype for the Eleanor Crosses." *Burlington Magazine* 91 (1949): 96.

"Ninety Years Ago." *Antiquity* 23 (1949): 115.

Cluniac Art of the Romanesque Period. Cambridge: Cambridge University Press, 1950.

"Cluny, centre d'art medieval." *Médicine de France* 12 (1950): 17.

"L'Iconographie clunisienne." In *Congrès Scientifique*, edited by A Cluny. Dijon: n.p., 1950.

Translator. *Illuminated Initials in Medieval Manuscripts,* by E. van Moé. London: n.p., 1950.

"Millais' Drawings of 1853." *Burlington Magazine* 92 (1950): 198.

"Sir Arthur Evans and Knossos." *Archaeology* 3 (September 1950): 134–39.

Style in Ornament. London: Oxford University Press, 1950.

"The Wilton Diptych Reconsidered." *Archaeological Journal* 105 (1950): 1.

"The Royal Archaeological Institute: A Retrospect." *Archaeological Journal* 106 (1951): 1.

"Archaeology in 1851." *Archaeological Journal* 107 (1952): 1.

Dress in Medieval France. Oxford: Clarendon Press, 1952.

A History of Jewellery, 1100–1870. London: Faber and Faber, 1953; rev. ed., 1970.

John Ruskin. London: Jonathan Cape, 1954.

Editor. *An Adventure,* by C. A. E. Moberly and E. F. Jourdain. 5th ed. London: Faber and Faber, 1955.

The Endless Web: John Dickinson & Co. Ltd, 1804–1954. London: Jonathan Cape, 1955.

"A Note on the Rheims Resurrection 'Reliquary.'" *Antiquaries Journal* 35 (1955): 52.

Translator. *Romanesque Wall Paintings in France,* by P. Michel. London, 1955.

With N. Cook. "A Statue of Christ from the Ruins of Mercers' Hall." *Archaeological Journal* 111 (1955): 168.

Editor with J. H. Whitehouse. *The Diaries of John Ruskin.* 3 vols. Oxford: Clarendon Press, 1956–59.

A History of the Society of Antiquaries. Oxford: Oxford University Press for the Society of Antiquaries, 1956.

"The Embassy of the Fourth Duke of Bedford to Paris, 1762–3." *Archaeological Journal* 113 (1957): 137.

"An English Alabaster from Montpezat." *Antiquaries Journal* 36 (1957): 73.
With N. Cook. "A Statue from the Minories." *Archaeological Journal* 113 (1957): 102.
Foreword to *The Trianon Adventure: A Symposium*. London: Museum Press, 1958.
Editor. *The Lamp of Beauty: Selections from John Ruskin's Writings on Art*. London: Phaidon, 1959.
Madame Royale. London: Museum Press, 1959.
"Anniversary Address." *Antiquaries Journal* 40 (1960): 125.
"Anniversary Address." *Antiquaries Journal* 41 (1961): 149.
"Anniversary Address." *Antiquaries Journal* 42 (1962): 141.
"Anniversary Address." *Antiquaries Journal* 43 (1963): 185.
"An English Alabaster at Muret, Haut Garonne." *Antiquaries Journal* 43 (1963): 284.
"Anniversary Address." *Antiquaries Journal* 44 (1964): 117.
Monastic Architecture in France from the Renaissance to the Revolution. Cambridge: Cambridge University Press, 1964.
Prelude and Fugue: An Autobiography. London: Museum Press, 1964.
The Conways: A History of Three Generations. London: Museum Press, 1966.
Editor. *The Flowering of the Middle Ages*. 1966. Reprint, London: Thames and Hudson, 1985, 2000.
The Victorians. Cambridge: Cambridge University Press, 1966.
Monastic Iconography in France: From the Renaissance to the Revolution. Cambridge: Cambridge University Press, 1970.
"An End to *An Adventure*." *Encounter* 47 (October 1976): 33.

Works Cited

Alexander, J., and P. Binski, eds., *Age of Chivalry*. London: Royal Academy, 1987. Exhibition catalog.
Blunt, A. Review of *Monastic Architecture in France from the Renaissance to the Revolution*, by J. Evans. *Burlington Magazine* 106 (1964): 467–68.
Brooke, C. N. L. "Dame Joan Evans." *Antiquaries Journal* 58 (1979): 9.
Bury, S. *Jewellery Gallery Summary Catalogue*. London: Victoria and Albert Museum, 1982.
Childe, V. R., ed. *Oxford Poetry*. Oxford: Oxford University Press, 1917.
Coldstream, N. "Le Decorated Style: Recherches recentes." *Bulletin Monumental* 147 (1989): 55–80.
———. *The Decorated Style. Architecture and Ornament, 1240–1360*. London: British Museum Press, 1994.
———. *Medieval Architecture*. Oxford: Oxford University Press, 2002.
Conant, K. J. "Medieval Academy Excavations at Cluny: I. The Season of 1928." *Speculum* 4 (1929): 5–6.
Coope, Rosalys. Review of *Monastic Architecture in France from the Renaissance to the Revolution*, by Joan Evans. *Antiquaries Journal* 44 (1964): 267–70.
Daniel, G. Editorial. *Antiquity* 51 (1977): 179.
Dickinson, J. C. Review of *English Art*, by J. Evans. *Antiquaries Journal* 31 (1951): 90–92.
Frankl, P. *The Gothic: Sources and Literary Interpretations through Eight Centuries*. Princeton, N.J.: Princeton University Press, 1960.
Givens, J. "The Leaves of Southwell Revisited." In *Southwell and Nottinghamshire Medieval Art, Architecture, and Industry,* edited by J. Alexander, British Archaeological Association Conference Transactions 21, 60–65. Leeds: British Archaeological Association, 1998.

Granville Fell, H. Review of *Art in Medieval France*, by Joan Evans. *Connoisseur* 125 (1950): 62.

Haskell, F. *Patrons and Painters: A Study in the Relations between Italian Art and Society in the Age of the Baroque*. London: Chatto and Windus, 1963.

Hawkes, J. *Mortimer Wheeler: Adventurer in Archaeology*. London: Weidenfeld and Nicolson, 1992. Reprint, London: Sphere Books, 1994.

Hildburgh, W. L. Review of *English Art*, by J. Evans. *Journal of the British Archaeological Association*, 3d ser., 13 (1950): 53–55.

Iremonger, L. *The Ghosts of Versailles: Miss Moberly and Miss Jourdain and Their Adventure: A Critical Study*. London: Faber and Faber, 1957.

J[ourdain, M]. Review of *English Art*, by J. Evans. *Apollo* 50 (1949): 178.

Kidson, P. "Bourges after Branner." *Gesta* 39 (2000): 156.

Lees-Milne, J. *A Mingled Measure: Diaries, 1953–72*. London: John Murray, 1994.

Leighton, H. G. M. "Memoir." *Transactions of the Bristol and Gloucester Archaeological Society* 95 (1977): 123.

MacGillivray, J. A. *Minotaur: Sir Arthur Evans and the Archaeology of the Minoan Myth*. London: Jonathan Cape, 2000.

Mann, J. "Anniversary Address." *Antiquaries Journal* 31 (1951): 130.

Moberly, C. A. E., and E. F. Jourdain. *An Adventure*. London: Faber and Faber, 1911; 5th ed., edited by Joan Evans, London: Faber and Faber, 1955.

Montague, J. Review of *Monastic Iconography in France from the Renaissance to the Revolution*, by J. Evans. *Art Bulletin* 54 (1972): 219.

Morris, R. K. "European Prodigy or Regional Eccentric? The Rebuilding of Saint Augustine's Abbey Church, Bristol." In *Almost the Richest City: Bristol in the Middle Ages*, edited by L. Keen, British Archaeological Association Conference Transactions 19, 51. London: British Archaeological Association, 1997.

Pevsner, N. Review of *Art in Medieval France*. *Architectural Review* 106 (1949): 334.

———. Review of *English Art*, by J. Evans. *Times Literary Supplement* (1950): 17–18.

Platt, C. *The Architecture of Medieval Britain: A Social History*. New Haven, Conn.: Yale University Press, 1990.

Quicherat, J. E. J. *Histoire du costume*. Paris: Hachette, 1877.

Simpson, A. *The Connections between English and Bohemian Painting during the Second Half of the Fourteenth Century*. New York: Garland, 1984.

Spurling, H. *Ivy: The Life of I. Compton-Burnett*. London: Richard Cohen Books, 1995.

Staniland, K. "Extravagance or Regal Necessity? The Clothing of Richard II." In *The Regal Image of Richard II and the Wilton Diptych*, edited by D. Gordon, L. Monnas, and C. Elam. London: Harvey Miller, 1997.

Tonnochy, A. B. Review of *Art in Medieval France*, by Joan Evans. *Antiquaries Journal* 30 (1950): 96–97.

Trickett, R. "Dame Joan Evans." *Saint Hugh's College Chronicle* 50 (1977–78): 33.

Viollet-le-Duc, E. E. *Dictionnaire raisonné du mobilier français de l'époque Carlovingienne à la Renaissance*. Paris: V. A. Morel and Co., 1873.

Wagner, A. *A Herald's World*. London: privately published, 1988.

Waterhouse, H. *The British School at Athens: The First Hundred Years*. London: British School at Athens, 1986.

CHAPTER 30

Dorothy L. Sayers (1893–1957)
Medieval Mystery Maker

MITZI M. BRUNSDALE

DOROTHY L. SAYERS believed that everyone was "either 'gothic' or 'classical'" by instinct, and there was no question where she herself stood.[1] Born amidst the "dreaming spires" of old Oxford, her spiritual home, and gifted with a keen intelligence and love of languages, she followed her own "gothic" instinct through a long, varied, and distinguished literary career that began and ended with translations of medieval French poetry. Her first and enduring literary love was poetic romance, epitomized in the figure of the Christian knight nobly championing the cause of Good and frequently, like Roland, losing against eternal Evil. That hero, and his mortal conflict, dominated nearly everything she wrote.

Dorothy Sayers was a precocious only child born 13 June 1893 to a scholarly music-loving Anglican clergyman and his patient wife, both older than the child-rearing average and doting on, though probably often bemused by, a daughter who gloried in Latin from the age of six and by thirteen had not only read Dumas's *Three Musketeers* in French but was conversant with the linguistic intricacies of the fourth-century Athanasian Creed, which she "hugged as a secret delight."[2] Much later Sayers observed that "complications of morphology and syntax released in me some kind of low cunning which today finds expression in the solving of crossword puzzles."[3] It probably also contributed significantly to the successful detective fiction for which she is best known.

Dorothy Sayers had a miserable stay from 1909 to 1911 at Godolphin School, a Low Church institution near Salisbury. She detested sports, but she caused her French teacher "to reel under the shock of hearing the subjunctive placed properly for the first time in her life from the lower fifth form," a combination that surely aroused

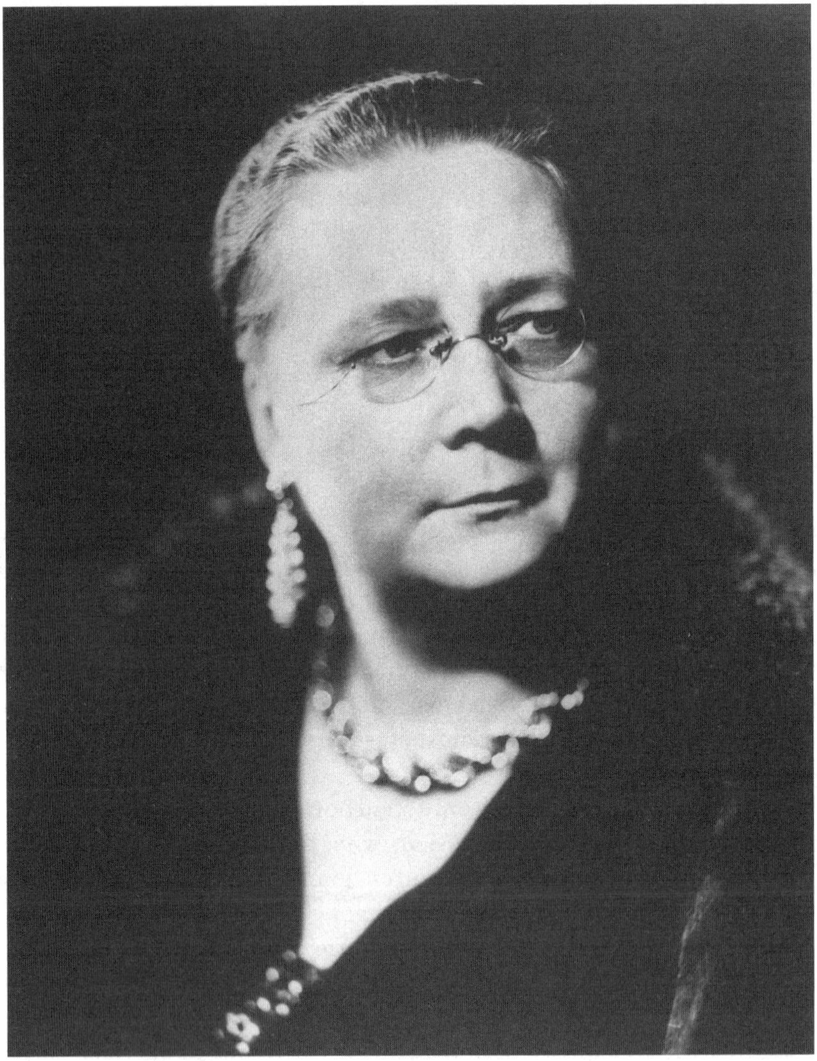

considerable animosity among her classmates.[4] When Sayers entered Oxford's all-woman Somerville College in 1912 bearing an illustrious Gilchrist Scholarship, however, she found not only friends she would cherish for the rest of her life but the superb guidance of Mildred Katherine Pope, under whom she took first-class honors in French in 1915. Miss Pope held a doctorate from the University of Paris and was a noted medieval scholar of her day. Her influence on Dorothy Sayers lasted from the start of Sayers's literary career, when she dedicated her translation of Thomas of Britain's *Tristan,* begun at Oxford, to Miss Pope, until its close, when in her introduction to her translation of *The Song of Roland,* she praised Miss Pope's "every encouragement and much practical help."[5]

After Sayers finished her studies, said farewell to her closest female friends, the all-girl Mutual Admiration Society, and "went down" from Oxford in the middle of World War I, she first tried teaching at Hull, then editing at Blackwell's in Oxford, and later secretarial work at an exclusive boys' prep school in Normandy, the while becoming unhappily involved with a succession of men who each, like Thomas's Tristan, had major flaws of character. After being dumped first by egotistical Eric Whelpton and then by Artist with a capital *A* John Cournos, and finally left pregnant and unwed by a mechanic she identified only as "Bill," Sayers had to support herself and the son whose parentage she kept secret for her entire life. To do so, she turned her considerable talents to mystery fiction, a craze raging in early roaring-twenties England.

Sayers was convinced that the modern detective was "the true successor of Roland and Lancelot," a knight errant who protected the weak and brought the wicked to justice.[6] Between 1921 and 1937 she featured her sleuth, the dashing Lord Peter Wimsey, in numerous short stories and a series of novels that remain classics of the golden age of detective fiction. As she developed Wimsey from "a worldly-wise Bertie Wooster with brains" into "something approximating a Christian hero trying to save the world from war and a virtuous lord representing the highest ideals of English life," Sayers was becoming increasingly absorbed with the theological problem of evil, that mystery of wickedness responsible for the deliberate choice of wrongdoing that separates men and women from their Maker.[7]

As a conservative Anglo-Catholic, Sayers felt that the Christian artist had an obligation to insist that the mystery of wickedness was central to the human condition, and that working to overcome it with God's grace was necessary for salvation. She herself worked thus, in no uncertain terms. Beginning in 1937, she published a series of religious plays addressing the question, "Why does everything we do go wrong and pile itself into some 'monstrous consummation'?" She counterpointed her plays with theological essays unequivocally stating her "Unpopular Opinions," the title of one of the three essay collections published by 1947 in which she expanded on "the Christian answer" to that thorny question: simply "Sin."[8]

For Sayers, as for medieval Christians, Lucifer's sin of pride was central to all the other deadly sins by which people choose to cut themselves off from God.[9] When her home at Witham fell under Nazi bombs in August 1944, Sayers providentially snatched for air-raid shelter reading the one book whose illumination of sin, purgation, and salvation would dominate the rest of her life, Dante's *Divine Comedy*. Totally smitten, Sayers taught herself to read medieval Italian, undertook a demanding *terza rima* translation of the *Commedia,* and created some of the most lucid notes and commentaries ever written on that medieval masterpiece. Sayers's *Hell* appeared in 1949, *Purgatory* in 1945, and *Paradise* in 1962, completed after Sayers's sudden death in 1957 by her friend and fellow scholar Barbara Reynolds.

The year of Sayers's death also saw the publication of her translation of *The Song of Roland,* a project she had worked on sporadically for forty years. It celebrated the common denominator of all her works, a medieval steadfastness, like Roland's, in the face of a world that chooses to be deaf to God's call to doing good. Throughout her life Dorothy Sayers practiced what she preached: that the greatest torment of hell is work that has no purpose, and that work that fits the pieces of the puzzle of human existence into one shining vision of salvation is nothing less than a sacrament that allows its maker to "feel like God on the seventh day," the one, the only, way that humanity can mirror its Maker.[10]

Sayers seemed to regret not pursuing her medieval studies more fully. Well after she had become a famous mystery author, Dorothy Sayers remarked publicly in February 1934, "I am a scholar gone wrong."[11] Today it appears that she had not gone wrong as a scholar so much as her times and situation were wrong for her to have made her mark as one. When she left Oxford in 1915, women were still five years from being able to receive Oxford degrees, so that even brilliant graduates like Dorothy Sayers were marooned in second- or third-rate backwaters of British academia. Furthermore, Sayers was both fiercely independent and relatively poor, lacking the resources and connections to build a reputation in the male-dominated scholarly world of the early twentieth century, though she gave it the best try she could.

While struggling at entry-level jobs like "a Derby winner hitched to a coal cart," Sayers did produce two slim volumes of verse with medieval overtones, *Op. 1,* published in 1916 while she was unhappily teaching at Hull, and *Catholic Tales and Christian Songs,* brought out while she was working at Blackwell's in 1918.[12] A *Times Literary Supplement* reviewer damned the latter with faint praise as "graceful religious fantasies" with "the childlike spirit and familiar intimacy with Christ characteristic of the Middle Ages."[13] Sayers in fact maintained this position vis-à-vis Christ throughout most, if not all, of her religious writing.

While at Blackwell's Sayers also continued translating the extant fragments of the Tristan romance written by the twelfth-century Anglo-Norman monk Thomas of Britain. Under Mildred Pope, Sayers had traced this passionate tale of illicit love back to its most primitive origins, but she was most captivated by the "strange power and poignancy" that she felt had made Thomas's version "one of the great stories of the world," and it probably fueled her own romantic imagination.[14] Women students had been ferociously segregated from men in pre–World War I Oxford, where male university officials denounced even a glimpse of a shapely female ankle as an unacceptable distraction for their susceptible male charges. After she left Oxford, Sayers's longing to find a twentieth-century knight to inspire and adore was running rampant, leading her into ungovernable and near-ruinous infatuations.

Literarily Dorothy Sayers keenly appreciated the strong appeal to reason, the remarkable interest in character, and the utter lack of puritanical disdain for the unhallowed love he depicted that she found in the work of Thomas of Britain.[15] She also set herself the formidable intellectual challenge of turning her translation into poetry, linking the fragments together with a smooth, high-spirited prose narrative. Mildred Pope convinced her to send two translated fragments to *Modern Languages,* whose editor, Eric Underwood, published them in the June and August 1920 issues, with a note praising Sayers for capturing "with singular freshness and simplicity the grace and pathos of the original" as well as for "a thing seldom achieved by even the most skillful of translators—a rendering which is in itself a poem."[16] Sir John Squire, editor of *London Mercury,* courteously but firmly refused Sayers's whole translation, *Tristan in Brittany,* however, though eventually Ernest Benn published it in 1929 with an introduction Sayers had elicited from the eminent scholar George Saintsbury.

Sayers's own introduction to *Tristan in Brittany* paid enthusiastic homage to Joseph Bédier, "that distinguished mediaevalist," for "his profound scholarship" and "fine poetic insight."[17] She also revealed her own fascination with the beauty and terror of overwhelming passion: "[T]he exasperating behaviour of the lovers conforms to the ordinary, [*sic*] human developments of that exasperating passion [which has] . . . a kind of desperate beauty faithful through years of sin and unfaith [*sic*] on both sides, and careless of lies and shifts and incredible dishonour."[18] From Thomas's penetrating psychological analysis of guilty love and from her own painful experience of the wages of such sins, Sayers was learning to measure the magnitude of the mystery of wickedness.[19]

While Dorothy Sayers was suffering the aftermath of her unrequited love for Eric Whelpton in 1920, she was also beginning to contemplate mayhem and murder, at least the literary variety that had become fashionable enough in Britain to be castigated as "bad reading" by London's *Evening Standard:* "Many are the crimes brought about by the disordered imagination of a reader of sensational and often immoral rubbish, while many a home is neglected and uncared for owing to the all-absorbed, novel-reading wife."[20] Out of Dorothy Sayers's need for money and her own orderly but unconventional imagination came her first mystery novel, *Whose Body?* (1923), opening on an uncircumcised corpse clad only in a pince-nez and floating in a bathtub, a scene of "instant appealing vulgarity" that became one of the trademarks of Sayers's immediately successful detective fiction.[21]

Sayers's detective novels fall into two chronologically overlapping groups. The earlier ones, born out of her financial need and featuring the noble latter-day knight in shining moral armor who brought her fame and fortune, Lord Peter Wimsey, accompanied her truncated infatuation with Cournos, her on-the-rebound pregnancy, and her subsequent marriage in 1926 to World War I veteran Atherton Fleming ("Mac").

After *Whose Body?* this group includes *Clouds of Witness* (1926), *Unnatural Death* (1927), *The Documents in the Case* (1930), *Five Red Herrings* (1931), *Murder Must Advertise* (1933), and the acclaimed *The Nine Tailors* (1934). By the end of the 1920s, though, Sayers was becoming bored with Wimsey and set about trying to kill him off through marriage to her fictional alter ego, Harriet Vane. The Peter-and-Harriet novels include *Strong Poison* (1930); *Have His Carcase* (1932); *Hangman's Holiday* (1933); *Gaudy Night* (1936), often considered Sayers's masterpiece; *Busman's Honeymoon* (1937), originally a stage play; and the unpublished fragment "Thrones, Dominations," written in 1938–39.

In creating a detective worthy of being "the true successor to Roland and Lancelot," Sayers endowed Lord Peter Wimsey, younger brother to a duke of the realm, with the aristocratic luxuries of body and mind she craved but could never have afforded in her youth. Wimsey shared Dorothy Sayers's flair for clothes, music, books, and dramatic color in his palatial London flat, which held a primrose-painted sitting room and glistening ebony grand piano. He was a bilingual connoisseur of fine foods and vintages as well as a collector of rare medieval tomes—in *Whose Body?* he purchases a folio *Divina Commedia* at a cost exceeding his valet Bunter's annual salary, and in *Unnatural Death* he demonstrates "a taste for collating the manuscripts of *Tristan*" (p. 38).[22] Early on, Lord Peter exhibited some maddening silly-ass mannerisms, but Sayers also gave him the chivalric qualities of the quintessential English gentleman—courtesy toward women, scrupulosity in keeping his word, playing fair even while dueling with the ungodly, never counting his change, and thoroughly enjoying his quest for justice, as long as it remained a game.

As her detective novels progressed, however, Sayers lifted her chevalier out of his medieval tapestry and gave him a modern moral dimension. Whatever chivalric black-and-white ideal of warfare Wimsey might originally have held, he abandoned it forever in the horrifying trenches of the Western Front, and Sayers sentenced him ever after to view even the murderers he pursued as perplexing mixtures of good and evil. Sayers and Wimsey both maintained the traditional Christian position that all human souls possess freedom of choice, which means that the wicked snare themselves, usually through their overweening pride. In the course of the Peter-and-Harriet novels, Peter increasingly torments himself over the deaths of innocent victims and becomes increasingly guilt-ridden over his role in bringing the perpetrators to justice, to the extent of collapsing in Harriet's arms on the eve of the criminal's hanging in *Busman's Honeymoon*.

Harriet Vane, the lady Sayers created to heal her knight's psychic wounds, also had much in common with Sayers herself. By 1928 Sayers was developing a profound theory of the postwar detective novel as requiring "a higher level of writing and a more competent delineation of character" than heretofore, as well as a "tenderer human feeling" beneath the hero's frivolous or ruthlessly efficient exterior. For Sayers, though, "tenderer" hardly involved frothy romanticized love affairs, since she scorned "heroes who insist on fooling about after young women instead of solving crimes."[23] In *Strong Poison,* Peter falls in love with Harriet Vane while Harriet is on trial for her life, accused of poisoning her former Artist with a capital *A* lover. Through this group of novels

Sayers showed the relationship between Peter and Harriet moving from a kind of hell where their pride keeps them apart, through a period in which they have to purge themselves of that pride, to reach at last a state of heavenly wedded bliss, a pattern similar to the great medieval vision that the last literary love of Sayers's life, Dante Alighieri, fleshed out in his towering *Commedia*.[24]

Around 1930, when Sayers was working on *Strong Poison*, her portrayal of evil seems to have become more like Dante's.[25] Harriet and Peter each make their own hells through pride, because here Peter's detecting game carries sinfully high stakes—the life of Harriet, the woman he loves. Harriet rejects his lordly hand in marriage because her pride will not allow her to accept what she mistakenly believes is his pity and charity. This hell of separated lovers darkens in the next Peter-and-Harriet novel, *Have His Carcase*, for which Sayers conceived of villains emerging, she wrote, "from a narrower and deeper and more intimate inferno; because we have realized only too well that kingdom of hell is within us."[26] When Harriet accuses Peter of humiliating her with his chivalry, he demands the same "common honesty" from her that she claimed she had always been seeking. Not only did this novel unmask one of Sayers's most distasteful murderers, it forced Harriet and Peter to acknowledge the pride that had been keeping them apart. Once they each can jettison it, they can work together to trap a killer who had sordidly betrayed a trust, the worst sin in the traditional landscape of hell. Peter and Harriet then escape the inferno of selfish pride that had kept them apart, but they had to be cleansed before they could achieve their own garden of earthly delights.

For medieval Christians purgatory was a place of necessary soul-cleaning preparatory to salvation, not a realm of torture similar, though finite, to the infinite torment of hell. In *Gaudy Night* Peter and Harriet once and for all purge themselves of pride. Sayers has Peter confess all his frailties to Harriet as they punt down Oxford's sacred Isis: his physical conceit, his regret over the debilitation of his aristocratic caste, his "cursed hankering" after the old values that had inspired Roland at Roncevaux.[27] For her part Harriet has to realize that she cannot solve the novel's poison-pen crimes without Peter's help. She has to root out as sickeningly false her image of him as "King Cophetua" giving alms to a beggar maid—herself—that has poisoned her love for him for so long. At the close of *Gaudy Night* they climb together to the top of the Radcliffe Camera, looking out over Sayers's "holy city" with a renewed vision of an earthly paradise: "All the kingdoms of the world and the glory of them."[28] Edith Hamilton observed in applauding the "ease and grace" with which Sayers married the love story to detection that Harriet was "a wish-fulfillment, what every scholastic woman wants to be . . . able, and in her thirties too—to work havoc in an undergraduate heart and hold to herself firmly, through year after year of refusals, a rich and noble lover . . . 'Oh, these are the dreams that visit women's pillows.'"[29]

Dreams of heavenly connubial bliss came true for Harriet and Peter in *Busman's Honeymoon*, Sayers's vision of heaven as a marriage between two independent minds and spirits, brought together in solving yet another juicy murder. In 1937 she described the union between Peter and Harriet as a metaphor for artistic creation, with Peter as "the interpretative artist, the romantic soul at war with the realistic brain," and Harriet, "with her lively and inquisitive mind and her soul grounded upon reality, as his complement, the creative artist."[30] As she would later prove in *The Mind of the Maker,* her treatise on the Trinity, humanity shares a minute spark of the divine ability to create, so Sayers thus endowed Harriet and the man she claimed on their wedding night as "My Lord!" an honest foretaste of paradise. Sayers's unfinished novel, "Thrones, Dominations," (a reference to the third and fourth orders of angels in the medieval hierarchy of heaven) promised not a human comedy but what she called a "tragedy" that would contrast the Wimseys' idyllic marriage with a desperately unhappy one, "a drama of agonized souls . . . with odd and alluring complications."[31] Sayers set this project aside in 1939, and occupied with her religious plays and essays and distracted by the opening of the Second World War, she never completed it.

By 1937 the Wimsey novels had been translated into eleven languages and were selling phenomenally well, and Dorothy Sayers was able to pension Lord Peter off with his panache and her intellectual integrity intact. Her own marriage had stabilized, though she had no romantic illusions about it, and now she could turn to the kind of writing she had been itching to do for some time—plays and theological essays.

Even as a child, Dorothy Sayers had exhibited a flair for drama, staging home plays about Dumas's three musketeers by dragooning her family and their servants into roles supporting her dashing portrayal of Athos, with his air of unhealed sorrows. Toward the end of the 1930s, she experimented with romantic plays such as the first version of *Busman's Honeymoon* (1936) and *Love All* (19390, but as the storm clouds of World War II gathered, she turned to far more profound matters.

Most of Sayers's religious dramas were set in the Middle Ages she loved. She wrote four plays for cathedral festivals: *The Zeal of Thy House,* the story of medieval architect William of Sens, was presented at Canterbury in 1937; *The Devil to Pay,* Sayers's reworking of the Faust legend, was also for Canterbury Cathedral, in 1939; and *The Just Vengeance,* featuring an RAF pilot close to meeting his Maker, was commissioned for Lichfield Cathedral's 750th anniversary in 1946. *The Emperor Constantine* was presented at Colchester Cathedral in 1951, a huge production centered on the Council of Nicaea, where Bishop Athanasius established the official doctrine of the Trinity. Sayers also wrote highly successful radio dramas based on the life of Christ: *He That Should Come* (1938) was an hour-long Nativity play, and her powerful twelve-part series *The Man Born to be King,* broadcast in 1942, recounted Christ's human life and death, which Sayers called "the greatest tragic irony in fact or fiction."[32]

Although the historical settings and circumstances of Sayers's religious dramas differ, one constant proved essential to their creation and their success: Sayers's heroes are all knights in shining armor, true successors to Roland and Lancelot, sharing the chivalric ideals and the pangs of conscience that had made Lord Peter Wimsey such a magnetic figure. Every one of them battles the sin of pride. William of Sens declares the choir he rebuilt at Canterbury Cathedral so good that not even God could equal it—and topples from a crane to spend the rest of his life paralyzed and repenting: "The work is sound, Lord God, no rottenness there— / Only in me."[33] Sayers's Faust, a talented reformer who grandly tossed away his immortal soul to save humanity from its sufferings, chose his own fate, hell, because he felt that "He [God] is there also."[34] The doomed pilot of *The Just Vengeance*, like the hero of *Sir Gawain and the Green Knight*, accepts his need for atonement even though he fought bravely for his king, and Bishop Athanasius in *The Emperor Constantine* successfully wins his theological duel with the heretic Bishop Arius, who denied Christ's divinity. Athanasius purges the church council of Arius's prideful evil and redeems Christ's church.

The most powerful knightly hero in Sayers's dramas, though, is her human Christ. She staunchly insisted on the truth of the Christian creeds, that Christ was both God and man, dealing with humanity's everyday problems. To use Christ as a speaking character in *The Man Born to be King*, a dramatic technique that British stage convention had not allowed since the Middle Ages, Sayers had to battle not only the BBC but the Protestant Truth Society and the Lord's Day Observance Society, whose spokesman howled that "[f]or sinful man to personify the Deity is approaching blasphemy."[35] Aired despite such objections, Sayers's portrayal of the human Christ proved meticulously accurate historically and theologically sound. It also proved to be irresistible theater. She refused to water down his story, relying on the Gospel of John, Christ's favorite disciple, for eyewitness accounts, and making Judas's betrayal yet another example of the sin of the noble mind that convinces itself it knows better than its Creator how to save mankind.

Sayers believed that the corollary to the sin of pride was the desire to alleviate all human suffering. This was for her the sin of modern times and the heart of the false doctrine of progress, which she saw as sapping the strength of Western civilization. Between 1937 and 1944 she addressed that complex theological issue in brilliantly argued essays that she hoped would also reinforce the British will to destroy godless fascism. *Begin Here,* written in 1939, exhibits Sayers's Athos-like romantic streak. She addressed nearly every kind of evil assaulting the modern world, which was happening, she said, because people are too lazy to resist it. She insisted as well that all people had the right and the responsibility to use their minds creatively to defeat those evils, and typically she minced no words: "It is to flatter a generation of mental sluggards that the lickspittles of public life make a virtue of imbecility."[36]

Willful sloppiness always roused Sayers to fury, and she could wield the English language like a barbed lance. In her preface to *The Mind of the Maker* (1941), her greatest theological achievement, she denounced "the slatternly habit of illiterate reading," which she held responsible for ignorance or misconceptions about official Christian dogma as announced in the church's accepted creeds.[37] She intended that *The Mind of the Maker* illuminate the process of creation, which according to the Book of Genesis is the one ability humanity shares with God. There she postulated a synthesis of Christian doctrine and human creativity that makes work give meaning to human life, insisting that through work, man can overcome evil and turn it into good. In the same year Sayers also delivered an address at Westminster, "The Other Six Deadly Sins," in which she declared that lust, wrath, gluttony, covetousness, envy, and sloth, in the descending order of wickedness church tradition had maintained since the sixth century, all derive from pride. With her thoroughgoing research for her religious plays, her theological essays laid the foundation for the next great absorption of her life, Dante's *Divine Comedy*, the masterpiece of the Middle Ages.

Although she must have been acquainted with the general pattern of the *Divine Comedy* at Oxford, Dorothy Sayers was over fifty when she declared that she "still knew Dante chiefly by repute."[38] Her deeper experience of Dante's work came through the esoteric and charismatic lecturer and Arthurian author Charles Williams, with whom she had been acquainted since the mid-1930s. In the winter of 1943–44, Sayers, by then an immensely successful writer, visited Williams at Oxford to advise him on becoming published. Twenty-four hours later, she "was his disciple, sitting at his feet."[39] Williams was somewhat less impressed, writing to his wife, who had stayed on in London, "I like the old dear [Sayers], but she's rather heavy going . . . but what can one do?"[40]

Under the influence of Williams's *The Figure of Beatrice*, a study of the complex meaning that Beatrice Portinari represented for Dante, itself heavy abstract going indeed, Dorothy Sayers was immediately smitten when she read *The Divine Comedy* in the Witham bomb shelter that August 1944: "What a writer! God's body and bones, what a writer!"[41] She later recalled, "I can remember nothing like it since I first read *The Three Musketeers* at the age of thirteen. . . . I bolted my meals, neglected my sleep, work and correspondence, drove my friends crazy, and paid only a distracted attention to the doodle-bugs [Nazi buzz-bombs] which happened to be infesting the neighbourhood at the time, until I had panted my way through the Three Realms of the dead from top to bottom and from bottom to top."[42]

Sayers felt that each piece of great literature should be first read at its own best age, not necessarily when one is young.[43] Evidently 1944, near the close of the war, was precisely right for her experience of *The Divine Comedy*, because it dominated the rest of her life. According to Barbara Reynolds, Sayers's mention of her thirteen-year-old self is "revealing," since it indicates that Sayers' "creative talent . . . for living in an imagined world had not deserted her," and that after nearly forty years, "her mature imaginative and intellectual powers were rejuvenated by an epiphany of delight."[44]

Sayers initially poured out her rapture over Dante, "the most incomparable storyteller who ever set pen to paper," in a series of remarkable letters to Charles Williams.[45] By Christmas of 1944 she had begun to translate *The Divine Comedy*, for which nearly everything in her scholarly life had prepared her: her knowledge of Latin, which allowed her to learn medieval Italian in only a few weeks; her long-standing passion for the Middle Ages; her voluminous reading; and her conservative theological orientation.[46] Besides her intellectual preoccupations, however, Dorothy Sayers experienced intense joy in discovering her ultimate "knight in shining armor," Dante the traveler who traced the most exciting journey a Christian soul could ever take, the road to salvation, and Dante the master storyteller who had created him. Dorothy Sayers was in love again, and this time the man was worthy of her.

In March 1945, Dorothy Sayers's friend Muriel St. Clare Byrne told E. V. Rieu, editor of the Penguin Classics, that Sayers was translating *The Divine Comedy*. It happened Rieu was looking for a new English version of it, and the next month he offered Sayers a contract to complete her translation by 1948. Because of other commitments and her husband's declining health, she could not meet that deadline, but before her death in late 1957, she had completed *Hell, Purgatory,* and twenty cantos of *Paradise*.

Sayers also produced numerous lectures and essays on Dante. Dr. George Purkis, head of Modern Languages at the Colchester Royal Grammar School, invited her to lecture at the Summer School of the Society of Italian Studies, Cambridge, where she met Barbara Reynolds, and she and Reynolds became close friends. Reynolds recalls that Sayers considered her work on Dante a sacred mission. When the dean of Chichester Cathedral approached Sayers about a festival play for 1947, he observed that many people had already translated Dante, but very few could equal Sayers's "particular dramatic gift." She turned him down, replying, "But how many people read him [Dante] in those translations?"[47] The inexpensive Penguin editions enjoyed a highly effective distribution to a war-weary reading public, and furthermore, Sayers insisted, the Dante translation was "as Tennyson observed, 'one clear call' for me."[48]

Just as she had done with *Tristan in Brittany*, Sayers chose to translate *The Divine Comedy* in verse, the demanding *terza rima* so resonant in Italian and so excruciatingly difficult to reproduce in English. She bluntly stated in her Introduction to *Hell* that "no translation could ever be Dante," but she felt that an English *terza rima* version would best reproduce the unity and momentum of the original. The aba bcb rhyme pattern possessed her to such an extent that often while peeling potatoes or washing the dishes whole Italian passages would seep into her consciousness, "to pop up fully formed in English *terza rima* in the middle of some later night."[49]

Sayers equipped her *Hell* with some of the most practical, even indispensable, adjuncts ever produced for *The Divine Comedy*: voluminous clear-headed notes, an appendix treating medieval cosmology, a historical chronology, a glossary of proper names, lists of secondary reading, brief portraits of "the Greater Images" of the work, and illustrative diagrams drawn by Dorothy Sayers's old friend C. W. Scott-Giles, who had designed the Wimsey coat of arms. Her supporting material has received wide praise, but overall, scholars have disputed the quality of Sayers's translation of *The Divine Comedy*.

No matter what heroic efforts Sayers made to correct the unfortunate general opinion, growing ever more prevalent with the decay of educational standards, that *The Divine Comedy* is unreadable, or in Sayers's words "full of awful sublimity and unmitigated Grimth," scholars tended to fault awkward stretches in her translation that may have been caused by the limitations of the English language.[50] This was particularly true of her *Hell*, which reads less smoothly than her *Purgatory*. Italian specialists, too, predictably resented the intrusion of a detective novelist—and a woman, at that—

into the most sacred of their precincts.[51] According to *The Times* Sayers's translations "of *Inferno* [*sic*] and *Purgatorio* [*sic*] caught the directness of the original but failed . . . to catch the poetry."[52] Barbara Reynolds's initial estimate noted that Dante wrote for ordinary people, not the scholars, and that scholarship had forced a *"seconda morte"* [second death] on him, from which Sayers had revived "the living Dante, not the biographer's Dante, but the poet alive in his writing."[53] Sayers herself knew that her translations would be successful only as long as they were suitable for their own time, but today's general opinion is that probably "it will be a long time before [her] notes on Dante are surpassed."[54]

Sayers always insisted that God condemns no one to everlasting torment; sinners choose hell for themselves through the sin of pride. Living as she did through World War II, Sayers compared Dante's City of Dis, the demarcation line between Upper and Lower Hell, to modern society. When Britain and Europe, with aid from the United States, began to rebuild their bombed-out cities, she maintained that "the road to restoration and the Earthly Paradise lies . . . through the understanding of Hell" as the corruption of the human intellect.[55] Sayers realized such opinions were not popular. She also believed that hell was work that had no meaning, while purgatory represented work that affirms, work with the sacramental function of salvation. Her paradise affirms God's plan for humanity, where humble redeemed souls revel in "the song, the shouting, the celestial dance . . . the laughter of the rejoicing universe."[56]

Although translating *The Divine Comedy* consumed most of Sayers's last years, she kept up a wicked pace with other projects, among them *The Emperor Constantine,* her lectures on Dante at the Cambridge Summer School, and her activities as chair of the advisory council of Saint Anne's House, an experiment in bringing Anglo-Catholicism to "thinking pagans" in downtown London.[57] Her husband's alcoholism and high blood pressure also took its toll on Sayers's own stamina, but after ten years of slogging through *Hell* and *Purgatory* and the constant domestic emergencies caused by Mac's drinking, Sayers asked E. V. Rieu for a change of pace, since two-thirds of the way through *Paradise,* she "felt compelled to devote herself also to the starkness and the directness of Roland," which she had begun to translate at Oxford.[58] She observed that "[i]t was nice to get something finished that had been lying about for forty years or so."[59]

For about two years Sayers happily immersed herself in the rules of Carolingian battle and the equipage of warhorses and the glory of a lost cause valiantly fought and immortalized in an epic form that was itself passing away, like the feudal system that was beginning to disintegrate when the poem took its written shape. In her introduction Sayers demonstrated that the poem's central conflict was a clash between good and evil, exactly the straightforward hand-to-hand combat she enjoyed most. "So he rides out, into that new-washed world of clear sun and glittering colour which we call the Middle Age [*sic*] . . . which has perhaps a better right than the blown summer of the Renaissance to be called the Age of Re-Birth. . . . Anyone who sees gleams of brightness in that [medieval] world is accused of romantic nostalgia for a

Golden Age which never existed. But the figure of Roland stands there to give us the lie: he is the Young Age as that age saw itself."[60] Sayers's Penguin Classics translation of *The Song of Roland* appeared a few months before her death.

Dorothy L. Sayers's religious plays, her theological essays, and her translations all share with her Wimsey novels that uncompromising figure of the knightly hero who suffers because he will not relinquish his convictions or his ideals. In a modern world where the certainties of the Christian Middle Ages no longer hold, Sayers's detective novels remain her best-loved works, where good and evil struggle for human souls, and the hero must fight his duels within himself as well as without. Sayers's knights, including her magnificent figure of the human side of Christ, earn their privileges by defending God's truth with their own heart's blood.

So did Dorothy Sayers. In the Service of Thanksgiving offered at Canterbury Cathedral thirty years after her death, the Very Reverend John Simpson recounted her achievements: "Not many in this century have made truth and excellence their pursuit. We are only too familiar with the pursuits of self fulfillment, of power, of compassion, kindness, even of a form of justice [which are] at best only pale reflections, and at worst perversions, of what in God's plan they are meant to be, unless underpinned by truth and excellence. . . . We give thanks to God for Dorothy L. Sayers, a woman of great scholarship, talent, Christian faith, and, above all, commitment to truth."[61]

Notes

1. Dale, *Maker and Craftsman*, 3.
2. Sayers, *Mind of the Maker*, 149–50.
3. Sayers, "Ignorance and Dissatisfaction," 179.
4. Sayers, "Cat o'Mary," unpublished autobiographical fragment quoted in Brabazon, *Dorothy L. Sayers*, 33.
5. Sayers, *Song of Roland*, 45.
6. Sayers, "Omnibus of Crime," 76.
7. Brown, *Seven Deadly Sins*, 3.
8. Letter from Dorothy L. Sayers to the Rev. J. W. Welch, 11 November 1941, quoted in Brown, *Seven Deadly Sins*, 1.
9. Brown, *Seven Deadly Sins*, 15.
10. Sayers, *Gaudy Night*, 149.
11. Hone, *Dorothy L. Sayers*, 58.
12. Quotation from Sayers, *Gaudy Night*, 45.
13. *Times Literary Supplement*, 21 November 1918, 570–71.
14. Sayers, "Ignorance and Dissatisfaction," 72.
15. Regarding the elements Sayers admired, see Loomis, *Romance of Tristram and Ysolt*, xxix–xxx. Eric Whelpton, the first man to throw Dorothy Sayers over, admired her translation of *Tristan* most of all her works—he never read her detective novels—possibly because he and she had explored some of Thomas's more daring passages together at Oxford. See Reynolds, *Dorothy L. Sayers*, 186.
16. Quoted in Reynolds, *Dorothy L. Sayers*, 186.

17. Sayers, introduction (unpaginated) to *Tristan in Brittany*.
18. Ibid.
19. The Arthurian scholar Lewis Thorpe has commented, "The uncontrolled violence and the unremitting strength of the passion of Tristan and Iseut appealed to something strong and primitive that lay beneath Dorothy Sayers's scholarly intellect." See Thorpe, "Dorothy L. Sayers as a Translator," 110. That "strong and primitive" element Thorpe saw in Sayers's personality might explain her actions after being jilted by John Cournos in October 1922. That December Dorothy announced to her mother she was coming home for Christmas "with a man and a motorcycle." The relationship thus begun resulted in John Anthony, born 3 January 1924 and later given Sayers's husband's family name of Fleming.
20. Quoted in Mann, *Deadlier Than the Male*, 27.
21. Brabazon, *Dorothy L. Sayers*, 87.
22. Reynolds, *Dorothy L. Sayers*, 189.
23. Sayers, "Omnibus of Crime," 72.
24. For a longer discussion of this pattern in Sayers's works, see chapter 6, "Human Comedies," in Brunsdale, *Dorothy L. Sayers*, 121–31.
25. Stock and Stock, "Agents of Evil and Justice," 15.
26. Sayers, introduction to *Great Short Stories of Detection, Mystery and Horror*, 20.
27. Sayers, *Gaudy Night*, 238.
28. Ibid., 381.
29. Hamilton, "Gaudeamus Igitur," 6.
30. Sayers, "Gaudy Night" (essay), 53.
31. The manuscript of "Thrones, Dominations" is in the Wade Collection of Wheaton College, Wheaton, Illinois. The novel published as *Thrones, Dominations*, "by Dorothy L. Sayers and Jill Paton Walsh," falls short of Sayers's promise of "alluring complications."
32. Sayers, *Man Born to be King*, 135.
33. Sayers, *Zeal of Thy House*, 68.
34. Sayers, *Devil to Pay*, 108.
35. Regarding this stage convention, see Hone, *Dorothy L. Sayers*, 102. The quotation regarding "blasphemy" is taken from Sayers's letter to Maurice Reckitt dated 20 October 20 1945, quoted in Brabazon, *Dorothy L. Sayers*, 202–3 and 204 n. 16.
36. Sayers, *Begin Here*, unpaginated preface.
37. Sayers, *Mind of the Maker*, ix.
38. Quoted in Carpenter, *Inklings*, 208.
39. This observation was made by Anne Spaulding, Williams's Oxford landlady; quoted in Brabazon, *Dorothy L. Sayers*, 160, 225.
40. Carpenter, *Inklings*, 208.
41. Dorothy L. Sayers, letter to Charles Williams, 26 September 1944. Also see Brabazon, *Dorothy L. Sayers*, 229.
42. Quoted in Reynolds, *Dorothy L. Sayers*, 354.
43. Sayers, introduction to *Further Papers on Dante*, vii.
44. Reynolds, *Dorothy L. Sayers*, 354. For a discussion of all Sayers's work on Dante, see Reynolds, *Passionate Intellect*.
45. Sayers, "And Telling You a Story," 1. Williams had intended to publish these letters to heighten public interest in Dante's work, but he died before he could do so. Portions of his

correspondence with Sayers about Dante, eleven letters from Williams and nineteen from Sayers, are discussed in detail in Reynolds, *Passionate Intellect*.

    46. Hone, *Dorothy L. Sayers*, 147.
    47. Reynolds, *Dorothy L. Sayers*, 355.
    48. Ibid.
    49. First quotation: Sayers, introduction to *The Comedy of Dante Alighieri the Florentine: Cantica I, Hell*, 56. Second quotation: Brabazon, *Dorothy L. Sayers*, 234.
    50. Sayers, "Comedy of *The Comedy*," 151.
    51. Hone, *Dorothy L. Sayers*, 185.
    52. Quoted in Hone, *Dorothy L. Sayers*, 185.
    53. Barbara Reynolds, preface to *Introductory Papers on Dante*, by Dorothy L. Sayers, vii–viii.
    54. Brabazon, *Dorothy L. Sayers*, 276.
    55. Sayers, "City of Dis," 151.
    56. Sayers, "Comedy of *The Comedy*," 174.
    57. Brabazon, *Dorothy L. Sayers*, 240.
    58. Hone, *Dorothy L. Sayers*, 183.
    59. Quoted in Hone, *Dorothy L. Sayers*, 183.
    60. Sayers, *Song of Roland*, 17.
    61. Quoted in Brunsdale, *Dorothy L. Sayers*, 209.

Select Bibliography of Works by Dorothy L. Sayers

Whose Body? London: T. Fisher Unwin, 1923.
Clouds of Witness. London: T. Fisher Unwin, 1926.
Unnatural Death. London: Ernest Benn, 1927.
Lord Peter Views the Body. London: Gollancz, 1928. Short fiction.
The Unpleasantness at the Bellona Club. London: Ernest Benn, 1928.
Tristan in Brittany. London: Ernest Benn, 1929. Includes brief prose condensations of Joseph Bedier's 1902–5 summary
With Robert Eustace. *The Documents in the Case.* London: Ernest Benn, 1930. Collaborative novel.
Strong Poison. London: Gollancz, 1930.
The Five Red Herrings. London: Gollancz, 1931.
Have His Carcase. London: Gollancz, 1932.
"My Edwardian Childhood." Fragment, thirty-three pages, ca. 1932. The Wade Collection, Wheaton College, Wheaton, Illinois.
Hangman's Holiday. London: Gollancz, 1933. Short fiction.
Murder Must Advertise. London: Gollancz, 1933.
"Cat o'Mary." Fragmentary autobiographical novel, 209 pages, ca. 1934. The Wade Collection, Wheaton College, Wheaton, Ill.
Introduction to *Great Short Stories of Detection, Mystery, and Horror.* Third Series. London: Gollancz, 1934.
The Nine Tailors. London: Gollancz, 1934.
Gaudy Night. London: Gollancz, 1936.
With Muriel St. Clare Byrne. *Busman's Honeymoon.* London: Gollancz, 1937. Detective comedy.
Busman's Honeymoon. London: Gollancz, 1937. Novel adaptation of play by Sayers.

The Zeal of Thy House. London: Gollancz, 1937. Religious drama on twelfth-century architect William of Sens, for Canterbury Cathedral Festival.

"Thrones, Dominations." Six chapters of unfinished novel, written ca. 1938–39. Manuscript in the Wade Center, Wheaton College, Wheaton, Illinois.

The Devil to Pay. London: Gollancz, 1939. Religious drama on the Faust legend, for Canterbury Cathedral Festival.

He That Should Come. London: Gollancz, 1939. Radio nativity play.

Begin Here: A Wartime Essay. London: Gollancz, 1940. Wartime essays.

Love All. Kent, Ohio: Kent State University Press, 1940. Romantic comedy.

The Man Born to be King. London: Gollancz, 1943. Twelve-part radio play on the life of Christ.

"Gaudy Night." In *The Art of the Mystery Story,* edited by Howard Haycraft. New York: Simon and Schuster, 1946.

The Heart of Stone. Witham, Essex, Eng.: J. H. Clarke, 1946. Four canzoni of Dante's "Pietra" group.

The Just Vengeance. London: Gollancz, 1946. Religious play for Lichfield Cathedral Festival.

"The Omnibus of Crime." In *The Art of the Mystery Story,* edited by Howard Haycraft. New York: Simon and Schuster, 1946.

Unpopular Opinions. London: Gollancz, 1946. Theological, political, and critical essays.

"And Telling You a Story." In *Essays Presented to Charles Williams,* edited by C. S. Lewis. Oxford: Oxford University Press, 1947.

Creed or Chaos? London: Methuen, 1947. Theological essays.

The Mind of the Maker. London: Methuen, 1941. Theological-aesthetic essays.

Translator. *The Comedy of Dante Alighieri, the Florentine.* Harmondsworth, Eng.: Penguin Books, 1949–63. *Terza rima* translation with notes and commentaries: *Hell,* 1949; *Purgatory,* 1955; *Paradise,* completed by Barbara Reynolds, 1963.

The Emperor Constantine. London: Gollancz, 1951. Religious play for Colchester Cathedral Festival.

"Ignorance and Dissatisfaction." *Latin Teaching* 28 (October 1952). Reprinted under the title "The Teaching of Latin: A New Approach," in Dorothy L. Sayers, *The Poetry of Search and the Poetry of Statement* (London: Gollancz, 1963), 177–99.

"The City of Dis." In *Introductory Papers on Dante.* New York: Harper, 1954.

"The Comedy of The Comedy." In *Introductory Papers on Dante.* New York: Harper, 1954.

Further Papers on Dante. London: Methuen, 1957. Intended for nonscholarly audiences.

Introductory Papers on Dante. London: Methuen, 1954. Essays first delivered to student audiences.

Translator. *The Song of Roland.* Harmondsworth: Penguin Books, 1957.

The Poetry of Search and the Poetry of Statement. London: Gollancz, 1963. Twelve essays for general audiences, five of them on Dante.

The Letters of Dorothy L. Sayers. Chosen and edited by Barbara Reynolds. 4 vols. New York: St. Martin's Press, 1995–2000.

Completed by Jill Paton Walsh. *Thrones, Dominations.* New York: St. Martin's Press, 1998. Sayers's unfinished manuscript completed by Walsh.

Works Cited

N.B.: Editions other than originals are cited here for reasons of accessibility.

Brabazon, James. *Dorothy L. Sayers: A Biography.* New York: Scribners, 1981.

Brown, Janice. *The Seven Deadly Sins in the World of Dorothy L. Sayers.* Kent, Ohio: Kent State University Press, 1998.

Brunsdale, Mitzi. *Dorothy L. Sayers: Solving the Mystery of Wickedness.* Oxford: Berg Publishers, 1990.

Carpenter, Humphrey. *The Inklings.* New York: Ballantine Books, 1981.

Dale, Alzina Stone. *Maker and Craftsman: The Story of Dorothy L. Sayers.* Grand Rapids, Michigan: Eerdmans, 1978.

Hamilton, Edith. "Gaudeamus Igitur," review of *Gaudy Night. Saturday Review of Literature* 13 (22 February 1936): 3–6.

Hone, Ralph. *Dorothy L. Sayers: A Literary Biography.* Kent, Ohio: Kent State University Press, 1979.

Loomis, Roger Sherman, trans. *The Romance of Tristram and Ysolt,* by Thomas of Britain. New York: Dutton, 1951.

Mann, Jessica. *Deadlier Than the Male.* New York: Macmillan, 1981.

Reynolds, Barbara. *Dorothy L. Sayers: Her Life and Soul.* New York: St. Martin's Press, 1993.

———. *The Passionate Intellect: Dorothy L. Sayers' Encounter with Dante.* Kent, Ohio; Kent State University Press, 1989.

Stock, R. D., and Barbara Stock. "The Agents of Evil and Justice in the Novels of Dorothy L. Sayers." In *As Her Whimsy Took Her,* edited by Margaret Hannay. Kent, Ohio: Kent State University Press, 1979.

Thorpe, Lewis. "Dorothy L. Sayers as a Translator of *Le Roman de Tristan* and *La Chanson de Roland.*" In *As Her Whimsy Took Her,* edited by Margaret Hannay. Kent, Ohio: Kent State University Press, 1979.

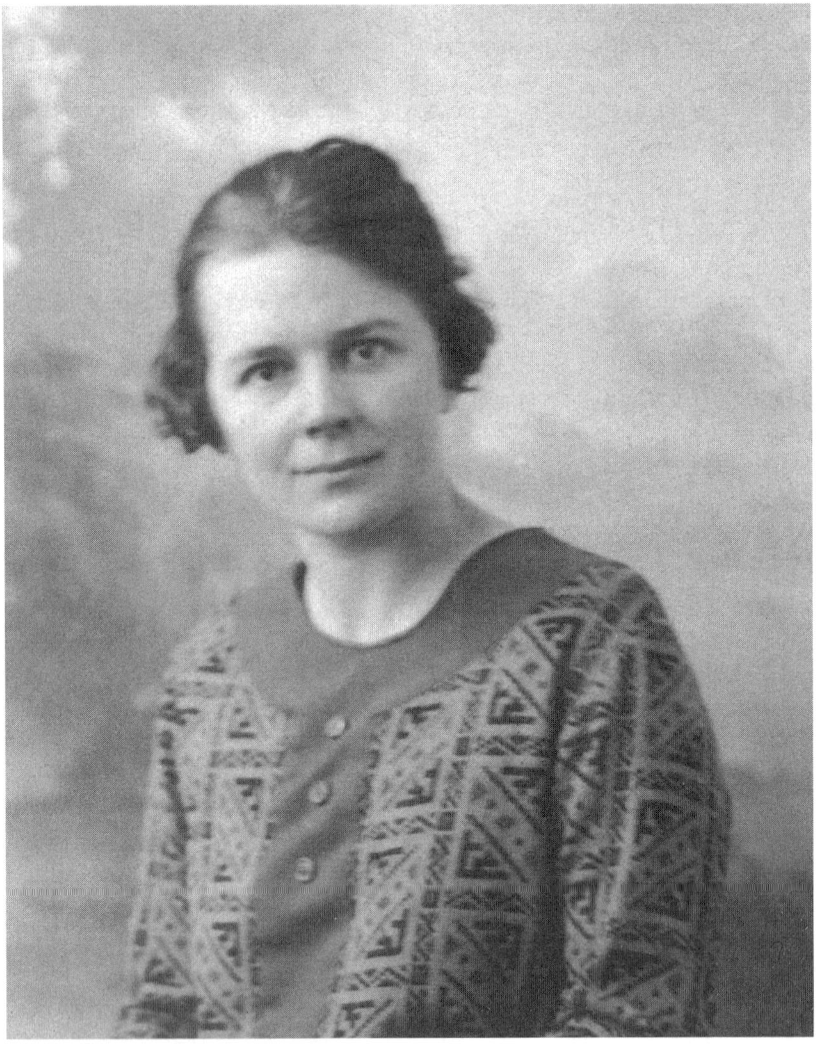

CHAPTER 31

Doris Mary Stenton (1894–1971)
The Legal Records and the Historian

PATRICIA R. ORR

By 1952, when Doris Mary Stenton published "The Pipe Rolls and the Historians," she had been arguing the importance of printing a wide variety of legal records as historical sources for the greater part of a lifetime. Although printing of the legal records began in 1835, the labor and expense restricted the selection of rolls to be printed and caused long lapses in their appearance.[1] With her capacity for unstinting work, impeccable standards, and discriminating legal intelligence, Lady Stenton created a monumental legacy of printed records in previously unimagined variety, with "masterly" introductions and notes that serve well as legal texts.[2] Her acute observations of medieval law and society gave insights into the character of King John that reshaped views of that vexed monarch, brought her to write a path-breaking work on women throughout English history, and served as a foundation for an enduring work of social history. In the midst of these achievements, she gave equal energy to her marriage to Sir Frank Stenton, distinguished historian of Anglo-Saxon England. Doris managed all the practical aspects of their lives, and her care and devotion made it possible for him to reach the full extent of his powers. One memorialist, commenting that Frank's output would have been impossible had he been subject to ordinary distractions, gave a fitting tribute to Doris's labors.[3]

As she bicycled to Reading University from her home village of Woodbury in 1912, the then Doris Mary Parsons probably had little idea of entering a notable academic career. Born on 27 August 1894, the daughter of a carpenter, she received a country girl's upbringing that she remembered all her life. A telling example appears in *The English Woman in History,* when she admires Lady Mary Coke's agility in getting a cow uphill.[4] It was a frugal and exacting life; she later commented that, in respect to finances, she had been "brought up hard."[5] She attended the Abbey School, which apparently did not discern the special abilities she was later to display.[6] But when she moved on to Reading University and attended the history lectures of Frank Merry Stenton (1880–1967), who had been appointed to a history chair at Reading in 1912, she felt that his teaching was like "the opening of windows" and declared that she immediately became "a dedicated historian." Moreover, she noted that he made no distinction among students, male or female.[7] For his part, Frank Stenton very soon recognized her lively intellect, guiding her research for her examinations and having her transcribe twelfth-century charters. In 1916 she won a first class in her examination for her degree (375, 396).

Doris soon demonstrated her capacity for hard work. Although after her graduation Frank Stenton found a grant of £100 for her in the hope that he could "save her from teaching" and give her free time for her research, her load as assistant lecturer at Reading increased, and such time was hard to find.[8] At the same time she was honing her research skills by working in the archives at Lincolnshire under the direction of Canon Charles Wilmer Foster, a founder of the Lincoln Record Society. She was fortunate to come of age academically at a time of renewed activity in the publishing of legal records and to have Canon Foster, a progenitor of the movement, as mentor. Doris Stenton later praised his inborn sense of scholarship, passion for truth, high academic standards, and instinct to record and spread knowledge, values she herself possessed and he nurtured in her.[9] Her labors produced two articles in the *English Historical Review* in 1917, in which she displayed her command of analytical skills and ability to extract the maximum of information from source material.[10]

Even her leisure activity was energetic, and in recording her bicycling trips she produced a charming if succinct journal that gives a sense of some of her central characteristics: energy, acuity, and reticence. In the summers of 1917 and 1918 she undertook day trips as long as sixty-four miles, many with Frank, often with other companions or alone. Longer trips involved overnight stays and the occasional company of friends. She persisted over bad roads and through rainstorms, and her sharp eye alerted her to "most beautiful fat thistles" and strawberries on the roadsides. Her reactions were strong and forthright, whether to wretched villages with uncared-for children or to fine vistas. She explored Roman roads, found ancient villages, and located sites mentioned in the documents she was working with. In all, she was firming up the knowledge of English geography that was to sharpen her understanding of the workings of medieval law.[11]

The quality of reticence marked her entire life. Journal entries are spare and unadorned, with little of an intimate nature and nothing about her developing relationship with Frank. She was similarly reserved in her personal letters. Forthright in her opinions about inflation or the new coinage, she said little about her personal life. Even her memorial to Frank, in which she apologized, "It is difficult to keep myself out of the story," tells very little about her.[12] Though they entertained often, the Stentons were private individuals; a colleague once urged them to come more often into the Senior Common Room, fearing that they had retired into seclusion (338). According to Cecil Slade, "[H]er main characteristic was self-sufficiency, and there was an inner core of thought and feeling that she kept from others." Late in life she was encouraged to write her autobiography, but she flatly refused, saying, "That's about the least useful thing I could do."[13] It is fortunate that her papers and the differing perspectives of her three memorialists are witness to her life.

At first Frank and Doris were probably no more to each other than historians admiring each other's work, and Slade believes Frank was attracted to her as a promising historian long before he saw her as a prospective wife.[14] It is true that he found opportunities for her to work and stretch her skills, but he did as much for other exceptional students, and Frank's mentors had found similar opportunities for him.[15] However, Frank soon saw her as more than a student. He was often her companion on those day trips on the bicycle, and by 1918 she was managing the logistics of his life with the same vigor she gave to her work, finding new living quarters for him when he needed them and cooking for him on a gas ring often enough that a letter from his mother remarks on his frequent mention of bacon and eggs (378, 379). They could not marry because of his concern for his mother, who, though financially independent during her long widowhood, depended more and more heavily on Frank for moral and practical support. Her health began to decline in 1918, and Frank went to stay with her until she died in the fall of that year. Doris never met Frank's mother, but admired her as "a woman of no ordinary type" who had raised Frank from a boy of delicate health to "a scholar of recognized reputation" (329, 279).

Frank and Doris were married in 1919 and began a life of such close association that, as Doris said, they "did everything together."[16] They moved into the back half of a seventeenth-century cottage and continued to take bicycle trips. Doris took over the entire management of the household, even becoming the couple's chauffeur; Frank never drove. She was particularly noted for her excellent cooking, a distinct advantage when they entertained. Above all, they engaged in the pursuit of history. Though they worked in different fields, each enthusiastically cooperated in, for example, searching for books the other needed. It was Doris's opinion that Frank's personality made everything they did, play or work, fun (338, 379). However, they never collaborated on a publication; their interests coincided, but their work remained independent.[17]

Doris's first major task was to take part in the resuscitation of the Pipe Roll Society and continue its publications. Pipe rolls, so named because they resemble pipes when rolled for storage, are financial records of the medieval monarchy. They are immensely valuable to historians, but before they were printed, access to them was limited and locating information in them was exceedingly difficult. Lengthy and complex, they require broad knowledge and concentrated application to edit properly. The Pipe Roll Society, formed in 1883 for the purpose of publishing them, suffered periodic stoppages and in 1914 suspended publication. The Stentons and Canon Foster worked to revive the society, and in 1925 they decided that Doris Stenton would become its honorary secretary and general editor, a post that she held until she retired in 1962.

She was an inspired choice. Her skills as a historian were already highly developed; she recognized the need for the highest standards in editing, indexing, and transcription; and she energetically recruited members and searched for grant money. An excellent delegator, she also knew when it was best to dig in and do the work herself. She produced an edition each year for most of the years between 1925 and 1949, an accomplishment to rival the production of the original records.[18]

Doris Stenton's talents made the most of the pipe rolls as a historical source. Her extensive indices made information easy to locate, but it was her introductions that focused attention on the unique value of each volume. She created a close-up view of historical events and clarified previously obscure points, demonstrating, for example, that the disturbances in Richard's reign caused by John's revolt were much more widespread and the justices' efforts to defeat him and hold the country for Richard much more strenuous than the chronicles indicate. She identified the contemporary chroniclers who reported events accurately and those who relied on the inaccuracies of gossip.[19] She worked out the itineraries of kings and justices, giving new understanding of the growth of the royal administrative and judicial systems.[20] Even a roll she found not "of outstanding interest" underlined King John's "readiness to sell whatever he could induce anyone to buy."[21] She was alert to the women in the rolls: the large amount paid by the countess of Aumale to remain unmarried, the execution by burning of a woman who had killed her husband, and the active part Eleanor of Aquitaine played in Richard's reign.[22] She had a taste for what she called "matters of real interest, if not of profound importance" that bring into sharp focus the aspects of otherwise obscure medieval life, such as the description of a newly built hunting lodge or the beginnings of the London river police.[23] She collected and preserved "the great diversity of matters" that, taken together, "suggest the ebb and flow of a rich and varied social and political life."[24]

Earlier, in 1921, Doris Stenton had begun work on her other major field of endeavor, the records of cases heard in the English courts of justice. Medieval English legal records survive from an earlier date and in greater profusion than do any others in Europe, with the exception of those of the papal courts, and give a unique perspective on a litigious and active people. Relatively few of the earliest records are extant[25] and Doris believed that all surviving records are invaluable, reflecting as they do a time when English law was assimilating Henry II's innovations and producing more of its own, including transforming the jury into a more rapid, direct, and rational way of settling both civil and criminal cases. Beyond this, these records reflect at first hand the events of John's reign and his dealings with his subjects. Doris's goal was to make them as widely accessible as possible, for they are an unparalleled source of information about individuals, society, and economics, and indeed about every possible area of the study of history. With her characteristic application and efficiency, she was able to produce editions of legal records concurrently with her ongoing volumes from the Pipe Roll Society.

First was *The Earliest Lincolnshire Assize Rolls, A.D. 1202–1209*, the records of cases heard in Lincolnshire by itinerant justices on eyre.[26] Eyre courts, royal courts of justice staffed by the king's judges but held in the county courts, brought the king's legal system into the local areas. Though feared for their multiple financial exactions, they became popular venues for people who could not spare the time and expense to go to the central court at Westminster. They contain most of the criminal cases and the majority of proceedings on the new legal actions of Henry II's reign. Still, eyres were considered by present-day historians to be of secondary importance, and the monumental series of the Curia Regis Rolls, for reasons of expense, chose to print only the cases heard at Westminster.[27] With few exceptions, eyre records were left inaccessible to all but those who could visit the archives.[28] This was a serious omission; without the eyre rolls, Doris Stenton argued, the picture of the English law would be incomplete. The Lincolnshire Record Society, founded by Canon Foster with the help of the Stentons, worked to rectify the omission and engaged Doris to edit the earliest of the county's eyre records.

Doris Stenton's fundamental requirement for publication was to print the original Latin text, an English translation, and extensive notes to explain points of law, but budget considerations forced a compromise. One solution is to omit the Latin text and its difficulties. Rendering the Latin of early legal records into intelligible form is laborious and expensive. The rolls are heavily abbreviated and often hastily written, with many interlinings, on inferior parchment. They can be fragmentary, nearly illegible, and of ambiguous or impenetrable meaning, and they require a system of symbols to indicate interlinings, cancellations, and marginal notations. Nevertheless, Doris deplored the practice of printing only translations, arguing that printing the Latin gave readers an opportunity to weigh decisions of translation themselves. In *The Earliest Lincolnshire Assize Rolls,* after much deliberation, it was the English translation that was omitted for the sake of economy. Doris printed the Latin text with explanatory notes to make clear the workings of the law.[29] The result is a workable and informative text, but one that requires some proficiency in basic Latin, an obstacle to those not working in medieval fields of study.

Doris Stenton's notes and introduction, however, go far to aid any reader to understand the rolls, the legal practices, and the people and actions involved. She described the context of the eyres and explained particular points about this one, and thus she created a primer for readers unversed in the law and instruction for those who know it well. In *The Earliest Northamptonshire Assize Rolls, A.D. 1202–1203* she investigates at length the careers and itineraries of justices of the eyre, giving a clear picture of busy and important men attending to the largest and most minute concerns of the court and building the law as they went.[30] She clarifies the inner workings of the county court and its humble officials.[31] Going deeply into the implications of individual cases, she sheds further light on life and law.[32] Her clarity and thoroughness make this and her other introductions, as a colleague described them, masterly.[33] A beginner in the study of thirteenth-century English law would do well to read any or all of her introductions.

Editions of eyre rolls continued to appear concurrently with volumes of the Pipe Roll series, each with its unique points of interest and insights into history and the law. In *The Earliest Lincolnshire Assize Rolls* Doris Stenton noted that most of the rolls surviving from John's reign recorded cases heard before Simon of Patishall, a clear indication of Simon's influence in a time when judicial rolls were usually destroyed once they had yielded their financial information at the Exchequer.[34] In *The Earliest Northamptonshire Assize Rolls, A.D. 1202–1203* she noted the unique importance of Northamptonshire, which, near to London, saw the conclusion of many cases initiated elsewhere, thus giving a broad view of English life and legal development. In both works she describes and clarifies court procedure as it stood before the first iteration of the Magna Carta and the loss of the ordeal as a means of trial, both of which occurred in 1215.[35] As she worked, she took stock of King John and prepared to prove that previous assessments of him had been wrong.

Doris Stenton's next publications of early eyre rolls, published by the Selden Society, deal with the years immediately after the revolt, when a child was on the throne, a regency ruled the country, and justice was only tentatively returning to the shires after the war.[36] Her 1934 work, concerning Lincolnshire and Worcestershire, is from the first general eyre after the revolt and shows the country's administration, uniquely without a single ruling figure at its head, dealing with legal change and the resolution of disputes exacerbated by the recent hostilities. These rolls are liberally marked by the compiler of the great legal treatise known by the name of Bracton, which, published in the middle of the thirteenth century, influenced English law for the rest of the Middle Ages.[37] Many of the cases do not appear in the working compilation known as *Bracton's Note Book* or are modified there, so these cases make a useful supplement to that work.[38] Everyday life appears here: widespread poverty resulting from the war, a wandering mason, a clerk who has gone off to school at Paris, a rural dean moving his two cartloads of books (lxiii, lxxiii). Disappointingly, the Lincolnshire crown pleas (i.e., the criminal cases) have been lost, so these rolls can tell little about the effect of the loss of the ordeal, a means of proof that, though disapproved of by reform clerics, nevertheless provided a way to deal with the accused.[39] But Doris Stenton's detective work shows an unbroken line of distinguished justices and their activities in an unquiet time (xxiv, lxxiii).

The subject of her next volume of eyre rolls, the violent county of Yorkshire, had many criminal cases, a problem when there was no recourse to the ordeal. Doris Stenton calculates that sessions started in November 1218, but the king's council did not reach a decision about handling criminal cases until late January 1219.[40] The eventual solution, using the jury, was by no means obvious, and the king's council did not suggest that it be used. The jury had been used by defendants to establish a flaw in criminal charges, usually that they were based on the malice of the accuser rather than on fact, and the courts hesitated to depend on it for a statement of guilt or innocence. Doris shows in great detail that the movement toward the jury, though "no more than foreshadowed" in the procedures at York, was a viable possibility.[41] The last of this series follows the eyre to later sittings in Gloucestershire, Warwickshire, and Shropshire and shows the court depending more on the jury to decide criminal cases, though it was reluctant to hang a man on the statement of the jury alone.[42] Doris Stenton's painstaking work brings order out of the welter of detail and makes it possible to view the ongoing process of legal change.[43]

She continued to produce editions of the Pipe rolls, leaving only the editions of 1935 and 1939 to others. She retained her skill at delegating work and was always grateful for the labor of others who aided the ongoing publication of the Pipe rolls by transcribing the rolls, preparing indices, and the like. Each volume, nonetheless, called for the scholarly equivalent of backbreaking labor on her part, and even those that came out under the names of others absorbed much of her time, labor, and skill, given that she was the general editor, responsible not only for oversight but for such matters as setting up schedules and working with printers to assure timely publication.[44]

Stringencies of World War II slowed production; Doris Stenton produced only two volumes in 1940 and a Pipe Roll edition in 1942. After the war she continued to produce volumes of primary sources: Pipe Roll editions in 1947, 1949, and 1953 and *Sir Christopher Hatton's Book of Seals,* a facsimile edition of a beautiful seventeenth-century transcription of medieval charters that was undertaken to honor Frank Stenton. She retained her position as honorary secretary and general editor of the Pipe Roll Society and all the duties of supervision it entailed. But changes were taking place. Others took up her labors of production of Pipe Roll editions. Her command of her historical period assured that she was in demand for more reflective work, articles and books explicating her insights into history and reviews of the work of others.

Pleas before the King and His Justices, four volumes of previously unpublished judicial records for the Selden Society, was a culmination of the principles that had always driven her work. It was an article of faith with her that records should be printed whole and complete to show the context of medieval life and legal activity.[45] With these volumes she completed the publication of all existing records of their time. Along with records of court cases, she included essoins, relentlessly repetitive excuses for nonappearance by parties to a lawsuit.[46] Essoins take up lengthy sections of the plea rolls and, because they exhibit no significant points of law, generally were not printed.[47] Doris Stenton asserted that omitting them leaves long gaps in a case's chronology and prevents readers from following a case in its entirety; she made them fully available in print for the first time. She made points about the law, such as the development of writs and the legal actions, and about society: the harsh life in Yorkshire and the poverty in remote Cornwall that reveals itself in the many land pleas there concerning only one acre.[48] She provided a new explanation of the meaning of Magna Carta 17 (1215), which provided that common pleas (e.g., lawsuits that do not involve the king) should be held in *aliquo loco certo,* "in some settled place." This had been taken to mean that such cases should be concluded at Westminster, but Doris Stenton argued that it meant that cases not completed on eyre had to be continued at a specific location so that the plaintiff would not have to follow the court on its travels for an indefinite period of time.⁴⁹ In all this she demonstrates the "essential unity of Royal Justice" (1, 2, 150), a picture of thoughtful judges and royal administrators moving, though often in an ad hoc way, toward the creation of a coherent legal system.

English Society in the Early Middle Ages, volume 3 in the *Pelican History of England,* was Doris Stenton's first full-fledged work of social history. Her methodology was to take elements of the English population and describe, in close and loving detail, the people and activities that comprised them. She described life in the aggregate, barons as barons and foresters as foresters. Then she narrowed the focus to individual lives to round out the picture of social life: the difficulties John faced, and posed, when his brother Richard I was captured; the elusiveness of an "evildoer" named William of Drayton; and an amusing story about the petulant servant of a saint.⁵⁰ Her exhaustive knowledge of historical sources and minute knowledge of English geography and placenames made this possible; her sure and guiding intellect gave coherence and lucidity. Practical and factual, intended for students, the work has much to tell even seasoned scholars.

The Pipe Rolls and the Historians expresses, if indirectly, Doris Stenton's sense of the value of the Pipe rolls and other records to understanding English history. She traces the career of these records, often neglected and misunderstood, sometimes in peril of disintegration. Always understood to be of value, the rolls were nevertheless little used, even by such scholars as the great John Selden.⁵¹ In the seventeenth century a minor clerk, "drunk with the delight of using" them, was first to study them thoroughly. Only in 1774 did Joseph Ayloffe declare that "civil and ecclesiastical history" cannot be written without "our national records," citing works of various historians to prove his point.⁵² From 1793 to 1819 the records were in sacks at Somerset House; then they were moved to a dark, damp, dirty repository under the care of an incompetent keeper who, among other abuses, cut seals off to make the documents easier to fold (286–87). In 1831 a scholarly new keeper was appointed and began the search for a better location; even so, they suffered further vicissitudes before the Pipe Roll Society was formed in 1883 (286–88, 291–92). Perhaps it is warranted to notice in the title an allusion to J. R. R. Tolkien's groundbreaking article "Beowulf: The Monsters and the Critics," surely well known to the wife of a great Anglo-Saxonist, which argued that the monsters in the poem, far from being irrelevant to its development, were central to its purpose.⁵³ In any case, her factual account of the records celebrates their central importance to history, in spite of centuries of neglect and misunderstanding.

Using a previously unknown charter, Doris Stenton cleared up the mystery of the identity of the author of *Gesta Regis Henrici secundi Benedicti Abbatis,* a reliable but unpolished chronicle known informally as *Benedict* after the abbot who commissioned it.⁵⁴ Her charter placed Roger of Howden, author of an equally reliable but more polished chronicle, at the siege of Acre with Richard I, an event of which *Benedict* displayed firsthand knowledge.⁵⁵ With the charter, internal evidence from both chronicles, and her own broad knowledge, she showed that the same author wrote both chronicles, that "Benedict" was actually written by Howden himself, an identification that continues to convince other historians (580–81).

A departure from Doris Stenton's usual work, *The English Woman in History* examined the life of women in England from earliest recorded times to the late nineteenth century. Frank and Doris shared a strong interest in the place of women in society; and over the years they accumulated an admirable collection of mainly primary sources, housed today in the Stenton Library.[56] Doris takes up and expands Frank's thesis that Anglo-Saxon women had been autonomous and influential, but the Norman Conquest and the introduction of feudalism drastically lowered their status.[57] But she deals less with Frank's thesis than with sharp observation of hundreds of women and the meaning of their lives in a historical context. Doris restricted herself to women whose contributions were unknown or inadequately discussed before she wrote; surprisingly, even Eleanor of Aquitaine fell into that category at the time of writing. Through lenses of all these lives, Doris found a pattern of rise and fall in women's fortunes over time. She accepts Frank's argument but considers the change under the Normans to be a difference of degree rather than of kind, and she notes the presence of assertive women under the Norman regime.[58] A worse period for women, in her opinion, was the seventeenth century, when, after acceptance of learning for women in the Renaissance, a severe reaction pictured women as vain, idle, and inferior and demanded their thorough subjection (129–43). This opinion, in Doris's view, was sufficiently widespread to inhibit both learning and autonomy for women and, even, insidiously, to persuade women themselves of its truth (145–46). After some recovery, women suffered a setback in the nineteenth century when women's rights were associated with socialism. Even so, among her multitudinous examples Doris finds "a continuous line of women, including farm women, who have left their mark on English life," whose "succession was never broken," and who avoided what she calls "the state of irresponsible subjection to men" (349). Though much has been done on the subject since then, her book has the freshness of her sense of discovery and the richness of the stories of many women. Still, Doris Stenton preferred to work within the medieval period and may have felt the book had taken her far from that calling: "I wish I could get back to some real history," she commented as she worked on it.[59]

English Justice between the Norman Conquest and the Great Charter, 1066–1215 combined "King John and the Courts of Justice," an article that had grown out of her Raleigh Lecture of 1958, with the Jayne Lectures she gave to the American Philosophical Society.[60] The Jayne Lectures use documents and incidents to support some of her conclusions. A sworn inquest in the time of Henry I, most of whose participants were of Anglo-Saxon descent, illustrates the dependence of Norman justice on its Anglo-Saxon heritage. Strong demand for royal writs and chirographs (formal records of agreements made in court) belies chroniclers' accounts of the burdensomeness of royal justice, and the traces of a developing legal profession appear during the reign of John.[61] These and other examples reveal and support some of her assumptions: that judges' motivations at least partly included the fundamental desire for good justice and that they felt a spirit of engagement with the law equal to her own. In "King John and the Courts of Justice" she demolished an outdated but persistent view: that King John had little or no respect for the law. Doris Stenton found ample evidence that he took a close personal interest in the rightful workings of the law, directing justices and sheriffs to deal with cases according to law and custom and consulting with his justices before resolving cases with no clear solution in law. He tirelessly heard cases as he moved about England, and he conceived of his judges as a core of experts who could hear cases in his presence or be dispatched wherever needed. He kept the court functioning well into the civil war and worked to make sure that the law took account of the special circumstances of "the helpless, women, children, the poor, and the idiot" (89, 90–93, 96, 97, 109–14). She argued that he had much to do with the development of the common law during his reign, and with her careful marshaling of evidence, she demonstrated that, whatever his lapses, he kept up a close and often surprisingly altruistic supervision of the law and the courts. King John as seen in the legal records was not a different king; his flaws remain, but the records reveal an unsuspected capacity in his character.

This was an output any historian could envy, and yet Doris Stenton dedicated equal energy to her marriage. The practical aspects of life were entirely her responsibility. When they married, she promised Frank he would never have to do any more gardening, a promise she kept, and it appears he was equally free of other domestic duties.[62] What Doris did not do herself she delegated to servants, managing even after World War II to keep a staff of several people, including a cook-housekeeper.[63] She worried over Frank's poor appetite and delicate health and augmented his austere meals; an egg with his Friday tea became a custom (7). She did everything from caring for the car to managing the finances. She bought his clothes, cut his hair, and scrupulously observed his wishes, never having a dog in the house or going to the hairdresser, for example (5). She tried to mitigate Frank's fears about money, which persisted even when they became relatively prosperous. He denied himself books and never bought a piano for their last home, even though he was a musician and composer. "I fought this as much as I could," Doris said, "even with trepidation buying him an occasional expensive book I knew he wanted."[64] Doris was equally devoted to Frank's welfare in his professional life. He accumulated honors, chaired historical organizations, and was awarded a title; she saw to the mundane details of his academic life, managing appointments and collecting student papers. Many meetings took place in their home, where she entertained Frank's confreres as guests. Cecil Slade summed it up thus: "[H]is splendid output in historical writing and his sustained contribution to the organization of history were possible only in the absence of mundane distractions."[65] Never, however, did she give any sign of strain, and they never ceased to delight in each other.

Doris Stenton's letters, written on the infrequent occasions when they were apart, give a rare glimpse of their life together. The letters are practical, full of comments on train journeys, an "immense lunch," and news about friends, but they sparkle with endearments and affection. Frank and Doris had nicknames they used only between themselves: he was Pupus and she was Pupa, Latin for "boy" and "girl," but perhaps from some other derivation since she often signed her letters with the initials "PPA." In a letter written while she was hospitalized, she apologizes for having dismissed him abruptly, says she is better now, and "Pupa does love Pupus." Usually there is no sense of even this much stress. "I have no news for Pupus except that he is a darling" or a line drawing of Frank in the garden having tea, accompanied by their cats, are more typical expressions. The mix of practicality and devotion reflects the deepest-running aspects of her character.[66]

The same qualities are seen in Doris Stenton's friendships. She found time for correspondence and visits with friends; her friendship with Dorothy Whitelock is a good example. Dorothy initiated a correspondence, not with Doris but with Frank, asking for advice on *Anglo-Saxon Wills*.[67] Her letters were formal, a young scholar addressing a scholar already eminent in his field, but after she met Doris some years later the correspondence began to change.[68] Dorothy wrote to Doris instead of to Frank, and the women were on a first-name basis long before Dorothy left off calling Frank "Professor Stenton."[69] They shared news about academic projects, personal news, and views on academic bureaucracies. They shared a horror of academic politics and of historians who did not meet their own high standards as well as a deep concern for friends. "He is so generous and nice he ought to be happier," Dorothy said of a mutual friend.[70] They exchanged visits when they found time in busy academic schedules. Finally most of Dorothy's letters were to Doris. Dorothy continued to rely on Frank's advice, though more and more she relayed her questions through Doris.[71] They corresponded regularly and affectionately to the end of Doris's life.

When Frank died in 1967 at the age of eighty-seven, Doris, aged seventy-three, faced both grief and new demands on her talents. She was asked to complete the third edition of Frank's classic *Anglo-Saxon England*, begun before his death; edit and publish his papers; and write a memorial of him for the *Proceedings of the British Academy*. Her energy, though lessened, did not fail her, and her old friend Dorothy Whitelock, by this time a distinguished Anglo-Saxonist, was ready to help her prepare Frank's work for publication. At Dorothy's suggestion, they decided to make only those changes in *Anglo-Saxon England* that could be justified from Frank's own notes and drafts; there would be no change for the sake of change. The pressure of work was nearly unbearable, but Doris felt it was comforting working with Dorothy, whose affection for her fellow Anglo-Saxon scholar, in Doris's words, "lasts so substantially."[72] They must often have "put on a spurt," in Dorothy's useful phrase, because *Preparatory to Anglo-Saxon England* and *Frank Merry Stenton, 1880–1967*, Doris's memoir of Frank, came out in 1970 and the third edition of *Anglo-Saxon England* in 1971.[73]

In all the rush Doris Stenton managed to achieve some comfort in her life. She was satisfied with the works she produced after Frank's death, especially with the memorial to Frank, which allowed her to "re-live their past and recall what he himself had told her of his earlier days." She gave it what was for her a high accolade: "I think he would have liked it."⁷⁴ She created an apartment on the first floor of their home to provide lodging for worthy graduate students and, on the lighter side, got a Jack Russell terrier and started going to the hairdresser (5). She continued with her work but also with the lighter reading that she and Frank had both enjoyed; the house was full of works of history but had plenty of room for mysteries. She had suffered from heart trouble for some years, and in December 1971, at the age of seventy-seven, not long after the revised edition of *Anglo-Saxon England* was published, she suffered a stroke and died without regaining consciousness.

Her solid accomplishments won Doris recognition and distinctions, but in some sense she remained in Frank's shadow during his life. In the early days of her career such authorities as J. H. Round and Maurice Powicke, the latter of whom she advised and corrected on some points about John's reign, praised her work.⁷⁵ She became the first D.Litt. at Reading University, the first to receive the degree on the basis of her published work, and one of the university's first readers. Glasgow University made her an honorary Doctor of Laws, and Oxford awarded her an honorary Doctor of Letters. When she retired as secretary of the Pipe Roll Society, members edited a collection of previously unpublished medieval manuscripts in her honor and "for her pleasure."⁷⁶ She was a fellow of the British Academy, served on the Council of the Selden Society, and also served on the Royal Historical Society, for which she was vice president. She presented the Raleigh Lecture for the British Academy in 1958 and gave the Jayne Lectures at the American Philosophical Society in 1963, for which occasion Frank traveled to Philadelphia with her.⁷⁷ A variety of publications, popular and scholarly, gave her admiring reviews, and, as a recognized authority in her field, she was sought after to review other scholars' works.⁷⁸ But some persons seem to have had reservations, and only after Frank's death was she listed in the *Dictionary of National Biography* for her scholarly merit. Previous editions gave her only a brief paragraph in his entry.⁷⁹ A former student may have expressed a widely held opinion when he said, "As a historian (Frank) was far superior to Doris."⁸⁰ Frank had inspired his readers and structured his work with theory and interpretation; Doris never strayed far from her sources and what she could derive from them. Her concern was all for the evidence, and she made certain that it be presented in full. Nothing was to be left out. She avowed Frank's theories but suppressed nothing that contradicted them, remarking only that here was an exception to the rule.

This is not to say, however, that there was no theoretical understanding in her work but rather that such understanding was cumulative, emerging as she presented the mass of evidence and then shaped it to point to what she saw as inherent themes. The wealth of detail may obscure an abstract thesis but bars hasty and superficial stereotypes. Unstated but implicit are the genuine efforts of judicial officials, from John on down, to achieve justice according to their homeland's good customs and the worthiness of the justice that was sometimes achieved. Doris Stenton crafted an overview in which justices, plaintiffs, and defendants, not free from self-interest but sensing the value of reasonably sound justice, built a flawed but vital legal system.

As she did this, she created works that are fundamental to understanding the reigns of Richard I and John and lucidly explain previously obscure legal operations that were essential to the court system, employing meticulous standards of publication that demand equal care from later editors. Her art of reading and presentation may well last as theories are superseded and forgotten.

But Doris Stenton would probably have cared little for a comparison of her work with Frank's or with anyone else's. She carved out a position that is unique in scholarly endeavor. Frank's career was as much a work of her art, in the support she gave him, as any of her writings. Their work was separate and independent; her role as wife and scholar was united and indivisible. We know her as the sustenance of her husband's scholarly life and the one who did much to introduce historians to the legal records and show what could be done with them. And her greatest gift may be that she brings the court to life before our eyes and puts the laws into the context of medieval society, not as dry rules, but as a living, changing component of a growing sense of justice that has become part of our heritage.

Notes

My deepest gratitude goes to G. Michael C. Bott, archivist at the Stenton Archives in the Reading University Library for his knowledge of the sources that would best bring this project into being and his unfailing attention to researchers' needs, and to Verity Andrews for her unstinting work and her gift for making the impossible become possible. I also thank David Bates and Jane Read for their consideration and aid. I owe more than I can say to Beth and Shannon, whose expertise, generous assistance, and loving support were indispensable to this work, to Sean, always a stalwart supporter and advisor, and to Terry for his unfailing generosity and love.

1. *Rotuli Curiae Regis.*
2. Regarding her introductions, see Holt, "Doris Mary Stenton," 266.
3. Slade, *"Liber Memorialis."*
4. D. M. Stenton, *English Woman*, 291.
5. Letter to C. W. Blunt, 1968, hereafter cited as Doris Mary Stenton to C. Blunt.
6. Major, "Doris Mary Stenton," 525.
7. D. M. Stenton, *Frank Merry Stenton*, 367. Subsequent citations of this work in the paragraph are given as page numbers in parentheses in the text..
8. Major, "Doris Mary Stenton," 525.
9. D. M. Stenton, "Charles Wilmer Foster," 216–18; Holt, "Doris Mary Stenton," 266; Major, "Doris Mary Stenton," 525–26.
10. D. M. Stenton, "Two Southern Sokes in the Twelfth Century"; "A Hitherto Unprinted Charter of David I."
11. Journal, held in the Stenton Collection, University of Reading: summer 1917; 25 June, 2, 25, 26, 30 July, 25 August 1918.
12. D. M. Stenton, *Frank Merry Stenton*, 379. The subsequent citation of this work in the paragraph is given as a page number in parentheses in the text..
13. Slade, *"Liber Memorialis,"* 5, 9.
14. Slade, *"Liber Memorialis,"* 5.

15. D. M. Stenton, *Frank Merry Stenton,* 363, 373, passim. Subsequent citations of this work in the paragraph are given as page numbers in parentheses in the text.

16. D. M. Stenton, *Frank Merry Stenton,* 338, 379. Subsequent citations of this work in the paragraph are given as page numbers in parentheses in the text.

17. Holt, "Doris Mary Stenton," 265.

18. Slade, *"Liber Memorialis,"* 8, D. M. Stenton, *Frank Merry Stenton,* 386.

19. D. M. Stenton, *Great Roll of the Pipe for the Second Year of the Reign of King John,* n.s., 3, xiii; passim. Pipe rolls will be cited hereafter by volume number, e.g., Pipe Roll, n.s., 3, xiii.

20. Pipe Roll, n.s., 7 and 8 passim.

21. Pipe Roll, n.s., 12, xviii.

22. Pipe Roll, n.s., 2, xv, xix; 5, xxxiv; 14, xv

23. Pipe Roll, n.s., 7, xxv.

24. Pipe Roll, n.s., 14, xix.

25. Pipe Roll, n.s., 7, xvi.

26. D. M. Stenton, *Earliest Lincolnshire Assize Rolls,* xi, hereafter cited as *ELAR.*

27. *Curia Regis Rolls Preserved in the Public Record Office.*

28. For an example of an exception, see Maitland, *Pleas of the Crown.*

29. *ELAR,* xi.

30. D. M. Stenton, *Earliest Northamptonshire Assize Rolls,* lii–liii, hereafter cited as *ENAR.*

31. *ELAR,* xlv, lxiii.

32. *ENAR,* xlix–lxxviii.

33. Holt, "Doris Mary Stenton," 265.

34. *ELAR,* xxii–xxiii.

35. Holt, *Magna Carta,* 292.

36. D. M. Stenton, *Rolls of the Justices in Eyre for Lincolnshire, Worcestershire,* hereafter cited as *RJELW;* D. M. Stenton, *Rolls of the Justices in Eyre for Yorkshire,* hereafter cited as *RJEY; Rolls of the Justices in Eyre for Gloucestershire, Warwickshire, and Staffordshire,* hereafter cited as *RJEGWS.*

37. *Bracton on the Laws and Customs of England.*

38. For supplementary cases, see *RJELW,* vii, xi, xii. Subsequent citations of this work in the paragraph are given as page numbers in parentheses in the text.

39. Bartlett, *Trial by Fire and Water,* 99–102. See also Pollock and Maitland, *History of the English Law,* 616–32 Milsom, *Historical Foundations of the Common Law,* 410–11.

40. *RJEY,* xl.

41. *RJEY,* xli–xlvii.

42. *RJEGWS,* liv, lvii.

43. *RJEGWS,* xxxiv–xxxv, passim.

44. Slade, *"Liber Memorialis,"* 27.

45. Slade, *"Liber Memorialis,"* 2.

46. Pollock and Maitland, *History of English Law,* 562–63.

47. Plucknett, *Concise History of the Common Law,* 383–84.

48. D. M. Stenton, *Pleas before the King,* 1:136; Yorkshire wildness is wittily suggested in the title of Hugh Thomas's *Vassals, Heiresses, Crusaders, and Thugs,* and see p. 59.

49. D. M. Stenton, *Pleas before the King,* 1:3. Subsequent citations of this work in the paragraph are given as page numbers in parentheses in the text.

50. D. M. Stenton, *English Society,* 44, 116, 214, passim.
51. D. M. Stenton, "Pipe Rolls and the Historians," 271.
52. D. M. Stenton, "Pipe Rolls and the Historians," 271–75. Subsequent citations of this work in the paragraph are given as page numbers in parentheses in the text.
53. Tolkien, "Beowulf," 245–95.
54. D. M. Stenton, "Roger of Howden and *Benedict.*"
55. D. M. Stenton, "Roger of Howden and *Benedict,*" 574, 577. The subsequent citation of this work in the paragraph is given as page numbers in parentheses in the text.
56. D. M. Stenton, *English Woman,* vii.
57. Regarding Doris Stenton's expansion of Frank Stenton's thesis, see James, "Translation and Study of the *Chronicon Monasterii* of Abingdon," 50–52. Frank Stenton's thesis is presented in his "Place of Women in Anglo-Saxon Society," passim.
58. D. M. Stenton, *English Woman,* vii, 35–37. Subsequent citations of this work in the paragraph are given as page numbers in parentheses in the text.
59. Slade, *"Liber Memorialis,"* 3.
60. D. M. Stenton, "King John and the Courts of Justice."
61. D. M. Stenton, *English Justice,* 18–21, 49–53, 85–87. Subsequent citations of this work in the paragraph are given as page numbers in parentheses in the text.
62. Regarding the gardening, see D. M. Stenton, *Frank Stenton,* 327–28.
63. Slade, *"Liber Memorialis,"* 7. Subsequent citations of this work in the paragraph are given as page numbers in parentheses in the text.
64. Doris Mary Stenton to C. Blunt.
65. Slade, *"Liber Memorialis,"* 5.
66. Stenton correspondence, held in the Stenton Archives at the University of Reading, Reading, United Kingdom, letters from Doris Mary Stenton to Frank Stenton, dates: 18 December 1934, 18 June 1936; undated letters: archive references 8/1, 12, 15, 30. Frank's letters to Doris do not survive, though she mentions receiving them (19 June 1940).
67. Whitelock, *Anglo-Saxon Wills.*
68. Stenton correspondence, letters between Dorothy Whitelock and the Stentons, 5 and 29 September, 6 and 31 October 1928, hereafter cited as Dorothy Whitelock to Frank Merry Stenton, Dorothy Whitelock to Doris Mary Stenton, Doris Mary Stenton to Dorothy Whitelock.
69. Dorothy Whitelock to Frank Merry Stenton, 23 May 1940; Dorothy Whitelock to Doris Mary Stenton, 27 August 1939.
70. Dorothy Whitelock to Doris Mary Stenton, 4 December 1951; 11 June 1961 inter alia.
71. Dorothy Whitelock to Doris Mary Stenton, 28 January 1967.
72. Doris Mary Stenton to Dorothy Whitelock, 9 February 1968, 12 February 1969.
73. Quotation from Dorothy Whitelock to Doris Mary Stenton, 19 November 1964.
74. Slade, *"Liber Memorialis,"* 4. The subsequent citation of this work in the paragraph is given as a page number in parentheses in the text.
75. Holt, "Doris Mary Stenton," 266; Slade, *"Liber Memorialis,"* 1.
76. Barnes and Slade, *Medieval Miscellany for Doris Mary Stenton.*
77. Major, "Doris Mary Stenton," 528.
78. Examples of positive reviews include *Observer* (London), 10 March 1957; *Times Literary Supplement,* 7 December 1951, 28 March 1965, 23 December 1965; *American Journal of Legal*

History 9 (1965): 179–81. Margaret Lane commented that Virginia Woolf, who had remarked that nothing had been written about women who lived before the eighteenth century, would have found *The English Woman in History* "useful and surprising" (*New Statesman and Nation*, 23 March 1957). Regarding Doris Stenton's recognition in her field, see Slade, "Liber Memorialis," 4.

79. *Dictionary of National Biography, 1961–1970*, s.v.; *Dictionary of National Biography, 1971–1980*, s.v.

80. Slade, "Liber Memorialis," 5.

Select Bibliography of Works by Doris Mary Stenton

The Stenton papers and correspondence are held in the Stenton Archive, and the Stentons' working book collection is held in the Stenton Library. Both are at Reading University, in the United Kingdom.

"A Hitherto Unprinted Charter of David I." *Scottish Historical Review* 14 (1917): 370–72.

"Two Southern Sokes in the Twelfth Century." *English Historical Review* 32 (1917): 245–48.

"Roger of Salisbury, Regni Angliæ Procurator." *English Historical Review* 41 (1924): 79–80.

The Great Roll of the Pipe for the Second Year of the Reign of King Richard I. Pipe Roll Society, n.s., 1. London: J. Ruddock and Sons, 1925.

The Earliest Lincolnshire Assize Rolls, A.D. 1202–1209. Publications of the Lincoln Record Society, v. 22. Lincoln, Eng.: Printed for the Lincoln Record Society, 1926.

The Great Rolls of the Pipe for the Third and Fourth Year of the Reign of King Richard I. Pipe Roll Society, n.s., 2. London: J. Ruddock and Sons, 1926.

"England, Henry II." In *Cambridge Medieval History*, 5:554–90.

The Great Roll of the Pipe for the Fifth Year of the Reign of King Richard I. Pipe Roll Society, n.s., 3. London: J. Ruddock and Sons, 1927.

The Great Roll of the Pipe for the Sixth Year of the Reign of King Richard I. Pipe Roll Society, n.s., 5. London: J. Ruddock and Sons, 1928.

The Great Roll of the Pipe for the Seventh Year of the Reign of King Richard I. Pipe Roll Society, n.s., 6. London: J. Ruddock and Sons, 1929.

The Chancellor's Roll for the Eighth Year of the Reign of King Richard I. Pipe Roll Society, n.s., 7. London: J. Ruddock and Sons, 1930.

The Earliest Northamptonshire Assize Rolls, A.D. 1202 and 1203. Northamptonshire Record Society 5. London: J. W. Ruddock and Sons, 1930.

The Great Roll of the Pipe for the Ninth Year of the Reign of King Richard I. Pipe Roll Society, n.s., 8. London: J. Ruddock and Sons, 1931.

The Great Roll of the Pipe for the Tenth Year of the Reign of King Richard I. Pipe Roll Society, n.s., 9. London: J. Ruddock and Sons, 1932.

The Great Roll of the Pipe for the First Year of the Reign of King John. Pipe Roll Society, n.s., 10. London: J. Ruddock and Sons, 1933.

The Great Roll of the Pipe for the Second Year of the Reign of King John. Pipe Roll Society, n.s., 12. London: J. Ruddock and Sons, 1934.

Rolls of the Justices in Eyre for Lincolnshire, 1218–19, and Worcestershire, 1221. Selden Society, 53. London: Bernard Quaritch, 1934.

"Charles Wilmer Foster." *Lincolnshire Magazine* 2, no. 8 (1935): 215–18.

The Great Roll of the Pipe for the Third Year of the Reign of King John. Pipe Roll Society, n.s., 14. London: J. Ruddock and Sons, 1936.

The Great Roll of the Pipe for the Fourth Year of the Reign of King John. Pipe Roll Society, n.s., 15. London: J. Ruddock and Sons, 1937.

Rolls of the Justices in Eyre for Yorkshire, 1218–19. Selden Society, 56. London: Bernard Quaritch, 1937.

The Great Roll of the Pipe for the Fifth Year of the Reign of King John. Pipe Roll Society, n.s., 16. London: J. Ruddock and Sons, 1938.

The Great Roll of the Pipe for the Sixth Year of the Reign of King John. Pipe Roll Society, n.s., 18. London: J. Ruddock and Sons, 1940.

Rolls of the Justices in Eyre for Gloucestershire, Warwickshire and Staffordshire, 1221, 1222. Selden Society, 59. London: Bernard Quaritch, 1940.

The Great Roll of the Pipe for the Eighth Year of the Reign of King John. Pipe Roll Society, n.s., 20. London: J. Ruddock and Sons, 1942.

The Great Roll of the Pipe for the Tenth Year of the Reign of King John. Pipe Roll Society, n.s., 23. London: J. Ruddock and Sons, 1947.

The Great Roll of the Pipe for the Eleventh Year of the Reign of King John. Pipe Roll Society, n.s., 24. London: J. Ruddock and Sons, 1949.

With Lewis C. Loyd. *Sir Christopher Hatton's Book of Seals, Presented to F. M. Stenton.* Oxford: Clarendon Press, 1950.

English Society in the Early Middle Ages (1066–1307). Vol. 3 of *Pelican History of England.* Middlesex, Eng.: Penguin, 1951; 2d ed., with notes, 1952; 3d ed., 1962.

"The Pipe Rolls and the Historians, 1660–1883." *Cambridge Historical Journal* 10, no. 3 (1952): 271–92.

Pleas before the King or His Justices, 1198–1202. Vol. 2. Selden Society, 58. London: Bernard Quaritch, 1952.

The Great Roll of the Pipe for the Thirteenth Year of the Reign of King John. Pipe Roll Society, n.s., 28. London: J. Ruddock and Sons, 1953.

Pleas before the King or His Justices, 1198–1202. Vol. 1. Selden Society, 57. London: Bernard Quaritch, 1953.

"Roger of Howden and *Benedict.*" *English Historical Review* 68 (1953): 574–82.

The English Woman in History. London: George Allen and Unwin, 1957.

"King John and the Courts of Justice" (Raleigh Lecture on History). *Proceedings of the British Academy* (1958): 103–27.

After Runnymede: Magna Carta in the Middle Ages. Magna Carta Essays. Charlottesville: University Press of Virginia, 1964.

English Justice between the Norman Conquest and the Great Charter, 1066–1215. Philadelphia, Memoirs of the American Philosophical Society, vol. 60. London: Allen and Unwin, 1965. The Jayne Lectures for 1963.

Pleas before the King or His Justices, 1198–1202. Vols. 3 and 4. Selden Society, 83, 84. London: Bernard Quaritch, 1967.

Frank Merry Stenton, 1880–1967. Reprinted from *The Proceedings of the British Academy.* Oxford: Oxford University Press, 1970.

Editor. *Preparatory to Anglo-Saxon England, Being the Collected Papers of Frank Merry Stenton.* Oxford: Clarendon Press, 1970.

Editor with Dorothy Whitelock. *Anglo-Saxon England,* by the late F. M. Stenton. 3d ed. Oxford: Oxford University Press, 1971.

Works Cited

Barnes, Patricia M., and C. F. Slade, eds. *A Medieval Miscellany for Doris Mary Stenton.* Pipe Roll Society, n.s., 36. London: J. Ruddock and Sons, 1960.

Bartlett, Robert. *Trial by Fire and Water: The Medieval Judicial Ordeal.* Oxford: Clarendon Press, 1986.

Bracton on the Laws and Customs of England. Edited and translated by Samuel E. Thorne. 4 vols. Cambridge: Cambridge University Press, 1968–77

Bracton's Note Book. Edited by Frederick William Maitland. 3 vols. London: C. J. Clay, 1887; reprint, Littleton, Col.: Fred B. Rothman and Co., 1983.

Curia Regis Rolls Preserved in the Public Record Office. Vols. 1–18. London: Her Majesty's Stationery Office, 1922–99.

Flower, C. T. *Introduction to the Curia Regis Rules, 1199–1230 A.D.* Selden Society, 62. London: Professional Books, 1972.

Holt, J. C. "Doris Mary Stenton." *American Historical Review* 29 (1974): 265–66.

———. *Magna Carta.* Cambridge: Cambridge University Press, 1965.

James, Darryl Dean. "A Translation and Study of the *Chronicon Monasterii* of Abingdon." Ph.D. diss., Rice University, 1988.

Lyon, Bryce. *A Constitutional and Legal History of Medieval England.* New York: W. W. Norton, 1960.

Maitland, Frederick William, ed. *Pleas of the Crown for the County of Gloucestershire.* London: Macmillan and Co., 1884.

Major, Kathleen. "Doris Mary Stenton, 1894–1971." *Proceedings of the British Academy* 58 (1972): 524–35.

Milsom, S. F. C. *Historical Foundations of the Common Law.* Toronto: Butterworth's, 1981.

Plucknett, Theodore F. T. *A Concise History of the Common Law.* Boston: Little, Brown, 1956.

Pollock, Frederick, and Frederick William Maitland. *The History of the English Law before the Time of Edward I.* 2 vols. Cambridge: Cambridge University Press, 1895; 2d. ed., 1898; reissued 1968.

Rotuli Curiae Regis. Edited by Francis Palgrave. 2 vols. Printed for the Record Commission. London: G. Eyre and A. Spottiswoode, 1835.

Slade, Cecil. "*Liber Memorialis*: Doris Mary Stenton, Honorary Secretary to the Pipe Roll Society, 1894–1971." Pipe Roll Society, n.s., 41. London: J. Ruddock and Sons, 1976.

Stenton, Frank Merry. *Anglo-Saxon England.* Oxford: Oxford University Press, 1943; 3d ed., Oxford: Clarendon Press, 1971.

———. "The Place of Women in Anglo-Saxon Society." *Transactions of the Royal Historical Society,* 4th ser., 25 (1943): 1–13.

Sutherland, Donald W. *The Assize of Novel Disseisin.* Oxford: Clarendon Press, 1973.

Thomas, Hugh. *Vassals, Heiresses, Crusaders, and Thugs: The Gentry of Angevin Yorkshire, 1154–1216.* Philadelphia: University of Pennsylvania Press, 1993.

Tolkien, J. R. R. "Beowulf: The Monsters and the Critics." *Proceedings of the British Academy* 22 (1936): 245–95.

The Treatise on the Laws and Customs of England Commonly Known as Glanvill. Edited and translated by G. D. G. Hall. London: Thomas Nelson and Sons, 1965.

Whitelock, Dorothy, ed. and trans. *Anglo-Saxon Wills.* Cambridge: Cambridge University Press, 1930.

CHAPTER 32

Helen M. Roe (1895–1988)
Champion of Medieval Irish Art and Iconography

Rory O'Farrell and Christine Bromwich

In considering the life of an Irish woman scholar in the early twentieth century, it is impossible to dissociate the personal biography from the general context of the political history of Ireland and society's pressure on women to be carers, which impeded women's inclusion in the academy. In spite of nonacademic responsibilities, Helen Maybury Roe (1895–1988) was instrumental in developing interest in the study of early Christian and medieval Ireland through years of great political turbulence and social change in the twentieth century.

Shortly after the close of World War I, the counties of southern Ireland reached a form of independence from the United Kingdom. As with all countries achieving independence, this new country was faced with the desire to reinvent itself, severing many of the overt links with its previous form of governance. For many years Ireland had had a two-tier society, for historical reasons largely demarcated by religion. The established state religion, the religion of the minority of the people, had been, until its formal disestablishment in 1869, the Protestant Church of Ireland, a branch of the Anglican Communion. The religion of the majority of the people was the Roman Catholic Church, even though this had been proscribed in varying degrees until the Catholic Emancipation Bill of 1829. Thus Protestants were often closer to the seat of power than Catholics, and they were often better educated because of the traditions of their church. With the advent of independence in 1921, a movement motivated over many preceding years largely by a Protestant intelligentsia, a bloody civil war ensued. This ultimately resulted in various political parties of more or less nationalistic leanings and a nationwide movement to disassociate the new country from historical links with Britain, seen as the oppressor of the past eight hundred years.

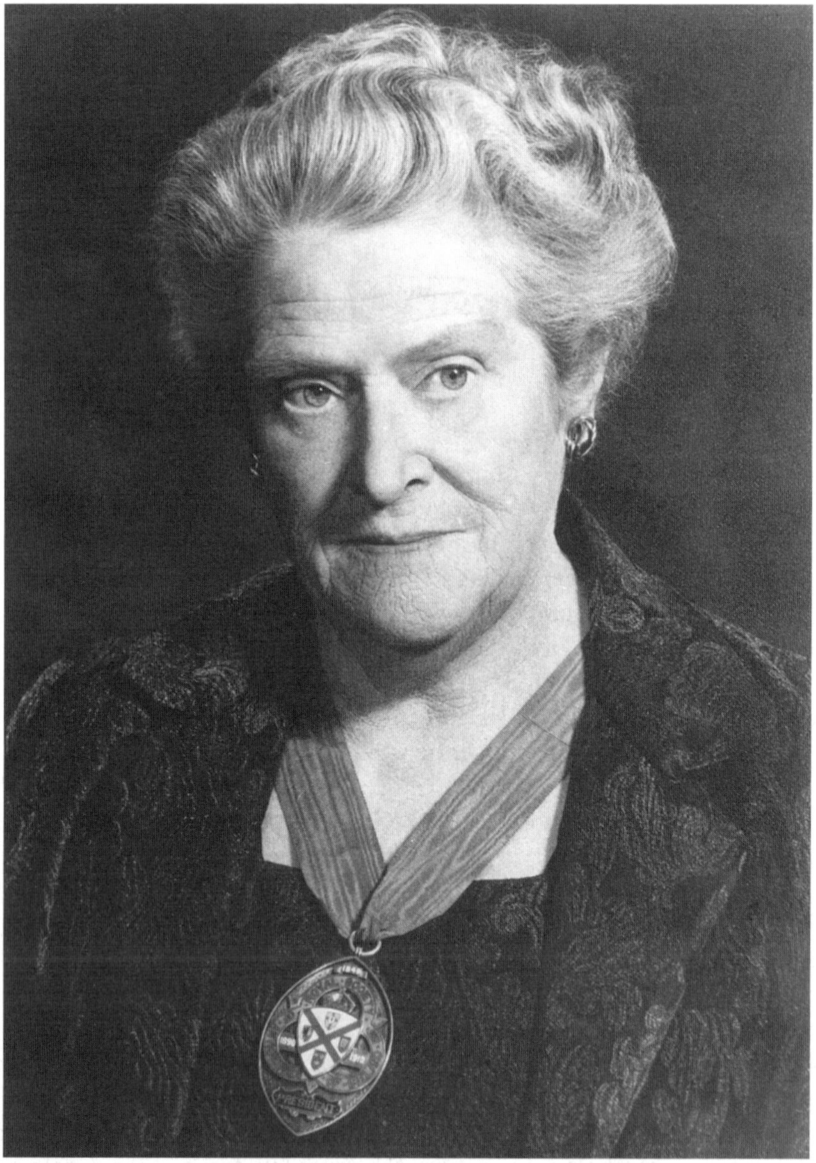

In consequence, at the time of World War II it was politically inappropriate for the country to ally itself with either side. Social links were mostly with the United Kingdom and the United States of America because of the large-scale emigration that had taken place during and since the great famine of the late 1840s, and the social pressures thus favored alliance with those countries. But the political need to disassociate from Britain, "the hated oppressor," would not permit any entry into the war on the side of the Allies. The philosophy of the political thinkers was closer to what they saw as a similar philosophy leading to the construction of new societies in Germany and in Spain. So the path chosen was neutrality, cleaving to the nationalist political philosophy that had developed of Sinn Féin, "Ourselves alone!" The disassociation from the existing state of affairs led to Protestants often being actively discriminated against on account of their perceived closeness to the now replaced establishment. Such was the background against which lived and worked the remarkable woman Helen Maybury Roe who, in contrast, took a stand for Ireland from when only twenty-one years old.

The early life of Roe reflects both her Irish nationalism and her attempt to construct an academic career while carrying alone burdens her male peers shared with spouses. She was born in provincial Ireland in 1895, in the small town of Mountrath, to the owner of the mill in that town. For several generations her Protestant family had owned the mill, and they were people of privilege and consequence in the town. She (an only child) was educated locally, and when World War I started, she joined, as expected of someone in her social position, the Saint John's Ambulance Corps, where she was concerned with support services such as rolling bandages and working as a volunteer in Cambridge Military Hospital. She tried to enlist for medical service in this military hospital at Aldershot (the center of British army power) but ended up working there, not as a nurse, but as a cook. This experience changed her allegiance. Heather King, archaeologist at Duchas, the Irish Government Department of Heritage, refers to Roe as "nationalist through and through and her slightly jaundiced view of the English attitude to Ireland [was] occasioned by the treatment she received from British soldiers while serving in Aldershot, England. At the time of the 1916 Easter Rising some British soldiers spat at her for being Irish."[1] This alienated her from any British identity one might presume from her membership by birth in the Protestant tradition and ascendancy community. She remarked later, "The great big gobs! I'll never forgive that" (as reported in an article in the *Irish Times* by Elgy Gillespie, 21 June 1985). Returned to Ireland—in her own words, "nearly a Republican"—she served in the British Military Hospital at Bray, County Wicklow, Ireland (where most of the wounded soldiers were Irish) until the end of the war. Then she entered Trinity College, Dublin, where she studied modern languages and took her B.A. degree in 1921 and an M.A. in 1924. There she was on an equal footing with men, some returned from warfare, and they all ducked when machine guns sprayed the lecture room during the civil war that followed the ceasefire with Britain. She subsequently taught for short periods in Dungannon and in Dublin and then joined the Carnegie Library service, spending some time as an assistant to Hubert Butler in Coleraine in the Protestant Northern Ireland at the time of the painful partition of north from south. The failure of her father's business necessitated her return (as expected of a single daughter) to Mountrath to contribute to the upkeep of her parents; she was able to transfer to the area in the southern Free State, working at first in the library in nearby Thurles as an assistant. In 1926 she became county librarian for Laois County, where she remained until 1939, when she left the library service. She was of the first generation of women who expected to live single lives and support themselves after the slaughter of so many contemporary Irish men, Protestant and Catholic, in the British army in World War I. The life expectancy of a young officer in the trenches of Flanders had been only six weeks.

While working in Northern Ireland (ruled by Britain) in her early days in the library service, her interest had been aroused by the standing stones and stone circles of the area, a pre-Christian and early Christian common heritage before the Reformation. Her ability to drive, and possession of a car, allowed her to visit the various antiquities of the area, and her knowledge of the classification systems of the libraries allowed her to investigate the background of these remains. When she returned to Portlaoise (in the independent part of Ireland) as county librarian, she published an official report on the service, using the Irish spelling of her name, Eibhlín Ní Ruaidh (a statement of nationalism itself). She was frequently asked for information on the antiquities of the area. This prompted her to start a series of traveling lectures, given to schools and local meetings, on the history of the local antiquities. Stories are told of her traveling to a school, having to black out the classroom in an ad hoc way and remove the battery from her car to drive the "magic lantern," which she herself operated as she lectured. Indeed, to the end of her days she remained a magnificent lecturer, with a carefully considered text delivered apparently extempore and a number of carefully chosen slides (often specially commissioned). Viewed against the increasingly nationalist background of the politics of the period, one can see that her talks would have added greatly to the local "sense of place." In 1937 she published an article for the first time in the *Journal of the Royal Society of Antiquaries of Ireland* (*JRSAI*) on a local monument.

The delayed opportunity for Roe's start in serious scholarship came when, in 1939 at the age of forty-four, she retired from the library service. (She had been the only Protestant county librarian in the Free State; members of the Protestant minority had either become reconciled to the new nation or emigrated, some burned out of their houses.) Free now from the burden of supporting her parents, she moved to Dublin, where she purchased a half-built house and a large garden. During World War II (when neutral Ireland's economy suffered), she was able to supplement her meager income by growing fruit and vegetables in her garden. With time on her hands she researched medieval matters, a luxury she had not had much time for while working in the library service. Needing practical experience in archaeology, she worked as a volunteer on several archaeological digs, including Fourknocks under P. J. Hartnett and

Knowth (with John Bromwich, archaeologist, and Rachel Bromwich, Celtic scholar) under R. A. S. MacAlister. She wrote part of the report on the latter site for the *Journal of the Royal Society of Antiquaries of Ireland*. She joined the Royal Society of Antiquaries of Ireland and became a regular frequenter of its evening lectures and reader in its library in Dublin. She formed a friendship with Nora Ní Shuilibhín, an assistant in the Department of Education, whom she taught to drive. Nora's interest was in photography, and the combination of this with driving brought the two of them to many antiquarian sites.

Roe's lectures given on local antiquities in Laois and her familiarity with the Bible and classical writings caused her to question the local uninformed attributions of many of the figure subjects of the early Christian sites she visited. Her biblical knowledge led her to recognize alternative attributions for some of these figure subjects on the early Irish High Crosses. These are major stone monuments, picture sermons, of cultural standing equal to illustrated bibles such as the Book of Kells and smaller artifacts such as the Ardagh Chalice and so are among Ireland's greatest contributions to European art of the early Middle Ages, according to Peter Harbison, Member of the Royal Irish Academy and author of *Irish High Crosses with Figure Sculptures Explained* (1994). In the library service she had been constrained, writing reports required by her employment and a few articles of local interest published in local newspapers, often under a pseudonym. From the time of her move to Dublin she started to write reports of archaeological and antiquarian finds in her home county. Her interest in the early Irish High Crosses led her to research Continental sources. In 1949 (the year the Free State of Ireland left the British Commonwealth for full independence), she published a seminal article, "The 'David Cycle' in Early Irish Art," tying Irish culture to Continental culture, not just to Britain. She firmly related many of the figure scenes on Irish High Crosses to a distinct Old Testament biblical sequence, disproving the fanciful interpretations of (inter alia) Eric Sexton and Kingsley Porter.

Roe's first major contribution to medieval scholarship was this theory that the panels of many Irish High Crosses depicted scenes from the David Cycle. It caused her to look systematically and in detail at most of these. As High Crosses are situated for the most part on church lands, naturally she also visited the adjoining church and took an interest in the carvings therein and in the ornate tombstones in the graveyard. She visited the Armagh area in the early 1950s and published the first systematic survey of the High Crosses of that region in 1954 and 1955 in *Seanchas Ardmhacha*. Although from the Protestant tradition, in her repeated visits to that area she was often driven around the locality by a young Catholic curate, whom she always referred to as "Father Tom." In later years he was a distinguished historian, better known as Cardinal Thomas O'Fíach, archbishop of Armagh (head of the Catholic Church in all Ireland). The social divisions in the republic were starting to change: being Irish was starting to become more important than the Christian tradition one might belong to. Having covered the High Crosses of that area of Northern Ireland, she then turned her attention to the south, publishing surveys of those of the Kilkenny area in 1958 and of the Kells area in 1959. She was careful to keep these publications compact and affordable (conscious from her librarian days of the thirst for knowledge in the general population living at a low economic level because of British economic sanctions). In addition she continued to publish many shorter articles in various local antiquarian publications and in the *Journal of the Royal Society of Antiquaries of Ireland*. She also was in great demand as a lecturer, speaking to local antiquarian societies. As one of her friends wrote, "If there is an interested audience for things medieval in Ireland today it is as much due to Miss Roe's research and lecturing as to any one other factor."[2]

As Roe came to influence more scholars of the younger generation, her fields of interest branched out from early Christian High Crosses and expanded to include medieval tomb sculpture, medieval fonts, the various pilgrimages of the Middle Ages, ornate tombstones of any period—all were grist to her mill. Her library was remarkable, containing almost every book published on Irish archaeology or antiquarian studies. Gifted with phenomenal recall, she could turn to her shelves and take down a book she had last read many years before and open to the section proving or disputing her point. Siobhán de hOir states, "An evening with Miss Roe in her home might last long into the night as she dispensed good food and practical advice or while she found yet another reference from her large library. One might notice plastic bags behind a chair. This was her filing system for her articles. She made notes on what ever paper came to hand—the back of envelopes and cigarette packets, on margins of notices to shareholders—and all this material was stuffed into the plastic bags. An article might be as much as three full plastic bags."[3] Not only did she lecture to any society that approached her to do so, but she was also most generous with her time and her advice for young scholars. Many of them talked through the subject of their thesis with her and were often put back on the rails after reaching an apparent impasse.

In time many scholars of the generations Roe mentored became eminent in the field both south and north of the border. Ann Hamlin, until recently director of Built Heritage for the Department of the Environment in Northern Ireland, testifies from personal experience to Roe's unfailing generosity to younger scholars, when sharing her great experience and knowledge. Patrick F. Wallace, director of the National Museum of Ireland, celebrates Roe as "one of Ireland's great mediaevalists. A thorough and well published scholar particularly in the iconography of our carved stone crosses and of the physical evidence for medieval Christian devotion, Roe was remarkably generous with her knowledge and celebrated for her encouragement of young archaeologists, art historians and genealogists whom she inspired."[4] Mairéad Dunlevy, keeper at the National Museum, Art and Industry Division at Collins Barracks, reinforces Roe's status as a scholar and mentor who encouraged the interest of the young in the life and art of the medieval period and used her enthusiasm to relax the student in the enjoyment of her great insights.[5] John Bradley, senior lecturer in the Department of Modern History at the National University at Maynooth, mentions in a letter that "[i]n the global development of medieval studies over the past half century, tea and truffles may seem irrelevant but in their own small way they typify Helen Roe the scholar. To a young student . . . she was generous, kind, indulgent and unfailingly helpful. Whenever I wrote to her with a problem there was a letter, not just informative but generally witty, by return of post. She expected you to work hard, think about the relevant data, master it but like the truffle, there was a reward, this time an intellectual one, a new understanding, a new insight, a new discovery."[6]

Full recognition as a scholar came later in life to Roe, delayed by her fulfilling her daughter/carer role. Roe served on the Council of the Royal Society of Antiquaries of Ireland, and in 1965–68 (starting at the age of seventy years) she served as its president, the first woman to hold that office. She continued to publish and lecture, frequently revisiting her earlier subjects to add new discoveries and always expanding her area of interest. She worked assiduously for many years on the Library Committee of the Royal Society of Antiquaries of Ireland and also on the preparation of the next volume of the index to the *Journal of the Royal Society of Antiquaries of Ireland*. Roe chaired the library committee for some years when it was cataloged, revamped, and brought up to modern standards. As one of her colleagues wrote, "Miss Roe was a marvellous conversationalist, full of anecdotes and stories, and could, when she wished, dominate any dinner table. The evening meetings of the library committee were ones that every member looked forward to."[7] In 1981, at the age of eighty-six, she published another booklet on High Crosses, this time on the High Crosses of Monasterboice. Rory O'Farrell, chairman of the trustees of the Cambrian Archaeological Association, collaborated with her on that publication and provided many of the illustrations for it. In 1984, at the age of ninety, she was elected a member of the Royal Irish Academy, an honor many felt was very long overdue.

Roe was an Irish scholar in a different medium, the spoken word, still much stronger in Ireland. In the bibliography accompanying this essay, some publications will be outdated by later works, a fact that would give her great pleasure, as she always felt that the work of a scholar was to make a contribution on which other generations could build. What her bibliography does not show is the extraordinary number of her lectures and talks to local and student societies. The intensity of her delivery, the concise focus of her treatment of her subject, the extraordinary relevance of her few carefully chosen illustrations, and the unfailingly lively discussions afterward, whether by way of questions to the speaker or informally over refreshments, can only be shown by the verdicts of scholars she mentored. Wallace notes that "[n]obody spoke as engagingly, as wittily or as eloquently at monuments on field trips."[8] Siobhán de hOir writes, "Unlike many lecturers, she kept the same title, but always had new and exciting material to delight her audience—and we came away singing. . . . Talking was her forte, whether in a lecture hall or on an excursion, whether to an audience of one or a group numbering a hundred."[9] Heather King reports on her "commanding presence, . . . style and panache that belied the amount of preparation in research. Giving a lecture on the monuments in Kildare Cathedral, she slapped Bishop Wellesley on the thigh and remarked 'good old Bishop Wellesley' as if he had been one of her own relatives. She had an affinity and familiarity with these long dead men and women that enabled the listener to glimpse the humanity of these figures cast in stone."¹⁰ Roe is widely credited with an eloquence that carries forward the oral tradition still so strong in Ireland, where the spoken word has not yet given way to the tyranny of print.

King gives us an account of an affectionate celebration of Roe's contribution to Irish scholarship in a European context.

> Papers written in her honour, subsequently published as a (Festschrift) book entitled *Figures from the Past,* were presented to her on her ninetieth birthday. The day was marked by . . . a day long seminar . . . at which many contributors presented a synopsis of their papers. It was followed by dinner in the University Club. It was decided that we should do something about the menu to make it a little more appropriate to the occasion. Hence the Consommé Coolfin related to her address; Potage St. Michel and the Trinité des Legumes referred to her papers on St Michael and her work on the descriptions of the Holy Trinity [*JRSAI* 1979 and 1976]; and Fruits Maybury and Gateaux Belle Hélène speak for themselves. Timothy O'Neill [one of Ireland's leading calligraphers and a noted historian on the later medieval period] wrote out the menu. Gerard Crotty [genealogist] researched Miss Roe's coat of arms and Heather King made a cake with these in marzipan. Miss Roe enjoyed this immensely with a photo with Professor Etienne Rynne and the late Professor George Mitchell blowing out the candles and making a speech.¹¹

On this occasion celebrating her scholarship and lecturing style, Peter Harbison praised, in addition, her "charming prose which reflects the warmth of that personality which has made Miss Roe one of our most captivating antiquarians, so widely loved far beyond the bounds of her native land."¹²

What was the achievement of this remarkable woman? In the words of a senior Irish professor of archaeology, one of her protégés in his youth, Etienne Rynne, "She made the study of the Early Christian and Medieval periods respectable."¹³ She inspired three whole generations of young archaeologists, historians, and antiquaries. To them she showed that we should look outside the narrow confines of nationalism, reading widely through international works and turning always to original sources, never hesitating to interpret these for ourselves, but always questioning derivative works. John Bradley sets her in place with her contemporary scholars, along with Margaret Stokes and Françoise Henry.¹⁴ "Miss Roe's contribution was twofold. Firstly she broadened the study of early Irish art so that it included the Anglo-Norman tradition and the later Middle Ages [in a series of papers in *JRSAI*]. Secondly, she deepened the body of information that had been gathered by Stokes and Henry, by focusing attention on the iconography of Irish art before 1170 [published in a series of studies of High Crosses]. This was exceptionally farsighted and set an agenda for the study of medieval art that is still relevant today."¹⁵

King agrees that Roe had been "forging a new path" in her research into the later medieval period with the article *Two Baptismal Fonts in County Laoighis* in 1947 and her presidential address, *Some Aspects of Medieval Culture in Ireland,* in 1966.[16] Roe's publication *The Medieval Fonts of Meath,* written in 1968, has not yet been matched for other counties in Ireland. Commenting on her influence and style of scholarship, John Bradley continues, "Her approach was multi-disciplinary, incorporating archaeology, architectural history, heraldry, history and iconography, while her knowledge of European art history enabled her to set mediaeval Irish art within its broader context. Together with John Hunt, she was the first to contextualise Irish art of the later Middle Ages and to demonstrate its distinctiveness within the wider European tradition."[17] From the 1950s Roe steered her studies toward art-historical subjects—away from the early excavation of Knowth with MacAlister—and collaborated with Joseph Raftery on a number of sites. Even so she pointed out the necessity of more excavation on the later-medieval sites. De hOir places Roe "outside the mainstream academic scene."[18] She recalls that Roe welcomed amateurs also among the scholars she shared her knowledge with. Roe included British and foreign scholars in her welcome but could be nationalist in her reaction to them sometimes. King reminds us of "[h]er very strong anti-British views. . . . forcibly enunciated [to a few close friends] when a [visiting English Medieval Society's] president gave a rather lukewarm farewell and thank you speech."[19] Christine Bromwich believes that Roe said on that occasion in 1982, "May the road rise before you, as the IRA said to the Black and Tans." "Black and Tans" was the derogatory nickname for the British military police, often traumatized former soldiers, used to enforce order in Ireland in the years following the 1916 nationalist uprising, who on occasions used excessive brutality.

In Roe's latter years, she was unable to visit sites but enjoyed hearing about them. She was able to remember more clearly the inscriptions and depictions than did the people who had recently observed the monument. To the end her scholarship was meticulous, and she published important articles in *JRSAI* on the depictions of the Trinity (1979, 1980, 1981) in her eighth decade. Rory O'Farrell concludes that her death in 1988 at the age of ninety-three, after a short illness, marked the passing of an era. Irish medievalists lost a friend, a stimulus, and the antiquarian world was a poorer place. She is buried in her native town of Mountrath, under a specially designed and executed recumbent tombstone, as befits a distinguished student of funerary monuments.

Notes

Rory O'Farrell wrote the main body of this paper, with the factual items of chronology of Roe's life and the outline judgment of her contribution to scholarship and mentoring. Christine Bromwich set Roe's life against Irish history, giving details of personal indebtedness of younger scholars, now established senior medievalists.

Edwin Phelan, Helen Roe's present successor in the County Library at Portlaoise, very kindly made relevant archive material available to Christine Bromwich, and Patrick Healy, John Bradley, and Peter Harbison gave help with individual entries. Miss Roe's own assistance was invaluable.

1. Heather King, letter to Christine Bromwich, 19 August 2001.
2. Siobhán de hOir, letter to Christine Bromwich, n.d., August 2001.

3. de hOir, letter to Bromwich, n.d.
4. Patrick Wallace, letter to Christine Bromwich, 21 July 2001.
5. MairJad Dunlevy, letter to Bromwich, 18 July 2001.
6. John Bradley, letter to Christine Bromwich, 28 August 2001.
7. Bradley, letter to Bromwich.
8. Patrick Wallace, letter to Christine Bromwich, 21 July 2001.
9. de hOir, letter to Bromwich.
10. King, letter to Bromwich.
11. King, letter to Bromwich.
12. Harbison, "Date of the Crucifixion Slabs," p. 73.
13. Etienne Rynne, conversation with Rory O'Farrell, 1992 post obit.
14. Bradley gives details in a letter to Bromwich, August 2001: Margaret Stokes founded the discipline with *Early Christian Art* and *Early Irish Architecture* (1878). Francoise Henry built on this with *La Sculpture Irlandaise* (1932) and her three-volume history, *Irish Art in the Early Christian Period (to 800 A.D.)* (1965), *Irish Art during the Viking Invasions (800–1020 A.D.)* (1967), and *Irish Art in the Romanesque Period (1020 to 1170 A.D.)* (1970).
15. Bradley, letter to Bromwich.
16. King, letter to Bromwich.
17. Bradley, letter to Bromwich.
18. de hOir, letter to Bromwich.
19. King, letter to Bromwich.

Select Bibliography of Works by Helen M. Roe

Reports of the Laoighis County Library Service, 1926–1939. The service was established early in 1926, and Roe was appointed first county librarian and secretary of the county library committee. In this capacity she produced two reports each year for fourteen years, until her retirement in January 1940. These reports were printed (generally verbatim) in the *Leinster Express* on the Saturday following the half-yearly committee meetings at which the reports were presented (i.e., the last Tuesday in June and January). These half-yearly reports were also printed and issued as separate pamphlets, but a complete series in this format does not appear to exist. From 1926 to 1930 the reports are signed "Helen M. Roe"; thereafter, this becomes "Eibhlín Ní Ruaidh."

In addition to her regular half-yearly reports, the librarian wrote or compiled a number of special reports, book lists, and so on, some of which are listed individually. Some others are reviewed or mentioned in the pages of *An Leabharlann* or may be found among the collections of the County Library in Portlaoise. Most are unsigned; many are undated and ephemeral publications. At this time Roe also contributed occasional articles to the local press, in particular the *Leinster Express, Leinster Leader,* and *Carlow Nationalist,* but no listing of these can be given.

"The Rock of Dunamase and the Dysart Hills." *Irish Travel* 4 (October 1928): 28 and 30.
"A Hosting into Ossory." *Irish Travel* 5 (November 1929): 69–70.
Laoighis: Official Guide. Dublin: Irish Tourist Association, n.d. [ca. 1930].
Saint Patrick and Laoighis County. Maryborough, Ire.: Laoighis County Library Service, 1932.
"Laoighis County Libraries: A Seven Year Survey." *An Leabharlann* 3 (1933): 7–9.
[Eibhlín Ní Ruaidh]. *Laoighis County Library Service, 1926–1936*. Maryborough, Ire.: Leinster Express Printing Works, 1936.

"Double Cist with Cremations, Ironmills, County Laoighis." *JRSAI* 67 (1937): 295–98.
"Tales, Customs, and Beliefs from Laoighis." *Béaloideas* 9 (1939): 21–35.
"Tales of Saint Fintan of Clonenagh and Saint Brigid." *Béaloideas* 11 (1941): 189–90.
"The Summit Structure." Contributed to "A Preliminary Report on the Excavation of Knowth," by R. A. S. MacAlister, in vol. 49 C of the *Proceedings of the Royal Irish Academy*. Dublin: Falconer, 1943.
"An Interpretation of Certain Symbolic Sculptures of Early Christian Ireland." *JRSAI* 75 (1945): 1–23.
"A Mediaeval Bronze Gaming Piece from Laoighis." *JRSAI* 75 (1945): 156–59.
"A Stone Head from Killavilla, County Offaly." *JRSAI* 75 (1945): 263–66.
"The Beginning of History: A Film." *JRSAI* 76 (1946): 220–22.
"An Encrusted Urn from Shanahoe, County Laoighis." *JRSAI* 76 (1946): 210–12.
With Ellen Prendergast. "Excavation of a Mound at Blessington, County Wicklow." *JRSAI* 76 (1946): 1–12.
"Two Baptismal Fonts in County Laoighis." *JRSAI* 77 (1947): 81–83.
"Why a Local Museum?" *Carloviana* 1 (1948): 85.
"The 'David Cycle' in Early Irish Art." *JRSAI* 79 (1949): 39–59.
"Antiquities of the Archdiocese of Armagh: A Photographic Survey with Notes on the Monuments. Part I: The High Crosses of County Louth." *Seanchas Ardmhacha* 1, no. 1 (1954): 101–14.
"Antiquities of the Archdiocese of Armagh. Part II: The High Crosses of County Armagh." *Seanchas Ardmhacha* 1, no. 2 (1955): 107–14.
"Antiquities of the Archdiocese of Armagh. Part III: The High Crosses of East Tyrone." *Seanchas Ardmhacha* 2, no. 1 (1956): 79–89.
The High Crosses of Western Ossory. Longford, Ire.: Kilkenny Archaeological Society, 1958; 2d ed., revised and enlarged, 1962; reprinted 1969, 1976, and 1982.
The High Crosses of Kells. Longford: Meath Archaeological and Historical Society, 1959; 2d ed., revised, 1966; reprinted 1975 and 1981.
"Going Places with the I.C.A.; I: New Grange." *An Grianán News Quarterly*, April 1960, 13–15.
"Going Places with the I.C.A.; II: Termonfechin and Duleek." *An Grianán News Quarterly*, July 1960, 25–28.
"A Stone Cross at Clogher, County Tyrone." *JRSAI* 90 (1960): 191–206.
"Ahenny's North Cross: An Open Letter to Patrick Lagan." *Irish Press*, 28 August 1962.
"Faces in Stone." *Ireland of the Welcomes* 12, no. 2 (July/August 1963): 18–24. Translated into German as "Gesichter in Stein," *Speculum Artis* 17, no. 3 (March 1965): 23–8.
"Muiredach's Cross, Monasterboice." *Ireland of the Welcomes* 11, no. 5 (January/February 1963): 16–20.
"The Irish High Cross: Morphology and Iconography." *JRSAI* 95 (1965): 213–26.
Review of *Irish High Crosses*, by Françoise Henry (1964). *Studia Hibernica* 5 (1965): 180–82.
"Some Irish Romanesque Doorways." *Ireland of the Welcomes* 13, no. 6 (March/April 1965): 27–32.
"Some Aspects of Medieval Culture in Ireland" (presidential address). *JRSAI* 96 (1966): 105–9.
"The Roscrea Pillar." In *North Munster Studies: Essays in Commemoration of Monsignor Michael Moloney*, edited by Etienne Rynne. Limerick: Thomond Archaeological Society, 1967.
"A Carved Stone at Castledermot, County Kildare." *JRSAI* 97 (1967): 179–80.
"High Crosses," "Grave Slabs," and "Irish Romanesque." In *Encyclopaedia of Ireland*, edited by Victor Meally. Dublin: Allen Figgis, 1968.

Medieval Fonts of Meath. Navan, Ire.: Meath Archaeological and Historical Society, 1968.
"Cadaver Effigial Monuments in Ireland." *JRSAI* 99 (1969): 119.
"The Orans in Irish Christian Art." *JRSAI* 100 (1970): 212–21.
"Ireland and the Archangel Michael." In *Culte de Saint Michel et pèlerinages au Mont,* edited by Marcel Baudot, vol. 3 of *Millénaire monastique du Mont Saint Michel.* Paris: Bibliothèque d'Histoire et d'Archaeologie Chrétiennes, 1971.
"A Medieval Alabaster Figure, Black Abbey, Kilkenny." *Old Kilkenny Review,* 24 (1972): 33–36.
"The Cult of Saint Michael in Ireland." In *Folk and Farm: Essays in Honour of Anthony T. Lucas* : edited by Caomhin O. Danachair. Dublin: RSAI, 1976.
"Two Decorated Fonts in Drogheda, County Louth." *County Louth Archaeological and Historical Journal* 18 (1976): 255–62.
"Illustrations of the Holy Trinity in Ireland, Thirteenth to Seventeenth Centuries." *JRSAI* 109 (1979): 101–50.
"Illustrations of the Holy Trinity in Ireland: Additamenta." *JRSAI* 110 (1980): 155–57.
"The Effigial Tomb at Castlemartin." In *The Restoration of the Church of Saint Mary, Castlemartin, County Kildare,* edited by Sean Landers. Castlemartin, County Kildare: A. J. O'Reilly (Dublin), 1981.
"Illustrations of the Holy Trinity in Ireland: A Further Note." *JRSAI* 111 (1981): 123.
Monasterboice and Its Monuments. Dundalk, Ire.: County Louth Archaeological and Historical Society, 1981.
"Instruments of the Passion: Notes towards a Survey of Their Illustration and Distribution in Ireland." *Old Kilkenny Review,* n.s., 2, no. 5 (1983): 527–34.

Works Cited

Gillespie, Elgy Gillespie. "From Army Cookhouses to High Crosses." *Irish Times* (Dublin), 1 June 1985.
Harbison, Peter. "The Date of the Crucifixion Slabs from Duvillaun More and Inishkea North, County Mayo." In *Figures from the Past: Studies on Figurative Art in Christian Ireland in honour of Helen M Roe,* edited by Etienne Rynne. Dublin: Glendale Press, 1987.
———. *Irish High Crosses with Figure Sculptures Explained.* Drogheda: Boyne Valley Honey Company, 1994.
Henry, Francoise. *La Sculpture Irlandaise.* Dublin: Librairie Ernest Leroux, 1932
Porter, Arthur Kingsley: *The Crosses and Culture of Ireland.* New Haven, Conn.: Yale University Press, 1931.
Sexton, Eric H. L. *Irish Figure Sculptures of the Early Christian Period.* Portland, Maine: Southworth-Anthoensen Press 1946.
Stokes, Margaret. *Early Christian Architecture in Ireland.* London: George Bell, 1894.
———. *Notes on Irish Architecture.* London: George Bell, 1875.

CHAPTER 33

Suzanne Solente (1895–1978)
A Life in the Manuscript Department of the Bibliothèque Nationale

MARIE-HÉLÈNE TESNIÈRE
Translated by Robyn Fréchet

SUZANNE-MARGUERITE-GERMAINE SOLENTE was born 12 May 1895. A brilliant student, at the age of twenty-two she headed the seventeen candidates who had passed the competitive examination for admittance to the Ecole des chartes. This was 1917, a year marked by the death of the great Romance-language scholar Paul Meyer. Wartime France meant that some of her fellow students were mobilized. In 1921, still top student of her class, she received her degree as archivist paleographer with a thesis titled "Le Livre des Fais et bonne meurs de Charles V," defended in early February during the centenary year of the Ecole des chartes. "The centenary class was nothing if not curious: a woman in first position, a woman in the last, four women in all among the 17 successful candidates.... Enough to make the Lacabanes and the Guérards of 1821 go crazy," wrote one of their fellow colleagues, Charles Du Bus, in his diary.[1]

The Ecole des chartes celebrated its hundred years in a solemn session at the Sorbonne at which the president of the republic, Alexandre Millerand, presided, and a banquet followed bringing together personalities and fellows. Among the 192 archivist-paleographers, there were four young women. It was only recently (as from 1910) that "those graceful feminine heads," as the count Paul Durrieu so elegantly described them, had begun "to pore over the *chartes* to be decoded."[2] And in a rather more ironic tone, M. Servois, honorary president of the Société de l'Ecole des chartes commented: "[H]aven't we noticed each year a somewhat unexpected turn of events, the successful integration of those earnest young women clutching their bachelor diploma or degree and in whom I recognize the heritage, not, doubtless to say, of a Philaminte, Armande or Bélise, but of the true scholar of times past, Madame Dacier,

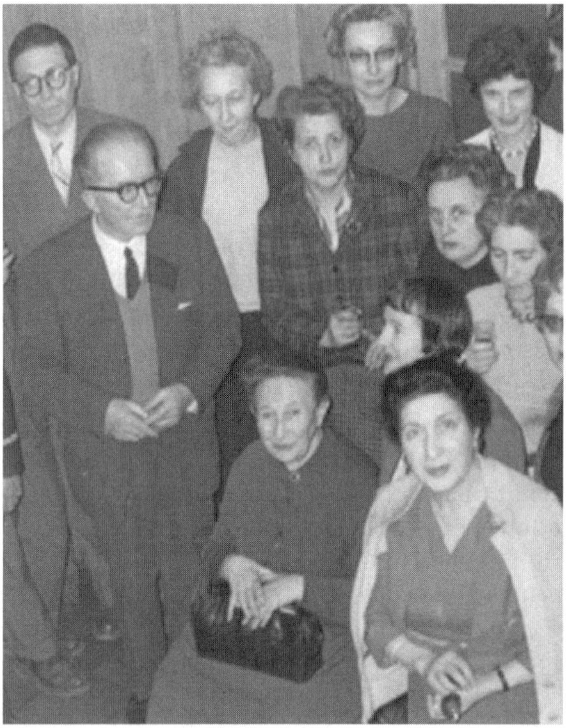

for example, that celebrated Dacier to whom, in a feminist moment, La Bruyère thought to open the gates of the Academy."³

The Ecole des chartes had been founded by Louis XVIII with a decree dated 22 February 1821. But the idea had been instigated by Baron de Gérando, secretary-general for the minister of the interior, who wished to create a school where young *pensionnaires* would be trained in the study of charters, in order to do learned research on archival documents, a school where, in a word, one learned to write history. The Ecole des chartes was established in the precincts of the Sorbonne in 1921, and the courses were dispensed for groups of up to twenty students in paleography, diplomatics (paleographic and critical study of old documents, history of institutions and of law, archaeology, Romance languages philology, sources in French history, and bibliography, all elements fundamental to reading, understanding, explaining, criticizing, and editing a document. It was a school devoted to the science of documents where one learned rigor, method, precision, clarity—in a word, as was hitherto recorded, "research devoted to truth." It trained archivists and librarians; Maurice Prou was the director of the school.

In March 1921 Suzanne Solente was appointed trainee in the manuscript department of the Bibliothèque nationale. She would remain there throughout her career, passing, according to the usual cursus, from librarian to assistant curator, then to curator responsible for French manuscripts. This essay will consider her in this context rather than seek other insights into her personality, for the reason that "the historian is wholly reflected in his history."⁴

Historical Collections

Suzanne Solente developed her talents in the manuscript department by initially working on the historical collections, which over and above the literary papers have been esteemed the wealth of the department. First in line were the papers of the military engineers Jean-Jacques and Louis Du Portal; she presented these fundamental writings for the military history of the reigns of Louis XIV and XV to the scientific community in the *Bibliothèque de l'Ecole des chartes*—the research publication to which she would contribute throughout her career.⁵

Having established the index tables for the Dupuy collection cataloged by Léon Dorez, she produced a fascinating article on the manuscripts of the Dupuy brothers.⁶ Her qualities as a historian are already evident in this article, which remains the standard reference today: her erudition and dispassionate objectivity are blended with precision and conciseness, a taste for the history of intellectual exchange, and interest in the history of transmission through collections. Solente, relying on direct reading of documents, provides a precise biographical study of Claude Dupuy (1546–94) and his sons, Pierre and Jacques, eminent scholars and guardians of the royal library, setting them in context with generous citations from the erudition of their period. She establishes methodically the catalog listings of their collections, which treat in particular the rights of the Gallican Church and of the king of France and follow step by step the vicissitudes of their donations to the king—the Dupuy collection would not enter the Bibliothèque Royale until 1754. She edits as an appendix the most important documents pertaining to the history of this collection.

Solente followed this research on the royal library with a study on the manuscripts of Colbert's librarian, Pierre de Carcavi, and then on the manuscripts of Béthune in an unpublished text, of which a typed copy is available for consultation in the manuscript department.[7]

Toward the end of her life as a graciously elderly lady dressed all in black, she was still working at a tiny desk alongside the entrance to the manuscript department, writing the card index of the first five hundred manuscripts in the Joly de Fleury collection, for which her colleague and friend Paul-Martin Bondois had established a manuscript inventory.[8] The Joly de Fleury card index may now be consulted in the manuscript reading room.

Manuscript Studies

Apart from the study of historical collections, Solente produced about twelve articles in which she presented her discoveries related to particular manuscripts. Although these small texts may appear today relatively austere, it must be remembered that their discovery represents a daily pleasure over a number of years spent in direct contact with manuscripts. Every facet of her chartist training (i.e., former student of the Ecole des chartes) is represented: diplomatics (paleographic and critical study of old documents, paleography, sources for the history of France, and codicology. As a diplomatist and Latinist, she published an early-twelfth-century *charte-partie,* or chirograph, from the abbey Saint-Amand as well as inventories of a collection of charters from the fifteenth to the nineteenth century.[9] As a paleographer, she transcribed for her colleague Ferdinand Lot a record of the parishes circa 1585 and helped two members of the medical profession present a manuscript of the writings of Guillaume Rondelet, the famous doctor from Montpellier and friend of Rabelais.[10] To the corpus of sources for French history she added two unpublished documents: a letter, partially autograph, from Marguerite de Valois, first wife of Henri IV, and an Italian commentary on the battle of Saint-Quentin in 1557.[11] As a worthy follower of Leopold Delisle, she took a vital interest in codicological considerations, those material aspects of the manuscript, mentions of ownership possessors, traces of fragments or pastedowns bound into the book bindings, added leaves, and so forth. In this context she discovered two new manuscripts from the abbeys of Mortemer and Foucarmont in the iocese of Rouen.[12] She also added a new manuscript to the library of Jean le Bègue, successor to Gilles Malet for the Librairie royale, and discovered in a binding pastedown an unknown manuscript relating the burning of the church of Saint-Amand.[13] She discovered at the end of a Latin manuscript a thirteenth-century *pastourelle* that she published with her Romance languages colleague Långfors.[14] And last, a spontaneous interest for literary history lies behind her pleasure in announcing the arrival in the Bibliothèque nationale manuscript collections of the famous La Clayette miscellany, the chimerical manuscript of thirteenth-century literary works that Paul Meyer had long sought to locate. With the measured sobriety, attention to detail, and bibliographical exactitude that so characterized her work she described the content of this manuscript in detail, particularly the writings of Pierre de Beauvais and a series of Latin and French songs with musical notation.[15]

Cataloging Collections

A considerable part of Solente's work in the manuscript department of the Bibliothèque nationale involved with the catalogs (anonymous descriptions) of the Nouvelles acquisitions françaises (new French acquisitions) appearing regularly in the *Bibliothèque de l'Ecole des chartes*, cataloging that may be followed in greater detail from 1946 on, when she was in charge of French manuscripts and described those collections recently entered by gift, legacy, or acquisition.[16] She assembled the papers of such learned philologists as Lucien Auvray, Anthoine Thomas, and Paul Meyer; of historians such as Joseph Reinach (historian of the Dreyfus Affair); and of nineteenth-century writers such as René Boylesve, George Sand, Benjamin Constant, and Victor Hugo.[17] When the big commemorative literary exhibitions began to be launched at the Bibliothèque nationale in the 1950s, she was accorded responsibility for the great Victor Hugo exhibition. This is a vitally important collection since Hugo had willed all his manuscripts and drawings to the "Bibliothèque nationale de Paris to be called one day the Bibliothèque des Etats-Unis d'Europ."[18] She would later take responsibility for the manuscripts exhibited for "Malherbe et les poètes de son temps."[19]

Christine de Pizan

Solente's most appreciable undertaking remains, without question, her contribution to introducing Christine de Pizan to the cultivated public. It all began with Charles V. At a time when Robert Delachenal was working to refine his monumental *Histoire de Charles V,* Solente was defending her thesis, "Introduction historique à l'édition du *Livre des Fais et bonnes meurs du sage roy Charles V* de Christine de Pisan." Biography, listing and dating of works, literary and historic sources, and description of the four known manuscripts make up the essentials of her study. A clear and precise mind and uncompromising judgment were necessary for an edition of this text, "since despite its pedantic form and cumbersome citations it is the only one to provide us with information on the life of the 'wise' king and to relate anecdotes that allow us to glimpse the character of Charles V."[20] A few years later, moreover, she identified six parchment folios, found in a binding pastedown from the Archives of Haute-Garonne, as belonging to the *Miroir aux dames,* by Durand de Champagne, with the signature of Charles V. A highlight of her discovery was her delivery of a paper on this subject before the most esteemed members of the Institute of France in a meeting on 28 January 1927.[21] But it was already less Charles V and rather more Christine de Pizan who had her attention. Her thesis not yet published, Solente had already written an essential article on Christine; she retraced for the first time the biography of this woman who, *seulette* on the death of her husband, must live by her pen.[22] Without a grain of romanticism here, Solente concentrates on defining Christine's protectors and insists on the foreign origins of Christine; she indicates two works hitherto unknown, spiritual works of consolation: *Les Heures de contemplation sur la Passion Nostre Seigneur* and, in particular, the *Epistre de la prison de vie humaine*, a work on the dead of the battle of Agincourt, dedicated to Marie, daughter of the Duc de Berry. She also discovers sources (Petrarch and Jacques Bauchant) and edits major passages from them.

Pursuing her exploration of Christine's writings, Solente contributed to a review of Marie-Josèphe Pinet's biography on Christine two cornerstones to the structure: the dating (1410) of the *Livre des Fais d'armes et de chevalerie* and mention of the *Avision du coq*, a treatise offered to Louis de Guyenne in 1413.[23] She does not hesitate to warn the biographer against evoking a literary culture that does not rely on a study of the work's sources. She worked herself to establish first the chronological order of the writings: in 1933 she established the dating of two other works, *Le Livre de Prod'homie* and the *Livre du corps de Policie*.[24] She wrote a study on the reception of Christine's writings in the fifteenth century, studying more particularly two works directly inspired by her, the *Enseignemens* (MS fr. 19919) and *La Louenge de Mariage*, printed in 1523.[25]

All these years of training in the work of Christine de Pizan culminated in Solente's great edition for the Société de l'Histoire de France of the *Livre des Fais et bonnes meurs de Charles V*. This work had been commissioned from Christine de Pizan by Philippe le Hardi to serve in educating the dauphin. It is a kind of teaching manual destined for the use of the kings of France, evoking in three sections the *noblece de courage*, the *sagece*, and the *chevalerie* of the dead king: a somewhat idealized tribute to Charles V. Christine offers it to the Duc de Berry for New Year 1405, the duke of Burgundy having died in the interim. Solente presents this work in a rich introduction: she retraces the career of Christine's father, Thomas de Pizan, astrologer to Charles V, and briefly evokes Christine's life, recalling that she had to become a man to head the ship; Solente particularly emphasizes Christine's financial difficulties and her search for protectors among the princes. She bases her statements on direct knowledge of the not-yet-edited manuscripts of Christine's most biographical writings: *L'Avision* (MS fr. 1176), the *Mutacion de Fortune* (MS fr. 603), and the *Livre des trois vertus* (MS fr. 1180). She explains the political motives for the writings: Philippe le Hardi intervened before Louis d'Orléans as continuator of his brother's program. She analyzes the writings and deduces their written sources (essentially based on the Vatican manuscript Vat. lat. 4791) and oral sources (Bureau de la Rivière, Gilles Malet, Jean de Montaigu). Finally, she passes judgment on the historical authority of Christine, recognizing that, although all her dates may be false, she is generally accurate regarding events. There follows a description of the six existing manuscripts and then the vast edition after the presentation manuscript for the duke of Burgundy (MS fr. 10135). Again a meticulously detailed edition is endowed with a mass of historical notes, leaving no stone unturned concerning the historical context of Charles V. This monumental work won the Bordin Prize of the Académie des Inscriptions et Belles-Lettres.

But Solente was already working on an edition of the *Livre de la mutacion de Fortune*, publication of which Maurice Roy had envisaged for the Société des Anciens Textes Français. This poem, over twenty-thousand lines long, is a kind of universal history in verse in which Christine tells first "how from woman becomes man" (*comment de femme homme devins*), the terrible "mutation" of widowhood that lends its name to the work's title.[26] She reaches the chateau of Fortune, which, held by Wealth (*Richesse*), Hope (*Espérance*), Poverty (*Pauvreté*), and Atropos, turns relentlessly on an icy rock in the middle of the Sea "of Great Peril" (*de grant Peril*). Four roads lead to the high fortress of Wealth: "Great Pride" (*Grant Orgueil*), "Great Maliciousness" (*Grant Malice*), "Great Knowledge" (*Grant Science*), and "Righteous Life" (*Juste Vie*). Under inspiration from the *Jeu des échecs moralisés* of Jacques de Cessoles, Christine describes *les sieges et condicions* (the seats and states) of those who lodge there.[27] Then follows treatment of the various sciences, the vast history of those whose actions Fortune considered worthy of being painted on the walls of the *Salle Merveilleuse*—from Adam and Eve, the ancient Jews, the Trojans, the Greeks, the Romans—up to her contemporaries. She herself prefers to avoid *Meseur,* or Misfortune, and leads a life hidden and solitary:

> J'ay choisie pour toute joye,
> (Quelqu'aultre l'ait), telle est la moye,
> Paix, solitude volumtaire
> Et vie astracte [et] solitaire.
>
> [I have chosen for happiness as a whole—
> but everybody can make another choice—mine is
> peace, voluntary loncliness,
> life apart and on one's own.][28]

Solente produced a magnificent edition of this text in four volumes published between 1959 and 1966, accompanied by an analysis, a study of the sources, an index, and a glossary. This publication received a recommendation from the Académie des Inscriptions et Belles-Lettres. She received in 1961 the Gustave Mendel Prize and in 1965 the George de la Grange Prize.

Solente's ultimate recognition as woman researcher came when she was invited to write the chapter devoted to Christine de Pizan in the *Histoire Littéraire de la France*. This was the culmination of Solente's work. She treats the subject within the traditional format of this collection, including the biography, the writings, and the writings falsely attributed to Christine: it is a monumental project considering the abundance of Christine's production. For each of Christine's writings, particularly those that had not yet been published, Solente provides an analysis, indicates the sources, and cites the known manuscripts. She also studies Christine's culture, language, rhythmic form, and influence. Solente's appreciation is subtle. Christine is the author who introduces Dante to the French; Christine's patriotism is touching. Solente paints a picture of the instruction that Christine might have received from her father and evokes her feminism in very measured terms: "Yet Christine de Pizan's feminism will not exceed the limits imposed by tradition and the ideas current in her period. She does not seek equality of the sexes. She simply wishes that women might fulfill their duties according to status and condition." Uplifted by Christine's learned lyricism, Solente adds, "She who defended in such manly fashion the reputation of women seems undeniably worthy by her fine and noble character to be admitted and seated among the chosen in the ideal retreat that is the *Cité des dames*."[29]

Solente spent the last years of her life accompanied by the *Livre du chemin de long estude* (The path of long study).[30] It is touching to reflect today on the penciled annotations—discreet witness to a bygone period—that are scattered through the manuscript fr. 1188, a presentation manuscript offered by Christine to the Duc de Berry.[31] And at the time of her death, Solente might have had in mind these lines from her *chère* Christine addressing the Sybil of Cumae:

> Moult m'avez fait grant cortoisie
> Qui a long estude menee
> M'avez, car je sui destinee
> A y user toute ma vie.
> Ne jamais je n'aray envie
> De saillir hors de ceste voie
> Qui a tout soulaz me convoie.

> [You showed great courtesy to me,
> you who guide me to such long study,
> as it is my destiny to spend my whole life to learn,
> and never would I have the desire
> to escape this path
> that gives me such happiness.][32]

Solente died on 15 November 1978. She was a chevalier of the Legion of Honor and an Officer of the Decoration, given by the Ministry of Education. The admiration of Suzanne Solente for Christine de Pizan became shortly shared overseas by other scholars such as Charity Cannon Willard. Since the seventies all over the world researchers have joined their efforts to proclaim Christine de Pizan as the first woman writer of French language.

Notes

1. Charles de Bus, Diary, Paris, BNF, Ms. Nouv. acq. fr. 12906, fol. 189v and fol. 186v.
2. *Centenaire de l'Ecole des chartes,* 37.
3. Ibid., 5.
4. Henri-Irénée Marrou, "Comment comprendre le métier d'historien," in *L'Histoire et ses méthodes,* sous la direction de Charles Samaran (Paris: Gallimard, 1973), 1465–539, particularly p. 1505.
5. Suzanne Solente, *Les Papiers des ingénieurs militaires Du Portal au département des manuscrits de la Bibliothèque nationale [Mss Nouv. acq. fr. 23102–054]* (Paris: Champion, 1924).
6. For the catalog and index, see, respectively, Leon Dorez, *Catalogue de la Collection Dupuy* (Paris : Leroux, 1899); Suzanne Solente, *Table alphabétique* (Paris: E. Leroux, 1928). Solente's article on the manuscripts appeared as "Les manuscrits des Dupuy à la Bibliothèque nationale," *Bibliothèque de l'Ecole des chartes* 88 (1927): 177–250.
7. For the Carcavi manuscripts, see Solente, "Nouveaux détails sur la vie et les manuscrits de Pierre de Carcavi." For the Béthune manuscripts, see Département des Manuscrits, Archives Modernes 696.
8. Suzanne Solente, "Paul-Martin Bondois (1885–1971)," *Bibliothèque de l'Ecole des chartes* 130 (1972): 672–77.
9. Suzanne Solente, "Une Charte-partie de 1107 dans un manuscrit de Saint-Amand" [Ms. Latin 2012], *Bibliothèque de l'Ecole des chartes* 94 (1933): 213–17; Suzanne Solente, "Chartes, lettres, et actes envoyés par M. Etienne . . . pour être offerts à la Bibliothèque nationale: Inventaire [Ms. Nouv. acq. fr. 23090]," *Bulletin philologique et historique jusqu'à 1715* 28 (1925): 251–57.
10. For her transcription for Lot, see Suzanne Solente, "Etat des paroisses par élections et diocèses vers 1585 [Ms. fr. 6413, fol. 125–26]," *Bibliothèque de l'Ecole des chartes* 90 (1929): 311–14. For her work on Rondelet, see Suzanne Solente, in collaboration with E. Jeanselme and Dr. M. Lanselle, "Un Manuscrit médical du XVIe siècle contenant principalement les œuvres de Guillaume Rondelet: Notes bibliographiques et biographiques," *Bulletin de la société française d'histoire de la médecine* 20 (1926): 3–30.
11. Suzanne Solente, "Une Lettre inédite de Marguerite de Valois [Nouv. acq. fr. 24253, fol. 275]," *Revue belge de philologie et d'histoire* 25, nos. 3 and 4 (1946–47): 612–18; Suzanne Solente, "Une Lettre du cardinal de Ferrare à propos de la défaite de Saint-Quentin, 30 août 1557 [Ms. Nouv. acq. fr. 25119]," *Bibliothèque de l'Ecole des chartes* 120 (1962): 178–85.
12. Suzanne Solente, "Deux nouveaux manuscrits provenant des abbayes de Foucarmont [Ms. Latin 65] et de Mortemer [Ms. Latin 92]," *Bibliothèque de l'Ecole des chartes* 94 (1933): 422–23.
13. Regarding the Jean le Bègue manuscript, see Suzanne Solente, "La Bible de Jean Le Bègue [Ms. Latin 24]," *Bibliothèque de l'Ecole des chartes* 89 (1928): 454–55. For the manuscript recounting the burning of the church of Saint-Amand, see Suzanne Solente, "Fragments du poème de Gilbert, *De incendio S. Amandi Elnonensis* [Ms. Latin 1709]," *Bibliothèque de l'Ecole des chartes* 92 (1931): 246–47.
14. Suzanne Solente, in collaboration with Arthur Långfors, "Une Pastourelle nouvellement découverte [Ms. Latin 193, fol. 58] et son modèle [Oxford, Bodleian Library, Douce 308]," *Neuphilologische Mitteilungen* 30 (1929): 215–25.
15. Solente, "Le Grand Recueil La Clayette." See also "Notice sur un manuscrit contenant des fragments littéraires [Nouv. acq. fr. 24398]," *Bibliothèque de l'Ecole des chartes* 108 (1949–50): 126–29.

16. Suzanne Solente "Nouvelles acquisitions françaises du Département des manuscrits : Nouv. acq. fr. 11272–3004 et 22426–4218," *Bibliothèque de l'Ecole des chartes* (1924, 1931, 1935, 1941, 1945–46).

17. Suzanne Solente, "Nouvelles Acquisitions latines et françaises du Département des manuscrits pendant les années 1946–50: Inventaire sommaire," *Bibliothèque de l'Ecole des chartes* 112 (1954): 182–246; and "Nouvelles Acquisitions latines et françaises du Département des manuscrits pendant les années 1951–1957: Inventaire sommaire," *Bibliothèque de l'Ecole des chartes* 117 (1959): 135–73.

18. Suzanne Solente, "Les Manuscrits de Victor-Hugo conservés à la Bibliothèque nationale," in *Victor Hugo, exposition organisée pour commémorer le cent cinquantième anniversaire de sa naissance* (Paris: Bibliothèque Nationale, 1952), xv–xxiv.

19. Suzanne Solente, *Malherbe et les poètes de son temps, exposition organisée pour le 4e centenaire de la naissance de Malherbe* (Paris: Bibliothèque Nationale, 1955).

20. Suzanne Solente, "Introduction historique à l'édition du *Livre des Fais et bonnes meurs du sage roy Charles V* de Christine de Pisan," in *Ecole nationale des chartes: Positions des thèses soutenues par les élèves de la promotion 1921 pours obtenir le diplôme d'archiviste-paléographe* (Paris: A. Picard, 1921), 107–12.

21. Mentioned in *Académie des Inscriptions et Belles-Lettres, comptes-rendus des séances*, (1927): 30; and "Fragments d'un nouveau manuscrit de la Bibliothèque de Charles V [Ms. Nouv. acq. fr. 23285]," *Bibliothèque de l'Ecole des chartes* 88 (1927): 43–49.

22. Solente, "Un traité inédit de Christine de Pisan."

23. Suzanne Solente, "A propos d'un livre récent sur Christine de Pisan: [Marie-Josèphe Pinet, *Christine de Pisan (1364–1430), Etude biographique et littéraire*, Paris, Champion, 1927]," *Revue belge de philologie et d'histoire* 8 (1929): 350–59.

24. Suzanne Solente, "Date de *La Prod'homie de l'homme* et du *Livre du corps de Policie*," *Bibliothèque de l'Ecole des chartes* 94 (1933): 422.

25. Suzanne Solente, "Deux chapitres de l'influence littéraire de Christine de Pisan," *Bibliothèque de l'Ecole des chartes* 94 (1933): 27–45.

26. Solente, *Le Livre de la mutacion de Fortune par Christine de Pisan*, vol. 1, verse 1029.

27. Solente, "*Le Jeu des échecs moralisés*, source de la *Mutacion de Fortune*."

28. Solente, *Le Livre de la mutacion de Fortune par Christine de Pisan*, vol. 4, verses 23,633–36.

30. Solente, "Christine de Pisan," 335–422.

29. Solente, "Un Nouveau Manuscrit de présentation du *Livre du chemin de long estude* de Christine de Pisan" (on the occasion of the issuing of the medal engraved by Aleth Guzman-Nageotte).

31. Ibid., 415.

32. Ms. fr. 1188, fol. 20.

Select Bibliography of Works by Suzanne Solente

"Introduction historique à l'édition du *Livre des Fais et bonnes meurs du sage roy Charles V* de Christine de Pisan." In *Ecole nationale des chartes: Positions des thèses soutenues par les élèves de la promotion 1921 pour obtenir le diplôme d'archiviste-paléographe*. Paris: A. Picard, 1921.

"Un Traité inédit de Christine de Pisan: *L'Epistre de la prison de vie humaine*." *Bibliothèque de l'Ecole des chartes* 85 (1924): 263–301.

"Fragments d'un nouveau manuscrit de la Bibliothèque de Charles V [Ms. Nouv. acq. fr. 23285]." *Bibliothèque de l'Ecole des chartes* 88 (1927): 43–49.

Le Livre des Fais et bonnes meurs du sage roy Charles V par Christine de Pisan. 2 vols. Société de l'Histoire de France. Paris: H. Champion, 1936–40. Reprint, in 1 vol., Genève: Slatkine, 1977.

"Le Grand Recueil La Clayette [Ms. Nouv. acq. fr. 13521] à la Bibliothèque nationale." *Scriptorium* 7 (1953): 226–34.

"Nouveaux détails sur la vie et les manuscrits de Pierre de Carcavi." *Bibliothèque de l'Ecole des chartes* 111 (1954): 124–39.

"Le Jeu des échecs moralisés, source de La Mutacion de Fortune." In *Recueil des travaux offerts à M. Clovis Brunel.* Paris: Société de l'Ecole des chartes, 1955.

Le "Livre de la mutacion de Fortune" par Christine de Pisan publié d'après les manuscrits. 4 vols. Société des Anciens Textes Français. Paris: A. et J. Picard, 1959–66.

"Christine de Pisan." In *Histoire Littéraire de la France*, vol. 40, extrait. Paris: Imprimerie Nationale et C. Klincksieck, 1969. Reprinted in a complete volume, 1974.

"Un Nouveau Manuscrit de présentation du *Livre du chemin de long estude* de Christine de Pisan." *Le Club Français de la médaille*, bulletin no. 50 (1st trimester 1976): 48–51.

Works Cited

Centenaire de l'Ecole des chartes, 1821–1921, compte-rendu de la journée du 22 février 1921. Paris: Nogent-le-Rotrou, printed by Daupeley-Gouverneur, 1921.

L'Histoire et ses méthodes. Edited by Charles Samaran. Paris: Gallimard, 1961 (Encyclopédie de la Pléiade, 11).

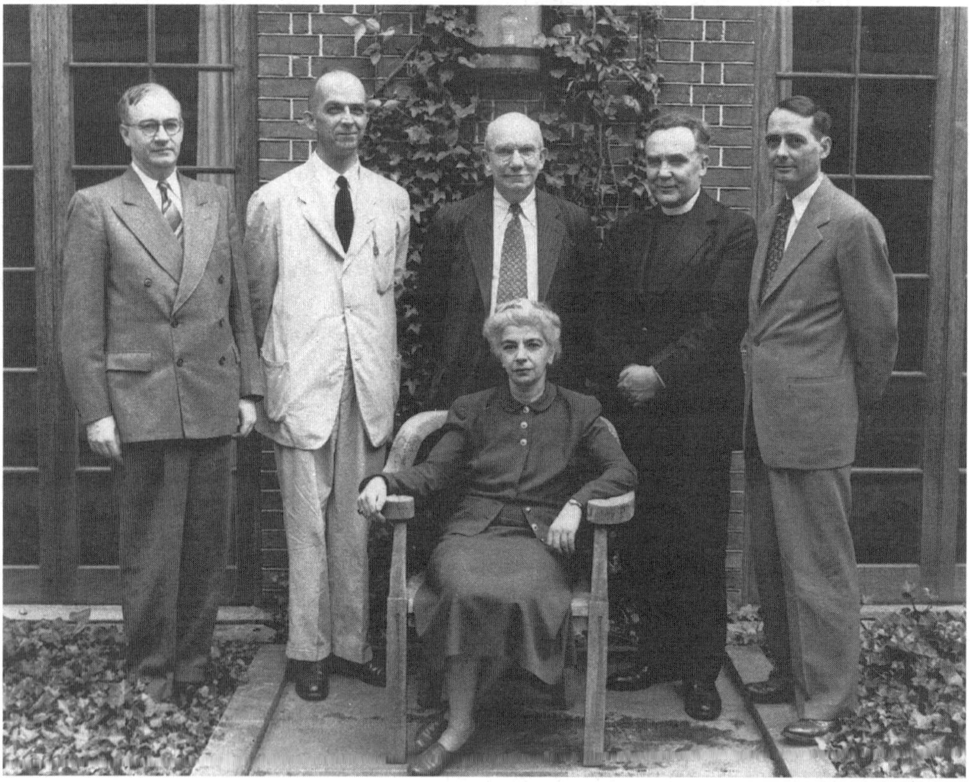

CHAPTER 34

Sirarpie Der Nersessian (1896–1989)
Pioneer of Armenian Art History

Dickran Kouymjian

Sirarpie Der Nersessian was the world's foremost authority on Armenian art as well as a renowned specialist in Byzantine art. It is she who established the principles for the study of Armenian manuscript illuminations and developed its methodology. She was the discipline's real pioneer and its most illustrious representative. She was a tireless researcher and writer with fifteen books, one hundred articles, and forty reviews; she contributed articles in festschrifts for most of the eminent medieval, Byzantine, and Armenian scholars of the twentieth century.[1]

Der Nersessian was born to an upper-middle-class family in Constantinople in 1896; her father, Mihran, was a well-known printer in the Ottoman capital and her mother, Akabi, the sister of Archbishop Maghakia Ormanian, patriarch of Constantinople and a distinguished church scholar and historian who lived with the family.[2] Orphaned at a young age, Der Nersessian and her older sister, Arax, fled to Bulgaria with an aunt—in the wake of the Turkish genocide of the Armenians in 1915—and then on to Geneva, Switzerland. Her uncle, Archbishop Ormanian, had an enormous influence on her life, as she so often mentioned, and he inspired her to become a historian. As the Armenian patriarch from 1896 to 1908, he was the official leader of the entire Armenian community in the Ottoman Empire and answered directly to the sultan. In 1910 he went to the Armenian monastery of St James in Jerusalem to complete the third and final volume of his massive *History of the Armenian Nation*.[3] He returned to Constantinople in 1918 and died the same year after his nieces were already settled in Paris. Unfortunately, his death and that of their aunt in the same year left the young Der Nersessian girls without resources or relatives except for their older brother, Boghos, who stayed in Constantinople. Supporting herself during college, very unusual for a woman in those years, Der Nersessian went from the University

483

of Geneva to the École des hautes études in Paris, where, through her great tenacity, she pursued her distinguished academic career.

Der Nersessian's teachers were the great figures of Byzantine and medieval studies of the time. In 1922 she was taken on as an assistant by Gabriel Millet, the renowned early Christian and Byzantine art historian, to help organize the world's foremost photographic archive of early Christian and Byzantine archaeology and iconography at the École des hautes études, inspiring her gradual drift from history to art history. She also studied with such luminaries as Henri Focillon, Charles Diehl, and Emile Mâle, the leading scholars in medieval art and art history, as well as with the linguist and Armenologist Antoine Meillet. Her main access to Armenian scholarship was through the impressive works of her uncle. It was principally with Gabriel Millet that her career was shaped toward Byzantine and, secondarily, Armenian art, especially manuscript illumination. In 1929, together with Millet, she published her first major study on the illustrations of the Armenian Psalter.[4] Five years later, after completing a series of long articles on Byzantine miniatures, she returned to Armenian art to examine the very beginnings of manuscript illumination in her first English-language article, "The Date of the Initial Miniatures of the Etchmiadzin Gospel."[5] Forty years after her first article, she again attacked the study of Byzantine psalm books, this time publishing an entire volume devoted to the famous eleventh-century marginal psalter in the British Library.[6] One of her two doctoral theses was also on the miniatures of Barlaam and Joasaph in the Byzantine tradition.[7] In between there were dozens of articles on Byzantine art, including a major study of the eleventh-century Menologium of Basil II.[8] Her precocious engagement in the interwar period made Der Nersessian one of the pioneers in the study of Byzantine illumination, a discipline just beginning to establish itself in the broad domain of Byzantine art, then considered a subdiscipline of early Christian and medieval art.

After some years of teaching as an assistant at the École des hautes études, she was invited in 1930 to join the art history faculty of Wellesley College near Boston. She eventually became chairperson of the art history department and director of the university's Farnsworth Museum. In 1946 she was invited to Dumbarton Oaks, the newly established Byzantine center of Harvard University in Washington, D.C., as one of its first senior fellows and resident scholar, which reinforced her research in Byzantine studies. She held that post as well as that of professor at Harvard University until her retirement in 1963, after which she moved back to Paris.

One must, however, consider her personal specialty as Armenian art, particularly the discipline she pioneered, the interrelations of Armenian and Byzantine art, especially in manuscript illumination. Already during the war years she gave a series of lectures in New York at the Pierpoint Morgan Library in French under the auspices of New York University and the École libre des hautes études, the "resistance movement" of exiled French intellectuals. These lectures were eventually published in 1945 by Harvard University Press under the title *Armenia and the Byzantine Empire*.

It is tempting to think of Sirarpie Der Nersessian as a feminist before feminism.

I do not think she would have approved of such a description, even though she never married and much of her adult life, in the personal realm, was shared with women. Motherless at age nine, fatherless at eighteen, she lived with her aunt (1914–18) and her sister, Arax, until the latter's marriage, but the untimely death of her sister's husband in 1947 brought the sisters together again. Arax died a few years before Sirarpie after a long illness. The Der Nersessian sisters shared a common house at Dumbarton Oaks (1947–63), known afterward as the "Der Nersessian house," and an apartment in the sixteenth arrondissement of Paris. Though she was regarded by students and even colleagues as an extremely well organized teacher, researcher, and administrator, she was also known for her keen sense of humor; for example, during a social gathering when she was asked, "Where is your husband, Professor Der Nersessian?" she quipped, "I am the husband."[9]

Though she was a pioneer as a female medievalist, she never made much of it. She was the first woman to teach Byzantine art in a woman's college, the first woman to be decorated with the very distinguished medal of Saint Gregory the Illuminator by His Holiness Catholicos Vazgen I (1960), the first woman invited to lecture at the prestigious Collège de France in Paris, the only woman in her time to gain full professorship at Dumbarton Oaks, and the second woman to be honored with a gold medal from the Society of Antiquaries of London (1970).

While teaching in America, she finally completed her French doctorate with the required two major dissertations, both published in 1936–37: one devoted to Byzantine manuscript illumination, *L'Illustration du "Roman de Barlaam et Joasaph,"* and the other to Armenian miniatures, *Manuscrits arméniens illustrés des 12e, 13e, et 14e siècles de la Bibliothèque des Pères Mekhitharistes de Venise*. Each of these books received a special prize.[10] Thus, Byzantine and Armenian manuscript studies were to be the poles of a career extending over six decades.

Though scholars before her had studied Armenian manuscript art—notably Father and later Catholicos Garegin Yovsēp'ian—it was Der Nersessian who established the parameters of the discipline and provided a conceptualization of its scope and characteristics. She was always known for her sense of organization and order. Because she was so firmly grounded in Byzantine and European art with a fine appreciation of Islamic painting as well, Der Nersessian was able to demonstrate that Armenian art was not just a provincial offshoot of Byzantine art but a distinct cultural expression with its own characteristics. Building on the studies of Yovsēp'ian and always using clear language replete with concrete references, she laid out the essentials of Armenian iconography, defined the styles of various periods, reconstructed numerous workshops, and revealed the characteristic features of the most prolific painters. This was often done in conjunction with the publication of catalogs of important collections of illuminated Armenian manuscripts: the Mekhitarist Library Collection in Venice (partial); the Chester Beatty Collection, Dublin; the Freer Gallery of Art, Washington, D.C.; the Walters Gallery of Art, Baltimore; the Library of the Armenian Prelacy, New Julfa, Isfahan.[11]

Der Nersessian's early historical training and her excellent command of classical, Western, and oriental languages inclined her toward providing at every step of the way a textual basis in her art-historical research. The text of manuscripts, especially the colophons of scribes and painters, were as important to her as the images. More than once she wrote pure history or analyses of liturgical and other texts. Her historical scholarship was not only impeccable but also methodologically exemplary and always based on primary sources.

I believe it would be more instructive to trace the way Der Nersessian treated some of the problems in her last book as a paradigm of her approach to scholarship than to provide an annotated catalog of her important works (see the bibliography). For years she spoke to close colleagues about a major study on Cilician Armenian art. This last monograph in two volumes, titled *Miniature Painting in the Armenian Kingdom of Cilicia from the Twelfth to the Fourteenth Century,* was issued posthumously in 1993. Her first book on Armenian art, published sixty years earlier, was already deeply immersed in precisely the same period. During the decades between them, Der Nersessian meticulously gathered notes and photographs of the 150 surviving illustrated manuscripts and fragments executed by artists working in Cilician Armenia. Many of the major monuments she had already analyzed in separate articles or as chapters in books and catalogs, including two of the most densely illustrated manuscripts of the most distinguished artist of the period, T'oros Roslin. After retiring she worked tirelessly on this major opus, but other commitments, the care of her sister, Arax, during the very long illness before her death, and, finally, her own age delayed its completion until the end of her life. She died while reviewing and revising the final manuscript with the help of art historian and late disciple Sylvia Agemian.

Sumptuously printed with 666 black-and-white illustrations and 51 color plates, *Miniature Painting of the Armenian Kingdom of Cilicia* is a vast chronological investigation of the history of Cilician book art. Yet, it has neither introduction nor conclusion. Explanation of the massive data and insights or generalities to be derived from them are given as the author moves through section after section, discussing artists and patrons and schools and monasteries. One suspects it was a matter of time, and none was left for such niceties as beginnings and endings or even in some cases, notes. But there is continuity throughout, as the story of Cilician illumination moves along from decade to decade. Of the six chapters, the last is devoted entirely to portraiture and the other five to the history of Cilician art from start to finish. The fifth chapter is principally about the prolific artist-scribe Sargis Pidsak and the slow decline in painting in the fourteenth century paralleling the gradual diminishing of the power of the Armenian kings.

The initial chapter of the book treats the beginning of Cilician painting in the first decades of the twelfth century. Der Nersessian starts by establishing in clear terms the necessity to reject received notions based on faulty information: "The general picture of the early stages of miniature painting in Cilicia had been distorted through the erroneous dating and attribution of the Gospels of the University of

Tübingen, MA.XIII.I, supposed to have been illustrated in 1113 at the monastery of Drazark. In his publication, Josef Strzygowski had relied on the information provided by the dealer.... Like many others I had accepted the date and provenance of this manuscript.... [However] the entire copy of the colophon of the Tübingen Gospels is a falsification."[12] Rather than a Cilician work of 1113, the miniatures show stylistically the manuscript and its illustrations to be of the late twelfth or early thirteenth century from Greater Armenia to the northeast. Ironically, the first authentic illustrated Cilician manuscript is in fact dated 1113 and is a gospel copied at Drazark, a poorly executed manuscript by a scribe-artist who had little experience and access only to inadequate models. Thus, the illumination is unskilled and the book unconventionally laid out. Despite its rudimentary quality, Der Nersessian treats the codex in great depth simply because it is the only known illustrated work from Cilicia in the first half of the twelfth century. She concludes her analysis judiciously: "[I]n the absence of contemporary illustrated manuscripts we have no way of knowing whether or not this mediocre work is representative of Cilician miniature painting in the first half of the twelfth century."[13]

With such deliberate caution she moves forward at a steady pace, tying together various threads to create a solid fabric, one that reconstructs the relationship between scribe, artist, and patron that produced the whole cloth of artistic and intellectual life of Armenian Cilicia. The flowering of the school was in the second half of the thirteenth century, but Der Nersessian chooses not to rush to it in order to enhance the achievements of the previous century, which made it possible. Each step on the way is clear and carefully considered. A lesser scholar might have been tempted to signal, in anticipation, what was to come.

Chapters 1 and 2A, presenting successively the second half of the twelfth and the first half of the thirteenth century, could have served as introductory material to the brilliance of the following fifty years. Such an approach held little interest for Sirarpie Der Nersessian. In her scholarship there is never exaggeration or sensation. I often recall her polite remonstrances toward some of my own more fanciful conjectures on the iconography of Armenian Pentecost when I discussed them with her more than twenty-five years ago and how she guided me quite calmly away from hypotheses that she knew would be unproductive, yet without the slightest bit of elevated authority.[14] Such firm yet sober language is at the very core of her method.

In analyzing the painting in the Armenian kingdom from 1150 to 1250, Der Nersessian took into consideration even the artistically least significant works, carefully assessing how or why an artist had failed in technique or in iconographic comprehension of a scene, but without denigrating an untalented scribe or monk with useless adjectives on the poor quality of his art. She just explains carefully, yet with great economy, why a painting or an artist's work falls short or why it is exceptional, always providing the source of the artist's inspiration, the relation of his work to that of the entire period and to neighboring scriptoria, and the place of a certain illuminated gospel in the context of the artist-scribe's entire output.

For such a balanced view, Der Nersessian has no equal in Armenian art studies. When she speaks of the production of an artist or scribe, she provides as background virtually everything there is to know about the person: all manuscripts (illustrated or not) copied by the scribe, including lost codices; the period of the artist's flourishing; the monasteries and teachers who formed his skills; his patrons (in the Cilician period almost exclusively aristocratic or upper clergy); and exhaustive bibliographical information, often of the most obscure variety.

Such is the case, for example, of a certain scribe named Kozma, who is responsible for four gospels copied on the northern fringes of Cilicia in the first decades of the thirteenth century. Der Nersessian creates a persona for Kozma: "We do not know where Kozma had been trained. He probably had come to Hromkla (the seat of the Catholicos of All Armenians) from Armenia, for the portraits show closer affinities with the miniatures of manuscripts copied in the mother country . . . than they do with the elegant style developed in Cilicia."[15] Yet, she is careful to point out that Kozma should not be confused with his namesake, another scribe who is a near contemporary. Thus, she is able to bring together four gospel books, which she attributes to Kozma on a careful comparison of style, without failing to mention other manuscripts, which were by another Kozma.

A more striking example of the startling results that Der Nersessian achieves through careful scholarship combined with the imagination of a detective concerns a group of three undated gospel manuscripts of the late twelfth or the early thirteenth century and their relation to one another, otherwise unclear because of disparate scenes and iconographic elements in them. Because of her familiarity with all periods of Armenian painting, she was able to bring to the discussion a late-sixteenth-century gospel painted at Khizan by a certain Martiros with iconographical elements from each of the three manuscripts painted four hundred years earlier, but which the three did not share with one another. Her almost understated remarks follow: "One of the models used by Martiros of Hizan, directly or indirectly, must have been the common prototype of our three Gospels, for it would be a very strange coincidence indeed if among the manuscripts to which he had access there happened to be one related" to each of the gospels.[16]

Throughout the book Der Nersessian carefully corrects her rare mistakes of the past and those of others, never passing judgment on earlier scholarship, just providing the reasons why previous opinions were in error and what new data have modified the accepted position. She is also remarkably objective in her judgments, with no trace of nationalism of any sort. This is exemplary scholarship for someone who had spent an entire life defining and developing the new field of Armenian miniature painting. Where others are quick to show that a certain feature is an Armenian "first" (but of course this curious sort of chauvinism does not apply only to members of small nations), she is content to point out new departures in restrained terms, as exemplified in her description of the fragments of the lost gospel reused as guard sheets in a later manuscript:

I have dwelt at some length on the miniatures of the two flyleaves, because their interest transcends the limits of Cilician art, bringing, as they do, a notable contribution toward the study of the Stavronikita type of evangelist portraits. Among the East Christians, the Armenians appear to have been the only ones interested in these types; no corresponding examples are known in Syriac or Coptic Gospels, nor, strangely enough, in Georgian manuscripts where the illustrations are remarkably close to the Byzantine models.... Insofar as the study of Cilician painting is concerned, the miniatures of the flyleaves have a somewhat marginal role. They testify to the skill of the painter who faithfully reproduced the Greek model, but ... are less interesting than ... the Lwów Gospels, which, based also on Greek models, show the translation of their style into a different idiom.[17]

A final example will underline her economy of expression—perhaps modesty is a better word. In the section devoted to Armenian painting's most brilliant and famous artist, T'oros Roslin (active 1256–68)—the longest part of the book devoted to a single individual, about whom Der Nersessian had written over and again—she underlines "Roslin's ability to convey deep emotion without undue emphasis," which appropriately defines her own personality. She, too, was for understatement, the idea that less is often more. Her most extravagant claims or praise for Cilician art come in this chapter. Here is her description of a painting of the descent from the cross: "This composition, in which Roslin's hand can be recognized without hesitation, surpasses in artistic quality the contemporary Byzantine examples." Or for another scene by Roslin, she writes, "Christ enthroned between the Virgin and St. John the Baptist—a figure comparable in its noble grandeur to the finest medieval examples—is no longer the severe judge but the compassionate Savior." And for yet another, "The compositional design, the delicate modeling of the individual figures, and the subtle color harmonies show Roslin's work at its best, equaling in artistic quality some of the finest Byzantine miniatures."[18]

Miniature Painting in the Armenian Kingdom of Cilicia is incontestably her magnum opus. It is at once a precise and ample study of the period and an encyclopedic compendium on Armenian art in general and the history of the medieval Armenian kingdom.

It has been impossible in this context to compare Der Nersessian's earlier positions on Armenian art with corrected or augmented ones in her final study, though an example was given earlier concerning the Tübingen Gospels. The specialized iconographic or paleographic background necessary to understand each point would have required much more space. Rather, I have emphasized her methodology. I do not mean to suggest that others before and contemporary to Der Nersessian did not uphold the same rigorous standards. But few are the scholars from any period and in any discipline who are able to combine such diverse personal resources and bring the benefit of such erudition so gracefully to the exposition of their research. Her comments on art are in part so convincing because they are grounded firmly on paleography, codicology, and historical texts, especially colophons. Through these scribal annotations she was able to piece together the story of Armenian manuscript production, and in this she followed her admired older friend Catholicos Garegin Yovsēp'ian, who, in addition to studying Armenian art, also published in 1913 the first systematic illustrated survey of Armenian paleography and, at the end of his life in 1951, the first systematic collection of Armenian manuscript colophons, the latter volume a constant companion of Der Nersessian.[19]

Though it is true that few scholars have had the good fortune to actively publish into their nineties, it is also true that few of us, given that chance, could lay claim to the integrity and thoroughness of Der Nersessian's labor. Her students at Wellesley were in awe of her knowledge, sophistication, generosity, and teaching skills. Because of her research post at Dumbarton Oaks, she produced few graduate students, though she was always ready to receive young scholars; she answered letters of inquiry promptly and amply. She always encouraged newer scholars and helped generously with her knowledge and experience. In her last decades in Paris her apartment was always open to old colleagues and students. She never refused to invite anyone who needed her help for afternoon tea, usually offering a thick demitasse of Armenian coffee. To the end the patter of her quick steps on the parquet floors of the avenue de Versailles apartment as she came to greet her guests announced the wonderful accepting smile that was to greet them as the door opened. She kept up the pace in her nineties and even began to indulge herself with an occasional cigarette, a chocolate, and discussions of current Armenian and world affairs. Yet, but for a few close friends, Sirarpie Der Nersessian will be remembered for her books and articles, glowing with a timeless purity both in method and in the credibility of the data. They will serve as paradigms of expression and refined analysis for generations of future art scholars.

Notes

Elements of this chapter were presented at the Thirty-Fifth International Congress of Orientalists, Budapest, July 1997, the theme of that year's congress being distinguished Orientalists of the past. Research on Sirarpie Der Nersessian was carried out in part under a grant from the Bertha and John Garabedian Charitable Foundation, Fresno, California.

1. A select bibliography is included at the end of this essay. Among the scholar friends she honored with essays are Gustave Schlumberger, Nicolas Iorga, Henri Focillon, Paul Peters, Henri Grégoire, Bella da Costa Greene, A. M. Friend Jr., Alexander Vasiliev, Robert Pierce Casey, George Ostrogorsky, Francis Dvornik, V. N. Lazarev, Otto Demus, Dorothy E. Minor, and Haïg Berbérian. A complete bibliography of Sirarpie Der Nersessian's works can be found in the following references: *Revue des études arméniennes*, n.s., 3 (1966): 3–6; Der Nersessian, *Études byzantines et arméniennes. Byzantine and Armenian Studies*, 2:167–70; and *Revue des études arméniennes*, n.s., 21 (1988–89): 8–11.

2. Details on Der Nersessian's life and career can be found in the carefully prepared biography by Jelisaveta Stanojevich Allen, "Sirarpie Der Nersessian." Obituaries appeared, inter alia, in Mahé and Garsoïan, "Sirarpie Der Nersessian 1896–1989"; J. Allen et al., "Sirarpie Der Nersessian 1896–1989"; and a number of Armenian newspapers and scientific journals. For her

publications, see note 5 and the bibliography. A newly published work, the first in a projected three volume series, provides the scholar's systematic archives on Armenian painting with all her unpublished notes, as well as a biography lavished with photographs in the form of a chronology (Agémian, *Archives Sirarpie Der Nersessian, Catalogue*).

3. Ormanean, *Azgapatum*.
4. Der Nersessian with Millet, "Le Psautier arménien illustré."
5. The articles on Byzantine miniatures are conveniently listed in the bibliography of Sirarpie Der Nersessian published on the occasion of her seventieth birthday in *Revue des études arméniennes*, n.s., 3 (1966): 3–6. The bibliography was brought up to date in Der Nersessian, *Études byzantines et arméniennes. Byzantine and Armenian Studies* 2:167–70, and again after her death in *Revue des études arméniennes*, n.s., 21 (1988–89): 8–11.
6. Der Nersessian, *L'Illustration des psautiers grecs.*
7. Der Nersessian, *L'Illustration du "Roman de Barlaam et Joasaph."* Der Nersessian, "Illustrations of the Homilies of Gregory of Nazianzus."
8. Der Nersessian, "Remarks on the Date of the Menologium and the Psalter Written for Basil II," *Byzantion* 15 (1940–41), pp. 104–25, reprinted in *Etudes byzantine et arméniennes*, 1:113–28.
9. J. S. Allen, "Sirarpie Der Nersessian," 337.
10. The first volume, *Roman de Barlaam et Joasaph*, received the Fould Prize of the Académie des Inscriptions et Belles Lettres, Paris, and the second, *Manuscrits arméniennes illustrès*, received the Prize of the Association des Études greques, Paris.
11. These are listed in the bibliography.
12. Der Nersessian, *Miniature Painting*, 1.
13. Der Nersessian, *Miniature Painting*, 3.
14. Kouymjian, "Problem of the Zoomorphic Figure."
15. Der Nersessian, *Miniature Painting*, 3, 11 n. 86, 12.
16. Ibid., 29.
17. Ibid., 35
18. Ibid., 59, 63a, 63b.
19. Yovsēp'ian, *Album of Armenian Paleography*. For a recent discussion of his paleographic insights, see Kouymjian, "Garegin Yovsēp'ian"; see also Yovsēp'ian's *Colophons of Manuscripts*.

SELECT BIBLIOGRAPHY OF WORKS BY SIRARPIE DER NERSESSIAN

"Illustrations de Nicéphore Phocas et de l'épopée Byzantine: Répertoire méthodique." In *Mélanges offerts à Gustave Schlumberger*. Paris: P. Geuthner, 1924.
With Gabriel Millet. "Le Psautier arménien illustré." *Revue des études arméniennes* 9 (1929): 137–81.
"The Date of the Initial Miniatures of the Etchmiadzin Gospel." *Art Bulletin* 15, no. 4 (1933): 327–60. Reprinted in Der Nersessian, *Études byzantines et arméniennes*, 1: 533–58.
L'Illustration du "Roman de Barlaam et Joasaph." 2 vols. Paris: Librairie E. de Boccard, 1936–37.
Manuscrits arméniens illustrès des XIIe, XIIIe et XIVe siècles de la Bibliothèque des Pères Mekhitaristes de Venise. 2 vols. Paris: Librairie E. de Boccard, 1937.
"The Direct Approach in the Study of Art History." *College Art Journal* 1 (1942): 54–60.
"Une apologie des images du septième siècle." *Byzantion* 14 (1944/45): 58–87. Reprinted in Der Nersessian, *Études byzantines et arméniennes*, 1: 379–404.

Armenia and the Byzantine Empire. Cambridge, Mass.: Harvard University Press, 1947.

The Chester Beatty Library: A Catalogue of the Armenian Manuscripts, with an Introduction on the History of Armenian Art. 2 vols. Dublin: Hodges, Figgis and Co., 1958.

"The Illustrations of the Homilies of Gregory of Nazianzus, Paris Gr. 510. A Study of the Connections between Text and Images." *Dumbarton Oaks Papers* 16 (1962): 195–228. Reprinted in Der Nersessian, *Études byzantines et arméniennes,* 77–107.

"The Kingdom of Cilician Armenia." In *A History of the Crusades,* edited by K. M. Setton, vol. 2, edited by R. L. Wolff and H. W. Hazard. Philadelphia: University of Pennsylvania Press, 1962. Reprinted in Der Nersessian, *Études byzantines et arméniennes,* 1: 329–52.

Armenian Manuscripts in the Freer Gallery of Art. Freer Gallery of Art Oriental Series, 6. Washington, D.C.: Smithsonian Institution, 1963.

"La peinture arménienne au VIIe siècle et les miniatures de l'Évangile d'Etchmiadzin." In *Actes du XIIe Congrès international d'etudes byzantines, Ochrid, 10–16 septembre, 1961.* Belgrade: n.p., 1964. Reprinted in Der Nersessian, *Études byzantines et arméniennes,* 1: 525–32.

Aght'amar: Church of the Holy Cross. Harvard Armenian Texts and Studies, 1. Cambridge, Mass.: Harvard University Press, 1965.

"Armenia in the Tenth and Eleventh Centuries." In *Proceedings of the Thirteenth International Congress of Byzantine Studies, Oxford, 5–10 September 1966,* edited by J. M. Hussey, D. Obolensky, and S. Runciman. London: n.p., 1967. Reprinted in Der Nersessian, *Études byzantines et arméniennes,* 1: 323–27.

The Armenians. Ancient Peoples and Places. London: Thames and Hudson, 1969.

L'Illustration des Psautiers grecs du Moyen Âge. II. Londres Add. 19352. Bibliothèque des Cahiers Archéologiques, 5. Paris: Éditions Klincksick, 1970.

Armenian Manuscripts in the Walters Art Gallery. Baltimore: Trustees Walters Art Gallery, 1973.

Études byzantines et arméniennes, Byzantine and Armenian Studies, (Collection of Sirarpie der Nersessian's essays). 2 vols. Louvain: Calouste Gulbenkian Foundation/Peeters, 1973.

"Le reliquaire de Skévra et l'orfèvrerie cilicienne aux XIIIe et XIVe siècles." In *Revue des etudes arméniennes,* n.s., 1 (1964): 121–47. Reprinted in Der Nersessian, *Études byzantines et arméniennes,* 705–22.

With Herman Vahramian. *Aght'amar* (in English, Italian, Armenian). Documenti di Architettura Armena, vol. 8. Milan: Edizioni Ares, 1974.

"Program and Iconography of the Frescoes of the Parecclesion." In Paul A. Underwood, *The Kariye Djami,* 4: 305–49. New York: Bollingen, 1975.

L'Art arménien. Paris: Flammarion, 1977. Translated under the title *Armenian Art* (London: Thames and Hudson, 1978).

"L'évangile du roi Gagik de Kars: Jérusalem no. 2556." *Revue des études arméniennes* 18 (1984): 85–107.

With Arpag Mekhitarian. *Armenian Miniatures from Isfahan.* Brussels: Les Editeurs d'Art Associés, 1986.

"Les portraits d'Esayi Nč'ec'i Supérieur de Glajor." In *Armenian Studies, Études arméniennes: In Memorium Haïg Berbérian,* edited by Dickran Kouymjian. Armenian Library of the Calouste Gulbenkian Foundation. Lisbon: Gulbenkian Foundation/Coimbra, 1986.

"Two Miracles of the Virgin in the Poems of Gautier de Coincy." *Dumbarton Oaks Papers* 41 (1987): 157–63.

With Sylvia Agemian. *Miniature Painting in the Armenian Kingdom of Cilicia from the Twelfth to the Fourteenth Century*. Introduction by Annemarie Weyl Carr. 2 vols. Dumbarton Oaks Studies, vol. 31. Washington, D.C.: Dumbarton Oaks, 1993.

Works Cited

Agémian, Sylvia. *Archives Sirarpie Der Nersessian, Catalogue*, vol. 1, Bibliothèque arménienne de la Fondation Calouste Gulbenkian. Antelias, Lebanon: Armenian Catholicosate of Cilicia, 2003.

Allen, J., N. Garsoïan, I. Ševčenko, and R. W. Thomson. "Sirarpie Der Nersessian 1896–1989." *Dumbarton Oaks Papers* 43 (1989): ix–xi.

Allen, Jelisaveta Stanojevich. "Sirarpie Der Nersessian (b. 1896): Educator and Scholar in Byzantine and Armenian Art." In *Women as Interpreters of the Visual Arts, 1820–1979*, edited by Claire Richter Sherman with Adele M. Holcomb, 321–56. Westport, Conn.: Greenwood Press, 1981.

Kouymjian, Dickran. "Garegin Yovsēp'ian." In *Album of Armenian Paleography*, edited by M. Stone, D. Kouymjian, and H. Lehmann, 33–35. Århus, Denmark: Århus University Press, 2002.

———. "The Problem of the Zoomorphic Figure in the Iconography of Armenian Pentecost: A Preliminary Report." In *Atti del Primo Simposio Internazionale de Arte Armena, Bergamo, 1975*, 403–13. Venice: Mekhitarist Press, San Lazzaro, 1978.

Mahé, J.-P., and N. Garsoïan. "Sirarpie Der Nersessian 1896–1989." *Revue des Études arméniennes*, n.s., 21 (1988–89): 5–7.

Ormanean, Maghak'ia. *Azgapatum* (History of the nation). 3 vols. Constantinople: Armenian Patriarchate, 1912, 1914; Jerusalem: St James Monastery, 1927. Reprint, Beirut: Sevan, 1959; Antelias, Lebanon: Cilician Catholicosate, 2002.

Yovsēp'ian, Garegin. *Album of Armenian Paleography* (in Armenian). Etchmiadzin: Armenian Catholicosate, 1913.

———. *Colophons of Manuscripts* (in Armenian). Vol. 1. Antelias: Press of the Catholicosate of the Great House of Cilicia, 1951. Armenian colophons to 1250 A.D., all published.

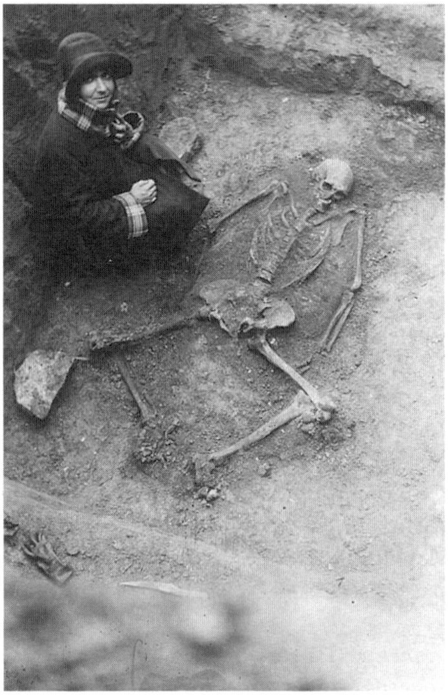

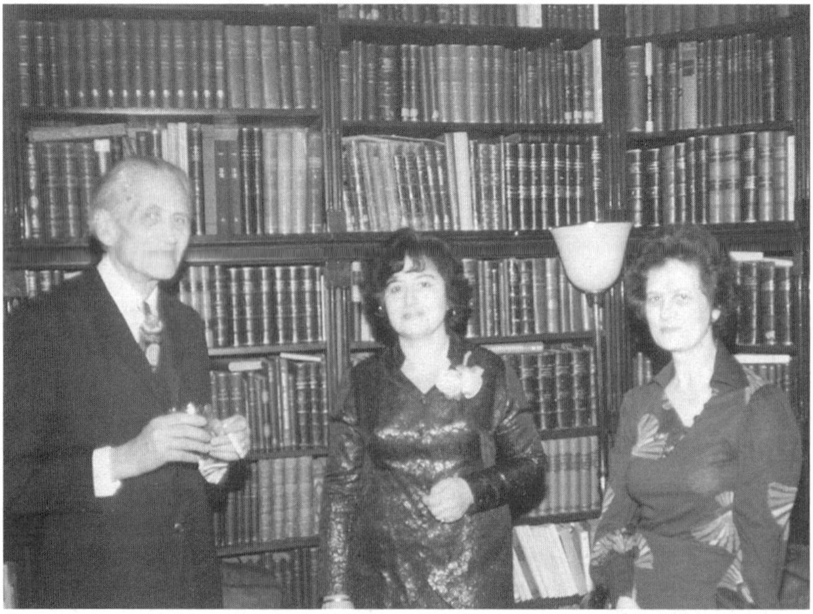

CHAPTER 35

Women and Medieval Scholarship in Bulgaria

Vera Ivanova-Mavrodinova (1896–1987) and Vasilka Tapkova-Zaimova (1924–)

LILIANA V. SIMEONOVA, WITH A MEMOIR BY VASILKA TAPKOVA-ZAIMOVA, TRANSLATED BY LILIANA V. SIMEONOVA

Part 1. Storming Academia's Heights

LILIANA V. SIMEONOVA

WHEN THE EDITOR OF THIS VOLUME, Professor Jane Chance of Rice University, contacted me and asked me to write an essay on Bulgarian women medievalists who were historians and were born before the year 1935, my immediate response was that there were no such women in Bulgaria. I went on to explain that the first women medievalists in my country were—by education and professional training—not historians but philologists, whether Slavic or classical; that they "arrived" at medieval studies either via the indirect routes of the so-called—at least until the early 1980s—auxiliary historical disciplines (archaeology, paleography, and epigraphy) or through their work as translators of medieval written sources; that history—and especially medieval history—remained, until not so long ago, an "exclusive gentlemen's club"; and that it was only in the mid-1970s that the first three or four women with M.A. degrees in history were enrolled in doctoral programs in medieval history.

Editor Chance and I then reached a compromise: inasmuch as the early Bulgarian women medievalists had succeeded in becoming leading specialists in their respective fields of medieval studies, they did not have to be historians. I suggested two case studies: those of Professor Vera Ivanova-Mavrodinova (1896–1987) and Professor Vasilka Tapkova-Zaimova (b. 1924). Although they belong to different generations of scholars, the two women have much in common. They both chose to step, so to speak, into their fathers' shoes by taking degrees in Slavic and classical philology, respectively;

both of them became leading specialists in their fields: Vera Ivanova-Mavrodinova in medieval archaeology and medieval Slavic epigraphy and paleography and Vasilka Tapkova-Zaimova in Byzantine studies. What is more, Ivanova-Mavrodinova is rightly considered to have been the first woman archaeologist in the Balkans, while Tapkova-Zaimova is the first woman Byzantinist in Bulgaria. Last but not least, they both married men who belonged to the same professional circles and whose academic careers developed, more or less, along parallel lines with those of their emancipated wives. While recounting the two women's life stories, the essay was going to show how they—through their successful careers—contributed to the breaking down of some of the traditional barriers that prevented women from entering into the male-dominated field of medieval studies in Bulgaria.

As a historian, however, I found it impossible to embark on writing a biographical essay without attempting to place my heroines in an appropriate historical setting. And then, understandably, my original plan was confounded by the questions that started coming up, one after another: When were women admitted, for the first time, into higher education? What happened to female college graduates who found themselves in the job market? When did college-educated women begin to show interest in medieval history? Why did they choose to become historical-fiction writers rather than scholars? Why were the first women medievalists philologists and not historians? The number of questions kept growing until I no longer knew how far back into history I should go, looking for answers.

One way or another, in its final version, the essay presents a brief survey of the processes and events that led to the entry of college-educated women into the arts and literature as well as, somewhat later, into scholarship. Chronologically, the entry of women into academia roughly coincides with the extension of political suffrage to women in the 1930s, which leads me to believe that the appearance of women scholars on the scene must have been the result, albeit an indirect one, of the same processes of emancipation of women in Bulgarian society that guaranteed the happy ending of the suffragist movement. At the same time, the story of women's joining the ranks of academics is closely linked to the development of the nation's oldest and most prestigious academic institutions, the Bulgarian Academy of Sciences (BAS; founded in 1869) and Sofia University (SU; founded in 1888), and the nation's oldest museum, the National Archaeological Museum (founded in 1893).

Let us first look into the processes that contributed, whether directly or indirectly, to the emergence of a relatively high number of college-educated women in Bulgaria in the interwar period (1919–39). As will be seen, college-educated women had difficulties finding jobs in certain fields of the national economy. Some of these difficulties stemmed from the post–World War I crisis; others were rooted in the then prevalent mentality. Eventually, in 1924, the Association of College-Educated Women was founded: its main goal was to help women with academic degrees "enter into the more prestigious professions." Indeed, the so-called prestigious, or well-paid, jobs remained by and large within a reserved perimeter of men. Particularly hard for women to join was the bar association, regardless of the fact that there had been women lawyers in Bulgaria since the 1840s. The medical profession, too, remained, at least until the 1920s, a field altogether reserved for men; while women surgeons had worked on the front line during the Russo-Turkish War (1877–78) and World War I and had been decorated as war heroes, women doctors continued to be a fairly rare phenomenon in Bulgaria of the 1920s. At the same time, college-educated women could find jobs as school teachers (especially in the elementary schools), museum curators, journalists, and translators: it was the lower pay that kept college-educated men away from certain intellectual spheres, thus allowing women to step in. An identical phenomenon could be observed even in spheres in which a lesser degree of education or professional training was required: women were employed as secretaries, typists, post office workers, and so forth, simply because many men who had the same qualifications would not go for such not-so-well-paid jobs. Still, in times of economic crises, female employees were the first ones to lose their jobs. This happened during the 1890s crisis and then again during the crisis that occurred right after World War I.

Another factor that prevented women from finding well-paid jobs was the unequal treatment of men and women by the existing laws. On one hand, the so-called Tirnovo Constitution (i.e., Bulgaria's constitution of 1879) proclaimed the formal equality of all Bulgarian citizens before the law; on the other, this constitution contained certain formulations that placed women in a lower category. Thus, while women had the same property rights and were subject to the same taxation as men, they were discriminated against by other laws, such as the ones referring to the right of high school education of young people or the ones guaranteeing the voting rights of Bulgarian citizens.

Because the struggle for women's education and emancipation seems to have been going hand in hand with the struggle for granting voting rights to women, I will make a short detour into the history of the Bulgarian feminist movement. As will be seen, the reformed education for girls (1897) and the subsequent enrollment of the first female students in Sofia University (1904), along with the extension of political suffrage to women (1937), eventually broke down most of the traditional barriers separating women from men in Bulgarian society. This, in turn, enabled a greater number of professional women to gain access to "prestigious" jobs, including those that had formerly been considered "a man's territory."

Let us begin with the voting rights of women and the high school and college education of girls. While the constitution of 1879 granted voting rights "to all Bulgarian citizens," women remained disenfranchised: borrowed from the *Code civile* (i.e., the French Civil Code), the very definition of citizen that the Tirnovo Constitution used was gendered to the core.[1] Women, however, profited from other "human rights" that were guaranteed by that constitution. Among them was "the universal right to [elementary] education," which was made mandatory for children of both sexes and of all social and ethnic backgrounds. Also, there was the constitutionally guaranteed right of all people to freely assemble and form unions of all kinds: the Bulgarian feminist movement, whose origins could be traced back to the 1850s, benefited from this, the result being that women's organizations continued to grow and multiply in the last quarter of the nineteenth century.[2]

Still, in the 1880s and 1890s women's organizations went on recruiting their members mostly from among the women of the upper classes, as they had done in the previous three decades. Before long, however, it became obvious that the feminist movement would become more efficient if all the women's organizations were brought under the same leadership and began to coordinate their actions on a nationwide scale. For this reason, in 1901 the Bulgarian Women's Union (BWU) was founded, with twenty-seven women's organizations becoming its collective cofounder. The emergence of BWU gave an impetus to the women's emancipation movement while continuing the work of the nineteenth-century women's organizations.

Initially, the BWU was dominated by the ideas of the political Left. Soon, however, its membership split along the lines of "traditionalism" (or "conservatism") and "socialism," since most of its activists shared the political views of their respective husbands, who were, in most cases, prominent intellectuals, scientists, or politicians. Thus, the "traditionalist" (or "conservative") trend in the BWU emphasized the need of continuing the philanthropist and educational traditions in the work of the women's organizations. The "socialist" trend, for its part, claimed to be voicing the grievances of the Bulgarian working-class women, regardless of the fact that its members were—without exception—educated, middle-class women: while they fought for higher wages and reduced working hours for female workers, they also talked about working-class women's participation in the world class struggle.

Eventually, the BWU ceased to exist, and two new women's unions took its place: the conservative *Ravnopravie* (Equality, 1909) and the leftist *Union of Women Socialists* (1914). Despite their different political orientation, however, both unions continued their struggle for enfranchising women.[3] In 1901 the Bulgarian Parliament, pressured by the women's organizations, had granted women the right to run for the elective boards of trustees of schools. But it was only in 1909 that the first women candidates got elected. The Balkan Wars (1911–13) and World War I put the suffragist movement on hold, with the 1920s and 1930s bearing witness to its renewal in Bulgaria as well as in all of Europe. In 1937 for the first time in Bulgarian history, the constitutionally guaranteed "universal voting rights" were extended to women, albeit not to all of them: one needed to have had a child born in wedlock in order to be allowed to cast a vote in the municipal elections held at the end of that year. Nevertheless, the participation of women in the 1937 communal elections was a major victory for the Bulgarian feminist movement, which had spent nearly sixty years struggling for the extension of political suffrage to women.[4]

As regards the reformation of the core curricula of the high schools for girls, it too was initiated mostly thanks to the concerted efforts of the Bulgarian women's organizations. While the Tirnovo Constitution guaranteed every child's right to an elementary education, at the next level of education boys and girls were treated differently. Since the 1830s almost every town and city in Bulgaria had come up with a girls' school of sorts. Girls' high schools, however, offered a four- or five-year course of education, whereas the high schools for boys offered the complete seven- or eight-year course. Besides, the curricula of the girls' schools primarily focused on subjects that would help young women become better wives and mothers, whereas the boys' schools offered math, physics, chemistry, biology, and the rest of the disciplines that eventually made one eligible for higher education.

In order to get the formal education that would enable them to apply for college, some ambitious young women went to boarding schools in Central and Western Europe as well as in Russia and Romania. Many of those female high school graduates later continued their education in European universities. This costly maneuver, however, could only be undertaken by young women of higher social standing and considerable means or by those who had been lucky enough to get some sponsorship.

In 1897 the core curricula of the boys' and the girls' high schools in Bulgaria were finally equalized: now young people of both sexes could attend seven- or eight-year high schools in which they could study pretty much the same disciplines. In this way the 1897 school reform practically eliminated the formal obstacles that prevented graduates of the Bulgarian high schools for girls from applying for college. Seven years later, in 1904, the nation's oldest and most prestigious institution of higher education, Sofia University, accepted its first female students. However, not all the faculties opened their doors to women: for example, female students were accepted by the School of Education but not by the law school.

In January 1907, Sofia University was closed with a royal decree: King Ferdinand I (1887–1918) was unable to swallow the humiliation he had suffered earlier that month when university students jeered at him in the National Theater, protesting against his increasingly tyrannical rule. When he threatened to take punitive action against the student body, most of the university professors chose to side with their students rather than with their king. The closure of Sofia University provoked public anger. one of the most influential national institutions, the Bulgarian Academy of Sciences, openly took the side of the fired university professors. The Academy of Sciences was soon followed by a large number of prominent intellectuals, journalists, and politicians. Unable to resist the mounting pressure, King Ferdinand reopened the university, which soon turned, to an even higher degree than before, into a hotbed of radicalism and liberalism. Also, its enrollment policies became somewhat liberalized, in the sense that most of the departments now opened for women. In the following years the number of female students continued to grow. This, in turn, led to a quick rise in the total number of college-educated women in Bulgaria. Once they got their academic degrees, however, these young women came to face the harsh reality of the job market.

College jobs were practically inaccessible to women. Regardless of the fast-growing number of female college graduates, scientific research and college-level teaching remained—even in the 1920s, 1930s, and throughout most of the 1940s—a field almost completely reserved for men. Thus, in the year 1944, when Communism began to get established in Bulgaria, the total number of women teaching at Sofia University was twenty-six: of them, twenty-three were assistant professors, two were lecturers (both taught foreign languages but not history in the history department), and only one was tenured (she was an associate professor in the physics department, with a Ph.D. from Vienna, and a former Yarrow Research Fellow of Girton College at Cambridge).[5]

Journalism, on the other hand, was one of the first intellectual fields to let women into its professional circles. Women began writing for newspapers and magazines as early as the 1850s and 1860s, but only in the 1880s and 1890s, with the growth of the publishing business and the emergence of newspapers, magazines, and journals that addressed the problems of women, women were able to enter into the journalistic profession.

Literature, along with the performing and fine arts, also opened for women fairly early, in the 1880s and 1890s. Women artists, actresses, writers, and musicians cut popular figures in the intellectual circles of that time period. It was socially acceptable for a young woman to get some vocational training and dedicate herself to the arts; a woman scientist, however, seemed to be a different matter. Women with college degrees, especially in philology, often turned to writing poetry or fiction in order to find some realization of their professional skills and dreams.[6]

Let us now take a look at women in historical studies. In the absence of official statistics, it is hard to say exactly when the first female students were enrolled in the Department of History, which was—until 1948—part of the huge historical-philological faculty at Sofia University.[7] To the best of my knowledge, in the interwar period very few women took degrees in history, and they became, without exception, school teachers. The first doctoral programs in history were offered by both Sofia University and the reformed Bulgarian Academy of Sciences in 1948.[8] In the early 1950s a handful of women embarked on writing dissertations in history; none of them, however, focused on the Middle Ages. At the same time, the medieval studies department at the newly founded Institute of Bulgarian History at the Academy of Sciences had two female "assistants" holding master's degrees in classical philology but no female doctoral students, whether in history or classical philology. As I mentioned earlier in this study, it was not until the mid-1970s that the first women with master's degrees in history were enrolled in Ph.D. programs in medieval studies, whether at Sofia University or at the Academy of Sciences.

Why did women stray from history for such a long time? The fact that until the mid-1940s the female students of the historical-philological faculty preferred to enroll en masse in the philological departments rather than in the history department could probably be explained through the specifics of both the then prevalent mentality and the job market: for a woman, to find a job as a foreign language teacher or a college-level foreign-language lecturer was much easier than to find a job as a history teacher, let alone a college professor in that discipline. Historical studies—which in that period focused on political rather than socioeconomic or cultural history—were traditionally considered male-dominated fields where women did not belong.

Still, history was "raided" by college-educated women as early as the later 1920s. Two venues lay before the woman who wished to dedicate herself to history: she could become a historical-fiction writer or a museum employee. Let us first explore the writer's venue. In Europe the post–World War I years bore witness to a boom of historical-fiction writing. This literary fashion came to Bulgaria too and provided women with a passage into the realm of historical research.[9] The most striking example of a Bulgarian woman novelist who was regarded as a historian of the Middle Ages not just by her readers but also by the professional community is that of Fani Popova-Mutafova (1902–77). To this day she is considered by many to have been the best-selling Bulgarian historical-fiction author of all time: in the 1930s and early 1940s her books sold in record numbers, such as fifteen thousand copies at a time. Popova is worth being mentioned here for yet another reason: her literary success paved the way for women who wished to join the Bulgarian medievalists' circles.

Fani Popova spent her formative years in Turin (Italy). There, little Fani took piano lessons and learned Italian. Her knowledge of that language proved very useful at a later stage of her life: under Communism, when she could no longer publish historical fiction, she translated books and plays from the Italian for a living. In 1922 Popova enrolled in Sofia University as a philosophy major. Soon, however, she married and had to accompany her husband, Tchavdar Mutafov, to Munich, where he studied architecture. In Germany Popova-Mutafova signed up for courses in art history at Munich University and took piano lessons in Professor Meilbeck's class (1923–25). Upon their return to Bulgaria the couple had their first child. The care for the baby, however, could not deter Popova-Mutafova from continuing her intellectual pursuits: she joined the *Streletz* (Archer) literary society, founded by Professor Ivan Galabov, the linguist, and her husband.[10]

Popova-Mutafova began contributing to Bulgarian literary journals while still living in Germany: her first short stories were published in *Vestnik za Zhenata* (A woman's newspaper) in 1924. Upon her return to Bulgaria she quickly gained access to the most prestigious literary journals: for example, *Zlatorog*, *Zlatostruj*, and others. Initially she wrote short stories whose heroines were women. Soon, however, Popova-Mutafova turned to historical fiction. Her very first historical novel, the two-volume *The Wonder-Worker of Salonica* (1929/30) was a tremendous success. It was followed by *John Assen* (1938), *The Last of the Assenids* (1939), and *Kalojan's Daughter* (1942). Chronologically, the three novels are situated in the epoch of the Assenid dynasty, in the early 1200s. Popova-Mutafova's mastery in describing the early-thirteenth-century Bulgarian court and customs is so great that even professional historians regarded her as a "colleague historian." She also published several collections of short stories based on historical legends.[11]

While in the 1930s and early 1940s Popova-Mutafova's work provided an example of a successful woman writer's career, what she wrote on behalf of "the new Bulgarian woman" was ultraconservative. She basically propagated the "return" of modern women to the traditional values of patriarchal society. During World War II Popova-Mutafova wrote some nationalistic articles that after the war were used by the Communists against her: she was accused of having propagated chauvinistic and fascist ideas and was even briefly jailed; also, her historical-fiction works were blacklisted. The ban on their publication was lifted only in the early 1960s; shortly afterward she was admitted into the Bulgarian Writers' Union.

It is worth noting that, even at the peak of her literary career, Popova-Mutafova did not attempt to challenge the then prevalent concept of a woman writer: until the establishment of the Communist regime in the mid- to late 1940s, she remained—in the eyes of society—an upper-middle-class housewife who dedicated her leisure time to writing. It was another woman, poet, and historical-fiction writer, Yana Yazova, who challenged this conservative view of women writers. Yazova was a widely traveled intellectual, journeying on her own, visiting the historic sites she would later describe, lecturing before a variety of audiences, being the 1990s type of an intellectual woman rather than a woman author of the later 1930s and early 1940s.

Yana Yazova was the pen name of Liuba T. Gantcheva (1912–74): a young and gifted poet who published her first collection of poems four years before she took her master's degree in Slavic philology (Sofia University, 1935). In 1940 she published a historical drama, *The Last of the Pagans,* and an adventure novel, *The Captain,* both of which became very popular. In 1942/43, she coedited—together with the famous classicist, translator, and publicist Professor Alexander Balabanov (1879–1955), who was also her intellectual mentor and lover—the children's magazine *Blok*. In 1943 she married another man without breaking off her relationship with Balabanov, who remained her intellectual mentor and most devoted friend until his death in 1955.[12]

As one French literary critic put it, Yazova was both "beautiful and eccentric"; she was also highly intellectual and very talented, but, above all, she was a rebel. Whether sponsored by wealthy individuals, women's organizations, or the International Pen Club, she journeyed to Turkey, Syria, Palestine, Egypt, Greece, Yugoslavia, Austria, Germany, and elsewhere. In *The Captain,* which is the first Bulgarian novel dealing with drug trafficking, one comes across breathtaking, exotic landscapes, wild adventure, and plenty of drama. While the work no doubt reflects its author's rebellion against traditional morality and prejudice, it also poses one important question: Could one become a victim of Fate?

Yazova's quest for new horizons—geographical, historical, and philosophical—did not end with that novel. The historic sites that she visited in Greece, Turkey, and the Middle East are described in the first of her historical novels, *Alexander of Macedon:* a masterful mixture of fact and fiction, it conveys much of the authentic atmosphere of Alexander the Great's epoch. This work of Yazova's remained unpublished in her lifetime and was only recently edited and submitted for publication. Although *The Captain* and *Alexander of Macedon* formally belong to different genres, the two works display a number of similarities: for example, they both contain fascinating descriptions of exotic places, in both of them the protagonist strives to reach beyond the physical and intellectual horizons of his contemporaries, and both of them are filled with drama. Most important of all, both works pose the same philosophical questions: Did great men become tragic victims of the epoch in which they lived? Could one become the victim of history?

In a bitter twist of irony, it was Yazova's own life that provided her with an answer to those questions. She found herself trapped in a situation that turned her into a victim of the turbulent times in which she happened to live. Upon the establishment of the new, Communist regime, she was pressured to denounce her previous writings and start writing odes to Communism. Yazova's independent and rebellious nature, however, did not allow her to compromise her principles. In 1952 she chose to withdraw herself from society rather than become an occasional poetry writer. Her withdrawal was complete. In self-imposed isolation she embarked on writing her trilogy, *Balkans,* dedicated to the nineteenth-century national liberation movement. It, too, remained unpublished in her lifetime: two of the three volumes were published posthumously, in 1987 and 1988 respectively; the third one—*Wars*—was published only in 2002. Again, the pervading theme of the trilogy is the romantic role that great men played in history and their inevitably tragic end.

The way in which Yazova left this world adds a tragic touch to the drama of her life. It was in August 1974: one day Sofia was shocked by the news of Yana Yazova's having been found murdered in her home. At that point in time, I was a high school student who believed that Yazova was a writer of children's books—I had read *The Captain* as a child—and that she had lived and worked when my mother was little, one thousand years ago. It had never crossed my mind that she might still be alive, living only a few blocks from where we lived. Having spent over twenty years in isolation, she seemed to have been forgotten by everyone. I cannot remember all the details of that dreadful story; what I remember is that even the medical examiner could not say with certainty how much time had elapsed since she had died. Her spacious apartment was cluttered with memorabilia—mostly exotic souvenirs of her long-distance trips—and books and papers, along with the typescripts of her historical-fiction works, waiting to be published and read by the generations to come.

In the interwar period the second venue to historical scholarship was that of becoming a museum employee. In the 1920s and 1930s institutions such as the National Archeological Museum (NAM) and the Ethnological Museum (founded in 1906) opened their doors to women. Vera Ivanova-Mavrodinova—an archaeologist, paleographer, and epigraphist—was, to the best of my knowledge, the first young woman employed by NAM. She was outspoken and tough, hardworking and extremely dedicated to her profession. Her work spans over a sixty-five-year period of time, with her last studies being submitted for publication only shortly before her death at age ninety-one. (When, at age eighty-three, she arose and walked after she had spent six months in bed with a broken hip, she said, "I managed to score a temporary victory in my combat with the other world"; when celebrating her ninetieth birthday, Vera casually remarked, "I no longer have enemies, alive.")

Vera Ivanova was the daughter of Professor Yordan Ivanov (1871–1947), the well-known medievalist, paleographer, literary historian, and archaeologist. Unlike her brother, a decorated World War I veteran who chose to go to a law school, young Vera was fascinated with her father's scholarly pursuits and wished to become a paleo-Slavicist and epigraphist like him. She took a master's degree in Slavic philology (Sofia University, 1921) but never considered teaching as a possibility. In her own words she preferred archaeological sites to classroom discussions. When, after her father's death in 1947, she was asked to fill in his vacated position in Slavic paleography at Sofia University, she turned down the offer.

An ambitious young woman, Vera Ivanova made painstaking efforts to prove that she should be considered a scholar in her own right and not just her father's daughter. Even when both father and daughter found themselves in Paris—with him teaching at the École des langues orientales vivantes (1927–30) and her taking courses at the École des hautes études at the Sorbonne and the École de Louvre (1926–28)—she only met with him twice, to dine out; during the rest of the time, they communicated through written messages.

Vera Ivanova's career as a museum employee had started three years prior to that, in 1923, when she was appointed "assistant" at the medieval department of NAM. At that point in time the museum had five departments: prehistory, ancient history, medieval history, numismatics, and fine arts. The director was then the well-known archaeologist Professor Andrej Protic. Apart from their work with the fast-growing museum holdings, the museum employees were also engaged in working on archaeological sites. As for the material that they excavated or that came into their hands through other channels, the museum workers were primarily responsible for cataloging it, while another institution, the Bulgarian Archaeological Institute (founded in 1901 as the Bulgarian Archeological Society), was largely responsible for its study and publication. However, this "division of labor" between the two archaeological institutions existed in theory rather than in practice, as people from both institutions produced scholarly publications.[13]

Upon her appointment at the museum, Vera Ivanova became acquainted with the future French Byzantinist Andre Grabar. In 1920–22 he was a young Russian émigré, a recent graduate of Saint Petersburg University, who lived in Sofia and contributed to the medieval studies department by doing research on the murals of Bulgarian medieval churches. A few years later, in France, he published his first monograph, *La peinture religieuse de Bulgarie* (1928).

As for young Vera Ivanova, her first assignment at the National Archeological Museum was to compile a catalog of all the late-antique and medieval churches in Bulgaria; the catalog was to contain a list of the known sites, supported by references in the surviving written sources. The result, "Old Churches and Monasteries in the Bulgarian Lands, Fourth-Twelfth Century," was an impressive corpus of early-Christian and medieval ecclesiastical architecture in Bulgaria that has remained in use ever since.[14] Later this work of Vera Ivanova earned her the prestigious award of the Berlinov Fund for Science (1933).

In 1926 Vera Ivanova left for Paris, where she spent two years taking classes in Byzantine history (with Ch. Diehl) and Byzantine art and architecture (with G. Millet); also, she took classes in Romanesque art (with H. Focillon) and history of the Eastern heresies (with A. Bayet). Apart from going to the Sorbonne, she also took courses at the École de Louvre (for example, she enrolled in Dussot's class in biblical archaeology). In Paris Vera Ivanova made friends with three female fellow-students: one young Japanese woman, a young Polish woman (the future Polish Byzantinist C. Osieczkowska), and the future U.S. Byzantinist Sirarpie Der Nersessian, who later became a fellow of the Dumbarton Oaks Center of Byzantine Studies.

On returning to Sofia in 1928 Vera Ivanova was promoted to the rank of curator at the newly founded early-medieval department of NAM. She continued her work on ecclesiastical architecture and was now given a license to carry out archaeological excavations, her publications of what she managed to unearth appearing shortly afterward.

My purpose here is not to present a detailed account of Vera Ivanova's contributions to the study of ecclesiastical architecture as well as to Slavic epigraphy and paleography.[15] However, because Vera Ivanova-Mavrodinova is something of a legendary figure among Balkan archaeologists, I should say a few words about that aspect of her career. In the 1920s, when she became an archaeologist, archaeology was still considered a man's profession, not just in Bulgaria but in Europe as a whole. Women like the American Garrett, who paid a visit to prehistoric sites in Bulgaria in the mid-1930s, were regarded as eccentric. On returning from Paris, however, Vera Ivanova embarked on carrying out excavations without fear of being the first and only woman archaeologist in those parts of the world. Initially she made excavations on some late-antique sites: thus, she excavated and immediately publicized through articles submitted to scholarly journals the early Christian basilicas in Ivaniane (near Sofia), Sofia, Hissaria (in Southern Bulgaria), and elsewhere. Further, she continued her work on cataloging the early Christian monuments in western Bulgaria, which resulted in her "Unpublished Churches of Western Bulgaria."[16]

Vera Ivanova was also interested in the early-medieval capitals of Bulgaria, Pliska and Preslav. It was in 1930 that she paid her first visit to Preslav and even worked briefly as a substitute for Professor Krustijo Mijatev, the chair of the early-medieval department of NAM, who was the person in charge of those excavations. While at Preslav Ivanova worked on the excavation of the basilica in the Gebe-klise area, which had been started by Karel Skorpil in the early 1900s. She also visited Pliska in order to become acquainted with the findings of earlier expeditions headed by Karel Skorpil and Fedor I. Uspensky.

Despite her great interest in the two early-medieval Bulgarian capitals, in the 1930s Ivanova was not able to work there: poor funding was one of the main reasons why the two sites remained insufficiently studied in the interwar period. In 1931 Vera Ivanova married a young employee of the National Archeological Museum and a recent graduate of the University at Liège (Belgium), Nikola Mavrodinov (1904–58).[17] The birth of their daughter, Liliana, in the following year could not distract Ivanova from continuing her work as an archaeologist.

The year 1935 marked the beginning of the internationally sponsored archaeological expeditions in Bulgaria: U.S., German, and Italian teams worked on various sites in the country in the mid- to later 1930s. World War II, however, interrupted the work of archaeologists in Bulgaria and elsewhere in Europe. From December 1943 onward the Anglo-American bombing raids began to inflict serious damage on the nation's capital, Sofia. Rather than leave town, the employees of various museums began working day and night trying to move the museum holdings and documentation to a safer place. Vera Ivanova, too, worked hard for the evacuation of the medieval department at NAM and succeeded in moving its most precious artifacts to the basement of the neighboring Bulgarian National Bank. Eventually a bomb fell on the museum building; another one fell only a few meters away from the bank. Other museums were also destroyed: for example, the National Ethnological Museum, whose holdings had not been evacuated, was completely destroyed.

In September 1944 Soviet troops invaded Bulgaria, which, according to the Yalta agreement, fell into the Soviet zone of influence in postwar Europe. In the new political situation N. Mavrodinov—who was a Communist—became director of the National Archeological Museum. He proved to be an energetic administrator: in those hungry postwar years he managed to find sufficient funding for a renewal of the excavation of Pliska and Preslav. In 1945 Vera Ivanova became the person in charge of the Preslav excavations and dedicated the next twenty years of her life to that site: she retired in 1966.

In 1947 the Bulgarian Parliament passed the Bulgarian Academy of Sciences Reformation Act: BAS was to be remodeled after the fashion of the Academy of Sciences of the USSR. A number of institutes and museums, which had existed as independent institutions before the war, now became part of the Bulgarian Academy of Sciences; also, a series of new institutes was founded. BAS became the nation's center of "fundamental research," that is, a giant research institution with its own Ph.D. programs.[18] In a way this reform gave an impetus to the development of medieval studies: apart from the extensive archaeological work, which was now carried out—and partially funded—by the Academy of Sciences, the conduct of medieval studies was also undertaken by the newly founded Institute of Bulgarian History at BAS. Those two institutes opened for women researchers, thus increasing the number of women in the medievalists' circles.

In 1950 Vera Ivanova-Mavrodinova got her tenure, but, senior research associate or not, she continued to spend two-thirds of the year in Preslav. Her dedication was legendary and has, quite understandably, become part of the student lore. Also, she succeeded in transferring to BAS the property rights over a spacious old building: a former episcopal residence, located in an old walnut-tree park, which was subsequently turned into an archeological base. In 1955, however, its bathing facilities were still under reconstruction, and the archaeology students, architects, and artists, who had arrived from Sofia to work on the site, had nowhere to shower or bathe. Says Professor Vasil Gjuzelev:

> Upon our arrival, I and the late Peiyo Berbenliev were immediately summoned to appear before the archeologist in charge: Mrs. Mavrodinova. It only took a minute or two for us to realize that she was absolutely fascinated with Preslav and regarded it as the cultural nexus of tenth-century Bulgaria. She told us that we would not be allowed to work on the digs unless we familiarized ourselves with all the surviving written sources and the available publications on Preslav. After a week of maniacal reading, Berbenliev and I sat for an oral exam: the jury consisted of Mrs. Mavrodinova herself and her associates. We passed the exam and were admitted into the team, for a period of two months.
>
> With Mrs. Mavrodinova, there never was a problem with work discipline or hygiene. The day we arrived she told us that, because the bathing facilities were under reconstruction, we needed to walk to a Turkish bathhouse, which was located in the nearby town of Preslav, about 3 km away from the site of the medieval town. The bathhouse was owned by some local man, an ethnic Turk, and was the only public bathhouse in the area. During our first conversation, Mrs. Mavrodinova made it clear that our daily visits to that facility were a must.
>
> In the morning, we had to get up at 5 A.M. and walk to the site on which we were currently working. The first month, I worked on the site of the Patleina monastic complex, with its workshops for glazed ceramic tiles. My supervisor was Mrs. Ivanka Akrabova-Zhandova, one of Mrs. Mavrodinova's associates. Every morning, we walked 7 km to Patleina. During my second month on the digs, I worked on a different site: the necropolis of medieval Preslav. There, the archeologist in charge was Stantcho Vaklinov. The idea behind our being moved around from site to site was that college students should get to know about Preslav as much as possible.[19]

By the mid-1950s a number of women had already entered medieval archaeology and art history. Vera Ivanova-Mavrodinova, for example, had several women assistants at the medieval department at AIM, whose chair she was. One of them was Ivanka Akrabova-Zhandova (b. 1901), who, upon getting a doctorate in art history in Rome in the mid-1930s, was appointed an assistant at the National Archeological Museum. When I visited her at her Sofian home in January 2002, Akrabova-Zhandova, already in her nineties, was continuing her work on Preslav's ceramic tiles, preparing some article for publication. Another one of Vera Ivanova-Mavrodinova's associates, Zhivka Vazharova (b. 1916, year of death unknown), with a master's degree in Slavic philology (Sofia University, 1943) and a Ph.D. in Slavic archaeology (the Academy of Sciences of the USSR, 1952), later became chair of the medieval department at AIM (1971). Yordanka Tchangova, the medieval archaeologist, was also one of Ivanova-Mavrodinova's female associates in the 1950s and 1960s.

Unlike medieval archaeology and art history, however, medieval history remained a male-dominated field much longer than any other field in the social sciences and the humanities. Thus, between 1948 and 1965 the total number of doctoral students at the Department of Bulgarian History (which during that period was part of the faculty of philosophy and history at SU) amounted to twenty-seven. Of them, there was only one woman, the late Professor Bistra Tzvetkova, who enrolled in a doctoral program in Ottoman studies (fifteenth–eighteenth centuries), while no woman was enrolled in a medieval studies doctoral program. Both SU and BAS had their first female students enrolled in doctoral programs in medieval history only in the mid- to late 1970s.[20]

Still, in the 1950s and 1960s women used roundabout routes to arrive at researchers' positions in medieval history. Initially it was the translator's venue that granted women access to research. Thus, at the moment it was founded (1947), the Institute of Bulgarian History (since 1960, Institute of History) at BAS had two women with M.A. degrees in classical philology; they were appointed to work on the team whose task was to translate the extant Greek and Latin sources of Bulgarian medieval history. These two women were the late Genoveva Tzankova-Petkova (b. 1913, exact year of death unknown) and Vasilka Tapkova-Zaimova (b. 1924). While the resultant multivolume corpus of the *Fontes historiae Bulgaricae* (FHB) is in itself a major accomplishment with respect to historical scholarship in Bulgaria, the process of its compilation—with all the translation work and the commentaries and references involved—eventually launched the younger people working on that assignment into the higher realm of research and made them eligible for tenured positions. Thus, in 1966 Tapkova-Zaimova published her first monograph: dedicated to the "barbaric" invasions in the Balkans in the sixth and seventh centuries, it remains—to this day—the most authoritative study of the ethnic and demographic changes that took place in southeastern Europe in late antiquity.

In the meantime Tapkova-Zaimova had become the cofounder of another research institute at the Bulgarian Academy of Sciences: the Institute of Balkan Studies (1964), which is truly interdisciplinary. While teaching courses in Byzantine history and literature at several Bulgarian universities, she continued her research at BAS. Among her books the most cited ones are her monograph on Byzantium's Danubian limes in the eleventh and twelfth centuries (Sofia, 1976) as well as the monograph, which she coauthored with A. Miltenova, on Byzantine and Slavonic apocalyptic literature (Sofia, 1996). Here, I cannot afford to recount all her scholarly contributions.[21]

Rather than embark on describing Tapkova-Zaimova's career as an internationally recognized scholar and college professor, it would be wiser, I think, to enclose a few selected passages of her memoirs.[22] They give a fairly good idea of how the Institute of Bulgarian History grew out of a small team initially engaged in the translation of foreign-language sources of Bulgarian history to become a fully fledged research institution; how the establishment of Communism and the so-called ideological debates of the late 1940s and early 1950s affected life in academia; and how a young female assistant felt in the company of older and higher-ranking scholars.

Part 2. The Beginning

VASILKA TAPKOVA-ZAIMOVA, SELECTION AND TRANSLATION FROM BULGARIAN
BY LILIANA SIMEONOVA

I was standing in front of the building of the Bulgarian Academy of Sciences, happy yet not daring to go in. I had just learned that, out of twenty-seven candidates, I was the one selected by the search committee for the junior associate's position—back then we were called assistants, not junior associates—at the newly founded Institute of Bulgarian History at the Academy of Sciences. I had applied for this position out of desperation, not really expecting to get the job, yet hoping to be given a chance to get away from a supervisor whom I feared and despised.

Upon my graduation from Sofia University earlier that year, I had been appointed "candidate-teacher," that is, a student teacher, in Latin at Boys' Gymnasium No. 3 in Sofia. (In Bulgaria, high schools are called gymnasia.) To my ultimate dismay, the school appointed as my supervisor the same man who, in 1940, had fired my father for political reasons. Having spent a lifetime teaching Latin, my father could not get over this and shortly afterward became seriously ill and died.

It was on the following day that I summoned enough courage to go in and sign my appointment papers. That day was 10 December 1947. The Institute of Bulgarian History was a successor to the Committee for the Publication of Sources of Bulgarian History, which had been founded, at the Academy of Sciences, two years earlier. It occupied a single room on the ground floor of what is now BAS-Central.

Initially, there were only four of us who were full-time employees of the institute, the others being "external" (or part-time) fellows. Most of the "externals" were professors at Sofia University who had worked for the Sources Committee prior to its transformation into an institute. By December 1947 some of those professors had already been fired from the university for political reasons. The first director of the institute was Professor Ivan Snegarov, an academician, that is, a full member of the Academy of Sciences. He worked in close collaboration with two other professors, specialists in the classics: Dimitar Detschew (also an academician) and Vesselin Besevliev (a corresponding member of the academy and a former professor at Sofia University who had been fired in 1944 on account of his "bourgeois" views). Mikhail Vojnov, a classicist who was a well-known compiler of classical Greek and Latin dictionaries, was going to be my supervisor.

There was only one other woman on the team: Genoveva Cankova-Petkova, who was some ten or eleven years older than I and who had worked prior to her appointment at the institute as a high school teacher in classical languages. In the course of time the number of the "external" fellows grew, mostly at the expense of people who were professors at Sofia University....

I no longer remember all the minute details of our work, but I clearly remember how the two "editorial staffs" on the team functioned: one of the "staffs" busied themselves with the Latin sources and the other with the Greek ones. It was at some point in 1949 that a third "staff" was assembled. They were called "the Slavonic staff," but their work practically amounted to the translation, into modern Bulgarian, of one single Slavonic source: *The Russian Primary Chronicle.* This translation was never published.

Let me say a few words about our work: it focused on the preparation of bilingual (Latin-Bulgarian and Greek-Bulgarian) editions of medieval sources of Bulgarian history. The members of both "staffs" were real professionals. In about two years we managed to select and translate into Bulgarian an impressive number of excerpts from Medieval Greek and Latin authors. Despite the high quality of our translations, however, nothing was getting published. There were several reasons for that. First, there were the difficulties that stemmed from the new ideological requirements we had to observe. We also had to abide by the ideas propagated by the contemporary Soviet historiography. Thus, in the years 1948–49 in Bulgaria the prevalent tendency was to altogether ignore the Proto-Bulgarians' role in Bulgaria's early medieval history and to exaggerate the Slavs' role at the same time. For example, once there was a formal discussion held at the Academy of Sciences: I do not remember what the main topic of that discussion was, but I vividly remember the discussion itself. Professor Assen Kisselintchev made an emotional speech, "erasing from the face of the earth" all of Professor Besevliev's contributions to the study of the Proto-Bulgarian inscriptions. The atmosphere became even more oppressive when Professor Alexander Burmov took the floor: following the same anti-Proto-Bulgarian line, he insisted on the exclusion from our sourcebook of all passages by the fifth-century historian Priscus that contained direct or indirect references to the Proto-Bulgarians. But how could we eliminate Priscus when those excerpts had already been prepared, by Ivan Dujcev, for publication in volume 1 of the future *Fontes Graeci*? Discussions such as this one brought about uncertainty, fears, and delays.

Still, the greatest difficulties we encountered in the process of our work were of a technical nature. Up to that point nobody in Bulgaria had undertaken the systematic publication of a large corpus of historical sources. Even Vesselin Besevliev and Ivan Dujcev, with all their professionalism, had no experience in the publication of such a *magnum corpus* of sources. Our work was often interrupted by arguments and disagreements that became even more frequent when, a couple of years later, Alexander Burmov came to chair the newly formed Department of Medieval History at the institute. For one thing, the new chair was an argumentative person; for another, he knew nothing about this type of work. Volume 1 of the *Fontes Graeci* appeared only in 1954, with Dujcev as editor-in-chief and Besevliev as a technical editor. I, for my part, wrote a short review of this volume for the *Vetcherni Novini* (Evening news). In the review I called the volume a "significant contribution" to the study of Bulgarian history, but the truth is that we did not even like it: there were typographical errors that had been overlooked by the publisher, we did not approve of the layout of the volume, and so forth. Things became somewhat better only when Mikhail Vojnov took over the organization of the work. He had some experience with the publication of sources because he had worked, together with other colleagues, on the compilation of classical Greek-Bulgarian and Latin-Bulgarian dictionaries. Now we could finally see the big picture of the multivolume corpus that was to be titled *Fontes historiae Bulgaricae* [(FHB)] and that was to include not just Greek and Latin but also Turkish, Hebraic, German, Czech, and other foreign sources of Bulgarian history. (Organized in series according to the original language of the documents, all those volumes of the huge *FHB* corpus later appeared in the book market and sold quite well.)

Along with all the difficulties and disagreements, in those early years we also had some fun. It would be interesting, I think, to mention a few funny stories. For example, one of the current jokes among us originated in the ideological instructions that our coworker Strashimir Lishev had been given "from above": "Medieval sources must be examined through a Marxist ocular."

I have already mentioned Ivan Dujcev's name several times. At that point in time he was not yet formally appointed to our team, although he had submitted several translations to the *FHB*. Eventually his formal appointment was somehow associated with the appearance on the scene of the colorful figure of Vsevolod Nikolaev. Vsevolod liked to title himself a "professor": he claimed that that title had been conferred on him during the war in Italy, but it remained an enigma at which university and in which year he had become a "professor." The important thing was that Vsevolod had "ideas." He had managed to make a great impression on Academician Todor Pavlov, the president of the Bulgarian Academy of Sciences, and had even become something of a protégé of Pavlov's. Vsevolod had also befriended another important figure, Academician Tzvetan Kristanov, the director of the Bulgarian Academy of Sciences Press.

Vsevolod was a big yet very energetic man. One day this person just burst into our room, presenting himself in a few words and handing out several typewritten copies of a paper on the Relief of Madara he had written. He said that the paper needed to be reviewed and subjected to scholarly discussion by the institute's associates in order to get academic approval and be accepted for publication. But the discussion, which was held in the spring of 1948, turned into a quarrel. Vsevolod Nikolaev's thesis was that the Relief of Madara was built by the Persian king Darius, during his campaign against the Scythians in 514 B.C. A detailed account of that discussion, in which the associates of the Institute of Archaeology played the most active part, can be found in Ivan Venedikov's memoirs titled *Know Them by Their Deeds* (Sofia, 1993). Here I would like to give an idea of the general atmosphere in which it was held. Academician Krustjo Mijatev, the archaeologist, spoke in a strictly academic manner, as usual. The other archaeologist, Professor Nikola Mavrodinov, was openly sarcastic. He was followed by Professor Vesselin Besevliev, who spoke unemotionally, presenting his own solid arguments in favor of the Proto-Bulgarian origin of the relief. What I could never forget about that discussion, however, is the "speech" of Vladimir Gueorgiev, the linguist. This polite and very refined man—he had not yet become an academician—made a real show. He demonstrated that, by applying Vsevolod's methods of research to the Greek inscriptions at the bottom of the relief, one could actually read the word "Bucephalus," the name of Alexander the Great's horse; the relief was, therefore, to be considered a work commissioned by no other than Alexander himself. On hearing this, everybody burst into laughter. But the president of the Academy of Sciences, Todor Pavlov, who was getting increasingly annoyed with the discussion, now became furious. In the break he yelled at Vladimir Gueorgiev in my presence.

In the meantime our Institute of Bulgarian History had been moved to Rakovsky Street, in the not-very-spacious apartment above the Institute of Archaeology. To the best of my knowledge, both apartments—the one where we had moved and the other where the archaeologists were—had once belonged to the Filovs.[23] However, we did not have a chance to occupy that apartment very long because Vsevolod came up with another "idea." He did not seem upset by the fact that his paper on the Relief of Madara had been turned down. One day not long after the failed discussion, he came to work and said that he had just been appointed "head curator" (*sic*!) at the Institute of Bulgarian History. But this was not all. Because, at that point in time, the institute could not afford a secretary, Vsevolod ordered the youngest of the associates—that is, me—to sit at the typewriter and start typing. I obeyed. He started dictating a letter to Ivan Dujcev, informing him that he, too, was going to get an appointment at the institute. I do not remember what bureaucratic procedure followed the dispatch of that letter, but I remember that shortly afterward Dujcev became a part-time associate of the institute. Later he became a full-time senior research associate. The whole story of how Dujcev was initially discriminated against by the Communist regime and how he eventually got this appointment at the institute is related in *Historians on Trial* (Sofia, 1995), edited by Vera Mutaftchieva and Vessela Tchitchovska (see esp. p. 385).

But let me go back to the story of the Rakovsky Street apartment. One day not long after we had moved in, "the head curator" Vsevolod said that he did not like the "ambience" that that apartment provided: he was going to find a better place for us. Lo and behold, in no time he managed to find a better "ambience." (Vsevolod Nikolaev was very proud of his French: he had graduated from the college of the Assomptionistes near Plovdiv and often resorted to French words when speaking Bulgarian.) So, we moved again, this time to 21 Marin Drinov Street. It was the second-floor apartment of a beautiful house that had once belonged to a Jew, a well-to-do man, who had been the representative of Osram in Bulgaria before and during the war. (Osram was a producer of electric bulbs.) Upon its owner's emigration to Israel in 1947, the house had been nationalized, and its first floor rented out to the consulate of Turkey. Anyway, not long after we moved in, the first floor was turned into a restaurant of the Council of Ministers and its employees. We could see cabinet members arriving in big cars driven by chauffeurs; some of the cabinet members brought with them canisters for take-outs from the restaurant. On several occasions I could catch a glimpse of the future Prime Minister Vulko Tchervenkov, dressed up in a gray coat and wide trousers, as was then fashionable.[24]

Our moving to 21 Marin Drinov Street roughly coincided with Ivan Dujcev's appointment as a part-time associate. We were very happy to have him on the team because we admired his courageous behavior in the face of Marxists' attacks: several months earlier, during the Meeting of Historians, of which I will tell a little bit later, Dujcev had been severely criticized by Alexander Burmov, mostly on account of his book titled *The Rila Saint and His Dwelling* (Sofia, 1947). At the institute Dujcev was assigned two tasks: to organize the publication of the *Fontes* and to gather material for an economic history of medieval Bulgaria. But as I have already mentioned, things were not going smoothly. Most of the responsibilities were bestowed on us, the younger and less experienced members of the team, while even the older and more experienced members, such as Dujcev, had next to no experience with the publication of medieval sources. The disagreements continued. It was only when volume 1 of *Fontes Latini historiae Bulgaricae* (Sofia, 1958) was published that our work became somewhat more rhythmical and less stressful. . . .

In 1947 the Parliament passed a new Act of the Bulgarian Academy of Sciences. It provided the legal basis for a reorganization of the academy. In the following years the newly established institutes of the academy were reorganized. In 1949/50 the Institute of Bulgarian History, too, underwent certain changes. . . . It now had two departments: the Department of Modern and Contemporary History (with five junior research associates in it) and the Department of Medieval History (with three junior and two senior research associates).

In the summer of 1950 the first doctoral students were enrolled. Dimitar Kossev, then a forty-seven-year-old associate professor, had just become the new director of the institute. Kossev was a kind and soft-spoken man, never saying as much as one rude word to anybody. But he seemed to be well aware of how inexperienced his associates were. One day I heard him speak with one of the few older associates, a man who had been working at the Ministry of Education for many years. Said Kossev, "You must help me, Comrade Lambrev! Can't you see that most of my employees are mere kids?!" I remember one scene at our department that shocked the new director. One day Ivan Dujcev and Vsevolod Nikolaev were having an argument about the Thracians in Late Antiquity. In his characteristically blunt manner Vsevolod was criticizing some article of Dujcev's, while Dujcev was fervently defending his views. Suddenly Vsevolod grabbed a chair and flung it at his friend, but Professor Snegarov managed to intercept the flying chair before it could hit anyone. Then Snegarov succeeded in putting an end to the fight. Director Kossev, who had become an involuntary witness of that scene, just stood there, unable to move or speak. . . .

In the early 1950s the institute continued to grow. I was happy to see other young women being appointed to researcher's positions or enrolled in doctoral programs. As early as 1949 the modern and contemporary history department appointed Elena Dilovska. Two young women of approximately my age were enrolled in that department as doctoral students: first, Tzvetana Todorova and, then, Virginia Paskaleva. Still, the institute remained predominantly male. Not that this mattered: what mattered was people's willingness, or unwillingness, to embrace the Marxist ideas. The institute now had a general, long-term plan of work: apart from the publication of the *FHB*, we had to come up with a two-volume *History of Bulgaria*, covering the period from Antiquity to the end of World War II and the subsequent establishment of Communism. The methodology used was to be that of historical materialism. Also, the institute was to start publishing a periodical: an annual titled *Izvestija na Instituta za Bulgarska Istorija* (Bulletin of the Institute of Bulgarian History). . . .

In the 1950s the practice of relying on the expertise of "external" fellows continued. As before, these were mostly people from Sofia University. They participated in the reviewing and editing of the articles submitted for publication in "the Bulletin" as well as in the work on the two-volume *History of Bulgaria*. Some of them also sat on our academic council, thus participating in the decision making and the employment policies of the institute. But all the contacts between the "externals" and the institute's full-time employees were taking place on the premises of the institute, not in Sofia University. It was considered ideologically unsafe for the young and inexperienced minds of the university students to be brought in touch with some "ideologically disoriented" people who were employed as researchers by the institute (respectively, the Academy of Sciences). I, for example, was labeled "ideologically unreliable": a euphemism for being a non-Communist. They would not let me give a single talk in front of the students at Sofia University. Another "ideologically unreliable" person employed by our institute was Professor Borislav Primov, the medievalist: if I remember correctly, he was kicked out of Sofia University in 1954 but shortly afterward was offered a researcher's position in our medieval studies department.

Speaking of the way in which the new, Communist ideology was being introduced into Eastern European scholarship and higher education, I should say a few words about what we in Eastern Europe call "the years of debate." In our country it was the year 1948 that marked the beginning of this process. The first "debate," which happened to be of the longest duration and which also had the deepest ideological impact on the work of Bulgarian historians, took place during the so-called Meeting of Historians, organized by the Committee of Science, Art, and Culture (March–April 1948). It aimed at setting up the ideological goals that historians in Bulgaria should strive to accomplish in their future work. These so-called goals were drafted by Professor Toushe Vlachov: copies of his paper had been handed out to all participants in advance; those were some large-size sheets of paper, with the text occupying only the right half of the sheet while the left half was left empty, to be filled in with notes. I did fill in the empty spaces with notes, in fine handwriting, practically summarizing the entire debate that followed Vlachov's presentation. Here there is no need for me to refer you to my notes because all the documents related to that debate have already been cited in *Historians on Trial* (pp. 203 ff.). Instead, I would like to give my personal impressions of that "meeting."

It was considered a gesture of goodwill on the part of the organizers that people like me should be allowed to attend it. All the sessions took place in the *aula* of Sofia

University. I attended all of them, squeezed in one corner of the crowded hall. I could overhear the comments that the non-Communist intellectuals, sitting or standing close to me, made in subdued voices. Another segment of my impressions refers to the participants in "the discussion": those were people who considered themselves representatives of "the new [i.e., Marxist] scholarship."

The sessions were presided over by Vulko Tchervenkov, who, characteristically, would not sit still but would jump to his feet every time he had to give the floor to a new speaker. The president of the Academy of Sciences, Todor Pavlov, was often late for the sessions, sat still most of the time, and altogether appeared to disagree with Tchervenkov. In spite of being colleagues who had worked together closely and had even coauthored joint publications in the not-so-distant past, some of the speakers hurled abuse at each other, accusing each other of using an "unscientific" (that is, "un-Marxist") approach to their subject matter. Some spoke in a relatively moderate fashion, while others—such as Nikola Mavrodinov, who had a sharp tongue—were downright sarcastic. (Mavrodinov, however, had his own style: he was a Communist and a "representative of the new scholarship," yet—when volume 1 of *History of Bulgaria* finally came out—he wrote a critical review, arguing that it was professionalism rather than Marxism that was needed for that type of work.)

As I have pointed out, my goal here is not to review and summarize all the critical remarks that were made in the course of that "debate." Suffice it to say that all the historical studies conducted and published before 1947 were said to be suffering from "bourgeois helplessness" on account of the methods used. At the same time the ideological directives that were being drawn were expected to set Bulgarian historiography on new "Marxist rails." Anyway, what seems to have impressed me most about that "meeting"—and continues to strike me as particularly repugnant as I look at the notes I took during its sessions—was the ease with which certain scholars embraced Marxism in order to keep their teaching or researcher's positions.

Another ideological "debate" of those days, which has left a deep impression on me, was the so-called Session of the Archeological Institute with a Museum (1949). This session showed people in an even worse light than the meeting I have just described. In a way I feel sorry for all those colleagues who back then seemed to consider it appropriate to subject their own views and former writings to adverse criticism while fervently making promises for their future work: as an auxiliary historical discipline, archaeology, too, was going to be set on "Marxist rails." As a result the atmosphere in which the "session" was being carried out became so unbearable that the elderly Professor Andrej Protic, who was known as a "big mouth," said, "Now I will make a confession but, for the record, please note that this is not going to be an attempted self-flagellation." . . .

While some of the episodes of those so-called ideological debates may appear funny, the purges that started in the early 1950s were not funny at all. Eastern European academia needed to get its ranks purged of all the "bourgeois elements." Our Institute of Bulgarian History was still occupying that single room on the ground floor of the Academy of Sciences building when we found out that the doorman and his wife, who worked as a cleaning woman, were by far not the only informers whom the Communist secret police had recruited from among the academy's employees. In the Academy of Sciences there was a group of "Robespierres" who openly disagreed with the president of the academy, Todor Pavlov, a man known to all the academy employees as agreeable and unbiased. Scholars who had worked under the previous regime were now labeled non-Marxists and were subject to persecution. One of those scholars, who were fired from the academy without prior notification, was my supervisor, Mikhail Vojnov. In order to survive he started work at a carpenter's workshop. But a year later Academician Pavlov managed to get him back, first appointing him to a part-time position, then restoring him to his full-time senior associate's position.

In those days it was not unusual for an academy employee to not show up at work: people would then start whispering among themselves that this person must have been "summoned to a certain place"; in most cases it only took a day or two for this person to come back to work. But the general atmosphere at the academy was oppressive. Among the names of scholars who were being mentioned as possible "suspects" were those of Academician Stefan Romanski, Ivan Dujcev, and Petar Koledarov (who was then a secretary of our institute). Of course, the associates of the academy had no concrete information about what was going on: it was just rumors. In 1952 my supervisor, Mikhail Vojnov, disappeared too. His wife had no idea what might have happened to him. The funny thing is that, out of the two of us, it was poor inexperienced me who figured out where Vojnov might be and what needed to be done to get him out of there. I called Academician Dimitar Detschew, and he then made phone calls to some "big shots" at the Academy of Sciences; they, in turn, must have called someone else. One way or another, by the evening of the same day Vojnov was released.

The weirdest and maybe the scariest events were, however, associated with our co-worker Vsevolod. At one point in time he disappeared for more than three months— we suspected that he had been arrested—and then he came back and resumed work, without saying a word about where he had been. Sadly smiling, Vojnov would sometimes joke about "Vsevolod's one hundred days." In 1957, under Academician Sava Ganovsky as president of the Academy of Sciences, Vsevolod was fired. A brief note in volume 7 of "the Bulletin" (p. 440) said that Vsevolod Nikolaev had been dismissed from the position of a senior research associate of the institute (respectively, the Academy of Sciences) on account of his fraudulent use of documents, disregard of work discipline, and systematic plagiarism of the works of other medievalists. Vsevolod filed a lawsuit against the Academy of Sciences but before long disappeared again.... Later we heard that he had left the country by secretly crossing the border with Yugoslavia.

By the early 1960s the research activities of the Institute of History, as our institute began to be called, had already resulted in the publication of an impressive number of works that, despite the use of some standard Marxist terms, presented a serious contribution to modern scholarship. These works were being cited by both Bulgarian and foreign scholars. Our medieval studies department too had begun to work in a more productive manner.

By that time the number of associates had increased considerably. We, the younger women at the institute, did not necessarily share the same political views and, as a rule, refrained from openly discussing politics. Nonetheless, we formed a kind of friendly circle. In the course of time, I met—and became friends with—the young historians Tzvetana Todorova, Virginia Paskaleva, Krumka Sharova, Vera Mutafthchieva, and Emilia Kostova, who was the institute's librarian. Only Bistra Tzvetkova, the Ottoman historian, kept her distance from us. In those years even feeding our little children was often a problem. Still, we never talked about the difficulties we encountered in our everyday life. Our conversations focused on the books we had read as well as on our own research and publications. Once Dujcev, who had no children of his own, said, condescendingly, "Your index cards, my dears, are the diapers of your babies." Oh, we did not think so: young and ambitious, we worked hard, and we also helped each other. We even lent one another money when one of us had to make a down payment toward buying an apartment....

In the late 1950s and early 1960s our institute hosted quite a few visiting scholars from the German Democratic Republic, Czechoslovakia, Belgium, and the USSR. Our contacts and our collaboration with the international historians' community were growing. We collaborated with a number of European research centers and were very active in acquiring archival material from other nations' depositories and manuscript collections, while the results of our own research were often published abroad. At the same time a new series of administrative changes was being introduced into the Bulgarian Academy of Sciences. Some of them were initiated by new bills passed by the Parliament; others were the result of decisions made at international meetings. Thus, in 1962, on the initiative of the Romanian UNESCO committee, a meeting of scholars from all the Balkan countries was held in Romania. At this meeting national committees for the promotion of Balkan studies were founded. A little bit later in each Southeastern European country an interdisciplinary research institute of Balkan, or Southeast European, studies came into being. In Bulgaria toward the end of 1963 was founded the Institute of Balkan Studies: its nucleus consisted of former research associates of the Institute of History. When Professor Vladimir Gueorgiev, vice president of the Academy of Sciences, asked me whether I would like to work at the new institute, I replied that I would be happy to. Shortly afterward, our former colleague from the Institute of History, Nikolay Todorov, became director of the new Institute of Balkan Studies, while Professor Vesselin Besevliev and I formed a team whose task was to explore the ethnogenesis of the Balkan nations. Also, a national Balkan Studies Committee was formed, and I became its secretary. These two events marked a new phase in my career and my life.

Notes

1. K. Daskalova, "Women, Nationalism and Nation-State in Bulgaria, 1800s–1940," in *Women's History in Southeastern Europe,* ed. S. Naumovic and M. Jovanovic (Belgrade, 2001).

2. On the Bulgarian feminist movement during the last phase of the National Revival period, see M. Tcholakova, *Bulgarskoto zhensko dvizhenie prez Vuzrazhdaneto (1857–1878)* (The Bulgarian feminist movement during the National Revival Period, 1857–1878) (Sofia: Albo, 1994). On how the basic human rights applied to Bulgarian women in the period between the Russo-Turkish War (1877/78) and the rise of Communists to power, see K. Daskalova, "Smislite na grazhdanstvoto: Grazhdani i grazhdanski prava v Bulgaria (1878–1944)," in *Granici na grazhdanstvoto: Evropejskite zheni mezhdu tradicijata i modernostta* (Boundaries of citizenship: European women between tradition and modernity), ed. K. Daskalova and R. Gavrilova (Sofia, 2001), 226 ff.

3. K. Daskalova, "Feminizum i ravnopravie v bulgarskija XX vek," in *Majki i dushteri: Pokolenija i posoki v bulgarskija feminizum* (Mothers and daughters: Generations and trends in Bulgarian feminism), ed. R. Mukharska (Sofia: Polis, 1999), 80–105.

4. On the women's emancipation and education movement, see *Ot sjankata na istorijata: Zhenite v bulgarskoto obshtestvo i kultura (1840–1940)* (Out of the shadow of history: Women in Bulgarian society and culture, 1840–1940), comp. and ed. K. Daskalova (Sofia: Lik, 1998), 11–41. See also K. Daskalova, "Bulgarian Women in Movements, Laws, Discourses, 1840s–1940s," *Bulgarian Historical Review* 27 (1999): fasc. 1–2, 180–96.

5. K. Daskalova, "Zhenite i bulgarskata knizhnina, 1878–1944," *Annuaire de l'Université de Sofia, Centre de culturologie* (Sofia: Universitetsko Izdatelstvo "Sv. Kliment Okhridski") 86 (1993): 71–93.

6. For example, in the period between 1878 and 1944, 356 women authors appeared in the Bulgarian book market, with a total of 982 titles of books (out of a total of 55,851 titles published in that period). It was, however, in the 1920s and 1930s that the number of women authors marked a considerable growth: statistics show that, while in the forty-year period between 1878 and 1919 there were only 56 women writers, in the following twenty years (i.e., between 1919 and 1939) their number grew to exceed 300. The bulk of their literary production and the prestige it carried also increased. As for the nature of their works, women authors wrote fiction and poetry as well as textbooks and manuals but no scholarly monographs. For further information on women writers and poets, see Daskalova, "Zhenite i bulgarskata knizhnina."

7. R. Donkov, "Sto godini specialnost istorija v Sofijskija universitet," *Annuaire de l'Université de Sofia: Faculté d'Histoire* (Sofia: Universitetsko Izdatelstvo "Sv. Kliment Okhridski") 80 (1992): 5–38; in his study dedicated to the one-hundred-year history of the history department at Sofia University, R. Donkov does not dwell on the problem of enrollment of female students in that department.

8. R. Komsalova, *Socialno-ikonomitcheskite problemi na srednovekovna Bulgaria v bulgarskata medievistika sled Vtorata svetovna vojna* (The socioeconomic problems of medieval Bulgaria in post–World War II Bulgarian medieval scholarship) (Plovdiv: IMN, 2000), 57–58.

9. On the boom of Bulgarian historical-fiction writing in the 1920s and 1930s, see G. Tsanev, *Istoritcheskijat roman v bulgarskata literatura* (The historical novel in Bulgarian literature) (Sofia: Bulgarski Pisatel, 1977); and *Stranici ot istorijata na bulgarskata literatura* (Pages from the history of Bulgarian literature), vol. 4 (Sofia: Nauka i Izkustvo, 1975).

10. Tchavdar Mutafov (1889–1959) was a person of versatile interests: the son of a socialist

publisher, he was a talented architect; also, he was an avant-garde writer who experimented with the techniques of literary expressionism. In terms of literary success, however, he could not compete with his wife, who soon became Bulgaria's favorite historical-fiction writer. On Fani Popova-Mutafova's life, see K. Daskalova, "A Life in History: Fani Mutafova," in *Gender and History*, vol. 14/2 (2002).

11. On Fani Popova-Mutafova as a historical-fiction writer, see B. Kasabova, *Tchudotvorkata: Shtrikhi ot portreta na Fani Popova-Mutafova* (The wonder-worker: A contribution to the portrait of F. Popova-Mutafova) (Sofia: K and M, 2000).

12. Tsv. Trifonova and P. Velitchkov, eds. *Moira: Epistoljarnijat roman na Yana Yazova i Alexander Balabanov* (Mo and Ra: The epistolary romance of Yana Yazova and Al. Balabanov) (Sofia: Akademichno Izdatelstvo "M. Drinov," 1996).

13. In 1948 the museum and the institute merged to become a joint institution, Archeological Institute with a Museum (AIM), which—in turn—became part of the reformed Bulgarian Academy of Sciences. On the history of NAM and AIM, see the Ph.D. thesis proposal of M. Stamenova, "Prinos kum istorijata na AIM kum BAN: dostizhenija i perspektivi (1893–2001)" (A contribution to the history of AIM at BAS: Accomplishments and perspectives, 1893–2001).

14. See *Godishnik na Narodnija arkheologitcheski muzej* (Annual of the National Archeological Museum) 4 (1922–25): 429–583.

15. A list of Vera Ivanova-Mavrodinova's publications is available in the volume published in honor of her eightieth birthday: *Preslav II: Receuil* (Sofia: Dukhovna Kultura, 1976), 10–11. An updated list of her works is available in *Kirilo-metodievska enciklopedia* (Cyrillo-Methodian Encyclopedia), vol. 2 (Sofia: Akademichno Izdatelstvo "M. Drinov," 1995), 40–42. Her last work—a study of Bulgarian medieval manuscript illumination, which she coauthored with her daughter, Liliana Mavrodinova—was published twelve years after her death: see *Cyrillo-Methodian Studies,* vol. 12 (Sofia: Akademichno Izdatelstvo "M. Drinov," 1999).

16. In *Godishnik na Narodnija arkheologitcheski muzej* (Annual of the National Archeological Museum) 5 (1926–31).

17. The future authority on medieval art and architecture, a visiting professor at the Sorbonne (1936–37), a full professor at the Higher Institute of Architecture and Civil Engineering (1953–58) and the Academy of Fine Arts (1955–58) in Sofia, director of the National Archaeological Museum (1944–48), and a corresponding member of the Bulgarian Academy of Sciences (since 1946).

18. St. Bozhkov, V. Vasilev, V. Paskaleva, and Tsv. Todorova, *Istorija na Bulgarskata Akademija na Naukite (1869–1969)* (History of the Bulgarian Academy of Sciences, 1869–1969) (Sofia: Izdatelstvo na BAN, 1971).

19. Professor Gjuzelev shared his memories of Vera Mavrodinova with me in a conversation, in the summer of 2001.

20. Komsalova, *Socialno-ikonomitcheskite problemi,* 57.

21. For the sake of reference, Tapkova-Zaimova's accomplishments are listed in her *Bio-bibliographia* (V. Turnovo: Universitetsko Izdatelstvo "Sv. Sv. Kiril i Metodij," 1985); the list of her publications for the years 1951 to 1995 is available in the volume dedicated to her seventieth birthday: *Obshtoto i specifitchnoto v balkanskite kulturi do kraia na XIX vek* (Common traits and specifics of Balkan cultures until the end of the nineteenth century) (Sofia: Universitetsko Izdatelstvo "Sv. Kl. Okhridski," 1997), 13–38.

22. See V. Tapkova-Zaimova, "Natchaloto," in *Istoritcheski Pregled,* vol. 54 (1998), fasc. 1-2, 51-63. The following excerpts were selected and translated from Bulgarian by Liliana Simeonova with V. Tapkova's permission.

23. Bogdan Filov (1883-1945): professor in archaeology, member of the Bulgarian Academy of Sciences, prime minister of Bulgaria (February 1940-April 1942), regent for the young King Simeon II.

24. Vulko Tchervenkov (1900-1980): a Bulgarian communist who emigrated to the USSR (1925) and, after World War II, returned to Bulgaria to participate in the puppet regime imposed on Bulgaria by the Soviets; prime minister of Bulgaria (1950-56).

SELECT BIBLIOGRAPHY OF WORKS BY VERA IVANOVA-MAVRODINOVA

Kirilo-metodievska enciklopedia, vol. 2. Sofia: Akademichno izdatelstvo "M. Drinov," 1995. 40-42.
Preslav II: Recueil. Sofia: Dukhovna kultura, 1976. 10-11.
With L. Mavrodinova. "Ukrasata na starobulgarskite rukopisi do kraja na XI v." In *Cyrillo-Methodian Studies*, vol. 12. Sofia: Akademichko Izdatelstvo "M. Drinov," 1999.

SELECT BIBLIOGRAPHY OF WORKS BY VASILKA TAPKOVA-ZAIMOVA

Biobibliographia. V. Turnovo: Universitetsko izdatelstvo "Sv. Sv. Kiril i Metodij," 1985.
"Natchaloto." *Istoritcheski pregled* (1998), Fasc. 1-2, 51-63.
Obshtoto i specifitchnoto v balkanskite kulturi do kraja na XIX vek. Sofia: Universitetsko izdatelstvo "Sv. K. Okhridski," 1997: 13-38.

WORKS CITED

Bozhkov, St., V. Vasilev, V. Paskaleva, and Tsv. Todorova. *Istorija na Bulgarskata Akademija na Naukite (1869-1969)*. Sofia: Izdatelstvo na BAN, 1971.
Daskalova, K. "Bulgarian women in movements, laws, discourses, 1840s-1940s." *Bulgarian Historical Review* 27 (1999), fasc. 1-2.
———. "Feminizum i ravnopravie v bulgarskija XX vek." In *Majki i dushteri: Pokolenija i posoki v bulgarskija feminizum*, ed. R. Mukharska. Sofia: Polis, 1999.
———. "A Life in History: Fani Mutafova." In *Gender and History* 14 (2002).
———. "Smislite na grazhdanstvoto: Grazhdani i grazhdanski prava v Bulgaria (1878-1944)." In *Granici na grazhdanstvoto: evropejskite zheni mezhdu tradicijata i modernostta*. Eds. K. Daskalova and R. Gavrilova. Sofia: Lik, 2001.
———. "Women, Nationalism and Nation-State in Bulgaria, 1840s-1940s." In *Women's History in Southeastern Europe*. Eds. S. Naumovic and M. Jovanovic. Belgrade, 2001.
———. "Zhenite i bulgarskata knizhnina, 1878-1944." In *Anuaire de l'Universite de Sofia, Centre de Culturologie*. Sofia: Universitetsko Izdatelstvo "Sv. K. Okhridski," 1973.
———, ed. *Ot sjankata na istorijata: Zhenite v bulgarskoto obshtestvo i kultura (1840-1940)*. Sofia: Lik, 1998.
Donkov, R. "Sto godini specialnost istorija v Sofijskija universitet." In *Annuaire de l'Université de Sofia: Faculté d'Histoire*, 80. Sofia: Universitetsko izdatelstvo "Sv. K. Okhridski," 1992.
Kasabova, B. *Tchudotvorkata: Shtrikhi ot portreta na Fani Popova-Mutafova*. Sofia: K and M, 2000.
Komsalova, R. *Socialno-ikonomitcheskite problemi na srednovekvna Bulgaria v bulgarskata medievistika sled Vtorata svetovna vojna*. Plovdiv: IMN, 2000.

Stamenova, M. "Prinos kum istorijata na AIM kum BAN: Dostizhenija i perspektivi (1893–2001)." unpublished Ph.D. diss.
Tcholakova, M. *Bulgarskoto zhensko dvizhenie prez Vuzrazhdaneto (1857–1878)*. Sofia: Albo, 1994.
Trifonova, Tsv., and P. Velitchkov, eds. *Moira: Epstoljarnijat roman na Yana Yazova i Alexander Balabanov*. Sofia: Akademichno izdatelstvo "M. Drinov," 1996.
Tsanev, G. *Istoritcheskijat roman v bulgarskata literatura*. Sofia: Bulgarski pisatel, 1977.
———. *Stranici ot istorijata na bulgarskata literatura*, vol. 4. Sofia: Nauka i izkustvo, 1975.

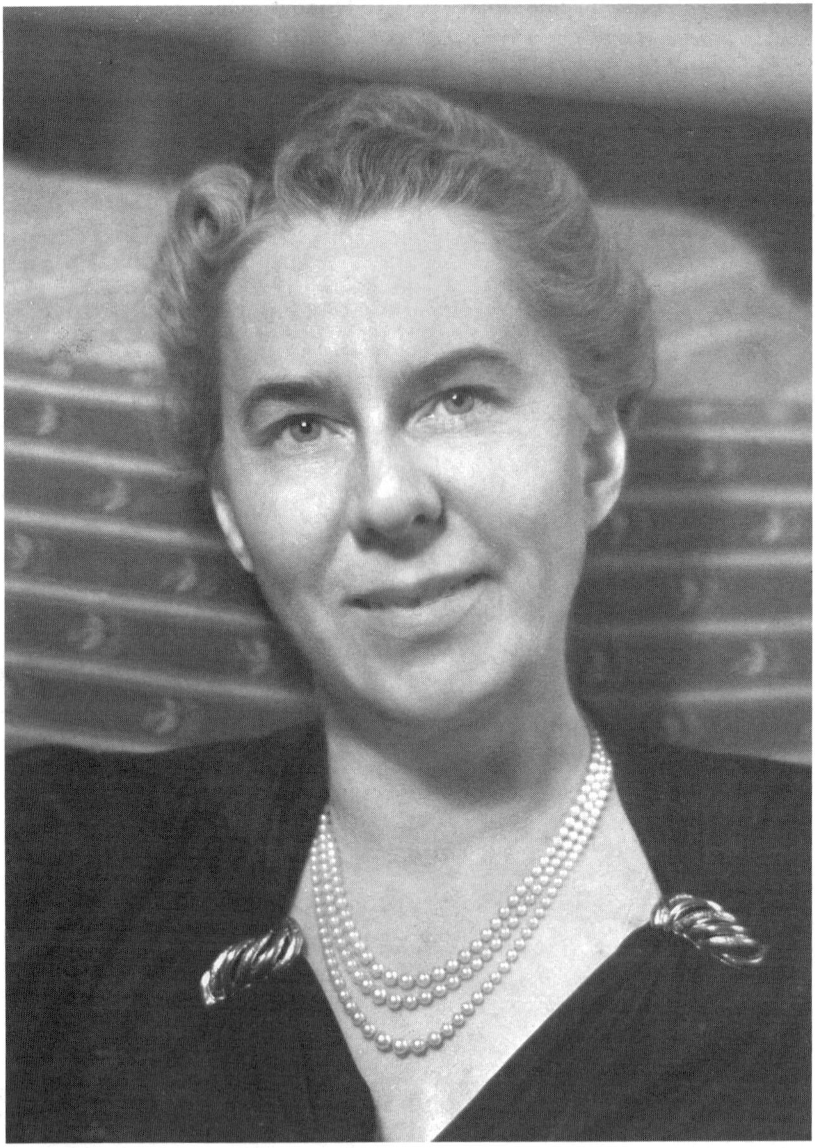

CHAPTER 36

Margaret Schlauch (1898–1986)

Christine M. Rose

PROFESSOR PREFERS IRON CURTAIN LAND

Dr. Margaret Schlauch, N.Y.U. English Instructor,
to Teach at Warsaw University

SHE ASSAILS U.S. POLICIES

Letter to Dean Recalls Happy Years Here and Generous
Treatment on Campus

THUS READ THE INCENDIARY headings on the long, above-the-fold article in section A of the 6 February 1951 issue of the *New York Times.* A smiling and attractive photo of Margaret Schlauch accompanied the piece, with the caption "Leaves N.Y.U. Post."[1] At the time of her resignation, Schlauch had been a professor of English at Washington Square College, New York University, for twenty-seven years, virtually all her scholarly life after her graduation from Columbia with the Ph.D. in 1927. The reporter says that Schlauch "announced her intention to live behind the Iron Curtain and teach at the University of Warsaw."

For myself, familiar with Schlauch's many and diverse admirable works of medieval studies—her *Chaucer's Constance and Accused Queens* (1927) was actually the first piece I remember reading for my dissertation—this glimpse into Schlauch's political life, and what must have been a torturous decision to make, came as a surprise tinged by a good deal of sadness. Hounded by the specter of McCarthyism and the House Un-American Activities Committee's (HUAC) inquisition into her political activism,

Schlauch evaded their subpoena and decamped, seemingly suddenly, for Poland. The university chose to go public in the *New York Times* with her decision to leave in advance of her tending a formal resignation, in order "to forestall its use as Communist propaganda." In a letter quoted in that *Times* article written from Stockholm to Oscar Cargill, chair of New York University's English department, subsequent to her flight, Schlauch speaks of her anguish about having to resolve—perhaps forever—to flee to Poland: "I am very aware, of course, that in the present phase of world history my transfer to Poland may mean an irrevocable step; at least a long absence until international affairs have ameliorated (through what intermediary stages one hesitates to contemplate). Awareness of this has torn me in a manner difficult to describe." The newspaper quotes more of her letter under the heading, "Cites Her Marxist Stand": "I am afraid that the economic and political future at home is not auspicious, not even for a Chaucer specialist, if such a person has been and still is a Marxist (no matter how undogmatic) and doesn't intend to deny it: and if she moreover condemns the foreign policy leading to war for the control of Asia through Chiang Kai-shek, and feels an obligation, sooner or later, to engage in active opposition to that policy." Yet, despite her beliefs in the wrong-headedness of American foreign policy, beliefs that would soon surely have been maligned by HUAC and used against her in her academic position, and despite her securing a position at a prestigious Eastern European university, Schlauch's decision was not without its attendant sorrow: "Now comes the part that is hardest to write, because I have to take time out and dry my eyes between sentences. I have been so very happy at N.Y.U.! I can't begin to say how grateful I've been for the generous treatment I've received. As I look back, I recall so much happiness for my work and my associations that I cannot possibly do justice to it in words."

When asked to comment for the *New York Times* about Schlauch's defection, Thomas C. Pollack, dean of Washington Square College, offered that "Miss Schlauch was a good teacher of Anglo-Saxon and philology" (the "Miss" is disconcerting). He noted students never complained "that she had injected her political opinions into her classroom lectures." Pollack declares to his interviewer that "under our American system of academic freedom, no disciplinary action was taken against her because of her political beliefs as long as there was no evidence that they interfered with her scholarship and classroom teaching." But, says Pollack, his remarks taking on perhaps a disdainful tenor, "We will be interested in this 'Journey for Margaret' and we will be interested to learn whether in years to come she will enjoy equal freedom at the University of Warsaw as a teacher there." The *New York Times* reporter observes that Schlauch had worked for the War Department during World War II preparing a manual of Icelandic. And, he says, Schlauch had been "one of a score of public school and college teachers accused of Communist leanings during the Rapp-Coudert committee's investigation of subversive activities in the city school system in 1941. At that time she replied [to the investigators] that 'I am not and never have been a member of the Communist Party.'"

At age fifty-two Schlauch, medievalist/Marxist/feminist, was starting her life over, a pariah to some, a heroine—I imagine—to many, living by her convictions, a victim of the Cold War. She remained an active and prolific scholar (at least 140 publications in her lifetime), lionized in Poland and regularly included in publications such as the *Who's Who of American Women, 1958–59; Who's Who in Socialist Countries, 1978, 1979;* or *Who's Who in the World, 1974–75.*[2] From 1954 to 1975 she was a member of the editorial board of *Kwartalnik Neofilologiczny.* She continued to produce during her Polish years the kind of rigorous scholarship in medieval studies, comparative literature, and linguistics that characterized her New York University period.

Joining the Polish Communist Party soon after her arrival in Poland, Schlauch took up her position teaching English in Warsaw, and from all accounts, throughout her subsequent career she was respected by her colleagues and beloved of her students for her rigorous intellect and munificence of spirit. In 1954 Schlauch became head of the Department of English and retained this position until her retirement in 1965. She also headed the Department of General Linguistics from 1954 to 1956. Her Polish students found her enthusiastic and her classes lively and inspiring. Professor Jacek Fisiak recalls that during his days as a graduate student she was generous with her time and egalitarian, always ready to include him, even when he remained tongue-tied with awe in lunches and conversations she was having with important scholars.[3] Fisiak says indeed her benevolence extended to subscribing on her own to English and American journals, then turning them over to the university library for student use when the library could not afford them, as well as regularly lending or giving her own books to students.

The Polish Academy elected her a corresponding member in 1961. A festschrift was published on the occasion of the fortieth anniversary of the beginning of her scholarly career (1966), to which prominent American, British, Polish, Icelandic, Welsh, Scottish, Japanese, Hungarian, Dutch, Czech, Soviet, and German linguists and medieval literary scholars contributed.[4] Fisiak says of her, "She has educated several generations of Polish anglicists and has laid the foundations for modern studies of English in Poland."[5] Schlauch remained part of the international medievalist scholarly community, retaining active membership in professional organizations like the Modern Language Association, the Society for the Advancement of Scandinavian Studies, the American Association of University Women (AAUW), and the Medieval Academy, journeying to the United States on various occasions to lecture or study. She visited at Vassar in 1968 and the University of Connecticut in 1970, where she taught undergraduate medieval literature and graduate Anglo-Saxon courses. But she never returned to live in her home country. Summers she often spent in research at the British Museum.[6] She remained unmarried all her life, although with a circle of family, former students, and friends who regarded her warmly. From the evidence of what few letters of hers survive, she suffered what must have been a stroke in 1974 that gradually made her more housebound and dependent upon a cane and outside helpers.[7] The letters from her later years show her, in probable deference to the ever-present censors, still supporting her decision to reside in Poland and even including admiring words about the general in power in the 1980s, hopeful he would solve the problem of shortages and long lines for even the most ordinary food staples, like bread, butter, and sugar.[8] Despite the dreadful winters of which she complained and her days circumscribed by her infirmities and lack of Western comforts, her letters remained upbeat.[9] Schlauch kept up her reading, writing, and reviewing into her eighties; she died in Warsaw in 1986 at age eighty-eight. Grateful former student Fisiak—since he left Warsaw University, both minister of education and president of Adam Mickiewicz University in Poznan, where he is now head of the School of English—gave the eulogy at her funeral on behalf of the scholarly community in Poland. Sadly, no one from her department at Warsaw came to represent the colleagues there to honor her and speak of her scholarly achievements on that rainy morning in July.

McCarthyism deprived the United States and the West of Schlauch's learned contribution in any conversation about the relationship of Marxism to medieval literature. Her removal to Poland and her apparent censorship and surveillance by Polish authorities surely kept her from any real dialogue in print about politics and literary study. U.S. scholarship and medieval studies of the 1950s, 1960s, and 1970s were impoverished because her voice as a member of the academic establishment was so effectively silenced by the events of 1951. It would have been interesting to see, had HUAC never happened, what turn her medieval scholarship might have taken: Would it have been more political, or not? As it was, her academic writings during her time at New York University as well as during her Communist years in the East display her Marxist philosophy only tepidly, despite what was, at least in New York, a life filled with socialist activism. According to Annette Rubinstein, former student and fellow activist, Schlauch was in her New York University days "the dynamic center of an informal Marxist study group." Moreover, she took on the chairmanship of the Greenwich Village American Labor Party, a group that included among its membership local longshoremen.[10] Her writings for the Marxist journal *Science and Society*, to which I will turn later, reflect a more fervent and doctrinaire Schlauch, evincing admiration for Soviet society and Marxist principles as applied to literary, historical, and linguistic study. It is clear from looking at her life that, aside from her accomplishments as a medievalist and linguist, Schlauch was always a feminist, ardently in favor of women's rights, and in light of her Marxist beliefs, she championed the rights of workers and oppressed peoples everywhere.[11]

Born in Philadelphia on 25 September 1898, the daughter of an Irish Catholic mother (who later abandoned her church altogether) and a "freethinking German professor," Margaret Schlauch was educated at Barnard College (A.B. 1918) and Columbia (A.M. 1919, Ph.D. 1927).[12] During her graduate studies she spent a year at the University of Munich (1923–24) on the Anna C. Brackett Fellowship from the American Association of University Women.[13] This represents a distinguished record for a young woman in the 1920s. She taught high-school English from 1920 to 1923 at Theodore Roosevelt High in New York, and in 1924 New York University hired her as an instructor, promoted her to assistant professor in 1927, associate professor in 1931, and granted her full professorship in the English department in 1940, where she taught until her resignation and flight in 1951. One summer she spent as visiting assistant professor of German at the University of Chicago (1937) and another as visiting associate professor of English at the Johns Hopkins University (1939). Perhaps the most important year for her scholarship, 1929–30, she spent as a Guggenheim fellow. Her official listing was as a fellow in German literature, but indeed her year abroad was one crammed with language and manuscript study that far exceeded the epithet of "German literature."

On her application to the Guggenheim Foundation, when asked for her language proficiency, Schlauch describes her abilities thus: "I can read, write and speak: French, German. I can read and speak: Dutch, Italian, Danish. I can read: Latin, Greek, Hebrew, Old Icelandic (and other early Germanic dialects such as Gothic, Old English, Middle High German and early Flemish)." In a later correspondence (1932) with the foundation she recounts how she learned Swedish and Norwegian: "Since I approached these languages from a background in Old Norse, my only aids were a tutor [for elementary instruction], a reader, and a dictionary. After that I began to read Ibsen." This marvelous linguistic expertise—attested to in her recommendation letters and by her subsequent career, which showcased her daunting language skills—is surely what gave her the ease to work with the Icelandic sagas (which some scholars say is her most important work), Chaucer, folklore, manuscripts of ancient texts, and Old and Middle English works, to name only a few of the areas of her wide expertise (see the select bibliography accompanying this essay).

At the time of her application to the foundation in 1928, she was already a productive scholar of serious proportions, having published her dissertation on the *märchen* and romance analogues of Chaucer's "Man of Law's Tale," *Chaucer's Constance and Accused Queens,* with New York University Press in 1927. This book, well reviewed when it appeared and since reprinted, continues to be cited in virtually every scholarly piece on "The Man of Law's Tale." Other publications she notes on her application are her second book, *Medieval Narrative: A Book of Translations* (1928), and seven articles, dating from 1923 to 1928, including pieces in *Publications of the Modern Language Association (PMLA),* the *English Journal, Romanic Review,* and *Germanic Review.* Her "Statement of Work Already Done" justifying her need for the fellowship reinforces the awesome breadth and depth of her scholarship. As I read all this, I was forced to remind myself that this was a woman only one year past the Ph.D.! In the years she spent at Columbia (1918–27), she specialized in medieval comparative literature and Germanic philology, working with Professor George P. Krapp (of Krapp and Dobbie) among other notable teachers, in her Old and Middle English studies. During 1923–24 at the University of Munich on the AAUW fellowship, she studied palaeography, which she made good use of in her work with manuscripts in a multitude of European libraries during that year and during the subsequent Guggenheim period of 1929–30.

The project she proposed for the year of her Guggenheim grant was "Folklore in the Icelandic Sagas: An Investigation of the Survivals of Primitive Superstition and Belief in the Medieval Literature of Iceland." Her application states that she intended to conduct, mainly in the Royal Library at Copenhagen, using rare manuscripts and printed books, a "scientific study of the field—a large part of which has never been treated," to discover "traces of primitive thought-ways, such as belief in sympathetic magic, external soul, witchcraft, spirits of nature (Naturdämonen), other-worldly creatures, and the like" and to recover information about early native Scandinavian myths and folklore not studied previously. She was interested in demonstrating how foreign models (French, Celtic) were adapted to Scandinavian tradition and fashioned into folklore in the lesser Icelandic romantic sagas. It is essentially a sources-and-analogues study of a complex sort, requiring her to learn Celtic—which she did in Berlin—as she was convinced of the Irish literary influence on Icelandic. She wanted "to put at the disposal of students of folklore the material at present buried in these obscure texts," to be of significance to "anyone who would understand the more primitive antecedents of our own attempts at thinking" about our world.

Schlauch received overwhelming endorsements for her work from the nine (!) letters of recommendation for the foundation. Her recommenders included both her supervisors at Columbia and prominent scholars such as Carleton Brown of New York University. Their letters—some quite lengthy—included such testaments as "wide learning, sound judgment, and great industry," "intense eagerness," "ideal candidate," "abundantly demonstrated" scholarship, "excellent," "unreserved recommendation," "distinguished scholarly investigation," "the most promising scholar in my department," "the most brilliant linguist," "stimulating influence upon her associates," "very highly developed eagerness," "unusual linguistic discipline," "competent and important" plan of study, "one of the most remarkable women I have ever met," and must have made her a shoo-in for the grant. A letter says, "I cannot speak too highly of Miss Schlauch's thoroughness as a scholar or of her indefatigable ambition in literary research," and another observes how his (the writers were all men) high hopes for her future achievement have "since been more than realized." In fact, besides acknowledging her brilliance, admiration for her "industry," "enthusiasm," or such like assets stands as the most common likeness among the recommenders' letters. One also says, rather sweetly, "In manners and appearance, she is a charming lady and will be an excellent representative abroad of American culture." On the foundation's part, Henry Allen Moe, then the chief executive, declares in a later correspondence, "[T]here never was a doubt in our minds about Miss Schlauch." It is relevant to note that of the sixty-three fellowships granted in 1929, only eight were awarded to women (although the names of a few candidates do not disclose their gender).[14]

Subsequent to her receipt of the grant monies of twenty-five hundred dollars, a considerable sum in 1929 dollars, Schlauch's early correspondence with the Guggenheim Foundation evinces a tone of wonder and rejoicing at the riches she has been enabled to study. Her messages are charming, energetic, and gracious. A letter from Berlin of 11 October 1929 to Moe speaks of her delight in her summer's work in the

Royal Library in Copenhagen and of the warmth of the Danes (as opposed to the Berliners she was then among). Significantly, she recounts her first visit to Russia in June of that year, and of her imagination's refusal to "envisage so different a civilization and to accept it as real." She also describes her admiration of the history and art of Russia, her appreciation of the bravery of the Russian people, who had been through so much "war, famine, terror, and civil strife," and notes an all-too-brief meeting with a professor who was working on Marxism and Hegelian philosophy. It may be that this vision of the brave Russian revolutionaries and the fledgling state's hopes sustained her in her decision to remove to the Communist East in 1951. Certainly, admiration of the Russian system figured large in her later writings for *Science and Society*. Near the end of the 1929 letter, mentioning the report of her work so far, which she must soon send to the foundation, she enthuses, "I could write two reports: one formal, one lyrical."

The formal "First Report to the J. S. Guggenheim Foundation" (November 1929), a meticulously handwritten document, manifests Schlauch's ardor for studying Old Welsh and philology in Berlin with Professor J. Pokorny, who, in his own report to the foundation in 1930, calls her "a very gifted and diligent student . . . using her time well." She also undertook private lessons in Old Irish to supplement her study of foreign influences on Old Icelandic literature. Her report recounts the wonderful finds of as-yet-unedited and perhaps unknown sagas in the Copenhagen Royal Library to which she yearns to return. Again, she profusely thanks the foundation for its generosity in giving her a scholarly opportunity, time to explore ancient Denmark and to absorb the culture of Germany. Succeeding reports (February and May 1930) show her still hard at work on her study of philology and the saga materials. As her year ended, she journeyed to Iceland for a month, and continued to discover formerly unknown sagas (*lygisögur*). The six-page handwritten final report of August 1930 details the results of what she terms an incredibly fruitful year of scholarship. Schlauch found that her work revealed, at least in part, the debts of the Icelandic sagas to classical antiquity, to French romances and to Celtic influence, and manifested connections with the Orient. These areas were the focus of what she intended to pursue (and did indeed pursue) in her subsequent scholarly research, because she wanted "to emphasize the significance of the lygisögur as sources for the study of medieval thought and culture," in order to clarify what she sees as a "little-regarded period" in Scandinavia. She mentions her gratitude to the foundation for the time in Iceland, since she had the chance to speak the language, thereby feeling closer to the sagas. She ends her last report with "It has been the richest year of my life."

Schlauch continued her correspondence with Moe and the foundation for a dozen years or so. The last letter in the archive is dated 1943. In the archives are attestations of Schlauch's achievement in her year off such as a letter to the foundation (1931) written by Columbia University professor E. H. Wright, praising a lecture given by Schlauch on her research as impressive scholarship and "remarkable." Schlauch herself reports in 1931 of two forthcoming articles arising from her research, in *PMLA* and *Journal of English and Germanic Philology*.[15] Her book *Romance in Iceland* (1934), a highly praised work on early Icelandic literature, was the result of her Guggenheim Fellowship year and established her as a, if not *the,* world authority. The foundation occasionally asked her to referee applications for fellowships during the 1930s and early 1940s, and in 1943 she recommended one of her own Ph.D. students, Lillian Hornstein, for a fellowship, along with a colleague at *Science and Society,* Samuel Bernstein.[16]

Even early in her career Schlauch was a masterful, surely dazzling, teacher. Her Guggenheim recommenders, in documents from the archive, comment on aspects of her teaching at New York University in 1929: "She comes close to being the best teacher in the department"; "She is the kind of teacher whom students follow out of the class room eager to get more, and while she is at her desk she is usually in conference with some student or discussing some problems of scholarship with another member of the department." Her approach to teaching was said to be filled with "genuine buoyancy and delight in the task," and her students speak of her "in the highest terms." From the documents I was able to obtain, it is clear (and odd) that at some time during the 1940s and certainly in 1943 Schlauch was teaching mathematics, since she complains to Henry Moe of the hampering of her research because "I am teaching mathematics much of the time—but I still use my summers for medieval studies."[17] *The Gift of Tongues* (1942), her book on the study of linguistics for a nonspecialist reader, had just been published, so teaching outside her area had not wholly restricted her writing and research.

One of the most intriguing pieces in Schlauch's oeuvre emanating from her political beliefs appeared in 1935, in response to the rise in Germany of the fascist Aryan-superiority movement. Schlauch wrote for the Anti-Fascist Literature Committee of New York a thirty-page pamphlet, *Who Are the Aryans?*, a sincerely-felt work deploring racial hatred of all kinds. Schlauch writes to demystify the term "Aryan" as used by the Nazis to designate the Germans as the master race and thus other races as inferior, a classification that they used to justify taking jobs away from Jews and putting them in concentration camps, leading to, of course, the terrible consequences of that racial hatred, the Holocaust. She introduces her argument by saying, "Anyone who understands the real causes of racial hatred and race persecution must wish to fight against them. But to do so, he must know better than those people who are deceived into hatred. He must be able to refute lies and misstatements; he must be able to tell what the words really mean."

Knowledge of terminology, says Schlauch, is power to rout xenophobic thinking. The pamphlet in most sane and clear language, for the nonspecialist, explains the origins of the term "Aryan," which Schlauch points out is a language term, not a racial term. She discusses the geographic locales that may have given rise to such a language and notes the impossibility of scholars (let alone the Nazis) ever being able to designate any people now living as the pure descendants of such a race so widely dispersed and whose origins are so disputed by anthropologists and linguists. Carefully and clearly Schlauch outlines the study of language families like Indo-European (Aryan) and claims that the speakers of the earliest language were not likely all of the same racial background, since some peoples would speak the language of their conquerors or neighbors without sharing, perhaps, facial shape, skin, or hair color. She also debunks the Nazi use of the swastika as "purely Aryan," saying, "[T]he claim is, however, an absurd mistake" (13), since the motif was found in India long before any speakers of ancient Sanskrit (the Aryan language of the north) had reached that country. The piece is both scholarly in its evidence and written at a level to convince any literate reader of its authority. It begins with a denunciation of capitalism as the root of racial hatred: the real enemies are those who oppress the people economically, giving rise to their lashing out at the innocent because they do not know the real cause of their suffering. She scoffs at imagining such a thing as a superior or inferior race: "There is almost no scientific evidence to support the claims made daily by this or that section of the white family of races for the position of highest in talent and ability. When such claims are made, they are usually a result of ignorant prejudice" (27). Her words are poignant, and the material she wrestles with, of course, still relevant. The work ends idealistically, with a paean to the possibility of a (Marxist) state from which all racial hatred, exploitation, and pogrom mentality has been removed, when all individuals develop to the level of which they are capable and contribute their talents to the good of the state. *Who Are the Aryans?* combines Schlauch's talents in linguistics and her lucid style in the service of her political beliefs.

Her other overtly Marxist writings were in the journal *Science and Society (S&S)*. While at New York University, Schlauch became one of its founding editors. The journal's inaugural issue of 1936–37 describes itself as "dedicated to the growth of Marxian scholarship," demonstrating how "Marxism integrates the various scientific disciplines and illuminates the interdependence of Science and Society." Early volumes intended to include articles by those who have "accepted and applied Marxian principles to their research" and those who are "exploring its possibilities."[18] Deploring academics' disregard of Marxist methodology, the editors strove to remedy "the pointed neglect of Marxist theory in scholarly circles, the easy disparagement, distorting and shunting to footnotes of a movement of such importance" (ii). Schlauch was an editor and contributor to the journal for fifteen years, until her defection in 1951. Among the first editors of *S&S* was Edwin Berry Burgum, also of New York University, who shortly after Schlauch's defection was dismissed from his job after a faculty committee hearing concerning his refusal to answer U.S. Senate subcommittee queries on his Communist Party ties. He was "the first tenured faculty member at a private college to fall victim to the cold war witch hunt."[19] Schlauch's contributions to the journal were doctrinaire scholarly pieces, ranging from a study of recent Soviet linguistics, to a Marxist analysis of the English Peasant's Revolt of 1381, to the language of James Joyce, to Soviet folklore. She also supplied book reviews and overt political pieces on Scandinavia, Soviet historiography, and semantics as "social evasion" (see the select bibliography for some of her *S&S* articles). Throughout her sincere and relatively idealistic essays she advocates the importance of the literary scholar acting within his or her community and the interconnection between theory and practice, between the intellectual and the ordinary worker. She especially lauds Marxism as a flexible and realistic doctrine adaptable to "the traditions and historical conditions of each people," and she claims that it endeavors to transform human irrationality into rationality. Her praise of the Soviet system's version of Marxism, now proven so horribly flawed, is that it "offers the clearest example of a prideful and solicitous development of national cultures."[20] Writing of the revolt of 1381 in England, she argues, invoking Engels, that only when viewed through the lens of historical materialism does one find a "coherent interpretation of these baffling events" in which an odd coalition of classes of workers and aristocrats united against feudal strictures.[21]

The variety and number of published works over the long course of Schlauch's career is formidable. Many of her works were reprinted and translated and are still consulted by scholars. Intellectual curiosity and clarity of mind characterize her style. A selection from her corpus, focusing especially on her work as a medievalist, is here appended as a select bibliography. Her most important contributions seem to me, as a medievalist, to be her discoveries of new sources or analogues of various English medieval narratives. The study of sources, influences, and analogues remains a vital tool of medieval literature scholars, and Schlauch found folktale sources or analogues for tales of Chaucer, for Icelandic Eddas, for Old English poetry, and for other works. But her expertise was not limited to this type of study, nor would scholars today agree on which was her most significant work. There was so much! She published on topics in education and pedagogy while she taught both in the United States and later in Poland. Her bibliography reflects an extensive linguistic expertise, and her books include translations into English of Norse sagas and Icelandic narratives. She wrote on an array of medieval subjects besides Chaucer, such as Arthurian legends, Wycliffe, romances, *Beowulf*, Old Scandinavian rhetoric, Thomas Usk, Lydgate, and Skelton. But she threw a wider net too, publishing on James Joyce, Sherwood Anderson, Emily Dickinson, Hollywood slang, folklore topics, the antecedents of the English novel, and the history of the English language. Especially during her Polish years, when her students studying English would have needed them, she produced volumes of a more general nature, surveying English medieval literature, English poetry, or the study of the English language. Aside from her famous work on Constance, her excellent specialist-medievalist articles, and her much-praised work on the sagas, it is her book *English Medieval Literature and Its Social Foundations* (1956) that makes a lasting contribution to scholarship. Though some of its historical analyses may be dated, this book is one to learn from, and I recommend it to students who need an overview of the period, of both its literature and its historical context. Written during the aftermath of wartime, when she could not even travel to libraries to confirm her citations were accurate and to obtain the illustrations she wanted, this volume nonetheless stands as a clearly written, cogent, engaging panorama of medieval literature, of both its familiar works and some that *should* be familiar but are not.[22] Although she addresses the book to "students and amateurs" of the field, even experienced medievalists would do well to peruse it for its scope and inclusiveness. In her foreword, Schlauch characteristically laments the "cult of medievalism" used for political purposes, such as to justify "the fascist corporate state in Italy," or "medieval orderliness" used as an escapist strategy from present anxieties (xv). She encourages readers to see the period without the veil of either academic enthusiasm or skepticism about a barbarous age.

Of course, it is apparent that, as Sheila Delany observes, Schlauch's study of the exiled innocent queens in romances, such as Chaucer's Constance in "The Man of Law's Tale," has eerie echoes for her own life lived in exile, sent away by a tyrannous regime, her virtue sorely tried—even though the accusation against Schlauch was not exactly false. She herself, however, did prove as constant in her convictions as was Constance. Unlike Constance, however, Schlauch did not make the round trip back home but remained an expatriate. At least at first Schlauch may have been lonely in Poland. She relocated knowing that her sister Helen, who had married Leopold Infeld, a physicist and student of Einstein's and who was associated with the Los Alamos project, was there.[23] Suspected of spying, Infeld was now a Polish resident. So, there was some familial support system for her in Warsaw. But, despite her linguistic agility, she did not know Polish at first well enough to use it at official meetings, and, as an outsider, a Communist with a distinguished research record, she had to have been the object of jealousy. With academic qualifications superior to any Polish professors, she was quickly made head of the department. Was she better, or just a showpiece of the Communist Party? could have been the attitude of her colleagues when she arrived in Warsaw. Some were Poles whose declarations of party loyalty might have been convenient, though not entirely sincere. Certainly, some felt that the plum job of a professorship should have been given to a Pole. Her status as a female administrator—not the norm—plus her idealism and enthusiasm for the system were certainly reasons for suspicion from people in the ranks, while her preferment to a professorship, richly deserved or not, was bound to gnaw. Her move from a nation enjoying a high standard of living to one of some deprivation, where she might not have accepted the life the Communist Party insisted on, could also have caused questioning of her sincerity.[24] And after all, as a foreigner, even though a party member, she was certainly under police scrutiny at all times and subject to arrest for the least violation of allegiance. Rubinstein notes in her obituary of Schlauch for *Science and Society* that it was five years before any invitation to a meal or to their homes was tendered by colleagues, although after a time she became as popular with her associates as she had been at New York University.

Schlauch was provided with a pleasant apartment in Old Town Warsaw with a balcony overlooking the Vistula River, but it was not a luxury unit. The unpretentious building housed many workers, and the apartment was small. A modest state pension supported her from her retirement in 1965 until her death in 1986. In her last extant letter to the Robbinses (5 February 1982), she waxes poetic, and medieval, over her view: "I look forward to the warm days when I'll be able to sit out on my balcony and look over the fabulous Vistula River. It may be less impressive than the Hudson—but what history it has seen!... I can imagine the Vikings sailing down it in the early Middle Ages, en route to Russia." After her death, the new tenants of her apartment sold all her books and destroyed or discarded her papers. Little trace remains of Schlauch or her life there.[25]

The 22 July 1986 obituary in the *New York Times* remarks that Schlauch was an "American scholar who left the U.S. in 1951 saying she wished to avoid persecution for pro-Communist views." She "often voiced pro-Soviet sympathies in the 1930's and was among New York City public school and college teachers accused of Communist leanings in 1940. At that time she said she had not been a member of the Communist Party." Among her accomplishments the obit mentions *The Gift of Tongues* and her award from the Polish government, the Order of Reborn Poland (Polonia Restituta). But there was so much more. She was brilliant, courageous, and interesting. Her groundbreaking scholarship in medieval studies and linguistics is her lasting legacy. Her life story, even as little as I discovered, has made her even more estimable to me as a feminist, a medievalist, a person of convictions who lived by them, and a woman scholar to emulate. I wish I had known her.

Notes

Thanks are due to Sheila Delany, who suggested that I write this chapter on Margaret Schlauch. Delany's own piece in *Medieval Feminist Forum* inspired my interest in Schlauch's biography. She generously provided encouragement and important materials about Schlauch for my research, also seeing to it that I was invited to the symposium in Poznan, a distinction I greatly appreciate and a valuable intellectual experience I will not forget. Seeing Schlauch's adopted homeland and speaking to a few who knew her provided invaluable background. Thanks also to Jane Chance, the editor, for her patience, for her good humor, and for the marvelous idea for this volume honoring our medievalist "mothers." Portland State University provided essential travel monies for my trip to Poland. As always, my husband, John Coldewey, was a sounding board for my ideas and an insightful reader of my prose. I offer this essay to honor the memory of Margaret Schlauch.

1. The photo accompanying this essay is the one that appeared in the *New York Times*. Reproduced courtesy of New York University Archives.

2. References to Schlauch are also found in *The International Who's Who* (1974–83); *Index to Women of the World* (1970); *International Authors and Writers Who's Who*, 8th and 9th eds. (1977–78); *Literary Exiles in the Twentieth Century*, ed. Martin Tucker (New York: Greenwood, 1991); and other works citing notable persons in their fields.

3. See Jacek Fisiak's account of Schlauch's Polish scholarly life in "Obituaries of Distinguished Scholars." I am indebted to his essay for factual material presented here about Schlauch's time at Warsaw and grateful to Fisiak for his conversations with me about Schlauch's life, from his perspective as a former student and scholarly colleague. With Sheila Delany of Simon Fraser University, Fisiak organized in 12–15 May 2002 an international symposium to honor Schlauch's scholarship: "Medieval Literature, Languages, and Culture: A Symposium in Memory of Professor Margaret Schlauch (1898–1986)" at Adam Mickiewicz University in Poznan, Poland, sponsored by the School of English there. The papers, all of which had some overt or implicit link to Schlauch's work, ranged from technical linguistic analyses to literary readings,

from feminism to historicism to Marxism—critical approaches both traditional and modern that Schlauch might have been delighted to hear from. The scholars present all had benefited in one way or another from Schlauch's pioneering and multitudinous writings on the language and literature of the Middle Ages. Fisiak and Delany created a fitting memorial indeed. As a member of the symposium, I know there was much important contact there between American, Australian, Polish, and other Eastern European scholars, representing the two geographical halves of Schlauch's career, finally united in dialogue.

4. Brahmer, Helsztynski, and Krzyzanowski, eds. *Studies in Language and Literature in Honour of Margaret Schlauch.*

5. Fisiak, "Obituaries of Distinguished Scholars," 293.

6. Obituary by Annette T. Rubinstein, friend, fellow activist, editor of *Science and Society*, and former student: "Margaret Schlauch," 389.

7. Sheila Delany kindly allowed me to read copies in her possession of several letters from Schlauch to Rossell Hope Robbins and his wife, Helen Ann, from 1968 to 1982, in some of which Schlauch complains of her ill health during the 1970s and 1980s, especially in a letter of 22 October 1981.

8. 1980 letter to Rossell Hope Robbins and Helen Ann Robbins. In one letter Schlauch asks the Robbinses for powdered coffee and toothpaste and any other small items they might send on to make the privations a bit less harsh.

9. Although she does say, "The relative isolation in which I live is naturally somewhat depressing" (Margaret Schlauch, letter to the Robbinses, 22 October 1981).

10. Rubinstein, "Margaret Schlauch," 387–88.

11. Two recent articles in the *Medieval Feminist Forum* voice different slants on Schlauch's integration of her life and work. Granting Schlauch's enormous influence and scholarly talents, Sheila Delany has written a memoir of her own days as a Marxist medievalist and compares Schlauch's career status as an outcast with her own ups and downs in the academy and her limitations because of her Marxist beliefs (see her "Feminist Legacies"; also see her "Marxist Medievalists"). Delany sees Schlauch as unable or unwilling in her era to infuse her works of literary history with the militant socialist activism she so obviously espoused. She recounts poignant anecdotes of Schlauch's activist days taken from Annette Rubinstein's unpublished memoir of Schlauch. But Delany notes that although Schlauch was a fervid (and idealistic) Marxist, her Marxism kept a low profile in her medieval scholarship, which was the Communist Party strategy in that era. So Delany, who looked to Schlauch as a model for integrating Marxist ideas into her own medieval scholarship, finds Schlauch wanting and not forceful enough in promoting her politics. Delany's piece is revealing about how things change and still are the same (dangerous) for academic political activists. Laura Mestayer Rogers, also writing in *Medieval Feminist Forum*, seeks in *Chaucer's Constance and Accused Queens,* and especially in its preface, the key to understanding Schlauch as a feminist, and in prefaces to some of her other works finds a positive statement of her feminism ("Embarking with Constance").

12. Quotation from the typescript of a short memoir of Schlauch by Annette Rubinstein, lent to me by Sheila Delany.

13. This information—and much else in this essay—comes from Schlauch's application to the John Simon Guggenheim Memorial Foundation in 1929. Documents from the foundation's archives relating to Schlauch were graciously provided to me by G. Thomas Tanselle, senior vice president. The materials proved a treasure trove of information, much of it in her

own words, about Schlauch's education, aspirations for her research, and early scholarly career. The Guggenheim papers include extensive professional correspondence over many years between Schlauch and the foundation's director at the time, Henry Allen Moe. All materials cited here about Schlauch and the foundation are quoted from these papers. Permission to quote from Moe's letters is by courtesy of the John Simon Guggenheim Memorial Foundation. It was a shame that the AAUW did not have such an archive, since had it yielded Schlauch's application for the fellowship she won during her dissertation research, given the nature of the funding group, such materials might speak to gender issues and to Schlauch's position as a woman scholar.

14. Guggenheim fellows are listed by year on the foundation's Web site: http://www.gf.org.

15. Schlauch, "Wídsíth, Viðförull, and Other Analogues" and "The Pound of Flesh Story in the North."

16. Schlauch might have been saddened to see that even the Guggenheim Foundation was not immune from HUAC. In 1953 the *New York Times* reported the recipients of fellowships, adding that the foundation, "lauding recipient Dr. F. Browder, denies he is or was Communist" (*New York Times,* 26 May 1953, p. 16, col. 5). And in the same vein, "Dr. Lewis loses Fulbright award after wife refuses to answer Sen. [McCarthy] subcommittee queries on alleged Communist party membership" (*New York Times,* 20 June 1953, p. 1, col.7).

17. Letter of 6 October 1943 from Schlauch to Henry Moe, from the Guggenheim archives on Schlauch.

18. *Science and Society* 1 (summer 1936): i; the page number for the subsequent citation of this work in the paragraph is given in parentheses in the text. The first editors were Albert E. Blumberg, of Johns Hopkins University, V. J. McGill of Hunter College, Bernhard J. Stern of Columbia, and Margaret Schlauch and Edwin Berry Burgum of New York University. The journal, still published today, is issued from Cambridge, Mass.

19. Rubinstein, "Margaret Schlauch," 388. The *New York Times* of 1 May 1953: p. 12, col. 3, says, "M. Johnson and H. A. Philbrick call him Communist." Burgum was still on the editorial board of *S&S* into the 1970s. Interestingly, an article of 6 May 1953, p.15, col. 4, notes that "W. Olsen refuses to answer subcommittee queries on party ties, association with Profs. Burgum and Schlauch and other issues." Refusing to name names, Olsen submitted his resignation. It is clear that Schlauch's name was still synonymous with traitor. The New York University Archives contain the files labeled the "Edwin Berry Burgum Academic Freedom Case, 1934–1961," which I was unable to consult for any mentions of his association with Schlauch.

20. Schlauch, review of *It Is Later than You Think,* 533, 532.

21. Margaret Schlauch, "The Revolt of 1381 in England," 416.

22. Regarding the limits on travel, see Schlauch, *English Medieval Literature and Its Social Foundations,* xvi. She pleads the exigencies of wartime in Poland for any inaccuracies the work may contain. But there is, by the way, a wonderfully ample selection of plates from secondary sources. In particular her discussion of the ideology of Early Latin literature in England is most illuminating. Even her brief description of the origins of *amor courtois*—while perhaps not au courant in its complexity—is a fine place from which to begin a study of courtly literature.

23. Helen Schlauch Infeld was also a remarkable woman for her times, it seems, having received her Ph.D. in mathematics from Cornell. Schlauch speaks in her letters with great fondness for Helen, who visited her often, and with pride in her niece and nephew, Joan and Eric.

24. This material derived from a note from Jacek Fisiak responding to Sheila Delany's query about Schlauch's Polish years, which Delany shared with me.

25. E-mail from Jacek Fisiak to Jane Chance, 1 March 2001.

SELECT BIBLIOGRAPHY OF WORKS BY MARGARET SCHLAUCH

Further bibliographic citations (to 1964) are listed by Jacek Niecko in Schlauch's 1966 festschrift, *Studies in Language and Literature in Honour of Margaret Schlauch,* ed. Brahmer, Helsztynski, and Krzyzanowski, 9–20, and (to 1976) in Rogers, "Embarking with Constance," 41–43. The festschrift bibliography also mentions the reviews of many of her books and notes reviews that she wrote. Only first editions of books are cited here; some have since been reprinted.

"Literary Exchange between Angevin England and Sicily." *Romanic Review* 14 (1923): 168–88.

"Putting Ideas into Their Heads." *Education* 46 (1925): 96–101.

Chaucer's Constance and Accused Queens. New York: New York University Press, 1927.

Medieval Narrative: A Book of Translations. New York: Prentice-Hall, 1928.

"The Historical Background of *Fergus and Galiene.*" *PMLA* 44 (1929): 360–76.

"The Danish Volksbücher." *Germanic Review* 5 (1930): 378–96.

The "Saga of the Volsungs," "The Saga of Ragnar Lodbrok," Together with "The Lay of Kraka." New York: American-Scandinavian Foundation; W. W. Norton and Co., 1930.

"The Palace of Hugon de Constantinople." *Speculum* 7 (1931): 500–514.

"The Pound of Flesh Story in the North." *Journal of English and German Philology* 30 (1931): 348–60.

"A Russian Study of the Tristan Legend." *Romanic Review* 24 (1933): 37–45.

"Chaucer's *Merchant's Tale* and a Russian Legend of King Solomon." *Modern Language Notes* 49 (1934): 229–32.

Romance in Iceland. Princeton: Princeton University Press; American-Scandinavian Foundation, 1934.

"Literature of the Folk." *Soviet Russia Today* 4, no. 9 (1935): 89–91.

Who Are the Aryans? New York: Anti-Fascist Literature Committee, 1935.

"The Social Basis of Linguistics." *Science and Society* 1, no. 1 (fall 1936–7): 18–44.

"Chaucer's *Merchant's Tale* and Courtly Love." *ELH* 4 (1937): 201–12.

"The *Dámusta Saga* and French Romance." *Modern Philology* 35 (1937): 1–13.

"Recent Soviet Linguistics." *Science and Society* 1, no. 2 (summer 1937): 152–67.

"The Allegory of Church and Synagogue." *Speculum* 14 (1939): 448–64.

"The Language of James Joyce." *Science and Society* 3, no. 4 (fall 1939): 482–97.

Review of *It Is Later than You Think,* by Max Lerner. *Science and Society* 3, no. 4 (fall 1939): 530–33.

"Widsith, Viðförull, and Other Analogues." *PMLA* 46 (1939): 969–87.

With John J. Parry. "A Bibliography of Critical Arthurian Literature for the Years 1936–1939." *Modern Language Quarterly* 1 (1940): 129–74.

"*The Dream of the Rood* as Prosopopoeia." In *Essays and Studies in Honor of Carleton Brown,* edited by P. W. Long. New York: New York University Press; London: H. Milford; Oxford: Oxford University Press, 1940.

"The Revolt of 1381 in England," *Science and Society,* 4, no. 4 (fall 1940): 414–32.

"The Man of Law's Tale." In *Sources and Analogues of Chaucer's "Canterbury Tales,"* edited by W. F. Bryan and G. Dempster. Chicago: University of Chicago Press, 1941.

"An Old English *Encomium Urbis.*" *JEGP* 40 (1941): 14–28.

The Gift of Tongues. New York: Modern Age Books, 1942. 4th ed. published as *The Gift of Language* (New York: Dover Publications, 1955).

"Russian People's Wars in 1812 and 1941: Recent Soviet Historiography." *Science and Society* 6, no. 1 (winter 1942): 24–33.

"The Women of the Icelandic Sagas." *American Scandinavian Review* 31 (winter 1943): 333–40.

"Folklore in the Soviet Union." *Science and Society* 8, no. 3 (summer 1944): 205–22.

"Chaucer's Doctrine of Kings and Tyrants." *Speculum* 20 (1945): 133–56.

"Scandinavia: The Dilemma of the Middle Way." *Science and Society* 9, no. 2 (spring 1945): 97–124.

"Early Behavioral Psychology and Contemporary Linguistics." *Word* 2 (1946): 25–36.

"The Marital Dilemma in the *Wife of Bath's Tale*." *PMLA* 61 (1946): 416–30.

"Mechanism and Historical Materialism in Semantic Studies." *Science and Society* 11 (1947): 144–67.

"The Soviet Linguistics Controversy." In *Marxism and Linguistics,* by Joseph Stalin. New York: International Publisher's Company, 1951.

"Chaucer's Colloquial English: Its Structural Traits." *PMLA* 67 (1952): 1, 103–16.

Outline History of the English Language: 1400 to the Present. Warsaw: Sanstwowego Wydawnictwa Naukowego, 1952.

English Medieval Literature and Its Social Foundations. Warsaw: PWN, Polish Scientific Publishers, 1956.

Modern English and American Poetry: Techniques and Ideologies. London: Watts, 1956.

"On Teaching English Historical Syntax to Slavic-Speaking Students." *Zeitschrift für Anglistik und Amerikanistik* 5 (1957): 57–67.

"A Polish Vernacular Eulogy of Wycliff." *Journal of Ecclesiastical History* 8 (1958): 58–73.

Antecedents of the English Novel, 1400–1600: From Chaucer to Deloney. Warsaw: PWN, Polish Scientific Publishers; London: Oxford University Press, 1963.

"Linguistic Aspects of Emily Dickinson's Style." *Prace Filologiczne* 18 (1963): 201–15.

"Mary of Nijmeghen (The Female Faust) in an English Prose Version of the Early Tudor Period." *Philologica Pragensia* 6 (1963): 4–11.

"Realism and Convention in Medieval Literature." *Kwartalnik Neofilologiczny* 11 (1964): 3–12.

The English Language in Modern Times (since 1400). Warsaw: PWN, Polish Scientific Publishers, 1967.

Language and the Study of Languages Today. Warsaw: PWN, Polish Scientific Publishers; London: Oxford University Press, 1967.

"Stylistic Attributes of John Lydgate's Prose." In *To Honor Roman Jakobson: Essays on the Occasion of His Seventieth Birthday, 11 October 1966.* Janua linguarum. Series maior; 31, 32, 33. The Hague and Paris: Mouton, 1967.

"John Skelton, Satirist and Court Poet (as Seen in the Light of Recent Studies)." *Kwartalnik Neofilologiczny* 16 (1969): 125–35.

"The Rhetoric of Public Speeches in Old Scandinavia (Chiefly Icelandic)." *Scandinavian Studies* 41 (1969): 297–314.

"The Doctrine of 'Vera Nobilitas' as Developed After Chaucer." *Kwartalnik Neofilologiczny* 17 (1970): 119–27.

"Polynices and Gunnlaug Serpent-Tongue: A Parallel." In *Essays and Studies 1972 in Honour of Beatrice White,* edited by T. S. Dorsch and Geoffrey Harlow. London: English Association, 1972.

"A Polish Analogue of the *Man of Law's Tale*." In *Chaucer and Middle English Studies in Honour of Rossell Hope Robbins,* edited by Beryl Rowland. London: Allen and Unwin, 1974.

"A Late Icelandic Saga as Parallel to Old French Literary Parody." *Kwartalnik Neofilologiczny* 23 (1976): 217–23.

Works Cited

Brahmer, Mieczyslaw, Stanislaw Helsztynski, and Julian Krzyzanowski, eds. *Studies in Language and Literature in Honour of Margaret Schlauch.* Warsaw: PWN, Polish Scientific Publishers, 1966.

Delany, Sheila. "Feminist Legacies: Female Medieval Scholars and the Academy." *Medieval Feminist Forum* 30 (fall 2000): 9–15.

———. "Marxist Medievalists: A Tradition." *Science and Society* 68 (2004): 206–15.

Fisiak, Jacek. "Obituaries of Distinguished Scholars." In *Medieval English Studies Past and Present,* edited by A. Oizumi and T. Takamiya. Tokyo: Eichosha Co., 1990. Originally published in *Poetica,* 28 (1988): 1–4.

Rogers, Laura Mestayer. "Embarking with Constance: Margaret Schlauch." *Medieval Feminist Forum* 31 (spring 2001): 36–43.

Rubinstein, Annette T. "Margaret Schlauch 1898–1986." *Science and Society* 50, no. 4 (fall 1987): 387–89.

———. Memoir. Typescript.

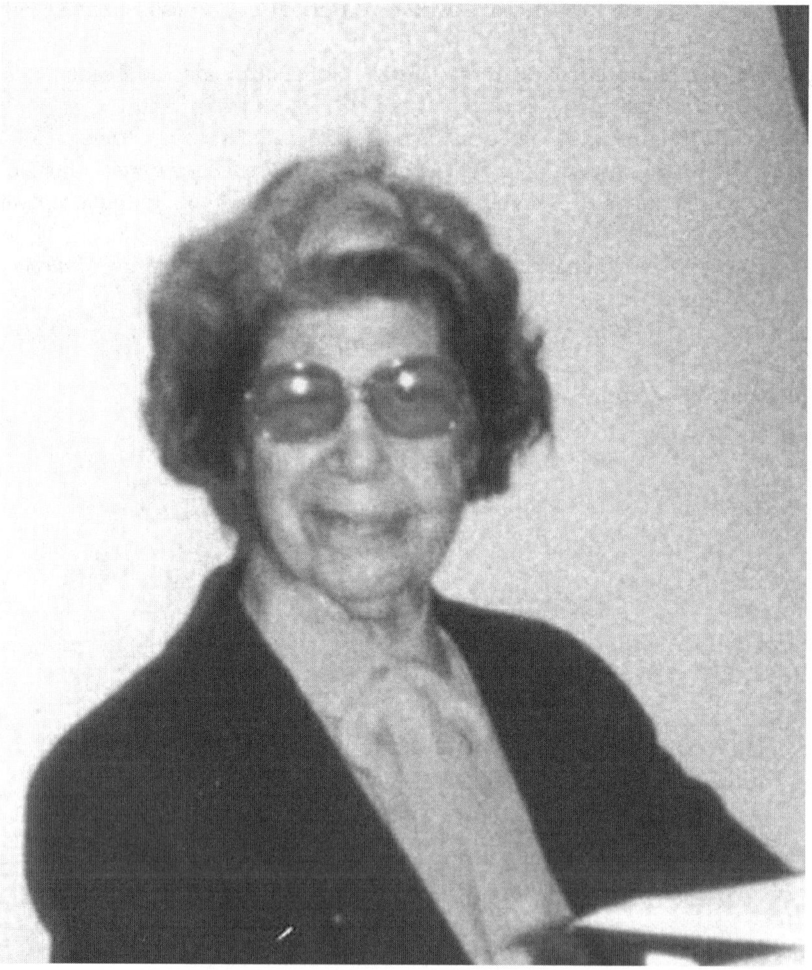

CHAPTER 37

Pearl Kibre (1900–1985)
Manuscript Hunter and Historian of Medieval Science and the Universities

Elspeth Whitney and Irving A. Kelter

Pearl Kibre was born in Philadelphia on 2 September 1900 and died in New York City on 15 July 1985.[1] A productive and much admired scholar and teacher throughout her long career, she helped lay the foundations for the contemporary study of medieval science and of medieval universities. As an undergraduate she first attended the southern branch of the University of California, later to become UCLA in 1921. She received her B.A. from Berkeley in 1924, an M.A. from Berkeley in 1925, and her doctorate from Columbia University in 1936. After receiving her degree, Kibre taught at Hunter College and, beginning in 1964, at the Graduate School of the City University of New York, where she helped found the doctoral program in history. She retired from teaching in 1971, though she remained an active scholar until the last days of her life.

Kibre left little information about her relationships with family and friends, as she was intensely private about her personal life. Born in Philadelphia, Kibre spent her childhood and early life in southern California, where her father, Kenneth Kibre, an optometrist, and mother, Jane du Pione Kibre, moved when Pearl was a young child. She never married. Although almost nothing is known about her later relationships with her family, Kibre did keep in touch with her sister, Adele, who also attended the southern branch of the University of California. Adele Kibre was a classicist and received a doctorate from the Department of Latin Language and Literature of the University of Chicago in 1930. Adele remained an independent scholar, spending much of her time in Europe, and Pearl Kibre occasionally relied on her for information about particular manuscripts and cited Adele in her notes.

Professor Kibre's closest relationships seem to have been with her colleagues and students, as well as with her beloved cat Tubby. Both colleagues and students not only held her in great esteem as a scholar but remember her with deep affection. She was unfailingly generous with her time and scholarly advice to others working in the field of medieval studies, including passing graduate students she encountered during her long stints at European libraries. She was also on close terms with the members of library staffs across Europe and in the United States, where she was a welcome and frequent visitor at the British Museum, the Bibliothèque nationale, the Vatican Library, and the Bodleian Library, among others. Her students include some of the most eminent American medieval and Renaissance historians, including Phyllis B. Roberts, historian of the medieval English Church and medieval sermons, and Nancy G. Siraisi and Luke Demaitre, both Kibre's protégés at the Graduate School of CUNY and both noted specialists in the fields of medieval and Renaissance medicine. All have remarked on Kibre's kindness, concern, and generosity.

Phyllis Roberts, who worked under Kibre's direction as a student in Hunter College's master's program in history, remembers the hours spent with Kibre going over the translation of John of Salisbury's *Entheticus,* which served as Roberts's thesis. When this thesis won the annual George Shuster Award for Best Master's Thesis in 1959, Kibre was overjoyed, not only because her student had won the award but also because history had beaten out the sciences that year.[2] In the same vein Nancy Siraisi recalls how early in her own career she was coauthoring an article with Kibre for the prestigious *Bulletin of the History of Medicine.* When the *Bulletin* required revisions before publication, Siraisi, then inexperienced and nervous about meeting the *Bulletin*'s deadline, kept Kibre in her office until 1 A.M. making the required changes.[3] Of course, looking back, one realizes that Kibre, who made her own decisions, was only too happy to stay that late working to help launch her student's career as a scholar. As Luke Demaitre has remarked, Kibre also shepherded her fledgling historians to conferences such as the International Congress on Medieval Studies at Kalamazoo, Michigan, so that they could give papers under her watchful eye.[4] Today students at the Graduate School of CUNY gather in the Pearl Kibre Medieval Study, dedicated in 1972 in recognition of Kibre's long-term support of student endeavors.

An unassuming and warm personality, Kibre was nevertheless demanding in terms of scholarly devotion both of herself and of others. Famous for attending every session at conferences, she worked up until the very last days of her life, with a major book appearing shortly before her death and two new articles published posthumously. Siraisi has said of her, "Dedication to scholarly research was the central focus of Pearl Kibre's life."[5]

Kibre's intellectual life was in many ways shaped by circumstances surrounding women's education in the 1920s and 1930s. She attended high school at the Manual Arts High School in Los Angeles and then matriculated at the southern branch of the University of California. Here she was among a small group of students in the Department of History, founded in 1919. Although women students were in many subtle and not-so-subtle ways discriminated against and the university as a whole had few women faculty, the University of California had been founded as a normal school and had a well-established tradition of coeducation. This seems to have been especially true at the southern branch, where women were a strong presence, perhaps in part because of the newness of the school. In the academic year 1925–26, for example, women outnumbered men in the College of Letters and Science by more than two to one, and all seven of the individuals receiving a B.A. in history were women.[6]

After three years on the southern campus, Kibre moved to Berkeley, where the history department was larger and had more resources for European history. At Berkeley also, women undergraduates in history, as well as in other fields, outnumbered men by a ratio of about 3 to 1 (exceptions seem to have been in engineering, agriculture, law, and the physical sciences, but not life sciences and mathematics). In the academic year 1924–25, there were only 34 male graduate students in history but 135 women.[7] Such an atmosphere must have been encouraging to budding female scholars. As indicated earlier, Kibre earned a B.A. in history in 1924 and then an M.A. in 1925 under the direction of noted medievalist Louis John Paetow, then chair of the history department. As an undergraduate she was a member of Sigma Kappa Alpha, a history honor society. While a graduate student, Kibre did her practice teaching and served as president of the Women's History Honor Society, among other activities. Her tenure as president of the society was later described by her long-time friend from graduate school, Gray C. Boyce, as one of "serenity . . . but [one managed] with a necessarily firm hand."[8]

Paetow was instrumental in sparking Kibre's interest in the history of medieval universities, libraries, and intellectual history and her determination to pursue a doctoral degree. After a brief return to southern California to teach at Pasadena Junior College, she began to investigate graduate programs. Her first choice was to study at Harvard University with Charles Homer Haskins, Paetow's mentor and one of the founders of medieval studies in the United States, particularly known for his exacting seminars in paleography. Kibre was extremely disappointed and dismayed to discover that Harvard did not accept women and she would have to matriculate at Radcliffe. She never forgave Harvard for this discriminatory policy. Instead, she chose to apply to Columbia University, like Harvard a leader in the fields of medieval intellectual history and history of science. Columbia had begun admitting women to its graduate programs in 1897, over the protests of John William Burgess, head of the faculty of political science, under which the Department of History was administered. Burgess was convinced that the scholarship and attention of his male students would be injured by the admission of women.[9] Outmaneuvered by President Seth Low, however, Burgess was forced to admit women to graduate courses in history and economics but continued to bar them from courses in public law, his own field, until his retirement in 1912.[10]

In the late 1920s and 1930s the vast majority of students at Columbia pursuing doctoral degrees in fields other than education were still male, but niches existed within which female doctoral students could flourish. Kibre found her mentor in the person of Lynn Thorndike (1882–1965), one of the most important and innovative historians of medieval and Renaissance science of his time. Accepted in 1928, she became one of a continuous stream of Thorndike's students, including Marshall Clagett, C. Doris Hellman, Richard Lemay, Edward Rosen, Kenneth Setton, and Charles Trinkaus. All of these scholars became important historians of medieval and Renaissance science and intellectual history. On the historiographical debate concerning the importance of the Renaissance in intellectual history, Kibre never wavered from upholding her mentor's view that "the so-called Renaissance" was a faulty historical concept. She was most certainly part of what Wallace K. Ferguson termed "the revolt of the medievalists."[11] Others, most notably Rosen, sharply critiqued Thorndike in this regard and upheld the overriding historical significance of Renaissance thought. These disagreements did not prevent Kibre and Rosen from maintaining a cordial relationship as members of the history faculty at the Graduate School of CUNY and each contributed to the other's festschrift.

Thorndike, who had received his own Ph.D. from Columbia and taught there from 1928 to 1950, was a pioneer not only in his willingness to take the history of magic and the so-called occult sciences seriously and on their own terms but also in his devotion to unearthing and cataloging manuscript sources throughout Europe. Kibre became especially close to Thorndike, for whom she worked first as a longtime research assistant and finally as a full collaborator in her own right. In the obituary for Thorndike for *Speculum,* written with Marshall Clagett and Gaines Post, Kibre recalled that her teacher "alternately awed, stimulated by example, and goaded [his students] to greater effort, caution, and achievement, by the scope and depth of his own knowledge and scholarly productions, by his ability to recall significant details, and by his constant and probing insistence upon concrete evidence from the sources."[12] Kibre took the example of Thorndike to heart and her own scholarly work was characterized by meticulousness, precision, superb technical skills, and a thorough grounding in the manuscript and printed sources.

On Thorndike's behalf she made numerous trips to European libraries in the 1930s, setting a pattern she was to follow throughout her life. This history of collaboration bore fruit in the publication in 1937 of the *Catalogue of Incipits of Mediaeval Scientific Writings in Latin,* a massive listing of over ten thousand items, many of them previously unidentified, which she coauthored with Thorndike. The *Catalogue of Incipits,* often referred to as "TK," was immediately hailed as "a very precious contribution to the study of the history of science in the middle ages" and remains over sixty years later "the single most important research tool for the study of medieval science."[13] Kibre and Thorndike continued to collaborate for over a quarter-century on additions and revisions to TK, which was republished in 1963 in an augmented and revised edition. Kibre alone published an article of "further addenda and corrigenda" in *Speculum* in 1968, three years after Thorndike's death. Current work on a digitized version of TK, which will be available on the Internet, demonstrates its continued importance as an essential research tool.[14]

Kibre's scholarly interests were certainly shaped by those of her mentors, but she without doubt retained her intellectual independence. Paetow undeniably inspired her interest in the medieval universities. Thorndike certainly stimulated her focus on the cataloging of manuscripts and may have been one influence behind Kibre's later work on the alchemical treatises of Albertus Magnus. Neither Thorndike nor Paetow, however, had done any significant work in the history of medieval medicine, which became one of Kibre's primary fields of research, possibly because of her father's profession.

Kibre made two important contributions to the history of medicine. First, she opened up this area to further research by beginning the enormous task of identifying relevant manuscript material, first in TK and later in her *Hippocrates Latinus: Repertorium of Hippocratic Writings in the Latin Middle Ages*. These two catalogs not only laid the groundwork for a systematic study of medieval medical texts but also provided a model for further research tools, such as the catalog of Old and Middle English scientific and medical manuscripts by Linda Ehrsam Voigts and Patricia Deery Kurtz.[15] Second, she also laid the foundations for the social history of medicine. In a series of articles she examined the institutional settings for the teaching and practice of medicine and uncovered the tracks of little-known physicians, including Dominicus de Ragusa, Lewis of Caerleon, and Cristoforo Barzizza, concentrating on what is known of their careers as well as on their written works and intellectual interests. Although Kibre did not typically consider gender in her work, in a 1953 article, "The Faculty of Medicine at Paris, Charlatanism and Unlicensed Medical Practice in the Later Middle Ages," she analyzed two cases of female physicians accused of practicing illegally. Her account of their trials, based on the records of the University of Paris and other archival sources, is one of the earliest studies of female physicians in the Middle Ages.

Kibre's research on the history of universities therefore served to complement and give depth to her study of the history of medicine by bringing an institutional and social dimension to her work. Her passion for the medieval universities and those university corporations of masters or students, known as the "nations," was first inspired when she was a member of Paetow's seminar on the University of Paris. Here one could see "at first hand the vigorous, boisterous, often bellicose societies of scholars" she so loved and admired in the Middle Ages and in her own day.[16] She pursued this line of research in her two major books on the institutional history of medieval universities, *The Nations in the Medieval Universities* (1948; rpt., 1962) and *Scholarly Privileges in the Middle Ages* (1961; rpt., 1962), for which she was awarded the Haskins Medal from the Medieval Academy in 1964. A review of *The Nations* in the *American Historical Review* hailed it as a "model" of institutional history, while the review of *Scholarly Privileges* in the same distinguished journal noted its "luxurious wealth of scholarly detail" and judged that "it will long remain a definitive work on its subject."[17] Decades later Kibre's writings on the universities of Europe were still the authoritative works on her subjects. As Alan B. Cobban observed in 1988 concerning the matter of the dearth of information about nations at Cambridge University, "[Even] Kibre ... can supply only one paragraph on the Cambridge nations."[18]

Kibre was in every sense of the word a true bibliophile. Her love of manuscripts in and of themselves fueled the extraordinary energy she brought to identifying and recording thousands of manuscripts in libraries across Europe and the United Kingdom. She also appreciated the aesthetic qualities of manuscripts. Indeed, she preferred manuscripts to printed books in part because she found them more aesthetically pleasing. Always careful to note illuminations and marginal decorations in the manuscripts she examined, as well as the physical condition of the manuscript itself, she was tireless in tracking down the provenance and history of individual manuscripts as well as the editorial history of the text itself. She also expressed an enduring interest in libraries and what they reflected about the intellectual interests of their owners.

Finally, we should note that she was protective of the rights of scholars and authors, a connection to her award-winning work on scholarly privileges. Her own book on the library of Pico della Mirandola (1936) was sold in 1966 by Columbia University Press to AMS Press without her knowledge or consent, an omission that angered her for years afterward. On at least one occasion, she autographed a copy of the reprint by noting it had been published "without the knowledge of the author."[19]

In the course of her career Kibre received many honors and awards. She received the Haskins Medal, the most prestigious award for medievalists in the United States, in 1964 for *Scholarly Privileges*. Elected a fellow of the Medieval Academy in 1964, she served as vice president and a member of the Haskins Medal Committee and was elected president of the fellows in 1975. She was also president of the Medieval Club of New York (1959–60). She was an active member of a number of other scholarly bodies and sat on the boards of *Medieval and Renaissance Latin Translations and Commentaries* and the United States Subcommission for the History of Universities (International Committee of Historical Sciences). She was named a corresponding member of l'Académie d'histoire des sciences in 1959.

Kibre was a recipient of a number of important grants, including a grant from the American Council of Learned Societies (1936), a Guggenheim Fellowship (1950–51), and a grant from the American Philosophical Society (1955–56). Although these grants helped finance her frequent trips to European libraries and archives, she also depended on her salary from Hunter College and, in some instances, family money. She also received grants for publication costs from the Carnegie Corporation of New York, the American Council of Learned Societies, and the John Simon Guggenheim Memorial Foundation.[20]

Pearl Kibre's work is distinguished by its enduring value to historians. The *Catalogue of Incipits* remains an invaluable research tool that has never been supplanted. It is symptomatic of the quality of her research, grounded as it was in a profound knowledge of the manuscript and printed sources, that all of her books, even her dissertation, have been reprinted, often decades after their original publication date. Her love of books has been amply repaid in the value in which her own books are still held. It is most fitting and proper that we conclude this analysis and appreciation of the career and achievements of Pearl Kibre by quoting the very same lines of Richard de Bury's *Philobiblion* that she used to begin her own first work: "All things are corrupted and decay in time; Saturn ceases not to devour the children that he generates; all the glory of the world would be buried in oblivion, unless God had provided mortals with the remedy of books."[21]

Acknowledgments

Many helped in the writing of this essay. To all of Pearl Kibre's students who shared their memories of her with us we wish to express our deepest gratitude. Here we must name Janice Gordon-Kelter, also of our charmed circle of medievalists from the Graduate School of the City University of New York. Dr. Gordon-Kelter is a dear friend and, to Irving Kelter, much more than that. She added to the content of this essay and was always an astute critic of our prose.

We would also like to thank Betty Einerman, administrative assistant in the doctoral program in history of the Graduate School and University Center of the City University of New York. Ms. Einerman goes back to our student days there, and she is as much a part of that program as any student who went there or historian who taught there. We must also thank Rosamond W. Dana of the Office of the Provost of the Graduate School of CUNY, who supplied us with information concerning the founding of the doctoral program in history.

A number of librarians assisted us in the preparation of this work. We wish to cite the efforts of Dennis Citterlich of the University Archives of UCLA and William Roberts of the Bancroft Library, University of California, Berkeley. We were lucky to be able to constantly turn to Lisa McNamara and Rachel Matre, both superb librarians at the Doherty Library of the University of Saint Thomas, Houston.

Finally, Irving Kelter would like to express his deep thanks to a wonderful student assistant at the University of Saint Thomas, Julianna Arnim.

Of course, the authors take full responsibility for any errors or deficiencies found in the essay.

Notes

1. The year of Pearl Kibre's birth is disputed. We have chosen to give 1900, as that is the year given by the United States Social Security Administration.
2. Personal interview of Phyllis B. Roberts by Irving A. Kelter, 23 March 2002.
3. E-mail to authors from Nancy G. Siraisi, 4 March 2002.
4. E-mail to authors from Luke Demaitre, 16 June 2002.
5. Siraisi, "Pearl Kibre (1902–1985)."
6. Minutes, Council of the Southern Branch, 65.
7. *Register, 1924–25*, 2: 7.
8. Boyce, "Dedicatory Preface," 68.
9. Hoxie et al., *History of the Faculty of Political Science, Columbia University*, 65.
10. Ibid., 67.
11. Kibre, *Library of Pico*, 4; Ferguson, *Renaissance in Historical Thought*, 329–85.
12. Kibre, Clagett, and Post, "Lynn Thorndike," 598.

13. Welborn, review of *A Catalogue of Incipits of Mediaeval Scientific Writings in Latin*, 140; Voigts, "Multitudes of Middle English Medical Manuscripts," 185.

14. E-mail to authors from Luke Demaitre, 19 May 2002.

15. Voigts and Kurtz, eds., *Scientific and Medical Writings in Old and Middle English.*

16. Kibre, *Nations in the Mediaeval Universities,* xi.

17. Post, review of *The Nations in the Mediaeval Universities*, 572 Daly, review of *Scholarly Privileges in the Middle Ages,* 1,024–25.

18. Cobban, *Medieval English Universities,* 103 n. 168.

19. This copy of the *Library of Pico* is the personal possession of Irving Kelter.

20. Doviak, "Pearl Kibre," 244–45.

21. Kibre, *Library of Pico,* 3.

SELECT BIBLIOGRAPHY OF WORKS BY PEARL KIBRE

The Library of Pico della Mirandola. New York: Columbia University Press, 1936. Reprint, New York: AMS Press, 1966.

With Lynn Thorndike. *A Catalogue of Incipits of Mediaeval Scientific Writings in Latin.* Cambridge, Mass.: Mediaeval Academy of America, 1937, revised and augmented edition, 1963.

"Hitherto Unnoted Medical Writings by Dominicus de Ragusa (1424–1425 A.D.)." *Bulletin of the History of Medicine* 7 (1939): 990–95.

"The Alkimia Minor Ascribed to Albertus Magnus." *Isis* 32 (1941): 267–300.

"A Fourteenth-Century Scholastic Miscellany." *New Scholasticism* 15 (1941): 261–71.

"Alchemical Writings Ascribed to Albertus Magnus." *Speculum* 17 (1942): 499–518.

"Cristoforo Barzizza, Professor of Medicine at Padua." *Bulletin of the History of Medicine* 11 (1942): 389–98.

With Lynn Thorndike. "More Incipits of Mediaeval Scientific Writings in Latin." *Speculum* 17 (1942): 342–66.

"An Alchemical Tract Attributed to Albertus Magnus." *Isis* 35 (1944): 303–16.

"Hippocratic Writings in the Middle Ages." *Bulletin of the History of Medicine* 18 (1945): 371–412. Reprinted in *Hippocrates in the Arabic Tradition: Texts and Studies,* ed. Fuat Sezgin. Frankfurt am Main: Institute for the History of Arabic-Islamic Science at Johann Wolfgang Goethe University, 1996.

"The Intellectual Interests Reflected in Libraries of the Fourteenth and Fifteenth Centuries." *Journal of the History of Ideas* 7 (1946): 257–97.

The Nations in the Mediaeval Universities. Cambridge, Mass.: Mediaeval Academy of America, 1948. Reprint, Cambridge, Mass.: Mediaeval Academy of America, 1962.

"Lewis of Caerleon, Doctor of Medicine, Astronomer, and Mathematician (d. 1494?)." *Isis* 43 (1952): 100–108.

"The Faculty of Medicine at Paris: Charlatanism, and Unlicensed Medical Practices in the Later Middle Ages." *Bulletin of the History of Medicine* 27 (1953): 1–20. Reprinted in *Legacies in Law and Medicine,* ed. C. R. Burnes. New York: Science History Publications, 1977.

"The De Occultis Naturae Attributed to Albertus Magnus." *Osiris* 11 (1954): 23–29.

"Lynn Thorndike (with Bibliography Portrait)." *Osiris* 11 (1954): 5–22.

Coeditor. *Osiris* 11 (1954). Dedicated to Lynn Thorndike.

"Scholarly Privileges: Their Roman Origins and Medieval Expression." *American Historical Review* 59 (1954): 543–67.

"The University of Paris and the Stationarii in the Thirteenth and Fourteenth Centuries." *Columbia University Columns* 4 (1954): 13–18.

"Academic Oaths at the University of Paris in the Middle Ages." In *Essays in Medieval Life and Thought: Essays in Honour of Austin Patterson Evans,* edited by John H. Mundy, Richard W. Emery, and Benjamin N. Nelson. New York: Columbia University Press, 1955.

"Albertus Magnus, De Occultis Nature." *Osiris* 13 (1957): 157–83.

"Further Manuscripts Containing Alchemical Tracts Attributed to Albertus Magnus." *Speculum* 34 (1959): 238–47.

"Two Alchemical Miscellanies: Vatican Latin MSS 4091, 4092." *Ambix* 8 (1960): 167–76.

Scholarly Privileges in the Middle Ages: The Rights, Privileges, and Immunities of Scholars and Universities at Bologna, Padua, Paris and Oxford. London: Mediaeval Academy of America, 1961; London and Cambridge, Mass.: Medieval Academy of America, 1961, 1962.

"Cardinal Domenico Grimani, 'Questio de intentione et remissione qualitatis': A Commentary of the Tractate of That Title by Richard Suiseth (Calculator)." In *Didascaliae: Studies in Honor of Anselm M. Albareda,* edited by Sesto Prete. New York: B. M. Rosenthal, 1961.

"The Christian: Augustine." In *The Educated Man: Studies in the History of Educational Thought,* edited by Paul Nash et al. New York: John Wiley, 1965. Reprint, Huntington, N.Y.: R. E. Krieger Publishing Co, 1980.

With Marshall Clagett and Gaines Post. "Lynn Thorndike." *Speculum* 41 (1966): 598–99.

"Giovanni Garzoni of Bologna (1419–1505), Professor of Medicine and Defender of Astrology." *Isis* 58 (1967): 504–14.

"Thorndike, Lynn (1882–1965), in Memoriam." *Archives internationales d'histoire des sciences* 20 (1967): 285–88.

"Further Addenda and Corrigenda to the Revised Edition of Lynn Thorndike and Pearl Kibre: A Catalogue of Incipits of Mediaeval Scientific Writings in Latin, 1963." *Speculum* 43 (1968): 78–114.

"The Quadrivium in Thirteenth-Century Universities (with Special Reference to Paris)." In *Arts libéraux et philosophie au Moyen Âge: Actes du quatrième Congrès international de philosophie médiévale, Université de Montréal, Canada, 27 août–2 septembre, 1967.* Montreal: Institut d'Études Médiévales; Paris: Librairie Philosophique J. Vrin, 1969.

"Dominicus de Ragus, Bolognese Doctor of Arts and Medicine." *Bulletin of the History of Medicine* 45 (1971): 383–86.

"Hippocrates Latinus: Repertorium of Hippocratic Writings in the Latin Middle Ages. Fasc. I." *Traditio* 31 (1975): 99–126.

With Nancy G. Siraisi. "Matheolus of Perugia's Commentary on the Preface to the *Aphorisms* of Hippocrates." *Bulletin of the History of Medicine* 49 (1975): 405–28.

"Hippocrates Latinus. Fasc. II." *Traditio* 32 (1976): 257–92.

"Hippocrates Latinus. Fasc. III." *Traditio* 33 (1977): 253–95.

"Arts and Medicine in the Universities of the Later Middle Ages." In *Les Universités a la fin du Moyen Âge,* edited by J. Paquet and J. Ijsewijn. Louvain, Belg.: Institut d'Etudes Médiévales U.C.L., 1978.

"*Astronomia* or *Astrologia* Ypocratis." In *Science and History: Studies in Honor of Edward Rosen,* edited by Erna Hilfstein et al. Wroclaw, Pol.: Ossolineum, 1978; New York: Science History Publications, 1978.

"Hippocrates Latinus. Fasc. IV." *Traditio* 34 (1978): 193–226.

With Nancy G. Siraisi. "The Institutional Setting: The Universities." In *Science in the Middle Ages,* edited by David Lindberg. Chicago: University of Chicago Press, 1978.
"Hippocrates Latinus. Fasc. V." *Traditio* 35 (1979): 273–302.
"Albertus Magnus on Alchemy." In *Albertus Magnus and the Sciences: Commemorative Essays 1980,* edited by J. A. Weisheipl, O.P. Toronto: Pontifical Institute of Mediaeval Studies, 1980.
"Hippocrates Latinus. Fasc. VI." *Traditio* 36 (1980): 347–72.
"Hippocrates Latinus. Fasc. VII." *Traditio* 37 (1981): 267–89.
"The Boethian *De Insitutione Arithmetica* and the *Quadrivium* in the Thirteenth-Century University Milieu at Paris." In *Boethius and the Liberal Arts,* edited by M. Masi. Berne: Peter Lang, 1981.
"Hippocrates Latinus. Fasc. VIII: Conclusion and Indexes of Treatises, Translators, and Commentators." *Traditio* 38 (1982): 165–92.
Studies in Medieval Science: Alchemy, Astrology, Mathematics and Medicine. London: Hambledon Press, 1984.
Hippocrates Latinus: Repertorium of Hippocratic Writings in the Latin Middle Ages. Rev. ed. New York: Fordham University Press, 1985.
With Irving A. Kelter. "Galen's *Methodus Medendi* in the Middle Ages." *History and Philosophy of the Life Sciences* 9 (1987): 17–36.
"A List of Latin Manuscripts Containing Medieval Versions of the *Methodus Medendi.*" In *Galen's Method of Healing: Proceedings of the 1982 Galen Symposium,* edited by Fridolf Kudlien and Richard J. Durling. Leiden: E. J. Brill, 1991.

WORKS CITED

Boyce, Gray C. "Dedicatory Preface." In *Manuscripta* 20 (1976): 68–70. This appeared as a special volume in two parts with the title *Science, Medicine and the University: 1200–1550: Essays in Honor of Pearl Kibre,* ed. Nancy G. Siraisi and Luke Demaitre. Saint Louis: Saint Louis University Library, 1976.
Cobban, A. B. *The Medieval English Universities: Oxford and Cambridge to c. 1500.* Berkeley: University of California Press, 1988.
Daly, Lowrie J., S.J. Review of *Scholarly Privileges in the Middle Ages: The Rights, Privileges, and Immunities, of Scholars and Universities at Bologna, Padua, Paris, and Oxford,* by Pearl Kibre. *American Historical Review* 68 (1963): 1,024–25.
Doviak, Ronald. "Pearl Kibre: Bio-Bibliography." *Manuscripta* 20 (1976): 244–50.
Ferguson, W. K. *The Renaissance in Historical Thought.* Cambridge, Mass.: Houghton Mifflin, 1948.
Hoxie, R. Gordon, et al. *A History of the Faculty of Political Science, Columbia University.* New York: Columbia University Press, 1955.
Minutes, Council of the Southern Branch, January 22, 1926. Powell Library, Department of Special Collections, University of California, Los Angeles. Typescript.
Post, Gaines. Review of *The Nations in the Mediaeval Universities,* by Pearl Kibre. *American Historical Review* 54 (1949): 572.
Register, 1924–25, with Announcements for 1925–26, Summary of Students, 1924–25, University of California. Vol. 2. Berkeley: University of California Press, 1926.
Siraisi, Nancy G. "Pearl Kibre (1902–1985)." *Bulletin of the History of Medicine* 59 (1985): 521.
Voigts, Linda Ehrsam. "Multitudes of Middle English Medical Manuscripts, or the Englishing

of Science and Medicine." In *Manuscript Sources of Medieval Medicine: A Book of Essays,* edited by Margaret R. Schleissner. New York: Garland Publishing, 1995.

Voigts, Linda Ehrsam, and Patricia Deery Kurtz, eds. *Scientific and Medical Writings in Old and Middle English: An Electronic Reference.* Ann Arbor: University of Michigan Press, 2000.

Welborn, Mary Catherine. Review of *A Catalogue of Incipits of Mediaeval Scientific Writings in Latin,* by Lynn Thorndike and Pearl Kibre. *Isis* 29 (1938): 140–41.

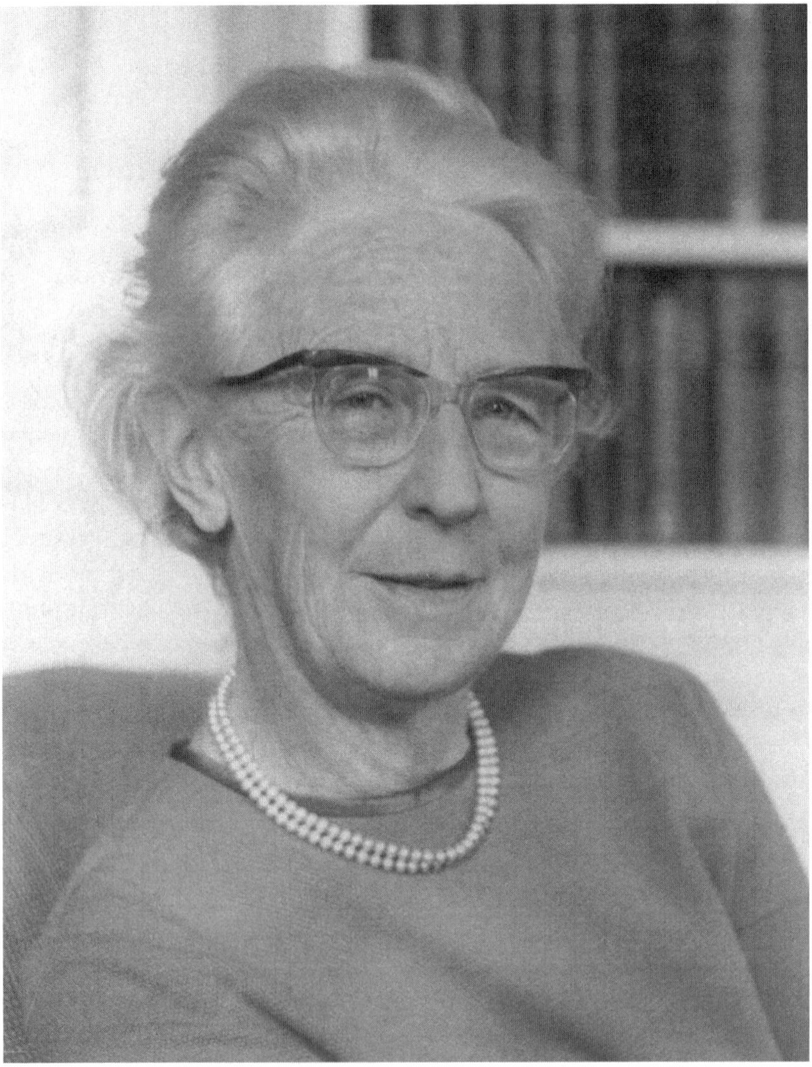

CHAPTER 38

❦

An Anglo-Saxonist at Oxford and Cambridge
Dorothy Whitelock (1901–1982)

JANA K. SCHULMAN

Dorothy Whitelock, admired and respected for her skills as an Anglo-Saxon historian, linguist, and diplomatist, entered the world in Leeds, on 11 November 1901. The daughter of Edward Whitelock and his second wife, Emmeline Dawson, she was the youngest of six children. Her father died in 1903, and her mother, impoverished, did the best she could for the family. Whitelock first studied the humanities at her local grammar school, Leeds Girls' High School. An excellent student, she received a place at Newnham College, Cambridge; she went there in 1921 and read for section B of the English Tripos (a university examination leading to an honors B.A.). She attended classes taught by Professor Hector M. Chadwick, who in 1919–20 had lobbied to change the focus of the English Tripos. Instead of balancing the amount of time devoted to the study of "Teutonic and English Philology" with that of "Old English and Old Icelandic," he opted to emphasize the "historical and cultural background" of the latter over the former.[1] Whitelock was particularly enamored of his interdisciplinary approach to the study of pre-Conquest Britain, appreciating the opportunity to study language, literature, history, and archaeology. Her formidable skills shone through, and she achieved a First in the first part of the Tripos in 1923 and a Second in the second part in 1924.

She continued to build an impressive list of undergraduate successes. Encouraged by Chadwick to undertake research, she worried that there would be no subjects left worth exploring. Fortunately, she ignored her fears and pressed on, spending six years as a research student. She was Marion Kennedy Student at Newnham (1924–26), Cambridge University Scandinavian Student at Uppsala (1927–29), and the first woman awarded the Allen Scholarship at the University of Cambridge (1929–30). The result of these years of research was her edition of the surviving Anglo-Saxon wills, published in 1930, which was her first work on primary sources. This book, *Anglo-Saxon Wills,* "followed the Chadwickian tradition of setting linguistic skills to serve cultural ends"[2] and shows Whitelock's command of Old English, Old Norse, and Anglo-Saxon history and her knowledge of modern diplomatic technique.

Although there were few academic positions for women in the late 1920s, Whitelock's skills made her an excellent candidate. In 1930 she became a lecturer in English language at St. Hilda's College, Oxford. The next seven years she devoted herself to her teaching. In 1935 she became a tutor; in 1937 a full fellow; and in 1951, in recognition of her services to the college, she was elected vice principal. During these years she taught undergraduates Old English, Old Norse, some Middle English, and philology. Awarded her M.A. from Cambridge in 1928, she was awarded the M.A. of the University of Oxford by decree in 1932. In 1940, as a result of her research, she was elected a Leverhulme Fellow.

However, even as Whitelock rose in the academic ranks of Oxford, the women's colleges still did not have the same privileges as the men's. As late as 1944 St. Hilda's College still had not managed to become self-governing and independent. In *The Centenary History of St. Hilda's College, Oxford,* the author discusses the tension between the principal and the fellows at St. Hilda's. The former, Miss Mann, supported the status quo; on the other hand, the fellows, led by Dorothy Whitelock and Helen Gardner with external encouragement, sought change.[3] Highly frustrated, Whitelock applied for a chair at Liverpool in early 1944. In a letter to Sir Frank Stenton dated 29 May 1944, she thanks him for supporting her application and goes on to write: "I know that I have hardly the remotest chance of getting it, and I don't know if I really want it. I should find it very difficult to tear myself away from St. Hilda's—from my room and its view. But I don't like the English school here & I am getting very tired of having no say in the running of it, its examinations & syllabuses etc."[4]

Beginning in 1947, through their meetings "the Fellows made it clear that they were ready—and anxious—to lose the country house image of the College ... and win for it acceptance as a college of Oxford, fully acknowledged by all the others."[5] However, not until 1959 did the women's societies become full colleges of the university, with the same privileges as the men's colleges.

In 1944 Whitelock applied for a sabbatical leave of absence to care for her aged and ailing mother. The council granted her request in May 1944, and she was on sabbatical from October 1944 to Easter 1945. While her concern for her mother probably motivated her to think about resigning from St. Hilda's, her dissatisfaction with the circumstances at the college also exacerbated the situation. She must have conveyed her feelings in a letter to the Stentons because Sir Frank wrote back, with uncharacteristic emotion, in a letter dated 19 March 1945, urging her not to resign:

> What I want to say is that to the best of my knowledge ... your resignation for this reason would be a serious injury to the interests of women in academic life. What is keeping women back from the consideration which many of them deserve is not "sex

prejudice" (except among a few eccentrics). It is a doubt whether women can stay the course as well as men. There is no question about scholarship involved. But there is a feeling that through ill-health or marriage or family troubles a woman is not unlikely to throw up her academic work just when she is fairly in the swing of it, and that she can't be relied on for the steady, long-term course of routine, on which all institutions depend. Your resignation would give a telling argument to those whom for this purpose you, like myself, regard as the enemy. The distinction of your work and your reputation among scholars would from this point of view merely underline the fact that you had fallen out of the regular course of teaching and college life.

Please forgive me for writing like this. It isn't a habit of mine. But Doris [his wife] is distressed and I won't pretend that I am happy.[6]

Many things are made clear from Dorothy's response to Sir Frank, dated 21 March 1945: her reliance on Sir Frank as her mentor and friend; his influence (in this letter she tells him, "You know that I value your judgment more than anybody's"); her love of the academic life; and her new awareness of the problems that exist for women in academia. She writes: "Your letter put a point of view that hadn't occurred to me. I recognise its validity & am glad to have something concrete to bolster up the feeling I've had all along that I should be doing something wrong in resigning. It would be an act of sheer tiredness and weakness, I believe, for it would probably not add to mother's eventual happiness, as I don't believe I should be strong enough to do it with a really good grace."[7] Whitelock herself said, years later, "I never had that feminine desire to run a home," and she never married.[8] When her sabbatical drew to a close, and with her sister Phyllis's blessing, Whitelock arranged for a housekeeper to care for their mother and returned to St. Hilda's for the next term.

In March 1946 she applied for the Rawlinson and Bosworth Professorship of Anglo-Saxon at the University of Oxford. Confident in her position as a teacher—she had had sole charge of the language side of the English school since her appointment in 1930—and as a scholar, with two books and approximately nine well-received articles to her credit, and with references from Hector M. Chadwick, F. Maurice Powicke, and Bruce Dickins, she (and the Stentons) expected that she would receive the appointment. Stenton and Kenneth Sisam voted for her, but the other three members of the committee (including J. R. R. Tolkien) voted against her and for C. L. Wrenn. Sir Frank's wife, Doris, wrote Dorothy on 16 April 1946, after the decision was made, to let her know:

Those who knew something of the subject all agreed with your merits—and a notably second rate person was put in because he enjoyed the inestimable privilege of masculinity. In a way I'm glad it's Wrenn and not Alistair Campbell for no one could think Wrenn beat you by scholarship.

You have good health and all being well should in the next 10 years acquire so high a reputation that when you next put in for a Chair it will be all right and even sex obsessed old gentlemen will not be able to stand against the shattering weight of your broadside. After all, perhaps we were expecting too much of the ancient university of Oxford. . . . One of the old chairs is very different.[9]

In a letter dated Easter Sunday, 1946, Lady Stenton summed up the situation for women in academia: "[I]f [Frank] and Sisam couldn't do it I really don't think it could be at this moment. But every incident of this sort shakes the barriers of prejudice in the older universities."[10]

Although disappointed, Whitelock remained at St. Hilda's. In 1946 she became a lecturer at the University of Oxford; in 1955 she became lecturer in Old English there. In 1948 she joined her alma mater, Newnham College, where she had maintained her contacts, as an associate of the college. The University of Cambridge awarded her the degree of Doctor of Literature in 1950, and she was elected a Professorial Fellow of Newnham College when she returned to Cambridge in 1957 as the Elrington and Bosworth Professor of Anglo-Saxon.

During her early years at St. Hilda's, Whitelock focused on her teaching; she believed that teaching was as much her work as writing and publishing were: "It always irritates me when people say 'How do you find time for your own work?' (meaning writing) as if bringing on the next generation was not part of my own work."[11] Throughout the years she worked hard to help her students with the intricacies of Old English, lending a sympathetic ear as well to students who regarded Beowulf not as a hero but as a nightmare. Students at all levels of study remember her lectures and her tutorials fondly.[12]

Like all students who then become professors, Whitelock had to learn the trade; not only did she refine her teaching skills during those first seven years, but she honed her literary sensibilities, too, by tutoring—as her later publications show. Her first book came out in 1930, and Whitelock began publishing again in 1937, when she published the first of a number of articles on Wulfstan, the archbishop of York, "A Note on Wulfstan the Homilist." She followed that up with an edition of Wulfstan's *Sermo Lupi ad Anglos* (1939, rev. eds. 1952, 1963), "Wulfstan and the So-Called Laws of Edward and Guthrum" (1941), "Archbishop Wulfstan, Homilist and Statesman" (1942), "Two Notes on Ælfric and Wulfstan" (1943), "Wulfstan and the Laws of Cnut" (1948), and several others. In the introduction to the edition of *Sermo Lupi ad Anglos,* she discusses Wulfstan's career, his education, and his role as a homilist. The articles, among other things, disprove the idea of a "Wulfstan imitator," demonstrate Wulfstan's importance as an advisor to kings (both Æthelred the Unready and his successor, the Danish Canute), his role as a statesman, and his contribution to the laws of the early eleventh century. The edition and articles reveal Whitelock's expertise in Old English, her historical interests, and her interdisciplinary approach to language, history, and primary sources.

In the article "Anglo-Saxon Poetry and the Historian" (1949), Whitelock discusses the importance of literary sources for understanding history, especially social history.

Her next article, "The Interpretation of the 'Seafarer'" (1950), is a detailed analysis of the poem; she concludes that the poem belongs in the Christian tradition of penance and exile. In 1951 she published a book, *The Audience of Beowulf,* which she had originally presented as a series of three lectures at London University. This book combines her literary and historical interests beautifully in that she uses the poem to discuss the historical background of the poet and his audience. Her argument for a late-eighth- to early-ninth-century origin for the poem is still convincing.

Her next publications mark her as one of the leading historians in Anglo-Saxon studies. Asked by editors at Penguin to contribute a book on the Anglo-Saxon period to their series on social history, she responded with *The Beginnings of English Society* (1952). Although the book has no footnotes, a fact that Whitelock herself later bemoaned, it is a wonderful introduction to all aspects of life in early England, written for the nonspecialist. Using literary and historical sources as evidence, Whitelock synthesized a picture of daily life, focusing on marriage and family and on law and property.

In 1954 she produced a facsimile edition of one of the manuscripts of the Anglo-Saxon chronicle *The Peterborough Chronicle,* which bears "witness to Dr. Whitelock's extensive knowledge of Anglo-Saxon historical sources, and is characterized by the exact scholarship and acute criticism typical of her work."[13] Good and useful as this book was (and is), her next book, *English Historical Documents* (1955, rev. 1979)—which made Latin and Old English documents from ca. 500 to 1042 available in translation and provided an introduction and context for each one—transformed primary source studies in departments around the world. Divided into three parts, the book includes a section on secular narrative sources (Asser's *Life of Alfred* and the *Anglo-Saxon Chronicle*, among others), one on charters and laws, and one on ecclesiastical sources (including Bede's *Ecclesiastical History* and saints' lives, for instance).

The next year, 1957, about eleven years after Lady Stenton wrote that she would get a chair, she was elected as Elrington and Bosworth Professor of Anglo-Saxon at Cambridge, the first woman ever (and still) to hold that position. In her inaugural lecture, *Changing Currents in Anglo-Saxon Studies,* she discusses pre-Conquest England, presenting an overview of Anglo-Saxon studies and their importance. Not surprisingly, given her own wide-ranging interests, she touches on numismatics, archaeology, history, law, placename studies, and literature, blending together her commentary so as synthesize these into an elegant summary of the inclusiveness and current state of Anglo-Saxon studies.

In an interview shortly after Whitelock took up her post, she identified herself as an Anglo-Saxon historian. Obviously her peers and publishers regarded her thusly. Some time after arriving at Cambridge, she was approached to write a biography of Alfred the Great. Much of her subsequent work centers on Alfred and his circle; she examined the primary sources available to him, the translations he himself undertook or had others do. She evaluated Asser's *Life of Alfred*, the primary source for information on the king, defending his authenticity. While she worked on Alfred's biography, she continued to publish on other subjects. She revised Henry Sweet's *Anglo-Saxon Reader* in 1967 and wrote several articles on Bede. Lord Rennell approached her to translate and comment on the tenth-century will of an Anglo-Saxon noblewoman, published by the Roxburghe Club in 1968 as the *Will of Æthelgifu*. In addition, she participated in several professional societies.

Over the years Whitelock held many offices and received many honors. She served as president of the Viking Society for Northern Research (1939–41) and editor of their publication (*Saga-Book*) beginning in 1940. She was a member of the Council of the Royal Historical Society (1945–49); a member of the Council of the Yorkshire Archaeological Society (1948–57); and vice president of the Society for Medieval Archaeology (1957–64). She was elected a Fellow of the British Academy in 1956; an Honorary Fellow of St. Hilda's College, Oxford, in 1957 and of Newnham College, Cambridge, in 1970. In 1964 Whitelock was recognized for her significant contributions to the field of Anglo-Saxon studies and was made Commander of the Order of the British Empire. Upon the death of Sir Stenton in 1967, Whitelock succeeded him as president of the English Place-Name Society (1967–79) and as chairman of the British Academy Committee for the Sylloge of Coins in the British Isles (1967–78).

Her correspondence reveals how busy these committees kept her. Her position as chair of the Sylloge Committee took an incredible amount of time and diplomacy. She wrote letters soliciting benefactors, worked on establishing a realistic publishing schedule and lining up contributors, and negotiated with a museum in Estonia to publish a book about its coin collection. This last involved a certain delicacy and an awareness of the political situation there. Furthermore, she ran interference for her own colleagues, often consulting her friends for the best way to present their cases to the British Museum.

Always willing to answer questions, Whitelock received many letters from students, fellow scholars, and local churches over the years. She kept copies of her replies, which show the attention to detail that so many people mention when they speak of her work. It is in these letters that Whitelock reveals that she has little tolerance for fools, regardless of their positions. However, she corresponded with many colleagues over the years, whether she agreed with their line of reasoning or not, answering their questions and asking for answers to some of her own. Her relationship with the numismatists was a particularly beneficial one; she provided them with historical data (such as regnal lists), and they reciprocated. She often turned to Neil Ker for help with scribal hands, admitting in a letter dated 18 January 1963, "I am no paleographer."[14] R. R. Darlington, Michael Dolley, Kenneth Sisam, Dom Paul Meyvaert, Christopher Blunt, Henry Loyn, Steward Lyon, Janet Nelson, and Janet Bately all consulted her at various times. Helmut Gneuss, in a letter dated 14 December 1976, probably summed up many peoples' feelings when he wrote, "I should like to thank you so much once again, not only for your letter, from which I have learned so many things, but for all that I have been able to learn from those numerous works of yours which I have on my shelves and to which I am turning again and again."[15]

Her letters to and from Stenton and his wife, Doris, document a relationship that began when she was a student and ended only after the deaths of both Stentons (he in 1967, she in 1971). Whitelock admired Sir Frank and considered him the best historian of his time. She often consulted him, and their early letters, addressed to Miss Whitelock and Professor Stenton, reveal their common interests in Anglo-Saxon history. Sometime after 1941, but before 1945, the address and tone of the letters change. Miss Whitelock becomes "My Dear Dorothy" and the subjects include some more personal ones. Stenton even suggested the title for her inaugural lecture (in a letter dated 20 January 1958) and gave her advice about the contents—suggesting that discussing social history in such a venue would be a bad idea and that she should include material about the Danish wars and settlements. After hearing the lecture, he reassured Whitelock, who was concerned, that neither he nor his wife had found the lecture dull.

Just as Stenton encouraged and helped Whitelock, she, too, helped him, occasionally providing insight into and observations on the language of charters and laws as well as on literary works. They reviewed some of each other's works (always positively) but did not hesitate to point out areas with which they disagreed. Their scholarly relationship benefited them both, he from her linguistic expertise, she from his historical acumen. After his death, Lady Stenton took over the revision of the third edition of his opus, *Anglo-Saxon England*. In the preface to that edition, she writes: "To Miss Whitelock, in particular, I am grateful for continued support and encouragement, for care in going through the book with a view to noting places where change might be necessary and where new editions of old authorities should be referred to, and for her support in not making changes where we both felt sure that my husband would not have wished it. Only a Saxonist of the highest standing could have done what she has done; only a close friend would have taken so much time from her own work to do it."[16]

In addition to revising Stenton's book, providing detailed responses to those who sought her help, writing reviews of literary and historical works, and working on her biography of Alfred the Great and other pieces, Whitelock also found time to serve on university committees at Cambridge and to build up an excellent Department of Anglo-Saxon and Kindred Studies. She worked closely with Peter Hunter Blair, Peter Clemoes (who later succeeded her in the chair), and Raymond Page (later chair of Scandinavian Studies) to recruit students. Together with Kathleen Hughes, who taught Celtic studies, they created as "fine a training ground for undergraduates interested in the language and history of Britain and Ireland in the early Middle Ages as was to be found anywhere in the world."[17]

In 1967, two years before she retired, Whitelock decided to negotiate with the university to move the Department of Anglo-Saxon and Kindred Studies out of the Archaeology and Anthropology Faculty—where it had been since 1927—and back into the English School. The *Cambridge University Reporter* (22 March 1967) makes it clear that, while not everyone in the university supported the move, the entire faculty of the English school and the Anglo-Saxon and Kindred Studies department did.

Whitelock explained that the primary reasons for this move were, first, to join a faculty that concerned itself with "the study of languages, literature, and documentary sources" and, second, to reconnect the "study of the earliest English language, literature, and history" with that of Middle English.[18] The General Board of the University of Cambridge granted that request, and Whitelock brought Anglo-Saxon back where it belonged. Today the department is part of the faculty of English, and its name is the Department of Anglo-Saxon, Norse, and Celtic.

Dorothy Whitelock's successes in academia—as a student, teacher, administrator, and scholar—are all the more impressive when one considers how few opportunities there were for women when she began her college career in 1921. In 1893 a Newnham student had been the first woman appointed to a University of Cambridge teaching post; in 1913 there were about 120 women in such posts, but they had no say in decision making, syllabus setting, and marking of exams—in other words, the running of their departments or colleges.[19] In 1946 at Cambridge "two women were Professors, twenty were University Lecturers and two were Heads of Departments, yet they were barred from voting, even on matters affecting their own Departments."[20] Whitelock's appointment as the Elrington and Bosworth Chair of Anglo-Saxon studies in 1957, therefore, is a testament, among other things, to the quality of her scholarship. After all, seventeen years later, "[i]n 1974, less than 3 per cent [sic] of Professors and 7 per cent of Readers were women. Of all University appointments at Cambridge, only 7 per cent were held by women."[21]

In 1979, at the age of seventy-eight, Whitelock revised her book *English Historical Documents*. In 1980 she proofed her contribution (translations of all the earliest material up to 1066) to the second volume of *Councils and Synods,* which she also helped edit. She also completed the manuscript of her biography of Alfred the Great. Unfortunately, later that year she had a stroke that impaired her ability to communicate; the Alfred biography remains unpublished to this day.[22] On 14 August 1982 she died in a Cambridge nursing home.

Given her contribution to Anglo-Saxon studies, it is not at all surprising that many of the works she authored grace Anglo-Saxon scholars' bookshelves today. As one of her friends and colleagues, Henry Loyn, said in an essay: "[W]e turn to her for authoritative statements on the *Chronicle, Beowulf,* the work of Wulfstan, the achievements of King Alfred, the social content of laws, charters, and wills."[23] It is also a testimony to her contributions at both Oxford and Cambridge that they each offer a Dorothy Whitelock prize to students. St. Hilda's College, Oxford, established the Whitelock Prize in 1982 with funds given to the college in her memory. Awarded first in 1983, it is given annually to an undergraduate at the college for the best performance in Anglo-Saxon. Newnham College, Cambridge, awards the Dorothy Whitelock Studentship. This award was founded in 1986 to honor Whitelock's contribution to Anglo-Saxon and Kindred Studies; it is given to graduate students working in or applying to the Department of Anglo-Saxon, Norse, and Celtic. Unlike the one at Oxford, both men and women may apply for it.

At her funeral the program, most probably put together by two of her former students, Peter Clemoes and Simon Keynes, included a selection of a letter from Alcuin to Arno of Salzburg, the closing prayer of Bede's *Ecclesiastical History,* and a reading from Byrhtnoth at the *Battle of Maldon* (991). It seems only fitting to end this essay with the quote from the *Battle of Maldon* because her delight in things Anglo-Saxon brought that material to many: "[Ic] geðance ðe, ðeoda Waldend, ealra ðæra wynna ðe ic on worulde gebad." [O God, ruler of peoples, I thank you for all the joys I have experienced in the world.]

Notes

I would like to thank the following people who helped me gather the information with which to write this essay: Joanna Ball, Andrew Lambert, and Jonathan Smith, Wren Library, Trinity College, Cambridge; Elizabeth Boardman, archivist, St. Hilda's College, Oxford; G. Michael Bott, keeper of the archives and manuscripts, Reading University Library; Simon Keynes, Elrington and Bosworth Professor of Anglo-Saxon, Trinity College, Cambridge (keeper of Dorothy Whitelock's papers); and Anne Thomson, archivist, Newnham College, Cambridge.

1. McWilliams Tullberg, *Women at Cambridge,* 215 n. 73.
2. Clark, "Dorothy Whitelock."
3. Rayner, *Centenary History of St. Hilda's College, Oxford,* 87.
4. Dorothy Whitelock to Sir Frank Stenton, 29 May 1944, copy in Dorothy Whitelock's papers in the keeping of Simon Keynes, Trinity College, Cambridge.
5. Rayner, *Centenary History of St. Hilda's College, Oxford,* 88.
6. Sir Frank Stenton to Dorothy Whitelock, 19 March 1945, in Dorothy Whitelock's papers in the keeping of Simon Keynes, Trinity College, Cambridge.
7. Dorothy Whitelock to Sir Frank Stenton, 21 March 1945, copy in Dorothy Whitelock's papers in the keeping of Simon Keynes, Trinity College, Cambridge.
8. John Cunningham, "Waiting for Alfred," 9.
9. Lady Doris Stenton to Dorothy Whitelock, 16 April 1946, in Dorothy Whitelock's papers in the keeping of Simon Keynes, Trinity College, Cambridge.
10. Lady Doris Stenton to Dorothy Whitelock, Easter Sunday 1946, in Dorothy Whitelock's papers in the keeping of Simon Keynes, Trinity College, Cambridge.
11. Cunningham, "Waiting for Alfred," 9.
12. Henry Loyn, "Dorothy Whitelock, 1901–1982," 545–46; conversations with Simon Keynes, 16 August 2001, and Alisoun Gardner-Medwin, 17 August 2001.
13. Harmer, review of *The Peterborough Chronicle.*
14. Dorothy Whitelock to Neil Ker, 18 January 1963, copy in Dorothy Whitelock's papers in the keeping of Simon Keynes, Trinity College, Cambridge.
15. Helmut Gneuss to Dorothy Whitelock, 14 December 1976, in Dorothy Whitelock's papers in the keeping of Simon Keynes, Trinity College, Cambridge.
16. Stenton, *Anglo-Saxon England,* vii.
17. Loyn, "Dorothy Whitelock (1901–1982)," 292.
18. *Cambridge University Reporter* (22 March 1967): 1: 174.
19. McWilliams Tullberg, *Women at Cambridge,* 120, 132.
20. McWilliams Tullberg, *Women at Cambridge,* 181–82.
21. McWilliams Tullberg, *Women at Cambridge,* 188.

22. The typescript can be found in Dorothy Whitelock's papers in the keeping of Simon Keynes, Trinity College, Cambridge.

23. Loyn, "Dorothy Whitelock (1901–1982)," 295.

Select Bibliography of Works by Dorothy Whitelock

For a bibliography of Dorothy Whitelock's books, articles, and reviews through 1970, see *England before the Conquest: Studies in Primary Sources Presented to Dorothy Whitelock*, ed. Peter Clemoes and Kathleen Hughes (Cambridge: Cambridge University Press, 1971). For the more recent works, see Loyn's essay, "Dorothy Whitelock (1901–1982)." Many of her articles and lectures have been reprinted in two volumes: *From Bede to Alfred: Studies in Early Anglo-Saxon Literature and History* (London: Variorum Reprints, 1980); *History, Law and Literature in Tenth–Eleventh Century England* (London: Variorum Reprints, 1981).

Anglo-Saxon Wills. Cambridge: Cambridge University Press, 1930.

"A Note on Wulfstan the Homilist." *English Historical Review* 52 (1937): 460–65.

Editor. *Sermo Lupi ad Anglos.* London: Methuen, 1939.

"Wulfstan and the So-Called Laws of Edward and Guthrum." *English Historical Review* 56 (1941): 1–21.

"Archbishop Wulfstan, Homilist and Statesman." *Transactions of the Royal Historical Society*, 4th ser., 24 (1942): 25–45.

"Two Notes on Ælfric and Wulfstan." *Modern Language Review* 38 (1943): 122–26.

"Wulfstan and the Laws of Cnut." *English Historical Review* 63 (1948): 433–52.

"Anglo-Saxon Poetry and the Historian." *Transactions of the Royal Historical Society*, 4th ser., 31 (1949): 75–94.

"The Interpretation of the 'Seafarer.'" In *The Early Cultures of North-West Europe: H. M. Chadwick Memorial Studies*, edited by Cyril Fox and Bruce Dickins. Cambridge: Cambridge University Press, 1950.

The Audience of Beowulf. Oxford: Clarendon Press, 1951.

The Beginnings of English Society. Harmondsworth, Eng.: Penguin, 1952.

Editor. *The Peterborough Chronicle.* Early English Manuscripts in Facsimile, 4. Copenhagen: Rosenkilde and Bagger, 1954.

Editor. *English Historical Documents I: c. 500–1042.* 1955. 2nd rev. ed., London: Eyre and Spottiswoode, 1979.

Changing Currents in Anglo-Saxon Studies: An Inaugural Lecture. Cambridge: Cambridge University Press, 1958.

Editor. *Sweet's Anglo-Saxon Reader: In Prose and Verse.* 15th ed. Oxford: Oxford University Press, 1967.

"Florence Elizabeth Harmer." *Girton Review* 183 (Lent Term 1968): 26–27.

The Genuine Asser. 1967 Stenton Lecture. Reading, Eng.: University of Reading, 1968.

Translator and examiner, with Neil Ker and Lord Rennell. *The Will of Æthelgifu. A Tenth Century Anglo-Saxon Manuscript.* Oxford: Oxford University Press for the Roxburghe Club, 1968.

"The English Kingdoms." *History of the English Speaking Peoples* 1, no. 5 (1969): 156–63.

"Epic of St. Boniface." *History of the English Speaking Peoples* 1, no. 5 (1969): 175–76.

"England's Defense." *History of the English Speaking Peoples* 1, no. 7 (1969): 227–31.

"Anglo-Saxon Chronicle." *History of the English Speaking Peoples* 1, no. 7 (1969): 232–33.

"The English Place-Name Society 1923–1973." *English Place-Name Society Journal* 5 (1972–73): 6–14.

Review of *Anglo-Saxon England 2,* edited by Peter Clemoes. *Antiquity* 48 (1974): 162–63.

Review of *An Introduction to English Runes,* by R. I. Page. *Antiquaries Journal* 54, no. 2 (1974): 340–41.

Review of *Britain before the Norman Conquest,* by C. W. Phillips. *Antiquity* 49 (1975): 147–48.

Review of *Untersuchungen zu Inhalt, Stil und Technik angelsächsischer Gesetz und Rechtsbücher des 6. bis 12. Jahrhunderts,* by Dirk Korte. *Cambridge Law Journal* (1975): 328–30.

"Dr. Olaf von Feilitzen." *English Place-Name Society Journal* 9 (1976–77): 1–2.

"Dr. Kathleen Winifred Hughes." *Cambridge Review* (10 June 1977): 168–69.

"In Memoriam. Dr. Kathleen Winifred Hughes, 1926–1977." *Newnham College Roll Letter* (1978): 41–44.

Editor with M. Brett and C. N. L. Brooke. *Councils and Synods: With Other Documents Relating to the English Church, 1: A.D. 871–1204.* Oxford: Clarendon Press, 1981.

Works Cited

Clark, Cecily. "Dorothy Whitelock." *Nomina* 6 (1982): 2.

Cunningham, John. "Waiting for Alfred." *Guardian,* 18 August 1978.

Harmer, F. E. Review of *The Peterborough Chronicle,* edited by Dorothy Whitelock. *Review of English Studies* 8 (1957): 51.

Loyn, Henry. "Dorothy Whitelock, 1901–1982." *Proceedings of the British Academy* 70 (1984): 541–53.

———. "Dorothy Whitelock (1901–1982)." In *Medieval Scholarship: Biographical Studies on the Formation of a Discipline,* vol. 1, edited by Helen Damico and Joseph B. Zavadil. New York: Garland, 1995.

McWilliams Tullberg, Rita. *Women at Cambridge.* 1975. Rev. ed., Cambridge: Cambridge University Press, 1998.

Rayner, Margaret E. *The Centenary History of St. Hilda's College, Oxford.* [Great Britain]: Lindsay Ross, 1993.

Stenton, Frank M. *Anglo Saxon England.* 3rd ed. Oxford: Clarendon Press, 1971.

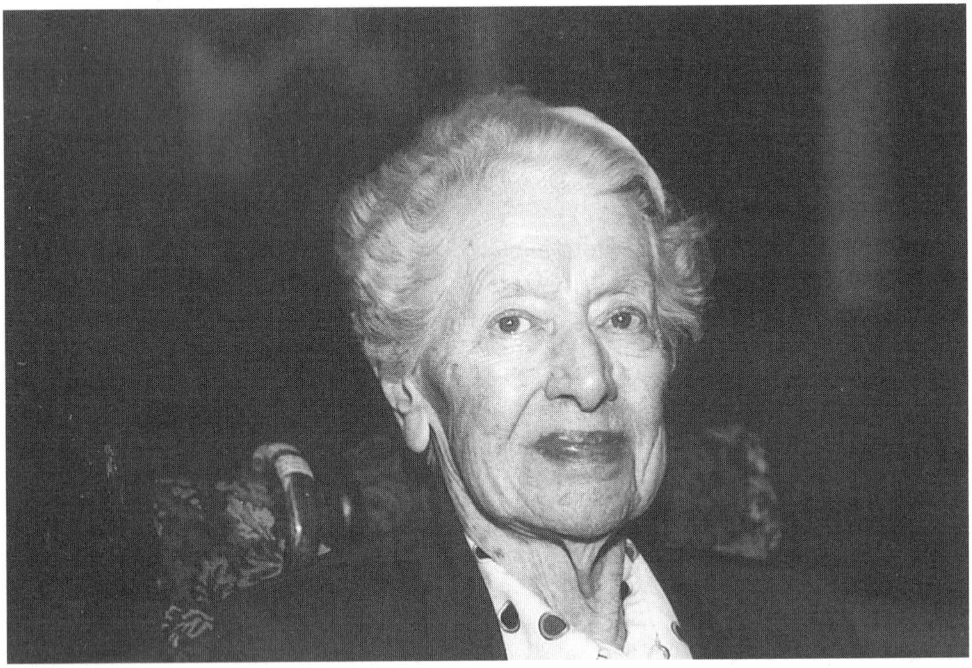

CHAPTER 39

Ruth J. Dean (1902–2003)
"Dean" of Anglo-Norman Studies

Kevin J. Harty

A STEPCHILD, A CINDERELLA, a poor relation, an ornament, a contributory element—at one time, doubtless all characterizations by the male-dominated academy (medieval and otherwise) of the role of women medievalists. These characterizations come, however, not from an article about women medievalists but from an article by a notable woman medievalist about Anglo-Norman studies, which in 1954 she characterized as a "fair field needing folk."[1]

When I came to the University of Pennsylvania as a first-year graduate student in September 1970, there were no tenured women in the English department. There was, however, a woman with presence in the department as well as in a number of other humanities departments. She was Ruth J. Dean, emerita professor of French language and literature at Mount Holyoke College. In her "retirement" Dean had moved to Philadelphia and joined the faculty of the University of Pennsylvania, variously serving as the university library's medieval bibliographer, lecturer in the Departments of English and Romance Languages, chair of the Medieval Studies Program, and visiting professor (and subsequently professor emerita—for a second time) in the Graduate School of Arts and Sciences (1969–74).

At Penn Dean also coordinated the development of the Middle Atlantic States Archive of Medieval Manuscripts on Microfilm, an invaluable resource for scholars, especially in the days before the advent of personal computers, online remote access to distant libraries and archives, and the development of the World Wide Web. In recognition of her service to the university and to the field of medieval studies, Penn awarded her an L.H.D. in 1979. That service was consistently to make the scholarship of others possible through her own scholarship.

The standard (off the record) comment about Dean's status at Penn was not that her male colleagues would tenure her but that she might tenure them if she were so inclined. At the time Penn's English department was a center for medieval studies—home to, among others, R. M. Lumiansky, Robert Pratt, James Rosier, Edward Irving, and the by-then retired Albert Baugh. Complementing the faculty in English were tenured medievalists (all male, of course) in history, in the classical and modern languages (notably William Roach), in philosophy, and in other fields. And the only woman to whom they all deferred was Ruth J. Dean.

I met Ruth Dean as soon as I came to Penn because I had the good fortune to be assigned to her as a research assistant—as part of the financial-aid package Penn awarded me. When I first went to see her in her principal office in Penn's Van Pelt Library, I knew two relevant things: that she was the only woman teaching in the graduate program in which I had just enrolled and that I knew nothing about Anglo-Norman or the literature written in it. In the next four years I was to learn a great deal about Dean and about Anglo-Norman and the literature of "the fair field." She was a formidable scholar without being a formidable person. While a number of her male colleagues cultivated unapproachable personae, Dean had an unbridled enthusiasm for scholarship—her own, her colleagues', and her students'. When I asked her to serve as second reader on my dissertation, she gladly agreed.

Ruth Josephine Dean was born in New York City on 10 March 1902. Her education was the best the academy in the first half of the twentieth century was prepared to allow women. She attended Wellesley College, earning a B.A. in 1922. She subsequently attended Saint Hugh's College, Oxford University, earning a B.A. (honors) in 1924, an M.A. in 1928, and a D.Phil. in 1938.

While a student at Oxford, Dean was research assistant to the eminent paleographer E. A. Lowe of Corpus Christi College. For her doctorate she studied with Mildred K. Pope of Somerville College, where she met a fellow student, M. Dominica Legge, with whom she later coedited *The Rule of Saint Benedict* (1964). For her thesis she was able to combine her knowledge of paleography with her love of the history of the French language. Her topic was a study of the Anglo-Norman *Cronicles* of Nicholas Trevet under the supervision of Alfred Ewert. Her love for her chosen topic, one of the finest and most influential pieces of Anglo-Norman literature, was infectious and genuine.

From this thesis came several articles, including "The Manuscripts of Nicholas Trevet's Anglo-Norman *Cronicles*" (1962) and "Nicholas Trevet, Historian" (1976). For more than half a century Dean was an unstinting advocate for the study of Anglo-Norman both as a language and as a body of literature, challenging other medievalists to move beyond any narrow constructs of Anglo-Norman as some "stepchild, Cinderella, poor relation, even barbarian" in the world of French and to see Anglo-Norman literature as a "varied body of material . . . to be reckoned with in the study not only of French and English, but also of comparative European literature."[2] Her advocacy for Anglo-Norman was literary as well as linguistic. She consistently encouraged scholars to become familiar with the three languages and the three literary traditions of medieval England.[3]

The pioneering study of Anglo-Norman had been Johan Vising's 1923 *Anglo-Norman Language and Literature*. Dean's lifework was to study the manuscripts and other materials that Vising catalogued in "his deceptively small book."[4] Her research took her to the Bodleian Library, to the British Museum, and to other libraries throughout Europe and North America. While Vising had organized his study from secondary sources, Dean examined in situ the hundreds of manuscripts containing Anglo-Norman texts. The results of her work, carried out with the good company and support of her longtime companion, the Renaissance scholar Eleanor Rosenberg of Barnard College (d. 1998), were published in 1999 with the collaboration of Maureen B. M. Bolton as *Anglo-Norman Literature: A Guide to Texts and Manuscripts,* a guide that supersedes Vising's catalog in every way and that is a major reference work in medieval studies.

We tend today to forget how marginalized both women and certain areas of medieval studies once were. Dean's tutor at Oxford, Mildred K. Pope, became a tutor at Somerville in 1894. But Pope herself was not admitted to full membership in the university until after World War I, and the Modern Language School, in which she taught Old French, was not established until 1903. In 1939 the University of Bordeaux awarded Pope an honorary doctorate; she was the first woman to be so honored by a French university. From the beginning the field studied (Old French in its various forms) and those who studied it seem to have held parallel marginalized statuses.

When she returned to the United States to teach, Dean came to Mount Holyoke College, where she would be a member of the faculty in the Department of French Language and Literature from 1933 to 1967; she served as department chair from 1951 to 1954. In 1950 she was appointed to the rank of professor. In 1966 she was named Mary Lyon Professor. In 1967 she was honored with emerita status.

Over the years Dean accumulated well-earned fellowships and well-deserved honors: she was a Fanny Bullock Workman Fellow (1937–38), a John Gamble Fund Researcher (1937–38), an Alice Freeman Palmer Fellow (1943–44), a member of the Institute of Advanced Study in Princeton (1943–44 and 1950–51), a John Simon Guggenheim Fellow (1948–49), the recipient of a grant-in-aid from the American Philosophical Society (1966), and a National Endowment for the Humanities Senior Fellow (1967–68).

In 1946 Wellesley College elected Dean as a distinguished alumna to Phi Beta Kappa. She was decorated as a chevalier of the Ordre des Palmes Académiques in 1949 and named an *officier* in 1963. She served as president of the Medieval Academy of America from 1973 to 1974. She was a member and officer of the Modern Language Association, the Modern Humanities Research Association, the American Association of Teachers, and the American Association of University Professors. She served as a member of the editorial boards of *PMLA* and *L'Esprit créateur* and an advisor to the College Board, to the National Council for the Junior Year Abroad, and to the American Council of Learned Societies.

There is, on one level, a kind of schizophrenic nature (not atypical for women medievalists at one time) to Dean's career and life, though clearly her career as an Anglo-Normanist came to define her life in the most meaningful way. The major part of her career was not spent at a major research university. She was a master teacher at a solid liberal arts college for women. But summers found her in major research centers across North America and Europe, carrying out the kind of close, hands-on work necessary for other kinds of serious research. Her focus was on Anglo-Norman studies, and her work in that fair field yielded an abundant harvest—as *Anglo-Norman Literature* clearly demonstrates. The impressive scope of her accomplishment in this volume will be obvious from my summary of the volume's contents later in this essay. The importance of Dean's work in Anglo-Norman studies cannot be overstated; her magnum opus makes possible and encourages future work in that fair field. *Anglo-Norman Literature* is a reminder to us all not to overlook an important corpus of literature from medieval England. Because of this meticulous study—the result of a lifetime of scholarly activity—we can all better appreciate the wealth of literature that is Anglo-Norman. Dean's work shows that the supposedly narrow field of Anglo-Norman studies has depth and breadth.

A no-nonsense study by a no-nonsense scholar, *Anglo-Norman Literature* begins by cataloguing a literary tradition that includes the earliest surviving chronicle in the French vernacular, Geffrei Gaimar's *L'Estoire des engleis,* which was composed sometime before 1140. Gaimar's work covers the period from the settlements of the Anglo-Saxons to the death of William Rufus; it was, however, soon surpassed in popularity on both sides of the Channel by a better-known and influential Anglo-Norman text, the *Roman de Brut* by Wace, finished in 1155 and based in large part on Geoffrey of Monmouth's *Historia Regum Britanniae* (1135–38). Abridgments of Geoffrey or of Wace (or of both) continued to be popular texts for Anglo-Norman writers. Historiographical texts indebted to them include the *Royal Brut* (fourteenth century), the *Conquests of England* (fifteenth century), *Le Livere de reis de Brittanie* (thirteenth century), the Harley *Brut* (thirteenth century), the *Brut Chronicle* (fourteenth century), the *Prose Brut to 1272,* the *Prose Brut to 1332,* and *Le Petit Bruit* by Rauf de Boun (fourteenth century).

What follows is a brief catalog of what other literary works *Anglo-Norman Literature* also surveys. Other Anglo-Norman historiographical texts in verse and in prose include chronicles of the dukes of Normandy (twelfth and thirteenth centuries), descriptions of England (twelfth century), noble and royal genealogies from France and England (thirteenth and fourteenth centuries), various versions of the prophecies of Merlin (thirteenth and fourteenth centuries), records of laws established by William the Conqueror (twelfth century), a 1215 translation of the Magna Carta ("the first document of political importance known to have been issued in the vernacular"), John of Canterbury's *Polistoire* (fourteenth century), histories of the Third Crusade (twelfth and thirteenth centuries), biographies of William the Marshall (thirteenth century) and of the Black Prince (fourteenth century), and, perhaps of most interest to Dean, the fourteenth-century *Les Cronicles* of Nicholas Trevet, O.P.[5] Trevet presents a history of the world from the Creation to the death of John XXII. For his sources Trevet used an Anglo-Norman *Brut,* Latin chronicles, and the Bible. His *Cronicles* in turn influenced later genealogists and chroniclers and has been studied in relation to the works of Chaucer and John Gower.

Anglo-Norman texts make important contributions to the chanson de geste tradition. The twelfth-century Oxford *Chanson de Roland* is the oldest surviving copy of the epic. Other Anglo-Norman chansons from the Charlemagne cycle include the *Chanson d'Aspremont* (thirteenth century), the only complete copy of *Otinel* (thirteenth century), a prose version of the *Pseudo-Turpin Chronicle* (fourteenth century), the mock-heroic *Pelerinage de Charlemagne* (thirteenth century), *La Destructioun de Rome* (thirteenth century), and *Fierabras* (fourteenth century).

Anglo-Norman political verse survives in a *Song of the Barons* and a *Lament for Simon de Montfort* (both thirteenth century), elegies for Edward I and Edward II and a rebuke of Queen Isabella (all fourteenth century), a *Prayer for Victory* arguing Edward III's claim to the throne of France (fourteenth century), an account of the treason of Thomas of Tuberville (before 1297), three satirical songs against the Scottish enemies of Edward I (fourteenth century), satires on the clergy (thirteenth and fourteenth centuries), and *The Devil's Contract,* a parodic attack on the privileged (thirteenth century).

Musicologists have long had an interest in Anglo-Norman songs for good reason. *Anglo-Norman Literature* catalogs love songs, humorous songs, rondeaux, virelays, a recruiting song for the Second Crusade, hymns, laments by the rejected and the imprisoned, *reverdies,* debates, drinking songs, and carols (twelfth century on).

The popularity of medieval romance extends to the canon of Anglo-Norman literature. In Anglo-Norman, Dean's catalog reminds us, we can find *Horn* (twelfth century), *Haveloc* (around 1200), *Boeve de Haumtone* and *Gui de Warewic* (both thirteenth century), *Waldef* (thirteenth or fourteenth century), *Fouke Le Fitz Waryn* (fourteenth century), *Amis et Amiloun* (thirteenth century), Thomas's *Tristan* (twelfth century), several versions of *La Foilie Tristan* (thirteenth century), *Amadas et Ydoine* (thirteenth century), *Ipomedon* (thirteenth century), *Protheselaus* (thirteenth century), *Floire et Blancheflor* (thirteenth century), the legends of Alexander (thirteenth and fourteenth centuries), *Fergus* (thirteenth century), Chrétien de Troyes's *Perceval* (fourteenth century), the prose *Lancelot* (fourteenth century), *Partonopeus de Blois* (thirteenth century), and *Octavian et Dagobert* (thirteenth century). Other Anglo-Norman courtly texts include the *Lais* and *Fables* of Marie de France (twelfth century), the contemporary *Lai du Cor* by Robert Biket, and various *contes, dits,* and fabliaux (all thirteenth and fourteenth centuries).

Anglo-Norman writers were partial to social and moral satire, and they have left us texts that both evidence and counter the medieval penchant for antifeminism; that warn of the dangers of wine, jealousy, boasting, and usury; and that discuss chess, fortune-telling, conduct for boys and young men, manners at table, courtly love, and physiognomy. These last texts (thirteenth and fourteenth centuries) reflect a tradition dating back to Aristotle's treatises for the education of Alexander the Great.

More than two dozen Anglo-Norman proverbial texts survive, including translations of the *Distichs* of Cato (twelfth century on), the *Liber Parabolarum* of Alain de Lille (thirteenth century), continental collections of anonymous proverbs in verse and in prose (twelfth and thirteenth centuries), *Les Aprises Salamon* (thirteenth or fourteenth century), the *Disciplina clericalis* of Petrus Alfonsi (thirteenth century), *Le Petit Plet* of Chardri (twelfth or thirteenth century), and a series of lines of verse traditionally said to have been engraved on the sword of Sir Gawain (thirteenth and fourteenth centuries).

The tenuous place that Anglo-Norman had in the linguistic history of England is reflected in the more than three dozens texts devoted to the teaching and learning of French in medieval England. These texts include a manual of French conversation revised around the year 1400; collections of simple phrases for teaching French to children (fifteenth century); observations comparing English with French (fifteenth century); a French vocabulary in the form of a guide for the care of infants (thirteenth century); a similar work in the form of guide to good manners for young people (fourteenth century); orthographic texts with guides to pronunciation (fourteenth and fifteenth centuries); multiple lists of conjugations of verbs and of declensional endings for nouns and pronouns (thirteenth, fourteenth, and fifteenth centuries); bilingual and trilingual medicinal, herbal, botanical, military, and legal texts and glossaries (thirteenth and fourteenth centuries); and several versions and adaptations of the *Ars dictaminis* (fourteenth and fifteenth centuries).

Anglo-Norman scientific and technological texts include *Le Petite Philosophie* (thirteenth century); a translation of separate texts of *L'Image du Monde* by Gossuin of Metz and by Perot Garbelei (fourteenth century); treatises on surveying land, on geography, and on algorism (thirteenth and fourteenth centuries); redactions of a report requested by Pope Innocent III from the Patriarch of Jerusalem that was intended to provide crusaders with a survey of Saracen lands (fourteenth century); an itinerary, in the hand of Matthew Paris, from London to Jerusalem by way of France and Italy, noting alternate routes (thirteenth century); guides to sacred cities in the Holy Land and descriptions of routes for pilgrimages (fourteenth century); a letter from Prester John to Emperor Frederick (thirteenth century); details of the travels of Marco Polo and of Sir John Mandeville (fourteenth century); instructions for calculating Easter (thirteenth century); the *Bestiarie* of Phillippe de Thaon (twelfth century—the oldest surviving bestiary in French); multiple lapidaries (twelfth century on); astrological tables and texts (thirteenth and fourteenth centuries); texts filled with predictions and prognostications (thirteenth and fourteenth centuries); alchemical texts (fourteenth century); directions for preparing paints and dyes (thirteenth and fourteenth centuries); heraldic treatises (thirteenth century on); sets of rules for estate and household management and treatises on husbandry composed by, among others, Bishop Robert Grosseteste (thirteenth and fourteenth centuries); cookbooks (thirteenth and fourteenth centuries); works on falconry (thirteenth and fourteenth centuries), and a dialogue between a knight and a huntsman on the art of venery (fourteenth century).

Anglo-Norman medical texts include versions of an apocryphal letter from Hippocrates to Caesar (thirteenth century on), translations of ancient medical texts (thirteenth and fourteenth centuries), discussions of the four humors (fourteenth and fifteenth centuries), gynecological texts (thirteenth century), guides to cosmetics and to phlebotomy (thirteenth century on), instructions for preparing ointments (fourteenth century), and numerous prescriptions and pharmaceutical texts (thirteenth century on).

Anglo-Norman biblical texts include translations and adaptations of (and commentaries on) Genesis, Judges, Psalms, Tobit, Proverbs, the Song of Songs, and Revelation as well as complete versions of the Old and New Testaments (twelfth century on). The most famous of these works may be the *Holkam Bible Picture Book,* composed before 1350. As early as 1200 biblical apocrypha were also a popular source for Anglo-Norman texts: there are translations of the *Infancy Gospels,* the *Testament of the Twelve Patriarchs,* the *Lives of the Virgin,* the *Gospel of Nicodemus,* and the *Passion of Judas.*

Anglo-Norman hagiographic texts date from Benedeit's *The Voyage of Saint Brendan,* composed circa 1106. Later texts include often multiple lives of Saint Alexis, Saint Alban, Saint Thomas Becket, Saint Gregory the Great, Saint Andrew, Saint Benedict, Saint Clement, Saint Cradoc, Saint Edmund, Saint Edward the Confessor, Saint Francis of Assisi, Saint George, Saint Giles, Saint Godric, Saint Hugh of Lincoln, Saint John the Baptist, Saint Josaphat, Saint John of Alexandria, Saint Lawrence, Saint Melor, Saint Nicholas, Saint Paul the Hermit, Saint Eustace, Saint Richard of Chichester, the Twelve Apostles, Saint Patrick, Saint Paul, Saint Audrey, the Virgin Mary, Saint Catherine of Alexandria, Saint Margaret, Saint Mary of Egypt, Saint Mary Magdalen, Saint Modwenna, Saint Osyth, and, for good measure, Antichrist.

Homiletic texts include sermons and other religious works by Maurice de Sully, bishop of Paris; by Robert of Greatham; by Nicholas Bozon, O.F.M.; by Simon of Caermarthen, O.S.A.; by Origen; by Thomas of Hales, O.F.M.; by Guischart de Beauliu; by Hélinant, monk of Froidmont; by Richard Rolle; by Robert Grosseteste; by John of Howden; by Saint Edmund Rich of Abingdon and Canterbury; by Peter of Peckham; by William of Waddington; by Odo of Cheriton; by Pierre de Blois, archdeacon of Bath; by Saint Gregory the Great; by Henry of Lancaster; by Alexander, monk of Canterbury and secretary to the archbishop; and by John Gower (all thirteenth century on). In Anglo-Norman we can also find versions of the *Ancrene Wisse* and of the rules of Saint Augustine, of Saint Benedict (another of Dean's favorite Anglo-Norman texts), and of the Hospitalers (thirteenth and fourteenth centuries). And from the twelfth century we have two important early religious dramatic texts, *Le Jeu d'Adam* and *La Seinte Resurreccion.*

Anglo-Norman Literature catalogs more than 260 devotional texts. These entries include meditations during and prayers at the Mass or for feast days; Marian devotional texts; the *Office of the Dead;* the canonical hours, the *Hours of the Virgin,* and sections of the breviary; popular hymns to the Trinity; reflections on and versions of the Pater Noster and the Ave Maria; prayers and hymns to Saints Anne and Joachim, to

Saint Catherine, to Saint Francis of Assisi, to Saint Giles, to Saint John the Evangelist, to Saint Margaret, and to Saint Thomas Beckett; and texts for the Stations of the Cross (all thirteenth century on). *Anglo-Norman Literature* concludes with a concordance to Vising and indices of manuscripts, incipits, titles, authors, sources, and patrons.

Few scholars have been so singular in their devotion to a field of study as Dean was to Anglo-Norman. Thanks in no small part to her life's work, Anglo-Norman can no longer be considered "an unimportant adjunct to English in an uncouth form of French."[6] Her legacy to the comparative interdisciplinary study of the Middle Ages is her most recent publication, the comprehensive and definitive *Anglo-Norman Literature*. That work synthesizes previous work in what Dean herself christened the "fair field" of Anglo-Norman and lays the ground for future spadework. *Anglo-Norman Literature* challenges current and future scholars to continue tilling the soil to bring forth future harvests of serious, in-depth studies of what was once dismissed as England's third literature written in a corrupt dialect of Old French. Such future studies will be part of the continuing legacy of this gracious, generous, and devoted teacher and scholar. For several generations Ruth J. Dean was rightly recognized—both in North America and abroad—as (no pun intended) the *dean* of Anglo-Norman studies. *Anglo-Norman Literature* is a lasting testimony to the important and pioneering scholarship done by Ruth J. Dean and by women medievalists in general.

Notes

1. Dean, "Fair Field Needing Folk."
2. First quotation: Dean, "Fair Field Needing Folk," 965: second quotation: Dean, "Fair Field of Anglo-Norman," 279.
3. Dean, "What Is Anglo-Norman?"
4. Dean with Boulton. *Anglo-Norman Literature,* vii.
5. Regarding the Magna Carta, see Dean with Boulton, *Anglo-Norman Literature*, 24.
6. Dean with Boulton, *Anglo-Norman Literature*, vii.

Select Bibliography of Works by Ruth J. Dean

"An Early Fragment of a Manuscript of Saint Augustine's Sermons on the Gospel according to Saint John." *Journal of Theological Studies* 36 (April 1935): 113–22.

"A Missing Chapter of the *Vie de Tobie*." *Modern Philology* 33 (August 1935): 13–19.

With E. A. Lowe. "Nouvelle liste de *Membra Disiecta*." *Revue Benedictine* 47 (October 1935): 305–11.

"An Anglo-Norman Version of Grosseteste: Part of His Suidas and *Testamenta XII Patriarcharum*." *PMLA* 51 (September 1936): 607–20.

"Manuscripts of Saint Elizabeth of Schönau in England." *Modern Language Review* 32 (January 1937): 62–71.

"Jean Baudoin's Version of *Testamenta XII Patriarcharum*." *Modern Language Notes* 53 (November 1938): 486–93.

"Nicholas Trevet: A Study of His Life and Works, with Special Reference to His Anglo-Norman

Chronicle." Ph.D. diss., Oxford University, 1938. Abstract in *Abstracts of Dissertations for the Degree of Doctor of Philosophy* 11 (1939): 116–19.

"Anglo-Norman Studies." *Romanic Review* 30 (February 1939): 3–14.

"An Essay in Anglo-Norman Paleography." In *Studies in French Language and Mediaeval Literature Presented to Professor Mildred K. Pope by Pupils, Colleagues, and Friends.* Manchester, Eng.: Manchester University Press, 1939.

"Un Manuscrit du *Roman de la Rose* a Jersey." *Romania* 65 (April 1939): 233–37.

"Ms. Bodl. 292 and the Canon of Nicholas Trevet's Works." *Speculum* 17 (April 1942): 243–49.

"A Fourteenth-Century Manuscript of *Le Roman de la Rose* and a Fragment of *Le Compot*: Huntington Manuscript 902." *Medium Aevum* 12 (1943): 18–24.

"Elizabeth, Abbess of Schönau, and Roger of Ford." *Modern Philology* 41 (May 1944): 209–20.

"Latin Paleography: 1929–1943." *Progress of Medieval and Renaissance Studies in the United States and Canada* 18 (June 1944): 6–18.

"The Earliest Known Commentary on Livy Is by Nicholas Trevet." *Medievalia et Humanistica* 3 (1945): 86–98.

"Chronicles and Memoires—Fourteenth and Fifteenth Centuries: 1314–1498." In *The Medieval Period,* edited by Urban Tigner Holmes Jr., vol. 1 of *A Critical Bibliography of French Literature,* edited by D. C. Cabeen. Syracuse: Syracuse University Press, 1947, 1952.

"Cultural Relations in the Middle Ages: Nicholas Trevet and Nicholas of Prato." *Studies in Philology* 65 (October 1948): 541–64.

"Unnoticed Commentaries on the *Bissasio Valerii* of Walter Map." *Mediaeval and Renaissance Studies* 2 (1950): 128–50.

"A Fair Field Needing Folk: Anglo-Norman." *PMLA* 69 (September 1954): 965–78.

"The Science and Art of Paleography." In *Literature and Science: Proceedings of the Sixth Triennial Congress, Oxford, 1954,* issued by the International Federation for Modern Languages and Literatures. Oxford: Basil Blackwell, 1955.

"The Manuscripts of Nicholas Trevet's Anglo-Norman *Cronicles*." *Medievalia et Humanistica* 14 (1962): 95–105.

"Nicolas Trevet." In *Dictionaire des lettres françaises: Le Moyen Âge,* edited by Georges Grente. Paris: Fayard, 1964.

Editor with M. Dominica Legge. *The Rule of Saint Benedict: A Norman Prose Version.* Medium Aevum Monographs, 7. Oxford: Basil Blackwell, 1964.

"What Is Anglo-Norman?" *Annuale Mediaevale* 6 (1965): 29–46.

"The Dedication of Nicholas Trevet's Commentary on Boethius." *Studies in Philology* 63 (1966): 593–603.

"An Early Treatise on Heraldry in Anglo-Norman." In *Romance Studies in Memory of Edward Billings Ham,* edited by Urban Tigner Holmes. Hayward: California State College Publications, 1967.

"The Fair Field of Anglo-Norman: Recent Cultivation." *Medievalia et Humanistica,* n.s., 3 (1972): 279–97.

With Elspeth Kennedy. "Un Fragment anglo-normand de la *Folie Tristan* de Berne." *Le Moyen Âge* 79 (1973): 57–72.

With Jeanne Krochalis. "Henry of Lancaster's *Livre de Seyntz Medicines*: New Fragments of an Anglo-Norman Work." *National Library of Wales Journal* 18 (1973): 87–94.

With Samuel G. Armistead. "A Fifteenth-Century Spanish Book List." In *Bibliographical Studies in Honor of Rudolf Hirsch*, edited by William E. Miller et al. Philadelphia: University of Pennsylvania Library, 1975.

"Nicholas Trevet, Historian." In *Medieval Learning and Literature: Essays Presented to Richard William Hunt*, ed. J. J. G. Alexander and M. T. Gibson. Oxford: Clarendon Press, 1976.

With Peter T. Collins. "Saint Deiniol Cathedral's Manuscript of John de Burgh's *Pupilla Oculi*." *Library Chronicle* (University of Pennsylvania) 43 (1979): 194–96.

With Maureen B. M. Boulton. *Anglo-Norman Literature: A Guide to Texts and Manuscripts*. London: Anglo-Norman Text Society, 1999.

CHAPTER 40

James Bruce Ross (1902–1995) and the Sources for Medieval and Renaissance History

CONSTANCE HOFFMAN BERMAN

JAMES BRUCE ROSS (known as J. B. to her friends and Miss Ross to her students) was born in Independence, Missouri, 3 July 1902, the youngest of a large family. She died at age ninety-three at the Collington Life Care Community near Washington, D.C., on 10 December 1995.[1] Much of her professional career was tied to Vassar College. She was a member of the class of 1925 of Vassar, with study at Cambridge University in 1922–23. She did her graduate study at the University of Chicago and received a master's degree in 1927 and a Ph.D. in 1934. In 1935 she was appointed a substitute instructor at Vassar, where she taught for two years. There was then a two-year interval at Wellesley (1937–39) before she returned to Vassar in 1940 as an instructor; in 1943 she became an assistant professor. In 1944–48 she served as assistant dean of the college. She then had a year's leave for research in Europe as a faculty fellow (1948–49). In 1949 she returned to full-time teaching as associate professor of history. In 1955 she was promoted to full professor with a year's leave again in 1955–56. In 1962 she was appointed to the Lucy Maynard Salmon Chair of History, which she held until her retirement in 1966.

Ross's skill and qualities as a teacher were much remarked, and she trained a number of important women scholars, among them several went on to become academics with expertise in the Middle Ages and the Renaissance.[2] The Vassar faculty memorial minute written in 1993 for Ross by colleagues and friends there remarks on her election in 1962 to the Lucy Maynard Salmon Chair:

> A particularly appropriate occupant of a chair honoring her former teacher, she continued as she had remained throughout her teaching career wholeheartedly dedicated

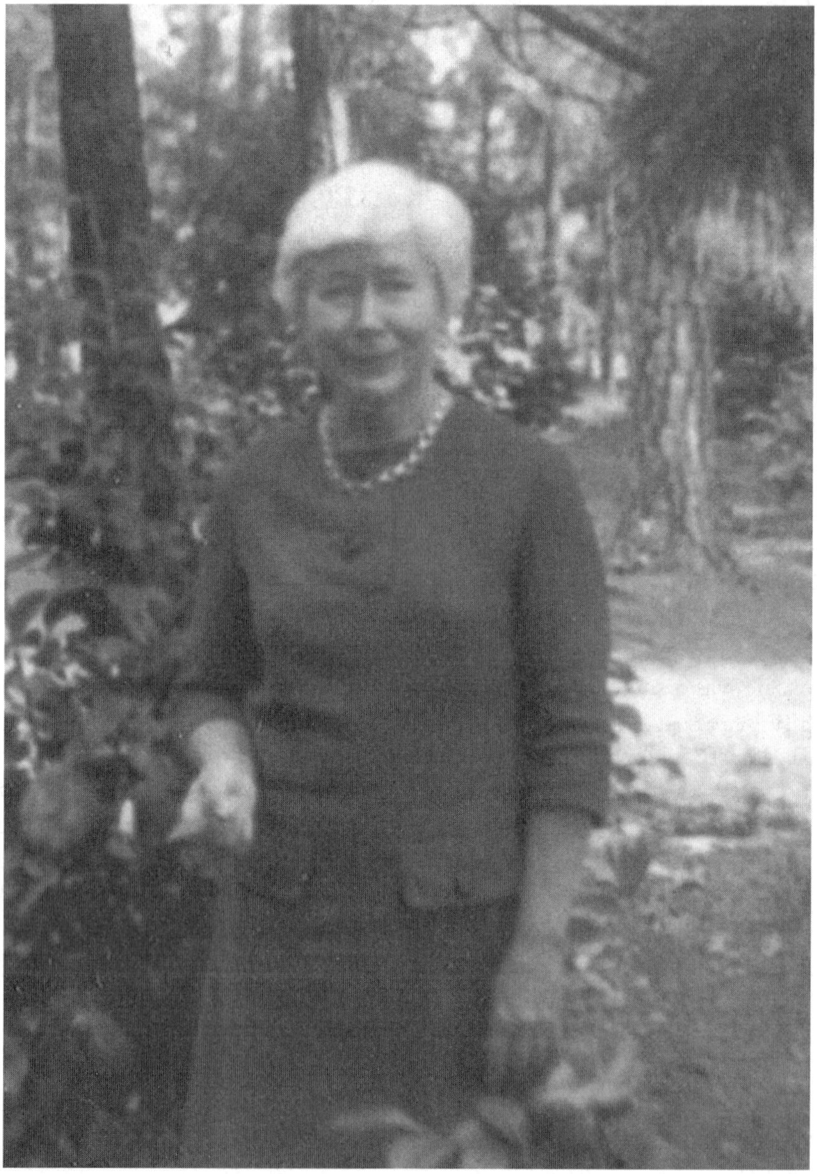

> to their shared goals.... J. B. Ross saw the relationship between teacher and students as that of "comrades in a quest," and she extended this quest most creatively to the especially challenging pursuit of knowledge and understanding of a more distant past. Discussing it specifically in relation to her enduring concern with beginning students, in a talk to an alumnae committee that she chaired, she stressed as a major goal "the intensifying of that life of the mind which the student has come here to experience." ... This has always been and remains the ideal of instruction at Vassar College.[3]

In remarks about her made at a memorial service in Washington, D.C., one of her students, Gloria Kury, wrote,

> It was during an educational experiment—the Renaissance Seminar of 1963–1964—that our relations became so rich.... I had in that Seminar the most compelling intellectual experience of my life.... We approached the Renaissance with a set of open-ended questions about patterns of continuity and change in the cultural and socio-political life of central Italy from the thirteenth through the sixteenth centuries. In some classes, the focus was on crisis and setback: for instance, we examined the Black Death's impact on demography, the mental climate, and the arts.... Others took up the growth of the commune and the imagery of "the good city." ... Spring Recess the whole group, students and teachers, went to Italy to visit the cities and the monuments we had been studying.... We were awestruck, of course, but could jump past first timers' wonder because of the months spent back in Poughkeepsie preparing us to meet the complex demands of the Renaissance heritage.[4]

Ross's teaching skill was matched by her scholarly rigor in attacking historiographical problems and the diversity of languages and bibliography that she brought to whatever topic she treated. It is difficult not to conclude that her first and last love in her scholarly work was the Renaissance humanist. In 1927, almost before embarking on her Ph.D., she published a learned article, "On the Early History of Leontius' Translation of Homer," in *Classical Philology*. One is reminded of Harriet Vane's lament for the life of the mind and the importance of correcting a single iota-subscript in Dorothy Sayers's *Gaudy Night* in Ross's approach to truth here and in all her other writing. Here there is a careful reconsideration of all the evidence about the precise date at which translations of Homer were made by the Greek Leontius and then transcribed for Petrarch and forwarded to Boccaccio. Starting, as many of her writings do, with a statement of what is known, in this case about the dating of Leontius's translation, Ross then gracefully points out the errors and contradictions in discussion of further points. Her firm conclusions are based on a collection of all possible evidence. The clear, decisive style and the linguistic accomplishments of a true scholar are already notable here in this early work.

Ross would expand her interests in things medieval, while retaining those in things Italian with her doctoral dissertation written at the University of Chicago and defended in 1934, "A Study of the Mediaeval Attitude toward Antiquities." Parts were published as her contribution to a collection of essays in honor of James Westfall Thompson, "A Study of Twelfth-Century Interest in the Antiquities of Rome." The opening paragraphs of this essay reflect her trenchant style and revisionism:

> It has long been assumed by historians that the men of the Middle Ages in western Europe viewed the relics and monuments of classical antiquity with no sense of their historical or aesthetic value but either neglected them entirely, except where they possessed intrinsic worth, or regarded them through a veil of superstition and legend. . . . [T]he current opinion must be rejected in favor of a broader view of the subject. (302–3)

She continues:

> In general it can be said that instances of genuine antiquarian interests, such as have been defined above, seem to increase from century to century during the Middle Ages and to be especially notable in the Carolingian age and in the twelfth century, two periods often designated by the term "Renaissance." (303–4)

She then marshals her evidence to defend the proposition that Rome in particular was appreciated for its antiquities already in the twelfth century. Among her examples are several that have become more familiar to my generation because we can now teach from an edition of the *Mirabilia urbis Romae,* usually attributed to Benedict, canon of Saint Peter's. Indeed, there was an entire National Endowment for the Humanities (NEH) summer seminar at the American Academy in Rome in 1999 dedicated to that text and the remains of Rome to which it referred.[5] In using this text in her dissertation, Ross was far ahead of her time. It is interesting, too, that she cites my own favorite contract from Rome from this period, which records the solution to a dispute involving the abbess of Saint-Cyriac over the ownership of Trajan's column, which was visited by twelfth-century pilgrims, possibly because from the top one gets such a good view of the ancient fora. It was the revived Roman Senate of the mid-twelfth century, of the time of Arnold of Brescia, that resolved this dispute, and for that reason this document has received much attention.[6] Ross's noting of this important Roman abbess makes it no surprise that forty years later the "Medieval Religious Women's Lives and Communities" project would begin with Latium.[7] Such knowledge of twelfth-century Rome's antiquities must certainly have added to the admiration of her erudition by Richard Krautheimer, her colleague for a number of years at Vassar.

In 1945 Ross produced the first of two articles published in *Speculum*. "Two Neglected Paladins of Charlemagne, Erich of Friuli and Gerold of Bavaria" is a study of two knights involved in Charlemagne's southeastern campaigns against the Avars that one can still read with interest today. Here one sees not only the relationship of her work to that of James W. Thompson but also Ross's continued concern with righting the historical record. As she puts it, "an attempt to bring together the scattered materials relating to the careers of these notable but neglected Carolingian figures seems peculiarly fitting at the present time because of the prominent, though somewhat obscure, role they played in the Carolingian *Ostpolitik*, the first conscious step in the historic Germanic push to the East" (212). As she says in the first note on page 213, "I have tried to examine the sources anew, in order to present a fresh account and interpretation of the subject." Within the exhaustive erudition of this article, Ross corrects some of what she calls the "racial" theories of German history written after 1933.

This concern with the details and causes of military conflict is found in her best-known work, her translation and notes on *The Murder of Charles the Good, Count of Flanders,* by Galbert of Bruges, a notary's vivid account of the events surrounding the murder in 1127 of the count by his vassals while he knelt in prayer. Published by the Columbia Records of Civilization series in 1959, then reissued in the Medieval Academy MART series of republished texts, and now again to be published by the Columbia series, *The Murder of Charles the Good* remains a perpetual favorite for classroom discussion of the violent upheavals in the burgeoning towns of the twelfth century. This translation of a Latin text edited by Henri Pirenne is published with a seventy-five-page introduction, appendices, and extensive notes at the foot of each page. It includes a good plan of the castle of Bruges and the church inside, genealogical tables, and a map of Flanders, which, along with the introduction, show a remarkable percipience for the things necessary for making this text accessible to students.

The drama of the events is evidenced in Ross's second *Speculum* article, "The Rise and Fall of a Flemish Clan: The Erembalds and the Murder of Count Charles of Flanders, 1127–28," which followed her publication of that text. Again, the opening words of that article cannot fail to convey the immediacy that she brought to those events: "At dawn on 2 March 1127, as he knelt in prayer in his castral church at Bruges, Count Charles of Flanders was struck down by a band of swordsmen led by his own vassals. The sense of horror aroused throughout Europe by this act of treachery was heightened by the fact that the victim perished 'in a holy place and in holy prayer, and in holy piety of spirit, and in the holy time of Lent, and in the holy act of almsgiving, and before the sacred altar and the sacred relics of the saints'" (367).

This is crime reporting at its best or a radio report from the battlefield.

The immediacy that Ross brings to this text perhaps reflects a now almost forgotten event (forgotten by all but her) of her early years as a teacher at Vassar, an event reported by her colleagues in the Vassar memorial:

> Whatever may have been the tensions of this first year of college teaching, they were nothing compared with the lasting impact of a trip to Spain with her friend and colleague, Leila Barber, of the art department, in the summer of 1936. Unaware, like most foreigners, of the impending civil war, they arrived in Granada on July 19th, only to learn of the sudden *coup* of the fascist General Francisco Franco. Cut off from all direct communication with the outside world, they were trapped in Granada for nineteen

days during its siege and ultimate capture by Franco's army. . . . The bombing of their hotel on August 7 and the death of several inhabitants marked the climax of an experience so vivid in the memory of J. B. Ross that describing it some fifty-five years later, she could still "hear the whistling bomb."[8]

The publication of the Galbert of Bruges account, however, was only the culmination of a larger project of presenting the voices of the medieval and Renaissance past directly to the classroom.

With her collaborator, Mary Martin McLaughlin, Ross also published two volumes of source readings, *The Portable Medieval Reader* in 1949 and *The Portable Renaissance Reader* in 1953. These were important contributions to teaching because many of the selections were their own translations of texts otherwise not available in English. Both still in print, their usefulness is evident from the frequent hits found in any Internet search for references to them. According to Mary McLaughlin their popularity may stem from the pure enjoyment that was had in their creation and from the fact that the introduction of such sources was part of Ross's approach to teaching, which aimed at "the cultivation of the intellectual gifts of her students."[9] The project is set out particularly in the introduction of the earlier volume, the *Portable Medieval Reader,* which appeared in 1949, and is best described in their own words:

> In our "modern times" we seldom have occasion to lament the hold of the past on the present, and we rarely feel dwarfed by its greatness. . . . We are often still further divorced from our remoter history by a grandiose conception of progress in which our own role looms large and that of the future larger still. This orientation is a common one, although the optimistic theory on which it rests has grown somewhat threadbare in an age when human advancement appears more and more as "a slow crablike movement sideways." (2)
>
> The focus of the *Medieval Reader* is the culture of Latin Christendom, which was an entity both larger and smaller than the Roman Empire it replaced in the West, just as it was both more and less in theory and in fact than the Europe of modern times. (11)
>
> In letters like those of Heloise to Abelard, and that of Peter the Venerable telling Heloise of Abelard's last days and death, there is a direct revelation of the personalities and relationships of these individuals. (15)
>
> Where an important or revealing record was not yet translated, we have tried to remedy that lack. (22).

It is difficult to distinguish the voices of Ross and McLaughlin, enjoying this endeavor as they did.

Following her retirement, Ross continued actively pursuing two interests. One was a return to her concern about Italian humanism and education. The first work to appear was a study based on published and unpublished family papers, most notably the Florentine *Ricordi,* as sources for "The Middle-Class Italian Child, Fourteenth to

Early Sixteenth Century," an article that appeared in *The History of Childhood,* edited by Lloyd de Mauss in 1974.[10] Again we see a typical rhetorical opening under "The First Years": "What were the infant's first contacts with the world outside the womb? Birth in the parental bed, bath in the same room and baptism in the parish church were followed almost at once by delivery in the hands of a *balia* or wet-nurse" (184). Her vivid picture of the sadness of childhood still remembered as an adult by one diarist is typical of her analytical use of such sources:

> By means of verbal portraits the Florentine Giovanni Morelli in his private journal, written mostly in his thirties, evoked vivid images of those whom he loved most in the family constellation, treating as shadowy figures the others. He idealizes his father, whom he lost at three years, as a "poor abandoned boy," left at the *balia*'s until ten or twelve years, who never saw his father, but who by courage and virtue triumphed over paternal neglect and fraternal indifference to become head of the family. (198)
>
> In his history of the family, Morelli, abandoned at four by a "cruel mother" notes in every case whether a widow remarried or stayed with her children. He gives elaborate direction to his heirs how to ensure in their wills that the mother should not leave the offspring. (201)

This article also considers the treatment and education of children in the treatises of the humanists, and the last three articles she published concentrate on such related topics as education of youths, friendship, and career patterns, particularly in Venice.

Two articles—"Gasparo Contarini and His Friends," which appeared in *Studies in the Renaissance* in 1970, and "The Emergence of Gasparo Contarini," in *Church History*, 1972—draw on newly found letters of Contarini concerning the internal religious and intellectual conflict of this Renaissance humanist/Counter-Reformation Catholic. The *Church History* article is a brilliant review of the literature and an outline for further study, complete in its grasp of the historiography, unrelenting in its search for excellence, it does not fail to complain of the inaccessibility of certain materials on Contarini that had rested too long in a scholar's study. A related article is the final publication, "Venetian Schools and Teachers, Fourteenth to Early Sixteen Century. A Survey and a Study of Giovanni Battista Egnazio," which appeared in *Renaissance Quarterly* in 1975. In Ross's typical rhetorical style, this work opens with a question: "What do we know about the education of boys and young men in Venice of this period?" She then examines the state of the literature and the possibilities for additional work.

But there was a second project that Ross began in collaboration with Mary McLaughlin, possible only once the articles on Renaissance humanists were completed. This was the consideration of medieval women as actors threatened in their own time and by an often hostile historiography. This concern to acknowledge the role of women as scholars, mystics, and leaders of monastic communities during the Middle Ages would be an abiding intellectual interest during the last two decades of her life, when she made her home in Washington, D.C. Her attention had come to be focused on the problem in the early 1970s. At the scholarly conference on Abelard held at Cluny in 1972 (where Giles Constable reports first getting to know her), Ross must have been convinced of the necessity that women scholars give their serious attention to the study of medieval women. It was a moment of serious crisis for our understanding of medieval women, in part because a series of articles by John F. Benton and others began appearing, purporting to show that Eleanor of Aquitaine and Marie of Champagne, her daughter, had had no relationship whatsoever, that the *Trotula* was not written by a woman, and that Heloise had not written her part of the Heloise/Abelard correspondence.[11] At the Abelard conference Heloise's voice in the Abelard/Heloise correspondence came under serious debate. The most important of the very limited female voices in the *Readers* was under attack. Ross became a paladin for Heloise and other medieval women. She would be a strong supporter of the Medieval Women's Communities and Lives Project, founded by Mary Martin McLaughlin and Suzanne Wemple, which began its work with an attempt to count the houses of nuns and the numbers of nuns in Rome. Ross also pursued medieval women's history on her own during her weekly trips to do research at the Library of Congress and at the time of her death was at work with Mary Martin McLaughlin on *Perilous Quests: Women's Initiatives in Western History from Late Antiquity to the Fifteenth Century*, still unpublished.

I came to know Ross only in my own years in Washington, where she moved to live with her sister after her retirement. She was petite, extremely elegant and proper in her dress, sweet-voiced but strong-minded, and a font of knowledge—concerned about her friends and about the choices we were facing. I remember her keen interest in the details of my pregnancy and the birth and infancy of my son, Benjamin, and I suspect that she was more aware than I of how soon, like those women and children of the Renaissance she had studied, I would be faced with compromises in order to manage a child and a career. It was always a pleasure to see her at receptions at Dumbarton Oaks or at the Library of Congress, where we had some memorable lunches. I remember the keen light in her eyes as she discussed with me the work of Herrad of Hohenburg or the depictions of women in the Dance of Death.

Her closest friends report that her interest in plants was legendary and described enjoyable visits with her at her sanctuary on Captiva Island. Mary McLaughlin describes her as a "gardener of the heart," with her "wise concern for the well-being of others, the generosity of spirit so variously bestowed on those whose lives she shared, her loving and unfailing devotion to her family and her friends."[12] Her abiding interest in her students, her friends, and her colleagues, as well as her determination to understand rightly the history of the men and women and children who were the subjects of her research, were her gifts to us all.

NOTES

1. Much of my information on James Bruce Ross comes from the "Vassar Faculty Memorial Minute," drafted by Pamela Askew, Miriam Cohen, Mary Martin McLaughlin, and Robert

Pounder, and from other tributes presented at the memorial service for her in Washington, D.C., by Elizabeth Eisenstein, Giles Constable, Gloria Kury, and Mary Martin McLaughlin. I am grateful to Mary Martin McLaughlin for sharing these with me and for allowing me to act as the facilitator as much as the author of this piece. There has always been speculation about her name, and indeed my own students, having heard my stories about Miss Ross when I introduced the Galbert of Bruges text, were outraged to discover that the latest printing (1998) for the MART series of the Medieval Academy of America referred to her on the cover as "he." The entire blurb is worth quoting as an example of how copyediting can garble things, since Ross in fact wrote on medieval Flanders, among other things, and on Renaissance Italy: "James Bruce Ross was for many years professor of History at Vassar College. He [sic] has written books and articles on Medieval and Renaissance Flanders and Italy and is co-editor of the *Portable Medieval Reader* and the *Portable Renaissance Reader.*" We are told in the "Vassar Memorial Minute" that, "named for her father, she was the youngest of six daughters in a family of seven siblings, the eldest her brother, Charles, the friend and press secretary of President Harry S. Truman."

2. Among them were Cecily d'Autremont Angleton, who went on to do a Ph.D. at Catholic University of America in the 1980s; Joan Cadden, now professor of medieval history at University of California, Davis; Sheila ffolliott, professor of art history at George Mason University; and Gloria Kury, now an editor for Penn State Press.

3. Askew et al., "Vassar Faculty Memorial Minute," 3–4.

4. Gloria Kury, remarks from memorial "Remembering J. B. Ross," [1996], private communication, Mary Martin McLaughlin.

5. I was one of the participants in this NEH summer seminar on the *Mirabilia urbis Romae*, directed by Dale Kinney, Bryn Mawr, and Birgitta Wohl, University of California, at the American Academy in Rome, summer 1999; Kinney was, of course, the student of Richard Krautheimer.

6. Ross, "Study of Twelfth-Century Interest," 311; the larger political context is also discussed by Benson in "Political Renovatio."

7. This project was originally created by Mary Martin McLaughlin and Suzanne Wemple, funded by NEH, and housed at Barnard College, Columbia; it has now become a Web-based project: http://monasticmatrix.org/dematrice/index.php, which describes itself as a scholarly resource for the study of women's religious communities from 400–1600 C.E.

8. Askew et al., "Vassar Memorial Minute," 2.

9. Mary Martin McLaughlin, "James Bruce Ross," a memorial tribute, 20 January 1996.

10. I find myself often recommending it along with the companion piece in that same volume by McLaughlin, "Survivors and Surrogates," 101–81), because Ross's work is the best place for important information on wet nurses ("Middle-Class Italian Child," 183–228).

11. On this, see collected publications by Benton, *Culture, Power, and Personality in Medieval France;* the conference in Cluny was published as Pierre Abélard, *Pierre le Vénérable.*

12. Mary Martin McLaughlin, memorial tribute.

SELECT BIBLIOGRAPHY OF WORKS BY JAMES BRUCE ROSS

"On the Early History of Leontius' Translation of Homer." *Classical Philology* 22 (1927): 341–55.

"A Study of Twelfth-Century Interest in the Antiquities of Rome." In *Medieval and Historiographical Essays in Honor of James Westfall Thompson,* edited by James Lea Cate and Eugene N. Anderson. Chicago: University of Chicago Press, 1938.

"Two Neglected Paladins of Charlemagne, Erich of Friuli and Gerold of Bavaria." *Speculum* 20 (1945): 212–35.

Editor, with Mary Martin McLaughlin. *The Portable Medieval Reader.* New York: Viking Press, 1949; reprint, Viking Penguin, 1977–.

Editor, with Mary Martin McLaughlin. *The Portable Renaissance Reader.* New York: Viking Press, 1953; reprint, Viking Penguin, 1977–.

Editor and translator. *The Murder of Charles the Good, Count of Flanders,* by Galbert of Bruges. Records of Civilization. New York: Columbia University Press, 1959, 2002; New York: Harper and Row, Harper Torchbooks, 1967–82; Medieval Academy Reprint for Teaching, Toronto: University of Toronto Press, 1982.

"The Rise and Fall of a Flemish Clan: The Erembalds and the Murder of Count Charles of Flanders, 1127–28." *Speculum* 34 (1959): 367–90.

"The Middle-Class Italian Child, Fourteenth to Early Sixteenth Century." In *The History of Childhood,* edited by Lloyd deMause. New York: Psychohistory Press, 1974; Harper and Row, Harper Torchbooks, 1975.

"Gasparo Contarini and His Friends." *Studies in the Renaissance* 17 (1970): 192–232.

"The Emergence of Gasparo Contarini: A Bibliographical Essay." *Church History* 41 (1972): 22–45.

"Venetian Schools and Teachers, Fourteenth to Sixteenth Century: A Survey and a Study of Giovanni Battista Egnazio." *Renaissance Quarterly* 39 (1975): 521–66.

Works Cited

Askew, Pamela, Miriam Cohen, Mary Martin McLaughlin, and Robert Pounder. "Vassar Faculty Memorial Minute." [1996] Vassar College Archives.

Benson, Robert. "Political Renovatio: Two Models from Roman Antiquity." In *Renaissance and Renewal in the Twelfth Century,* edited by Robert L. Benson and Giles Constable, with Carol D. Lanham, 339–86. Cambridge, Mass.: Harvard University Press, 1982.

Benton, John F. *Culture, Power, and Personality in Medieval France.* Edited by Thomas N. Bisson. London: Hambledon Press, 1991.

Kury, Gloria. "Remembering J. B. Ross." [1996.] Private communication from Mary Martin McLaughlin.

McLaughlin, Mary Martin. "Survivors and Surrogates: Children and Parents from the Ninth to the Thirteenth Centuries." In *The History of Childhood,* edited by Lloyd de Mause. New York: Psychohistory Press, 1974; Harper and Row, Harper Torchbooks, 1975.

Medieval Women's Lives and Communities Project, now Matrix: http://monasticmatrix.org/dematrice/index.php

Mirabilia urbis Romae, published in English as The Marvels of Rome. Trans. Francis Morgan Nichols. Edited by Eileen Gardiner. New York, Italica Press, 1986.

Pierre Abélard. *Pierre le Vénérable: Les courants philosophiques, littéraires, et artistiques en Occident au milieu du XIIe siècle: Actes et mémoires du Colloque international, Abbaye de Cluny, 2 au 9 juillet 1972.* Paris: Éditions du Centre National de la Recherche Scientifique, 1975.

Sayers, Dorothy. *Gaudy Night.* London: Four Square editions, 1936; reprint. 1963.

CHAPTER 41

Marie-Thérèse d'Alverny (1903–1991)
The History of Ideas in the Middle Ages in the Mediterranean Basin

CHARLES S. F. BURNETT

MARIE-THÉRÈSE D'ALVERNY was born into the minor nobility. Among her near relatives were the Comtes d'Harcourt, who owned the medieval monastery of Bec, which had supplied England with two archbishops. But her immediate family showed a strong Catholic and missionary zeal; a cousin, André, served with the Jesuits in Lebanon and was the author of several religious books. She herself enrolled as an auxiliary nurse in the Second World War.[1]

D'Alverny was born on 25 January 1903 in the little town of Boën-sur-Lignon near Montbrison in the Department of Loire and spent her childhood in Aix-en-Provence and Strasbourg, where her father was a civil servant. She took her first degree (Licence ès-lettres), in philosophy, at the University of Strasbourg. Here she came under the spell of Étienne Gilson, who transformed the study of the philosophy of the Middle Ages from the hackneyed Thomism of Roman Catholic seminaries into a rich and lively discipline within the history of ideas; he was to have a profound influence over her life.[2] In 1924, in spite of some pressure to pursue occupations more fitting for a young lady of her class, she persisted in continuing in academic life and entered the École des chartes in Paris, which had already acquired a fine reputation as Europe's leading center for the study of manuscripts. She obtained the degree of Archiviste paléographe, with a thesis on the ascetic Franciscan Pierre-Jean Olieu, which was awarded the prix Auguste Molinier in 1928.[3] The thesis was never published, but her interest in poverty and Christian charity remained with her throughout her life. The École des chartes encouraged her to use primary documents, especially those that were unedited.

Immediately after graduation d'Alverny joined the staff of the Bibliothèque nationale (now Bibliothèque nationale de France), first, in the Department of Printed Books,

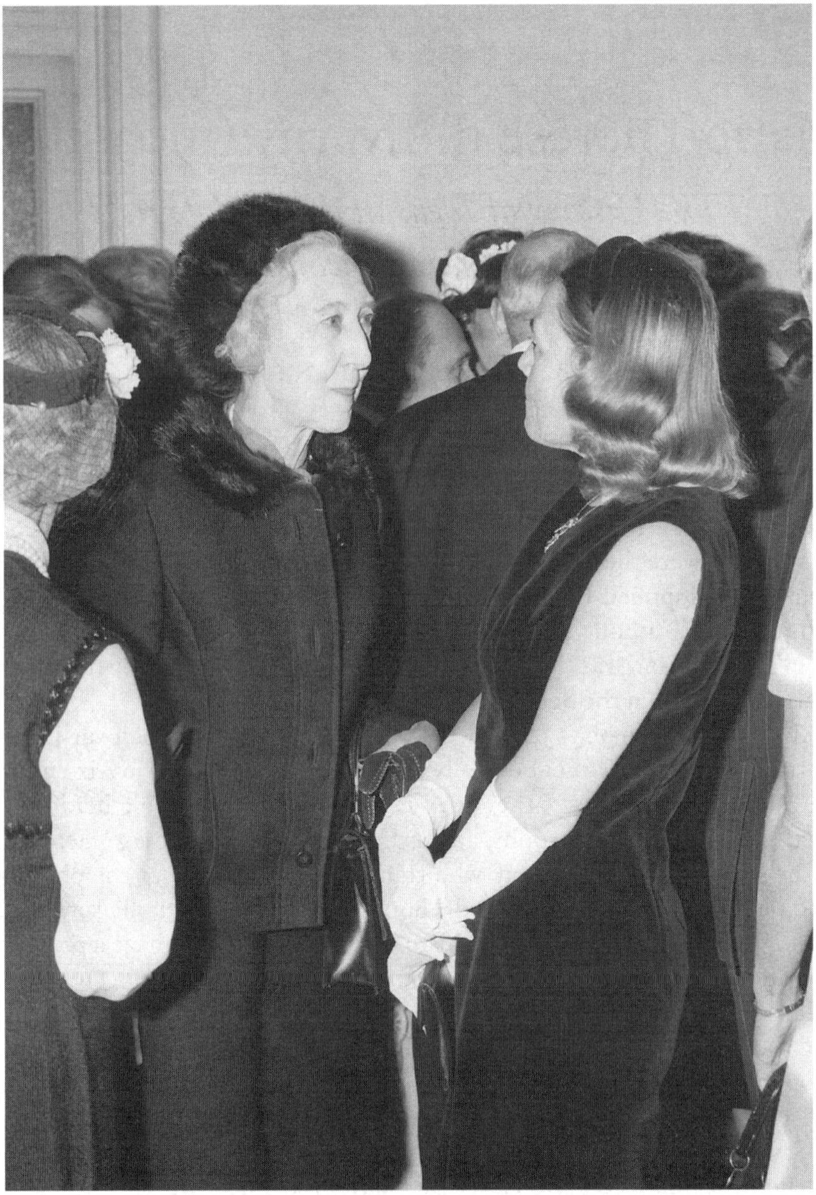

but soon in the Department of Western Manuscripts (Cabinet des manuscrits), where she was to become a familiar and welcoming figure for countless visiting scholars. Here she revived and supervised the publication of the *Catalogue général des manuscrits latins* (volumes 3, 4, and 5, 1952–66) and assumed responsibility for three volumes on the dated manuscripts in the collection.[4] However, she also maintained her primary interest in philosophy and was quite innovative in mounting exhibitions at the library on philosophers such as Descartes and Malebranche. In the meantime she pursued studies at the École pratique des hautes études, for which she wrote a thesis, "Les pérégrinations de l'âme dans l'autre monde d'après un anonyme de la fin du XIIe siècle." This work, published as the first of her many articles in *Archives d'histoire doctrinale et littéraire du Moyen Âge,* exhibits her interest in the influence of Arabic writings on Latin literature, for the anonymous author, in describing the ascent of the soul to the Infinite Being and Cause of Causes, cited the *Liber de causis* (an Arabic Neoplatonic text on metaphysics, largely dependent on Proclus), the *Metaphysics* of Avicenna and Algazel, and the *Fons vitae* of Ibn Gabirol and may have modeled his account on the well-known Islamic account of the prophet Muhammad's ascent to heaven, known as the *Mirāj.* It also showed her interest in the visual depiction of doctrine, since the text was illustrated by an image of souls clambering through the spheres of existence to God, first cause and creator of all things. To complete her academic qualifications she wrote a dissertation on one of the most innovative and influential thinkers of the late twelfth century, Alan of Lille; this became her book *Alain de Lille: Textes inédits.* She describes this book as being almost the result of chance: because of her professional duties and her insatiable curiosity, she "did not always find what she was looking for," but "kept coming across unpublished works of Alain de Lille."[5] The result is a complete account of the works of Alain (with a special chapter dedicated to his exposition of the conundrum "God is an intelligible sphere whose center is everywhere, but whose circumference is nowhere"), followed by nearly 150 pages of editions of previously unedited texts.

While pursuing her doctoral research d'Alverny started to learn Arabic and established contact with Arabic scholars, such as her colleague at the Bibliothèque nationale, Georges Vajda (the director of the Arabic and Hebrew sections of the Institut de recherche et d'histoire des textes), Louis Massignon at the École pratique des hautes études, and the doyen of Arabic philosophy, Father Georges Anawati, O.P., of the Institut dominicain des études orientales in Cairo. My own introduction to the comparative study of Arabic texts and their Latin translations was a weekly class of the Arabist Gérard Troupeau at the École pratique des hautes études, in which d'Alverny and Troupeau read together the Arabic and Latin versions of the same text, usually transcribed directly from manuscript.[6]

To her disappointment and to many people's surprise d'Alverny was not invited to become the director of the Department of Manuscripts when the position became vacant in 1962, since she was obviously the most qualified person for this post. Just as when she had experienced opposition applying for the École des Chartes so many years before, so now, her being a woman was seen to count against her.[7] But her failure to gain this position prompted her to apply, in 1962, to the Centre national de la recherche scientifique (CNRS), where she was accepted first as *maître* and eventually as *directeur* of research (1962–73).

Her position at the CNRS involved no teaching and did not even offer the opportunity of mixing regularly with scholars, which she had in the Bibliothèque Nationale. She welcomed, therefore, the invitation, in 1957, to teach at the Centre d'études supérieures de civilisation médiévale at Poitiers. This unique institute was founded in 1953 in order to encourage the study of the Middle Ages (in particular the Romanesque period, from the tenth to the twelfth centuries) by means of seminars throughout the year and a five-week summer school to which participants from all over the world were invited. In 1958 its directors, René Crozet and Edmond–René Labande, founded the periodical *Cahiers de civilisation médiévale* whose aim was interdisciplinary, to give a rounded picture of "a period in history."[8] At approximately the same time they realized that what was needed at the center was someone who understood the intellectual history of the Middle Ages. The history of ideas was a subject virtually unknown in France. The initiative of Gilson had found little support in his own country, and this had encouraged him in 1929 to found the Institute (later Pontifical Institute) of Medieval Studies in Toronto. D'Alverny was not only the most appropriate but arguably the only scholar in France who could have taken the position at Poitiers, which she held until 1978. Here she delighted in teaching aspiring medievalists both from France and from other countries. A note on her courses for 1975–76 may be representative:

> 1°. Codicology, viz. history of manuscripts . . . scribes, scriptoria, university scribes and bookshops . . . practical training: description of manuscripts of the Poitiers Library. 2°. History of philosophy and science in the M.A. The topic for this academic year . . . is *Islam and the West*: the impact of Arabic culture on Western culture. 1. The knowledge of Islam in the West. First contacts in Spain. Study of the tracts of Eulogius Cordubensis and Alvarus Cordubensis (IX cent.). 2. Question of possible influence of Arabic Spanish poetry on European poetry. Technique and major themes. 3. Penetration of Arabic science in the West, Xth–XIth cent. Arabic numbers; astronomy, astrology, the astrolabe. 4. Study of Petrus Alphonsi (early XIIth cent.): accurate information on the Moslem faith and customs; the Arabic scientific tradition; transmission of folklore tales.[9]

Another important strand in her academic life was her direction of the *Archives d'histoire doctrinale et littéraire du Moyen Âge*. This periodical was founded by Étienne Gilson and Gérard Théry in 1926 specifically to demonstrate the cultural and philosophical richness of the Middle Ages. D'Alverny's name first appeared on the cover in 1953, beside those of the founders, and for the next thirty years she effectively directed the journal, attracting to it articles of the highest caliber, reading and checking Latin texts, and compiling the indexes. Through this journal, as through her teaching, she maintained contact with an international community of scholars.

One result of her transfer from the Bibliothèque nationale to the CNRS was that she was able to travel more easily. She enjoyed attending conferences, which took her not only to Europe and America, but also to Islamic countries, including Iraq, Egypt, Morocco, and Syria. She regularly attended the meetings of the Union internationale d'histoire des sciences, for which she served as president of the Commission for Bibliography (that is, in this case, for the sources of the history of science), and the International Society for the Study of Medieval Philosophy, for which she was president of the commission on editions of medieval texts. She was particularly fond of the United States and Poland. She taught at Columbia University and Barnard College in New York and at the University of California at Berkeley, was twice a member of the Institute for Advanced Study at Princeton, and in 1967 was elected a foreign member of the Mediaeval Academy of America. Amongst her closest friends were Poles, who included Alexander Birkenmajer and Sophie Wlodek, and she received an honorary degree from the University of Cracow. In England she received an honorary fellowship at the College of Saint Hilda's, Oxford (where her dear friend Beryl Smalley was a fellow), and was elected a corresponding fellow of the British Academy. Her reputation abroad, however, was not matched by recognition in her own country, for she was never elected to the Académie Française.

After retirement, she continued writing, attending conferences and encouraging scholars until a stroke in 1988 forced her to leave her apartment and her books and enter the residential care of the Hôpital Sainte-Périne. Accepting with stoicism her reduced circumstances, she discussed the arrangements for the completion of her unfinished work by younger scholars and received with dignity the visits of many admirers, including a Japanese scholar with whom she found solace in learning about Zen Buddhism.

D'Alverny's main aim in life was the understanding of the philosophical thought and religious belief of the twelfth and thirteenth centuries through the study of texts. Most of her articles are based on particular texts, consisting either of editions or of analyses of those texts. The format of the *Archives d'histoire doctrinale et littéraire de Moyen Âge* was particularly conducive to this, since each issue comprised, specifically, a section on "texts" and a section on "études." She was fascinated about what was new in this period—how certain authors strayed from the writings of the Church Fathers and dared to explore those of Muslims and Jews. Hence she wrote her still fundamental article on the translations of the Koran in the twelfth and thirteenth centuries and embarked on the study of the Muslim philosophers who most profoundly influenced Western thought: al-Kindī (Alkindi), Ibn Sīnā (Avicenna), and al-Ghazālī (Algazel). In the case of Alkindi she opened up a completely new facet of scholarship on this "Philosopher of the Arabs," for she introduced and edited (with her student Françoise Hudry) a text, surviving only in Latin, that gave the philosophical and cosmological underpinnings of the working of magic: the *De radiis*. This study has changed the course of Alkindi scholarship as much among Arabists as among Latin scholars.[10] In respect to Algazel, she brought together all the information she had gathered over many years in one of the last articles she published: "Algazel dans l'occident latin." In this work she traces, among other things, the knowledge in the West of Algazel's refutation of Avicenna's philosophy.

It is to Avicenna that d'Alverny devoted most of her energy. Although belonging to the Aristotelian tradition, Avicenna provided an independent account of the whole of philosophy, which covered many subjects not treated by Aristotle and incorporated advances in scientific learning made since Aristotle's time. His works were popular among both Arabic and Jewish philosophers, and several parts of the most comprehensive of his philosophical works, the *Shifā'*, or "Cure (from ignorance)," were translated into Latin and had a profound effect on Western scholars.[11] Over a period of eleven years d'Alverny published a series of catalogs of Latin manuscripts containing these portions of Avicenna's work. They followed the model of the two volumes of descriptions of the manuscripts containing Aristotle's works (*Aristoteles Latinus: Codices,* edited by G. Lacombe et al.) and provided the basis for the editions of Avicenna made by d'Alverny's friend Simone van Riet. Unfortunately, d'Alverny's own contribution to *Avicenna Latinus,* that of the book on logic from the *Shifā',* was left incomplete at the time of her death, but she wrote several important articles on the Latin Avicenna, including the definitive description of the portions of the *Shifā'* translated into Latin.[12] She found a kindred soul in Avicenna, who carefully thought through every aspect of the Greek philosophical and medical tradition, and she had great respect for the translators in Spain who tried to make the thought of a Persian Muslim philosopher writing in Arabic accessible to a Christian Latin reader. At the beginning of one of her articles she asked: "How could the Shaykh al-Rais, a physician, doctor, and vizier, become one of the masters of Western thought? What could have been known of his life and work? What routes did his teaching take before it became integrated more or less openly in the teaching of the schools? What were the agencies and places of transmission? Finally, if one may mention here a pictorial witness to his popularity, under what kind of appearance was Avicenna represented?"[13]

D'Alverny used her vast erudition to compose what was to become the most authoritative account of the activity of translation and the role of the translators in the twelfth century, which was appropriately included in the proceedings of a conference commemorating the fiftieth anniversary of the publication of *The Renaissance of the Twelfth Century* of her illustrious precursor, Charles Haskins.[14] This article, above all, confirmed her reputation among English-reading scholars.

Her interest in the translations of Arabic texts led naturally to her study of the earliest works to be influenced by these texts. Her article on the wanderings of the soul in the other world has already been mentioned, but she also wrote about the *Liber de causis primis et secundis,* a curious blend of John Scot Eriugena and Avicenna (*Avicenne en Occident,* article 11); Eudes of Champagne's defense of astrology, as reported in Hélinand of Froidmont's *Chronicon* (*La transmission des textes philosophiques et scientifiques au Moyen Âge,* article 16); and Raymond of Marseilles's *Liber iudiciorum,* which she had identified, and which provides the earliest example of the use of the astrological translations from Arabic made by John of Seville (*La transmission des textes philosophiques et scientifiques au Moyen Âge,* article 15, in which the logical discussion of Abelard concerning future contingents is compared with Raymond's statements about the validity of astrological prediction). All these studies were based on texts that she was preparing for publication, but it was left to her pupils and admirers to complete them: the *De causis primis et secundis,* by Marek Procop (as yet unpublished), Eudes's *Libellus de efficatia artis astrologice,* by Malgorzata Malewicz, and Raymond's *Liber iudiciorum* by Emmanuel Poulle and others (to be published in the series *Belles Lettres*). Finally, she did not forget the renewal of interest in the Arabic sources of Western science in the Renaissance and wrote two articles on Andrea Alpago, the sixteenth-century physician, who attended the Venetian ambassador in Damascus and searched out there Arabic manuscripts of Avicenna, by which he could correct the twelfth-century translation of Avicenna's Canon of Medicine and add new texts to the Latin corpus of Avicenna's works; he also was the first to introduce the West to Sufism and the whirling dervishes (*Avicenne en occident,* articles 12–14).

Many people will remember the unpretentious flat in 58, rue de Vaugirard, entered by a rickety back staircase, where the floor tipped at a giddy angle and the main room was dominated by an out-of-control rubber plant. In this flat d'Alverny's library of books, successive drafts of her articles, photographs of manuscripts, and a voluminous correspondence accumulated, endangering further the infrastructure. She lived very much as a student, unconcerned about the quality of her crockery or the amenities of her kitchen and bathroom. There are tales like that of the English visitor for whom she kindly cooked an egg, who could not decide whether the egg was meant to be on a plate or was still in the pan that it had been cooked in. It was here that she held an open house every Thursday afternoon, serving tea from a samovar to her guests sitting on a couch that served also as a bed. She would discuss anything from the peculiarities of the script of a particular twelfth-century writer to the way the English drank tea. She rarely took on the role of a teacher on these occasions but rather participated in discussion as an equal. On one occasion an English student (David d'Avray, now professor of medieval history at University College, London) invented a game that involved guessing the date of a manuscript; d'Alverny won outright! She exhibited a childlike enthusiasm, with her eyes sparkling and frequently blinking, and she would lace her conversation, as she did her articles, with gentle humor. Typical is her remark concerning medieval scribes, that "we shall leave aside the saintly man who limits himself to requesting the prayers of his readers and heavenly rewards . . . in order to examine his successors who demand more frequently Falernian wine and even a *pulchra puella* when they have finished their task."[15]

D'Alverny enjoyed the sense of being part of an international community of scholars, with whom she communicated in their own languages (she spoke English, Italian, and Spanish with fluency), and with whom she entered into dialogue in her articles and her reviews (especially numerous in the *Bibliothèque de l'École des chartes* and *Bulletin des bibliothèques de France*). She was instrumental, together with Edmond René Labande and his wife, in setting up a directory of medieval scholars and their interests, of which new editions continue to be produced.[16] She wrote moving obituaries for Alexander Birkenmajer, Étienne Gilson, Francis Wormald, Richard Hunt, and Marie-Dominique Chenu.[17] She was so much in demand as a contributor to her colleagues' festschriften that she eventually made a public declaration that she would not write anything for anybody's festschrift. But such was her desire to honor her fellow paleographer Bernhard Bischoff that she succumbed for his festschrift but insisted that her name as author should be omitted.[18]

Throughout her life d'Alverny followed the same routine: she would spend most of the year in her Paris apartment, which, though cramped, was near the Sorbonne (being on the edge of the Jardins de Luxembourg). Every summer, however, she would retreat to a family house in the south of France, in Languedoc-Roussillon, close to the places of activity of several of the Arabic-Latin translators she studied, and there she would continue with her research in tranquillity.

D'Alverny's research was not so much a career as an extension of her spiritual life. She shared with members of her family a close personal interest in the Islamic world. Her brother, François, before his premature death, had served in North Africa, and her cousin, André, while serving as a Jesuit priest in Lebanon, had edited the Arabic and Latin texts of Qusṭa b. Lūqā's *On the Difference between the Spirit and the Soul*, which d'Alverny had intended to complete. Père D'Alverny, because of his sympathy for the Orient, had adopted the Melchite rite for his own worship in Lebanon, and it was in the Melchite church in Paris—Saint Julien-le-Pauvre—that d'Alverny found her spiritual home. She would regularly take part in the liturgy of Saint Chrysostom, performed for the most part in Arabic, and she would listen to the Oriental intonations of the a cappella choir. It was appropriate that her memorial service was held in this church on 16 May 1991 (she had passed away on 26 April), and the many friends and colleagues who attended that service will remember the sensitive appreciation of her life given by the officiating priest, Monsignor Joseph Nasrallah.

In her scholarship d'Alverny sought not to bring out the bloody conflicts between different religions or the internecine strife within Christendom but rather to show how attempts were made by Christians to understand Islam, and how scholars in the late twelfth and thirteenth centuries tried to use Arabic, and indeed Islamic, doctrines and revelations to corroborate their own Christian faith. She was in sympathy more with scholars than with potentates and, among scholars, with those who sought reconciliation, like Peter the Venerable, who wished to fight Islam "not with arms, but with words."[19] Hence her sympathy, too, for translators and their attempts to be exactly faithful to the original texts, for example, John of Segovia, who, in 1455, persuaded the leader of the Muslim community in Segovia, Isa Gidelli, to pass some time in his priory in Savoy in the Alps, in order to help him make the definitive translation into Latin of the Koran.[20] In her work on Arabic/Islamic influence, she combined her philological expertise with her concern about mutual understanding. She deplored "the barrier that separates medievalists from Orientalists" and wished, as far as she was able, "to contribute to tearing down this barrier."[21] In her life, as in her scholarship, she brought together East and West, and though she was not involved in politics herself, she has provided an example of the mutual understanding that is possible for all those who share the same Mediterranean Sea.

NOTES

In compiling this biography the author is grateful for the help of Danielle Jacquart, Elizabeth McGrath, Anne-Marie Meyer, Henrietta Leyser, and especially Patricia Stirnemann.

1. For her service to the sick and wounded during the war she received "la médaille de guerre de la Croix-Rouge."

2. D'Alverny expressed her admiration for Gilson in several articles written at the time of his death in 1978, e.g., "Actualité de la pensée d'Étienne Gilson."

3. "Les écrits théoriques concernant la pauvreté évangélique depuis Pierre-Jean Olieu jusqu'à la bulle 'Cum inter nonnullos' (12 novembre 1323)." A copy of this thesis has been deposited in the Archives nationales.

4. In *Catalogue des manuscrits en écriture latine portant des indications de date, de lieu, ou de copiste.*

5. D'Alverny, *Alain de Lille: Textes inédits,* 7: "Le livre que nous offrons aux médiévistes est presque le fruit du hasard. Ayant été amenée, par devoir professionnel et curiosité invincible à explorer un grand nombre de collections de manuscrits, nous n'avons pas toujours trouvé ce que nous cherchions, mais nous avons rencontré, un peu partout, les œuvres de [Alain de Lille]."

6. A sample of the fruitful results of this class is the bilingual text of Ibn al-Masawaih's *Aphorisms,* edited by Jacquart and Troupeau. Jacquart, a student of d'Alverny's and herself now the professor of the history of medieval science at the École pratique des hautes études, has fulfilled and passed on to her own students d'Alverny's ideals of close philological analysis of the Latin translations of Arabic texts.

7. It is perhaps worth noting that she did not adopt a feminist stance in the face of the opposition she met and expressed reluctance to write the one article that might seem to touch on a feminist issue: "Comment les théologiens et les philosophes voient la femme."

8. See "liminaire" to the first volume, 6: "La présente revue se consacrera donc, non à une discipline, mais à un temps de l'histoire."

9. The excerpt is an abbreviated copy of d'Alverny's own description of her course, written in English, presumably because a large number of her students were not French speaking.

10. Two works that take their starting-point from d'Alverny's pioneering research are Wiesner, "Cosmology of al-Kindi"; and Travaglia, *Magic, Causality and Intentionality.*

11. The most recent work to demonstrate this effect in detail is Hasse, *Avicenna's "De Anima" in the Latin West.* Hasse highlights d'Alverny's contribution to Avicennian scholarship (alongside that of Simone Van Riet) on p. vi: "The credit for raising our knowledge of Avicenna's impact on Western thought to a higher level [than that of Gilson and his successors] by giving it a firm philological grounding, goes to Marie-Thérèse d'Alverny, who produced a catalogue of manuscripts, and Simone Van Riet."

12. The descriptions of manuscripts have recently been brought together into one volume (with much previously unpublished material) by van Riet and Jodogne, under the title *Avicenna Latinus,* while the other articles relevant to Avicenna have been published in the volume

Avicenn en Occident, Études de philosophie médiévale 71 (Paris: Libraire philosophique J. Vrin, 1993). The latter includes "Notes sur les traductions médiévales d'Avicenne," which is still the essential guide to the extant Latin sections of the *Shifā'*.

13. The beginning of the article "Les traductions d'Avicenne (Moyen Âge et Renaissance)" in *Avicenn en Occident*, article 5, p. 71: "Comment le Shaykh al-Rais, médecin, philosophe et ministre, est-il devenu l'un des maîtres de la pensée occidentale? Qu'a-t-on connu de sa personne et de son œuvre? Quels chemins a pris son enseignement avant d'être intégré plus ou moins ouvertement dans celui des Ecoles? Quels ont été les agents et les lieux de transmission? Enfin, s'il est permis de mentionner ici un témoignage pittoresque de sa popularité, sous quel aspect l'a-t-on représenté?" Following d'Alverny's lead in the last theme Dag Hasse has recently written "King Avicenna: the Iconographic Consequences of a Mistranslation."

14. D'Alverny, "Translations and Translators."

15. In "Notes et observations au sujet des éditions de textes médiévaux," 42: "Nous laisserons de côté ce saint homme, qui se borne à demander les prières des lecteurs, et les récompenses célestes: *Dentur pro penna scriptori caelica regna*, pour examiner ses successeurs qui réclament plus fréquemment du vin de Falerne et même une *pulchra puella* à la fin de leur labeur."

16. D'Alverny, with Labande-Mailfert and Labande, *Répertoire des médiévistes européens*.

17. D'Alverny, "In memoriam Alexandre Birkenmajer (1890–1967)"; "Étienne Gilson"; "F. Wormald (1904–72)"; "Memoirs of Fellows and Corresponding Fellows of the Medieval Academy of America. Richard William Hunt"; "In memoriam M-D. Chenu, O.P. (1895–1990)."

18. "'Novus regnat Salomon in diebus malis.'" Her name is revealed in the reprint of her article in *Pensée médiévale en Occident*.

19. Peter the Venerable, "Summa contra sectam sive haeresim Saracenorum," in Kritzeck, *Peter the Venerable and Islam,* 231.

20. D'Alverny tells this story in her "Les traductions à deux interprètes, d'arabe en langue vernaculaire et de langue vernaculaire en latin." For the full story of Isa Gidelli, see Wiegers, "Yça Gidelli (fl. 1450)."

21. D'Alverny, "Deux traductions latines du Coran au Moyen Âge" 96: "Nous déplorons, une fois de plus, la barrière qui sépare les médiévistes des orientalistes, et que nous voudrions, dans la mesure de nos moyens, contribuer à abattre."

Selected Bibliography of Works by Marie-Therèse d'Alverny

For d'Alverny's bibliography, see *Archives d'histoire littéraire et doctrinale du Moyen Âge* 149 (1991): 279–89, with the supplement in *La transmission des textes philosophiques et scientifiques au Moyen Âge,* xi–xvi. D'Alverny tended to write articles rather than books. In spite of repeated suggestions that she should collect her articles into a book, she refused, preferring to complete new work. After her death, however, her most important articles were included as indicated in the works listed at the end of this bibliography.

Editor. *Exposition organisée pour le IIIe centenaire du* [Descartes's] *"Discours de la Méthode."* Paris: Bibliothèque Nationale, 1937.

Editor. "Catalogue de l'exposition Malebranche, Paris, 1938." *Revue d'histoire de la philosophie et d'histoire génerale de la civilisation* 25 (1939): 1–13.

"Les pérégrinations de l'âme dans l'autre monde d'après un anonyme de la fin du xiie siècle." *Archives d'histoire doctrinale et littéraire du Moyen Âge* 15–17 (1942): 239–99. Reprinted in *Études sur le symbolisme de la Sagesse et sur l'iconographie,* article 5.

"Deux traductions latines du Coran au Moyen Âge." *Archives d'histoire doctrinale et littéraire du Moyen Âge* 16 (1948): 69–131. Reprinted in *La connaissance de l'Islam dans l'Occident medieval,* article 1.

Editor. *Catalogue général des manuscrits latins.* Vols. 3–5. Paris: La Bibliothéque, 1952–66.

"Notes sur les traductions médiévales d'Avicenne." *Archives d'histoire doctrinale et littéraire du Moyen Âge* 19 (1952): 337–58. Reprinted in *Avicenne en Occident,* article 4.

Editor. *Catalogue général des manuscrits latins.* Vols. 3–5. Paris: La Bibliothèque, 1953–66.

Editor with Yvonne Labande-Mailfert and Edmond René Labande. *Répertoire des médiévistes européens.* Poitiers: Centre d'études supérieures de civilisation médiévale, 1960.

Editor. *Catalogue des manuscrits en écriture latine portant des indications de date, de lieu, ou de copiste.* Vols. 2–4.1. Paris: Centre national de la recherche scientifique, 1962–81.

Editor. *Alain de Lille: Textes inédits.* Paris: Libraire philosophique J. Vrin, 1965.

"In memoriam Alexandre Birkenmajer (1890–1967)." *Archives internationales d'histoire des sciences* 21, nos. 84–85 (1968): 306–8.

"'Novus regnat Salomon in diebus malis' : Une satire contre Innocent III." In *Festschrift Bernhard Bischoff zu seinem 65. Geburtstag,* edited by Johanne Autenrieth and Franz Brunhölzl, 372–90. Stuttgart: A. Hirsemann, 1971. Reprinted in *Pensée médiévale en Occident,* article 14.

"F. Wormald (1904–72)." *Cahiers de civilisation médiévale* 15 (1972): 347–48.

"Comment les théologiens et les philosophes voient la femme." In *La femme dans les civilisations des Xe–XIIIe siècles, Cahiers de civilisation médiévales* 20 (1977): 105–28. Reprinted in *Pensée médiévale en Occident,* article 11.

"Notes et observations au sujet des éditions de textes médiévaux." In *Probleme der Edition mittel- und neulateinischer Texte, Deutsche Forschungsgemeinschaft,* edited by Ludwig Hödl and Dieter Wuttke 41–58. Boppard am Rhein: Harald Boldt Verlag, 1978. Reprinted in *Pensée médiévale en Occident,* article 1.

"Actualité de la pensée d'Étienne Gilson." *Cahiers de civilisation médiévale* 22 (1979): 431–35.

"Étienne Gilson." *Cahiers de civilisation médiévale* 22 (1979): 425–30.

In collaboration. "Memoirs of Fellows and Corresponding Fellows of the Medieval Academy of America: Richard William Hunt." *Speculum* 55 (1980): 647–48.

"Translations and Translators," in *Renaissance and Renewal in the Twelfth Century,* ed. R. L. Benson and G. Constable (Cambridge, Mass.: Harvard University Press, 1982), 421–62. Reprinted in *La transmission des textes philosophiques et scientifiques au Moyen Âge,* article 2.

"Algazel dans l'occident latin." In *Académie du royaume du Maroc, session de novembre 1985.* Rabat: l'Imprimerie El maarif al jadida for Academie du royaume du Maroc, 1986. Reprinted in *La transmission des textes philosophiques et scientifiques au Moyen Âge,* article 7.

"Les traductions a deux interprètes, d'arabe en langue vernaculaire et de langue vernaculaire en latin." In *Traduction et traducteurs au Moyen Âge, Colloques internationaux du Centre national de la recherche scientifique, Institut de recherche et histoire des textes, 26–28 mai 1986,* edited by Geneviève Contamine, 193–206. Paris: Editions du Centre national de la recherche scientifique, 1989. Reprinted in *La transmission des textes philosophiques et scientifiques au Moyen Âge,* article 3.

"In memoriam M-D. Chenu, O.P. (1895–1990)." *Archives d'histoire littéraire et doctrinale du Moyen Âge* 57 (1990): 9–10.

Avicenne en Occident. Études de philosophie médiévale, 71. Paris: Libraire philosophique J. Vrin, 1993. This volume includes the articles that arose out of her research on the manuscripts of the Latin Avicenna.

Études sur le symbolisme de la Sagesse et sur l'iconographie. Variorum Collected Studies series, CS421. Aldershot, Eng.: Variorum, 1993. This volume includes her important studies on the personification of Wisdom in the art, poetry, and philosophy of the Middle Ages, together with the symbolic use of the cosmos and the angels revolving the spheres within it.

Avicenna Latinus. Edited by Simone van Riet and Pierre Jodogne. Louvain-la-Neuve, Belg.: E. Peeters; Leiden: E. J. Brill, 1994. A collection of all her articles on the manuscripts of the Latin translations of portions of Avicenna's philosophical encyclopedia, the *Shifā'*, with addenda and corrigenda.

La connaissance de l'Islam dans l'Occident médiéval. Variorum Collected Studies series, CS445. Aldershot, Eng.: Variorum, 1994. This includes her seminal article on the translations of the Koran in the Middle Ages and her edition, together with Georges Vajda, of the religious texts of Ibn Tumart, the Mahdi of the Almohads, in Arabic and in Mark of Toledo's Latin translation.

La transmission des textes philosophiques et scientifiques au Moyen Âge. Variorum Collected Studies series, CS463. Aldershot, Eng.: Variorum, 1994. This includes her articles on the translations and translators of the twelfth century and on the practice of translating Arabic into Latin via a vernacular intermediary, together with studies of translations of the works of individual Arabic scholars, al-Kindī, al-Ghazālī, Ibn Rushd (Averroes), Pseudo-Aristotle, and Galen, and studies of texts on astrology and on cosmology.

Pensée médiévale en Occident. Variorum Collected Study series. Aldershot, Eng.: Variorum, 1995. This volume begins with d'Alverny's thoughts on editing medieval Latin texts, and includes articles on Alain de Lille written subsequent to her book on this scholar, articles on other theologians (Achard of Saint Victor, Humbertus de Balesma, Pierre de Roissy) and on magic, and a paleographical study of the writing of Bernard Itier.

Works Cited

Most informative on points of biography are the obituaries by André Vernet in *Archives d'histoire littéraire et doctrinale du Moyen Âge* 149 (1991): 5–8; by Guy Beaujouan in *Bibliothèque de l'École des chartes,* 150 (1992): 439–42; and by Marcia L. Colish, Giles Constable, and William J. Courtenay, in *Speculum* 67 (1992): 795–96. For an appreciation of d'Alverny's work, see Danielle Jacquart in "Avant-Propos" to *Avicenna en Occident,* v–vii; and Peter Dronke, preface to *Études sur le symbolisme de la Sagesse et sur l'iconographie,* ix–xii.

Crozet, René, and Edmond René Labande. "Liminaire." *Cahiers de civilisation médiévale* 1 (1958): 5–7.

Hasse, Dag N. *Avicenna's "De Anima" in the Latin West: The Formation of a Peripatetic Philosophy of the Soul 1160–1300.* London: Warburg Institute, Nino Aragno Editore, 2000.

———. "King Avicenna: the Iconographic Consequences of a Mistranslation." *Journal of the Warburg and Courtauld Institutes* 60 (1997): 230–34.

Jacquart, Danielle, and Gérard Troupeau. *Le livre des axiomes médicales,* by Ibn al-Masawaih. Geneva: Droz; Paris: Champion, 1980.

Kritzeck, James. *Peter the Venerable and Islam.* Princeton, N.J.: Princeton University Press, 1964.

Lacombe, G., et al, eds. *Aristoteles Latinus: Codices.* 2 vols. Rome: Librareria dello stato, 1939–45.

Malewicz, Malgorzata H., ed. "*Libellus de efficatia artis astrologice,* traité astrologique d'Eudes de Champagne XIIe siècle." *Mediaevalia Philosophica Polonorum* 20 (1974): 3–95.

Travaglia, Pinella. *Magic, Causality and Intentionality: The Doctrine of Rays in al-Kindī*. Micrologus' Library, 3. Florence: Società internazionale per lo studio del medioevo latino, Edizioni del Galluzzo, 1999.

Wiegers, G. A. "Yça Gidelli (fl. 1450), His Antecedents and Successors." Ph.D. diss., Leiden University, 1991.

Wiesner, Hillary S. "The Cosmology of al-Kindī." Ph.D. diss., Harvard University, 1993.

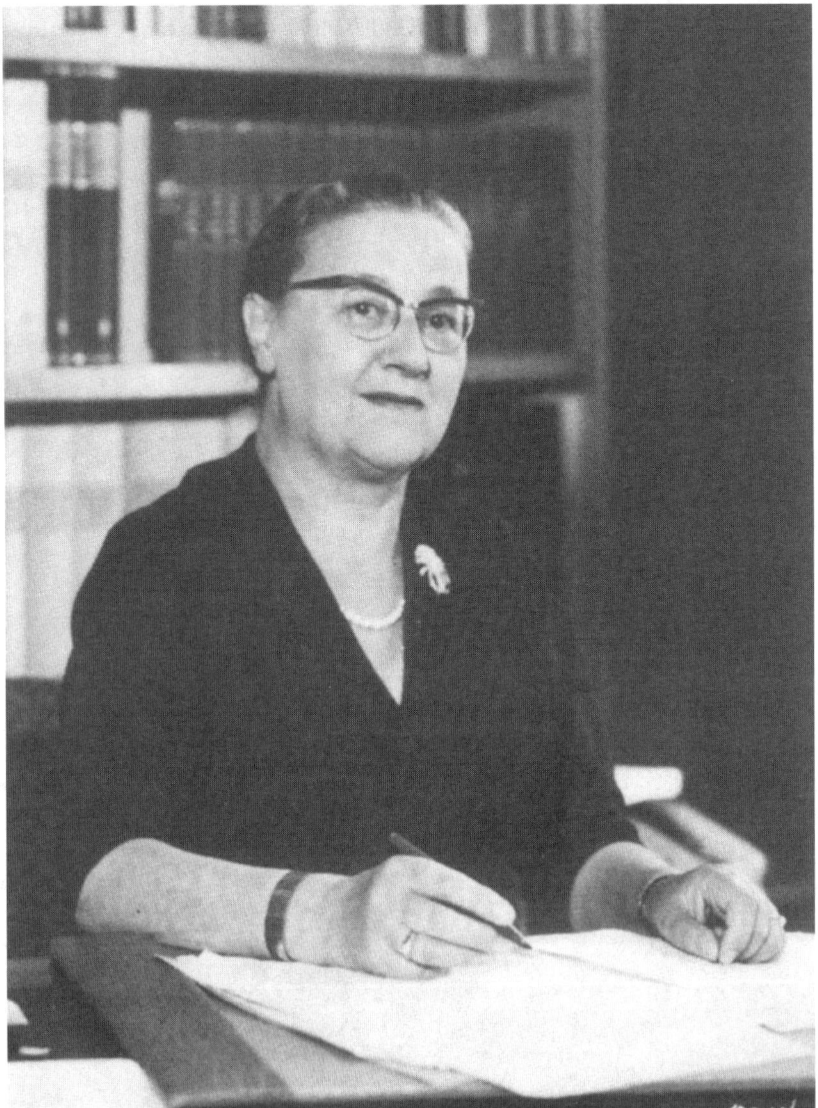

CHAPTER 42

Christine A. E. M. Mohrmann (1903–1988) and the Study of Christian Latin

CARMELA VIRCILLO FRANKLIN

CHRISTINE ANDRINE ELISABETH MARIE MOHRMANN, pioneering scholar of Christian and Medieval Latin, was born in Groningen on 1 August 1903 and died on 13 July 1988 at Nijmegen. Her family belonged to the well-to-do middle class of the city and, more significantly for the intellectual development of their daughter, to the Catholic minority of Holland. Mohrmann's parents supported the church and its institutions, but they also retained great liberalism and independence in the upbringing of their daughter. A frequently cited example of this family trait is her parents' disregard of their parish priest's contrary advice when they sent their clever and studious Tine, who had completed primary school and showed no interest in home economics, to pursue more academic subjects at the municipal lycée of Groningen and then at the one near Arnhem, where the family moved in 1917.[1]

It was at the Arnhem lycée that Christine began to develop the two dominant interests that shaped her life as a scholar, the study of ancient Greek and Latin and a passionate commitment to what she called the cultural emancipation of Dutch Catholics, who had not been fully represented in the intellectual elite of her country.[2] Her life and work exemplify the integration of her scholarly interests and her religious and cultural activism. She credited one of her teachers at the lycée in Arnhem, the classical philologist P. C. Groeneboom, with awakening her love of the ancient authors.[3] Mohrmann's professional relationship with Groeneboom, who followed his pupil's career with great encouragement and interest, foreshadows the bond she would forge with her university teacher and mentor, the Catholic priest Joseph Schrijnen, the founder of the Nijmegen School of Early Christian Latin.[4] Schrijnen was also one of the principal advocates for the establishment of the Catholic University of Nijmegen and its first rector.

In 1922 Mohrmann began her university studies in classics (Greek and Latin) at the (state) University of Utrecht while waiting for the opening of the new Catholic University of Nijmegen in 1923, from which she graduated in December 1925. Her academic training was strongly philological; there was little attention paid to the ancillary fields of classical studies, such as archaeology, history, or art history. But at the same time the study of Greek and Latin at Nijmegen during Mohrmann's career as a student stressed the methodologies of the newly founded discipline of linguistics, of which Schrijnen was an early exponent. While teaching at the Catholic lycée for girls in Venray and later at the one in Nijmegen, where she attained the rank of professor (1929), Mohrmann pursued her doctoral studies at Nijmegen's Catholic University, concentrating on Early Christian Latin. She defended her dissertation on the language of the sermons of Saint Augustine in 1932.

Mohrmann's dissertation, published as *Die altchristliche Sondersprache in den Sermones des hl. Augustin,* already amply illustrates her association with the scholarly agenda of the Nijmegen School and the intersection of her scholarly interest in the classical languages with the cultural patrimony of Catholicism. According to her own interpretation, the Nijmegen School grew out of the renewed interest in the second half of the nineteenth century among philologists and historians in patristic and early Christian texts, to which they applied the tools of text-criticism developed by classical philologists.[5] Schrijnen's fundamental methodological innovation was to connect the study of the Latinity of early Christian texts and documents with the tools provided by the fledgling discipline of linguistics. Schrijnen had followed Ferdinand de Saussure's courses in Paris while a doctoral student. He had also been one of the leading participants at the first congress of the Comité International Permanent de Linguistes that met at The Hague in 1928, marking the formal entrance of the discipline into the international scholarly world. Christine Mohrmann also attended the congress.[6]

In accordance with linguistic principles already formulated by Saussure, and especially under the influence of what would later be called sociolinguistics, Schrijnen was led to consider anew the changes that Christianity had introduced into Latin as the Christian community began to expand into the Western parts of the Roman Empire from its Greek roots. Mohrmann emphasizes that Schrijnen opposed the widely held belief that the forms of Latin found in ancient Christian texts, inscriptions, and other documents represented a decadent or debased form of classical Latin, a corruption of standard norms of grammar, syntax, and lexical usage. He also opposed the Romantic view that Christianity introduced a "reborn Latinity" into the ancient community.[7] He wanted to move the philological study of early Christian texts beyond the simple observations of theologians who had identified the new religion's influence on Latin only in the creation of neologisms, new words and expressions to accommodate concepts and institutions introduced by Christianity.[8] Rather, Schrijnen theorized the existence of a "special language" (*Sondersprache*) of Christians, a language that was the result of the social and cultural differentiation of early Christians from the larger social group. This special language of Christians was clearly visible in the early third century. The works of Tertullian (ca. 160–220) are its earliest literary expression, and despite classicizing resistance by contemporary Christian writers such as Minucius Felix, a generation later Cyprian (d. 258) would use Christian Latin without reserve.[9]

While the fundamental importance of Schrijnen in the creation of the theories of the Nijmegen School is widely acknowledged, it was left to his pupils to develop and substantiate his first theoretical concepts. After the death of the founder in 1938, the program of the Nijmegen School was led most visibly and successfully by Christine Mohrmann. This was done in three principal ways. First of all, Mohrmann and other followers of the Nijmegen School modified its early theories in response to criticism. Also, they concretized the theory by studying ancient texts to illustrate its workings in detail. Finally, they propagandized their work through a large list of publications and lectures. Mohrmann in particular was also keen to apply the teachings of the school to the religious life of contemporary society, primarily in the renewal of the liturgy.

The theory of the existence of a particular language among early Christians as proposed by the Nijmegen School was widely debated.[10] Discussions and criticisms led Mohrmann to refine and expand the theory as propounded by her teacher. The strongest criticisms that had been addressed to Schrijnen's formulation concerned the relationship between Christian Latin and common Latin, the language used by the community at large. Critics, while admitting the existence of characteristic lexical and semantic facts and morphological peculiarities in Early Christian Latin, had expostulated that the Latin of Christian texts and documents cannot be considered a language unto itself because it does not have its own phonetics or its own syntax. In Mohrmann's reformulation of the theory these criticisms are not appropriate because the Nijmegen School does not intend Early Christian Latin to be an autonomous language but rather a "special language," a "method of communication . . . that maintains its roots and feeds itself in the ground of the common language" (Schrijnen, *I caratteri*, 8). Christian Latin in Mohrmann's understanding is not a language within a language but the special language of a group that defines itself according to special social and cultural conditions. She illustrates the relationship between the special language of the Christians and the common language of the broader community most simply through the polysemic function assumed by certain words, or "direct Christianisms" (Mohrmann, "L'Étude du grec," 95). Hence, for example, *logos verbum* maintained for Christians the common Greek or Latin meaning as "word," but it also received a new semantic content derived from Christian ideology, becoming in effect a "semantic neologism." Even more important in Mohrmann's reformulation is the role of "indirect Christianisms," lexical and syntactical neologisms that do not have a direct relationship with Christian ideology yet are not found in the common language. Among lexical neologisms Mohrmann identified many words with particular derivations.[11] Among syntactical neologisms, she singled out in particular the use of the collective singular of words such as *opus* (to indicate works of mercy).[12] Many of these neologisms derive from biblical use. To emphasize this distinction from the theory as formulated by Schrijnen, Mohrmann preferred to use the term "Latin of the Christians" rather than "Christian Latin."[13]

In a series of studies of early Christian authors, Mohrmann examined specific manifestations of Early Christian Latin. Among these, most significant are her works on Augustine, in whom she maintained a lifelong interest, and Saint Patrick.[14] But she also wrote on Cyprian, Ambrose, Jerome, and numerous others.[15] Mohrmann also expanded significantly the scope of the application of the theories of the Nijmegen School by analyzing early translations of Greek and Hebrew texts into Latin. This work is particularly important because it expands the chronological development of Christian Latin to the period preceding Tertullian, who had been considered "the Father of Christian Latin." She was the first to recognize the importance of the early (pre-Jerome) translations of the Bible as manifestations of the Latinity of Christians.[16] She paid more attention to the influence of Christian Greek and of Hebrew, in particular through the Septuagint (i.e., the Greek translation of the Hebrew Scriptures), in the formation of Christian Latin.[17] She also was the first to exploit early Christian Latin writings that up to then had been completely neglected, such as the Latin translation of the letter of Clement to the Corinthians.[18]

Mohrmann expanded the field of the Nijmegen School to consider during the 1950s also ecclesiastical Latin and especially the Latin of the Christian liturgy. Her interest was certainly spurred by the Liturgical Movement, which led many Catholic intellectuals to study the ancient liturgical sources. She was the first to apply the term *Kunstsprache* (artificial, stylized speech) to the language of the liturgy. This term she borrowed from scholars who had used it to describe the language of the Homeric poems, an idiom that is detached from everyday speech or a community of speakers but rests rather on a collective tradition. Like the formulaic language of the *Iliad* and the *Odyssey*, so also the language of the liturgy, in Mohrmann's theory, is a mixture of archaisms, newer formulations, and varied dialectical expressions but results in a formal style that is unified and even rigid.[19]

Her interest in the language of Christian communities led her also to consider the linguistic expressions of early Latin monasticism. She wrote on the newly discovered early Latin translation of Athanasius's *Life of Antony* and on the *Rule* of Benedict.[20] Particularly important was her contribution to the debate over the dating of Benedict's *Rule* in relation to the *Rule of the Master*. Through lexical and morphological analysis of the manuscripts of the *Rule* of Benedict, she pointed out the evidence of its authentic, sixth-century language, which had been corrected during the Carolingian Reform to adhere more closely to classical standards.[21]

She also addressed the prejudice that considered Medieval Latin not as an autonomous phenomenon but simply as a language related to ancient literature. She criticized Ludwig Traube and W. Meyer, whose works had shaped the modern study of Medieval Latin, because they had emphasized the classical, profane tradition of medieval Latin literature and had ignored the Latin of the church, formed by the Latin Bible, the Fathers, and especially the liturgy. She devised a theory of Medieval Latin that emphasized its dualism, the classicism of the schools, on the one hand (as manifested, for example, in the Latin of the Carolingian Reform), and the Latin of the church, on the other. It was the vitality of Christian Latin, she insisted, that kept Medieval Latin from atrophy, so that it was able to become the language of a new abstract system of thought at the end of the Middle Ages, Scholasticism.[22]

Through her indefatigable activities as a teacher and lecturer, and through her writings primarily in French and German for scholars and in Dutch for her country's Catholics, Mohrmann made the theories of the Nijmegen School well known.[23] She became its principal representative in the international scholarly world. Alone of all her colleagues associated with the school, for example, Mohrmann lectured in the United States and Ireland, and some of her work also appeared in English.[24] A particularly important vehicle for the dissemination of learned studies of the Nijmegen School was the journal *Vigiliae christianae,* founded under Mohrmann's leadership in 1947. She also was the main impetus behind the series *Graecitas christianorum primaeva,* established in 1962 to parallel the older series *Latinitas christianorum primaeva,* started by Schrijnen in 1932.

From the very first Mohrmann was keen on widening the influence of the new field of linguistics on the study of the ancient languages and extending the discoveries of the School of Nijmegen to as broad a public as possible. While still teaching at the lycée, she wrote a Homeric grammar for secondary-school pupils with the purpose of "adapting the teaching of Homer's language in the lycées to modern linguistic concepts."[25] From 1935 to 1938 she regularly contributed materials on linguistics and early Christian literature to the newspaper *De Tijd.* In 1943 she coauthored a Greek grammar to introduce the contributions of linguistics to university students of the classical language.[26] She was also a very active member of the Comité International Permanent de Linguistes, serving as its general secretary from 1964 to 1977.

Most important, Mohrmann applied her scholarly expertise to the work of the liturgical renewal of the Roman Catholic Church in the twentieth century. When a new Latin translation of the Psalter—executed by Rome's Biblical Institute under the leadership of its rector and future cardinal, Agostino Bea—was authorized for private and choral prayer by Pope Pius XII on 24 March 1945, Mohrmann was strongly and publicly critical. She rebuked the new edition for abandoning the Christian Latin idioms and forms of the ancient Gallican Psalter in favor of classical norms of Latin usage—such as the substitution of *tabernaculum* with *tentorium* or of *ambulo* with *incedo.* The translators' belief that Early Christian Latin was a decadent form of Ciceronian Latin ignored the rich cultural and ideological reverberations of the older translation. She pointed out, for example, that the replacement in the new version of Latinized Greek words in favor of classical Latin expressions showed little understanding of the development of the Latin of the Bible. The new rendering of Psalm 105:21 as *qui fecit portenta in Aegypto* for the old *qui fecit magnalia in Aegypto* ignores that *magnalia,* regarded as "decadent Latin" by the translators, is a Christian coinage from the Greek to distinguish the Christian God's prodigies from the *portenta* of the pagan gods. Similarly, the use of the classical *laudare* by the new translators where the old translation had *confiteri* overlooks the specific meaning of "praise of God" that the word *confiteri* had in biblical and early Christian writers, most famously in Augustine.[27]

In the early 1950s, while engaged in her own scholarly studies of the early Christian Latin liturgy, she also participated vigorously in the debate over the translation of the liturgy into the vernacular. She compared the contemporary renewal and the search for a new language in liturgical and religious practice to the "consciousness of newness" of the first days of the church.[28] Her pronouncements on contemporary issues were always informed by her scholarship. In preparation for the translation into French of the Ordinary of the Mass under the sponsorship of the Centre de pastorale liturgique, she undertook a series of studies on the language and composition of this prayer.[29] And a decade later, when, as a result of the Second Vatican Council (1961–65), the translation of the entire liturgy into the vernacular became a necessity, she advocated the adherence to clear principles, based on scholarly understanding of the development and function of the language of prayer.[30] Her insistence on the relevance of her work to the broader Christian public is also illustrated by her Dutch translation of a selection of Augustine's sermons. Her purpose was to present texts "that might capture the attention of modern man" without sacrificing historical authenticity.[31] This was one of the goals of the Liturgical Movement.

Yet, despite Mohrmann's enormous contributions to the discussions of liturgical reform within international Roman Catholic circles, she is not popularly identified as one of the scholars of the Liturgical Movement. She has been discussed only within the more local concerns of Dutch Catholic emancipation. This stems at least partly from the fact that she was never appointed to a major papal commission or study group guiding the reforms within the Roman Catholic Church in the twentieth century. She was not invited to take part in an official capacity in the work of Vatican II, as male scholars were who served as expert consultants to the bishops. Her role in this arena awaits a thorough examination.

Mohrmann described the love that as a young girl she had developed for the classical languages and their literatures in almost romantic terms, a "pure" love, one that was completely disinterested.[32] Yet, it is significant that at the university she did not choose to follow the path of classical Greek and Latin philology but instead embraced the new subjects of Early Christian Latin and linguistics. She liked to reminisce to her students about the powerful impact that Schrijnen's inaugural lecture for the opening of the new Catholic University had on her, and she often stated that it was her teacher's influence that led her into these pioneering fields.[33] These statements, however, should not obscure other factors that may have also been influential. Mohrmann's choice of specialization, while certainly a reflection of her own scholarly and personal interests, might also have derived from the realization that a new field, a radical departure from the old and hence less bound by traditional restrictions, might offer more possibilities for work and advancement to a woman.

Similarly, her association with Joseph Schrijnen may be revealed to be more complex than the simple hierarchical teacher-pupil relationship many have described. Those who have written about Mohrmann claim that Schrijnen was extraordinarily influential on his young pupil. He is credited with transforming the shy, timid student who matriculated at the university into an energetic and confident scholar "with international connections, an emancipated woman and a convinced Christian."[34] In fact, it has even been claimed that, had it not been for Schrijnen, Mohrmann's timidity would have prevented her access to the national and international scholarly community.[35] Clearly there is much evidence for this view. Schrijnen was Mohrmann's teacher at Utrecht and then at the Catholic University of Nijmegen. He, very much senior and well established, provided opportunities for his young pupil. When he was elected secretary of the Comité International Permanent de Linguistes at its first meeting in 1928, she became the adjunct secretary, carrying out most of the practical duties of the office.[36] She fulfilled a similar role for the Federation of Catholic Universities, founded by Schrijnen and Agostino Gemelli of Milan's Università Cattolica del Sacro Cuore. Schrijnen's influence on his pupil is thought by many to have extended even over her personal life. Mohrmann's lifelong celibacy is attributed to a desire to follow Schrijnen's model.[37] Their daily familiarity was made easy by their dwelling only a few doors from each other.[38] Descriptions of Schrijnen's intellectual and religious interests could easily fit, mutatis mutandis, his pupil.[39] After the death of its founder, Mohrmann became completely identified with the School of Nijmegen.

Still, it is hard to accept that Mohrmann's timidity was not just the normal manifestation of youth and inexperience. Another picture of her emerges from the evidence, as a boisterous, jovial, cigar-smoking woman, a powerful and funny teacher, a great storyteller who very much enjoyed being at the center of attention and felt completely at ease among priests and ecclesiastics.[40] Personal choices attributed to Schrijnen's influence may in fact have been Mohrmann's deliberate accommodations to a system in which she wanted to succeed. Mohrmann frequently stated that she did not regret remaining celibate for the sake of scholarship, which she considered a vocation. But one should remember that the prejudice against married women in universities, especially Catholic ones, was felt, and is still felt, to be even stronger than that against single women.[41]

While Schrijnen's role as mentor is undisputed, it is clear that Mohrmann even when still a young student had a significant part in shaping Schrijnen's theories as he was formulating them and that she directly contributed to his work. While consulting the files of the *Thesaurus linguae latinae* at Munich for her dissertation on the language of the sermons of Augustine, Mohrmann realized the importance of the phenomenon of "indirect Christianisms." It is generally acknowledged that this discovery provided the first concrete confirmation of Schrijnen's theories that the new religion and the new outlook marked the use of language to such an extent that one can speak of structural changes.[42] That Mohrmann's discovery had an immediate impact on

Schrijnen's "manifesto" of the Nijmegen School, *Charakteristik des altchristlichen Latein*, is generally recognized.⁴³ This book was published in 1932, the same year Mohrmann completed her dissertation. Their joint publication in 1936 and 1937 of the two-volume study on the syntax of the letters of Cyprian is but a later, more public manifestation of their collaborative relationship.

Finally, one must note that Schrijnen was not able to secure for her the succession to his chair in Greek and Latin linguistics, which included Early Christian Latin, at Nijmegen. That long-delayed achievement was the result of the bishops' attitude toward Mohrmann's incontrovertible scholarly achievement and international prestige.⁴⁴ This episode shows both the discrimination to which she was subject as a woman as well as her determination to obtain what she and many of her colleagues felt she was entitled to.⁴⁵ The Catholic University of Nijmegen was governed by a board of Dutch bishops, the Radboudstichting. It was this board that dispensed teaching appointments. Immediately after she defended her dissertation, Mohrmann applied to the Radboudstichting to be admitted to teach general and Latin linguistics, with particular expertise in Early Christian Latin, as a *privaat-docente,* the lowest university teaching rank. The Radboudstichting refused the request, without providing any explanation. But in a private letter to Schrijnen, one of the members of the episcopal board indicated that the bishops feared that she would later claim a higher appointment if they admitted her to this rank. It is clear that the bishops did not want any woman teaching at the Catholic University of Nijmegen, for at that same time Hedwige Houben was also refused a license to teach Italian. Subsequent attempts by Schrijnen and the dean of the university's Faculty of Letters also failed.⁴⁶

It is clear that the Dutch bishops' position was reactionary and not the norm at other Catholic institutions in Europe. Agostino Gemelli—the rector of Milan's Catholic university "Sacro Cuore"—supported the appointment of women as teachers in the Catholic universities on the simple principle that women were already admitted as students. At Schrijnen's request Gemelli even consulted Pope Pius XII, and Rome made it clear to the Dutch bishops that the Congregation for the Universities, if asked, would not oppose the appointment of a woman at Nijmegen. But it was also made clear that Rome would not interfere on its own initiative but only reply to a direct question by the bishops. Hence, in effect the Radboudstichting was allowed to retain its discriminatory practice.⁴⁷ Mohrmann's papers, as discussed by A. A. R. Bastiaensen, suggest that she was deeply affected by this experience. Many years later, she began to write, but did not finish apparently, an account of these events.⁴⁸

Thwarted at Nijmegen, Mohrmann applied and received the teaching rank of *privaat-docente* at the state University of Utrecht in 1937.⁴⁹ In 1946 the University of Amsterdam appointed her to the *lectorat* and in 1955 to the position of "Extraordinary Professor." But already in 1953 Nijmegen had created for her a post as "Extraordinary Professor."⁵⁰ It was not until 1961, when she was almost sixty and long the recognized authority in her field, that Christine Mohrmann was finally granted the position many people felt she had deserved long before, that of holder as "Ordinary Professor" of the chair that had been first occupied by Schrijnen. She directed twenty-two dissertations at Nijmegen, which would solidify and further expand the work of the school.

Christine Mohrmann's publications constitute a very substantial and influential opus. They illustrate the tenacity of her scholarly interests, but also their evolution and the religious commitments in which they were anchored. Her early works are primarily concerned with the general characteristics of Christian Latinity, with semantic studies of words or expressions and the language and style of early Christian authors, especially Augustine. Increasingly, however, Mohrmann used her studies as vehicles for broader historical understanding. Her investigation of monastic terminology was the means by which she gained understanding of early monastic institutions. Her discussion of the language and style of Bernard of Clairvaux reveals the intellectual framework of the monastic reformer.[51] Her studies of the polysemic language of ancient prayer shed light on the spiritual world of early Christianity and are further made to bear on the contemporary efforts to render these ancient prayers in the vernacular.[52] She concluded her farewell lecture to her students and colleagues at Nijmegen by taking issue with Saussure's famous statement that the single object of linguistics is to understand language for itself and by itself. She protested that this assertion cannot apply to her work or that of the Nijmegen School. Rather, Mohrmann defined her use of linguistics in philological terms, as a means to understand ancient texts and through them to give life to the world that is behind the texts.[53]

While the theory of a *Sondersprache* as formulated by Schrijnen has largely been overcome, the work of Christine Mohrmann and of the School of Nijmegen under her leadership made a significant contribution to our understanding of the evolution of the Latin language by taking into account the role of Christianity and its ideology. The study of texts that had been largely marginalized was legitimized and given high visibility. Christine Mohrmann left a large archive of materials, including her correspondence with Joseph Schrijnen, to the Centre de documentation catholique at Nijmegen. These materials, as they become accessible, will make possible a full biography of the Dutch scholar, one that should provide a complete assessment of Mohrmann's scholarly work and also take into consideration her development as a lay Catholic and feminist intellectual.[54]

Notes

Basic treatments of Christine Mohrmann's life and work are L. J. Engels, "Christine A. E. M. Mohrmann (1903–1988): Une Vie de savant"; G. J. M. Bartelink, "L'Oeuvre scientifique de Christine Mohrmann (l'École de Nimègue)"; and A. A. R. Bastiaensen, "Schrijnen-Mohrmann: Collaboration et succession retardée." My essay is heavily indebted to these articles, which were delivered at the colloquium organized by the Société des études paléochrétiennes of the Catholic University of Nijmegen. I am also very grateful to Dr. H. E. G. Rose of the University of Utrecht, who made valuable comments on my essay. I refer to Mohrmann's articles as they appear in the four volumes of collected studies, *Études sur le latin des chrétiens* (hereafter cited as *Études*). All translations are my own.

1. Engels, "Une Vie," 14, refers to "her aversion for what we now call domestic or family studies" ("son aversion pour ce que nous appelons maintenant les études ménagères ou familiales").

2. Engels, "Une Vie," 14, and also Bastiaensen, "Schrijnen-Mohrmann," 46.

3. Engels, "Une Vie," 14.

4. This term is capitalized to emphasize that Early Christian Latin is considered a special language, as will be discussed later in this essay.

5. I am following Christine Mohrmann's evaluation of Schrijnen's thought as she presented it in her appendix ("Dopo quarant'anni") to the 1977 Italian translation of his *Charakteristik des altchristlichen Latein* that had appeared in 1932 (*I caratteri del Latino cristiano antico*, 91–119). The essay was included in German in the fourth volume of her collected studies ("Nach vierzig Jahren," in *Études*, 4:111–40). She also discussed the early development of the Nijmegen School in her farewell address upon retirement ("L'Étude du grec et du latin de l'antiquité chrétienne: Passé, présent, avenir," in *Études*, 4:91–110).

6. Ferdinand de Saussure is considered the "father of modern linguistics"; his principal work, *Cours de linguistique général*, appeared in 1915. Also influential on the School of Nijmegen were the contemporary Parisian linguists J. Vendryes and A. Meillet (Mohrmann, "L'Étude du grec," 92–93).

7. Such a view was attributed by Schrijnen to certain late-nineteenth-century writers, such as F. Ozanam (Mohrmann, "L'Étude du grec," 92).

8. Mohrmann, "L'Étude du grec," 93–94. These are called "christianismes lexicologiques directs" (Christine Mohrmann, "Quelques traits caractéristiques du latin des chrétiens," in *Études*, 1:22).

9. Mohrmann, "Dopo Quarant'anni," 99–104.

10. A useful summary of the critical debate is found in Burton, *Old Latin Gospels*, 153–54. Standard accounts of Christian Latin reflect the debate. See, for example, the classic survey, *The Latin Language*, by L. R. Palmer, published in 1954 in London (Faber and Faber) and much reprinted (181–205). Palmer criticizes Schrijnen's "terminological hair-splitting" and accepts the "existence of a special Christian idiom," established by study of "individual detail" (195). Palmer also supports Mohrmann's chronology of the development of Christian Latin (198–201).

11. For example, nouns formed with the suffix *tor* (*cooperator, miserator, operator*); verbs of the first conjugation in *ficare* (such as *clarificare, mortificare, glorificare*) (Mohrmann, "Quelques traits caracteristiques," 35).

12. Mohrmann, "Quelques traits caractéristiques," 36–37, where Mohrmann also discusses the criticisms of E. Löfstedt.

13. Mohrmann, "L'Étude du grec," 94–95. The contrast between the Nijmegen School advocates, who emphasized the role of Christianity in the transformation of Latin, and other contemporary philologists is clearly illustrated by Mohrmann's discussion of the history of the Latin word *gentes*. The Swedish philologist E. Löfstedt had illustrated the semantic transformation of *gentes*, by which the Romans designated peoples in contrast to the *populus romanus*, into a word with negative connotations and hence into its meaning as "pagans." Mohrmann points out that its "intellectual value in the language of the Christians is completely new (and inspired by Greek precedent)," even though it rests upon the "affective nuance of the word in the common language" of the Romans (Mohrmann, "Quelques traits caracteristiques," 26–27). See also Mohrmann's discussion of the transformation of the word *paganus* ("Encore une fois 'paganus,'" in *Études*, 3:277–89).

14. Each of the volumes of the *Études* contains articles on Augustine. For her work on Saint Patrick, see *Latin of Saint Patrick*.

15. See particularly Mohrmann, *Études*, 1:289–435, 2: 235–367, and 3: 379–411. She also was the general editor of the series Vite dei santi (Milan: Mondadori, 1974).

16. But see Burton's discussion, which tries to establish the priority of Biblical Latin (*Old Latin Gospels*, 154 and n. 9).

17. Bartelink, "L'Oeuvre scientifique," 28. But Christine Mohrmann criticized the notion of Hebrew borrowings through direct contact on the basis of the evidence of Jewish inscriptions in Latin ("Les Origines de la latinité chrétienne à Rome," in *Études*, 4:67–68). A very clear example of the subtler results achieved by her skillful use of all three biblical languages is found in "'Tertium Genus': Les Relations judaïsme, antiquité, christianisme reflétées dans la langue des chrétiens," in *Études*, 4:195–210. See especially her discussion of the semantic transformation of the Latin word *gloria* (198–203).

18. Mohrmann, "Les Origines"; also discussed by Bartelink, "L'Oeuvre scientifique," 28–29.

19. Christine Mohrmann, "Notes sur le latin liturgique," in *Études*, 2:93–107; and "Le Latin médiéval," *Études*, 2:181–232, particularly 194–95. Her most comprehensive discussion of liturgical language is found in *Liturgical Latin*.

20. For her work on Saint Anthony, see "Note sur la version latine la plus ancienne de la Vie de saint Antoine par saint Athanase."

21. Mohrmann, "La Latinité de saint Benoît: Étude linguistique sur la tradition de la *Règle*," in *Études*, 1:403–35; and "Étude sur la langue de saint Benoît," in *Études,* 2:325–45; Bartelink, "L'oeuvre scientifique," 34–35.

22. Mohrmann, "Le Latin médiévale," 184.

23. Mohrmann had written mostly in German and Dutch until 1939. After that, she did not publish in German again until 1954. See her bibliography in *Études* 1:xii–xix covering this period. Her activities during the war remain unexplored.

24. Mohrmann's lectures at the Catholic University of America on liturgical language were published in 1957, and those in Dublin on Saint Patrick's Latinity in 1961. See bibliography

25. Engels, "Une Vie," 16.

26. Mohrmann, with Brinkhoff, and Lagas, *Grieksche Grammatika*.

27. Mohrmann, "Quelques observations linguistiques à propos de la nouvelle version latine du Psautier," *Vigiliae christianae* 1 (1947): 114–28. Mohrmann wrote a follow-up article as well as a formal review in the same journal the following year (*Vigiliae christianae* 2 [1948]: 168–82). Both articles were combined into one in *Études*, 4:197–225. For her Dutch publication on this subject, see Bartelink, "L'Oeuvre scientifique," 35. See also Mohrmann "The New Latin Psalter: Its Diction and Style," in *Études,* 2:109–32.

28. Mohrmann, "The Ever-Recurring Problem of Language in the Church," in *Études,* 4:143–59 and especially 159; this paper was first presented at the Congress of the Theology of the Renewal of the Church in 1967 in Canada.

29. Mohrmann, "Quelques observations sur l'évolution stylistique du canon de la messe romaine," in *Études,* 3:227–44; with B. Botte, *L'Ordinaire de la Messe*.

30. Bartelink, "L'Oeuvre scientifique," 33. See Mohrmann's own discussion in "Ever-Recurring Problem."

31. Engels, "Une Vie," 17. Mohrmann was extremely critical of the misuse of history in contemporary religious debates. See her scathing criticism of Hans Küng in "L'Étude du grec," 98.

32. Bastiaensen, "Schrijnen-Mohrmann," 42 and notes.

33. Bastiaensen, "Schrijnen-Mohrmann," 42 and notes.

34. Engels, "Une Vie," 15; Bastiaensen, "Schrijnen-Mohrmann," 41–42.

35. "But it is evident that it is Joseph Schrijnen who opened for her the way into this domain [i.e., the national and international scholarly community], a domain that, had she been on her own, would have been little accessible because of her initial timidity" (Bastiaensen, "Schrijnen-Mohrmann," 44).

36. It is Mohrmann who appears on the title page of *L'Organisation et l'activité du Comité International Permanent de Linguistes.*

37. Bastiaensen, "Schrijnen-Mohrmann," 46. One must assume that Schrijnen's priestly celibacy is meant.

38. Apparently it was by chance that Mohrmann's family, moving from Arnhem to Nijmegen in 1923 when she enrolled at the university, occupied the house at 9 St. Annastraat. Schrijnen had moved into 17 St. Annastraat earlier that year (Bastiaensen, "Schrijnen-Mohrmann," 42–43).

39. See, for example, Bastiaensen's portrayal of Schrijnen ("Schrijnen-Mohrmann," 42).

40. Many who had only met her once or twice describe her in these terms and remark on her cigar-smoking habit. It was thus, for example, that Professor Jacqueline Hamesse of the Catholic University at Louvain described her to me in conversation and remarked that Mohrmann seemed perfectly at ease surrounded by prelates. Her courses are described by her students as "events," in which "one learned much, but also laughed much" (Engels, "Une Vie," 19–20).

41. In his efforts to get Mohrmann a teaching appointment at Nijmegen, Schrijnen emphasized that she was not married, as was proper for all women who aspired to such a career (Bastiaensen, "Schrijnen-Mohrmann," 52–53).

42. Late in her life Mohrmann herself appears to have wanted to emphasize the role of Schrijnen's pupils in the development of the Nijmegen School. In her farewell address at Nijmegen she noted that "the proof . . . that the new religion and the new mentality had marked the language to such a point that one could speak of structural changes . . . was delivered by Schrijnen only toward the end of his life." And again she stated that Schrijnen "had to rely on his students and successors" to establish in practice his theory ("L'Étude du grec," 93).

43. Bastiaensen, "Schrijnen-Mohrmann," 44–45. Schrijnen's earlier works had not been sufficiently developed (Bartelink, "L'Oeuvre scientifique," 23).

44. For a list of the honors bestowed on her, see [No author], "Avant-propos," *Sacris erudiri* 32, no. 1 (1991): 9. In what follows, I follow Bastiaensen, "Schrijnen-Mohrmann," 47–59, which is based on the unpublished materials in Mohrmann's archive, including her extensive correspondence with Schrijnen.

45. According to Rose's communication to me (e-mail message of 22 January 2002), other factors may have further complicated the negotiations to obtain Mohrmann's appointment, including Schrijnen's relationship to his colleagues at Nijmegen and the relations between the Dutch episcopate and Rome. Some of the papers relating to these negotiations will not be accessible to scholars for several decades.

46. Schrijnen tried without success to convince the president of the Fédération des Unions Féminines Catholiques to intervene with the bishops. His arguments used the (paternalistic?) Catholic argument that women who aspire to scholarly careers should not be denied in their own Catholic institutions (Bartelink, "Schrijnen-Mohrmann," 52–53). He was implying, most likely, that Catholic women would then turn to secular institutions, as Mohrmann was about to do.

47. Schrijnen and Mohrmann traveled to Italy during the Christmas break of 1937–38, and it was during this trip that Schrijnen first talked to Agostino Gemelli. He then wrote to him right before his death in January 1938, and Mohrmann as well as officers of the university pursued the correspondence with Gemelli.

48. There is a short piece by Christine Mohrmann titled "Mijn ervaringen" (My experiences) cited by Bastiaensen, "Schrijnen-Mohrmann," 56 and n. 44.

49. At the same time, Mohrmann continued to teach at the lycée until 1946.

50. This post was obtained by detaching the specialty of Early Christian Latin from the chair of Greek and Latin linguistics (i.e., Schrijnen's old chair), held since 1938 by H. H. Janssen, also a pupil of Schrijnen, but junior to Mohrmann, since he had just completed his dissertation in 1938.

51. Mohrmann, "Le Style de saint Bernard," in *Études,* 2:347–67.

52. In her farewell address, she movingly remarks on the loss of polysemic richness in contemporary liturgical language, especially in Italian and French, which lacked the liturgical and biblical vernacular tradition of English and German. As an example, she discusses the "Zwinglian" view of the Last Supper betrayed by the translation of the canon of the Mass into French. The words of consecration *Pensez à Moi* to translate *hoc facite in meam commemorationem* disregards the charged meaning of *commemoratio,* both in its biblical context (the Jewish Passover "in commemoration" of the departure from Egypt) and Christian interpretation (the "commemoration" of Christ's death and resurrection) ("L'Étude du grec," 95–96).

53. Mohrmann, "L'Étude du grec," 94.

54. As an example of the connection between these two important commitments, H. G. E. Rose pointed out to me (e-mail message of 22 January 2002) that Mohrmann's interest in Roman liturgical texts to the exclusion of other languages and traditions stemmed from her engagement in the contemporary debate about liturgical language. I am also informed that Rose is planning to write a biography of Mohrmann, whose work on liturgical language she analyzed in her dissertation ("Communitas in commemoratione: Liturgical Latin and Liturgical Commemoration in the Missale Gothicum [Vat. reg. lat. 317]" [Ph.D. diss., Utrecht: 2001]).

Select Bibliography of Works by Christine A. E. M. Mohrmann

A list of Mohrmann's publications from 1928 until 1977 is included in *Études,* 1:ix–xxii and 4:405–11. It contains 179 entries, excluding book reviews. The reader is referred to that list for a complete bibliography up to 1977. Here I include only what I consider most significant. The collection of her articles in the four volumes of *Études* published by Edizioni di Storia e Letteratura is the most important item in her bibliography; it includes all of her articles published in *Vigiliae christianae* and most of those published elsewhere. I have not therefore listed here single articles already contained in the *Études.*

Die altchristliche Sondersprache in den Sermones des hl. Augustin. Latinitas christianorum primaeva, 3. Nijmegen, Neth.: Dekker & v. d. Vegt en van Leeuwen, 1932.

L'Organisation et l'activité du Comité International Permanent de Linguistes. Comité International Permanent de Linguistes. Publications du Secrétariat general 1. Nijmegen, Neth.: Dekker & v. d. Vegt en van Leeuwen, 1933.

With Joseph Schrijnen. *Studien zur Syntax der Briefe des hl. Cyprian.* 2 vols. Latinitas christianorum primaeva, 5 and 6. Nijmegen, Neth.: Dekker & v. d. Vegt en van Leeuwen, 1936–37.

With J. Brinkhoff and R. Lagas. *Griekse Grammatika.* Maastricht, Neth.: n.p., 1943.

With B. Botte. *L'Ordinaire de la Messe: Texte critique, traduction, et études.* Études liturgiques, 2. Paris: Éditions du Cerf, 1953.

Latin vulgaire, Latin des chrétiens, Latin médiéval. Paris: Klincksieck, 1956.

"Note sur la version latine la plus ancienne de la Vie de saint Antoine par saint Athanase." *Studia anselmiana* 38 (1956): 35–44.

Liturgical Latin: Its Origins and Character: Three Lectures. Washington, D.C.: Catholic University Press, 1957. Reprint, London: n.p., 1959.

Études sur le latin des chrétiens. 4 vols. Rome: Edizioni di Storia e Letteratura, Raccolta di studi e testi, 1958; 1961; 1965; 1977.

With F. Van Der Meer. *Bildatlas der frühchristlichen Welt.* Gütersloh, Ger.: G. Mohn, 1959. Translated and edited by Mary F. Hedlund and H. H. Rowley under the title *Atlas of the Early Christian World* London: Nelson, 1966.

The Latin of Saint Patrick: Four Lectures. Dublin: Dublin Institute for Advanced Studies, 1961.

Works Cited

Bartelink, G. J. M. "L'Oeuvre scientifique de Christine Mohrmann (l'École de Nimègue)." *Sacris erudiri* 32, no. 1 (1991): 23–37.

Bastiaensen, A. A. R. "Schrijnen-Mohrmann: Collaboration et succession retardée." *Sacris erudiri* 32, no. 1 (1991): 39–59.

Burton, Philip. *The Old Latin Gospels.* Oxford: Oxford University Press, 2000.

Engels, L. J. "Christine A. E. M. Mohrmann (1903–1988): Une Vie de savant." *Sacris erudiri* 32, no.1 (1991): 15–22.

Schrijnen, Joseph. *I caratteri del Latino cristiano antico: Con un'appendice di Christine Mohrmann: Dopo quarant'anni.* Testi e manuali per l'insegnamento universitario del latino, 13. Bologna: Patron Editore, 1977, 1981.

———. *Charakteristik des altchristlichen Latein.* Latinitas christianorum primaeva, 1. Nijmegen, Neth.: n.p., 1932.

CHAPTER 43

Mary Dominica Legge (1905–1986)
Anglo-Norman Scholar

Harriet Spiegel

Mary Dominica Legge helped define Anglo-Norman language and literature and establish the field of Anglo-Norman studies. One of the founding members of the Anglo-Norman Text Society, she was a prolific scholar, editing five Anglo-Norman volumes and authoring two books and over seventy articles and chapters in areas of Anglo-Norman studies from law to history to philology.

Mary Dominica Legge came from a family already distinguished intellectually and noted for pursuing and defining new areas of study. Her Scottish grandfather, James Legge, was taught to read by a blind woman; he had, as Marjorie Chibnall comments, a medieval-style education, for his teacher used "as a school book the metrical psalms she herself knew by heart."[1] James Legge had a varied and perhaps exotic career—first as principal of the Anglo-Chinese College in Malacca, then moving the college and himself to Hong Kong. In Hong Kong he also established missionary schools, mastered the Chinese language and Chinese classics, and established himself as a translator from Chinese because, as he wrote, "it will greatly facilitate the labours of future missionaries that the entire book of Confucius should be published with a translation and notes."[2] He later became the first professor of Chinese at Oxford (hence his sobriquet "Chinese Legge"), and Oxford then became the family home.[3] Legge served on the Oxford Somerville Committee, which sought to establish a non-sectarian hall for women; this would later become Somerville College.[4] Somerville College would be an important home for Mary Dominica Legge throughout her life. Mary Dominica Legge's father, James Granville Legge, continued the family's interest in intellectual matters, serving as the first director of education for Liverpool.

Mary Dominica Legge was the second of four children. Because her expected birth date was 25 March, Lady Day, her parents planned to name her Mary. However, she

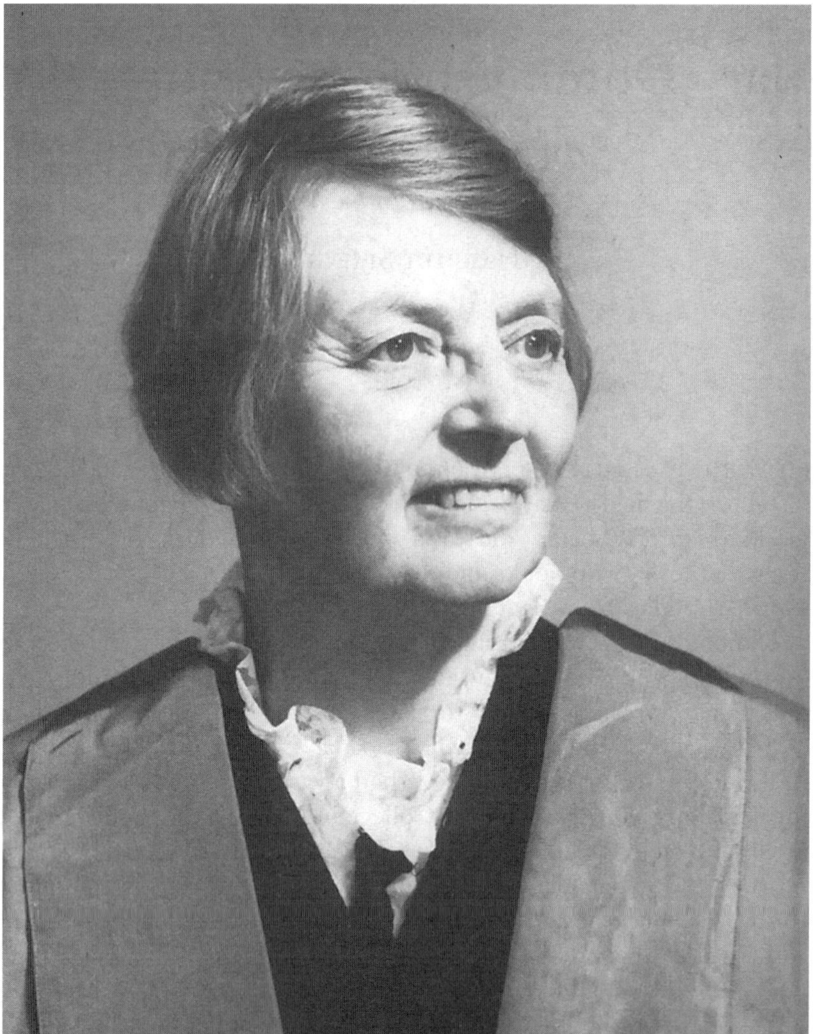

arrived a day later, on a Sunday. So her parents added the name Dominica, the name by which she was known throughout her life.[5] Thus, although some have assumed her name indicated she was a religious, in fact she was not. The family seems to have enjoyed exotic names for their daughters—Legge's two sisters were named Maréio and Pompilia; the only son was simply Harry (though perhaps with a wink toward the family surname). She grew up in an environment that was to shape her as a scholar. C. A. Robson notes, "In Dominica's company one never forgot the long Edwardian afternoon of her earliest childhood, when children were brought up in nurseries, not nursery schools, and girls read the same books as their brothers."[6] Hers was also a musical family. Her younger brother and sister became professional musicians. She herself studied violin but was better known for her lute playing; she also studied the musical settings of medieval poetry.[7]

Legge was a student at Somerville College, Oxford, the earliest Oxford college for women, where she read for the Oxford Honor School of Modern Languages in French.[8] Here she met Mildred K. Pope when she enrolled in her course "Elements of Romance Philology"; with Pope she subsequently took as her special subject Anglo-Norman language and literature, which was to become the subject of her thesis.

Pope was a lifelong inspiration and model for Legge. In a memorial tribute to Legge, Robson describes her admiration thus: "[A] great source of inspiration was Mildred Pope for whom Dominica entertained a veneration well on the far side of idolatry—perhaps I should say hyperdulia. One of her favorite expressions when any new fact was unearthed, or any new view canvassed, was 'But Miss Pope always knew that!'"[9]

Not only did Legge begin her formal study of Anglo-Norman in Pope's seminar; she also met there Ruth J. Dean, who remembers how Legge "happened to befriend this stray American" and how the Legges "welcomed [her] to teas and dinners." Dean relates that Legge "turned up in the final frantic weeks of finishing [her] thesis and gallantly proof-read all [her] typed-out transcriptions of Anglo-Norman texts and variants."[10] The two became lifelong friends.

The friendship of Legge, Dean, and Pope begun in Pope's seminar continued throughout their lives, one of the fruits being the formation of the Anglo-Norman Text Society (ANTS). Pope was instrumental in the formation of the society and became its first honorary secretary, and Legge and Dean were among its "founder members." The society pledged to be "devoted to promoting the study of Anglo-Norman language and literature . . . and concern itself with the publication of a series of Anglo-Norman texts of literary, linguistic, historical and legal value and interest," thus hoping to correct what had been seen as marginalization and neglect by Old French scholars.[11]

Legge's earliest publications, appearing in *Modern Language Review* in 1929, were drawn from her B.Litt. thesis, a description of the manuscripts of *La Lumiere as Lais* and a comparison of the poem with its Latin source.[12] Her first major publication was in collaboration with Sir William Holdsworth, a two-volume edition for the Selden Society of the *Year Books of Edward II, Vols. 20 and 21*. These were to be part of a large project by the Selden Society of publishing all the yearbooks, covering a period from approximately 1202 to 1535. Holdsworth prepared the case notes in the introduction and revised the translation, while Legge was responsible for the translations (from Anglo-Norman and Latin) and the preparation of the text. Here Legge makes a claim for the legitimacy of Anglo-Norman as a language distinct from law French and establishes her authority (and her sometimes acerbic wit as well as its champion):

> Law-French belongs to the interval between the discontinuance of French as a vernacular and its final disappearance as the vehicle of the Law in the course of the seventeenth century. It followed a development of its own undisturbed by outside influences, and could be modified for its single purpose.... The Anglo-norman of the earlier Year Books was the language of the Court, Parliament, the Universities, the grammar-schools, and of all people of consideration.... This language was not a patois, but was a dialect spoken and written by men as cultured as any in Europe.... The contemporary comment and ridicule which Anglo-norman excited in the Continent were due to political reasons, and the airs which Walter Map gave himself prove nothing more than his own conceit.[13]

These volumes, of interest to social as well as legal historians, merited a review in the *University of Pennsylvania Law Review*.[14]

Legge's next major publication, an edition of *Anglo-Norman Letters and Petitions*, consists of two main parts: the first, in Latin, contains ecclesiastical documents; the second, in French, is primarily governmental and private records. Legge had originally intended to serve as coeditor, assisting Somerville College historian Maude Clark by providing the linguistic introduction. Clark's untimely death in 1935 left Legge with full editing responsibilities, and the result was that she took on Clark's historical introduction but had to postpone her own linguistic analysis "for, since each document presents problems of its own, any treatment full enough to be of use would overweight the edition."[15] The year 1935 also saw Legge's election to the Mary Somerville Research Fellowship at Somerville College for a two-year tenure, "one of the most important senior research fellowships then open to women."[16]

The war years saw the launching of Legge's teaching career, first as assistant lecturer in French at Royal Holloway College in the University of London in 1938 and then, four years later, as assistant lecturer at University College, Dundee. She was active as a volunteer during the war, working at the Board of Trade. Also during this time she accepted an offer from Eugène Vinaver to prepare an edition of the *Roman de Balain*. In 1943 she accepted a lectureship at the University of Edinburgh, where she remained until her retirement in 1973 as professor emerita. After retirement she returned to Somerville College, where she was named an honorary fellow. Here she continued her research and writing and enjoyed many social evenings at college tables.[17]

While Legge was at Royal Holloway College, and in spite of war-related difficulties, she and Dean began working on a collaborative edition of a prose version of the

Rule of Saint Benedict. The preface to this edition relates the impediments encountered and overcome: "During the early years of the war the Douce manuscript was removed to a safe place 'for the duration,' and Miss Legge was obliged to work from transcripts of the text which Miss Dean made and sent across the Atlantic ten pages at a time. Only one envelope of the series was a victim of enemy action, and none was delayed by the censors, who opened every packet but forwarded all of them intact, recognizing that they were not an attempt to communicate in code. The possibility of having such 'normal' work as this to turn to during the war meant much to Miss Legge, the British editor."[18] The two ran into a slight problem when they realized that Legge's analysis of the text concluded that it was not, in fact, Anglo-Norman: "As Basil Blackwell was then the publisher of Anglo-Norman Texts, we consulted him about separate publication; but his solution was to include it in Medium Aevum Monographs," where it finally appeared in 1964.[19]

Legge notes similar war-related difficulties in her efforts to consult manuscripts in the editing of *Anglo-Norman Letters and Petitions:* "The preparation of this edition for the Press has met with minor delays owing to the war. Unfortunately, too, the MS. has not been available for reference since the text has been in proof, and it has not been possible to obtain a facsimile of the MS. for the frontispiece usual in this series. The material in the Public Record Office and the British Museum has also been inaccessible."[20]

Legge's first extended critical study, *Anglo-Norman in the Cloisters,* is, as she states in the introduction, "a short book, but . . . long in preparation."[21] Here Legge documents the extensive literary contributions made to Anglo-Norman England by members of religious orders in England, and she includes a brief comparison with similar works written by secular clergy. Her interest in the uses of the Anglo-Norman language, in preaching as well as in broader contexts, lays the groundwork for her later, major book, *Anglo-Norman Literature and Its Background.*

"Saluted even by a French reviewer as one of the most important works ever to appear on the history of medieval French literature,"[22] *Anglo-Norman Literature and Its Background* was immediately hailed as the first definitive study of Anglo-Norman literature: "For the first time a specialist in Anglo-Norman has made a comprehensive study of the three centuries of Anglo-Norman literature and devoted a book to it. Whereas previous writers on the subject have limited their scope or their point of view, Miss Legge has considered all the various forms taken by this literature and she has treated it as an independent subject."[23] The book is partly organized chronologically and partly by genres identified by Legge as being either uniquely or characteristically Anglo-Norman. The first third of the book, a historical survey of the three centuries of Anglo-Norman England, moves from the predominantly Norman tastes of the twelfth century toward what would emerge as distinctly English preferences by the end of the fourteenth century. Legge identifies two defining events: in history the loss of Normandy by John in 1204 and the subsequent separation of kingdom and duchy; and in religion the Fourth Lateran Council of 1215 and the resulting emphasis on instruction of the laity. This, she argues, led to the use of the Anglo-Norman vernacular (instead of Latin) and concurrently to a change in the tone of homiletic literature.

Turning to genres, Legge identifies as Anglo-Norman what she calls the "ancestral romance." These romances arose from the desire of the homesick Anglo-Norman aristocracy to establish an ancestral, legendary English home. Discussing Guillaume d'Angleterre, Waldef, Boeve de Haumtone, Fergus, Gui de Warewic, and Fouke Fitzwarin, Legge shows how these romances use a heroic exile and return formula, with the hero returning to the ancestral home, and how this home is marked by local and English historical and geographical details to "describe the founding of a family."[24] Legge looks at religious literature, saints' lives, chronicles, histories, drama, and lyric poetry. Her scope is broad, including not only texts defined by linguistic criteria but also those written for or read by an Anglo-Norman audience. Also important to Anglo-Norman literature are its precocity, a term she draws from Pope, and its patronage: "What counted for more than the quality or nationality of the writer was the taste, the power, and the riches of the patron."[25]

The book remains a landmark in Anglo-Norman studies for its comprehensive survey of Anglo-Norman texts as well as for its placement of these texts in historical and linguistic context. As such, Legge has clearly embodied the guiding principles of the Anglo-Norman Text Society to address the necessity of establishing "the centrality of Anglo-Norman for a proper understanding of the literary and linguistic culture of medieval Britain."[26]

Legge continued to be a prodigiously productive scholar throughout her life, publishing a total of seventy-four essays and fifty-eight reviews.[27] A glance at the twenty festschriften to which she contributed bears witness to her wide circle of friends, almost a who's who in Old French studies around the world: included are Mildred K. Pope, Rose Graham, John Orr, Angelo Monteverdi, A. Ewert, Maurice Delbouille, Eugène Vinaver, Margaret Schlauch, René Crozet, Rita Lejeune, Jean Frappier, Tatiana Fotitch, Teruo Sato, Pierre Le Gentil, Charles Rostaing, Edmond-René Labande, Jeanne Wathelet-Willem, Reto R. Bezzola, Jeanne Lods, and Lewis Thorpe.[28]

Anglo-Norman Literature and Its Background was Legge's final book, but it was by no means her final work. Her many subsequent articles serve, in a way, as additional chapters to her major work, as she continued to expand Anglo-Norman studies. No subject was beyond her scope. She dealt with the small details: "An English Allusion to Montaigne before 1595"; and she examined the grand genres: "Les Chansons de geste et la Grande Bretagne." She explored the ethereal: "Clouds and Rainbows in the Age of Allegory"; and she studied the earthly: "More about *Mouru*." In the latter piece, with a title curiously appropriate to her final published work, she argues that the analogical form *mouru* is more than a French teacher's headache; rather it is of particular interest because *est mort* means "is dead." This, she says, "is why the Polish statesman at the end of the Great War chose deliberately to say, "La Pologne a mouru trois fois, et chaque fois elle s'est ressuscitée'" (Poland died three times, and each time it came back from the dead).[29] This and all her contributions are marked by impressive learnedness and engaging wit. In "Toothache and Courtly Love," for example, she connects the agony of the courtly suitor tormented by a toothache with the noble suffering of a lover's sleepless nights and weighs these against the embarrassment of the loss of a front tooth. The loss of a back tooth, she notes, may be an inconvenience, but as it cannot be seen, it does not constitute embarrassment or disgrace. While Legge acknowledges that some may find this particular essay "frivolous," it is also broadly learned; in its few pages she refers to Jehan Renart's *Le Lai de l'ombre* and *L'Escoufle, Florence de Rome,* Matthew Paris's *Cronica majora,* Gerbert de Montreuil's *Le Roman de la Violette,* a song by Peire Vidal, *La Chastelaine de Vergi,* Guillaume de Lorris's *Roman de la Rose, Le Roman du comte de Poitiers, Le Roman d'Eneas,* Ovid, Chréstien's *Cligés,* and Piramus.

Legge was honored by many organizations throughout her life. In 1968 the University of Edinburgh created a personal professorship in Anglo-Norman studies. Legge was awarded Oxford's D.Litt. and was honored by the French government as an officer in l'Ordre des Palmes Académiques, as a fellow by the Royal Historical Society of Antiquaries and by the Scottish Society of Antiquaries, and in 1971 as a corresponding fellow of the Medieval Academy of America. The University of Edinburgh held a colloquium in her honor in 1973.[30] The University of Edinburgh also established the M. D. Legge Prize in French Medieval Studies. The British Academy elected her a fellow in 1974.

Some who met her might well have been intimidated by her intellectual demands and occasionally acerbic wit. "Many people found a trace of asperity in Dominica's manner. . . . her criticism of people was 'downright, uncompromising even abrasive, but never malicious.'"[31] Yet her passion for intellectual engagement won her many friends and made her a much-loved teacher. In her final days, blind and bedridden, she received visits from student volunteers who were to assist her in duties she could no longer perform. One such volunteer was a mathematics student. When Legge found out he was unfamiliar with Plato, she assigned him readings, and their times together were spent reading and discussing the works of Plato.[32]

Legge had a zest for travel and adventure; she attended conferences in Portugal (1962) and the United States (1965 and 1979). Her sense of humor and her own personal style matched her zeal for intellectual engagement. Marjorie Chibnall recounts a characteristic behavior: "In the last years of her life, when others of her sex arrived in taxis for the British Academy dinners, she invariably travelled by Underground, pinning up her long skirts to avoid catching them on the escalators."[33]

Mary Dominica Legge was a pioneer and champion of Anglo-Norman studies, and she has left her mark as a committed teacher, scholar, and friend. Her obituary in *Speculum* pays tribute thus: "She contributed vitally to our recognition that the French language and literature of medieval England are significant aspects of European history and not merely ill-expressed and negligible colonial offshoots, as French scholars used to imply."[34] No one can begin a study of Anglo-Norman without turning first to *Anglo-Norman Literature and Its Background.* And Legge has set the standard for medieval study in her ability to "bridge the gap between historians and philologists, to the lasting profit of both."[35]

NOTES

1. Chibnall, "Mary Dominica Legge," 389.
2. Biographical note by Lindsay Ride, in J. Legge, *Chinese Classics*, 1–25, cited by Chibnall, "Mary Dominica Legge," 390.
3. His nickname is noted in Robson, memorial remarks.
4. Adams, *Somerville for Women*, 12, 14.
5. Her publications are signed variously "M. Dominica Legge" (most commonly), "Mary Dominica Legge," and "M. D. Legge."
6. Robson, memorial remarks.
7. Legge's friend Ruth J. Dean mentions her lute playing, in "M. Dominica Legge," 410. The *Times* (London), however, comments that, to demonstrate medieval music to her students, Legge liked "to illustrate on the viol how medieval music might have sounded" (obituary notice).
8. For an excellent study of the history of Somerville College, including discussion of Legge as well as of Mildred K. Pope and Maude Clark, see Adams, *Somerville for Women*.
9. Robson, memorial remarks.
10. Dean, "M. Dominica Legge," 411.
11. Ian Short, introduction to *Anglo-Norman Anniversary Essays*, ix.
12. M. D. Legge, "Pierre de Peckham and His 'Lumiere as Lais,'"; see also "Lumiere as Lais." For a modern edition of this poem, see Hesketh, *La Lumiere as Lais*.
13. M. D. Legge and Holdsworth, *Year Books of Edward II*, 52: xxx.
14. Kirk, review of *Year Book of Edward II, Vol. 20*.
15. M. D. Legge, *Anglo-Norman Letters and Petitions*, v.
16. Chibnall, "Mary Dominica Legge," 393.
17. Robson, memorial remarks.
18. Dean and Legge, *Rule of Saint Benedict*, v.
19. Dean, "M. Dominica Legge," 411.
20. M. D. Legge, *Anglo-Norman Letters and Petitions*, v.
21. M. D. Legge, *Anglo-Norman in the Cloisters*, v.
22. Dean, "M. Dominica Legge," 409. The reference is presumably to Gallais, review of *Anglo-Norman Literature and Its Background*. Gallais deems this work "le premier ouvrage d'ensemble sur la littérature anglo-normande et l'un des ouvrages les plus importants qui aient paru depuis un siècle sur l'histoire de la littérature médiévale d'expression français." (The premier work covering all of Anglo-Norman literature and one of the most important works to have appeared for a century on the history of medieval French literature.)
23. Dean, review of *Anglo-Norman Literature and Its Background*.
24. M. D. Legge, *Anglo-Norman Literature*, 140–41.
25. Regarding Legge's use of the term "precocity," see her *Anglo-Norman Literature*, 362–64. Legge cites an unpublished paper by Mildred Pope, "The Precocity of Anglo-Norman Literature." Legge develops the concept further in "La Précocité de la littérature anglo-normande." For her comment on patronage, see Legge, *Anglo-Norman Literature*, 364.
26. Ian Short, introduction to *Anglo-Norman Anniversary Essays*, vii.
27. She gave offprints of all her published essays to the Somerville College Library; they

are now in the college archives. Also in the archives are a list of her book reviews and several photographs of Legge as stroke on the Somerville eight (a sport considered controversial for its likelihood to damage women's reproductive organs). A caption under a photograph of the Somerville Rowing Team appearing in the *Daily Express* (Oxford, 28 February 1925) reads: "The opinion expressed in Wales that rowing is too strenuous a form of exercise for women is not supported at Oxford, where University women are now in rigorous training."

28. *Studies Presented to M. K. Pope; Medieval Studies Presented to Rose Graham; Studies Presented to John Orr; Studi in onore di Angelo Monteverdi; Studies Presented to A. Ewert; Mélanges de linguistique romane et de philologie médiévale offerts à M. Maurice Delbouille; Medieval Miscellany Presented to Eugène Vinaver; Studies in Language and Literature in Honour of Margaret Schlauch; Mélanges offerts à René Crozet; Mélanges offerts à Rita Lejeune; Mélanges de langue et de littérature du Moyen Âge et de la Renaissance offerts à Jean Frappier; Studies in Honor of Tatiana Fotitch; Mélanges de langue et de littérature du Moyen Âge offerts à Teruo Sato; Mélanges de langue et de littérature médiévales offerts à Pierre Le Gentil; Mélanges d'histoire littéraire, de linguistique, et de philologie romanes offerts à Charles Rostaing; Mélanges offerts à Edmond-René Labande; Mélanges de philologie et de littératures romanes offerts à Jeanne Wathelet-Willem; Mélanges de langue et de littérature médiévales offerts à Reto Raduolf Bezzola; Mélanges de littérature du Moyen Âge au XXe siècle offerts à Mademoiselle Jeanne Lods; Arthurian Tapestry.*

29. "More about *Mouru*."

30. A list of papers from this colloquium together with Runnalls's "Hommage à Mary Dominica Legge" and "Bibliographie de Miss Mary Dominica Legge" were subsequently published in *Marche romane* 29, nos. 3–4 (1979): 109–17.

31. Robson, memorial remarks.

32. This was told to me by Pauline Adams in conversation at Somerville College, Oxford, on April 2002; it is also related in Chibnall, "Mary Dominica Legge," 401.

33. Chibnall, "Mary Dominica Legge," 402.

34. Dean et al., "Mary Dominica Legge," obituary notice.

35. Chibnall, "Mary Dominica Legge," 403.

Select Bibliography of Works by Mary Dominica Legge

Legge's archives, including offprints of her published essays, bibliographies of essays and reviews, photographs, and unpublished memorial remarks by C. A. Robson, are housed at Somerville College, Oxford. I am deeply grateful to Pauline Adams, Somerville College archivist, for access to the Legge archives and for her gracious and generous assistance.

For a bibliography of Legge's work up to 1976, see G. A. Runnalls, *Marche romane* 29 (1979): 115–17. Marjorie Chibnall completes this bibliography with the years 1978–86 in "Supplementary Bibliography," *Proceedings of the British Academy* 74 (1988): 403. A "Colloquium in Honour of Professor M. Dominica Legge" was held on 25 September 1973 at the University of Edinburgh. A list of papers presented was subsequently published in *Marche romane* 29 (1979): 111. An unpublished bound volume of these papers is in the Legge Archives, Somerville College.

"Pierre de Peckham and His 'Lumiere as Lais.'" *Modern Language Review* 24 (1929): 37–47; 153–71.

Editor with William Holdsworth. *The Year Books of Edward II, Vols. 20 and 21*. Year Books series, vol. 52. London: Bernard Quaritch for the Selden Society, 1934.

Editor with William Holdsworth. *The Year Books of Edward II, Vols. 20 and 21*. Year Books series, vol. 54. London: Bernard Quaritch for the Selden Society, 1935.

"Anglo-Norman and the Historian." *History* (December 1941): 162–75.

Editor. *Anglo-Norman Letters and Petitions from All Souls MS. 182.* With an introduction by Eugène Vinaver. Anglo-Norman Texts, 3. Oxford: B. Blackwell for the Anglo-Norman Text Society, 1941. Reprint, New York: Johnson Reprint Corporation, 1967.

Editor. *"Le Roman de Balain," A Prose Romance of the Thirteenth Century.* Manchester, Eng.: Manchester University Press, 1942.

Anglo-Norman in the Cloisters. Edinburgh: Edinburgh University Press, 1950.

"Anglo-Norman Studies Today." *Revue de linguistique romane* 17 (1950): 213–22.

"An English Allusion to Montaigne before 1595." *Review of English Studies,* n.s., 1. (1950): 340–44.

"The French Language and the English Cloister." In *Medieval Studies Presented to Rose Graham.* Oxford: Oxford University Press, 1950.

"Toothache and Courtly Love." *French Studies* 4 (1950): 50–54.

"'Lumiere as Lais': A Postscript." *Modern Language Review* 46 (1951): 191–95.

Anglo-Norman Literature and Its Background. Oxford: Oxford University Press, 1963.

"La Précocité de la littérature anglo-normande." *Cahiers de civilisation médiévale* 8 (1965): 327–49.

"Les origines de l'anglo-normand littéraire." *Revue de linguistique romane* 31 (1967): 44–57.

"Clouds and Rainbows in the Age of Allegory." In *Mélanges de langue et de littérature du Moyen Âge offerts à Teruo Sato par ses amis et ses collègues,* 79–83. Nagoya, Jap.: Centre d'Études Médiévales et Romanes, 1973.

"Anglo-Norman Hagiography and the Romances." *Medievalia et humanistica* (Cambridge University Press), n.s., 6 (1975): 41–49.

"Les Chansons de geste et la Grande Bretagne." In *Mélanges de philologie et de littératures romanes offerts à Jeanne Wathelet-Willem,* 353–55. Liège, Belg.: Cahiers de l'Association des romanistes de l'Université de Liège, 1978.

"Anglo-Norman as a Spoken Language." In *Proceedings of the Battle Conference in Anglo-Norman Studies II,* 1979, edited by Allen Brown. Woodbridge, Suffolk, UK: Boydell, 1980.

"More about *Mouru*." *French Studies Bulletin,* no. 16 (autumn 1985): 10.

Works Cited

Adams, Pauline. *Somerville for Women: An Oxford College, 1879–1993.* Oxford: Oxford University Press, 1966.

An Arthurian Tapestry: Essays in Memory of Lewis Thorpe, edited by Kenneth Varty. Glasgow: University of Glasgow Press, 1981.

Chibnall, Marjorie. "Mary Dominica Legge, 1905–1986." *Proceedings of the British Academy* 74 (1988): 388–403.

"Colloquium in Honor of Professor M. Dominica Legge." Unpublished bound volume in the Legge Archives, Somerville College, Oxford. From a colloquium held 25 September 1973, University of Edinburgh.

Dean, Ruth J. "M. Dominica Legge." In *Anglo-Norman Anniversary Essays,* edited by Ian Short, Anglo-Norman Text Society Occasional Publications Series, 2. London: Anglo-Norman Text Society from Birbeck College, 1993.

———. Review of *Anglo-Norman Literature and Its Background,* by M. Dominica Legge. *Speculum* 40, no. 1 (January 1969): 148–49.

Dean, Ruth J., and M. Dominica Legge, eds. *The Rule of Saint Benedict: A Norman Prose Version.* Medium Aevum Monographs 7. Oxford: Basil Blackwell, 1964.

Dean, Ruth J., et al. "Mary Dominica Legge." Obituary notice in *Speculum* 62: 3 (July 1987): 788–89.
Gallais, Pierre. Review of *Anglo-Norman Literature and Its Background,* by M. Dominica Legge. *Cahiers de civilisation médiévale* 9 (1966): 82–83.
Hesketh, Glynn, ed. *La Lumiere as Lais.* 3 vols. Anglo Norman Texts, nos. 54–58. London: Anglo-Norman Text Society from Birbeck College, 1996–2000.
Kirk, Marion S. Review of *Year Books of Edward II, Vol. 20,* edited by M. Dominica Legge and William Holdsworth. *University of Pennsylvania Law Review* 83 (1934–35): 402–5.
Legge, James. *The Chinese Classics.* Hong Kong: Hong Kong University Press, 1960.
Medieval Miscellany Presented to Eugène Vinaver, edited by F. Whitehead, A. H. Diverres, and F. Sutcliffe. Manchester, Eng.: Manchester University Press, 1965.
Medieval Studies Presented to Rose Graham, edited by Veronica Ruffer and A. J. Taylor. Oxford: Oxford University Press, 1950.
Mélanges de langue et de littérature du Moyen Âge et de la Renaissance offerts à Jean Frappier. 2 vols. Geneva: Droz, 1970.
Mélanges de langue et de littérature du Moyen Âge offerts à Teruo Sato par ses amis et ses collègues. 2 vols. Nagoya, Jap.: Centre d'Études Médiévales et Romanes, 1973.
Mélanges de langue et de littérature médiévales offerts à Pierre Le Gentil, edited by Jean Dufournet and Daniel Poirion. Paris: S.E.D.E.S. and C.D.U. Réunis, 1973.
Mélanges de langue et de littérature médiévales offerts à Reto Radulf Bezzola à l'occasion de son quatre-vingtième anniversaire, edited by Georges Guntert et al. Bern: Francke, 1978.
Mélanges de linguistique romane et de philologie médiévale offerts à M. Maurice Delbouille, edited by Jean Ransom. 2 vols. Gembloux, Belg.: J. Ducolot, 1964.
Mélanges de littérature du Moyen Âge au XXe siècle offerts à Mademoiselle Jeanne Lods. Paris: Collection de l'École Normale Supérieure de Jeunes Filles, 1978.
Mélanges de philologie et de littératures romanes offerts à Jeanne Wathelet-Willem, Jacques De Caluwe. Liège, Belg.: Cahiers de l'Association des Romanistes de l'Université de Liège, 1978.
Mélanges d'histoire littéraire, de linguistique, et de philologie romanes offerts à Charles Rostaing, edited by Jacques De Caluwe, Jean-Marie D'Heur, and René Domas. 2 vols. Liège, Belg.: Association des Romanistes de l'Université de Liège (*Marche Romaine*), 1974.
Mélanges offerts à Edmond-René Labande. Poitiers: Centre d'Études Supérieures de Civilisation Médiévale, 1974.
Mélanges offerts à René Crozet à l'occasion de son soixante-dixième anniversaire, edited by Pierre Gallais and Yves-Jean Riou. 2 vols. Poitiers: Societé d'Études Médiévales, 1966.
Mélanges offerts à Rita Lejeune. 2 vols. Gembloux, Belg.: Duculot, 1968.
Robson, C. A. Memorial remarks. Untitled typescript. Somerville College Archives.
Runnalls, G. A. "Hommage à Mary Dominica Legge." *Marche romane* 29 (1979): 109–18.
Short, Ian, ed. *Anglo-Norman Anniversary Essays.* Anglo-Norman Text Society Occasional Texts Series, 2. London: 1993.
Studi in onore di Angelo Monteverdi. 2 vols. Modena, It.: Società Tipografica Editrice Modenese, 1959.
Studies in Honour of Tatiana Fotitch, edited by Joseph M. Sola-Sole, Alessandro S. Crisafulli, and Siegfried A. Schulz. Washington, D.C.: Catholic University of America Press, in association with Consortium Press, 1973.

Studies in Language and Literature in Honour of Margaret Schlauch, edited by Mieczyslaw Brahmer, Stanislaw Helsztynski, and Julian Krzyzanowski. Warsaw: Panstwowe Wydawnictwo Naukowe, 1966.

Studies Presented to A. Ewert, edited by E. A. Frances. Oxford: Clarendon Press, 1961.

Studies Presented to John Orr. Manchester, Eng.: Manchester University Press, 1953.

Studies Presented to M. K. Pope, compiled by Olsen Rhys. Manchester, Eng.: Manchester University Press, 1939.

Times (London). Obituary notice. 16 December 1986.

CHAPTER 44

Daughter of Her Time
Anneliese Maier (1905–1971)
and the Study of Fourteenth-Century Philosophy

Alfonso Maierù and Edith Sylla

THE HIGH REGARD surrounding the name of Anneliese Maier is especially a result of her contribution to the study of the philosophy of nature and of fourteenth-century scientific thought collected in the five-volume *Studien zur Naturphilosophie der Spätscholastik* and in the three volumes of *Ausgehendes Mittelalter*.[1] To these should be added the second edition of her doctoral dissertation and the second edition of her research on the mechanization of the world picture in the seventeenth century published under the title *Zwei Untersuchungen zur nachscholastischen Philosophie*.[2] It is an imposing body of work, and one which to this day has exerted a profound influence on the study of medieval scientific and philosophical thought, as even the most cursory glance through the indexes of secondary sources will prove. But Maier's contribution to the study of late-medieval intellectual history goes far beyond this important specific sphere of interest and includes many and various other aspects, from codicology to epistemology and the definition of the principal trends (or "schools") of fourteenth-century thought within the overall context of doctrinal debate, taking into account the circulation of texts and the international contacts within medieval universities. Toward the end of her life Maier was engaged in a study of the debate on the beatific vision, which was stirred up by Pope John XXII in 1331–32 and brought to rest from a doctrinal point of view by Pope Benedict XII in 1336. To understand how this extraordinary body of work took shape and how it developed through relationships and exchanges of ideas between Maier and other scholars, it is perhaps opportune to examine both the intellectual work itself and the conditions in which it was carried out, thus leading to a fuller appreciation of Maier's achievement.

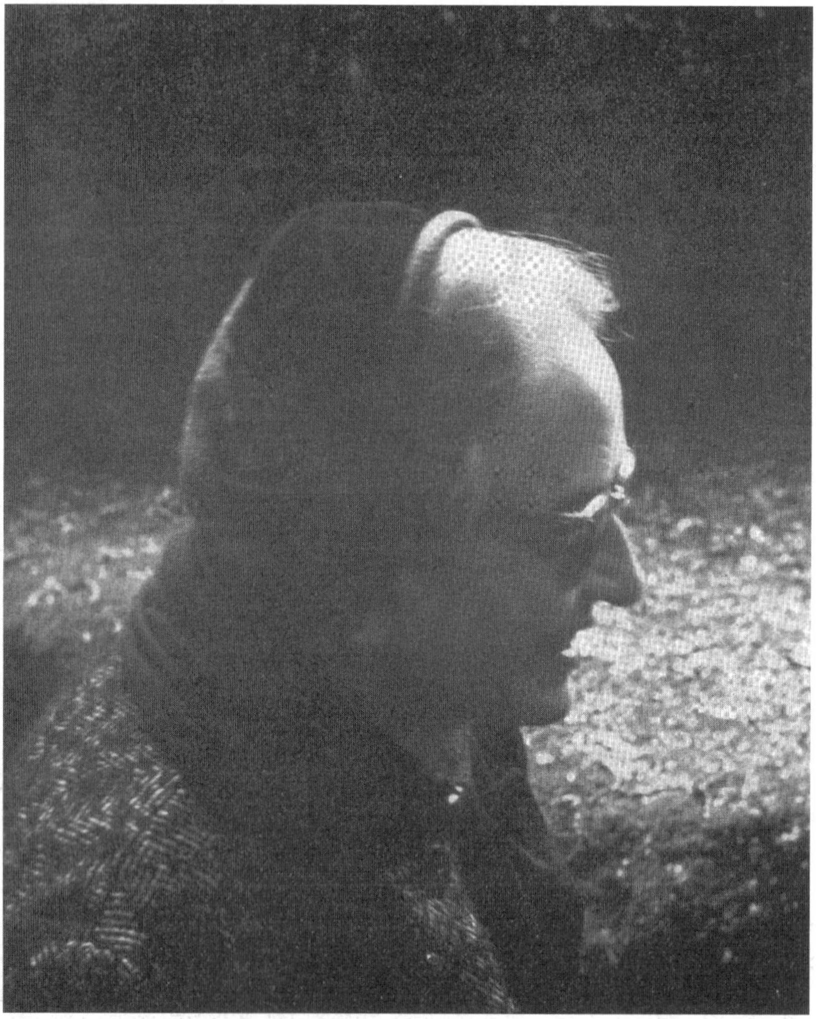

Anneliese Maier was born in Tübingen on 5 November 1905 and died in Rome on 2 December 1971.[3] At the time of her birth, her father, Heinrich Maier, was professor of philosophy at the University of Tübingen. As the family moved around Germany according to Heinrich Maier's academic appointments, Anneliese Maier attended schools in Göttingen (1912–18) and Heidelberg (1918–23). After high school Anneliese Maier began following courses in philosophy, mathematics, and theoretical physics (under the guidance of none other than Max Planck) at the University of Berlin, where she received her Ph.D. in 1930, completing her dissertation, under the supervision of her tutor Eduard Spranger, on Kant's categories of quality.[4] Following her Ph.D., Maier continued her studies to prepare her *Habilitation,* but she was forced to give this up in 1934 for political reasons.[5] Her attention then focussed on completing the publication of her father's *Philosophie der Wirklichkeit*, in process at the time of his death at the end of 1933.

Known above all for his three-volume work on Aristotle's syllogistic (1896–1900) and for his monograph on Socrates (1913), Anneliese Maier's father, Heinrich, had been a prolific scholar, who was also interested in Kant. He had held the post of secretary of the Kant-Gesellschaft and had published a book on the philosopher in 1924. In the final years of his life, Heinrich Maier was working on a three-volume work titled *Philosophie der Wirklichkeit,* in which he developed a philosophical system aimed at supplying "a scientific metaphysics, that is to say a science, well grounded from the logical and epistemological point of view, of the elementary categories and of the systematic, formal structures of reality."[6] Before his death Heinrich Maier had personally overseen the printing of the first volume (*Wahrheit und Wirklichkeit,* 1926) of this work and had completed most of the rest. After his death on 28 November 1933 Anneliese Maier took over the responsibility for editing and overseeing the publication of the rest (*Die physische Wirklichkeit,* in two parts, 1933–34; and *Die psychisch-geistige Wirklichkeit,* 1935).[7] In this way Anneliese Maier had the opportunity for further, profound reflection on the work of her venerated and much loved father, the father whose philosophical preoccupations had already provided the theme for her doctoral dissertation.[8] It is possible to understand the consideration that Anneliese Maier held for her father's philosophical and methodological concerns if one reads the article in *Philosophen-Lexikon* in 1937 that she dedicated to his work. Apart from an interest in particular philosophical concerns, Anneliese Maier inherited from her father above all an ideal of intellectual life that she translated into rigorous conceptual analysis and utter dedication to research.[9] To this ideal she dedicated her whole life, a life, moreover, that she lived in the utmost simplicity, if not poverty.

In 1936 Anneliese Maier received a grant from the Prussian Academy of Science in Berlin to carry out research on the letters of Leibniz contained in Italian libraries and archives as part of the preparation of the edition of Leibniz's works.[10] Once in Rome, Maier made the acquaintance of and subsequently became friends with Friedrich Bock, the secretary of the German Historical Institute. Bock was an expert on the Vatican Secret Archives, to which he introduced Maier and provided valuable early assistance as she began her research.[11] Maier also received advice from Monsignor Angelo Mercati, the prefect of the Vatican Archives.[12] In Rome, Maier was associated from 1937 with the Kaiser-Wilhelm-Institut für Kunst- und Kulturwissenschaft, housed in Palazzo Zuccari (Bibliotheca Hertziana). This institution awarded Maier a research grant.[13] In 1943 she became assistant in the Bibliotheca Hertziana.

From the very beginning of her time in Rome, Maier was a habitual visitor to the Vatican Library, which swiftly became her regular place of work. During her long hours in the library, she found many occasions to meet and exchange views with other scholars, some of whom became close friends. When the war caused funds from Germany to run out, Cardinal Giovanni Mercati, librarian and archivist of the Catholic Church (and brother of Angelo Mercati), took on Maier as a collaborator, from 1945 on paying her with funds at his disposal.[14] She was, however, never formally employed by the administration of the Vatican Library, with whom her relationship remained one of collaboration. Surrounded as she was by affectionate admiration, Maier worked on in the Vatican Library with great profit. Perhaps the welcome and support she found there during the Second World War played a part in her conversion in 1943 from the Lutheranism of her family to Catholicism. At the same time, the conversion made this competent and hard-working scholar yet more welcome to the library authorities.[15]

In the second part of 1949 Maier—who apparently never had a personal house in Rome and whose books had been taken from her house in Berlin by a Russian officer shortly after the end of the war—tried to obtain financial support for her research from the Max-Planck-Gesellschaft (this was the name given to the Kaiser-Wilhelm-Gesellschaft after the Second World War). She also suggested turning the *Kulturabteilung* (established in the Bibliotheca Hertziana in 1933) into a philosophical section, proposing herself as a candidate for that position. Maier succeeded in receiving financial support from 1950 on, but her suggestion of a philosophical section was not accepted. The Bibliotheca Hertziana had closed in fall 1943; it reopened in 1953 without any other section except history of art. On 14 December 1954 Maier was nominated as a fellow of the Max-Planck-Gesellschaft, and from then on was able to devote herself to her research without constant financial worry. She never, however, held a guaranteed permanent position.

In 1951 Maier accepted an invitation from Professor Josef Koch of the Thomas-Institut to deliver lectures at Cologne University. In July of that year she gave lectures on "the beginnings of philosophical and scientific thought in the thirteenth and fourteenth centuries."[16] Koch had great respect for Maier's work and on 3 August 1951 applied to the Ministry of Higher Education in Nordrhein-Westfalen for Maier to be granted the title of professor. The title was granted on 30 November, but Maier never was a member of the faculty at Cologne University, nor did she apply there for the *Habilitation*.[17] According to testimony from people who knew Maier well and who were in a position to be directly informed by Maier herself, she gave lectures at Cologne only in two summer semesters, because she "was in a hurry to get back to Rome."[18] Since 1945 Maier had been engaged in cataloging the Borghese manuscripts of the

Vatican Library, a catalog that was published in 1952. (She was the first woman to be given responsibility for a Vatican manuscript catalog.)[19] Again in 1957 Cardinal Mercati charged Maier with the task of cataloging the Vatican Latin manuscripts 1218–92; this catalog was published in 1961.[20]

In Rome from the wartime to her death, Maier lived first in one and then another house of nuns, both situated on the Gianiculum. In each house she had the use of a simple room. According to her friend and fellow scholar at the Vatican Jeanne Bignami Odier, Maier never expressed a desire to marry and always lived alone, although she was gifted in cultivating lasting friendships.[21] Mme. Bignami Odier, who met Maier when she arrived in Rome just having turned thirty, described her as a "young woman of pleasant appearance, whose magnificent forehead recalled that of Goethe."[22] To a member of the audience in Cologne who attended her lectures, the then forty-six-year-old appeared as "a very cultured woman of particularly fascinating charms."[23] In her final years, although she maintained her extraordinary capacity for hard work, Maier aged prematurely and somehow lost the spark of vitality that had previously marked her personality.[24] A woman of reserve, she was nonetheless generous with help to anyone who approached her in the Vatican Library.[25] She is remembered as an energetic person. A daughter of her time, Maier participated in the social opportunities offered, for instance, lectures at the Bibliotheca Hertziana, the Vatican Library's annual excursion, and seminars and excursions of the Görres-Gesellschaft, of whose advisory committee (*Beirat*) she became a member in 1954.

The Influences on Anneliese Maier's Work of Her Father, of August Pelzer, and of Giuseppe De Luca

Early on, Maier's development was primarily influenced by her father and by Friedrich Bock—particularly by her father.[26] Her friends in Rome also concede pride of place to Heinrich Maier, but immediately after him they point to August Pelzer as the person who helped steer her toward the study of medieval philosophy. Mention should also be made of Maier's friend Don Giuseppe De Luca, the founder of the specialist publishers Edizioni di Storia e Letteratura, who provided valuable assistance in publishing her research and in planning and editing her written work. To understand the traditions within which Anneliese Maier worked, it will be worthwhile to look in more detail at the relation of her work to that of these three men.

Heinrich Maier's *Philosophie der Wirklichkeit* was particularly notable for its study of the categories, including the spiritual as well as the physical.[27] Maier took as the basic problem of her doctoral dissertation the explication of Kant's Table of the Categories in the *Critique of Pure Reason,* where, under the category "Of Quality," Kant listed the subcategories "Reality," "Negation," and "Limitation." In particular the problem was how Kant could have understood the difference between his qualitative subcategory "Reality" (*Realität*) and reality in general (*Wirklickeit*). Maier solved this problem by tracing *Realität* back through eighteenth-century school philosophy to the Scotist concept of *realitas,* which could refer to an aspect of a larger entity, so that, for instance, within illuminations, light might be the reality and shadow the corresponding negation, while a finite degree of illumination expressed Kant's third subcategory, "Limitation."[28] In reaching this conclusion, Maier saw herself as confirming an idea that her father had previously proposed, reaching her solution through a study of the prehistory of the concept before it appeared in Kant's table.[29] Having found the concept of reality she needed in the Middle Ages, she proceeded to trace the path to Christian Wolff and eighteenth-century school philosophy, through which *realitas,* together with the concept of quality or intensive magnitude, came to Kant. The final sentence of the shortened second edition of the dissertation, published in 1968, ends with the ringing statement that Kant's position can only be explained by using a bit of the philosophy of the schools.[30]

With this background it is easy to see how Maier came to be interested in scholastic theories of intensive magnitudes, on which she published a monograph in 1939. Before that, moreover, she had published in Leipzig in 1938 *Die Mechanisierung des Weltbildes im 17. Jahrhundert.*[31] No doubt because of its publication in Germany during the war, this work never received the attention it deserved, though a second edition was published in Rome in 1968. In this work Maier acknowledged the pioneering work of Pierre Duhem and Constantin Michalski on fourteenth-century impetus theory, but said it was still an open question whether Duhem was correct in his claim that the Parisian dynamics of John Buridan and Nicole Oresme was well known to Italian scientists of the seventeenth century.[32] It was one of the strangest and most distinctive phenomena in the history of the new natural philosophy, she wrote, that impetus, or impressed force (*vis impressa*), was considered to be a quality in the normal scheme of things, although even Galileo was not clear about its nature.[33]

The framework that Maier laid out in *Die Mechanisierung des Weltbildes im 17. Jahrhundert* provided the basis for her later work on late-scholastic natural philosophy. The change that occurred in the new science of the seventeenth century was, she said, most of all a change of world picture and ontology, rather than a change in epistemology or scientific method.[34] The speculative shift to atomism preceded and led to developments in positive mathematical science rather than the reverse.[35] There were many paths to the new scientific developments, not a single one, although the adoption of atomism was fundamental. Atomism led to a turning away from the scholastic interest in qualities, which would, however, be rehabilitated to some extent in the work of Kant. Notably, *Die Mechanisierung des Weltbildes* described the shift from the qualitative to the mechanical in the work of a series of philosophers from Gassendi, Galileo, Digby, and Hobbes to Descartes, Malebranche, Huygens, Newton, Leibniz, Boyle, and Locke—without the usual value judgment against scholastic interest in qualities and in favor of the new mechanical science. Perhaps Maier's evenhanded description of what happened derived in part from her realization that qualities would reappear in a new guise in the theories of Kant and of her father.[36] Unlike Duhem, Maier considered the results of fourteenth-century natural philosophy as worthy of interest in their own right, not leading in a straight line to the new science of the seventeenth century, but rather more nearly reaching a dead end.

If Maier had already considered scholastic topics before moving to Rome, her concentration on the Middle Ages was no doubt reinforced by her location in the Vatican Library and association with August Pelzer. In order to understand better the influence on Maier exercised by Monsignor August Pelzer, it is opportune to look further at this learned prelate and scholar (*scrittore*) of the Vatican Library. Pelzer (1876–1958) was born to Belgian parents in Germany, where he lived until the age of twelve. He studied at the Institut supérieur de philosophie of the University of Louvain, where he obtained his doctorate. He then took holy orders and began collaborating with Alfred Chauchie and Maurice De Wulf. Invited to Rome by Cardinal Mercier to carry out research in medieval philosophy under Franz Ehrle, the prefect of the Vatican Library and an eminent scholar, Pelzer accepted gladly, and in 1907 he traveled to Rome, where he was to remain for the rest of his life.[37] We do not know precisely when Pelzer and Maier met, but it must have been toward the end of the 1930s. Under Pelzer's influence Maier's interests turned decisively toward Scholasticism (she was to include a note of thanks to Pelzer in a work published as early as 1939).[38] An important factor in strengthening the friendship between the two scholars was certainly that they had German as a common language.

It was Pelzer who proposed that Maier be appointed to catalog the manuscripts of the Borghese Collection in the Vatican Library, a task that led to many of her later publications, beyond the manuscript catalog itself. The collection, containing what remained of the papal library from Avignon, was acquired by Franz Erhle and well known to Pelzer.[39] The catalog was published in 1952, as we have seen, but Maier's writings on the Borghese Collection had begun appearing in 1946–48—with articles on the manuscript tradition of works by Siger of Brabant, Peter Johannis Olivi, Arnald of Villanova, William of Ockham, Thomas Wylton, and others—and were to continue until the final years of her life.[40] Pelzer may also have encouraged Maier to test on the basis of texts the ideas of Pierre Duhem on the medieval origins of seventeenth-century science. That Pelzer may have been involved in this project may be inferred from an essay written by Maier in 1950. The essay ("Die Anfänge des physikalischen Denkens im 14. Jahrhundert"), which Maier did not include in *Ausgehendes Mittelalter,* seems to lead in that direction. It includes the statement:

> Duhem's affirmations that the most important discoveries of seventeenth-century classical physics had been anticipated by fourteenth-century philosophy of nature were swiftly opposed by important voices, such as that of Franz Erhle, the learned researcher into Scholasticism, expressing serious doubts over this interpretation and calling for verification from the sources—because it seemed impossible a priori that certain all too modern ideas and theories should have been encountered within the framework of such differently oriented fields as scholastic metaphysics and philosophy of nature. Meanwhile, several separate lines of research have made much more material available

than Duhem was able to consult, and although this material is still incomplete, it allows us to make a definitive response to this fundamental question. It may be said that overall Cardinal Ehrle was right: Scholasticism did not make the great discoveries with which Duhem sought to credit it—the principle of inertia, laws of free fall, analytical geometry, graphical integration, the principle of virtual work, etc.—and it was not possible for it to do so. In this sense Duhem was certainly mistaken. However, he still has the great merit of being the first to have published information on this aspect of Scholastic philosophy, in doing so opening up for wider research a new field, which is interesting in many respects. His error was only the point of view from which he wished to judge it. The philosophy of nature of late Scholasticism is in itself sufficiently important without seeking to attribute to it a premonition of what later generations were to think. It was an attempt, for the first time in the history of Western thought, to conceive a true physics, that is to say to provide a complete and unitary explanation, based on a few principles of universal value, of the processes of inorganic nature known at that time.[41]

It would not seem excessive to give an autobiographical gloss to this passage. Pelzer may well have encouraged Maier to carry out the verification of Duhem's thesis, a task that had the approval of Cardinal Ehrle.[42] Maier was certainly well qualified for the duty thanks to her university studies of philosophy and science and the paleographical skills she had recently acquired during her research in the Vatican Library. Her work managed to establish on the most solid of bases (knowledge of the texts and precise attention to contexts) research into the philosophy of nature and discussion of the relationships between medieval thought and the scientific revolution—with the result that her studies became an essential reference point for this kind of research. But the long struggle with Duhem's ideas in the end worked in some ways to condition her approach and to limit her horizons: an important subject like divine omnipotence or a field of study like logic and *sophismata*, both of which have been broadly investigated by historians in recent decades, failed to obtain the attention from Maier that they deserved, at least in part because they failed to fit conceptions of what might be important in the history of science, conceptions that Maier partly shared with Duhem.[43]

Maier's work was also influenced by her relationship with Don Giuseppe De Luca (1898–1962), who was also an assiduous user of the Vatican Library, as was his younger sister, Maddalena, who later became a close friend of Anneliese.[44] Once his high-level cultural publishing activities had begun to get underway, De Luca would offer a chance of publication to the most talented scholars and intellectuals he happened to meet. This proved to Maier's advantage, as she was able to rework and examine more closely a series of her research studies that had already been published but that had appeared during the war and had as a result gone largely unnoticed. The index of her first book was in De Luca's hands by 1948, and the following year *Die Vorläufer Galileis im 14. Jahrhundert: Studien zur Naturphilosophie der Spätscholastik* was published.[45] In it Maier collected—and extended or sometimes shortened—some already published writings as well as included new material. In 1951 there followed *Zwei Grundprobleme der scholastischen Naturphilosophie,* a collection of her essays on intensive qualities and the theory of impetus, which had been separately published in 1939 and 1940. In 1952 it was the turn of *An der Grenze von Scholastik und Naturwissenschaft,* the first edition of which had been published at Leipzig in 1943. Maier's books must have proved an unusual success for those times, as on 11 December 1953 De Luca wrote to her that hers were "the biggest sellers in my scholarly series of publications."[46] Other volumes were to follow. The collection that goes under the title of *Ausgehendes Mittelalter* was suggested by De Luca, and the details of the project were worked out during one of the last meetings between De Luca and Maier.[47] In 1961 Maier suggested republishing two of her father's writings (the monograph on Socrates and a collection of *Kleinere Schriften*) through Storia e Letteratura, but neither book was published.

Don Giuseppe De Luca also put forward a project that was to occupy much of Maier's energies in the later years of her life: the publication of all the texts concerning the Avignon debate on beatific vision. De Luca planned to publish the entire corpus as volume 12 of the *Archivio italiano per la storia della pietà,* which he had founded; in 1959 he had written his plans to Pope John XXIII, who evidently in previous conversations had encouraged him to proceed with the work. (John XXIII's "approval" of the publication of the texts on beatific vision, which at times has been mentioned, was precisely this oral encouragement.)[48] After De Luca's death publication of the *Archivio* became irregular because of increasing financial difficulties. At the Storia e Letteratura publishers in or around 1970, perhaps at Maier's insistence, consideration was given to the idea of resuming the project to publish the texts on beatific vision in a special collection with Maier as the editor. In 1970 a brief presentation of the proposed collection was published, probably written by Maier herself.[49] For several years she had been working on the corpus and wrote a total of seven essays, publication of which started in 1965.[50] There is reasonable evidence to suggest Maier may also have been persuaded to study the texts on beatific vision by the Dominican friar Thomas Kaeppeli. Kaeppeli was another of Maier's close friends from the Vatican Library, and in that period he was preparing the first two volumes of *Scriptores Ordinis Praedicatorum,* which include articles on the Dominicans who took part in the debate on beatific vision: Armandus de Belloviso, Durandus de Sancto Porciano, and Johannes Regina de Neapoli.[51] Maier hoped to be able to continue working for another thirty years.[52] In October 1971, just before she died from complications of the flu, Maier was working on a text by Durandus de Sancto Porciano.[53]

The Reception of Anneliese Maier's Work among Historians of Science

E. J. Dijksterhuis may have been the first historian of science to recognize fully the merit of Anneliese Maier's studies in the field, even borrowing the title of the German translation of his own work *Die Mechanisierung des Weltbildes* (first appearing in

Dutch as *De Mechanisering van het Wereldbeeld* in 1950) from her 1938 monograph.[54] Dijksterhius wrote:

> That the conceptions to which [Aristotle's treatment of the phenomena concerned with falling bodies and projectiles] led the medieval thinkers are to some extent familiar to us today is due in the first place to the pioneering work of the French physicist and historian Pierre Duhem. . . . However, whereas some decades ago his works formed the only source from which those who had no opportunity of studying the manuscripts at first hand could derive their information, a good deal more has since become available through the investigations of C. Michalsky and Miss Anneliese Maier. Unfortunately the results of Michalsky's work are difficult of access. . . . Miss Maier, on the other hand, has laid down the fruits of her studies in a number of works written in German, which, thanks to the author's great knowledge of medieval manuscripts and her perspicacious expositions, now constitute the most important source of information on scholastic science.[55]

Coming then to his exposition of impetus theory, Dijksterhuis commented:

> A closer critical study, and there have been several—by Miss Maier among others—shows that it is dangerous to interpret ideas from scholastic philosophy too readily in the sense of classical mechanics and identify them with the sharply defined conceptions occurring in the latter.[56]

Likewise at a conference on critical problems in the history of science held at Madison, Wisconsin, in 1957, Dijksterhuis said:

> In the department of medieval dynamics, too, the pioneering work was performed by Duhem. . . . Since 1939, however, a considerable correction and extension of this was given by Miss Anneliese Maier, to whom everyone who is concerned with medieval science owes a debt of great gratitude. In five books and numerous treatises . . . she brought to light a large body of material previously buried in manuscripts, and on a great many points gave occasion to a revision of particular notions made current by Duhem. Owing to the work of Duhem and Miss Maier, and, though to a lesser extent, of the Polish scholar Michalsky (whose writings were chiefly published in Polish and consequently became less widely known), a keen interest is now universally evinced in medieval science in general, and that of the fourteenth century in particular.[57]

Whereas in the 1950s and 1960s there was much ferment and personal interchange among historians of science, Anneliese Maier seems to have remained relatively secluded at the Vatican, not traveling to international congresses or, except for her guest professorship at Cologne, taking on teaching positions. Among American historians of medieval science, it is perhaps Marshall Clagett who from the start most consistently emphasized the necessity of approaching the subject on the basis of the corrections that Anneliese Maier had made to the interpretive course first set out by Duhem.[58] Whereas Clagett had close collegial relations with many other historians of science, he seems to have known Maier's work primarily through her publications—of which he read as many as he could find after the end of the war—until in the 1960s and afterward, when he met her many times at the Vatican Library, while he was working there on his *Archimedes in the Middle Ages*.[59]

In the preface to his *The Science of Mechanics in the Middle Ages* (1959), Clagett expressed gratitude "To Anneliese Maier of the Vatican Library, whose careful and penetrating investigations must be the point of departure for any study of medieval mechanics, as they have been for mine."[60] The other two "eminent historians of mechanics" to whom Clagett expressed a debt were Alexandre Koyré, who had spent time at the Institute for Advanced Study at Princeton as well as taught at the Ecole pratique des hautes etudes of Paris, and with whom Clagett said he had had "in recent years . . . such a warm and intellectually profitable relationship," and Ernest Moody, his "friend and erstwhile collaborator," with whom Clagett had published *The Medieval Science of Weights* in 1952. In describing the recent historiography of medieval mechanics, Clagett emphasized Maier's corrections to Duhem:

> Thus it was actually reserved to one individual to change the investigation of medieval mechanics from an incidental bypath to a field of investigation where the principal objective of research was to estimate the views of the medieval schoolmen on mechanical problems. This was the eminent French scientist Pierre Duhem. . . . So rich were Duhem's investigations . . . that one can say that in a sense the succeeding study of medieval mechanics has been largely devoted to an extension or refutation of Duhem's work.
>
> But in spite of their obvious importance, Duhem's investigations were not without serious defects. He made extravagant claims for the modernity of medieval concepts. . . . It was only with the publication of Anneliese Maier's studies that Duhem's works were given a thoroughgoing review and re-evaluation. . . . Miss Maier's work has been based on detailed manuscript investigations. . . . The result of Maier's magnificent studies has been to place the mechanical ideas uncovered by Duhem in their proper medieval setting and to show their essential divergences from the later concepts of modern mechanics. . . . Furthermore, Miss Maier's studies opened up areas of medieval natural philosophy not studied by Duhem. The succeeding pages of this volume will demonstrate the great debt owed by me and all recent studies of medieval mechanics to Miss Maier's work.[61]

At a 1961 conference on scientific change held at the University of Oxford, Guy Beaujouan gave credit to Maier for penetrating, like a man of the fourteenth century, into the very heart of medieval natural philosophy:

> Thus, if we can believe Duhem, modern science was born in 1277. "No," replies Miss Anneliese Maier, "1277–1377 is not the first classical century as far as physics are

concerned, but it is certainly the classical century for natural philosophy." It would be mistaken to suppose that, in order to return the scientific revolution once more to the seventeenth century, Miss Maier has seriously contradicted Duhem. The merit of this great German historian seems to be above all else the resolute manner in which she has penetrated, like a man of the fourteenth-century, into the very heart of medieval natural philosophy, instead of adopting the inevitably artificial and anachronistic point of view of the history of science as seen in present-day terms.[62]

If Anneliese Maier was rarely or never present at international conferences at which her work was acknowledged from a distance, she had made her presence felt through critical reviews and reactions to the work of other historians of science.[63] Her reviews of Ernest Moody and Marshall Clagett's *The Medieval Science of Weights* and of H. Lamar Crosby Jr.'s *Thomas of Bradwardine, His Tractatus de Proportionibus* were published in *Isis* in 1955 and 1957, respectively. In the former review Maier challenged Moody and Clagett's assertion that the nine propositions appearing in various works on statics ascribed to Jordanus de Nemore may have stemmed not from Jordanus himself but from antiquity or the Arabs, with Jordanus being responsible only for a commentary appearing with them. But, Maier wrote in her review, the whole fourteenth century attributed these propositions to Jordanus, and she herself had always been of the opinion that *only* these propositions were to be attributed to Jordanus.[64] Clagett clearly took Maier's critique seriously. In *The Science of Mechanics in the Middle Ages,* Clagett included Maier's review of *The Medieval Science of Weights* in the bibliography, ascribed the suggestion that the propositions had an Arabic original to Moody and suggested as equally plausible that there might have been an entirely original *Elementa* of Jordanus.[65]

Moody was perhaps not so quick to accept Maier's criticisms of his work—except possibly that he did not publish some of the research he had done when he discovered that Maier had already published similar findings. In his "Galileo and Avempace: The Dynamics of the Leaning Tower Experiment," published in 1951, Moody cited Maier's 1946 article on the concept of function in the fourteenth century, *Die Vorläufer Galileis im 14. Jahrhundert,* and her work on the impetus theory of the Scholastics.[66] He said, however, that he had completed his study of scholastic discussions of Avempace's theory before he discovered that much of the same material had been covered by Maier in her *An der Grenze von Scholastik und Naturwissenschaft* (1943). In fact, Moody had written to Maier in late 1949 that he had been shocked to discover that his work for the previous five years, which he had hoped to publish, was superfluous, given Maier's earlier publication.[67] Maier, for her part, was relieved that she was ten years ahead of other scholars in the newly popular field of medieval natural philosophy and that she had scooped Moody rather than the reverse. At the same time she was glad that the Americans were coming to evaluations of medieval natural philosophy similar to her own.[68] Nevertheless, in *Zwischen Philosophie und Mechanik* (1958) Maier questioned Moody's claims about the relationship between Platonism and

Aristotelianism in "Galileo and Avempace."[69] In the 1975 preface to his collected papers, Moody responded laconically only that he was not "ready to make any retractions."[70]

Maier had been the first to understand thoroughly and to emphasize the proper interpretation of "Bradwardine's function" relating forces, resistances, and velocities in motions. A number of interchanges between Maier and other scholars involved the interpretation of texts that involved or might be thought to involve this function. In her review of Moody and Clagett's *The Science of Weights,* for example, Maier rejected the argument that certain commentaries on the science of weights belonged to the fourteenth century because they were familiar with Bradwardine's function: they did not involve the distinctive Bradwardinian view, Maier argued, and so reference to it could not furnish a *terminus post quem*.[71] When, under the direction of Ernest Moody at Columbia, H. Lamar Crosby Jr. edited as his doctoral dissertation and later published Bradwardine's *De proportionibus,* Maier recognized the importance of this publication in her review, corrected her own misinterpretation of some details of Bradwardine's work, but faulted Crosby for some misinterpretations of his own, particularly his claim that John Dumbleton took Bradwardine's view to imply that a constant force would produce an accelerated motion, saying that the means by which Crosby attempted to support this conclusion were not properly historical.[72]

Although most non-German-speaking historians of medieval science have found Maier's work profoundly useful because of the extent to which its discussion is couched in the original Latin terminology rather than in translation (as was Duhem's work), some historians of science, perhaps lacking language skills or patience, failed to appreciate what Maier had to offer. Proposed projects to translate Anneliese Maier's writings into English received only limited and belated success. In 1966 the MIT Press in Cambridge, Massachusetts, put forward the idea of printing a selection from the first volume of *Ausgehendes Mittelalter*, but this never happened. In 1968 Reidel Publishing in Dordrecht expressed an interest in translating *Die Vorläufer* and *An der Grenze* as well as other books from the *Studien*. The whole project was then passed on to the Johnson Reprint Corporation of New York, which in 1969 suggested that the work of translating the five volumes of *Studien* be given to William A. Wallace. Maier accepted the choice of translator willingly, but the project never came to fruition.[73] Finally, in 1982, at the suggestion of Edward Peters, the University of Pennsylvania Press published a translation by Steven D. Sargent of seven essays selected from Maier's work. All of this goes to show the interest aroused by Maier's work, which continued to grow throughout the 1950s and 1960s and beyond.

Maier's consolidated position as a respected scholar is also testified to by a number of recognitions from academic bodies. She became a corresponding member of the Academy of Sciences in Mainz (1949), Paris (1958), Göttingen (1962), and Munich (1966) and a fellow of the Medieval Academy of America in 1970. In 1966 she received the prestigious Sarton Medal of the American History of Science Society, the second woman to be so honored (Dorothea Waley Singer, together with her husband Charles Singer, had received the second Sarton medal ever given in 1956). Maier was also honorary fellow of the German Society for the History of Medicine, Natural Sciences, and Technology. In 1964 she was invited to take part in the Third International Congress of Medieval Philosophy, which took place in Passo della Mendola (Trento) and was dedicated to the theme of natural philosophy in the Middle Ages; she was repeatedly urged to present a paper on the philosophy of nature in the fourteenth century. Later Sofia Vanni Rovighi, who was in touch with her, admitted disconsolately, "I just couldn't persuade her to accept the invitation."[74]

If we consider, then, the impact on Maier's work of the fact that she was a woman, we might speculate that, had she been a man, she might more likely have become a professor at a German university.[75] She might also have traveled internationally to conferences and had more personal contacts with other scholars—though her contacts at the Vatican Library were not insignificant. As a woman of her time, she seems to have preferred her relatively enclosed life at the Vatican Library, a life that enabled her to do enormous amounts of research, although not to finish the project on the beatific vision, on which she was working at the end of her life. Thus, any limitations on Maier's chances that might have resulted from her social position as a woman did not deny her the scholarly achievement that would have made her father proud. The keenness of her intellect, the depth of her manuscript skills, and the breadth of her knowledge and insight led to publications on fourteenth-century natural philosophy and thought that remain unsurpassed even at the start of the twenty-first century.[76]

Notes

We would like to thank John Murdoch for his careful reading of this article. We also thank Christine Grafinger, Romana Guarnieri, Hermann Goldbrunner, and Matthias Quast for help in searching for information.

1. For a story of the title *Studien zur Naturphilosophie der Spätscholastik,* see Maierù, "Anneliese Maier e la filosofia della natura tardoscolastica," 304–5. See Maier's bibliography by Paravicini Bagliani in A. Maier, *Ausgehendes Mittelalter,* 3:615–26; reprinted with an additional item in *Studi sul XIV secolo in memoria di Anneliese Maier,* 15–23. The latter volume contains, on pp. 7–13, a brief appreciation by John Murdoch and Edith Sylla of Maier's contributions to the history of medieval science.

2. The original publications were *Kants Qualitätskategorien* and *Die Mechanisierung des Weltbildes im 17. Jahrhundert.*

3. A faithful reconstruction of Maier's life is that by Jeanne Bignami Odier, her friend from the Vatican Library: "Anneliese Maier."

4. Planck served as full professor of the University of Berlin from 1892 to 1926; from 1930 to 1935 he was president of the Kaiser-Wilhelm-Gesellschaft. Bignami Odier, whose source for this information about Maier's doctoral studies was Maier's sister-in-law, lists studies in philosophy, physics, and history of art at the Universities of Berlin and Zurich ("Anneliese Maier," 245); Josef Koch (letter of 3 August 1951 to the Ministry of Higher Education in Nordrhein-Westfalen), whose source must have been A. Maier herself, lists studies in philosophy, mathematics, and physics in Berlin, Zurich, and Paris. We thank Silvia Donati, who asked the archives of the University of Cologne for copies of that letter and of the minister's reply (30 November

1951), both press-marked "Zug 357/1," and Andreas Freitäger, archivist of the university, who allowed us to use these documents. We are following a short "curriculum vitae" (ten lines) included in a typewritten personal card (*Personalbogen*), signed by A. Maier (31 January 1955) and conserved in the Archives for the History of the Max-Planck-Gesellschaft, Berlin (MPG-Archiv, II. Abt., Rep. 1A, PA Maier). This document gives 1929 as the year of her Ph.D., and the same year is given by Koch, but Annette Vogt ("Maier, Anneliese," 92), gives the date 30 July 1930, with reference to Archive HUB (Humboldt University, Berlin), Phil. Fak. Nr. 704, Bl. 1–16; A. Maier's dissertation was published in 1930. Information about Planck's guidance of Anneliese's studies in physics is in a reference by Auguste Pelzer dated 15 December 1953 (MPG-Archiv, II. Abt., Rep. 1A, PA Maier), and cf. Maierù, "Anneliese Maier," 306 n. 12. We thank Marion Kazemi for sending copies of these two documents and of three letters by A. Maier (MPG-Archiv, II. Abt., Rep. 1A, PA Maier: to Nicolai Hartmann, 4 October 1949; to Otto Hahn, president of the Max-Planck-Gesellschaft, 14 January 1950; and to an unnamed "Herr Doktor," perhaps Ernst Telschow, 28 January 1950). We thank also Annette Vogt for information and advice.

5. Cf. A. Maier's "Personalbogen" (see n. 4): "Dann weitere Studien, Vorbereitung der Habilitation (auf die 1934 verzichtet musste, da politisch kompromittiert)." According to Annette Vogt (e-mail to A. Maierù 28 January 2002), between 1933 and 1938 women were not allowed—although it was not officially forbidden—to make their *Habilitation* at any German university.

6. See A. Maier, "Maier, Heinrich," 2d ed., 2: 99.

7. A. Maier, "Maier, Heinrich," 2:107; but Paravicini Bagliani, in A. Maier's bibliography reprinted in *Studi sul XIV secolo*, 15, gives 1934 as the year of publication of H. Maier's *Philosophie der Wirklichkeit*, vol. 2, parts 1 and 2: the Vatican Library copy fits the latter description, although it has a brief forward by Heinrich Maier dated April 1933. Evidently part 1 was published separately in 1933 and then together with part 2 in 1934.

8. Cf. Maierù, "Anneliese Maier," 306–7.

9. Cf. Heimsoeth, "Zum Lebenswerk von Anneliese Maier," 3: "[S]tarb … Anneliese Maier in Rom, wo sie in der Stille eines ausschliesslich ihrer Forschungsarbeit dargebrachten Daseins seit mehr als drei Jahrzehnten lebte." ("Anneliese Maier died … in Rome, where for more than three decades she [had] carried on a quiet life exclusively dedicated to her research work" [our translation].)

10. Regarding the archival research, see A. Maier, "Leibnizbriefe in Italienischen Bibliotheken und Archiven," *Quellen und Forschungen aus Italienischen Archiven und Bibliotheken* 27 (1937): 268. We do not know if somebody helped her on this occasion as on the next one (see n. 13).

11. Lehmann-Brockhaus, "Anneliese Maier," 10. A. Maier acknowledged her debt to Friederich Bock in "Leibnizbriefe," 274 n. 8.

12. Bignami Odier, "Anneliese Maier," 246.

13. Vogt, "Maier, Anneliese," 92. Grants were given from 1939 to 1940 and again at least in 1943–44; but Maier writes (letter of 14 January 1950 to the president of the Max-Planck-Gesellschaft; see n. 4) that she began her research twelve years before, "und zwar als 'Stipendiatin' des römischen Kaiser-Wilhelm-Instituts"; she received money till October 1944 (the last year through the German Embassy to the Holy See). In the letter to Hartmann, Maier gives the name of the person who helped her to obtain the grant ("Exzellenz Schmitt-Ott").

14. Bignami Odier, "Anneliese Maier," 246; and Maier's "Personalbogen" (see n. 4).

15. Bignami Odier, "Anneliese Maier," 247–48.

16. We owe information on Maier at Cologne to Prof. Albert Zimmermann, former director of the Thomas-Institut, who as young student attended Maier's lectures: "Die Anfänge des naturphilosophischen und physikalischen Denkens im 13. und 14. Jahrhundert" (letter of 26 June 2001 to Alfonso Maierù).

17. The information about her nonfaculty status is from A. Zimmermann, letter to Alfonso Maierù, 17 June 2001. Silvia Donati kindly checked the catalog of dissertations and *Habilitationen* of the Cologne University for that period.

18. Bignami Odier, "Anneliese Maier," 246. According to Pelzer (see n. 4), Maier was in Cologne in July 1952 and 1953 (actually the first year was 1951). In her "Personalbogen" (see n. 4), Maier includes the title of professor she received (1951), but not even the name of Cologne (Köln).

19. See Koch, letter to Ministry of Higher Education.

20. *Codices Vaticani latini. Codices, 2118–2192,* section VII: "Eminentissimus cardinalis Iohannes Mercati beata memoria codices Vaticanos latinos . . . recensendos mihi commisit"; instead, Bignami Odier writes that it was the prefect of the Vatican Library, Anselm M. Albareda ("Anneliese Maier," 247).

21. Bignami Odier, "Anneliese Maier," 248.

22. Bignami Odier, "Anneliese Maier," 247.

23. A. Zimmermann letter to Alfonso Maierù, 17 June 2001.

24. Bignami Odier, "Anneliese Maier," 247.

25. On her generosity, see g.d.l. [G. De Luca] in the periodical *Mater Dei* 5 (1958): 547. "A most patient and cheerful guide to anyone stumped in their research who turned to her." A. Maier edited in the same number of *Mater Dei* a partial transcription of a text by Guido Ebroicensis, "Un sermone sull'Assunta," 547–50, an item to be added to her bibliography. See also Vanni Rovighi, "Necrologio."

26. See Lehmann-Brockhaus, "Anneliese Maier," 9–10.

27. See Müller, "Heinrich Maier," 223–28.

28. A. Maier, *Kants Qualitätskategorien,* 2d ed., 77 (we quote from the second edition not only because of availability but because the text remained essentially the same, although sometimes shortened, in the second, as Maier herself stated in the preface, 7): "Stephanus Chauvin gibt für diesen Begriff in seinem *Lexicon rationale s. thesaurus philosophicus* (1692) folgende Erklärung: 'Realitas est diminutivum dictum a re. Et a Scotistis, qui primi vocis hujus inventores fuere, distinguitur a re; quod res sit id quod per se potest existere . . . et non sit pars rei; realitas autem sit aliquid minus re. Ideoque ponunt in unaquaque re plures realitates, quas alio nomine appellant formalitates.'" ("Stephen Clauvin, in his *Lexicon rationale sive thesaurus philosophicus* [1692] gives for this concept the following explanation: '*Realitas* is a diminutive based on *res* [thing]. And by the Scotists, who were the first inventors of this word, it is distinguished from *res* in the sense that a thing can exist by itself . . . and it is not a part of a thing; a reality [*realitas*], however, is something less than a thing. Therefore they posit in any given thing several realities, which by another name are called formalities [*formalitates*].'")

29. Regarding her confirmation of Heinrich Maier's idea, see A. Maier, *Kants Qualitätskategorien,* 72–73. She quoted her father as saying, "Dass hinter den Kantischen Qualitätskategorien sich die Apprehensionskategorien 'Qualität' und 'Intensität' verbergen." ("That behind the Kantian categories of quality are hidden the categories of apprehension 'quality' and 'intensity.'") For her use of the prehistory of the concept, see A. Maier, *Kants Qualitätskategorien,* 73.

30. A. Maier, *Kants Qualitätskategorien,* 147: "Der von ihm vertretene Standpunkt selbst lässt sich allerdings nur aus einem Stück alter Schulphilosophie heraus erklären."

31. Might either or both of the books that Maier published in the late 1930s have made use of research intended for her abandoned *Habilitation*?

32. Anneliese Maier, *Die Mechanisierung des Weltbildes,* 2d ed., 23 n; the text of the second edition remained essentially the same as that of the first, although sometimes shortened.

33. A. Maier, *Die Mechanisierung des Weltbildes,* 23–24.

34. A. Maier, *Die Mechanisierung des Weltbildes,* 13–14.

35. A. Maier, *Die Mechanisierung des Weltbildes,* 15–16.

36. See Müller, "Heinrich Maier," 226. For Heinrich Maier quality and intensity are *Apprehensionskategorien,* which, along with the *Anschauungskategorien* (space and time), are *präsentative,* as opposed to noetic, categories.

37. See Van Steenberghen, "Monseigneur Auguste Pelzer," 7–9.

38. A. Maier, *Das Problem der intensiven Grösse in der Scholastik,* 7 n. 2.

39. Bignami Odier, "Anneliese Maier," 246.

40. A. Maier, "Nouvelles Questions de Siger de Brabant sur la Physique d'Aristote," *Revue philosophique de Louvain* 44 (1946): 497–513; "Zur handschriftlichen Überlieferung der Quodlibeta des Petrus Johannis Olivi," *Recherches de théologie ancienne et médiévale* 14 (1947): 223–28; "Ein neues Ockham-Manuskript (Die Originalform der Expositio aurea?)," *Gregorianum* 28 (1947): 101–33; "Das Quodlibet des Thomas Wylton," *Recherches de théologie ancienne et médiévale* 14 (1947): 106–10; "Handschriftliches zu Arnaldus de Villanova und Petrus Johannis Olivi," *Analecta sacra Tarraconensia* 21 (1948): 53–74.

41. A. Maier, "Die Anfänge des physikalischen Denkens," 7–8 (our translation).

42. A. Maier, " Die Anfänge des physikalischen Denkens," 7 n. 2, gives reference to Ehrle, *Grundsätzliches zur neueren und neuesten Scholastik,* 2 n. 1; and Ehrle, *Der Sentenzenkommentar Peters von Candia,* 344–45.

43. Marshall Clagett also concentrated on topics with links to early modern science.

44. Cf. Vian, *Don Giuseppe De Luca e la cultura italiana del Novocento.*

45. Maierù, "Anneliese Maier," 305 n. 7.

46. Quoted by Bignami Odier, "Anneliese Maier," 247.

47. A. Maier, *Ausgehendes Mittelalter,* 1, item 7.

48. Capovilla, *Giovanni XXIII in alcuni scritti di don Giuseppe De Luca,* 96 (De Luca's letter of 26 June 1959). Cf. Trottmann, *La vision béatifique.*

49. See "Una nuova iniziativa di storia medievale," *Il pensiero politico* 3 (1970), 174; for the authorship of the anonymous text, see Bignami Odier, "Anneliese Maier," 247.

50. A. Maier, *Ausgehendes Mittelalter,* 3: articles 53 (1965), 54 (1967), 55 (1969), 56 (1969), 57 (1970), 58 (1971), 59 (1971), and see 544 n. 2.

51. Kaeppeli, *Scriptores Ordinis Praedicatorum.*

52. Bignami Odier, "Anneliese Maier," 248.

53. We owe this piece of information to Maddalena De Luca.

54. When Maier republished the work in 1968 along with her doctoral dissertation, *Kants Qualitatskategorien,* she noted ironically that the title remained unchanged from the first edition although in the meanwhile E. J. Dijksterhuis had used the same title, without limitation to the seventeenth century, for his own well-known survey. She noted that in the foreword of the German edition of his book Dijksterhuis had acknowledged borrowing the title from her,

so that there should be no misunderstanding if she used it again (A. Maier, *Zwei Untersuchungen,* 7–8).

55. Dijksterhuis, *Mechanization of the World Picture,* 176.

56. Dijksterhuis, *Mechanization of the World Picture,* 182. Dijksterhius refers to Maier again on p. 189, crediting her for drawing attention to what has come to be called "Bradwardine's function," and on pp. 198–99.

57. Dijksterhuis, "Origins of Classical Mechanics," 170.

58. In a letter of 4 January 2002 to Edith Sylla, Marshall Clagett writes that he is fairly sure he learned of Maier's work from Ernest Moody during his doctoral examination, when they were discussing Bradwardine's theory of the proportion of motions. In his dissertation, published in 1941 as *Giovanni Marliani and Late Medieval Physics,* Clagett cites Duhem many times but never mentions Maier. On Bradwardine's law, Clagett writes, "I might take this opportunity to mention Dr. Moody's help in interpreting Bradwardine's work" (131 n. 12).

59. Clagett, letter to Sylla.

60. Clagett, *Science of Mechanics,* x.

61. Clagett, *Science of Mechanics,* xxi.

62. Beaujouan, "Motives and Opportunities for Science in the Medieval Universities," 227–28.

63. Although Maier never had enough money for traveling, she met many scholars from abroad when they worked in the Vatican Library. We know nothing about her correspondence.

64. As reprinted in Anneliese Maier, *Ausgehendes Mittelalter,* 2: 456.

65. Clagett, *Science of Mechanics,* 73.

66. See the reprint of the article in Moody, *Studies in Medieval Philosophy,* 203–86.

67. In the letter of 14 January 1950 to a "sehr vererter Herr Doctor," perhaps Ernst Telschow of the Max-Planck-Gesellschaft (see n. 4), Maier wrote: "Es ist namlich so, dass die mittelalterliche Naturphilosophie und Naturwissenschaft nach dem Krieg auf einmal in der ganzen Welt, und besonders in Amerika, Mode geworden ist. Und da ich in der glücklichen Lage bin, vor den andern einen Vorsprung von zehn Jahren zu haben, sind meine Sachen unglaublich begehrt und haben einen Erfolg, der mir selber unheimlich ist. Vor ein paar Monaten schrieb mir Prof. Moodie von der Columbia-Universität, er habe meine Arbeiten— eben jene Abhandlungen der Kulturabteilung—erst jetzt kennen gelernt und sei ganz entsetzt feststellen zu müssen, dass seine eigenen Untersuchungen aus den letzten fünf Jahren, die er jetzt veröffentlichen wollte, dadurch überflüssig geworden seien. So kann es einem gehen; ich bin nur froh, dass der Fall nicht umgekehrt liegt. Erfreulich war mir besonders, dass die Amerikaner grundsätzlich zu denselben Auffassungen und Wertungen gekommen sind wie ich: immerhin eine Bestätigung, dass man auf dem richtigen Weg ist."

68. See letter quoted in preceding note.

69. A. Maier, "Platonische Einflüsse in der scholastischen Mechanik?" in *Zwischen Philosophie und Mechanik* (Rome: Edizioni di Storia e Letteratura, 1958), e.g., 244 n. 10.

70. Moody, *Studies in Medieval Philosophy,* xiv.

71. In Maier, *Ausgehendes Mittelalter,* 2: 457.

72. See A. Maier, *Zwischen Philosophie und Mechanik,* 242 n. 6, for two of the opinions that Bradwardine rejected. For Maier's critique of Crosby's interpretation, see A. Maier, *Ausgehendes Mittelalter,* 2:461 (review of Crosby's book). In his foreword to the edition Marshall Clagett had already questioned Crosby's suggestion on this point.

73. We owe all these pieces of information to Maddalena De Luca.

74. Vanni Rovighi, "Necrologio," 354.

75. By the 1950s Maier's scholarly focus may have been considered not broad enough to make her suitable for a professorial chair in a German university. Thanks to Prof. Wolfgang Kluxen for his letter of 26 April 2002 to Alfonso Maierù.

76. Bignami Odier, "Anneliese Maier," 245.

Select Bibliography of Works by Anneliese Maier

A complete list of the works published by Anneliese Maier was published by Agostino Paravicini Bagliani in A. Maier's *Ausgehendes Mittelalter*, 3:615–26, reprinted with an additional item in *Studi sul XIV secolo in memoria di Anneliese Maier*, 15–23. What follows is a select list of her most important works, with an emphasis on those concerned with late-medieval natural philosophy and including the items mentioned in this article.

Kants Qualitätskategorien. [Ph.D. diss.] Kant-Studien. Ergänzungshefte, 65. Edited by Paul Menzer and Arthur Liebert. Berlin: Pan-Verlag Kurt Metzner, 1930.

Editor. *Philosophie der Wirklichkeit*, by Heinrich Maier. Vols. 2 and 3. Tübingen: Mohr, 1933–35.

"Maier, Heinrich." In *Philosophen-Lexikon: Handwörterbuch der Philosophie nach Personen*, edited by Eugen Hauer, W. Ziegenfuss, and Gertrud Jung. Berlin: E. S. Mittler, 1937; 2d ed., Berlin: Walter de Gruyter, 1950.

Die Mechanisierung des Weltbildes im 17. Jahrhundert. Forschungen zur Geschichte der Philosophie und der Pädagogik, 18. Leipzig: Meiner, 1938. A second edition of this work, together with Maier's dissertation, was published as *Zwei Untersuchungen zur Nachscholastischen Philosophie* (Rome: Edizioni di Storia e Letteratura, 1968).

Das Problem der intensiven Grösse in der Scholastik (De intensione et remissione formarum). Veröffentlichungen des Kaiser Wilhelm-Instituts für Kulturwissenschaft im Palazzo Zuccari, Rom. Abhandlungen. Leipzig: Keller, 1939.

Die Impetustheorie der Scholastik. Veröffentlichungen des Kaiser Wilhelm-Instituts für Kulturwissenschaft im Palazzo Zuccari, Rom. Abhandlungen. Leipzig: Keller, 1939; Vienna: Schroll, 1940.

An der Grenze von Scholastik und Naturwissenschaft. Veröffentlichungen des Kaiser Wilhelm-Instituts für Kulturwissenschaft im Palazzo Zuccari, Rom. Abhandlungen. Essen: Essener Verlag-Amst, 1943.

Studien zur Naturphilosophie der Spätscholastik. 5 vols. Rome: Edizioni di Storia e Letteratura, 1949–58.

"Die Anfänge des physikalischen Denkens im 14. Jahrhundert." *Philosophia Naturalis* 1 (1950): 7–35.

Codices Burghesiani Bibliothecae Vaticanae. Studi e Testi, 170. Vatican City: Biblioteca Apostolica Vaticana, 1952.

Review of *The Medieval Science of Weights*, by E. A. Moody and M. Clagett. *Isis* 46 (1955): 297–300.

Review of *Thomas of Bradwardine: His Tractatus de proportionibus*, by H. Lamar Crosby Jr. *Isis* 48 (1957): 84–87.

Codices Vaticani latini. Codices, 2118–2192. Vatican City: Typis Polyglottis Vaticanis, 1961.

"Philosophy of Nature at the End of the Middle Ages." *Philosophy Today* 5 (1961): 92–107. Translation of "Ergebnisse der Spätscholastischen Naturphilosophie," *Scholastik* 35 (1960): 161–87.

Ausgehendes Mittelalter: Gesammelte Aufsätze zur Geistesgeschichte des 14. Jahrhunderts. Edited by A. Paravicini Bagliani. 3 vols. Rome: Edizioni di Storia e Letteratura, 1964–77.

On the Threshold of Exact Science: Selected Writings of Anneliese Maier on Late Medieval Natural Philosophy. Edited and translated by Steven D. Sargent. Philadelphia: University of Pennsylvania Press, 1982.

WORKS CITED

Beaujouan, Guy. "Motives and Opportunities for Science in the Medieval Universities." In *Scientific Change: Historical Studies in the Intellectual, Social and Technical Conditions for Scientific Discovery and Technical Invention, from Antiquity to the Present,* edited by A. C. Crombie. New York: Basic Books, 1963.

Bignami Odier, Jeanne. "Anneliese Maier (17 novembre 1905–2 décembre 1971)." *Rivista di storia della chiesa in Italia* 26 (1972): 245–48.

Capovilla, Loris, ed. *Giovanni XXIII in alcuni scritti di Don Giuseppe De Luca, con un saggio di corrispondenza inedita.* Brescia, It.: Morcelliana, 1963.

Clagett, Marshall. *Giovanni Marliani and Late-Medieval Physics.* New York: Columbia University Press, 1941.

———. *The Science of Mechanics in the Middle Ages.* Madison: University of Wisconsin Press; London: Oxford University Press, 1959.

Dijksterhuis, E. J. *The Mechanization of the World Picture.* Translated by C. Dikshoorn. Oxford: Clarendon Press, 1961.

———. "The Origins of Classical Mechanics." In *Critical Problems in the History of Science,* edited by Marshall Clagett. Madison: University of Wisconsin Press, 1962.

Ehrle, Franz. *Grundsätzliches zur neueren und neuesten Scholastik.* Freiburg, Ger.: Herder, 1918.

———. *Der Sentenzenkommentar Peters von Candia.* Franziskanische Studien, Beiheft 9. Münster: Aschendorff, 1925.

Heimsoeth, Heinz. "Zum Lebenswerk von Anneliese Maier." *Studi internazionali di filosofia* 4 (1972): 3–14.

Kaeppeli, Thomas. *Scriptores Ordinis Praedicatorum.* 2 vols. Rome: Istituto storico dei Domenicani, 1970–75.

Lehmann-Brockhaus, Otto. "Anneliese Maier, 17.11.1905–2.12.1971: Gedenkwort am Grabe (Rom, Campo Santo Teutonico)." *Mitteilungen aus der Max-Planck-Gesellschaft zur Foerderung der Wissenschaften* 1 (1972): 9–11.

Maierù, Alfonso. "Anneliese Maier e la filosofia della natura tardoscolastica." In *Gli studi di filosofia medievale tra Otto e Novecento: Contributo a un bilancio storiografico,* edited by Ruedi Imbach and A. Maierù. Rome: Edizioni di Storia e Letteratura, 1991.

Moody, Ernest A. *Studies in Medieval Philosophy, Science, and Logic: Collected Papers, 1933–1969.* Berkeley: University of California Press, 1975.

Müller, Ernst. "Heinrich Maier (1867–1933)." In *Schwäbische Profile.* Stuttgart: W. Kohlhammer Verlag, 1950.

Paravicini Bagliani, Agostino. "Anneliese Maier: Bibliographie." In *Ausgehendes Mittelalter: Gesammelte Aufsätze zur Geistesgeschichte del 14. Jahrhunderts,* by Anneliese Maier, edited by A. Paravicini Bagliani. Rome: Edizioni di Storia e Letteratura, 1977, 3:615–26. Reprinted with an additional item in *Studi sul XIV secolo in memoria di Anneliese Maier,* ed. A. Maierù and A. Paravicini Bagliani (Rome: Edizioni di Storia e Letteratura, 1981).

Trottmann, Christian. *La Vision béatifique des disputes scolastiques à sa définition par Benoît XII.* Rome: École Française, 1995.

Vanni Rovighi, Sofia. "Necrologio." *Rivista di filosofia neo scolastica* 64 (1972): 353–54.
Van Steenberghen, Fernand. "Monseigneur Auguste Pelzer." In *Études d'histoire littéraire sur la scolastique médiévale,* by A. Pelzer, edited by Adrien Pattin and Émile Van der Vyver. Louvain, Belg.: Béatrice-Nauwelaerts; Paris: Publications Universitaires, 1964.
Vian, Paolo, ed. *Don Giuseppe De Luca e la cultura italiana del Novecento.* Atti del convegno nel centenario della nascita, Roma, 22–24 ottobre 1998. Rome: Edizioni di Storia e Letteratura, 2001.
Vogt, Annette. "Maier, Anneliese." In *Wissenschaftlerinnen in Kaiser-Wilhelm-Instituten A–Z.* Berlin: Archiv zur Geschichte der Max-Planck Gesellschaft, 1999.

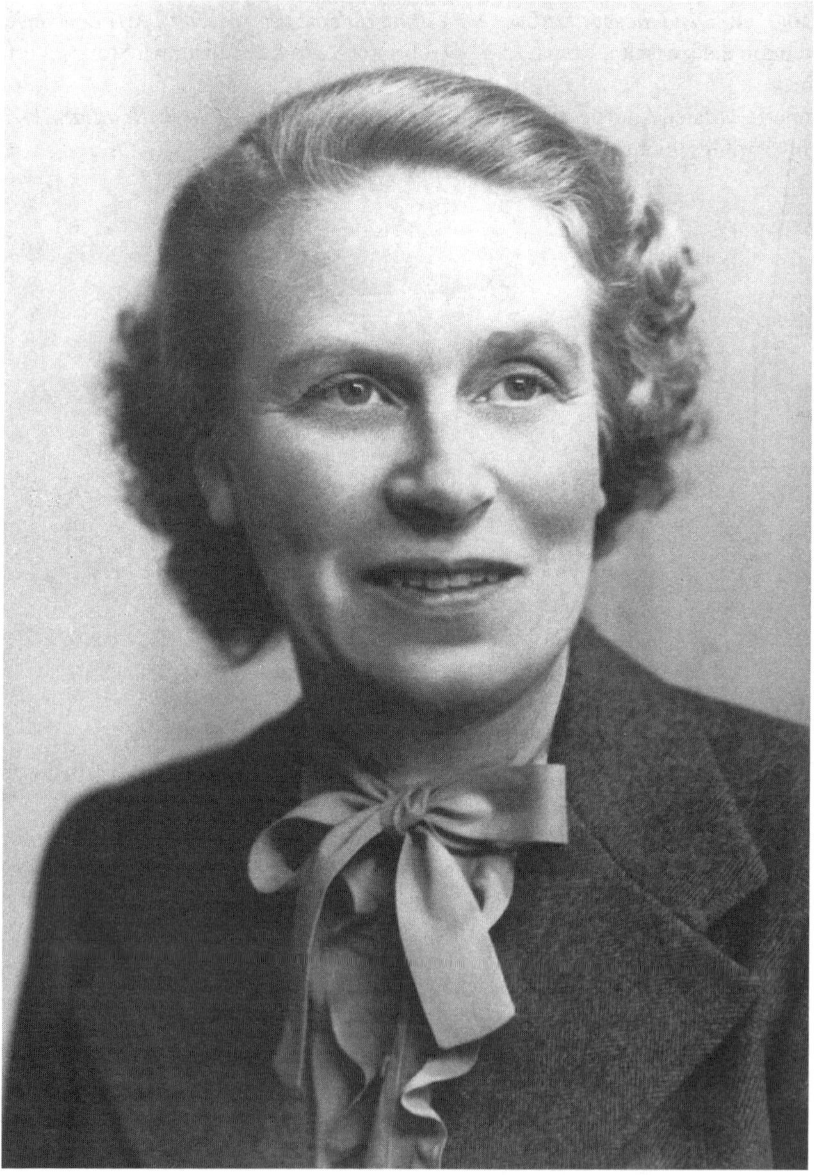

CHAPTER 45

A Woman Historian in Oxford (1905–2003)

MARJORIE ETHEL REEVES

I WAS A COUNTRY RABBIT from mid-Wiltshire when I came up in 1923 to read history at Saint Hugh's College, Oxford—with a pigtail in place of a bobtail. Saint Hugh's was then a women's college, founded by one of the earnest band of women who had campaigned so energetically (supported by a group of enlightened men) to secure degrees for women. This had just been achieved in 1921. Although constitutionally the college was still largely governed by men, academically and socially its members took a full part in university life. There were still some quaint rules, such as those that required that we take a woman don as chaperon when we went to tea in a man's rooms and that all colleges—men's as well as women's—shut their gates at a fixed time that was creeping toward midnight. The medieval time had been 9 P.M., still marked as Great Tom at Christchurch booms through the city at 9:05 P.M.

The eye opener for me was the intellectual freedom of Oxford. Whatever one's particular course, most lectures were open to all. You could pick them from the lecture lists (at least in the arts) without necessarily following your tutor's advice. I still remember the smell of breakfast in the Balliol hall where the distinguished historian A. L. Smith drew a great crowd at 10 A.M. We were assigned to both men and women dons as tutors according to their specialization and moved freely around the colleges for tutorials.

My chief inspiration came from Cecilia Ady, who had a considerable reputation in medieval and Renaissance Italian history. I went to her for the "special subject," the age of Dante, studied from Italian and Latin texts. I chose it because I knew nothing about Dante, except lurid engravings of the *Inferno* in an English translation of the *Comedy* possessed by my grandparents. The first thing I noticed when I went to Cecilia

Ady's house for my first tutorial was the walls lined with Alinari prints of Italian art and architecture. In that Victorian dining room at 40 Saint Margaret's Road, she recreated for me the vivid life of thirteenth-century Florence. When I recrossed to the college just opposite, the road would be full of proud Florentines flaunting their glory like peacocks in the narrow streets of that contentious city.

This gives a highly romantic impression, but in fact the set texts required close critical analysis. One of the notable features of the Oxford history school at that time was the writing of "gobbits," that is, comments on quotations from original sources, which required succinct elucidation of textual problems and historical significance. These exercises gave a marvelous training in getting quickly to the main point and catching it in a sharp phrase. I industriously wrote gobbits on Dante, Stubbs Charters, and political thought and loved it. Essays were required to be as short as was consistent with an adequate answer to the question. In both term work and examinations we wrote answers to questions rather than papers on topics. Engagement of the imagination and training in writing were Oxford's chief gifts to me.

After three years, "taking Schools," as the phrase went, was a ritual both formidable and exciting. We all dressed up in undergraduate gowns and subfusc. For women this was a black skirt, white top, and black shoes. Dressing up took our minds off reality, to concentrate on looking as fetching as possible, and of course, the requirement created amusing diversion when invigilators rejected, for instance, pink socks.

But Schools did demand fortitude. One was examined on the whole three year's work by about eleven papers involving two- or three-hour papers a day, with three or four questions to be answered on each—all in one week. This took place in the Examination Schools, where crowds of black-clad figures assembled each day. Compensation lay in the fact that for a week we were important people, gaped at by tourists, given precedence in restaurants, and treated to strawberry teas by attentive friends.

After taking the education diploma the following summer, I departed from Oxford to teach history in a southeast London grammar school. I took it for granted that this was the next step: there was then no automatic state provision for postgraduate research and few awards in Oxford for women. In any case, I had discovered already that I wanted to teach—in the sense that when I found new knowledge exciting I wanted to communicate it.

In the event, I spent ten years in London, and looking back, I would not have missed any of my London experience. Oxford has its special allure, but it is a mistake to stay there without a break. My two years in the Greenwich school were somewhat turbulent. The seasoned teachers had their individual methods of discipline, as I discovered painfully, trying to find my own approach. I remember a particularly shaming occasion in a class of twelve-year-olds while acting out the story of the Roman Horatius defending the bridge against Etruscan invaders. The whole bridge, constructed of chairs, came crashing down, evoking an angry intervention from the next door teacher: "What's going on here?" But the whole experience showed me the rich possibilities of history for schools.

However, during my second year of teaching I received a typically laconic letter from Barbara Gwyer, my principal at Saint Hugh's, saying, "I think you ought to apply for this." Pinned to it was an advertisement for a postgraduate studentship at Westfield College in Hampstead, which offered free board and lodging, supervision, and twenty pounds a term pocket money. I had kept vaguely in mind the idea of research in some medieval Italian field, so now I said to myself, "Why not have a go?" I went up to the British Museum Library, as it was called then, looked up some references, and concocted a very amateurish scheme on Lombard communes in the twelfth century. Without taking any advice, I sent in this half-cocked application and to my surprise won the studentship. Westfield was then still a comfortable Victorian-style women's college, part of London University, but mainly run by that dedicated generation of high-minded, serious academic women. It was housed in a Hampstead mansion entered through an impressive white portico adorned by two complacent stucco dogs. Various modern additions dotted the gardens, but the community still lived in the style of the old house, dressing for formal dinner on most nights and socializing in senior, middle, and junior common rooms.

I found that I was scheduled for a doctoral thesis on the Lombard communes. "Doctorate?" said I. "I just want to pursue a medieval research subject. I had not thought about getting a doctorate." We agreed that I might as well throw one in. I think my attitude was typical of Oxford at that time: further degrees were almost an irrelevance. Research was the thing. I remember quite late in my career eminent Oxford scholars who paraded their M.A. gowns, green with age, at public ceremonies, while others flaunted colorful doctoral gowns.

I duly took myself to the British Museum to explore those communes, only to find that I had burdened myself with a subject that eluded me. In the course of the wider reading, however, I stumbled on Emile Gebhart's *L'Italie mystique,* with its pioneering essay on Joachim of Fiore. Discovering the mysterious abbot was a moment of revelation. "That's what I'm going to do!" I exclaimed to myself. It has taken the rest of my researching life to meet this demand. I have often reflected on the varying and hidden processes by which scholars find their particular field of exploration. For some of us, at least, there is some kind of personal engagement even when we are still ignorant of what it is that excites us. It is a mysterious process, which Michael Polanyi has called "personal knowledge." The whole concept might be repudiated by those who prefer a scientific model for historical research. But unrepentantly I stand with those who find history requires a commitment of the imagination as well as of analytical skills (and, indeed, lately this is admitted by many scientists too).

There was rather a fuss in Westfield when I announced my intention. I was told that it would be difficult to find me a supervisor for such a marginal subject, and various historians said it would do my academic career no good to leave the field of "proper history" for its borders. Finally, Professor Edmund Gardner of University College took me on, his being the only person in this country who knew anything about Joachim. But I now wonder at my luck—rather than foresight. The latter half of the twentieth century saw a sea change in what constituted important history. As a result, intellectual, sociological, and psychological ways of exploring the past have come to the forefront competing with the institutional and political history of older convention. Not least the concern of the human mind with its own future is now seen as part of history. Joachim as a major medieval prophet stands now in a prominent position on the historical stage.

I found my leading question in the reasons for the abbot's remarkable later influence and duly joined the fellowship of readers in the famous Round Room at the British Museum. A special kind of silent noise—the rustling of papers and movement of chairs—pervaded it. We all engaged in the same rituals, circling the concentric rings of catalogs, handing in order slips to the dragon at the center, competing for our favorite chairs. Three of us from Westfield would collect stories of the eccentrics sitting next to us, to tell when we foregathered for a 2s. 6d. lunch at a small tea shop in Great Russell Street. At 4 P.M. readers were allowed tea and biscuits in the staff canteen. There were no restaurants for tourists. I remember walking rather quickly, on a dark November day, through the spooky gallery of Egyptian mummies to reach the ordinariness of the little tearoom. When the closing bell rang, we all trouped out together exchanging surmises about the odd characters whom we could never catch coming out. Back in Westfield one day Cicely Davies, one of our company, passed round her clever caricatures of some of these eccentrics.

Edmund Gardener was a delightful supervisor who left me almost entirely alone to find my own way into the subject. When I visited him in University College close to the British Museum, I walked past the upright embalmed figure of Jeremy Bentham (bequeathed by himself to the college). Once Gardener said to me, "Have you genuflected to the great utilitarian?" Gardener, deep in his Franciscan studies, was a strange figure in that "godless institution in Gower Street." He and I would converse amicably about medieval mysticism, and on occasion he generously lent me his sixteenth-century editions of Joachim's works.

In 1931 I left Westfield with the thesis half done, for my original question—Why did Venetian friars publish those Joachimist editions in the midst of Renaissance culture?—had led me into surprising new paths of late-medieval and Renaissance thought. I took a job as lecturer in history in a southeast training college for teachers, Saint Gabriel's. For a year I divided my interest between the thesis and elementary school education in run-down parts of London. A very civilized viva by two eminent medievalists revealed that I knew more about Joachim than they did, although they had to rebuke me for crashing mistakes on general background. With the Ph.D. duly confirmed in a mass ceremony in which rows of kneeling candidates were expertly lassoed into their doctoral hoods, I plunged back into the world of schools and teachers. The next eight years formed an absorbing experience of enthusiastic experimentation and much discussion of the educational future. At the same time there were gathering clouds of apprehensions, especially perhaps in my generation, as we drew toward the years of the Spanish civil war and the inexorable approach of Fascism and Nazism.

In 1938 I was faced with the possibility of two moves: one into general educational work with the Student Christian Movement, the other back to Oxford as a tutor in the Society of Home Students (later Saint Anne's College). Both drew me but Oxford won. I was writing my first lectures for the course called "Outlines of English Constitutional History" in the Radcliffe Camera when Neville Chamberlain returned from Munich with the infamous pact of "peace with honor"—a real irony, that.

Oxford in wartime is another story for another occasion. It was both tragic and comic: bombers went overhead to Coventry; evacuees poured out of London; students searched for their battle bowlers when summoned by the sirens to their fire-watching stations; elderly dons tried to apply their habits of exactitude to war work. Research took a back seat, but in the midst of this strange life, German scholars began to arrive, throwing our minds back to the academic quest that knows no frontiers. One of these, Otto Pächt, discovered some unknown *figurae* in a thirteenth-century manuscript, which Pächt described as "probably Joachimist." I got out the manuscript and within ten minutes had verified it—by comparison with references in the Franciscan chronicle of Salinbene—as the lost *Liber figurarum* of Abbot Joachim. I was sitting in Bodley's Duke Humphrey Library, overwhelmed by my luck, when another refugee scholar, Beatrice Hirsch-Reich, came and looked over my shoulder. She recognized the Joachimist character of these *figurae* at once. That was the start of a long and fruitful partnership in unraveling their meaning.

By the late forties Oxford University was in full swing again. Former servicemen and women were flooding back, thankful for this second chance. We were teaching undergraduates sometimes up to eighteen hours a week. Tutorials (in ones, twos, or threes) with these more mature young people were particularly exciting because their experiences added depth to our discussions of history. It was hectic but satisfying. I kept one day a week for research at Bodley. But teaching and research have always interacted for me. Each fertilizes the other, and I have always maintained that they should never be separated in higher education. For over twenty years—punctuated by two periods of sabbatical leave—this was roughly the pattern I followed. During our three eight-week terms, teaching and increasingly much begrudged administration ate up most of the week except for the one precious day collecting material in Bodley. Most of our three ample vacations I spent in my Wiltshire home writing. With Dr. Hirsch-Reich and Monsignor Tonddelli in Reggio Emilia I had helped to publish the *Liber figurarum* in 1950, but my own work saw daylight in print only in 1969. By that time it was a much bigger and better book than the original thesis. In spite of the present pressure to publish quickly, I would still say, "Don't publish half-baked theses!"

Although during my time Saint Anne's was a women's college, relationships with male colleagues in the university presented few problems. We sat on the History Board and other delegacies of the university, we shared responsibilities on examining boards, and we belonged to the same academic societies. There were some exclusive male and female social clubs, but during this period—just prior to the movement for going mixed—senior common rooms in men's colleges started inviting academic women to their formal guest nights, and the women reciprocated. For myself at this time my educational experience was widening: I sat on the academic planning boards of two new postwar universities and on the Central Advisory Council for Education, established by the government for postwar reconstruction; and I was appointed to the governing body of several schools and colleges outside Oxford. There was always a majority of men on these bodies, but this never seemed of much consequence. We acted as persons in our own right, and sex never seemed much of an issue.

It is appropriate here to mention personal contacts with three eminent academic women whom I knew. My remarks are anecdotal; others have commemorated them in full memoirs. First, Dorothy Whitelock. I knew her, of course, as a leading scholar in Anglo-Saxon literature, but my particular contact with her was on a distinctly non-academic and somewhat hilarious occasion. My home was a mile away from Edington, the site claimed for Alfred the Great's great victory over the Viking invaders at Elthandun. In our village we held this for truth and were much elated when this interpretation was "confirmed" by the learned Anglo-Saxon expert. So we asked her to honor our eleven hundredth celebration of the battle, held over the spring bank holiday in 1978. Behold her then first reading aloud her translation of *The Dream of the Rood* in the Edington church packed on Sunday afternoon by an enthusiastic but bemused village audience. Then came an "Anglo-Saxon feast" held in a barn belonging to the leading farmer of the area. I found myself instructing our host in the etiquette of the occasion, seating Dorothy Whitelock on his right and remembering to toast her. The "Anglo-Saxon-ness" of the feast consisted in devouring chicken joints and such with our fingers and quaffing something purporting to be mead. We, the yokels, had a jolly good time, and our guest surveyed the scene with an air of benign amusement. Next morning she and I judged the procession of tableaux on floats (flat-bottomed trucks). The most popular, of course, was Alfred burning the cakes, but we gave the prize for "historical accuracy" to Alfred learning to read surrounded by Anglo-Saxon ladies costumed with careful correctness. Finally the battle was refought with tremendous panache before a large audience seated on the steep slopes of a natural arena in the hills. I have told this story because it encapsulates the academic playing a public role with style.

My contact with Dame Helen Gardner can be recorded more briefly. I knew her, of course, as a weighty scholar and a powerful professorial figure in academic politics, particularly in pressing women to move from a teaching role to publishing their research. My personal contact arose, however, because for several years we met in the ladies' room at Middle Temple Hall prior to the British Academy's annual Fellows' Dinner. It was my privilege to pin her royal decoration on her evening frock—just so! Then I would watch her sweep into the distinguished throng with inimitable style.

Finally, my relationship with Beryl Smalley was a much more serious academic one. We were colleagues at Oxford in the History School. She was a complex character: dedicated to the highest academic standards and a formidable tutor; her great work,

The Study of the Bible in the Middle Ages, was yet infused with an imaginative insight that I felt she did not want to acknowledge. She disapproved of my choice of Joachim of Fiore as a subject of academic research because he was intellectually unimportant, a trivial figure in the medieval scene. We argued about this amicably. Latterly, after she retired from her official fellowship at Saint Hilda's College to a north Oxford house, we often met on a Sunday in Parks Road, she walking to Saint Hilda's for lunch, I coming back from the University Church. One day, as we greeted each other, she said, "Oh, Marjorie, I have changed my mind about the Abbot Joachim. I don't like him any better, but I acknowledge his influence as really important, so I have put him into the revised edition of *The Study of the Bible*." In her book *English Friars and Antiquity* (1960), I was struck by her confession that being "ambushed" by certain friars, the book she had intended to write changed into a different one. "This book was born in an ambush. . . . They (the Friars) surrounded me and barred my retreat" (p. 1). I think she was enthralled by her "conversation" with medieval religious (some of them). I would place her beside Sir Richard Southern (though her range was narrower) in their shared qualities of great scholarship and imaginative involvement with their subjects.

The last part of my academic life has had several foci—too many, some would say. But central to it has always been what I myself call the steady march of Joachim and Joachimism to a position of central interest among historians. I have traced my own involvement with this in an essay, "A Sixty-Year Pilgrimage with the Abbot Joachim." When I first visited Joachim's monastery, San Giovanni in Fiore, high in the Sila Mountains of Calabria, there were few remains of the abbey except one impressive arch across a street. The people of the little town, which tumbled down the hill above the site of the monastery, knew little about the abbot to whom they owed their existence. That was in 1950. The change when next I made the journey to this remote spot was remarkable. Stimulated by academics from Cosenza and by the accumulating literature on Joachim, a group of enthusiasts was developing a center for the study of Joachimism. In 1979 they boldly held the first Congresso Internazionale di Studi Gioachomiti. Although the little town was hung with the flags of many nations, I have to admit that a Geneva scholar, Henri Mottu, and I, were the only two non-Italians. But the enthusiasm was palpable. Academic papers and discussions were serious, but the unusual aspect of this conference was the participation of "the people." All sessions were open to anyone. I remember particularly one occasion when nonacademic passions took over in an argument between the clerical contingent and a gang of local journalists who seemed to be Communists over which group had the better claim to Joachim as a prophet. A brief intervention by local carabinieri prevented descent to fisticuffs.

Since then I have been to successive conferences, in 1984, 1988, and 1994, at San Giovanni. Each drew new international participants from Germany, France, Spain, and especially America. A highlight was the special occasion in 1988 when the abbot's relics were transferred from their temporary resting place to the crypt in the beautifully restored abbey church. Led by a cardinal from Rome and an array of bishops and clergy, the casket on a jeep was taken in procession round the town. Then the whole excited crowd, with their candles and torches, poured into the church for the special mass. "Joachim," I said to myself, "has at last been cleared of his semiheretical status and brought home."

These experiences as a historian point up the enrichment one receives in an academic career. There is a real fellowship of scholars working in the same field who soon became friends rather than just colleagues. The dialogues in which we engage range far more widely than just technical exchanges, and I have received much generous sharing of insights and discoveries. This is especially true of a group of American scholars who have contributed so much to the advance of Joachimist studies. I was especially delighted when these contacts led to my election as a corresponding fellow of the Medieval Academy of America. One of the bonuses of living in Oxford now is that so many academic friends come to visit me.

But being a historian has given me a second reward in the discovery that history now belongs to a much wider range of people. Perhaps I first recognized this in San Giovanni in Fiore when the *sindaco* (mayor) presented me with the freedom of the city because I had helped to give them back "their" abbot. History belongs to a wider fraternity than academics. It has gone public. It nourishes our self-identity by revealing our "roots"; it develops our capacity to engage with "difference" in exploring a rich variety of cultures and civilizations. Claiming history should begin in schools. I remember a discussion on the panel of history advisors brought together by the BBC, when I found myself saying with fervor, "I want school children to be able to sit down in a rich patch of history and explore it with delight." Out of my London teaching experience came the idea of "history patch books," which finally materialized in the *Then and There* series of school books, which I edited from the mid-fifties onward, writing a number of medieval and Renaissance ones myself. They became for me a fascinating alternative to academic research, and at one time the schools here were full of them. But there was a clear connection with academic standards, for the basis of these books was to stimulate an imaginative understanding through close contact with original sources. Today, some have predicted the death of history, yet it remains a bestseller. I have written elsewhere about the many shapes today that popular history takes. In these unstable days when tragically history can become the Devil—*damnosa hereditas* that ensnares fanatics—all the more do we need truthful, balanced, but also imaginative history. A fruitful relationship between academic scholars and responsible "popularists" of history is crucial. As I was writing this I received notice from the Royal Historical Society of a colloquium called for February 2002, "The Responsibilities of the Historian": To "Truth"? To the Advancement of Knowledge? To the Public? This is very apt.

I end with a personal memory. Once a fellow historian said to me (jokingly): "If you get to heaven and find the abbot Joachim and his disciples gathered in a special corner for Joachimites waiting for you, will you be able to look him in the face?" The idea took me aback. The only possible response would be, "I tried to be as truthful as possible." This surely goes for all of us.

Select Bibliography of Works by Marjorie Ethel Reeves

"The *Liber Figurarum* of Joachim of Fiore." *Medieval and Renaissance Studies* 2 (1950): 59–81.

"The Abbot Joachim's Disciples and the Cistercian Order." *Sophia* 19 (1951): 355–71.

With L. Tondelli and B. Hirsch-Reich. *Il Libro delle figure dell'Abate Gioachimo da Fiore II.* Torino, It.: Societa Editrice Internazionale, 1953.

With B. Hirsch-Reich. "The *Figurae* of Joachim of Fiore: Genuine and Spurious Collections." *Medieval and Renaissance Studies* 3 (1954): 170–99.

With Morton Bloomfield. "The Penetration of Joachimism into Northern Europe." *Speculum* 29 (1954): 772–93.

With B. Hirsch-Reich. "The Seven Seals in the Writings of Joachim of Fiore." *Recherches de théologie ancienne et mediévale* 25 (1954): 211–47.

Three Questions in Higher Education. New Haven, Conn.: Hazen Foundation, 1955.

"The *Arbores* of Joachim of Fiore." In *Studies in Italian Medieval History: Presented to Miss E. M. Jamison,* Papers of the British School at Rome 24, n.s., 11, 124–36. London: British School at Rome, 1956.

"Joachimist Expectations in the Order of Angustinian Hermits." *Recherches de théologie ancienne et mediévale* 25 (1958): 111–41.

"The Abbot Joachim and the Society of Jesus." *Medieval and Renaissance Studies* 5 (1961): 163–81.

"Joachimist Influence on the Idea of a Last World Emperor." *Traditio* 17 (1961): 323–70.

"Dante Alighieri and Marsilio of Padua." In *Trends in Medieval Political Thought,* edited by B. Smalley. Oxford: Blackwell, 1965.

"Joachim of Fiore." In *The Encyclopedia of Philosophy,* vol. 4, edited by Paul Edwards. New York: Macmillan and Free Press, 1967.

"The European University from Medieval Times, with Special Reference to Oxford and Cambridge." In *Higher Education: Demand and Response,* edited by W. R. Niblett. London: Tavistock Publications, 1969.

The Influence of Prophecy in the Later Middle Ages: A Study in Joachimism. Oxford: Clarendon Press, 1969; rev. ed., South Bend, Ind.: Notre Dame University Press, 1993; Millenium ed., Oxford: Clarendon Press, 1999.

With B. Hirsch-Reich. *The Figurae of Joachim of Fiore.* Oxford-Warburg Studies. Oxford: Clarendon Press, 1972.

"Some Popular Prophecies from the Fourteenth to the Seventeenth Centuries." In *Popular Belief and Practice: Studies in Church History,* vol. 8, edited by G. J. Cuming and D. Baker. Cambridge: Cambridge University Press, 1972.

"History and Eschatology: Medieval and Early Protestant Thought in Some English and Scottish Writings." *Medievalia et Humanistica,* n.s., 4 (1973): 99–123.

"History and Prophecy in Medieval Thought." *Medievalia et Humanistica,* n.s., 5 (1974): 51–75.

"Joachim of Fiore." In *The Encyclopedia Britannica,* 15th ed., 1974, 225.

With M. Bloomfield. "The Penetration of Joachimism into Northern Europe." "The Abbot Joachim's Disciples and the Cistercian Order," "The Abbot Joachim and the Society of Jesus," and "Joachimist Influences on the Idea of the Last World Emperor." In *Joachim of Fiore in Christian Thought,* edited by Delno C. West. New York: Burt Franklin, 1975.

Joachim of Fiore and the Prophetic Future. London: SPCK, 1976; rev. ed., Gloucester: Sutton: 1999.

"Dante and the Prophetic View of History." In *The World of Dante,* edited by C. Grayson. Oxford: Oxford University Press, 1980.

"How Original Was Joachim of Fiore's Theology of History?" In *Atti del I Congresso Internazionale di Studi Gioachimiti.* San Giovanni in Fiore, It.: Centro di Studi Giochimiti, 1980.

"The Originality and Influence of Joachim of Fiore." *Traditio* 36 (1980): 270–316.

"The Ideal, the Real and the Quest for Perfection." In *The Later Middle Ages: The Context of English Literature,* edited by S. Medcalf. London: Methuen, 1981.

"Joachim of Fiore." In *A Dictionary of Christian Spirituality,* edited by Gordon S. Wakefield. London: SCM Press, 1983.

"Roma profetica." In *La cittá dei segreti: Magia, astrologia, e cultura esoterica a Roma,* edited by F. Troncarelli. Milan: Franco Angeli, 1983.

"The Development of Apocalyptic Thought: Medieval Attitudes." In *The Apocalypse in English Renaissance Thought and Literature,* edited by C. A. Patrides and J. Wittreich. Manchester, Eng.: Manchester University Press, 1984.

"The Third Age: Dante's Debt to Gioacchino da Fiore." In *Atti del II Congresso Internazionale di Studi Gioachimiti.* San Giovanni in Fiore, Italy: Centro di Studi Gioachimiti, 1986.

With Warwick Gould. *Joachim of Fiore and the Myth of the Eternal Evangel in the Nineteenth and Twentieth Centuries.* Oxford: Clarendon Press, 1987; rev. ed., New York: Oxford University Press; Italian translation, forthcoming.

The Crisis in Higher Education: Competence, Delight, and the Common Good. Milton, Keynes, Eng.: SRHE and Open University Press, 1988.

"Joachim of Fiore, Dante and the Prophecy of the Last World Emperor." In *Kathegetria: Essays Presented to Joan Hussey for her Eightieth Birthday,* edited by J. Chrysostomides. Chamberley, Eng.: Porphyrogenitus, 1988.

With H. Lee and G. Silano. *Western Mediterranean Prophecy: The School of Joachim and the Fourteenth-Century Breviloquium.* Toronto: Pontifical Institute of Medieval Studies, 1989.

"Cardinal Egidio of Viterbo and the Abbot Joachim." In *Il Profetismo Gioachimità tra Quattrocento e Cinquecento,* edited by Gian Luca Potestà. Genova: Marietti, 1991.

"The Bible and Literary Authorship in the Middle Ages." In *Reading the Text, Biblical Criticism and Literary Theory,* edited by Stephen Prickett. Oxford: Blackwell, 1991.

Editing contributor. *Prophetic Rome in the High Renaissance Period.* Oxford: Clarendon Press, 1992.

"A Sixty-Year Pilgrimage with the Abbot Joachim." *Florensia* 6 (1992): 7–32.

'The Vaticinia de Summis Pontifiebus: A Question of Authorship." In *Intellectual Life in the Middle Ages: Essays Presented to Margaret Gibson,* edited by Lesley Smith and Benedicta Ward. London: Hambledon Press, 1992.

"Pattern and Purpose in History in the Late Medieval and Renaissance Periods." In *Apocalypse Theory and the Ends of the World,* edited by Malcolm Bull. Oxford: Blackwell, 1995.

"English Apocalyptic Thinkers (c. 1540–1620)." In *Storia e figure dell'Apocalisse fra '500 e '600: Atti del IV Congresso Internazionale di Studi Gioachimiti.* Rome: Viella, 1996.

"Joachim of Fiore." In *Dictionary of Biblical Interpretation,* edited by John H. Hayes. Nashville, Tenn.: Abingdon Press, 1999.

The Prophetic Sense of History in Medieval and Renaissance Europe. Variorum Collected Studies. Aldershot, Eng.: Ashgate, 1999.

CHAPTER 46

Beryl Smalley (1905–1984)
The Medieval Bible in the Modern Academy

HENRIETTA LEYSER AND DEEANA COPELAND KLEPPER

WHEN BERYL SMALLEY turned her attention to the study of medieval Bible commentary in the 1930s, she charted a course for herself that would in time utterly transform the landscape of medieval studies. It was not that Smalley was the first modern scholar to take such literature seriously; scholars of Christian and Jewish religious traditions had been exploring medieval Bible exegesis for some time. Rather, her achievement was to do so from within the discipline of history and to restore the Bible and related literature to its rightful place within medieval society and culture. As unusual as Smalley's intellectual path seemed to others in the academy during the early years of her career, the value of her work soon became apparent. Her disciples were many, and her sphere of influence extended far beyond her perch at Oxford. Many scholars across Europe and North America could echo Robert Lerner's sentiments when he wrote, "I never met Beryl Smalley, but I went to school with her. Perhaps one might even say I took refuge with her."[1] Beryl opened the way for new kinds of questions to be asked and answered, for new kinds of work to emerge alongside the old models. The extent to which her status as a woman in an overwhelmingly male field may have impacted on the direction of her career is hard to determine, but clearly she derived a certain amount of freedom from being an "outsider." With few preconceptions about how a medieval scholar ought to proceed, Smalley fearlessly set out on her own.

Beryl was born on 3 June 1905 at Cheadle in Cheshire, her parents' first child. There were to be three more children, a break during World War I, and then another two, but it was Beryl, the firstborn, who remained all her life a source of astonishment to her parents. Her father, Edgar, a successful Manchester businessman, dealt in cotton,

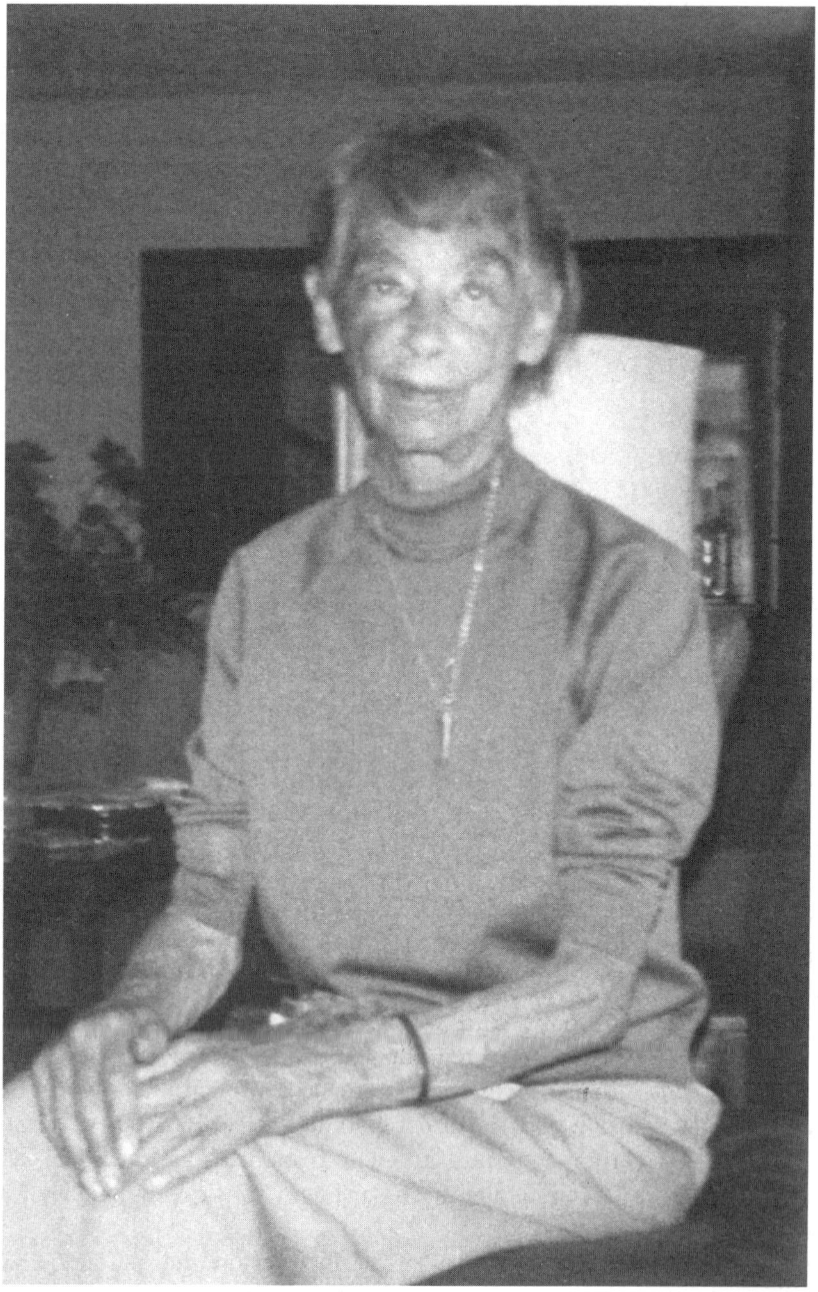

but his chief passion was horses. (Smalley's youngest brother, Richard, would later become the Grand National's starter.) Her mother, Lilian (nee Bowman), to whom she remained devoted until her death at the age of ninety-one, Beryl could sometimes shock—she turned up at the family home, by this time in Derbyshire, in the 1930s in a most outrageous hat from Paris, a pillbox creation no less—but more often Beryl simply perplexed her. There really was, her mother would say, no need for Beryl to work so hard; it was quite unnecessary (and not what was expected) to go to Oxford. Dances, parties, and marriage were the plan. Smalley, never for an instant stuffy, took to both the dances and the parties, but marriage was not part of her horizon. Her family—their marriages, children, and grandchildren—were close to her all her life. As the oldest child she had her own share of parenting early on. She would take the younger ones for walks, write poetry for them, read to them, even, when scarlet fever made school impossible, teach them. The young Smalleys had a nurse but no governess; Beryl had everything in hand. Years later she would attribute her powers of concentration to those nursery years. She grew accustomed to doing her own homework surrounded by clamorous siblings, keeping them satisfied and in order by regular helpings of "yes" and "no." As an established scholar in Oxford, she would punctuate her reading in the Bodleian by these habitual affirmative and negative utterances, much to the astonishment of others in the library.

At thirteen Smalley was sent away to Cheltenham Ladies' College. Cheltenham was, and in some ways still is, an austere, high-minded school. Discipline was rigorous: early-morning runs regardless of the weather, parade-ground-type inspections of clothing and appearance. But founded as it was by Miss Dorothea Beale, a pioneer of women's education and the founder also of Saint Hilda's, Oxford, where Smalley would later go, it was a school committed to academic excellence. Smalley was soon spotted to be a pupil of exceptional promise, and she was not allowed to forget it. The expectations were relentless. In 1923, her last year, Smalley was awarded a scholarship to read history at Saint Hilda's, but she paid a heavy price for the honor. Smalley's toughness had another side, an inner nervosity. Very few who knew her ever saw this, though they may have guessed at it, but her family always recognized the oncoming of crisis times when she would need to be allowed to collapse and to be succored. Today Smalley's condition would be described as anorexic, but back then it was not generally looked for in English society.

In 1924 the role of succorer fell to an aunt, who took Smalley to Rome for some months for a change of air and scenery. Rome supplied both—and something more. It laid the foundation for Smalley's conversion five years later to Catholicism. What it did for her anorexia it is more difficult and possibly unnecessary to know. All her life Smalley smoked heavily and ate little—she could be a most frustrating dinner guest, although sometimes culinary temptation was possible (with stewed red cabbage, for instance). Not that she was in any sense an ascetic. Her youngest sister, Suzanne, remembers well how Smalley, when at Oxford, came to visit her while she was still at school in Cheltenham and the look of horror on the housemistress's face at the full extent of the older sister's glamour, red nails included. As a tutor her elegance was legendary; her pupils felt quite dowdy in her presence. Her colleagues called her Queen Nefertiti, and even in her seventies she could be found asking about "what they are wearing now." It would be wrong to suggest that Smalley was frail. Suzanne remembers how easily her sister could outwalk her, how intrepid she was as a traveler, and friends testify to her zest for impromptu river swims.

As an undergraduate (1924–27) Smalley is an elusive figure: she made a fleeting but unforgettable appearance as the archangel Gabriel in a freshman Nativity play; she earned distinction in her first public examination (History Previous) and exemption from the notorious "divvers" (religious studies); she went to a galaxy of tutors around the university, but none supplanted Agnes Leys, Saint Hilda's medievalist, in her affection. Smalley's great disappointment was getting a second-class degree in her finals, and it was Agnes Leys who stood by her at that critical time. Why Smalley failed has remained a puzzle: some attribute it to her inability to master one of the compulsory texts for the political-science paper or to her distaste for the Stubbsian syllabus, with its heavy bias toward English constitutional and political history. Yet it was this syllabus, virtually unaltered, that she herself would come to teach for twenty-five years with unstinting dedication on succeeding Agnes Leys at Saint Hilda's in 1944. If it dismayed her as an undergraduate, this was not something she betrayed later to her pupils.

Smalley's training at Oxford laid the foundation for her later precision as a teacher. There was never a whisper of subversion of the Oxford syllabus in her tutorials, and those who persevered got their rewards. But to talk about Saint Bernard with Smalley was exhilarating in a way that 1066 had never been. Her tutorials were never sober or dull, but they were both awe inspiring and serious: no smoking (a sacrifice on Smalley's part, whatever it may have meant to her pupils), no backsliding, and you wore your gown. What mattered was scholarship and discipline.

The direction of Smalley's lifework was fixed in her final undergraduate year.[2] She had attended F. M. Powicke's Ford Lectures on Stephen Langton, and Agnes Leys saw to it that they met each other. At the time Powicke (later described by Smalley as "that leaper over academic walls") was beginning to be interested in the vast amount of Langton's work dating from his Paris days that remained unpublished and unstudied.[3] He founded "a little group of students" to carry the discussion further.[4] Smalley became one of the group, and in her first year after finals she served as his research student. Powicke, professor then at Manchester, was based close to Smalley's own home; she could in effect commute between Manchester and Buxton, where her family then lived. Her father was not sympathetic to this prolongation of her academic work; it may have come as a relief that the search for manuscripts took her not only to Cambridge and London but also in early 1929 to Paris.

Smalley's task as allotted by Powicke was the sorting out of Langton's commentaries on the Bible. The work was both pioneering and taxing; it demanded perseverance and exactitude. The manuscript tradition was confused and much of the content dreary. In Paris Smalley was helped and guided by Monsignor Georges Lacombe, a scholar whose subject was the commentaries of Langton's contemporary Prepositinus. In the work they published together in 1931, Smalley gives an impression of both the labors and the occasional rewards of their enterprise: "A very large proportion of Langton's work is composed of extracts from the Gloss, Biblical quotations, allegorical and moral excursions which recall the worst type of twelfth century sermon. It is often necessary to read through many folios of such material before arriving at an interesting *questio* or one of Langton's incomparably pithy *dicta.*"[5]

Reading these folios trained Smalley in manuscript scholarship, but she also found in Paris a new academic home. Subsequently her work would be published as often in French as in English journals. It was in Paris also that she began her friendship with Marie-Thérèse d'Alverny, an outstanding medievalist who, like Smalley, often found the world reluctant to give female scholars their due.

Her doctorate completed, Smalley got a job in 1931 lecturing at Royal Holloway College, London. She turned her scholarly attention to investigating the nature of the Gloss, so often used by Langton. The Gloss was assumed to be the work of the ninth-century German monk Walafrid Strabo; Smalley argued that it was in origin a product of the late eleventh and early twelfth centuries, masterminded at Laon under the aegis of Anselm. The complete story of the Gloss, known by the early thirteenth century as the Glossa ordinaria, may have eluded her—indeed it has yet to be told— but it was Smalley, in Richard Southern's words, who "laid the foundations and indicated the lines of inquiry for the future [and who] made the origins and a large part of the process clear for the first time."[6]

In 1935 Smalley became research fellow at Girton College, Cambridge, although she had not been Girton's first choice. She had published four articles (in addition to her work with Georges Lacombe), but her work was so unusual as to be considered eccentric. In her years at Cambridge Smalley had to validate once and for all the importance of her chosen field for all medieval scholars. It was at Cambridge that *The Study of the Bible in the Middle Ages* took shape. It was conceived, in Smalley's words, as "a history of the origins and development of biblical scholarship . . . through the Middle Ages up to c. 1300."[7] The hero of the book came to be Andrew of Saint Victor (d. ca. 1150). Medieval schoolmen had traditionally favored symbolic exegesis; Andrew's achievement was to begin a reevaluation of the literal meanings of the text: "No western commentator before him had set out to give a purely literal interpretation of the Old Testament, though many had attempted a purely spiritual one. There was general uncertainty as to the content of the letter. There were no rules for defining it, just as there were no rules for establishing one's text. Andrew would have to define how much the literal interpretation included for himself."[8]

In his quandaries Andrew turned to the Jews. It seemed a reasonable assumption that literalism and Jewish exegesis would go hand in hand—and he was right, though this had been so only since the late eleventh century. In her pursuit of Andrew and his methods Smalley herself would need to "go to school with the Jews."[9] As Southern has pointed out, it was for Smalley a considerable solace, in the late 1930s, to be in the position of needing the help of Jewish scholars.[10] Andrew's appeal to them had been made in comparable circumstances: his lifetime too had coincided with the rise of anti-Jewish activity in Europe.

There are perhaps further reasons why Andrew's approach may have appealed to Smalley, especially when set beside her response to Joachim of Fiore (the apocalyptic prophet and abbot). Andrew's literalist exegetical concerns appealed to Smalley's sensibilities; his work could be made to fit into the framework of modern intellectual culture, while Joachim's clearly could not. She never made any attempt to be "objective" about her characters. Writing about her commentators in the preface to *The Gospels in the Schools,* she defends her position: "The historian who studies characters has to establish some sort of contact with them. He has to come clean about his subjective impressions of them as persons. Many commentaries originated in lecture courses. Sitting in on a lecture cannot but make him admire or like, criticise or dislike the lecturer as such."[11]

Joachim was one of those she intensely disliked. In the third edition of *The Study of the Bible,* there is a note of repentance, but it is halfhearted. Joachim and Joachism were no longer "an attack of senile dementia in the spiritual exposition."' The spiritual exposition "in its old age" had, she conceded, "produced a thriving child." But, she continued, "it was not one that I would care to adopt."[12]

Smalley was passionately idealistic, but as the author of *The Study of the Bible* she had already rejected visions of any age to come, such as those Joachim favored. Her concerns had become more immediate and pragmatic. Asked once by her sister what her Marxism meant to her, she replied, "I met my charwoman in the High Street and I carried her baby."[13] Those who knew Smalley can imagine the relish with which she would have said this, a remark as meaningful on one level as it is absurd on another.

It was also at Cambridge and during the writing of *The Study of the Bible* that Smalley had to reconcile her Catholicism with Marxism. Although there is some discrepancy in the memories of her undergraduate contemporaries as to her position in the General Strike of 1926, there can be no doubt that for the best part of her adult life (and most probably for all of it) Smalley was a staunch left-winger.[14] Her conversion to Catholicism in no way represented a lurch to the right. On the contrary, her religious inspiration was derived from the radicals of the church, the Dominicans. Initially her work on *The Study of the Bible* dovetailed nicely with her newfound faith. Both represented a departure from the Protestant traditions of Cheltenham, Saint Hilda's, and Bishop Stubbs. Rome and Paris had offered horizons undreamed of in Derbyshire and only hinted at in the sheltered atmosphere Oxford provided for women in the 1920s. But the traumas of the 1930s demanded that all allegiances be reexamined. Were they adequate for the Herculean task of combating Nazi aggression in Europe? For some, especially after Munich, the Catholic Church became the ark where they could find shelter. Not so for Smalley. It was not so much that she renounced her faith; it simply faded away. The horrors of the here and now seemed to her to require an earthly savior. She turned toward Russia.

Smalley's communism was by no means uncommon in her day, though after the war it never ceased to amaze some of her colleagues at Saint Hilda's. She entertained frequently at high table; a murmured question would go round—Were the guests "h" or "c," historians or communists? Perhaps they were both. But the Hungarian rising of 1956 would change all that; its brutal suppression made it impossible for Smalley to support communism any longer. The lack of a creed, of a basis for social justice, whether religious or secular, she found as impoverishing as it was unavoidable.

The Study of the Bible in the Middle Ages was published in 1941. The middle of the war was a bad time for reviews; those that appeared were not enthusiastic. English scholarship was still insular—Continental interest in medieval learning had barely crossed the Channel—and the book soon went out of print. There was no new edition until 1952. With no permanent job Smalley returned to Oxford to work as a temporary assistant in the Department of Western Manuscripts in the Bodleian. Congenial as this job may have been, it was still a cause of relief and joy to her to be appointed in 1944 the successor to Agnes Leys at Saint Hilda's, where she remained until her retirement in 1969. From 1957 to 1969 Smalley was also vice principal of Saint Hilda's, an exacting office, but one she filled, according to her colleague and fellow historian Menna Prestwich, with a typical blend of irony and conscientiousness. Asked about her duties, she is said to have replied, "[O]ne attends to the seating for guest nights and conferences and sends flowers for illness—and of course for funerals."[15]

If Smalley was an enigma to her parents, so she was also to many of her colleagues and pupils. There were countless paradoxes. She was utterly loyal to her college and yet had no firm friends within it; she was a dedicated teacher, yet the center of her scholarly interests were far removed from nearly everything she taught; she had a heart of gold and could be relied on to give generously of herself to those in any kind of distress, yet it is her acerbic remarks that are the more often remembered. A pupil, for example, returning some work she had been lent, told Smalley she had found it so enthralling she had read it late into the night; the compliment was quickly crushed: "[M]y work is not for bedside reading."[16] She was an ardent socialist who looked as if she had stepped straight out of the pages of *Vogue*. To attempt to fathom such paradoxes would be foolhardy indeed, yet it is worth remembering that even Smalley's singularities had their contexts; it is perhaps her refusal to accommodate herself smoothly to them that gave both her scholarship and her personality their cutting edge and integrity. Her school, her church, her party, her university—each has on occasion drowned lesser mortals in their waters. Smalley, not one to make flamboyant gestures from the bank, would dive gracefully in and then swim against the current.

In 1944, when Smalley became a tutor at Saint Hilda's, the study of medieval manuscripts in England was still regarded as primarily "of antiquarian curiosity, interesting but hardly 'serious.'" M. R. James, best remembered by the general public for his ghost stories, had indeed inspired Eton pupils with a passion for manuscripts, among them Neil Ker and Roger Mynors. (As undergraduates neither had read history.) As scholars at Oxford these two, with Richard Hunt, Christopher Cheney, William Pantin, Richard

Southern, and Smalley, would come to "dominate medieval studies in Britain." The quotations here and the prosopography come from Richard and Mary Rouse's edition of the *Registrum Anglie de libris doctorum et auctorem veterum,* itself a long-awaited offspring.[17] It was within this loose circle that what the Rouses call a move away from "politico-institutional history" first took shape. Smalley's contribution to this development was considerable.

Smalley saw her own work as clustering around three main books, *The Study of the Bible in the Middle Ages* (1941, 1952, 1983), *English Friars and Antiquity in the Early Fourteenth Century* (1960), and *The Becket Conflict and the Schools* (1973). (She seems to have discounted somewhat a more "popular" book, *Historians in the Middle Ages* [1974], written for students and "the general reader," well loved though it is for its wit, lucidity, and idiosyncratic choice of historians.) Her two collections of essays, *Studies in Medieval Thought and Learning from Abelard to Wyclif* (1981) and *The Gospels in the Schools, c. 1100–c. 1280* (1985), were both intended to supplement the main books. Smalley, typically, is her own best critic. In the third edition of *The Study of the Bible,* she refers to her original text as "a period piece."[18] It is in fact a tribute to the work she herself either undertook or generated that it would have required on her own reckoning two volumes rather than one to bring it up to date. *The Gospels in the Schools* presents her major corrective; *The Study of the Bible* had given "only passing glances" to the New Testament.

The Gospels in the Schools, published posthumously, shows both the strengths and the self-imposed limitations of Smalley's work. Her concern, and her primary contribution, was to offer a methodology for scholarly inquiry. When Smalley started her research, the importance of both the Old and the New Testament for an understanding of the Middle Ages had in no way been recognized. In her own lifetime all that was written on biblical models of kingship, on the search for the *vita apostolica,* and on the revival of preaching and the spread among the laity of Franciscan-inspired piety bears witness to the growing realization of the Bible's many and crucial roles. Smalley herself remained committed to the ground level. In the foreword to *The Gospels* she writes that before discussing any commentator one must always ask, "who, when, and where?" next one must trace sources; finally, one can choose further questions: what these are "are his own business."[19] Though she pursues throughout the work a specific question concerning the development of an emerging approach within mendicant exegesis, the situating of the text for the reader—providing a model for study—matters almost as much.

Smalley's very questions—"who, when, where"—come straight from the pages of early-medieval exegesis, "persona, locus, tempus." It is as if she not only read but also internalized the outlook of her commentators. The words of Hugh of Saint Victor throw light on Smalley's methodology:

> It is not without value to call to mind what we see happen in the construction of buildings, when first the foundation is laid, then the structure is raised upon it, and finally, when the work is all finished, the house is decorated by the laying on of colour.

So too, in fact, must it be in your instruction. First you learn history and diligently commit to memory the truth of the deeds that have been performed, reviewing from beginning to end what has been done, where it has been done, and by whom it has been done. For these are the four things which are especially to be sought for in history—the person, the business done, the time and the place.... Do not look down upon these least things. The man who looks down on such smallest things slips little by little.... I know there are certain fellows who want to play the philosopher right away.... The knowledge of these fellows is like that of an ass.... The man who moves along step by step is the one who moves along best.[20]

Smalley would have been in no doubt that in her work on the Bible she was indeed far from "decorating the house"; she explicitly saw herself as offering "guide-lines to future research."[21]

But what of *English Friars and Antiquity*? What of *The Becket Conflict*? There is indeed much more a sense here of finished buildings, possibly because both books are presented as studies in lost causes. In *The Becket Conflict and the Schools,* subtitled *A Study of Intellectuals in Politics in the Twelfth Century* (and delivered in Oxford as the Ford Lectures), we are given an illuminating picture of Becket's circle, a nuanced interpretation of the interplay of principle and self-interest, of personality and theory. But once the drama is over and the blood is off the walls, the protagonists become bored; the quarrel now seems "stale and tiresome."[22] Similarly in *English Friars:* beguiled we may be—as were Smalley's friars (and the example is chosen at random) by tales of Virgil the wizard who "built a palace of clotted air, which reflected absolutely everything in the world"—we still finally have to be brought down to earth.[23] The friars' love of classics is an episode unto itself; the classicizing movement in England does not and could not have turned into humanism. To expect otherwise would be to behave like children planting orange pips, who watch the pips sprout and then are disappointed that they don't turn into fruit. The simile takes us back to the likeness between Smalley and her commentators. Her audience is never allowed to nod off. Her prose is crisp and compelling, and she is as capable as any thirteenth-century friar of introducing *exempla* to make her point: the "attitude to space" among the English public who heard her friars is illustrated by a snippet of conversation overheard in a Derbyshire bus, retold in broad dialect. The concreteness of such comparisons (a quality Smalley herself affectionately ascribes to the work of the Provençal friar Armand de Bezier) keeps us wide-awake and in touch with everyday reality. For historians this is essential—for historians must be levelheaded. They should not expect too much from their characters; on the other hand, they do not have to show much patience with those in their cast who themselves let grandiose ideas get the better of them. We have seen this already in the case of Joachim of Fiore; another example would be John Wycliffe, reprimanded for his refusal to accept Thomas Aquinas's "down-to-earth" solution to the problem of scriptural tenses; his belief that he can change the world leads him to end his life as "a mere bore, inventing fresh insults in default of new ideas."[24]

We can still hear Smalley's voice in the work of her pupils and colleagues. *The Bible in the Medieval World,* written in her honor but published, alas, only as a memorial volume, presents a sampler of the work of a whole generation of medievalists, deeply influenced by Smalley.[25] Not quite ten years after her death, Robert E. Lerner gathered together twenty-one scholars from five countries as participants in a colloquium at Munich's Historische Kolleg on medieval Bible studies with special reference to Smalley's scholarly legacy.[26] In an afterword to the published collection of essays that emerged from the proceedings, Lerner considered how each contribution functioned as a supplement to, complement to, or engagement with Smalley, demonstrating the continued relevance of her work at the close of the twentieth century, but also suggesting the diversity and richness of medieval Bible studies today. A less direct (though no less real) tribute to Smalley took shape around the same time in the formation of the Society for the Study of the Bible in the Middle Ages (SSBMA), a scholarly organization that not only facilitates communication and collaboration among its members but also encourages new scholarship in the field through its sponsorship of special sessions at the International Congress of Medieval Studies at Kalamazoo and the International Medieval Congress at Leeds each year. The society recently engaged in its first collaborative book project; under the leadership of Philip Krey and Lesley Smith, a group composed largely of SSBMA members published a collection of essays on the biblical exegesis of the fourteenth-century friar Nicholas of Lyra. Like the Munich colloquium the collection highlights both the centrality of Smalley to the field and the wide range of work currently being pursued.

Some recent scholarship bears the unmistakable imprint of Smalley herself: studies of Christian Hebraism and Christian use of Jewish exegesis, continued work on the Victorines and the friars from a variety of perspectives, explorations of the culture of Bible study in the earliest schools, and so on. If, in her later years, Smalley came to recognize some of the ways her work had been constrained and limited by her own predispositions, her admirers have managed simultaneously to embrace her work and her methods while pushing in new directions. The spiritual sense she disdained has received a great deal of attention from many scholars either through the examination of specific books (like the Song of Songs) or through the study of specific exegetes, such as Rupert of Deutz or Alexander Minorita. Joachim of Fiore himself and Joachim-inspired exegetes like Peter Olivi have now found a firm place within medieval scholarship, their importance and influence uncontested. New studies are connecting intellectual culture with visual culture through interdisciplinary explorations of medieval Bible illumination, while others are highlighting the importance of biblical interpretation in medieval political culture.[27]

Beyond Smalley's obvious achievement in paving the way for new studies of the medieval Bible, it is also important to recognize the mark she has made on other branches of medieval studies. Whereas once, as Southern found in Paris in the early 1930s, it was possible to study all the vicissitudes of the reign of Charles the Bald without for one moment considering the Old Testament imagery of his kingship, now biblical imagery is recognized as "a central influence in the conduct of business and in the concept of established government."[28] Medieval Europeans were indeed peoples of the book; we accept now that if we are to begin to understand how they thought and acted we must start by looking at their uses of the Bible. This is Smalley's legacy. But she left more besides, explicit pointers to further research: "[T]he comforting thought," as she wrote in her posthumously published *The Gospels in the Schools*, "is that one person's end may mark another's beginning."[29] It is clear that Beryl Smalley's exemplary scholarship—her unremitting journeys through "nettles and thickets," "through unknown, pathless ways"—has made it impossible ever again to marginalize either the Bible or its exegetes.[30]

In *The Medieval Theory of Authorship*, A. J. Minnis pays tribute to Smalley in words she would surely have cherished as an epitaph: she has become a "primary efficient cause," an "efficient cause" being, in Aristotelian terms, "the moving force which brought something from potentiality into actual being."[31] There had indeed been a time in Smalley's career, in the 1930s, when she alone had believed in the potential of her work. It is a measure of her achievement that by the time of her death, on 6 April 1984, it had become impossible to imagine a Middle Ages without the study of its Bible.

NOTES

An earlier version of some of this material appeared in Leyser, "Beryl Smalley (1905–1984)."

1. Lerner with Müller-Luckner, *Neue Richtungen*, 181.
2. For much of what follows, see Richard Southern's memoir, "Beryl Smalley, 1905–1984."
3. Quotation from Smalley, *Becket Conflict and the Schools*, 12.
4. Southern, "Beryl Smalley, 1905–1984," 456.
5. Southern, "Beryl Smalley, 1905–1984," 475.
6. Richard Southern, "Beryl Smalley and the Place of the Bible," 7.
7. Smalley, *Study of the Bible*, 3d ed., vii.
8. Smalley, *Study of the Bible*, 169.
9. Smalley, *Study of the Bible*, 156. Worthy of particular mention here is the important English scholar of Christian Hebraism Raphael Loewe, with whom Smalley enjoyed a long and fruitful collaboration.
10. Southern, "Beryl Smalley, 1905–1984," 460–61.
11. Beryl Smalley, *Gospels in the Schools*, vii.
12. Smalley, *Study of the Bible*, xiii.
13. Suzanne Pinset, Beryl Smalley's sister, conversation with Henrietta Leyser, Maugersburg, 1993.
14. Smalley's embrace of communism, combined with the mystique that seems to have surrounded her personal life generally, led to a widespread, persistent rumor that she went to Spain in the 1930s to assist the Loyalists in the Spanish Civil War. However, inquiries of numerous friends and students turned up nothing to confirm the episode. Beryl's sister Lesley Ling emphatically insists that Smalley never went to Spain, wherever her sympathies may have lain. Ling, telephone conversation with Henrietta Leyser, Oxford, May 2002.
15. Prestwich, "Beryl Smalley," 11.
16. Diana Wood, conversation with Henrietta Leyser, Oxford, 1993.

17. Rouse and Rouse, *Registrum Anglie de libris doctorum et auctorum veterum,* xxi, xxvi, xxvii.
18. Smalley, *Study of the Bible,* vii.
19. Smalley, *Gospels in the Schools,* ix.
20. *Didascalion,* book 6, chaps. 2–3, in Minnis and Scott with Wallace, *Medieval Literary Theory and Criticism,* 74.
21. Smalley, *Gospels and the Schools,* vii.
22. Smalley, *Becket Conflict and the Schools,* 215.
23. Smalley, *English Friars and Antiquity,* 231.
24. Smalley, *Studies in Medieval Thought,* 415.
25. Walsh and Wood, *Bible in the Medieval World.*
26. Lerner with Müller-Luckner, *Neue Richtungen.*
27. For specific titles, see the extensive bibliography at the end of Krey and Smith, *Nicholas of Lyra.* A directory of scholars working in the field, including selected publications, may be found on the SSBMA Web page: http://www.usfca.edu/org/ssbma/.
28. Southern, "Beryl Smalley and the Place of the Bible," 16.
29. Smalley, *Gospels in the Schools,* vii.
30. First quotation: Smalley, *Becket Conflict and the Schools,* 16; second quotation: Smalley, *Study of the Bible in the Middle Ages,* 357.
31. Minnis, *Medieval Theory of Authorship,* xviii, 28.

Select Bibliography of Works by Beryl Smalley

For a complete bibliography of Smalley's writing, see Henrietta Leyser, "Beryl Smalley," 323–24. For Smalley's assessment of her own work, see the preface to the 3d ed. of *The Study of the Bible in the Middle Ages.* In addition to the memorial volume edited by Walsh and Wood, *The Bible in the Medieval World,* see also Lerner with Müller-Luckner, *Neue Richtungen.*

With Georges Lacombe. "Studies on the Commentaries of Cardinal Stephen Langton." *Archives d'histoire doctrinale et littéraire du Moyen Âge* 5 (1930): 5–266.

Hebrew Scholarship among Christians in Thirteenth Century England as Illustrated by Some Hebrew-Latin Psalters. London: Shapiro, Vallentine, 1939.

The Study of the Bible in the Middle Ages. Oxford: Clarendon, 1941; 2d ed., Oxford: Blackwell, 1952; 3d ed., Oxford: Blackwell, 1983.

"Robert Bacon and the Early Dominican School at Oxford." *Transactions of the Royal Historical Society,* 4th ser., 30 (1948): 1–19.

"John Wyclif's *Postilla Super Totam Bibliam.*" *Bodleian Library Record* 4 (1952/53): 186–205.

English Friars and Antiquity in the Early Fourteenth Century. Oxford: Blackwell, 1960.

The Becket Conflict and the Schools: A Study of Intellectuals in Politics in the Twelfth Century. Oxford: Blackwell, 1973.

Historians in the Middle Ages. London: Thames and Hudson, 1974.

Studies in Medieval Thought and Learning from Abelard to Wyclif. London: Hambledon, 1981.

The Gospels in the Schools, c. 1100–c. 1280. London: Hambledon, 1985.

Works Cited

Krey, Philip D. W., and Lesley Smith, eds. *Nicholas of Lyra: The Senses of Scripture.* Leiden: Brill, 2000.

Lerner, Robert E., ed., with the assistance of Elisabeth Müller-Luckner. *Neue Richtungen in der hoch- und spätmittelalterlichen Bibelexegese.* Schriften des Historischen Kollegs: Kolloquien 32. Munich: R. Oldenbourg Verlag, 1996.

Leyser, Henrietta. "Beryl Smalley (1905–1984)." In *History,* vol. 1 of *Medieval Scholarship: Biographical Studies on the Formation of a Discipline,* edited by Helen Damico and Joseph B. Zavadil, 313–24. New York: Garland Publishing, 1995.

Minnis, A. J. *The Medieval Theory of Authorship: Scholastic Literary Attitudes in the Later Middle Ages.* 2d ed. Aldershot, Eng.: Wildwood House, 1988.

Minnis, A. J., and A. B. Scott, with the assistance of David Wallace, eds. *Medieval Literary Theory and Criticism, c. 1100–c. 1375: The Commentary-Tradition.* Oxford: Clarendon, 1988.

Prestwich, Menna. "Beryl Smalley." *Saint Hilda's College Record* (1984): 10–12.

Rouse, Richard, and Mary Rouse, eds. *Registrum Anglie de libris doctorum et auctorum veterum.* London: British Library, 1991.

Southern, R. W. "Beryl Smalley, 1905–1984." *Proceedings of the British Academy* 72 (1986): 455–71.

———. "Beryl Smalley and the Place of the Bible in Medieval Studies, 1927–84." In *The Bible in the Medieval World: Essays in Memory of Beryl Smalley,* edited by Katherine Walsh and Diana Wood. Oxford: Blackwell, 1985.

Walsh, Katherine, and Diana Wood, eds. *The Bible in the Medieval World: Essays in Memory of Beryl Smalley.* Oxford: Blackwell, 1985.

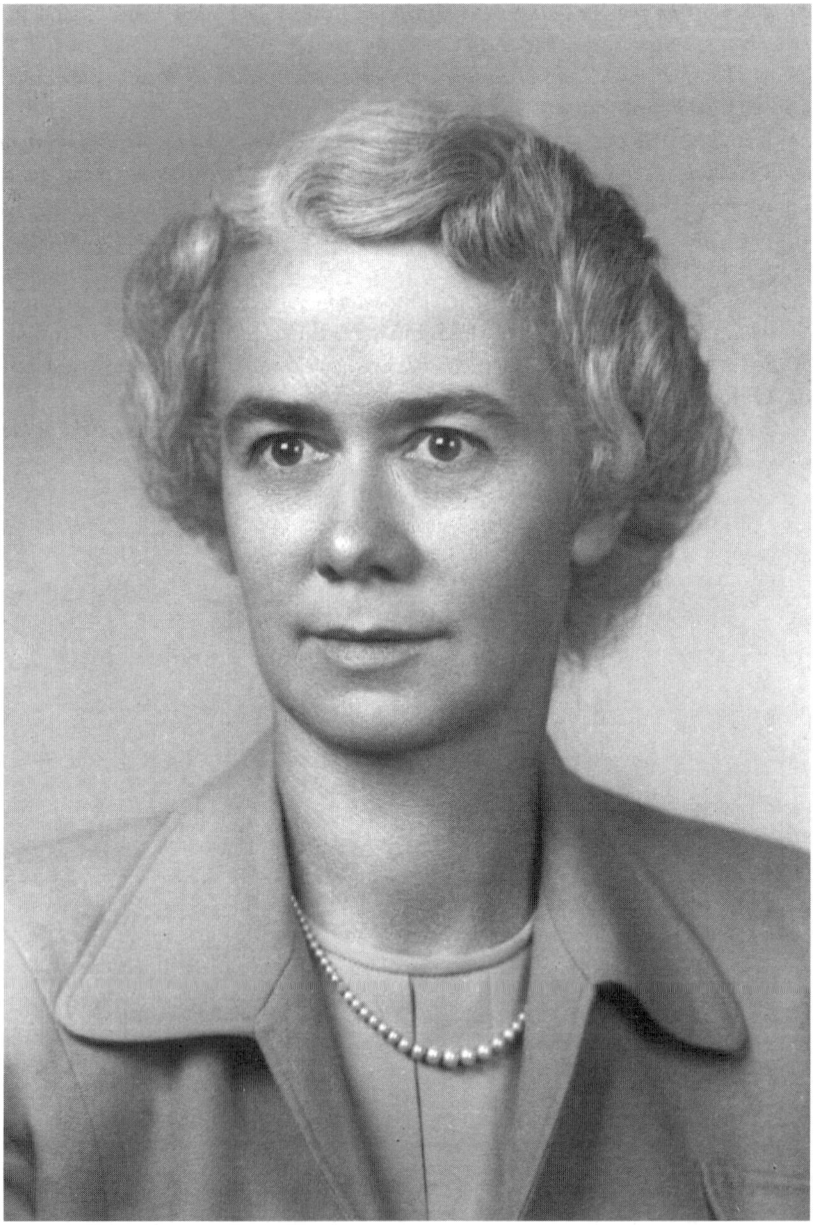

CHAPTER 47

Cora Elizabeth Lutz (1906–1985)
Magistra Egregii

Deanna Delmar Evans

PEOPLE USUALLY LOOK FORWARD to retirement as a time for doing what they please. For New Englanders this often includes a desire to move south in order to enjoy a more leisurely lifestyle in a warmer climate. Retirement from college teaching provided the late Professor Cora E. Lutz with time for doing what she pleased, but what pleased this New Englander was quite out of the ordinary. Instead of heading south, she moved north, returning to her native state of Connecticut, and her idea of a more leisurely lifestyle was to spend six years describing and cataloging pre-1600 manuscripts for the Beinecke Library at Yale. Her "leisure-time" activities consisted of writing many library articles and publishing three books. Thus, in retirement as throughout the earlier portions of her life, Cora Lutz ever demonstrated her "Yankee ingenuity."

Cora Elizabeth Lutz and her twin brother, Frank, were born on 23 October 1906 in Rockville, Connecticut, children of George W. and Cora Townsend Lutz.[1] The twins completed the Lutz family, which at the time of their birth included an older daughter, Hazel, born in 1902. Of the three Cora alone pursued a career in higher education, although her sister became an art supervisor in the Manchester School System in Connecticut. Her twin brother became the owner of a hardware store in Vernon, Connecticut. Despite their different career paths, the siblings remained close throughout their lives, even dying within months of one another. A victim of cancer, Cora Lutz died on 28 March 1985. Her sister preceded her in death by only two months, and her twin brother died in March of the following year.

None of the three ever married. Whatever the reasons for her siblings' choices, Cora's decision to remain single is hardly surprising; married women of her generation had few opportunities to advance in the academic world. She perceived that women could not "have it all," and so, according to Barbara A. Shailor, Lutz advised promising female students to avoid marriage if they were serious about their careers.[2] Yet on one occasion Lutz humorously acknowledged that having a spouse could be advantageous. Ann Matter, a graduate student at Yale during Lutz's years at the Beinecke, recalls that Lutz once remarked that she would have had an easier time in the academic world if she had had a wife. "Remember, dear," she said to Matter, "all those men you will work with will have wives doing their laundry and cooking their meals."[3]

Cora Lutz received all of her education in her native state; she was, as the writers of the memorial tribute to her in *Speculum* note, "first and last a Connecticut woman."[4] In 1923 Lutz entered Connecticut College for Women, and while there often used the nickname "Cody," acquired during her youth.[5] She graduated with an A.B. in 1927 and was named a Winthrop scholar for academic excellence.[6] She received many other collegiate honors, including election to Phi Beta Kappa; moreover, she received the Greek prize two years in a row. In her senior year she also was awarded the botany prize, an unexpected accomplishment for a student of classical languages, but the honor seems not to have been a fluke. Lutz maintained a lifelong interest in horticulture. Matter recalls that Lutz took pride in growing African violets, while John Cavadini, also a Yale graduate student when Lutz worked at the Beinecke, was hired to help her with gardening chores. Cavadini recalls her love of pink flowers: "She always had impatiens, and she always asked me to buy a flat or two 'in variegated shades of pink.'"[7] Lutz and Cavadini became good friends, often discussing academic as well as horticultural topics, and their friendship lasted throughout the remainder of Lutz's life.

Lutz was certified to teach Latin, Greek, archaeology, and ancient history when she graduated from Connecticut College. She put her expertise to use when she was hired as a teacher at Killingly High School in Danielson, Connecticut. She spent two years there (1927–29) teaching Latin, French, and ancient history. She left her job at Killingly to enroll in the graduate program in classical languages at Yale. Lutz also began her career as a college instructor at that time: in 1930 she was hired to teach sophomore Latin at Albertus Magnus College in New Haven.

Women students were a rarity in graduate programs at Yale in 1930. Cora Lutz found herself part of a select minority and, as such, sometimes endured gender bias. Years later she shared stories about her early Yale experiences with Barbara Shailor. One such story concerns a certain professor who would walk into the classroom, turn his back on the few women students huddled together, and then, facing the male students, would begin his lecture with the word "Gentlemen." Yet Lutz enjoyed happy experiences during her graduate student days as well. She lived in the Graduate House for Women on Prospect Street in New Haven and there made many lifelong friendships with women from a variety of disciplines.[8] Moreover, Lutz quickly proved her academic mettle: she was named a university scholar in classics and received her Ph.D. in 1935.

With her new doctorate in hand Cora Lutz in 1935 made her first and only move south: she had been hired as assistant professor of classics at Judson College in Marion, Alabama. Lutz taught at Judson for two years but then, perhaps because she missed the leaves of a New England autumn, packed her bags and headed north in 1937. The move was to Chambersburg, a quiet college town in central Pennsylvania.

The reason for Lutz's move was to assume a new position, assistant professor of classical languages at Wilson College. Lutz continued to teach Latin and Greek at Wilson for more than thirty years, until she took early retirement in 1969. She moved through the academic ranks, being promoted to associate professor of classics in 1944 and to professor in 1950; the same year she was elected chairperson of the Department of Classical Languages and held that office until her retirement.

From all accounts Lutz enjoyed teaching at Wilson. She had close friends among the faculty, including her longtime colleague Professor Ruth Hicks.[9] Another close friend at Wilson, according to Barbara Shailor, was Marian H. Mowatt, who taught at Wilson between 1937 and 1939; Lutz was godmother to Mowatt's daughter. As her scholarly reputation grew, Lutz had opportunities to move to larger universities where she could have taught in graduate programs, but she always declined such offers. When questioned about the reason, Shailor replied that Lutz chose to stay at Wilson because she believed that within the setting of a small liberal arts college for women, she could better influence women's lives. Indeed, Lutz did help shape the careers of many talented Wilson students, Shailor herself providing a case in point.[10]

Julia Billings, a member of the Wilson class of 1938, recalls studying with Lutz during the latter's assistant professor years: "We who knew her in the '30s valued her sympathetic interest in our lives, her attention to our problems, whether personal or academic, and her amused laughter at our escapades. She was the perfect model of a charming lady, but beneath the ladylike demeanor was an uncompromising scholar, unforgettable to students like myself, who quaked beneath her scorn of mediocrity."[11] Shailor, a Wilson student during Lutz's final years of teaching, concurs with Billings that Lutz demanded much of students, but adds that Lutz encouraged qualified students to participate in "study abroad" programs to Italy and Greece and to attend graduate school. Shailor remarked that Lutz was not likely to have described herself as a feminist, yet she frequently went out of her way to help women pursue their academic dreams.

It was out of gratitude to Lutz's strong interest in student development that the Wilson class of 1955 dedicated its yearbook to her. In addition Lutz's teaching excellence was recognized by her peers: at commencement in 1962 she received the Christian R. and Mary F. Lindback Foundation Award for Distinguished Teaching at Wilson College. Her excellence as a teacher was recognized at other women's colleges as well: in 1962 she was invited to deliver the Earle Lecture at Hunter College (a public lecture directed toward the encouragement of Greek). Lutz's desire to help women succeed in the academic world continued after she had moved on to her position at the Beinecke, where it was her policy to employ women students as her research assistants. Ann Matter, one Yale graduate student Lutz befriended, remembers her as "an elegant person of good taste; a lovely person, very kind, very encouraging to students."[12] Matter also found Lutz wise about academic politics. In discussing their friendship Matter commented that she had invited Lutz to serve on her dissertation committee, but Lutz declined, pointing out that as a library cataloger she would lack the power to help the younger woman if any of the professorial members of the committee, all men, engaged in gender politics.[13]

Cora Lutz was ever the scholar, evident at the outset of her professional career. In 1934–35 she was elected president of the Alabama Classical Association. Throughout her professional life, she maintained active memberships in several professional organizations, including the American Philological Association, the Medieval Academy of America, the Renaissance Society of America, the Classical Association of the Atlantic States, the Connecticut Academy of Arts and Sciences, and the American Association of University Women. Lutz spent many summers abroad engaged in research: she worked at the British Museum (1936), in Italy (1937), and at major libraries in Italy, Switzerland, Holland, and France (1951). During the spring of 1955, she was on sabbatical leave and traveled to England, where she did research at the British Museum and in libraries at Cambridge and Oxford Universities. To help finance her research, Lutz applied for highly competitive fellowships. She was awarded a Kellogg Research Fellowship (1943–44) and also achieved the rare distinction of twice receiving Guggenheim Fellowships (1949–50; 1954–55).

While teaching at Wilson, Lutz established her scholarly reputation. Because of her editions of Latin commentaries and several significant articles, she became recognized as an authority on the commentaries of Martianus Capella, the fifth-century North African Roman scholar best known for having authored *De nuptiis Philologiae et Mercurii* (On the marriage of Philology and Mercury). But Lutz's earliest edition of one of those commentaries met with some harsh criticism.

Iohannis Scotti: Annotationes in Marcianum, Lutz's first edition, was published by the Mediaeval Academy of America in 1939. Her book provides the complete transcription of the glosses made by John the Scot (John Scottus Eriugena), the ninth-century philosopher, on Martianus Capella. Dino Bigongiari of Columbia University reviewed that edition for *Classical Philology*. After years of hard work on her edition, Lutz must have been heartbroken as she read that 1941 review. Bigongiari says, "The reason why I call this publication unscholarly is that too often the editor shows herself unable to understand the text or incapable of dealing with the problems it presents."[14] Bigongiari complains that Lutz makes "unnecessary and erroneous emendations of sound passages," retains "faulty readings," and creates a "dislocation of the text through misleading punctuation" (74). He devotes the last five pages of the review to a list of perceived errors, proudly boasting that he was "able to detect [them] in the course of a hasty reading and with no access to the manuscript" (75).

Even though Bigongiari documents his criticism, one cannot help but wonder if he did not overemphasize the presence of errors because the editor of the manuscript was a young woman daring to tread on scholarly turf traditionally reserved for a few men. While my statement perhaps reflects the bias of a feminist biographer, it gains credibility, I believe, when Bigongiari's negative review is compared with another published during the same year.

No less of a scholar than E. K. Rand of Harvard University reviewed the edition for *Speculum*. Rand welcomes Lutz's volume as "a complete and satisfactory edition of a work of exceeding significance in the history of early mediaeval culture."[15] Moreover, he establishes himself as an authority on the manuscript, noting that he had studied it in 1899, "hoping at the time to publish the Commentary myself" (129–30), and he identifies Lutz's mentor on Martianus commentaries as Professor E. T. Silk (of Yale), for whom he shows great respect. Rand points out that Lutz's edition was based on the only extant manuscript, a "book of Corbie from the ninth century" (119), and that although parts of that manuscript had been published earlier, Lutz was the first to publish it in entirety.

In commenting about the edition specifically, Rand commends Lutz for having "carefully described" the manuscript and comments, "The text of the one manuscript is reproduced with its spellings (most commendably) but its text is treated to necessary emendation here and there" (130). He also compliments Lutz for her valuable introduction and her three appendices completing the book. Rand says that in the third appendix Lutz "successfully" refutes the once popular assumption that the commentary "was largely dependent on that of Dunchad" (131). Moreover, at the end of the review, Rand offers a note of encouragement: "We need a fresh examination of the two manuscripts . . . in which the commentary . . . is generally regarded as that of Remigius. But that inquiry must await another occasion, or, preferably, be undertaken by Dr Lutz or her master, Professor Silk" (131).[16] Eventually Lutz would produce that edition.

Lutz's second edition, *Dunchad: Glossae in Martianum* (Dunchad's glosses on Martianus), was published by the American Philological Association in 1944. Charles W. Jones of Cornell University reviewed it for *Speculum*. No doubt aware of the earlier assault on Lutz's scholarship, Jones acknowledges that Lutz has taken on "the thankless task of editing early medieval glosses" and acknowledges the value of her edition: it makes "available one more sample of the academic patterns of the ninth century, when the very foundation of our western educational tradition was being laid."[17] Jones adds that "[g]losses on the liberal arts require so catholic a knowledge that it is easy to quarrel with the inevitable unevenness of editing" (359). Among his harshest comments are that "the editor sees Neoplatonists lurking in the bushes" and makes an unlikely attribution to Bede (359).

Lutz, in spite of critical reviews, continued her research on the medieval commentary writers during the 1950s, devoting her attention to Remigius of Auxerre. Between 1955 and 1960 she published four articles on Remigius in distinguished journals: two focus specifically on Remigius and the seven liberal arts. Then in 1962 she published the first volume of her two-volume edition of Remigius's commentaries (*Commentum in Martianum Capellam*). With that edition she fulfilled the request

Rand had made some twenty years earlier. Yet again the reviewers were not entirely grateful.

The first volume of Remigius was reviewed for *Speculum* in 1964 by Marvin Colker of the University of Virginia. Finding Lutz's scholarly introduction valuable, Colker is less positive about her editing of the text; he believes that "certain weaknesses occur."[18] He also complains that Lutz lists only thirty-seven manuscripts of the commentary out of the more than seventy known to her: Colker indicates that "the full list would have been more instructive" (719). He concludes, however, that, in spite of the errors, "there is also evidence of painstaking effort, and the sections on the sources and influence of the commentary are particularly useful" (721).

Lutz's second volume of Remigius's commentaries was published in 1965 and reviewed for *Speculum* by Philip Levine of UCLA. Levine notes that this volume "completes a long-term project dealing with texts of ninth-century commentaries on staples of medieval education," bringing "the worthy enterprise to a successful conclusion."[19] But Levine also points out flaws: "Miss Lutz could have rendered an even greater service to scholars if, besides the explicit citations or allusions made by Remigius himself, she had identified and included among the testimonia also the numerous unacknowledged borrowings, or at least the more important of them, whether directly or indirectly transmitted from earlier writers" (394). Levine attempts to improve on Lutz's work by offering in the review a stemma, which he says he constructed out of "the basis of the evidence available in her apparatus" (395–96). Yet the review ends with a note of gratitude: "Lutz has produced an estimable scholarly edition of an important commentary that has lain too long neglected. This work will surely bring her the warm commendation and sincere gratitude of all those who have occasion to use it" (397).

This pastiche of critical remarks shows that with every edition she published Lutz had to endure criticism; it is hardly surprising that she refrained from editing the works of tenth-century "schoolmasters." Even on the "home front" her scholarly editions sometimes received only a lukewarm response. Ann Matter relates a story about such an occasion: "Miss Lutz told me once about a faculty meeting at Wilson when she published her book on Remigius of Auxerre. The President of Wilson went on and on about the young male faculty member whose wife had just had a baby—how big the baby was, what its name was, etc. Then he said dismissively, 'and Miss Lutz has just published another book—but you will have to ask her what it is called because I cannot pronounce the title!'" Matter concludes the tale with an insightful editorial comment: "She told me this story with scorn, even though she was a gentle person. She felt the slights of a woman in academe very personally."[20]

Although editing medieval commentaries took considerable time and effort, Lutz also devoted some of her scholarly energy to topics in the area of classical studies. In 1947 her edition and translation of the works of *Musonius Rufus: "The Roman Socrates"* was published by Yale University Press, and in the early 1950s she published three articles on various "Classical" topics: one she called a "footnote" on dogs in Homer; she also wrote an essay on Juvenal and another concerning Democritus and Heraclitus.

After more than thirty years of teaching at Wilson and making substantial contributions to scholarship, Lutz officially retired on 25 May 1969. But, as noted earlier, her academic career was far from over. She returned to Yale later that year, and then, for the next six years, undertook the challenging task of cataloging and describing pre-1600 manuscripts for the Beinecke Library. Marjorie G. Wynne, then reference librarian at the Beinecke, describes the magnitude of Lutz's task: "Since Elihu Yale's gift of the *Speculum humanae salvationis* in 1714, the library had acquired over 800 codices and several hundred single leaves, all unnumbered and uncatalogued.... From 1969 to 1975 Miss Lutz examined, sorted and for the first time described these manuscripts for the benefit of scholars everywhere, and her work provides the basis for the full-scale catalogue ... [subsequently] prepared and published by her assistant and successor, Barbara Shailor."[21]

When asked to describe the experience of working with Lutz on the catalog, Shailor noted that Lutz possessed the remarkable ability to transcribe, read, and translate at the same time and was not afraid to ask for information in subject areas where she herself lacked expertise. Describing her as an avid letter writer, Shailor noted that some of Lutz's favorite scholarly correspondents were Edward Cranz at Connecticut College and Paul Kristeller at Columbia University. The significance of Lutz's pioneer work on the Beinecke catalog is summed up in the Lutz "Memoirs" published in *Speculum:* "Her twelve-volume typewritten catalogue of pre-1600 manuscripts in the Beinecke Library was itself a major achievement and provided the groundwork for the finished catalogue."[22] Lutz also continued to receive academic honors. In 1970 she was awarded the Connecticut College Medal by her alma mater and in 1975 election to the Fellowship of the Medieval Academy of America.

While working on the Beinecke catalog and afterward, Lutz continued in her own scholarly endeavors, publishing three books and more than thirty articles. Most of the articles were inspired by her direct contact with manuscripts and rare books in the Beinecke and published in the *Yale University Library Gazette*. As Wynne observes, "[I]t was unlike Miss Lutz merely to count folios, identify texts, and analyze handwriting, in addition, she read the words themselves and then, in a series of felicitous essays, gave voice to manuscripts that would otherwise have remained mute."[23] Eventually Lutz republished many of these essays in book collections—*Essays on Manuscripts and Rare Books* (1975) and *The Oldest Library Motto and Other Library Essays* (1979).

During her retirement Lutz also published *Schoolmasters of the Tenth Century* (1977). In many ways this book serves as a "sequel" to Lutz's editions of ninth-century medieval commentaries. In *Schoolmasters* she provides a series of biographical portraits of several of the great scholars of the tenth century: some of those included are Aelfric, Bruno, Notker, Odo, Dunstan, and Oswald. For her efforts Lutz was awarded a Bollinger Fellowship. Moreover, she found particular enjoyment in writing this book. In a personal letter dated 2 March 1977, she remarks, "It was such a joyous experience to investigate these wonderful people that I may have been carried away sometimes."[24] Because *Schoolmasters* is largely expository in nature and clearly written, it is a valuable resource for general readers and highly suitable for undergraduate libraries. Lutz's intention in writing the book, in my opinion, was to draw on her own wealth of knowledge based on more than forty years of research and to make that knowledge available to a nonspecialized audience.

Not all of Lutz's scholarly attention during her retirement years was devoted to medieval and classical topics. She became interested in Ezra Stiles, an eighteenth-century New England Puritan who served as a president of Yale College. Lutz's curiosity about Stiles undoubtedly was tweaked by her Yale pride and her "Connecticut Yankee" heritage. She completed four essays on Stiles, the last published posthumously in the *Yale University Library Gazette* in 1999.[25] In that particular article Lutz describes a book written by Stiles on three of the men who had participated in the execution of the Stuart king Charles I. The regicides escaped prosecution by emigrating to Massachusetts and Connecticut, and one of them, Lutz argues, is the source for the New England myth known as "the angel" of Hadley.

Lutz retired from her work on the Beinecke catalog when her health began to decline. During her final years she enjoyed her home in Mount Carmel, Connecticut. Yet she continued to maintain her scholarly correspondence and enjoyed visiting with siblings, friends, former students, and Yale graduate students. John Cavadini was one who visited her regularly, often bringing his entire family with him. About those visits Cavadini, in an e-mail message dated 1 November 2001, writes: "She was not accustomed to being around children, but she discovered how much she actually enjoyed them, unexpectedly to her, I think. She always commented how all her life long she had in her mind berated 'doting grandmothers' who seemed to make such a fuss about their young grandchildren, but she said that now she could easily see herself becoming just such a doting grandmother (mutatis mutandis)."

Lutz's contributions as a woman medievalist were so many and so varied that it is impossible to list them all. Yet while I reread *Schoolmasters of the Tenth Century*, it became evident to me that Lutz, in that book, reveals her own values of what a teacher-scholar should be. What Lutz describes as the most admirable qualities in the medieval schoolmasters are the very qualities that she exhibited in her own life and work. In the first chapter of *Schoolmasters* Lutz explains that teachers of the arts in tenth-century church schools "experienced a sense of mission, a feeling of obligation to pass on their learning."[26] Lutz felt such a "sense of mission" in her own teaching, writing, scholarly editing, and in constructing a catalog for the Beinecke Library.

In the final chapter of *Schoolmasters* Lutz delineates what she calls "the legacy" of those great medieval teachers:

> These men were never mere passive links in the chain of scholars who bridge the chasm between Remigius of Auxerre in the ninth century and Fulbert of Chartres in the eleventh. The intellectual and spiritual legacy they left to their students and their age constitutes a truer measure of their real worth as teachers than the bare account of their schoolroom achievements. . . . [T]he most precious bequest of these teachers

was the light they brought to dispel the darkness of their times. . . . [T]hese men gave their lives to kindling torches to restore knowledge and virtue. . . . By kindling the light of learning, the schoolmasters became the benefactors of all of their people. In the more restricted field of teaching, they made at least three important bequests to scholarship: a concept of the teacher as an understanding guide to the young; some innovative methods for presenting the liberal arts; and the libraries which they were instrumental in assembling. (149–50)

When she died at the age of seventy-eight in Mount Carmel, Cora Elizabeth Lutz had herself left such a legacy. She was far more than a "passive link" in the American academic community between the Great Depression and the conclusion of the Vietnam War. Her "bequests to scholarship" may be seen to parallel those of the schoolmasters. As a classroom instructor and faculty advisor, she proved herself an "understanding guide to the young," especially young women. She used "innovative methods" in both her teaching and scholarship. Not only did she convey knowledge of the "liberal arts," but through her work on Remigius, she adds to our knowledge of that concept and its history. Then ever relying on her "Yankee ingenuity," she devised a plan that would result in a catalog of rare books and early manuscripts for the Beinecke Library, proving that she, like those men of old, could be "instrumental in assembling" a library. Truly Cora Lutz was one who devoted her life to kindling "the light of learning," thus becoming the benefactor of many.

Notes

1. The dates of birth and death for Lutz and her siblings were confirmed from the *Connecticut Death Index, 1949–1996,* Connecticut Department of Health, Hartford, Conn.[database online] [cited 15 August 2002]; available from Ancestry Plus, powered by Ancestry.com, Provo, Utah, available from http.//www.gale.ancestry.com/ggmain.htm.

2. Barbara Shailor, Yale University, personal interview with biographer, New Haven, Conn., 16 August 2001. All subsequent references to Shailor, unless specifically quoted from another source, are from this interview. I am indebted to Dr. Shailor, who generously loaned me a folder containing various documents pertaining to Cora Lutz's life, including a professional vita Lutz had filed with the Beinecke Library and an almost complete bibliography of her writings. Many of the details about Lutz's life mentioned in this essay are taken from that vita. I am further indebted to Dr. Shailor for reading through and correcting an earlier draft of this biographical essay.

3. E. Ann Matter, University of Pennsylvania, e-mail to biographer, 26 October 2001. I am grateful to Barbara Shailor for putting me in touch with Dr. Matter (see n. 2).

4. Cranz, Dean, and Robinson, "Cora E. Lutz," 263.

5. Catherine Phinizy, archivist at Connecticut College, e-mail to biographer, 6 August 2001; this information was confirmed by Barbara Shailor (see n. 2).

6. Wanda Finney, archivist at C. Elizabeth Boyd 1933 Archives, Wilson College, mailed to biographer with cover letter, dated 15 June 2001, several materials about Lutz's professional life. Among these documents were photocopies of Lutz's vita, one from 1962 and one ca. 1969; from these I draw most of my textual information about Lutz's academic career. I am most

grateful to Dr. Finney for making these and other documents available to me as well as for locating a suitable photograph for this publication; she also has replied to my queries through e-mail messages. Finally, I am indebted to her for putting me in contact with Barbara Shailor (see n. 2).

7. John Cavadini, Notre Dame University, e-mail to biographer, 1 November 2001; all subsequent references to Cavadini are based on this correspondence. I am grateful to E. Ann Matter for putting me in touch with Cavadini (see n. 3).

8. From a personal letter dated 24 May 1985, written by one of the women who resided with Lutz in the graduate house. I am grateful to Barbara Shailor for showing me this letter, addressed to her after Lutz's death.

9. Wanda Finney, telephone conversation with author, 6 August 2001.

10. Shailor currently is the director of the Rare Book and Manuscript Library at the Beinecke Library; earlier she enjoyed a successful teaching career in classics at Bucknell University and Rutgers University.

11. Billings, "Cora Lutz," 18. I am grateful to Wanda Finney for providing me with a copy of this obituary (see n. 9).

12. E. Ann Matter, e-mail to biographer, 26 October 2001; in an e-mail to biographer dated 16 November 2001, Matter observes, "Cora Lutz was always called—by all of us—Miss Lutz, never Dr. Lutz" because "the Yale world did not use Dr. for professors."

13. E. Ann Matter, in an informal discussion following biographer's presentation of a paper on Lutz at the Thirty-fifth International Congress on Medieval Studies, Western Michigan University, Kalamazoo, Michigan, 3 May 2002.

14. Bigongiari, review of *Johannis Scoti,* 73–74. Subsequent citations from this work in the paragraph are documented with page numbers in parentheses in the text.

15. Rand, review of *Iohannis Scotti,* 129. Subsequent citations from this work are documented with page numbers in parentheses in the text.

16. Even though Rand's review is largely positive, it is probable that Bigongiari's negative review helped pave the way for later scholars to validate the need for new editions of Martianus Capella: see, for example, James Willis, ed., *Martianus Capella* (Leipzig: B. G. Teubner, 1983).

17. Jones, review of *Dunchad: Glossae in Martianum,* 358–359. Subsequent citations from this work in the paragraph are documented with page numbers in parentheses in the text.

18. Colker, review of *Remigii Autissiodorensis Commentum in Martianum Capellam,* 719. Subsequent citations from this work in the paragraph are documented with page numbers in parentheses in the text.

19. Levine, review of *Remigii Autissiodorensis Commentum in Martianum Capellam,* 394. Subsequent citations from this work in the paragraph are documented with page numbers in parentheses in the text.

20. E. Ann Matter, e-mail to biographer, 26 October 2001.

21. Wynne, "Cora Elizabeth Lutz."

22. Cranz, Dean, and Robinson, "Cora E. Lutz," 763.

23. Wynne, "Cora Elizabeth Lutz," 9.

24. Quoted from Cranz, Dean, and Robinson, "Cora E. Lutz," 764.

25. My summary of "Ezra Stiles and the Legend of the Angel of Hadley," by Cora Lutz.

26. Lutz, *Schoolmasters of the Tenth Century,* 9. A subsequent citation from this work in the paragraph is documented with page numbers in the text.

Select Bibliography of Works by Cora Elizabeth Lutz

Iohannis Scotti: Annotationes in Marcianum. Cambridge, Mass.: Mediaeval Academy of America, 1939.

Dunchad: Glossae in Martianum. Lancaster, Pa.: American Philological Association, 1944.

Musonius Rufus: The Roman Socrates. Section of Yale Classical Studies, vol. 10. New Haven, Conn.: Yale University Press, 1947.

"Any Resemblance—Is Purely Coincidental": On Juvenal. *Classical Journal* 46 (1950): 115–21.

"Footnote to Professor Scott's *Dogs in Homer.*" *Classical Weekly* 43 (1950): 89–90.

"Democritus and Heraclitus." *Classical Journal* 49 (1954): 309–15.

"The Use of the Letters 'M' and 'N' in Certain Manuscripts of Remigius." *Athenaeum* 30 (1955): 343–44.

"Remigius' Ideas on the Origin of the Seven Liberal Arts." *Medievalia et Humanistica* 10 (1956): 37–49.

"Remigius' Ideas on the Classification of the Seven Liberal Arts." *Traditio* 12 (1956): 65–86.

"The Commentary of Remigius of Auxerre on Martianus Capella." *Mediaeval Studies* 19 (1957): 137–58.

"One Formula of *Accessus* in Remigius' Works." *Latomus* 19 (1960): 774–80.

Remigius Autissiodorensis: Commentum in Martianum Capellam. 2 vols. Leiden: Brill, 1962–65.

"Aesticampianus' Edition of the *Tabula* Attributed to Cebes." *Yale University Library Gazette* 45 (1971): 110–17.

"A Diamond and a Dürer in Dubravius' Commentary on Martianus Capella." *Yale University Library Gazette* 46 (1971): 89–96.

"Letaldus: A Wit of the Tenth Century." *Viator* 1 (1971): 97–106.

"Martianus Capella." *Catalogus translationum et commentariorum* 2 (1971): 367–81.

"Walter Burley's 'De vita et moribus philosophorum.'" *Yale University Library Gazette* 46 (1972): 247–52.

"Aesticampianus' Commentary on the *De Grammatica* of Martianus Capella." *Renaissance Quarterly* 26 (1973): 157–66.

"Johannes Climacus' *Ladder of Divine Ascent.*" *Yale University Library Gazette* 47 (1973): 224–27.

"A Manuscript from Bede's Monastery." *Yale University Library Gazette* 48 (1973): 135–38.

"A Manuscript of Charlemagne's *Homiliarium.*" *Yale University Library Gazette* 47 (1972): 100–102.

"A Medieval Textbook." *Yale University Library Gazette* 48 (1974): 212–16.

"The *Theriobulia* of Jan Dubravius." *Harvard Library Bulletin* 22 (1974): 36–46.

Essays on Manuscripts and Rare Books. New Haven, Conn.: Archon, 1975.

"The Letter of Lentulus Describing Christ." *Yale University Library Gazette* 50 (1975): 91–97.

"Manuscripts Copied from Printed Books." *Yale University Library Gazette* 49 (1975): 261–67.

Schoolmasters of the Tenth Century. New Haven, Conn.: Archon, 1977.

"The Clock of Eternal Wisdom." *Yale University Library Gazette* 53 (1978): 79–85.

"A Forged Manuscript in [N]oustrophedon." *Yale University Library Gazette* 53 (1978): 39–44.

"The 'Gentle Puritan' and the 'Angelic Doctor.'" *Yale University Library Gazette* 52 (1978): 122–26.

The Oldest Library Motto and Other Library Essays. New Haven, Conn.: Archon, 1979.

"The Salmasius-Elichmann Edition of the *Tabula* of Cebes." *Harvard Library Bulletin* 27 (1979): 165–71.

"Some Medieval Impressions of the Ostrich." *Yale University Library Gazette* 54 (1979): 18–25.

"Ezra Stiles and the Dark Day." *Yale University Library Gazette* 54 (1980): 163–67.

"Ezra Stiles and the Monument to Colonel John Dixwell." *Yale University Library Gazette* 55 (1981): 116–20.

"Ezra Stiles and the Legend of the Angel of Hadley." *Yale University Library Gazette* 73 (1999): 115–23.

Works Cited

Bigongiari, Dino. Review of *Johannis Scoti, Annotationes in Marcianum* (sic), edited by Cora E. Lutz. *Classical Philology* 36 (1941): 72–79.

Billings, Julia E. "Cora Lutz: 1906–1985." *Wilson Alumnae Quarterly* 58, no. 3 (summer 1985): 18–19.

Colker, Marvin L. Review of *Remigii Autissiodorensis Commentum in Martianum Capellam, Libri I–II*, edited by Cora E. Lutz. *Speculum* 39 (1964): 719–21.

Cranz, F. Edward, Ruth J. Dean, and Fred C. Robinson. "Cora E. Lutz." In "Memoirs of Fellows and Corresponding Fellows." *Speculum* 61 (1986): 763–64.

Jones, Charles W. Review of *Dunchad: Glossae in Martianum*, edited by Cora E. Lutz. *Speculum* 20 (1945): 357–59.

Levine, Philip. Review of *Remigii Autissiodorensis Commentum in Martianum Capellam, II: Libri III–IX*, edited by Cora E. Lutz. *Speculum* 43 (1967): 394–98.

Rand, E. K. Review of *Iohannis Scotti, Annotationes in Marcianum*, edited by Cora E. Lutz. *Speculum* 16 (1941): 129–31.

Wynne, Marjorie. "Cora Elizabeth Lutz: 1906–1985," *The Yale University Library Gazette* 60, nos. 1–2 (1985): 9–10.

CHAPTER 48

Voicing Silenced Rituals
The Unearthing of the Life Story of Arthurian Legend by Helaine Newstead (1906–1981)

GALE SIGAL

From the perspective of Morton Hunt, author of a lengthy and respectful *New Yorker* profile of the scholar Helaine Newstead, the Middle Ages was "a field already raked over with such thoroughness that anyone eager to contribute something original must really scratch around to find a bit of unexplored territory."[1] Professor Helaine Newstead, at the time the profile of her was published (1957), had made her mark: she had received a Guggenheim Foundation Fellowship (1948–49), and her scholarship had brought her to enough prominence to be elected president of the Medieval Club of New York (1950) and chair of the Arthurian Romances section of Modern Language Association (MLA) (1956–57). Like those of us in the field today, Newstead did not harbor the fear that medieval literature had little left to explore: "There is so much yet to do. Take one example — the thing I am interested in right now. That's the need to disentangle the Wagnerian influence and reveal the original Tristan story in its true light."[2]

Despite her prominence as a medievalist, Newstead did not hesitate to agree with Hunt that her work was rarified, an attitude reflected in his observation that "the claim that the medieval scholar finally stakes out for himself is so remote, and the fragments of learning it yields are so arcane, that the whole project becomes unintelligible to the outsider, who thereupon tends to dismiss it as pointless." Newstead accepted the accusation that humanists, especially those interested in the past, strive to "know more and more about less and less," but for her, knowing more, even "about less and less," was compelling: "I admit that many people can see no point to it, and I also admit that it produces no immediate results, like engineering or medical research. In fact, one of the best [anthropologists] . . . told me that I ought to switch over to

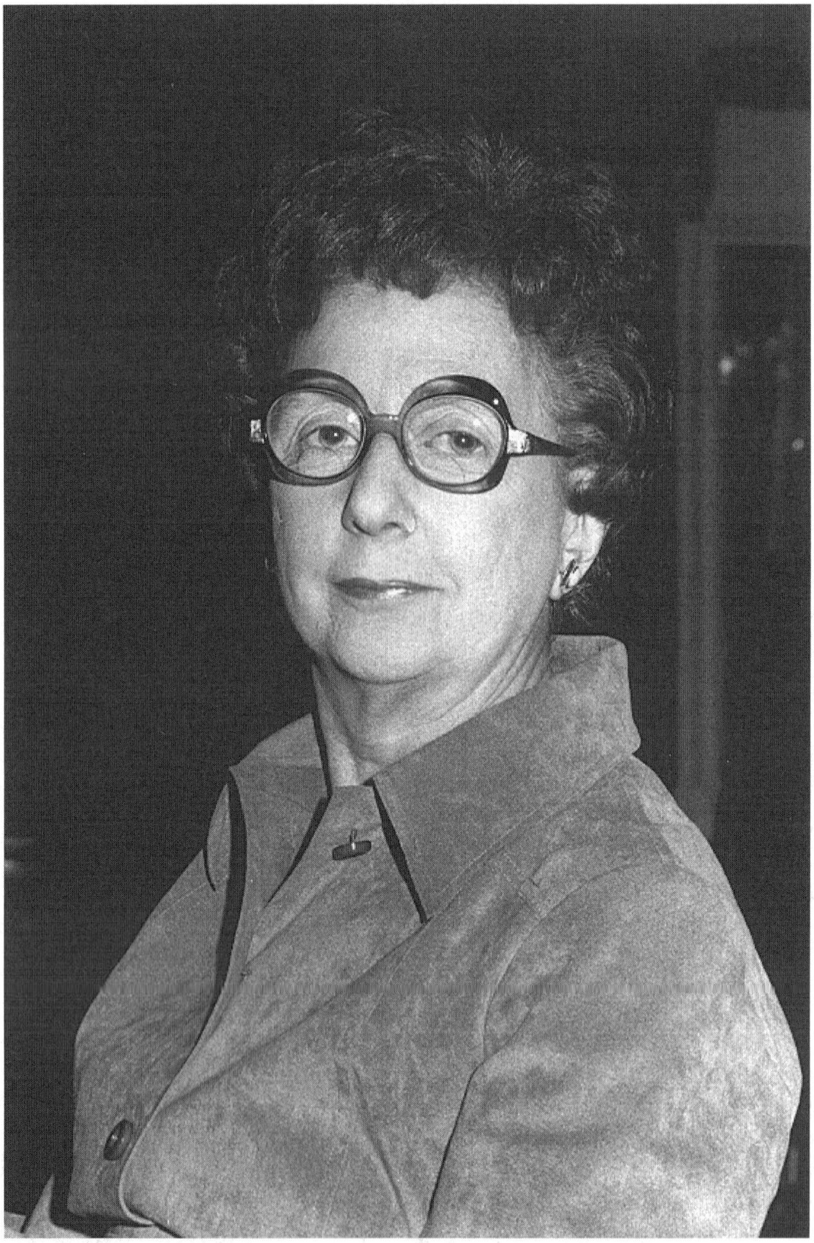

anthropology so that I could be dealing with something real. Well, my answer was, and is, that I *am* dealing with something real—the life history of a body of legend. Every new thing I learn about it tells us more about man himself. I suppose that's the final justification for scholarship. But personally I have never felt any need to justify it."[3]

Her plain-spoken comment reveals a characteristic independence of mind and her serious, practical, and modest approach. Her scholarship was balanced, unpretentious, and clear; her enjoyment of research, her well considered explanations, and her "cool and elegant prose" were "careful products of a life in which scholarship was the central, signifying activity, the essential act of community and self-fulfillment."[4]

Although medieval scholarship must have seemed alien to the *New Yorker* audience of forty-five years ago, Newstead was notable enough to merit a *New Yorker* profile, subtitled "A Giant in Her Field." For Newstead being a scholar meant playing a part, "a small part, to be sure . . . in preserving a record of man's cultural history."[5] The isolation of being a medievalist was compounded by the obvious fact that, as a woman, Newstead was even more singular; her achievements at a time when few women had the privilege of even attending college perhaps explains why, at the memorial service for her, colleague after colleague remarked that Professor Newstead's passing marked the end of an era. Widely regarded as a leading Arthurian, Newstead gradually made her way from college tutor to full professor to department head. She was both the first American and the first woman to be named president of the International Arthurian Society (1972–75). Leading a devoted academic life, dedicated to teaching at a public university, her consistently high standards and her efforts to educate women students in particular made her an exemplary model.

Born in New York City in 1906, Newstead grew up in what was then a middle-class Jewish neighborhood in Harlem. A talented pianist, she attended Juilliard while simultaneously a full-time student at Hunter College High School, but the strain of attending two schools at once put an end to her musical ambitions. She entered Hunter College, New York's fine women's college, in 1923, and excelled in language and literature courses. A self-described "longhair" during her college years, she loved attending concerts and the theatre. According to a college classmate, Newstead, by the age of twenty, "had a way of talking like a learned person": "She never went in for idle girl-talk, like the rest of us."[6]

The year after graduating magna cum laude (1927) Newstead undertook her M.A., writing a thesis on litotes in Anglo-Saxon poetry, while simultaneously joining the English faculty at Hunter College as a tutor. Those who knew her forceful personality after her career was established may have been surprised to read Newstead's confession in the *New Yorker* that during her early teaching years she was "terrified of [her] students. . . . a scared little rabbit."[7] Both her M.A. (1928) and her Ph.D. (1939) were taken at Columbia University, where she fell under the influence of the ranking American Arthurian R. S. Loomis. She became a prized student when she volunteered to summarize for him a collection of articles in German on the *Mabinogion*. Loomis, known to be begrudging in his praise, was nonetheless impressed by her proficient work, and for the next forty or so years Newstead was his protégé. Although Loomis was "rather strong willed, opinionated, and in more than one way controversial," Newstead revered him for his "brilliance, inexhaustible patience, and generously extended help."[8]

After achieving her doctorate and publishing her dissertation as *Bran the Blessed in Arthurian Romance* (1939), Newstead moved ahead in the New York academic hierarchy, holding a visiting professorship at Columbia University (1952), where in 1962, she became an adjunct professor as well as an active member of the well-known medieval studies seminar. In 1954 she was promoted to full professor at Hunter College, a singular achievement. By this time she had developed a repertory of courses. But when she moved to the Graduate Center of the City University of New York soon after it was founded, she was at last able to teach specialized courses in Arthurian literature; she also designed an interdisciplinary medieval studies seminar at a time when such a course was quite rare. At the Graduate Center she was chosen to serve as the first executive officer of the English doctoral program (1962 until 1969), and once that program was well established, she headed the comparative literature doctoral program (1974 until her retirement in 1976). She was named distinguished professor in 1971; after retiring in 1976 she continued to teach until 1981, the year of her death at age seventy-five.

Among Newstead's other distinctions were the Guggenheim Foundation Fellowship (1948–49); an honorary Doctor of Letters from the University of Wales (1969), where she studied Welsh; and the Hunter College President's Medal (1970). In the last year of her life she was awarded the City University's Chancellor's Medal, which honored her scholarly achievement, service, and commitment to students and literature.

Newstead's articles, book reviews, bibliographical studies, encyclopedia entries, and essays for the general reader are characterized by the thoughtfulness, breadth of knowledge, and care of a deeply read intellect and a meticulous scholar. Her expertise was enhanced by her gift for languages; she could read Anglo-Norman, Middle High German, Early Italian, Old English, Middle English, Old Norse, Old French, Old Irish, and Early Dutch as well as modern French, German, Italian, and Welsh. Newstead's approach to—as well as her research in—Arthurian studies have become so fully incorporated into our received view of the field that it is difficult to appreciate the challenge she confronted in advocating the importance of source studies of Arthurian romances. Loomis strove, against significant opposition, to prove that the substance of Arthurian romances derives more from early Celtic folk motifs and tales than from the creativity of French poets.[9] And Newstead's first published article, "The 'Joie de la Cort' Episode in *Erec* and the Horn of Bran" (published three years prior to completing her dissertation), was an extension of his approach. Newstead demonstrated that many puzzling references in the final episode of Chrétien de Troyes's *Erec* could be understood when the distinction between the words *cort* (court) and *cor* (horn) was sorted out. In demonstrating that the horn in the "Joie de la Cort" episode was the horn of plenty belonging to Bran, an ancient (and little studied) Welsh sea god,

Newstead also revealed how Chrétien de Troyes adopted Celtic figures. Her research was impressive enough for her paper, presented at the 1935 MLA Convention, to be published in *PMLA*.

Newstead's identification of Bran illuminated the final episode of *Erec;* in pursuing this line of research, Newstead became convinced that Bran was the source of the enigmatic Fisher King figure of the Grail romances. This subject became the focus of Newstead's doctoral dissertation, in which she found traces of the legendary sea god throughout the Arthurian corpus surviving in French, Latin, and German Arthurian texts. Resemblances to Bran were embedded in twenty-two Arthurian characters (including the wounded Grail King Anfortas), and echoes of his exploits appeared in a number of Arthurian feats, battles, castles, and miracles. In the process of doing this research Newstead developed the theory that the Welsh traditions served as the intermediary between Celtic tales and the songs of the Breton *conteurs* (who then transmitted the stories to the French). Her research strengthened the evidence that Welsh contributions to French Arthurian romances were not only present but central.

Published the year her doctoral degree was awarded as *Bran the Blessed in Arthurian Romance,* Newstead's book is considered a classic of Arthurian scholarship and continues to be consulted today. Although not all Arthurians were equally persuaded by her conclusions, none questioned the seriousness of Newstead's scholarship or her technical expertise. Newstead supplemented her work on Bran in "Perceval's Father and Welsh Tradition" (1945) by suggesting that Perceval's father, under various names, is another of Bran's descendants. As she confided to Hunt, the *New Yorker* interviewer, "Gradually it became apparent to me that the shadowy figure of Perceval's father bore some traits of the early Welsh sea-god named Bran. No one had ever noticed the similarity before. I felt just as thrilled as if I had found a lost manuscript in an attic."[10] In "The Grail Legend and Celtic Tradition" Newstead presented her theory to the nonspecialist that the name, characteristics, and attributes of the Grail King were derived from Welsh tradition. Although she wrote numerous essays, encyclopedia entries, and reviews during her career, *Bran the Blessed* was to be Newstead's only book-length work. Her balanced and well-researched scholarship produced a series of substantial, highly polished articles, a collection of which, especially her studies of the Tristan legend, would easily make a volume.

The basic premises of Newstead's work were that (a) a literary text, especially those concerning the *matière de Bretagne,* must not be seen as existing in a cultural vacuum; (b) any situation, episode, character, or motif arising in medieval literature was probably not invented by the author of the extant text; (c) some of the intermediate stages in the development of stories can be detected (or presumed); and (d) the search for literature's raw materials and their transmission into a work of art is in itself interesting and worthwhile.[11] Despite the fact that Newstead's output was narrowly focused and far from prolific, the very high quality of her output made her internationally known and respected: "The relative slowness of her production was, to be sure, due to her innate thoroughness and intellectual honesty—to the need she absolutely felt to read all those texts that fascinated her, plus their sources, in older Welsh and Irish, in Middle High German, in Classical and medieval Latin and in Old French."[12]

Tracing the life story of the Arthurian legend was a time-consuming undertaking. Although Newstead argued that researching the oral sources of the romance tradition was central to any comprehension of medieval romance literature, she saw her work as that of a literary scholar, not a historian: "Not being a medieval historian, Miss Newstead isn't the slightest bit interested in who or what the real Arthur was.... 'I'm not at all concerned with the facts of Arthur's life and deeds,' she says. 'I'm concerned only with the life story of the *legend* and what it reveals about creative man.'"[13] With her optimistic, "sharply focused," and "unintimidated" temperament, she—along with Loomis—"marched boldly into the immense unreadable wilderness of Arthurian sources."[14] The value and difficulty of Newstead's scholarship is detailed by her younger Graduate Center, CUNY colleague, Frederick Goldin, in his introduction to the essays in the *Voices in Translation* collection:

> In that thematic tangle [of Arthurian sources], Helaine Newstead blazed her own clarity. She studied the gratuitous episodes, the intricate and accidental accretions, the fragments of silenced rituals and the free-floating images in the material from which these romances were formed. To these details, fallen through many ancient generations into incoherence, she restored the dignity of their origins. In this work of restoration she not only solved many scholarly puzzles but also rendered the most profound homage to the great poets of the Middle Ages, particularly Chrétien de Troyes; for it was after she and others cleared the field that one could gauge the greatness of the poets' achievement.... [O]ut of this debris of dead images they created narratives that represented the culture and self-consciousness of the courtly class—and have enriched the repertory of narrative, the perception of experience, and the discovery of the individual in the Western world ever since.[15]

Newstead was convinced that by acknowledging the "tenacity of tradition," by taking into account how the fidelity of later romance writers to earlier Celtic tradition affected their treatment of Arthurian plots, subplots, and character traits, the critic would be able to more accurately assess the artistry of such writers.[16] As a consequence she vehemently opposed the fashionable symbolic and allegorical interpretations commonly put forth by her academic peers, considering them to be rash or romanticized readings based on mere opinion rather than learning.

Newstead's focus on the preliterary backgrounds to French romance led to an interest in the Old French romance *Partonopeus de Blois* and hence to her engagement with the character of Morgain la Fée. In "The Traditional Background of *Partonopeus de Blois*" (1946), Newstead theorized that the story blends various Celtic traditions connected to Morgan le Fay with reverberations of the classical legend of Cupid and Psyche. Examining Morgan also led Newstead to write "The Besieged Ladies in Arthurian Romance" (1948), in which she proposed that the Celtic traditions that shaped the legend of Morgan le Fay were adapted to the Arthurian stories of besieged ladies. Newstead surmised that the source of the plot pattern for the besieged ladies of Arthurian romance was found in the Irish tale "The Sickbed of Cuchulainn" and that the combining of love and war themes led to a variety of treatments of the besieged ladies plot element.[17]

Beginning in 1948 Newstead became fascinated by the Tristan legend, a subject that held her interest for the next twenty years. In her view Wagner was responsible for the fact that most people, including some scholars, consider the Tristan legend a solemn tragedy, with weighty oral significance. For her "the real Tristan legend was a rattling good story—full of adventures, hair-raising escapes, and moments of low farce. That's what originally made it so popular."[18] The Guggenheim Foundation Fellowship (1948–49) enabled her to study the origins of the Tristan legend so that she could flesh out her view of it. When, during that time, she was invited to join a rarified circle of distinguished medievalists on the faculty of Columbia University (who met once a month at the Men's Faculty Club), she felt honored: "It's wonderful, being with people like that. . . . Why, there are fifteen of us, and we put in one whole year just discussing the subject of courtly love!"[19] She took her turn reading her paper on King Mark's ears (which in some versions are said to have been those of a horse). In her article "King Mark of Cornwall" Newstead isolates the only Cornish element in Mark's legend, the tradition of human tribute.

Newstead's articles on the Tristan material, such as "Kaherdin and the Enchanted Pillow: An Episode in the Tristan Legend" (1950),"The Tryst beneath the Tree: An Episode in the Tristan Legend" (1955–56), and "Isolt of the White Hands and Tristan's Marriage" (1965–66), track down the origins of certain episodes or motifs: the faithful attendant, the soporific pillow, the lover's boasting of his beloved's surpassing beauty, the spying from a tree, the motif of the splashing (or audacious) water, and the motif of the separating sword. Newstead concluded that such episodes resulted from artistic fusions of early-twelfth-century Irish, Welsh, and Breton stories with Oriental fabliaux. In the process of her research Newstead discovered that the Celtic source of "the tryst beneath the tree episode" in Tristan is also the source of Boccaccio's *Decameron* 7.9 and the pear tree episode in Chaucer's "Merchant's Tale." The painstaking work of isolating the various motifs that comprise plot elements in Tristan helped Newstead demonstrate how romance writers like Thomas and Gottfried "enriched and refined the traditional material according to their modes of thought."[20] Newstead's careful research and lucid writing on the Tristan legend can be seen in her chapter "The Origin and Growth of the Tristan Legend" in Loomis's encyclopedic and groundbreaking "collaborative history" *Arthurian Literature in the Middle Ages* (1959).[21] In her section Newstead concisely traces the development of the Tristan story from the scattered evidence of the earliest sources, showing how Celtic, Arabic, and Oriental folk tales coalesced into the Tristan legend and how the legend itself was transmitted by Breton *conteurs* to the French romancers.

A comprehensive summary of the issues involved in the source-study approach to

Arthurian scholarship appears in Newstead's "Recent Perspectives on Arthurian Literature."[22] In this article Newstead considers two recently published Arthurian studies that represent common, but opposite, approaches: C. S. Lewis's article "The Anthropological Approach" and Kenneth Jackson's book *The International Popular Tale and Early Welsh Tradition*.[23] Newstead contrasts the article and the book as two convincing but ultimately distorted views. Newstead admonishes Lewis for favoring the direct critical response to the literary text over the more comprehensive understanding gained by knowledge of the preliterary sources. And while she praises Jackson for stressing the value of studying the international folktale (especially in early Welsh culture), she nonetheless notes that studying the folktale alone does not lead to a full appreciation of the literary texts that arose from it.[24]

Newstead takes Lewis to task for his denial of the relevance of sound scholarly investigation into the literary history of the stories that later developed into celebrated romances. Lewis's disparagement of "the anthropological explanation" that "cannot increase our understanding or enjoyment of one single sentence" in a literary work is countered by Newstead, who points out how Malory's methods are illuminated when we understand how he endeavors to explain and rationalize inherited motifs.[25] A strange feature in an Arthurian character or plot, such as Gawain's magically increasing strength at noontime, often evolves not from the author's own fertile imagination (as Lewis would assume), but from the author's "fidelity to the received tradition." By dismissing "the inconsistencies and irrational features in the Arthurian legend as irrelevant," Lewis misapprehends the evolution of Arthurian romance and the nature of its literary art, which makes his approach "misleading" and "highly subjective, even romantic."[26]

Lewis's importance as a scholar made it all the more necessary to caution the inexperienced student against being lured into a faulty belief that "only his unaided reading of the text is needed for full comprehension." Further, understanding the romance author's source narratives, the reader more fully appreciates his sophistication, humor, and stylistic virtuosity: "The critic who is more than a dilettante will be able to discriminate more accurately if he is aware of the traditional background and the poet's reliance on it."[27] So although Lewis makes "an eloquent plea for a direct response to the imaginative power of Arthurian romance," Newstead concludes that his enthusiasm leads him to champion an "uninformed response" that underestimates the value of scholarship.[28]

In contrast, Jackson's *International Popular Tale and Early Welsh Tradition* provides valuable insights into the oral and folklorist background of Arthurian romance. For Jackson the folklorist's work of sketching the "interchange of plot between written and oral versions" illuminates the "process whereby literary men adopted stories from folk sources and folktale tellers made use of material which they acquired in various ways from literary sources." In her balanced way Newstead convincingly argues that while neither the direct critical approach nor the folklorist one alone "is wholly satisfactory," the folklorist approach—when applied to a critical interpretation—produces a more refined and informed evaluation.[29]

Newstead occasionally wrote on subjects other than source studies, including the atypical polemical piece "The Blancheflor-Perceval Question Again," provoked by a scholarly disagreement over whether Blancheflor and Perceval in Chrétien's *Conte del Graal* behaved in a chaste or unchaste manner while spending a night together in Belrepaire Castle.[30] The scholarly debate over just what occurred that night and how to classify it "raged" between Newstead and Sister Amelia Klenke for nine years, and when Newstead declined to reengage, the cause was taken up by several other scholars. Another piece Newstead wrote on a subject far removed from the Tristan and Arthurian legends was nonetheless a source study. In "Some Observations on King Herla and the Herlething," Newstead traces a reference to King Herla and his troop made by Walter Map (in the miscellany *De Nugis Curialium*) back to "a composite of traditions about the Wild Hunt and a tale about a mortal's visit to the Otherworld realm of a pygmy king." Newstead tracks this ancient legend as far back as the Old English *Widsith*. According to Newstead, Map, who "was deeply interested in manifestations of the marvelous," embellishes the King Herla story with suggestions of hell and damnation in order to use it as an exemplum of the restlessness of the court in his own day: "[T]he doomed wanderers bequeathed their restlessness" to Map's contemporary court.[31]

In her last published essay Newstead dealt with the unusual subject (for her) "Narrative Techniques in Chrétien de Troyes's *Yvain*." Newstead provides a reading of the original audience's listening experience of *Yvain*, noting that romances "were intended to be read aloud to a . . . public outside the immediate circle of the original audience addressed by the poet," an audience that to some degree had to be imagined by the author.[32] In Newstead's view "the narrator's frequently deflating commentary prevents us from becoming so absorbed in the theme of love that we forget the progress of the action."[33] Underlying the love scenes' bravura rhetorical displays of "the language of amorous poetry, embellished with paradoxes, syllogisms, and scholastic arguments . . . is a narrative marked by deception and guile," the purpose of which is to downplay the prominence of love: "The pyrotechnics of language conceal without obliterating the moral issues to convey an ambiguous impression of love's invincibility." Through narrative structure, ironic commentary, and subtle nuances of technique, Chrétien differentiates the values of love and chivalry, privileging the values of the chivalric life over the prominence of love.[34]

In addition to her articles and book chapters Newstead authored critical introductions and notes for spoken-word records and cassettes on such varied subjects as the fairy tales of Ireland, medieval English drama, and *Idylls of the King*.[35] She was considered by Yakov Malkiel, the editor of *Romance Philology*, to have been "one of the finest book reviewers whom I could ever persuade to contribute"; he especially valued her skill, alertness, and precise appraisals of the more than fifty book reviews she contributed. At the same time Malkiel found that Newstead could be "humorless" and hypersensitive to editorial querying.[36] Yet her written work is not devoid of an understated, ironic sense of humor; after discussing a possible connection between two ancient tales, she observes, "These two stories are so divergent that one might well doubt any relationship between them, were it not for the inconvenient presence of the Grail as the central element in both."[37] Her "tough talk when provoked, her instant distrust of charm . . . her vigorous impatience with doubt, her antipathy to disorder, her sense of the immanence of corruption or dissolution" was balanced by "shyness," optimism, and "devotion to scholarly standards."[38] To feel the brunt of her "aggressive alertness in the presence of all facile innovations—short-cuts, formulas, selling personalities, everything that smacked of the new and improved" was a formidable and unfortunately all-too-memorable experience for some.[39] For those "whom she perceived as outlandish, as impostors, malingerers, invaders of her space. . . . she sometimes exercised the powers of martial law."[40] And yet, many of her students felt "her unstinting generosity . . . and for her supportive expectations that they would be as intellectually rigorous and profoundly curious as she was."[41] In brief, she was a vigorous champion of causes, a forceful ally, or a formidable opponent.

In the later years of her life Newstead was practically an institution to herself at the Graduate Center. Her judgment of what constituted good research and teaching were "uncompromising"; she "pulled no punches in demanding the highest quality" and violations of her standards were expressed "stridently."[42] Her students early learned the perils of imprecise thinking, careless commentary, and sketchy research, perpetrators of which could be reduced to tears. They had no choice but to elevate their discourse to her level, and they knew firsthand the consequences of losing their composure and professional demeanor. However, her students also learned from her the importance of independent thinking and creative, interdisciplinary study, as long as such work was upheld by careful scholarship.

At the time of her death the extraordinary outpouring of affection, respect, and admiration reflected what she had given to her colleagues and students. To the City University of New York Graduate Center she left her large personal library as well as an endowment that has sponsored a series of "Medieval Cities" conferences and created three Helaine Newstead Dissertation Fellowships, one each in the humanities, comparative literature, and English, which have been awarded for the last twenty years.

The *New Yorker* profile is particularly fascinating for its author's surprise at the cultural and social life of his subject. Admiring yet puzzled that such a scholar participated in activities or had interests outside of the Middle Ages, he describes his subject's nonscholarly appearance and her daily routines, as though a distinguished academic would appear more eccentric and devoid of cultural—or even normal—tastes:

> A small woman of fifty, Miss Newstead has almost none of the physical attributes that have come to be popularly associated with the scholar. A somewhat receding chin, a prominent nose, and thick glasses combine to give her a pleasantly birdlike appearance; she wears her brown hair short, and her comfortable middle-aged silhouette bears no hint of the ascetic. Unlike the cardboard scholar of the movies, she has been known to go swimming and take a walk in the country.[43]

What's more, she

> frequently bustles around town after dark to attend poetry readings, plays, operas, and concerts (she is likely to anticipate such occasions with a visit to her hairdresser, where a friend recently discovered her sitting under the dryer deeply absorbed in a volume on Pictish archeology) and she sometimes accepts (but almost as often declines) invitations from her many friends to join them at Sunday dinner. . . . But although no movie producer would type-cast Ms. Newstead as a scholar, she has established herself as an almost perfect example of one.[44]

Hunt's expectations of what the appearance and life of a serious female academic would be like (apparently derived from film rather than reality) reveal how rare a creature Newstead appeared to a contemporary and clearly sophisticated journalist. The *New Yorker* article, at sixteen pages, is at least twice as long as such an article would be today (would such an article be written). However, Hunt's respectful approach is distanced, almost as though he were examining an admirable anthropological curiosity. Despite his characterization of Newstead's articles as written "in an almost impenetrably learned prose that in no way reflects her inner elation," he seems to have had little difficulty himself in comprehending it, and he succinctly, accurately, and intelligently describes not only Newstead's work but the challenge of the scholarly life.[45] He is especially sensitive to (if not bemused by) the kind of painstaking effort such work involves when he notes that "the addition of one more tiny morsel to mankind's prodigious store of knowledge, and the fact that the morsel can be assimilated by fewer than five hundred persons throughout the world (Japan[,] incidentally, is a comparative hotbed of Arthurians) do not in the least diminish the excitement she derives from her accomplishment."[46]

In summing up the excitement she derived from her work, Newstead occasionally quoted Marjorie Nicolson, professor of English at Columbia, who recalled "moments of splendid isolation when each of us have had the momentary experience of being the only living person to know something that the world has never known or long forgotten."[47] Sharing the fruits of those solitary and hard-won moments, through her devoted teaching and her lucid essays, and taking a special but by no means exclusive interest in the education of her female students, Helaine Newstead has left a legacy to the world of scholarship that is as enduring as it is precious.

Notes

I am indebted to Deborah Sinnreich-Levi, William Coleman, David Manning, John Hopper, Gale Justin, and Laury Magnus for their interest and help in gathering information and the photo for this essay.

1. Hunt, "Profiles."
2. Hunt, "Profiles," 73.
3. Hunt, "Profiles," 39.

4. Proshansky, preface, xv.
5. Hunt, "Profiles," 39.
6. Hunt, "Profiles," 58.
7. Hunt, "Profiles," 62.
8. Malkiel and Sargent-Baur, "Necrology," 565.
9. Hunt, "Profiles," 62.
10. Hunt, "Profiles," 80.
11. Malkiel and Sargent-Baur, "Necrology," 570.
12. Malkiel and Sargent-Baur, "Necrology," 566.
13. Hunt, "Profiles," 39.
14. Goldin, introduction to *"Voices,"* xiv.
15. Goldin, introduction to *"Voices,"* xiv–xv.
16. Newstead, "Recent Perspectives," 879.
17. She was invited to summarize her findings in an entry for the *Dictionnaire de la littérature et des letters,* ed. Georges Grente (Paris: Fayard, 1949).
18. Hunt, "Profiles," 73.
19. Hunt, "Profiles," 39.
20. Newstead, "Isolt," 165.
21. Newstead, "Origin and Growth of the Tristan Legend," 122–33.
22. Newstead "Recent Perspectives," 877–83.
23. C. S. Lewis, "The Anthropological Approach," in *English and Medieval Studies, Presented to J. R. R. Tolkien on the Occasion of His Seventieth Birthday,* ed. Norman Davis and C. L. Wrenn (London: Allen & Unwin, 1962), 219–30; Kenneth Hurlstone Jackson, *The International Popular Tale and Early Welsh Tradition* (Cardiff: University of Wales Press, 1961).
24. Newstead, "Recent Perspectives," 878.
25. Newstead. "Recent Perspectives," 878–79.
26. Newstead, "Recent Perspectives," 879.
27. Newstead, "Recent Perspectives," 880.
28. Newstead, "Recent Perspectives," 881.
29. Newstead, "Recent Perspectives," 881.
30. Sister M. Amelia Klenke, "The Blancheflor-Perceval Question," *Romance Philology* 6 (1952): 173–78.
31. Newstead, "Some Observations on King Herla," 110.
32. Newstead, "Narrative Techniques," 431.
33. Newstead, "Narrative Techniques," 435.
34. Newstead, "Narrative Techniques," 441.
35. Newstead contributed general or introductory essays to *Colliers Encyclopedia* ("Arthurian Legends," "Grail Legends"), the *Magazine of the American Society of the French Legion of Honor* ("The Grail Legend and Celtic Tradition"), and the *Manual of Writings in Middle English* ("Romance" and "Arthurian Legends"); she edited and wrote the introduction for *Chaucer and His Contemporaries: Essays on Medieval Literature and Thought;* her chapter "Malory and Romance" was included in *Four Essays in Romance.*
36. Malkiel and Sargent-Baur, "Necrology," 566.
37. Hunt, "Profiles," 43.
38. Goldin, introduction to *Voices,* xvii–xviii.

39. Goldin, introduction to *Voices,* xvi.
40. Goldin, introduction to *Voices,* xvii.
41. "In Memorium," *Graduate School Newsreport* 6, no. 2 (published by the Graduate School and University Center of the City University of New York) (November/December 1981).
42. "In Memorium."
43. Hunt, "Profiles," 40.
44. Hunt, "Profiles," 42.
45. Hunt, "Profiles," 42
46. Hunt, "Profiles," 63.
47. Hunt, "Profiles," 63.

Select Bibliography of Works by Helaine Newstead

Tributes to Newstead include the *New Yorker* profile (1957), which makes fascinating reading for today's medievalists and women scholars, and an issue of *Romance Philology* published as a festschrift in her honor, including an "Analytical Bibliography of the Writings of Helaine Newstead" compiled by Harriet Brodey and Benjamin N. Woodbridge Jr. (*Romance Philology* 7, no. 3 [1964]: 527–34). After her death Yakov Malkiel and Barbara N. Sargent-Baur wrote the "Contributions of Newstead, Helaine." A posthumous collection of essays, *Voices in Translation: The Authority of 'Olde Bookes' in Medieval Literature,* edited by Deborah Sinnreich-Levy and Gale Sigal, was written in her honor. Sigmund Eisner contributed "Helaine Newstead: A 'Giant in her Field,'" to *On Arthurian Women: Essays in Memory of Maureen Fries,* edited by Bonnie Wheeler and Fiona Tolhurst (Dallas: Scriptorium Press, 2001).

"The 'Joie de la Cort' Episode in *Erec* and the Horn of Bran." *PMLA* 51 (1936): 13–25.

Bran the Blessed in Arthurian Romance. New York: Columbia University Press, 1939. Reprint, AMS Press 1966.

"The Grail Legend and Celtic Tradition." *Magazine of the American Society of the French Legion of Honor* 16 (1945): 219–34.

"Perceval's Father and Welsh Tradition." *Romanic Review* 36 (1945): 3–31.

"The Traditional Background of *Partonopeus de Blois.*" *PMLA* 61 (1946): 916–46.

"The Besieged Ladies in Arthurian Romance." *PMLA* 63 (1948): 803–30.

"Kaherdin and the Enchanted Pillow: An Episode in the Tristan Legend." *PMLA* 65 (1950). 290–312.

"The Blancheflor-Perceval Question Again." *Romance Philology* 7 (1953–54): 171–75.

"The Tryst beneath the Tree: An Episode in the Tristan Legend." *Romance Philology* 9 (1955–56): 269–84.

"King Mark of Cornwall." *Romance Philology* 11 (1957–58): 240–53.

"The Origin and Growth of the Tristan Legend." In *Arthurian Literature in the Middle Ages: A Collaborative History,* edited by R. S. Loomis. Oxford: Clarendon Press, 1959.

"The *Enfances* of Tristan and English Tradition." In *Studies in Medieval Literature in Honor of Professor Albert Croll Baugh,* edited by MacEdward Leach. Philadelphia: University of Pennsylvania Press, 1961.

"Isolt of the White Hands and Tristan's Marriage" *Romance Philology* 19 (1965): 155–66.

"Arthurian Legends." In *A Manual of the Writings in Middle English 1050–1500,* edited by J. Burke Severs. New Haven, Conn.: Yale University Press, 1967.

"Romance." In *A Manual of the Writings in Middle English 1050–1500,* edited by J. Burke Severs. New Haven, Conn.: Yale University Press, 1967.

Editor. *Chaucer and His Contemporaries: Essays on Medieval Literature and Thought.* Greenwich, Conn.: Fawcett Books, 1968.

"Recent Perspectives on Arthurian Literature." In *Mélanges de langue et de littérature du Moyen-Âge et de la Renaissance offerts à Jean Frappier, professeur à la Sorbonne.* 2 vols. Geneva: Droz, 1970.

"Narrative Techniques in Chrétien's *Yvain*." *Romance Philology* 30 (1971): 431–41.

"Some Observations on King Herla and the Herlething." In *Medieval Literature and Folklore Studies: Essays in Honor of Francis Lee Utley,* edited by Jerome Mandel and Bruce A. Rosenberg. New Brunswick, N.J.: Rutgers University Press, 1971.

Works Cited

Goldin, Frederick. Introduction to *Voices in Translation: The Authority of 'Olde Bookes' in Medieval Literature.* Edited by Deborah Sinnreich-Levy and Gale Sigal. New York: AMS Press, 1992.

Hunt, Morton N. "Profiles: A Giant in Her Field." *New Yorker,* 30 March 1957, 39–80.

Malkiel, Yakov, and Barbara N. Sargent-Baur. "Necrology: Contributions of Newstead, Helaine." *Romance Philology* 36, no. 4 (1983): 564–71.

Proshansky, Harold. Preface to *Voices in Translation: The Authority of 'Olde Bookes' in Medieval Literature.* Edited by Deborah Sinnreich-Levy and Gale Sigal. New York: AMS Press, 1992.

CHAPTER 49

Articulating the Middle English Lexicon

Margaret Ogden (1909–1988), Medieval Medical Texts, and the Middle English Dictionary

MICHAEL ADAMS

MARGARET SINCLAIR OGDEN was a textual scholar and philologist of outstanding insight and impeccable technique whose work profoundly influenced both the history of medical science and the historical study of English language and literature. She was a member of the staff of the *Middle English Dictionary* (*MED*) for over forty years, from 1933 to 1974, first as a full-time assistant and finally as a senior associate editor. During that period she contributed entries to every published fascicle covering the alphabetical range *A–I*, and she also served as the project's chief bibliographer, leading the team that compiled the *MED*'s complex, sophisticated working bibliography as well as the version published in 1954, both in a fascicle of the dictionary, titled *Plan and Bibliography,* and as a separate volume, titled *A Bibliography of Middle English Texts*. The published bibliography remains an essential resource for the study of Middle English, Middle English literature, and medieval manuscripts in English nearly fifty years after it first appeared in print.

But Ogden's contributions to those fields of study far exceeded her lexicography. She also edited the *Liber de Diversis Medicinis*, "a compendium of remedies for various ailments" included in the Thornton Manuscript. Her work on that text led her to Guy de Chauliac's *Inventarium sive chirurgia magna,* the most significant of medieval medical texts, the English translations of which she ultimately edited.[1] Although she never completed the volume of commentary meant to accompany her edition of Chauliac, Ogden made significant progress toward it and during her last years collaborated with Michael R. McVaugh on the commentary to an edition of Chauliac's Latin text.[2]

Margaret Ogden's scholarly temperament was bred in the bone and manifested itself even in her early years. Her mother, Elisabeth Sinclair, had earned a doctorate

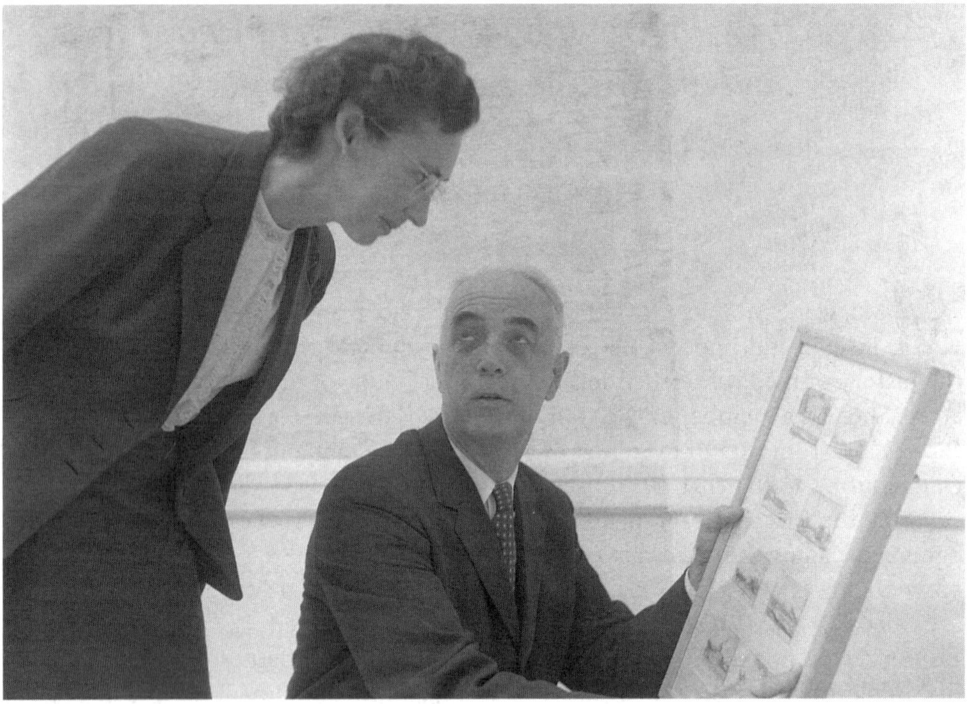

and taught history at Berea College, in Berea, Kentucky. Her father, Clement Holdeman, died when Ogden was two, a victim of tuberculosis; her stepfather, George Peck, also taught at Berea College.[3] Ogden graduated from high school at sixteen and matriculated at Berea College in 1924; she attended the University of Chicago during the summer quarter of 1925 but left for the University of Michigan in the fall, graduating with an A.B. in 1927. She took her A.M. at Michigan in 1928 and returned to Chicago to pursue her doctorate, awarded on 17 December 1935.[4]

She may have formed the idea of returning to Ann Arbor to work on the *MED* while studying for her Ph.D. at Chicago; her curriculum there was ideal preparation for an *MED* editor. She took courses on Chaucer, alliterative poetry, the metrical romances, and *Piers Plowman,* but she emphasized language study, taking courses in the elements of Old English, Old English poetry, *Beowulf,* advanced Old English grammar, early Middle English, northern English, Old English and the German dialects, advanced Old French, Gothic, and Icelandic.

Although University of Chicago transcripts do not record instructors, Ogden almost certainly took Icelandic with Sir William A. Craigie, one of the editors of the *Oxford English Dictionary,* editor of the *Dictionary of the Older Scottish Tongue,* then in progress, and of the *Dictionary of American English* (*DAE*), which he had come to Chicago to edit in 1925. Most important, she took courses titled "Dictionary of American English" and "Practical Lexicography," both very likely under Craigie's supervision or perhaps that of George Watson, one of the dictionary's assistant editors.[5] This indicates something hitherto unnoticed, that she contributed to the *DAE* in the early stages of its preparation, probably by reading material and excerpting quotations ultimately used to illustrate usage in the dictionary's entries.[6] In any event, when she was hired to assist with the *MED* in 1933, she had both the necessary intellectual equipment and firsthand experience of a historical dictionary project.

Ogden's dissertation, on the "Liber de Diversis Medicinis" in the Thornton Manuscript, became her first book, under the same title (1938). She was led to edit the text by Craigie and James Hulbert and completed the work while at the *MED,* where she was "allowed . . . free use of the facilities of the dictionary" and received "encouragement and advice," not only from Samuel Moore and Thomas A. Knott, successively the *MED*'s chief editors through 1944, but also from Sanford B. Meech, one the *MED*'s assistant editors, who was "able to draw upon his wide experience with fifteenth-century manuscripts for the solution of several cruces in the transcription," and Hope Emily Allen, an associate editor of the Early Modern English Dictionary (*EMED*), who "offered helpful suggestions, especially concerning the identification of Robert Thornton."[7]

Her edition was published by the Early English Text Society (EETS), a result Craigie probably expected when he and Hulbert proposed the project, as the original purpose of EETS volumes had been to supply accurate Middle English texts from which the *OED* could quote.[8] Well aware of the *MED*'s similar needs, Craigie and Hulbert encouraged Ogden in textual and philological work that, while significant in its own right, would ultimately prove Ogden well suited for Middle English lexicography and bibliography. Work on the Thornton Manuscript trained Ogden in paleography, the linguistic forms of later Middle English (especially the northern dialect), the disciplines of accurate transcription, and glossarial treatment of Middle English vocabulary. The edition also initiated her intensive, lifelong study of the Galenic medical tradition, the published fruits of which would significantly affect the historical study of medieval medicine.

Ogden began full-time work on the *MED* in 1933, according to the project's archives. She first worked under Moore, who died prematurely in 1934, and then continued under Knott, who assumed responsibility for the dictionary in 1935. While in graduate school she had married a fellow student, H. V. S. "Harry" Ogden, who accompanied her to Michigan and subsequently took a position in the Department of English. During her first decade on the staff, the project conspicuously lacked direction and was wracked with turmoil.[9] The staff toiled against those odds as well as against financial challenges presented by the Depression and the Second World War, without much to show for their effort.

A young woman without a faculty appointment, married to a junior member of the faculty, Ogden worked hard and kept her head down: except in lists of the staff she is ignored by the archival record during Knott's tenure. Howard Mumford Jones, who taught at Michigan in the mid-1930s, wrote that he "never felt professionally comfortable in Ann Arbor. There was too much pride of place, self-assurance, and emphasis on money and rank."[10] Frederic G. Cassidy, who worked on both the *MED* and *EMED* during this period, remembered that Hereward T. Price, associate editor of the *EMED*, interim editor of the *MED* in 1944, and professor of English, possessed a "strong sense of hierarchy," in which "instructors and graduate students, even assistant professors, were barely human."[11] In spite of her accomplishments and evident abilities, Ogden was not taken very seriously by her senior colleagues.

An exception was Hope Emily Allen, who had arrived in Ann Arbor somewhat earlier than the Ogdens, in 1931, as assistant editor of the *EMED*. She, too, may have felt less than fully appreciated by her male colleagues, both junior and senior. Though she had not earned a Ph.D., she was a credentialed medievalist and well connected among American, English, and Continental scholars. As Cassidy put it, "There were few women medievalists those days, at least in America, and certainly few who had made the kind of discovery that Hope Emily had done with the *Book of Margery Kempe*."[12] But when she investigated the etymological relations among "bug," "bug in one's ear," "bogey," and "booger," "some of the staff women were put off. For them the dominance of scholar over woman was not easy to accept."[13]

Allen's indelicacy did not bother Ogden, and they became close friends, "in spite of a certain formality which remained. [Ogden] and her husband called Hope 'Miss Allen,' even when she began to call them by their first name, and Hope maintained her position by courteously suggesting unpublished texts for Margaret Ogden to edit, a sign of confidence and friendship she extended to very few." Away from home and from all her other American friends, "a friendship with an intelligent, personable woman like Margaret Ogden gave [Allen] a pleasure during her years at Ann Arbor that no institution by itself could have afforded her."[14] Clearly, the appreciation was mutual, and Ogden must have been grateful not only to make a friend but to find a mentor who was both a medievalist and a woman. Allen was godmother to the Ogdens' daughter, Elisabeth Ogden Lampert; Hope Lampert Burnam, the Ogdens' granddaughter, was in turn Allen's namesake.[15]

Ogden's professional life and prospects changed significantly after Hans Kurath was hired to replace Knott as editor of the *MED* in 1945. Kurath appealed to the University of Michigan partly because he was director of the *Linguistic Atlas of the United States and Canada,* a vast, ambitious project that had already yielded the *Linguistic Atlas of New England* (1939–43) and the accompanying *Handbook of the Linguistic Geography of New England* (1939). Kurath had proven himself capable of managing complicated projects over long stretches of time and then bringing them to fruition. After fifteen years of the University of Michigan's financial support and the staff's labor, none of the *MED* had found its way into print.

Of course, one of Kurath's managerial strengths was to recognize, develop, and exploit the talents of staff members. He must have recognized Ogden's understated superiority more or less immediately on his arrival, as he entrusted to her responsibilities crucial to the project's success. In 1951, while justifying delays in publication, Kurath noted that the *MED*'s "bibliographical apparatus (which was most inadequate and out of date) had to be created from the ground up."[16] Whatever else had not been completed, Kurath could employ the past perfect because Ogden had organized a working bibliography by 1949. The task was a formidable one, and Ogden's success was so absolute that the "bibliographical apparatus" she designed remained unaltered throughout the dictionary's subsequent history.

The apparatus, however, was the least of Ogden's concerns. The dictionary required the best possible estimate of every Middle English manuscript cited in the dictionary: Ogden had to determine which of multiple witnesses of any given text was most authoritative, how other witnesses should be understood in relation to that text, which texts or witnesses of texts represented which Middle English dialects, what dates should be assigned to each manuscript, which texts were published in reliable editions, and of which texts the dictionary should procure photostatic copies because no reliable editions had been prepared.

By 1946 Ogden was corresponding with librarians, record keepers, textual scholars, and paleographers to answer these questions about nearly every text to be included in the bibliography. Previously published assumptions were confirmed or challenged and revised, manuscript by manuscript. Among others she consulted Allen, who wrote extensive responses to her queries in several letters dated 1947.[17] As a result of her work the dictionary's bibliography was the best yet compiled, and it remains a remarkably useful first point of reference for Middle English manuscript and textual study to the present day.

One innovative feature of the bibliography deserves special mention. It is unclear whether Kurath or Ogden first proposed it; it seems reasonable to conclude that they adopted it in consultation with each other, once they knew that they could gather information that would make it practicable. Because we have lost many original versions of Middle English manuscripts, we often confront the fact that a manuscript date is not the same as its text's date of composition. For the *MED*'s purposes, the difference between manuscript and composition dates is significant: a word or form of a word taken from a manuscript certainly represents English at the manuscript date; it may also represent the word or form of the word at the date of composition. When different witnesses to a text contain variants, the variants belong to the manuscript and must be dated with the manuscript, not with the text as originally written.

Most historical dictionaries are content to quote published editions of texts and date the texts at the point of composition, but the *MED*'s system of double dating allows much more precise historical linguistic conclusions. Such conclusions are available due partly to Ogden's vision and partly to the depth of her research into manuscript and textual dates; the *MED*'s system of double dating advances both manuscript bibliography and lexicographical technique.

Ogden had to adapt the results of her prodigious labor to useful application in the dictionary offices; she had to convert the bibliography in her mind into one that could be housed in a large filing cabinet. Thus each manuscript or printed text representing a manuscript, including untitled works identified by "incipit," was registered on an eight-by-five-inch card. Each card contained information relevant to an editor's use of the manuscript. First, it indicated the stencil, or abbreviated title, by which the manuscript would be identified in entries, for instance, "c1450 *Chauliac (1)* (Sln 3666: Wallner)" for Björn Wallner's edition of Chauliac's *Grande chirurgie*, published in several volumes from 1969 to 1988. The card also included the full title of the work, as printed in the published bibliography. Readings from the Sloane Manuscript are recorded among the variants in Wallner's edition, and the card included a field in which the relevant pages of all volumes comprising that edition were listed. The card noted the manuscript in question and indicated its date, as established by Ogden's research, and also provided space to record the date of composition, the manuscript's dialect, and a Latin or French original, when appropriate. Additionally, the card recorded the *OED*'s stencil, if the manuscript was quoted in the *OED*, cross-referenced the text to J. E. Wells's *Manual of the Writings in Middle English, 1050–1400* (1916–51) whenever relevant, provided the text's shelf number in the dictionary's library, and instructed editors on how to refer to the text in entries, in this case, for instance, by "book page/line." To what extent should an editor rely on the book in question? In the case of Wallner's edition, Ogden wrote, "Sl[oane MS] in this ed[ition] *Quote reluctantly*."

One might dismiss the card bibliography as merely advanced recordkeeping. But card by card, Ogden and her associates, Charles E. Palmer and Richard L. McKelvey, compiled many thousands of concrete data into a solid foundation on which the *MED*'s editors would subsequently build, from over three million citations, a towering dictionary of more than fifteen thousand pages. As Sherman M. Kuhn, one of the *MED*'s chief editors, explained, "If a bibliography containing all of the information needed for a specific dictionary is available, and it is complete and up-to-date, the lexicographer can use it for all references. But in the 1940's no such bibliography existed for M[iddle] E[nglish]."[18] With assistance from Palmer and McKelvey, Ogden organized that bibliography between 1945 and 1949 and, as Kuhn implies, supplied an essential work of reference, not only for lexicographers but for all students of Middle English language and literature as well as for medieval English culture generally.

The bibliography was published as the bulk of the dictionary's plan and bibliography in 1954. Entries in the published version, of course, did not include all of the information recorded on the cards. A typical entry is that for the romance *Amis and Amiloun:*

c1330   Amis (Auch): Amis and Amiloun, ed. M. Leach,
(?c1300) *EETS* 203 (1937), lines 97–2112, 2125–2395, and portions of other lines in fns. [W 1.110; BR 821].

The first date is that of the Auchinleck Manuscript, which includes the romance; the second is the hypothetical date of the romance's composition. The entry identifies precisely the lines in McEdward Leach's edition for the Early English Text Society that contain readings from that manuscript. The bracketed abbreviations refer to the entries in Wells's *Manual* and Carleton Brown and Rossell Hope Robbins's *Index of Middle English Verse* (1943). The Auchinleck Manuscript is the dictionary's preferred manuscript: several other manuscript versions of the poem (Sutherland, Douce, Harley) are entered underneath the Auchinleck Manuscript, an arrangement applied to all texts preserved in multiple witnesses, reflecting Ogden's judgment, given her research, on which manuscript best represents the text's original version. In all the bibliography comprises 2,985 such entries, while 1,272 incipits receive more cursory treatment.

Kurath, Ogden, and their colleagues recognized that the bibliography was self-sufficiently important and would serve scholars who did not subscribe to the *MED*, which was released in 128-page fascicles, usually four per year. So the dictionary's publisher, the University of Michigan Press, issued the bibliography separately, under the title *A Bibliography of Middle English Texts,* also in 1954. In his annual report for that year, Kurath asserted that "[t]he Bibliography itself may be regarded as a major contribution to medieval studies, since it includes all Middle English texts that have been edited as well as unedited manuscripts of the more important texts and of many unedited documents used by the Dictionary in Photostat or microfilm, each with precise bibliographical information."[19]

The scholarly community agreed with Kurath's estimate of Ogden and her colleagues' achievement. As *The Year's Work in English Studies* put it, the bibliography's "main use is, naturally, in connexion with the rest of the *Dictionary*. But it possesses considerable value in itself. There are 63 double-column pages of the titles of the works excerpted for the Dictionary, with the 'preferred manuscripts' and 'preferred editions' noted. There are also 20 similar pages of incipits of short verse pieces. The whole makes a most valuable reading list for the Middle English student."[20] Randolph Quirk concurred: "The long *Bibliography* by Mrs Ogden, Mr Palmer, and Mr McKelvey... is not only indispensable as an alphabetical guide to the abbreviated references in the *Dictionary*: it will be of immense service to medievalists in its own right by virtue of its completeness and its up-to-date information on editions, and MS dating and location. Scientifically consistent and concise, each entry manages to convey a wealth of tightly packed data."[21] Herbert Pilch considered the bibliography "impressive... and bidding fair to become a standard reference book on M[iddle] E[nglish] sources."[22] H. M. Flasdieck suggested that "[t]he revision of the manuscript dates undertaken by the *MED* with the generous support of the libraries holding the manuscripts is in itself of inestimable value."[23] And John Bromwich praised it as "a wonder of organisation and technical efficiency" and perhaps "the most thorough bibliography of any given period in any of the European languages."[24]

While compiling the *MED*'s bibliography, Ogden was also engaged in routine lexicography. Although the *MED* had inherited the *OED*'s Middle English slips, material collected by Clark Northup, of Cornell University, when he was editor of the *MED* from 1926 to 1929, and material collected by Ewald Flügel, of Stanford University, for his uncompleted Chaucer dictionary, editors daily collected new evidence of Middle English forms, meaning, and usage from texts either not read for those other projects or read inadequately. The reading program was very intensive under Moore and, given her training on the *DAE* and her relatively subordinate position under Moore and Knott, it is likely that Ogden spent considerable time during the 1930s and early 1940s excerpting texts.[25] Editors continued to add to the *MED*'s corpus of quotations throughout the project's history, and Ogden's expertise in medical literature was particularly valuable: "In the absence of good scientific and technical lexicons for most of the specialized fields of M[iddle] E[nglish], the *MED* resolved to treat all specialized fields of M[iddle] E[nglish]. By way of illustration, I need only refer to our handling of the anatomical and surgical terms found in the M[iddle] E[nglish] translations of Guy de Chauliac's treatises. These rich resources and others like them had been neglected for so long that there was no printed edition, old or new, good or bad; and we had to quote them wholly, from 1952 until recently, out of photostats of the manuscripts."[26] The method of quotation had changed "recently" because, after decades of work on the Chauliac manuscripts, Ogden had published an excellent edition.[27]

An editor's central responsibility, of course, was to prepare entries for each word included in the *MED*. Quotation slips were arranged alphabetically under entry words in large boxes; editors worked box by box, and since some boxes by the nature of their vocabulary took longer to edit than others, a fascicle's alphabetical range was fragmented among several editors. An editor would begin by writing rough definitions for the meaning of a word illustrated on each slip and then would engage in a complex process of "lumping" or "splitting" senses.[28] Ultimately the editor would arrange the senses of a word into a semantically "logical" analysis of the word's meaning.[29] An editor would then select quotations to illustrate the various senses, an unexpectedly formidable task: quotations convey a term's chronology, at twenty-five-year intervals, whenever possible, but they also indicate the registers in which a term appears (literary, documentary, technical, glossarial, and so forth), locate the term within dialects, and illustrate the term's grammar (something which, in a dictionary, can be accomplished only through quotation) and its idiomatic uses, especially those beyond the grasp of definition. The editor must also select those especially valuable quotations that define the term in question, whenever such are available.[30] In other words, an editor had to exercise considerable judgment in arranging a comprehensive, precise, and balanced entry.

After completion of the bibliography, from 1955 to 1964, Ogden worked half time at the *MED*. She had a full year's leave, from 1 July 1960 to 30 June 1961, while a Guggenheim Fellowship funded her work on Chauliac's English text. She received four grants from the Horace A. Rackham School of Graduate Studies at the University of Michigan "between 1959 and 1964 to defray the cost of travel, to buy microfilms and photographs, and to provide research assistance and clerical assistance" for what would become her edition, for the Early English Text Society, of *The Cyrurgie of Guy de Chauliac*.[31] In order to bring that work to fruition, she worked only quarter time at the *MED* during 1965 and through June 1966, from which point she took an extended leave, originally scheduled to end in 1968 but in fact lasting until her retirement in 1974.

Ogden based her edition on Bibliothèque nationale Paris MS Anglais 25, collating it principally against Cambridge University MS Dd.3.52 and New York Academy of Medicine MS 12, readings from which appear in notes. She transcribed and collated with remarkable precision, particularly conscious of cruces that reflected mistranslation of the various Latin manuscripts behind the independently translated English texts. Reviewing Björn Wallner's selection from Chauliac (1964), Ogden remarked that his reliance on Nicaise's nineteenth-century edition of Chauliac's French text was ill advised, as collation of that edition with actual Old French manuscripts "shows that it cannot be used as presumptively equivalent to any known Old French version."[32] She also noted that Wallner could not account adequately for several variants that derived from English mistranslation of Latin manuscripts that he had overlooked, such as Magdalen College Oxford MS 208.[33]

Ogden's work, on the other hand, reflected her firsthand knowledge not only of the English manuscripts but of all the Old French and Latin manuscripts, so that she was aware not only of English mistranslations but of Old French and Latin mistranslations from earlier Latin manuscripts that ultimately underlay variants among the English manuscripts.[34] This thorough familiarity with the manuscripts, editorial acumen, and an almost supernatural patience with a very long manuscript (her printed text runs to 639 pages) led to an edition that Wallner, in turn reviewing her work, called "truly impressive." "Most editors," he wrote, "are presumably disappointed when they see the finished product of their efforts in print. Mrs. Ogden, however, should not feel disappointed."[35]

Ogden had planned to provide not only the English text of Chauliac's *Inventarium* but a second volume of commentary, which would include notes on medieval medicine and pharmacology, or the matter of Chauliac's work, as well as detailed textual and etymological notes and a glossary. During the early 1970s she continued her work on the commentary under the aegis of a fellowship from the National Institutes of Health (NIH). "By 1981 Dr. Ogden had decided that she would be unable to complete the commentary volume, and she proposed that I should take it over," writes Michael R. McVaugh, of the University of North Carolina. "She and I had long had a personal connection, for I had known her when I was growing up in Ann Arbor while she was at work on the *Middle English Dictionary*, but I had only become aware at the end of my graduate training . . . that this mother of my high-school friends was at work in the same general area of scholarship—the history of medieval medicine—that I had come to mark out for myself."[36]

According to McVaugh, "Dr. Ogden had recognized from the beginning that her plans for the commentary were ambitious and that it might have to be altered or reduced in scope. . . . Realizing that her projected volume might be thought of as comprising one commentary on the Middle English and a second on the Latin Guy . . . I concluded that the two might be dissociated and published separately."[37] Thus McVaugh published an edition of Chauliac's *Inventarium* (1997), accompanied by a volume of commentary prepared, according to the title page, by McVaugh and Ogden. The commentary includes 2,680 entries, some very brief and others quite extensive. Ogden wrote several of the longer notes while editing the Middle English text, especially those to Chauliac's anatomy and his *antidotarium*, the Latin of which is particularly important to the Middle English medical lexicon. In all, these notes comprise only about 4 percent of the total entries, but measured by inches of printed text, Ogden's authorial contribution is really about 20 percent of the whole. McVaugh assures us, however, that Ogden's research influenced many entries not attributed to her.[38]

Ogden's edition of the Middle English *Cyrurgie*, her collaboration with McVaugh on the commentary to the *Inventarium*, and two seminal articles, "The Galenic Works Cited in Guy de Chauliac's *Chirurgia Magna*" (1973) and "Guy de Chauliac's *Theory of the Humors*" (1969), establish Ogden as a scholar of extraordinary importance and influence. The former article is a study in the transmission of ideas; according to McVaugh, "[H]istorians of translation and dissemination owe some of their sophistication" to Ogden's example in this article. The latter article, focused on the intellectual content of Chauliac's work, was unusual for its time because it "took the material seriously, divorced from any judgment of usefulness" and in so doing "anticipate[d] the sort of intellectual history of medical thought that subsequently became standard."[39]

Ogden's eminence, unusual for a woman of her generation, was not always easy for male colleagues to accept. Ogden apparently brought Sherman M. Kuhn, her contemporary at the University of Chicago, to Kurath's attention; Kurath hired Kuhn as associate editor of the *MED*, while Ogden, in spite of her seniority and accomplishment, remained an assistant editor. According to Robert N. Mory, one of Ogden's assistants under the NIH grant and subsequently an assistant editor himself, Kuhn and Ogden "were wary friends who had a high regard for each other," though he "resented her medical knowledge." Like Ogden, Kuhn was engaged on an ambitious edition, in his case of *The Vespasian Psalter,* the text of which he published in 1965; also like Ogden he was unable to complete the intended volume of commentary, though Kuhn found no one to carry on his work. Ironically, while Ogden's grants and leaves allowed her to study Chauliac intensively and continuously, Kuhn's superior position at the *MED* impeded his work. In his review of Ogden's edition of Chauliac's Middle English text (1972), Kuhn incorrectly accused her of an inappropriate emendation, because "he was so anxious to find fault."[40] Their rivalry, though far from malignant, was sometimes palpable.

Margaret Ogden had a loving, mutually supportive relationship with her husband, Harry. According to their son, John Ogden, "It is difficult to overstate the importance he had on her career or her importance to his work. There were things she didn't like to do or didn't feel she did well that he did for her, and work they shared, and work she did for him, and many things they wrote together. They of course published a book together, but that was only one aspect of their professional and intellectual partnership."[41] The book to which Ogden refers is *English Taste in Landscape in the Seventeenth Century* (1955), the research for which involved much travel among the country houses of England to view the pictures with which the study is principally concerned as well as collaboration on articles preliminary to the book.

According to Mory, Margaret Ogden "had will power and dedication that would astonish anyone. . . . [Librarians] used to quake when they saw her coming. She was not to be denied." Asked what he had learned from Ogden, Mory replied, "Her scholarship was so impeccable and she worked from such high standards. I learned most of all the importance of maintaining the very highest scholarship possible."[42] Ogden's ambition, determination, thoroughness, and precision endowed medieval studies with an impressive legacy, especially in the areas of Middle English bibliography and of medieval medicine and its lexicon.

Notes

1. Ogden, *Cyrurgie of Guy de Chauliac.*
2. Ogden with McVaugh, *Commentary.*
3. These facts about Margaret Ogden's family and early life were communicated to the author by Hope Lampert Burnam, Ogden's granddaughter, and Bruce Burnam, Hope Lampert Burnam's husband, in a letter dated 26 March 2002.
4. Information about Ogden's career at the University of Chicago was supplied by Andrew S. Hannah, acting university registrar, in a letter to the author dated 8 February 2002; the summary of her course work was compiled from photocopies of her transcripts sent to the author by Mr. Hannah.
5. Robert N. Mory, who assisted Ogden for several years while she prepared her edition of Chauliac and knew her well, suggested in a telephone interview with the author, on 28 August

2001, that Ogden had worked with Craigie. Regarding Watson's role in the *DAE*, see Mitford M. Mathews, "Of Matters Lexicographical," 122–23.

6. Mathews, "Of Matters Lexicographical," 51.

7. Ogden, *"Liber de Diversis Medicinis,"* v.

8. Benzie, *Dr. F. J. Furnivall,* 117.

9. For information about the early history of the *MED*, see Adams, "Sanford Brown Meech at the *Middle English Dictionary*"; and Adams, "Phantom Dictionaries."

10. Jones, *Howard Mumford Jones,* 149.

11. Cassidy made this remark during an interview with the author on 10 January 1991.

12. Cassidy, "Hope Emily Allen," 150.

13. Ibid., 150–51.

14. Hirsh, *Hope Emily Allen,* 112.

15. Information provided by Hope Lampert Burnam and Bruce Burnam in a letter to the author, dated 26 March 2002.

16. Kurath, "Report, [1]."

17. For a full account of these letters and their importance to the *MED*, see Adams, *"Dialect Dilemma."* The letters can be found among the *MED* archives in the Bentley Historical Library at the University of Michigan.

18. Kuhn, "On the Making of the *Middle English Dictionary*," 124.

19. Kurath's report can be found among the archives of the *MED* in the Bentley Historical Library at the University of Michigan. The quotation here is printed with permission.

20. White, *Year's Work in English Studies,* 244a.

21. Quirk, review of the *Middle English Dictionary,* 580.

22. Pilch, review of the *Middle English Dictionary,* 155.

23. Flasdieck, review of the *Middle English Dictionary,* 252.

24. Bromwich, "University Printing Today," 75a.

25. For a full account of the *MED*'s reading program, see Jost's two excellent articles, "Reading Program of the *Middle English Dictionary*"; and "Survey of the Reading Program of the *Middle English Dictionary*."

26. Kuhn, "On the Making of the *Middle English Dictionary*," 20.

27. Ogden, *Cyrurgie of Guy de Chauliac*."

28. Kuhn, "On the Making of the *Middle English Dictionary*," 27–33.

29. Ibid., 33–35.

30. Ibid., 35–36.

31. Ogden, *Cyrurgie of Guy de Chauliac,* xi.

32. Ogden, review of *The Middle English Translation of Guy de Chauliac's Anatomy,* 427.

33. Ibid., 427–28.

34. Michael R. McVaugh referred to this particular virtue of Ogden's work in a telephone interview with the author on 18 December 2001.

35. Wallner, review of *Cyrurgie of Guy de Chauliac,* 4, 3.

36. McVaugh, *Text,* vii.

37. Ibid., viii.

38. Ogden with McVaugh, *Commentary,* 1.43.

39. Michael R. McVaugh, telephone interview with the author, 18 December 2000.

40. Robert N. Mory, telephone interview with the author, 28 August 2001.

41. John Ogden, letter to the author dated 26 April 2002.
42. Robert N. Mory, telephone interview with the author, 28 August 2001.

Select Bibliography of Works by Margaret Ogden

Editor. *"Liber de Diversis Medicinis."* Early English Text Society Original Series, 207. London: Oxford University Press, 1938.

With Hans Kurath, Sherman M. Kuhn, et al. *Middle English Dictionary A–I*. Ann Arbor: University of Michigan Press, 1952–62.

With Charles E. Palmer and Richard L. McKelvey. *A Bibliography of Middle English Texts*. Ann Arbor: University of Michigan Press, 1954.

With H. V. S. Ogden. *English Taste in Seventeenth Century Landscape*. Ann Arbor: University of Michigan Press, 1955.

Review of *The Middle English Translation of Guy de Chauliac's Anatomy*, edited by Björn Wallner. *Review of English Studies* 17 (1966): 425–28.

"Guy de Chauliac's Theory of the Humors." *Journal of the History of Medicine and Allied Sciences* 25 (1969): 272–91.

Editor. *The Cyrurgie of Guy de Chauliac*. Early English Text Society, o.s., 265. London: Oxford University Press, 1971.

"The Galenic Works Cited in Guy de Chauliac's *Chirurgia Magna*." *Journal of the History of Medicine and Allied Sciences* 28 (1973): 24–33.

With Michael R. McVaugh. *Commentary*. Vol. 2 of *Inventarium sive chirurgia magna*, by Guy de Chauliac, edited by Michael McVaugh, Studies in Ancient Medicine, 14. Leiden: E. J. Brill, 1997.

Works Cited

Adams, Michael. "*Dialect Dilemma: The 'Middle English Dictionary' and Techniques of Historical Lexicography*." In preparation.

———. "Phantom Dictionaries: The *Middle English Dictionary* before Kurath." *Dictionaries* 23 (2002): 95–114.

———. "Sanford Brown Meech at the *Middle English Dictionary*." *Dictionaries* 16 (1995): 151–85.

Benzie, William. *Dr. F. J. Furnivall: A Victorian Scholar Adventurer*. Norman, Okla.: Pilgrim Books, 1983.

Bromwich, John. "University Printing Today." *Cambridge Review* 79 (26 October 1957): 72–75.

Brown, Carleton, and Rossell Hope Robbins. *The Index of Middle English Verse*. New York: Columbia University Press, 1943.

Cassidy, Frederic G. "Hope Emily Allen: A Personal Reminiscence." *Dictionaries* 11 (1989): 149–51.

Dictionary of American English. 4 vols. Edited by William A. Craigie, James R. Hulbert, et al. Chicago: University of Chicago Press, 1938–44.

Dictionary of the Older Scottish Tongue. Edited by William A. Craigie, A. J. Aitken, et al. Chicago: University of Chicago Press, 1933–2001.

Flasdieck, H. F. 1957. Review of the *Middle English Dictionary*. *Anglia* 74: 251–52.

Hirsh, John C. *Hope Emily Allen: Medieval Scholarship and Feminism*. Norman, Okla.: Pilgrim Books, 1988.

Jones, Howard Mumford. *Howard Mumford Jones: An Autobiography*. Madison: University of Wisconsin Press, 1979.

Jost, David. "The Reading Program of the *Middle English Dictionary:* Evaluation and Instructions." *Dictionaries* 6 (1984): 113–27.

———. "Survey of the Reading Program of the *Middle English Dictionary.*" *Dictionaries* 7 (1985): 201–13.

Kuhn, Sherman M. "On the Making of the *Middle English Dictionary.*" *Dictionaries* 4 (1982): 14–41.

———. Review of *The Cyrurgie of Guy de Chauliac,* by M. S. Ogden. *Speculum* 47 (1972): 544–48.

———, ed. *The Vespasian Psalter.* Ann Arbor: University of Michigan Press, 1965.

Kurath, Hans. "Report on the Middle English Dictionary, 1951." Bentley Historical Library, MED archives, currently uncatalogued. Quoted here with permission.

Kurath, Hans, et al. *Handbook to the Linguistic Geography of New England.* Providence, R.I.: Brown University Press, 1939.

———. *Linguistic Atlas of New England.* 3 vols. Providence, R.I.: Brown University Press, 1939–43.

Mathews, Mitford M. "Of Matters Lexicographical." *American Speech* 33 (1958): 51–55.

———. "Of Matters Lexicographical." *American Speech* 33 (1958): 119–24.

McVaugh, Michael R., ed. *Text.* Vol. 1 of *Inventarium sive chirurgia magna,* by Guy de Chauliac, edited by Michael R. McVaugh, Studies in Ancient Medicine, 14. Leiden: E. J. Brill, 1997.

Middle English Dictionary Records. Bentley Historical Library, University of Michigan.

Pilch, Herbert. Review of the *Middle English Dictionary. Word* 12 (1957): 151–56.

Quirk, Randolph. Review of the *Middle English Dictionary. Modern Language Review* 51 (1956): 578–81.

Wallner, Björn. *The Middle English Translation of Guy de Chauliac's "Anatomy."* Lund, Sw.: Gleerup, 1964.

———. Review of *The Cyrurgie of Guy de Chauliac,* by Margaret S. Ogden. *English Studies* 54 (1973): 1–4.

Wells, John E. *A Manual of the Writings in Middle English, 1050–1400.* 9 vols. New Haven, Conn.: Yale University Press, 1916–41.

White, Beatrice, ed. *The Year's Work in English Studies.* London: John Murray, for the English Association, 1956 (for 1954).

CHAPTER 50

Debunking the Myths, Transmitting Knowledge in Clear Language
Régine Pernoud (1909–1998)

Josette A. Wisman

Régine Pernoud was one of the most prolific medievalists in France in the twentieth century, and without a doubt, the one who did the most to further studies on Joan of Arc. Her numerous books and articles in popular magazines and newspapers, her participation as a historical consultant in documentaries and films for cinema and television, her radio and television interviews in France and abroad, her exhibitions in museums and libraries, her papers and lectures—all contributed to bringing to the general public, particularly in France, an awareness of the accomplishments of the Middle Ages. Régine Pernoud greatly helped change the narrow views many held of medieval times as merely an epoch of violence, ignorance, and superstition. Her life is an example of a dedicated historian who worked incessantly to make knowledge accessible to the layperson while also contributing to the scholarly community.

The Early Years

Régine Pernoud was born in Château-Chinon on 17 June 1909. Her father, Louis Pernoud, was a land surveyor and a part-time insurance man when he and Nelly Fournier married in 1901. While they resided at Pont-de-Beauvoisin in the Savoie region, their first son, René, was born. The family then moved to Château-Chinon in Burgundy, where the father bought a commission as an archivist at the courthouse of the town. Three children were born there: Paul, Jean, and then Régine. Louis Pernoud created what we would now call the tourism office there, and his daughter was later invited to become a member of the local "Académie" in homage to her father.[1] The

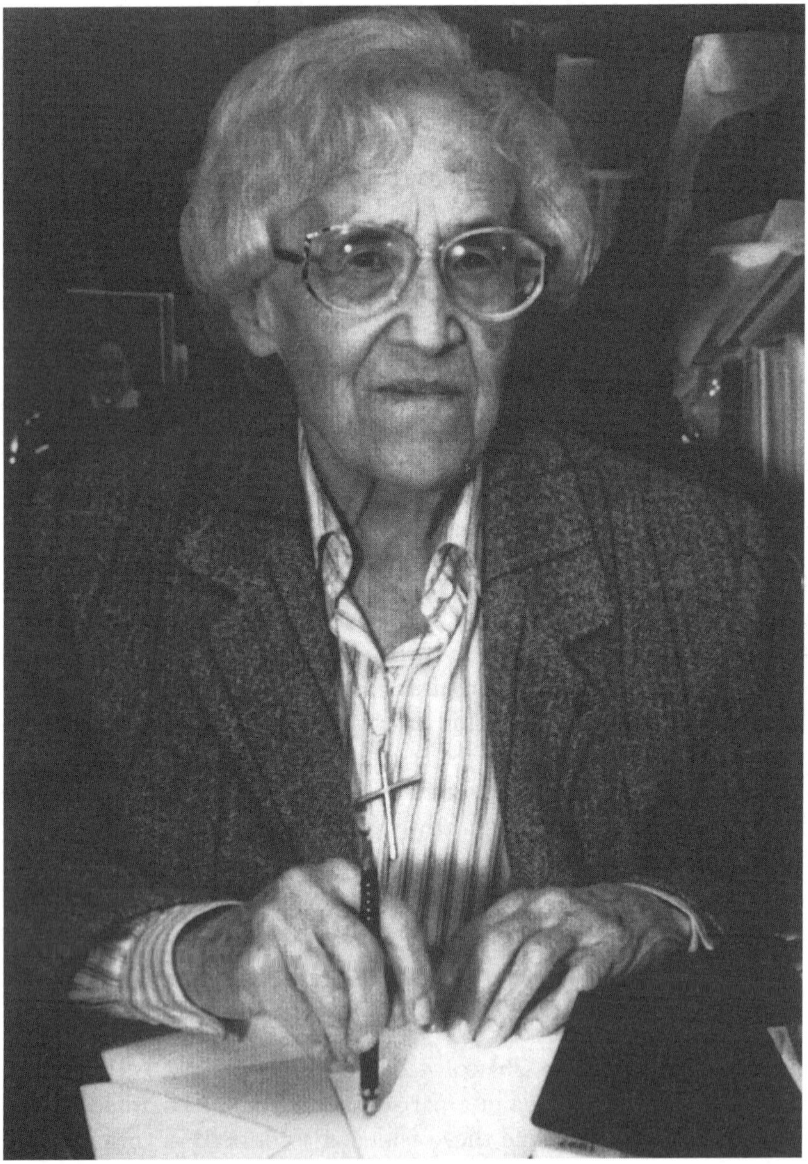

family lived ten stable and prosperous years there until 1912, the year when Louis Pernoud sold his commission and moved his wife and children to Marseille. There he served as archivist in the Bonasse Bank. Two other children were born after Régine: Madeleine and then Georges, with whom Régine would be especially close throughout her entire life.

The family did not fare well in Marseille, where they lived in semi-poverty for many years. Régine Pernoud wrote that her father was a dreamer, a man who did not know how to handle money matters. He was a stubborn man who liked to play the role of the paterfamilias in the home, a cold man toward his wife and children, not able to get along with any of his progeny. Outside the house he was a shy man who went on working for years at the bank without ever requesting a raise, leaving his household in continual financial difficulties. Understandably, this precarious situation hardly made for a happy family. Régine would later describe her insensitive father as "a father with a sad face."[2] Her mother, who did not have a formal education, had been raised by two aunts who encouraged her to read the classics of literature. She had been taught how to play the piano and had loved the theater. She would tell her children about the plays that she had seen in Paris when she visited relatives, and she made her children promise to get a good education "in order to be able to choose the life that they wanted later on."[3] Régine Pernoud expressed deep admiration for her mother, who worked as hard as she could to give her family a decent life although in dire straits.

Régine Pernoud got the reading bug from her mother and taught herself to read many years before she was sent to school at the rather late age of seven. At home the whole family, except for the father, would have heated discussions at the dinner table about the books that they were reading, and Régine Pernoud was fond of saying how her mother was sometimes obliged to close the windows for fear that the neighbors would think the worst when hearing all the loud voices. Both parents were devout Catholics and had decided that, in spite of the economic hardship that it represented, they would send all their children to Catholic schools.

Régine went to school at the Cours Sainte-Marthe and then to the Cours Notre-Dame-de-France, where the costs of her studies were largely paid by the institutions. She was a good student despite the fact that she started having hearing difficulties, which worsened with age. Régine said that she got along well with her schoolmates, who came mostly from wealthy Marseille families. But for some unclear reasons, during her high school years Régine developed a "strong antagonism towards the bourgeois families" of that city.[4]

Régine proved to be such a good student that she was ready to take her *baccalauréat*, the French national exam that serves as a gateway to university studies, at the tender age of fifteen. However, she was thought to be too young and forced to wait another year. But she was so highly thought of that the administrators at Notre-Dame-de-France offered her a teaching position while she was waiting for the permission to take the *bac*. She thus taught Greek and history to younger students when she was but fifteen. Régine passed the *baccalauréat* in 1924 and 1925, only a few years after it was first open to women, in 1920. After that she enrolled at the University of Aix-en-Provence for two years to pursue a *licence-ès-lettres*, a degree that she would complete in Paris.

In 1928 she came to Paris, having decided to prepare for a career as a librarian or an archivist by entering the famous École des chartes. She took preparatory classes at the Collège Sévigné and was accepted at the école in 1929. It is there that she discovered the Middle Ages, an age, as she said, "that represented for [her] a liberation.... [She] could see a very humane society which was not as obsessed as antiquity had been by military prowess, and full of scorn for the defeated; [she saw] a society which placed the highest importance on the individual."[5] Thus far, all of her teachers and professors had stressed the superiority of antiquity over the Middle Ages, but at the École des chartes, the emphasis was on the study of medieval documents, and most of the courses taught there dealt with the Middle Ages. Her teachers at Notre-Dame-de-France would later reproach her for "abandoning" the study of the greatness that was antiquity.

Fourteen Years in Limbo

In 1930, the Pernoud family moved to Fontenay-aux-Roses, near Paris, where they made friends with their neighbors, the famous medievalists Ferdinand Lot and his wife Myrrha Lot-Borodine who taught Russian to Régine. In 1933 she received her degree from the École des chartes, but she was not to have full-time employment using her competence before 1947. As she remarked, she was classified as an "unemployed intellectual" for fourteen years by the employment agencies. While working at various part-time jobs in Paris and in the suburbs, she decided to start studying for a doctorate in history at the Sorbonne. In 1936 she defended her dissertation, an edition of a thirteenth-century Latin manuscript on the port of Marseille, which she published as *Les Statuts municipaux de Marseille*.

From 1936 to 1940 she traveled intensely in Europe, and in 1938 she was able to secure another part-time job as an archivist for the private libraries of Jean Lebaudy, owner of a castle first built by Sully. In the castle, located in Rosny-sur-Seine, not very far from Paris, Régine Pernoud was given the task of writing forms describing in detail all the books and manuscripts held in the library. Lebaudy had another library in his home in Paris, and Pernoud was asked to do the same work there. Among the Lebaudy manuscripts she found several original texts that she published with the approval and help of Jean Lebaudy: a fifteenth-century guide for pilgrims going to the Holy Land; the letters of Suffren, who battled the English along the coasts of India in the eighteenth century; and various eighteenth-century documents pertaining to explorations in South America.

During the war Régine was allowed to bring her widowed and handicapped mother (victim of a stroke) and her sister to Rosny, where they lived until the beginning of

1943. They then moved to a house near Carcassonne, where they spent the rest of the war, and where Régine Pernoud started writing a book based on ten years of research on the Middle Ages. She wrote it, as she said, "to make known the serenity of the Romanesque abbeys, the lyricism of the Gothic cathedrals, the refinement of the courtly tradition, and also the deep and long-lasting equilibrium of the medieval society whose goal was to make the people blossom."[6] She wanted a large audience for her book and followed her brother Georges's advice to write for nonspecialists, people "who did not know."[7] She titled this first presentation of the medieval world to the lay reader *Lumière du Moyen Âge,* and Grasset published it in 1944. In this book Régine Pernoud clearly spelled out her views of the Middle Ages: first, that the term "Middle Ages," which encompasses one thousand years, was a misnomer, for it was not an intermediary period lost between the brilliance of antiquity and the Renaissance, but an original era that saw innovations and creations even more remarkable than those of these two periods. She also asserted that, thanks to Christianity, slavery and even servitude disappeared almost totally during the Middle Ages. She believed that feudalism was a mutual commitment based on trust and respect, and that it had given birth to the *commune,* far superior, to her mind, to the city of antiquity and the modern centralized state. She claimed that in the Middle Ages the bourgeoisie was not yet a caste, the guilds were not yet monopolies, chivalry was not just an honor society, the nobility was not yet an aristocracy, and the king not yet an absolute monarch.[8] The last words of her book rhapsodized the Middle Ages: "Overall, there is [in the Middle Ages] a trust in life, a *joie de vivre* that has no equivalent in any other civilization. . . . [I]n its philosophy, in its architecture, in its way of life, everywhere a powerful affirmation of the joy of living can be seen, something that reminds us of the delightful statement made by Louis VII, who was attacked for disliking pomp: 'At the French court, we only have bread, wine, and gaiety.'"[9]

The book was awarded the Fémina-Varesco Prize, and it was reviewed in newspapers. Not all were favorable. Many critics found that Régine Pernoud's enthusiasm for the beauty of the medieval civilization gave a far too rosy picture of these centuries. She had also made obvious her denial of the superiority of the Greek and Roman civilizations. For example, she could not understand—perhaps because of her profound Christian faith—why Saint Paul was not studied in religious schools as much as Horace. But in spite of the negative criticism, her book made her famous in the world of arts and letters. Both the poet Blaise Cendrars and the painter Henri Matisse highly praised her book. She went on to develop a deep and long-lasting friendship with the famous painter.

In 1945 she left her house near Carcassonne to go to Jouques, near Aix-en-Provence, in the hope of opening a bilingual (French-English) secondary school. The project never materialized, but while in Jouques she was asked by one of her former professors to give a series of lectures at the university on modern art, a subject of research that was new to her. Her lectures were very successful. They became the basis of her book *Les Grandes Epoques de l'art en Occident* that she would publish in 1954.

Recognition

In July 1946 she moved back to Paris with her family, thinking she might launch a new career as a museum curator. She enrolled in courses at the École du Louvre, where she was much influenced by one of her professors, the famous Georges-Henri Rivière. In March 1947, fourteen years after she graduated from the École des chartes, she found her first full-time position as the curator of the Reims Municipal Museum. Régine Pernoud put together several successful exhibitions, one of them on the role of the Champagne region during the Crusades. However, because she was very close to her mother, her sister, and her brother Georges, who had all remained in Paris, she was happy to return to live with them when offered a position as curator of the Museum of French History at the Archives nationales in 1949. Desirous of opening the museum to a large audience, she began renovating its rooms so as to be able to organize exhibits attracting visitors of all ages and social and educational backgrounds. Her first exhibit was to show the daily life of medieval people as well as the wealth of the nobility and the church as exemplified in seals and coats of arms. Although the show was favorably reviewed in the press in general, Régine Pernoud believed that to put together a show for the general audience had made her vulnerable to attacks from the erudite. Yet famous visitors came to the show: Matisse attended one morning, to be followed that same afternoon by the Swiss medievalist Reto Bezzola.

Régine Pernoud professed great admiration for Bezzola. She believed him to be unfairly neglected by French medievalists teaching in the universities. She especially admired his scholarly books on courtly love, a topic she thought most French medievalists unduly ignored or disdained. For example, they favored Jean de Meun's second professorial part of *The Romance of the Rose* over Guillaume de Lorris's first poetic part. Pernoud saw in Jean de Meun's writing "the emergence of the bourgeois and antifeminist spirit that would be put into action two centuries later, and that would gain more and more acceptance. It showed how [the] University, as soon as it was born, turned its back to the courtly tradition, which is a truly humanistic and poetical tradition, and the cradle of [French] literature, to the advantage of a rigid, dogmatic, and masculine form of learning."[10] These words are revealing: Régine Pernoud would, to her dying day, distrust university scholars in general for being too rationalistic, too bourgeois, but also for having a bias against women and people outside the profession.[11]

In 1951 she was responsible for the first part of the multivolume *Histoire du peuple français,* titled *Des origines au Moyen Âge*. It is a remarkable overview of the social and political history of France from its Celtic background up to the reign of Charles V. Noteworthy is that in the last part of her study Régine Pernoud reiterates her negative views of the bourgeoisie. She claims that the bourgeois Étienne Marcel's attempt at establishing a parliament was purely grounded on private interest. Noticeable also in this work is her omission of the role of women in history.

In 1952 Régine Pernoud was asked to write an article on Joan of Arc, which she agreed to do, although with some reluctance at the outset. She would later avow that until that invitation this historical character had never attracted her. She started reading about Joan and found a wealth of information on her. She soon became fascinated with her research topic, but the historian in her could not be content just to write a short piece when confronted with so much. She decided to write a book on the maid of Lorraine. Thus, her first book on Joan, *Vie et mort de Jeanne d'Arc: Les Témoignages du procès de réhabilitation* was published in 1953. It was to be followed by many others with Joan as the main subject.

Régine Pernoud lost her position as the curator of the Museum of French History, but she continued to work at the Archives nationales until 1974. During these years she put together several exhibitions on Joan in several locations, on Saint Louis at the Archives nationales, on Notre-Dame at the Sainte-Chapelle, and on Mont-Saint-Michel at the Palais de Justice in Paris, as well as others. This was a change from her work as archivist. She also made a one-hour documentary on the archives with the director Jean Vigne, with whom she was to collaborate again on films and books.

In 1954 she published her first book dealing with art, *Les Grandes Époques de l'art en Occident.* The title is misleading, for the book is a study of medieval art, and her defense of it against the common view of the time that Romanesque and Gothic arts were inferior to classical and Renaissance arts.

Régine Pernoud published her two volumes titled *Histoire de la bourgeoisie en France* in 1960 and 1962; this work took her eighteen years to research and write. It captured her long-held dislike of the bourgeoisie, which she saw as too materialistic, moralistic, and suppressive of what is original in all human beings. These sentiments had been kept alive by a promise that she and her siblings had made to one another on one 14 October in the 1920s not to become "surreptitiously bourgeois" themselves. Her book was dedicated to her two younger siblings in memory of that date. In the first volume, which dealt mostly with the Middle Ages, Régine Pernoud recognized the primordial role of the bourgeoisie in the creation and flourishing of cities. But she indicted them for losing their dynamism when they assumed power, and she was appalled at their taste for speculation and their search for personal gain.

In 1965 she was asked to become a historical advisor to the newly founded periodical *Archeologia,* and she stayed on the board of advisors until 1970.

Orléans: Fame and Controversy

In 1974 André Malraux, in his role as minister of culture, decided to establish a center where all the documents concerning Joan of Arc would be collected, stored, and available to whoever wanted to study them. He had met Régine Pernoud several times and asked her to assume the position of director of the newly created Centre Jeanne d'Arc in Orléans. The center's aim was and still is to gather all existing documentation on Joan of Arc, including contemporary documents, works of art, films, and realia. Its library has now gathered more than sixteen thousand books and documents. Régine Pernoud directed the center from its creation until 1985.

In 1976 her book *Pour en finir avec le Moyen Âge* gained her an unexpectedly wide audience. She posited that serious, accurate, and objective study of the Middle Ages had not reached a broader general audience because research had been confined to libraries that barred entry to those not affiliated with an institution of higher learning. In addition she wrote that university professors "have a physical incapacity to see what does not conform to the ideas that their brains have concocted."[12] She stressed the fact that, contrary to a widespread belief, the Greek and Roman civilizations were well known in the Middle Ages and were neither despised nor thrown aside. Medieval people were not pale imitators of the ancients as the Renaissance scholars and artists were to be. Instead, they exhibited an originality that had not been adequately appreciated. She also wrote a chapter to prove that the medieval church was never as repressive as it was to become in later centuries. She devoted a full chapter in *Pour en finir avec le Moyen Âge* to women in the Middle Ages, arguing that their position and their influence in society were very important. Moreover, they were highly respected by the church, as evidenced by the great number of female saints and religious women in charge of abbeys. Pernoud lamented the veritable absence of studies of women as a historical category and particularly the lack of research about women in the Middle Ages. She hoped that she had helped rectify this lacuna a few years later when she published *La Femme au temps des cathédrales* and *Visages de femmes au Moyen Âge* as well as other studies of women of the Middle Ages.

Statements that Pernoud made in *Pour en finir avec le Moyen Âge* provoked mixed reactions, in particular to her ideas that women were not victimized in the Middle Ages. Georges Duby challenged her theses in at least two books: first, in *Le Chevalier, la femme et le prêtre: Le Mariage dans la France féodale* published in 1981, and then in *Mâle Moyen Âge* published in 1986.[13] In the latter Duby asserted that "[t]he Middle Ages are male, definitely. All the voices that I hear and that inform me are male voices; they are convinced of the superiority of their sex. I only hear them. They talk mostly of their desire, so they talk about women. They are afraid of them, therefore they despise them."[14] He saw in courtly love a trumped game, where the courtly lover wanted to gain access to his lord rather than the love of his lord's wife. Duby believed that on the whole women in the Middle Ages did not agree to marriage willingly; most of the time their consent was wrested from them. In brief, medieval women were treated like commodities. If Régine Pernoud thought the Middle Ages were a golden age for women, Georges Duby, on the contrary, saw them as such for men.

Pernoud's biographies of famous women were counter to the trends in historical research being carried out at the *École des annales*. The *Annales* historians emphasized structure rather than narrative, made use of new data, such as topographical and historical maps, and documented and captured *mentalités*—the character of earlier attitudes, mental approaches, collective psychology, beliefs, and ritual expressions of them. They focused on *la longue durée*—long-term historical structures and dynamics; by contrast Régine Pernoud and the professors at the École des chartes—often called "positivistic historians" tressed the study of documents of an age as they were, although their interpretations often revealed their subjective predilections.

The Last Years

Régine Pernoud traveled a good deal during her lifetime, and she often remembered fondly her trips to the United States: she came to this country first in December 1949, armed with a Fulbright Scholarship to study the educational services that museums provided in America. This first visit lasted three months. In the 1970s and 1980s, she came back to teach courses at Bryn Mawr, later at Anna Maria College, and then at Laval University in Canada. She gave papers in many foreign countries, among them England, Canada, Italy, Germany, Chile, and Brazil. Her last paper presentation in America was at the International Congress on Medieval Studies in Kalamazoo in 1991; her topic was Hildegard of Bingen. She also went to Japan in 1982 to set up an exhibit on Joan of Arc.

After many years as head of the Centre Jeanne d'Arc in Orléans, Régine Pernoud retired in 1985. But this indefatigable woman did not rest on her laurels. For the remaining thirteen years of her life she continued writing and traveling. In 1986 and 1987, respectively, she published two important books: *Le Moyen Âge pour quoi faire?* with Raymond Latouche and Jean Gimpel, and *Jeanne d'Arc* with Marie-Véronique Clin. The latter work is widely considered one of the best books on Joan of Arc. It brings together information and insights from virtually all the research that had been carried out on Joan of Arc. The English translation of this work is superior to the original French, thanks to the translator and editors, Jeremy duQuesnay Adams and Bonnie Wheeler, who rectified some factual errors and wrote considerable supplementary information on Joan of Arc scholarship (with full approval of the two authors).[15]

Régine Pernoud also wrote many prefaces to books and was the advisor for many documentaries and feature films for television and movie theaters. She was the historical advisor for the movie *Jeanne la Pucelle* made by Jacques Rivette in 1998 with Sandrine Bonnaire in the title role. She wrote radio programs and was often interviewed on French and foreign radio and television. Many of her books were translated into various foreign languages. She received numerous awards during her lifetime, among them the Prix de la Ville de Paris (1978) for her entire oeuvre. Twice the Académie Française rewarded her for her books, first in 1981 and then in 1997. She was named doctor honoris causa by both Anna Maria College in Paxton, Massachusetts, and the University of Rio de Janeiro, Brazil. Régine Pernoud died in Paris on 23 April 1998. Her papers were donated to the Centre Jeanne d'Arc in Orléans.

Notes

1. R. Pernoud, *Villa Paradis*, 16. Most of my information on Régine Pernoud's life comes from this work, her memoirs, dictated to her nephew Jérôme Pernoud, interviews of her and Jean Tulard given to him in *Jeanne d'Arc, Napoléon,* and to Laetitia de Traversay in *Histoire et*

Lumière. I would like to thank Jérôme Pernoud and Olivier Bouzy, associate director of the Centre Jeanne d'Arc in Orléans, who have very kindly provided answers to my numerous questions regarding Régine Pernoud.

2. R. Pernoud, *Villa Paradis,* 16, all the quotations are my translation.
3. R. Pernoud, *Villa Paradis,* 10.
4. R. Pernoud, *Villa Paradis,* 63.
5. R. Pernoud, *Villa Paradis,* 93.
6. R. Pernoud, *Villa Paradis,* 189.
7. R. Pernoud, *Villa Paradis,* 194.
8. I paraphrase Pernoud's own words in *Lumière du Moyen Âge,* 7.
9. R. Pernoud, *Villa Paradis,* 258.
10. R. Pernoud, *Villa Paradis,* 245.
11. We can read in one of her last books, *Histoire et lumière,* the following words that could very well apply to her: "The university decided in the thirteenth century to monopolize knowledge in a way that excluded women from the erudite world, especially in France" (20), and: "The adverse effect of my desire to vulgarize has been that I am not accepted among 'the people to be admired' according to the university people" (21) (my translation).
12. R. Pernoud, *Pour en finir avec le Moyen Âge,* 10 (my translation).
13. Duby's *Le Chevalier, la femme et le prêtre* was published in English as *The Knight, the Lady, and the Priest.* His *Mâle Moyen Âge* was published in English as *Love and Marriage in the Middle Ages.*
14. Duby, *Mâle Moyen Âge,* 7 (my translation).
15. Olivier Bouzy in his article, "Transcriptions Errors in Texts of Joan of Arc's History," has also added much to the scholarship on Joan by questioning the way Jules Quicherat edited his four volumes on Joan's trials. He showed that Quicherat had not read all the manuscripts firsthand but had relied on readers, who made mistakes in transcription. Many critics had for years accepted Quicherat's work as the definitive edition without checking the original documents.

Select Bibliography of Works by Régine Pernoud

Régine Pernoud wrote: "I have never had an article in *Bibliothèque de l'École des chartes* or in any famous historical journal. Truly, I was not adding anything to erudition, my sole intention was to transmit knowledge in a clear language" (*Histoire et lumière,* 20–21). She published many articles in popular magazines such as *L'Oeil, Historia, Historama, Cadmos, Cahiers de la cinémathèque, Le Temps stratégique, La Vie, L'Express, Le Point,* and *Témoignage chrétien,* among others. She also wrote several children's books, numerous prefaces to books, and gave many speeches and lectures. Her papers at the Centre Jeanne d'Arc in Orléans testify to her many activities; unfortunately they have not yet been classified.

Régine Pernoud wrote and edited more than sixty books. The following list consists of those considered her most important works. Dates of the first French and English editions are given, but many of her books were later reprinted or appeared as a new and sometimes revised edition.

Un Guide du pèlerin de Terre Sainte au XVe siècle. Mantes, Fr.: Imprimerie du Petit Mantais, 1940.

Lumière du Moyen Âge. Paris: Grasset, 1945. Translated by Joyce Emerson as *The Glory of the Medieval World.* New York: Roy Publishers, 1950.

L'Unité française. Paris: Presses Universitaires de France, 1946. Reprinted as *La Formation de la France,* Paris: Presses Universitaires de France, 1966.

Les Origines de la bourgeoisie. Paris: Presses Universitaires de France, 1947. Reprinted as *La Bourgeoisie,* Paris: Presses Universitaires de France, 1985.

Des Origines au Moyen Âge (1er siècle avant J.-C.–1380). Vol. 1 of *Histoire du peuple français,* edited by Louis-Henri Parias. Paris: Nouvelle Librairie de France, 1951.

Vie et mort de Jeanne d'Arc: Les témoignages du procès de réhabilitation 1450–1456. Paris: Hachette, 1953. Translated by J. M. Cohen as *The Retrial of Jean d'Arc: The Evidence at the Trial for Her Rehabilitation 1450–1456,* intro. by Katherine Anne Porter. New York: Harcourt, Brace and Company, 1955.

Les Grandes Époques de l'art en occident. Paris: Editions du Chêne, 1954.

La Littérature médiévale. Vol. 3 of *Histoire des Littératures,* edited by Raymond Queneau. Paris: Gallimard, 1957.

Les Croisés. Paris: Hachette, 1959. Translated by Enid McLeod as *The Crusades.* New York: Putnam, 1962.

Histoire de la bourgeoisie en France. 2 vols. Paris: Editions du Seuil, 1960–62.

Jeanne D'Arc par elle-même et par ses témoins. Paris: Editions du Seuil, 1962. Translated by Edward Hyams as *Joan of Arc by Herself and Her Witnesses.* New York: Dorset Press, 1964.

Aliénor d'Aquitaine. Paris: Albin Michel, 1966. Translated by Peter Wiles as *Eleanor of Aquitaine.* London: Collins, 1968.

La Libération d'Orléans, 8 mai 1429. Paris: Gallimard, 1969.

Héloïse et Abélard. Paris: Albin Michel, 1970. Translated by Peter Wiles as *Heloise and Abelard.* London: Collins, 1973.

La Reine Blanche. Paris: Albin Michel, 1972. Translated by Henry Noël as *Blanche of Castille.* New York: Coward, McCann and Geoghegan, 1975.

Les Templiers. Paris: Presses Universitaires de France, 1974.

Pour en finir avec le Moyen Âge. Paris: Editions du Seuil, 1976. Translated by Anne Englund Nash as *Those Terrible Middle Ages: Debunking the Myths.* San Francisco: Ignatius Press, 2000.

La Femme au temps des cathédrales. Paris: Stock, 1980. Translated by Anne Côté-Harriss as *Women in the Days of the Cathedrals.* San Francisco: Ignatius Press, 1998.

Christine de Pisan. Paris: Calmann-Lévy, 1982.

With Georges Pernoud. *Le Tour de France médiéval.* Paris: Stock, 1982.

With Marie-Véronique Clin. *Jeanne d'Arc.* Paris: Fayard, 1986. Translated and revised by Jeremy duQuesnay Adams as *Joan of Arc: Her Story,* ed. Bonnie Wheeler. New York: St. Martin's Press, 1999.

With Raymond Delatouche and Jean Gimpel. *Le Moyen Âge pour quoi faire?* Paris: Stock, 1986.

La Femme au temps des croisades. Paris: Stock/Laurence Pernoud, 1990.

Villa Paradis: Souvenirs. Edited by Jérôme Pernoud. Paris: Stock, 1992.

Hildegarde de Bingen: Conscience inspirée du XIIe siècle. Monaco: Editions du Rocher, 1994. Translated by Paul Duggan as *Hildegard of Bingen: Inspired Conscience of the Twelfth Century.* New York: Marlowe, 1998.

J'ai nom Jeanne la Pucelle. Paris: Gallimard, 1994.

Réhabilitation de Jeanne d'Arc, reconquête de la France. Monaco: Editions du Rocher, 1995. Reprinted as *Jeanne d'Arc: La reconquête de la France,* Paris: Gallimard, 1997.

Les Templiers, chevaliers du Christ. Paris: Gallimard, 1995.

With Jean Tulard and Jérôme Pernoud. *Jeanne d'Arc, Napoléon: Le Paradoxe du biographe.* Monaco: Editions du Rocher, 1997.

With Laetitia de Traversay. *Histoire et Lumière*. Paris: Editions du Cerf, 1998.

Visages de femmes au Moyen Âge. Paris: Editions Zodiaque, 1998.

Works Cited

Bouzy, Olivier. "Transcriptions Errors in Texts of Joan of Arc's History." In *Fresh Verdicts on Joan of Arc,* edited by Bonnie Wheeler and Charles T. Wood, 73–83. New York: Garland, 1996.

Duby, Georges. *The Knight, the Lady, and the Priest: The Making of Modern Marriage in Medieval France*. Translated by Barbara Bray. New York: Pantheon Books, 1984.

——. *Mâle Moyen Âge*. Paris: Flammarion, 1988. Translated by Jane Dunnett as *Love and Marriage in the Middle Ages*. Chicago: University of Chicago Press, 1994.

Pernoud, Jerôme, Régine Pernoud, and Jean Tulard. *Jeanne d'Arc, Napoléon: Le Paradoxe du biographe*. Monaco: Editions du Rocher, 1997.

Traversay, Laetitia de, and Régine Pernoud. *Histoire et lumière*. Paris: Editions du Cerf, 1998.

CHAPTER 51

María Rosa Lida de Malkiel (1910–1962) and Medieval Spanish Literary Historiography

Ana M. Gómez-Bravo

THE YOUNGEST SIBLING born to a family of Eastern European (Polish) émigrés, María Rosa Lida was born in Buenos Aires on 7 November 1910, shortly after her family's arrival in Argentina. While embracing its adopted country and language, the Lida family kept a strong sense of their Jewish identity and the Yiddish language, which was the principal and native tongue of both parents. An avid reader since childhood, who is said to have spent her summers reading the Greek classics, María Rosa Lida attended the University of Buenos Aires during 1928–32, obtaining a degree and credential in secondary teaching and graduating with highest honors.[1] Pursuing her research interests and being recognized as a rising talent, she was invited to be part of the newly founded research center Instituto de Filología at the University of Buenos Aires, where she worked with influential intellectuals and authors such as Amado Alonso, Américo Castro, Pedro Henríquez Ureña, and Alfonso Reyes. Although the ideas and encouragement of these figures undoubtedly had an impact on her early formative years, her interests, writing, and work methodology had a highly individual character that was evident from the very start. She wrote her much-acclaimed dissertation on fifteenth-century Spanish poet Juan de Mena, later published as a book, and received her Ph.D. degree ("Doctora en filosofía y letras," summa cum laude) in 1947.[2]

Lida de Malkiel held various posts in Argentina from 1938 on, including teaching instructor at two Buenos Aires schools (1938–47); research associate and editorial assistant at the Instituto de Filología, University of Buenos Aires (1939–47); professor of classical Greek language and literature (1941–47), and concomitantly Spanish after 1944, at the Instituto Nacional del Profesorado; as well as lecturer at the Colegio Libre de Estudios Superiores in 1943, all in Buenos Aires. In 1947 she was awarded a

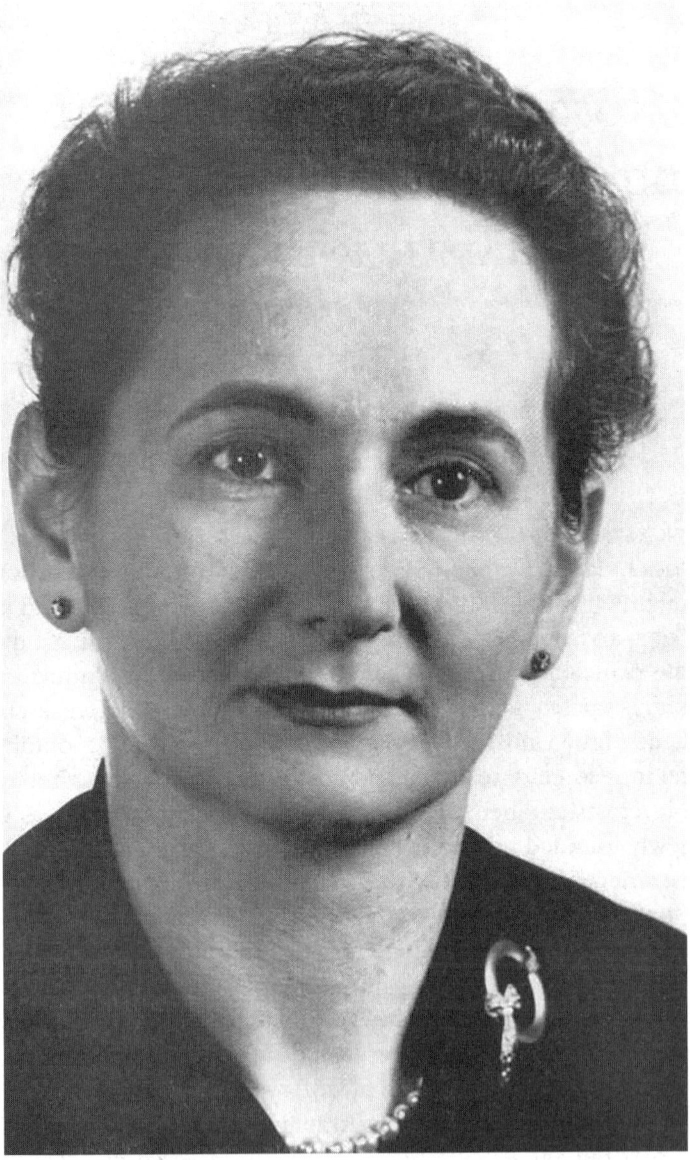

research fellowship in medieval Spanish literature by the Rockefeller Foundation, with residences first in Cambridge, Massachusetts, and subsequently in Berkeley, California. After corresponding by mail with Berkeley professor and world-renowned Romance philologist Yakov Malkiel, the two scholars finally met during Lida de Malkiel's stay in Cambridge. After she moved to Berkeley, the two were married in Oakland, California, on 2 March 1948. This event determined María Rosa Lida's permanent residence in the United States thereafter and Berkeley as her permanent home until her death in 1962, when she succumbed to cancer after a two-year battle. In 1948, 1950, and 1952, she was visiting lecturer during the summer sessions at the University of California, Berkeley. She was only on occasion professionally associated with Berkeley, but rather held a series of temporary positions at many prestigious universities around the United States and for a short period in Argentina. During 1949–51 she received a fellowship from the John Simon Guggenheim Memorial Foundation to study the legend of Alexander in medieval literature. This was followed by a string of visiting appointments at various prestigious universities, such as Ohio State University (summer 1953); Harvard University (one quarter, 1954); University of Wisconsin (special one-month appointment, 1955); University of California, Los Angeles (first summer session, 1958); University of Illinois, Urbana (Miller Visiting Professorship, 1959–60); Stanford University, Division of Modern European Languages (on a part-time basis, 1960–61 and part of 1962); University of Buenos Aires (second half of 1962); and University of California, Berkeley (first summer session, 1962). Her achievements were widely recognized in the field, and Lida de Malkiel was named a corresponding member of the Hispanic Society of America in 1952 and a corresponding member of the Spanish Real Academia de Córdoba de Ciencias, Bellas Letras y Nobles Artes in 1953. She also received an honorary degree (Litt.D.) from Smith College in 1955 and an achievement award from the American Association of University Women in 1958 and was elected as a corresponding member to the Academia Argentina de Letras in 1959. She was an advisor on the editorial board of two prestigious professional journals: *Nueva Revista de Filología Hispánica* (1947–), based in Mexico City, and *Hispanic Review* (1950–), published at the University of Pennsylvania.

These accomplishments show an indefatigable scholar and early and wide professional recognition of the groundbreaking quality of her work. Some of the originality of her work has been attributed to her thorough and early training in Greco-Latin classical letters. She was thus in the unique position of being able to identify and examine the impact of these classical texts in medieval, Golden Age, and later works. But her interests and abilities did not stop there. Her aptness at languages was fostered by years of firsthand contact with primary texts, through translations and readings. She was fluent in a number of European languages, though she used Spanish and English exclusively both in her publications and in her lectures. Lida de Malkiel's work methodology involved years of careful reading of primary and secondary sources, which she annotated in the margins. She took careful notes, which she used for the drafts that she wrote in her notebooks, and which she supplemented with additional citations in the form of slips of paper or file cards affixed to the relevant notebook. A particular piece would be subject to rewriting until the author considered it worthy of publication. This process was so painstakingly thorough and the material utilized by Lida de Malkiel so extensive that it often took several years for a piece to see the light in print form as a long article or book. This thoroughness and display of erudition was also her signature style for writing book reviews, which were often so extensive and meticulous that they were in reality review articles or even book drafts. Lida de Malkiel was not afraid of engaging in discussion or controversy with well-established scholars often regarded as leading authorities in the field, and she participated in such exchanges, often through one of her very thorough book reviews, with prominent figures such as Ramón Menéndez Pidal, Dámaso Alonso, or Ernst Robert Curtius. For this and her other work she earned a reputation as a discerning and firm critic who upheld the highest standards of scholarship. This was true in relation both to the work of others and to her own. Lida de Malkiel's numerous densely handwritten notebooks with drafts and notes of her books and articles are kept among the Yakov Malkiel papers at the University of California, Berkeley; various other materials, mostly articles and reviews, are kept at the University of California, Los Angeles.[3] Her notebooks are testament to her intense, unflagging, and diligent work through the years. Their careful preparation enabled her widower, Yakov Malkiel, to make their legacy known after Lida de Malkiel's untimely death, with minimum editorial interventions, often limited to the addition of a prologue or an addendum. This allowed some of Lida de Malkiel's pioneering work to be made known for over two decades after her death. For many years her work enriched the field of Hispanism in general and medieval studies in particular. Her posthumous publications also allowed for unusual coincidences, such as the reciprocal contribution of María Rosa Lida de Malkiel and Ramón Menéndez Pidal to each other's memorial volumes published by the journal *Romance Philology*.[4]

Lida de Malkiel's modus operandi reflected her meticulous and thorough research but also the wide variety of her interests and expertise. This approach to scholarship resulted in the striking fact that most of her more substantial contributions to the field, either in the form of long articles or books, were considered groundbreaking and took specialized studies in her areas of interest to a new level. These studies were, as evidenced by her notebooks, the product of many years of study and of careful revisions, as well as a reflection of her own trajectory of interests and a readjustment of the focus of her studies. Thus, Lida de Malkiel's early specialization in Greco-Roman classical literature, mostly developed during her formative years in Argentina, gave way to studies such as her book on Sophocles' theater and studies on Herodotus, Josephus, the classical tradition in Spain, or the highly original and widely acclaimed study on Dido in Spanish literature.[5] At the end of her time in Argentina, she took her research in a different direction, writing a dissertation on Spanish fifteenth-century poet Juan de Mena, a study that stemmed from what was becoming an extensive review of a book by Spanish scholar José Manuel Blecua.[6] This shift also occurred because materials on Spanish literature were more widely available to her than those on classical letters and also because of the well-established community of Hispanists in Argentina at the time and in particular at the Instituto de Filología at the University of Buenos Aires, where she worked. After finishing her dissertation, later published as a highly influential book, and her move to the United States under the auspices of the Rockefeller Foundation, she continued pursuing her interests and developing her expertise mainly, though by no means exclusively, in medieval Spanish literature. Lida de Malkiel had a novel view of later authors, such as Antonio de Guevara, Lope de Vega, Tirso de Molina, and even Bécquer, to cite but a few examples.[7]

Although firmly grounded in traditional historicist methodologies, she bore a personal interest to her research, which was related to different issues regarding various aspects of her ethnic, national, or gender identity. Although the bulk of the texts she studied pertained to European culture, she also paid close attention to Latin American literature, writing on Latin American folklore, material culture, and, in a most novel manner, the relation between classical and New World literature as a parallel tradition to the European adoption of classical themes and forms.[8] Her interest in Jewish intellectual history and identity was sustained for many years in the preparation of a major study on Josephus.[9] She found the figures of Philo and Josephus particularly appealing because of what she saw as the materialization of the perfect balance between the best of Greco-Roman and Judaic thought. Lida de Malkiel's explorations of issues of Jewish identity were extended to and combined with her interest in the impact of racial issues in the New World, as is evident from her study of the confusion of the Jews and the indigenous peoples of the Americas in Hispanic texts.[10] She also combined her interest in racial issues and classical Spanish literature, for instance, by analyzing their interconnectedness in texts by classical authors such as Lope de Vega.[11] These explorations are likely to be tied to the racially motivated obstacles to her being published in Germany during the Nazi regime or to the perishing of the European portion of her family that was unable to escape the Jewish massacre of the 1940s.[12] From her early writings it is also easy to see Lida de Malkiel's engagement in research topics that reflected issues of gender identity. Her translations of Emily Brontë and other noted female authors gave her much personal satisfaction. She dedicated monographic studies to noteworthy female figures of classical literature, for example, her studies on Helen of Troy and Sappho. Her much acclaimed book-length study of Virgil's work centered on the female figure Dido instead of the male protagonist, Aeneas. Dido, as a complex female figure who most likely spoke a dialect of classical Hebrew, must have struck a chord in Lida de Malkiel.[13] Her treatment of topics such as the "defense of women," for example, in relation to Dido is a novel and valuable contribution to the on-going scholarship on the subject of the pro- and anti-feminist debate through the centuries.[14] Her interests in these issues expanded to an inquiry on the establishment of individualism in literature, in regard both to a text and to an author, thus dispelling any potential approaches to medieval works as purely derivative products of classical texts.

Lida de Malkiel's major studies on medieval Spanish literature had a strong impact and managed to play a major role in the shaping of each of the individual subfields, most notably the literature of the fifteenth century, though she by no means confined herself to the late-medieval period. Her studies on *Libro de buen amor,* Rodríguez del Padrón, don Juan Manuel, Arthurian literature, *Celestina,* Juan de Mena, as well as those ranging from the idea of fame to the afterlife to the figure of the courtly lady, to name a few of her better-known works, marked a major turn in each on the individual subfields, particularly in the case of her studies on Mena and *Celestina.*[15] The end of the Middle Ages particularly interested her because of its complex nature as a period of change. She studied issues such as the impact of Greek and Latin literature and language on the vernacular and innovations in literary form, and significantly elaborated the idea of a pre-Renaissance in the fifteenth century. She was also interested in the period's changing politics and its impact on religious, social, and racial identities, particularly that of converted Jews, or *conversos,* in works such as Roja's *Celestina.* In this sense her interest in Josephus and Rojas and the similarities in their ethnic backgrounds and sociopolitical positions highlight common and relevant threads in her scholarship.

Clearly Lida de Malkiel opened new paths in some of the most important topics in medieval Spanish literature and in other areas. Her solid and wide knowledge of a variety of traditions, languages, and texts, together with her sharp memory and research methodologies, helped her introduce a highly original literary hermeneutics that set the path for contemporary and later scholars. Her personal background and engagement with the works she studied established a unique perspective that combined rigorous erudition, a comparatist eye, and an inquiry into issues as varied as courtly culture, religion, race, gender, and classicism, spanning many centuries and bringing together Roman and Greek classical Europe, Hebrew intellectual and literary tradition, and later European cultures and crossing over to colonial and contemporary Latin America. This placed her squarely at the forefront of Spanish literary studies, and her broad and powerful impact can be felt today in the work of contemporary scholars.

NOTES

1. Regarding her early interest in the classics, see Raimundo Lida's introduction to Lida de Malkiel, *Introducción al teatro de Sófocles,* 7.

2. See Lida de Malkiel, *Juan de Mena.*

3. Yakov Malkiel, Yakov Malkiel Papers, [ca. 1930–90], ca. 70 cartons, 1 tube, 1 oversize folder, Northern Regional Library Facility, Bancroft Library, UC Berkeley. María Rosa Lida de Malkiel [A collection of pamphlets on Romance philology, various pagings, 1940?-63?], articles and reviews; reprints and extracts from various periodicals, 1 v. (various pagings), Young Research Library, UCLA.

4. See *Romance Philology* 17 (1963) for Lida de Malkiel's memorial volume and *Romance Philology* 23 (1970) for Menéndez Pidal's.

5. See Lida de Malkiel, *Dido en la literatura española;* also Lida de Malkiel, "Earliest Trace of

Euripides in Spanish Literature"; Lida de Malkiel, *Introducción al teatro de Sófocles;* Lida de Malkiel, *La tradición clásica en España;* and her translation of Herodotus, *Los nueve libros de la historia.*

6. Lida de Malkiel, *Juan de Mena.* The book under review was the edition of Juan de Mena's *Laberinto de Fortuna* (Madrid: Espasa-Calpe, 1943).

7. See Lida de Malkiel, *Estudios de literatura española y comparada.*

8. See, among other examples, the treatment of these diverse materials in Lida de Malkiel, *Dido en la literatura española*; also Lida de Malkiel, *El cuento popular y otros ensayos.* See also Y. Malkiel, "María Rosa Lida de Malkiel como investigadora de las letras coloniales."

9. See, for example, Lida de Malkiel, "La dinastía de los Macabeos en Josefo y en la literatura española"; Lida de Malkiel, "En torno a Josefo y su influencia en la literatura española"; Lida de Malkiel, *Herodes*; Lida de Malkiel, *Jerusalén*; Lida de Malkiel, "La métrica en la Biblia"; Lida de Malkiel, "Las sectas judías y los 'procuradores' romanos." In his introductions to María Rosa Lida's posthumously published studies, Yakov Malkiel rightly emphasizes her personal and intellectual interest in Jewish figures and their influence on her choice of research topics.

10. See Lida de Malkiel with Y. Malkiel, "Jew and the Indian," 167–72.

11. See Lida de Malkiel, "Lope de Vega y los judíos"; and Lida de Malkiel, "El moro en las letras castellanas."

12. Regarding barriers to her publication in Germany, see Yakov Malkiel's introduction to Lida de Malkiel's *La tradición clásica en España,* 19 n. 5.

13. See, for example, Lida de Malkiel, "Cómo era Safo"; Lida de Malkiel, "Helena en los poemas homéricos"; Lida de Malkiel, "La mujer ante el lenguaje." Also relevant to her inquiries on gender and her own engagement in literary hermeneutics is her short but sharp article "Free Opportunity for Intellectual Pursuits."

14. Lida de Malkiel, *Dido en la literatura española,* 81–91.

15. See Lida de Malkiel, "El ambiente concreto en *La Celestina*"; Lida de Malkiel, "La dama como obra maestra de Dios"; Lida de Malkiel, *Estudios sobre la literatura española del Siglo XV;* Lida de Malkiel, "La hipérbole sagrada en la poesía castellana del siglo XV"; Lida de Malkiel, *Juan de Mena;* Lida de Malkiel, *La idea de la fama en la edad media castellana;* Lida de Malkiel, *Juan Ruiz;* Lida de Malkiel, *La originalidad artística de 'La Celestina';* Lida de Malkiel, "La técnica dramática de *La Celestina*"; Lida de Malkiel, *Two Spanish Masterpieces.* It is not possible here to offer a thorough review of Lida de Malkiel's extensive work. For a critical overview and introduction to the impact of Lida de Malkiel in the field of medieval Spanish, see, for example, Deyermond, *Historia y crítica de la Literatura Española,* vol. 1, *Edad Media;* and Deyermond, *Historia y crítica de la Literatura Española,* Primer Suplemento, vol. 1, *Edad Media.* For detailed and insightful information on her life and professional trajectory, see Yakov Malkiel's contribution to the memorial volume published in *Romance Philology* 17 (1963) after her death.

Select Bibliography of Works by María Rosa Lida de Malkiel

Because of the extensiveness of Lida de Malkiel's publications, only a selection of the most relevant ones is included here. For a more complete list, see María Rosa Lida de Malkiel's biography and initial bibliography in the memorial volume published by *Romance Philology* 17 (1963), updated by Margaret Sinclair Breslin in an appendix to Lida de Malkiel, *Herodes,* 220–44. Additional biobibliographical information may be found in Yakov Malkiel, *A Tentative Autobibliography. Romance Philology*, Special Issue, edited by Joseph J. Duggan and Charles B. Faulhaber

(Berkeley and Los Angeles: University of California Press, 1988–1989): nos. 763–778; and Y. Malkiel, "Supplement to *A Tentative Autobibliography.*" Other memorial volumes were published in *Filología* (Buenos Aires) 8 (1962); and in *Homenaje a María Rosa Lida de Malkiel y Raimundo Lida* (Buenos Aires: EDIGRAF, 1983).

"Cómo era Safo." *Revista Cubana* 8 (1937): 85–89.

"Helena en los poemas homéricos." *Cursos y Conferencias: Revista del Colegio Libre de Estudios Superiores de Buenos Aires* 11 (1937): 113–40.

"La mujer ante el lenguaje: Algunas opiniones de la Antigüedad y del Renacimiento." *Boletín de la Academia Argentina de Letras* (Buenos Aires) 5 (1937): 237–48.

"La hipérbole sagrada en la poesía castellana del siglo XV." *Revista de Filología Hispánica* 8 (1946): 121–30.

"La métrica en la Biblia: Un motivo de Josefo y San Jerónimo en la literatura española." In *Estudios hispánicos, homenaje a Archer M. Huntington,* 335–59. Wellesley, Mass.: Wellesley College, 1952.

Juan Segundo y la biografía de vários autores peninsulares del siglo XVI. Lisboa: Universidade de Lisboa, Faculdade de Letras, 1957.

"Free Opportunity for Intellectual Pursuits." *Journal of the American Association of University Women* (October 1958): 5–8.

"El moro en las letras castellanas." *Hispanic Review* 28 (1960): 350–58.

Two Spanish Masterpieces: The Book of Good Love, and The Celestina. Urbana: University of Illinois Press, 1961.

"Una anécdota de Facundo Quiroga." *Hispanic Review* 31 (1963): 61–64.

"Función del cuento popular en el *Lazarillo de Tormes.*" *Actas del Primer Congreso Internacional de Hispanistas,* edited by Frank Pierce and Cyril A. Jones, 349–59. Oxford: Dolphin Book Co. for the International Association of Hispanists, 1964.

With Yakov Malkiel. "The Jew and the Indian: Traces of a Confusion in the Hispanic Tradition." In *For Max Weinreich on His Seventieth Birthday: Studies in Jewish Languages, Literature, and Society,* 167–72. The Hague: Mouton, 1964.

"El ambiente concreto en *La Celestina.*" In *Estudios dedicados a James Homer Herriott,* 145–65. Madison: University of Wisconsin, 1966.

"Las infancias de Moisés y otros tres estudios." *Romance Philology* 23 (1970): 412–48.

La originalidad artística de "La Celestina." Buenos Aires: Editorial Universitaria de Buenos Aires, 1970.

"La dinastía de los Macabeos en Josefo y en la literatura española." *Bulletin of Hispanic Studies* 48 (1971): 289–97.

"Las sectas judías y los 'procuradores' romanos: En torno a Josefo y su influjo sobre la literatura española." *Hispanic Review* 39 (1971): 183–213.

"En torno a Josefo y su influencia en la literatura española: Precursores e inventores." In *Studia Hispanica in Honorem R. Lapesa,* 3 vols., 1:15–59. Madrid: Gredos-Seminario Menéndez Pidal, 1972–75.

Jerusalén: El tema literario de su cerco y destrucción por los romanos. Buenos Aires: Universidad de Buenos Aires, Facultad de Filosofía y Letras, Instituto de Filología y Literatura Hispánicas, 1972 [i.e. 1973].

"Elementos técnicos del teatro romano desechados en *La Celestina.*" *Romance Philology* 27 (1973): 1–12.

Juan Ruiz: Delección del 'Libro de buen amor', y estudios críticos. Buenos Aires: Editorial Universitaria de Buenos Aires, 1973.
"Lope de Vega y los judíos." *Bulletin Hispanique* 75 (1973): 73–113.
Dido en la literatura española: Su retrato y defensa. London: Tamesis, 1974.
"La dama como obra maestra de Dios." *Romance Philology* 28 (1975): 267–324.
La tradición clásica en España. Esplugues de Llobregat, Sp.: Ariel, 1975.
El cuento popular y otros ensayos. Buenos Aires: Losada, 1976.
Herodes: Su persona, reinado y dinastía. Madrid: Castalia, 1977.
Estudios sobre la literatura española del Siglo XV. Madrid: J. Porrúa Turanzas, 1978.
La idea de la fama en la edad media castellana. 1952. Reprint, Mexico City: Fondo de Cultura Económica, 1983.
Introducción al teatro de Sófocles. Barcelona: Paidós, 1983.
"La visión de trasmundo en las literaturas hispánicas." In *El otro mundo en la literatura medieval,* by Howard Rollin Patch, translated by Jorge Hernández Campos. Mexico City: Fondo de Cultura Económica, 1983.
Estudios de literatura española y comparada. Buenos Aires: Losada, 1984.
Juan de Mena, poeta del prerrenacimiento español. Mexico City: Centro de Estudios Lingüísticos y Literarios, Colegio de México, 1984.
"La técnica dramática de *La Celestina.*" In *Homenaje a Ana María Barrenechea,* edited by Lia Schwartz Lerner and Isaias Lerner, 281–92. Madrid: Castalia, 1984.
"The Earliest Trace of Euripides in Spanish Literature." Introduction by Yakov Malkiel. *Celestinesca: Boletin Informativo Internacional* 9 (1985): 75–79.

Works Cited

Deyermond, Alan, ed. *Historia y crítica de la Literatura Española.* Vol. 1, *Edad Media.* Barcelona: Crítica, 1980.
———, ed. *Historia y crítica de la Literatura Española.* Primer Suplemento. Vol. 1, *Edad Media.* Barcelona: Crítica, 1991.
Herodotus. *Los nueve libros de la historia.* Translated by María Rosa Lida. 2 vols. Barcelona: Lumen, 1981.
Malkiel, Yakov. "Antiquity, the Middle Ages, and the Renaissance as Seen through the Eyes of an Argentinian Scholar: The Buenos Aires Years of María Rosa Lida de Malkiel, 1910–62." In *The Classics in the Middle Ages: Papers of the Twentieth Annual Conference of the Center for Medieval and Early Renaissance Studies,* edited by Aldo S. Bernardo and Saul Levin, 237–52. Binghamton, N.Y.: Center for Medieval & Early Renaissance Studies, 1990.
———. "A Brief History of M. R. Lida de Malkiel's Celestina Studies." *Celestinesca: Boletin Informativo Internacional* 6 (1982): 3–13.
———. "Cómo trabajaba María Rosa Lida de Malkiel". In *Homenaje a Rodríguez-Moñino; Estudios de erudición que le ofrecen sus amigos o discípulos hispanistas norteamericanos,* 2 vols., 1:371–79. Madrid: Castalia, 1966.
———. "Las fuentes de los estudios josefinos de María Rosa Lida de Malkiel." *Cuadernos del Sur* (Universidad Nacional del Sur, Argentina) 11 (1972): 9–18.
———. "The Judaic Strain in María Rosa Lida de Malkiel." *Hebrew University Studies in Literature* 1(1973): 119–31.
———. "María Rosa Lida de Malkiel como investigadora de las letras coloniales." In *Homenaje*

a Don Agapito Rey, edited by Josep Roca-Pons, 357–73. Bloomington: Dept. of Spanish and Portuguese, Indiana University, 1980.

———. "M. R. Lida de Malkiel's Ur-'Celestina' (1949)." *Celestinesca: Boletin Informativo Internacional* 8 (1984): 14–28.

Reichenberger, Arnold G. "Herodotus in Spain: Comments on a Neglected Essay (1949) by María Rosa Lida de Malkiel." *Romance Philology* 19 (1965): 235–49.

CHAPTER 52

"To Open a Door upon the Past of Scotland"

Helena Mennie Shire (1912–1991)

JANET HADLEY WILLIAMS

A PLAQUE COMMEMORATING Helena Mennie Shire is placed at her birthplace, 98 Leslie Terrace, Aberdeen.[1] Its brief notice of her, as "scholar of the literature and music of Scotland," is direct and accessible. Aptly for Helena Shire, it also admits a subtler reading. In the word "scholar" the notice captures her character, at once eager pupil and learned teacher her life long. In naming her chief interests, it lays bare the breadth (and, implicitly, the certain challenges) of her research. What it also signals is Helena Shire's new way of seeing (well before interdisciplinary studies came to prominence) and thus the importance of her early contributions in two major fields of medieval and Renaissance scholarship.

Helena was the elder daughter of Jane Ewen Rae and her husband, John Henderson Mennie, a headmaster in Aberdeen. Her childhood was happy and stimulating, with an awareness of words and of music taking an integral part.[2] To the friend and visitor to the Mennie family (of her parents, an elder brother, Duncan, Helena, and a younger sister, Elma) the household was "warm, comforting, filled with laughter and wide-ranging chat."[3] Beyond the family home Helena Mennie showed executive and scholarly promise from an early age and fulfilled it.[4] She was head prefect of Aberdeen High School for Girls in 1928–29 and gained a bursary for further study.[5]

At Aberdeen University Helena Mennie began a double honors degree in English and modern languages. She won prizes for French and German but chose English language and literature, graduating with both a first-class honors degree (Early and Medieval English) and many prizes.[6] During these years she participated fully in university life. She entered (and won) the Literary Society's short-story competition in her first year; her story, titled "Corbeau," was published in that year's *Alma Mater*.[7] She was on

733

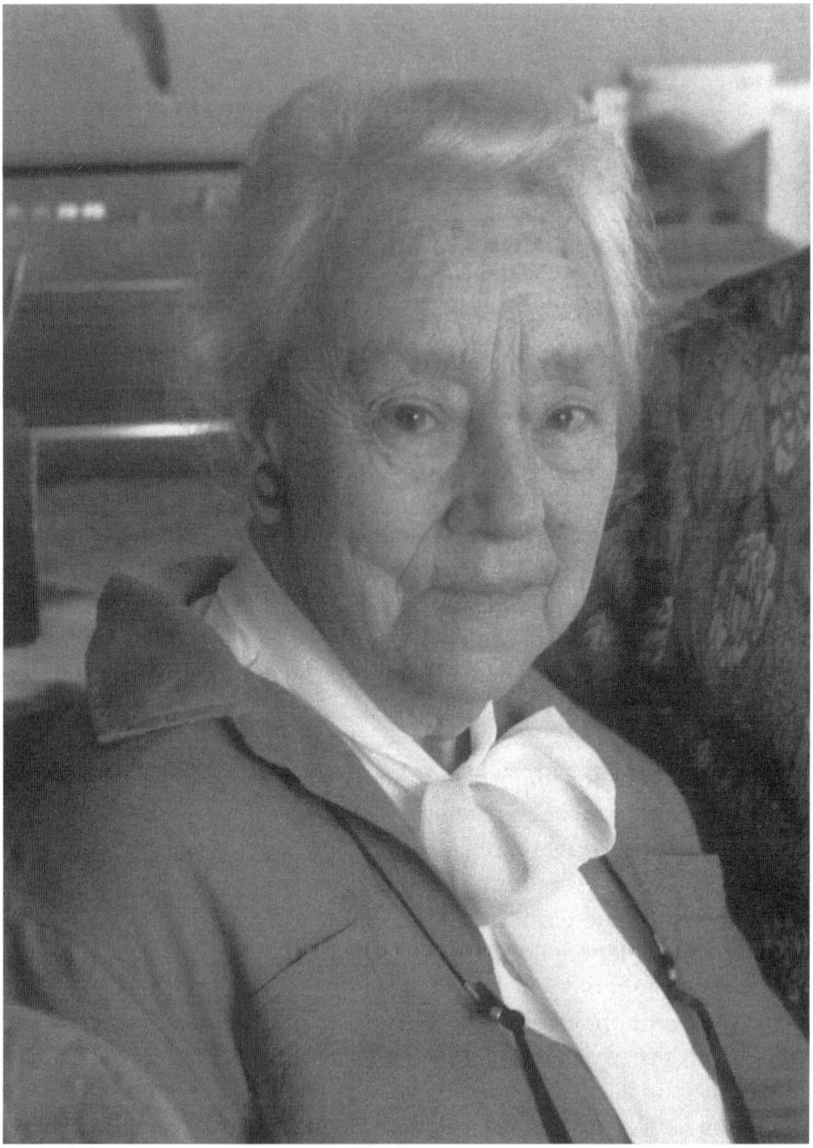

the *Alma Mater* editorial committee, was elected to the Student Representative Council, and was on the committees of the Inter-Varsity Debating, Scottish Nationalist, and Literary Societies, speaking frequently to and becoming president of the latter by 1933.[8] Helena Mennie's interest in early Scottish court song was kindled at this time, too, when the writer John R. Allan showed her a copy of the 1666 edition of an old music part book, John Forbes's *Cantus, Songs, and Fancies.* In this, as she noted later, Mennie found "the 'tunes' to which the words [of early Scottish writers] could be sung." It opened "a whole world of earlier music still to be explored, described and brought back into life" that was distinct and very different from the earliest (ballad) songs of Scotland she had heard of so far.[9]

A grant from the Reid Dean Trust and the Murray scholarship took Helena Mennie to the University of Cambridge.[10] There (in the days before women were permitted to take a degree) she was from 1933 to 1935 an affiliated student of Newnham College, with Enid Welsford and Nora Chadwick among her teachers. With a first in part 1, Helena Mennie was awarded a Gamble studentship in 1935. For the next two years she read part 2 of the English tripos, graduating with first-class honors (and a grounding in ballad study, linked romances, and broadside tunes of England and Scotland that was to complement and inform her subsequent work on court song and culture).[11] She kept alive the idea of searching for the "lost" repertory of Scottish court song during the following period, but her marriage in 1936 to a physicist and King's College fellow, Edward Shire, prevented her from continuing officially with her research. The birth of her first daughter in 1938 also gave her another immediate occupation.

The outbreak of war in 1939 brought further changes and then opportunities for Helena Shire, as for many women. Her husband's war service took him away from Cambridge. With her eighteen-month-old child she traveled north and stayed for part of the autumn in Inverness. What remained with her of this time was not so much the dark and cold of her attic lodgings but the fact that though "engaged every hour of the day with a small child [she] was screamingly under-employed and could not think of a way to be useful."[12] (This desire to be active in a larger sphere was a recurring motif of Helena Shire's life. Even in times of ill health or family sadness, she looked outward, at some considerable cost to herself, keeping on with her research and writing and with correspondence with colleagues about their work.)[13] From Inverness she went to Mudeford, on the south coast of England, where she spent several months near her husband. By 1941 she had returned to Cambridge.[14]

Her husband's newly widowed father, in uncertain health, came to live with the family (and was to prove a great help with the children). Soon Helena Shire was carrying a heavy load of teaching and supervision.[15] In 1940 she also became a lecturer for the Workers Educational Association, which involved traveling widely in East Anglia by train and bus.[16] In addition, although the care of a son, born in 1942, must have drawn further on her physical stamina and waking hours, she became assistant lecturer, teaching "Literature 800–1500" at Queen Mary College, London, (evacuated to Cambridge during the war) and assistant lecturer for the London School of Economics (LSE; also then in Cambridge), teaching "English for Foreign Students."[17] Many of her LSE students were Polish graduates who had come to Britain eager to join the Allied forces and were sent on army release to learn English. These students had French or, rarely, only Latin in common with her.[18] For them she made special efforts, studying Polish language and literature. Her level of proficiency later allowed her to translate Polish drama for performance and Polish folk-song repertory for BBC radio broadcasts and to interweave commentary on the sixteenth-century poet and humanist Jan Kochanowski into her important study of the lyric in western Europe during the late-medieval and Renaissance period.[19] (Her friendship with the Polish people was enduring. Much later, Helena Shire became a trustee of the Corbridge Trust, set up to foster Polish-British cultural relations. Her services to Poland were recognized in 1991 with the award of the Order of Merit of the Republic of Poland.)[20]

After the war effort Shire "relinquished lecturing," as she put it, for Queen Mary College, in order to devote herself to the family reunited in Cambridge.[21] She gave birth to a second daughter in 1946. For all that, she had not ceased supervising, at first for Fitzwilliam House and then other colleges, including Trinity and then King's. For the latter she became a college lecturer in 1969, teaching "the whole First Year—medieval, seventeenth century and eighteenth century, [and] Shakespeare."[22] Now, too, Helena Shire returned to her earlier ideas, formulating a plan to "find, collect and reassemble and have published the whole 'lost' repertory of music and song of medieval and Renaissance Scotland."[23] By 1952 (the year her youngest child began day school), Shire's report on her findings so far, given to the Women's Research Club of Girton and Newnham, drew the interest of Thurston Dart, harpsichordist and musicologist at Jesus College, Cambridge.[24] He saw in her work the promise of a volume for the Musica Britannica series (of which he was then committee secretary), and he encouraged her to continue and collaborate with him.[25] Thurston Dart's Ph.D. student Kenneth Elliott, who already had considerable knowledge of early Scottish sacred music, joined them in October 1954. (For the term in which Thurston Dart was on sabbatical leave Helena Shire became Kenneth Elliott's supervisor.)[26]

As "Scholars Inc.," their private joke, the three worked together closely and with evident enjoyment. For Helena Shire it was both exhilarating and a huge undertaking, "tracing lost documents, searching archives, laborious transcription and the frustration of documents withheld."[27] As work progressed, they also reported the discoveries. From 1954 to 1956 they gave several radio broadcasts. Shire's 8 July 1954 broadcast for the BBC Third Programme, "The Lost Songs of Scotland," gave the first public intimation that new discoveries were being made. In 1956 she gave two further talks for the BBC Third Programme, illustrated with song and harpsichord music to show the richness of the material coming to light: "Scots Song Discovered: 1. Sixteenth Century" (on 11 June) and "Scots Song Discovered: 2. Seventeenth Century" (21 June). The series was completed by David Daiches's talk in the same month, "Scots Song Discovered: 3. Eighteenth Century." In 1955 Helena Shire and Kenneth Elliott also spoke at Abbaye de Royaumont, France, on the three early medleys they had found and reconstructed.[28]

The gathered fruits of their work were published by Stainer and Bell in 1957 as a joint edition, *Music of Scotland, 1500–1700,* Musica Britannica 15. This work received an enthusiastic reception. The National Library of Scotland held an exhibition of the volume's sources.[29] There were concerts in Edinburgh, Cambridge, Paris, and Hanover. At last, with much of the music and many of the song texts of the Scottish medieval and Renaissance period established, the repertory could be placed within that of Britain and be set beside the repertories of other countries.[30]

The revised editions of *Music of Scotland, 1500–1700* (1964 and 1975) and a series of articles (some written with Kenneth Elliott) attest to Helena Shire's ongoing research for the project. Yet she now added considerably to that. A paper was given in June 1958 at the Colóquio de Estudos Etnograficos, in Oporto, on the remains in folk currency of festival interlude (fricasée) and ritual mime in Scotland and Portugal.[31] For the Saltire Society—a group keen to revitalize Scottish culture—Helena Shire edited *Alexander Montgomerie: A Selection from His Songs and Poems* in 1960. (Her careful choices of manuscripts and early prints as her text bases are confirmed in the most recent edition of the poet for the Scottish Text Society.)[32]

From material amassed for *Music of Scotland 1500–1700* she also wrote up "the literary aspects and the 'history of culture'" of the period. For this project she was supported by the Carnegie Trust for the Universities of Scotland, as a 1958–59 fellow and then as a 1961–63 senior research fellow.[33] The result, from Cambridge University Press in 1969, was *Song, Dance, and Poetry of the Court of Scotland under King James VI*. It quickly became and still is indispensable to literature and music scholars of that period and earlier.[34] Therein, for example, Shire drew attention to the Bannatyne Manuscript (National Library of Scotland, Adv. MS 1.1.6). She looked freshly at the implications of George Bannatyne's own title, "Ane Ballat Buik," for his organizing scheme and the place that music, as well as words, had in it. Among much more, she produced rich new material on the major poet and musician Alexander Scott, on the hitherto little-known sonneteer and song-writer "Murray" (of uncertain first name), and on Robert Ayton, royal secretary and "father of the Cavalier lyric."[35]

In 1971 Helena Shire traveled to California, New York, and Cambridge, Massachusetts, for further sources research, again assisted by the Carnegie Trust. During the 1970s she was elected a member of the council both of the Scottish Text Society (of which she became a vice president) and the Saltire Society.[36] She was preelected a founding fellow of Robinson College, Cambridge and by 1980 was an emeritus fellow of Robinson, a recognition of her friendship to fellow college members at all career stages and for her wise advice on the college's English teaching program and the new library.[37] At the same time Shire was lecturing in Cambridge. Although she was never given the university lectureship her teaching and published work merited, the response to one particular series of four lectures with slides, "Middle Ages to Renaissance: The Word and the Picture," was notably enthusiastic.[38] These, given in 1969 and repeated in 1970, drew ever-increasing numbers, for which, to Shire's great pleasure, a larger lecture theater had to be found.[39]

Shire also continued to supervise. Her gifts for teaching—especially for recognizing a pupil's particular abilities and for creating the kind of environment that stimulated each to give the very best—have been noted or attested to by many students over several generations. Among the diversely talented people who were her students are the United States–based poet Thom Gunn, the specialist librarian the late Susan Skilliter, and the fine printer Sebastian Carter.[40] To enable the latter student to produce his first example of fine work, Helena Shire set up, with herself as publisher, the limited edition series the Ninth of May. This was both practical and ingenious, a true collaboration, as their flyer for the first volume made plain: "Our aim is to extend knowledge and to delight the eye." In four distinctive monographs appearing between 1960 and 1973, she published the previously little known late-medieval and Renaissance poems she had rediscovered, carefully editing them and adding her own perceptive commentaries.[41] As a whole, the series helped to draw out the connections Shire saw to be vital, although neglected or misunderstood, between English, Scottish, Danish, and French poetry and song.[42]

The fourth Ninth of May volume, equaling the others in the quality of printing and the rarity of its contents, provides evidence of another kind of collaboration that was typical of Shire. On a visit to the Scottish Record Office (now National Archives of Scotland), she heard from one of the archivists, Marion Stewart, of her discovery in a basement storeroom of two sixteenth-century Scottish verse "taills" ("King Orphius" and "Sir Colling"). She invited Stewart (who already had published parts of these tales in articles for *Scottish Studies*) to share the editing of the next Ninth of May volume, so that full texts could be made available.[43] In this instance as in others Shire gave generously of time and friendship, working with scholars who were continuing their research outside the academy, or who were not her formal responsibility, always keeping in mind the cause of early Scottish culture.[44]

It must be added that if her dedicated cultivation of a new field of medieval and Renaissance studies and her encouragement to the upcoming or struggling "independent" researcher distinguished Helena Shire as a true scholar, that outlook also meant that she had high expectations of those who were her peers within the academy. She delighted in lively discussions with them and welcomed their work in print. For the same reason she could speak with fearless and passionate disappointment of colleagues' publications that, in her informed opinion, were not the result of a careful assessment of the evidence. Her few formal reviews were serious pieces of work. In one written in the 1970s Shire is both helpful and just as she comments on the book in question: "[I]t is bound to interest the student of the love-lyric as a verbal art . . . has much to offer the scholar who is watching the waning of the Middle Ages. . . . But the lover of court-song as words-and-music is not so well served."[45] She supports her stance in a proper questioning spirit, in this instance bringing into play her knowledge of many aspects of the poems under discussion: "[T]he rose here could be not the briar but the 'lenten rose,' a hellebore."[46] She uses findings from her own research: "[H]e has not, as Bannatyne did, gone to the manuscript music books available."[47]

Above all, she speaks for the practical needs of the reader: "[W]hy not tell [them] where the songs with their music could be found in modern editions?"[48]

It is not surprising that Helena Shire's next book was described as "the fruit of an intense commitment to the literature of the Middle Ages and the Renaissance."[49] *A Preface to Spenser,* her critical study of that poet's life and work, appeared in 1978. Its authority is the harvest of years of supervisions of part 2 special projects and "long essays" on Spenser (and, more informally, though highly revealing of the way in which Shire could capture attention, a "Read-In" of *The Faerie Queene,* book 2, in the 1970s).[50] Its balanced outlook is the result of a willingness to research far afield in Ireland.[51] It also is highly readable, acutely aware of the "the needs of a generation who know no Latin and can seldom 'derive' a word . . . to try to get at the poet's full meaning, who must seek many a mythological reference . . . but who have a serious interest in the past as relevant to the present."[52] Shire's explanatory commentary on number theory, for instance, gives her reader the keys to understanding Spenser's thought and writing. First touching with great skill on the philosophical and astronomical aspects of number, as then perceived, she links these specifically to aspects of poetry—metrical composition, relation to "nature," form, and total meaning.[53] Yet Shire ever assists without belittling, as a representative opening illustrates: "It is only fair at this point to recall to the modern reader what every literate Elizabethan knew."[54]

Once having seen *A Preface* through the press, Shire—though well into her sixties—traveled even more frequently. In the second half of 1978 she spoke on the topic "Le recit bref au Moyen Âge" at Amiens and on the topic of "Style King James V" at Strasbourg (the second meeting of the International Medieval and Renaissance Language and Literature conferences she was to support enthusiastically from the first in 1975 until 1990, when she could no longer travel). At Strasbourg she was invited to become a visiting fellow at the Australian National University, so that she might speak again on her innovative topic at the Humanities Research Centre's then-imminent "Waning of the Middle Ages" conference. She took up the invitation with alacrity.[55] In her Australian fellowship term Shire also gave a more informal presentation (in which she and others she had befriended sang some of Scotland's early court songs). As well, she encouraged two Australian postgraduate students of early Scottish literature and music, despite the fact that they were not formally under her supervision, giving in-depth advice on their written work.[56]

The death of her husband soon after the return from Australia was a blow from which Shire did not recover easily. The retrospection that naturally followed, however, gave her a desire to set the record straight for a Scottish friend and fellow-student of Aberdeen University days, the poet Olive Fraser, who had died in 1977 after years of illness misdiagnosed. In the next few years Helena Shire painstakingly collected Fraser's poems from many sources and pieced together the facts of her later life, publishing an annotated selection of the poems in *The Pure Account* (Aberdeen University Press) in 1981 and a full edition, *The Wrong Music: The Poems of Olive Fraser, 1909–77* (Canongate Press) in 1989. With her local knowledge, language training, and familiarity with classical, medieval, and Renaissance correspondences, she could explain the allusions in many of these pieces.[57]

There were several concurrent and diverse projects. Shire helped another close friend, Professor Jack Hamson, prepare a manuscript written during his wartime imprisonment in Crete and after his death in 1987 greatly assisted the work's progress into print.[58] She made a cassette in the Scotsoun Makars Series, writing and speaking the introduction to and sharing with Jack Aitken (then editor of the *Dictionary of the Older Scottish Tongue*) the readings of a selection of poems and songs by Alexander Montgomerie.[59] Here one of her greatest assets—her voice, which was full, yet musically soft, with a low register—was used to bring these works to life.[60] And she renewed her earlier suggestion to the present writer that they collaborate on a volume dedicated to the reign of James V of Scotland.[61] Although chiefly preoccupied with the editing of Olive Fraser's works, she discussed the plans for the volume in numerous letters.[62] (These also included comments on new books, ideas about early Scottish poems, and summaries of lectures heard in Cambridge: she understood how much they were needed by a scholar—probably similar to many with whom she kept in contact—who was distant from source materials or other help.)[63] Notwithstanding, when possible Helena Shire continued to pursue her own interests and projects with enthusiasm. Her papers at meetings in, for instance, Stirling (1981), Amiens (1983), Germersheim (1984), and Aberdeen (1985, 1987), building upon and adding to earlier research in medieval and Renaissance words-and-music, lit a way that was soon after traveled by others who had heard her speak.[64]

In 1988 Shire was awarded an honorary Doctor of Laws degree by Aberdeen University. Her generosity to younger scholars played its part even in this formal ceremony, as Professor James Laidlaw, whom she had encouraged long before as a student in Cambridge, delightedly presented her achievements to the vice chancellor and the others assembled.[65] Far from taking this honor as a signal to stop, Dr. Shire recast earlier plans for a "James V" volume. It now was tentatively titled "Style King James V: The Spirit of His Reign in Artefact and Address." Invitations to contribute were written to specialist scholars in early Scottish arts and letters. When her son fell desperately ill in March 1991, Helena Shire continued stoically, even after his death in June.[66] Hardly mentioning that her own ill health hampered her, Shire wrote a detailed article, especially for the book, on three distinctive architectural examples linked to James V's reign. At the time of her death, 16 November 1991, much was in hand, although the book as it appeared, *Stewart Style, 1513–1542: Essays on the Court of James V* (1996), was not altogether the volume of either earlier or later plans. This was in part to do with Helena Shire herself. Her lengthy typescripts on the music and poetry, the composers and writers, of James V's reign, written in the 1950s and 1960s during the work for *Music of Scotland, 1500–1700*, had come to light in the sorting of some of her papers for the Aberdeen University Archive in 1993. The quality of this work, as she must have known, was such that she could have revised it for publication (and, indeed, after her death, one long essay was edited for inclusion as "Music for 'Goddis Glore and the Kingis,'" 118–41). In her customary style, however, Helena Mennie Shire had chosen to look forward by encouraging other scholars to take up the baton.

NOTES

I wish to acknowledge Dr. Alisoun Gardner-Medwin's valuable advice and kind permission to consult and quote from her family's unpublished papers. My warm thanks also to Mrs. Myrtle Anderson-Smith, senior curator, Special Libraries and Archives, Historic Collections, University of Aberdeen, for her careful help.

The title quotation is from Shire, *Alexander Montgomerie*, 7.

1. Aberdeen City Council, *Commemorative Plaques of Aberdeen*.
2. This latter is revealed in Helena Shire's dedication of *Song, Dance, and Poetry*, ix: "To keep in mind my father and mother from whom I learned to love Scottish song, the words—John H. Mennie and the music—Jane E. Rae."
3. Garden, "Helena Mennie Shire," 5.
4. See further Gardner-Medwin, "Helena Mary Mennie," 47–53; Shire, "The Hame-made Quilt"; Shire, "Fifth Form Fever"; and "Ferlie."
5. See *Aberdeen High School Magazine*, n.s., 1, no. 6 (May 1929): 353.
6. See *Aberdeen High School Magazine*, n.s., 11, no. 5 (November 1933): 260.
7. She won again in 1933. This story was not published, but the win was noted in *Alma Mater* 50 (1932–33): 222. For the manuscript text see Helena Mennie Shire Papers, Aberdeen University Library (hereafter cited as AUL) MS 3407/3/1/3.
8. See Gardner-Medwin, "Helena Mary Mennie," 47; *Alma Mater*, 22 January 1931, 152; 18 February 1932, 212; 28 April 1932, 259; 27 October 1932, 32; 23 February 1933, 222.
9. See Shire, "As I Recall."
10. See Shire, curriculum vitae, 1971.
11. Shire, curriculum vitae, 1959. For her thesis, "*Tom o'Bedlam* Ballads," Shire Papers.
12. Shire, "As I Recall." Shire's "Collecting Folk-songs in War-Time" confirms that she kept up her scholarly interests.
13. Her decision to continue with a visit to Verona provides one example. Despite having been stung on the eyes by wasps as she was about to leave Cambridge, she was determined that her pain would not prevent her from attending graduation (Shire, letter to the author, undated [September 1989]). Another example is found in a letter to the author (29 November 1990) to tell of the death of her dearly loved sister. Helena Shire adds that because of her own state of health and course of medical treatment, she cannot attend the funeral (in Aberdeen), yet she continues: "To turn to business. I am still 'writing up' the heraldic ceiling and the Stirling palace. I translated the introduction on Cracow."
14. Shire, "As I Recall."
15. Shire, curriculum vitae, 1959: "Returning to Cambridge after 'Dunkirk' [1940] I took over the teaching and supervision of my former teacher, Lionel Elvin."
16. Shire, curriculum vitae, 1971.
17. Shire, curriculum vitae, 1959.
18. Shire, curriculum vitae, 1959, and curriculum vitae, ca. 1975.
19. One twentieth-century Polish play Helena Shire translated into Scots was Stefan Zeromsky's *The Castle Looks Down*, which was read at a Saltire Society meeting, Cambridge

Branch, in 1964. Regarding the translation for BBC radio, see Shire, curriculum vitae, 1959. For her commentary on Kochanowski, see "Lyric and the Renaissance."

20. Gardner-Medwin, "Helena Mary Mennie," 48.

21. Shire, curriculum vitae, 1959.

22. Shire, curriculum vitae, ca. 1975.

23. Shire, curriculum vitae, 1959.

24. Shire, curriculum vitae, 1959; Percival, "Robert Thurston Dart," 25.

25. Percival, "Robert Thurston Dart," 23.

26. Kenneth Elliott, letter to the author, 28 October 2001.

27. Shire, curriculum vitae, 1959. On the last, for example, Shire greatly regretted that she was not permitted to see the "Robert Taitt Music-Book" MS T1352 B7 24 (William Andrews Clark Memorial Library, University of California, Los Angeles). This was because W. H. Rubsamen, who hoped to publish the manuscript, would not agree to it. Although he had drawn on *Music of Scotland, 1500–1700* for his article "Scottish and English Music of the Renaissance in a Newly-Discovered Manuscript," he was willing to provide for Shire a copy of only three stanzas of verbal text; see further, Shire, *Song, Dance and Poetry,* 266.

28. Shire with Elliott, "La Fricassée en Écosse." Also in the same year (1955) were Thurston Dart's two talks, "Early Scottish Music," and "Les Rapports entre la musique française et écossaise pendant la renaissance"; and Kenneth Elliott's "Scottish Christmas Medley."

29. Shire and Elliott made the selection and wrote the descriptions for the catalog, National Library of Scotland, *Musica Scotica.*

30. See further, Shire, curriculum vitae; Gardner-Medwin, "Helena Mary Mennie," n. 33.

31. Kenneth Elliott, letter to the author, 28 October 2001; Elliott, "*Trip and Goe, Hey*, 'A Truly Scottish Song,'" 158.

32. See *Alexander Montgomerie: Poems,* 2: 8.

33. Shire, curriculum vitae, 1959.

34. The volume is cited extensively, for instance, in the latest (2001) edition of *Grove's Dictionary of Music and Musicians;* note also John Purser's description of it in *Scotland's Music* as "a most important . . . book" (281 n. 6).

35. See Shire, *Song, Dance, and Poetry,* 10–23, 44–66, 181–206, and 215–54.

36. Shire, curriculum vitae, 1971.

37. Gardner-Medwin, "Helena Mary Mennie," 49; Yates, "Helena Mennie Shire Papers," 107.

38. Shire applied for a university lectureship in 1959: Shire, curriculum vitae, 1959.

39. The title of this lecture is noted in *Cambridge University Reporter* 99, no. 1 (1969): 12; 100, no. 18 (1970): 785; 100, no. 30 (1970): 1321; 101, no. 7 (special number) (1971): 12; as are those of Shire's other lectures: "Late Medieval and Early Tudor Literature" (with others), *Cambridge University Reporter* 101, no. 2 (special number) (1970): 12; 101, no. 7 (special number) (1971): 12; and "Lyric, Ballad and the Medieval World Picture" (4 lectures), *Cambridge University Reporter* 103, no. 1 (special number) (1972): 15, and 103, no. 8 (special number) (1983): 14. See also Helen Mennie Shire Papers. Shire's delight at the need for a large theater is noted by Alisoun Gardner-Medwin, letter to the author, 17 June 2001.

40. See Gunn, *Occasions of Poetry,* 158–59. The information regarding Skilliter derives from Alisoun Gardner-Medwin, letter to the author, 27 November 2001. Carter's acknowledgment of Shire's help and influence came in the form of a beautifully printed flyer to advertise *A Day*

Estivall, a volume of essays written in Shire's honor, ed. A. Gardner-Medwin and J. Hadley Williams. On the Ninth of May imprint, see Crutchley, *Rampant Lions Press,* no. 22.

41. Shire also published as a broadside *The Sheath and the Knife or Leesome Brand.* This reprinted in a different format the new version of the ballad (Edinburgh, National Library of Scotland MS Panmure 11) appearing in the first of the Ninth of May series, *Poems from Panmure House.*

42. See, for example, the volumes *A Choice of Poems and Songs by Sir Robert Ayton,* in which Shire presents Ayton as "the last courtly poet of Scotland growing from northern roots, maturing under European influences to flower *in aula Britannica*" (3); and *The Thrissil, the Rois, and the Flour-de-Lys,* 25–31.

43. Marion Stewart, letter to the author, 8 November 2001.

44. One in the latter category is Donald Meek, now professor of Scottish and Gaelic studies, University of Edinburgh, who remembers Shire's kindness "to an exiled Scot" during his studies with Rachel Bromwich in Cambridge (Donald Meek, letter to the author, 15 November 2001).

45. Shire, review of *Ballattis,* 181.

46. Shire, review of *Ballattis,* 182.

47. Shire, review of *Ballattis,* 181.

48. Shire, review of *Ballattis,* 182–83.

49. Maurice Hussey, foreword to Shire, *Preface,* vii.

50. Shire, curriculum vitae, ca. 1975.

51. Shire sought to present Spenser's Irish, Spanish, and Gaelic connections; see *Preface,* vi and 18–64; Helena Shire, letter to the author (about the Spenser conference in Kilcolman), undated [?September 1977].

52. Shire, *Preface,* ix.

53. Shire, *Preface,* especially 76–81 and 165–77.

54. Shire, *Preface,* 176.

55. Shire, letter to the author, undated [July 1978], where she also describes the support given her by her family, whose plans had been disrupted.

56. Patricia Jackson and Janet Hadley Williams.

57. See, for example, "Desperate for Love," in Shire, *Wrong Music,* 212, and note to line 185.

58. Hamson, *Liber in Vinculis,* i–ii; and Helena Shire, letters to the author, 15 November 1987 and undated [late August 1989].

59. Shire with Aitken, *Alexander Montgomerie.*

60. Donald Meek, in a letter to the author, 15 November 2001, recalls that her "Scottish accent was unalloyed and beautiful."

61. Helena Shire, letter to the author, December 1979.

62. See Shire, "Languages of Scotland in Poems by Olive Fraser," 53–56.

63. Yates, "Shire Papers, AUL MS 3407," 107, mentions "the extensive correspondence in the collection" that bears witness to the "generations of pupils and colleagues whom she generously encouraged, befriended and fostered in scholarly careers."

64. Her 1981 talk on the Covenanter poet William Cleland, for instance, drew attention to the little known "Hallow My Fancie," which afterward took its place for the first time—though with no mention that Cleland had set it to well-known tunes (as Shire had pointed out)—in an anthology, Crawford, Hewitt, Law, *Longer Scottish Poems 2,* 1–6 and 356.

65. Laidlaw, "Helena Mennie Shire."

66. Alisoun Gardner-Medwin, letter to the author, 5 June 1991; Helena Shire, letter to the author, 8 June 1991.

Select Bibliography of Works by Helena Mennie Shire

"The Hame-made Quilt, A One-Act Play." *Aberdeen High School Magazine* 1, no. 3 (October 1927): 152–53.

"Fifth Form Fever." *Aberdeen High School Magazine*, n.s., 1, no. 4 (May 1928): 231.

"Corbeau." *Alma Mater* 47 (6 March 1930): 219–20.

"Ferlie." *Aberdeen High School Magazine*, n.s., 2, no. 3 (November 1932): 125.

"*Tom o'Bedlam* Ballads." Shire Papers, AUL MS 3407/3/3.

"Collecting Folk-Songs in War-Time." *Aberdeen University Review* 21, no. 92 (1945): 4–13.

With Phyllis M. Giles. "Court Song in Scotland after 1603: Aberdeenshire. I. The Tolquhon Cantus Part Book." *Edinburgh Bibliographical Society Transactions* 3, no. 3 (1951–52): 161–65.

"Court Song in Scotland after 1603: Aberdeenshire. II. The Forbes-Leith Music Books, 1611–1779." *Edinburgh Bibliographical Society Transactions* 3, no. 3 (1952–53): 165–68.

"The Lost Songs of Scotland." BBC Third Programme, 8 July 1954.

"Scottish Song-Book, 1611." *Saltire Review* 1, no. 2 (1954): 46–52.

"Court Song in Scotland after 1603: Aberdeenshire. III. Andro Melvill's Music Library: Aberdeen, 1637." *Edinburgh Bibliographical Society Transactions* 4, no. 1 (1955–56): 3–12.

With Kenneth Elliott. "Pleugh Song and Plough Play." *Saltire Review* 2, no. 6 (1955): 39–44.

With Alexander Fenton. "The Sweepings of Parnassus: Four Poems Transcribed from the Record Books of the Burgh Sasines of Aberdeen." *Aberdeen University Review* 36, no. 112 (1955): 43–54.

With Kenneth Elliott. "La Fricassée en Écosse et ses rapports avec Les Fêtes de la renaissance." In *Les Fêtes de la renaissance*, vol. 1, edited by Jean Jacquot, 335–45. Paris: Éditions du Centre National de la Recherche Scientifique, 1956.

"Scots Song Discovered: Sixteenth Century." BBC Third Programme, 11 June 1956.

"Scots Song Discovered: Seventeenth Century." BBC Third Programme, 21 June 1956.

Editor with Kenneth Elliot. *Music of Scotland, 1500–1700*. Musica Britannica, 15. London: Stainer and Bell, 1957.

Curriculum vitae, 1959. Original held among the family papers of Dr. Alisoun Gardner-Medwin, Newcastle-upon-Tyne.

"Musical Servitors to Queen Mary Stuart." *Music and Letters* 40 (1959): 15–18.

Editor. *Alexander Montgomerie: A Selection from His Songs and Poems.* Edinburgh: Oliver and Boyd for the Saltire Society, 1960.

Editor. *Poems from Panmure House.* Cambridge: The Ninth of May, 1960.

Editor. *A Choice of Poems and Songs by Sir Robert Ayton.* Cambridge: The Ninth of May, 1961.

"Robert Edwards' Commonplace Book and Scots Literary Tradition." *Scottish Studies* 5, pt. 1 (1961): 43–49.

Editor. *The Thrissil, the Rois and the Flour-de-Lys: A Sample-Book of State Poems and Love-Songs Showing Affinities between Scotland, England and France in the Sixteenth and Seventeenth Centuries.* Cambridge: The Ninth of May, 1962.

Editor with Marion Stewart. *"King Orphius," "Sir Colling," "The Brother's Lament," "Litel Musgray": Poems from Scottish Manuscripts of c. 1586 and c. 1630.* Cambridge: The Ninth of May, 1963.

"Alexander Montgomerie: The Oppositione of the Court to Conscience: 'Court and Conscience Walis Not Weill.'" *Studies in Scottish Literature* 3, no. 3 (1966): 144–50.

Song, Dance, and Poetry of the Court of Scotland under King James VI. Cambridge: Cambridge University Press, 1969.

Curriculum vitae, 1971. Shire Papers, AUL MS 3407/3/1.

Review of "*Ballattis of Luve: The Scottish Courtly Love Lyric, 1400–1700,*" edited by John MacQueen. *Medium Ævum* 41, no. 2 (1972): 180–84.

"The Lyric and the Renaissance." In *The Old World: Discovery and Rebirth,* vol. 3 of *Literature and Western Civilization,* edited by D. Daiches and A. Thorlby, 147–75. London: Aldus, 1974.

"A Scots Poet Rediscovered? R. Allane." *Scottish Literary Journal* 1, no. 2 (1974): 5–14.

The Sheath and the Knife or Leesome Brand [Broadside from Edinburgh, National Library of Scotland, MS Panmure 11]. Cambridge: The Ninth of May, 1974.

Curriculum vitae, ca. 1975. Original held among the family papers of Dr. Alisoun Gardner-Medwin, Newcastle-upon-Tyne.

Editor with Kenneth Elliot. *Music of Scotland, 1500–1700.* Musica Britannica, 15. Rev. ed. London: Stainer and Bell, 1975.

A Preface to Spenser. London: Longman, 1978.

"Style King James V." Paper presented at the Second International Conference on Scottish Language and Literature (Medieval and Renaissance), University of Strasbourg, 5–11 July 1978.

"Le Recit bref et la poesie lyrique medievale de langue anglaise." In *Le Recit bref au Moyen Âge: Actes du colloque des 27, 28, et 29 Avril 1979, Université de Picardie, Centre d'Etudes Medievales,* edited by Danielle Buschinger. Paris: Librairie Honoré Champion [1980].

With Jack Aitken. *Alexander Montgomerie (c. 1545–1611): Poems and Songs.* Scotsoun Makars Series, SSC 060. Glasgow: Scotsoun, 1981, audiocassette.

"The Case of Colonel Cleland." Paper presented at the Third International Conference on Scottish Language and Literature (Medieval and Renaissance), University of Stirling, 2–7 July 1981.

Editor. *The Pure Account: Poems by Olive Fraser (1909–1977).* Aberdeen: Aberdeen University Press, 1981.

"The Languages of Scotland in Poems of Olive Fraser." In *Gaelic and Scots in Harmony: Proceedings of the Second International Conference on the Languages of Scotland, University of Glasgow, 1988,* edited by Derick S. Thomson. Glasgow: Department of Celtic, University of Glasgow [1989].

Editor. *The Wrong Music: The Poems of Olive Fraser, 1909–1977.* Edinburgh: Canongate, 1989.

"The King in His House: Three Architectural Artefacts Belonging to the Reign of James V." In *Stewart Style, 1513–1542: Essays on the Court of James V,* edited by Janet Hadley Williams. East Linton, Scot.: Tuckwell Press, 1996.

"Music for 'Goddis Glore and the Kingis.'" In *Stewart Style, 1513–1542: Essays on the Court of James V,* edited by Janet Hadley Williams. East Linton: Tuckwell Press, 1996.

"As I Recall" [holograph autobiography]. Shire Papers, AUL MS 3407/1/2.

The Helena Mennie Shire Papers, Aberdeen University Library MS 3407.

Works Cited

Aberdeen City Council. *The Commemorative Plaques of Aberdeen.* No. 40. [Aberdeen]: Aberdeen City Council, n.d.

Crawford, Thomas, David Hewitt, and Alexander Law, eds. *Longer Scottish Poems 2: 1650–1830.* Edinburgh: Scottish Academic Press, 1987.

Crutchley, Brooke. *The Rampant Lions Press: A Printing Workshop through Five Decades.* Catalog of an exhibition at the Fitzwilliam Museum, Cambridge, 11 May–27 June 1982. Cambridge: Rampant Lions Press, 1982.

Dart, Thurston. "Early Scottish Music." BBC Third Programme, 8 June 1955.

———. "Les Rapports entre la musique française et écossaise pendant la renaissance." BBC French Service, 3 November 1955.

Elliott, Kenneth. "A Scottish Christmas Medley." BBC Third Programme, 28 December 1955.

———. *"Trip and Goe, Hey, 'A Truly Scottish Song.'"* In *Stewart Style, 1513–1542: Essays on the Court of James V.* Edited by Janet Hadley Williams. East Linton, Scot.: Tuckwell Press, 1996.

Garden, Dina. "Helena Mennie Shire: Portrait by a Friend." In *A Day Estivall,* edited by Alisoun Gardner-Medwin and Janet Hadley Williams, 5–8. Aberdeen: Aberdeen University Press, 1990.

Gardner-Medwin, Alisoun, and Janet Hadley Williams, eds. *A Day Estivall: Essays on the Music, Poetry and History of Scotland and England and Poems Previously Unpublished in Honour of Helena Mennie Shire.* Aberdeen: Aberdeen University Press, 1990.

———. "Helena Mary Mennie (Generation 2), 1912–1991." In "The Shire Family in Somerset." Unpublished manuscript compiled in 1996.

Gunn, Thom. *Occasions of Poetry. Essays in Criticism and Autobiography.* Edited by Clive Wilmer. London: Faber and Faber, 1982.

Hamson, C. J. *Liber in Vinculis, or The Mock Turtle's Adventure (Written in Captivity, 1941–1945).* Cambridge: Trinity College, 1989.

Laidlaw, J. C. "Helena Mennie Shire, Doctor of Laws, *Honoris Causa*." In *A Day Estivall,* edited by A. Gardner-Medwin and J. Hadley Williams, 9–12. Aberdeen: Aberdeen University Press, 1990.

Montgomerie, Alexander. *Alexander Montgomerie: Poems.* Vol. 2, *Notes.* Edited by David Parkinson. Edinburgh: Scottish Text Society, 2000.

National Library of Scotland. *Musica Scotica: An Exhibition of Scottish Music Books, 1500–1700.* [Edinburgh]: National Library of Scotland, 1971.

Percival, Allen. "Robert Thurston Dart." In *Source Materials and the Interpretation of Music: A Memorial Volume to Thurston Dart,* edited by Ian Bent. London: Stainer and Bell, 1981.

Purser, John. *Scotland's Music: A History of the Traditional and Classical Music of Scotland from the Earliest Times to the Present Day.* Edinburgh: Mainstream Publishing in conjunction with BBC Scotland, 1992.

Rubsamen, W. H. "Scottish and English Music of the Renaissance in a Newly-Discovered Manuscript". In *Festschrift Heinrich Besseler,* edited by Eberhardt Klemm. Leipzig: Veb Deutscher Verlag für Musik, 1961.

Yates, C. Sian. "The Helena Mennie Shire Papers, AUL MS 3407." *Northern Scotland* 18 (1998): 104–8.

CHAPTER 53

Memoir (1914–)

MARJORIE McCALLUM CHIBNALL

WHEN CARLO CIPOLLA was invited to write a short memoir describing how and why he had come to be a historian, he prefaced it by admitting that up to that time he had failed to acknowledge his "immense and incalculable debts to the mysterious personage whom, for want of better knowledge and more precise terminology, we call Fortuna or Chance."[1] He went on to describe the remarkable combination of circumstances that enabled him, after entering the University of Pavia with the intention of becoming a teacher of history and philosophy in a lyceum, to become a professor of economic history in California. I, too, owe an immense debt to Fortuna, which the invitation to write this short memoir now enables me to repay.

I was born in Shropshire during the First World War, into a family that had farmed for generations. Apart from my maternal grandmother, a Highland Scot who had been a primary-school teacher for a very short time before her marriage, no woman in my family had embarked on a profession. It was taken for granted that after leaving school girls would help their mothers until they married, and that if they remained single, their family would provide for them. I cannot remember a time when I did not want to write, and I scribbled a great deal during my school days, but my inclination was to poetry. If I had any ambition, it was to be an author of some kind, and writing could be done at home in the intervals of housekeeping.

Fortunately, my parents believed in education and sent me (after first lessons with a governess) to the local grammar school in Shrewsbury. It was small but had some good teachers, including a brilliant history mistress, and as I was happy there, I stayed through the sixth form and took the Higher School Certificate without any clear idea of what would come afterward. In the early 1930s agriculture was in the depths of depression, and all money had to be plowed back into the land for families

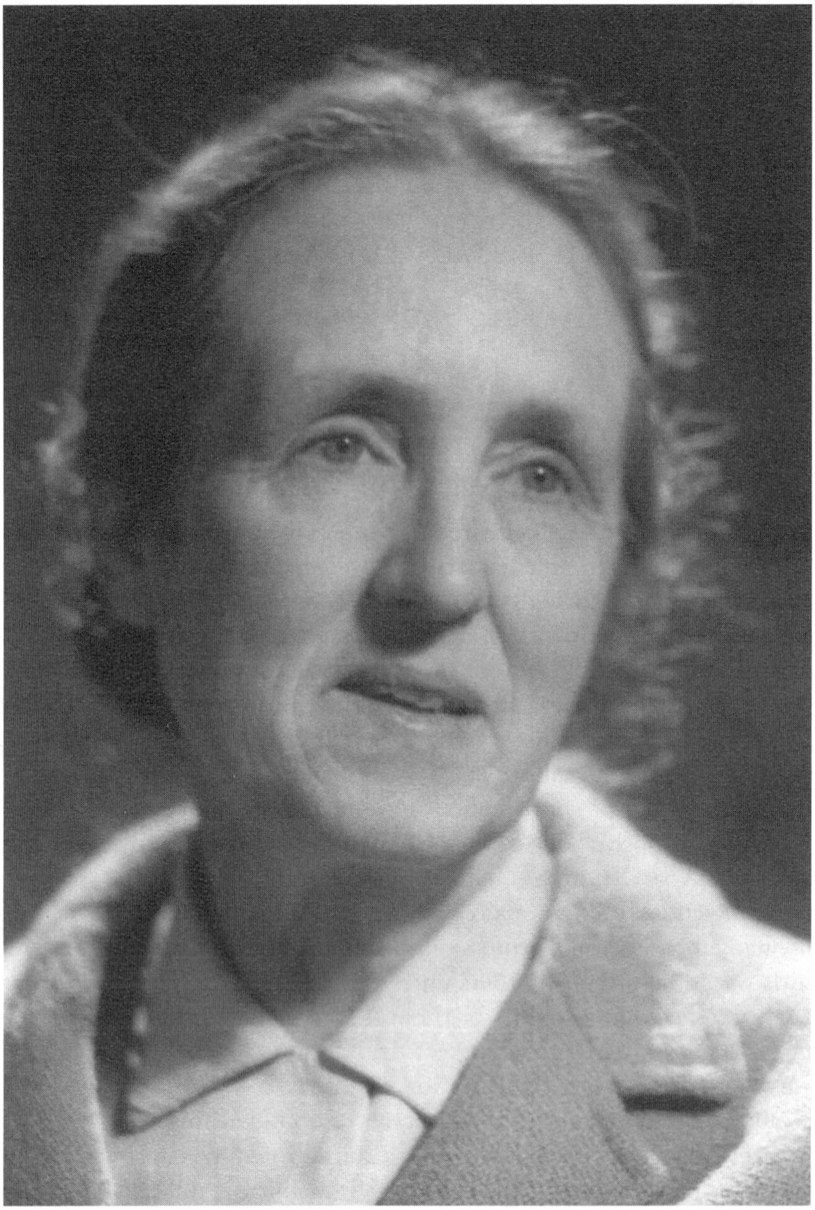

to survive, so nothing would have been available for further education. This was the moment for Fortuna to make her first appearance. When I saw the examination results I discovered that I had won a state scholarship; previously I had had no idea that such things existed. It meant that if I went on to university, all my expenses could be paid for three or four years. The doors of Oxford were open to me.

Up to the last moment I hesitated between history and English, but finally I sat the entrance examination in history for Lady Margaret Hall and just managed to gain a place. My interview with Evelyn Jamison, the remarkable woman who was to become my tutor, finally tipped the balance in favor of history. She was probably the most brilliant and certainly the most beautiful academic woman in Oxford at the time. My intention then was to concentrate on modern history; I thought rather vaguely that I might use the privilege of a university education—still rare for women in 1933—to find work in some organization that would promote peace and international understanding. The recent war and the economic depression that had brought appalling poverty were on the conscience of my generation. We were passionate idealists, debating and talking far into the night (when we were not making music or reading poetry) about world affairs and the ways of preventing war and alleviating ignorance and poverty. Modern history seemed to many of us to have more immediate relevance than medieval, and I chose for my special study of European history the most modern period then available, from 1815 to 1914. The Middle Ages, largely unknown territory for me, began to open up only in my first year.

Historical studies at Oxford were then in a phase of revival and renewal, particularly those in medieval history. The pattern stamped on the History School in the nineteenth century by William Stubbs still persisted; the mainstay of the syllabus had been English constitutional history with particular emphasis on parliamentary institutions. Now, thanks to the influence of a group of scholars who provided what has been called "the most remarkable combination of historical talent in England at that time," it was beginning to take in new, much wider, cultural history. Much was owed to two very different individuals: the Regius Professor F. M. Powicke, fresh from the work on Stephen Langton that had taken him into the study of medieval universities, and V. H. Galbraith, a Fellow of Balliol College with a background of solid documentary work both in the Public Record Office and on medieval chronicles. Both helped to build up a tradition of exact but never narrow scholarship. A new syllabus swept away the separate papers in constitutional and economic history and simply required three papers in English history "from the beginning to the present day." There was intensive study of a relatively short period in European history and, of course, a special subject. Political thought provided for some general theoretical study, together with a new paper on general historical ideas, whose probable contents were the subject of much speculation. For my generation, who were the guinea pigs, preparation meant reading theories of history in Benedetto Croce and (for me at least) attending the brilliant and entertaining lectures of R. G. Collingwood. The History School was unusual in providing a long period of peaceful study untroubled by examinations. After preliminary pass examinations in Latin, French, and economics, which were the essential tools of the trade and could be polished off in the first term, we plunged straight into work for finals, which were to be taken at the end of the third year. This did not suit everyone, but for someone as immature and ignorant as I was, the two and a half years of quiet study and deepening understanding were ideal.

The Oxford method of teaching was largely in individual tutorials, singly or in pairs. We wrote weekly essays and submitted or read them to our tutors. Lectures were numerous but not compulsory, which was fortunate because until the third year most of them were very dull indeed. The system involved punishing work for the tutors—as I myself discovered later—but for the students fortunate enough to have good tutors it was ideal. And I was fortunate; Evelyn Jamison, a specialist on the Normans in Italy, not only gave me a glimpse into the medieval world but also was the friend of some of the best tutors in the men's colleges and sent pupils to them. When I embarked on my finals work in English medieval history in my second term, I was sent to Balliol to work under V. H. Galbraith. It was an electrifying experience for me as for many others.

H. A. Cronne, one of Galbraith's numerous pupils, wrote later of his own experience in words that could have described mine: "A first tutorial with Galbraith was, for most undergraduates, an astonishing experience.... It was rather like being immersed in a bath of gin-and-tonic, from which one emerged relaxed, refreshed and tremendously stimulated.... For him the point of history was a personal encounter between the individual and the material."[2] Galbraith was the first to impress on me that history was "not anything you read in books: it's a method of thought. In time you won't even be able to look at a chair without seeing its history." Much later when, after beginning to think about research, I returned to him for revision in political thought, he gave me an impassioned account of what was involved in research. Walking round and round his study and practising golf strokes a few inches from my toes, he dwelt on the sheer nastiness of life in the Middle Ages and the hard struggle of a researcher to find a way through masses of documents, insisting that "you have to go through the long dark tunnel" and then ending on a note of triumph, "and you have to love the thing you write about." All this, however, was two years later.

My scholarship provided enough money over and above the termly expenses for a few weeks abroad in both long vacations. I took the opportunity of going to Germany to learn the language and study German literature as part of my work on nineteenth-century European history. I stayed in the house of Helene Koch in Jugendheim-an-der-Bergstrasse, in Hessen, and with her guidance read the literature of the German struggle toward unification from Goethe and Schiller onward. It was possible to see a production of Goethe's *Goetz von Berlichingen* magnificently staged in the as-yet-unbombed medieval heart of Frankfurt, and—more importantly—to try to understand the thought and history of the past century in Germany against the background of the twentieth-century revolution taking place all round me. It was, I think, in Germany that I first began to see the past in the present.

Hindenburg died in 1934 during my first visit; the mourning and despair all around me brought home to me how loyal Germans, who loved their country, dreaded the changes threatened by Hitler's rise to power. Hindenburg had seemed to them the last guardian of the traditions they valued; without him anything might happen. A year later I could see what they feared. Even in Jugendheim, a small village, notices were appearing on garden gates telling Jews to keep away; the swimming bath proclaimed itself a *Judenfreies Schwimmbad*. I was able to read Hitler's *Mein Kampf* in the full original; the only version readily available in England was a bowdlerized translation with the virulent attacks on the Jews and the French cut out. So garbled, it could be read as a plea on behalf of a new movement designed to lift Germany out of the poverty and misery caused by defeat, war reparations, and galloping inflation. The original showed the brutal and aggressive side of the Nazi movement; it was part of the propaganda bringing cruelty and persecution into the everyday life of a peaceful village. I saw how history could be distorted by propaganda. The way to fight propaganda seemed to me in my youthful innocence to be by teaching people the true history of the past and training their minds to be critical. My growing interest in the Middle Ages now appeared, not as a form of escapism, but as a way of promoting peace and tolerance. To those who have seen what the media can do even in democracies such ideas must seem very naive, but at that time it was widely believed that a proper understanding of the past could be the surest defense against oppression and war.

At the beginning of my third year at Oxford, I chose as my special subject a medieval topic taught by Professor Powicke: "Church and State in the Time of Edward I." Powicke was a very small, prematurely white-haired man; he lectured in a kind of luminous haze that was both impressive and inspiring. The sources for his chosen subject were of two kinds: theoretical, with a treatise by James of Viterbo to explain the principles behind medieval government; and practical, with records such as Archbishop Pecham's Register to show the actual workings of law and administration. Before Christmas I knew that I wanted to go on to medieval research. Evelyn Jamison was encouraging, with the proviso, "Of course, you will have to get a First." Fortunately I was able to clear the necessary hurdle.

Still uncertain about a subject, I was inclined toward church history, and Powicke suggested that I might tackle the thirteenth-century *sede vacante* records in the Canterbury Cathedral library. He hoped they might form part of a volume of documents on ecclesiastical courts that he was planning for possible publication by the Selden Society. An Oxford B. Litt thesis could be submitted after a year's work, and by the end of a year I knew that, though finding my way through thirteenth-century English church administration and canon law had been a useful discipline, it was not the kind of subject on which I hoped to spend my life. My supervisor, W. A. Pantin, drew my attention to a manuscript in the British Museum, MS Cotton Domitian A 11, which was concerned with the relations between the Norman Abbey of Bec and its English priories, and this seemed to offer a starting point. As an undergraduate I had been fascinated by the problems of Church and State, and the relations between

England and Normandy implied investigating the differences between medieval and modern nationalism. In time the realities of research in original sources brought me down to earth; the first step was to study the manuscripts in Paris and the Norman provincial archives, and this led me to apply for a residential scholarship offered by the British Federation of University Women at Reid Hall in Paris. This with additional support from Oxford University's Amy Mary Preston Reid Scholarship and a two-year Goldsmiths' Senior Studentship provided for all my needs.

Reid Hall was a delightful small international house just off the boulevard de Montparnasse, within walking distance of the Sorbonne and the Bibliothèque nationale. I was not attached formally to any institution; my time was spent in the manuscript room of the Bibliothèque, when not attending the valuable lectures of Gabriel Le Bras in the Law Faculty of the Sorbonne, and Étienne Gilson at the Collège de France or Frédéric Jouön des Longrais's classes on English law. After sampling a few lectures at the École des chartes I realized that they had little to offer anyone who had already studied diplomatics under Galbraith and paleography under E. A. Lowe at Oxford. It was a wonderful year for forming friendships with French and American scholars, as well as for enjoying music, theater, and art galleries (and even buying a little Parisian black suit that gave a touch of elegance to my official Oxford subfusc—a technical term for Oxford academic dress). Politics too were exciting; this was the year of Léon Blum's Popular Front government, and though the shadows of war threatened, they held off for a time and children continued to play in the Luxembourg Gardens. My summer travels in Normandy introduced me to the French provincial archives and took me to Caen. There, sitting in the glorious nave of the Abbey of Saint-Étienne, I began to feel certain that one day I would study the history of the men who were able to build such churches.

After my return to England to work in the libraries of London and Cambridge, my research took an unexpected turn. When the alien priories were dissolved, the very extensive estates owned by the Abbey of Bec in England were given to newly founded schools and colleges: enduring institutions that preserved their archives. Consequently, manorial documents had piled up in King's College Cambridge, Eton College, and the royal chapel at Windsor. In Cambridge I met Helen Cam, who introduced me by letter to Eileen Power (then professor of economic history at the London School of Economics [LSE]) and in person to Power's husband, "Munia" Postan. So I became immersed in manorial materials and returned to London to join the famous Power/Postan seminar in the Institute of Historical Research. It was a revolutionary introduction to a subject I had barely touched at Oxford. Among other changes the seminar brought some of the methods of the Annales school to England and used some of the techniques of sociology. I had not previously registered my work for a doctoral degree—Oxford in those days regarded such things as unnecessary—but I decided it would be sensible to do so and asked Eileen Power if she would be my supervisor. To my delight she agreed, and Oxford allowed me to register for a D.Phil. under a London supervisor, without any further residence in Oxford. So I joined a lively group including Nora Carus-Wilson, R. A. L. Smith, Edward Miller, Philippe Wolff, Dorothea Oschinsky, and Elizabeth Crittall. Eileen also drew me further into the study of changes in agrarian society by lending me her photocopy of the twelfth-century surveys of the Abbey of La Trinité, Caen, preserved in the Bibliothèque nationale. My plan was to edit the surveys after finishing my thesis, but this was a project that had to wait for forty years. The outbreak of war in September 1939 changed all our lives.

Postan left to work in the Ministry of Economic Warfare in London; Eileen moved with part of the LSE to Cambridge. The rest of us registered for war service and waited for our turn to be called up to come. The call-up, however, was slow. After trying in vain to find something more directly connected with the war (including a crash course in nursing—but there were no casualties—and training as an air-raid warden—but there were no air raids), I returned for a time to Cambridge, where the seminar was reassembling under Eileen. I began supervising some first-year Newnham undergraduates in economic history, with the result that for many years Cambridge regarded me, not without reason, as an economic historian. In May I was offered three months' work as a night nurse in the Royal Salop Infirmary. It was there that I received a bitter blow. News came of the sudden and tragic death of Eileen Power, then only fifty-one. When my spell of nursing ended, I went back to Cambridge for a brief period of work, and Postan replaced her as my supervisor. Their methods were totally different but complementary. Eileen worked with the grain: she understood her pupils as individuals and with great patience and learning pointed them in the direction they were able to go and drew out their potentialities. Postan was immensely stimulating; he poured out his ideas of economic change and development and left his pupils to use them as best they could. This, fortunately, was all that I needed by this time, for he could see me only on his rare visits to Cambridge to escape from the bombing in London. To both my totally different supervisors I owe much.

The seminar group slowly melted away as individuals were called up. I was the youngest, and before my time came, I was offered an assistant lectureship at University College, Southampton, as half of the replacement for a very hard-working professor who had gone to the BBC. The other half was Nicolai Rubinstein, and we two dedicated medievalists found ourselves teaching almost everything in English, European, and American history as well as giving short courses to RAF cadets. It was a baptism of fire: I hope my pupils learned as much as I did. The cadets in particular were a joy to teach, once we had realized that the only way to interest them in modern European history was to begin, not in 1815, but with the present day and to work backward so as to understand the conditions that had produced the Fascist and Communist regimes.

After two years student numbers were falling drastically, and I was beginning to seek an educational commission in the Women's Royal Navy Service, when a vacancy for an assistant in history occurred in Aberdeen. Once again Fortuna intervened, this time in the person of Professor Powicke. I wrote to ask him for a reference, while expressing doubts about whether it was right not to choose more active war service, and he replied with the best piece of advice I have ever been given: "It is no good weighing the pros and cons; you obviously want to go to Aberdeen, and the important thing is to do what you want to do, provided it is not immoral." I applied, went for an interview with Professor J. B. Black, and was appointed on the spot. So began some of the happiest years of my professional life.

Scottish universities accepted young students, and most could fit in two years of study before being called up. One further year of war service entitled them to a pass M.A. degree. They were keen, hard-working, enterprising, and friendly. The Ordinary Degree students liked to have lectures delivered at dictation speed; fortunately, my work with them was in small essay classes. All my lectures were in medieval history for Honors students, and they were prepared after some initial shocks to learn to take notes from lectures delivered at the normal speed. Some were very good indeed; one group of four men included a future ambassador to the United Nations, a future professor at the University of Saint Andrews, and a Nigerian student who became in succession a professor of history, then vice chancellor at Ibadan, and finally a Harvard professor.

My research work soon took a new turn. Vivian Galbraith had moved from Oxford to a chair in Edinburgh, and he introduced me to Peter Morrison, the learned and enlightened publisher with whom he had founded Nelson's Medieval Texts. This was the greatest enterprise of Galbraith's later years; he realized that, as Latin teaching in the schools declined, the great mass of students would never have full access to medieval sources without a crutch of some kind. If new, scholarly editions of medieval texts with readable English translations on the facing page were provided, they would be able to make some progress into the Latin original through the English. I agreed to undertake an edition and translation of John of Salisbury's *Historia Pontificalis*. After two years' teaching at Aberdeen, I was appointed to a newly-founded lectureship in medieval history and began to investigate early Scots history and to settle happily into both university and city; my spare-time work included extramural classes in surrounding villages, and I took part in so-called Brains' Trusts on current affairs in Aberdeen. Professor Black, who became a lifelong friend (and was to be the godfather of my first baby), said later that he had hoped I would succeed him in the chair of history. I might well have spent the remainder of my life in Aberdeen.

Fortuna, however, had other ideas for me. In March 1947 I was approached by the fellows of Girton College, who were looking for a successor to Helen Cam. Simultaneously and independently, I was becoming engaged to a Cambridge professor of biochemistry. The outcome was that a week after the end of the academic year in Aberdeen, I married Charles Chibnall and moved to Cambridge. Girton was kind and generous; although Helen Cam's first reaction when my future husband broke the news of our engagement was an anguished cry, "Why must these good women get married?" I was given a college lectureship. From that time Cambridge has been my home.

Looking back over my early career, I can state positively that before coming to Cambridge I had not suffered any disadvantage through being a woman. In Oxford it was firmly and I think rightly believed that the examiners in the schools were fair and impartial: I never heard any suggestion of the kind I was later to hear and even to share in Cambridge that some examiners were prejudiced against women. I gained my postgraduate awards, including an open university scholarship, and my Aberdeen lectureship in competition with men. At Aberdeen I participated fully and equally in all the work of university lecturers and was paid the same salary as a man. It took some years for me to grasp the very different conditions then prevailing in Cambridge. Women were not admitted to full degrees (instead of "titles to degrees") until 1948. The university appeared friendly and welcoming; the general atmosphere was chivalrous. It took time to appreciate that, though socially men stood back and opened doors for women to pass through, professionally they slammed them in their faces. For the first six or seven years I believed that in time I would be elected to a university lectureship, especially after I had given some short courses of lectures and been asked to take over Postan's special subject lectures for a term while he was on leave of absence. Only after two or three applications for university posts had produced nothing more than polite letters—regretting either that I had not been appointed but that the faculty was glad I was in Cambridge anyway or that I was unfortunately too senior for the post advertised—did I fully appreciate my position. I could carry on as a fellow and lecturer at Girton, but I would have no official standing in the history faculty.

At the time it was very disagreeable; looking back now—dispassionately, as a historian—I can appreciate the official outlook of the faculty (some individual members, notably Christopher Morris, "Otto" Smail, and David Joslin, were very helpful indeed). It brings to mind an illustration in the delightful memoirs of Darwin's granddaughter, Gwen Raverat, of her childhood in late-nineteenth-century Cambridge, when Gwen's Aunt Etty, a determined anti-Catholic, suddenly appeared at the foot of her bed, exclaiming with passion, "I could *swallow* the Pope of Rome, but what I can *not* swallow is the celibacy of the clergy."[3]

The history faculty in Cambridge could swallow women lecturers—indeed, it had swallowed four or five and not found them too indigestible—but it could not swallow married women lecturers. Attitudes have changed since then; married women may even be elected to chairs in history. But the change has been slow, and at the time I needed to consider my future. I chose not to hammer on a closed door but to build on what I had: my fellowship and teaching at Girton and my experience of editing and translating medieval texts. I might have sought a post in another university, but there was something I wanted to do more, which could be combined more easily with the supremely happy marriage that tied me to Cambridge. The day that I received the last discouraging letter, I wrote to Galbraith as general editor of Nelson's Medieval Texts and asked him if there was any hope of being allowed to edit the *Ecclesiastical History* of Orderic Vitalis, which I had been hankering to do for some time.

He replied almost by return of post on 17 July 1954, "Are you aware that I have been worrying my head off trying to find the right person to do Orderic for Nelson's—for say 7 years past? And here you have been hankering and never told me (you do know, I hope, how long it is!). It is the book of books that Morrison wants done or started before he dies, and I am in consequence very excited by your letter." Four days later Peter Morrison wrote to me, "A letter from Vivian Galbraith has given me immense pleasure. He tells me that you want to 'do' Orderic.... You have a double portion of my blessing for coming forward. Because it was Orderic who founded the Med Texts series! It was while wishing for a second Edition of the Shropshire lad that the idea came into my mind." My contract with Nelson's was signed on 31 August 1954. The edition ran to six volumes and took me twenty-five years. It was a labor of love, the principal work of my life, and the basis of much of my later historical writing. Moreover, it opened many doors outside Cambridge, in Europe and America. Election as a fellow of the British Academy in 1978 and as a corresponding fellow of the Medieval Academy of America in 1983 has meant a very great deal to me.

Orderic Vitalis spent over thirty years writing his *Ecclesiastical History,* which deals chiefly with England, Normandy, and the Normans elsewhere in the century before 1141. He was born in 1075 in Shropshire, two or three miles from my own birthplace, and was sent at the age of ten to become an oblate monk in the Norman monastery of Saint-Évroult, where he passed the remainder of his life. His great book brings in every aspect of the life of the monks and knights whom he knew, from liturgy and monastic studies to warfare and castle building, from the lives of saints to epic songs. It shows the aftermath of the Norman Conquest while changes were taking place and before anyone could tell what the final outcome was to be. It takes its readers into the dynamic of history and defies facile judgments. At times I think of Orderic as the last of the line of distinguished teachers under whom I have studied. He made me realize that many of the questions that university students were being required to answer were the wrong questions and could never produce satisfactory answers.[4] He pleads (in modern terminology) for taking a holistic view of history and for consensus rather than confrontation.

I continued to teach and undertake increasing college duties for ten years without having completed even the first volume of my edition. Clearly I would never finish the work at that rate, and I decided to resign my Girton fellowship. I took the decision alone and was relieved and encouraged by a characteristic letter of approval from Vivian Galbraith. He wrote on 21 December 1964, "I congratulate you—without qualification—on your impending retirement from Girton. I did it—coaching, tutorials and all that—at Balliol for ten years, and literally fled exhausted to Edinburgh. Properly done Oxford and Cambridge are the two most eviscerating universities in the world.... I found Edinburgh a rest cure.... My one word of caution is to make it plain—absolutely plain—to Girton that you really are going, even though the whole staff go sick or the skies fall."

Leaving Girton felt at first a little like amputating a limb, but it was the right decision for me. I settled down to fifteen more years' work, mainly on Orderic. By great good fortune Clare Hall, a research college founded shortly afterward, invited me into its fellowship in 1969, and it has provided support and stimulating companionship ever since. I continued to teach a few research students and an occasional undergraduate; I even gave a full course of Cambridge University lectures on the Norman Conquest to replace an absent lecturer. I love teaching, but I have never attempted to found a "school"; my aim has always been to help my pupils, who are men and women of very different interests and abilities, to understand what history is and to use their understanding in whatever career they decide to pursue.

Much of my work in the twenty years since Orderic was finished has arisen directly from it and has been on subjects connected with Norman and Anglo-Norman history and historiography. In 1978 my friend Allen Brown founded the Battle Conference on Anglo-Norman Studies, which has been held annually ever since, and I was deeply involved in it from the beginning. After his tragically early death I became director of the conference and edited *Anglo-Norman Studies* for five years. This brought many overseas contacts. In 1992 I took the conference to Palermo in collaboration with Patrizia Lendinara, Cataldo Roccaro, and the Officina di Studi Medievali. The ambition to write about the Normans, which first took shape when as a research student I first visited Caen, has been amply fulfilled.

These were years when other interests, too, could be taken further. Economic history was not forgotten; I was able at long last to edit for the British Academy the twelfth-century surveys of the English estates of the Abbey of La Trinité, Caen, which Eileen Power had hoped that I would do. An invitation to give the Prothero Lecture of the Royal Historical Society led me to turn my attention to the Empress Matilda, a remarkable women who had first impressed me when, as an undergraduate, I read her reactions to the Constitutions of Clarendon. It seemed to me that anyone who had lived through the turmoil of the Investiture Contest in Germany as the wife of the Emperor Henry V must have applied some of her experience of the relations between Church and State when her son was king of England. From there it was only a short step to writing her biography. Other books, papers, and editions have been connected with the Normans, with a particular slant recently toward historiography. Historians are fortunate in not needing laboratories, as do scientists; consequently they can continue to work long after formal retirement. I still have short-term plans for further writing; but it is not my intention to undertake anything likely to involve (as Orderic did) twenty-five years for completion.

NOTES

1. Cipolla, *"Fortuna plus homini quam consilium valet,"* 65–75.
2. Southern, "V. H. Galbraith," 397–425, 410.
3. Raverat, *Period Piece*, 133–34.
4. For an account of the changes, see Chibnall, *Debate on the Norman Conquest.*

Select Bibliography of Works by Marjorie McCallum Chibnall

A full bibliography to 1983 is printed in *Tradition and Change,* ed. Diana Greenway, Christopher Holdsworth, and Jane Sayers (Cambridge: Cambridge University Press, 1985), 263–69. A typed bibliography to 2000 is deposited with the British Academy.

As Marjorie Morgan

The English Lands of the Abbey of Bec. Oxford: Oxford University Press, 1947.

As Marjorie Chibnall

Editor. *Select Documents of the English Lands of the Abbey of Bec.* Camden Society, 3rd series, vol. 73. London: Royal Historical Society, 1951.
Editor and translator. *Joannis Sarisberiensis Historia Pontificalis: John of Salisbury's Memoirs of the Papal Court.* London: Nelson, 1956.
Editor and translator. *The Ecclesiastical History of Orderic Vitalis*, 6 vols. Oxford: Clarendon Press, 1969–80.
Editor. *Charters and Custumals of the Abbey of Holy Trinity Caen.* Records of Social and Economic History, n.s., vol. 5. London: British Academy, 1982.
The World of Orderic Vitalis. Oxford: Clarendon Press, 1984. Reprint, Woodbridge, Eng.: Boydell, 1995.
Anglo-Norman England 1066–1166. Oxford: Blackwell, 1986.
Editor. *Anglo-Norman Studies.* Vols. 12–16. Woodbridge, Eng.: Boydell, 1990–94.
The Empress Matilda: Queen Consort, Queen Mother and Lady of the English. Oxford: Blackwell, 1991.
Editor and translator with Leslie Watkiss. *The Waltham Chronicle.* Oxford: Clarendon Press, 1994.
Editor and translator with R. A. C. Davis. *The "Gesta Guillelmi" of Williams of Poitiers.* Oxford: Clarendon Press, 1998.
The Debate on the Norman Conquest. Studies in Historiography. Manchester: Manchester University Press, 1999.
The Normans. The Peoples of Europe. Oxford: Blackwell, 2000.
Piety, Power and History in Medieval England and Normandy. Variorum Series (reprints 31 articles from 1959 to 1997). Aldershot, Eng.: Ashgate, 2000.

Works Cited

Cipolla, Carlo M. "*Fortuna plus homini quam consilium valet.*" In *The Historian's Workshop*, ed. L. P. Curtis Jr., 65–75. New York: Alfred A. Knopf, 1970.
Raverat, Gwen. *Period Piece.* London: Faber & Faber, 1952.
Southern, R. W. "V. H. Galbraith." In *Proceedings of the British Academy* 64 (1978): 397–425, 410.

CHAPTER 54

∝

A Singular Career
College Professor and Army Wife (1914–)

CHARITY CANNON WILLARD

Not too long ago I had occasion to read Virginia Woolf's *A Room of One's Own*, which dwells on the discrepancy of educational opportunities for women as opposed to men, notably at Cambridge, where Woolf had recently lectured at two of the women's colleges. What struck me particularly was the evident difference between what was offered to women in England and what was offered to them in the United States at the time she was writing in the twenties. The difference between what she was describing and my own education in the thirties was notable. I never at any time felt that my educational opportunities were inferior to men's—at a small Midwestern coeducational college, at Smith, and even at Radcliffe, where most of my courses took place at Harvard, but where I was respected and well treated by my professors and my fellow students, to one of whom I was eventually married for half a century. My parents were both college teachers: my mother started teaching on a regular basis when I was four years old and my father held a higher academic rank than my mother, but both of them made notable contributions to their institution, Hiram College. But there were problems for women in the United States. Those problems arose from professional attitudes toward them in too many places.

My own career, however, started normally enough, even though I received my Ph.D. in French in June 1940, the week France fell to the German invaders. There was, of course, no possibility of getting to Europe to get on with the research on Christine de Pizan in which I had been involved for my Ph.D. thesis, but there was an abundant need for teachers to replace men who were being called to military duty.

I taught for three years, but then I married my Harvard man, who had by that time been drafted, sent to officer candidate school (OCS), and then immediately appointed

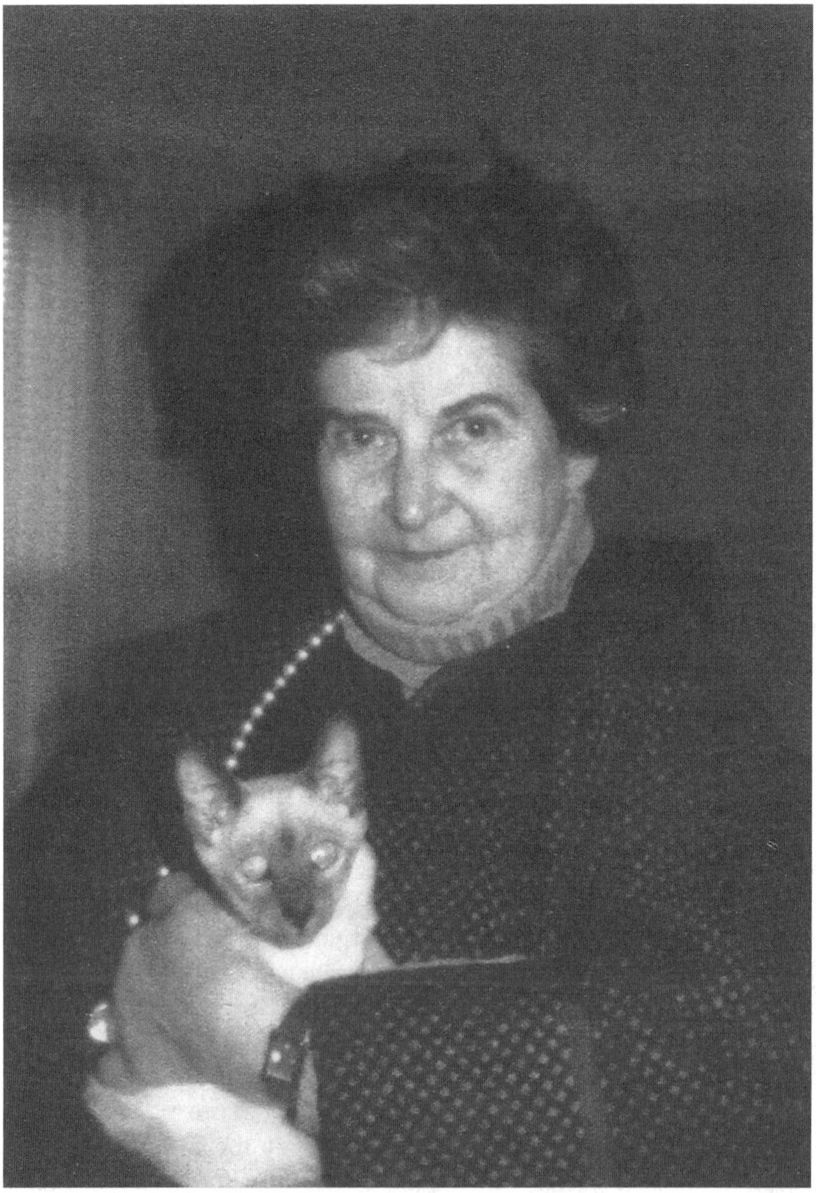

a language instructor at the United States Military Academy at West Point. Unfortunately there was no place available for a junior married officer to live at West Point or in the vicinity, so I taught for another year until we found an apartment in a neighboring town. That was the beginning of my problems, because army wives of that day were not expected to be educated and certainly not professional. The most constructive thing I could find to do was to sew for the Red Cross. In 1946, to be sure, I was offered a promising position in the French department at Brown University, but when my husband spoke of it to the head of the West Point language department, the colonel was highly disapproving. Not wanting to damage my husband's career, I turned down the position. The head of the Brown department did not speak to me at meetings for several years.

The following year, 1947, my husband, along with other temporary officers, prepared to leave the army, although there was a slight misadventure when my husband was on the point of accepting a civilian job before the army was prepared to release him. We could both have taught at Lawrence College in Wisconsin. Eventually, however, my husband accepted an appointment at the University of Vermont, where two contemporaries from graduate school were in the foreign language department, one of them as chairman. Being a New Englander, my husband was no doubt tempted to return to that part of the country, but unfortunately the university did not hire wives of faculty members. As school started that fall, there was need for an additional French instructor, but someone with an A.B. degree, who happened to be available, was hired, even though I had the same degree as three members of the department.

This was a difficult period in our lives in several respects, but especially because my husband's salary was less than his army pay as a captain had been, and we simply couldn't live on it. Others who had just left military service were having similar problems.

Eventually I got a job in the university archives, which was interesting enough, to be sure, for I was asked to file the papers Dorothy Canfield Fisher was giving to the university. It is not often recalled that Fisher was the first woman to receive a Ph.D. from Columbia University, producing an interesting thesis on the French classical theater. She had also done significant work as a volunteer in France during World War I. Getting to know her was a very pleasant experience, as I had read several of her books when I was younger. I paid several visits to her home in southern Vermont. But then a Radcliffe friend had the idea of proposing me as someone who could rescue college professors who had problems arranging leaves from their jobs. So it was that I taught at Bennington College, an especially interesting experience, and then a year at Saint Lawrence University, where I earned enough to contemplate a trip to France.

At about this time the Boston Public Library acquired an early manuscript of Christine de Pizan's *Livre des trois vertus,* written for the daughter of a duke of Burgundy who was about to be married to the heir to the French throne. The first part of this book discusses the duties that would be expected of this young noblewoman as she became queen of France and was expected to play a leading role at the French court. However, two other parts of the book are devoted to discussing proper lives for other women in society, from those in convents to wives of various sorts of professional men. It is a fascinating view of late-medieval French society, and as there are a number of surviving manuscripts as well as three early printed editions, it was obviously read by a number of women. I thought it would be very interesting to edit this text and so became involved in studying the manuscripts. As the Christine de Pizan manuscripts are scattered over a considerable number of libraries, this promised fairly extensive travels in Europe and contact with a number of libraries and archives. The archives, of course, give information not only about the early owners but also about the production of these manuscripts beginning with the scribes who copied them. The archives at Dijon and Lille would be especially important.

One interesting aspect of the *Livre des trois vertus* is that the duchess of Burgundy, Isabel of Portugal, sister of Henry the Navigator, had a Portuguese translation made for their niece, who was then queen of Portugal. Isabel had good reason to think that she was in need of advice. A slightly later princess had the text printed, one of the earliest books in Portugal. One finds this book in Lisbon, but the manuscript is in Madrid. The Spanish Queen Isabel was a close relative of these other royal ladies and apparently claimed the original manuscript.

When the Korean War heated up, my husband was called back to active military duty, again at West Point. Once we were settled there, this time in proper housing on the post, I spent two months in France, intensifying the extensive study of the Christine de Pizan manuscripts that has occupied me ever since.

Not long after our return to West Point, I was asked to rescue a situation at the Emma Willard School at Troy, New York, where a Spanish teacher had collapsed in her classroom shortly after the beginning of the second semester. I taught there for three years, but as the demands on me as an army wife increased, along with my husband's progression in rank, commuting simply became too difficult, and the school kept expecting more extracurricular service from me—so I resigned.

A crisis, the unexpected need for a teacher, occurred the following year in the local high school attended by army children, where I stepped in to help. Teaching there turned out to be unexpectedly interesting, for it was just as NATO was being established in Europe, and the children I taught knew that there was a good possibility of their living abroad, so they were eager to learn French, in particular, although I also taught Spanish to students who eventually lived in Spanish-speaking countries. Other students of mine have lived in France or Belgium. One has become a collector of eighteenth-century French antiques, and I frequently see another who, retired from the army, works for an international concern in Brussels. Another now teaches in the Air Force Academy. These were some of the brightest and most enthusiastic students I have ever taught.

Eventually, however, a new principal expected me to stay after school to do various duties that interfered with what I was expected to do at West Point. One must understand that army wives were then, even more than now, expected to do a variety of social and charitable duties. My husband's department by this time had some fifty members teaching seven languages. We were supposed to help maintain good relations among some hundred people and also to entertain visitors to the academy. My husband frequently interpreted for the superintendent of the academy when there were non-English-speaking dignitaries, and if they arrived with their wives, I was often expected to help. So it was that I assisted the superintendent's wife when she had to give a luncheon for the wife of the chief of staff of the Spanish army. We also attended a reception for the king of Morocco and his family, so we learned how to address royalty in French. There were several foreign exchange officers in the department, some of whom had wives who didn't speak much English. We were expected to help them adapt to life at West Point. When my husband became second in command in the department, I was once required to give a dinner for thirty-four visiting officers from the Naval Academy, representing four or five languages. We also had a cocktail party for a new French military attaché who chose to make a visit to West Point shortly before Christmas vacation. That was a real trial with the pre-Christmas duties at school, but we managed.

An especially amusing episode occurred at a dinner to honor a French officer who had just been appointed to teach at West Point, the first to be assigned there. Present at the dinner were the military attaché from the French embassy in Washington and an assistant, a colonel. We were delegated to entertain him and his wife at dinner, along with several cadets. As the party was breaking up, we were talking to the officer's wife while her husband was consulting with the attaché. A French instructor, who was one of the aides for the evening, came up and said to the Frenchwoman, "Do you know, Madame, that Madame Willard is a specialist in the writings of Christine de Pizan?" I expected some sort of polite noise from the lady, but she looked at me in surprise and said, "Why, that is one of my husband's ancestors!" When the officer returned, he also expressed surprise but told me a bit about the modern family, saying that there were eighty members in his generation. It is, of course, true that Christine's son, Jean du Castel, had three children, but this is still a rather astonishing statistic. The colonel was the nephew of the Madame du Castel who wrote a biography of Christine de Pizan some years ago.

My professional problems were eventually solved by a position at Ladycliffe, a small college just outside the gates of West Point. Its principal French teacher had suffered a spell of illness that prevented her from teaching. The Franciscan sisters who ran this school were outstanding administrators, and they understood the problems I had to contend with. It was never a question of my teaching schedule, but they were willing to adapt my other duties to demands at West Point. Furthermore, as I continued to teach there, they hired other West Point wives, several of whom have subsequently had very good professional careers. I should perhaps have preferred to teach at a more prestigious college, but I discovered that there was merit in holding a position where others at West Point could see me in action. When the superintendent of West Point would attend commencement, for instance, there I would be in academic regalia marching in the procession. I do think it helped to change the attitude toward army wives at West Point. I also observe with pleasure the careers of some of my former students. Several are now colonel's wives, who earlier taught in schools for army children in a variety of countries where they were stationed. Another former student has had an interesting international position based in Lyon, France, and recently I saw another who had started on her study of French as a young woman, and who is now teaching in the foreign language department at West Point.

At the time when West Point was undertaking to become more academic, the officers were expected to earn advanced degrees and also to participate in outside academic activities. So it was that my husband and I would attend professional meetings together, at least partly subsidized by the military, where I would frequently read a paper, and he would socialize. People still mention conversations they remember having had with him at various places. One of the organizers of a conference at the University of Lausanne, for instance, recalled a conversation in Bologna!

It was his position that made it possible for me to go to Europe regularly and to publish my Ph.D. dissertation, the edition of Christine de Pizan's *Livre de la paix,* as well as to hunt for the manuscripts that interested me. There were no research funds available to subsidize army wives. The army was not unique in not taking us seriously.

I naturally went first to Paris, although the earliest copy of the *Livre de la paix* is in the Royal Library in Brussels. I also naturally wanted to see other manuscripts of the *Livre des trois vertus.* In Paris I learned to cope with the complexities of the manuscript department of the Bibliothèque nationale, and in Brussels I became acquainted with the remarkable library of the dukes of Burgundy, now, for the most part, in the Bibliothèque Royale there. Not only did I find this library an especially pleasant place to work, but I became acquainted there with a remarkable member of the staff, L. M. J. Delaissé, a notable codicologist. My contact with him taught me a great deal about looking at the physical characteristics of manuscripts: writing, marginal notations, illustrations, not to mention the parchment or paper on which they were written. Examining these late-medieval manuscripts, primarily from the fifteenth century, opened a whole new world to me. This is a most interesting way of studying history, especially identifying and learning about their original owners. It is indeed exciting to hold in one's own hands these books read by queens and duchesses.

It was my good fortune that, when what became the Bunting Institute at Radcliffe College was founded to help professional women return to interrupted professions, I was given a grant in the second group. I was also given leave from Ladycliff for two years and greatly enjoyed once more the facilities of Harvard. Another advantage was that I had a respectable and known institution from which to publish, so it was at this point that I started publishing a number of articles. It was also my good fortune that while I was at the institute, Delaissé, by then attached to an Oxford college, was a visiting professor. I not only attended his seminars but made interesting contacts with other students of manuscripts. This was all a most valuable and enjoyable experience.

This experience also gave me a desire for greener pastures. My husband had then completed twenty years of military service and could retire with a pension. We were discussing future plans when he was suddenly informed that he was in line to be the next head of the foreign language department at West Point, something he certainly never expected, not being a West Point graduate. He was, however, appointed to the position so that there was no longer any question of our leaving the military academy. We were, however, given two different years of leave in Europe, one in Paris and one in Brussels, from which I benefited greatly, of course.

Our year in Paris turned out to be a rather unexpected experience. It started out normally enough, with much time spent in the Bibliothèque nationale. I also had the opportunity to participate in a seminar at the École des hautes études devoted to manuscript study. This was directed by Gilbert Ouy from the Bibliothèque nationale, who has since published a good deal on the subject. He has been especially interested in the manuscripts from the period of Christine de Pizan as well as the Christine manuscripts themselves.

Toward spring of that year, 1968, propaganda from Vietnam, where the French were still involved despite the United States' embroilment in war, began to be more and more apparent in public places. Then demonstrations, notably by university students, began to take place, until a full-scale revolt began, with demonstrations in the streets and the fear of worse. University classes were cancelled, and many institutions, including the Bibliothèque nationale, closed their doors for nearly a month. Because a part of the National Radio was housed on the street where we lived, the riot police occupied our neighborhood for this same period. On a couple of occasions we were obliged to show identification in order to enter the street! One amusing aspect of the situation was that strangers spoke to one another on the street in a way I have never seen in Paris before or since. If one had a newspaper under one's arm, perfect strangers would inquire about the latest news and exchange comments about it. Of course all this prepared us for the student protests against the war in Vietnam that took place in the United States the following year.

During our year in Brussels my husband had as a project the translation of Christine de Pizan's *Livre des faits d'armes et de chevalerie*, which I edited. It was published in 1999, as some of you undoubtedly know. I have recently finished editing the French text, an undertaking started that same year, and it is now awaiting publication.

My husband's duties and connections also took us on some other interesting expeditions—to Turkey, Morocco, and Tunisia, as well as to Spain and Portugal, where former members of the foreign language department were on duty. He was well suited for the position, and I do not regret that he carried it out. Professional army officers with good linguistic capabilities certainly make an important contribution to the country, as we had ample opportunity to observe on these trips. One is especially pleased at the present time to think that Arabic has been taught at West Point for a number of years.

We both arrived at the point of retirement at about the same time and by chance found an agreeable house in a town north of West Point on the Hudson River. From there we continued frequent travels, but I also found leisure to publish the books I had never had time to take through the final stages while I was teaching. Since retirement I have published five books and have finished the edition of the *Faits d'armes* of which I spoke earlier.

My husband and I were good people to work on this *Faits d'armes,* as it is a book of advice on military matters written by Christine de Pizan for Louis de Guyenne in 1410, at a time when France was in a rather sorry state in this respect. She explains that she had the advice of professional military men, but her manner of giving advice to the young prince is impressive. Although her advice on siege warfare and firing stones from cannons is obsolete, what she has to say about military leadership and organizing troops is not too different from what is taught to cadets at West Point today. It was interesting to discover that one of the manuscripts at the Bibliothèque nationale has Napoleon's coat of arms on the cover, and one now in Harvard's Houghton Library bears the signature of his chief of staff.

Unfortunately, after about fifteen years of very agreeable life with yearly travels, during which time we celebrated our golden wedding anniversary, my husband's health failed, and he died quite unexpectedly. Of course, my life is no longer as agreeable, but my work makes it livable. I am very grateful to be educated and to have the society of Christine de Pizan. A good deal has been said about the passage in her *Mutacion de fortune* concerning her transformation into a man who had to guide the ship they had been sailing after her husband's untimely death. She also says in her advice to widows in the *Livre des trois vertus* that if one loses one's husband one "must take on the heart of a man" (191). When I was left alone to look after all my affairs, I had a new understanding of what Christine was saying.

As I have said, it is having work to do, making contacts with others with similar interests, and seeing old friends at meetings that have made life reasonably agreeable. I come from a long-lived family, so perhaps I shall be able to finish my half-written biography of Isabel of Portugal, from which I have been distracted by the great interest in Christine de Pizan. When we were first back at West Point, I made an effort to go frequently to work at the Morgan Library in New York. There I would encounter Curt Bühler, curator of early printed books, who was editing the Middle English translation of Christine de Pizan's *Epître d'Othéa*. He would greet me jauntily and say, "You know, Mrs. Willard, I think you and I are the only people in the United States who are interested in Christine de Pizan." How times have changed!

SELECT BIBLIOGRAPHY OF WORKS BY CHARITY CANNON WILLARD

"The 'Three Virtues' of Christine de Pizan." *Boston Public Library Quarterly* 2 (1950): 201–305.
Le Livre de la paix, by Christine de Pizan. Edition critique. The Hague: Mouton, 1958.
"Christine de Pizan's 'Clock of Temperance.'" *L'Esprit Créateur* 2 (1962): 149–54.
"An Autograph Manuscript of Christine de Pizan." *Studi Francesi* 78 (1965): 452–57.
"A Portuguese Translation of Christine de Pizan's *Livre des trois vertus*." *PMLA* 78 (1965): 452–57.
"The Manuscript Tradition of *Le Livre des trois vertus* and Christine de Pizan's Audience." *Journal of the History of Ideas* 27 (1966): 433–44.

"Christine de Pizan's Treatise on the Art of Medieval Warfare." In *Essays in Honor of L. F. Solano,* edited by Raymond Cormier and Urban Holmes. Chapel Hill: University of North Carolina Press, 1970.

"An Unknown Manuscript of Christine de Pizan's *Livre de la paix.*" *Studi Francesi* 64 (1978): 90–97.

"Christine de Pizan: The Astrologer's Daughter." In *Moyen Âge et Renaissance,* edited by Jonathan Beck and Gianni Mombello, vol. 1 of *Mélanges à la mémoire de Franco Simone: France et Italie dans la culture européenne.* Geneva: Slatkine, 1980.

"Christine de Pizan and the Order of the Rose" and "Christine de Pizan's *Livre des trois vertus*: Feminine Ideal or Practical Advice?" In *Ideals for Women in the Works of Christine de Pizan,* edited by Diane Bornstein, Michigan Consortium of Medieval and Early Modern Studies Monograph Series 1. East Lansing: Michigan Consortium for Medieval and Early Modern Studies, 1981.

Christine de Pizan: Her Life and Works. New York: Persea Books, 1985.

Text established in collaboration with Eric Hicks. *Le Livre des trois vertus.* Paris: Champion, 1989.

Translator. *A Medieval Woman's Mirror of Honor: The Treasury of the City of Ladies.* Edited by Madeleine Pelner Cosman. New York: Persea Books, 1989.

"Christine de Pizan." In vol. 2 of *An Encyclopedia of Continental Women Writers,* edited by Katherina M. Wilson. New York: Garland, 1991.

Editor. *The Writings of Christine de Pizan.* New York: Persea Books, 1993.

Editor. *The Book of Arms and of Chivalry,* by Christine de Pizan. Translated by B. G. Sumner Willard. University Park: Pennsylvania State University Press, 1999.

Editor. *Les Faits d'armes et de chevalerie.* Edition critique. Forthcoming.

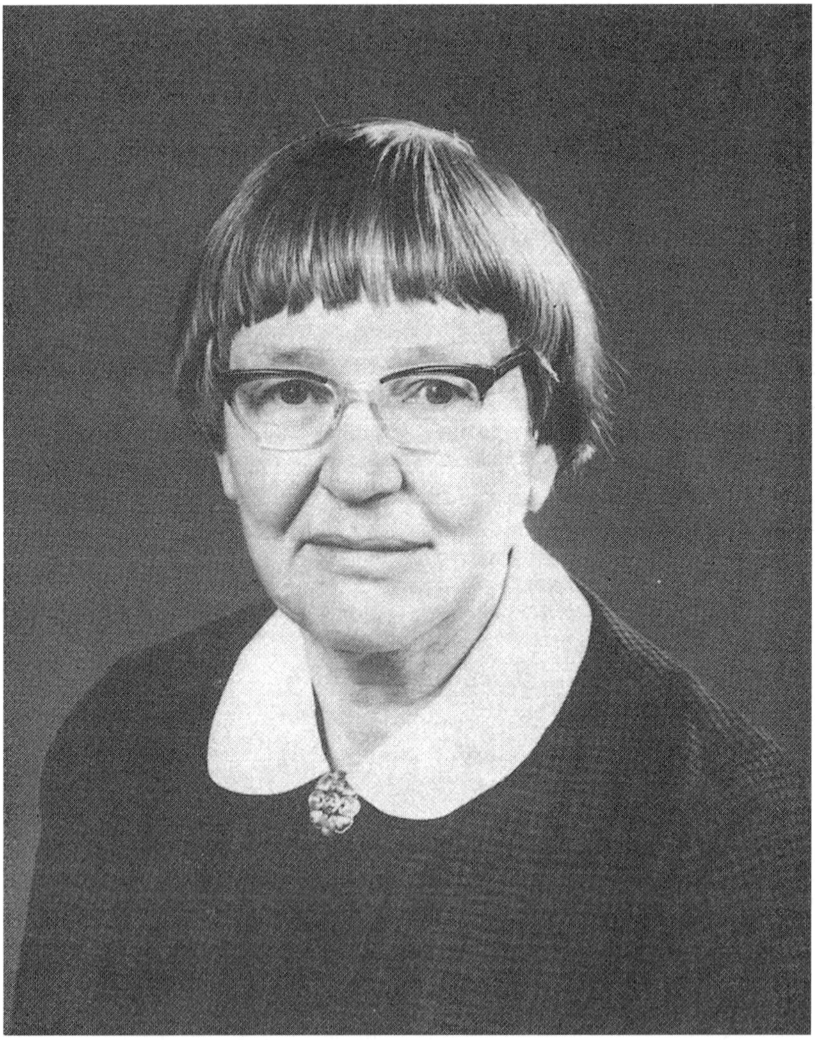

CHAPTER 55

A Scholar of Early Britain
Rachel Bromwich (1915–)

GERALD MORGAN

RACHEL BROMWICH (nee Amos) was born in 1915 in the town of Hove on the English south coast. Her father, Maurice Amos, was an adviser on international law to the Egyptian government, then very much under British influence, and served as a judge in Cairo; on retirement he was knighted for his services. His specialization was international marriage law, in which field his work is still quoted. His wife, by the unwritten rules of the age, followed him to Egypt, but children were often born at home in England, and Hove, which was never the Bromwich family home, happened to be convenient at the time. Rachel was the fourth of five children, three girls and two boys, of an English father and a Scots mother with strong Quaker connections. She lost both her brothers prematurely, one to illness, the other to the Second World War.

Childhood for the offspring of overseas civil servants was rarely settled. As an infant Rachel was able to be with her parents in Egypt, but the need for schooling in Britain meant separation from her father and mother at the age of seven, save only for summer holidays, for the next ten years. Her first school was at Cuckfield, a little town deep in rural Sussex, a countryside still at its most rich and beautiful, with at the time little of the exploitative farming, heavy traffic, and commuter suburbia that now blight much of southeast England. She then spent time at a school in Westmoreland, near her parents' retirement home in mountainous Cumbria. From there she followed her elder sister, Margaret, to the Mount School at York, a well-known Quaker foundation, which in a later generation educated the novelist sisters Antonia Byatt and Margaret Drabble and the actress Judy Dench. Boarding school was not an experience she enjoyed; even now Rachel much prefers the company of a few to the hurly-burly of the many, and she missed home, feeling to this day that her parents were under too much pressure and separated from their children for too long for her to know them well. Of the many books she read during her childhood and adolescence, perhaps the most influential was an edition of Arthurian tales from Malory, illustrated by the extraordinary artist Arthur Rackham. Her warm response to the "Matter of Britain," the legends of Arthur, has lasted her lifetime.

There was academic ambition in the Amos household, and the elder sister, Margaret, went to Newnham College, Cambridge, but then chose marriage rather than a career. Their father saw this, in the way of his time, as a waste, and expected Rachel to become a village schoolteacher, without the bother and expense of Cambridge, for which he did not feel she had the ability. He insisted that she spend six months with a French family in Paris, attending French classes. She was disappointed to discover that the teacher would not give her lessons in medieval French; she had been given a copy of her relation C. K. Scott-Montcrieff's translation of *Le Chanson de Roland* and longed to read the original. Then, after some months with her family in London, her father agreed that she should have coaching for the Cambridge entrance examination, and Rachel Amos went to Newnham College, Cambridge, in 1934. There she read for the first year of the English tripos, encouraged by an admired Scots teacher, Dorothy Hoare, and eagerly took on Anglo-Saxon, inspired, as she feels, by a desire not only to learn the language and its literature, but to know more of the early history of England.[1] This interest had been augmented by her father's decision, on his retirement from service in Egypt in 1925, to return to the Cumbrian Lake District in northwest England (though he also spent time in Cambridge). Cumbria, uniquely in England, was enriched over the centuries by powerful Celtic, Norse, and Anglo-Saxon influences. For the Welsh it is part of the "Old North," reminiscent of the post-Roman period when British, the ancestor language of Welsh, Cornish, and Breton, was spoken from Edinburgh to Vannes. It was in Cumbria that Rachel spent many of her adolescent school holidays home from boarding school, and her love of mountains, lakes, and streams has lasted throughout her lifetime.

Rachel Amos's Cambridge encounter with Anglo-Saxon was all-important, for it brought a decision to move from English to the entirely separate department of archaeology and anthropology, whose section B, now itself a separate department, provided courses in Anglo-Saxon, Old Norse, and Celtic, acronymically known as ASNAC. This discipline was the personal creation of a giant of British scholarship, Hector Munro Chadwick, author of *The Heroic Age* (1912) and with his wife Nora of *The Growth of Literature* (1932–40).[2] Anglo-Saxon, Old Norse, and Celtic may sound parochial to the ignorant, but Chadwick was a man whose cultural boundaries knew few limits, and his wife shared his interest in world literature; their masterpiece *The Growth of Literature* includes treatments of early European, Hebrew, and Indian literatures and the oral literatures of the Tartars, Polynesians, and some African peoples.[3] Rachel Amos was taught medieval Welsh by the remarkable young scholar Kenneth Jackson, an Englishman who had already studied Welsh at Bangor and Irish in Dublin and who held the newly created post of lecturer in Celtic languages and literature.[4]

It is not easy to re-create in the imagination the condition of Welsh studies in 1930s Britain. Welsh speakers, already a minority among the people of Wales, were virtually invisible on the British cultural and political landscape, despite the charisma of the Welsh-speaking British prime minister and world statesman David Lloyd George earlier in the century. Much of Wales was in deep economic depression, and there was heavy migration to England in search of work. The rich literary tradition of the Welsh language, reaching back to the sixth century A.D., was not well known beyond the boundaries of Wales, though some major English, Irish, French, German, and Danish scholars had done important work in the field. The only chair of Celtic in an English university was at Oxford, now named after its first holder, Sir John Rhys (1840–1915); its establishment had been inspired by Matthew Arnold. In the 1930s, however, the chair was occupied by a Scot who left no great reputation behind him. There was a lectureship in Welsh in the University of Liverpool and a tradition of Welsh interest in the University of Manchester. Four colleges of the federal University of Wales—Aberystwyth, Bangor, Cardiff, and Swansea—had departments of Welsh with chaired professors, but the departments were tiny, and the task before the staff was enormous. Their main resources were the splendid collections of Welsh literary manuscripts at the National Library of Wales, in the Cardiff Free Library and the Jesus College manuscript collection, and the facilities of the University of Wales Press, the third largest university press in Britain.

The Welsh literary heritage that seized Rachel Amos's imagination was a complex one. The great treasures of medieval Welsh prose were well known through Lady Charlotte Guest's 1846 translation, *The Mabinogion,* but before 1920 little had been done by way of textual analysis and linguistic study. Despite the pioneering work of the eighteenth-century curate-scholar Evan Evans, the riches of early Welsh poetry, including the works attributed to Aneirin and Taliesin, had not been critically edited.[5] The difficult texts of the poets of the Welsh princes (1080–1284) were available in print, but unedited. Only selections of the work of the greatest of Welsh poets, Dafydd ap Gwilym, and of his contemporaries were available in a scholarly edition of 1914.[6] When a pioneering Dutch scholar, Theodore M. Chotzen, produced a remarkable and voluminous study of Dafydd ap Gwilym, *Récherches sur la poesie de Dafydd ap Gwilym* (Amsterdam, 1927), he had had to visit Aberystwyth to copy most of the poems from an unscholarly edition of 1789. Particularly frustrating for Welsh scholars was the absence of a proper Welsh-English dictionary on lexicographical principles; such a work only began publication in 1950 and is at the time of writing still not quite complete.

For Rachel Amos a special lack was serious analysis of the relationship between Welsh literature and the legend of King Arthur. So effectively had medieval poets and pseudohistorians developed an English Arthur, a French Arthur, a German Arthur, a Latin Arthur, and indeed a European Arthur that the Welsh roots of the figure of Arthur himself and his early associates Cei (Sir Kay) and Bedwyr (Sir Bedevere) were little understood. Welsh scholars had not yet sought to edit the Welsh Arthurian tales of *Culhwch ac Olwen, Breuddwyd Rhonabwy, Geraint ac Enid, Peredur,* and *Owein,* and the obviously close relationship between the three last-named and three of the poems of Chrétien de Troyes was not (and is still not) fully explained. Throughout Rachel Bromwich's scholarly career the riddles of Arthurian origins, and the associated Tristan and Merlin legends, have exercised her intellect and imagination.

To revert to her career: first-class honors at Cambridge meant that in 1938, following her teacher Kenneth Jackson's example, she was able to move to the University College of Wales, Bangor, to study with the greatest of living Welsh scholars, Ifor Williams, later knighted for his contribution to learning.[7] Ifor Williams had a grounding in Greek and Latin that served him well in his painstaking analysis of the vocabulary of early Welsh inscriptions and literature. He had succeeded Sir John Morris-Jones as professor and head of his small but busy department, and as well as bearing a heavy teaching load, he had recently reached the climax of a lifetime of editing early Welsh texts, a period that lasted from 1908 until 1962. The 1930s had seen the publication of three of his masterpieces: *Pedeir Keinc y Mabinogi* (1930), *Canu Llywarch Hen* (1935), and *Canu Aneirin* (1937). Rachel Bromwich found him a man of great sympathy and kindness; she flourished for a year under his guidance and would have enjoyed a second year but for the interference of the outbreak of World War II in 1939. It was Ifor Williams who suggested that she might edit the Welsh triads, the extraordinary cryptic medieval triple-groupings of legendary figures from the Welsh past, which became the major work of her scholarly career. This suggestion in itself demonstrates his confidence in her ability. Williams was a man less affected than most by academic misogyny. One must realize that hitherto the study of Welsh literature and its texts had been almost entirely a masculine monopoly. No woman had ever been appointed lecturer in a university department of Welsh (they were rare enough in most disciplines). Inspired by her teacher, determined to justify his confidence in her, she set out to copy the manuscript texts of the triads.

It was at this troubled beginning of war in 1939 that Rachel Amos married John Bromwich, a brilliant man of eclectic tastes and abilities, who had been a fellow student of hers at Cambridge. He was quickly called to the British army and posted to Northern Ireland, where Rachel followed him, and where their only child, Brian, was born. Rachel had been working hard on her triads, but the only copy of the first draft of her study of the triads was destroyed in a German bombing raid on Belfast, which fortunately she survived unscathed. However, she had had the good fortune during her time in Ireland to study Irish at Queen's University, Belfast, with Michael O'Brien. When her husband was posted overseas in 1942, Rachel and Brian returned to Cumbria, where she did her best to keep up her studies while rearing her son in difficult wartime circumstances. John Bromwich meanwhile followed a brilliant but difficult and dangerous military career, first in Italy and then in Greece, where he was deeply involved in the effort to prevent the Communist and royalist partisans from slaughtering each other and was decorated for his services. He was severely affected by these experiences, and although Rachel cared for him devotedly through bouts of illness, their ways parted in 1971.

With the end of the war in 1945, Rachel Bromwich was invited to return to Cambridge as lecturer in Celtic languages and literature; the lectureship had been vacant during the war, following the departure of Kenneth Jackson for Harvard in 1939. Rachel Bromwich held the post for thirty-one years, teaching medieval Welsh and Irish; she was eventually honored with the university title of reader and retired in 1976. The house that many of her students knew as her home, 153 Huntingdon Road, whose door was always open to them, had been sold by the time of her retirement. Instead of remaining in Cambridge, she moved with her library to Tyddyn Sabel, a romantic little mountain farmhouse on the high slopes of Snowdonia above the village of Bethesda, with superb views over the isle of Anglesey, but sometimes cut off by deep winter snows.

This house had been found for her by Idris Foster, another former student of Sir Ifor Williams at Bangor, who had been appointed to the Oxford Sir John Rhys Chair of Celtic in 1948 and was eventually knighted for his services to Welsh culture. Idris Foster was a polymath and a man happily at home both in the highest reaches of Oxford's intelligentsia and among the Welsh-speaking slate workers of Bethesda, where he had grown up. His students used to speculate on the number of disciplines in which he could have filled a university lectureship.[8] He and Rachel had long been warm friends, and she was able to spend the year 1974–75 at Oxford as Sir John Rhys Fellow. It was during her time at Bangor that she was given the degree of D.Litt. by the University of Wales, presented by the university's chancellor, Prince Charles, prince of Wales. Rachel has been invited to give titled lectures on several occasions; the most recent was the 1993 inaugural Van Hamel Lecture in Amsterdam.

Rachel Bromwich's years at her mountain nest in Tyddyn Sabel eventually had to end, a move forced on her by the difficulties of the rough track to the house and the inclement winters. After a brief time at a small house lower down the mountain, and following the death of Sir Idris Foster in 1984, she decided to move to Aberystwyth. Although for many years Bangor would have disputed this claim, there can be no doubt that Aberystwyth is the epicenter of Welsh and Celtic studies in Wales—indeed, in the United Kingdom. The university has chairs in Welsh and in Celtic Studies, and the National Library of Wales, itself a major scholarly center, has as its closest neighbor the University of Wales Centre for Advanced Welsh and Celtic Studies, which has developed into a substantial engine room of scholarship, with a large number of full-time fellows and at least six major scholarly projects already completed or under way. The center's first director, Emeritus Professor Caerwyn Williams, who had known Rachel Bromwich since her time at Bangor in 1938, dedicated to her volume 13 (1985) of his remarkable series of volumes of literary essays, *Ysgrifau Beirniadol,* complete with a bibliography of three full pages in small print. At Aberystwyth Rachel Bromwich has continued academic publication into her ninth decade and at the time of writing is revising her scholarly masterpiece, *Trioedd Ynys Prydein,* for its third edition.

It is time to review, however inadequately, the extraordinary range of publications Rachel Bromwich has produced since her first venture, on the triads, in the *Bulletin of the Board of Celtic Studies* for 1946.⁹ During the next four years she produced three important articles in the wider Celtic field, one about the Breton and Welsh legends of a sunken land, the others about Irish literature. Then in 1954 came a splendid study, "The Character of the Early Welsh Tradition," in Nora Chadwick's volume *Studies in Early British History.* This detailed chapter was the profoundest review of its subject that had yet appeared and still repays careful reading despite all that has been published since. Its original inspiration had, of course, been the work she was engaged in on the Welsh triads, eventually published as *Trioedd Ynys Prydein* (henceforth *TYP*) in 1961 by the University of Wales Press, revised and updated edition 1978.

Lesser mortals might have looked at the comparatively brief manuscript texts of the triads as something to be got out of the way with a short introduction and notes, totaling perhaps no more than 150 pages. Rachel Bromwich had seen, almost from the start, that the triads were more than just another literary text; they were a summary of a huge range of mythical, legendary, and literary knowledge, knowledge that would have been on the tongues of generations of Welsh poets and of the narrators of the Welsh prose tales. It may assist the reader to quote an example: "Three Generous Men of the Island of Britain: Nudd the Generous, son of Senyllt; Mordaf the Generous, son of Serwan; Rhydderch the Generous, son of Tudwal Tudglyd."[10] This translation fails to convey the brevity of the original; seventeen words of Welsh necessitate twenty-seven words of English. Not every triad is so laconic. Many individuals and incidents are glossed with explanations and a few with a summary of the legend attached to a particular individual or incident. Some triads have a fourth individual or incident added; thus to the "three exalted prisoners" is added the name of a fourth "who was more exalted than the three of them" (p. 140) There are occasional strokes of grim humor. One of the Three Fortunate Assassinations was that of the two birds of Gwenddoleu, who would eat two corpses of the Welsh for their dinner and two for their supper (p. 68). It must be added that not every character named is entirely Welsh. A number are classical in origin; for example, the three women who received the beauty of Eve are Dido, Helen, and Polixena (p. 128). It may be objected that they are not "of the island of Britain," but they appear in the manuscript texts and were part of the standard repertory of the poets. Several triads contain references to historical figures. Among the "three bulwarks of battle" (p. 42) the name of Gilbert de Clare occurs; more than one man of that name existed among the Norman aristocrats involved in the twelfth-century assault on Welsh independence, but it may be that Gilbert who was lord of Ceredigion at that time.

The triads deal with incidents and groups as well as individuals; thus we have "three fortunate concealments of the island of Britain," "three oppressions that came to this island," "three faithful warbands of the island of Britain" (pp. 88, 84, 57). Some triads exist in pairs; for example, there is also a triad of "faithless warbands (p. 58)" Some appear to be duplicates but are not; thus "three faithful wives" and "three faithful women" (p. 174) of the island of Britain contain different names. Arthur and his associates figure in many of the triads. No single text contains all the triads that seemed significant. The oldest text is of several "triads of horses" that appear in the *Black Book of Carmarthen*, before 1300 (pp. 97–101). Some triads are found only in later manuscripts—in a few cases as late as the work of eighteenth-century copyists. *TYP* identifies ninety-six triads as significant; it must be understood that other writers, such as those who worked on the medieval Welsh law texts, also delighted in the triadic form, but their significance is legal.

The body of historical triads, brief as it is, spans the whole range of Welsh history and legend, somewhat resembling the haunting medieval Welsh poem "The Stanzas of the Graves."[11] In both texts can be found personages from the earliest layers of Welsh mythology, from the legendary history of Wales and from Arthur's court. Arthur even appears as a poet, singing a verse to "the three favourites of Arthur's court, and three battle-horsemen" (p.31); and as one of the "three frivolous bards" (p.21) of the Island of Britain. Arthur possesses the three tribal thrones of the Island of Britain at Menevia, Celliwig, and Pen Rhionydd (p.211).

The editorial method chosen for this unique text had itself to be unique. The triads are dealt with individually or in their pairs; text and translation are followed by manuscript variants and notes that are linguistic or relevant only to the individual triad and the places named therein. The whole assemblage of triads is then followed by 260 pages of "Notes to Personal Names," running the entire alphabetical gamut of Welsh myth and legend. There are also five appendices of brief medieval texts relevant to the triads and to Welsh medieval legend, all carefully edited and annotated. The notes to personal names are the most generally valuable part of *TYP*; they are used by scholars far beyond those interested in the triads as such. They form a veritable dictionary of Welsh legendary biography. The third edition, when ready, will have incorporated hundreds of additional references to material made available since the second edition, which itself had enlarged on the original.

Following the major success of *TYP*, Rachel Bromwich did not abandon the subject but returned to it in several later publications. She also turned her eye to a new subject, the poetry of Dafydd ap Gwilym, the major fourteenth-century Welsh poet referred to earlier in this essay. Dafydd's poetry covers a wide range of themes, some reminiscent of the common stock of European poetry. He is best known as a poet of love and of nature, two themes that he often celebrated together, as in his poem "The Woodland Mass." He also delighted to appear as the victim of love: a wayward girl refuses to open her door to him and leaves him standing in the rain; a tavern maid offers him her bed, but in the dark he falls over the furniture, awakening the whole house, including "three Saxons in their stinking pit," and has to flee. On another occasion he attends church with the aim of ogling the girls, only to have to endure their mortifying comments on his effeminate appearance and lustful nature.

A magisterial edition of 150 of Dafydd's poems had been produced in 1952 by Sir Thomas Parry. This work was widely accepted by scholars as representing the canon of the poet's work, and it enabled scholars and readers to approach the poetry anew.[12] Rachel Bromwich was able to bring to her study of Dafydd ap Gwilym a wide familiarity with medieval European literature, which enabled her to improve our understanding of the broader context of the poet's work, an understanding pioneered by L. C. Stern and T. M. Chotzen of Germany and the Netherlands, respectively.[13] She had to master the extraordinary nuances of Welsh classical poetic technique, the *cynghanedd* ("consonantal chime," as it was memorably christened by Gerard Manley Hopkins). Not only did she bring a new depth of understanding to appreciation of Dafydd's poetry of love and nature; she gave it a new popularity through her edition, with literal translations, of fifty of his poems, published in Wales in 1980 and reprinted by Penguin. Her various papers on Dafydd's poetry were brought together in a volume published in 1986, which was very well received. Moreover, in more recent years she produced invaluable ten-page reviews (not included in the bibliography) of later studies and editions by Helen Fulton and Huw Meirion Edwards. She is, it should be said, the most thorough and painstaking of reviewers.

The death of Sir Idris Foster in 1984 brought Rachel Bromwich a new responsibility. As a student in the early 1930s, Foster had worked on a massive and admired University of Wales M.A. thesis dealing with the earliest of all Arthurian tales in any language, the extraordinary *Culhwch and Olwen*. Unfortunately, for complex reasons he was never able to complete the edition that had been expected of him, and this lacuna in Welsh scholarship had become a source of some embarrassment to him and to his fellow scholars. After his death Rachel Bromwich and her friend D. Simon Evans, emeritus professor of Welsh at Lampeter, at the request of the University of Wales Board of Celtic Studies, began work on the text and editorial material that Foster had prepared before his death. The eventual result was bibliographically complex. Welsh and English versions of Foster's work were published. Then English and Welsh editions with a great deal of additional material by the editors appeared. At the same period Rachel was collaborating with Professors Brynley F. Roberts and A. O. H. Jarman in editing *The Arthur of the Welsh*, a splendid series of studies of virtually all the Welsh-language Arthurian materials, which has not yet fully received its due.

The Welsh-language edition of *Culhwch and Olwen* was the culmination of several publications by Rachel Bromwich in Welsh. All the important items in this group are listed in the bibliography. Although Rachel Bromwich speaks Welsh somewhat hesitantly, regretting that before her retirement she had never been immersed in a milieu where the daily speaking of Welsh was essential, she reads and writes the language with fluency. Some critics have regretted the devotion of Welsh scholars to publishing in the Welsh language. But these women and men are not simply scholars; they are members of an embattled society for whom publishing scholarly work in Welsh is a matter of maintaining a great tradition as well as a matter of personal identity. Rachel Bromwich, while never forgetting her Anglo-Scottish roots, has been happy to make her contribution. She also made a valuable contribution to Welsh studies, as an act of *pietas* to her great teacher, by collecting together the English-language papers of Sir Ifor Williams and preparing an English translation of Williams's edition of the tenth-century prophetic poem *Armes Prydein*, both published in 1972.

I would like to end on a personal note. It was in 1958 that I first encountered Mrs. Bromwich, as she was then respectfully known to her students. Born in England to Welsh parents, I had made several unsuccessful efforts to learn the language of my forebears before reaching my final year in the Cambridge English tripos, when I found that Medieval Welsh was an alternative to the compulsory language paper in finals. I went to call on Rachel Bromwich at 153 Huntingdon Road. It must be understood that from the age of eight to that time I had been entirely taught in male-only schools, followed by two years in the army and then two years in a men-only college at Cambridge. I had had hardly any experience of being taught by women—none at all after the age of eleven. Rachel appeared to me as a shy person, indeed, as what I had imagined a truly unworldly scholar might be. I was soon to revise my opinion; gently but firmly she set out to replace my essay-based aestheticism with some real understanding of how to read difficult texts and discuss them and with an exciting realization of the extent and nature of the Welsh tradition. It was typical of her kindness that she took me on as a student during what was supposed to be a sabbatical year devoted to the preparation for the press of her study of the triads, published in 1961. Typical too was her acceptance of my naive student offer to help read the proofs of this scholarly masterpiece; she kindly acknowledged this help in the foreword, although the hours I spent on this enjoyably awesome task only resulted in the discovery of a single misprint that others had not noted! Rachel's former students, many of them holding distinguished academic posts in Britain, Ireland, and North America, speak as I do with great warmth both of her skill as a teacher and tutor in small classes and of her many personal kindnesses. I was to benefit greatly by her recommendation that I should pursue Celtic studies with Professor Idris Foster at Oxford; in effect, she changed the whole direction of my life for the better, and my debt to her is immense.

Visiting Rachel Bromwich at her Aberystwyth home has been a weekly pleasure for me for many years. Her living room cum study is filled with books; the portrait of a delightful nineteenth-century female Scott-Montcrieff ancestor looks down from the chimneypiece. There are papers, books, magazines, and correspondence every where, yet in order. She takes a warm interest in her former students' careers, their families, and their children and grandchildren, and she will readily discuss all kinds of subjects, from current affairs to the Quaker meetings that she attended for many years, from the novels of Sir Walter Scott to the latest scholarly publication, often with lively humor. Best of all for some of us, she will give what are in effect impromptu seminars on the topics that have exercised her for so many years: the triads and their origins; the Four Branches of the Mabinogi; Dafydd ap Gwilym; and the origins, development, and transmission of the Arthurian legend. The depth of her knowledge and the breadth of her publications have made her the doyenne of living Celtic scholars. It is to be hoped that she will be able to overcome health problems to finish the third edition of *Trioedd Ynys Prydein,* a work that one cannot imagine ever being replaced.

Notes

I am grateful to Morfydd Owen for much help with this text; to Brian and Christine Bromwich, Rachel's son and daughter-in-law; to Michael de Navarro; and to Chris Grooms, who has paid his own tribute to Rachel: "The Girl from Cumbria."

1. Dorothy Hoare (1901–1987), fellow of Newnham College, Cambridge, and university lecturer in English (married to J. M. de Navarro).

2. For Hector Munro Chadwick (1870–1947), see de Navarro's "Memoir for Hector Munro Chadwick." This essay describes the development of Section B of the medieval and modern languages tripos, as established in 1894, to the much broader ASNAC courses available today, originally drawn up by Chadwick in 1907 and 1917. He had a powerful ally in Arthur Quiller-Couch, the professor of English. Chadwick himself taught Welsh until the appointment of Kenneth Jackson.

3. For Nora Kershaw Chadwick (1891–1972), lecturer in early history and culture of the British Isles at Cambridge, see Owen, "Memoir for Nora Kershaw Chadwick"; and Jackson, "Memoir for Nora Kershaw Chadwick."

4. For Kenneth H. Jackson, see Williams, "Memoir for Kenneth H. Jackson."

5. Evan Evans (1731–88) produced his trilingual masterpiece *Some Specimens of the Poetry of the Antient Welsh Bards,* partly as a riposte to the fantasies of Macpherson's *Ossian.* For the first time passages from Aneirin's *Gododdin* were printed in the original and translated. The second part of the volume, "De Bardis Dissertatio," was the first attempt at a history of Welsh poetry.

6. *Dafydd ap Gwilym a'i Gyfoeswyr.*

7. For Sir Ifor Williams, see Foster, "Memoir for Sir Ifor Williams."

8. For Sir Idris Foster, see Bromwich, "Idris Foster, 1911–84."

9. Bibliographical information on all publications referred to, other than reviews, is to be found in the select bibliography.

10. Bromwich, *Trioedd Ynys Prydein,* 5.

11. Thomas Jones, "The Stanzas of the Graves," *Proceedings of the British Academy* 53 (1967, 97–137).

12. Parry, ed., *Gwaith Dafydd ap Gwilym.* A new edition of Dafydd's poetry is in preparation by a consortium of Welsh scholars.

13. Stern, *Davydd ap Gwilym.*

Select Bibliography of Works by Rachel Bromwich

"The Historical Triads, with Special Reference to Peniarth MS. 16." *Bulletin of the Board of Celtic Studies* 12 (1946): 1–15.

"The Continuity of Gaelic Tradition in Eighteenth-Century Ireland." *Transactions of the Yorkshire Society for Celtic Studies* (1947–48): 2–28.

"The Keen for Art O'Leary: Its Background and Its Place in Gaelic Keening Tradition." *Éigse* 5, part 4 (1947): 236–52.

"Cantre'r Gwaelod and Ker Is." In *The Early Cultures of North-West Europe,* edited by Cyril Fox and Bruce Dickins. H. M. Chadwick Memorial volume. Cambridge: Cambridge University Press, 1950.

"The Character of the Early Welsh Tradition." In *Studies in Early British History,* edited by Nora K. Chadwick. Cambridge: Cambridge University Press, 1954.

"Some Remarks on the Celtic Sources of 'Tristan.'" *Transactions of the Honourable Society of Cymmrodorion* (1955): 32–60.

"The Welsh Triads." In *Arthurian Literature in the Middle Ages,* edited by R. S. Loomis. Oxford: Oxford University Press, 1959.

"Celtic Dynastic Themes and the Breton Lays." *Études Celtiques* 9 (1961): 439–74.

Trioedd Ynys Prydein: The Welsh Triads. Cardiff: University of Wales Press, 1961. 2nd augmented ed., Cardiff: University of Wales Press, 1978.

"Chwedlau'r Greal." *Llên Cymru* 8 (1964): 47–57.

Matthew Arnold and Celtic Literature: A Retrospect, 1865–1965. O'Donnell Lecture, Oxford University, 1964. Oxford: Oxford University Press, 1965.

"Tradition and Innovation in the Poetry of Dafydd ap Gwilym." *Transactions of the Honourable Society of Cymmrodorion* (1964): 9–40. Reprinted separately twice, Cardiff: University of Wales Press, 1967, 1972.

"The Celtic Inheritance of Medieval Literature." *Modern Language Quarterly* 26 (1965): 203–27.

"Y Cynfeirdd a'r Traddodiad Cymraeg." *Bulletin of the Board of Celtic Studies* 22, (1966): 30–37.

"'Trioedd Ynys Prydein: The Myvyrian Third Series'. Part I," *Transactions of the Honourable Society of Cymmrodorion* (1968): 299–338; Part II, *Transactions of the Honourable Society of Cymmrodorion* (1969): 127–56.

"'Trioedd Ynys Prydein' in Welsh Literature and Scholarship." G. J. Williams Memorial Lecture for 1968. Cardiff: University of Wales Press, 1969.

"The Celtic Literatures." In *Literature in Celtic Countries,* edited by J. E. Caerwyn Williams. Cardiff: University of Wales Press, 1971.

Translator. *Armes Prydein.* Edited by Ifor Williams. Dublin: Dublin Institute for Advanced Studies, 1972.

The Beginnings of Welsh Poetry: Studies by Sir Ifor Williams. Cardiff: University of Wales Press, 1972.

"Y Llenyddiaethau Celtaidd." *Y Traethodydd* 128 (1973): 47–73.

Dafydd ap Gwilym. Writers of Wales series. Cardiff: University of Wales Press, 1974. This work was awarded a prize by the Arts Council of Wales.

Medieval Celtic Literature: A Select Bibliography. Toronto Medieval Bibliographies, 5. Toronto: Toronto University Press, 1974.

"Traddodiad Llafar y Chwedlau" and "Dwy Chwedl a Thair Rhamant." In *Y Traddodiad Rhyddiaith yn yr Oesau Canol,* edited by Geraint Bowen. Llandysul, Wales: Gomer Press, 1974.

"Dafydd ap Gwilym: Y Traddodiad Islenyddol." In *Dafydd ap Gwilym a Chanu Serch yr Oesoedd Canol,* edited by John Rowlands. Cardiff: University of Wales Press, 1975.

"Concepts of Arthur." *Studia Celtica* 10/11 (1976): 163–81.

"Gwaith Einion Offeiriad a Barddoniaeth Dafydd ap Gwilym." In *Ysgrifau Beirniadol,* vol. 10, edited by J. E. Caerwyn Williams. Denbigh, Wales: Gwasg Gee, 1977.

Editor with R. Brinley Jones. "Cynon fab Clydno." In *Astudiaethau ar yr Hengerdd: Studies in Old Welsh Poetry Presented to Sir Idris Foster.* Cardiff: University of Wales Press, 1978.

"Dafydd ap Gwilym" and "The Earlier *Cywyddwyr*: Poets Contemporary with Dafydd ap Gwilym." In *A Guide to Welsh Literature,* vol. 2, edited by A. O. H. Jarman and Gwilym Rees Hughes. Swansea: Christopher Davies, 1979.

"The 'Tristan' Poem in the Black Book of Carmarthen." *Studia Celtica* 14–15 (1980): 54–65.

"Cyfeiriadau Dafydd ap Gwilym at Chwedl a Rhamant." In *Ysgrifau Beirniadol* 12, edited by J. E. Caerwyn Williams. Denbigh, Wales: Gwasg Gee, 1982.

Dafydd ap Gwilym: A Selection of His Poems. Llandysul, Wales: Gomer Press, 1982. Reprint, Harmondsworth, Eng.: Penguin, 1985.

"Idris Foster, 1911–84." *Studia Celtica* 20–21 (1985–86): 221–29.

Aspects of the Poetry of Dafydd ap Gwilym: Collected Papers. Cardiff: University of Wales Press, 1986.

"The Mabinogion and Lady Charlotte Guest." *Transactions of the Honourable Society of Cymmrodorion* (1986): 127–41.

Editor with D. Simon Evans. *Culhwch ac Olwen: Testun Syr Idris Foster.* Cardiff: University of Wales Press, 1988.

"Le Conte de Culhwch et Olwen." *Journées d'Études sur la Bretagne et les Pays Celtiques* 1 (1990–91): 17–28.

Editor with A. O. H. Jarman and Brynley F. Roberts. *The Arthur of the Welsh.* Cardiff: University of Wales Press, 1991. Reprint pb., 1995.

Editor with D. Simon Evans. *Culhwch and Olwen: An Edition and Study of the Oldest Arthurian Tale.* Cardiff: University of Wales Press, 1992.

"Dafydd ap Gwilym." [The Van Hamel Memorial Lecture, 1993.] In *Welsh and Breton Studies in Memory of Th. M. Th. Chotzen,* by the A. G. van Hamel Foundation for Celtic Studies (Colloquium). Utrecht: Celtic Dragon, 1995.

Medieval Welsh Literature to c.1400, including Arthurian Studies: A Personal Guide to University of Wales Publications. Cardiff: University of Wales Press, 1996.

Editor with D. Simon Evans. *Culhwch ac Olwen.* Cardiff: University of Wales Press, 1997. This is a much fuller Welsh edition of the work first published in 1988.

"The Triads of the Horses." In *The Horse in Celtic Culture: Medieval Welsh Perspectives,* edited by Sioned Davies and Nerys Ann Jones. Cardiff: University of Wales Press, 1997.

Works Cited

de Navarro, J. M. "Memoir for Hector Munro Chadwick." *Proceedings of the British Academy* 33 (1947): 307–30.

Evans, Evan. *Some Specimens of the Poetry of the Antient Welsh Bards.* London, 1764.

Foster, Idris. Memoir for Sir Ifor Williams. *Proceedings of the British Academy* 53 (1967): 361–78.

Grooms, Chris. "The Girl from Cumbria." In *On Arthurian Women: Essays in Memory of Maureen Fries,* edited by Fiona Tolhurst and Bonnie Wheeler, 369–72. Dallas: Scriptorium Press, 2001.

Jackson, Kenneth H. "Memoir for Nora Kershaw Chadwick." *Proceedings of the British Academy* 58 (1972): 537–49.

Owen, Morfydd E. "Memoir for Nora Kershaw Chadwick." *Studia Celtica* 8/9 (1973–74): 319–24.

Parry, Thomas, ed. *Gwaith Dafydd ap Gwilym.* Cardiff: University of Wales Press, 1952.

Stern, Ludwig Christian. *Davydd ap Gwilym: Ein Walischer minnesänger.* Halle, Ger.: Max Niemayer, 1909.

Williams, Ifor, and Thomas Roberts, eds. *Dafydd ap Gwilym a'i Gyfoeswyr.* Bangor, Wales: Evan Thomas, 1914.

Williams, J. E. Caerwyn. "Memoir for Kenneth H. Jackson." *Studia Celtica* 14/15 (1979–80): 1–11.

CHAPTER 56

Jane Hayward (1918–1994)
"Radiance and Reflection"

MARILYN J. STOKSTAD

"Radiance and Reflection," the title of one of the Metropolitan Museum of Art's most noteworthy exhibitions, organized by Jane Hayward and her colleagues, included the finest medieval stained glass in any American private collection, the Raymond Pitcairn Collection at Glencairn in Bryn Athyn, Pennsylvania. The evocative title of the exhibition and catalog also characterizes Hayward's contribution to medieval studies: the "radiance" of her scholarship as North America's leading expert on the art of stained glass and the "reflection" of her ideas and principles in the work of her students and colleagues. Her forceful personality and forthright manner, her clear-headed focus on essentials, and what William Wixom (then chairman of medieval art at the museum) called "her commanding intellect" made her a formidable scholar and an invaluable colleague. As a member of boards and committees she also served the profession and the community with great distinction. In 1980 after her third election to the Board of Trustees of Stonehill College (North Easton, Massachusetts), the college honored her with an honorary doctor of arts degree. In recognition of her leadership and contributions to the organization, the directors of the International Center of Medieval Art (ICMA) made her a fellow for life in 1987.

As the guiding spirit behind the study of stained glass in the United States, Hayward served as president of the American section of the *Corpus Vitrearum Medii Aevi* committee (known simply as the Corpus Vitrearum). When she died in 1994, she had nearly finished her monumental study of the medieval and Renaissance stained glass in the collection of the Metropolitan Museum of Art.

Like many people of her generation, Hayward had her life interrupted by World War II. After graduating from the Pennsylvania Academy of Fine Arts, where she had

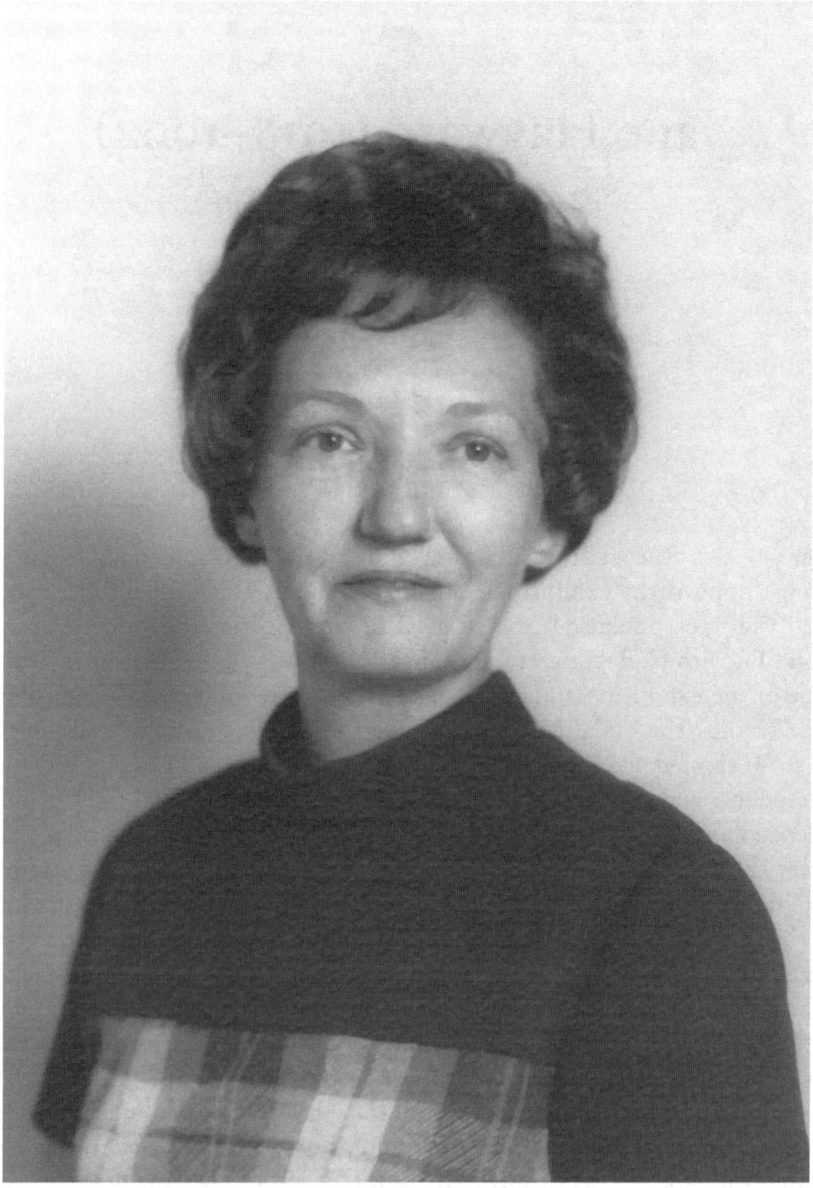

studied from 1936 to 1942, and after taking an engineering drawing course at the Bock Vocational School in Philadelphia (1941–42), she went to work as a draftsperson in the machine-design section of the Fourth Naval District, Philadelphia (1942–45). With the return of peace, she left the navy to work as a technical illustrator, teacher, and author of training manuals at the American Viscose Corporation (1945–54). Her skill as an expert draftsperson and illustrator would serve her well when she turned to the study of stained glass, where she recorded her subjects with meticulous drawings as well as photographs.

In 1946 Hayward began her preparation in the history of art by taking evening classes at the University of Pennsylvania School of Fine Arts, where she graduated with a bachelor of fine arts degree in 1952. Two more years in the graduate school of the university resulted in a master's degree in art history with a specialty in American and Renaissance art. In 1954 she entered Yale, and four years later Hayward earned her Ph.D. in art history. Her achievement was all the more impressive since in the 1950s the study of art history at the graduate level—as well as employment in colleges and universities—was essentially a male preserve. While many women studied "art appreciation" as undergraduates, they seldom continued graduate work beyond the M.A. or M.F.A. degrees. Those women who persisted in the field could look forward to becoming junior curators in museums or instructors in art history departments. They staffed the slide libraries and photograph archives, and some became distinguished art librarians and curators of manuscript collections. Jane Hayward not only attained the doctoral degree in 1958, with Yale's great medievalist Sumner McKnight Crosby as her mentor; she went on to establish the field of stained-glass studies in the United States. The entry of women into advanced graduate study and senior positions in art history has been one of the noteworthy developments in the profession in the second half of the twentieth century.

In 1953, the year before Hayward began her doctoral studies with Crosby, European scholars of the International Committee for the History of Art founded the Corpus Vitrearum, an international organization formed to locate and catalog the surviving stained glass of the medieval and Renaissance periods (defined as stained-glass dating before 1700). Crosby, who was engaged in the excavation and study of the abbey church of Saint Denis in the outskirts of Paris, became involved in these efforts. He sent his student, Jane Hayward, to France to study with the experts in the field, Louis Grodecki and Jean Lafond. Hayward's dissertation, "The Angevine Style of Glass Painting in the Twelfth and Thirteenth Centuries," was the first scholarly study of the medium by an American. Stained glass had not been popular with collectors and museums in the United States, probably because, like architectural sculpture, it was an integral part of a building's structure and not easily acquired or displayed in a private or domestic setting. The situation changed with the emergence of collectors like George Grey Barnard (whose collection formed the Cloisters) and Raymond Pitcairn, most of whose collection with the exception of loans to the Philadelphia Museum of Art remained in his home in Bryn Athyn, Pennsylvania.

The impact that Hayward and her research would have on medieval studies was not immediately apparent. After earning her doctoral degree, she stayed at Yale as a research assistant in the Yale Art Gallery in the Department of American Decorative Arts (1958–61). Then from 1961 to 1965 she was the curator of the Lyman Allyn Museum and taught at Connecticut College in New London, where she held the rank of instructor from 1961 to 1964 and assistant professor from 1964 to 1967. In 1967 she began her association with the Metropolitan Museum of Art, first as the Clawson Mills Fellow (1967–69) to catalog stained glass for the Corpus Vitrearum and then as an associate curator at the Cloisters (the medieval branch of the Metropolitan Museum). By the time she finally achieved a permanent position and could devote herself to significant scholarly work, Hayward was over fifty years old. Less determined scholars might have been thinking about retirement.

In 1971 Hayward became an adjunct professor at Columbia University in New York, where her association went back to her graduate-school days and her friendship with Robert Branner. Branner, Columbia University's architectural historian and distinguished medievalist, was a fair-minded advocate of women in the academy. Branner had earned his own Ph.D. at Yale, and shortly after arriving at Columbia from the University of Kansas in 1957, Sumner Crosby asked him to serve on Hayward's doctoral oral examination committee. In 1975 Hayward more than repaid Crosby and Branner's faith in her when she delivered the Mathews Lectures at Columbia. She spoke on a subject dear to both men, "Early Gothic Stained Glass from Abbot Suger through the Reign of Saint Louis." In these (unpublished) lectures she analyzed regional styles in French medieval glass and brought lesser-known examples of stained-glass windows to the attention of the international scholarly community.

In 1974 Hayward became a full curator at the Cloisters, a position she held for the rest of her life. Her study of medieval stained glass in the collection of the Metropolitan Museum of Art was a lifetime commitment, but she also seemed to know every fragment of stained glass in North America. While Hayward wrote less than many scholars, she generously shared all her knowledge with fellow curators and scholars. She presented her research in short, pithy catalog entries and bulletin articles. Although her groundbreaking exhibition, "Stained Glass of the Middle Ages and Renaissance" (1971–72), had brought attention to the importance of collections in the United States, as a true team worker, she devoted as much energy to the projects of others as she gave to her own. She contributed essays and catalog entries on stained glass to major exhibitions organized in collaboration with her colleagues. Among the exhibitions and catalogs for which the Metropolitan Museum is justly famous—all with many important works by Hayward—are Carmen Gomez-Moreno's "Medieval Art from Private Collections" (1968); the masterful collaborative work "The Year 1200" (1970); "The Secular Spirit: Art and Life at the End of the Middle Ages" (1975) with Timothy Husband; "The Royal Abbey of Saint Denis in the Time of Abbot Suger" (1981) with Sumner McKnight Crosby, Charles Little, and William Wixom; "Gothic and Renaissance Art in Nuremberg" (1986); and "Radiance and Reflection: Medieval Art from the Raymond Pitcairn Collection" (1982) with Walter Cahn. After her death in 1994, her monumental catalog of the medieval and Renaissance stained-glass holdings of the Metropolitan Museum of Art and the Cloisters was completed and prepared for publication by her colleague Mary B. Shepard.

Although she never lost her focus on stained glass in the collection of the Metropolitan Museum, Hayward's great opportunity (and what proved to be a defining moment in stained-glass studies) came in 1977 when she was invited to catalog the stained glass in the Raymond Pitcairn collection of medieval art in Glencairn, Bryn Athyn, Pennsylvania. Her work resulted in the exhibition and catalog "Radiance and Reflection," and along the way she also transformed this very important but almost inaccessible private collection into a museum open to the public. She used this and other opportunities to lead people like Michael Cothren, Linda Papanicolaou, Mary Shepard, and others into the field. They soon made their own significant contributions to medieval studies.

The Corpus Vitrearum eventually became the focus of Hayward's work. In 1953 European scholars had formed an international committee to produce the multivolume *Corpus Vitrearum Medii Aevi*. In 1970 Hayward became the American delegate, the first representative of the committee in the United States. As the moving force behind the formation of an American committee, she became its president in 1982. Under her inspiration the work of locating and cataloging medieval and Renaissance stained glass for the Corpus Vitrearum turned into a national effort. In volume after volume Hayward, now ably seconded by her colleague and coauthor Madeline Caviness and others, published works about stained glass in museums from Maine to California. Hayward and Caviness collaborated on four volumes, published in 1985, 1987, 1989, and 1991.

Hayward was not content to devote herself to the European Middle Ages. Her passion extended to the discovery and scholarly study of stained glass wherever it was made and used. After all, she had begun her graduate study and her career as an art historian in American art and American decorative arts, and she recognized that the study of European stained glass in American museums, while a worthy project, should be expanded to include modern stained glass made in the United States. American interpretations of the medium needed study. The very existence of many fine examples of American stained glass was endangered by lack of information and public interest. In 1979 Hayward began a project to record these new treasures. With her characteristic energy she became a founder and member of the Board of Governors of the Census of Stained Glass in America.

Jane Hayward understood the importance of associations and professional societies as well as the power of group action in committees. In the United States historians of medieval art often led intellectually isolated lives in academic institutions and museums, where they worked alone in departments filled with modernists and Americanists. They had few colleagues to share their enthusiasm for what seemed to others to be esoteric subjects, and they had few venues where they could meet and discuss the results of their research. To overcome the lack of opportunities for the exchange of ideas, professional societies emerged to provide both social interchange and an avenue for group action.

Hayward founded, joined, or revitalized several associations, none more lively than the ICMA, where her sharp intellect and vigorous participation made an impact. She began to take an active role in the ICMA in 1973. The ICMA had begun as a Franco-American association of men who appreciated French medieval art almost as much as they loved French wine. They met in Burgundy and New York, a convivial mix of professionals and amateurs. Then, as interest in the semisocial society began to fade, some of the members turned it into the International Center of Medieval Art. Given a permanent home in New York in the Cloisters, the ICMA grew into a true scholarly society under the watchful eyes of people like Jane Hayward. Nevertheless, for many years, and abetted by Hayward, the festive celebration of the Feast of Saint Polycarp recalled the social origins of the society. Through her service on the board of directors of the ICMA (as a director in 1977–82 and 1984–86 and as an advisor in 1973–76 and 1982–84), Hayward became one of the people who established the future direction of the organization and its journal, *Gesta*. It is perhaps significant that she chose to have her research appear in publications sponsored by institutions to which she was devoted: the Metropolitan Museum, the Corpus Vitrearum, and the ICMA.

During these years another medievalist also began to make an impact on the profession outside the traditional scholarly realm. Professor Otto Gründler organized a local conference of medievalists at Western Michigan University in Kalamazoo, Michigan. From modest beginnings, the congress grew into the largest professional gathering of medievalists in the world. With over four hundred sessions held over a period of five days, the congress became a veritable free-for-all of ideas sponsored by interest groups as well as by professional associations. Soon Hayward was organizing her colleagues and students to make the annual pilgrimage to western Michigan. The directors of the ICMA saw how they could take advantage of the organizational work and facilities provided by Gründler, and they began holding sessions and board meetings in Kalamazoo. The Hayward delegation, and Jane's sharp comments on papers and sessions, did much to ensure the scholarly success of the congress (known affectionately as "K'zoo"). Later, the ICMA also affiliated with the College Art Association (CAA). Each winter the ICMA organized sessions and held the annual members' meeting at the CAA's conference. Hayward's perceptive understanding of the national role the ICMA could play through the conferences organized by larger, more encompassing groups helped make the ICMA a national as well as international society.

Even in her leisure activities Hayward worked with formidable energy. Like so many scholars she turned to her garden and her cats for relaxation. How appropriate that a new daylily, bred by Greg Piotrowski of the New York Botanical Garden, should be named for her, the *Hemerocallis* "Jane Hayward."

As a leading scholar of stained glass, Jane Hayward contributed significantly to medieval studies in the United States. She was able to make an impact through her work as a curator, as an informal teacher, and as an administrator without portfolio. Her enduring legacy is the collection she created in a great public museum—the Metropolitan Museum of Art in New York. Seeking perfection, she possessed a vision that was overarching. She could present the arcane details of meticulously researched scholarship effectively in part because she never lost sight of her goals—the creation of an educated and appreciative public and the re-creation of the brilliant, light-filled chapels of the Middle Ages, chapels and walls that reflect the glory of stained-glass windows in radiant detail. As we stand in the galleries of the medieval department of the Metropolitan Museum or walk through the Cloisters, the medieval and Renaissance windows above and around us recall the uncompromising scholarship and the impeccable taste and imagination of Jane Hayward.

Select Bibliography of Works by Jane Hayward

"Identification of the Crucifixion Window." *Bulletin of the City Art Museum of Saint Louis* 3 (1957): 18–22.

"The Angevine Style of Glass Painting in the Twelfth and Thirteenth Centuries." Ph.D. diss., Yale University, 1958.

Review of *Peter Hemmel Glasmaler von Andlau*, by Paul Frankl. *Art Bulletin* 40 (1958): 75–78.

"Roman Mold-Blown Glass at Yale University." *Journal of Glass Studies* 4 (1962): 49–60.

With Louis Grodecki. "Les Vitraux de la cathedrale d'Angers." *Bulletin Monumental* 124 (1966): 7–76.

Entries on stained glass, nos. 174–97. In *Medieval Art from Private Collections*, edited by Carmen Gomez-Moreno. New York: Metropolitan Museum of Art, 1968.

"Stained Glass Windows from the Carmelite Church at Boppard-am-Rhein: A Reconstruction of the Glazing Program of the North Nave." *Metropolitan Museum Journal* 2 (1969): 75–114.

Entries on stained glass, nos. 200–237. In *The Year 1200: The Exhibition,* edited by Konrad Hoffman. New York: The Metropolitan Museum of Art, 1970.

"The Seven Sleepers from Rouen." *Bulletin of the Worcester Art Museum* 35 (1970).

"Sacred Vestments as They Developed in the Middle Ages." *Metropolitan Museum of Art Bulletin* 29 (1971): 299–309.

"Glazed Cloisters and Their Development in the Houses of the Cistercian Order." *Gesta* 12 (1973): 93–109.

"History of Stained Glass." In *Encyclopedia Americana* 25, 1973.

Review of *Die Architecktonische Rahmung des Hochgotischen Bildfensters,* by Rudiger Becksmann. *Speculum* 48 (1973): 110–12.

Review of *Les Vitraux de l'eglise Saint-Ouen de Rouen,* by Jean Lafond. *Art Bulletin* 40 (1973): 293–96.

With Timothy B. Husband. *The Secular Spirit: Life and Art at the End of the Middle Ages.* New York: Metropolitan Museum of Art, 1975.

"The Choir Windows of Saint-Serge and Their Glazing Atelier." *Gesta* 15 (1976): 255–64.

"Installation of Medieval Stained Glass at the Cloisters." *Verres et refractaires: Documentation* 30 (1976): 77–79.

Review of "Canterbury Comes to New York." *Glass* 5 (1977): 16–18, 35.

"Stained Glass." *World Book Encyclopedia.* 1980.

Entries on stained glass, nos. 10–22. In *The Royal Abbey of Saint-Denis in the Time of Abbot Suger.* New York: Metropolitan Museum of Art, 1981.

"The Lost Noah Window from Poitiers." Essays in Honor of Harry Bober, *Gesta* 20 (1981): 129–39.

"The Redemption Windows of the Loire Valley." In *Etudes d'art medieval offertes a Louis Grodecki,* edited by Sumner McKnight Crosby et al., 129–44. Paris: Ophrys, 1981.

With Walter Cahn et al. *Radiance and Reflection: Medieval Art from the Raymond Pitcairn Collection.* New York: Metropolitan Museum of Art, 1982.

With Madeline H. Caviness. Introduction and entries for Connecticut, New York, and Rhode Island in "Stained Glass before 1700 in American Collections: New England and New York." *Studies in the History of Art* 15 (1985) (Corpus Vitrearum, checklist 1): 10–19, 22–29, 87–88, 89–91, 92–178, 180–86, 191–92, 211–12.

Introduction to *Studies on Medieval Stained Glass.* Edited by Madeline H. Caviness and Timothy B. Husband. Corpus Vitrearum United States, Occasional Papers, 1. New York: 1985.

Entries on stained glass, nos. 65–66, 157–59, 172, 264. In *Gothic and Renaissance Art in Nuremberg, 1300–1550,* 206–7, 339–41, 356, 454–55. New York: Metropolitan Museum of Art, 1986.

With Madeline H. Caviness. Introduction and entries for Florida, Maryland, North Carolina, and South Carolina in "Stained Glass before 1700 in American Collections: Mid-Atlantic and Southeastern Seaboard States." *Studies in the History of Art* 23 (1987) (Corpus Vitrearum, checklist 2): 9–20, 42–46, 47, 48, 49, 50, 60, 62–69, 92–94, 95–97, 98, 186–89.

With Madeline H. Caviness. Introduction and entries for California, Indiana, Kentucky, Tennessee, with additions to entries for New York, North Carolina, and South Carolina, in "Stained Glass before 1700 in American Collections: Midwestern and Western States." *Studies in the History of Art* 28 (1989) (Corpus Vitrearum, checklist 3): 11–36, 44–81, 90–93, 130–32, 140–48, 224–25, 257–61, 266–68, 274, 276, 292.

"Neue Funde zur Glasmalerei aus der Karmeliterkirche zu Boppard-am-Rhein." In *Bau- und Bildkunst im Spiegel internationaler Forschung* (Festschrift zum 80. Geburtstag von Prof. Dr. Edgar Lehmann), 182–93. Berlin: Verlaug für Bauwesen, 1989.

With Madeline H. Caviness. Foreword to "Stained Glass before 1700 in American Collections: Silver-Stained Roundels and Unipartite Panels." *Studies in the History of Art* 39 (1991) (Corpus Vitrearum, checklist 4): 9–11.

"Two Grisaille Glass Panels from Saint-Denis at the Cloisters." In *The Cloisters: Studies in Honor of the Fiftieth Anniversary,* edited by Elizabeth C. Parker with Mary B. Shepard. New York: 1992.

Metropolitan Museum of Art, *English and French Medieval Stained Glass in the Collection of the Metropolitan Museum of Art.* Revised and edited by Mary B. Shepard and Cynthia Clark, with an introduction by Mary B. Shepard. Corpus Vitrearum, United States of America. New York: Metropolitan Museum of Art and Harvey Miller Publisherss, 2003.

Tributes

"Remembrances of Jane Hayward." In "Essays on Stained Glass in Memory of Jane Hayward (1918–1994),"edited by Michael W. Cothren and Mary B. Shepard. *Gesta* 37/2 (1998): 127–32; complete bibliography.

CHAPTER 57

Getting It All Together (1923–)

MARIE BORROFF

I HAVE NEVER thought of myself as a medievalist in the full, honorific sense of that word, nor have I ever devoted myself full-time to scholarship in the medieval field. I entered it late, as an unforeseen result of the doctoral studies in philology at Yale I embarked on, six years after receiving an M.A. in comparative literature at the University of Chicago.

In June 1951 I had just resigned from Smith College, having served a three-year term there as assistant professor of English. I was twenty-seven years old. I had graduated from Chicago with a Ph.B. in 1943. This degree, which has since been abandoned, signified my completion of a two-year course of study instituted by Robert Maynard Hutchins, then president of the university, and intended by him to give all citizens, once they had graduated from high school, a general education in the liberal arts. Each student would then either go into vocational training or continue for three years leading to a master's degree in an elected major field. I enrolled in a graduate program run by a faculty group, chaired by R. S. Crane, that called itself the Committee on Comparative Studies in Literature and the Arts. My chosen field of concentration was lyric poetry from the Renaissance to the twentieth century, which I studied primarily in English, but also, less intensively, in French, and still less intensively in German. At that time the faculty of the university was almost exclusively male (there was a single woman professor of English named Gladys Campbell, whom I met only once). Accordingly the teachers who influenced and befriended me were male: Crane, Norman Maclean, and Elder Olson. These three, with a few others, had founded the "Chicago School" of criticism; the method of literary analysis they propounded and practiced has sometimes, rather reductively, been called neo-Aristotelianism. I have

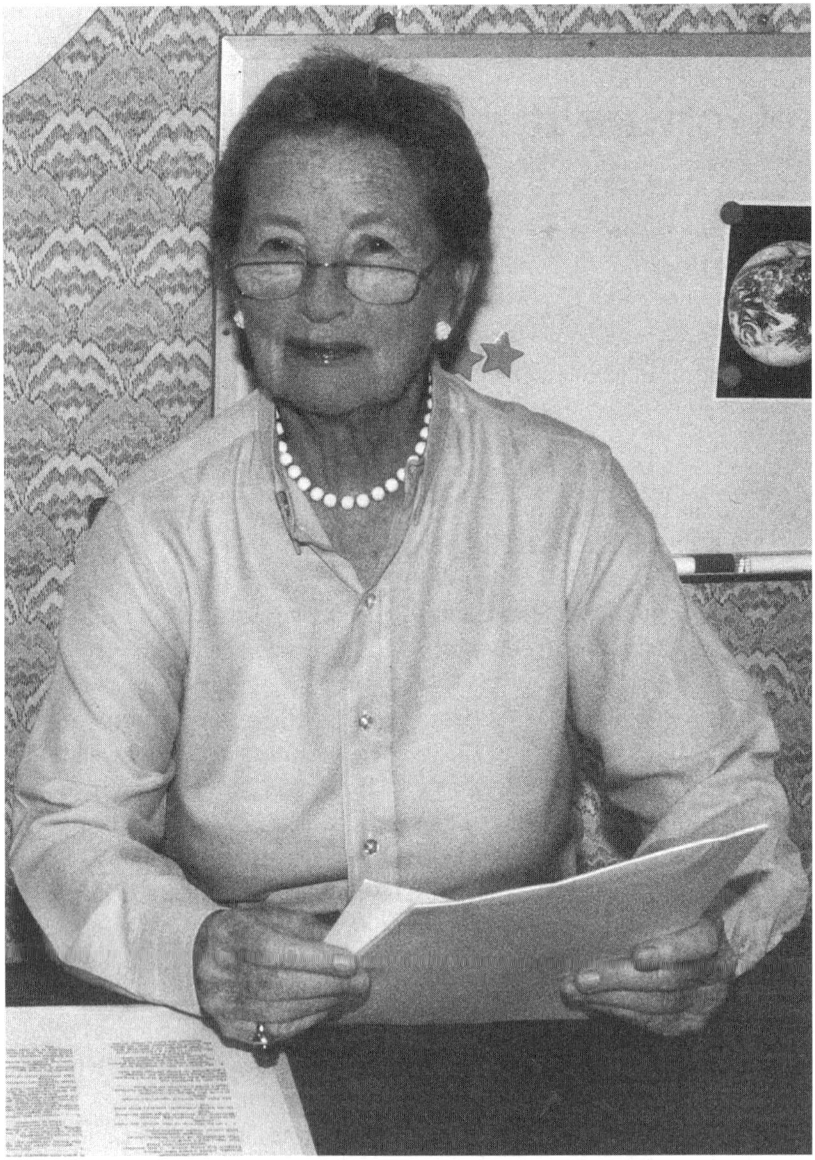

always been grateful for the training I received at their hands and have been proud to identify myself as a "Chicago critic."

My studies under the committee did include courses with several female teachers, though not teachers of English: elementary German was taught by Viola Manderfeld, and *études de style* by a woman, her white hair invariably crowned by a black tricorne, whom we knew only as "Mademoiselle." This latter course was a prerequisite for a year of in-depth *explication de texte* taught by the formidable Professor Robert Vigneron. I also had a series of tutorial sessions with Professor Helena Gamer of the German department; in these I mainly read German lyrics aloud so that she could correct my pronunciation. I remember her wanting me to pronounce the German vowel spelled *a* in two different ways, depending on which word it appeared in, and my feeling of frustration at being unable to tell which one was correct in a given case. This would, of course, have required philological knowledge of which I was totally innocent and concerning which, strange as it seems to me now, I had no curiosity whatsoever. My only encounter at Chicago with the sounds of words and their historical development took place in a course in the history of the English language taught by Professor James Hulbert. I found it dull as ditchwater, and my performance in it was, to put it charitably, mediocre.

In 1945–46, during my last year in the program, I wrote a master's thesis that had what I see in retrospect as a prophetic title: "The Theory of the Translation of Poetry." In it I defined and discussed the changing standards by which translations into English verse were evaluated in the Renaissance, the Augustan, Romantic, and Victorian periods, and the early twentieth century (at that time, the history of English literature ended with Eliot's *The Waste Land*).

Two other components of this early mix were to figure importantly in my later work: the writing of original poems (always in meter and rhyme) and the study of metrics. I have always felt that my lifelong training as a musician helped me to understand the all-too-often neglected temporal aspect of metrical patterning. Fortunately, a course in metrics was offered by Professor Olson, who had written a treatise on the subject. I had written poems from early childhood on and was still writing them when I began my college studies. But Norman Maclean's course in the lyric, which I took as a freshman, opened my eyes to expressive effects and powers in poetic language that I had previously had no inkling of. As a result I stopped writing poems for two years. A group of the more mature poems that I then started to write won the university's annual poetry prize; other poems were accepted for publication in the 1940s by *Poetry*, the *American Scholar*, and the *Yale Review*. During the decades that followed I continued to be a practicing poet and to place my poems in periodicals, though I have not yet published them as a book.

In 1948, having returned to the States after a year abroad, I needed a job, and I accepted an offer from Smith College of a three-year instructorship in English. During the first year I taught only freshman composition, but in my second and third years I was given the creative writing course for sophomores. The basic plan of this course called for the writing of a short story every two weeks, but the assignments also included an imitation of prose style, the author to be chosen by each student. A number of the young women in my class found this undertaking difficult; they came to me wanting to know what was meant by style, how they could detect its manifestations in the writings of a given author, and how they could imitate it. My attempts at answering them were, I felt, too general and superficial to be of much help. I tried to find a published handbook containing a systematic and literal description of stylistic features that they could make use of in writing their imitations, but to no avail. I then decided that I would write something myself. But as I tried to do so, I felt myself floundering. I thought I ought to say something about the kinds of differences among words that made the style of Hemingway easily distinguishable from that of D. H. Lawrence. I knew, if only because I had read in Ivanhoe about the difference between native English pig and calf and French pork and veal, that "native" words tended to be plainer and more homely than their French counterparts. But when I cast about for particular instances (having been trained at Chicago to utter no generalization without supporting examples), I was baffled by the etymologies I found in my 1949 edition of *Webster's New Collegiate Dictionary*. "Speak," for example, was said to come from "AS," or "Anglo-Saxon," *specan, sprecan,* and "converse" from "OF," or "Old French," *converser.* So far, so good. But the origin of "talk" was simply "ME," or "Middle English," *talken.* Why was the word not in the language earlier? Where did it come from? More confusing still, "chat" turned out to come from "chatter," which was simply labeled "imitative" (I now recognize it as a sound-symbolic coinage of the "frequentative" type). I won't expand this list of examples; suffice it to say that I ended by realizing that I knew nothing about "Anglo-Saxon," or how "Middle English" grew out of it, or how or why words like "chat" and "chatter" came into being. If I wanted to write the kind of essay my students needed—and more and more I found myself interested in doing so—I needed to study the history of the English language.

In 1951, to return to the date at which I began my story, I resigned from Smith and went to live for a year in New York City. I eked out my savings by working as a professional pianist, accompanying for classes in singing and dancing while looking, somewhat half-heartedly, for a job at a magazine or a publishing house. After a few months I realized that my dream of working as an editor to support myself as a poet was impractical. At the same time I found myself pulled in the direction of further graduate study leading to a Ph.D. and a career of college or university teaching. Specifically, I wanted to acquire the historical knowledge I knew I needed if I were to develop my nascent concept of literary style. Style, I had come to think, was something that could be sensed intuitively in an author's writings but was also grounded in features of language that it should be possible to describe and observe in factual terms. In addition I wanted to study and write about the distinctive language of two poets I had come to admire, Wallace Stevens and Marianne Moore, combining my ideas about style with the method of literary criticism I had learned at Chicago.

I had kept in touch with R. S. Crane after going east, and when I wrote him about these aspirations, he replied that he had heard of a professor of English at Yale University, a philologist named Helge Kökeritz. Kökeritz, Crane said, was writing on Shakespeare and seemed interested in combining stylistic criticism with the study of language, as I wished to do. Following Crane's lead I wrote to Kökeritz and arranged to see him in New Haven. He advised me to apply for admission to a program sponsored by the Yale English department in which one could earn a joint Ph.D. in English literature and English philology. (I was later to learn that I was the only person who ever actually elected this program.)

At that time the Faculty of Arts and Sciences at Yale, whose five-hundred-odd members taught in the college and the graduate school, was exclusively male. At Yale, as earlier at Chicago, I was befriended and encouraged by a group of male professors: by Kökeritz, of course, but also, to my great good fortune, by John C. Pope and E. T. Donaldson. During my first three years there I took the year-long introductory course in Old English (Yale's name for Anglo-Saxon), which was then required of all first-year students and was taught by Pope. I studied Chaucer, whom I had never read, with Donaldson. I later took courses in advanced Old English (with Pope), Old English dialects (with Kökeritz), and Renaissance English (also with Kökeritz). I had known that the expertise I sought could be acquired only at the price of a lot of hard work, and I had turned to my new studies with a will. What I had not expected was the delight that overcame me when I first contemplated the spelling and pronunciation and grammatical paradigms of Old English words, and that sustained me unfailingly through my four years in the program—and the years that followed. I realized that I had entered a place I had always belonged to without knowing it, where an endless store of knowledge waited to be mined and treasured.

After passing the required general oral examination on English literature and English philology, I cast about for a dissertation subject. I wanted to apply both my training as a literary critic at Chicago and my newly acquired philological expertise to a work or body of literature, preferably poetry, but I was daunted by the profusion of published criticism on Chaucer and Shakespeare and could think of no other possibility. Then, happily, I went to see John Pope. After I had explained to him the sort of thing I wanted to do, he submerged himself for a few moments in one of the silences I had learned were characteristic of him, bowing his head, and withdrawing into thought. After a few moments he looked up, smiling, and said, "Why don't you write something about *Sir Gawain and the Green Knight?*" Out of my vast ignorance of medieval English literature other than Chaucer, I responded with, "What is *Sir Gawain and the Green Knight?*" Pope explained that it was an Arthurian romance of superb literary quality, that little had been written about its style, and that its alliterative meter had been variously analyzed. I bought a copy of the poem on my way back to the graduate women's dormitory and began my reading of it that night, drawing up lists of hitherto unknown Middle English words and their definitions in the glossary.

In the dissertation I wrote the following year, I was able to accomplish what I had hoped my studies at Yale would enable me to accomplish. The first part of it was devoted to the language and style of *Sir Gawain;* the second to an analysis of its alliterative and rhymed verse. I identified certain kinds of facts about the words making up the poet's Late Middle English vocabulary that correlated credibly with stylistic values: their positioning in the metrical patterns of the poem; their earlier use by Old English poets; their presence in, or absence from, the language of Chaucer; and their descent, or failure to descend, into present-day English. I approached my analysis of the poem's metrics from the point of view of the history of pronunciation, with regard especially to the sounding (as in Chaucer's verse) or silencing of "final -*e*." My findings led me to conclude that "final -*e*" never counted as a syllable within the long alliterative line as the *Gawain* poet wrote it. This in turn enabled me to adjudicate, to my own satisfaction at least, between the two interpretations of the meter of the line that figured most prominently in scholarly writings on the subject.

I had decided that while completing the dissertation I would not look for a teaching job. Instead, I applied for, and was awarded, a fellowship from the American Association of University Women that would support me for the following academic year (1956–57). During that year, I returned to my studies of style and language in Marianne Moore and Wallace Stevens, adding a third poet, Robert Frost.

When I went on the job market during the following year, it was with the expectation that I would teach in a women's college. Not only did the men's colleges, such as Yale, have exclusively male faculties, but men outnumbered women on the faculties of co-ed colleges and of most, if not all, colleges for women. Among the several women's colleges that offered me jobs, I decided on Smith; I had come to know and like the countryside in that part of Massachusetts, and I still had friends among the faculty. But during the first year of my second stint there, something quite unexpected happened: when Helge Kökeritz went to Sweden on sabbatical, I was invited to teach his graduate course in Renaissance English. (At that time a course in philology, in addition to a year of Old English, was required of every student in the Ph.D. program. The presence nearby, in Kökeritz's absence, of someone suitably trained in philology and known to the department was a boon.) Despite a deep-seated conviction that I was unequal to so exalted a task, I accepted the invitation. I commuted weekly that year (1957–58) between Smith and Yale and learned, after completing the course, that it had in fact been very well received.

The following autumn, out of the blue, I had a phone call from Helge Kökeritz. With a mixture of agitation and incredulity, he told me that "they wanted me," and that I would soon be receiving an invitation to come down to New Haven to talk about the possibility of my teaching at Yale. The offer that resulted pushed me once again toward medieval scholarship. I was to be appointed a visiting associate professor for the following year; my work for the department would consist of one course, a seminar in the analysis of poetry in which I could teach whatever poems I liked. I would have no committee or other departmental responsibilities. This light schedule was designed to give me time to revise my dissertation. Despite the fact that I had

had a letter from Yale University Press inviting me to submit a revised version of it for publication, it had languished in a desk drawer and would have remained there had the department not made its proposal. I was told that if I completed the revision by the end of the academic year and the book was accepted by the Press, I could join the department as an associate professor on term. So I left Smith for Yale, where, as things turned out, I happily spent the rest of my professional life. *Sir Gawain and the Green Knight: A Stylistic and Metrical Study* was published in 1962; two years later I received tenure. I was one of the first two women to join the Faculty of Arts and Sciences, the other being the late Mary Clabaugh Wright, a specialist in the history of modern China.

As I look back on the Yale English department's pathbreaking decision to invite me to join it, I see it as having two causes: the curricular needs of the department and the enlightened attitudes of several of its key figures. As I have said, a strong philological requirement was then still in force. Kökeritz, whose courses fulfilled the requirement in tandem with John Pope's Old English, was a kindly man but an inept teacher. Though he wrote clearly, his explanations in class were not merely unhelpful but hopelessly confusing. When I began to teach at Yale, the enrollment in his undergraduate course in the history of the English language had dwindled to two. Moreover, by the time I embarked on my graduate studies, his health had begun to decline. He published little or nothing after *Shakespeare's Pronunciation* (1953), and he died a few years after I joined the department.

As for the attitudes of those who hired me, I did not, of course, know at the time, nor was I told later, how the Yale English department arrived at its decision. It was surely preceded by a discussion in a meeting of the full professors, perhaps in more than one. My guess, in retrospect, is that Talbot Donaldson took the initiative, with John Pope and Helge Kökeritz supporting him from the sidelines. (Talbot had once said to me, in my graduate-student days, "I know you could teach boys"—a remark whose purport I now understand but then wholly failed to grasp.) I also have reason to think that Louis Martz and Maynard Mack were enthusiastic advocates of the idea of "coeducating the department," especially since the department could at the same time acquire an effective teacher of philological courses. Both these men were prominent on the Yale scene; Martz, in fact, was departmental chairman. At any rate, during my first years of teaching at Yale I never sensed any resentment toward me on the part of my colleagues as an intruder on previously all-male turf. As for social relationships, I remained friends with Donaldson, Pope, and Kökeritz, but our socializing took the form of the occasional dinner party (at the Donaldsons' or the Popes') or dinner at the Faculty Club (with Kökeritz). There was in any case little day-to-day departmental camaraderie, and I took no part in what there was of it—in informal lunches at Mory's or Naples Pizza or shoptalk over coffee at George and Harry's. I never gave this a thought. I was away from New Haven most weekends, and the time I spent there was more than fully occupied in teaching, preparing my classes, attending committee meetings, and trying to get on with my scholarship. I did have a concerned and wise mentor in the person of Talbot Donaldson. With his support and his advice as to how to proceed, I applied for and received my promotion from associate to full professor in 1965.

As was and is true of Yale professors generally, at least in English, I was allowed to teach whatever courses interested me, and my range expanded as the department's philological requirements were dropped. For fifteen years or more I taught two undergraduate lecture courses in alternation, one in the history of the English language to 1500, the other in twentieth-century poetry. I also taught a seminar in which an adventurous group of undergraduates read the works of the *Gawain* poet in the original. I designed a course in stylistic analysis, in which pairs of authors who wrote during the same period and in the same genre, but in conspicuously different styles, were studied comparatively. This course always led off with the sixteenth-century narratives of Thomas Deloney and Thomas Nash and ended with a pair of twentieth-century essayists, journalists, or political speakers. One year, I remember, these latter were Harry Truman and Douglas MacArthur. In the graduate school I taught courses in the language and style of Chaucer, the *Gawain* poet, and Shakespeare.

A single anecdote will suffice to convey the kind of generosity with which I was treated. A senior professor, whose seminar in the analysis of lyric poetry I had taken over after he had taught it for many years, once told me that he had been talking with a student of mine who, after praising my course to the skies, asked, "Why haven't they given it before?" He considered me for a moment, unsmiling, then added, "It's a good thing I have no pride."

Shortly after writing my dissertation, when I was teaching at Smith for the second time, I began to realize, with growing excitement, that I might be able to compose a verse translation of *Sir Gawain and the Green Knight* that would be both more like the original than any that had been published previously and, or so I dared to hope, superior poetically. My first idea was to reproduce all the words of the poem, spelling those that had become obsolete as they would have been spelled if they had descended into present-day English. But when the passages on which I tried out this method simply sounded eccentric, I abandoned that plan and started translating in earnest. My progress was sporadic—as everyone knows, verse, unlike prose, cannot be composed at will—and it took me several years to finish the project to my satisfaction. I showed the completed translation to Talbot Donaldson, who was then the editor of the medieval section of the *Norton Anthology of English Literature*. He brought it to the attention of his Norton editors and helped me work out the financial details of a contract according to which it would be published both as a book and, under Norton's exclusive aegis, as part of the anthology. The book appeared in 1967.

Shortly thereafter, Donaldson, on Norton's behalf, proposed to me that I should translate the *Gawain* poet's *Pearl*. I immediately turned this idea down flat, telling him that the demands of the rhyme scheme of *Pearl* made it impossible to produce a modern translation that would be poetically effective. But then I began to think that the technical difficulties posed by the multiple rhymes might be alleviated by the use of eye rhymes and slant rhymes. "Wear," "her," "were," "peer," "dear," and "bear" suggested themselves for use in the first stanza, and I was hooked. I finished the translation four years later; it was published in 1977.

To translate *Sir Gawain* and then *Pearl* was the happiest of all possible undertakings, calling into play, and richly rewarding, all my training and all my talents. To begin with, my philological investigations into the poem's language had convinced me, as I said earlier, that the syllabic "final -e" familiar to students of Chaucer never appeared within the "long alliterative lines" of *Sir Gawain*. This fact had an important and exciting corollary: the metrical patterns of the poem as I understood them could be not merely approximated but reproduced in contemporary English, so that the verse of the translation would have the same varied yet continuous movement as that of the original. My intensive philological study of the poem had also taught me much about the expressive nuances of its wording, including relevant meanings in Middle English, now obsolete, of words still in use in the present. In addition I had at my command the craft of verse, acquired in the course of many years of writing poems in traditional meter and rhyme. The success of my translation was due, I am sure, to this unusual mix of qualifications.

During the late 1960s and 1970s I again turned my attention to the poetry of Stevens, Frost, and Moore, carrying out comparative analyses of language and style that were published first in part in journals, then as a book, *Language and the Poet* (1979). In the 1980s I published two substantial essays on the works of the *Gawain* poet: one on *Sir Gawain*, the other on *Pearl*. I also became interested in sound symbolism and its uses, particularly in the language of poetry. I had become more and more aware, as I continued to teach the history of the language, of the importance of sound-symbolic "motivation," both in the coinage of new words by inventive speakers of English and in choices made by English speakers generally among existent grammatical, lexical, and phonic alternatives. I had also come to see that what I termed "systematic" (as opposed to "mimetic") sound symbolism gave an expressiveness above and beyond meaning to the linking of identical sounds, both in end rhyme and in the "initial rhyme" of alliteration. This line of inquiry bore fruit in a pair of essays titled "Sound Symbolism as Drama in the Poetry of Wallace Stevens" and "Sound Symbolism as Drama in the Poetry of Robert Frost." I also investigated visual symbolism in an essay titled "Questions of Design in [William Carlos] Williams and Moore," in which I compared the two in terms of the effects produced by the layout of their poems on the printed page. When I was asked to participate in a symposium on English historical metrics at the University of Manchester in England, I contributed an essay, "Systematic Sound Symbolism in the Long Alliterative Line in *Beowulf* and *Sir Gawain and the Green Knight*." Later I wrote an article titled "Chaucer's English Rhymes" for a festschrift for my colleague Fred C. Robinson.

I should include in this essay an account of two of my administrative assignments at Yale. One was my contribution as "wordsmith" to the Committee on the Education of Women, chaired by Professor Donald Crothers, which had been appointed by

President A. Bartlett Giamatti in 1983. This committee was charged with looking into the situation of women at Yale, including faculty as well as students, evaluating it, and making whatever recommendations for improvement it deemed advisable. The committee's report, submitted in April 1984, was based on extensive research, including a questionnaire I sent out to women faculty at a number of other colleges and universities, and was shaped in the course of a long period of discussions. Its final section consisted of a numbered list of recommendations, many of which, unfortunately, were never put into effect.

Late in the spring of 1992 Yale's unpopular president, Benno Schmidt, suddenly resigned. Professor Howard Lamar of the Department of History was asked to serve as acting president of the university in 1992–93, at the end of which time a search committee appointed by the Yale incorporators was to have submitted the name of a candidate or a ranked list of candidates. Many of those concerned felt that the appointment of President Schmidt had been put through with undue haste, that his performance in earlier administrative roles had not been checked with sufficient care, and that the pool of potential candidates had not been fully canvassed. Every effort, accordingly, was made in forming the committee and giving it its charge to ensure that the search for Yale's next president would yield the most satisfactory possible result. The committee's chair was the estimable Dr. Robert Lynn of the Yale Corporation; its membership was drawn from both the corporation and the faculty. (This was, I believe, the first time faculty had ever been officially involved in a presidential search.)

Early in the summer of 1992 I received telephone calls from both Professor Lamar and Dr. Lynn. I accepted their invitation to serve in an innovative capacity: as liaison with the Yale faculty, responsible for hearing their views as to what the qualifications of the next president should be and what needs of the university he should address. I was also to receive nominations of candidates at or outside of Yale, and to hear opinions concerning candidates who were presumably already under consideration. I would transmit my findings in written form to the chair of the committee, and he, at his discretion, would communicate them to the others. I myself would not be a voting member of the committee, but I would attend its meetings and participate in its discussions. My title would be "faculty counselor." That fall I composed a letter, a copy of which went by first-class mail to every member of the faculty, inviting all those who wished to come and talk with me. I signed the letters individually and wrote an additional note to everyone I knew personally. This stratagem drew in well over a hundred people. I told each of my interlocutors that he or she could speak either on or off the record, and that I would keep off-the-record remarks in absolute confidence. As a result I heard some negative opinions about seemingly unexceptionable candidates from people who might otherwise have remained silent. Every member of the committee worked long and hard, and its final decision was arrived at by a long and at times painful process of deliberation. That it was the right decision has been proven by the performance over the past eight years of President Richard Levin.

I continued to teach into the 1990s, going on phased retirement in 1991 and retiring completely in 1994. In 1992 I was awarded a Sterling Professorship, joining, as another Sterling professor put it in a note of congratulation, "Yale's most exclusive club." During the 1990s I continued my scholarly work in both the medieval period and the twentieth century. I made a set of six videotaped lectures for what was then called the "Yale Great Teachers Series," sponsored by the Association of Yale Alumni. I called these "To Hear Their Voices"; two were on Chaucer, two on Shakespeare, and two on Robert Frost. In them I interpreted "voice" both literally, as the way each poet spoke the English language, and figuratively, as each one's way of conveying in language his vision of human experience. The tapes are now part of the materials studied in an on-line course for Yale alumni, with the same title, that I began teaching in 1999. It will be offered in 2001–2 by the "Alliance for Lifelong Learning," a newly formed consortium aimed at the promotion of "distance learning" and made up of Yale, Stanford, and Harvard Universities and the University of Oxford.

My teaching of Chaucer at the graduate level had left me eager to explore an aspect of the *Canterbury Tales* that had increasingly piqued my interest. Trying to arrive at an interpretation of this or that tale before discussing it with my students, I had again and again found that its meaning, at the deepest level, was at once signified in veiled fashion and left implicit. The poet seemed to have used this means of protecting himself in the society, dominated by a tyrannical king and fraught with religious controversy, at whose center he lived. My thinking along these lines accorded, I found, with the views of certain of the "new historicists" who had become prominent in medieval studies in the 1980s. The first product of my new investigations was an essay on "The Merchant's Tale" in which I argued that the culminating event of the tale, even though Chaucer did not refer to it explicitly, was the impregnation of the heroine. When phased retirement gave me more leisure, I turned to "The Summoner's Tale," following up on a hunch that blasphemy, though mentioned only once toward the end, was central to the tale's meaning. This led me straight to Chaucer's contemporary, the religious reformer John Wycliffe, of whose writings I was largely ignorant. My study of Wycliffe enabled me to write two essays. In one I interpreted "The Summoner's Tale" against its historical background in antifraternal polemic and Wycliffe's antifraternal writings in particular. In the other I argued for unexpressed yet crucial meanings in "The Merchant's Tale," "The Reeve's Tale," and "The Pardoner's Tale," each in some way reflecting concealed reformist sympathies on Chaucer's part. These essays, together with one I have written more recently titled "Contrast and Complementarity in the Design of *Pearl*," will appear in a collection of my essays on medieval subjects to be published by Yale University Press.

In the early 1990s I turned again to the task of translating the works of the *Gawain* poet and finished a modern version of *Patience*, in which he retells the Old Testament story of Jonah and the whale. Two more translations lie ahead: of *Cleanness*, which is usually ascribed to that poet, and *Saint Erkenwald*, a poem of disputed authorship that I have long believed to be the *Gawain* poet's work. *Erkenwald* also presents me with a compelling scholarly project: an essay in which I hope to argue convincingly for the *Gawain* poet's authorship, or at least to show that the evidence that has been adduced against it fails to hold up under close scrutiny. When I look back, remembering that I started out in comparative literature with the intention of spending my life as a poet, I am reminded of the statement in *Sir Gawain* that "first things and final conform but seldom." When I find myself thinking that I could have done more as a medievalist if I had not devoted so much time to twentieth-century poetry, including my own, I think of Wallace Stevens's statement, "It was not a choice between, but of." I am well aware that I have had good fortune in both fields, in the activity and in the outcome.

Select Bibliography of Works by Marie Borroff

A festschrift in honor of Borroff appeared in 1995: *The Endless Knot: Essays on Old and Middle English in Honor of Marie Borroff*, ed. M. Teresa Tavormina and R. F. Yeager (Rochester, N.Y.: Boydell and Brewer).

"The Seeking" [poem]. *Poetry* (October 1943): 27.

"The Seeking," "Guerilla," "The Task," "The Faith" [poems]. In *The John Billings Fiske Prize Poems*. Chicago: University of Chicago Press, 1943.

"The Stranger," "The Dwelling," "Ars Poetica," "Next Moment" [poems]. *The American Scholar.* (October 1947): 456–57.

"'Tom Fool at Jamaica' by Marianne Moore: Meaning and Structure." *College English* (May 1956): 466–69.

"Dramatic Structure in the Poetry of Marianne Moore." *The Literary Review* (autumn 1958): 112–23.

"What a Poem Is: For Instance, 'Snow.'" *Essays in Criticism* (October 1958): 393–404.

"'Snow' and Poetic Theory." *Essays in Criticism* (October 1959): 450–51.

Sir Gawain and the Green Knight: A Stylistic and Metrical Study. Yale Studies in English 152. New Haven, Conn.: Yale University Press, 1962. Reprint, Hamden, Conn.: Archon Books, 1973.

Dialogues from Sir Gawain and the Green Knight and Pearl. Read in Middle English with J. B. Bessinger Jr. New York: Caedmon Records TC 1192, 1965. Audiocassette published by Harper and Row. Recording.

Sir Gawain and the Green Knight: A New Verse Translation. New York: W. W. Norton, 1967.

"The Computer as Poet." *Yale Alumni Magazine*. January 1971, 22–25. Accompanied by a series of excerpts from computer-generated poetry titled "The Meditation of IBM 7094–7040 DCS."

"Creativity, Poetic Language, and the Computer." *Yale Review* (summer 1971): 481–513.

"Five Poems from the Chinese," "New York" [computer-generated poems]. In *Computer Poems,* edited by Richard W. Bailey, 3–4. Drummond Island, Mich.: Potagannissing Press, 1973.

"Broken Thumb," "Floating" [poems]. *The Virginia Quarterly Review* (autumn 1974): 568.

Pearl: A New Verse Translation. New York: W. W. Norton, 1977.

Language and the Poet: Verbal Artistry in Frost, Stevens, and Moore. Chicago: University of Chicago Press, 1979.

"William Carlos Williams: The Diagnostic Eye." In *Medicine and Literature,* edited by Enid Rhodes Peschel, 56–65. New York: Neale Watson, 1980.

"Sound Symbolism as Drama in the Poetry of Wallace Stevens." *ELH* (winter 1981): 914–34.

"*Pearl's Maynful Mone:* Crux, Simile, and Structure." In *Acts of Interpretation: The Text in Its Contexts, 700–1600: Essays on Medieval and Renaissance Literature in Honor of E. Talbot Donaldson,* edited by Mary J. Carruthers and Elizabeth D. Kirk, 159–72. Norman, Okla.: Pilgrim Books, 1982.

"Fowler and the Rest." *Yale Review* (spring 1985): 353–67. On guides to usage and standards of correctness in English.

"Reading the Poem Aloud." In *Approaches to Teaching "Sir Gawain and the Green Knight,"* edited by Miriam Youngerman Miller and Jane Chance 191–98 Approaches to Teaching Masterpieces of World Literature. Modern Language Association of America, 1986.

"Understanding Poetry" [poem]. *Poetry* (July 1986): 194.

"Rafting down the Grand Canyon: A Meditation." *Virginia Quarterly Review* (summer 1987): 498–514.

"A Cipher in *Hamlet.*" In *Philologia Anglica: Essays Presented to Professor Yoshio Terasawa on the Occasion of His Sixtieth Birthday,* edited by Kinshiro Oshitari et al., 320–27. Tokyo: Kenkyusha, 1988.

"Questions of Design in Williams and Moore." *William Carlos Williams Review* (spring 1988): 104–15.

"*Sir Gawain and the Green Knight:* The Passing of Judgment." In *The Passing of Arthur: New Essays in Arthurian Tradition,* edited by Christopher Baswell and William Sharpe, 105–28. New York: Garland, 1988.

"'Loves Hete' in the 'Prioress's Prologue' and 'Tale.'" In *The Olde Daunce: Love, Friendship, Sex, and Marriage in the Medieval World,* edited by Robert R. Edwards and Stephen Spector, 229–35. Albany, N.Y.: State University of New York Press, 1991.

"Sound Symbolism as Drama in the Poetry of Robert Frost." *PMLA* 107 (1992): 131–44.

"The Achievement of Norman Maclean." *Yale Review* (April 1994): 118–32.

To Hear Their Voices: Chaucer, Shakespeare and Frost. Yale Great Teachers Series. Florence, Kentucky: Brenzel Publishing, 1995. Videotaped lectures with readings from the *Canterbury Tales* on audiocassette and a booklet containing essays titled "The Language of Chaucer's Poetry" and "The Language of Shakespeare's Stage."

"At Seventy, the Tools" [poem]. *Quarterly West* (autumn/winter 1996–97): 119.

"Systematic Sound Symbolism in the Long Alliterative Line in *Beowulf* and *Sir Gawain and the Green Knight.*" In *English Historical Metrics,* edited by C. B. McCully and J. J. Anderson, 120–33. Cambridge: Cambridge University Press, 1996.

"Origination" [poem]. *The Yale Review* (April 1997): 41–42.

"Chaucer's English Rhymes." In *Words and Works: Studies in Medieval English in Honour of Fred C. Robinson,* edited by Peter S. Baker and Nicholas Howe, 223–42. Toronto: University of Toronto Press, 1998.

Sir Gawain and the Green Knight, Patience, Pearl: Verse Translations. New York: W. W. Norton, 2001.

Essays, Chiefly Medieval. New Haven, Conn.: Yale University Press, forthcoming.

Works Cited

Kökeritz, Helge. *Shakespeare's Pronunciation.* New Haven, Conn.: Yale University Press, 1953.

Webster's New Collegiate Dictionary. 1949.

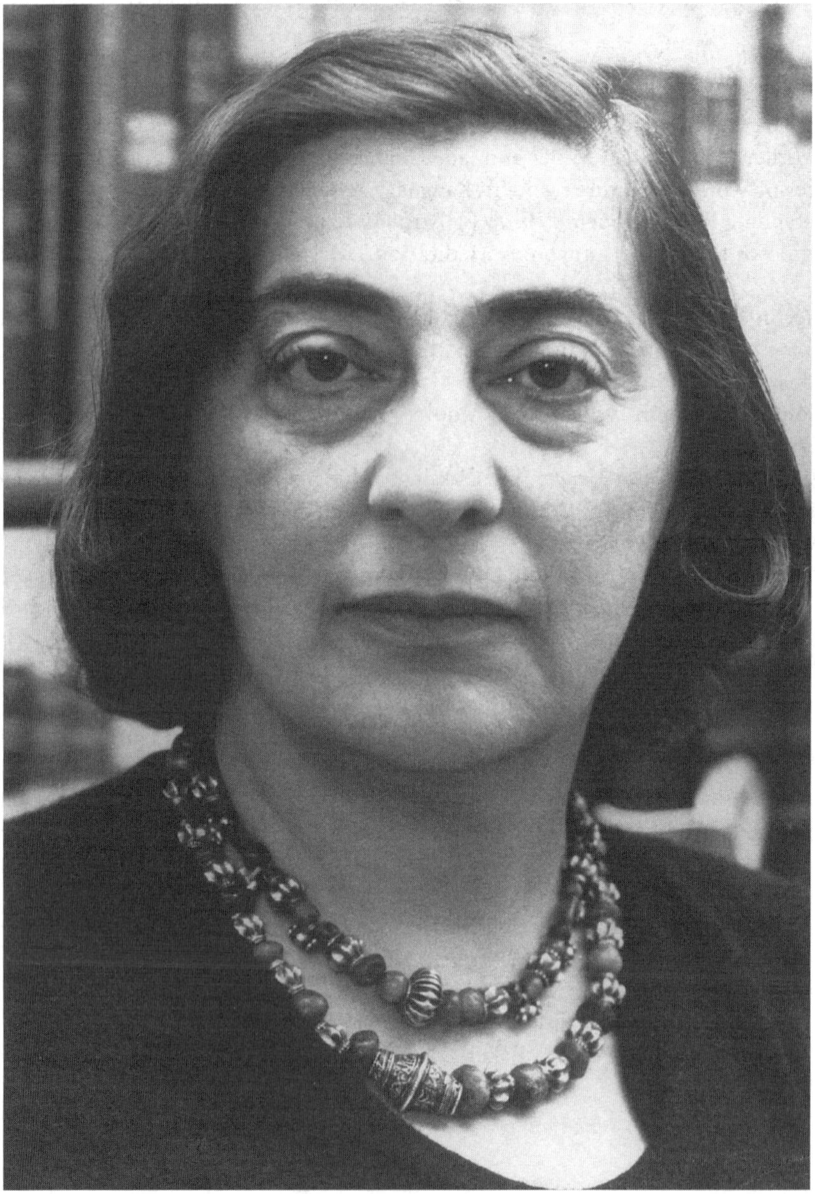

CHAPTER 58

"Magistra Studentorum per Armeniam et Byzantium"
Nina G. Garsoïan (1923–)

LEVON AVDOYAN

FOR ANY WOMAN to have had both the temerity and the courage to enter the long-established field of medieval studies in twentieth-century American academic life and to prove herself was a daunting task, indeed. Success was admitted only grudgingly by those long in possession of the discipline. Yet even more daring was for one fascinated by and dedicated to two ancillary subjects—Armenian and Byzantine studies, areas undervalued by both male and female practitioners of the academy—to dedicate her life's work to their study. This, in essence, is what Nina G. Garsoïan, professor emerita of Armenian history and civilization and of Byzantine history at Columbia University, set out to do; her efforts have been so highly successful they have paved the way for several generations of present and future scholars in those fields.

The past has always figured heavily in Garsoïan's thoughts and works as it coalesced with her present. Garsoïan has always paid homage to the many remarkable personalities of her own past while acknowledging with typical graciousness the very real influence of those now in her life. Her first book was dedicated quite simply "To My Mother," Ina Garsoïan, a gifted painter trained in prerevolutionary Russia, whose paintings now hang in several galleries in the United States, Italy and France, and several European countries.[1] A strong female presence with a lively spirit of independence, style, and dedication to her own craft, then dominated by men, she was a perfect parental role model for her inquisitive and equally gifted daughter. In typical fashion Nina Garsoïan's latest work pays tribute and acknowledges the debt owed to her three academic parents:

Á la mémoire des maîtres
Elias Bickerman
Sirarpie Der Nersessian
Garrett Mattingly
Qui me donnèrent la formation et l'amour de mon métier d'historien
(To my teachers
Elias Bickerman
Sirarpie Der Nersession
Garrett Mattingly
Who molded me and gave me the love of my craft as an historian).[2]

The present was acknowledged in 1993 in her remarks delivered at a symposium held on the occasion of her retirement from Columbia University, as she paid tribute to her many students whom she had mentored and from whom she claimed she had learned much. Both her past and that present have merged since her retirement into a future that has led not to rest but to yet more scholarly achievements.

Garsoïan was born on 11 April 1923 in Paris "into a milieu of émigrés"; "[she was] bilingual from infancy, and transported before [her] teens to the New World." She recalls, "I have never managed to achieve a single minded or whole hearted patriotism. I have been comfortable in and loved especially Paris and Venice, but also Moscow and Tiflis, Nantucket, New England and New York, but none of them has been my exclusive home. Insofar as limited information and the abomination of Nazi insanities on racial purity permit, I presume that I am ethnically as completely Armenian as is possible."[3] Her mother's family came from the Armenian community in the Crimea; her father's family was from Tiflis, the administrative capital of the Russian Empire's Transcaucasian Republics. Conditions following World War I and the Russian Revolution led the family to immigrate to France, where their daughter was born. Her father died in 1925, leaving her in the care of her mother and her redoubtable maternal grandmother. Exposed early to music on account of her mother's connections to the Parisian artistic communities, Garsoïan began studying the piano, eventually becoming a student of the renowned French pianist Robert Cassadesus and training to become a concert pianist. Her plans, however, were later to change abruptly following an accident that injured her hand severely enough to cause the loss of facility and dexterity needed for such a career. Of greater importance was the rise to power of Hitler, which prompted her maternal uncle, then living in New York, to persuade the three—grandmother, mother, and child—to join him in that city on 5 October 1933. Speaking French and Russian only, the young Garsoïan took up residence in the United States and began her formal education.

After earning her diploma from the Brearley School in New York in 1940, Garsoïan then received a baccalauréat in 1941 from the Lycée Français de New York. She went to Bryn Mawr College, where in 1943 she received her B.A. with honors in the fields of classical archaeology and ancient history. Her love of the ancient world led her to pursue and receive an M.A. in classical archaeology in 1946 from Columbia University, where she continued her graduate studies. After she was appointed an instructor of history at Smith College, she commuted between New York and Northampton, Massachusetts. In 1958 she received her Ph.D. in Armenian, Byzantine, and mediaeval history from Columbia, after defending a dissertation on the heresy of the Paulicians, directed by the brilliant yet severe—at least on his crusty surface—Elias Bickerman. She often recalls her defense when, twenty minutes after its commencement, one committee member asked in a fairly disparaging tone of voice, "Now tell me, Miss Garsoïan, do your really think your argument is convincing?" Before the young scholar could reply, Bickerman gruffly answered in her stead, "Convinced me." The defense concluded successfully within minutes.

From 1961 to 1962 she continued postdoctoral studies in classical Armenian at the Institut Catholique in Paris, under Father Charles Mercier, and in Iranian dialectology at the École des hautes études of the University of Paris, under Emile Benveniste. Here her formal education ended. Her prior academic pursuits in the classical, Byzantine, and western European worlds were now complemented by training in classical Armenian and Iranian studies. The background indispensable for her groundbreaking reinterpretation of the basic nature of Armenian history and culture in the ancient and Byzantine periods was now hers.[4]

In 1962, while still teaching at Smith College in Massachusetts, Garsoïan became visiting associate professor of Armenian studies at Columbia University. After leaving Smith in 1965, where she had risen to the position of associate professor, she remained, with one relatively brief interruption, both in the Department of Middle Eastern Languages and Cultures and in the Department of History at Columbia University until her retirement in 1993. Despite the fact that she was one of only two women professors in each of those departments in the 1960s, her advancement was rapid. In 1965 she became associate professor of Armenian studies and history; in 1969 a tenured professorship was hers. Throughout her career at Columbia she served and was a member of all committees having to do with the status of women scholars at the university. Attracting many students, she began the creation of one of the most formidable centers of Armenian and of Byzantine Studies in the West, while at the same time producing monographs and articles of such depth and intricacy that they would help reshape the discipline for decades to come.

Her career altered when, in 1973, she became the chair of the Department of Middle Eastern Languages and Cultures; she continued in that role until she was offered and persuaded to take the position of dean of the graduate school at Princeton University, the first woman to hold that position. Nonetheless, her colleagues Jean-Pierre Mahé and Robert Thomson rather gently maintain that "administration . . . was not to be Nina Garsoïan's future career for which her [then] colleagues [were] very thankful."[5] Her antipathy to administration was happily alleviated when, after a successful fund-raising campaign at Columbia University, a chair of Armenian studies was created. In 1979 Nina G. Garsoïan became the first Centennial, afterward renamed

Gevork M. Avedissian, professor of Armenian History and Civilization. Not known for a paucity of energy, she continued as well as professor of Byzantine history in the Department of History. Throughout this period she also intermittently served as visiting professor in several European universities: 1985, 1990, and 1992 saw her at the University of Rome-La Sapienza; 1986, at the Sorbonne in Paris; 1992, at the Collège de France; and 1994, as *directeur d'études* at the University of Paris, École des hautes études.

In addition to her role as scholar and teacher Garsoïan became an active trustee for the Ford Foundation in 1977 and continued in this capacity until 1989. She was a great traveler in her own right, and her duties to the foundation took her along the silk route through Afghanistan and Pakistan into India.[6] Among other highlights of her professional activities are her election as a fellow of the Medieval Academy of America in 1992; her role as a founding member of the United States–based Society for Armenian Studies; she also served as a board member (1980–88) and vice chair (1989–93) of the American Council of Learned Societies, as editor (1984–89) and director (1989–) of the influential *Revue des études arméniennes,* and as an associate member of the Centre de recherche d'histoire et de civilisation de Byzance of the Collège de France.[7] The latest, however, in the series of acknowledgments of her superior contributions to scholarship was her election in July 2002 as corresponding fellow of the British Academy, the highest such academic honor accorded to a non-British citizen.

All of this is the beginning and the end of the story, that is, a litany of the events of her life and training and the rewards reaped from her efforts, but such a narrative risks obscuring her many contributions to her students, to her colleagues, and to the field. Among Garsoïan's many talents is her ability to communicate superbly and eloquently, both as an author and as a lecturer. This skill made her an ideal teacher, whether in general history, Byzantine history, or her seminal work in Armenian studies. Her activities drew a great number of students to her for the study of these disciplines, so much so that an argument can be made that she, a women operating in a still very patriarchal Middle Eastern society, nonetheless had the capacity to create the most successful and influential chair for the study of Armenian history in the West. In a record unsurpassed outside the Republic of Armenia, Garsoïan directed fourteen doctorates and numerous masters in the field. Many of these students have gone on to fill chairs and take up other positions in the field. Her success as a teacher was recognized by the Armenian community in 1989, when she was awarded the Dadian Heritage Award by the Armenian Students' Association.[8]

Her students soon learned that she was there not only as a teacher, an advisor, and a director but also as a mentor. Those with no place to live in the summers were offered her apartment while she traveled. Those who were themselves fortunate enough to be in the same place as she in her travels—whether Paris, Venice, or Rome—found that they had a willing, energetic, and extremely able tour guide. Those who found themselves in New York at Easter were invited to a traditional Caucasian Easter feast with enough native dishes and vodka to foster conversations both elevated and not.

Yet as important as her contribution as scholarly parent to these future scholars was, it is in the products of her impeccable scholarship that her renown lies. Garsoïan studied lands whose history and culture had from the beginning of modern scholarship on the medieval world been interpreted through Western eyes. This Eurocentric school of thought more often than not obscured the accurate nature of these societies; only a few scholars had studied the requisite native languages in which most of the primary source materials had been composed. Through a series of publications of original monographs, articles, and translations, Garsoïan has gone far to restore the balance and elucidate the nature of ancient and medieval Armenia in particular and of the region of Anatolia and Iran in general. She first subjected all topics, whether political or religious or artistic in nature, to a rigorous examination of the extant primary sources. When none was available, consultation with colleagues followed. Garsoïan was always eager to benefit from the learning of others; her questions were legion and her graciously expressed thanks numerous.

This gratitude to the past and present is amply displayed by a series of translations Garsoïan produced of monographic works of distinguished Armenian scholars; in so doing she implicitly recognized the high level of scholarship being produced in Armenia. These translations, it must be understood, were not slavishly done but were always augmented and brought up to date, using the most rigorous academic standards. In 1965 she published a translation of the still unsurpassed study by H. A. Manandian, *The Trade and Cities of Armenia in Relation to Ancient World Trade*. In 1970 the English edition of Nicholas Adontz's *Armenia in the Period of Justinian: The Political Conditions Based on the Naxarar System* appeared. Its subtitle states that Garsoïan translated the work "with partial revisions, a bibliographic note and appendices." In point of fact, she had more than doubled the length of the original, providing what were to become the hallmarks of all her works and publications: extensive and exacting notes, the texts and elucidation of key historical and legal primary source materials, and a toponymic index, which is still consulted for the wealth and great variety of information it contains. No mere study of Armenia in the sixth century, the work is now used to good effect by everyone who studies the Byzantine Empire in that period and especially Justinian's reign and his failed actions to reconstitute the old Roman Empire. In 1976 she published a translation of Aram Ter Ghevondyan's *The Arab Emirates in Bagratid Armenia*, again a work published in the Soviet Republic of Armenia on a subject little studied in the West. Its importance has been underscored by the events of 11 September 2002 and the resulting demands for resources on Islam, Christianity, and the Middle Eastern countries.

It was in 1989, however, with the appearance of her translation of the classical Armenian text of what was almost universally thought to be a history of Armenia ascribed to a certain P'awstos Byzand, that her activities as translator reached their apogee. In an extended and cogent introduction, she argues that the work's attribution is incorrect and that it is, indeed, an early repository of history, folklore, and oral traditions known as the *Buzandaran Patmut'iwnk'* (Epic histories).[9] The text is presented in a clear, grammatical, yet literal translation. In this work she followed her own instructions to her students not to apologize for the text by smoothing over its faults; what results is not a great work of literature but rather an accurate version of a work important for the study of the early-Christian period in Armenia and for what it teaches us about the true nature of the earliest periods of Armenian Christianity, a period at one more with the Syrian tradition and Iranian worlds than with the later Greek Orthodox strata added after the victories of the West.

Garsoïan's original monographs and articles all reflect the same exactitude displayed in her translations: detailed and meticulous research of both primary and secondary materials in all formats; honest critique of previous scholarship on the subject, without resorting to ad hominem or ad feminam attacks; lengthy and exacting footnotes, supplemented with massive appendices, to arm the researcher interested in going even further with a topic; and a literary style attuned to the scholarship of the past that maintained that works of history are also literature.

These original works are most important for the new interpretations they bring to bear on the topics at hand. Garsoïan is an iconoclastic observer of the past, a skeptic who maintains that a constant reassessment based on whatever new evidence is available is needed to reach any sort of a synthesis. Especially in Armenian studies, a discipline dominated by orthodox and pseudorthodox traditions, her works on occasion have led, side by side with praise, to condemnation.[10]

Her first major exploration was her dissertation, a detailed examination of the heresy known as Paulicianism. After a careful discussion of the primary source materials related to this sect and then of the origins of Christianity in Armenia itself, Garsoïan is led to conclude, "The sect first developed in Armenia whence it passed to the eastern provinces of the Byzantine Empire and was probably imported into the Balkans."[11]

Political, social, and military history also figure prominently in her output. Many of Garsoïan's students had reason to be thankful for the detailed lectures she delivered on the run of Armenian history from ancient times to the Russian conquest in the early nineteenth century, and not a few bragged that they were still able to use their notes while fashioning their own lectures. Her studies led her to correct again the rather Eurocentric interpretation of that history and to restore the greater importance of the Anatolian and Iranian milieus in which Armenia grew and thrived. The best written record, until recently, of her reinterpretation of the ancient and medieval periods was published in the *Dictionary of the Middle Ages*.[12] A conclusion succinctly stated at the beginning of this influential article is known now to many of her students and colleagues as Garsoïan's law: "From antiquity, Armenia's geographical position at the meeting point of the Greco-Roman and Iranian worlds created a situation that favored the country's cultural life, enriching it with two major traditions but playing havoc with the continuity of its political history. As a general pattern, therefore, Armenia flourished only when the contending forces on either side were in near equilibrium and neither was in a position to dominate it entirely."[13] Since 1997 researchers have had at their disposal several chapters she authored about Armenia in the ancient and Byzantine eras that provide a more extensive and updated narration of Armenian history.[14]

Early Christianity in Armenia and the evolving nature of the Armenian Church and its institutions in its earliest and formative periods have been of special interest to Garsoïan. This examination of Christianity and Christian institutions has both coexisted with and complemented her political, historical, and cultural studies of Armenia and Iran and their relations since the mid-sixth century B.C. A series of influential articles on this subject was capped in 1999 by the publication of her work on the Armenian Church and "the Great Schism" of the East."[15] A detailed examination of the history of Armenia and of its church from the fourth century up to its break with the Church of Georgia in the early seventh century, it offers a fresh and challenging interpretation of the growth of the anti-Chalcedonian aspect of Armenia's national church and its nature, which was increasingly unacceptable when viewed through the eyes of the Chalcedonian churches of the West. Among this work's many important contributions guaranteeing its importance for decades to come in academic circles are appendices that present to the Western world translations from important classical Armenian religious texts, most notably from the collection of ecclesiastical letters known as the *Girk' t'lt'oc'* (Book of letters), many of which have been previously inaccessible to Western scholarship. In typical fashion, implicitly requesting a scholarly dialogue on the subject, Garsoïan maintains that her conclusions are provisional, pending the results of her further research into the topic.

In 1998 the excellence her scholarship earned her the Anania Širakac'i Award, rarely bestowed by the Academy of Sciences of Armenia on a foreign scholar. In 1993 she was awarded the Mesrop Maštoc' Medal for academic excellence by Katholikos (Patriarch) Garegin I of the Katholikate of the Great House of Cilicia. Yet iconoclastic interpreters of national histories do not fare well and are often condemned by the more ethnocentric interpreters of that history: "A prophet is without honor in her home town." With her emphasis on the centrifugal nature of the lands of the Armenians and the fragmentation of those lands; with her stance on the origins of the Armenian people and their ethnicity; with her inviolable rule that the sources should speak for themselves and that all forms of primary source materials must be examined and used and never, ever altered; with her demand for as strict an objectivity as is possible and her belief that apologetics are not needed for any interpretation of Armenian history; and most of all, as with Socrates, with her passing these tenets on to her students, she (and many of her colleagues) has received harsh criticism in the Republic of Armenia following its declaration of independence from the USSR in 1991. With freedom a new national consciousness awoke in all the former Soviet republics, and in each, in small yet potent circles, ethnocentric schools have arisen to condemn anyone who does not maintain a rigid orthodoxy of the racial purity of the people and their autochthony. It is then all the more fitting that Garsoïan's last published article, to date, is her assessment of the present state of Armenian studies both in the Republic of Armenia and in the Armenian diaspora in the West.[16]

As this essay goes to press, Garsoïan is crafting a reinterpretation of the Armenian frontier zone while continuing her latest grand exploration—a reexamination of the growth of early monasticism and monastic institutions in Armenia. It will no doubt be a unique excursion that will enlighten as well as provoke.

Essays cannot do justice to a person; the biographer's task is unenviable, for it must attempt to be comprehensive yet fair, laudatory yet seemingly objective. It is difficult, nonetheless, to overestimate the contributions of Nina G. Garsoïan. Her impact on the study of ancient and medieval Armenia and on Byzantine studies should by this point be evident. Her influence on her students and her constant interaction with them and her colleagues in the United State, in her native France, and, yes, even in Armenia, continues. A lively dialogue flows as the constant examination proceeds.

Yet if one had to choose the one achievement that outshines all others, it is the fact that she and her colleagues have created a corpus of works of the highest scholarly caliber on Armenian translations, analyses, and syntheses, which has made the study of Armenia—the land, its people, and their culture—finally accessible to Western scholarship. These publications have gone a long way toward alleviating if not eliminating the bias against these disciplines; their influence and the standards they display will be long felt, just as certainly as the acknowledgment of Nina Garsoïan's role in this success is assured.

Notes

1. Garsoïan, *Paulician Heresy*, 5. The title of this essay parallels the *Magister militum per orientem et Armeniam*, the honorific of the Justinianic official responsible for military affairs in the East and in Armenia.

2. Garsoïan, *L'Église arménienne et le grand schisme d'orient*. On Garsoïan's friend and mentor, the great art historian Sirarpie Der Nersessian, see Dickran Kouymjian's essay in the present volume and Garsoïan, "Sirarpie Der Nersessian." Elias Bickerman, the avowed misogynist, became Garsoïan's doctoral advisor at Columbia University and a strong advocate for her position at Columbia. A testament to her thirst for knowledge and admiration for all historic inquiry is that, although Mattingly's historical studies in the Renaissance and Counter Reformation were outside her own, she nonetheless attended his lectures at Columbia for the sheer brilliance of his approach; she often credits his continuing influence on her written style.

3. Quoted from an unpublished memoir of her early years that Nina Garsoïan kindly sent to me for use in the present study. Although ostensibly a record of her life from birth through her early studies and first trip to her beloved Venice in the late 1940s, this intriguing document paints a brilliant portrait of the lives of the Armenian nobility and bourgeoisie who lived in prerevolutionary Russia and follows them into exile to Europe and beyond.

4. Garsoïan has received many fellowships, grants, and awards throughout her career, chief among which were a Fulbright for study in Italy (1952–53); an American Association of University Women Fellowship to France (1961–62); a grant from the American Council of Learned Societies/Academy of Sciences of the USSR Senior Exchange Program (1970, 1976); a grant from the National Endowment for the Humanities (1970–71, 1984–86); and a John Simon Guggenheim Memorial Fellowship (1985–86).

5. Mahé and Thomson, *From Byzantium to Iran,* xv.

6. Again from her unpublished memoir, 1: "My friend Norma who knows me best maintains that I shall die with my bags packed."

7. *Revue des études arméniennes* is arguably the most important of the Western academic journals dedicated to the study of Armenian history and civilization.

8. The award recognizes "individuals who have made an outstanding contribution to the preservation and presentation of the Armenian heritage to the world community."

9. Garsoïan, *Epic Histories Attributed to P'awstos Buzand.*

10. See Avdoyan, *Pseudo-Yovhannēs Mamikonean,* ix–x, especially note 3, for a discussion of the orthodox, iconoclastic, and pseudorthodox Armenological circles. "Pseudorthodox" is a handy word borrowed from the writings of the brilliant Morton Smith: "But everywhere there are persistent efforts to square the facts of the OT [for us, Armenian history] as far as possible with the traditional teachings of the institutions and even more, to make them serviceable for homiletic [in our case, chauvinistic] presentation." See Morton Smith, "The Present State of Old Testament Studies," *The Journal of Biblical Literature* 88 (1969): 21.

11. Garsoïan, *The Paulician Heresy,* 232. Never fearful of altering her position on a subject and changing her conclusions in reply to criticisms of certain aspects of her thesis that she deemed justifiable, she published "Byzantine Heresy: A Re-Interpretation." Both works are still considered the state of the question on the subject by most reputable scholars.

12. See "Armenia: History of," in *Dictionary of the Middle Ages,* 1:471–88. Garsoïan was an associate editor of this massive and indispensable reference work; as a result, it is one of the first works on the medieval period to include major articles on the lands and peoples of the Middle East on an equal footing with those concerning the lands and peoples of Europe.

13. Ibid., 474.

14. See chapters 3–8, in Hovannisian, *Armenian People from Ancient to Modern Times,* 1:37–198.

15. Garsoïan, *L'Église arménienne et le grand schisme d'orien.*

16. Garsoïan, "Evolution et crise dans l'historiographie recente de l'Arménie médiévale."

SELECT BIBLIOGRAPHY OF WORKS BY NINA G. GARSOÏAN

Translator. *The Trade and Cities of Armenia in Relation to Ancient World Trade,* by H. A. Manandian. Lisbon: Livraria Bertrand, 1965.
The Paulician Heresy: A Study of the Origin and Development of Paulicianism in Armenia and the Eastern Provinces of the Byzantine Empire. The Hague: Mouton, 1967.
"Politique ou orthodoxie? L'Arménie au quatrième siècle." *Revue des études arméniennes,* n.s., 4 (1967): 297–32.
"Quidam Narsaeus: A Note on the Mission of Saint Nerses the Great." In *Armeniaca: Mélanges d'études arméniennes,* 148–64. Venice: San Lazaro, 1969.
Translator and reviser. *Armenia in the Period of Justinian: The Political Conditions Based on the Naxarar System,* by Nicholas Adontz. Louvain, Belg.: Calouste Gulbenkian Foundation, 1970.
"Armenia in the Fourth Century: An Attempt to Redefine the Concepts of 'Armenia' and 'Loyalty.'" *Revue des études arméniennes,* n.s., 8 (1971): 341–52.
"Byzantine Heresy: A Re-interpretation." *Dumbarton Oaks Papers* 25 (1971): 85–113.
"Le Rôle de la hiérarchie chrétienne dans les rapports diplomatiques entre Byzance et les Sassanides." *Revue des études arméniennes,* n.s., 10 (1973): 119–38.

Translator. *The Arab Emirates in Bagratid Armenia,* by Aram Ter Ghevondyan. Lisbon: Calouste Gulbenkian Foundation, 1976.

"Prolegomena to a Study of the Iranian Elements in Arsacid Armenia." *Handēs Amsōreay* 90 1976): 177–234.

"The Locus of the Death of Kings: Armenia the Inverted Image." In *The Armenian Image in History and Literature,* edited by R. G. Hovannisian, 27–64. Malibu, Cal.: Undena Publications, 1981.

"Sur le titre de 'Protecteur des pauvres.'" *Revue des études arméniennes,* n.s., 15 (1981): 21–31.

"The Iranian Substratum of the Agat'angełos Cycle." In *East of Byzantium: Syria and Armenia in the Formative Period,* edited by N. G. Garsoian, T. F. Mathews and R. W. Thomson, 151–98. Washington, D.C.: Dumbarton Oaks, 1982.

"Nersēs le Grand, Basile de Césarée et Eustathe de Sébaste." *Revue des études arméniennes,* n.s., 17 (1983): 145–69.

"The Early Mediaeval City: An Alien Element?" In *Ancient Studies in Memory of Elias Bickerman [Special Issue]. Journal of the Ancient Near East Society* 16–17 (1984–85 [1987]): 67–83.

"Secular Jurisdiction over the Armenian Church (Fourth–Seventh Centuries)." In *Okeanos: Essays Presented to Ihor Ševčenko on His Sixtieth Birthday [Special Issue],* edited by C. Mango. *Harvard Ukrainian Studies* 7 (1984): 220–50.

"The Enigmatic Figure of Šahak of Manazkert." *Handēs Amsōreay* 101 (1987): 883–95.

"'T'agaworanist kayeank' kam 'Banak' ark'uni': Les residences royale des Arsacides arméniens." *Revue des études arméniennes,* n.s., 21 (1988–89): 251–70.

The Epic Histories Attributed to P'awstos Buzand: Buzandaran Patmut'iwnk'. Cambridge, Mass: Harvard University Press, 1989.

"L'art iranien comme témoin de l'armement arménien sous les Arsacides." In *Atti del V Simposio Internazionale di Arte Armena,* edited by Boghos Levon Zekiyan, 385–400. Venice: San Lazzaro, 1991.

With B. Martin-Hisard. "Unité et diversité de la Caucasie médiévale (IXe–Xe siècle)." In *Il Caucaso: Cerniera fra culture dal Mediterraneo alla Persia (secoli IV–XI),* Settimane di studio del Centro italiano di Studi sull' alto medioevo, 43 (20–26 April 1995). Spoleto: Centro Italiano di Studi Sull' Alto Medievo, 1996. 1: 275–347.

"The Two Voices of Armenian Mediaeval Historiography: The Iranian Index." *Studia Iranica* 25/1 (1996): 7–43.

With J.-P. Mahé. *Des Parthes au Califat: Quatre leçons sur la formation de l'identité arménienne.* Centre de recherche d'histoire et de civilization de Byzantine du Collège de France. Travaux et mémoires: Monographies 10. Paris: De Boccard, 1997.

"The Problem of Armenian Integration into the Byzantine Empire." In *Studies on the Internal Diaspora of the Byzantine Empire,* edited by Hélène Ahrweiler and Angeliki E. Laiou, 53–124. Washington, D.C.: Dumbarton Oaks, 1998.

L'Église arménienne et le grande schisme d'orient. Corpus Scriptorum Christianorum Orientalium, vol. 574, subsidia tom. 100. Louvain, Belg.: Peeters, 1999.

"Sirarpie Der Nersessian." In *Medieval Scholarship: Biographical Studies on the Formation of a Discipline,* edited by H. Damico, 3:287–305. New York: Garland, 1999.

"Evolution et crise dans l'historiographie recente de l'Arménie médiévale." *Revue du monde arménien moderne et contemporaine* 6 (2002): 727–37.

Works Cited

Avdoyan, Levon. *Pseudo-Yovhannēs Mamikonean: The History of Tarōn (Patmut'iwn Tarōnoy): Historical Investigation, Critical Translation, and Historical and Textual Commentaries.* Columbia University Program in Armenian Studies. Suren D. Fesjian Academic Publications, no. 6. Atlanta: Scholars Press, 1993.

The Dictionary of the Middle Ages. Edited by Joseph R. Strayer. 12 vols. New York: Charles Scribner's Sons, 1982–87.

Hovannisian, R. G., ed. *The Armenian People from Ancient to Modern Times.* 2 vols. New York: St. Martin's Press, 1997.

Mahé, Jean-Pierre, and Robert Thomson, eds. *From Byzantium to Iran: Armenian Studies in Honour of Nina G. Garsoïan.* Columbia University Program in Armenian Studies. Suren D. Fesjian Academic Publications, no. 5. Atlanta: Scholars Press, 1996.

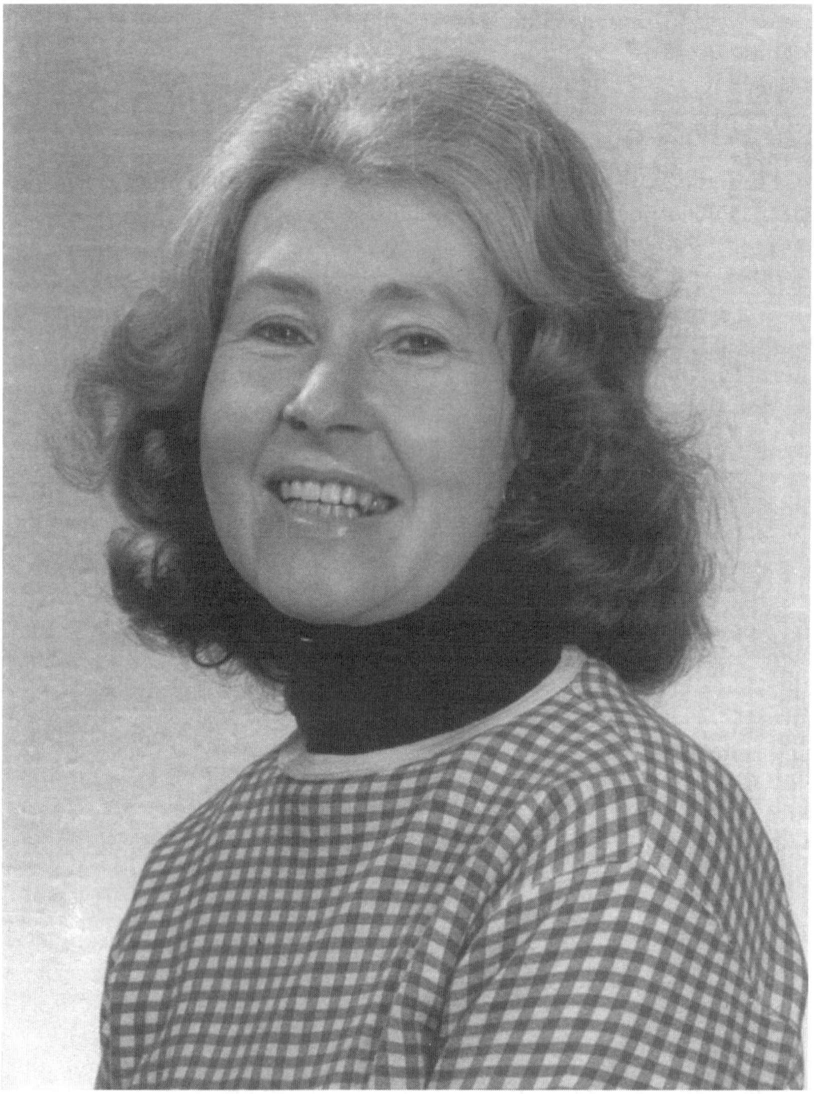

CHAPTER 59

Elizabeth Salter (1925–1980)
Teacher and Scholar of Middle English Literature

JULIA BOFFEY

To EXPLORE ELIZABETH SALTER's published work and the spheres in which her influence as a teacher was most telling offers the opportunity to trace the development of medieval studies as a discipline in Britain over three decades and to appreciate the significance of her formative role in this.[1] Such exploration also reveals how her interests both proliferated and yet continued to return to certain questions that for her remained persistently compelling. The work she was engaged in shortly before her death from cancer in 1980 still wrestles with issues that had prompted some of her undergraduate lecture courses in the early 1950s, and one can see in the sophisticated and wide-ranging analysis of "The Annunciation to the Shepherds in Later Medieval Art and Drama" (published in *English and International* in 1988) a development of the themes of lectures on the natural world in medieval painting and poetry given thirty years before. The subjects of her published books and articles, some completed posthumously by her literary executors Nicolette Zeeman and Derek Pearsall, illustrate these lasting concerns: medieval religious writing; Langland and alliterative poetry; Chaucer and his fourteenth-century context; relationships between art and literature in the Middle Ages.

Like a number of other medievalists of her generation, Elizabeth Jones, as she was born, was the product of a grammar-school system of English education that no longer exists.[2] She was born on 23 February 1925 at Bream in Gloucestershire, situated between the Severn Estuary and the Wye Valley in the area close to the Welsh border known as the Forest of Dean, and educated at secondary level at the grammar school in Lydney. Her mother taught at the village school in Bream, and her father worked for the Forestry Commission and as a printer. From Lydney she proceeded in 1943 to university in London, at Bedford College—a women's foundation, with buildings located in and around Regent's Park.[3] Like the other original women's foundations in the University of London (Westfield College in Hampstead and Royal Holloway College in Egham), Bedford had a strong reputation for scholarship in all areas.[4] In the prewar years the English department had been led successively by Caroline Spurgeon (the first woman professor in the University of London), Lascelles Abercrombie, and F. P. Wilson, and its teaching staff in the 1940s included Una Ellis-Fermor and Kathleen Tillotson.

It was still wartime, and like other parts of the University of London, Bedford had arranged for the partial evacuation of its staff and students to institutions outside London. Bedford's arrangement was with Newnham College in Cambridge, another women's foundation, where Elizabeth Jones spent a year of her undergraduate career before receiving her B.A. degree in 1946 with first-class honors. After a year working for the civil service, she returned to Bedford College for an M.A., at that stage in the University of London a degree gained by research and a substantial thesis and much more like the modern Ph.D. than the taught master's degrees currently offered in British universities.[5] Working under the supervision of Phyllis Hodgson on Nicholas Love's *Myrrour of the Blessed Lyf of Jesu Christ,* a Middle English prose translation of the pseudo-Bonaventuran *Meditationes vitae Christi,* she produced a study that reviewed the manuscripts and circulation of the *Myrrour,* its context in the tradition of medieval lives of Christ, and the specifics of Love's prose style.[6] Much of the thesis remains essential reading for anyone working on Middle English religious prose, and although some of its conclusions were published in the form of early articles, in 1974 it was published in toto (with minor revisions) as a volume of *Analecta Cartusiana.*[7]

The scholarly solidity and depth of this early work owes much to the traditions of Middle English scholarship in the University of London in the postwar years. The history of Middle English prose was a central interest for many London scholars: R. W. Chambers of University College, London, for example, had written influentially on the continuity of English prose and furnished an introduction to the edition of *The Book of Margery Kempe* published in 1936.[8] London was also rich in editors, and alongside Salter's supervisor Phyllis Hodgson were George Kane at University College, who completed in 1946 as a Ph.D. thesis a critical edition of *passus* 18–20 of the B-text of *Piers Plowman,* and Mabel Day at King's.[9] Women scholars were important to the traditions of London Middle English: Marjorie Daunt had worked with R. W. Chambers on *A Book of London English;* Beatrice White, then at Westfield College in Hampstead, was another prominent figure.[10] Having gained her M.A. in 1949 (examined by Beatrice White and Phyllis Hodgson), Elizabeth Jones taught part-time at Westfield College and was appointed to an assistant lectureship at King's College in the Strand, where the Department of English then included G. N. Garmonsway.[11] Although teaching in London was at this time largely college based, the examining system for the awarding of degrees necessitated a federal board of studies and considerable contact between teachers at the different constituent institutions; and the university also fostered interdisciplinary interests through some of its special institutes, such as the Warburg Institute and the Institute of Historical Research. Such an environment would surely have been formative for a graduate student and then a young teacher starting an academic career.

In 1950 her marriage to the mathematician Christopher Zeeman brought about not just a change of name for Elizabeth Jones but also a move to Cambridge, where she apparently intended to teach part-time and continue work for a London Ph.D. But the Cambridge teaching led to various research studentships at Newnham College from 1951 to 1954, a fellowship at Girton from 1955, a university assistant lectureship (1954–58), and then a lectureship (1958–63), and the Ph.D. was overtaken by events.[12] These years saw the publication of a number of significant articles, some on Nicholas Love, others branching out into new areas—notably *Piers Plowman*—and the birth of a daughter, Nicolette Zeeman, in 1956.[13] The lectures she gave during this period cover topics that were to remain central to her research interests: "The Natural World in Medieval Painting and Poetry," "Langland's *Piers Plowman* and the Medieval Poetic Tradition," "Medieval Religious Literature," and "Medieval Aesthetics" are among the series that she regularly offered.[14] Noticeable too in her activities during this period is an interest in teaching methods and in ways of bringing alive the literature of a culture that for many undergraduates might seem incomprehensible, if not repellent. The lectures on art and aesthetics were accompanied by slides; some sessions (such as those in a series on "Early Middle English Literature") took the form of seminars—unusual in the context of Cambridge teaching in the 1950s; and a series of lectures titled "The Sound of Medieval Poetry" promised readings and recordings.[15]

Such innovative teaching may have suggested itself as part of an effort to illuminate the particular emphases of the Cambridge English tripos, which was titled "Literature, Life and Thought." Although teaching in the faculty during this period in practice followed a variety of approaches (including the Leavisite), medieval and early-modern studies retained an essentially historical and historicizing base, contextualizing literature as broadly as possible in the culture of its period.[16] The books that Elizabeth Zeeman worked on during her years in Cambridge—a study of "The Knight's Tale" and "The Clerk's Tale" and an introduction to *Piers Plowman*—combine the characteristically wide scholarship of this approach with an intense engagement in the experience that medieval texts offered and continue to offer to their readers and with a willingness to confront what can, especially for modern audiences, seem intractable issues or points of interpretation.[17]

Divorce and remarriage to David Salter, in 1960, followed by the birth of a son, Mark, heralded a change of direction. In 1963 Elizabeth Salter spent a year at the University of Connecticut in Storrs on a visiting appointment before returning to take up a readership at the University of York, one of the new institutions founded in the early 1960s at the time when the Robbins Committee, founded to review the pattern of full-time higher education in Great Britain, was preparing its report.[18] As in the other new foundations, the English department at York was able to draw up its own principles for the curriculum and its delivery. In line with the university's mission "to encourage the growth of an academic community that is alive to the needs of society at large," the teaching of English here was designed to encourage "close study of selected topics in related disciplines," and the university's students of English were expected to read broadly and ideally to gain expertise in languages not their own.[19] By 1968–69 the department's name had changed from "English" to "English and Related Literature." Some of the new teaching staff were already known to Elizabeth Salter from Cambridge: the Shakespeare scholar Philip Brockbank had been a fellow assistant lecturer and was appointed to head the new department at York; a number of the other new members of the staff had been Cambridge students, and the Cambridge connection was further strengthened in 1966 by the appointment of F. R. Leavis as visiting professor. Within the parameters of its new curriculum, much of what was taught at and fostered in the new English department at York retained both the Leavisite dimension and the focus on "literature, life, and thought" that characterized the teaching of English in Cambridge.

Elizabeth Salter's work during these early years at York maintained the interest in Langland and Chaucer that she had begun to explore during the previous decade, with the publication of important articles titled "The Alliterative Revival" and "Piers Plowman and 'The Simonie,'" and with an analysis of *Troilus and Criseyde* written to honor C. S. Lewis, who was professor of medieval English in Cambridge from 1954 and so for most of her years there.[20] At the same time that she was writing these articles, though, she was continuing to explore and develop ideas about the relationship of literature and the visual arts that had stimulated some of her first undergraduate lectures in the 1950s. Special options available to undergraduates in York included a course on medieval iconography and later one on art and literature in the Middle Ages. The environment in York, where art history figured in the offerings of several departments, and where the art historian Kenneth Clark was to become chancellor of the university in 1970, must have been especially congenial for this kind of research, which bore fruit in a number of studies published in the late 1960s. Her essay "Medieval Poetry and the Visual Arts," which manages deftly to combine both theoretical spadework and sensitive critical analysis, remains essential reading for any consideration of the possible relationships between word and image in the Middle Ages; some of the ideas advanced here were pursued with more specificity in a published British Academy lecture "Medieval Poetry and the Figural View of Reality" and an article "*Piers Plowman* and the Visual Arts."

As the department grew, so did its strengths in the medieval area. Derek Pearsall moved to a lectureship in York from King's College, London, in 1965, and Karen Hodder, S. A. Bradley, Ruth Ellison, and N. R. Haveley took up teaching posts there. A new initiative was the series of teaching editions known as York Medieval Texts—according to the general introduction for all volumes, "designed for undergraduates and, where the text is appropriate, for upper forms of schools. Its aim is to provide editions of major pieces of Middle English writing in a form which will make them accessible without loss of historical authenticity"[21]—undertaken by the publisher Edward Arnold with Elizabeth Salter and Derek Pearsall as general editors. One of the first volumes to be published was a selection of extracts from the C-text of *Piers Plowman,* on which Salter and Pearsall collaborated.[22] This continuing collaboration, which drew together different but productively complementary sets of skills and interests, was to be of immense significance for medieval studies at York, generating many new initiatives in teaching and research and cultivating a stimulating context for the training of new scholars and teachers. A significant number of Elizabeth Salter's former students now hold distinguished academic posts.

Graduate teaching at York had been a part of the department's activities from the beginning, and this offered opportunities that very well matched the range and depth of Elizabeth Salter's interests. As the university grew, the possibilities of interdisciplinary teaching and research at an advanced level—drawing together especially the interests of teachers in the fields of English, history, and art history—were carefully explored. In 1968, largely through Salter's single-minded energy, the Centre for Medieval Studies came into being, with the aim of integrating these subjects in a one-year master's degree (at this stage in York termed a B.Phil. rather than an M.A.). By 1974 the center had its own independent quarters in the King's Manor, a complex of historic buildings in the center of York that had for a time housed the whole English department while the new campus was under construction, and it continued to offer a taught one-year degree in medieval studies as well as supervision for the higher degrees of M.Phil. and D.Phil.[23]

The courses that were developed at this new center—the first of its kind in Britain—built on and extended the model of interdisciplinarity that increasingly informed Elizabeth Salter's published work. Students registered for one of a number of different pathways and were taught by means of seminars that involved two, sometimes three, teachers from the different disciplines of English, history, and art history. The fruits of this joint teaching are perceptible in a good deal of Salter's work from the 1970s (some of which was published only posthumously): the chapters in *English and International* (1988) that constitute the section called "An Obsession with the Continent," like the chapter "Mappings" in *Fourteenth-Century English Poetry* (1983), reflect material that fed into teaching for an option on Anglo-French culture; the detailed art-historical research contributed to the introduction to the facsimile of the Corpus manuscript of *Troilus and Criseyde* draws on work undertaken in connection with a long-running option on the court of Richard II.[24]

Other work that Salter undertook and published in the 1970s demonstrates the stimulus furnished by collaborative ventures of different kinds. In two chapters—"Courts and Courtly Love" and "The Medieval Lyric"—contributed to the multivolume survey *Literature and Western Civilization*, edited by a former Cambridge colleague, David Daiches, Salter ventured into areas in which she had not previously published. She was on the advisory committee of the *Index of Middle English Prose* and gave a paper on the manuscripts of Love's *Myrrour* at the conference held in Cambridge in the summer of 1978 to launch the project.²⁵ A book called *Landscapes and Seasons of the Medieval World* gave her the opportunity to work with Derek Pearsall on an extended survey of the connections between art and literature in the Middle Ages, searching back to the classical traditions that informed such medieval topoi as the enclosed garden and providing alongside scholarly detail and perceptive critical reading a rich anthology of images and verse extracts. The same collaboration, together with work on the *Troilus* manuscript, also generated a study of the role of prefatory pictures in manuscripts of late medieval texts.²⁶

Just as *Landscapes and Images* enabled Elizabeth Salter to combine the research and thinking of several decades with the original insights called forth by collaboration, so a number of her published articles in the 1970s demonstrate the ways in which new currents of various kinds (some perhaps springing from her supervision of Ph.D. students, others from new publications in fields of relevance to medieval literature) prompted fresh scrutiny of texts she had known and worked on throughout her scholarly life.²⁷ In particular she seems to have wished to explore the pressing social and economic concerns voiced by Langland and other anonymous alliterative poets: she wrote "The Timeliness of *Wynnere and Wastoure*" and, in an extraordinarily productive contextualization, rescued the short poem known as "A Complaint against Blacksmiths."²⁸ The questions asked of this anonymous piece, which survives only in the form of an obscure manuscript addition to an earlier collection of unrelated material, concentrate on the recovery of its "affiliations"—a word that figures both explicitly and implicitly in much of Salter's later work—and stress that "the business of attempting recovery in this case illustrates particularly well the nature of the problems often set for us by medieval vernacular texts, in which an impression of strong but unlocalized life urges us to work towards reducing some of the uncertainties of authorship, intention and status."²⁹

Sensitivity to such impressions of "strong but unlocalized life" seems perhaps the most characteristic feature of Salter's scholarly work, prompting the various directions in which research was to take her and drawing forth the tough analyses and arguments that were to be articulated in her writings. For her colleagues and students and for the audiences of her lectures, this receptivity to the life of medieval texts was immediately and powerfully infectious, all the more so when communicated by someone of her zest and personal warmth. For readers of her published work the breadth and vigor of her engagement with the texts she studied are still palpable and provocative.

Notes

1. Pearsall, ed. *Essays in Memory of Elizabeth Salter*, includes a memoir by Derek Pearsall and a bibliography of Elizabeth Salter's writings. The latter is reprinted in Salter, *English and International*, 353–54.

2. Some other products of this system are considered by D. S. Brewer in his preface to *Medieval Literature and Historical Inquiry*, vii.

3. For an account of Bedford College's early years, see Tuke, *History of Bedford College for Women*. In the 1980s, by which time it was no longer a women's college, Bedford merged with another school of the University of London, Royal Holloway College, and now (as a mixed-sex college) forms part of what is known as Royal Holloway, University of London.

4. See Gillian Sutherland, "The Plainest Principles of Justice," 35–56.

5. Other graduate students in London at approximately the same time included Marjory Morgan (also at Bedford), working on an edition of Rolle's *Meditations on the Passion;* Geoffrey Shepherd, completing an M.A. thesis titled "Medieval Lyrics with Special Reference to the Devotion of Our Lady" (see D. S. Brewer, "Geoffrey Thomas Shepherd, 1918–1982," in Oizumi and Takamiya, *Medieval English Studies,* 294–99); Claude Luttrell, working on "The Scandinavian Element in some NW Midland Alliterative Poems"; and Randolph Quirk, beginning M.A. and later Ph.D. research on diphthongal spellings in Old English. Details of these projects are contained in the minutes of the Higher Degrees Sub-Committee of the Board of Studies in English, University of London (UL Archives AC 8/20/1/3–4).

6. Hodgson, *Deonise hid diuinite, The Cloud of Unknowing,* and *The Orcherd of Syon.*

7. Salter, *Nicholas Love's "Myrrour of the Blessed Lyf of Jesu Christ"*; Zeeman, "Nicholas Love"; Zeeman, "Continuity in Middle English Devotional Prose"; Zeeman, "Punctuation in an Early Manuscript of Love's *Mirror*"; Zeeman, "Continuity and Change in Middle English Versions of the *Meditationes vitae Christi.*"

8. See Chambers, *Nicholas Harpsfield's Life of Sir Thomas More.*

9. Kane taught at University College and later at Royal Holloway College and King's College; see the biographical details in Kennedy, Waldron, and Wittig, *Medieval English Studies Presented to George Kane.* Regarding Mabel Day, see, for instance, her edition of *English Text of the Ancrene Riwle*; Steele and Day, *Mum and the Sothsegger;* and Steele and Day, *English Poems of Charles d'Orleans.*

10. Chambers and Daunt, *Book of London English;* Beatrice White was appointed lecturer in 1939, reader in 1945, and professor in 1967, before retiring in 1969; see Sondheimer, *Castle Adamant in Hampstead.* Other members of Westfield at this time included the ecclesiastical historian Rosalind Hill, appointed lecturer in 1937, reader in 1955, and to a personal chair in 1971.

11. See Pearsall and Waldron, *Medieval Literature and Civilization.*

12. According to the Newnham College Register, Salter was Marion Kennedy Student in 1951 and Gamble Student in 1952. She received a Cambridge M.A. in 1954. She held the Pfeiffer Research Fellowship at Girton from 1955 onward.

13. For her work in new areas, see Zeeman, "Two Middle English Versions of a Prayer to the Sacrament"; Zeeman, "*Piers Plowman* and the Pilgrimage to Truth."

14. As listed in the *Cambridge University Reporter* for the years 1954–61.

15. This approach to teaching was an interest to be developed in the "Sussex tapes" and commercial recordings for Argo, which Elizabeth Salter undertook in the 1960s and 1970s.

16. For some discussion of teaching in Cambridge during this period, see the recollections of Daiches, "Place of English Studies in the Sussex Scheme," 81–99, especially 85–86. For a brief history of Cambridge Middle English scholarship, see Richard Beadle, "Medieval English Studies in Cambridge," in Oizumi and Takamiya, *Medieval English Studies,* 50–55.

17. Salter, *Chaucer: "The Knight's Tale" and "The Clerk's Tale"; Piers Plowman: An Introduction.*

18. The committee reported in 1963. The "new" universities that developed in the light of the Robbins Report were York (1963), Lancaster (1964), Warwick (1965), East Anglia (1963),

Essex (1964), Sussex (1961), and Kent (1965). (Keele's charter was granted in 1962, but it began life, as the University College of North Staffordshire in 1950).

19. Phrases are quoted from the University's Undergraduate Prospectus for 1964–65.

20. Salter, "Alliterative Revival"; Salter, "Piers Plowman and 'The Simonie'"; Salter, "'Troilus and Criseyde': A Reconsideration."

21. The general introduction appears in all the volumes of the York Medieval Texts.

22. Salter with Pearsall, *Piers Plowman: Selections from the C-Text*.

23. See Pearsall, "Teaching Medieval Studies," 217–30.

24. Salter with Parkes, introduction to *Troilus and Criseyde*.

25. Salter, "Manuscripts of Nicholas Love's *Myrrour of the Blessed Lyf of Jesu Christ* and Related Texts."

26. Salter with Pearsall, "Pictorial Illustration of Late Medieval Poetic Texts."

27. Rodney Hilton's work on the English peasantry in the Middle Ages, published in the 1960s and 1970s, seems to have been one notable influence; David Aers's work on Langland, both while a graduate student at York and afterward, another.

28. Salter, "Timeliness of *Wynnere and Wastoure*"; Salter, "Complaint against Blacksmiths."

29. Salter, "A Complaint against Blacksmiths," in *English and International*, 199.

Select Bibliography of Works by Elizabeth Salter

As Elizabeth Zeeman

"Nicholas Love: A Fifteenth-Century Translator." *Review of English Studies*, n.s., 6 (1955): 113–27.

"Continuity in Middle English Devotional Prose." *Journal of English and Germanic Philology* 55 (1956): 417–22.

"Punctuation in an Early Manuscript of Love's *Mirror.*" *Review of English Studies*, n.s., 7 (1956): 11–18.

"Continuity and Change in Middle English Versions of the *Meditationes vitae Christi.*" *Medium Aevum* 26 (1957): 25–31.

"Two Middle English Versions of a Prayer to the Sacrament." *Archiv* 194 (1957): 113–21.

"*Piers Plowman* and the Pilgrimage to Truth." *Essays and Studies* 11 (1958): 1–16.

As Elizabeth Salter

Chaucer: "The Knight's Tale" and "The Clerk's Tale." Studies in English Literature, 5. London: Edward Arnold, 1962.

Piers Plowman: An Introduction. Oxford: Blackwell, 1963.

"The Alliterative Revival." *Modern Philology* 64 (1966): 146–50, 233–37.

"'Troilus and Criseyde': A Reconsideration." In *Patterns of Love and Courtesy: Essays in Memory of C. S. Lewis,* edited by John Lawlor. London: Edward Arnold, 1966.

Editor with Derek Pearsall. *Piers Plowman: Selections from the C-Text,* by William Langland. York Medieval Texts. London: Edward Arnold, 1967.

"Piers Plowman and 'The Simonie.'" *Archiv* 203 (1967): 241–54.

"Medieval Poetry and the Figural View of Reality." Sir Israel Gollancz Memorial Lecture, British Academy, 1968. *Proceedings of the British Academy* 54 (1968): 73–92.

"Medieval Poetry and the Visual Arts." *Essays and Studies* 22 (1969): 16–32.

"*Piers Plowman* and the Visual Arts." In *Encounters: Essays on Literature and the Visual Arts,* edited by John Dixon Hunt. London: Studio Vista, 1971.

"Courts and Courtly Love" and "The Medieval Lyric." In *The Medieval World,* edited by D. Daiches and A. Thorlby. London: Aldus, 1973.

With Derek Pearsall. *Landscapes and Seasons of the Medieval World.* London: Elek, 1973.

Nicholas Love's "Myrrour of the Blessed Lyf of Jesu Christ." Analecta Cartusiana, 10. Salzburg: Institut für englische Sprache und Literatur, Universität Salzburg, 1974.

With M. B. Parkes. Introduction. *Troilus and Criseyde: A Facsimile of Corpus Christi College, Cambridge, MS 61.* Cambridge: D. S. Brewer, 1978.

"The Timeliness of *Wynnere and Wastoure.*" *Medium Aevum* 47 (1978): 40–65.

"A Complaint against Blacksmiths." *Literature and History* 5 (1979): 194–215. Reprinted in *English and International*, 199–214.

"Langland and the Contexts of *Piers Plowman.*" *Essays and Studies* 32 (1979): 19–25.

With Derek Pearsall. "Pictorial Illustration of Late Medieval Poetic Texts: The Role of the Frontispiece or Prefatory Picture." In *Medieval Iconography and Narrative: A Symposium,* edited by Flemming G. Andersen et al. Odense, Den.: Odense University Press, 1980.

"The Manuscripts of Nicholas Love's *Myrrour of the Blessed Lyf of Jesu Christ* and Related Texts." In *Middle English Prose: Essays on Bibliographical Problems,* edited by A. S. G. Edwards and D. Pearsall. New York: Garland, 1981.

"Mappings." In *Fourteenth-Century English Poetry: Contexts and Readings.* Edited by Derek Pearsall and Nicolette Zeeman. Oxford: Clarendon Press, 1983.

English and International: Studies in the Literature, Art, and Patronage of Medieval England. Edited by Derek Pearsall and Nicolette Zeeman. Cambridge: Cambridge University Press, 1988.

"The Annunciation to the Shepherds in Later Medieval Art and Drama." In *English and International*, 272–92.

Works Cited

Brewer, D. S. Preface to *Medieval Literature and Historical Inquiry: Essays in Honor of Derek Pearsall*, edited by David Aers. Cambridge: D. S. Brewer, 2000.

Chambers, R. W., ed. *Nicholas Harpsfield's Life of Sir Thomas More.* EETS, o.s., 186. London: Oxford University Press, 1932.

Chambers, R. W., and Marjorie Daunt, eds. *A Book of London English, 1384–1425.* Oxford: Clarendon Press, 1931.

Daiches, D. "The Place of English Studies in the Sussex Scheme." In *The Idea of a New University: An Experiment in Sussex,* edited by D. Daiches, 2d ed. London: Andre Deutsch, 1970.

Day, Mabel, ed. *The English Text of the Ancrene Riwle . . . from Cotton MS Nero A. xiv.* EETS, o.s., 225. London: Oxford University Press, 1952.

Day, Mabel, and Robert Steele, eds. *Mum and the Sothsegger.* EETS, o.s., 199. London: Oxford University Press, 1936.

Hodgson, Phyllis, ed. *The Cloud of Unknowing and Book of Privy Counselling.* EETS, o.s., 218. London: Oxford University Press, 1944.

———, ed. *Deonise hid diuinite.* EETS, o.s., 231. London: Oxford University Press, 1955.

———, ed. *The Orchard of Syon.* EETS, o.s., 258. London: Oxford University Press, 1966.

Kennedy, Edward Donald, Ronald Waldron, and Joseph S. Wittig. *Medieval English Studies Presented to George Kane.* Woodbridge: D. S. Brewer, 1988.

Oizumi, Akio, and Toshiyuki Takamiya, eds. *Medieval English Studies, Past and Present.* Tokyo: Tokyo Centre for Medieval Studies, 1990.

Pearsall, Derek. "Teaching Medieval Studies: The York Experience." In *The Past and Future of Medieval Studies,* edited by J. H. van Enghen. Notre Dame, Ind.: University of Notre Dame Press, 1994.

Pearsall, Derek, ed. *Essays in Memory of Elizabeth Salter.* Leeds Studies in English, n.s., 14. Leeds: University of Leeds, School of English, 1983.

Pearsall, Derek, and R. A. Waldron. *Medieval Literature and Civilization: Studies in Memory of G. N. Garmonsway.* London: Athlone Press, 1969.

Sondheimer, Janet. *Castle Adamant in Hampstead: A History of Westfield College: 1882–1982.* London: Westfield College, 1983.

Steele, Robert, and Mable Day, eds. *The English Poems of Charles d'Orleans.* EETS, o.s., 215, 220. London: Oxford University Press, 1941, 1946.

Sutherland, Gillian. "The Plainest Principles of Justice: The University of London and the Higher Education of Women." In *The University of London and the World of Learning 1836–1986,* edited by F. M. L. Thompson. London: Hambledon Press, 1990.

Tuke, Margaret J. *A History of Bedford College for Women, 1849–1937.* London: Oxford University Press, 1939.

CHAPTER 60

Rosemary Estelle Woolf (1925–1978)
A Serious Scholar

JOYCE BORO

Rosemary Woolf was born on 27 December 1925 to Gladys Capua and C. M. Woolf. She grew up in Hampstead, London, and attended Saint George's School, a small Anglican boarding school in Ascot. Excelling in hockey and show jumping, as well as performing very well academically, Woolf was an active member of her school. She was a clever and responsible girl, and her father was very enthusiastic about her decision to attend university. She was the first woman in her family to do so. Her father died on New Year's Eve of 1942, not living long enough to see Woolf's success, but it is unlikely that he doubted her potential: his will provided amply for Woolf's education and guaranteed her financial independence.[1]

Woolf entered Saint Hugh's Hall, Oxford, in the autumn of 1943 to read English.[2] At that time Saint Hugh's was one of four Oxford "colleges" that admitted women.[3] In the 1940s men and women attended separate colleges, but the courses and quality of education were identical: Woolf went to the same lectures, took the same exams, and was awarded the same degree as the men in her year.[4] But while academic matters remained equal, certain societies, like the Oxford Union and the University Drama Society, were still closed to women, and women and their colleges were subject to special university regulations.[5] Rachel Trickett, Woolf's lifelong friend, comments: "Life for women undergraduates in the 1930s was not very different from life for women undergraduates in the 1950s. Chaperonage had been dropped, girls were not confined to their own colleges either socially or academically . . . but [the women's colleges'] own gate rules were often stricter than those of the men's colleges, [and] their atmosphere was inevitably more protective, sometimes more defensive. To someone like myself, who had come up as an undergraduate during the Second World

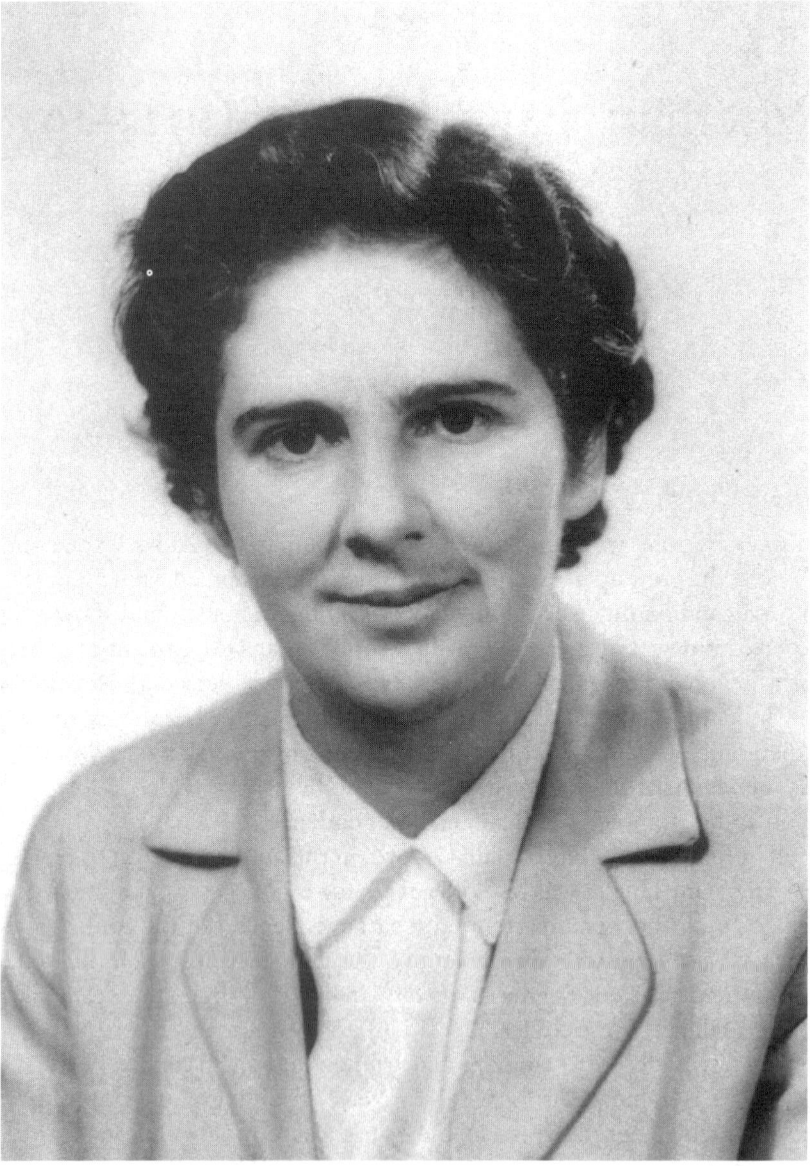

War, there was, however, no sense of academic restriction and certainly no feeling of discrimination against women."[6]

Woolf and her female peers, such as Trickett, were fortunate to have been in Oxford during the war: at that time the most oppressive restrictions were not gender related. In *Saint Hugh's: One Hundred Years of Women's Education in Oxford,* Woolf's contemporaries reminisce about strict food and clothes rationing; frequent air raids; blackouts that forced all libraries (with the exception of the Radcliffe Camera) to shut early; fire-watching duties; and the need to carry gas masks everywhere, even to lectures.[7] Most of the men resident in Oxford in the early forties were not students or dons, but soldiers, medics, the ill, and those exempted from service. With so many of the university's men at war, the female population within the university must have seemed greater and more secure. Because of the absence of male dons, women were increasingly asked to examine, supervise, or take on university administrative duties.[8] Although these activities were not formally sanctioned, the women who performed them helped to create the atmosphere that Trickett remembers. This positive image of women doing the same work as men, and doing it well, also may have encouraged young women such as Woolf to seriously contemplate academic careers.

Also because of the war, Saint Hugh's and other college and university buildings were assigned for military use. Until her final year Woolf did not live in college but resided in Holywell Manor, sharing a set of rooms with Heather Martin-Hawking, another English student.[9] Saint Hugh's was used as a military hospital, and it was closed to students, with the exception of the library, which was shared by students, doctors, patients, and soldiers.[10] While unable to enjoy traditional college life, other social and academic aspects of Oxford were open to Woolf and her peers. Woolf was enthusiastic about film and drama. She often went to the Walton Street Cinema (now the Phoenix Picture House) and took advantage of the many active theater troupes in Oxford, including the drama society at Saint Hugh's. Clubs and societies of all sorts thrived, including the English Society, to which Woolf belonged, and the Socratic Club, whose meetings she attended regularly. In the Socratic Club Woolf met C. S. Lewis, with whom she was very impressed and whose lectures she attended. She also went to lectures by J. R. R. Tolkien on Old English literature and Lord David Cecil on Shakespeare.[11] Within college her tutors were Mary Seaton and Daisy Clark, and she may have been instructed by Hugo Dyson at Merton, to whom many women from Saint Hugh's were sent.[12] On a more personal level, during these years Woolf was undergoing a profound spiritual change. It was while at Saint Hugh's that she converted from Judaism to the Anglican faith. She was instructed by Dick Milford, the vicar of the university church, Saint Mary's. Woolf was baptized and confirmed in Christ Church Cathedral on 14 June 1945, and she remained a devout Anglican until her death.[13]

With the autumn of 1945 came a return to the college premises for Saint Hugh's, finally allowing Woolf and others in her year to experience real college life. That year also signaled the beginning of very harsh, cramped conditions at the university. From

1945 to 1947, on top of regular admissions, former servicemen flooded to Oxford to resume abandoned studies, as did those who had deferred entrance during the war. The atmosphere changed as Woolf and her peers were joined by new, older, and much more experienced students. Overcrowding was endemic. Pubs, lecture theatres, and colleges were full, and Oxford was revitalized; yet simultaneously food, clothing, fuel, and coal shortages persisted. Colleges were unable to cope with their inflated numbers and were plagued by a shortage of teachers, books, library desks, and lecture rooms.[14] As the Oxford correspondent for the *Somerville College Report* (1945/46) observed, "Queues form before 9 o'clock at the doors of all the libraries; by 9.05 every seat is taken."[15] This was the climate of Woolf's final year at Oxford, but despite problems getting the books she needed and finding places to study and the discomfort of being crammed into cold, damp lecture theaters, she successfully completed her degree in the spring of 1946, achieving a second class.

Over the course of the next two years she remained at Saint Hugh's, studying for the degree of B.Litt., which she received in 1948. Her thesis, supervised by C. L. Wrenn, was an edition of the Old English poem *Juliana*. It was published by Methuen in 1955.[16] The edition was intended to replace Strunk's of 1904, which was "now antiquated" and out of print.[17] The introduction to *Juliana* explores the manuscript, dialect, date, author, runic signature, sources, and literary and grammatical style. It "presents a clear and readable account of present-day opinion on these matters."[18] Where Woolf diverges from prior scholarship is in dating the poem in the ninth century: earlier editors opted for a date in the eighth. While the revised date has its basis in Kenneth Sisam's work, Woolf's arguments, based on grammatical, linguistic, and literary evidence, are her own.[19] The edition itself is conservative and accurate, with several new useful emendations, and the glossary is supplemented by an appendix that treats more problematic words.[20] As J. Turville-Petre concludes, "[T]he edition is serviceable and it provides a welcome reassessment in light of modern knowledge."[21]

By the time the edition emerged, Woolf had begun her first job and published two articles.[22] The influx of students in 1945–47, as noted earlier, affected all British universities as they struggled to find enough well-qualified instructors for all the new pupils. Academic employment rates rose to match the growing student bodies, and in 1948 Woolf was one of many young, talented scholars to be hired by University College, Hull.[23] She was first appointed as assistant lecturer in 1948 and in 1950 was promoted to the post of lecturer, which she filled until 1961. At around the same time Hull also employed Rachel Trickett, Lucy Brown, George Hunter, and Alastair Smart, who, with Woolf, quickly formed a close-knit social unit. They were all young and talented and greatly invigorated their department while motivating one another and their pupils.[24] For Woolf these years at Hull were joyous and inspirational, filled with long walks in the countryside, trips to the Continent, and productive academic work. According to Rachel Trickett in the 1950s Hull was a good place to be a female academic. She writes, "The eight years during which I taught at the then University College of Hull revealed no trace of prejudice against women as teachers or as lecturers."[25]

While Woolf spent twelve good years in Hull, surrounded by intimate friends, her heart remained in Oxford: vacations were spent in the Bodleian and socializing with Oxford friends. She must have been pleased when she was hired by Somerville College, Oxford, in 1961 as an English tutor.[26] As in Hull, Woolf was again surrounded by gifted individuals who were friends and supportive colleagues. For most of her time at Somerville she lived in a handsome set of rooms at college, with a bedroom and a spacious and bright study. Her corridor was lined with bookshelves overflowing with detective fiction, one of her great passions. It was only toward the end of her life that she moved out of the college premises to a house in North Oxford, which she shared with Lotte Labowsky. At Somerville Woolf taught Old and Middle English literature and the history of the English language. She also lectured in the English faculty—her lectures on *Piers Plowman* were especially memorable. A former student writes: "There was not a great deal of first-class criticism on Langland in print at that date, and her lectures were expertly prepared and seemed almost ready for publication. In 1968 she had published her 'Tearing of the Pardon' and was perfectly equipped, especially through her work on the religious lyric, to approach Langland in the most brilliant and well-informed ways. I think these lectures might have evolved into a major book."[27]

Woolf's corpus consists of two books, one edition, and seventeen articles. Not only was she instrumental in the evolution of medieval literary studies into a modern discipline, but her articles and books continue to be appreciated as valuable contributions to the field. Woolf's work exhibits a conviction that a literary work is a cultural artifact, inextricably linked to other art and literary forms and to contemporary scientific, religious, and philosophical systems of belief. Woolf was, of course, not the only critic of her time who felt that a greater historical understanding could lead to a more profound literary appreciation of literature: the work of C. S. Lewis, E. K. Chambers, J. A. W. Bennett, and Rosemund Tuve is very relevant in this context. But Woolf's approach is broader: she embraces the formal, doctrinal, and historical qualities of literature equally. "Her application of extra-textual learning is always subservient to the text itself: she uses it to develop an understanding of the period, to dispel readings based on historical ignorance or misunderstanding, and, fundamentally, as the soundest basis from which to attempt literary judgements."[28] The art historian Aby Warburg was an important influence on Woolf's scholarship.[29] Woolf shared Warburg's interest in iconography and interdisciplinarity, and as it did for Warburg, European art, religion, philosophy, and sociology provided her with the detailed cultural awareness that formed the lens through which she examined literature.[30] Woolf differs from Warburg in that she never neglects formal or stylistic analysis: for her the textual and extratextual are neither distinct nor separable.

It is in her first major book, *The English Religious Lyric in the Middle Ages,* that the full extent of her potential and her critical methodology is apparent. This book is remarkable for its fresh approach to the lyric, which combines an evaluation of the lyrics' poetic aspects with a discussion of the cultural and theological matrix that instigated their development and evolution. The two aspects are inextricably linked: the book "combines a history of the lyric with a history of Christian spirituality in Western Europe in such a way as to make them interdependent and mutually illuminating."[31]

Woolf's definition of the lyric distinguishes this book from other studies of the genre, as it limits both the focus and the range of works discussed. She proposes a definition of the lyrics "in terms of content and not of form" and concludes that "[w]hen approached in this way the lyrics can immediately be recognised as meditative poems."[32] By "meditative" she means poems that evoke a deep religious response in the reader; in contrast to metaphysical poetry, where the focus is on the poets' feelings. The lyrics are neither purely narrative nor versified prayers nor carols that "are public, celebratory poems, designed for singing, in contrast to the religious lyric, which was private poetry."[33] Furthermore, nonmeditative lyrics and carols and meditative lyrics have different sources, influences, and effects, and as these are the aspects of the lyric that Woolf seeks to explore, only the meditative lyrics fall under the rubric of her book. While her definition of the lyric as meditative has occasionally been criticized, it is what allows her to investigate the lyrics in such depth: "'Meditative' . . . enables Miss Woolf to bring out a quality, perhaps the central quality, in a large number of indisputably fine poems."[34]

In light of the absence of earlier scholarly material, the magnitude of Woolf's project is striking. Of course, the publication of Carlton Brown's lyric anthologies, R. L. Greene's edition of the carols, and especially *The Index of Middle English Verse* by Brown and Rossell Hope Robbins did much to make her work possible, and Louis Martz's *The Poetry of Meditation* greatly influenced Woolf's concept of the lyric.[35] We must not forget, however, that in 1955 the only substantial work on the medieval genre was George Kane's.[36] An established tradition of literary criticism for the lyric did not yet exist: works such as Woolf's, Douglas Gray's, and Peter Dronke's were still in the making, and so in many respects Woolf had to pave her own way.[37]

The next few years were taken up by teaching duties and the composition and publication of several articles on Old and Middle English literature. It was not until she was granted a leave of absence from Hull in the academic year 1960–61, which she spent in Oxford, that her book could be finished. By May 1961 Woolf's description of the project matches the book that we know: "The aim of the present book is to discuss the lyric as part of the literature of medieval devotion, and in particular to trace its origins in the theology and theories of meditation of the twelfth century, to distinguish its meditative function, and to define its characteristic qualities against the background of the contemporary lyric in Latin, French and Italian."[38] In the final book Woolf posits that meditativeness is the central quality of the lyrics, deriving from a combined appeal to, and use of, emotion, reason, and will. Woolf uses this quality to explain their style, measure their effect, identify their sources and analogues, and explore their theological and doctrinal roots. Reading the lyrics as meditations necessitates a huge degree of cultural displacement for the modern reader, and such a leap can only be made through an understanding of the doctrine informing the poems: this is provided. Never afraid to articulate the distance between us and the poetry, she uses these sites of difference to gain a greater understanding of the period and the literature: as the gap is defined, medieval culture, and thus the literature, becomes closer and more readily comprehensible. Woolf writes, "[A] history of the religious lyric that seeks to be comprehensive must become in part a history of medieval meditation and devotion."[39] Literary appreciation and evaluation of the lyrics necessitates an awareness of religious history. In rooting the lyrics in the tradition of Latin meditation, she argues that their aims are similar, and so to be poetically successful they must be effective meditations; thus, if we cannot evaluate a meditation we cannot appraise a lyric. Stylistic factors typical of the genre are also related to the meditative tradition: their plain style, unadorned language, unity of theme, simple content, and avoidance of intellectual ideas link them to, and contribute to their effectiveness as, meditations. Both this relationship between style and effect and the cultural, linguistic, and theological factors that lead the lyrics to exhibit these stylistic features are explored in this book.

The English Mystery Plays (1972) increased Woolf's scholarly reputation of serious erudition and thoroughness. The reviews were unanimously positive, and the book continues to have an important place in medieval drama studies. When one reviewer wrote, "*The English Mystery Plays* will clearly take its place beside the classical works of reference on the medieval drama library shelf, for the value of its presentation of the cultural context, and is in no danger of being displaced," he was not mistaken.[40] The book is divided into two main parts, followed by a concluding section and appendices. The first part provides the background material necessary to appreciate the plays, which are explored in detail in the second part.

The book begins by illustrating the impact of liturgical drama on the mystery plays; but while earlier scholars argued that the latter evolved out of the former, Woolf concludes that while the liturgy itself was crucial to the development of the mystery plays, liturgical drama was not. Liturgical drama served a different function, and its role, and the role of other literary genres and theological texts, is used to shed light on the mystery plays and to explain their position within medieval society. Nonliturgical drama is taken up in chapter 2. By examining a vast range of disparate evidence, Woolf shows how drama was interpreted by an early medieval audience. Knowledge of classical drama in the Middle Ages is surveyed to show that the mystery plays had a unique literary identity—they were perceived as more than an extension of liturgical drama. Here as elsewhere Woolf's range of sources and examples is impressive, and this chapter is invaluable for gathering such a large corpus of material on medieval attitudes to drama. In many ways the fifth chapter complements the second: it is an insightful and useful survey of English and Continental objections to drama, from eleventh-century theologians, through the Lollards, to Protestant Reformers. Aside from its extensiveness, what distinguishes this chapter from earlier, similar work is that from those condemnations and criticisms Woolf draws conclusions regarding aspects of audience response, performance history and conditions, clerical decorum, and the value of images in religious education. Chapters 3 and 4 are characterized by the same high standard of erudition and scholarship. In the former she discusses twelfth-century, noncyclical, European drama, arguing against common practices of categorizing the plays according to their language, musicality, or the time and place of performance. Moving closer to the mystery plays themselves, chapter 4 explores the development of the cycles offering probable explanations for the biblical episodes they habitually include. From this initial section the importance of iconography to understand the plays surfaces. Woolf writes, "The conception of the plays as speaking pictures is therefore useful in enabling us to reconstruct the medieval understanding of biblical drama, and is helpful to us nowadays as is any definition of a genre to which a given work belongs. It cannot of course replace the critic's investigation of the literary skill of the authors, but it defines expectation, the expectation of what to find, and, even more importantly, of what not to find."[41]

It is, appropriately, with these words that the first part of the book concludes and a discussion of the plays themselves begins. The plays are considered according to theme or matter, rather than cycle. Such an approach has the inherent trap of treating the plays as discrete units, which they are not, yet Woolf avoids this snare masterfully, discussing how each play's cyclic position controls interpretation and dramatic effect. While this thematic division is not original, the detail and thoroughness with which the plays are discussed certainly is.[42] The plays are subjected to close, rigorous analysis, with attention to iconography, sources, and literary components such as structure, characterization, performance, and dialogue. The method is comparative and detailed as she demonstrates how the interplay of language and iconography elicits specific audience responses. The cycles are compared to each other, to Continental drama, and to other literary and artistic genres. Through the contrasts and parallels that emerge, dramatic effect, the advantages and disadvantages to the varied approaches, and medieval attitudes to drama, art, and religion are illuminated. The motion is one of ebb and flow: she moves away from the plays to explore other artistic and religious representations, advancing and explaining their allegorical interpretations and relevant theological and cultural points, and then she returns to the plays with a sharpened focus, reading the plays from a new, heightened perspective. As in *Lyrics,* the literary and doctrinal qualities of the drama are not divorced from each other, and neither aspect is privileged. Woolf "indicate[s] the vast mass of material which is common not only to the mystery plays but to the instructional and devotional writings of the late medieval period."[43] The book ends by offering general observations on the four cycles and by discussing the decline of the plays. Both the deterioration of the literary and dramatic qualities of the plays and the drop in performances are explored as she describes how ideas of classical decorum and humanist and Protestant ideas adversely affected the plays.

Woolf's literary approach is typified by a fascination with sources, analogues, and iconographic detail. Characteristic of her work is the way she continually and adeptly contextualizes literature by examining contemporary and antecedent European literature, art, culture, and religion, allowing different genres and disciplines to illuminate one another: "On the whole, Miss Woolf sees much more than pictorial representations; she always looks for the parallel, the analogy, the deeper significance of the apparently simple and superficial, though she is not carried to extremes."[44] Equally praiseworthy is Woolf's attitude to earlier scholarship. She is neither defensive, self-effacing, nor condescending to those with different opinions and approaches. From her writing one gets the sense that she has read and carefully considered all that has come before, and without being dismissive or repetitive she shows how her knowledge supplements and moves beyond received interpretations, providing fresh evidence and new explanations. This attitude was equally characteristic of her teaching methodology and behavior in scholarly circles. In academic gatherings she would listen attentively, ponder, and then speak. Her words were serious, measured, rarely negative, and generally constructive. Students remember her similarly in lectures and tutorials, treating them and other scholars with the utmost respect.

Colleagues, students, and friends all remember her as a serious woman and a serious scholar. In speaking to those who knew her, "very serious" and "quite shy" are common refrains. Yet while she was quiet, humble, and very private, she is also remembered as friendly and supportive to her colleagues, with a great laugh and intense, expressive eyes. Work was her priority, and she did work hard, but she had a tremendous capacity for fun and took time to enjoy life. Animals and children were known to bring out a rarely seen giggly, playful side in her. She was very fond of travel, cinema, and theatre, and holidays frequently involved research trips to churches and cathedrals where she would examine images down to their most minute details. Detective fiction was a great passion: former students and colleagues vividly recall its prominent place on her bookshelves. Although she had an affluent upbringing, Woolf lived modestly, enjoying the simple pleasures of life. Her final years were plagued by illness, and she died of cancer on 13 April 1978. Despite the emotional and physical pain she experienced, she never complained, rarely discussed her condition, and she worked until she was physically unable to, even having students visit her at home when she was unable to make it into college. As a testament to her academic and personal strength, nearly twenty-five years after her death Woolf and her work are still respected and esteemed, and her reputation as a serious scholar and as a serious woman remains intact.

Notes

I would like to thank Pauline Adams, John Bowers, Katherine Duncan-Jones, and Douglas Gray, without whom this essay could not have been written. All errors and misinterpretations are, however, my own.

1. Spevack-Husmann, "Rosemary Woolf (1925–1978)," 339–440.
2. Saint Hugh's Hall was later to become Saint Hugh's College. The women's "colleges" were societies until 1959. See Howarth, "Women," 352; Adams, *Somerville for Women,* 266–67; Brittain, *Women at Oxford,* 238.
3. The other three were Lady Margaret Hall, Somerville, and Saint Hilda's.
4. On how women achieved these rights, see Howarth, "Women," 348–51; Adams, *Somerville for Women,* 265; Byrne and Mansfield, *Somerville College,* 57–71; R. Trickett, "Women's

Education," 7; Kemp, "Early History of Saint Hugh's College," 15–47; Rogers, *Degrees by Degrees*, 105–7.

5. For specific examples, see Howarth, "Women," 355ff.; R. Trickett, "Women's Education," 9; Adams, *Somerville for Women*, 265, 272.

6. R. Trickett, "Women's Education," 9.

7. West, "Reminiscences of Seven Decades," 130ff; Adams, *Somerville for Women*, 239–51.

8. R. Trickett, "Women's Education," 10. Female dons were allowed to serve on faculty boards and lecture under the auspices of the faculties as of 1920. Women had been lecturing before this date, however, because of shortages of suitable lecturers during the First World War. Howarth, "Women," 349; Rogers, *Degrees by Degrees*, 105–7.

9. West, "Reminiscences of Seven Decades," 125–26; Spevack-Husmann, "Rosemary Woolf (1925–1978)," 440.

10. West, "Reminiscences of Seven Decades," 125–26.

11. West, "Reminiscences of Seven Decades," 126; Spevack-Husmann, "Rosemary Woolf (1925–1978)," 440.

12. West, "Reminiscences of Seven Decades," 148–49.

13. Spevack-Husmann, "Rosemary Woolf (1925–1978)," 440.

14. West, "Reminiscences of Seven Decades,"141–49; Adams, *Somerville for Women*, 254.

15. Quoted in Adams, *Somerville for Women*, 255.

16. It was reprinted by the University of Exeter Press in 1977, 1981, and 1993.

17. Woolf, *Juliana*, v.

18. Dobbie, review of *Juliana*, 538.

19. Dobbie, review of *Juliana*, 538; Kenneth Sisam, "Cynewulf and His Poetry," Sir Israel Gollancz Memorial Lecture, in *Proceedings of the British Academy*, vol. 18 (London: Humphrey Milford Amen House, 1932).

20. For a detailed discussion of the emendations, see Dobbie, review of *Juliana*; Turville-Petre, review of *Juliana*.

21. Turville-Petre, review of *Juliana*, 58.

22. Fourteen out of Woolf's seventeen articles have been collected in *Art and Doctrine*. In Heather O'Donoghue's introduction she discusses each essay individually, explaining its impact on medieval studies. To do so here would only be repetitive and derivative. For an appraisal of some of the articles that differs from O'Donoghue's, see Frankis, review of *Art and Doctrine*. Many of Woolf's articles are deemed classic studies, and a glance at the bibliography of her works will reveal her impressive range of expertise.

23. It became Hull University in 1954. The student population at Hull was rapidly escalating: it went from 116 students in 1944–45 to 769 in 1948–49, the year Woolf was hired, to 917 in 1950–51. See Bamford, *University of Hull*, 148.

24. Spevack-Husmann, "Rosemary Woolf (1925–1978)," 440.

25. R. Trickett, "Women's Education," 13.

26. For information on Woolf's time at Somerville I am much beholden to Professor Katherine Duncan-Jones, who graciously showed me Woolf's old rooms and took the time to reminisce about Rosemary Woolf with me.

27. John Bowers, personal correspondence with the author, 14 March 2001. I am grateful to Bowers for his numerous informative e-mails on his memories of Woolf, who was his B.Phil. supervisor.

28. Heather O'Donoghue, introduction to *Art and Doctrine,* by Rosemary Woolf, x.

29. I would like to thank Professor Douglas Gray for alerting me to the importance of Warburg's work to Woolf's career, as well as for the time he took to talk and write to me about Woolf's life and career, providing me with invaluable information, references, and encouragement. On Warburg, see Ferretti, *Cassirer, Panofsky, and Warburg;* Gombrich, *Aby Warburg.*

30. Iconology developed from iconography, but the latter prescribes that the viewer seek to understand the symbolic and conceptual levels of the object's meaning through the images, rather than through study of the history of imagery or thematic representations.

31. Stevens, review of *The English Religious Lyric in the Middle Ages,* 74.

32. Woolf, *English Religious Lyric,* 3.

33. Woolf, *English Religious Lyric,* 385.

34. For criticisms and modifications, see Davies, review of *The English Religious Lyric in the Middle Ages;* Davies, review of *Themes and Images in the Middle English Religious Lyric;* Robbins, review of *The English Religious Lyric in the Middle Ages;* and Stevens, review of *The English Religious Lyric in the Middle Ages.* Quotation from Stevens, review of *The English Religious Lyric in the Middle Ages,* 74. Interestingly, to judge from two of Woolf's research proposals, the idea to focus on the meditativeness of the lyric came quite late. Cf. letter from Woolf to the president of Somerville College, Janet Vaughan, 27 February 1955, and "Present Research," Woolf's research proposal sent to Janet Vaughan at Somerville College, 17 May 1961. I am indebted to Pauline Adams, the librarian and archivist at Somerville College, for granting me access to these and other papers in Woolf's file.

35. Cf. Davies regarding the usefulness of these published works for Woolf's undertaking. Still, Rosemary also includes unprinted lyrics.

36. George Kane, *Middle English Literature: A Critical Study of the Romance, the Religious Lyrics, "Piers Plowman"* (London: Methuen, 1951).

37. Dronke, *Medieval Latin and the Rise of the European Love Lyric;* Dronke, *Medieval Lyric;* Dronke, *Medieval Poet and His World;* Gray, *Themes and Images in the Medieval English Religious Lyric.*

38. Woolf, "Present Research."

39. Woolf, *English Religious Lyric,* 13.

40. Denny, review of *The English Mystery Plays,* 84.

41. Woolf, *English Mystery Plays,* 101.

42. Denny, review of *The English Mystery Plays,* 85.

43. Barbara Raw, review of *The English Mystery Plays,* 344.

44. Rigby, review of *The English Mystery Plays,* 71.

Select Bibliography of Works by Rosemary Estelle Woolf

"The Devil in Old English Poetry." *Review of English Studies,* n.s., 4 (1953): 1–12.

Editor. *Juliana.* London: Methuen, 1955.

"The Lost Opening to the *Judith.*" *Modern Language Review* 50 (1955): 168–72.

"The Effect of Typology on the English Medieval Plays of Abraham and Isaac." *Speculum* 32 (1957): 802–25.

"Doctrinal Influences on *The Dream of the Rood.*" *Medium Aevum* 27 (1958): 137–53.

"Chaucer as Satirist in the General Prologue to the *Canterbury Tales.*" *Critical Quarterly* 1 (1959): 150–57.

"Some Non-Medieval Qualities of *Piers Plowman.*" *Essays in Criticism* 12 (1962): 111–25.
"The Theme of Christ the Lover-Knight in Medieval English Literature." *Review of English Studies,* n.s., 13 (1962): 1–16.
"The Fall of Man in Genesis B and the Mystere d'Adam." In *Studies in Old English Literature in Honor of Arthur G. Brodeur,* edited by Stanley B. Greenfield. Eugene: University of Oregon Press, 1963.
"Saints' Lives." In *Continuations and Beginnings: Studies in Old English Literature,* edited by Eric G. Stanley. London: Nelson, 1966.
The English Religious Lyric in the Middle Ages. Oxford: Clarendon Press, 1968.
"The Construction of *In a Fryht as Y Con Fare Fremede.*" *Medium Aevum* 38 (1969): 55–59.
"The Tearing of the Pardon." In *Piers Plowman: Critical Approaches,* edited by S. S. Hussey. London: Methuen; New York: Barnes and Noble, 1969.
"Later Poetry: The Popular Tradition." In *History of Literature in the English Language,* edited by W. F. Bolton, vol. 1. London: Barrie and Jenkins, 1970.
The English Mystery Plays. London: Routledge and Kegan Paul, 1972.
"The Influence of the Mystery Plays upon the Popular Tragedies of the 1560's." *Renaissance Drama,* n.s., 6 (1973): 89–105.
"English Imitations of the Homelia Origenis de Maria Magdalena." In *Chaucer and Middle English Studies in Honour of Rossel Hope Robbins,* edited by Beryl Rowland and Lloyd A. Duchemin. London: Allen and Unwin, 1974.
"*The Wanderer, The Seafarer,* and the Genre of *Planctus.*" In *Anglo-Saxon Poetry: Essays in Appreciation for John C. McGalliard,* edited by Lewis E. Nicholson, Dolores Warwick Frese, and John C. Gerber. Notre Dame, Ind.: University of Notre Dame Press, 1975.
"The Ideal of Men Dying with Their Lord in the *Germania* and in *The Battle of Maldon.*" *Anglo-Saxon England* 5 (1976): 63–81.
"Moral Chaucer and Kindly Gower." In *J. R. R. Tolkien, Scholar and Storyteller: Essays in Memoriam,* edited by Mary Salu, Robert T. Farrell, and Humphrey Carpenter. Ithaca, N.Y.: Cornell University Press, 1979.
Art and Doctrine: Essays On Medieval Literature. Edited by Heather O'Donoghue. London: Hambeldon Press, 1986.

Works Cited

Adams, Pauline. *Somerville for Women: An Oxford College, 1879–1993.* Oxford: Oxford University Press, 1996.
Bamford, T. N. *The University of Hull: The First Fifty Years.* Oxford: Oxford University Press, 1978.
Brittain, Vera. *The Women at Oxford: A Fragment of History.* London: Harrap, 1960.
Brown, Carlton. *Religious Lyrics of the Fifteenth Century.* Oxford: Clarendon Press, 1939.
——. *Religious Lyrics of the Fourteenth Century.* Oxford: Clarendon Press, 1924.
——, ed. *English Lyrics of the Thirteenth Century.* Oxford: Clarendon Press, 1932.
Brown, Carlton, and R. H. Robbins. *The Index of Middle English Verse.* New York: Columbia University Press, 1943.
Byrne, Muriel St. Clare, and Catherine Hope Godfrey Mansfield. *Somerville College, 1879–1921.* Oxford: Oxford University Press, 1922.
Davies, R. T. Review of *The English Religious Lyric in the Middle Ages,* by Rosemary Woolf. *Modern Language Review* 65 (1970): 365–67.

———. Review of *Themes and Images in the Middle English Religious Lyric,* by Douglas Gray. *Notes and Queries* 20 (1973): 299–301.
Denny, Neville. Review of *The English Mystery Plays,* by Rosemary Woolf. *Medium Aevum* 43 (1974): 84–87.
Dobbie, Elliott V. K. Review of *Juliana,* edited by Rosemary Woolf. *Modern Language Notes* 62 (1957): 538–39.
Dronke, Peter. *Medieval Latin and the Rise of the European Love Lyric.* Oxford: Oxford University Press, 1968.
———. *The Medieval Lyric.* Cambridge: Brewer, 1968.
———. *The Medieval Poet and His World.* Rome: Storia e Letteratura, 1984.
Ferretti, S. *Cassirer, Panofsky, and Warburg: Symbol, Art, and History.* Translated by R. Pierce. London: Yale University Press, 1989.
Frankis, John. Review of *Art and Doctrine: Essays on Medieval Literature,* by Rosemary Woolf. *Review of English Studies* 40 (1989): 399–400.
Gombrich, E. H. *Aby Warburg: An Intellectual Biography: With a Memoir on the History of the Library by F. Saxl.* London: Warburg Institute, 1970.
Gray, Douglas. *Themes and Images in the Medieval English Religious Lyric.* London: Routledge and Kegan Paul, 1972.
Greene, R. L., ed. *The Early English Carols.* Oxford: Clarendon Press, 1935.
Griffin, Penny, ed. *Saint Hugh's: One Hundred Years of Women's Education in Oxford.* London: Macmillan, 1986.
Howarth, Janet. "Women." In *The History of the University of Oxford,* edited by Brian Harrison, vol. 8. Oxford: Clarendon Press, 1994.
Kemp, Betty. "The Early History of Saint Hugh's College." In *Saint Hugh's: One Hundred Years of Women's Education in Oxford,* edited by Penny Griffin. London: Macmillan, 1986.
Martz, Louis. *The Poetry of Meditation: A Study in English Religious Literature of the Seventeenth Century.* New Haven: Yale University Press, 1954.
Raw, Barbara. Review of *The English Mystery Plays,* by Rosemary Woolf. *Notes and Queries* 20 (1973): 344–45.
Rigby, Marjory. Review of *The English Mystery Plays,* by Rosemary Woolf. *Review of English Studies* 25 (1974): 70–72.
Robbins, Rossell Hope. Review of *The English Religious Lyric in the Middle Ages,* by Rosemary Woolf. *Speculum* 45 (1970): 337–38.
Rogers, Annie M. A. H. *Degrees by Degrees: The Story of the Admission of Oxford Women Students to Membership of the University.* Oxford: Oxford University Press, 1938.
Somerville College. *Somerville College Register.* Oxford: Parchment, 1972.
Spevack-Husmann, Helga. "Rosemary Woolf (1925–1978)." In *Medieval Scholarship: Biographical Studies on the Formation of a Discipline,* edited by Helen Damico, vol. 2. New York: Garland, 1998.
Stevens, John. Review of *The English Religious Lyric in the Middle Ages,* by Rosemary Woolf. *Medium Aevum* 40 (1971): 72–74.
Trickett, M. R. "Memorial Service for Rosemary Estelle Woolf in Somerville College Chapel on 3 June 1978." Somerville College Archives.
Trickett, Rachel. "Rosemary Woolf's Obituary." *Times* (London). 19 April 1978, 18.
———. "Women's Education." In *Saint Hugh's: One Hundred Years of Women's Education in Oxford,* edited by Penny Griffin. London: Macmillan, 1986.

Turville-Petre, J. Review of *Juliana,* edited by Rosemary Woolf. *Medium Aevum* 26 (1957): 57–58.

West, Priscilla. "Reminiscences of Seven Decades." In *Saint Hugh's: One Hundred Years of Women's Education in Oxford,* edited by Penny Griffin. London: Macmillan, 1986.

Woolf, Rosemary. Letter from Rosemary Woolf to Janet Vaughan, president of Somerville College. 27 February 1955.

———. "Present Research." Research proposal sent to Janet Vaughan at Somerville College. 17 May 1961.

CHAPTER 61

Historian of Art (1928–)

ILENE H. FORSYTH

It started with stone. I remember the coolness of it as I sat on the marble floor of the basilica of San Apollinare Nuovo in Ravenna. The smooth, silken touch of a chancel screen also comes back vividly. I dared to stroke its relief panels when the fierce woman who guarded San Vitale was not looking. The stone, in varied form, was the frame for figures that were bedazzling to my young eyes. I had never seen or imagined anything like them. They appeared remote yet penetrating and oddly personal, for their eyes followed me insistently. They made me feel reverential as I moved through the spaces in which they hovered. These spaces seemed at once brilliant, because of the shimmer of the golden mosaics enveloping them, yet dark, because of the stern looks of their mysterious inhabitants.

It was the early fifties, and I was encountering Byzantine art for the first time. It was a surprise. I had recently graduated with an A.B. degree, having majored in English, and was on a *Wanderjahr* with young friends in Europe. I was not totally ignorant of the art of the western tradition. I had had a good number of history of art courses as a student at the University of Michigan. Though these classes had not included study of Byzantium, they had featured substantial doses of Western cathedrals. I had already visited the major ones and had spent a number of months in Paris, regularly frequenting the Louvre and luxuriating on occasion in the gorgeous stained glass of the Sainte Chapelle. In the usual way I had toured France, Germany, Austria, the Low Countries, England, and Italy, yet none of these experiences had turned me as irrevocably toward art as the days in Ravenna, where I felt for the first time totally enveloped by an expansive and expressive Byzantine space.

As I sat on the marble, I began making drawings of conch shells, doves, grapevines, hanging jewels, and lilting figures in ritual dances. My clumsy sketches helped me to

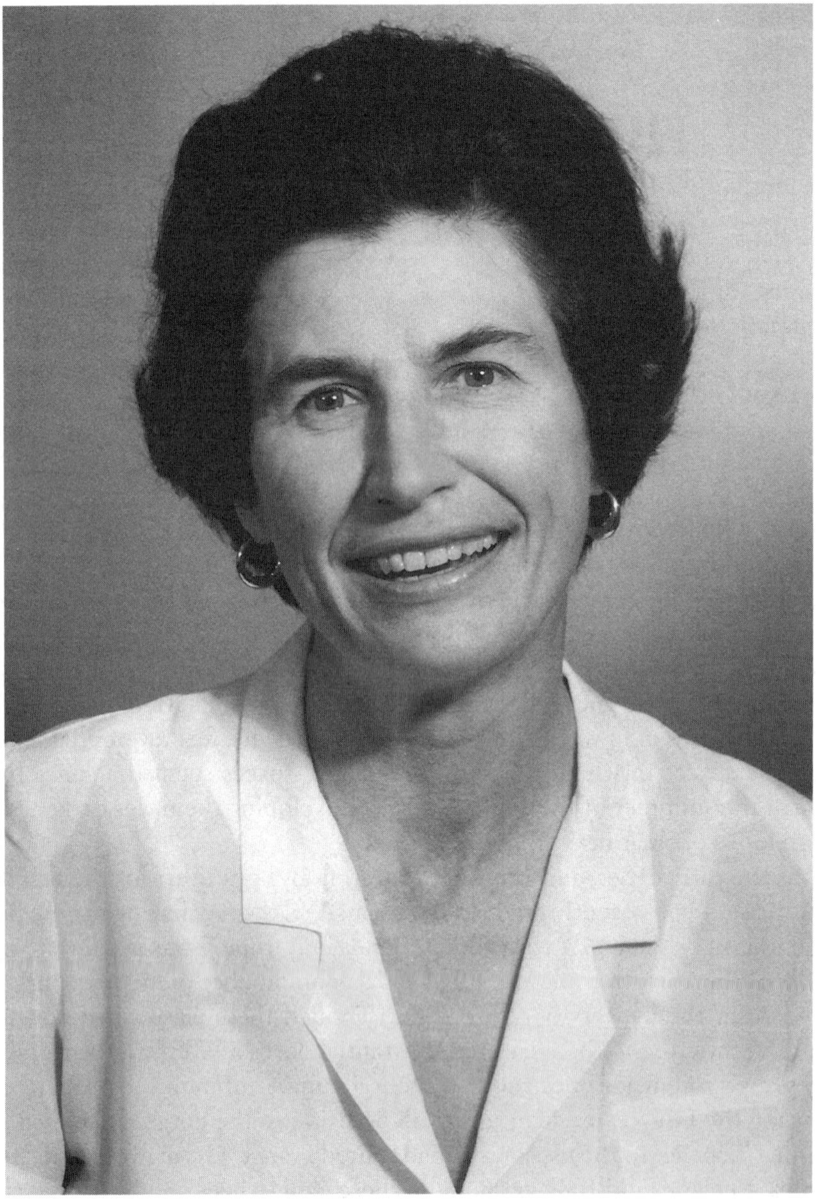

know them better. I felt it imperative to know what they meant. I had to learn the secret of their power to mesmerize. How had they functioned in their original context, and why did they still seem so strong? It was an emotional thing, of course, as critical decisions in life often are, yet I felt sure that at last I had found a goal worthy of the devotion of a life's energies. I knew that I must become a Byzantinist. I must understand this art.

To my callow view it seemed predestined then, when I traveled on to Rome, that I should accidentally stumble upon a copy of Otto Demus's *Byzantine Mosaic Decoration* at a street stall. I hardly realized at the time that I would one day come to know as well as admire this distinguished scholar, though I never lost the awe I felt over what he had put into my hands. Yes, according to his claims, the images configuring the interiors of these churches were designed for enlightened viewers and did make programmatic sense. Totally engaged by the conception of this little book, I determinedly journeyed to as many of the churches noted in Demus's work as possible, seeking them out in Rome, Naples, Milan, and then Palermo, Monreale, and Cefalù, and later on in Greece for the stirring works at Daphni and Hosios Loukas. After these firsthand experiences of close though not yet enlightened looking, I firmly decided to return to the United States, enter the best graduate school possible, and pursue this aim as avidly as only a youthful mind could imagine. I could not have guessed that in almost another decade I would find myself repeatedly on scaffolds *facia-a-facia* with the grandest yet still very little known mosaics surviving from the time of Justinian—in the bemas of Hagia Sophia in Istanbul and at the monastery Church of Saint Catherine at Mount Sinai.

As I set about applying for admission to a graduate program where I could train for the realization of this new vision of myself, I was advised that Princeton was the leading place for serious training in Byzantine studies, and I naively mailed my request for application forms. I promptly received a polite but curt response indicating that, as my name seemed female, I should be aware that Princeton only admitted males, even to its graduate Department of Art and Archaeology. Indeed, women were not included in that program until almost a quarter-century later! Thus it was that, in the fall of 1952, I enrolled in Columbia University's Department of Art History and Archaeology, met Marion Lawrence, Meyer Schapiro, and Emerson Swift, in addition to many other highly distinguished lights, and began intensive study of both Greek and Medieval Latin languages. To that point I had only western European languages plus classical Latin in my dossier.

The courses devoted to medieval art at Columbia at that time were numerous by today's standards. I took them all. They primarily covered the early Byzantine world, including the great stone churches of the Syrian desert, Hagia Sophia (Swift), the painting of early Syriac manuscripts, the mosaics of major sites—at that time chiefly thought to be Rome and Ravenna—a few Coptic sites of early date, a rushed survey of the churches of the medieval West, and a lot of sarcophagi (Lawrence and Schapiro). What ironies there turned out to be in all of this! Had I been admitted to Princeton, there would not have been an entire term devoted to Hagia Sophia; more important, my scholarly thinking might have taken a very different tack, though I doubt that I should ever have lost sight of the fact that it was the intimate, direct confrontation with medieval art itself, not slides or pictures or talk about it, that had first kindled in me the fire that favored the Middle Ages and that enlivened my intellectual life. Most significantly, had I been admitted to Princeton, I might never have become a student of Meyer Schapiro.

With Schapiro I found a mentor who passionately believed that important insights about art normally issue from the work of art itself, as had been the case with the genesis of my own enthusiasm for *mediaevalia*. At the time of my study Schapiro served Columbia as a historian of both Byzantine and Western medieval art. Initially I was certain that things Byzantine would always be uppermost in my mind, and they were ever inspiring. Yet, Schapiro introduced me to another, captivating unknown: Romanesque sculpture. Perhaps I was attracted by the elegance and finesse of the twelfth-century sculptors' working of the stone medium, indeed their superb mastery of the challenge of directly attacking the limestone block with the chisel, an achievement that still awes contemporary sculptors; or the humor of many of the carvings; or their ultimate objective—a human expressiveness that fully indulged both metaphor and paradox. The high-minded, awesome beauty of their creations, as at Moissac, framed by the allure of France, became a lifelong obsession for me.

One of my first assignments for Schapiro, a "long paper" in my initial course on Romanesque sculpture, investigated the topic of narrative order. Ever unwary, I ardently pursued this work. When the results were considered promising for further development, I believed that the topic could yield original results and be solidly grounded only if I were able to extend the investigation at firsthand in various medieval centers in western Europe. I sailed to France and settled in at sites such as Moissac and Toulouse, plus many others where I could witness (and even touch!— with my eyes at least) the narrative sculptures themselves and examine them in my own way. Sketches, diagrams, and elaborate photography accompanied my sustained search for the elusive order governing the sequences of episodes presented to viewers in what I thought then must have been Romanesque storytelling. The presumption in the literature was that the purpose of these figural carvings was to narrate stories from Christian history.

My attention focused particularly on the scenes carved on the capitals of Romanesque cloisters. Sometimes these were vexingly enigmatic. Occasionally they were accompanied by carved letters that formed words aiding their decipherment, but often these inscriptions seemed "vagrant" or "decomposed" (as Schapiro called them). The long painted cycles within the interiors of churches and the relief sculptures elsewhere—particularly at portals, as in bronze doors as well as in stone portal enframements—were easier to analyze, but the capitals engrossed me. This work occupied the summer of 1954 and developed during the following year into a master's essay ("Narrative Order in Romanesque Sculpture") that qualified me for an M.A. degree in 1955. The major fruit of this research was the growing realization that, in the Romanesque world, narratives were not very regular and programs—if they existed at all, particularly in cloisters—were not likely to be orderly or to follow generally held presumptions about didactic purpose. Conventional storytelling was probably not at all the aim of the producers or the expectation of the viewers of these works. It was to be a very positive negative conclusion for me to discover.

After more advanced study back at Columbia, some teaching at Barnard, regular research travel, lots of photography, and, finally, prelims, I was still uncertain whether to settle on a Byzantine or a Romanesque topic for a dissertation. Though I did not realize it at the time, the subject that I finally hit upon curiously combined my double-pronged interest in both East and West. Again, my choice of subject was more decidedly influenced by my immediate and frequent contact with medieval sculpture than by the suggestions of mentors. Living in Morningside Heights for my work at Columbia meant ready access to the Metropolitan Museum of Art. I regularly spent long hours in the museum, always feeling particularly attracted by the early medieval collections. As a young preceptor and then as an instructor at Barnard, I had responsibility for teaching many classes at the Met and necessarily gave much structured attention to the art in its grand medieval galleries. Among its masterworks the enthroned wood figures of the Romanesque Madonna and Child in Majesty drew me. They were sometimes called "cult statues," probably because their hieratic poses and elaborate linear draperies evoked exotic idols of distant cultures. Among them were some particularly fine pieces, such as the sculpture I later dubbed *The Morgan Madonna* (fig. 60) and the poignant Autun Majesty atop the altar in the Langon Chapel at the Met's uptown subsidiary, the Cloisters. Perhaps in their iconic rigidity they suggested more tangible versions of the Byzantine images that had moved me years earlier. These, too, were commanding, imperious figures and simulated imposing presences. They had an aura about them. The power that a function within the rituals of medieval life must have ceded them still seemed to emanate from them. How was that achieved? As frontally seated and enthroned embodiments of the conception of a divine *sedes sapientiae* (the seat or throne of wisdom) and often considered miracle workers, the statues began to seem to me western analogues to the "miraculous" icons of the East, and I began thinking of them as icons in the round. As vehicles for prayer, they were transmitters as well as recipients of religious devotions. How could an artist manage to instill the expression of such lofty functions in his work? Was it all sham, or was there a discernible ingredient that made these particular figures particularly effective carriers of transcendent goals? I liked the cool remoteness and linearity of their style and thought it might have played a part. Although carved of wood, the wood was elegantly worked, and it was the wood that gave rise to the intriguing matter of their portability. Was that critical as well?

The choice of that material meant that both the viewers and the viewed were mobile and could move through changing viewing situations. There was the further fascination that many of these figures contained relics, surely an essential factor in

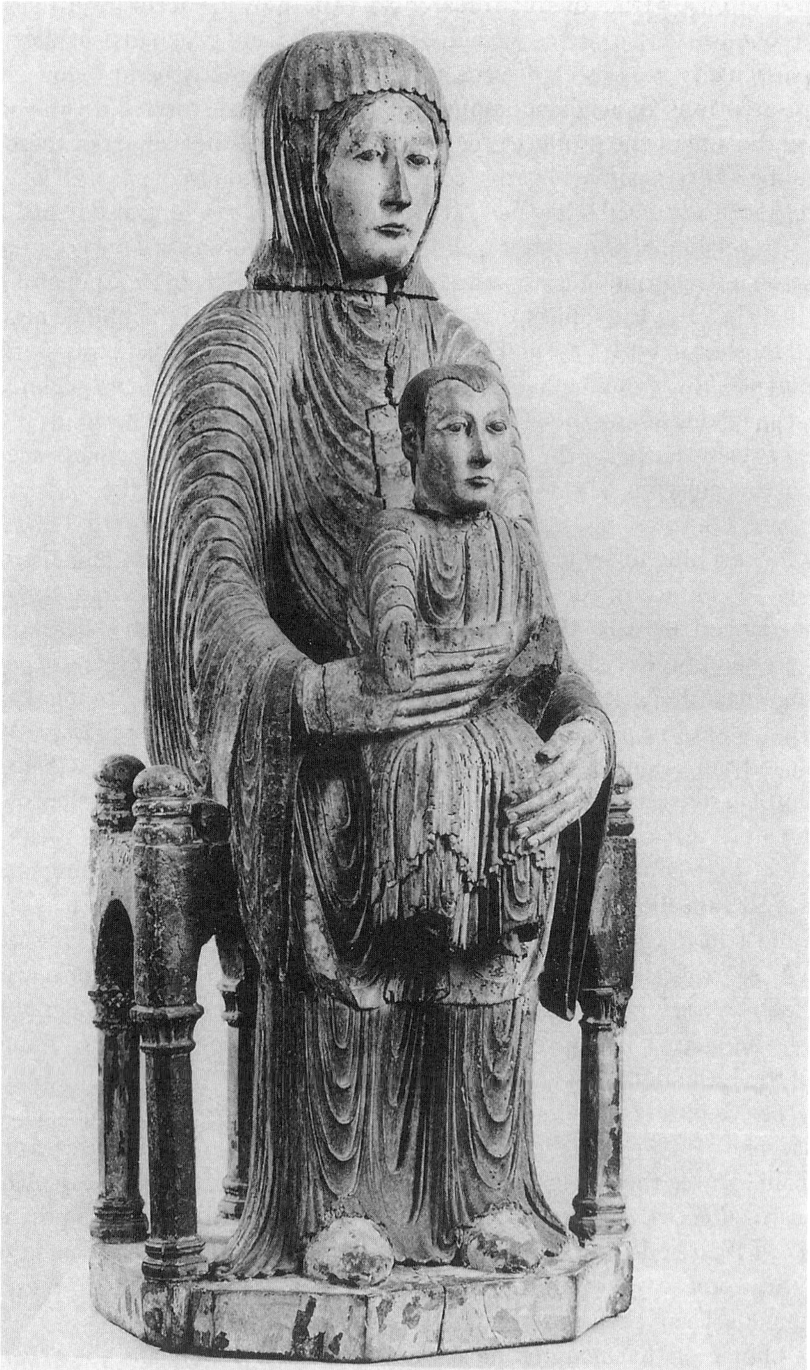

explaining the religious energy they seemed to embody and the high regard they enjoyed. Were they really the major works that could be thought of as freestanding statues prior to Donatello? Why was sculpture in the round seemingly proscribed in the early Christian period only to reappear in *this* form? Why was there such an apparent East-West divide on this issue, with the "cult of icons" characteristic of the Christian East and the "cult of relics," and its interesting corollary the creation of "speaking reliquaries," a feature of the medieval West? These matters all had to be probed. I was eager to explore them and to determine the varied functions the Throne of Wisdom statues assumed within multiple contexts from both religious and civil spheres of medieval life. Their genesis and widespread development, despite iconoclastic proscriptions regarding freestanding statuary in the early Middle Ages, seemed an enigma awaiting thorough research and analysis. The topic was challenging, and it required an interdisciplinary approach. Perhaps it was even risky. Could the questions be answered? And was I with my modest learning and capacity up to it?

Schapiro had suggested something quite different, the topic of Byzantine figure sculpture. Thinking of the pearly marble from which these shallow reliefs were usually carved, I obviously liked this subject as well, but there was still very little figural relief from Byzantine spheres known at the time. The history of the more tactile *sedes sapientiae* in the early-medieval West seemed to me to offer a project at once more viable and profound. And it was a topic that I had conceived independently. Surely that was key to the total latitude I was accorded in pursuing it. Though Schapiro readily agreed to my choice of subject, it was considered rather edgy by a number of my other mentors, who perhaps thought it would venture too far from traditional art history in its anthropological, religious, and practical consequences. I was aware that it would take me away from the question of what coherence might undergird the programs for Romanesque architectural sculpture, a question that had guided my narrative studies; it would also take me away from stone, yet it would fully immerse me in the big question, the question of the power of images, and that question was what had generated my early ardor for *mediaevalia*.

After requisite preparations in New York I was fortunate in winning financial support for my project, sailed again for Europe, embarked on the complexities of a scholarly life abroad, and "chased Virgins" (as my friends teasingly said) throughout western Europe. Driving my tiny car, though often on foot, I found them in small villages as well as towns, often after trekking through pastures, clambering over stiles, and hiking up narrow paths. The dust and the smells of European churches, archives, and libraries became my favorite scents. Further research, analysis, and writing took place the following hectic year back at Columbia, a year also marked by a profound change in my personal life. A whirlwind courtship took place, primarily at the annual Byzantine Symposium at Dumbarton Oaks in May, while my readers were assessing my doctoral tomes. Then a happy confluence of events overtook me. I defended my work, and the Ph.D. was awarded on 3 June 1960. On June 4 I was wed to George H. Forsyth Jr. in Saint Paul's Chapel on the Columbia campus. Immediately afterward

I was asked to inscribe my name in the chapel's marriage book (Ilene: "Which name should I write?"[After all, I had just established my scholarly identity the day before, using my maiden name. Was I perhaps prescient in being reluctant to give it up?] Mother: "Do we have to repeat the wedding ceremony?"). A reception followed at the Women's Faculty Club across the street; then we were off—the destination: Egypt and the Sinai Peninsula. My new husband, George, archaeologist and architectural historian from the University of Michigan, was the only one who understood that I would leave well before he did, departing soon after the wedding, flying from Cape Cod to Europe and making a lengthy stop in Germany in order to photograph some newly uncovered works of Ottonian sculpture, while he traveled several weeks later by ship to Naples. There we met for the last leg of the voyage to Alexandria. We were joined by other members of the expedition team as well as by the accompanying archaeological freight that had traveled with George all the way from Ann Arbor.

The work at the Sinai fortress was exhilarating. For me it meant a return to study of mosaic. Sinai's *Transfiguration* in the apse of the monastery's church and the related scenes of Moses on either side of the chancel at its east end were simply stunning. As the highest quality wall mosaics that survive from the time of Justinian, they represent the summa of this first golden age of Byzantine mosaic art. The monks graciously allowed us to set up the scaffold brought from Michigan in the sanctuary. It was essential for the conservation, photography, and other study carried out in the bema area of the church. It was also key to many insights that came during those weeks of study. It was a special privilege for me to assist Paul Underwood during this 1960 visit and to learn from him and from this special, close-range investigation many secrets regarding mosaic facture. I quickly became a mosaic snob, believing that if one had not studied a wall mosaic from scaffolding one simply did not know it. For me, from then on, it had to be a nose-to-nose experience. Ernest Hawkins also became a friend at this time and a little later taught me much from the scaffolds in Istanbul, in Hagia Sophia, the Fethiye Camii, and the Kariye Camii. Peter Megaw and Robert Van Nice were also mentors who kindly shared their unique perceptions regarding Justinianic art. They were all stars in my personal pantheon of great Byzantinists. For me there were later, similar forays from Ann Arbor to the churches of Istanbul and Athens, where I was able to interact with these and other Byzantinists. I became particularly drawn during the next few years to the mosaics of northern Greece, where I concentrated on the stunning mosaic programs in Thessaloníki, especially those in the rotunda known as Hagios Georgios.

George was field director of the Sinai expeditions, and although he was always totally occupied with his own work, the 1960 expedition, following our marriage, was one of the rare times when we could be together in the field. George was committed to the challenge of producing the first measured architectural survey of the monastery. It was a daunting task because of the size of the monastic fortress and its veritable warren of sixth-century structures with interlarding levels and inchoate additions. A compensating factor to offset the enormity of the project and its topographic difficulties was the fact that the inscriptions of the church's ceiling allowed an unequivocal dating of the church and, by extension, the surviving, related buildings of the fortress—to circa 548–565. The Sinai icons, the province of Kurt Weitzmann, who represented the Princeton part of Michigan's partnership with Princeton University in the Sinai expeditions, were another matter. They survived in abundance, as did the famous Sinai manuscripts. Both came from varied periods of Byzantine painting. The mosaics were of greater interest to me, and I devoted myself wholeheartedly to them, as I had only a few weeks to study them before being obliged to leave Sinai to return to my teaching duties at Columbia. George and the other members of the archaeological team remained there for additional months. This was only one of George's many missions to the mountain. He carried out his architectural work there with a dedication to exactitude that awed me. It took five expeditions to gather the huge amounts of data he believed essential to the accuracy of his work. In consequence he produced a large number of measured drawings and plans of the many parts of the monastery, as well as the whole, some now being widely dispersed in handbooks, others awaiting posthumous publication, and he was thereby able to probe effectively many of the secrets of its curious features. Although we spent the first fourteen months of our marriage at separate venues, including separate universities, as a proto double-household couple, I turned away from New York and Columbia the following year when invited to take up a post at the University of Michigan and moved to Ann Arbor.

As my teaching career unfolded, I taught courses of all sizes, ranging from huge introductory surveys to small, specialized seminars in both Eastern and Western areas of the Middle Ages. Among my courses—first at Barnard, then at Columbia, and finally at Michigan—there were those dealing with Byzantine art (Justinianic, especially as at Mount Sinai, but also pre-Justinianic mosaics, as in Thessaloníki, plus posticonoclastic mural programs, as in Ohrid, Nerezi, and Kurbinovo). There were also courses dealing with Western medieval art, particularly Carolingian, Ottonian, Romanesque, and Early Gothic seminars, some dealing with *ars sacra*, or the sacred, sumptuary arts, such as ivories, portable altars, and reliquaries, while others treated more monumental, site-specific subjects, such as Cluny, Chartres, Saint-Denis, and Toulouse, or problems regarding pilgrimage, programming, narrative, and related themes. Later special attention was given to monasticism's impact on the arts. Problems or issues always provided the structuring framework for the course, and the style was always Socratic. Summers and leaves from teaching were devoted to extensive field trips that allowed sustained study of medieval monuments (e.g., in the area then known as Yugoslavia, plus Greece, Turkey, Libya, and Egypt, as well as sites in France, Germany, Spain, and Italy), all to be incorporated into the training of students in the classroom, while some were to be developed into detailed research projects. There were stimulating breaks in my hectic teaching schedule afforded by research and sabbatical leaves as well as by invitations to teach as a guest professor at Harvard (1980), the University of Pittsburgh (1981), and the University of California at Berkeley (1996). It was an exciting moment when I was named Arthur F. Thurnau Professor of the History of

Art at the University of Michigan in 1984, as I was told that it was the first time that the university had appointed a woman to a chair not specifically designated for women. Happily, there is no longer any novelty in such an appointment.

I was particularly fortunate in having unusually gifted students in my seminars at Michigan. The design I favored assigned each a problem related to an aspect of the driving question of the theme under review, and I placed particular stress on a dialectical critique of the literature to date along with a search for new approaches to the issues that clustered about the theme. I asked that every point be evidenced through reference to the specific works of art being studied; these were kept in constant view through the use of detailed photographs that always fully littered the seminar table. Because of the seriousness of the students, I remember that the discussions in these seminars often rose far beyond my expectations with regard to the level of sophistication and originality, and, I believe, they stimulated exciting intellectual growth for all of us. I continually preached what seemed to me the three essentials to high-quality scholarship: frequent travel to the original works of art ("Don't stop looking at your monument"); intense use of detailed photographs of the original works of art under review ("Prop these up about you on your desk as you write"); and patience (*sitzfleiß*) in libraries and archives ("Remember that the documentary support for your work will always be like an iceberg; only a little of it may show but its depth should be enormous"). Emphasis on context, interdisciplinarity, and the theoretical underpinnings of interpretation was always present, for these were what had brought me to the study of medieval art.

Young colleagues in the Romanesque field whose careers developed during the same time span as mine were, among others, Walter Cahn at Yale, Charles Little and William Wixom at the Metropolitan, Elizabeth Parker at Fordham, Linda Seidel at Chicago, and O. Karl Werckmeister, lately at Northwestern. We met at meetings of the International Center of Medieval Art and at College Art Association conventions, and we listened to one another's papers at Kalamazoo and elsewhere ("Current Studies on Cluny, 1986" [1988]). The field will always be indebted to each of these distinguished scholars for their pathfinding contributions to Romanesque studies and for their work in developing centers of interest in medieval art that have drawn newcomers to this area of study.

As my own career developed and in the time that academic life allowed for research and publication, my preoccupation with mosaic during the sixties was shared with my investigations of how the early-medieval art of the West might relate to broader spheres of twelfth-century life, such as the ritualized time spent in the offices and services of the church, particularly in the experience of the church's liturgy or on special feast days via liturgical dramas. Such festival dramas, played out in church sanctuaries with members of religious communities impersonating sacred figures of history, began to monopolize my researches. It need hardly be said that just as religious subject matter dominated the art of the Middle Ages, plays within the church constituted the leading theater of the period. Particularly delightful to me was my discovery that, though there was normally a serious religious armature for the main themes of these plays, there were also numerous humorous asides. Sometimes there were extended tropes or interpolations that led to high hilarity of a secular sort. For example, as I discovered later, when Balaam's she-ass was to speak suddenly with a human voice in the *Play of the Prophets,* the play's stage directions indicated that the ass's words might be voiced by a young religious strapped under the animal, the animal being either simulated or real (just as a *Palmesel* might be a wood sculpture on wheels or a local animal), surely eliciting comic effect. Or when the impersonators of the three Marys (usually young monks or clerics) in the *Visitatio sepulchri* play were to act out their visit to the tomb of Christ on Easter morning, they might be directed to stop for a long haggle with an impersonator of a perfume merchant to discuss the price of the unguents they wished to buy to anoint the body of their Lord. The form of the play helps explain why Romanesque sculptures that treat this same, basic Easter subject might also present to viewers commercial details of such visits, including the merchant's weighing or pinching of the coins paid by the Marys, with simulations of the coins' exact denominations, and/or the women's reaction to the merchant's wily use of the scales. That the relationship between the liturgical texts and the sculptures might be significant was instilled in my mind by Schapiro. Interestingly, liturgical drama was hardly taken up by him in his published work on Romanesque sculpture, though it was discussed in his late lectures. It was also an interest of Emile Mâle, in his book on the twelfth century. The question for me, however, was just what significance might lodge in that relationship. It grew in importance for me as I began to forage in the writings of clerics that would help explain some peculiarities of Romanesque sculpture.

I found that the rubrics accompanying the dialogues of the players in the medieval texts that form the surviving "playbooks" sometimes directed the use of portable images of Mary and the Christ Child. These were usually to be set upon altars. The rubrics sometimes referred to them as images within baldachins, from which curtains were to hang, and indicated that the curtains should be parted to reveal the figures at the critical moment of the drama. I believed these textual references must have applied to images that were figures of wood or the Madonna and Child statues of the *sedes sapientiae* type that I had studied. This hypothesis resulted in a first tentative publication titled "Magi and Majesty: A Study of Romanesque Sculpture and Liturgical Drama" (1968). The wood figures coordinated particularly well with the plays that dramatized the presentation of gifts by the Three Kings at sanctuary altars in the Christmas season, particularly in the *Officium stellae,* or Office of the Star. In these holiday reenactments of the story of the Magi, monks and canons might impersonate the shepherds, kings, and assorted extras moving along the naves of the churches, as required by the plays, but the wondrous chief protagonists of the story, the Child Jesus and Mary, the mother of God, to whom the gifts were presented, were represented by simulacra or formal images. As the curtains were parted, these commanding, freestanding figures afforded convincing visual reference to the enthroned seat of wisdom and hence assured the presence of God. I argued that such a liturgical as well as dramatic function helped explain the hieratic style of the figures and that the use of wood facilitated the mobility essential to the dramatic experience. Mobility allowed changing roles and changing meanings in multiple contexts. The statues might function in Epiphany plays and in other dramatizations such as the *Play of the Shepherds,* the *Play of the Prophets,* the Saint Nicholas plays, or those featuring Saint Luke. As they were portable, they could be carried in processions or be present at ceremonies such as baptisms and dedications, or they might be focal presences in civil ceremonies such as the taking of oaths, particularly those dealing with vassalage and the pledging of gifts or the transfer of property.

As I sought to understand the genesis of these wood statues in relation to the revival of sculpture in the round, I penetrated more deeply into the matter of the figures' possible role as reliquaries, a function that would enhance the aura of their presence. Study of their styles, their varying attributes, and technical considerations such as the materials, tools, and methods used in the making and carving of them also taught me much about the organizations of workshops and helped to identify some of the sculptors who worked in them. The consequence of these various investigations was the realization that the Romanesque concept of the *sedes sapientiae* was as multifaceted as it was complex. Mary was understood as both the Mother of God and the *cathedra,* or "seat," of the Logos incarnate. The concept combines the humanity and divinity of Christ and is powerful in imaging this fusion in a freestanding, tactile form that, being mobile, shared the viewer's space in various venues. The sculpture thus allowed viewers firsthand confrontation with and experience of its essential meaning. That seemed to me to be given even greater immediacy through the enmeshing of these special statues with the rituals of medieval life. My study of them became the book titled the *Throne of Wisdom,* published in 1972.

While the book manuscript was in press, I turned to the stone sculpture of Romanesque France, eager to take up again the puzzling questions that revolved about the Romanesque invention of the historiated capital that had first engrossed me. Because capitals are forms of architectural sculpture, only portions of them can be seen at any one moment. The reading of their subjects unfolds as an observer moves about, along the side aisle of a church, say, where three-sided capitals crown the engaged columns of piers, or along the gallery of a cloister, where the capitals are likely to be atop freestanding columns and therefore quadripartite, or four-sided. Especially intriguing is the fact that while a capital's curious configuration of bent surfaces seems to offer an intractable field for narration, carvers were redoubtable in responding to this challenge. The sculptors clearly realized that when a capital's surfaces are historiated, its story can impress itself upon a viewer's attention in particularly effective ways. Because it thrusts itself into a viewer's space, a capital's special qualities could be exploited to enhance meaning. In a cloister where capitals are often four-sided, they are also normally at eye level and visually very accessible. Along the cloister walk the angular projecting corners of the capitals could be privileged locations for particularly dramatic forms within the design. Also, while full comprehension of a capital's story would seem to have required a twelfth-century observer to move all the way around its perimeter, this was usually impossible because of the low socle walls—used for sitting, reading, and ruminating on texts—that lined the walkways of the cloisters and allowed only limited passage into the courtyards beyond where the "fourth" side of the capital could be seen. Analysis indicates that the narratives were designed with this simple fact in mind. Rather than a progressive unfolding of a story, the episodes forming a narrative might be presented in sequences contrary to conventional expectations, with dramatic disruptions and curiously selected emphases or combinations of themes on a single capital. The "fourth" side, that side visible only from the courtyard, might shift the action, double, ambiguate, or pluralize it, or offer an unusually uplifting finale. These highly expressive manipulations seemed to me to call for deeper study. Their discovery made me keen to search for underlying agendas that would explain such departures from orderly narration. The search led to varied studies of capital sculptures and found some resolution later in a work on Samson ("The Samson Monolith," 1991, fig. 61).

Study also revealed that many of the subjects carved on the capitals represented a creative fusion of secular and sacred subject matter while showing a penchant for lodging complex thought within apparently simple forms. Deeply serious themes might be presented with a childlike directness, yielding a lightness and a humor that combined poignantly with the profundity of the subject matter. Study of these qualities led to "Children in Early Medieval Art, Ninth through Twelfth Centuries" (1976) and "The Ganymede Capital at Vézelay" (1976).

Exploration of secular/sacred antitheses that I found in Romanesque themes—particularly on Burgundian historiated capitals, as at Saulieu, where I was also conducting a monographic study—led to publications such as "The Theme of Cockfighting" (1978) and "The Ass of Balaam" (1981). In these the analysis noted the use of paradoxical metaphors in Romanesque expression. I sensed that the liking for such paradox could reach an extraordinarily high level of sophistication, a sophistication that goes beyond the incorporation of multivalent references or allusion to multiple senses or visual correlations to a number of possible socioreligious factors. In my view such sophistication evidences an awareness of the usefulness of equivocality in a work of art. Intentional ambiguity might bring together in one theme the opposites of, say, salvation and condemnation, or life and death, as in the utter, loving, to-the-death commitment of the cocks in the cockfighting scenes. These depict gruesome violence that is simultaneously a celebration of committed love yielding a joyful, triumphal, eternal renewal of life. The play off one another of the obtuse and the visionary, as in the ignorant prophet Balaam and his clear-eyed mount, the ass, also produced an antithetical albeit delightful profundity, a type of divine comedy. I found just such ambiguous, antithetical truths expressed in Romanesque poetry and in the thinking of Romanesque theologians as I scoured their writings in an effort to know as intimately as possible the educated communities of that milieu and to demonstrate thereby the prevalence of a taste for the sophistication of equivocality and ambiguity in the intellectual climate of the Romanesque period. It is obvious in the writing of Bernard of Clairvaux—as brilliantly demonstrated in 1947 by Schapiro—but in many other writers as well.

Monasteries, houses of canons, and the new *collégiales* that sprouted widely at this time, with their well-organized, closed, communal structures and their importance as centers of learning, seemed to me likely natural crucibles for the generation of such high-minded thinking ("The Vita Apostolica," 1986). Inspiration for this line of research came from the work of Léon Pressouyre, Jean Leclercq, Paul Meyvaert, Marie-Dominique Chenu, and Giles Constable, among others. The religious in these twelfth-century institutions were, of course, the intellectual elite of the period. Their emphasis on reading, writing, and rumination over texts *(lectio divina)* was reinforced by homiletic and parenetical literature. As I worked with this material, I realized that the meanings I suspected were embedded in the sculptures of this period were often elusive and lacked programmatic coherence and narrative orderliness because of differing modes and patterns of thought and reception. The subjects that are fragmented into units, then altered, varied, and re-treated, as well as the ornamental motifs that are turned through multiple variations—all of these seem playfully manipulated in an endless kaleidoscope of change. Like Protean ruminations in the cloister, Romanesque visual forms suffer inversions, reversals, repetitions, and metamorphoses as well as decomposition. Analogues may be created through pairings or visual rhymes; they may be foiled by asymmetrical symmetries or dualities of apposite opposites. Fanciful effects may interlard with inscriptions and floral or figural forms, in a mix of fantasy and fable, making the sculptures delightfully enigmatic. At their best these tendencies produce tightly knotted patterns like fugues, recalcitrant in yielding their meanings but visually and intellectually challenging. I suggest now that this evident Romanesque predilection for continual permutation of form was purposeful. Its cultivation and appreciation might relieve some of the *otium* of the cloister. The mental exercise required to unravel the visual riddles could only be salutary. Close viewers might be rewarded with aggregations or clusters of visual references rather than single-minded interpretations. The equivocal, antithetical, or overlapping implications might result in richer, more fully textured, closer approximations of more perfect truths than could spring from consistent, linear, syllogistic visual argument. Hopelessly entangled figures, moving in two or more directions at once while simultaneously expressing both, mark this art. The ability to keep the oppositions in a tense equilibrium while striving for sublime truths seems youthful, exuberant, endlessly playful, yet the tension or the striving of the *play* itself seems to have been the aim. These thoughts have led to publications such as "The Romanesque Cloister" (1992) and "Permutations of Cluny-Paradigms at Savigny" (1994).

In addition to these musings, a love of the materiality of stone has continued to surface in my work. It has been accompanied by an eagerness to understand myriad aspects of Romanesque sculptural facture, to know such things as where the stone came from; what qualities of density, brittleness, color, and precision it offered the carver; and what tools and methods were used to enhance its natural appeal. Fuller comprehension of some of these matters could be aided by testing sample specimens of the stone with the techniques of neutron activation analysis. That has proved useful in a number of ways, particularly in settling questions relevant to churches that used stone from quarries in regions of Paris and Burgundy. Determining the origins of handsome sculptures now in American collections that are totally disconnected from their original locations can be a daunting task. In fact, conventional art historical methods may lead to faulty conclusions (viz. Gesta 1988 and Gesta 1994 . Charles Little, Jean French, and Pamela Blum have pioneered with the exciting work of incorporating neutron activation analysis into art historical study. The Limestone Sculpture Provenance Project continues now under the direction of Georgia Wright. I have been most grateful for the assistance of the Brookhaven laboratory, and Lore Holmes in particular, in bringing closure to some nagging questions that have bedeviled my own researches at Savigny: "Five Sculptures from a Single Limestone Formation" (1994) and "The Dumbarton Oaks Agnus Dei" (1995). The promise of this line of study is very real. It can have significant historiographic value. It also points to highly discriminating and knowledgeable uses of stone in the twelfth century.

From my office windows I enjoyed for many years a full view of the beautiful, honey-colored, rough-hewn, seam-face granite used for the buildings of the Michigan Law School across the street. Then, during the senior phase of my time at Michigan, these buildings became a research topic for me. That meant a turn to a study of the medievalism that produced this Collegiate-Gothic ensemble during the 1920s and 1930s. The shift to a case study on my own campus was invigorating. The modern world took on new importance for me. The project became especially serious when I was invited to deliver the Distinguished Senior Faculty Lecture Series at Michigan. Fearing that protracted discourse on the twelfth century would attract few listeners, I devised a medieval-modern dialectic that turned on local history. I expected that some of my thinking about Romanesque cloisters would inevitably seep through, and I hoped that such a series would interest a wide audience and stimulate within the broader academic community a sense of collegiality. I also thought of the double subject as an appropriate vehicle to convey my thanks to the university for the insights engendered by my years of rich experience at Michigan. The project resulted in a little book titled *The Uses of Art: Medieval Metaphor in the Michigan Law Quadrangle* (1993).

The research for this work was a special pleasure. It could be pursued by consulting an abundance of unpublished documents, including original drawings, specification books, contracts, receipts, and correspondence between the patron and his architect, along with comments on intention by both the patron and various officers of the university, all in English, most of it clearly typewritten, scattered in archives in various locations, to be sure, but nearly all of them in or near Ann Arbor. These were extraordinary luxuries. I would have given my "eye-teeth" to have had them for the twelfth, not the twentieth, century. They created a medievalist's dream. I had in my hands written, autographic evidence of a patron's intentions. In addition the patron's personality, an unforgettable blend of curmudgeonly irascibility and outrageous, sardonic wit, provided an absorbing distraction that leavened the year following my husband's death. For a Romanesque scholar it is fortifying to realize that the form of a twelfth-century cloister and some of its attendant meaning, particularly when articulated in stone, could speak across continents and centuries of the liberating forces of learning.

Except for time needed to prepare a book that presents to the academic community my late husband's scholarly legacy regarding his work at Mount Sinai, my study currently continues with problems that issue from my researches on Romanesque sites at Saulieu, Savigny, and Moissac. These investigations turn on the creative uses in art of images and words—words cut in stone, as in inscriptions—particularly when the words and images are arranged in sequences. Sculpture, as ever, is the lodestar.

I like to think that good art history comes from the application of as many sub-disciplines as possible in the study of a work of art. It should obviously include analyses of form, along with study of style, sources, and provenience; deep study of history; incorporation of archaeological data; reliance on textual evidences and other forms of documentary resources; consideration of function; awareness of political and socioeconomic factors; knowledge of current theoretical thinking; and especially serious consideration of contexts along with the possibility of multiple audiences and varied intentions and receptions. Fresh thinking has always seemed to me to be stimulated by study of the work of colleagues from other, related disciplines and direct interactions with them. As important as all of these considerations are, I believe that for us intimate contact with original works of art must always be respected as primary. That seems to me to constitute the unique core of our discipline.

Select Bibliography of Works by Ilene H. Forsyth

"Magi and Majesty: A Study of Romanesque Sculpture and Liturgical Drama." *The Art Bulletin* 50 (September 1968): 215–22.

The Throne of Wisdom: Wood Sculptures of the Madonna in Romanesque France. Princeton, N.J.: Princeton University Press, 1972. Presented the Charles Rufus Morey Book Award by the College Art Association, 1974.

"Children in Early Medieval Art, Ninth through Twelfth Centuries." *History of Childhood Quarterly: The Journal of Psychohistory* 4 (summer 1976): 31–70.

"The Ganymede Capital at Vézelay." *Gesta* 15 (1976): 241–46.

"The Theme of Cockfighting in Burgundian Romanesque Sculpture." *Speculum: A Journal of Medieval Studies* 50 (April 1978): 252–82.

"The Romanesque Portal of the Church of Saint-Andoche, Saulieu (Côte d'Or)." *Gesta* 19 (1980): 83–94.

"The Ass of Balaam in Romanesque Sculpture." *Gesta* 20 (1981): 59–65.

"The '*Vita Apostolica*' and Romanesque Sculpture." *Gesta* 25 (1986): 75–82.

Editor with W. Cahn and W. Clark. *Current Studies on Cluny*. Special double issue of *Gesta* 27. New York: International Center of Medieval Art, 1988.

"The Samson Monolith," In *The Duke University Museum of Art: The Brummer Collection of Medieval Art,* edited by C. Bruzelius, 21–55. Durham, N.C.: Duke University Press, 1991.

"The Monumental Arts of the Romanesque Period: Recent Research. The Romanesque Cloister." *The Cloisters: Studies in Honor of the Fiftieth Anniversary,* edited by E. Parker with M. Shepard, 2–25. New York: Metropolitan Museum of Art, 1992.

The Uses of Art: Medieval Metaphor in the Michigan Law Quadrangle. Ann Arbor: University of Michigan Press, 1993. Presented the Annie Award for Excellence in the Arts, 1994.

"Five Sculptures from a Single Limestone Formation: The Case of Savigny." *Gesta* 33 (1994): 47–52.

"Permutations of Cluny-Paradigms at Savigny: Problems of Historiation in Rhône Valley Sculpture." In *Studien zur Geschichte der europäischen Skulptur im 12./13. Jahrhunderts,* edited by H. Beck and K. Hengevoss-Dürkop, 333–49, pls. 183–95. Frankfurt am Main: Schriften des Liebieghauses, 1994.

"Art with History: The Role of *Spolia* in the Cumulative Work of Art." In *Byzantine East, Latin West: Art Historical Studies in Honor of Kurt Weitzmann,* edited by C. Moss and K. Kiefer, 153–58. Princeton, N.J.: Princeton University Press, 1995.

"The Dumbarton Oaks *Agnus Dei*." In *Catalogue of the Sculpture in the Dumbarton Oaks Collection,* edited by G. Vikan, 115–23. Washington, D.C.: Dumbarton Oaks, 1995.

"Words and Images Carved in Stone." *Center for Advanced Study in the Visual Arts, Reports* 19 (1998–99): 62–65.

"Narrative at Moissac: Schapiro's Legacy." *Gesta* 41 (2002): 71–93.

Works Cited

Blum, P., et al. *Neutron Activation Analysis and Medieval Limestone Sculpture, Gesta* 33/1. New York: International Center of Medieval Art, 1994.

Chenu, M. D. *Nature, Man and Society in the Twelfth Century.* Translated by Lester K. Little. Chicago: University of Chicago Press, 1968. Originally published as *La théologie au douzième siècle* (Paris: J. Vrin, 1957).

Constable, G. "Monachisme et pèlerinage au Moyen Âge." *Revue historique* 256 (1977): 3–27.

———. "Opposition to Pilgrimage in the Middle Ages." *Mélanges G. Fransen I, Studia Gratiana* 19 (1976): 125–46.

———. "Renewal and Reform in Religious Life: Concepts and Realities." In *Renaissance and Renewal in the Twelfth Century,* edited by R. L. Benson and G. Constable with C. Lanham, 37–67. Cambridge, Mass: Harvard University Press, 1982.

Demus, O. *Byzantine Mosaic Decoration.* London: Kegan Paul, 1947.

Forsyth, G., and K. Weitzmann. *The Monastery of Saint Catherine at Mount Sinai: The Church and Fortress of Justinian.* Ann Arbor: University of Michigan Press, 1973.

Leclercq, J. *The Love of Learning and the Desire for God: A Study of Monastic Culture.* Translated by C. Misrahi. New York: Fordham University Press, 1961.

———. "Monachisme et pérégrination du IXe au XIIe siècle." *Studia monastica* 3 (1961): 33–52.

Mâle, E. *L'Art religieux du XIIe siècle en France.* Paris: Armand Colin, 1922.

Meyvaert, P. "The Medieval Monastic Claustrum." *Gesta* 12 (1973): 53–59.

Pressouyre, Léon. "Saint Bernard to Saint Francis: Monastic Ideals and Iconographic Programs in the Cloister." *Gesta* 12 (1973): 71–92.

Schapiro, M. *Romanesque Art.* New York: Braziller, 1977.

CHAPTER 62

Elisabeth Gössmann (1928–)
Overcoming Obstacles

Rebecca L. R. Garber

Maria Elisabeth Gössmann was born in Osnabrück in 1928, the eldest child of a Catholic-Protestant union. In accordance with her parents' marriage vows, both she and her younger brother were baptized and raised in her mother's Catholic faith.[1] Gössmann proved to be a precocious child and noticed at an early age that there were differences in Catholic and Lutheran practices, both at home and in church. As an adult Gössmann realized that the majority of these childhood distinctions were only superficial: her father did not cross himself before meals, and her Catholic and Protestant relatives preferred different locations around Osnabrück for their weekends gatherings. She confessed freely that she preferred the Catholic Mass to the Lutheran or Reformed Protestant services, taking childish delight in the pageantry of the Corpus Christi processions and the mysterious cherubim and seraphim of the accompanying hymn; yet she also felt guilty for preferring the Gothic style of the Protestant Marienkirche to the Catholic cathedral in Osnabrück.[2]

Her first theological debates took place at age seven with her playmates, Friedel and Günter, who lived in the house across the courtyard and opposite Gössmann's family. Accused by them of "adoring Mary," she refuted this Lutheran conception of Catholicism with the help of the "small school catechism" (*kleiner Schulkatechismus*).[3] All three children employed this part of the catechism to further their curiosity about religious beliefs. Gössmann recalls with amusement that this early interest in religious differences rarely moved beyond the physical to the transcendent: when confronted with the question on the size of God, Friedel and Günter imagined stacks of furniture, while Gössmann used the height of the pear tree in the courtyard and the old chestnut by the Hegertor, the old city gate, as references, believing that a living tree was a more appropriate comparison than lifeless furniture.[4]

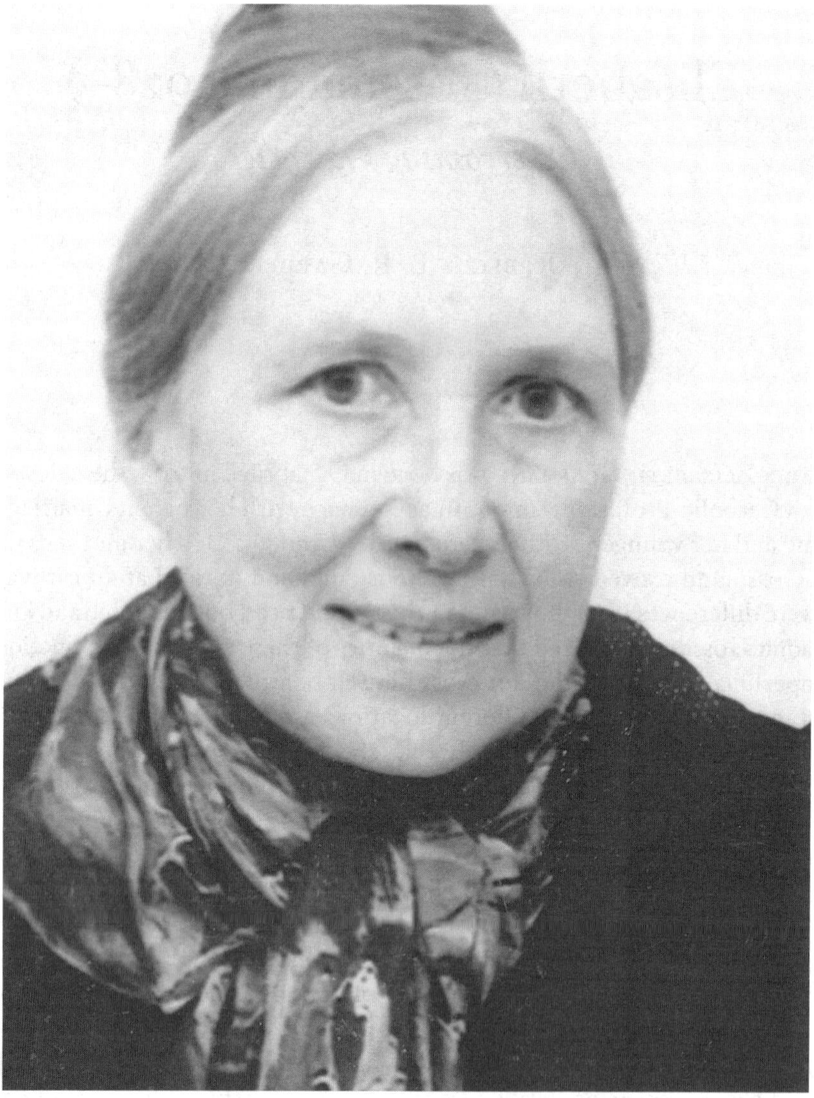

The gender inequities of Christianity and society also arose in these early childhood debates. Although the size of God was defined by Friedel as "bigger than our father," the boys demonstrated no apparent interest in parallel questions, or answers, about women.[5] As Friedel and Günter's mother was pregnant at the time, this inexplicable enlargement of feminine body puzzled the young girl and caused her to brood about questions of identity, subjectivity, and biological difference. Her questions and statements from this period appear to have worried her mother, who confided to her husband that "the child's nerves are sometimes overstimulated."[6]

In 1938 the family moved to Dortmund. Gössmann's father had finally received a promotion in the civil service as a customs agent, one long delayed because of his suspect "Catholic family." One year earlier, in 1937, he had joined the National Socialist Party for career reasons, and the promotion may have been a reward for an active show of political correctness. According to Gössmann he had been enlisted without his permission in the SA (Sturmabteilung) several years earlier, which he had passively endured, probably for the same economic and career reasons.[7] He was drafted by the Wehrmacht, the army, in 1943.

At the beginning of 1943, when the allied bombing attacks began successfully targeting the industrial areas of Germany, including Dortmund, the lower classes at Gössmann's school, the secondary school for girls in Dortmund, were evacuated to Oberammergau in a children's evacuation program (KLV, *Kinderlandverschickung*).[8] Many European countries sent children from urban areas to the countryside in order to protect them from enemy air attacks during the war. Gössmann's class was housed in a small pension run by a highly religious Catholic family in Oberammergau, with the other seven classes from her school lodged in different hotels in the area. Interestingly enough, most of the teachers who accompanied their pupils did not indoctrinate the children with National Socialist ideology, nor did the leaders of the BDM (*Bund deutscher Mädel*, "league of German girls") who were responsible for the girls in the afternoon.[9] The only National Socialist presence appears to have been a mandatory Hitler Youth meeting each Sunday morning, which conflicted with the time of Catholic Mass. When the girls went to the priest with their complaint, he agreed to hold a special mass for them, which became known locally as the Mass for the Evacuated Children (*KLV-Messe*).

Gössmann was transferred to several different small cities and villages during the following years as the war turned against Germany. At the end of 1944 she found herself, along with her mother and younger brother, just behind the front lines at Rhede-an-der-Ems, which lies quite close to the border with the Netherlands and only 40 kilometers (24 miles) from the north German coast line. The fifteen- and sixteen-year-old girls from the village of Rhede dug trenches and also cooked for the soldiers. Gössmann's family and the inhabitants of Rhede watched the village fall to the Allies from a farmer's house, which was situated in the swampland outside the village. They had been evacuated from Rhede before the final artillery battle, which took place in early 1945. Rhede was completely destroyed in the fight, and Gössmann and her family lost the last of their belongings as well as their provisional shelter.

The farmers of Rhede set up Quonset huts to shelter themselves and the evacuated families, the girls of the village filled in the defensive trenches they had dug, and Gössmann had her first opportunity to practice her English as she translated for the farmers and the Allied forces occupying Rhede. It was a very tense time, as the few German soldiers who had survived the battle were separated from the civilian population and sent to prisoner-of-war camps, and many of the civilians, especially the girls who had aided the soldiers, feared that they would also be transported by the Allies to internment camps.

Gössmann's father was reunited with the family in autumn of 1945, when he was released from a POW camp. Their relief was short lived, as a few weeks later he lost his job in the customs service due to his membership in the National Socialist Party. In addition the family's bank accounts were frozen, although they were allowed to withdraw three hundred marks per month to live on. With no other sources of income Gössmann recalled that it was quite easy to calculate how long the money would last.

Her father explained to her that they could only afford to pay for her education if she wrote her *Abitur* by spring of 1947.[10] Had the war not intervened, 1947 would have been the year she would have written these all important exams; however, the interruptions and numerous evacuations had left gaps in her education. She spent the fall in the Quonset hut, studying foreign languages with a young woman from Rhede, who had studied at the Universität Münster. After they managed to find a mathematics textbook, her father tutored her in the higher levels of math, stealing time away from his obligatory duties in the fields.

In 1946, Gössmann enrolled in the eighth class (the final secondary school level) in the secondary school for girls in Leer, where she had been a student during the war.[11] However, one teacher noticed her educational gaps and wanted her placed in the seventh class, which, considering the family's monetary difficulties, was not acceptable. Gössmann's mother traded a golden brooch, the last of her inheritance from her own mother, for bacon, which she then took to Leer to "convince" the teacher of her daughter's educational fitness. However, the teacher had, that very day, been visited with the same fate as Gössmann's father and had been relieved of his teaching duties due to his political membership. After enduring a cold winter without coal for heating, Gössmann wrote her *Abitur* as planned, in the spring of 1947.

By this time her father had been classified as denazified by the Allied forces, and Gössmann was permitted to enroll at the university in Münster. After all that she had endured during the war—the fear in the bombshelters, the bodies of dead soldiers during the assault on Rhede, the destruction of Osnabrück and Dortmund—she determined to focus on the eternal, rather than depend on the temporal, which had proven itself to be easily destroyed by external forces. Thus, she chose to study theology and philosophy, and, to appease her father by studying something "safe," she chose German literature as her third major field. With this in mind she attended all lectures and seminars with a metaphysical theme, which she noted were rather common in the post-war period, as both academics and students grappled with the intellectual inheritance of the Nazi period.

Gössmann notes that she and her university colleagues at Münster were remarkably uncritical of the church's role in the Nazi period, in part because the theology taught at the university was spiritually and intellectually more open and responsive to criticism than the polemical religious instruction required under the Nazis, and in part because her generation was determinedly anti-political. They firmly believed that, if the church had been allowed its freedom, then it, as a social institution of immense influence, would have been able to prevent atrocities, such as the crimes of the Nazi government. At the time Gössmann and her colleagues could point to the numbers of priests and ministers who had died in the concentration camps to support this belief. In hindsight the complicity of the Catholic and Protestant churches with the Nazi leaders appears readily visible, but these activities were not yet public knowledge in the late forties and early fifties.[12] The question of whether it was possible to conceive of a "theology after Auschwitz" had not yet been raised.[13] In 1952 Gössmann passed her *Staatsexamen* in theology, philosophy, and German literature, which completed her studies at Münster.[14]

The decades following the Second World War were a time of upheaval in Germany, both socially and politically, and, more important for Gössmann personally, academically, as one generation of scholars began to retire from positions, and the younger generation, whose maturity was gained during air raids, began to receive university appointments. Among other changes made in the German universities at this time, the requirements for gaining a doctoral degree in Catholic theology at the Ludwig-Maximilians-Universität-München (LMU-Munich) had changed, and the candidates were no longer "required to have been consecrated as a deacon."[15] As women could not become deacons in the Catholic Church, this new "lack" opened a door for Gössmann and her female colleagues. In order to be sure, though, she and a comrade had hitchhiked to Munich during spring break of 1951 and consulted with Dr. Michael Schmaus, who would later become her dissertation advisor. In answer to their question as to whether this now meant that they, women, could attain a doctoral degree in theology, Gössmann reports that he answered, "Yes, but only if you turn in a work of better than average quality; otherwise there will certainly be difficulties."[16] The LMU thus accepted female postgraduates into its Catholic theology department at least ten years earlier than other German universities. Five semesters after enrolling at the LMU in Munich, in November 1954, Gössmann and one female colleague became the first women to complete their *Doktorarbeit* and the series of exams required for gaining the degree of Doctor of Theology at a German university.[17]

The Catholic theological faculty at the Universität Münster and at the LMU included a number of gifted teachers and thinkers who laid the groundwork for much of the reformulation of theological thought in Germany. Johann Peter Steffes and Thomas Ohm, O.S.B., in Münster, along with Gottlieb Söhngen and Josef Schmid at the LMU, were among those who actively combined knowledge of non-Christian religions with Christian theological instruction, producing not only ecumenical dialogues among Christian denominations but also some of the first inter-religious exchanges of the post-war years.[18] Existentialism and dialectic theology, the theories and vocabularies of contemporary philosophy, appeared in combination with exegetical theory in Gössmann's seminars, especially in those conducted by Hermann Volk, a specialist in dogmatics and the history of dogma at Münster.[19]

Gössmann had spent most of the years 1952–54 at the Grabmann Institute for Research in the Philosophy and Theology of the Middle Ages, under the direction of Dr. Michael Schmaus.[20] She notes that her studies at the institute involved a "return to historicity" in theology. This should not be interpreted as a sign that she lost her interest in metaphysics, but that she, like many of her generation, was exposed to the new current of theological debate, which sought to ground biblical statements within historical contexts.

In Munich Dr. Josef Schmid was the primary proponent of this type of historically contextualized reading, which radically alters the interpretation of the bible, as it denies an ahistorical, eternally consistent reading and replaces the former with a mutable, socially and historically influenced reception of the biblical texts.[21] Inspired by such readings, Gössmann and her female colleagues noted with delight that the phrase "Mulier taceat in Ecclesia" (Let the women remain silent in the Church, 1 Cor. 14:34), which had been drummed into their heads since childhood, had thus lost its eternal validity and no longer applied, as social constructs had changed since it was recorded.[22]

This concept, that even biblical and theological texts were grounded in the historical context of their inception, and that modern understanding is furthered when this historical background is understood, was of particular interest to Michael Schmaus.[23] His seminars on the theology presented by the early scholastics, the mystics, the Franciscans, and others exposed his students to a number of the medieval developments of Christian theology and required them to recognize that the same theological term did not retain its meaning between theological schools or across centuries. Schmaus taught his students that, in order to understand theologians of the past, they must translate the earlier concepts into modern speech, a process which reveals changes in linguistics as well as theology. Gössmann notes with amusement that before the term "paradigm shift" had entered the collective vocabulary, Schmaus was instructing his students in the means of recognizing and examining such changes through the use of contextualized reading, another term invented later.

During these years at the Grabmann Institute, Gössmann read a number of texts by women.[24] In seminars at the institute she reports a consistent reaction to Hildegard's texts by both her professors and her fellow students: "She appears to be not merely (!) a mystic, but a mature theologian."[25] Yet, except for Gössmann's contributions, the religious writings by medieval women were not incorporated into the theology seminars: she read most of the women's texts in seminars on German literature and later through her own research into German, English, and French medieval religious material.

In her own doctoral writing Gössmann obeyed this theological gender split. Although she had discovered in her dissertation research (*Forschung zur Doktorarbeit*) on the Annunciation (Luke 1:26–38) that the theology presented in medieval women's texts had been tightly interwoven into the male, Franciscan theological tradition, she did not dare to set the women's texts on an equal level with the men's as "theological commentaries."[26] Therefore, she introduced them to her argument through the literary side door of "spiritual poetry."[27] Only in the section devoted to "Meister Eckhart and the [male] Mystics" did she include some short analyses of texts by Mechthild von Hackeborn, Gertrud von Helfta, Margarete Ebner, Adelheid Langmann, and Birgitta von Schweden, in comparison with or in support of the men's works.

Although reassured by Schmaus about the relevance of these women writers, Gössmann feared that her incorporation of women's writings, which were not even included as possible transmitters of historical tradition in theology, would lead to the dismissal of her *Doktorarbeit,* as such texts had to be approved by a number of the professors in the Catholic theology department at the LMU before they could be accepted. Yet she also hoped, in what she describes as "the naiveté of youth," that if her research were positively accepted and valued, then the female tradition in Christianity might become a subject for investigation by other theologians. Both her hopes and fears would come to pass: nearly thirty years would separate the publication of her *Doktorarbeit* from her first teaching position at a German university, where, in the last two decades of the twentieth century, the works of female religious writers have attracted the interest of theologians and literary scholars.[28]

Gössmann's fellow students at the Grabmann Institute were also quite gifted, as their later careers demonstrate. She attended seminars and conducted research alongside the young men who would become leaders in the Catholic Church, like Joseph Ratzinger, Cardinal and later Prefect of the Congregation for the Doctrine of the Faith; Alfred Bengsch, the late Cardinal of Berlin; Friedrich Wetter, Cardinal of Munich; and Hubert Luthe, Bishop of Essen. Many of Gössmann's male colleagues were offered teaching positions before they had done more than begin their *Habilitationsschrift* while hers was already well underway, a memory that always evokes some justifiable bitterness.[29] When all thirty-seven of her applications to teaching positions in theology and philosophy were rejected, Gössmann was plagued by self-doubt and even self-hatred. Her dissertation advisor's black-humored comment on the rejections, "Birth defect: female," served as a reminder that he never doubted her intelligence and ability.[30]

In 1955, two months after the birth of their first daughter, Gössmann accepted a teaching position at a Women's University in Tokyo, and later on in the German department at the Sophia University in Tokyo, where her husband, Wilhelm Gössmann, held a position. The couple's second daughter was born in Tokyo in 1957. Because the couple received enough social support, Gössmann was able to teach and continue her research even while their daughters were small.

The years in Tokyo were fruitful ones. Gössmann taught not only German language and literature at the Sophia University but also offered courses at the Seishin Women's University, where she lectured in English on medieval philosophy and modern Christian philosophy. Because she spoke English as a second language, and therefore slowly and with precise enunciation, many of the international students understood her better than her American and British colleagues, whose speech was more fluent but also faster.

After five years in Japan, in 1960, the family returned to Munich. Gössmann's work on her *Habilitationsschrift*, in which she was researching the *Summa Theologica* (a compendium of theological knowledge) redacted by the Franciscan Alexander Halensis, required the resources available in the *Staatsbibliothek* in Munich. Schmaus offered her a position as a researcher at the Grabmann Institute, and she was able to pursue her studies as well, during which she increased her understanding of the differences between the various Scholastic schools of thought.

Gössmann submitted her *Habilitationsschrift* in fulfillment of the requirements of *Habilitation* in theology in the fall of 1962 to Schmaus, who knew something of the expected outcome of Vatican II (1962) and had attempted to prepare the theology faculty to grant *Habilitation* to a layperson, one who had not been consecrated as a priest or even as a deacon.[31] However, it quickly became clear that the bishops' conference of Germany raised some objections, as up to that time all faculty members of university theology departments were consecrated priests. Rather than have Gössmann's *Habilitationsschrift* publicly failed because of her status as a layperson, which would have made a later acceptance of her work impossible, Schmaus withdrew her text from submission to the Catholic theology faculty at the LMU. His attempts to have her *Habilitationsschrift* accepted at another university in Germany or Austria proved as disappointing.

Yet the possibility that a later submission might pass was made clear to Gössmann by Cardinal Julius Döpfner (Munich/Freising), who assured her that the fault did not lie in her abilities but rather explained that "We bishops do not know what to do with lay professors in the theology faculty."[32] Gössmann describes her reaction to this statement as positive, as it was her status as a layperson, not as a woman, that the bishops and faculty found at that time an insurmountable obstacle, and that attitude would likely change, in consequence of the shifts taking place following Vatican II. Since that time a number of laymen have had their *Habilitationsschrift* accepted and, more recently, a handful of women; however, Gössmann is not among them. Her *Habilitationsschrift*, in addition to her later scholarly works on medieval philosophy, were accepted by the philosophy department of the LMU for her *Habilitation* in 1978, fourteen years after its publication, thus making one of Germany's most famous female theologians, academically at least, a philosopher.[33]

Following the refusal of her *Habilitation*, Gössmann returned to Tokyo with her two daughters in 1963. She continued teaching at both the Sophia and Seishin Universities, published her *Habilitationsschrift* and other books, remained current in European theological debates, and began research into Japanese religious practices.

Modern Japanese society is overwhelmingly secular, with religious roots in Shintoism, Mahayâna-Buddhism, and Confucianism. Gössmann had the opportunity to observe these religious practices as an outsider, and to compare them with both her own modern Catholic traditions and with medieval Christian theology. Her research into Japan's religious past led to publications on the history of Christianity in Japan, in which she concentrated on religious history after 1549, the year Saint Francis Xavier landed in Japan, as well as the recuperation of historical female figures, such as the Christian martyr Gracia Hosokawa Tama (d. 1600).[34]

In 1967 Gössmann was appointed director of the "Humanities in English" department at Seishin Women's University. In Japan at the time the "humanities" as college subject matter had been imported from the United States, and focused primarily on literature, history, and philosophy, with some social science as well. Her favorite course was a two-year cycle of "Great Books of World Literature," which included German, English, Spanish, French, Italian, and Russian works, which she organized with colleagues from the respective departments or embassies. By 1968 she had achieved an appointment as *Kyôju*, or "full professor." She describes the following seven years as relatively happy ones in which she developed professionally and academically and enjoyed teaching her internationally mixed students.[35]

However, Japan's universities did not retain their ability to attract international students, and in 1974 the "Humanities in English" department was dissolved because of low enrollments. Gössmann had previously recognized that her future as an academic in Tokyo would require her to teach in Japanese, a language that she had acquired during her years in Japan, but also one in which she had had no formal language instruction. During the 1974 spring semester break she began the arduous task of preparing her lectures in Japanese. One of the students, a young Japanese woman, resided with Gössmann and her daughters at this time and assisted her in addressing questions of style.[36] Gössmann's university appointment at Seishin Women's University was transferred to the Department of Western Philosophy (*Seiyô tetsugaku*), which included a section on Christian Studies, where she later became section director. Here Gössmann had the opportunity to teach Greek, the New Testament, Greek and Roman philosophy, as well as Christian Theology and women in the Christian tradition. She and her Japanese colleagues from the department continue to maintain a cordial relationship, expressed most clearly in their mutually cooperative translation efforts.

In 1977 Professor Eugen Biser (LMU) offered to evaluate her medieval publications, including her original *Habilitationsschrift,* as a basis for awarding Gössmann her *Habilitation* in philosophy. To attain this degree she was required to submit three theses to the committee and prepare a substantive written lecture on each one as part of the final requirements for the *Habilitation*.[37] Thus, as she "commuted" between Munich and Tokyo, she found herself constantly filling her suitcases with books and photocopies to prepare for the theses and the final *Habilitation* lecture; carrying these materials with her was a nerve-wracking experience, as she flew Aeroflot via Moscow, and the Soviets were interested in limiting the transportation of printed material within their borders.³⁸ In the winter term 1978/79 Elisabeth Gössmann received her *Habilitation* at the LMU in the Department of Philosophy.

Although she was now qualified to teach at German universities, her academic life remained in Japan, because no German university would hire her. While initially depressing, her position in Japan allowed her to teach seminars based on her initial interest in medieval texts, written by women as well as men. This would not have been the case in Germany, which lagged behind Japan and the United States in offering courses in Women's Studies. Her research on historical women, their texts, and their actions, by which means they influenced and corrected current androcentric theories about women, also encouraged Gössmann to overcome her own resignation and continue to strive for the recognition that women had always been involved in the transmission and transformation of theological thought. In 1984 the first volume in her series, "Archiv für philosophie- und theologiegeschichtliche Frauenforschung," appeared in Munich, published by Iudicium.³⁹

In 1985 Gössmann received an honorary degree (Dr. h.c., Doctor honoris causa) in Theology from the Universität Graz, Austria, and the following year she was invited to teach as a guest professor at the Universität Münster and also at the LMU. Because the semesters in Europe and Japan do not overlap, she was able to accept the invitations. For the first time in three decades of teaching at the university level, Gössmann lectured in her native tongue and was astonished at how quickly one could prepare for classes. Other guest professorships in Austria and Switzerland followed; however, she credits her students from Munich for gaining her a non-tenure-track professorship at the LMU. Her students petitioned for her to serve as their exam director, for which she would require a permanent position in Germany, and they were supported in their petition by the faculty of the philosophy department and Professor Werner Beierwaltes at the LMU. Such a position could only be created for her because she had passed her *Habilitation* in philosophy, however late that had occurred.

The position at the LMU required that she give up her full professorship in Tokyo; however, the university there offered her an honorary professorship, which allowed her to retain certain responsibilities, as well as to lecture, teach, and publish in Japan. After so many years of teaching required courses, including language, she now allows herself the freedom to teach only those courses that interest her personally and contribute to her own research.

When she first began teaching in Germany, her seminars were usually filled by female students. Her first male students appeared when she began offering courses regularly at the LMU. She notes that at the beginning of the nineties, these male students behaved in class like the few female theological students in the forties and early fifties: they remained practically silent. She is encouraged that this has changed, and that both men and women in her courses feel free to exchange ideas. In addition she has visited the United States a number of times to give conference papers on Hildegard von Bingen and finds further encouragement in the scholarly engagement that this German mystic has found in the English-speaking academy.⁴⁰

Gössmann has since been honored with a festschrift (1993) and another honorary degree, this one being that of a Doctor of Philosophy from the Johann Wolfgang Goethe-Universität, Frankfurt am Main, in 1994.[41] On 12 June 2001 the Catholic Theology Department of the University of Graz in Austria awarded the first Elisabeth Gössmann Prizes for superior scholarship in the fields of Women's and Gender Studies in Theology. Dr. Silvia Arzt and Maria Katharina Moser, M.A., received the awards for their respective theses, which both "critically address elements and tendencies of discrimination against women, or discrimination based on gender, in Christian or other religious traditions, or in other broadly based philosophical traditions."[42] The recognition that Prof. Dr. Gössmann has received in the last two decades of the twentieth century is long overdue in a professional life marked by gender-based obstacles and setbacks.

Gössmann currently alternates her time between Tokyo and Munich, where she lectures and offers seminars at a number of universities. She remains active in research and teaching, in which her interests remain the recuperation of women into the historical, Christian theological tradition, investigations into gender-based differences in societies and religions, and medieval doctrinal theories about the relationships of human beings, both male and female, with the Godhead.

Notes

1. Much of the information about Elisabeth Gössmann's early life stems from her own *Lebenslauf*, which is a narrative description of the course or progress of one's life and is also a standard text that accompanies résumés in the German speaking world. When Gössmann wrote her *Lebenslauf* in 1999, she punningly titled it *Hindernislauf*, "the obstacle course" of her life. "Hindernislauf," 91.

2. Another source for information about Gössmann's life stems from a series of radio interviews, which were broadcast by Hessischer Rundfunk in 2000 and were then edited and published by Lothar Bauerochse and Klaus Hofmeister; see Gössmann, "Elisabeth Gössmann," 46.

3. "Adoring Mary" meant adoration in the technical sense of worshipping the Virgin Mary, or honoring her in a fashion that the Protestant groups find excessive and that should be reserved for God alone. The attitude of the Catholic Church toward Mary and the saints has been misinterpreted or misrepresented by Protestant groups since the Reformation. These misconceptions persist into the present day.

4 "In Gedanken stellten Friedel und Günter viele Schränke und Tische übereinander, um Gottes Größe zu ermessen, und ich bemühte mich, den großen Birnbaum auf unserem Hof oder den alten Kastanianbaum auf dem Hegertor gelegentlich dazwischen zu schieben, da mir Bäume 'göttlicher' erschienen als das tote Holz." Gössmann, "Hindernislauf," 91.

5. Günter's question, "Wie groß ist der liebe Gott?" was answered by Friedel as "größer als unser Vater." Gössmann noted that, for her friends, "'Unser Mutter' war von solchen Vergleichen ausgeklammert" ("Our mother" [Friedel and Günter's mother] was bracketed from such comparisons). Gössmann, "Hindernislauf," 91.

6. "[Die Mutter] darauf, . . . am Abend zum Vater: 'Das Kind ist manchmal etwas überspannt.'" Gössmann, "Hindernislauf," 91.

7. "Er war im Herbst 1937, nachdem er schon viel früher ohne sein Zutun vom 'Stahlhelm' in die 'SA' überführt worden war, in die Partei eingetreten, aus Karrieregründen" Gössmann, "Hindernislauf," 91. The name *Stahlhelm* (steel helmet) comes from the headgear worn by the German army since 1916. This group was later absorbed into the SA and its membership transferred to that body. The Sturm Abteilung (storm troopers) was a quasi-military group with police-like functions, designed to intimidate those who disagreed with the National Socialists. After the institution of the SS (*Schutzstaffel*), the elite police/military group, the SA lost importance.

8. Gössmann's school was the Goethe-Oberschule für Mädchen.

9. "Wir wurden von unseren mitverschickten Lehrerinnen (mit einer Ausnahme) nicht etwa nationalsozialistisch indoktriniert, eigentlich auch nicht von den BDM-Führerinnen." Gössmann, "Hindernislauf," 92.

10. The *Abitur* is the high-school final exam that qualifies students to study at a university.

11. At that time there were only eight years of secondary education required for university-bound students. Two years later a ninth class year was added.

12. Gössmann, "Theologiegeschichtliche Frauenforschung," 71.

13. Revelations about the Nazi's comprehensive misuse of theology, history, literature, culture, biology, and science led many Germans in the late fifties to question the ability of knowledge, art, or philosophy to comprehend or express the horrors of Auschwitz. The question, "Could there be literature, science, art, philosophy *'nach Auschwitz'*?" was commonly answered in the negative. It took a full generation for Germans, Germanists, and especially theologians to begin to answer this question positively.

14. *Staatsexamen*, or state exams, are required for graduate study at a German university and also serve as the final fulfillment of the requirements for a teaching position at a German secondary school (*Gymnasium*).

15. Among the requirements the sentence "Der Kandidat müsse bereits die Diakonatsweihe empfangen haben" had been dropped. Gössmann, "Hindernislauf," 94.

16. "Ja, aber nur, wenn Ihr nicht mit einer durchschnittlichen Arbeit kommt, sonst gibt es sicher Schwierigkeiten" Gössmann, "Hindernislauf," 94. According to a later radio interview, Schmaus warned, "Ihr müßt am Anfang mindestens doppelt so viel leisten, wie Männer, sonst bringen wir euch nicht durch" (At the beginning, you would have to work at least twice as hard as the men; otherwise we will not be able to get you through.) Gössmann, "Prof. Dr. Elisabeth Gössmann im Gespräch mit Wolfgang Küpper."

17. A *Doktorarbeit* serves as the first graduate dissertation and, along with the doctoral exams, is required in order to gain for the successful candidate the title of Doctor of Theology. Those wishing to teach at the professorial level must continue in their studies and complete a second dissertation, the *Habilitationsschrift*.

18. Seminal texts by Gössmann's professors, which demonstrate the reformulations and new directions of post-war theological scholarship, include Steffes, *Christliche Existenz inmitten der Welt;* Steffes, *Glaubensbegründung;* Ohm, *Die Liebe zu Gott in den nichtchristlichen Religionen;* and Söhngen, *Philosophische Einübung in die Theologie*.

19. For an example of the combination of dialectics, philosophy, exegetics, and history, see Volk, *Das neue Marien-Dogma*.

20. Grabmann-Institut zur Erforschung der Philosophie und Theologie des Mittelalters. The institute was founded by Schmaus in memory of his dissertation advisor (*Doktorvater*), Martin Grabmann.

21. For historically grounded readings of the gospels, see Schmid, *Das Evangelium nach Matthäus;* Schmid, *Das Evangelium nach Lukas;* Schmid, *Das Evangelium nach Markus.*

22. "Uns Theologiestudentinnen ging ein Licht auf, dass das 'Mulier taceat', das uns immer noch an den Kopf geworfen wurde, wohl nicht für alle Zeiten galt und auch nicht zur ersten Botschaft aus der Jesus-Bewegung gehörte." Gössmann, "Theologiegeschichtliche Frauenforschung," 70.

23. Schmaus, *Der Glaube der Kirche;* Schmaus, *Dogma.*

24. In particular Gössmann notes that she read Hildegard von Bingen, whose texts she found in volume 197 of J.- P. Migne's *Patrologia Latina* (Paris: Garnier Fratres, 1882), in which she is listed as one of the "Patres Latini," or Latin Fathers. Vol. 197 contains the *Vita S. Hildegardis, Epistolae, Scivias, Liber divinorum operum, Physica,* and several short works.

25. "Das scheint ja nicht bloß (!) eine Mystikerin, sondern eine 'gestandene' Theologin gewesen zu sein." Gössmann, "Theologiegeschichtliche Frauenforschung," 72.

26. "Aber es war in einer theologischen Arbeit alles andere als selbstverständlich, neben den Kommentaren aus männlicher Feder auch weibliche Äußerungen zu dieser Thematik zu zitieren." (In a theological study it was anything but acceptable to cite women's statements on this theme next to the commentaries that flowed from masculine pens.) Gössmann, "Theologiegeschichtliche Frauenforschung," 72–73.

27. "[Ich habe] die Frauentexte damals nicht in die Rubrik 'theologisches Schrifttum,' sondern in die über geistliche Dichtung eingeordnet." (At that time I did not organize the women's texts within the rubric of "theological commentary," but rather under "spiritual poetry.") Gössmann, "Theologiegeschichtliche Frauenforschung," 73.

28. Gössmann's *Doktorarbeit* was published in accordance with German university degree requirements as *Die Verkündigung an Maria im dogmatischen Verständnis des Mittelalters.*

29. Gössmann's record of the sexual bias, which affected her so directly, appears in her autobiographical article, "Theologiegeschichtliche Frauenforschung." "In den sechziger Jahren wurde so mancher Kollege am Institut auf einen Lehrstuhl berufen, noch ohne mit seiner Habil-Schrift so recht begonnen zu haben. Kurz nach Abschluss der Ausbildung am Institut waren alle meine dortigen Kollegen Professoren oder Bischöfe—bis auf die wenigen Frauen." (In the sixties a number of my male colleagues at the [Grabmann] Institute were offered teaching positions [at universities] even though [an individual] had not yet begun his *Habil-Schrift.* Shortly after the completion of [our] education at the Institute, all of my [male] colleagues from there were professors or bishops, except for the few women.) Gössmann, "Theologiegeschichtliche Frauenforschung," 69.

30. "Geburtsfehler: weiblich." Gössmann, "Hindernislauf," 90.

31. "[O]bwohl Schmaus im Rom, im Aufwind der ersten Sitzungsperiode des II. Vaticanum, versucht hatte, allerwärts 'gutes Wetter' für die 'Laienhabilitation' (Habilitation von Nichtpriestern) zu machen." (Although Schmaus had attempted in Rome, under the impetus of the first session of Vatican II, to create 'good weather [smooth sailing]' for the acceptance of lay-*Habilitations* [*Habilitationsschrift* written by nonpriests].) Gössmann, "Hindernislauf," 95.

32. "Wir Bischöfe wissen ja noch nicht, was wir mit habilitierten Laien in der Theologie anfangen sollen." Gössmann, "Hindernislauf," 95; Alpha Forum (shortened form from note 16).

33. Gössmann's *Habilitationsschrift* was published as *Metaphysik und Heilsgeschichte. Eine theologische Untersuchung der Summa Halensis.*

34. Gössmann, *Religiöse Herkunft, profane Zukunft? Das Christentum in Japan.* Gössmann's

research on Gracia Hosokawa Tama appears much later, in the collection of essays *Japan—ein Land der Frauen?*

35. "Dazu gehört auch ein zweijähriger Kurs, 'Great Books of World Literature,' den zu organisieren mir viel Spass machte. . . . Das waren sieben relativ glücklich verlaufende und Berufsfreude erweckende Jahre, die auch durch die bunt gemischte Studentinnenschaft viel Anregung gaben." Gössmann, "Hindernislauf," 94.

36. "Nächtelang sass ich an der Vorbereitung, wobei ich die Hilfe einer bei uns wohnenden Studentin in Anspruch nehmen musste." Gössmann, "Hindernislauf," 95. According to Gössmann she never "translated" lectures from one language to another but instead prepared them directly in the language of delivery. Elisabeth Gössmann, letter to author, 5 September 2002.

37. All those seeking the degree of *Habilitation* need only hold one lecture; however, they must prepare three and are informed shortly before their scheduled date as to which topic has been chosen. Because Gössmann was residing and lecturing in Tokyo, this requirement caused her a number of difficulties not normally encountered by applicants in a similar position in Germany.

38. "In Moskau . . . musste man damals noch auf einen Fragebogen die Titel aller Bücher und Zeitschriften eintragen, die man mit sich führte. Ich hatte aber nichts als Bücher und Kopien zur Vorbereitung meiner drei Themen im Gepäck. . . . Ich wagte es, ein leeres Blatt abzugeben. . . . Auf dem Rückweg ging es genauso, allerdings mit viel Herzklopfen, aus Furcht, dass mir etwas Notwendiges abgenommen werden könnte" (At that time in Moscow, you had to complete a [customs] form and record all of the titles of all of the books and journals/magazines that you had in your luggage. However, I had nothing but books and photocopies for the preparation of my three theses in my luggage. . . . I risked turning in a blank page. . . . It was the same on the return trip, which [I endured] with great heart palpitations out of fear that something absolutely necessary [to my theses] could be confiscated from me). Gössmann, "Hindernislauf," 95.

39. Gössmann, *Das wohlgelahrte Frauenzimmer.* A second revised and expanded edition of the text was published in 1998.

40. Gössmann read papers on Hildegard von Bingen at the International Medieval Congress in Kalamazoo, Michigan, in 1986, 1987, 1988, and 1991 and also participated in the Hildegard-Congress in Burlington, Vermont, in 1998.

41. For Gössmann's festschrift, see Schneider and Schüngel-Straumann, *Theologie zwischen Zeiten und Kontinenten.*

42. "Die Katholisch-Theologische Fakultät der Universität Graz hat einen Preis für hervorragende Arbeiten zur Frauen- und Geschlechterforschung eingerichtet und ihn nach Frau Prof. Dr. theol., Dr. phil. habil., Dr. h.c. mult. Elisabeth Gössmann benannt. . . . Die Arbeiten können aus allen theologischen Fachdisziplinen kommen. Sie sollen sich kritisch mit frauen- und geschlechterdiskriminierenden Elementen und Tendenzen in den christlichen oder anderen religiösen oder weltanschaulichen Traditionen auseinandersetzen und zugleich kreative Neuentwürfe entwickeln. Erwartet werden Arbeiten mit einem explizit feministischen Ansatz." http://www.uni-graz.at/ainst/news/news_01/goessmann.html.

SELECT BIBLIOGRAPHY OF WORKS BY ELISABETH GÖSSMANN

Die Verkündigung an Maria im dogmatischen Verständnis des Mittelalters. Munich: Hueber, 1957.
"Der Christologietraktat in der *Summa Halensis,* bei Bonaventura und Thomas von Aquin." *Münchener Theologische Zeitschrift* 12 (1961): 175–91.

Mann und Frau in Familie und Öffentlichkeit. Munich: Hueber, 1964.

Metaphysik und Heilsgeschichte. Eine theologische Untersuchung der "Summa Halensis." Grabmann-Institut zur Erforschung der Mittelalterlichen Theologie und Philosophie. Mitteilungen. Special Issue. Munich: Hueber, 1964.

Religiöse Herkunft, profane Zukunft? Das Christentum in Japan. Munich: Hueber, 1965.

Glaube und Gotteserkenntnis im Mittelalter. Freiburg: Herder, 1971.

Antiqui und Moderni im Mittelalter. Eine geschichtliche Standortbestimmung. Veröffentlichungen des Grabmann-Instituts zur Erforschung der mittelalterlichen Theologie und Philosophie; n.F., 23. Paderborn: F. Schöningh, 1974.

"Dialektische und rhetorische Implikationen der Auseinandersetzung zwischen Abaelard und Bernhard von Clairvaux um die Gotteserkenntnis." In *Sprache und Erkenntnis im Mittelalter.* Edited by Wolfgang Kluxen. *Miscellanea Mediaevalia* 13. 890–902. Berlin: de Gruyter, 1981.

Die streitbaren Schwestern: Was will die Feministische Theologie? Freiburg: Herder, 1981.

Editor. *Das wohlgelahrte Frauenzimmer.* Archiv für philosophie- und theologiegeschichtliche Frauenforschung, 1. Munich: Iudicium, 1984, 1998.

Editor. *Eva—Gottes Meisterwerk.* Archiv für philosophie- und theologiegeschichtliche Frauenforschung, 2. Munich: Iudicium, 1985, 2000.

Editor. *Johann Caspar Eberti: "Eröffnetes Cabinet deß gelehrten Frauen-Zimmers," unveränderter Nachdruck der Ausgabe Frankfurt und Leipzig, 1706.* Archiv für philosophie- und theologiegeschichtliche Frauenforschung, 3. Munich: Iudicium, 1986, 1990.

Editor with Günter Zobel. *Das Gold im Wachs. Festschrift für Thomas Immoos zum 70. Geburtstag.* Munich: Iudicium, 1988.

Editor. *Ob die Weiber Menschen seyn, oder nicht?* Archiv für philosophie- und theologiegeschichtliche Frauenforschung, 4. Munich: Iudicium, 1988, 1996.

Editor with Dieter R. Bauer. *Maria, für alle Frauen oder über allen Frauen?* Reihe Frauenforum. Freiburg: Herder, 1989.

Editor. *Japan—Ein Land der Frauen?* Munich: Iudicium, 1991.

Editor with others. *Wörterbuch der Feministischen Theologie.* Gütersloh: Gütersloher Verlagshaus Gerd Mohn, 1991, 2002.

"'Naturaliter femina est subiecta viro.' Die Frau—Ein verminderter Mann? Thomas von Aquin." In *Wie Theologen Frauen sehen—Von der Macht der Bilder.* Edited by Renate Jost and Ursula Kubera. 37–56. Freiburg: Herder, 1993.

Editor. *Kennt der Geist kein Geschlecht?* Archiv für philosophie- und theologiegeschichtliche Frauenforschung, 6. Munich: Iudicium, 1994.

Editor. *Mulier Papa. Der Skandal eines weiblichen Papstes. Zur Rezeptionsgeschichte der Gestalt der Päpstin Johanna.* Archiv für philosophie- und theologiegeschichtliche Frauenforschung, 5. Munich: Iudicium, 1994.

Hildegard of Bingen: Four Papers. Peregrina Papers series, no. 5. Toronto: Peregrina Publishing, 1995.

Editor. *Hildegard von Bingen. Versuche einer Annäherung.* Archiv für philosophie- und theologiegeschichtliche Frauenforschung. Special Issue. Munich: Iudicidum, 1995.

"Theologiegeschichtliche Frauenforschung—Eine Bedrohung für die etablierte Theologie?" In *Zäsur: Generationswechsel in der katholischen Theologie.* Edited by Gebhard Fürst. 69–86. Stuttgart: Akademie der Diözese Rottenburg-Stuttgart, 1997.

Editor. *Johann Heinrich Feustking: Gynaeceum haeretico fanaticum, Oder Historie und Beschreibung*

Der falschen Prophetinnen / Quäckerinnen / Schwärmerinnen / und andern sectirischen und begeisterten Weibes-Personen. Nachdruck der Ausgabe Frankfurt u. Leipzig, Zimmermann, 1704. Mit einer Einleitung von Ruth Albrecht. Archiv für philosophie- und theologiegeschichtliche Frauenforschung, 7. Munich: Iudicium, 1998.

"Prof. Dr. Elisabeth Gössmann im Gespräch mit Wolfgang Küpper." *Alpha Forum.* Bayrischer Rundfunk (Bavarian Radio). Interview by Wolfgang Küpper. 24 August 1998. Available from http://www.br-online.de/alpha/forum/vor9808/19980824_i.html.

"Hindernislauf." *Widerspruch: Münchner Zeitschrift für Philosophie* 36 (2000): 90–99.

"Elisabeth Gössmann." In *Wie sie wurden, was sie sind—Zeitgenössische Theologinnen und Theologen im Portrait.* Edited by Lothar Bauerochse and Klaus Hofmeister. 45–61. Gütersloh: Gütersloher Verlagshaus, 2001.

Works Cited

Migne, J.- P., ed. *Patrologia Latina.* Vol. 197. Paris: Garnier Fratres, 1882.

Ohm, Thomas, O.S.B. *Die Liebe zu Gott in den nichtchristlichen Religionen.* Freiburg: Erich Wewel Verlag, 1950.

Schmaus, Michael. *Der Glaube der Kirche. Handbuch katholischer Dogmatik.* Vols. 1–4. 1938–41. Reprint, Munich: Hueber, 1969–70.

———. *Dogma.* Vols. 1–6. Edited by T. Patrick Burke. Translated by Ann Laeuchli, Mary Lederer, et al. London: Sheed and Ward, 1971–77.

Schmid, Josef. *Das Evangelium nach Matthäus.* Regensburg: Pustet, 1959.

———. *Das Evangelium nach Lukas.* Regensburg: Pustet, 1960.

———. *Das Evangelium nach Markus.* Regensburg: Pustet, 1963.

Schneider, Theodor, and Helen Schüngel-Straumann, eds. *Theologie zwischen Zeiten und Kontinenten. Für Elisabeth Gössmann.* Freiburg i. Br.: Herder, 1993.

Söhngen, Gottlieb. *Philosophische Einübung in die Theologie. Erkennen—Wissen—Glauben.* Freiburg i. Br.: K. Alber, 1955.

Steffes, Johann Peter. *Christliche Existenz inmitten der Welt. Die Bildung zum christlichen Menschen.* Düsseldorf: Patmos, 1947.

———. *Glaubensbegründung. Christlicher Gottesglaube in Grundlegung und Abwehr.* Edited by Ludwig Deimel. Vol. 1. Mainz: Grünewald, 1958.

Universität Graz. Ausseninstitut Kurzmeldung. "Elisabeth Gössmann-Preis erstmalig vergeben." http://www.uni-graz.at/ainst/news/news_01/goessmann.html. 2001. Katholische Fakultät. Universität Graz.

Volk, Hermann. *Das neue Marien-Dogma: Inhalt, Begründung, Bedeutung.* Münster: Verlag Regensberg, 1951.

CHAPTER 63

My Way with Misericords (1929–)

ELAINE C. BLOCK

IT IS DIFFICULT for me to believe that I am living a fairy-tale life. I divide my time between Paris and New York; I travel extensively over my favorite medieval routes in Europe; I have friends all over the world; and I have time to do what I wish to do—study and write about medieval misericords. This stage of my life took many years to form and on the way I passed many critical moments.

The Très riches heures du Duc de Berry

Never in my life had I seen such a beautiful painting. I stood before this reproduction of a calendar page from the *Très riches heures du Duc de Berry,* astounded by the landscapes, the castles, the tiny people in their homes and on the land. I wondered how I might spend the rest of my life looking at and studying this work of art. It took me twenty years to find a way.

I was a graduate student in Paris, recipient of a scholarship from the French government. Following my graduation from Cornell University, as an English major, my father promised me a year's graduate study at the university of my choice, but he never dreamed that my choice would be the Sorbonne. I thus investigated possibilities myself, and when I announced I had a scholarship to the university of my choice, my father canceled his objections, mainly that his twenty-year-old daughter was going forth to an unknown land at a difficult time.

It was just after the war, and I was probably the first American student, except for several thousand former GIs, to land in France. I was also the youngest graduate student in the scholarship group and was therefore given a G-3 ration card, which

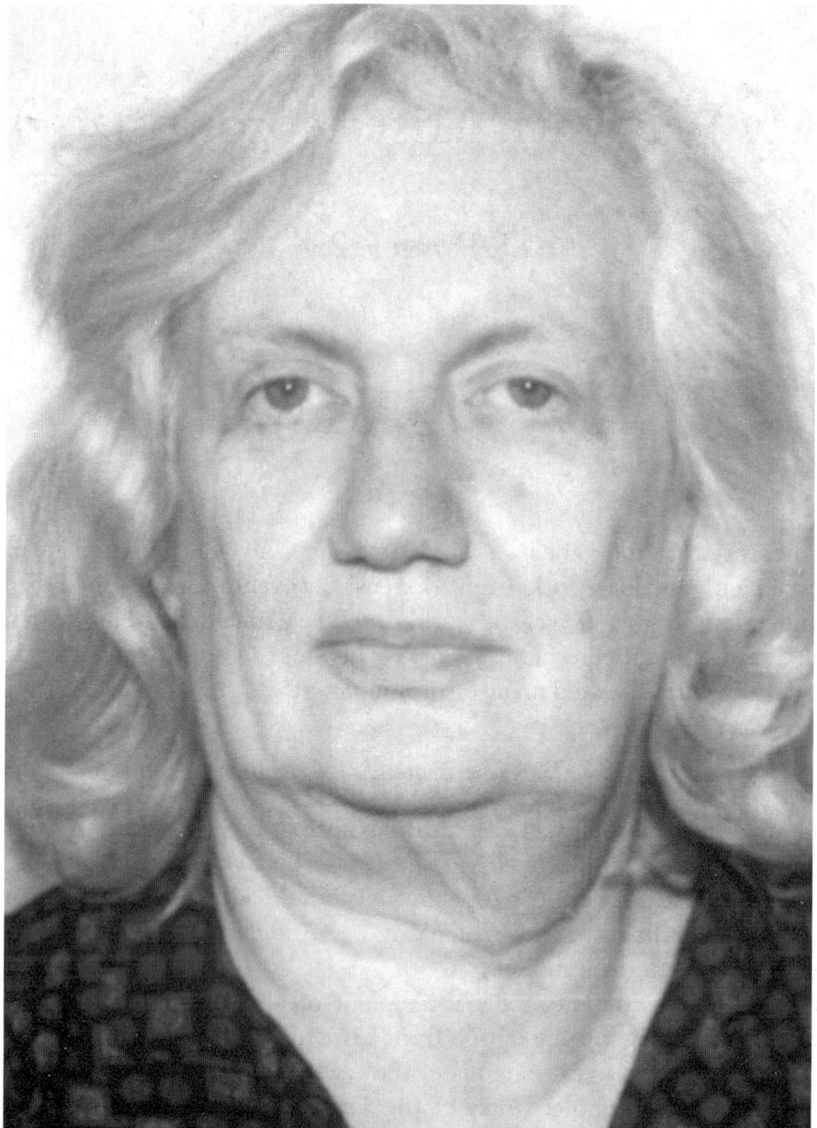

entitled me to a glass of milk every other day and a bar of chocolate a month, but no cigarettes.

I was not especially interested in the Middle Ages until I saw the copy of the *Très riches heures* manuscript at the Musee Condé at Chantilly. After lectures on French literature and on art history at the Louvre, I hung around the galleries on the Left Bank. I became aquainted with contemporary artists and started my collection of graphics. I traveled wherever it was possible to go, but my main love was France with its exquisite countryside and more medieval monuments than I could possibly see in one lifetime. I extended my stay in Paris for two years, returned to the United States, and married one of the former GIs. With a husband who was still a student and my son on the way, I realized I would have to contribute to the family income. I became a teacher and taught at an inner-city school in New York.

Folio 92 of *The Hours of Catherine of Cleves*

One Christmas, many years later, I received a gift of a facsimile edition of *The Hours of Catherine of Cleves*. I was almost as fascinated with these illuminations as I was with the *Très riches heures*. When I turned to folio 92, I realized I had the answer to my twenty-year-old question. The illumination showed the Holy Family in a workroom. Joseph was carving lumber, Mary was weaving, and the baby was learning to walk in a walker. There were beams on the ceiling, panes of glass on the window, and dishes on shelves, and on the next folio, Joseph was resting on a barrel chair. This was the life not of the Holy Family in the Holy Land but of a bourgeois family in medieval France. What a wonderful way to teach about medieval life! Works of art could be the primary source materials to learn about the civilization that produced them. Until now my main goal in teaching had been to incorporate art in many ways into the elementary school curriculum. I now had a Ph.D. in education from the University of Wisconsin, had returned to New York, had three children, and was teaching at Hunter College. I was director of Project Muse, where we developed materials to teach reading through the arts to children who were nonreaders. We found, for example, that many children could read songs better than ordinary prose. Reading directions for a craft project provided immediate satisfaction since the reader had a kite or a puppet in hand as a result of reading the directions.

After that Christmas vacation I presented a new course proposal to my chairperson: *Teaching Civilization through the Arts*. I intended to cover ancient China: Han to Tang, Aztecs, and nineteenth-century America as well as the European Middle Ages. While my chair was reading my proposal, her telephone rang. The education department of the Metropolitan Museum of Art was looking for a social-science specialist to work with them. Obviously I was the choice.

For the next three years I taught a graduate course at the Metropolitan Museum along with members of their education staff. We modified my proposed course outline and limited it to a study of the Middle Ages. Each session of the course covered one topic, such as childhood, married life, urban occupations, war, and calendars. I presented the topic illustrated with slides and then we analyzed selected works of art in the museum that illustrated these topics. I was able to incorporate the *Très riches heures* and other similar manuscripts into many sessions of the course. I soon encountered misericords, the carvings under the seats of choir stalls, and realized that they, better than any other art media—tapestries, manuscript illuminations, capitals of Romanesque columns—provided insights into the daily life and thought of the Middle Ages. I still have thousands of medieval slides, taken mainly from books, but they are in a closet and I use them only as comparison materials for my studies on misericords.

I visited the archives of the Monuments historiques (a government agency that has archives and a library in Paris and about twenty regional centers) and asked if there was a list of medieval choir stalls with misericords. They had no such list but offered to make me one. Two weeks later I returned for the list and was allowed to look at it but not to keep it. A bit of persistence led me to the head of department, who said of course I could have the list, but I would have to pay for it. I was more than happy to do that, and for fifteen francs, one for each page, I had the biggest bargain to start my research. In addition there was a good book—1910—on Belgian misericords and records of misericords in a series of government publications from Switzerland and Germany. A catalog of English misericords was replete with errors.

The Reynardian Society

My department was not particularly interested in my research. They knew that I went to Europe on every possible occasion, kept a car there, and roamed from one church to another to study and photograph the carvings on choir stalls. Another department, however, invited me to give an informal talk on my research. After the presentation, in which I used some of my by-now-extensive supply of slides, one colleague, Maurice Martinez, said my work would make a fine film. Martinez juggled his interests in filmmaking and jazz cello with his job of teaching sociology of education. We made a fine team, often hollering at each other when we disagreed and scaring the technician who worked with us, but always ending with a better version than either of us had originally proposed. Hunter College lent us their equipment when it was not being used by students. That meant we often worked late into the night, several times sleeping on the floor in our offices.

As we made the hour-long film, we applied for a grant from the U.S. Office of Education so that we could incorporate live shots of the churches and choir stalls in addition to the zooms and pans of my slides. In connection with this proposal I asked for a letter of recommendation from Christine Reno at Vassar College. Reno not only wrote a fine letter (we were not funded anyway) but also invited me to give a talk at the Mid-Hudson Valley Medieval Club. This might sound like small potatoes, but the other presenters were Meradith McMunn and Charity Cannon Willard, both close friends since that date. Willard asked if I knew Kenneth Varty. While I had read his books on foxes, including those on English misericords, I had never met him. I knew he was scheduled to talk soon at the Medieval Club of New York. Varty was president of the Reynard Society and Willard suggested that I give my mid-Hudson paper at their next meeting in August at Lausanne, Switzerland. My paper was accepted, and I met Varty at his talk in New York. He still talks of the invitation to my brownstone since he thought that was some kind of a gemstone. A few weeks afterward he saw a play, *Street Scene* by Elmer Rice, that took place in front of a brownstone. He and his wife, Hety, beamed to think they had actually been in one.

Lausanne, August 1990

I felt this was my first important entrance into the medieval world. About fifty people were there, and I knew only Kenneth, the president, and Willard, the star. On that first day I spent most of my time between sessions in the ladies room since I had no one to talk to. On the second day an excursion to the cathedral was scheduled. I told Kenneth I was going there early since I knew there were misericords. These were in a small chapel closed to the public. I asked to have it opened and explained my professional purpose. Among the misericords was a cock eating a sleeping fox. It probably represented the episode in the epic when the fox pretends to be asleep and swallows his prey when they get too close. What a real discovery for a Reynardian. When Kenneth arrived, I showed it to him. He told a few others, who in turn told the rest. My life has not been the same since that moment. I was seized by the members of this group who wanted to know how I knew the fox and cock were there and what else I knew about misericords. I felt I had come out, fully grown, from the closet since by now I had seen almost every misericord in twelve countries in Europe and had over fifty thousand slides. I had published a very few articles in esoteric journals so very few people knew that I was doing this research.

I was amazed mainly that this erudite group of people knew so little about misericords yet were fascinated when they saw these images that were in fact central to their work. I knew I had a lot of work to do just to present this area to medievalists. The general public, farther removed from these medieval tales, would have to be further enticed to add misericords to their cultural lives. Since the Lausanne meeting I have attended each Reynard meeting and presented a paper that suited the subject of the sly fox. There are, for example, fox preachers on misericords, fox thieves, and also fox physicians, musicians, teachers, and hunters, composing a topsy-turvy world.

That evening in Lausanne my recently completed film was shown, and attendance was 100 percent. I have since made five other films, one half hour each, an introduction and four focusing on the mirrors of Vincent of Beauvais. These films, two years in the making, each end with the words "This film was made with no grants from anybody"; they are distributed by the Museum of Modern Art in New York.

By the following day everyone knew me. I presented my paper on animals and proverbs on misericords and was swamped afterward with questions and comments.

Most of my friends—Brian Levy of Hull, Hisara Kondo of Kanasawa, Japan, Ettie Niebur of Amsterdam, Elizabeth Porges-Watson of Nottingham, Baudouin Van de Abeele of Louvain, Wilfried Schouwink of Heidelberg, and many others date from that conference.

My paper appeared in the *Reynardus* journal the following year, followed by others on the Green Man, the Triple Head, the Renaissance, and the Stalls of Gaillon and so forth.

Misericordia International

At one of the Reynardian conferences, Varty suggested that I start a misericord organization. Since Varty had started the Reynardian Society twenty years before, he was an expert at conference organization and administration. He advised a focus that was not too limited. Misericords alone would not be broad enough; we decided to include other profane arts and media such as tapestries, manuscript illuminations, and music. And so Misericordia International, a nonprofit organization registered in France and in the United States, was born.

Our first colloquium was in Paris and the Oise Valley in 1993. I sent out flyers, and the first person to contact me was Menahen Erez from Israel, whose wife was writing a thesis on the choir stalls of André Sulpice. While no one had yet applied for a place in the colloquium, Erez wanted to make sure a spot would be reserved for him and his wife, Ariela. And so I met an artist who is also a pilot for El Al and am grateful to him for the sketches he graciously makes for our various misericord publications.

The first colloquium consisted mainly of excursions to see choir stalls, with commentaries at each site. As I arranged for entry and photography in the church of Saint-Gervais in Paris, I realized that the monk I was speaking to, Brother Bradford, was an American from Virginia. He arranged for us to use the monastic meeting room, with kitchen, so we could breakfast together as we listened to Brother Bradford tell the history of the church. In return I gave a talk to the monks on the misericords in their choir stalls. When I last saw Brother Bradford, he was in charge of Vézelay Basilica and invited me to visit the choir or consult archives as I wished. My eleven-year-old grandson was visiting at the time, and after his amazement at the monks' friendly greeting subsided, he decided that everyone in France knew his grandma. Everyone, that is, on the misericord trail.

Of course, we planned much too much at our first colloquium and had to omit sites like Presles, L'Isle-Adam, and Saint-Denis. However, the colloquium served the purpose of bringing together those interested in misericords, and we printed—thanks to Brian Levy—a little book with a list and description of all the misericords on our route.

We sponsored several other colloquia: one in Barcelona organized by Wilfried Schouwink; one in Cologne and the Rhineland, also by Schouwink; one in Picardy, organized by Frédéric Billiet and Kristiane Lemé; and one in Angers, organized by Frederic Billiet and Patrick Barbier. In 2003 we had a colloquium in Sheffield, England, organized by Malcolm Jones, and in 2006 will have one in Basel, under the direction of Baudouin Van den Abeele.

At first a newsletter was prepared for Misericordia International members with lists of recent publications and announcements of relevant meetings. By 1994 this became a biannual publication called *Profane Arts / Arts profanes*. By the year 2000 the journal had become an annual in larger format and with improved design.

Conques: *Le Miroir des miséricordes*

A few year after the Lausanne conference, when I was in New York, I received a flyer from Varty in Glasgow. It was an announcement he had received of a conference to be held in the near future, organized by Claude Rivals at the University of Toulouse. I immediately replied to Toulouse, offering a paper and any help they might need with the conference. There was no reply.

In May of that year, once more in Paris, I received a telephone call from Marie Grèzes. She had recently completed a master's degree at Toulouse and was involved with the colloquium. When we met at my apartment, she brought her thesis, an inventory of misericords in Haute Normandy. I was delighted with this encounter since I had seen all her misericords and had similar photographs. Here was someone with whom I could share ideas on choir-stall iconography. The following day Pierre Bureau, also connected with the Toulouse conference, phoned, and we met; he was exploring the theme of the fight to see who wears the pants in the family. I had also seen all his misericords.

I realized that Grèzes and Bureau were like the spies from Canaan (a popular misericord theme). They had been sent by the Toulouse conference organizers to find out if I really knew anything about misericords, or if I was just bluffing. After all I was from America, a region notably deficient in medieval misericords. Following the two visits, my paper was accepted, and I attended the conference at beautiful Conques under the sponsorship of the Centre europeen d' art et de civilisation medievale. This was the first time I presented a paper in French. I had not as yet retired, and my time in France was limited. However, with two huge dictionaries, four books on grammar, and a number of friends on call, I managed to write the paper. My computer is French and automatically corrects minor errors. Friends corrected the grammar, and I practiced several times before the final performance. I have accepted the fact that I will always have an American accent, which some of my French friends find charming. I have a general and a technical vocabulary, and I dare not let my work be translated by an ordinary translator; he or she probably will not know a number of the words I use.

This colloquium was never publicized, and only a dozen or so people attended. However, the publication of the proceedings, *Le Miroir des miséricordes,* is now a standard reference in this field, and students working on theses frequently contact me and consult my misericord archives.

After I gave my Conques paper on Flemish proverbs on misericords, I descended the steps from the platform to see a tall young man, pen and notebook in hand, waiting for me. Since I had been introduced on stage, he knew my name, so he just asked for my address and phone number. He said he had written a book on music on the choir stalls at Amiens Cathedral and offered me a copy. I smiled and said I already had a copy and knew the book well. That was the start of my collaboration with Frédéric Billiet, recently appointed to the post of professor of early music at the University of Paris IV-Sorbonne (one of the several subuniversities of the University of Paris located in Paris or suburbs). I was honored to be a member of the jury for his habilitation at the University of Rouen.

Billiet and I have conducted a number of round tables on choir-stall iconography, organized sessions at Kalamazoo and Leeds, organized special misericord meetings, and collaborated on a number of publications. The years 2002–4 saw our collaboration on *Misericordes: Images profanes des lieux sacrés,* a bilingual lexicon, and a book on the choir stalls of Rouen Cathedral.

GIRS

After the Conques colloquium and several other conferences, I realized that I probably knew most of the students in France and in Belgium who were working on choir-stall iconography. One even contacted me by Internet. I invited all these students to a meeting so they could become acquainted and we could help one another. Sylvie Bethmont, one of the students—and this was her second or third career—offered her house at Moret-sur-Loing, near Fontainebleau. Ten of us met there and worked for three days. Bethmont's family organized our meals, and everyone brought some edibles with them. Between sessions we feasted. The family left for the weekend, so we had room to stay overnight.

It was soon obvious that the students had been working in a vacuum. Their thesis directors knew little or nothing of the field, which was not quite a field of study. They were just happy to talk to one another and comment on their common problems. Since misericord iconography is such an underdeveloped field, each student had begun from scratch by inventing terminology, descriptions, and even the names for different parts of choir stalls. We decided together to tackle several problems.

Our first job was to decide on a system to identify each seat in a set of choir stalls. That was necessary so that we would know what everyone was talking about. Some systems numbered seats from west to east and others from east to west. Still others numbered seats from northeast straight around a horseshoe-shaped arrangement to southeast. We decided on numbers from west, the usual entrance to the choir, to east, by the altar.

We decided on the letter *H* to indicate the rear row or the high row of stalls, should there be a double row. The *H* would also apply in French, standing for the *stalles hautes.* The letter *B* was adopted to indicate the base stalls, or *stalles basses.* The suggestion to have lowercase letters for the base stalls and uppercase for the high stalls was rejected since there would be problems with Internet communication.

While this work may seem primitive and unimportant, it shows the state of research in this field. We were reasonably satisfied with our numbering system, and I think we all use it now. We also felt the need for a name for our group, and after a night of reflection I suggested GIRS: Groupe international de recherche sur les stalles. Bethmont named the members the "stallologues."

The next problem we tackled was nomenclature. There was no name in French for certain parts of choir stalls: for example, misericords in Great Britain generally have side scenes called supporters, a heraldic term. Since there are rarely side scenes on French stalls, there is no word for them. We adopted the word *tenant,* which is also a heraldic term and matches the meaning of "supporter." The French word *jouée* has no equivalent in English, which uses the more generic term of "end panel." The French word was adopted and used to describe the English as well as the French panels.

Our lexicon became a more demanding project as we worked. Several meetings were held in Paris and at Billiet's house in Picardy, also large enough to house us all. The lexicon, about 175 pages, included an introduction, two iconographic sections, and four hundred illustrations; it was published by Brepols in 2004. Unfortunately, the group was divided by several conflicts and is not now active. Subgroups, however, still work together, and we expect further publications.

The Fire at Saint-Claude

In 1981, on one of my yearly meanderings on misericord routes, I took extensive notes on the choir stalls of Saint-Claude in the Jura. I had a new camera and was not sure if my photographs succeeded in the blackness of this cathedral. As it turned out my photos were blurry, but I still had my notes. It was only two years later that I heard of the fire that carbonized the south stalls of Saint-Claude. I returned to Saint-Claude at that time and asked if I could be of help in the reconstruction of these stalls. I was told that the project was well under way; the architect and sculptors had all the documents they needed. Many tourists had sent in photographs; no one had sent in notes.

Several years later I heard that the new south stalls were to be installed. I of course drove to the easternmost corner of France to participate in this great event. What I saw in the cathedral choir was nine misericords out of the original forty. What happened to the others? The guide told me there was not sufficient documentation, even with photographs contributed by tourists, to know where each misericord should be placed. And I had all the notes indicating the themes and details and the placement of each misericord. I spoke at length to the conservator of historic monuments in Franche Comte and offered her my notes on the Saint-Claude choir stalls. Gabrielle Devergramme was happy to accept them.

Those notes opened for me the doors to the workshop under the supervision of the family Fancelli, sculptors since the Renaissance. I even flew to Pisa to see the master carver at work. I was able to see the clay models and the plaster casts and participated in the decisions they made with the chief architect, Eric Pallot. When the stalls were ready to be installed, I was back at Saint-Claude to watch as each piece was placed in order. I was one of the honored guests, with police escort no less, at the celebration of the installation and was publicly thanked by the director of the province of the Jura. I devoted one issue of the *Profane arts* to the stalls of Saint-Claude, and the sacristan still smiles when he opens the grill to the choir on my visits to Saint-Claude.

Patrimony Day

The third weekend in September celebrates Patrimony Day in France. As far as I am concerned, this is the best time of the year to visit France. Many cultural monuments closed during the year are open to the public on these days, and other monuments, usually open, plan special events. Other countries now celebrate their patrimony, but on different days. I am possibly the only American to work in French monuments on Patrimony Day. Naturally, I talk to visitors about medieval life as revealed on choir stalls and guide them through a part of the church usually barred to the public.

I have been asked by a number of churches to be the misericord guide on Patrimony Day. Unfortunately I cannot cut myself in pieces. I am hoping that the graduate students in this field will take up the staff and offer to show misericords to the interested public.

I started my patrimony work at the Basilica Saint-Denis when I was writing a yet unpublished book on the Gaillon choir stalls, now in a dark corner of the nave of the basilica. The administrator of the basilica organized the patrimony program into fifteen-minute sessions so that visitors could choose one of several themes and follow a guide for no more than a half hour. They could then choose another theme and tour again. The royal tombs, the west portal sculptures, and the early excavations are some of the topics. I proposed that the daily life shown on medieval misericords be added. Thus every Patrimony Day for the past ten years or so I have guided groups—five or six each afternoon—and I show the exquisite stalls that were commissioned by Cardinal George d'Amboise for the archbishop of Rouen's summer palace. One woman returns each year. I used to guide both Saturday and Sunday, but now I have to divide my time. Several years ago I guided tours at Saint-Martin-aux-Bois, a little church that is all that remains of a great monastery with twenty-five of its original misericords that would be superb if they were repaired and cleaned. Windows were broken during a recent storm, and pigeons fly into the church but cannot find their way out. You can imagine the mess on the choir stalls. I have also been asked to guide groups at Rouen Cathedral and hope to do this on Patrimony Saturday, returning to the basilica for Sunday.

The Gaillon stalls are exceptionally important because they show the entrance of the Renaissance into France—before the School of Fontainebleau. My book on these stalls has been rejected by several publishers because "Gaillon is not the Sistine Chapel." But I have not given up. One day the general public, who may not be able to get easily to Saint-Denis, will enjoy seeing the miniature artists working on the armrests, medieval court musicians and musical putti playing on their Gothic or Renaissance partitions, and realistic Gothic and fantastic Renaissance groupings on the misericords. Sibyls and Virtues personified as women inhabit the first marquetry panels in France, while carvings of John the Baptist and Saint George overlook all the carvings below.

Choir stalls and their misericords are still generally ignored in churches. Usually, the seats are lowered, and it is not at all obvious that there are carvings below. While some churches leave the seats raised so that visitors can appreciate the glories normally hidden, other churches, especially in England, place heavy petit-point cushions, difficult to lift, on the seats. Those carvings are rarely seen. However, everyone who knows me heads for the choir and lifts these little seats. They send a postcard, a sketch, or a description. "Do I know this one?" Only once has a misericord been introduced to me this way.

By now I have traveled through thirteen countries in Europe, mainly through towns that have churches with misericords. I waited through three services in Flemish to see the choir stalls at Saint-Sauveur in Bruges. I was locked in the castle chapel at Cappenberg and scared the cleaning woman, who thought I was a phantom. I crawled under a piano in the Bolshoi Museum in Moscow, where I spotted a row of four misericords—from France. The church alarm system was turned off so I could study the misericords at Saint-Gertrude in Louvain. A nun photographed for me in a cloistered chapel in Spain. Since many churches, especially in France, are now locked, I know where to find most of the keys. The most difficult country to work in is Spain, and although I have managed to photograph, by hook or by crook, the misericords, there are many other carvings on Spanish choir stalls and a glance with a group of tourists, generally in the dark, is not sufficient as a base for study.

While I have been called obsessed with misericords, I think this term is not appropriate. A passion, yes, and one that has enriched my life immensely. A number of scholars have told me that I have created a field of study with its own language and its own lines of research. Perhaps. However, my main goals are to assist students in advancing this field and in making these sculptures available to the public so that their lives, too, can be enriched by the carvers' view of medieval life around them. I continue the misericord routes.

Afterword

On 9/11 everyone mentioned in this memoir telephoned me or sent an e-mail. In addition many members of their families also phoned—sisters, parents, aunts, and uncles. Some, not sure where I was at the moment, tried to contact me in Paris and in New York. On that day I happened to be at Rouen Cathedral working on the program for Patrimony Day. The program, along with all other celebrations of patrimony programs in 2001 was canceled. I look forward to many more Patrimony Days.

Select Bibliography of Works by Elaine C. Block

"A Hidden Pageant from the Middle Ages." *New York Times,* Travel Section, 30 December 1984.

"Bell the Cat and Gnaw the Bone: Animals and Proverbs on Misericords." *Renardus* 4 (1991): 41–50.

"Half Angel Half Beast: Images of Woman on Misericords." *Renardus* 5 (June 1992): 17–34, 235–45.

Misericords: Hidden Mirrors of Medieval Life. New York: Museum of Modern Art of New York, 1992. A series of 5 videotapes, each 30 minutes.

"Rural and Urban Occupations on Misericords." *Romance Language Annual* 3 (1992): 8–14.

With Kenneth Varty. "Dance Macabre on a Misericord." *Profane Arts* 5, no. 2 (autumn 1993): pages.

Misericords in Paris and the Oise Valley. Hull, Eng.: Hull University Press, 1993.

"The Devil at Saint-Katherine's." *Profane Arts* 2, no. 2. (autumn 1994): 9–13.

"The Choir Stalls of the Chateau of Gaillon: The Cutting Edge of the Renaissance in France." *Profane Arts* 4, no. 1 (spring 1995): 9–28.

"Judaic Images on Medieval Misericords." *Renardus* 8 (1995): 25–47, 225–35.

Misericords in the Rhineland. Cleveland: Shelden Enterprises, 1995.

"Reading the Choir Stalls of Saint-Claude." *Profane Arts* 4, no. 2 (autumn 1995): 35–60.

"Proverbs on Choir Stalls in the Rhineland." *Profane Arts* 5, no. 1 (spring 1996): 25–45.

"Visions of Hell on the Choir Stalls from the Chateau of Gaillon: A Note." *Profane Arts* 5, no. 2 (autumn 1996): 208–17.

"Hell under the Seats of the Choir Stalls." In *Les Animaux dans la littérature,* edited by H. Matsubara, S. Suzuki, N. Fukumoto, and N. Harano. Tokyo: Keio University Press, 1997.

"The Misericords of Saint-Martin-aux-Bois." *Profane Arts* 6, no. 1 (spring 1997): 26–38.

"Iconography of Choir Stalls in Barcelona." *Profane Arts* 6, no. 2 (autumn 1997): 240–57.

"The Triple Head Motif in Medieval Art and Literature." *Renardus* 10 (September 1997): 45–57.

"Physical and Social Inversions in the Topsy-Turvy World." *Profane Arts* 7, no. 1, (spring 1998): 8–28.

"Les Stalles de choeur du château de Gaillon: Leurs secrets." In *La Vie castrale au Moyen Âge,* edited by M. Pastré. Rouen: Université de Rouen Press, 1998.

"Les culbuteurs de Vendôme." In *Art sacré,* no. 12, Stalles et miséricordes, Spiritualité et truculence, colloque de Vendôme, 1999, Cahiers de Rencontre avec le Patrimoine Religieux, 83–95. Vendome, Fr.: Cahiers de Rencontre avec le Patrimoine Religieux, 1999.

Miséricordes: Images profanes des lieux sacres. Paris : Leopard d'Or, 2002.

Corpus of Medieval Misericords I: France. London: Brepols, 2003.

"Liturgical and Anti-Liturgical Elements on Medieval Choir Stalls." In *The Word, the Object: Art in the Service of the Liturgy.* Princeton, N.J.: Princeton University Press, 2003.

Editor with Frédéric Billiet. *Les Stalles de la cathédrale de Rouen.* Rouen: Publications of the University of Rouen, 2003.

Corpus of Medieval Misericords II: Iberia. London: Brepols, 2004.

Author and editor with GIRS. *Lexicon of Medieval Choir Stalls.* London: Brepols, 2004.

CHAPTER 64

Professor Rosemary Cramp (1929–)
The Hild of Durham

Phyllis R. Brown

On 28 June 2001, shortly after presiding for the first time as president at a meeting of the Society of Antiquaries of London, Professor Emerita of Archaeology at the University of Durham Rosemary Cramp was presented with a festschrift, *Image and Power in the Archaeology of Early Medieval Britain: Essays in Honour of Rosemary Cramp*.[1] Appropriately, the extensive list of Cramp's publications Derek Craig compiled to conclude *Image and Power* is called "an interim bibliography" because Cramp's ability to keep up a grueling schedule of research, writing, editing, and presentation of her findings at conferences and symposia in local, national, and international venues, along with her work for a variety of museums, boards, councils, panels, and societies since she retired from full-time teaching in 1990, seems not to have abated at all. Although Cramp has seen the end of some terms of office in long term commitments, such as trustee of the British Museum (1978–98), member of the Advisory Board for Redundant Churches (1984–98), commissioner on the Royal Commission on Ancient and Historical Monuments of Scotland (1975–99), and a founding commissioner of the Historic Buildings and Monuments Commission of English Heritage (1984–89), in the 1990s she took on many new responsibilities, and she continues to serve on the Reviewing Committee on Export of Works of Art, as honorary vice president of the Council for British Archaeology, in the Society for Church Archaeology, and as president of the Durham and Northumberland Architectural and Archaeological Society, to name a few.

These positions, along with her more scholarly roles such as general editor of the *Corpus of Anglo-Saxon Stone Sculpture*, allow her to have a significant influence on the future of archaeological studies, in a sense continuing her long and fruitful career as

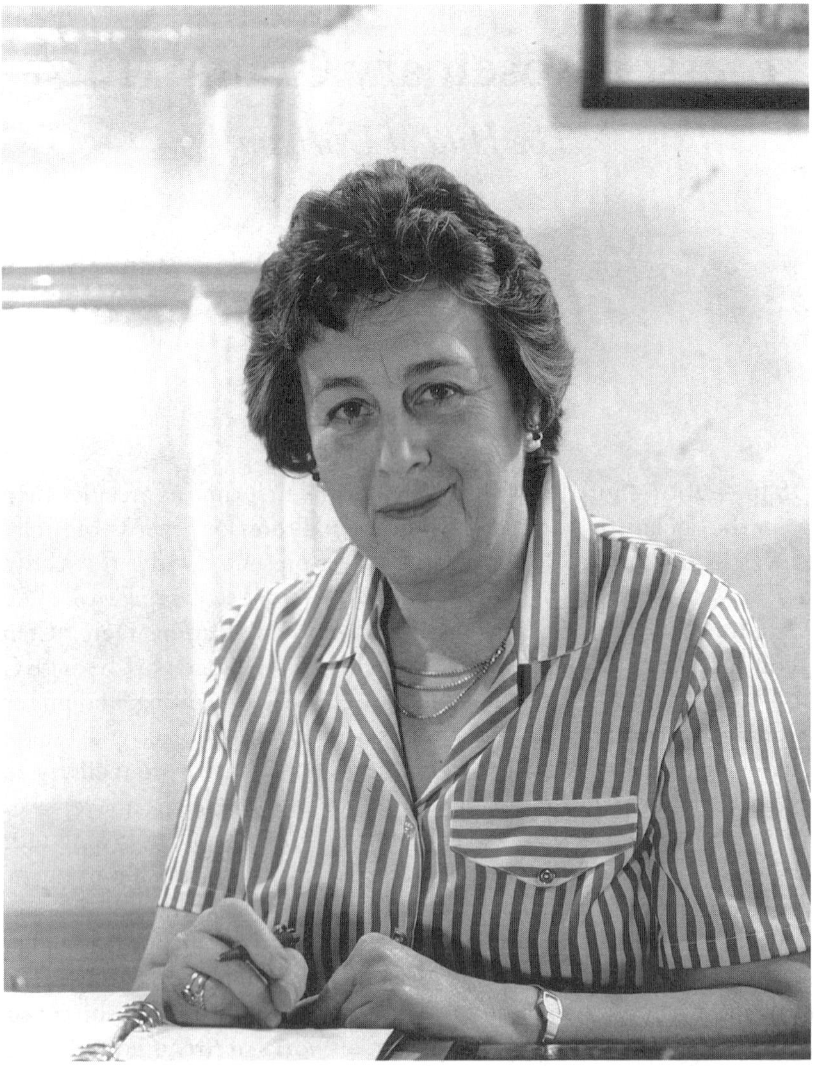

a teacher in a national and international as well as a university context. A colleague and friend at Durham has remarked a similarity between Professor Rosemary Cramp of Durham and the seventh-century Abbess Hild of Whitby: Cramp's contributions to archaeology and more generally to Anglo-Saxon studies shape the present and future of medieval studies in ways very like Hild's influences in Anglo-Saxon England. According to Bede the Venerable, Hild's prudence was so great that "not only ordinary folk, but kings and princes used to come and ask her advice in their difficulties and take it." Bede goes on to say five men trained under her supervision went on to become bishops.[2] In England today many people likewise seek out Rosemary Cramp's advice—and take it—and many of Cramp's students have gone on to distinguished careers in medieval studies, especially archaeology.

Cramp's extraordinary contributions to the scholarship and field research of Anglo-Saxon archaeology and her work as a teacher and administrator are closely interwoven strands of a career striking not only for what she herself has accomplished but also on account of her sensitivity to the interdisciplinarity of medieval studies and her ability to facilitate collaboration.

Cramp is particularly well known for her archaeological research and publications relating to early medieval monasticism, especially in the north of England; the settlement and cultures of Northumbria; Anglo-Saxon and early-medieval stone sculpture; and the medieval glass excavated at Monkwearmouth and Jarrow. *Studies in Anglo-Saxon Sculpture* conveniently brings together seventeen of her most important essays on stone sculpture published over a period of thirty years, between 1961 and 1989. The year 1984 saw the publication of volume 1 of *Corpus of Anglo-Saxon Stone Sculpture,* which includes not only a reliable and comprehensive catalog of carved stones found in County Durham and Northumberland but also Cramp's general introduction to the series of volumes, for which Cramp is the general editor. Volume 2, on Cumberland, Westmorland, and Lancashire North-of-the-Sands, which Cramp coauthored with Richard Bailey, appeared in 1988. The sixth volume (Northern Yorkshire) was published during the summer of 2001. When completed, *Corpus of Anglo-Saxon Stone Sculpture* will include another ten volumes (several of which are currently being prepared; Cramp is actively involved in writing two of the forthcoming volumes) and will provide descriptions, discussions, and photographs of each carved stone surviving from the pre-Conquest period in England, as well as a full bibliography.

Imagining the difficulties nonspecialists would encounter when trying to understand the materials made available by *Corpus,* Cramp devised a system of description for the patterns of carving that appear on the stones; in 1991 she published *Grammar of Anglo-Saxon Ornament: A General Introduction to the Corpus of Anglo-Saxon Stone Sculpture* (initially published as part of the *Corpus* volumes, but in 1999 reprinted as a separate volume), a handbook of descriptive reference that classifies the forms, shapes, and decoration and describes techniques of carving and methods for dating stones. Due largely to Cramp's sponsorship, grantsmanship, and ability to keep a team of archaeologists working together, this monumental project (which other distinguished archaeologists had unsuccessfully attempted in the past) has been supported since 1981 by the British Academy. In 1999 the Arts and Humanities Research Board granted the project a major award that funds the long-term archiving for curation by the Archaeology Data Service and the publication of a digital version, making the full contents of *Corpus* available on the World Wide Web (at http://www.dur.ac.uk/corpus/index.htm).

The *Corpus* project in many ways represents Cramp's philosophy of scholarship and teaching by making all the physical evidence that survives available for students and scholars to work with. Its availability is already changing the way specialists think about Anglo-Saxon England, for instance, by demonstrating the variety of material evidence that survives from sites, therefore making easy generalizations and simplifications less believable. Articles she published during the years *Corpus* was coming into being and since the first volume appeared clarify that Cramp's work has international as well as regional and national implications. Colloquia at Mainz, the UISPP Congress at Nice, a Spoleto seminar, meetings of the International Society of Anglo-Saxonists (over which Cramp presided in 1988–89), meetings of the Medieval Academy of America (which made her a corresponding fellow in 1994), as well as numerous invited lectures in places as far-flung as Texas, New Mexico, and upstate New York have allowed Cramp to disseminate information about Anglo-Saxon archaeology as well as about stone sculpture and the *Corpus* project itself.

One of Cramp's earliest publications, a brief report on Saint Peter's Church, Monkwearmouth, published in 1959, signals the beginning of a project approaching completion in 2005: the publication of *Monkwearmouth and Jarrow* for English Heritage, volumes chronicling and documenting the excavation of monastic sites important not only because of their association with the Venerable Bede, their most famous inhabitant, but also because their founding abbot Benedict Biscop built them, as Bede tells us in the *Ecclesiastical History,* "in the Roman manner." Working from the data (and destruction) of nineteenth-century excavations, Cramp has revealed similarities between Roman and Gaulish monastic sites and the layout at Wearmouth (founded ca. 673) and Jarrow (founded ca. 681).[3] In her 1965 Jarrow Lecture Cramp pointed out,

> When one looks today at the remnants of stone carving in these main centres [Wearmouth, Jarrow, York, and others] or the fragments of crosses in many of our remote parish churches, one should not forget what an immense achievement it was for the English to step outside their tradition of abstract non-monumental decorative art, and to produce under the stimulus of Mediterranean and late antique models what Kendrick calls justly "a premature variety of Romanesque art." It was indeed the love of earlier Christian culture such as Bede related of Benedict Biscop which produced that special contribution from the British Isles, that so early brought Christ and his Saints out of the surroundings of the Church and majestically mounted them as a symbol of Christ's Victory in the wild open places of Northumbria.[4]

Cramp also excavated large quantities of colored and plain window glass, substantiating with archaeological evidence Bede's report that Abbot Biscop had sent to the Continent for glaziers to provide windows for Wearmouth and to instruct his native workers in the Mediterranean craft of glassmaking. Remains of buildings on the waterfront at Jarrow have been interpreted as having "flimsy workshops attached, in which metal- and glass-working took place."[5] The English Heritage publication will include information about every item excavated, over seven thousand pieces for Jarrow alone, as well as extensive photographs and drawings clarifying the information.

Another result of Cramp's work at Wearmouth and Jarrow is Bede's World, an Anglo-Saxon experimental farm and a museum with a permanent exhibition, *The Age of Bede,* both on the land immediately adjacent to the church at Jarrow. On the farm, cattle, sheep, pigs, and geese are being bred and ancient strains of wheat and vegetables are being grown, using medieval methods, to approximate the animals and crops that were probably cultivated in Anglo-Saxon England. The farm also features full-size reconstructions of buildings such as a timber hall, a pit-house, and a monastic cell, all created on the basis of archaeological evidence with materials available in Bede's lifetime. In addition to presenting information about life in Northumbria during the age of Bede and about writing and book production for which the monasteries were famous, the museum displays some of the first colored window glass made in England. Cramp herself pieced together for the display the broken bits she had excavated, working from what she believes are representations of a head, a foot, and arms and her knowledge of proportion to create a reconstruction that fits one of the window apertures at Jarrow. Cramp's interest in medieval glass and glassmaking extends beyond her work with Wearmouth-Jarrow to her article, for example, on window glass at Whithorn and Saint Ninian, published in 1997.

Complementing the work on monastic sites, Cramp's publications on archaeology and Anglo-Saxon literature explore the implications of archaeological finds and details in literature for our understanding of Anglo-Saxon culture. Cramp's career as a scholar began with her 1957 publication "*Beowulf* and Archaeology," in which she explores the extent to which archaeological evidence can alter as well as contribute to our understanding *Beowulf.* In that essay Cramp presents archaeological evidence to clarify literary critical understanding of helmets, swords, and houses. Moreover, in the absence of specific material evidence, she speculates about what architectural features the *Beowulf* poet refers to when he describes Hroðgar's approach to view Grendel's arm in Heorot:

> he to healle geong
> stod on stapole, geseah steapne hrof
> golde fahne ond Grendles hond.
>   (lines 925b–27)

Drawing on what archaeologists did know about buildings, she hypothesized that *stapol* might refer to "a step or small landing at the entrance to the hall."[6] Thirty-six years later, in "The Hall in *Beowulf* and in Archaeology," Cramp reported that newly uncovered evidence for a raised floor inside the building at Cowder's Down provided material evidence to support her earlier reading of *Beowulf*.[7] In "The Hall in *Beowulf* and in Archaeology" and in subsequent publications, Cramp uses new evidence of archaeology to open up our understanding of the material world depicted in Anglo-Saxon poetry.

Similar evidence of the results Cramp achieves from interdisciplinary approaches can be seen, for example, in three essays published in the last fifteen years. In 1983 Cramp presented a paper (published in 1992) that draws on Bede's *Ecclesiastical History* and other writings relating to Anglo-Saxon monasticism, the Anglo-Saxon poem "Deor," Anglo-Saxon laws, historical research, and archaeological research "to examine in detail the manner in which the Irish and the Anglo-Saxons supported their craftsmen and maintained production centers for specialized goods."[8] Cramp concludes that in addition to looking to the Mediterranean for economic and religious models, the Anglo-Saxons in Northumbria also looked to Ireland, and that craftsmen of different races worked together within monasteries to achieve high standards of craftsmanship. By drawing on a variety of resources available to monastic churchmen and craftsmen, Northumbria achieved what is commonly called a golden age; Cramp's high achievement similarly depends on familiarity with multidisciplinary resources.

However, Cramp warns medievalists in "Not Why but How," her contribution to the 1991 meeting of the International Society of Anglo-Saxonists (published in 1997), that approaches to the material evidence (including ecological evidence such as "seeds and pollen, animal, bird, and fish bones, remains of insects, parasites, copralites"[9] as well as landscape and archeological artifacts) had better be different from approaches to the written records that survive. She is wary not only of the excessive enthusiasm of David Austin (who avers in "The 'Proper Study' of Medieval Archaeology" that "archaeologists rather than historians or students of literature are '*better* [emphasis added] placed to see the creative mind and the individual will active within society'") but also of the conservative view that archaeology serves primarily to clarify our understanding of written documents.[10] Simply to use archaeological evidence to confirm the understanding of medieval culture acquired from the historical and literary texts is to risk entrapment in circular arguments. Cramp points out,

> The foundations of our study of Anglo-Saxon England, as defined annually in the periodical of that name, have been largely documentary, and the temporal and physical boundaries of the subject are defined by the currency of Old English, although a wider intellectual framework is provided by sources in Early Medieval Latin. The documents in both languages provide an indispensable insight into the individual and collective attitudes, the social organization and political events of Anglo-Saxon England, but they are nonetheless selective in their social and topographic reference and they are an incalculable remnant of a larger body of evidence. They are spread over six hundred years, and there is sometimes the tendency to see their evidence as more coherent and continuous than it can possibly be.[11]

After immediately pointing out that "archaeological evidence is likewise patchy, incoherent, and non-selective (save in the materials that survive best in the ground)," Cramp goes on to give examples of contradictions between what the documentary records and the material artifacts tell medievalists about Anglo-Saxon culture. For example, rural land use did not change significantly after the withdrawal of the Roman army from Northumbria, as one might expect after reading documents relating to the departure of the Romans. Moreover, extensive excavation sometimes reveals that sites first identified with one category provide evidence that flies in the face of preconceptions about that category, and marked similarities are increasingly being seen in the material evidence from sites that documentary evidence suggests should fall into very different categories. Generalizing too quickly or easily from either documentary or material evidence will result in oversimplified understanding of Anglo-Saxon culture. Cramp concludes, "I do not feel that we can reconstruct individual lives through archaeological evidence, and though archaeologists constantly interrogate their evidence as to why it is so, I do not believe that they can offer more than an opinion as to *why* events in the past which produced their evidence took place. Their opinions here have no more validity than those from any other discipline. What they can offer is an increasingly informative account of *how* events took place and an increasingly clear account of what those events were."[12] Cramp can imagine a future for medieval studies in which the temporal and/or social patterns or fashions defined by archaeology might open up new contexts for textual studies and agendas for medievalists and medieval symposia, in which archaeology, drawing on creativity and a variety of intellectual resources, is recognized as more than a technique in the service of history. One result might be more nuanced understandings of medieval culture and a greater willingness to acknowledge the differences not only across time and space but even within a single community in a short period of time.

In "The Northumbrian Identity," the opening essay in *Northumbria's Golden Age,* Cramp considers the question "Why should Northumbria's identity differ from that of western Wessex for example?" with particular attention to the ways archaeological, art historical, and textual evidence contribute to an understanding of the acculturation and assimilation of various peoples that resulted in the Northumbrian golden age. Cramp invites readers to reconsider assumptions and rethink what they know about this period of medieval history in light of recent excavations such as the one at Catterick, a site for which Roman, native, and Anglo-Saxon documentary evidence survives. The perceptive analysis and reflection of these three essays especially characterize not only Cramp's work on medieval monastic sites—such as those at Wearmouth, Jarrow, Whithorn, Lindisfarne, Tynemouth, Hartelpool, and Whitby—but also her less well known work on nonmonastic sites such as the Hirsel and on metalwork from the pagan Saxon period.

It seems likely that Cramp's understanding of the complexity of Anglo-Saxon culture derives more from her rich experiences with education as a student, teacher, administrator, and community leader than from research leaves, which have been few and widely spaced in her career (the first in 1965 and the coveted fellowship at Oxford's All Souls College in 1992). Cramp's work as a teacher began at Oxford University's Saint Anne's College, immediately after she completed her honors degree in English language and literature there in 1950. When she set out to attend university, Cramp's aspirations were far from medieval literature; she thought reading literature would contribute to a future career in journalism. Fortunately for later generations of medievalists, Dorothy Whitelock noticed her aptitude and encouraged her to specialize in the early period. Cramp recollects a significant time when C. L. Wrenn was weeding out students for whom the study of early English did not seem to be suitable. Although he remarked (with some condescension) the interest Cramp had expressed in studying journalism and that her "mind was not sufficiently in the literature," he allowed her to stay in the course.

While Cramp read early language and literature at Oxford, one important way she filled in the background was through time spent with the Archaeological Society. Cramp recounts that many of the officers in the society, such as Andrew Saunders, Dorothy Charlesworth, and Christopher Gowing, went on to important careers in archaeology. Senior archaeologists such as Richard Atkinson, Christopher Hawkes, and Donald Harden were mentors to the members of the Archaeological Society. Cramp remembers, "They visited us and we would gather in their houses, and we ran our own digs. I went on some of Atkinson's and the Ashmolean was our centre. There was no Department; we taught each other."[13]

Cramp's interest in archaeology preceded her matriculation at Oxford. She remembers arriving at Oxford, thinking she was an archaeologist. After all, the *Market Harborough Advertiser* had run an article celebrating her finding and excavating a Roman site, and the find had been reported in *The Journal of Roman Studies* "Roman Britain in 1945" and "Roman Britain in 1947." Cramp recollects that her interest began after a bank on the family land near Market Harborough collapsed and she and her sister found part of a Roman villa. Believing they had discovered something important, Cramp consulted the local rector, the most learned person she knew, and her encyclopedia. The encyclopedia convinced her that the "indications of a house—flue tiles, stone slates, tesserae, and walling" were Roman; the rector helped her dig a trench and took away some hypocaust for his rockery.[14] Cramp also wrote to Kathleen Kenyon to inquire what ought to be done. Kenyon's response announced that Cramp had found "evidence" that ought to be turned over to a museum. Before Cramp left for Oxford, she had the opportunity to work with a local amateur archaeologist laying out a trench and to see how he drew the site.

Shortly after going up to Oxford, Cramp received a letter from M. B. Taylor at the Ashmolean, asking Cramp to come and see her. Taylor, who turned out to be eminent historian and archeologist Francis John Haverfield's secretary and research assistant, was appalled by the idea of an untrained person digging a trench into a site, even with the help of local pundits. After making the young Cramp feel utterly ridiculous, she announced that Miss Cramp had better be trained and arranged for her to participate in a dig at the University of Durham archaeological training site at Corbridge.

From 1950 to 1955 Cramp taught Old and Middle English and the history of language at Saint Anne's and four other Oxford colleges. During those years she began to be known as someone interested in the background of the early period, interest that grew into her work for the B.Litt., which Cramp completed in 1957 without any research period free of teaching. The interdisciplinary nature of her B.Litt., revised and published as "*Beowulf* and Archaeology," is characteristic of her teaching as well as of her scholarly career. When she accepted the position teaching at the University of Durham in 1955, she was expected to teach the whole subject of Anglo-Saxon archaeology, architecture, language, literature, and history.

At Durham Cramp continued to teach English literature, but she had much greater opportunities for pursuing her other love, archaeology. Before she left Oxford, V. E. Nash-Williams, the keeper of archaeology at the National Museum of Wales, told Cramp he hoped while she was at Durham she would do something on Anglo-Saxon stone sculpture. After she arrived, Eric Birley, professor of archaeology, greeted her by saying, "We're now a department because there are two of us, as well as John Gillam, who lectures half time at Newcastle." (Newcastle and Durham were one university until September 1963.) They also had the luxury of one technician. Cramp describes the "hut" in which the department first was located as being "like an Anglo-Saxon house with one big room and a small private room at the end, and a large stove in the middle."[15]

At first forming only a research department (not offering undergraduate degrees in archaeology), Birley and Cramp offered courses in archaeology for students reading English, classics, and history. Although in its early days many saw the archaeology department as a refuge for eccentrics, Cramp almost immediately began attracting research students to Durham, whose distinguished careers are a testimony to her accomplishments as a teacher and later as an administrator. While the number of important archaeologists who have trained with Cramp exceeds the number of Anglo-Saxon bishops trained under the supervision of Hild at Whitby, the effect is similar. The list of contributors to her festschrift provides a good sample: Professor Richard Bailey, Pro-Vice-Chancellors' Office, University of Newcastle upon Tyne; Professor Martin Carver, University of York; Dr. Nancy Edwards, University of Wales, Bangor; Dr. Catherine Hills, University of Cambridge; Dr. Christopher Loveluck, University of Southampton; Dr. Arthur MacGregor, Ashmolean Museum, University of Oxford; Professor Christopher Morris, University of Glasgow; and Deirdre O'Sullivan, University of Leicester. Moreover, Cramp's "Abbess Hild effect" extends beyond the influence of students who have gone on to be important archaeologists. Christopher Morris writes,

> It should be emphasized that Rosemary always expected students to engage with the primary material and, as a true pedagogue, expected more from students than they could necessarily give at a particular stage. For most students, the experience in tutorials was

that they responded to the expectation and "raised their game." Of course, Rosemary would then simply expect an even greater improvement, but any one who experienced this sort of education through personal expectation, could not but improve. In essence, of course, this experience is based in part upon the labour-intensive system of tutorials, and in part upon time spent handling material or going out on field-visits. Its foundation was also the philosophy of the fundamental interaction of personal research and teaching which, while by no means unique to Rosemary, was exemplified at its best in her.[16]

In Durham one frequently meets former undergraduate and graduate students of Cramp, who seem always to have a tale to tell of a dig they participated in or a tutorial that changed their lives for the better; the warmth of affection and respect that permeates the conversation is a reminder of how very influential teachers can be.

During those early years Cramp was a tutor at Saint Mary's College, Durham's first residential college for women. Saint Mary's College originated as the Women's Hostel, founded in 1899 to satisfy the University Senate resolutions passed in May 1881, stipulating that female students "shall be admissible to the Public Examinations and the first degree in Arts of the University" and that "private individuals" should establish a residential college or house for "such students."[17] The eighteen-year delay resulted in part from the verdict in 1886 that the earlier senate vote to confer degrees on women had been illegal and in part from the subsequent vote to reject a proposal that Hatfield Lodge at 3 South Bailey be converted into a college for women. In 1895 the University Senate finally obtained a supplementary charter permitting admission of women to the university and opening all degrees except divinity to women; four years later, a large house at 33 Claypath was rented, furnished, and equipped by the bursar of University College, and the newly appointed principal moved in during summer term with two students. After one term the only domestic help left, saying she couldn't face a winter in that house![18] In 1901 the Women's Hostel was moved to Abbey House on Palace Green after "the throats and other ailments became so frequent it was clear something was wrong."[19] Finally, in 1920 the Women's Hostel gained full collegiate status, was renamed Saint Mary's College, and moved into larger quarters in the Cathedral Precincts (buildings now housing the Choir School). One staff member in the thirties remembers that "ninety students were housed in six houses: Abbey House, the Cottage in Dun Cow Lane, 39 North Bailey, 8 and 13 South Bailey, with the present Choir School as St. Mary's."[20] After the war a new Saint Mary's, "at last a purpose-built accommodation under one roof," became a reality; students began moving in during 1951.[21]

During Cramp's first ten years at Durham, both Saint Mary's College and the University of Durham grew rapidly in numbers and in outlook. As a "moral tutor" at Saint Mary's, Cramp became known for her entertaining and informative part in the induction of "freshers"; she is reputed to have concluded her remarks with the reminder, "And if you don't work, then you fail and you just get thrown out!"[22] In 1962 Saint Mary's expanded into a new building, and in the spring of 1964 women students were admitted for the first time to the University Union Society (a Saint Mary's student was the first woman to join, three days before she graduated; the Junior Common Room planned to join en bloc the following fall). Early in 1966 Mary Holdsworth, principal of Saint Mary's between 1962 and 1974 and first woman pro-vice-chancellor at Durham, reflected on the problems of university expansion in a year when her college had 258 students in residence: "To choose learning—whether by probing enquiry or by perceptive assimilation of concepts—is still today to answer an inner compulsion in much the same way as it was in earlier centuries. The country's wealth, its needs, the attitudes of society have mitigated the threadbare poverty of Chaucer's Clerke of Oxenford, but his deliberate choice—'Of studie took he most cure and most hede'—must remain the basic attitude of the student always and everywhere." After another paragraph concerned with teaching priorities and methods, Holdsworth continued:

> So much for university life generally. But what is there to add about being a student specifically in Durham? In the first place, to spend one's university years in a city where the Venerable Bede is buried and in the countryside where he lived and wrote, can be an inspiration and a symbol. Bede, England's first indigenous historian, compiling the record of Christianity in this land and subjecting his work to the critical tools of painstaking scholarship, can well be taken as a pattern by students for the rigour with which to re-appraise their inherited and perhaps partially understood beliefs, not to mention other beliefs and disbeliefs which they will meet. Moreover, Bede's physical memorial is not just a tomb, but the church where he prayed and worked is still a structural part of St. Paul's parish in Jarrow, seen against a skyline of pylons, derricks and a timber yard.[23]

In 1965 Rosemary Cramp had given the Jarrow lecture in that parish church, Saint Paul's in Jarrow; by then Cramp's archaeological work at Monkwearmouth and Jarrow was well underway. Holdsworth and Cramp were close friends who regularly spoke together about their work. Moreover, Saint Mary's was home to Cramp's archaeology students whenever they were engaged in digs. Clearly Cramp's influence permeated education at the University of Durham.

After giving her Jarrow lecture, Cramp had the first research leave of her career, during which she studied Merovingian and Carolingian sculpture in France. The following year she was promoted to senior lecturer. During those years the archaeology department was growing and changing as well. Not long after Cramp arrived, it moved from the "hut" (which was later torn down to build tennis courts for Hatfield College) to the Old Fulling Mill on the bank of the river Wear, directly below the cathedral; by 1977 it had outgrown the Fulling Mill and moved to 46 Saddler Street, where it remained until 1996, when it moved to the Science Site on Elvet Hill. As the faculty grew to include more and more specialties, as the general degree course of study in archaeology was approved and then, finally, in 1974, the honors degree, Rosemary

Cramp's vision and leadership were vital. Resounding confidence in her leadership was expressed in 1972 when she was elected to succeed Professor Eric Birley in the chair of archaeology—the first woman to be elected professor at Durham.

While the University of Durham changed, archaeology became increasingly professional. In 1926 a report of the Society of Antiquaries specified: "No work should be begun without the supervision of an archaeologist competent by reason of his experience and general knowledge to direct every detail. Provision must be made for complete and accurate record by measurements, drawings and photographs of all evidence disclosed. Supervision must be continuous. And a necessary condition of all such work must be that its results must be published as promptly and completely as possible. Where an excavation extends over a series of years, annual reports giving a summary of the progress made should be issued, leaving the full record to appear at the close of operations."[24] Cramp, who was elected a fellow of the Society of Antiquaries in 1959, has followed this vision of archaeology throughout her years at Durham and taught generations of students to do the same. The carefully controlled rage in her description of the absence of such care at Whitby, which, she writes, "seems to have been excavated by remotely supervised Ministry of Works workmen who maintained a record of the finds but little else," is characteristically expressed in the context of work with other archaeologists that manages to salvage a remarkable amount of information from the site in spite of the incompetence of official authorities.[25]

The transformation of archaeology from a field dominated by amateurs into an academic discipline during the second half of the twentieth century shaped Cramp's career, while she herself has contributed to the growth and development of archaeology, most notably at the University of Durham. The teaching staff there has grown from two and a half to twenty-four, and the subspecialties now include not only scientific aspects of archaeology but also all geographic areas and periods. Christopher Morris writes that through all the discussions and negotiations, Cramp never lost sight of her main aim: "to establish, alongside a re-energized postgraduate school, an undergraduate school that could compete for students wishing to take Archaeology on equal terms with the longer established centres such as London, Cambridge, Cardiff, Edinburgh, and the newer Departments of repute such as Sheffield and Southampton."[26]

Cramp was not content, however, with the influence she could wield within her own college and department. As a young lecturer she and others "managed to get the University to establish an Academic Electoral Assembly to enfranchize the younger staff through election to the Senate—an institution that still survives."[27] She is still indefatigably engaged with empowering younger academics all the while she is working to convince local organizations and governmental agencies and representatives of the value and significance of archaeology—so that the new generation of archaeologists will have more opportunities than her generation had. And since retiring Cramp has continued to have confidence in her younger colleagues, to be open to their new ways of thinking about medieval studies, and to open up for them opportunities that come her way because of her authority and experience.

Rosemary Cramp, the Hild of Durham, has shaped and continues to shape the future of medieval studies through the example of her research, writing, teaching, and administrative service, all of which extend beyond her academic center at Durham. Perhaps her greatest influence, however, is on the fortunate individuals whose lives she has touched in friendship.

NOTES

1. Hamerow and MacGregor, *Image and Power in the Archaeology of Early Medieval Britain: Essays in Honour of Rosemary Cramp.*
2. Bede, *History of the English Church and People,* 247.
3. Christopher D. Morris writes, "When the final report on these sites is published, we shall all be able to appreciate the major logistical problems she overcame simply in getting access to these sites, and then in excavating them, and in managing the large teams that assisted her over the many years of excavation" ("From *Beowulf* to Binford," 159).
4. Cramp, *Early Northumbrian Sculpture.*
5. Cramp, "Monkwearmouth (or Wearmouth) and Jarrow," 325.
6. Cramp, "*Beowulf* and Archaeology," 137–38.
7. Cramp, "Hall in *Beowulf* and in Archaeology," 340.
8. Originally presented at the International Congress on Medieval Studies at Western Michigan University, the paper was later published as "Northumberland and Ireland," 186.
9. Cramp, "Not Why but How," 278.
10. Cramp, "Not Why but How," 274.
11. Cramp, "Not Why but How," 272.
12. Cramp, "Not Why but How," 281.
13. Quoted in Gerard, *Another Country,* 103.
14. Cramp, "Roman Britain in 1947," 89.
15. Quoted in Gerard, *Another Country,* 105.
16. Morris, "From *Beowulf* to Binford," 150.
17. *Question of Degree,* item 4.
18. *Question of Degree,* item 19.
19. *Question of Degree,* item 20.
20. *Question of Degree,* item 21b.
21. *Question of Degree,* item 21c.
22. Quoted in Morris, "From *Beowulf* to Binford," 148.
23. *Saint Mary's College Durham Newsletter.*
24. Quoted in Evans, *History of the Society of Antiquaries,* 401.
25. Cramp, "Anglo-Saxon Monasteries of the North," 112.
26. Morris, "From *Beowulf* to Binford," 152.
27. Morris, "From *Beowulf* to Binford," 150.

SELECT BIBLIOGRAPHY OF WORKS BY ROSEMARY CRAMP

"Roman Britain in 1947." *Journal of Roman Studies* 38 (1948): 89.
"*Beowulf* and Archaeology." *Medieval Archaeology* 1 (1957): 57–77. Reprinted in *The 'Beowulf' Poet: A Collection of Critical Essays,* ed. D. K. Fry, 114–40. Englewood Cliffs, N.J.: Prentice Hall, 1968.
Early Northumbrian Sculpture. Jarrow Lecture, 1965. Jarrow, Eng.: Parish of Jarrow, 1965. Reprinted

in *Studies in Anglo-Saxon Sculpture,* 21–38; and in vol. 1 of *Bede and His World: The Jarrow Lectures 1958–1993,* ed. Michael Lapidge, 133–52. Aldershot, Eng.: Variorum, 1994.

With Bertram Colgrave. *Saint Peter's Church, Wearmouth.* Gloucester, Eng.: British Publishing, 1965.

"Glass Finds from the Anglo-Saxon Monastery of Monkwearmouth and Jarrow." In *Studies in Glass History and Design,* edited by R. Charleston, W. Evans, and A. E. Werner. Sheffield, Eng.: Society of Glass Technology, 1970.

"Anglo-Saxon Monasteries of the North." *Scottish Archaeology Forum* 5 (1974): 104–24.

"Early Northumbrian Sculpture at Hexham." In *Saint Wilfrid at Hexham,* edited by D. P. Kirby, 115–40. Newcastle upon Tyne, Eng.: Oriel Press, 1974. Reprinted in *Studies in Anglo-Saxon Sculpture,* 95–139.

"Window Glass from the Monastic Site of Jarrow: Problems of Interpretation." *Journal of Glass Studies* 17 (1975): 88–96.

"Monastic Sites." In *The Archaeology of Anglo-Saxon England,* edited by D. M. Wilson, 201–52. London: Methuen, 1976.

"Monkwearmouth and Jarrow: The Archaeological Evidence." In *Famulus Christi: Essays in Commemoration of the Thirteenth Centenary of the Birth of the Venerable Bede,* edited by Gerald Bonner, 5–18. London: SPCK, 1976.

With C. Douglas-Home. "New Discoveries at The Hirsel, Coldstream, Berwickshire." *Proceedings of the Society of Antiquities in Scotland* 109 (1977–78): 223–32.

The Background to Saint Cuthbert's Life, Delivered in the Prior's Hall at Durham, 14 March 1980. Durham Cathedral Lecture. Durham, Eng.: Dean and Chapter of Durham, 1980.

"The Viking Image." In *The Vikings,* edited by R. T. Farrell, 8–19. London: Phillimore, 1982.

"The Anglian Sculptures from Jedburgh." In *From the Stone Age to the 'Forty-Five: Studies Presented to R. B. K. Stevenson, Former Keeper, National Museum of Antiquities of Scotland,* edited by A. O'Connor and D. V. Clarke, 269–84. Edinburgh: John Donald, 1983.

"Anglo-Saxon Settlement." In *Settlement in North Britain, 1000 B.C. to A.D. 1000: Papers Presented to George Jobey, Newcastle upon Tyne, December 1982,* edited by J. C. Chapman and H. C. Mytum, 263–97. Oxford: BAR, 1983.

County Durham and Northumberland. Vol. 1 of *Corpus of Anglo-Saxon Stone Sculpture.* Oxford: Oxford University Press, 1984.

"The Furnishing and Sculptural Decoration of Anglo-Saxon Churches." In *The Anglo-Saxon Church: Papers on History, Architecture and Archaeology in Honour of Dr. H. M. Taylor,* edited by L. A. S. Butler and R. K. Morris, 101–4. London: Council for British Archaeology. Reprinted in *Studies in Anglo-Saxon Sculpture,* 289–97.

"Northumbria and Ireland." In *Sources of Anglo-Saxon Culture,* edited by P. Szarmach with V. D. Oggins, Studies in Medieval Culture 20, 185–201. Kalamazoo, Mich.: Medieval Institute Publications, 1986. Reprinted in *Studies in Anglo-Saxon Sculpture,* 272–88.

With R. Daniels. "New Finds from the Anglo-Saxon Monastery at Hartlepool, Cleveland." *Antiquity* 61 (1987): 424–32.

With Richard N. Bailey. *Cumberland, Westmorland, and Lancashire North-of-the-Sands.* Vol. 2 of *Corpus of Anglo-Saxon Stone Sculpture.* Oxford: Oxford University Press, 1988.

"Northumbria: The Archaeological Evidence." In *Power and Politics in Early Medieval Britain and Ireland,* edited by S. T. Driscoll and M. R. Nieke, 69–78. Edinburgh: Edinburgh University Press, 1988.

"The Artistic Influence of Lindisfarne within Northumbria." In *Saint Cuthbert, His Cult and*

His Community to A.D. *1200,* edited by G. Bonner, D. Rollason, and C. Stancliffe, 213–28. Woodbridge, Eng.: Boydell Press, 1989. Reprinted in *Studies in Anglo-Saxon Sculpture,* 329–44.
Grammar of Anglo-Saxon Ornament: A General Introduction to the Corpus of Anglo-Saxon Stone Sculpture. Oxford: Oxford University Press, 1991.
"Northumberland and Ireland." In *Sources of Anglo-Saxon Culture.* Kalamazoo, Mich.: Medieval Institute Publications, 1992.
Studies in Anglo-Saxon Sculpture. London: Pindar Press, 1992.
"The Hall in Beowulf and in Archaeology." In *Heroic Poetry in the Anglo-Saxon Period: Studies in Honor of Jess B. Bessinger, Jr.,* edited by Helen Damico and John Leyerle, Studies in Medieval Culture 32, 331–46. Kalamazoo, Mich.: Medieval Institute Publications, 1993.
"A Reconsideration of the Monastic Site of Whitby." In *The Age of Migrating Ideas: Early Medieval Art in Northern Britain and Ireland,* edited by R. M. Spearman and J. Higgitt, 64–73. Edinburgh: Sutton Publishing, 1993.
"Monkwearmouth and Jarrow in Their Continental Context." In *"Churches Built in Ancient Times": Recent Studies in Early Christian Archaeology,* edited by K. Painter, Society of Antiquaries, London, Occasional Paper 16, and Specialist Studies on the Mediterranean 1, 279–94. London: Society of Antiquaries, 1994. Reprinted in *The Archaeology of Anglo-Saxon England: Basic Readings,* ed. Catherine. E. Karkov, Basic Readings in Anglo-Saxon England 7, 137–53. New York: Garland Publishing, 1999.
"The Making of Oswald's Northumbria." In *Oswald: Northumbrian King to European Saint,* edited by Clare Stancliffe and Eric Cambridge, 17–32. Stamford, Eng.: Paul Watkins, 1995.
"Nature Redeemed." In *The Sense of the Sacramental: Movement and Measure in Art and Music, Place and Time,* edited by D. Brown and A. Loades, 122–36. London: SPCK, 1995.
"The Insular Tradition: An Overview." In *The Insular Tradition,* edited by Catherine E. Karkov, Robert T. Farrell, and M. Ryan, SUNY Series in Medieval Studies, 283–99. Albany: State University of New York Press, 1997.
"Not Why but How: The Contribution Of Archaeological Evidence to the Understanding of Anglo-Saxon England." In *The Preservation and Transmission of Anglo-Saxon Culture: Selected Papers from the 1991 Meeting of the International Society of Anglo-Saxonists,* edited by Paul E. Szarmach and Joel T. Rosenthal, Studies in Medieval Culture 40, 271–86. Kalamazoo, Mich.: Medieval Institute Publications, 1997.
"The Window Glass." In *Whithorn and Saint Ninian: The Excavation of a Monastic Town 1984–91,* edited by P. Hill, 326–32. Stroud, Eng.: Sutton Publishing, 1997.
"Monkwearmouth (or Wearmouth) and Jarrow." In *The Blackwell Encyclopaedia of Anglo-Saxon England,* edited by M. Lapidge et al. Oxford: Blackwell, 1999.
"The Northumbrian Identity." In *Northumbria's Golden Age,* edited by Jane Hawkes and Susan Mills, 1–11. Stroud, Eng.: Sutton Publishing, 1999.
"The Pre-Conquest Sculptures of Glastonbury Monastery." In *New Offerings, Ancient Treasures: Studies in Medieval Art for George Henderson,* edited by Paul Binski and William Noel, 148–62. Stroud, Eng.: Sutton Publishing, 2001.

Works Cited

A Question of Degree: An Exhibition to Celebrate One Hundred Years of Degrees for Women at Durham University. Compiled by Jane Hogan, Becky Mead, and Beth Rainey. Durham, Eng.: Durham University Library, 1995.

Bede. *A History of the English Church and People.* Translated by Leo Sherley-Price. London: Penguin, 1975.

Evans, Joan. *A History of the Society of Antiquaries.* Oxford: Oxford University Press, 1956.

Gerard, David. *Another Country: A Season in Archaeology.* Wilmslow, Eng.: Elvet, 1974.

Hamerow, Helena, and Arthur MacGregor, eds. *Image and Power in the Archaeology of Early Medieval Britain: Essays in Honour of Rosemary Cramp.* Oxford: Oxbow, 2001.

Holliday, Fred. Foreword to *Corpus of Anglo-Saxon Stone Sculpture 1: County Durham and Northumberland.* Oxford: Oxford University Press, 1984.

Morris, Christopher. "From Beowulf to Binford: Sketches of an Archaeological Career." In *Image and Power in the Archaeology of Early Medieval Britain: Essays in Honour of Rosemary Cramp,* edited by Helena Hamerow and Arthur MacGregor. Oxford: Oxbow, 2001.

Saint Mary's College Durham Newsletter (1967): 3–4.

CHAPTER 65

The Networked Life (1931–)

JO ANN McNAMARA

"SISTERHOOD IS POWERFUL," we used to say in the 1970s. I define my own life as a medievalist by the assistance, guidance, and warm friendship of the many women (and sympathetic men) who have transformed the historical discipline and its practitioners. When I was born, in 1931, and while I was growing up during the Depression and World War II, a generation of women were struggling to secure their places as citizens and as educated professionals, and I believed that this would be my own future. As a child I was a precursor of the mobile American culture that has developed in the later twentieth century. Then, as the daughter of a General Motors executive, I was virtually alone in moving from town to town every few years. A childhood spent adjusting to new schools in Kansas, California, New York, Delaware, and Pennsylvania accustomed me to a sense of self-sufficiency and nurtured a love of solitary pleasures that no doubt turned me in the direction of a scholarly career.

The fifties, when I was an undergraduate, were something of a lost decade for traditional feminists. The generation of women who first enjoyed the vote and who began to register a meaningful presence in the academic world were then passing the midpoint of their careers. Role models were scarce and so were ambitious contemporaries. The only female teachers I remember at the University of Pennsylvania and then at Columbia were young instructors, not destined for the professoriat at those institutions. The campuses of the postwar period were deluged by returning veterans seeking career opportunities with the aid of the G.I. Bill of Rights. All too many of the women might best be characterized by my first college roommate, a Southern belle from Savannah, Georgia, who explained to me that she wanted a schedule that would enable her to get her beauty sleep in the mornings and complement her

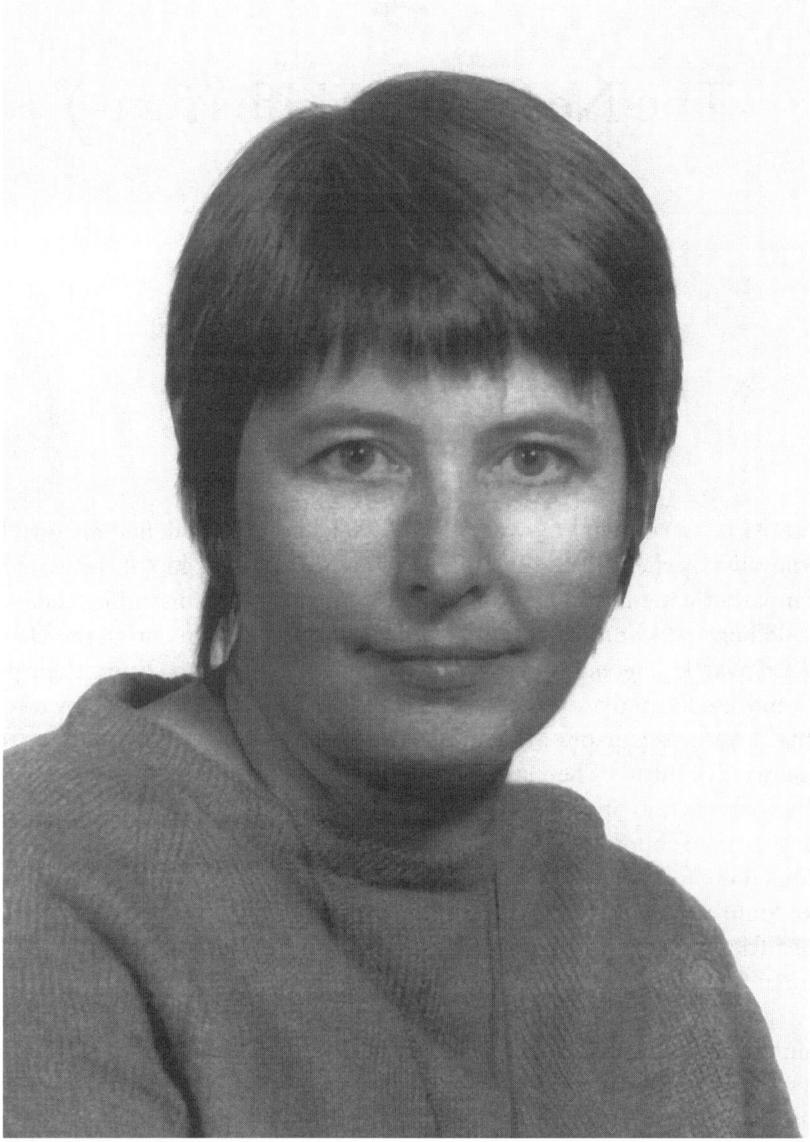

husband-hunting interests. My own sights were not too steady. Through the fifties I pursued a meandering process of typing my way through school, one or two courses at a time, in Columbia's School of General Studies while flirting with the possibility of some sort of theatrical career. I finally graduated as an English major in 1956 and spent some time out of school catching up on my finances by working for the army as an entertainment director in France. Thus, when I finally made up my mind, my credentials to undertake the study of medieval history were less than impressive.

When I look back, I am amazed that I could even have contemplated starting out with no meaningful background in my discipline and no linguistic or other equipment save a working knowledge of French. I am even more amazed that Columbia accepted me into their graduate program in 1957. Thinking about it now, I suppose that I simply fell between two periods in academic history. I was still sailing along with the veterans into an expanding academic environment ill equipped to deal with the large numbers of people suddenly interested in advanced study. And I was doing it at a moment when colleges everywhere were expanding to meet unprecedented enrollments. When that job market contracted, the rigor of graduate study steadily increased.

In brief, Columbia accepted a degree candidate with no discernible qualifications but a bachelor's degree and excellent secretarial skills. In addition to a lack of academic background, I found myself there without the mentoring of an undergraduate department or even the support of a cohort of classmates from my undergraduate experience. What saved me, probably, was my profound ignorance of the extent of my inadequacies. As for the university, their attitude in those days seemed to be that a decent college record entitled just about anyone who asked and who could pay what was then a fairly modest tuition to an opportunity to start the course. Stamina, optimism, and some degree of intelligence would presumably do the rest. The fainthearted and the inadequate would fall out along the way. Most of the remainder would get their degrees, and throughout the sixties there were jobs waiting for nearly all. The overdetermined or the financially independent gradually lapsed into the handful of perpetual graduate students who labored on in the library long past retirement age, paying their research fees every semester while they polished and perfected the dissertation of a lifetime. It was an odd world but a world adapted to someone like me, painfully typing my way along, fitting classes in around my job and eventually my marriage and my baby. I took classes, I learned languages, I read medieval books to my son while feeding him, and little by little, I amassed credits and made my way toward the Ph.D. seminar that changed my life.

Allow me, briefly, to skip ahead to a vantage point a few years later. One afternoon I found myself sitting on a familiar bench outside my advisor's office waiting to keep an appointment to discuss progress on my dissertation. Those meetings usually consisted of a brief report on what I was doing that semester, a nod of approval, and instructions to come back when I had completed the work outlined. They were dispiriting and depressing but served to keep me moving along. While I was waiting,

I unavoidably eavesdropped on the conversation that floated out the transom along with a heady combination of pipe and cigarette smoke. My sponsor, John Mundy, was talking with a young man who had entered our seminar a year or so after I started. The conversation was spirited and meaty, involving Machiavelli and the urban politics of late medieval Italy. It spoke to one of my favorite fantasies—that I myself would one day be engaged in such conversations with the great scholars who lectured to me daily. While I sat there, I felt a crushing certainty that it would never happen, and, all at once, I was sure that the reason was that I was a woman.

Life is full of twists and turns. In time I did indeed have those conversations with Professor Mundy and enjoyed them very much.[1] But it is more to the point to recount an incident later still in my career. A good ten years or so after that depressing day, I was attending a conference at the college where my seminar colleague worked, and I accepted his invitation to dinner. The conversation turned, naturally enough, to reminiscences of our graduate-student days. Imagine my surprise when he began to complain of the chilly indifference and neglect to which he had been subjected. He and the others of his cohort had felt isolated and rejected. Moreover, he claimed, "You and Suzanne Wemple and Phyllis Barzillay [now Roberts] had everything sewn up. You dominated the seminar, and you were the favorites and the rest of us felt totally shut out." In turn I told my story, and we all had a good laugh at the echoes of *Rashomon* in academia.

But I have often pondered this incident, never more deeply than when I hear the tales of other feminist women about the rejection and indifference they suffered in similar circumstances. It is easy enough to recognize that the men who seemed to have such advantages over us were equally insecure and unhappy. But the twist to the story is the appearance that I and my friends projected of self-assurance and exclusivity. Suzanne, Phyllis, and I entered the seminar at the same time, and, for a variety of reasons, there were no old-timers in that cohort. We all felt that we were in over our heads, and each recognized qualities in the others that we felt we lacked. Early in the semester I met Suzanne in the library, and after some conversation she proposed that we make up a study group to share the enormous reading list we had been given in preparation for our oral examinations. We invited Phyllis to join us, and she readily agreed. Thereafter, once a week, rain or shine, we met, taking turns sharing notes from our reading, slowly munching our way through the bibliography. Sometimes we met after hours in the geology department office, where I had a job as a typist. Or we met in a small reading room in Paterno Library that Suzanne could reserve as a member of the library staff. Or we met in Phyllis's dormitory room. Later on, when we had finished our course work, we met in one another's homes.

Years went by. We held one another's hands through the orals and into the dissertation writing period. We were together through Phyllis's divorce and Suzanne's second child and my only child. We were still together when we got our first jobs as adjuncts. Briefly we added a couple of other people including Blanche Wiesen (now Cook), a closet medievalist writing her dissertation in American history, who then taught with Suzanne at Stern College for Women (the auxiliary of Yeshiva). Eventually dissertation research and teaching commitments put an end to the weekly meetings, but the friendships continued and still continue to bear fruit. Without question, the sense of belonging, the air of authority, the impression that we were the favored children of the graduate student set derived from the solidarity of that friendship.

In those days there were no feminists among us, and feminist scholarship was unimaginable. Like the moment of shock I suffered on that bench outside my advisor's door, there were times when each of us wondered, even out loud, whether or not sex was a factor that might create serious difficulties in our careers. It was obvious that the preservation of our personal lives demanded that we seek jobs that could conform to the demands of our families. When I married just after registering my master's degree in 1959, it was almost unheard-of that I should keep my own name. After long discussions with my husband-to-be, I did so because I could not face the effort of trying to impose a new name on the Columbia bureaucracy and the fragile memories of my teachers and acquaintances. Ironically, that problem reversed itself in latter days when I began to introduce my budding historian son, Edmund Clingan, to my colleagues and friends in his later profession.

My friends and I sometimes conferred on how to make ourselves fit into a male world while maintaining a female identity. We prided ourselves on keeping the difficulties of our private lives out of the work place. Babies, husbands, housekeeping, and even financial problems were not supposed to intrude on keeping up our responsibilities as students. It was an unusual exception to the rule that Suzanne had to curtail one teaching assignment by a couple of weeks when she had her second child. Even then, she saw it as her responsibility to supply me as a pinch hitter in her course. The books we read and the courses we originally taught omitted all mention of women except for the occasional queen. All three of us wrote dissertations on male figures in the context of a male polity.[2] If anyone had thought to ask us, we probably would have said that this was just as it should be.

Primarily this is a story of sisterhood. But in time we were all to find that we had mothers as well. For both Phyllis and me the mothers were associated with Hunter College, then the female partner-school of the City College of New York. Pearl Kibre discovered Phyllis when she was seeking advanced credits with a view to certifying in the New York public school system. Learning that she had been a classics major as an undergraduate, Pearl urged Phyllis to undertake the master's degree in medieval history and then go on to Columbia. It was Phyllis's extensive understanding of manuscript study, which she learned under Pearl's tutelage, that drew us to her in our seminar.

Hunter, in those days, was virtually a matriarchy. Women reigned as deans and department heads, and finally, during my early years there, a woman became president. Only in the early seventies, when the Coordinating Committee for Women in the Historical Profession undertook a nationwide survey of the staffing of history departments, did I learn that Hunter's was the only department in the United States with a female faculty of over 50 percent. The "blue-haired ladies," as some of the younger people called them, who first interviewed me in 1963 were a formidable lot, and now, as I picture them, I realize that they looked then as I look now—something like a ship of the line under full sail to Trafalgar.

Younger and smaller, and hoping for a modest position as an adjunct to teach surveys of ancient and medieval history at night, I confronted them in all their majesty a year after I had had my baby and begun work on my dissertation. The first question came from the chair, Dorothy Ganfield Fowler, and it seemed like a dreadful one. She wanted to know whether I was Miss or Mrs. McNamara. Clutching at a straw, I answered that I hoped soon to be Dr. McNamara, but she obliged me to admit that McNamara was my maiden name despite the wedding ring and all the rest. With that, she broke into what I can only call a giggle, turned to her colleagues, and said, "Did you hear that, girls?" Everyone laughed appreciatively, and at last she deigned to relieve my mounting anxiety. She told me that she had originally been hired at the depth of the Depression when the City of New York had instituted a practice of firing all married women in order to protect the jobs of married men. When she married, she had tried to keep her maiden name, but the city insisted she change her name, and then they fired her. "But," she smiled wickedly, "I came back, didn't I?"

Well, gentle reader, the rest is obvious. I got the job, and they liked me and kept me on full time after I finished my dissertation, and, in fact, it turned out to be the only academic job I ever had. There was an old-girl's network, even though it was a limited one. Fowler once told me that she always made it a practice of choosing the woman over the equally qualified man because every other college in her experience did the opposite. That was undoubtedly true, though the great expansion of the sixties greatly reduced the odds against us and left enough of us in tenured positions to try to even them when the job crunch came in the seventies. The practices that now ensure a far more impartial and open job market were not then in place. No one thought it odd that a person like me could be hired in response to a letter of inquiry without open advertising and that I could eventually be retained and given tenure in 1969 because the department liked my work.

The first of the great injustices that women confronted in those days was reversed through the energy of that same Dorothy Fowler and her cohort. New York labor law aimed at the "protection" of pregnant women. We were all required in those days to report to our chairs as soon as we knew we were pregnant and accept being dismissed as soon as practically possible—usually at the end of the current semester. Such a dismissal automatically broke an untenured individual's service so that, if she were rehired after the baby was born, she would have to begin again. Nor did she have any legal claim to be rehired. More than one woman who achieved future eminence as a scholar was caught in this trap and delayed in her career progress as a result. No one can tell how many lost their purchase on a career altogether. Our department at that time boasted a whole cohort of young women, many, like me, with young children and many who might and some who did get pregnant. When that happened, our blue-haired ladies confronted Albany with all the political support and all the persuasive measures they could muster and got the law changed before any of that new generation could be penalized. The Hunter history department in those years sometimes seemed like a day-care center as our children became accustomed to sitting in our offices when the baby-sitters failed to show up. As a result my own son became so addicted to the academic life that he grew up to become a historian in his turn.

When the feminist movement began to formulate new ideas about how the workplace should function and how business relationships should be developed, I realized with amazement that they need only look to Hunter College for their inspiration. Collegiality was the motto in my department, and despite differences of opinion over the years, that spirit saw us through decades of student uprisings, financial crises, and the claustrophobia born of long attrition. Most of the people whose children grew up with mine and who sat with me in department meetings over all the years were still there to wish me well at my retirement party and are still central to my social calendar.

In the meantime Blanche Wiesen had become Blanche Wiesen Cook and joined activist political activities to her weakening avocation as a part-time medievalist. As I was then married to a politician in the ferment of the Lindsay years, Blanche and I often met outside the academic setting, and it was no surprise when she approached me with news of a new network forming to join the two sectors.

Bernice Carroll originated the Coordinating Committee for Women in the Historical Profession (CCWHP). She was then engaged in a struggle with a midwestern university over the nepotism rules that were standard in so many institutions at the time. She had applied for and won a job that would enable her to move to the same institution that employed her then-fiancé. But when she made the mistake of telling her new colleagues about her engagement, they rescinded the appointment on the basis of a rule that married persons could not both be employed by the institution. At this stage, in the late sixties, with the Civil Rights movement in full bloom, the time was ripe for feminist organizing, and Bernice was able fairly swiftly to marshal a strong body of supporters in her effort to overturn the rule. The CCWHP took shape as an avowedly feminist interest group, and we soon had chapters all over the country and a central executive committee to carry our resolutions to the American Historical Association.

In New York the CCWHP grew very rapidly from a small handful of politically active women to a large group bound together by professional interests that spanned a wide spectrum of political positions. Graduate students and tenured faculty were brought together at the frequent meetings where broad policies and individual grievances were taken up. Appeals came in from colleges up and down the East Coast from students and faculty members who claimed a variety of personal grievances. Our better-established leaders became advocates, inquiring into the questions and sometimes helping to secure arbitration for individuals or general legal advice from sympathetic jurists. We formulated a broad agenda for fairer hiring practices and against sexual harassment that has since become part of a national standard. All over the city we regularly carried off the circus clown trick of jamming more people into the limited spaces of our apartments than any observer would ever have believed they would hold.

How odd it seems now to see those passionately held principles branded as "PC" by critics who seem no longer to have any conception of how deeply implanted the old practices were. As I look back, sorting out the confusion that occurred as we advanced our cause in the full flood of the political passions of the late sixties and early seventies, it is a credit to our entire profession that so many of our programs for a fairer and more open working environment were met speedily and generously. Obviously, we did not achieve a perfect world, and it remains a matter of deep concern that many people in positions of influence and authority blame affirmative action concerns rather than professional choices on a lot of hiring decisions that go against young white men. But there can be no question that the face of the profession has changed dramatically, and I nourish the hope that nothing will ever turn back that tide.

For myself those meetings brought me out of my relatively small circle of friends from Columbia and Hunter and introduced me to the rich and busy world of women who worked in the other eighteen history departments at CUNY and the bevy of private-college and SUNY campuses in the neighborhood. For nearly twenty years every semester opened with the "welcome back" CCWHP party, usually at Dorothy Helly's, and even now that we have let attrition have its way with the chapter, we continue to maintain the friendships that grew out of it.

In the early days of the CCWHP meetings used to take place in a small study parlor at Barnard, where we would slide boxes of cookies back and forth across the table. Sandi Cooper, one of our first leaders, was also the first to introduce us to a larger network of women historians. I still remember her entering a meeting, lit up with excitement, declaring, "Ladies, I have found our grandmothers." She was referring to the Berkshire Conference of Women Historians, a group already some decades old that met annually in the spring at an inn in the Berkshire Mountains to gossip, drink, and exchange professional information and scholarly reports. The group originated with women in the Seven Sisters colleges who had grown tired of being excluded from "old boy" outings and determined to establish a tradition of their own. From the twenties until the eighties, the Berks met regularly with no charter, no treasury, and only a skeletal volunteer set of organizers. Its most prestigious offering was the trillium award, a double shot of whiskey awarded to the hiker who spotted the first purple trillium of the season. Today, as the Berks has expanded to its present eminence, the trillium remains its symbol.

Our cohort of feminists and activists entered into the Berks enthusiastically. The organization has maintained its original social and intellectual mission, vastly expanded by the organization of the "Big Berks" triennial conference on women's history, which has achieved an attendance of thousands from all over the world. The success of the conference necessitated a more formal structure, particularly a complex financial system, for the mother organization. But the "little Berks" has clung to its function as a network organization for women practitioners of every sort of history. My entire generation treasures the memories of hiking, boating, and partying that have sustained our friendships over the years.

By the mid-seventies feminist historians were thick on the ground, making a political and intellectual impact on institutions all over the country. But we needed all our determination and newly won political skills to counter the backlash that accompanied the deepening job crisis that persisted until the retirement of my generation and, to some extent, even beyond. The crisis was most traumatic in New York, where it was coupled with the city's financial crisis. President Gerald Ford's "Drop Dead" speech ended the city's policy of free university tuition forever. In one blow in 1976 every nontenured faculty member in the entire system was dropped, and those of us who remained were given much heavier teaching loads to compensate. For roughly a decade thereafter our energies were consumed by attempts to find some remedies for these disasters.[3]

Our own group of feminist historians looked for ways to use grant monies from governmental and other nonacademic institutions to fund projects for historians. One of our young adjuncts at Hunter, Marjorie Lightman, devised the notion of establishing an Institute for Research in History—funded by dues from employed faculty—to act as an umbrella for scholars whose unemployment deprived them of eligibility for grants as well. The Institute soon became a major player in the competition for grants of various sorts, and a core of active members served to generate a multiplicity of projects that provided employment and overhead to pay office expenses. One of the more successful programs was a grant-funded series of seminars called "Scholars in Transition," headed by Mary Somers, that helped unemployed scholars refashion their talents for employment in the corporate world.

Time has healed the immediate wounds of the crisis, and many of the original political problems that feminist historians set out to solve have given way to different agenda. The CCWHP has metamorphosed into a permanent committee of the American Historical Association, and the Institute for Research in History is but a fond memory, though I still attend monthly meetings of two discussion groups that grew out of it. Looking back, I see clearly that the most permanent and dramatic impact of feminism on academia has been the implantation of women's studies in the curriculum. In my own discipline women not only form the subject of specific courses but have been steadily integrated into the mainstream, fundamentally changing the way we formulate every aspect of history. Moreover, gender analysis has been fruitfully applied to almost every field of study. The social and political networks I have been describing were vital to the formation of feminist scholarship by combining intellectual exploration with academic politics.

Hunter College was again in the front rank of this enterprise. When I began teaching there in 1962, Barbara Welter was already giving courses on women in American history. A decade had gone by when Suzanne approached me with a call for papers from the Berkshire Conference, which had determined to sponsor a daylong conference on women's history, a field just beginning to formulate itself. Our paper was the only medieval entry among the handful of panels that formed that first meeting, and it was chosen for publication in one of the first issues of *Feminist Studies,* a journal established by a group of women from CCWHP and other feminist groups in New York.[4] Since then the conferences, called the "Big Berks" by members of the mother organization, have been held triennially with thousands of participants. I was privileged to be on the program committee for no less than seven of these meetings, once as cochair of the whole conference, and thereby I was able to extend my network to medievalists entering the field of women's history throughout the country.[5]

Sarah Pomeroy was another participant from Hunter in that first Berks. She was already well along in writing her classic survey of women in ancient Greece and Rome. She took the initiative in forming a committee to establish a program in women's studies at Hunter, and this enterprise engaged a number of us for years to come.[6] Outside of Hunter our intellectual formation continued in close connection with our political lives. The CCWHP customarily included reports from some of the members on their current research in its monthly meetings. Looking for an even more formal venue, some of the CCWHP group formed a seminar that still meets under the umbrella of Columbia University's seminars. Scholars from many disciplines were brought together there to learn from one another. One of the first organizers of the seminar, Renate Bridenthal, joined forces with Claudia Koonz to design a textbook for courses on women in European history, and Suzanne and I were invited to collaborate once more on a chapter covering the early Middle Ages.[7] The textbook, *Becoming Visible,* has continued through repeated revisions to be a leader in the field.

The institute also formed a series of study groups where the members met regularly as a complement to the larger business meetings. Many of these research groups have outlived the institute itself, and I still attend two of them regularly. The family history group reaches across periods and is devoted to reading and discussing new work in the field as recommended by our members in turn. The hagiography group, informally known as Friends of the Saints, is generally devoted to presentation of new research by members. It includes members from other disciplines drawn from most of the New York colleges as well as some from New Jersey. Older members regularly refer their graduate students, who use the group as an early venue for presenting papers in a friendly atmosphere.[8]

My early ventures in women's history brought me into an even more far-reaching network when Sister Lillian Thomas Shank wrote me from the Abbey of Our Lady of the Mississippi, where she was novice mistress. Sister Lillian was writing to scholars in various periods, hoping to interest them in contributing to a collection outlining the history of nuns, particularly Cistercians, originally intended for use in her novitiate. As she joined forces with John Nichols from Slippery Rock University, this project grew into a four-volume anthology focusing on nuns in the Middle Ages.[9] It produced a cottage industry among medievalists and permanently shifted the course of my own scholarly career. For twenty years the bulk of my research time was consumed by work on a small monograph followed by a large history of Roman Catholic nuns over two millennia.[10] As a result, also, my experience of sisterhood has broadly expanded among the bands of modern sisters, particularly those with an interest in their own history who have formed the Network for the History of Women Religious and who regularly communicate in cyberspace over Sister-L.

When I first took up women's history, I imagined that it was an unmined field. Only a few trips to the library were needed to reveal that we had many foremothers, only a handful of whom can be accommodated by this one collection of essays. The books lined many shelves, gathering dust, waiting for the heirs to their legacies. It was clear enough what had happened. Few of these authors ever found a firm foothold in academia. They had no graduate students, and no one endowed chairs to carry on their research. The male professoriat went on pursuing its own interests. The work of their female colleagues only entered into their bibliographies and their footnotes if it contributed to subjects that they considered pertinent. Thanks to the success of our networking activities over the course of my lifetime, I do not think that this will happen again.

The increase of women interested in higher education has been bolstered by the success of feminist activists in ensuring them a fair share of the tenured positions available. Feminist scholars have taken a strong interest in mentoring their younger colleagues, and feminist organizations like the Medieval Feminists—with their newsletter, their e-mail list, and the conference panels that produced the core of this volume—have consolidated our informal networks and ensure us the stimulation of exchanged ideas. Programs in women's studies have produced a body of scholarship that has spread into every discipline. In recent years women's studies has spawned gender studies and men's studies, which have progressively begun to transform even the most resistant corners of our disciplines.[11]

Today I look back at the women who befriended me in graduate school, the women who hired me, and the innumerable women I knew and those I never knew who have struggled in my lifetime to secure our place in the academy and to advance a scholarship that gives us the means to understand our own experiences. Sisterhood is powerful indeed, and it provides a working model for all humanity.

NOTES

1. My contribution to his festschrift testifies to these enduring ties; see "Legacy of Miracles."

2. From the dissertation I drew an article, "Simon de Beaulieu and *Clericis Laicos.*" It was ultimately published as *Gilles Aycelin: The Servant of Two Masters.*

3. In that pressured atmosphere I began to devote my "spare" time to translation projects, more readily accomplished than original writings. Out of this came *Daily Life in the World of Charlemagne,* translated from the French, *La vie quotidienne de l'empire carolingienne,* by Pierre Riché. In addition I worked on two Latin collections: McNamara and Halborg, *Ordeal of Community;* and McNamara with Halborg and Whatley, *Sainted Women in the Dark Ages.*

4. McNamara with Wemple, "Power of Women through the Family," was reprinted in *Clio's Consciousness Raised* and again in *Women and Power.* A retrospective paper written for the Fordham

conference, *Women and Power Revisited*, appears in *Gendering the Master Narrative: Women and Power in the Middle Ages*, ed. Mary C. Erler and Maryanne Kowaleski (Ithaca: Cornell University Press, 2003), 17–30. Several other papers were also first introduced at the Berkshire Conference, including McNamara, "Sexual Equality and the Cult of Virginity in Early Christian Thought"; "Wives and Widows in Early Christian Thought"; *"De Quibusdam Mulieribus."*

5. The 1980 conference, which we chaired, produced McNamara with Harris, *Women and the Structures of Society: Selected Research from the Fifth Berkshire Conference on the History of Women.*

6. The Hunter Collective eventually produced a textbook titled *Women's Reality, Women's Choices* (New York: Oxford University Press, 1985).

7. McNamara with Wemple, "Sanctity and Power." For later editions we divided our task, and I turned to the earlier period, McNamara "Matres Patriae/Matres Ecclesiae: Women in the Roman Empire," in *Becoming Visible*, ed. Renate Bridenthal, Claudia Koonz, and Susan Stuard, new rev. ed. (New York: Houghton Mifflin, 1987). Suzanne and I collaborated on a third article, "Marriage and Divorce in the Frankish Kingdom."

8. This group provided me with an introductory venue for several papers: "The Need to Give"; "The Rhetoric of Orthodoxy"; *"Imitatio Helenae";* and a couple of translation projects: "Dado of Rouen"; and *The Life of Yvette of Huy.*

9. I contributed to the first two volumes: "Muffled Voices"; and "Living Sermons."

10. McNamara, *New Song,* which has been translated into Dutch (*Zusters ten Strijde: Tweeduizend Jaar Nonnen* [Amsterdam: Calnbach, 1997]), Spanish (*Hermanas en Arma* [Barcelona: Herder, 1999]), and Italian *(Sorrelle in Armi* [Casale Monferrato: Edizione Piemme, 2000]).

11. A conference held at Fordham University in 1991 gave forceful impetus to the study of men in the Middle Ages. I gave the keynote, which was subsequently published in a collection of essays from the conference; see "Herrenfrage." Since then I have devoted much of my time to the problem, publishing several articles: "Canossa"; "City Air Makes Men Free and Women Bound"; "Gendering Virtue"; "Unresolved Syllogism"; "Chastity as a Third Gender in the History and Hagiography of Gregory of Tours"; "Chastity as a Manly Virtue."

Select Bibliography of Works by Jo Ann McNamara

"Simon de Beaulieu and *Clericis Laicos.*" *Traditio* 25 (1969): 155–170.

Gilles Aycelin: A Servant of Two Masters. Syracuse: Syracuse University Press, 1973.

With Suzanne Wemple. "The Power of Women through the Family," *Feminist Studies* 2 (1973): 126–41. Reprinted in *Clio's Consciousness Raised,* ed. Mary Hartman and Lois Banner (New York: Harper and Row, 1974), 103–18 and in *Women and Power,* ed. Maryanne Kowaleski and Mary Erler (Athens: University of Georgia Press, 1988), 83–101.

With Suzanne Wemple. "Marriage and Divorce in the Frankish Kingdom." In *Women in Medieval Society,* edited by Susan M. Stuard, 95–124. Philadelphia: University of Pennsylvania Press, 1976.

"Sexual Equality and the Cult of Virginity in Early Christian Thought. *Feminist Studies* 3, nos. 3/4 (1976): 145–58. Reprinted in *Women in Early Christianity, Studies in Early Christianity,* ed. David M. Scholer, vol. 14 (New York: Garland, 1993).

With Suzanne Wemple. "Sanctity and Power: The Dual Pursuit of Medieval Women." Chapter 4 of *Becoming Visible,* edited by Renate Bridenthal and Claudia Koonz. New York: Houghton Mifflin, 1977.

Translator. *Daily Life in the World of Charlemagne,* by Pierre Riché. Philadelphia: University of

Pennsylvania Press, 1978; 2nd ed., 1987. Originally published as *La vie quotidienne de l'empire carolingienne.*

"Wives and Widows in Early Christian Thought." *International Journal of Women's Studies* 2, no. 6 (1979): 575–92.

"Chaste Marriage and Clerical Celibacy." In *Sexual Practices and the Medieval Church,* edited by Vern L. Bullough and James A. Brundage, 22–33. Buffalo, N.Y.: Prometheus, 1981.

A New Song: Celibate Women in the First Three Christian Centuries. New York: Haworth Press, 1983. Reprint, New York: Harrington Park Press, 1986.

"Cornelia's Daughters: Paula and Eustochium." In *Women's Studies,* edited by Hope Phyllis Weissman, 9–27. London: Gordon and Breach, 1984.

"Muffled Voices: The Lives of Consecrated Women in the Christian Empire." In *Distant Echoes: Medieval Religious Women,* edited by John A. Nichols and Sr. Lilian Thomas Shank, 11–30. Kalamazoo, Mich.: Cistercian Publications, 1984.

Editor with Barbara J. Harris. *Women and the Structures of Society: Selected Research from the Fifth Berkshire Conference on the History of Women.* Durham, N.C.: Duke University Press, 1984.

"A Legacy of Miracles: Hagiography and Nunneries in Merovingian Gaul." In *Women of the Medieval World: Essays in Honor of John H. Mundy,* edited by Julius Kirshner and Suzanne F. Wemple, 36–53. London: Basil Blackwell, 1985.

"Living Sermons: Consecrated Women in the Conversion of Europe." In vol. 2 of *Peace Weavers: Medieval Religious Women,* edited by John A. Nichols and Sr. Lillian Thomas Shank, 19–37. Kalamazoo, Mich.: Cistercian Publications, 1987.

"Matres Patriae/Matres Ecclesiae: Women in the Roman Empire." In *Becoming Visible,* edited by Renate Bridenthal, Claudia Koonz, and Susan Stuard. New rev. ed. New York: Houghton Mifflin, 1987.

Translator with John E. Halborg. *The Ordeal of Community: Saints as Disciplinarians in Merovingian Convents, with "The Rule of Donatus of Besançon," and "An Anonymous Rule for Virgins attributed to Waldebert of Luxeuil."* Kalamazoo, Mich.: Cistercian Publications, 1987; 2nd ed., Toronto: Peregrina Press, 1994.

"*De Quibusdam Mulieribus:* Reading Women's History from Hostile Sources." In *Medieval Women and the Sources of Medieval History,* edited by Joel T. Rosenthal, 237–58. Athens: University of Georgia Press, 1990.

"The Need to Give: Suffering and Female Sanctity in the Middle Ages." In *Images of Sainthood in Medieval and Renaissance Europe,* edited by Renate Blumenfeld-Kosinski and Timea Szell, 199–221. Ithaca, N.Y.: Cornell University Press, 1991.

With John E. Halborg and Gordon Whatley. *Sainted Women of the Dark Ages.* Durham, N.C.: Duke University Press, 1992.

"The Rhetoric of Orthodoxy." In *Maps of Flesh and Light,* edited by Ulrike Wiethaus, 9–27. Syracuse, N.Y.: Syracuse University Press, 1993.

"The Herrenfrage: The Restructuring of the Gender System, 1050–1150." In *Medieval Masculinities,* edited by Clare A. Lees, 3–29. Minneapolis: University of Minnesota Press, 1994.

"Canossa: The Ungendered Man and the Anthropomorphized Institution." In *Render Unto Caesar,* edited by Sabrina Petra Ramet and Donald Treadgold, 131–50. Washington, D.C.: American University Press, 1995.

"*Imitatio Helenae:* Sainthood as an Attribute of Queenship in the Early Middle Ages." In *Saints: Studies in Hagiography,* edited by Sandro Sticca, 51–81. Binghamton, N.Y.: MRTS, 1996.

Sisters in Arms: Catholic Nuns through Two Millennia. Cambridge, Mass.: Harvard University Press, 1996.

"City Air Makes Men Free and Women Bound." In *Text and Territory: Geography and Literature in the European Middle Ages,* edited by Sylvia Tomasch and Sealy Gilles, 143–58. Philadelphia: University of Pennsylvania Press, 1997.

"Gendering Virtue." In *Plutarch's Advice to the Bride and Groom and A Consolation to His Wife: English Translations, Commentary, Interpretive Essays and Bibliography,* edited by Sarah B. Pomeroy, 151–61. Oxford: Oxford University Press, 1999.

Translator. *The Life of Yvette of Huy.* Annotated and with an introduction by Jo Ann McNamara. Toronto: Peregrina Press, 1999.

"An Unresolved Syllogism: The Search for a Christian Gender System." In *Conflicted Identities and Multiple Masculinities: Men in the Medieval West,* edited by Jacqueline Murray, 1–24. New York: Garland Press, 1999.

Translator. "Dado of Rouen, Life of Saint Eligius of Noyon," with an introduction. In *Medieval Hagiography: An Anthology,* edited by Thomas Head, 137–68. New York: Garland Press, 2000.

"Forward to the Past: Hildegard of Bingen and Monastic Reform." Afterword to *Hildegard's Explication of the Rule of Saint Benedict,* translated by Hugh Feiss. Toronto: Peregrina Press, 2000.

"Chastity as a Third Gender in the History and Hagiography of Gregory of Tours." In *The World of Gregory of Tours,* edited by Kathleen Mitchell and Ian Wood, 182–99. Leiden: Brill, 2002.

"Chastity as a Manly Virtue: Odo of Cluny and Gerald of Aurillac," For James Brundage's festschrift. Forthcoming.

CHAPTER 66

⟨∽

Another Perspective on Alterity and the Grotesque (1932–)

ELIZABETH A. R. BROWN

HONORED AS I WAS to be asked to contribute a memoir to this volume, the invitation presented a daunting challenge. On the one hand, with my seventieth birthday fast approaching (on 16 February 2002) I felt moved as a historian to record some of my recollections of the half-century I have devoted to the medieval past. On the other hand, setting down random memories of my experiences as a woman scholar who has worked on medieval Europe seemed to me unproductive. Despite the professor in graduate school who remarked wistfully in 1955, "If only you were a man" (and with whom, at the time, to my shame I agreed), I have not felt that being a woman has particularly helped or hindered my career. Nor do I believe that my outlook and perspective as a woman have perceptibly affected my research and writing. Do not mistake me. I am convinced that many women (including myself) possess certain qualities that many men lack. Among these I include an inclination to realistic practicality, attentiveness to detail, humility in the face of complexity, caution in generalizing, wariness of ex cathedra pronouncements, and sensitivity to the varying emotions and developmental patterns of individual human beings. Nonetheless, I am not prepared to characterize these qualities as essentially, much less exclusively, female, since I know many women who do not have them, and many males who do, and whose research reflects their influence.

Having decided to contribute to this volume, I was, in short, trying to find an appropriate angle, focus, and perspective for presenting my reflections. One quickly suggested itself: my disagreement with the provocative assessments three eminent American medieval historians have given of the past and future of the discipline we share, and their visions of the goals they think medievalists have pursued and are

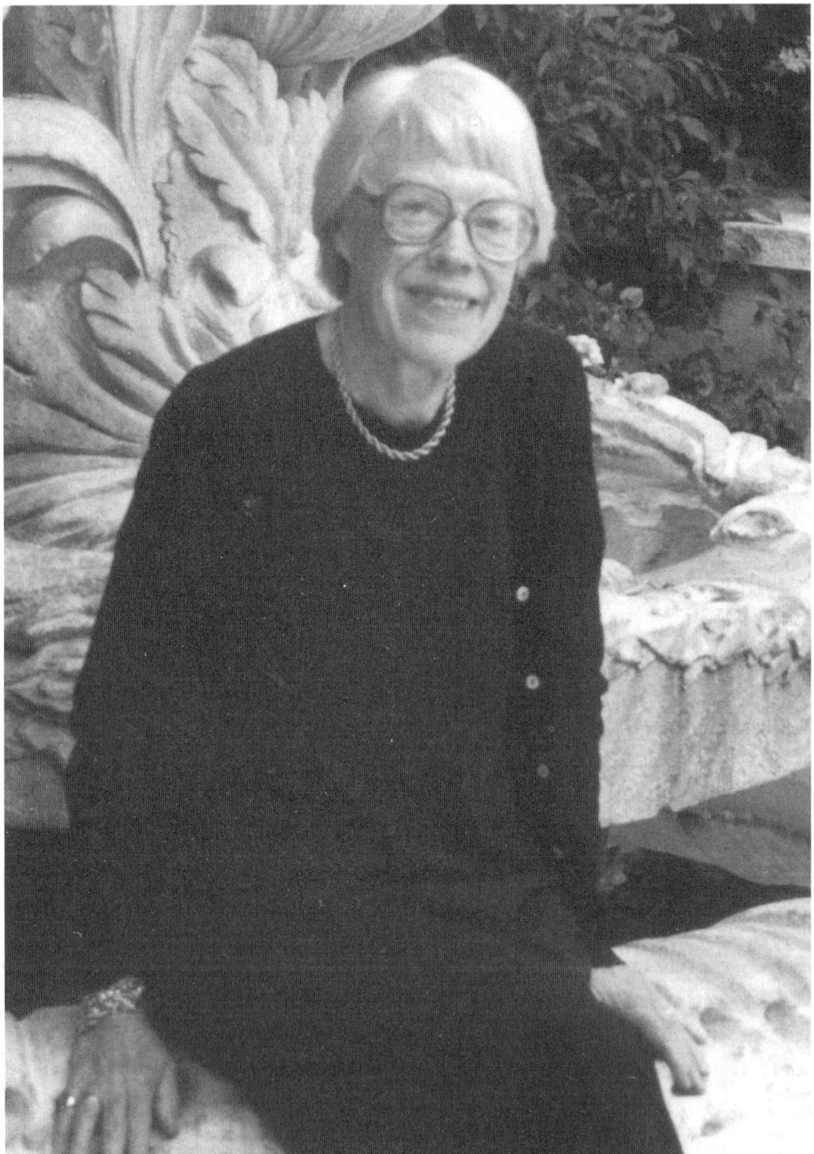

pursuing. The dramatic hypotheses they advance involve individuals I have known, times through which I have lived, movements in which I have participated, and events that have influenced me. Their impressions contrast markedly with my own. Led by them to reflect on my own experiences, I should like to present my own view of the evolution of medieval historiography during the past fifty years, since 1950 (when, at eighteen, I entered Swarthmore College and commenced my work in medieval history with Mary Albertson, Helen North, John Teall, and—rather osmotically—George Peddie Cuttino). I leave it to others to judge the extent to which my opinions and my work as a medievalist have been influenced by my childhood in Louisville, Kentucky; the years from 1939 to 1942 I spent as an "army brat" in Pass Christian, Mississippi, and Fort Leavenworth, Kansas; the conservatism of my parents; my own conversion to liberalism (and Episcopalianism); my very distant descent from immigrants; and the fact that I am a woman.

The first of the historians whose ideas concern me is Norman Cantor, who in 1991 published his controversial book *Inventing the Middle Ages: The Lives, Works, and Ideas of the Great Medievalists of the Twentieth Century*. Cantor's bold analysis of the process by which medieval historical writing developed between 1895 and 1965 was widely read and debated. Infuriating to many, the book influenced the thinking of Paul Freedman and Gabrielle Spiegel, the other two historians whose opinions I shall discuss. Both were investigating the evolution of medieval historiography in America when Cantor's book appeared. Freedman's paper, "The Return of the Grotesque in Medieval Historiography," was delivered in 1993 and published in 1995.[1] His ideas resonated with hypotheses Spiegel was developing, which she set out in an essay titled "In the Mirror's Eye: The Writing of Medieval History in North America."[2] Collaboration ensued, and in June 1998 Freedman and Spiegel published a joint article, "Medievalisms Old and New: The Rediscovery of Alterity in North American Medieval Studies."[3]

The views that Freedman and Spiegel set forth recall those of Cantor. Following Cantor, Freedman and Spiegel present Charles Homer Haskins (1870–1937) and Joseph R. Strayer (1904–87) as dominating the study and practice of medieval history in the United States.[4] They see both men as modernizers of the Middle Ages who espoused the "modernizing paradigms" and the "model of total identification" that had long characterized American views of the Middle Ages.[5] Both men were activists who were eager to make medieval history relevant to their own societies. Wilsonian progressivists, they aimed to demonstrate the compatibility of "medieval governmental history... with American democratic principles."[6] Their students (including myself) are said to be "centrally concerned with questions of legal/constitutional history in relation to issues of both feudalism and state formation."[7] We are credited with having spread the masters' vision during the 1950s and 1960s. John F. Benton (who investigated individuality and rationality) and Charles M. Radding (who studies cognitive development)—both students of Strayer, although Freedman and Spiegel do not mention this—are judged to have advanced "a rational and optimistic image of the twelfth century" and, in so doing, to have made the "period intelligible in contemporary terms."[8] Thus, like Haskins and Strayer, their students "shap[ed professional medievalism in America] with notions of scientific methodology, rationality, and progressive ideology."[9]

Since the 1970s, in Freedman's and Spiegel's view, the profession and the practice of medieval historiography have undergone radical change: "reiterated strangeness," "the suppressed, the odd, the fragmentary, and the marginal" have come to the fore, and "optimistic belief in a progressive Middle Ages" has been cast aside.[10] The new scholarship privileges the "grotesque" and "strange and extreme forms of belief and behavior."[11] Its practitioners study the irresponsible use of power and intimidation, persecution of sexual and ethnic minorities, the degradation of women, marginal groups and the powerless, heresy, incest, masochism, rape, transvestism, postcolonialism, and the grotesque—or, in Freedman's and Spiegel's summary characterization—"death, pus, contagion, defilement, blood, abjection, disgust and humiliation, castration, pain, and autopsy."[12] These orientations reflect a sense of the Middle Ages as different, as "other," but also as "darkly familiar, the analogue of a negatively construed modern West."[13] Thus, the new medievalists, like the old, interpret the past in terms of their own present.

Freedman and Spiegel associate the changes with broader, more general movements, which they label postmodern and link with Michel Foucault, Jacques Derrida, and Clifford Geertz: the emergence of feminism and gender studies; the rejection of positivism and disenchantment with the search for origins; and realization that documents are "texts" and provide "images" rather than "truth."[14] Freedman and Spiegel associate these shifts with alterations in political sentiments: frustration with the inferior status of women and blacks; anger at warfare considered unjust; skepticism regarding the virtue of pluralism and the efficacy of human reason; widespread disillusionment with the state; and pessimism regarding the future.[15] Spiegel is particularly interested in the backgrounds of the new medievalists.[16] She acknowledges that some are social and political conservatives, but those who practice the new medieval history, she thinks, are not. She links the novel trends in medieval historiography with the changing composition of the historical profession in the 1960s and 1970s. During these decades more "women and blacks," as well as a wider variety of "ethnic groups" including Jews, refugees, and immigrants, became historians. Many felt ambivalence toward the European past, she believes, and this led them to aim to master it and also to recognize that it had vanished forever. Recognizing the European Middle Ages as other and different, the new medievalists have reinterpreted the medieval past in light of their own experience, which has led them to focus on aspects of the past their more optimistic predecessors disregarded or avoided.[17]

I should like to turn now from the views of Freedman and Spiegel to my own experience. I shall begin by contesting the central importance that Cantor, Freedman, and Spiegel accord to Haskins and Strayer and go on to describe the aims and values my contemporaries and I espoused in the 1950s and 1960s, which differ from those

Freedman and Spiegel attribute to us. Finally I shall discuss my own and my contemporaries' interest in the aberrant, the other, and propose that changes in the questions we and others ask about the past reflect shifts in attitude in the world in which we live.

The love of the Middle Ages that my studies at Swarthmore nourished propelled me to graduate studies at Harvard and Radcliffe in 1954. The world of medieval studies that I entered was dominated by Charles Holt Taylor, Haskins's student and Strayer's slightly older contemporary—and also by Herbert Bloch, Harry Wolfson, Robert Lee Wolff, and the legendary Helen Maud Cam, who by her presence had proved that a woman historian could succeed at Harvard. Gaines Post, fellow graduate student of Taylor and Strayer, was, like Strayer, a presence intellectually. So too were Ernst Kantorowicz and Erwin Panofsky, whose works we read, and who visited to lecture. Like most college students in the 1950s, I had first become acquainted with Strayer through one of his textbooks. Long before I met him, I read most of what he had written and learned much about him from fellow graduate students (notably Fredric Cheyette and John Henneman) who had studied with him as undergraduates.

Haskins died when I was five, and I never knew him—although I met his long-lived contemporary Charles Howard McIlwain, who shared some but not all of his views, and who by all accounts was far more likable.[18] My fellow students and I indeed felt Haskins' presence at Harvard. We came to know him as a person principally through Charles Taylor. Haskins, we learned, was "the Iron Duke," who "took no hostages." He never compromised. He had "an exterior of granite and a heart of steel." On Christmas Eve he roamed the stacks of Widener Library checking to see if his students were working. Of course we read his books, but we read them skeptically, for his writings revealed that he was as stern a taskmaster and disciplinarian in dealing with the past as he was in handling his students. He was a regulator, a master creator of system and discipline. We took the Norman invention of the feudal system and the twelfth-century Renaissance with a grain of salt, although we dutifully parroted one or the other (if not both) on our exams. But we wondered.

Why were we skeptical? Charles Taylor's experience as a military historian during World War II led him to respect recalcitrant facts and recognize the importance of the contingent and the unpredictable. A fox to Strayer's hedgehog, a splitter who distrusted lumpers, he introduced us to microhistory and goaded us to ruminate as long and hard as he did over the evidence.[19] Constantly rethinking his own assumptions, he taught us to be wary of system and to avoid the hasty conclusion. He appreciated the importance of other disciplines, and he inculcated in us respect for collaborative scholarship. He encouraged us to grapple with Erik Erikson's work and heed William L. Langer's call to historians to utilize psychoanalytic insights.[20] He opened our eyes to the significance of the work of Gaines Post on the canon and civil law. Most important, he transmitted to us his love of archives and parchment. Our slightly older contemporaries Anne Freeman and Giles Constable made us aware of the challenges of editing texts, lessons reinforced when Samuel E. Thorne arrived at Harvard in 1956. On my first research trip to Europe, in 1958, Robert Fawtier drove this point home, declaring to me that the editions and inventories of texts he was then preparing were "what would live forever"—not his narrative and analytical publications.

Many of us elected to investigate political and institutional history, topics to which, as a good student of Haskins and McIlwain, Taylor introduced us. But neither we nor he believed that medieval institutions were by their nature good, or that we should view and interpret them as distant ancestors of modern American institutions. Our admiration for our own institutions was hardly unbounded. The Korean war, the execution of Ethel and Julius Rosenberg, the McCarthy hearings, the brutalities associated with the early Civil Rights movement, the hostility and disdain that greeted the publication of Simone de Beauvoir's *The Second Sex*—all these events marked the 1950s, and they affected our attitude to our world and, inevitably, to the past.

We recognized with regret the impossibility of attaining objectivity but determined to do our best to avoid projecting our own ideas and values onto the past.[21] Pondering the responsibilities of the profession we were preparing to enter, we staunchly opposed the contamination of the past by present concerns. We shunned imputing present value to our exploration of the past. Rather, we considered it our calling to investigate the vestiges of the past as honestly, as imaginatively, and as responsibly as we could. We believed that political activity should be channeled into present causes, not past ones. Crusading we considered well and good, but if we were to crusade as scholars, we determined to do so in order to refine and correct misapprehensions about the past—not to utilize the past in the service of the present, an aim that we disdained. We learned to tolerate with equanimity the idea that we were studying the Middle Ages quite simply because the period interested us. This conviction, at odds with the views of Haskins and Strayer, was one that, at Swarthmore, Mary Albertson had expressed with commonsensical vigor.[22]

My fellow graduate students and I valued the critical standards we worked hard to develop. We earned our (rather meager) livings by grading papers for the senior professors and teaching "the great historians" (whom we were at liberty to select) and "the philosophy of history" (which we had, somehow, to master). Reading Herodotus, Thucydides, Morton White, and Isaiah Berlin sharpened our perceptions and honed our critical faculties. Rather cowed, we nonetheless dreamed of putting into practice the theory we had absorbed and tried to pass on to our students. This was the scholarly activism that inspired us.

To what extent did we believe in scientific methodology? To what extent were we positivists? We demanded of ourselves the same rigor and precision we expected of scientists, and we used the word "cause" with extreme care, but we rejected the notion that we could produce laws of historical development. Recognizing that our findings and our theses would be replaced by those of future scholars, we determined to do our best to ensure that our work assist (and even, we hoped, inspire), rather than impede or mislead, those who were to follow.

As to the object of our study, we accepted the notion that we were engaged in investigating something real and actual that was different from our own world.[23] But not entirely lacking in common sense, we never believed that we could encounter or recover the medieval world that had once existed. We resigned ourselves to achieving fragmentary and fleeting glimpses of a past we would never fully know. How could this be otherwise when Sam Thorne told us repeatedly about his frustration in being unable (even through spiritualistic strategies) to discover from Bracton what some of that English medieval legist's more puzzling statements signified? To Bracton, as to Thorne, it was all so long ago, and when Bracton turned to Glanvill for assistance, he found Glanvill's memory as faulty as his own.

We learned these lessons as well from what we read. Some of us questioned the appropriateness of Carl Becker's title "Everyman His Own Historian" and wondered where the women were. But we accepted his view of history as "an imaginative creation"; "an unstable pattern of remembered things," which changed from age to age and person to person; a reconstruction that was obviously affected by the "literary discourse" in which it had its only "negotiable existence."[24]

We read not only Becker but also Marc Bloch, whose magisterial book *The Historian's Craft* appeared in 1954 (with an introduction, interestingly enough, by Joseph Strayer).[25] Given Strayer's own predilections, it did not surprise us that he emphasized Bloch's comments on the use of history, his vision of history as a whole ("the larger framework of the history of human society"), his concern for "all aspects of history"—and that he mentioned approvingly Bloch's having taught a course on United States economic history.[26] Strayer's assessment was not entirely laudatory. According to Norman Cantor, Strayer told his graduate students "that, compared to [Robert] Fawtier, Bloch was second-rate" and did not mention Bloch's work in the undergraduate lectures on medieval history he gave between 1955 and 1960.[27] We perceived Bloch differently. We appreciated his sensitivity to the interaction between present and past. We took to heart his attack on the search for origins and his discussion of documentary criticism. I was particularly affected by his analysis of "nomenclature" and the questions he posed regarding the appropriateness of terms like "feudalism" and "feudal system," labels he had used in his work *La société féodale*, which Strayer, predictably, praised, but which many of us thought far less impressive than *The Historian's Craft* or his study of the healing powers of kings.[28]

My fellow students and I were not unsophisticated. One thing, however, we lacked: encouragement to regard documents as artifacts or, following Freedman and Spiegel, as "texts" rather than repositories of "facts." We were fact grubbers. We were interested in manuscripts and documents because of the data they contain, not as objects deserving analysis for themselves. Because of the unprecedented opportunities we had to work in archives and to visit them vicariously through microfilm, we were perhaps more convinced of the importance of "primary sources" than were our mentors. But we were naive in our approach to the texts. Had we been more conversant with "the New Criticism," we might have employed the new critics' strategies in analyzing the texts we studied, but we did not.

Freedman and Spiegel link the changed attitude to manuscripts that now exists with postmodernism and the 1970s, but I think it began to develop much earlier, prompted by the work of paleographers, diplomaticists, and codicologists. My colleagues and I, alas, remained largely unaffected until the 1960s. Why Harvard should have been the backwater it was, I do not know. The study of paleography had long flourished in the United States. Since 1936 the subject had been taught at the Pontifical Institute in Toronto, and our contemporaries there and at Cornell received training that we, sadly, were denied.[29] The career of E. A. Lowe, who did not die until 1969, exemplified the cooperation and collaboration between Europe and North America that has promoted the progress of such studies.[30]

At Harvard rather than study paleography we transcribed facsimiles of documents related to the topics of our dissertations, so that we would not be completely lost when we entered archives and libraries abroad. We needed to be able to make some sense of the sources, which involved first of all reading them. We were dedicated to the search for facts, although in the actual presence of the documents and manuscripts our opinions of them slowly changed. In 1958 evenings spent in Paris discussing with Walter Goffart the vagaries of medieval punctuation and capitalization and the motivations of medieval forgers made me realize that there was more to studying sources than transcribing them. Robert Fawtier and François Maillard made it possible for me to see original acts and registers at the Archives nationales. Marie-Thérèse d'Alverny helped me at the Cabinet des manuscrits of the Bibliothèque nationale. Thus I became aware as I had never been before of seals, erasures, prickings, marginal notations, and rulings—and increasingly contemptuous of the microfilms Maurice Keen and I (like all our fellow *chercheurs*) were ordinarily forced to use at the Archives nationales. These experiences prepared the way. Encountering the work of Pierre Chaplais and Leonard Boyle fully converted me to a new vision of and respect for the texts with which I worked. Reading Foucault and Derrida years later simply reinforced the perspective I had found in the field. There I had come to recognize the document as critical actor in and delimiter of the historian's craft.

Marked change has indeed occurred, not only in medievalists' views of the sources but also in the topics we elect to study. We have become less interested in the state and politics. We are more concerned with spirituality and sexuality. We are exploring topics that may still be considered, as they were fifty years ago, "bizarre" and even "grotesque"—although, *pace* Freedman and Spiegel, I would not so characterize death (or dying).

Why have these changes occurred? In my view this question is ultimately unanswerable. Still, our altered agenda can be related to transformations that are culture-wide. They parallel analogous shifts in a variety of disciplines. Take, for example, music and opera. When asked to comment on Handel's current popularity, the opera director Francisco Negrin appealed in 1997 to "a resurgence of interest in 'the sacred'" and in "spiritual things, which," he believes, "were left aside in the 19th century and the early part of this century." Gone are the days, he said, when people were "interested in building nations or progressing technologically."³¹ Similarly, writing in the *Wall Street Journal* in 1998, Daniel Akst noted current novelists' lack of interest in money and business, and he commented that "[i]f love and work are the things that give our lives value, . . . it's strange that the literature of the day should only cover half the list."³² Foucault reminded us in 1966 that eras change mysteriously, and thoughts and values with them.³³ In 1970 Thomas Kuhn similarly emphasized the inexorability with which assumptions and world-views mutate.³⁴ Neither attempted to explain why such changes occur—for good reason. Involved in the shifts as we are, we can only attempt to discern them and record them. We have lost Vico's confidence that since human beings have made the world of nations, human beings can comprehend it.³⁵

In 1997 Caroline Walker Bynum quoted in her presidential address to the American Historical Association a Parisian student slogan of the 1960s, "Toute vue des choses qui n'est pas étrange est fausse" [Every view of things that is not strange is false].³⁶ Bynum saw in this statement a reflection of her own desire "to jolt my listeners and readers into an encounter with a past that is unexpected and strange." This, she implies, leads her to investigate the "bizarre and unheard of."³⁷ In another article, published in 1995, she expressed her commitment to writing "about what is other—radically, terrifyingly, fascinatingly other"—the very alterity on which Freedman and Spiegel focus.³⁸ Bynum does not attempt to explain why she herself is attracted to alterity, although her interest is doubtless prompted by impulses deeper than her wish to respond to our contemporaries' fascination with the grotesque and her desire to shock.

I myself am intrigued by phenomena that seem strange, bizarre, and grotesque because they challenge my experience of the normal. I doubt that my reaction is unique. As apparently recalcitrant data, such phenomena force us to recognize that we do not understand the past—or human nature—as fully as we might. This awareness spurs us not simply to describe the phenomena but also to explore the contexts in which they occurred or were manifested and also to seek traces and resonances in similar contemporary practices that may give us some insight into the past. In helping us to comprehend the phenomena, these strategies inevitably reduce the sense of grotesqueness they initially generate.

I should like to give two examples from my own experience. The first is predictable in a student descended directly from Charles Homer Haskins and Charles Taylor and indirectly from Joseph Strayer. It involves taxation and government and the reign of Philip the Fair of France (r. 1285–1314). The bizarre and puzzling phenomenon that aroused my interest was the decision of that reputedly calculating and "modern" monarch not only to cancel a tax imposed in 1313 to support an attack on the Flemings that was halted by a truce but also to return all his agents had collected. Investigating Philip's decision made me aware of the importance past rulers and their advisers accorded to philosophical and juristic principles, as it became clear that the reason for Philip's act of self-denial lay in his (and his subjects') commitment to the principle, "When the cause ceases, so should the effect."³⁹ This is not all. My findings changed my view of Philip the Fair himself, convincing me that he was far more rigidly religious and punctilious, far more determined to emulate and exceed his grandfather Saint Louis (who had been a stickler for restitution), and far more troubled by the prospect of God's final judgment than I had ever thought.[40] This led me to reevaluate the significance of the extraordinary lavishness of Philip's testamentary bequests and to recognize the unprecedented daring of the steps his heir and his executors took, shortly after his death, to modify the terms of his will and soften its impact on the kingdom's treasury.[41]

When I discussed Philip's restitution of taxes in 1313 at the Annual Meeting of the American Historical Association in Washington in 1969, the evident appeal of the notion to tax-weary Americans resulted in an article in the *Washington Post* titled "Historians Delve into Era When Taxation Was Sinful." "Hundreds of persons journeyed vicariously into the past here yesterday," Martin Weil wrote, "reaching a real but strange world . . . where rulers felt it so sinful to collect taxes that they sometimes stopped." For Weil the world I described seemed "strange" because of the "contrast with contemporary experience" offered by "revocation and even refunding of taxes."[42] I have since come to realize that restitution, although rare, is sometimes ordered by present-day governments. Nonetheless, Philip the Fair's actions at the end of his life remain unusual and cry out for explanation.

Another of my forays into the strange and grotesque was occasioned, yet again, by Philip the Fair. This time I was baffled by his determination to have his body divided after death, in order to permit his heart to be interred in a site of his own choosing, apart from his body, which, like those of his predecessors, would lie in the royal mausoleum of Saint-Denis. Investigation of what initially appeared an exceedingly curious practice revealed how widespread desire for division once was and also how popular it remained, well into the twentieth century. The particular ways in which people ordered themselves divided (or decreed against division) provided suggestive insights into their characters, personalities, motivations, and sensibilities.[43] Focusing on the transplantation of organs, Caroline Bynum has drawn analogies with our own times, and Katharine Park has related the attitudes to the body reflected in desire for and antipathy toward division to a wide range of feelings about corpses prevalent above and below the Alps, not only in the Middle Ages but also in modern times.[44]

Such research as this inevitably mitigates the sense of difference, of alterity, between ourselves and the past. Still, the chasm between past and present, the gulf separating us from those who have lived before is untraversable. There is no question that this is so. Nonetheless, our fascination with and dedication to exploring the past belie the logic we endorse. We continue to say, with Marianne Moore,

> If you will tell me why the fen
> appears impassable, I then
> will tell you why I think that I
> can get across it if I try.[45]

In this connection I should like to reconsider the French slogan from the sixties that Caroline Bynum quoted: "Toute vue des choses qui n'est pas étrange est fausse." As I read these words, it is the *vue,* not the *choses,* that must be *étrange* in order not to be false. If this is right, what could produce the "strangeness" of the "view" that would, because of its strangeness, be unfalse—and hence true? As I see it, the novelty, the originality, the freshness of the perspectives and techniques we bring to the *choses* we study. John Paul II's exhortation in *Fides et Ratio* seems particularly apt: to marshal, in our passion for ultimate truth and our eagerness to search for it, the audacity to forge new paths in its pursuit.[46]

The new and imaginative strategies that medievalists now employ have venerable roots and precedents. The advances made in the last fifty years are nevertheless strikingly impressive. What the future holds is as unknowable as the range of topics historians will choose to study, responding to their own and their societies' interests and concerns. One thing, however, is sure. Fresh generations of medieval historians will approach the subjects they select, whatever they are, with a sophistication and an array of tools, methodologies, and insights undreamed of when I began my exploration of the medieval past. I envy them, and with all my heart, I wish them well.

NOTES

1. Freedman, "Return of the Grotesque," 9–19. For the delivery of the paper at Santiago, a conference Spiegel attended, see Freedman and Spiegel, "Medievalisms," 704. The paper Spiegel presented at Santiago became the basis for the third chapter ("Towards a Theory of the Middle Ground") of her *Past as Text,* ix, 44–56.

2. Spiegel, *Past as Text*, 57–80, with notes on 230–38, and see also her discussion of the essay in the introduction, xxxi. In the spring of 1997 Spiegel presented a series of lectures on this topic at the École des hautes études en sciences sociales.

3. Slightly more than half of "Medievalisms" repeats material Freedman and Spiegel published in their independent articles, the bulk of it (a bit over 80 percent of the reused material, as I calculate it) being drawn from Spiegel's essay.

4. For Cantor's views of Haskins and Strayer, see *Inventing the Middle Ages,* 37–38, 245–86. Cantor (36–37, 283–84) links the radicalism of the 1960s with the emergence of historians concerned with "medieval alternative cultures and disempowered groups," "antistatist and socially irrational behavior, including juvenile delinquency, petty crime, and familial disorder, as structurally representative of antiestablishment, protomodern revolution"; see 413, for his depiction of the 1970s and 1980s as characterized by "antihumanistic rages." He connects interest in medieval "expression[s] of self-interested power" with the ideas of Jacques Derrida and Michel Foucault (367). For Spiegel's use of Cantor, see Spiegel, "In the Mirror's Eye," in *The Past as Text,* 66–67, 71, 232 (nn. 18–20), 234 (n. 30), and 235 (nn. 32 and 39, where the page reference should be corrected from 254 to 255). Freedman does not refer to Cantor in "Return of the Grotesque," although his use of the phrase "American triumphalism" (15) recalls Cantor's references to "American exceptionalism" (*Inventing the Middle Ages,* 37–38, 263). In their joint article Freedman and Spiegel simply cite Cantor on Haskins and Strayer ("Medievalisms," 682 n. 17, corresponding to Spiegel's first reference to Cantor in "In the Mirror's Eye," in *The Past as Text*).

5. Freedman and Spiegel, "Medievalisms," 679, 703.

6. Freedman and Spiegel, "Medievalisms," 687–88; cf. Spiegel, "In the Mirror's Eye," *The Past as Text*, 67–71 (characterizing Strayer's work as "Americanizing" medieval royal history and noting his emphasis on the virtues of medieval kingship and the laicization of society in the thirteenth century, points that are omitted in the joint article).

7. Freedman and Spiegel, "Medievalisms," 689; cf. Spiegel, "In the Mirror's Eye," *The Past as Text*, 71.

8. Freedman and Spiegel, "Medievalisms," 691–93, with the quoted phrases found on 691 and 693; cf. Freedman, "Return," 15–16.

9. Freedman and Spiegel, "Medievalisms," 689.

10. Freedman and Spiegel, "Medievalisms," 693.

11. Freedman and Spiegel, "Medievalisms," 677 n. 1, 679–81, 693, 703. In "Return of the Grotesque" Freedman insists that the Middle Ages were generally characterized as grotesque before the twentieth century, but he mentions only Victor Hugo and Gibbon by name (11) and for the rest invokes "nineteenth-century Gothic tale[s]" (11), "Romantic and Gothic ghosts that never really died" (14), and "venerable Gothic clichés" (18). Freedman asserts that "a long history of representing the period as progressive or rational does not exist" (13) and suggests that for this reason scholars have found it easier to perceive the grotesque in the Middle Ages than in the Renaissance or in modern United States history.

12. Freedman and Spiegel, "Medievalisms," 690, 695–96, 698–700, with the quoted phrases taken from 699.

13. Freedman and Spiegel, "Medievalisms," 702.

14. Freedman and Spiegel, "Medievalisms," 694–97.

15. Freedman and Spiegel, "Medievalisms," 690, 702–3.

16. Spiegel, "In the Mirror's Eye," 72, 78–79; cf. Freedman and Spiegel, "Medievalisms," 702; and Freedman, "Return of the Grotesque," 13.

17. Freedman holds that the new approach may lead (1) to exaggeration of differences between medieval and modern times; (2) to projection of a different, grotesque set of modern values onto the past; and (3) to the search for medieval examples to serve different current agendas. For the first point, see Freedman, "Return of the Grotesque," 10–11 ("a sophisticated anthropological appreciation [may] merely [reproduce] a nineteenth-century Gothic tale"; esp. n. 7), 17 ("[t]he liminal, the extreme, the grotesque may become magnified disproportionately and cut off from their cultural context"), 18 ("a return to a grotesque Middle Ages [may] produce a sophisticated version of venerable Gothic clichés"), and 19 ("[t]he strange and disturbing aspects of the medieval have a way of shaping themselves into lurid forms of Gothicism"). For the second point, see Freedman, "Return of the Grotesque," 11–12, 13, and esp. 17 ("Now that the project of modernity is widely equated with hegemony, rape and colonialism, the contested Middle Ages is made to serve a new contemporary master"; "the medieval becomes . . . a Foucaultian panopticon of discipline and colonization" [a phrase that Spiegel quotes in "In the Mirror's Eye," 77, and that reappears in "Medievalisms," 698—in both cases with the spelling "Foucauldian"]; "its repressive physical and discursive practices [anticipating] the negatively represented modern West"; cf. Freedman and Spiegel, "Medievalisms," 702 ["negatively constructed modern West"]). For the third point, see Freedman, "Return of the Grotesque," 18–19 (citing Lee Patterson and Judith M. Bennett).

18. Freedman and Spiegel perceptively analyze the changes in McIlwain's views on historical objectivity, in "Medievalisms," 687, esp. n. 36. When Charles Taylor lectured on the relationship

between lord and man, McIlwain was one of the two men he had known to whom he said he would willingly have done homage.

19. See Berlin, *Hedgehog and the Fox*.

20. Langer's presidential address to the American Historical Association was published as "The Next Assignment." It sparked hours of heated debate among graduate students and young instructors at Harvard.

21. Cf. the similar views expressed by Cantor, *Inventing the Middle Ages,* 17, 27–28, 37.

22. Strayer opposed what he termed antiquarianism and in 1969 accused his colleagues of "spend[ing] time on trivial problems," "accumulat[ing] odds and ends of esoteric learning of interest only to themselves," and "[sometimes letting new] techniques become ends in themselves": see his essay, "The Future of Medieval History," esp. 179–80, 188. Strayer had advanced much the same views in his article "What Is Medieval History?" (*Social Education* 9 [November 1945]: 295–98). In 1948 Strayer despaired of the study of ancient history ("ancient history is almost a lost cause") in his essay "United States History and World History" (orig. pub. in *The Journal of General Education* 22 [1948]: 144–48, reprinted in Strayer, *Medieval Statecraft,* 379–86, quotation from 382).

23. Cf. the similar views expressed by Cantor, *Inventing the Middle Ages,* 28–39, 414.

24. Becker, "Everyman His Own Historian," esp. 227–38, 233–34, 235. Freedman and Spiegel ("Medievalisms," 687) follow Peter Novick in analyzing medievalists' rejection of Becker's relativism before World War II and their conversion to his position as a result of the war.

25. Bloch, *Historian's Craft*. The work is now available in a critical edition, edited by Bloch's son Étienne, *Apologie pour l'histoire ou Métier d'historien*.

26. Strayer, introduction to Bloch, *Historian's Craft,* vii–xii (esp. vii–viii, x–xi). In a letter dated 19 November 1998, Norman Cantor reminded me that Bloch taught American economic history because, holding as he did the chair of economic history at the Sorbonne, he was obligated to do so. See Fink, *Marc Bloch,* 183–204 (who does not, however, mention the lectures, although Professor Cantor remembers reading them in mimeographed form in the series regularly published at the time by the Sorbonne). Fink notes (260) that among the projects Bloch was planning in the spring of 1941 was a study "of the settlement of the United States"—as well as a murder mystery. On Strayer, who prided himself on having taught every course in the Princeton history department except Latin American history between 1930 and 1951, see the *Daily Princetonian,* Wednesday, 2 May 1973, 1, 3, and also the obituary of Strayer, written for the Princeton faculty by Jerome Blum, Michael S. Mahoney, Robert L. Tignor, and William C. Jordan (chair). Strayer's publications ranged from United States history to world history, to Russia, to Roman history; he was especially concerned with pedagogy. See his *Medieval Statecraft,* 321–98.

27. Norman Cantor, who was Strayer's research assistant between 1954 and 1960, communicated these observations to me in a personal letter written on 19 November 1998.

28. See Strayer's comments in his introduction to Bloch, *Historian's Craft,* x; for publication data, see Fink, *Marc Bloch,* 347–48.

29. For background, see Rouse, "Latin Paleography," 307–27. I am grateful to Richard Rouse for a letter he wrote on 23 November 1997 describing his studies with Stuart Hoyt at the University of Iowa, his work at Cornell, and the encouragement he received from Bernard Bischoff, Richard Hunt, and Neil Ker.

30. See Brown, "E. A. Lowe."

31. An interview with Negrin, who was directing a new production of *Partenope* at the New York City Opera, appeared in *Stagebill,* 22 September 1998, 22, 24.

32. Akst, "Money Vanishes."

33. Foucault, foreword to the English edition of *Les mots et les choses,* ix–xiv (esp. xii–xiii).

34. S. Kuhn, *Structure of Scientific Revolutions,* esp. 111–43.

35. Vico, *New Science,* 96–97 (Section 3, Principles [1.1–3]).

36. Bynum, "Wonder," 702 n. 84.

37. Bynum, "Wonder," 1, 25–26.

38. Bynum, "Why All the Fuss about the Body?" 31.

39. This principle was even more widely endorsed than I realized when I published my article *"Cessante Causa";* see also my article "Taxation and Morality." John Bell Henneman included excerpts from two papers on the topic that I presented in 1966 in *Medieval French Monarchy,* 111–19. Richard Helmholz gives additional examples of the invocation of the principle in *Spirit of Classical Canon Law,* 57. Kenneth Pennington gives even more in his review of this book; see "Spirit of Legal History," esp. 1,007–8.

40. See my articles "Prince Is Father"; "Philippe le Bel"; "Royal Salvation"; and "Persona et Gesta."

41. Brown, "Royal Salvation," which is a radically revised version of an article I wrote for *Order and Innovation in the Medieval West,* 365–83, 541–61.

42. Weil, "Historians Delve into Era." Weil also presented Jeffrey B. Russell's paper on witchcraft as "reality" in the Middle Ages as additional evidence of the strangeness of the medieval world. He ended by discussing the meeting of eighty women historians to discuss the problems faced by women in the profession and the need "for courses in 'women's history.'"

43. Brown, "Death and the Human Body in the Later Middle Ages"; for Philip the Fair, see Brown, "Prince Is Father," 310–11.

44. See esp. Caroline Walker Bynum, "Material Continuity, Personal Survival and the Resurrection of the Body: A Scholastic Discussion in Its Medieval and Modern Contexts," in her *Fragmentation and Redemption,* 239–97. Park, "Sensitive Corpse"; and Park, "Life of the Corpse."

45. Moore, *Complete Poems,* 178. The poem is titled "I May, I Might, I Must" and was first published in 1959 (in a collection of Moore's poems titled *O To Be a Dragon*). I am grateful to the estate of Marianne Moore and to Viking Press for giving me permission to publish the poem here.

46. *New York Times,* Friday, 16 October 1998, A1, A10, section 56 ("The lesson of history in this millennium now drawing to a close shows that this is the path to follow: it is necessary not to abandon the passion for ultimate truth, the eagerness to search for it or the audacity to forge new paths in the search").

Select Bibliography of Works by Elizabeth A. R. Brown

"Cessante Causa and the Taxes of the Last Capetians: The Political Applications of a Philosophical Maxim." *Studia Gratiana* 15 (*Post Scripta*) (1972): 567–87. Reprinted in *Politics and Institutions in Capetian France.* Variorum Collected Studies, CS350. Aldershot, Eng.: Variorum, 1991, no. 2.

"Taxation and Morality in the Thirteenth and Fourteenth Centuries: Conscience and Political Power and the Kings of France." *French Historical Studies* 8 (1973): 1–28. Reprinted in *Politics and Institutions in Capetian France.* Variorum Collected Studies, CS350. Aldershot, Eng.: Variorum, 1991, no. 3.

"The Tyranny of a Construct: Feudalism and Historians of Medieval Europe." *American Historical Review* 79 (1974): 1,063–88.

"Royal Salvation and Needs of State in Late Capetian France." In *Order and Innovation in the Medieval West: Essays in Honor of Joseph R. Strayer*, edited by William C. Jordan, Bruce McNab, and Teofilo F. Ruiz. Princeton, N.J.: Princeton University Press, 1976. Reprinted in *The Monarchy of Capetian France and Royal Ceremonial*. Variorum Collected Studies, CS 345. Aldershot, Eng.: Variorum, 1991, no. 4.

"Philippe le Bel and the Remains of Saint Louis." *Gazette des Beaux-Arts* 115 (1980): 175–82. Reprinted in *The Monarchy of Capetian France and Royal Ceremonial*. Variorum Collected Studies, CS 345. Aldershot, Eng.: Variorum, 1991, no. 3.

"Death and the Human Body in the Later Middle Ages: The Legislation of Boniface VIII on the Division of the Corpse." *Viator* 12 (1981): 221–70. Reprinted in *The Monarchy of Capetian France and Royal Ceremonial*. Variorum Collected Studies, CS 345. Aldershot, Eng.: Variorum, 1991, no. 6.

"The Prince Is Father of the King: The Character and Childhood of Philip IV of France." *Mediaeval Studies* 49 (1987): 282–334. Reprinted in *The Monarchy of Capetian France and Royal Ceremonial*. Variorum Collected Studies, CS 345. Aldershot, Eng.: Variorum, 1991, no. 2.

The Oxford Collection of the Drawings of Roger de Gaignières and the Royal Tombs of Saint-Denis. Transactions of the American Philosophical Society, vol. 78, pt. 5. Philadelphia: American Philosophical Society, 1988.

"Persona et Gesta: The Image and Deeds of the Thirteenth-Century Capetians: 3, The Case of Philip the Fair." *Viator* 19 (1988): 219–46. Reprinted in *The Monarchy of Capetian France and Royal Ceremonial*. Variorum Collected Studies, CS 345. Aldershot: Variorum, 1991, no. 5.

The Monarchy of Capetian France and Royal Ceremonial. Aldershot, Eng.: Variorum, 1991.

Politics and Institutions in Capetian France. Aldershot, Eng.: Variorum, 1991.

Customary Aids and Royal Finances in Capetian France: The Marriage Aid of Philip the Fair. Medieval Academy Books, no. 100. Cambridge, Mass.: Medieval Academy of America, 1992.

"Franks, Burgundians, and Aquitanians" *and the Royal Coronation Ceremony in France*. Transactions of the American Philosophical Society, vol. 82, pt. 7. Philadelphia: American Philosophical Society, 1992.

Jean du Tillet and the French Wars of Religion: Five Tracts, 1562–1569. Medieval and Renaissance Texts and Studies, 108. Binghamton, N.Y.: Medieval and Renaissance Texts and Studies, 1994.

With Richard C. Famiglietti. *The Lit de Justice: Semantics, Ceremonial, and the Parlement of Paris, 1300–1600*. Beiheft der Francia, vol. 31. Sigmaringen, Ger.: Jan Thorbecke, 1994.

"Le greffe civil du Parlement de Paris au XVIe siècle: Jean du Tillet et les registres des plaidoiries." *Bibliothèque de l'École des chartes* 153 (1995): 325–72.

"The Dinteville Family and the Allegory of *Moses and Aaron before Pharaoh*." *Metropolitan Museum of Art Journal* 34 (1999): 73–100.

Saint-Denis: La basilique. La Pierre-qui-Vire, Fr.: Éditions Zodiaque, 2001.

Works Cited

Akst, Daniel. "The Money Vanishes: Novelists Used to Care about Capital and Commerce. Not Anymore." *Wall Street Journal*, 9 October 1998, W13.

Becker, Carl. "Everyman His Own Historian." *American Historical Review* 37 (1932): 221–36.

Berlin, Isaiah. *The Hedgehog and the Fox: An Essay on Tolstoy's View of History*. 1953. Reprint, New York: Mentor Books, 1957.
Bloch, Marc. *Apologie pour l'histoire ou Métier d'historien*. Edited by Étienne Bloch. Paris: Armand Colin, 1993.
———. *The Historian's Craft*. Translated by Peter Putnam. Manchester, Eng.: Manchester University Press, 1954.
———. *Les Rois thaumaturges: Étude sur le caractère surnaturel attribué à la puissance royale particulièrement en France et en Angleterre*. Publications de la Faculté des lettres de l'Université de Strasbourg, 19. Strasbourg: Istra, 1924.
———. *La Société féodale*. 2 vols. L'évolution de l'humanité, synthèse collective, 24. Paris: Albin Michel, 1939. Translated by L. A. Manyon under the title *Feudal Society*. London: Routledge, 1961.
Blum, Jerome, Michael S. Mahoney, Robert L. Tignor, and William C. Jordan. "Joseph Reese Strayer, August 20, 1904–July 2, 1987." Unpublished obituary, written for the faculty of Princeton University. Copy owned by William Jordan, History Department, Princeton University.
Brown, Julian. "E. A. Lowe and *Codices Latini Antiquiores*." *Scrittura e civiltà* 1 (1977): 177–97.
Bynum, Caroline Walker. *Fragmentation and Redemption: Essays on Gender and the Human Body in Medieval Religion*. New York: Zone Books, 1991.
———. "Why All the Fuss about the Body? A Medievalist's Perspective." *Critical Inquiry* 22 (1995): 1–33.
———. "Wonder." *American Historical Review* 102 (1997): 1–26.
Cantor, Norman. *Inventing the Middle Ages: The Lives, Works, and Ideas of the Great Medievalists of the Twentieth Century*. New York: William Morrow, 1991.
Fink, Carole. *Marc Bloch: A Life in History*. Cambridge: Cambridge University Press, 1989.
Foucault, Michel. *Les mots et les choses*. Paris: Gallimard, 1966. [No translator listed.] Translated under the title *The Order of Things: An Archaeology of the Human Sciences* (New York: Vintage Books, 1971).
Freedman, Paul. "The Return of the Grotesque in Medieval Historiography." In *Historia a Debate: Medieval*, edited by Carlos Barros. Santiago de Compostela, Sp.: HAD, 1995.
Freedman, Paul, and Gabrielle M. Spiegel. "Medievalisms Old and New: The Rediscovery of Alterity in North American Medieval Studies." *American Historical Review* 103 (1998): 677–704.
Goldstein, Joel. "Medievalist Strayer to Deliver Last Lecture Today." *Daily Princetonian*, 2 May 1973, 1, 3.
Helmholz, Richard. *The Spirit of Classical Canon Law*. The Spirit of the Laws Series. Athens: University of Georgia Press, 1996.
Henneman, John Bell. *The Medieval French Monarchy*. European Problem Studies. Hinsdale, Ill.: Dryden, 1973.
Kuhn, Thomas S. *The Structure of Scientific Revolutions*. 2d ed. International Encyclopedia of Unified Science, Foundations of the Unity of Science, 2, pt. 2. Chicago: University of Chicago Press, 1970.
Langer, William L. "The Next Assignment." *American Historical Review* 63 (1958): 283–304.
Moore, Marianne. *The Complete Poems of Marianne Moore*. New York: Macmillan, 1982.
Negrin, Francisco. Interview in *Stagebill*, 22 September 1998, 22, 24.

Park, Katharine. "The Life of the Corpse: Division and Dissection in Late-Medieval Europe." *Journal of the History of Medicine and Allied Sciences* 50 (1995): 111–32.

———. "The Sensitive Corpse: Body and Self in Renaissance Medicine." *Fenway Court, 1990–91: Isabella Stewart Gardner Museum* (1992): 77–87.

Pennington, Kenneth. "The Spirit of Legal History." *University of Chicago Law Review* 64 (1997): 1,097–116.

Rouse, Richard H. "Latin Paleography and Manuscript Studies in North America." In *Un secolo di paleografia e diplomatica (1887–1986): Per il centenario dell'Istituto di paleografia dell'Università di Roma,* edited by Armando Petrucci and Alessandro Pratesi. Rome: Gela Editrice, 1988.

Spiegel, Gabrielle M. *The Past as Text: The Theory and Practice of Medieval Historiography.* Parallax: Re-visions of Culture and Society. Baltimore: Johns Hopkins University Press, 1997.

———. "In the Mirror's Eye: The Writing of Medieval History in America." Reprinted in *Imagined Histories: American Historians Interpret the Past,* edited by Anthony Molho and Gordon S. Wood, 238–63. Princeton: Princeton University Press, 1998.

Strayer, Joseph R. "The Future of Medieval History." *Medievalia et Humanistica: Studies in Medieval and Renaissance Culture,* n.s., 2 (1971): 179–88.

———. *Medieval Statecraft and the Perspectives of History: Essays by Joseph R. Strayer.* Edited by John F. Benton and Thomas N. Bisson. Princeton, N.J.: Princeton University Press, 1971.

Vico, Giambattista. *The New Science of Giambattista Vico: Unabridged Translation of the Third Edition (1744) with the Addition of "Practic of the New Science."* Translated by Thomas Goddard Bergin and Max Harold Fisch. Rev. ed. Ithaca, N.Y.: Cornell University Press, 1968, 1984.

Weil, Martin. "Historians Delve into Era When Taxation Was Sinful." *Washington Post,* 30 December 1969.

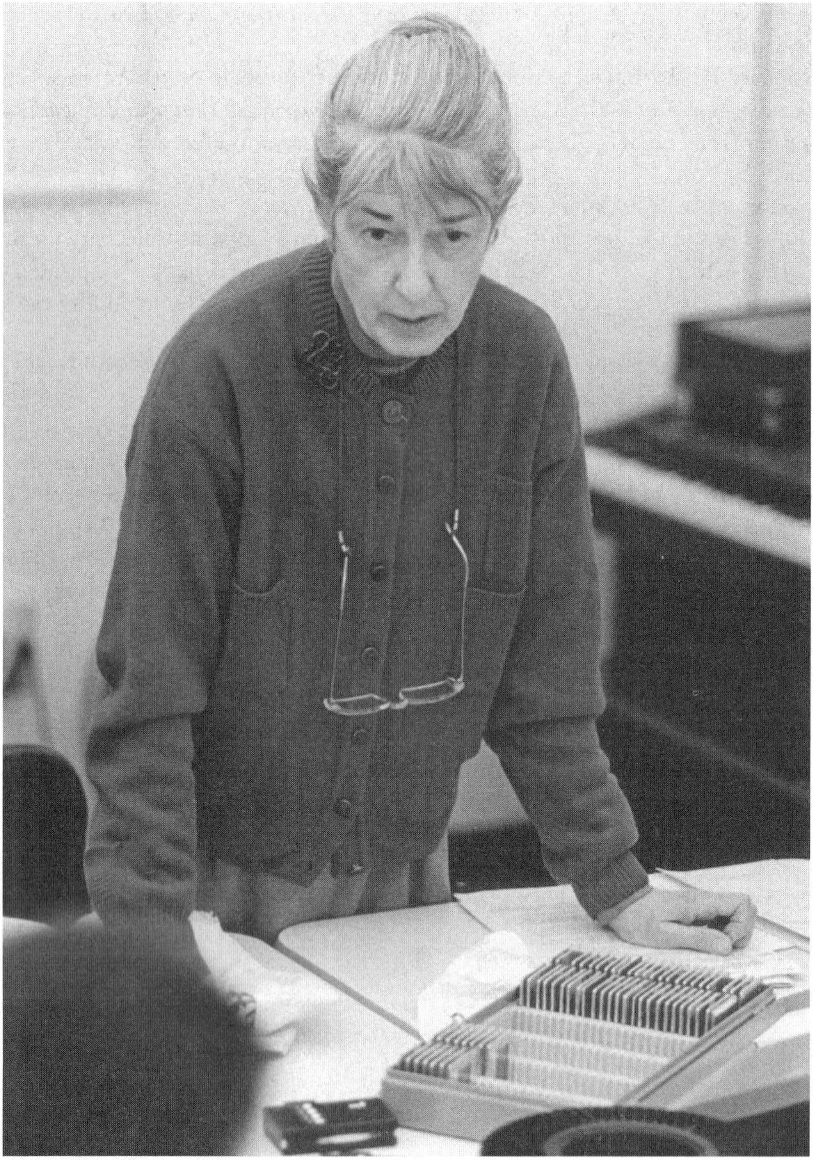

CHAPTER 67

Ars Longa, Vita Brevis (1932–)

MEREDITH PARSONS LILLICH

ONCE UPON A TIME there was no penicillin, no plastic, and no pizza. No interstate highways and no jet planes; no microwaves, no frozen foods or freezers, no clothes dryers. No nylon, acrylic, Lycra, polyester; no videos or even TV, no long-playing records (and that was before tape cassettes). No battery wristwatches or ballpoint pens. No Xerox machines (just carbon paper), no electric typewriters; no fax machines, and, of course, no e-mail.

I was a child of the Second World War—born during the Depression in an unquestionably middle-class neighborhood that no longer exists on the south side of Chicago. A child of this land: my father's family had arrived in Massachusetts in 1635, and my mother's in Quebec about the same time, Normandy peasants serving the Jesuits. My parents had both graduated from the University of Illinois—the first of their families, as far as I know, to go to college. My father, who employed his journalistic training to run a small advertising business, became interested in modern design when I was small; in his enthusiasm he actually bought a couple pieces of Noguchi furniture (which I still have) and hired John Lloyd Wright (son of Frank) to remodel a small summer cottage near Valparaiso, Indiana.[1] Polio having arrived at the Chicago beaches, I spent all my summers there from age four to seventeen. My mother was a lifelong homemaker who did my father's bookkeeping but never received a paycheck in her life. When I was very young she learned to weave at Hull House; as a suburbanite much, much later in life, she gave classes for ladies and studied at the school of the Art Institute—where Lenore Tawney once arranged for her to "substitute teach" her classes.[2]

Growing up smart and female presented challenges. My grandmother and mother taught me that women had to make the family decisions but that the real trick was to learn how to plant the ideas with the head of the house and get him to think they were his own. The girls' magazines of the day cautioned me to hide my brain whenever possible and offered me the career choices that, they decreed, were the only ones available to females who could not be full-time homemakers: nurse, teacher, or librarian. Nursing repelled me only slightly more than school teaching, but since I loved books I assumed I would have to be a librarian.

The city elementary schools solved the problem I presented by skipping me ahead, a semester at a time (since during the war years there were classes starting in September and again in January), until at the fourth skip my parents complained. I missed the multiplication tables, which I had to drill with my father, and the geography of the states (forty-eight in those days), which I never did learn. I was, however, allowed to give the valedictory speech when my primary class moved to high school—something to do with the Founding Fathers and America as the melting pot and Chicago as the hog-butcher of the world, as I recall.

The public high school's solution was different. In place of free or study periods in my schedule, I was enrolled in more major courses, ultimately six instead of the usual three or four. When graduation time arrived, I was again, statistically, the valedictorian, but since I was female—and the next candidate was male—we reigned as covaledictorians.

I flew to Oberlin College like a bird out of a cage. Oberlin, with its venerable history as the first college to grant undergraduate degrees to women, was a rare and special place in the early 1950s; later it seemed to me as if they didn't notice whether you were a boy or a girl until you graduated. For the first time in my life everything I really cherished was not only tolerated but enthusiastically encouraged and rewarded. I felt that I had been born. Not reborn; life-before-Oberlin seemed a gray, disquieting morass from which I had emerged, unexpectedly, into the full sunlight. I had gone to Oberlin as a good school where I could also pursue voice lessons, since singing had been an acceptable activity for a midwestern girl-child, but as a freshman I couldn't pass required music theory; I was tutored and given a C, provided I would drop the major. What Oberlin provided to fill the void was serious and quality instruction in art history from mentors such as Wolfgang Stechow and Ellen Johnson.[3] When I graduated Phi Beta Kappa with a double major in art history and English, the only thought in my head was to go to Europe—something not possible during the war. My mentors helped me apply for and win one of the early Fulbrights—to Belgium, since I spoke French, and they thought I would have a better chance than in the heavy competition for France. I did also apply for and get a French government grant to Paris, but my mother insisted on Belgium because Fulbrights were "safer"—chaperoned by the United States government. My mentors had helped me craft a research project about the Belgian painter James Ensor, but when I arrived in Brussels at age twenty-one, the Belgian Fulbright committee would not hear of it and enrolled me in the Université libre de Bruxelles.

The university had no more light, heat, or amenities than the rest of Europe in those years, and several of my professors made the trip up from the Sorbonne once every three or four weeks to lecture. My salvation was the local Belgian professor in my schedule: Suzanne Sulzberger, a specialist in sixteenth-century northern painting.[4] I found out many decades later that her brother had died in a Nazi concentration camp. She took one look at this young American naïve, and told me I was *not* to stick around the cold dark halls in Brussels but to *travel.* In postwar Europe third-class train travel was cheap, and travel I did, visiting those museums, cathedrals, and monuments that were then open from Oslo to Rome, Granada to occupied Vienna. When I got back from one of my trips, Mlle. Sulzberger and I would have tea, and the quiz would begin: "Where did you go?" "Venice." "Did you go to the Accadèmia?" "Yes." "What's in the first room? The second room?"

So far the Middle Ages have not been mentioned in this story. There weren't any in Chicago; my father had enrolled me in a children's art class with the Bauhaus theorist Laszlo Moholy-Nagy, and I had haunted the Art Institute during the period it was housing the world-class Picassos and Matisses of the Chester Dale collection.[5] My art history training at Oberlin had centered on early Renaissance through baroque (Stechow) and modern painting (Johnson). Traveling throughout Europe as a twenty-one-year-old Fulbright, I saw my first Gothic vaulted spaces. My life's research has been devoted to stained glass, and I can still vividly recall the first medieval windows I ever saw—it was on an early trip across the channel, in Canterbury—the north ambulatory windows, as I remember. I was transfixed. I had never dreamed anything so magnificent existed on earth, and when I found old sepia postcards of those windows for sale in the nave and read the captions, my only thought was "You can actually *study* these gorgeous things?" Some traveling buddy told me about the Sainte-Chapelle, where I went on my next trip out. And the rest, as they say, is history.

Well, not quite. On my return from the Fulbright, married to Richard Lillich, an Oberlin classmate, we headed for Cornell, where my husband attended law school.[6] I worked in the art museum and then the art library, earning what was in those days called my "PH.T.": Putting Hubby Through. As we would be there three—and only three—years, I took one course a semester, two during summer schools, and eked out an M.A. degree in art history during the same period my husband was in law school. I was their first grad student, and since no one knew much about the Middle Ages, much less about stained glass, they really didn't know what to do with me. I did research papers in undergrad courses and wrote my thesis from books, self-taught, and nobody knew enough to seriously criticize it. Cornell was not particularly supportive. One semester I had had a large and unexpected dental bill and couldn't pay my one-course tuition, so I went to the administration to plead my case, my grades record, and my three-year deadline. I was seated in the dean's office, and his first words to me were "Why do you want this degree? You're married!" Nothing in my Oberlin years had prepared me for such a confrontation, and I don't really recall what I did, except that it approached the hysterical. I got the course tuition money.

In 1958, with my husband's law degree and my M.A.—and a new baby daughter—we headed for New York and his beginning law-firm job. Very shortly, however, my husband became restless with that routine and began a two-year program at New York University for a doctorate in law, preparatory to a law teaching career. I applied to Columbia's art history program, dirt poor and with a baby to mind, proposing to do my required work for the Ph.D. one course at a time and in the summers, as at Cornell. Part-time students were then as rare at Columbia as they had been at Cornell. Miraculously I was accepted. The chair was then Rudolf Wittkower, and many years later I learned that my Oberlin mentor, Stechow, who had known Wittkower in exile at the Warburg Institute in London, wrote to him and said, "Rudi, take care of her."[7] And Rudi did. In order to make my two-year deadline I was allowed to break or bend every regulation in the graduate manual, postponing requirements that could be done from a distance—such as language exams—and concentrating on those for which residence was of the essence.

To my immense good fortune, Robert Branner was beginning his brilliant career as Columbia's medievalist, and Wittkower must have instructed him concerning my off-the-record special status.[8] "Mr. B" (I could never bring myself to call him by his first name) was my height (five feet two inches) and living a research life at white heat. Role model, mentor, ultimately he was—as he identified himself in a phone call just before his tragically premature death—my "guardian angel." I had the great honor and responsibility to be the graduate student who spoke at his Columbia memorial service.

Branner was no feminist; our relationship existed on some other plane. One incident says it all. One day as we were returning to the campus from some seminar trip, he got on the subject of female graduate students and voiced the opinion that they should be encouraged to become art librarians, where they could best provide services for the (real) scholars in the field. Why is he telling me this? I thought with alarm! But as the conversation unfolded it became clear that *I* was not in his category of "female grad students."

Mr. B insisted on training me in Gothic architecture and sculpture and instructed me in the mysteries of the old Bibliothèque nationale reading room, the Sorbonne (how, and at what hour, to approach scholars like Marcel Aubert), and the photo archives of the postwar Monuments historiques. For stained glass, my heart's desire, he was content to arrange an interview with Louis Grodecki during one of the latter's trips to the United States. Grodecki was the most influential scholar, and nearly the only one, working in the field of French stained glass.[9] The interview was in French and intended to produce a dissertation topic for me. After introductions Grodecki said to me: "What do you want to work on?" I responded that I wanted a single monument, and not in the early or High Gothic period but perhaps in the later thirteenth century. He said, "Saint-Père de Chartres." And that was to become my dissertation, my first book, and ultimately the root of my magnum opus on western French glass of 1250 to 1325.[10] Grodecki promised to help me get photographs, and the interview was over. He returned to France, and I was on my own.

The dissertation took eleven years to come to term—another broken record in the Columbia art history department—and in that time my life was to make a 180-degree turn.

We arrived in 1960 at Syracuse University, where my husband was to teach law. I was to be a "faculty wife" and shortly to have a second daughter. Work on my dissertation and various postponed Columbia exams went forward as time, money, and the fatigue level allowed. We spent the year 1963 in England, my husband on a research grant to London and Cambridge, the toddler in Montessori schools, the baby with a part-time nanny, and me (via Wittkower's letters of introduction) putting in a few precious hours on my dissertation at the Warburg Institute and then Cambridge University Library. There, since I was typing at that point, they installed me in the little-used but frigid Lord Acton collection ("Power corrupts and absolute power corrupts absolutely.") I typed chapter 1 on my nine-pound, portable, manual typewriter, in those gloves with the fingers cut off that street musicians use.

Upon our return to Syracuse we bought a little house (where I still live), and my husband left me.[11] I was faced with raising children aged about eight and four, a mortgaged house, a car held together by spit and Scotch tape, a folder full of my husband's debts, and—oh yes—an unfinished dissertation. It was time for another miracle.

And lo! It came to pass. Into the chaos came a phone call from the chair of the Syracuse University art history department, William Fleming.[12] He introduced himself and said that he needed someone to teach a graduate seminar in medieval art, had called Rudolf Wittkower at Columbia, and had received the response: "Do you know Mrs. Lillich? She lives in Syracuse, New York." (No Equal-Opportunity-Affirmative-Action in those days!) I taught the seminar (on Chartres sculpture) and was hired the following year (1968) full-time as an instructor (not having a Ph.D.); over a third of a century later I am still there, teaching medieval art and architecture. In time my daughters were both in school for the full day, and my dissertation was finally defended in 1969, when they were about eleven and seven. I thought then and have often thought since about an early study of academic women by the sociologist Eli Ginzberg, which concluded that women with two children had a chance for a career, but those with three or more most probably not.[13]

The 1970s and 1980s were, from our present perspective, a golden age for the support of scholarly research. While my children were young, we spent every summer abroad: Paris, of course, Poitiers, Dublin, the beach at Ostend, a small village in French Switzerland, the rugged Normandy coast, where the wind comes straight from Boston, a farmhouse in the peach fields outside of Verona, even the London suburbs one year. I took a graduate student along as a helper, and the requirements were that we could manage in French or English and rent a vacation house or apartment of some kind. During the month of the summer that my daughters spent with their father, I was free to devote myself to my summer research grant, and I had repeats of all kinds: American Philosophical Society, National Endowment for the Humanities, American Council of Learned Societies.

Through Grodecki, who wanted to know what everyone in stained glass was up to, I had met Jean Lafond, the French scholar who is installed in my pantheon of heroes.[14] I first came across his limpid French prose when locked in my ivory tower at Cornell producing my master's thesis. Lafond never held a teaching position, since he wrote but was never allowed to defend his Sorbonne dissertation. His family controlled the newspapers in Rouen, which had editorialized for the Vichy government. As I heard the story, which may be apocryphal, when Lafond handed in his doctoral thesis, his mentor put it on his desk where it was to remain—unread. Beyond Lafond's graceful writing style, his uncanny and never-failing eye, and his total devotion to stained glass, what I loved in him was his old-world graciousness and his indomitable spirit. When I discovered that, in the face of his difficulties, he had published something every single year but one, I made that my goal. (Well, some years it has been just a book review.) I felt, and feel, that I somehow owed it to him for his great skill, for his unfailing kindness, and for his example.

As everywhere in American academic life, medieval studies have waxed and waned at Syracuse University, as have graduate programs, medieval/Renaissance majors and students, research support, library resources, and so on. I quickly abandoned any idea of administrative power when, as appointed chair of a committee, I learned that the committee members (all male) had held a "smoker" the previous evening to decide what they would vote for. For the majority of my Syracuse years, women were exploited, poorly paid, and not readily promoted. Promotions I have achieved through my publication and grants records, but salary is something else. Academic poverty, of course, is always with us, but at a certain level it impacts on one's ability to seize opportunities for research and for high-profile career advancement. Scholarly publication has therefore been my arena. The university was moderately supportive of my requests for leaves for fellowships and with honorary awards (for graduate teaching in 1987, service to one's field in 1989, and exceptional academic achievement in 1999). Salary would have been more useful. Thus, for me the university has been a safe haven from which to raise my children and to plot my research, with that occasional bonus of self-education that comes along with the routine of teaching and, of course, the reward of the unpredictable appearance of a brilliant student.

When my children were launched into prep school and beyond, I was able to apply for research fellowships involving travel and residence elsewhere: the National Endowment for the Humanities (1976), the American Council of Learned Societies (1980–81), a senior Fulbright to Paris (1983), the Center for Advanced Study in the Visual Arts at the National Gallery in Washington, D.C. (1987–88), and the Institute for Advanced Study at Princeton (1988).[15] And I was able to teach in my university's programs abroad, twice in Strasbourg (1984, 1991) and once in Florence (1985).

After my children (and now my four grandchildren), my research in French Gothic stained glass has always been the glue that holds my life together. The epiphany I experienced standing before that first Canterbury window in 1953 was not so much a new beginning as the final denouement of a Sherlock Holmes story, where all the chaotic pieces fall succinctly into place to reveal the truth. I was born with a medieval aesthetic sense. If a thirteenth-century Frenchman wished to explain something beautiful he had seen, aesthetic language not yet having been developed, he would first tell you how much it cost, he would describe it as intricate and multicolored (many colors being automatically more beautiful than only one), and, finally, in desperation, he would impress upon you that it was light-passing or light-reflecting, shiny, translucent. Glass is the most beautiful and profound thing the Middle Ages produced, on their own terms, and so it has always seemed to me. Translucence is better! As a child I filled my room with tiny colored bottles and mirrors. The full-page illustration of gems in my children's dictionary was my favorite page. In the Museum of Science and Industry in Chicago, one of my frequent haunts, I always saved the "jewel room" for last, absorbing all that light and color and sparkle before reeling out the door homeward. Canterbury and the Sainte-Chapelle finally put a name and a direction to this inborn passion.

Stained glass is the monumental painting of the Gothic period, but it is much more than that. The medium of glass *is* the message.[16] Two Christian metaphors are at play: God is light, and the church is the City of God, the heavenly Jerusalem. "Ego sum lux," said Christ. Light symbolism is basic to Augustine, and Scholasticism refined the differences between *lux* and *lumen*; light is not only the symbol of God but also his attribute, the action of God. Three themes are present: the mystery of translucence, the marvelous gemlike richness of glass, and the ideal of a building made with walls of light. Concerning translucence, if light is matter and glass is also another matter, how can one pass through the other without breaking it? Glass however is a matter different from others because it does not stop the light but allows itself to be penetrated. The connection to the Incarnation had been made by the mid-twelfth century. As for gemlike preciousness, everything about medieval glass encouraged this idea. Red stained glass was called ruby; the blue was called sapphire (for example, by Abbot Suger of Saint-Denis). Made of sand and wood ash transformed, via an unapproachable molten state, to the hard brilliance of gems (and nearly as expensive), glass assumed qualities associated with gems: magic powers, as described in the lapidaries, and sacred meaning, as in the pectoral of Aaron. The idea of a building with walls of light is a venerable biblical theme (Isaiah 54:11–12, Tobias 13:20, Apocalypse 21:18ff.), which returns us to the concept of the church (or any church) as God's abode, the heavenly Jerusalem. This conceit was extended to romances and the Grail literature (such as von Eschenbach's *Parzifal*), where chapels have walls of precious stones. The (contemporary) Sainte-Chapelle is such an artifact. For the first century of Gothic art, moreover, by "light" one did not mean foot-candles, intensity, wattage. As masons were able to enlarge window openings more and more, the glass that filled them became darker and more color-saturated. The concept of Dionysius the Pseudo-Areopagite is at work, identifying the light of God as incomprehensible, God as the Divine Gloom.

It is not really so surprising that I have worked and learned in isolation, since at the time I first saw that Canterbury window in 1953, the study of medieval stained glass was in its infancy. The reasons are obvious, if one thinks about it. The discipline of art history itself is no older than photography, since serious visual comparison requires accurate images. The early decades of photography produced exquisitely precise exterior views of medieval monuments but scarcely anything useful for interiors because the available light was inadequate. Stained glass is normally located far from the eye, in nearly inaccessible locations, and shining artificial light on it (when interior lighting became available) is pointless and counterproductive. Glass lit from the front (that is, by surface light) turns dull and opaque to the eye.

The destruction of World War I alerted European nations in possession of stained glass treasures to remove and store them whenever time and circumstances allowed in the late l930s, providing (during and after the war) the first chance for close-up photography under studio conditions, panel by panel. In France—which has more medieval stained glass than the rest of the world combined—this archive of photographs was only gradually being processed and made available for study during the 1950s. These were the photographs of Saint-Père de Chartres that Grodecki promised to obtain for me, in our interview in 1959, and he did so. Panel by panel, I mounted them myself, with my household iron, into vast montages identical to those in the Monuments historiques—and I still have them in an upstairs closet.

Modern scholarship on stained glass dates from the founding of the international Corpus Vitrearum, established in 1952 by European medievalists from Austria, France, Germany, and Switzerland. The aim was to take advantage of the wartime photography noted earlier, to create a published "database" of stained glass, dealing with questions of authenticity, condition, history and documentation, bibliography, and photo archives.[17] I have been a member of the United States committee since it joined the Corpus in 1982. Thirteen countries now participate, with over fifty volumes already published and many more to come. The hope has always been that trustworthy information about stained glass will encourage medievalists to include it in their scholarly venue. As Madeline Caviness puts it, "Those who venture into the field to make their own observations are encouraged to take a Corpus volume and a pair of binoculars!"[18]

The Corpus endeavor was in its infancy when I had my interview with Grodecki in which he named my dissertation topic, the Benedictine abbey church of Saint-Père in Chartres. His choice was fortuitous beyond anyone's (certainly including his) expectations, since it proved to be the kingpin of a regional type of stained glass that occupied me for decades. I published my recast dissertation materials (1978), without the chapter that had stretched in that direction, and thereafter began the study and publication of the related western French monuments, one by one, grant by grant. My book on them, the Gothic school of the West, finally dragged through publication as a Centennial Book at Berkeley in 1994 (*The Armor of Light*). As most authors know, by the time it finally materialized I had long since finished (what I had thought would be) my life's work on the West, given myself twelve months to decide what to do with myself (Should I learn to play the organ? Go to med school?), and faced the fact that Gothic stained glass was as necessary to me as breathing. I looked around to avoid where other scholars were, by that era, working, and decided to begin at the northeastern francophone border and look at Lorraine and Champagne. The francophone line goes down the Vosges Mountains and has not moved over three miles since the early Middle Ages. I hoped to produce another book, on eastern France, but it soon became obvious that the wars in that area—every thirty years since Caesar—had erased the evidence. Lorraine and Champagne undoubtedly were related, but the proofs are gone. So I wrote up my work on Lorraine (*Rainbow like an Emerald*, 1991) and have been devoting myself to Champagne ever since, circling and closing in on Reims Cathedral, with the goal to attempt to place that supremely famous medieval achievement within its regional milieu and to comprehend its familial, as well as its magnificently unique, character. If I live long enough, after Champagne, as I have always intended, I will move my campaign of attack to a third regional front. At seventy-two years of age I am superstitious enough not to tempt fate by identifying it here.

NOTES

1. On the Noguchi table, manufactured 1947–53, see Hiesinger and Marcus, *Landmarks of Twentieth-Century Design*, 159, no. 193. On Wright's Indiana houses ca. 1936–1939, see Chappell and Van Zanten, *Barry Byrne, John Lloyd Wright*, 52–56, 70; our house, not mentioned, may have been among those whose archives were lost in Wright's studio fire of the winter 1938/39 (56).

2. A Hull House weaver appears in Johnson, *Many Faces of Hull-House*, no.11. Weaving was "de-emphasized" in 1938 (Bryan and Davis, *100 Years at Hull-House*, 225). That was about the time my mother began studying weaving with Marli Ehrmann at Moholy-Nagy's School of Design (see n. 5). On the Chicago period of Lenore Tawney, who also trained there under Ehrmann, see Mangan, *Lenore Tawney*, 17–20, 151.

3. Obituary of Wolfgang Stechow. Obituary of Ellen Johnson.

4. Obituary of Suzanne Sulzberger.

5. Moholy-Nagy, *Moholy-Nagy*, 171–72. On Moholy-Nagy, see Margolin, *Struggle for Utopia*. Regarding the Dale collection, see *Twentieth Century French Paintings from the Chester Dale Collection*. These paintings were loaned to the National Gallery of Art in Washington, D.C., in 1952 and, upon Dale's death in 1962, were bequeathed to that museum. See "Dale Pictures Leave Chicago for Washington"; "National Gallery of Art, Washington, D.C."

6. See n. 11.

7. Obituary of Rudolf Wittkower.

8. Obituary of Robert Branner.

9. Caviness, obituary of Louis Grodecki.

10. See the last paragraph of this essay.

11. Obituary of Richard Lillich (1933–1996). He married twice more and had one more daughter before dying at age sixty-three.

12. *Directory of American Scholars*, 7th ed., s.v. "Fleming, William." See also obituary of William Fleming.

13. I recall this as a statement in Ginzberg et al., *Life Styles of Educated Women*. In looking through this volume a third of a century later, I cannot put my finger on the statement, but see the chart on p. 102 ("High and Good Achievement Levels").

14. Jean Lafond (1888–1975): see biographical note and bibliography in the handsome new edition, by Françoise Perrot, of his book *Le Vitrail*, 209–14.

15. The two Fulbrights I have held, one as a rank beginner and the other as a prestigious senior scholar, both provided giant boosts to my career, and I had the joy of writing as much to the senator before he died and of receiving his predictably generous, warm reply. Senator Fulbright died in 1995 at the age of ninety.

16. The initial scholarship on this area was by Louis Grodecki, in Marcel Aubert et al., *Le Vitrail français,* 39–45. See also Meredith Lillich, "Monastic Stained Glass: Patronage and Style," in *Monasticism and the Arts,* ed. Timothy Verdon (Syracuse, N.Y.: Syracuse University Press, 1984), 207–54, reprinted in Lillich, *Studies in Medieval Stained Glass and Monasticism,* 302–54. For a more recent bibliography, see Caviness, *Stained Glass Windows,* 58.

17. A succinct sketch of the Corpus Vitrearum is in Caviness, *Stained Glass Windows,* 67–69, with a full list of volumes then published and projected on pp. 30–38. Several countries are publishing initial census volumes; twenty-three of the fifty states of the United States of America appeared in 1985–89 (see bibliography). The glass cataloged in the United States of America dates up to 1700 and arrived via the art market.

18. Caviness, *Stained Glass Windows,* 10.

Select Bibliography of Works by Meredith Parsons Lillich

Omitted here are those articles reprinted in *Studies in Medieval Stained Glass and Monasticism* (2001).

"Les Vitraux de la nef, Saint-Père de Chartres: Analyse stylistique." *Bulletin des Sociétés archéologiques d'Eure-et-Loir. Mémoires* 115 (1st trimester 1971): 207–37.

"Les Donateurs de quelques vitraux de la nef de Saint-Père de Chartres." *Bulletin des Sociétés archéologiques d'Eure-et-Loir. Mémoires* 116 (3d trimester 1972): 11–18.

Editor and organizer. *Medieval Art in Upstate New York.* Syracuse, N.Y.: Everson Museum of Art, 1974. Exhibition catalog.

"The Choir Clerestory Windows of La Trinité at Vendôme: Dating and Patronage." *Journal of the Society of Architectural Historians* 34, no. 3 (October 1975): 238–50.

"Les Vitraux de Saint-Pierre de Chartres." *Les Monuments historiques de la France* 1 (1977): 52–57.

The Stained Glass of Saint-Père de Chartres. Middletown, Conn.: Wesleyan University Press, 1978.

Editor for illustrations and contributor. "A Note on Cistercian Art." In *The Abbey Psalter: The Book of Psalms Used by the Trappist Monks of Genesee Abbey.* Facsimile ed. Ramsey, N.J.: Paulist Press, 1981.

Editor of series. *Studies in Cistercian Art and Architecture.* 6 vols. Kalamazoo, Mich.: Cistercian Publications, 1982–.

"Stained Glass from Western France (1250–1325) in American Collections." *Journal of Glass Studies* 25 (1983): 121–28.

"Bishops from Evron." In *Studies on Medieval Stained Glass,* edited by Madeline Caviness and Timothy Husband, Corpus Vitrearum United States, Occasional Papers 1. New York: Metropolitan Museum of Art, 1985.

Contributor. *Stained Glass before 1700 in American Collections.* Studies in the History of Art series. Corpus Vitrearum United States. Washington, D.C.: National Gallery of Art. Checklist 1, vol. l5 (1985); checklist 2, vol. 23 (1987); checklist 3, vol. 28 (1989).

"Gothic Heraldry and Name Punning: Secular Iconography on a Box of Limoges Enamel." *Journal of Medieval History* 12, no. 3 (September 1986): 239–51.

"Les Vitraux de la cathédrale de Sées à Los Angeles et dans d'autres musées américains." *Annales de Normandie,* 40th year, nos. 3–4 (July–October 1990): 151–75.

Rainbow like an Emerald: Stained Glass in Lorraine in the Thirteenth and Early Fourteenth Centuries. College Art Association Monograph, no. 47. University Park: Pennsylvania State University Press, 1991.

The Armor of Light: Stained Glass in Western France, 1250–1325. California Studies in the History of Art, 23. Centennial Book. Berkeley: University of California Press, 1994.

Editor and author of notes and captions for the posthumously published essay by Jane Hayward. "The Church of Saint-Urbain at Troyes and Its Glazing Program." *Gesta* 37 (1998): 165–77.

"Gifts of the Lords of Brienne: Gothic Windows in Champagne, Donors from Cyprus." *Arte medievale,* 2d ser., 12–13 (1998–99): 173–92.

The Queen of Sicily and Gothic Stained Glass in Mussy and Tonnerre. Transactions, vol. 88, pt. 3. Philadelphia: American Philosophical Society, 1998.

Studies in Medieval Stained Glass and Monasticism. London: Pindar Press, 2001.

"La 'rose verte' de la Cathédrale de Châlons." *Cahiers archéologiques* 49 (2001): 117–42.

"The Genesis Rose Window of Reims Cathedral." *Arte medievale* 17 (2003): 41–63.

Stained Glass Before 1700 in Upstate New York. Corpus Vitrearum United States of America, II/1. London: Harvey Miller, Brepols, 2004.

Works Cited

Aubert, Marcel, et al. *Le Vitrail français.* Paris: Editions des Deux Mondes, 1958.

Bryan, Mary, and Allen Davis, eds. *One Hundred Years at Hull-House.* Bloomington: Indiana University Press, 1990.

Caviness, Madeline. Obituary of Louis Grodecki (1910–1982). *Gesta* 21, no. 2 (1982): 157–58.

———. *Stained Glass Windows.* Typologie des sources du Moyen Âge occidental, fasc. 76. Turnhout, Belg.: Brepols, 1996.

Chappell, Sally, and Ann Van Zanten. *Barry Byrne, John Lloyd Wright: Architecture and Design.* Chicago: University of Chicago Press, 1982.

"Dale Pictures Leave Chicago for Washington." *Art News* 51 (September 1952): 7.

Ginzberg, Eli, et al. *Life Styles of Educated Women.* New York: Columbia University Press, 1966.

Hiesinger, Kathryn, and George Marcus. *Landmarks of Twentieth-Century Design.* New York: Abbeville, 1993.

Johnson, Mary Ann, ed. *The Many Faces of Hull-House: The Photographs of Wallace Kirkland.* Urbana: University of Illinois Press, 1989.

Lafond, Jean. *Le Vitrail: Origines, technique, destinées.* Edited by Françoise Perrot. Lyon: La Manufacture, 1988.

Mangan, Kathleen, ed. *Lenore Tawney: A Retrospective: American Craft Museum, New York.* New York: Rizzoli, 1990.

Margolin, Victor. *The Struggle for Utopia: Rodchenko, Lissitzky, Moholy-Nagy, 1917–1946.* Chicago: University of Chicago Press, 1997.

Moholy-Nagy, Sibyl. *Moholy-Nagy: Experiment in Totality.* 2d ed. Cambridge, Mass.: MIT Press, 1969.

"National Gallery of Art, Washington, D.C.: Chester Dale Bequest." *Burlington Magazine* 107 (July 1965): 396–98.

Obituary of Ellen Johnson (1910–1992). *New York Times,* 24 March 1992, D-21.

Obituary of Richard Lillich (1933–1996). *New York Times,* 11 August 1996, 13.
Obituary of Robert Branner (1927–1973). *New York Times,* 28 November 1973, 48.
Obituary of Rudolf Wittkower (1901–1971). *New York Times,* 12 October 1971, 47.
Obituary of Suzanne Sulzberger (1903–1990). *Revue belge d'archéologie et d'histoire de l'art* 59 (1990): 173.
Obituary of William Fleming (1909–2001). *Syracuse Post-Standard,* 8 May 2001, B-4.
Obituary of Wolfgang Stechow (1896–1974). *New York Times,* 14 October 1974, 36.
Twentieth-Century French Paintings from the Chester Dale Collection. Chicago: Art Institute, 1946.

CHAPTER 68

Benedicta Ward, S.L.G. (1933–)
The Love of Learning and the Love of God

Debra L. Stoudt

Benedicta Ward numbers among the vanguard of modern women medievalists whose works not only offer insights into the medieval way of thinking and way of life but also suggest a bond between modern and medieval existence. In her scholarly study of the writings of notable early Christians, she allows the texts to speak for themselves—and encourages her readers to do likewise.

Born on 4 February 1933, Benedicta Ward attended grammar schools in Rotheram and Crediton as well as the Bolton School near Manchester.[1] In 1955 she earned her Bachelor of Arts with honors in history from Manchester University. That same year she became a permanent member of the Community of the Sisters of the Love of God (S.L.G.) at Fairacres, Oxford, an Anglican contemplative religious order; throughout her career the impact of her vocation on her scholarship has been self-evident. From 1972 to 1978 Sister Benedicta studied at Saint Anne's College, Oxford University, earning her doctoral degree in theology. Sir Richard W. Southern supervised her doctoral thesis on miracles and miracle collections and has served as her mentor in a number of her research projects.

From 1979 to 1981 Benedicta Ward was a member of Wolfson College. Since 1982 she has taught in a nonsalaried position at Oxford for the theology and history faculties. In 1991 she became a fellow of the Royal Historical Society. From 1991 to 1995 she served as associate director of Manchester College. She was an honorary lecturer of Harris-Manchester College from 1995 to 1999, and since 1999 she has been a supernumerary fellow of the college. In the same year she also began to serve as a reader in the history of Christian spirituality at the University of Oxford. Sister Benedicta has taught courses on church history in the early, medieval, and reformation periods

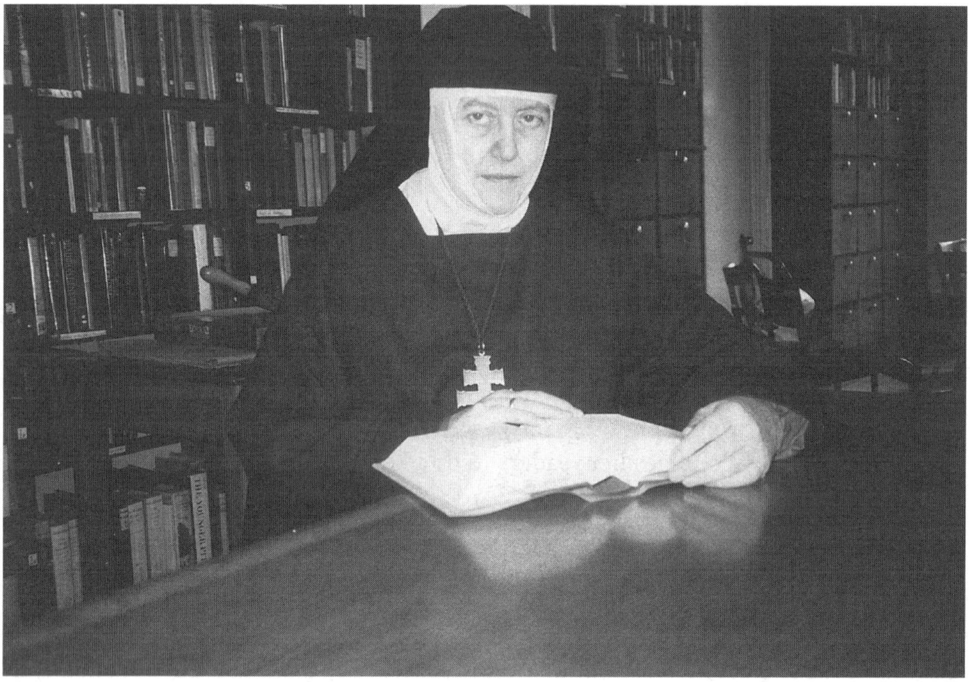

as well as on medieval church historiography, Julian of Norwich, and Teresa of Avila. She has lectured widely throughout Britain as well as in France, Belgium, Denmark, Ireland, and the United States.

Sister Benedicta's scholarly production to date includes fourteen books in addition to numerous articles and book chapters on various aspects of early and medieval church history. In the foreword to *Signs and Wonders* (1992), a collection of her previously published essays, she identifies three directions that her examinations of the concept of Christian holiness from late antiquity to the High Middle Ages had taken to that point in her career.[2] Her study of aspects of early Christian monasticism has resulted in various translations of and commentaries on the writings of the desert fathers; she published the translated texts themselves in the 1970s, with additional commentary appearing in the 1980s. Sister Benedicta has acknowledged the encouragement of Dom David Knowles, Metropolitan Anthony of Sourohz, and members of her religious community in fostering her work in this area. The interest expressed by Dom Jean Leclercq and by Benedictine and Cistercian communities in Belgium and America gave rise to a second direction of her scholarly inquiry that focuses on work begun with her dissertation and later published as *Miracles and the Medieval Mind* (1982). The third direction, strongly affected by Sir Richard Southern, concerns two pillars of the English monastic tradition: Anselm of Canterbury (1033–1109) and the Venerable Bede (673–735). Sister Benedicta's work on these two churchmen, like that on the desert fathers, consists of translations as well as commentaries on their writings. At present she is pursuing her translation work with an edition of the *Exordium Magnum Cisterciense* and building on her interest in miracles with a study of relics in the Middle Ages.

Chronologically, it is the third direction that is the focus of Sister Benedicta's earliest scholarly endeavors. In 1973 *The Prayers and Meditations of Saint Anselm* was published in the Penguin Classics series; Richard Southern, her mentor and doctoral thesis adviser, penned the foreword. The volume offers a translation in unrhymed verse form of the abbot's prayers and a prose translation of his meditations; Sister Benedicta focuses a great deal of attention on the rhythm of the language she employs and on the nuances of punctuation in her English rendition, since both are so significant in the Latin original. Preceding the translations of Anselm's texts, which date primarily from between 1070 and 1080, are comments that contextualize the abbot's understanding of the nature of prayer and the content of the works; the appendix offers evidence of the reception of the works in its discussion of the circulation and influence of the prayers.

Sister Benedicta emphasizes the importance of Anselm's prayers in the development of Christian spirituality. Their content is influenced by the formal traditions that shape his life—the divine office, the calendar of the liturgical year as established at the community of Bec in Normandy, and the Mass—as well as private prayer practices recorded in prayer books beginning already in the fifth century. Indeed, the earliest prayers by the abbot accompanied such prayer books that consisted of selections from the Psalms; around 1104, when Anselm sent the complete collection to Countess Mathilda of Tuscany, his works began to circulate separately.[3] Addressed to individual saints, they express emotional and personal appeals in florid language rich in imagery. Sister Benedicta notes that "the prayers are meant to be said in solitude, and the aim is to stir the mind out of its inertia to know itself thoroughly and so come to contrition and the love of God."[4] They are intended for personal rather than public recitation and sometimes are written for use by the laity, including women of wealth and power such as Princess Adelaide, daughter of William the Conqueror, and Countess Mathilda. Anselm himself comments on the length of the individual prayers, stating that "[i]t is not intended that the reader should feel impelled to read the whole, but only as much as will stir up the affections to prayer."[5] The fact that Sister Benedicta's translation work was reissued in the Penguin series in 1984 offers evidence that readers centuries later still are stirred by the abbot's words.

Almost concurrently with the original translation of Anselm's works, Sister Benedicta published an expanded version of a paper given to the Anselm Society at Saint Augustine's College, Canterbury, titled *Anselm of Canterbury: A Monastic Scholar* (1973; revised and enlarged 1977 and 1980), in which she examined the relationship between Anselm's scholarship and his life as a monk. Sister Benedicta positions Anselm between Augustine of Hippo and Bernard of Clairvaux in the Western spiritual tradition, providing a careful study of how his intellectual training and his monastic experiences shaped his theological and spiritual ideas. Her purpose is to see Anselm not only as a religious or an intellectual figure but also as an individual in the broader context of his society. Thus, the editor of the Fairacres publication series, in which the paper appeared, comments in his introduction that her approach "suggests that Anselm's understanding of the connection between reason and faith, thought and prayer, can be relevant to Christian scholarship in any age."[6] Sister Benedicta renewed her scholarly involvement with Anselm by preparing the introduction to a recent Italian translation of his prayers and meditations.[7]

Sister Benedicta's subsequent translation work underscores the relevance today of the writings of other luminaries of the early church. *The Sayings of the Desert Fathers,* published in 1975, was the first of three works she devoted to the desert fathers and mothers. The collection of sayings, attributed to individual desert fathers, is a translation of the Greek alphabetical series as found in the *Series graeca* of Jacques-Paul Migne's *Patrologiae cursus completus* and transcribed from a twelfth-century manuscript. In her foreword Sister Benedicta characterizes Egypt as the fourth-century center of monasticism and identifies the various types of eremitic life that flourished in this environment. The sayings represent the folk wisdom of the early Fathers concerning the monastic life, wisdom recorded by later generations in simple language. The words are attributed to leaders, teachers, and ascetics such as Anthony the Great, Cassian, and Theodora. They offer advice about how to successfully lead a monastic life; the advice commonly appears in the form of anecdotes, such as the story of the theft of Father Gelasius's Bible, and proverblike sayings like Silvanus's statement, "Unhappy is the man whose reputation is greater than his work."[8] Both Sister Benedicta in her foreword and Metropolitan Anthony of Sourozh in his preface comment on the resonance these words and ideas have centuries later. Their opinion is reinforced by the popularity of the collection, which was reprinted in the mid-1980s. The year the work first appeared Macmillan Publishers also published it under the title *The Desert Christian* and with a different introduction for inclusion in their series that consisted of C. S. Lewis's *The Joyful Christian,* Dorothy L. Sayers's *The Whimsical Christian,* J. B. Phillips's *The Newborn Christian,* and Fulton J. Sheen's *The Electronic Christian*. All the volumes in this series present readers with texts of a meditative nature.

The introduction of *The Desert Christian* was taken from *The Wisdom of the Desert Fathers,* which appeared in 1975, the same year as *The Sayings of the Desert Fathers. The Wisdom of the Desert Fathers* is a translation of the *Apophthegmata Patrum* from the Anonymous Series and functions as a companion piece to the *Sayings*. Both collections derive from the same tradition, but the *Wisdom* material is grouped under subject headings, whereas the *Sayings* are attributed to specific individuals and cataloged alphabetically according to the purported author. Sister Benedicta's volume contains 239 sayings culled from the Greek texts published by François Nau in *Le Revue de l'Orient chrétien* between 1908 and 1913. Most sayings consist of a few sentences in a single paragraph and are translated in prose form. The subjects focus on virtues of the monastic life that are to be pursued, but these attributes are equally desirable for lay persons, as, for example, the saying regarding humility: "An old man was asked, 'What is humility?' He replied, 'It is when your brother sins against you and you forgive him before he comes to ask for forgiveness.'"[9] As with the previous translated works, the purpose here is to make accessible in English works that reflect the foundations and basic traditions of monastic spirituality. There is ample evidence of the success of Sister Benedicta's translations and of their popularity among audiences today. Since the publication of the original editions, she has produced for a general readership several briefer compilations of quotations and maxims attributed to the desert fathers.[10] A translation of the desert fathers based on the Latin sources of the apothegmata appeared in the Penguin Classics series in 2003.

Appearing more than a decade later but still part of the corpus devoted to the earliest Christians is *Harlots of the Desert* (1987). Here Sister Benedicta's focus shifts to early Christian women and the theme of repentance; she recounts the lives of sinful women by translating and interpolating various texts about them. The idea for this volume stemmed from Sister Benedicta's meeting with Maria, a young prostitute in London, who asked for advice on how to abandon the life she was leading; the book is dedicated to the young woman. *Harlots of the Desert* recounts the lives of Saint Mary Magdalene, Saint Mary of Egypt, Pelagia, Thaïs, and Maria, the niece of Abraham; much of the biographical information is derived from sources such as the *Acta Sanctorum Bollandiana, Bibliotheca Hagiographica Graeca, Bibliotheca Hagiographica Latina,* Migne's collections, *Sources chrétiennes,* and works by and attributed to the desert fathers. In addition Sister Benedicta translates less familiar texts: the *Life of Saint*

Mary of Egypt, by Sophronius, bishop of Jerusalem; the *Life of Saint Pelagia the Harlot,* by Deacon James; the *Life of Saint Thaïs the Harlot,* from a Latin translation of a Greek text by an anonymous author; and the *Life of Maria the Harlot,* by Archdeacon Ephraim.

Sister Benedicta's translations of wisdom from the desert fathers and mothers and her vitae of early Christian women have attracted substantial academic attention in recent years, most manifestly in Laura Swan's *The Forgotten Desert Mothers: Sayings, Lives, and Stories of Early Christian Women,* published in 2001. Swan cites Sister Benedicta's volume in her bibliography but draws directly from *The Sayings of the Desert Fathers,* which serves to some extent as a prototype for this Paulist Press volume. In addition her translations of the writings of these early leaders of the church have themselves been translated into an array of languages, including Arabic, Chinese, French, Icelandic, Italian, Polish, Rumanian, and Spanish.

For Sister Benedicta the process of translating is particularly meaningful. In her article titled "Translator's Charity," she states, "To undertake translation is in itself a part of charity. . . . It is a service, a way of offering treasure to others."[11] The treasure consists of a translation that is transparent but also readable and usable. In her translations Sister Benedicta strives to place the past in the hands of the present and to provide her readers with a balance of love and truth.[12] Her intention is the same as the one she defines for Christian literature itself in the original language: "[I]t is designed for the purpose of aiding conversion of the heart towards God."[13]

Complementing the translations and studies of the works of early Christian heroes and heroines is Sister Benedicta's examination of the medieval reception of such individuals, in particular the veneration shown them by religious and lay persons in the Middle Ages. Her dissertation titled "Miracles and Miracle Collections, 1015–1215" is the earliest result of her forays into this area. From the doctoral and subsequent research on the theory of miracles and on miraculous acts and events in practical contexts emerged *Miracles and the Medieval Mind: Theory, Record, and Event 1000–1215* (1982, revised 1987), which Sister Benedicta dedicated to Sir Richard and Lady Southern and which deals primarily with miraculous phenomena in France and England. The volume appeared in the University of Pennsylvania's Middle Ages series, a series devoted to persons, events, and themes central to the shaping of the Western Middle Ages. In straightforward style she provides readers with numerous anecdotes concerning saints' lives and accomplishments and challenges readers to consider how the medieval mind perceived these miraculous events and attempted to integrate them into the pattern of the daily routine. Of special significance in the volume are the relationship between miracles and sanctity and how miracles relate to their historical context and geographic environment. Sister Benedicta describes in detail the miracles of the Virgin and those of Saint Thomas of Canterbury. In addition she characterizes in depth the miracles at the traditional shrines of Saint Faith, Saint Benedict, and Saint Cuthbert, as well as those at the three twelfth-century shrines of Saint William, Saint Godric, and Saint Frideswide. She frequently cites from insular hagiographical reports often neglected by Continental scholars.[14] Throughout her study Sister Benedicta notes the impact of miracles on culture, asserting that they provide "a way to approach the ordinary day-to-day life of men and women in all kinds of situations and in all ranks of society."[15] Both the "moments of greatness" and the little miracles exert an influence on the lives of medieval men and women, facilitating a connection between the divine and the human and characterizing miracles as "the ordinary life of heaven made manifest in earthly affairs."[16]

In 1988 Sister Benedicta presented a lecture at Saint Julian's Church following the mass celebrated on the Saturday after the eighth of May, the date of the *Showings* of Julian of Norwich. Her lecture examined Julian's personal background and appeared along with the 1987 lecture of Kenneth Leech in *Julian Reconsidered* (1988). Sister Benedicta takes issue with the idea that Julian was a professed nun and puts forth the theory that "when Julian received the Revelations and wrote her short account of them, she was a young widow living in her own house with her servants and her mother."[17] Given the significance of the theme of motherhood and the symbolism of God as Mother in Julian's *Showings,* such a circumstance is especially consequential to the interpretation of Julian's work. Sister Benedicta draws attention to the paucity of evidence in the records of nearby priories and nunneries that might substantiate Julian's association with them; likewise, Julian's short text of the *Showings*, the focus of Sister Benedicta's study, is devoid of references to monastic practices or the cloistered life, which further substantiates her thesis.

In the early 1990s Sister Benedicta turned her attention once again to luminaries of the early church. She was chosen to present the Jarrow Lecture in 1991, and her presentation focused on Bede and the Psalter. In the same year she completed a book-length study on the Venerable Bede, in which she examined this doctor of the church in the context of his times; of particular import are his role as teacher, his method of biblical commentary, his description of the English in the *Ecclesiastical History of the English People,* and his status as a great Christian thinker.[18] Fittingly, the volume appeared as part of the Outstanding Christian Thinkers series; it was reprinted in 1997 by Cistercian Publications.

Sister Benedicta prefaces her essay collection *Signs and Wonders* with a brief introduction concerning hagiography and history. Her understanding of the significance of saints' lives is revelatory for much of her own work dealing with the accomplishments of influential Christian figures from Bede to Julian of Norwich. She notes that Christians "are saints insofar as they have 'put on the Lord Jesus.'"[19] She asserts that "[t]he central purpose of a hagiography is to present this Christ-likeness to others who run the same race, as encouragement, as assurance that they are surrounded by a great cloud of witnesses and that with God all things are possible. The question for the Christian is not how can I enjoy myself, do good, help others, get rich, happy, balanced or respected, but, how can I receive the gift of Christ most completely."[20] Through her scholarship Sister Benedicta has sought to mediate to modern readers the gift of Christ proffered by medieval Christian saints.

Recently Sister Benedicta has shifted her scholarly attention to Christian spirituality in more general terms. With *High King of Heaven: Aspects of Early English Spirituality* (1999) she focuses on early English piety in the first centuries after conversion. She draws on her work on Bede, frequently citing his commentary on the subject. Central to the study is the mingling of Celtic and Roman influences with Anglo-Saxon tendencies and the primacy of prayer in the devotional life of the early English. Excerpting from this early tradition, Sister Benedicta published *Christ within Me: Texts for Anglo-Saxon Spirituality*, which contains a compilation of texts translated from Anglo-Saxon and from Latin and presented for meditative purposes.

Sister Benedicta also has been active as an editor of essay collections. The first volume, *The Influence of Saint Bernard: Anglican Essays* (1976), consisted of seven essays dedicated to brothers in the Cistercian order and to Dom Jean Leclercq, who wrote the introduction; it appeared as part of the Fairacres series. Sister Benedicta also contributed to the volume herself with the brief essay "Apophthegmata Bernardi: Some Aspects of Saint Bernard of Clairvaux" (pp. 135–43). Although there is no extant collection of Saint Bernard's apothegmata, Sister Benedicta proposes that one can gain an understanding of Bernard through his words and actions as they were recorded by his fellow Cistercians "in a way parallel to that of the communication of sanctity in the desert."[21] Sister Benedicta coedited a second volume, *Intellectual Life in the Middle Ages: Essays Presented to Margaret Gibson* (1992), with Lesley Smith. The twenty-one essays were presented to Margaret Gibson in recognition of her contribution to the study of medieval thought and learning. In this volume Sister Benedicta combines her interest in miracles and relics with a brief examination of two letters concerning the relics of Saint Thomas of Canterbury.[22] With Ralph Waller she edited a third selection of essays on various aspects of Christian spirituality in 1999.[23] To this volume she herself contributed an essay on the English mystics from Richard Rolle to Julian of Norwich. Not surprisingly, the emphases of the volume lie in discussions of the significance of prayer and the English spiritual tradition.

Throughout her career Sister Benedicta's scholarship has served to increase understanding of early Christian spirituality, especially the spiritual tradition that flourished in England during the Middle Ages. Her work also has enhanced interest in the early years of the Cistercian movement; for this reason it is not surprising that a number of her studies—*The Venerable Bede, Harlots of the Desert, World of the Desert Fathers, Sayings of the Desert Fathers, High King of Heaven: Aspects of Early English Spirituality*—appear in the Cistercian Publications series.

Sister Benedicta's own community, the Sisters of the Love of God, has been particularly supportive of her work throughout her career, as she acknowledges in the foreword or preface of most of her publications. Fairacres Press has published many of her studies, including numerous works devoted to meditative practices. The sisters, as well as other friends and mentors, serve as Sister Benedicta's "cloud of witnesses" with their encouragement, criticism, and advice.

Sister Benedicta's devotion to the eremitic life that she herself has embraced as a member of the Community of the Sisters of the Love of God has inspired and shaped her scholarly career. Her work demonstrates that men and women today, lay and religious, can glean direction for their own lives and obtain solace for their own futures by examining the lives and the words of blessed models from the past and by considering in solitude, in meditation, and in prayer their own spiritual well-being.

NOTES

1. In June 2001 Sister Benedicta provided me with a copy of her vita, which outlined her career, teaching experience, and publications. The vita served as the primary source for the biographical information included in this essay.
2. Ward, *Signs and Wonders,* x.
3. Ward, *Prayers and Meditations of Saint Anselm,* 277.
4. Ibid., 51.
5. Ward, trans., letter to Countess Mathilda of Tuscany before the preface to the collection of prayers and meditations, in *Prayers and Meditations of Saint Anselm,* 90.
6. Ward, *Anselm of Canterbury,* 2.
7. *Orazioni e meditazioni,* trans. Giorgio Maschio (Milan: Jaca Books, 1997).
8. For the story of the Bible theft, see Ward, *Sayings of the Desert Fathers: The Alphabetical Collection,* 46. The quotation from Silvanus may be found on p. 224 of that work.
9. Ward, *Wisdom of the Desert Fathers,* no. 171, 48.
10. These popular collections, which are about half as long as the original editions, include *Daily Readings with the Desert Fathers* and *Wisdom of the Desert Fathers* (Oxford: Lion Publications, 1998).
11. Benedicta Ward, "Translator's Charity," in *The Translator's Art: Essays in Honour of Betty Radice,* ed. William Radice and Barbara Reynolds (Harmondsworth, Eng.: Penguin, 1987), 209 and 210. The article is reprinted in *Signs and Wonders* as number 14; the original pagination has been retained.
12. Ibid., 215 and 207.
13. Ibid., 207.
14. Joseph-Claude Poulin makes this point in his review of *Miracles and the Medieval Mind,* 452.
15. Ward, *Miracles and the Medieval Mind: Theory, Record, and Event, 1000–1215,* 214.
16. Ibid., 216.
17. Ward with Leech, *Julian Reconsidered,* 27.
18. Ward, *Venerable Bede.*
19. Ward, *Signs and Wonders,* xiv.
20. Ibid., xiv.
21. Ward, *Influence of Saint Bernard,* 137.
22. Benedicta Ward, "Two Letters Relating to Relics of Saint Thomas of Canterbury," in *Intellectual Life in the Middle Ages,* ed. Benedicta Ward and Lesley Smith, 175–78.
23. Ward with Waller, *Introduction to Christian Spirituality.* A Fourth volume appeared in 2003: Ward with Waller, *Joy of Heaven.*

SELECT BIBLIOGRAPHY OF WORKS BY BENEDICTA WARD, S.L.G.

Liturgy Today: The Divine Office and the Eucharist. 1971. Reprint, Oxford: SLG Press, 1981.
Anselm of Canterbury: A Monastic Scholar. 1973. Rev. and enlarged ed., Oxford: SLG Press, 1990.
Translator. *The Prayers and Meditations of Saint Anselm.* 1973. Reprint, Harmondsworth, Eng.: Penguin, 1992.

Translator. *The Desert Christian: Sayings of the Desert Fathers, the Alphabetical Collection.* London: Mowbray, 1975. Reprint, New York: Macmillan, 1992.

Translator. *The Sayings of the Desert Fathers: The Alphabetical Collection.* Cistercian Studies Series 59. Oxford: Mowbray; Kalamazoo, Mich.: Cistercian Publications, 1975. Rev. ed., Kalamazoo, Mich.: Cistercian Publications, 1984.

Translator. *The Wisdom of the Desert Fathers: The Apophthegmata Patrum.* The Anonymous Series. 1975. Reprint, Oxford: SLG Press, 1990.

Editor. *The Influence of Saint Bernard: Anglican Essays.* Oxford: SLG Press, 1976.

Introduction to *Lives of the Desert Fathers.* Translated by Norman Russell. 1981. Reprint, Kalamazoo, Mich.: Cistercian Studies, 1991.

Miracles and the Medieval Mind: Theory, Record, and Event, 1000–1215. London: Scolar Press, 1982. Rev. ed., Philadelphia: University of Pennsylvania Press, 1987.

Harlots of the Desert: A Study of Repentance of Early Monastic Sources. Oxford: Mowbray, 1987. Reprint, Kalamazoo, Mich.: Cistercian Publications, 1993.

Daily Readings with the Desert Fathers. 1988. Reprint, Springfield, Ill.: Templegate, 1990.

With Kenneth Leech. *Julian Reconsidered.* Oxford: SLG Press, 1988. Reprint, Oxford: SLG Press, 1995.

The Desert of the Heart: Selections from the Desert Fathers. 1990. Reprint, London: Darton, Longman and Todd, 1994.

Bede and the Psalter. Jarrow Lecture, 1991. Newcastle upon Tyne, Eng.: n.p., 1992. Reprint, Oxford: SLG Press, 2002.

The Venerable Bede. Outstanding Christian Thinkers series. London: Geoffrey Chapman Publishers, 1991. Reprint, Kalamazoo, Mich.: Cistercian Publications, 1998. Reprint, London: Continuum, 2002.

Editor with Lesley Smith. *Intellectual Life in the Middle Ages: Essays Presented to Margaret Gibson.* London: Hambledon Press, 1992.

Signs and Wonders: Saints, Miracles, and Prayers from the Fourth Century to the Fourteenth. Hampshire, Eng.: Variorum; Brookfield, Vt.: Ashgate Publishing, 1992.

The Spirituality of Saint Cuthbert. Oxford: SLG Press, 1992.

Editor. *Wisdom of the Desert.* Oxford: Lion Publications, 1998.

Editor. *Christ within Me: Texts for Anglo-Saxon Spirituality.* London: Darton, Longman and Todd, 1999.

Editor. *High King of Heaven: Aspects of Early English Spirituality.* Kalamazoo, Mich.: Cistercian Publications, 1999.

Editor with Ralph Waller. *An Introduction to Christian Spirituality.* London: Society for Promoting Christian Knowledge, 1999.

Pilgrimage of the Heart. Fairacres, Eng.: SLG Press, 2001.

Translator. *The Desert Fathers: Sayings of the Early Christian Monks.* London and New York: Penguin 2003.

Editor, with Ralph Waller. *Joy of Heaven: Spring of Christian Sprituality.* London: SPCK, 2003.

WORKS CITED

Poulin, Joseph-Claude. Review of *Miracles and the Medieval Mind: Theory, Record, and Event, 1000–1215. Speculum* 59 (1984): 450–53.

Swan, Laura. *The Forgotten Desert Mothers: Sayings, Lives, and Stories of Early Christian Women.* New York: Paulist Press, 2001.

CHAPTER 69

Latent Feminist Loosed on Medieval History (1935–)

SUSAN MOSHER STUARD

IT TOOK ONLY a few turns pacing the living-room rug to set my future course in 1970. Belatedly, somewhat haltingly, but with high anticipation, the idea of a medieval history about women lay before me if I had the temerity to grasp it. With that prospect, anxiety over my future career faded, my horizons enlarged, every optimistic cliché ever uttered seemed right for the moment. Feminism was a given with my background—more on that later—but I was sufficiently well read to know that others before me had tried to compose women's history and failed. Matilda Gage, 1826–98, proposing to write women's history on a vast scale in three volumes, had given up in sheer frustration. Except for scurrilous allegations and some rare women worthies, her researches found little to go on. Gage realized that historians defined what was historical, and they had relegated most women to ahistorical status, with lives so unchanging over the centuries and the millennia that there was no compelling reason to tell their story. In the face of this monumental dismissal, other daring souls had made only small inroads or thrown up their hands in defeat. Professionalization of the discipline had strengthened opposition to a meaningful women's history. Women's religious orders, women's rights movements, or women rulers might receive occasional lines of text, but these were intriguing asides in the magisterial, moving stream of objectivist history. Women did not affect interpretation.

"Documents of practice" composed the core of my archival experience up to 1970. I had studied these records under the instruction of Robert S. Lopez at Yale, but it had never been my intention to add scholarly footnotes to another's thesis. My Ph.D. had been too hard-won to point me in that direction. Notarial records, which were private contracts not intended for the historian's prying eyes, were largely unexamined

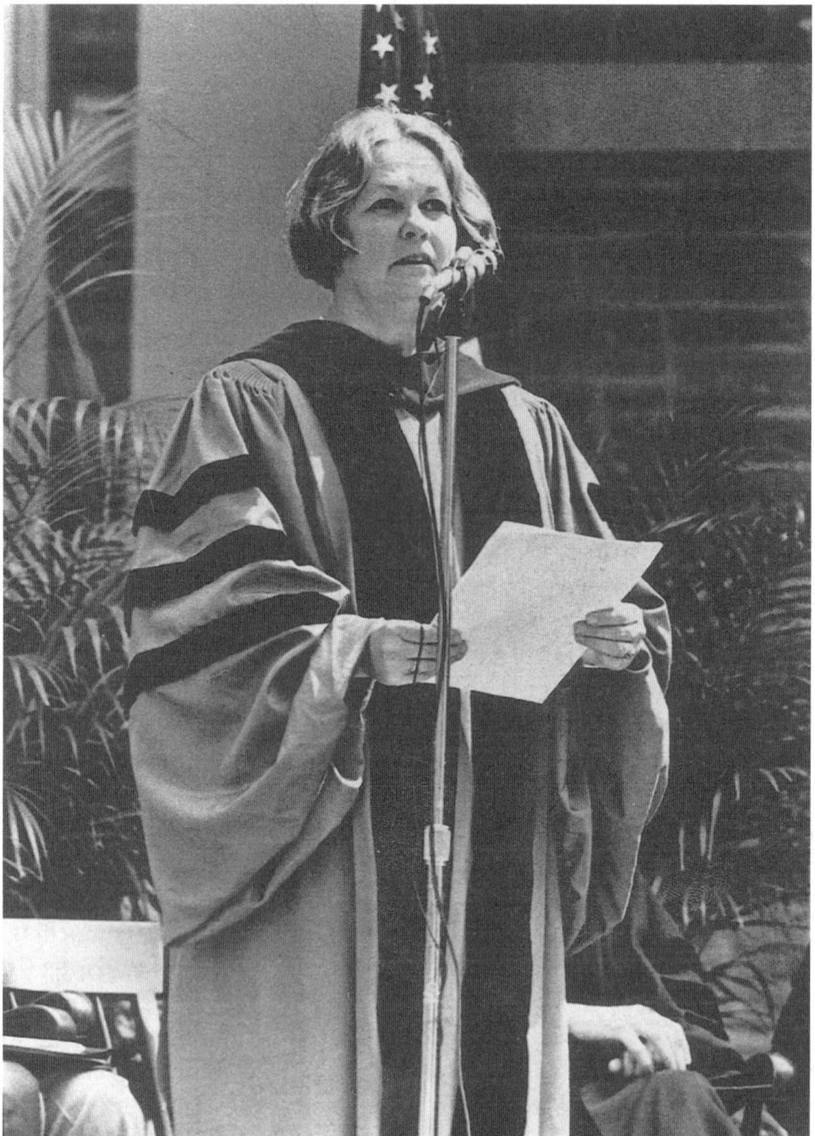

but of inestimable value for learning about lives in medieval times. If long-term analysis of the ways women made a living were to become the focus of my research, then I would be well served by these primary sources. Centuries-long series of awarded dowries were collated together in urban archives. *Testamenta* (wills) gave gifts to women's heirs as to men's heirs; these might be compared. Women initiated lawsuits that left records, or they were sued in court. Women worked, and on occasion this left a record. I believed the rendering of women's labor to families, to communities, and to long-term economic development was a matter of primary importance. I was convinced women's work was time-sensitive rather than an abiding uniformity. Division of labor between men and women evolved over time; innovations, technology, and rights to control one's wealth might tip the equilibrium between women and men in any age. When those moments occurred, the way in which changes dissipated out through the social order revealed vital intelligence about an era. The evidence for constructing a dynamic women's history lay in ordinary lives, thus in the documents of practice. Today I can laugh at my 1970 self; I had no inkling of the momentous changes that lay waiting.

A long-standing interest in historiography played into my 1970 decision. Since my junior year at Smith College, when I was introduced to historians from Herodotus and Thucydides to the present, I had marveled at the evolving concerns of dominant schools of history and the periodic creation of new canons of historical significance. History was not poured in concrete no matter how solid a monolith it appeared to be. Still, I underestimated the far-reaching effects of simply questioning evidentiary criteria applied by practicing historians. In the first volume of *Signs* I published a brief note titled "Dame Trot." In it I looked at the provenance of two early medical treatises traditionally ascribed to eleventh-century Dame Trotula of Salerno. After reviewing opinion, and almost as an aside, I noted that on more slender evidence than this the authority of eleventh-century men of letters is generally accepted today. Why then doubt Dame Trot? Medieval people had believed in her. How could I have anticipated that a bright graduate student at Princeton named Monica Green would read that note, make that search, and then, with her skill at manuscript attribution, untangle the authority of the Trotula treatises? Could verities be challenged this easily? Make no mistake: manuscript ascription is difficult, time-consuming work, but I had learned the lesson that objectivist historians react when the parity of their empirical standards is impugned. Many of us jumped into the fray, which was just as well since medieval women of letters had been often dispossessed of their texts when modern scholars had reattributed their works to men.[1]

A small portion of the work of constructing a new women's history might be accomplished by simply challenging equity in applying the rules of evidence, but of course this was not adequate for composing a meaningful history. The new history must be constructed from the bottom up, and in 1976 I completed work editing *Women in Medieval Society,* a volume devoted to archival findings about women's lives. Going to conferences, listening to others, sharing ideas, and reading each other's work produced this joint effort. Originally one discreet goal drove the project: convince readers that evidence about women exists in medieval archives. This limited aim in no way explains the long and robust history of the volume. For some years it was the best-selling history book from the University of Pennsylvania Press. It earned royalties for contributors over twenty years; indeed, small royalties trickle in to this day. Moreover the volume sells about as well abroad as at home. My introduction to that collection has been anthologized at least twice, although all I intended to do was to raise a few questions about what should be investigated to understand the lives of medieval women. That book and the others like it of multiple authorship give some idea of a strategy that succeeded in those early years. Somehow our combined voices were more persuasive than any one voice. Challenging prevailing interpretation, a project in which we were joined, was abetted by composing, then combining, brief, thesis-driven analyses. Essays began with one version or another of the phrase "until now it has been generally accepted," then proceeded to examine a familiar historical tenet in the light of what women's history reveals.

This led in very short order to another surprise. Women's history began to be taken seriously, not just by publishers who knew women's history sold well, but by established historians. Eminent men in the field began to read what we wrote, so those brief essays, which were certainly "quick reads," won over an audience. The new history, previously a Berkshire Conference concern, was suddenly mainstreamed.[2] I tend to favor Gabrielle Spiegel's tart retort about this sudden, unanticipated interest in women's history: "And why not? This is the only radical discourse remaining on our college campuses!"[3] But misgivings arose when we ceased to be the black sheep of the profession and suddenly became pet lambs. Unanticipated attention made many of us suspicious and increasingly wary, yet conference-corridor encounters with our new fans required forbearance. When racing for a session and accosted by a scholar of eminence seeking answers, it was a mistake to blurt out, "Well, yes, that is a question I frequently hear from freshmen." Was it really necessary to expend valuable time on rudimentary queries posed by our wisest and most discerning colleagues? At meetings we furthered our field by attending the few women's history sessions that had made it onto the program, and the intense discussions that ensued were our self-styled seminars, now that exchange was jeopardized. All people without histories must be torn by similar quandaries when a tyro, especially a respected and eminent one, suddenly discovers their relevance and demands to be brought up to date. To advance understandings or gain women's history a sympathetic hearing was a trade-off; as I recall, no one expressed satisfaction at the balance struck.

But urgency was in the air. A new women's history was emerging at once and altogether, and time was always a pressing matter. Bringing along fellow historians, who now contemplated placing women within the framework of their history while we struggled to create new frameworks, new language, and a more encompassing vision, tried us to the limit. Whether to burrow more deeply into records or build vast schemes and new canons of significance was a topic we actually debated. The growing corps of scholars writing about women tended to be well trained in the discipline, so it was widely recognized that, properly speaking, good history requires constant interplay between uncovering new evidence and rethinking received interpretation. We had embarked on our project idealistic, committed, and remarkably naive. We would create a more meaningful history, and such were the demands we placed on ourselves that we would compose that history in record time. Controversies and challenges on matters of priority appeared at every turn. Women's history was born in debate and disputation.

Yet I cannot remember a soul encountering that challenge with anything less than unalloyed enthusiasm. The joy of it lay in the process. I was working out a history in concert with others, gratified with each new completed project in research and interpretation. State University of New York research grants sent me back to the archives. I organized and offered my first women's history course with Robert Smith at the State University College at Brockport. Any depth I have gained in teaching advanced subjects came in those early years of college teaching. I transferred my teaching to Haverford College and met a groundswell of interest in women's history. I spent a wonderful year as a fellow at the Institute for Advanced Study, where years of pent-up scholarship finally saw the light of day.

Textbooks, vehicles for conveying the historically tried and true, took on a new task. Since there was a pressing need to create long-term synthesis for students eager to learn some women's history, where no accepted synthesis had yet appeared, a textbook bore the weight of presenting one. I joined Renate Bridenthal and Claudia Koonz in editing *Becoming Visible* in the 1980s; the first edition of their textbook already held the reputation of groundbreaking scholarship and interpretation about women over the centuries.[4] It had received critical attention as serious as that lavished on monographs directed at an audience of scholars when it had first appeared in 1976. We expected the second edition to be reviewed just as seriously, and indeed, that edition of *Becoming Visible* was regarded as a litmus test of the current state of the field of women's history in 1987. So a volume designed for undergraduate instruction answered demands for sophisticated and novel interpretation. A vehicle for transmitting historical discoveries was created out of a pedagogical tool. In chapter 6 of *Becoming Visible* I proposed to investigate how ideas about gender transferred from the scholarly page into popular beliefs that affected medieval women's lives, rights, and livelihoods. This entailed discussion of canon law and lawyers and the scholastic curriculum for clergy and physicians, who then applied Aristotelian ideas about women to the conduct of their daily work with the laity. This was received as a departure in interpretation.[5] Should students' requirements for simple, clear presentation be jettisoned in the interests of a highly trained audience determined to regard a college textbook as new scholarship? Was writing for both audiences in one text even possible?

The general line of questioning taken in the 1980s helps to explain the interpretive task imposed on pedagogical tools like a women's-history textbook. Frequently I would be asked this vexing question: "When was the worst moment for women in the West?" It legitimately called into question inherited periodization, but unfortunately this was also the relativist question about women's status and power in relation to men in a given age. It was simply unanswerable. I understood why a medievalist would be so queried: the pejorative use of "medieval" in the popular press—the *New York Times* in particular—had led the curious to imagine a gruesome early history for women. And admittedly I was a textbook author and a self-proclaimed economic historian with an ardent interest in social change, as titles of my books and articles betrayed. Still, I had no ready answers. Was the nadir for women the early modern era with its witch hunts? Possibly so, but count the number of women who sat on European thrones in that age. And what about women who entered new fields of endeavor like printing or set off to colonize Crete and, not so long after that, settled the Atlantic islands, New Spain, and New France? Was the nineteenth century most restrictive of women's legal rights? Certainly the arm of the law had lengthened by that date, but challenges to marriage and divorce laws became some of the most important reform agendas of nineteenth-century Europe. I had no new periodization to offer that allowed history to be read as progress from one age to the next. At times women's history appeared to be counterprogressive, or at the least, what progress occurred was purchased at great cost, and women bore a disproportionate part of that cost. What were we to think of the right of consent to marry granted in medieval canon law? Was it a legal right as modern feminism defined rights? Was it ever enforceable? And was it a boon to women? How often I stated that relativist arguments based on twentieth-century assumptions seldom produced better historical understanding.

Yet the historical study of women was revolutionary in its implications. By the 1980s the corpus of new interpretation might be regarded in the light of other twentieth-century historical schools of thought that had consciously fomented change within the discipline. The Annales School, with its between-war embattled stance against establishment history as pursued on the Continent, provided one possible precedent. Annales historians repudiated diplomatic history as "what one clerk said to another" and in its stead favored material life, study of the masses, geophysical structuralism, investigation of the "mental equipment" of a given era, and a dazzling vision of total history. Was such a rethinking of terms what thoroughgoing revisionist history demanded? I read Marc Bloch and Fernand Braudel and studied Lucien Febvre's method of investigation in *The Problem of Unbelief in the Sixteenth Century* with great care. From its inception women's history had maintained a dialogue with histories of minorities and the exploited. Could a model be found for all these concerns in the Annales ideal of constructing a total history, that is, inclusive and responsive to the condition of all peoples? But the masses as Annales writers conceived them were largely undifferentiated; they were acted upon and seldom actors with the capacity to effect change of any sort. Indeed, Annales history was sadly lacking in historical agency of any kind. In vain I sought in early Annales histories for women, who must, assuredly, be part of any vision of total history; they were not present.[6] No matter how thought-provoking the Annales agenda, radical their new methods of investigation, or encompassing their vision, this history had little to offer by way of a model.[7]

Bloch had raised one question in *Feudal Society* and in his essays that could profitably be tested by reference to women's historical experience. He asserted that medieval Europe differed fundamentally from the antique world because of the demise of ancient slavery. By the latter half of the twentieth century, this had become a tenet of interpretation for medieval studies, more broadly for the evolution of Western society. A belief that the rendering of agricultural labor did not favor deployment of slaves in the West, resulting in the decline and disappearance of the institution itself, held widespread appeal. Basic Western institutions rather than intent had produced beneficent change. Bloch bequeathed a hopeful message to his French compatriots and to the West generally in the aftermath of two brutal world wars by arguing that humane solutions were ingrained in the very attributes of Western culture. But did the experience of slavery for women bear out this sanguine interpretation?

In the archives of Dubrovnik (medieval Ragusa), I had come across a series of contracts legitimating sales of Balkan women to local householders or to visiting merchants from Italy. Wilhelm Heyd had first commented on these and like records, expressing surprise that a medieval traffic in slaves moved from the East to the West. Charles Verlinden had studied the revived Mediterranean slave-trade documentation as well. He concluded that close to 90 percent of traded slaves were women. Sales of slaves destined for domestic service in European towns revived in the thirteenth century and continued strong for centuries to come. I had uncovered ideal evidence for studying this revived institution that relied on traffic in women.[8] Soon I expanded the purview to study the fate of domestic slaves in medieval communities that distinguished *servus* (male slave but also serf) from *ancilla* (female slave), not only in terms of division of labor but in regard to custom and to rights in canon and civic law. Whereas the word *servus* evolved in meaning as church lawyers argued for the paternal rights of *servi* over their offspring, *ancillae* and their offspring remained the chattels of owners in law and practice throughout the medieval era. The disparity was glaring, and while the evolving condition of *servi* might substantiate Bloch's demise argument, the historical condition of the *ancillae* did not.

Now I had thoroughly assimilated the lesson that women have a dynamic history, marked by significant change rather than unending sameness, and I had spoken or written on that matter. I registered shock on encountering stability of meaning over the medieval centuries in regard to *ancillae*. Not only was this the case, but notarial charters provided me extensive anecdotal evidence that this remarkable stability of meaning had embedded itself in legal discourse and was enforced in communities where women served as slaves. Women slaves or their offspring might be treated humanely by householders, they might even be manumitted, but that was never a given; manumission required a conscious act on the part of the chattel slave's owner. The child of an *ancilla* was the possession of the *ancilla*'s owner; parental rights did not pertain. On reflection it became clear that women's experience of medieval slavery rather than men's squared with what was known of the transport of slaves to serve in the plantation economy of the modern era. Slavery's utility, along with the practices associated with the *ancilla,* were proved in the sugar fields of Crete; then slaves were transported for intensive agriculture to other Mediterranean and Atlantic islands and finally into the New World. Slavery had not died out; it was in good running order because of the revival of medieval domestic slavery that preceded it. The sad history of medieval women slaves had preserved the institution for later use; this was a particularly grim instance of women's experience affecting the general course of history.

Women's history incorporated into general historical interpretation provided dramatic new perspectives on the past. On occasion new answers came to light, or conclusions were modified in that light. When *Past and Present* published "Ancillary Evidence on the Decline of Medieval Slavery," the study set off a scholarly debate that continues until today.[9] Women's history does not lie outside the concerns of mainstream history; it is part of the totality, and after two decades we are still only in the initial phases of learning about women.

Today, as I research the fourteenth-century advent of fashion in costume that stimulated demand for goods in Italy, I am constantly struck by women's pivotal role. Urban sumptuary laws limited women, while men remained unrestrained in their consumption. But women did not sit idly by; they invented new fashions at home. Despite the strong arm of the law, women in cities became trendsetters, and this in turn stimulated consumption markets. Despite efforts to curb them, despite their lack of direct access to luxury markets, women found ways to be fashionable, to turn eyes, and so to influence the taste of others. Wealthy women and their clever serving maids were important components of new consumer markets where taste and fashion influenced demand. Their acts of dress did not occur in a vacuum but resounded in society and affected the economy.[10]

Yet each of us is much more than the conscious decisions that direct our choices, and chance may well play a significant role. In 1935 I was born at North Haven, a Quaker-founded home for unwed mothers in Rochester, New York. I was "placed," as luck and the preferences of the institution prescribed, with a family possessing Quaker roots in nearby Auburn, New York. The Mosher family had settled early in Cayuga County (the Military Tract) in company with like-minded Quaker neighbors, and they proved to have a strong penchant for women's rights. Both Sarah and Phoebe Mosher signed the Women's Right's Declaration at Seneca Falls, New York. Eliza Mosher, she "of the booming voice," numbered among the first women physicians, and the University of Michigan honors her as such.[11] Clelia Mosher, also a woman physician, composed the Stanford Report, in which she explored nineteenth-century American women's attitudes toward their sexuality. There were women entrepreneurs in the family tree—even one inventor (of an early antiperspirant, no less). In my small town one female cousin practiced law, and others were widely respected teachers. Since no one made much of this—my parents merely joked about how many "lady" doctors, lawyers, and old-maid schoolteachers appeared in the family tree—I assumed that when I grew up I would just follow along. Midcentury America may have conveyed entirely different messages to other girls, but insulated as I was, I never doubted that I would pursue a profession.

Not that I showed much early talent for it. In nursery school I was assigned the job of consoling the miserable ones and coaxing them into the circle. I was the easygoing, good-natured younger child, sensitive to the needs of others, in contrast to my more high-strung and nervy older sister. I could sit contentedly for hours if someone would read to me, and I always asked for my favorite story, "Living in Whales," from the "Told under the Umbrella" series. Years later I found that story, to discover that it was a satire of the cranky literalism of Fabian socialists. I considered it hilarious as a child and wonder to this day if my delight in it held any predictive power.

It was a relief to all parties when I learned to read for myself. This finally occurred in third grade, quite late, admittedly, probably the result of an undiagnosed dyslexia. It was so liberating to read that I went off the scale of the tests administered by the state. No one, much less I, grasped what had happened, but I read every book in sight, such was the pleasure at overcoming my earlier disability. I read so much, and talked so much about what I read, that I was accused of telling "tall tales" at the dinner table. I learned to borrow books from school to prove that I had not made it all up.

I lived in a prosperous, stable home with caring parents. My mother had graduated from Smith College in 1924 and prized her literary background. She directed theatricals, in which I played small parts, and gave gratis elocution lessons while I sat on the stairs and listened. To this day I can rattle off reams of nineteenth-century poetry, psalms, and long passages of the New Testament. Doris Sherman Mosher founded a book club that has lasted more than half a century, and she read everything that C. S. Lewis ever wrote. But knowledge and poetry were embellishments to a privileged life as a cherished small-town daughter and wife, so her erudition was always an amateur pursuit. In my naiveté I failed to realize that my paternal kin were remarkable women, and my mother's reticence about pursuing serious learning, despite great interest, was more typical of the times. In turn my headlong pursuit of any new book, field of study, or idea frightened her mightily. My enthusiasms, and they were many, were simply unsuitable in a girl.

But my father indulged me in this, as he supported and indulged my mother and older sister in their choices. Charles Hull Mosher was the true nurturing presence in my early life, and I spent every available minute I could with him. He never preached, which I would later learn was a trait of Quakerism; my father taught by example, as he had been taught. His formal education had been slighted because of the decline and early death of his own father, so all his advanced education was gained through correspondence courses. His Aunt Emma had convinced him to tithe very early in his prosperous business career, saying, "Try it for a year, and if you miss the money you can stop." He never missed the money, and local charities learned to rely on his generosity. I had an inflated idea of our family wealth because we gave away more money than others. I basked in reflected approbation, but such a fine example ultimately exacts recompense, so I tithe today.

My parents lived a pleasant small-town existence. Summer vacations took us to Murray Island in the Thousand Islands. My father traveled extensively for business, and my mother accompanied him whenever she could. She loved staying at private reserves in the Poconos, at the Breakers in Palm Beach, and in fine New York City hotels. I have them caught in a snapshot by a street photographer in New York City: they walk along the street, an elegant and handsome couple. I can see why they sprang for the photo: it is pleasant to measure up to urbanity in the great metropolis. Charles and Doris Mosher maintained their striking social presence well into their eighties. One day I caught my three children calling them "Darling Doris and Charming Charles." They had just been exposed to their grandparents working a crowd and had been suitably impressed.

In truth, most of my early learning occurred outside of school after my extraordinary breakthrough in deciphering print in third grade. I did learn passable French and excellent Latin at school, but my academic high school was far more interested in cramming us up into the high nineties for our Regents exams than in presenting us with any sort of a stiff learning challenge. So I went to the town library and read about Chief Logan, William H. Seward, and Harriet Tubman, whose lives provided the town with its proud heritage. I found a dusty old Victorian series—the Lives of the Elizabeths, the Marys, and the Catherines—in which I found biographies of historical women whose lives just astonished me. The Marys were fine women all, as were the Elizabeths, what with all the queens in their midst, but the Catherines were truly inspiring for me, no matter how they spelled their name. I do not have the faintest idea how sheltered Victorian daughters in Auburn, New York, were expected to react to these spine-stiffening role models, but I concluded that the sky was the limit if women from earlier times reacted with such spunk. I dreamed about what I would do.

A secure and comfortable childhood in which to explore can breed complacency, and I make no claim to having escaped, but a privileged upbringing also led me to question the conditions in my safe world. This took two forms, both of them distressing to my mother. I wanted to work; initially this meant odd jobs or baby-sitting for pay or gratis, which opened all sorts of windows into other households and other lives. I satisfied some of my insatiable curiosity in this fashion. Next I wanted a "real" job, and to my mother's and sister's alarm I went to work for the Columbian Rope Company as a filing clerk. My father had pulled strings for me because he thought it was fine if I wanted to do it; and as was his habit, he patiently answered my endless list of questions, now about "business." The files I combed through were a treasure. Ships from all over the world were represented there, including my favorites, the doughty fleets of harbor tugboats that ordered quantities of line and giant hawsers. I learned why company families we knew had been incarcerated under horrible conditions in the Philippines during World War II. It was all because of manila, grown there, not here. There was also the problem of hemp, which was illegal to grow in the United

States, so the company imported it. I learned that the America's Cup winner, the *Columbia*, had received all its line free from the company because of its name: it was good advertising. I learned about obsolescence with the invention of wire rope and how this might be counteracted by producing nylon rope with a wire-rope core. I talked the office staff blue in the face and asked everyone about his or her work. I would take on any job they entrusted to me.

More ominous, I became interested in politics. Auburn had a tiny Socialist Party consisting of ministers from nonestablishment churches, a few wild-haired but articulate elderly ladies of wealthy background, and some intense labor leaders from the town's factories. These people analyzed social structure and kept tabs on the economy. I learned about their programs of social reform, Eugene Debs, and the endless presidential candidacy of Norman Thomas, who could claim at the end of his life that most of his platform had been incorporated into law despite his constant defeats. Socialism looked at the economy and society as a whole and sought amelioration of conditions, which appealed to my youthful idealism. I developed an interest in welfare programs, the loss of local jobs to the South, and the impact of the Marshall Plan. This was not learning as a social embellishment, and the very unpoetic nature of my intellectual pursuits aroused concern at home. Why did I always want to challenge the status quo? Wasn't what I learned in social studies class enough to satisfy me? I questioned the conservative Republican politics of my family. I proved difficult.

So it was a relief to my family when I took my subversive self off to college. Now my mother could explain to friends that I was just "very liberal" without having to specify what outrageous opinion I held at the moment. I arrived at Smith College still in time to be taught by that generation of refugee European intellectuals who had immigrated to America to escape Fascism. The brilliance of mind and commitment to values that they represented convinced me that academia was the best of all possible worlds. My instructors demanded rigorous work, for which the reward was inclusion in their discussions, the great honor of having one's own views taken seriously. My future as a college teacher was sealed in those years; I wanted to be like my professors. When I look back today on my highly rewarding career in teaching, I credit the excellent faculty who educated me and set standards that have inspired me ever since.

Yet in those years we were known to our faculty as the Silent Generation, and we resented the label. When I announced at graduation that I was to be married the next day, Donald Sheehan of the history faculty said to me, "Well, now you will never know how good you are at history." It was a slap in the face that expressed the deep frustration of a faculty who wondered about our commitments. I never forgot his words. They probably carried me through a master's degree program and gave me the determination to pursue my Ph.D. at Yale. I was not about to be eliminated on the grounds of marriage and a family. Why not have both? It creates a nice balance in life. My husband and I both have professions; we both worked hard at our careers; we tried to support each other. Our children gained an idea of how a person accomplishes work because, like so many other professional women, I brought my work home and they had firsthand experience of it.

But silent? That was never the case. My peers and I, among us Smith College women from the Silent Generation, found our commitments, and we have spoken out. We continue to speak out, loud and often. I wonder at that epithet, Silent Generation: Wasn't it just a matter of taking time until we figured out what it was we wanted to say?

NOTES

1. Green, *Trotula*. There are actually three treatises in the Trotula corpus according to Green; only one of them may be attributed to Trotula of Salerno.

2. The Berkshire Conference on Women's History grew out of a gathering of women historians from primarily women's colleges that was held each year in the Berkshire Mountains. The history conference meets every three years in the spring.

3. This quotation emerged from a conversation with Gabrielle Spiegel, a professor of history at the Johns Hopkins University and a medievalist.

4. Renate Bridenthal and Claudia Koonz, *Becoming Visible*, 1st. ed. (Boston: Macmillan, 1976).

5. Stuard, "Dominion of Gender," 129–50.

6. Over the course of the 1980s Christiane Klapisch-Zuber would change that with her extensive study of Florentine women, families, servants, and prevailing attitudes toward women. See Klapisch-Zuber, *Women, Family and Ritual in Renaissance Florence*. The work she accomplished with David Herlihy on the cadasto of 1427 stands as the most far-reaching investigation of medieval archival material undertaken to date. See Herlihy and Klapisch-Zuber, *Les Toscans et leurs familles*.

7. See Stuard, "American Feminism and the Annales School," 135–43.

8. Stuard, "To Town to Serve," 39–55.

9. Stuard, "Ancillary Evidence on the Decline of Medieval Slavery," 3–28. This work received the Berkshire Conference of Women Historians Prize for a women's history (article) in 1996. For the ensuing debate, see, for example, Jean-Pierre Devroey, "Men and Women in Early Medieval Serfdom," *Past and Present* 166 (February 2000): 3–30.

10. Stuard, *Gilding the Market in Fourteenth-Century Italy*.

11. Evans et al., "Dictionary of Quaker Biography," s.v. "Mosher, Eliza."

SELECT BIBLIOGRAPHY OF WORKS BY SUSAN MOSHER STUARD

"Dame Trot." *Signs: Journal of Women in Culture and Society* 1 (1976): 537–43.
Women in Medieval Society. Philadelphia: University of Pennsylvania Press, 1976.
"American Feminism and the Annales School." *Signs: Journal of Women in Culture and Society* 6 (1981): 152–55.
"Dowry Increase and Increments of Wealth in Medieval Ragusa (Dubrovnik)." *Journal of Economic History* 41 (1981): 795–811.
"Domestic Slavery in Medieval Ragusa." *Journal of Medieval History* 9 (1983): 155–71.
Editor with Renate Bridenthal and Claudia Koonz. *Becoming Visible*. Boston: Houghton Mifflin, 2d ed., 1987; 3d ed., 1998.
"Dominion of Gender." In *Becoming Visible*, edited by Susan Mosher Stuard, Renate Bridenthal, and Claudia Koonz. Boston: Houghton Mifflin, 2d ed., 1987; 3d ed., 1998.

"To Town to Serve." In *Women and Work in Pre-Industrial Europe,* edited by Barbara Hanawalt. Bloomington: Indiana University Press, 1987.

Women in Medieval History and Historiography. Philadelphia: University of Pennsylvania Press, 1987.

"From Women to Woman: New Thinking about Gender." *Thought* 64 (1989): 208–19.

"A New Dimension: North American Scholars Contribute Their Perspective on Medieval Women." In *American Medievalism.* Binghamton, N.Y.: CEMERS, 1989.

"The Chase after Theory." *Gender and History* 4 (1992): 135–46.

A State of Deference: Ragusa (Dubrovnik) in the Medieval Centuries. Philadelphia: University of Pennsylvania Press, 1992.

"Burdens of Matrimony: Husbanding and Gender in Medieval Italy." In *Medieval Masculinities,* edited by Claire Lees, 61–71. Minneapolis: University of Minnesota Press, 1994.

"Ancillary Evidence on the Decline of Medieval Slavery." In *Past and Present* 149 (November 1995): 3–32.

Gilding the Market in Fourteenth-Century Italy. Philadelphia: University of Pennsylvania Press, 2004.

Works Cited

Bloch, Marc. *Feudal Society.* Translated by L. A. Manyon. 2 vols. Chicago: University of Chicago Press, 1964.

Evans, William Bacon, et al. "Dictionary of Quaker Biography." Quaker Collection, Haverford College. Typescript.

Febvre, Lucien. *The Problem of Unbelief in the Sixteenth Century.* Translated by Beatrice Gottlieb. Cambridge, Mass.: Harvard University Press, 1982.

Green, Monica. *The Trotula: A Medieval Compendium of Women's Medicine.* Philadelphia: University of Pennsylvania Press, 2001.

Herlihy, David, and Christiane Klapisch-Zuber. *Les Toscans et leurs familles.* Paris: SEVPEN, 1978.

Heyd, Wilhelm. *Histoire du commerce du Levant au Moyen Âge.* 6th ed. 2 vols. Amsterdam: O. Harrassawit, 1855.

Klapisch-Zuber, Christiane. *Women, Family and Ritual in Renaissance Florence.* Translated by Lydia Cochrane. Chicago: University of Chicago Press, 1985.

Verlinden, Charles. *L'Esclavage dans l'Europe médiévale.* 2 vols. Bruges: De Tempel, 1955–77.

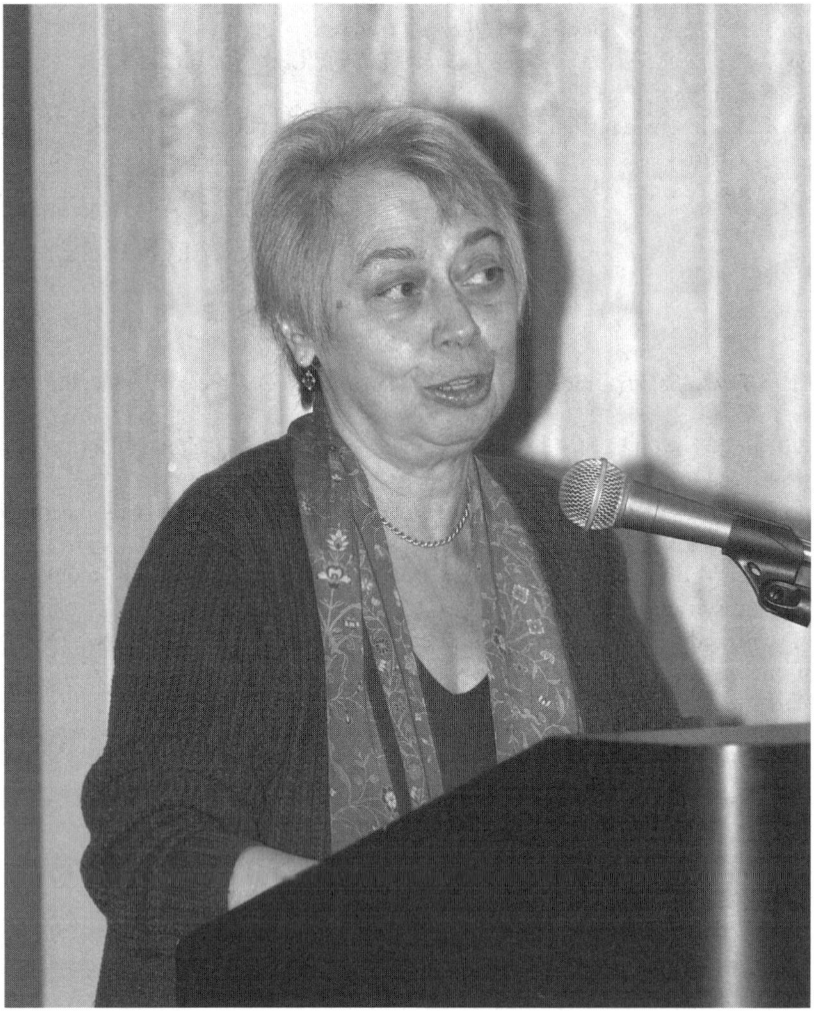

CHAPTER 70

Joan M. Ferrante (1936–)
Going the Distance in Life and Literature

JULIE CROSBY

WHENEVER POSSIBLE JOAN FERRANTE likes to walk a considerable distance in Riverside Park, which her apartment near the Columbia University campus in New York City overlooks. One July afternoon we were walking through the park at a clip, and although I was breathless, Ferrante apologized for not being able to go faster. "It's my knee—an old football injury," she explained with a smile, her voice matching the increasing speed of her step. The scene is perhaps emblematic of Ferrante's life: a life that is breathtaking in its commitment to going the distance; a life that acknowledges and then overpowers the difficulties; a life that consistently takes delight in whatever the moment brings.

Ferrante describes herself as something of a dilettante in her approach to intellectual undertakings: "I sort of flit over things," she says. However, her career portrays a distinctly different image, one in which there is a very determined focus on languages, including Latin, Greek, Italian, French, Provençal, German, Russian, Serbo-Croatian, and Arabic. Ferrante says, "For me, the only way into a culture is through language, or at least without language, I can't even begin to understand the culture." The sheer breadth of her linguistic interests coupled with the depth in which she considers each language's nuance seem to betray the "dilettante" label and undoubtedly set a standard for comparative studies in the medieval period and beyond.

The standard was set early for Ferrante herself, by a family who encouraged her to embrace wholeheartedly whatever challenge came her way, whether in the shape of a football or a thousand years of literary history. She was reared in New York City as the only child of American-born Josephine Pisacane and Italian-born Nicolas Ferrante, and the first grandchild of an Italian man who—defying the stereotype—greatly preferred daughters to sons. She was taught that she could do anything she wanted to do, except perhaps to be pope, and she continues today to live by the principle.

In part Ferrante's parents steered her toward a study of languages by their own example. Her father first worked as a pharmacist, but after going blind at age forty-three, when Joan was fourteen, he spent over twenty years as a social worker at the Lighthouse, a school for the blind in Manhattan. Ferrante notes, "My father originally went to the Lighthouse to learn Braille. He spoke Italian, Spanish, and some French, and he did so well that they saw in him a great boon and offered him a job." Equally determined was Ferrante's mother, who dropped out of college during the Depression to help her family but later took a job as a secretary in Columbia's School of Law and simultaneously worked on her degree in Columbia's general studies program, eventually graduating a member of Phi Beta Kappa and teaching Italian in general studies.

Ferrante attended public school until the sixth grade, when her parents enrolled her in Foxwood in Flushing, Queens. The small Quaker school armed Ferrante with French and Latin and prepared her to succeed at the Brearley School, a private girls' high school in Manhattan. Brearley had gained a considerable reputation for academic excellence under the guidance of Millicent McIntosh, a woman who had left Brearley three years before Ferrante's arrival to head Barnard College and who would later become Ferrante's mother-in-law. At Brearley, Ferrante learned Greek, a feat instigated by her mother: "My mother always said I was going to go to a high school that teaches Greek. She said I didn't have to take Greek if I didn't want to, but what would be the point of that? Of course, I was going to take it." She credits Brearley with fostering her pride in being an intellectual, and her attachment to the school later resulted in an eight-year appointment to its board of trustees.

After graduating from Brearley in 1954, Ferrante spent a year at Radcliffe, where she found herself at odds with her dorm mates' general preoccupation with marriage and wealth rather than with more intellectual matters. She happily returned to New York City to attend Barnard College. Although her early education had been speckled with the usual fickleness—she thought alternatively of being a sportscaster, an anthropologist, a concert pianist, and a medical doctor—her focus continually returned to languages, and she graduated from Barnard College in 1958 after majoring in Italian and taking a number of medieval studies courses, including several graduate seminars.

Ferrante picked up other languages more casually. German "seemed important" to her, so she learned it on her own during summers as a teenager, aided in part by her maternal grandmother, who had grown up in a German neighborhood. During college Ferrante went on an expedition to Mexico with the parents of a friend who were investigating the effects of hallucinogenic mushrooms. During this anthropological jaunt the friend's mother, a pediatrician from Russia, taught Ferrante some Russian, and she continued in her fashion to study the language.

In 1958 Ferrante entered graduate school at Columbia University and began expanding her already impressive command of languages. She learned enough Serbo-Croatian to study oral epics with Stavros Skendi, who taught her alone for two hours each week. She laughs as she says, "I would sit, and he would march up and down in front of me lecturing about Serbo-Croatian epics—which were full of the most horrifying atrocities I've ever known to be practiced against a people—and then he would take me for tea." She also studied Provençal with Kurt Lewent, a German refugee and scholar. Ferrante says: "Lewent worked downtown as a clerk, and on Friday nights he taught Provençal to a few of us at Columbia. He taught the class in the old-fashioned philological way, which is that you did not read literature *qua* literature, but you read the poem parsing it to see how the language was put together. He sometimes taught at his house, and after class his wife would provide drinks and cakes, and well, it was all quite elegant."

The study of languages helped to shape the trajectory of Ferrante's early literary studies. By the time she entered graduate school, she was keenly interested in working on oral traditions. She found that the medieval chansons de geste seemed to be posing many of the same stock descriptions and formulae as the Serbo-Croatian epics she had studied with Skendi, but she was diverted from pursuing a more comprehensive comparison. Ferrante recalls: "This was all very unpopular in Western medieval studies at the time. The academy didn't like thinking of the Western tradition as oral."

The diversion from the oral tradition came largely in the shape of William T. H. Jackson, a well-known scholar in the field of comparative literature and Ferrante's mentor since her days at Barnard. He persuaded her to work instead on the Tristan romances, a topic that she confesses interested Jackson more than it did her at that point. However, Ferrante notes, "Jackson was probably right in the sense that I was better equipped to handle it." The sophisticated comparison of various Tristan texts was, in 1973, to become Ferrante's first published book, *The Conflict of Love and Honor: The Medieval Tristan Legend in France, Germany, and Italy*.

In 1963, a mere five years after entering graduate school, Ferrante earned her doctorate. She was determined to remain a resident of New York City, even preferring the idea of driving a taxi to moving off the island. Given the rumors that Ferrante's presence behind a wheel is what gave rise to the seat-belt laws, it is perhaps fortunate that Jackson helped her to get her first job as a lecturer in general studies at Columbia. Ferrante recalls: "Jackson picked up the phone and called G. S. and said he had the perfect person to fill the medievalist position. I went for the interview in the comparative literature department. In the small committee was Alice Frendman, who had taught my mother, and she remembered my mother telling her that I was learning Russian. I told her that Russian was no longer my focus, but it did give me an entrée into speaking about languages, which they really cared about at that time. So they were impressed. I had a very strong recommendation from Jackson—the quintessential old boy's network—and I got the job." After Ferrante joined the general studies faculty in 1963, Jackson continued to be supportive by asking her to teach Medieval Latin and participate in doctoral oral exams in the graduate school, at a time when precious few women were teaching there.

Jackson also later encouraged Ferrante to return to her study of oral traditions by commissioning for the Records of Civilization a translation of four poems from the most extensive epic cycle of the Western Middle Ages. These twelfth-century poems celebrating the hero and later monk William of Orange were based on legends transmitted orally from at least the ninth century. Ferrante's edition of *Guillaume d'Orange: Four Epics* was first published in 1974, reprinted in 1991, and remains today the definitive English translation. In her introduction to the work, Ferrante insists, "Oral traditions persist and grow, even in literate societies."

Ferrante's voice has itself persisted and resonated most profoundly through her work on medieval women. In addition to numerous articles, her book *Woman as Image in Medieval Literature from the Twelfth Century to Dante*—first published in 1975 and reprinted in 1985—is undisputedly a seminal text in medieval feminist studies. Ferrante credits Carolyn Heilbrun, her longtime friend and colleague, with inspiring the work during their fierce discussions about life and literature; Ferrante repeatedly asserted that medieval women were often perceived—for better or worse—in much the same way as modern women, and Heilbrun finally insisted that she prove it in writing. With her usual attention to detail Ferrante recalls the book in critical terms. In addition to a small mistake with pronoun usage—"the sort of thing that can bother you for the rest of your life," she laments—the title remains a source of embarrassment. "It was written in an era when everyone spoke of woman as image. Now we look at women in a much more realistic and historic way. We're moving in the right direction."

The direction of Ferrante's subsequent scholarship was indeed right. She teamed up with another dear friend and colleague, Robert Hanning, to produce an edition and translation of the *Lais* of Marie de France, first published in 1978, reprinted in 1982, and still in print. The volume not only remains authoritative in terms of scholarship but also in terms of collaboration between academics. Ferrante and Hanning both recall the experience with mutual glee, and they echo each other verbatim when separately recounting various comic adventures with the publishers. Their extraordinary camaraderie continues today to impress and instruct their students, who are fortunate to find in both professors a constant readiness to share their time, expertise, and good humor.

The spirit of collaboration also pervades Ferrante's latest and perhaps her greatest venture—an enormous digital project called *Epistolae*. The growing collection now features about two thousand letters written in Latin to and by women during the fourth to the thirteenth century, which are being translated, contexualized, and put online. The project is both a labor of love—Ferrante derives no remuneration from it—and an obsession that has commandeered her attention for over fifteen years. She began collecting the letters after being asked to contribute a volume to Indiana University's Women of Letters series, a request that eventually led to the 1997 publication of *To the Glory of Her Sex: Women's Roles in the Composition of Medieval Texts*. The book itself is monumental—a compelling analysis of countless historical and literary texts written by or at the request of medieval women. The letters in particular led Ferrante to believe that "while misogyny was strong as theory throughout the Middle Ages, it had much less influence on practical reality than is frequently claimed." In an effort to change the frequency of those claims, Ferrante teamed up with the Columbia Center for New Media to put online the collection of letters in an easily searchable format that is accessible free of charge to people of any educational background. She also began urging other scholars in the field to contribute additional letters, translations, corrections, and clarifying notes, all in the hope that *Epistolae* will become "a living resource that will get larger and more accurate all the time."

Fittingly, Ferrante's interest in medieval women's underrecognized authority in political, religious, and social arenas, as evidenced by the letters, grew concurrently with her involvement in the human rights movement. In 1986 she began working at Columbia's Center for the Study of Human Rights, staring with an appointment to its board. Ferrante is an unapologetic atheist, yet she devotes her teaching commitment at the center to a course on women, religion, and human rights, primarily because she sees religion as a source of many problems in women's rights. "Not religion itself necessarily," Ferrante clarifies, "but the way the patriarchy has used religion to oppress women, and religions have allowed themselves to be used as tools to oppress women. This is particularly true I think of Christianity and Islam. The documents were written down long after Mohammed or Christ said anything—so the texts are at best approximations and the product of fallible human memory—and still, given all of that, the fact is that both Christ and Mohammed were very progressive on the subject of women. If their followers had actually followed them, we would have a very different situation." In the same way that Ferrante sees the *Epistolae* project as a means of reclaiming women's authority in medieval life and literature, she wishes her work in human rights could help women in contemporary religious traditions to regain the rights taken away by centuries of patriarchal exegesis and practice.

For the past eight years Ferrante has taught "Women, Religion and Human Rights," assuaging her appetite for languages in the process—in her sixties, she began the serious study of Arabic in order to further her understanding of the Koran. More significantly, however, the course reflects Ferrante's prominent concern with justice and social responsibility. It is a concern that readily surfaces in the 1984 publication of *The Political Vision of the Divine Comedy,* a work that was rapidly deemed one of the most original and useful Dante studies produced in twenty years. She reads the *Comedy* as a document of justice, injustice, and corruption rather than as a religious poem. More specifically, Ferrante says, "Dante's moral universe is structured on what we do to others—how our actions affect our society for good or ill—rather than on what we do to ourselves." Ferrante is unsure whether Dante helped to shape her concern for justice or whether her concern made her alert to Dante's political program, but in either case she actively opposes injustice wherever she encounters it, in both life and literature.

Life at Columbia University has often proven a source of moral outrage, and Ferrante has certainly experienced her fair share of it. In 1968, during the notorious riots between an administration out of step with the times and student protestors demanding rapid change, Ferrante joined the Ad Hoc Faculty Committee, a group of concerned professors seeking to find some common ground between the warring parties. It was a brave move on Ferrante's part, especially since she did not yet have tenure. The Ad Hoc Faculty Committee evolved into the Columbia University Senate, which Ferrante eagerly joined shortly after its inception. At first she focused primarily on women's issues through the Commission on the Status of Women; later she focused more generally on faculty rights, chairing several major senate committees. Ferrante had some direct experience in these areas: a departmental administrator had requested that she postpone her tenure decision in favor of a weaker male colleague. Ferrante refused, and she was granted tenure in 1970. She continued, however, to advance, but considerably slower in rank and salary than her male colleagues—like all the women then in arts and sciences. Eventually her colleague Robert Hanning took the extraordinary step in a private university of revealing his salary and authorizing Ferrante to use the information, so she and Carolyn Heilbrun were able to make the point with the administration and have some adjustments made.

After years of fighting the administration on various types of injustice, including inequities in salary and tenure procedures, Ferrante temporarily lost her seat on the Columbia University Senate in a rigged election. Robert Hanning recalls, "She is the only known member of the Senate to lose an election in which there were more votes reported for her opponents than total votes cast." Ferrante's experiences with the administration are memorialized not only in the pantheon of dirty politics but also on the equally cutthroat football field. In the late 1970s Ferrante regularly played Saturday morning football with graduate students and faculty members. She was a formidable quarterback, despite her petite size, and an expert passer. In tribute to her experience in the Columbia University Senate, Ferrante devised the still famous "Columbia Administration Play," which involved staging a considerable degree of chaos, with several receivers reversing direction and one moving in a complete circle.

At the same time Ferrante makes light of certain administrative punting, she more seriously questions the long-term success of her own efforts on the Columbia University Senate and during her tenure as chair of the Department of English and Comparative Literature (1988-91) and as the department's director of graduate studies (1974-77, 1999-2000). Ferrante says, "The central administration is heavily male, macho male, and they are bullies. Our department is still fiercely male dominated. Even today, by and large, the women who speak out on women's issues are ostracized. They don't trust us. They refuse to come to grips with their own prejudices. There are still a lot of places where it's a mess, and on balance, I would say things haven't improved a lot."

Ferrante's frustration with the lack of institutional justice is conspicuous, but she is frustrated on behalf of others rather than for herself. Columbia has consistently capitalized on Ferrante's efficiency and intelligence through her administrative service in the Department of English and Comparative Literature; as director of Casa

Italiana, Center for Italian Studies (1977–80); and as acting chair of the Department of Spanish and Portuguese (1985–87). However, Columbia has just as consistently denied her the same honors, awards, and recognition that it has bestowed readily on men with far fewer scholarly contributions and considerably less humanity. Ferrante takes full responsibility for the phenomenon: "I chose early on to fight unpopular battles, which isn't wise if you want to rise within the university." While her colleagues and students often remark on the lack of respect she is shown by the administration, Ferrante adamantly refuses to acknowledge it, preferring instead to focus on what she does have: "I have a tremendous backlog of support where it matters most. The men in my life have been incredibly supportive—my father, grandfather, Carey [McIntosh, husband], and Bob [Hanning]. When you have that in your most personal life, it makes things much easier. It allows me to say to hell with those other guys."

With characteristic determination Ferrante chooses not only to dwell on the good guys but also to overpower the bad ones, a feat that seems managed in part by pure psychological fortitude. "It is just part of my mentality that focuses on the positive rather than the negative," Ferrante says. "It doesn't mean that the negative isn't there. I just don't see any point in focusing on the negative. What's the use of it? It only gets in the way. I don't think I'm suppressing information that I need in order to cope with life." It is this mental vision that allows her to dwarf the bad guys at Columbia under a heap of giant accomplishments in scholarship and in rewarding service outside the august institution. She has repeatedly risen to the top positions within organizations outside Columbia, including president of the Medieval Academy of America (2000–2001), president of the Dante Society of America (1985–91), and president of the National Society of Phi Beta Kappa (1991–94). Ferrante takes great, almost giddy pleasure in the fact that colleagues she respects have deemed her fit to hold these positions.

For any normal person Ferrante's giant accomplishments in scholarship and in service would be sufficient cause for exhaustion. But Ferrante seems positively energized by it all, and she adds daily to her list of passions, which include gourmet cooking and, as she merrily describes "gardening, growing vegetables, weeding—it's very satisfying to pull the bad guys out, an image I thought of when I was gardening during the worst part of my political struggles. And there's nothing like producing an eggplant." In her abundant spare time she also plays the piano and viola, the first with substantial talent, according to those who would know, and the second with enthusiasm, according to her own report. Her parents encouraged her to learn to play the piano, and she attended the prestigious Julliard Preparatory School for nine years as a child. After high school she polished her playing at Fontainebleau, the summer program of the Paris Conservatory. She continues today to take lessons and perform chamber music pieces with equally accomplished friends and family. Her living room holds two grand pianos, a rather amazing detail for anyone familiar with real estate in Manhattan. Ferrante's fondness for grand pianos is matched by her fondness for grand music, favoring the intellectual and emotional complexities of Brahms, Beethoven, Schubert, Dvorak, and Mozart.

That Ferrante's favorite music is lush and romantic is perhaps sentimentally significant, since she met her future husband because of a shared passion for the genre. Carey McIntosh is a gifted violinist and violist who holds a Ph.D. in eighteenth-century English literature. He taught at Harvard, was tenured at Rochester University, and spent ten years as a dean at Brown University. Acquainted years earlier, the couple grew to know each other when they showed up at the same music camp by accident in 1986. After the camp they continued to meet and play chamber music.

Ferrante's marriage to McIntosh surprised everyone, including Ferrante. "When I was young, I thought that I would get married and have children, but later I always cut off any relationship before it got too serious," she recalls. "I always said, after my first book, after I get tenure, after I do x, y, and z, then I'll think about these other things more seriously. But I finally faced that fact that I enjoyed my life, and I was quite happy with it." When Carey proposed marriage, Ferrante was still opposed to the idea. "I thought it was a patriarchal institution, and I didn't want anything to do with it," she remembers. "But then Carey said, 'But marriage is family, and I want you to be part of my family.' Well, it's a hell of a family to be part of, and I was enormously pleased to be invited into it."

The McIntosh clan is indeed most impressive, especially in terms of its deep-seated support of and admiration for its female members. Carey's mother, Millicent McIntosh, who died in January 2001 at age 102, was first the headmistress of the Brearley School. She later served as Barnard College's dean, then president, from 1947 to 1962, feats that she managed while raising five children, all of whom followed her and their father into academic life. Carey's great aunt and namesake, M. Carey Thomas, served for twenty-eight years as the second president of Bryn Mawr College.

McIntosh has two sons, and Ferrante confesses to being besotted with their two grandchildren, perhaps because, as she once explained to Robert Hanning, she sometimes thinks she has the soul of a four-year-old boy. Her fondness runs deep for the family at large, regardless of age. "We share the same values—social values—and a deep commitment to real liberalism," Ferrante says. "It is nice to sit down at a family dinner with any one of them and say what I think and feel and know that they understand."

Ferrante and McIntosh planned a wedding that incorporated their shared beliefs and passions. The wedding took place in Ferrante's living room on 11 April 1987. They had arranged for a female judge, so that the event might be as unpatriarchal as possible, and cut all religious references from the ceremony—"It was very short," Ferrante remarks with a laugh. The five McIntosh siblings played one movement of Brahms' Clarinet Quintet, and then Ferrante joined the family to play a movement of Schubert's Trout Quintet. The couple made the cake themselves, which was meant to be a skyscraper as a symbol of Ferrante and urban culture, but "it leaned slightly during the ceremony, and so it looked like the Tower of Pisa." Urban landmarks aside, when asked whether there were noticeable changes in her life after the wedding, Ferrante remarked without hesitation, "Well the quality of the chamber music went up considerably."

There is another change. Since the wedding McIntosh has altered the direction of some of Ferrante's walks. The couple hikes as often as possible over some rough, non-urban terrain, including treks in the Rockies, the Dolomites, and the Pecos Wilderness in New Mexico. Any lingering effects of the old football injury—or other harms that came her way during the unruly days of the Columbia Administration Play—are resolutely ignored. Indeed, if the walks in Riverside Park are a reliable indicator, then I am convinced that Joan Ferrante hikes where she pleases, at a breathless pace, with a ready smile. And surely anyone who is fortunate enough to cross one of her many prominent paths is profoundly impressed by the distance she has so purposefully traveled.

Notes

This article is based largely on interviews that I conducted with Joan Ferrante on 27 and 30 July 2001, as well as on conversations held while I was her student at Columbia University. I was further informed by a printed version of Ferrante's lecture "They Were There All the Time," delivered at the Thirty-sixth International Congress on Medieval Studies (2001).

In addition Robert W. Hanning provided valuable insight during an interview conducted on 31 July 2001 and by generously sharing with me a printed version of his warm and witty remarks in honor of Ferrante's sixty-fifth birthday celebration, held at Columbia University on 10 November 2001. The conference was organized by Teodolinda Barolini, Ferrante's former student and now colleague, and featured distinguished former students of Joan Ferrante.

Select Bibliography of Works by Joan M. Ferrante

"The Frame Characters of the Decameron: A Progression of Virtues." *Romance Philology* 19 (1965): 212–26.

"The Malebolge as the Key to the Structure of Dante's Inferno." *Romance Philology* 20 (1967): 456–66.

"The Relation of Speech to Sin in the Inferno." *Dante Studies* 87 (1969): 33–46.

The Conflict of Love and Honor: The Medieval Tristan Legend in France, Germany, and Italy. De proprietatibus litterarum. The Hague: Mouton, 1973.

Translator. *Guillaume d'Orange: Four Epics* (with commentary). Records of Civilization. New York: Columbia University Press, 1974. Reprint in paper, 1991.

Editor with George D. Economou. *In Pursuit of Perfection: Courtly Love in Medieval Literature.* Port Washington, N.Y.: Kennikat Press, 1975.

Woman as Image in Medieval Literature from the Twelfth Century to Dante. New York: Columbia University, 1975. Reprint in paper, Durham, N.C.: Labyrinth Press, 1985.

"Florence and Rome: The Two Cities of Man in the Divine Comedy." *Acta, Binghamton Conference on the Early Renaissance* 5 (1978): 1–19.

Translator with Robert W. Hanning. *The Lais of Marie de France* (with commentary). New York: Dutton, 1978. Reprint in paper, Durham, N.C.: Labyrinth, 1982.

"Narrative Patterns in the Decameron." *Romance Philology* 31 (1978): 585–604.

"Ab joi mou lo vers e'l comens." In *The Interpretation of the Medieval Lyric,* edited by W. T. H. Jackson. New York: Macmillan, 1979.

"Artist Figures in the Tristan Stories." *Tristania* 4 (1979): 25–34.

"Some Thoughts on the Application of Modern Critical Methods to Medieval Literature." *Yearbook of Comparative and General Literature* 28 (1979): 5–9.

"Cortes' Amor in Medieval Texts." *Speculum* 55 (1980): 686–95.

"The Education of Women in the Middle Ages, in Theory, Fact, and Fantasy." In *Beyond Their Sex: Learned Women of the European Past,* edited by Patricia A. Labalme. New York: New York University, 1980. Reprint in paper, 1984.

"Is Vernacular Poetic Practice a Response to Latin Language Theory?" *Romance Philology* 35 (1982): 586–600.

"Farai un vers de dreyt nien: The Craft of the Early Trobadors." In *Vernacular Poetics in the Middle Ages,* edited by Lois Ebin. Kalamazoo, Mich.: Medieval Institute, 1983.

"Words and Images in the Paradiso: Reflections of the Divine." In *Dante, Petrarch, Boccaccio: Studies in the Italian Trecento in Honor of Charles S. Singleton,* edited by Aldo Bernardo and Anthony Pellegrini, 115–32. Binghamton, N.Y.: Center for Medieval and Early Renaissance Studies, 1983.

"The French Courtly Poet: Marie de France." In *Medieval Women Writers,* edited by Katharina M. Wilson. Athens: University of Georgia Press, 1984.

"Male Fantasy and Female Reality in Courtly Literature." *Women's Studies* 11 (1984): 67–97.

The Political Vision of the Divine Comedy. Princeton, N.J.: Princeton University Press, 1984.

"The Self-Imprisonment of Man and Society in Courtly Codes." In *Mellon Lectures.* New Orleans: Tulane University Press, 1984.

Editor with R. W. Hanning. *W. T. H. Jackson: The Challenge of the Medieval Text: Studies in Genre and Interpretation.* New York: Columbia University Press, 1985.

"The Court in Medieval Literature: The Center of the Problem." In *The Medieval Court in Europe,* edited by Edward E. Haymes, German Studies 6. Munich: Wilhelm Fink, 1986.

"Good Thieves and Bad Thieves: A Reading of *Inferno* XXIV." *Dante Studies* 104 (1986): 83–98.

"Public Postures and Private Manoeuvres: Roles Medieval Women Play." In *Women and Power in the Middle Ages,* edited by Mary Erler and Maryanne Kowaleski. Athens: University of Georgia Press, 1988.

"Usi e abusi della Bibbia nella letteratura medievale." In *Dante e la Bibbia,* Atti del Convegno Internazionale, 213–25. Florence: Olschki, 1988.

"Notes towards the Study of a Female Rhetoric in the Trobairitz." In *The Voice of the Trobairitz,* edited by William Paden. Philadelphia: University of Pennsylvania Press, 1989.

Translator. "Parole e immagini nel *Paradiso*: Riflessi del Divino." In *Studi Americani su Dante,* edited by Gian Carlo Alessio and Robert Hollander. Milan: Franco Angeli, 1989.

"A Woman's Voice in England: Marie de France." In *The Harvard History of French Literature,* edited by Denis Hollier. Cambridge: Harvard University, 1989. French translation in press. Paperback edition of English version in press.

"'Ez ist ein zunge, dunket mich': Fiction, Deception, and Self-Deception in Gottfried's Tristan." In *Gottfried von Strassburg and the Medieval Tristan Legend,* edited by Adrian Stevens and Roy Wisbey. Cambridge: D. S. Brewer, 1990.

"Images of the Cloister: Haven or Prison." In *A Miscellany of Medieval and Renaissance Studies in Honor of Aldo Bernardo,* edited by Anthony L. Pellegrini and Bernard S. Levy, 57–66. *Medievalia* (1986, pub. 1990).

"The Bible as Thesaurus in Medieval Literature." In *Acta of the Conference on the Bible in the Middle Ages,* edited by Bernard S. Levy. Albany: State University of New York Press, 1992.

"Dante's Beatrice: Priest of an Androgynous God." Cemers Occasional Papers, 2. Binghamton, N.Y.: Medieval and Renaissance Texts and Studies, 1992.

"Alatiel, Politics, Finance, and Feminism in *Decameron* II, 7." *Studi su Boccaccio* (1993): 51–74.

"A Poetics of Chaos and Harmony." In *Cambridge Companion to Dante*, edited by Rachel Jacoff. Cambridge: Cambridge University Press, 1993.

"Why Did Dante Write the Comedy?" *Dante Studies* (1993): 9–18.

"Beyond the Borders of Nation and Discipline." In *Papers on the Future of Medieval French Studies,* edited by William Paden. Gainesville: University Press of Florida, 1994.

"Whose Voice? The Influence of Women Patrons on Courtly Romances." In *Literary Aspects of Courtly Culture,* ed. Donald Maddox and Sara Sturm-Maddox. Rochester, N.Y.: Boydell and Brewer, 1994.

"Hell as the Mirror Image of Paradise." In *Dante's Inferno: The Indiana Critical Edition,* edited by Mark Musa. Bloomington: Indiana University Press, 1995.

"Women's Role in Latin Letters from the Fourth to the Early Twelfth Century." In *The Cultural Patronage of Medieval Women,* edited by June Hall McCash. Athens: University of Georgia Press, 1995.

"Dante and Politics." In *Dante: Contemporary Perspectives,* edited by Amilcare Iannucci, Major Authors Series. Toronto: University of Toronto Press, 1997.

To the Glory of Her Sex: Women's Roles in the Composition of Medieval Texts. Bloomington: Indiana University Press, 1997.

"Hildegard as Correspondent." In *Hildegard of Bingen: Voice of the Living Light,* edited by Barbara Newman. Berkeley: University of California Press, 1998.

With Robert W. Hanning. "Introduction to Medieval Scholarship, 2." In *Literature and Philology.* New York: Garland, 1998.

"A Reading of Canto XXIV." In *California Lectura Dantis, 1. Hell,* edited by Anthony Oldcorn. Berkeley: University of California Press, 1998.

"'Scribe quae vides et audis,': Hildegard, Her Language and Her Secretaries." In *The Tongue of the Fathers,* edited by David Townsend. Philadelphia: University of Pennsylvania Press, 1998.

"Earthly Love in a Spiritual Setting: The Language of Friendship among Religious" and "Spiritual Love in an Earthly Context: Religious Allusions in Courtly Love Texts." *Sewanee Medieval Studies* 8 (1999).

"History Is Myth, Myth Is History." In *Dante, Mito e Poesia*, Atti del Convegno del Secondo Seminario Dantesco Internazionale, edited by M. Picone and T. Crivelli. Florence: Franco Cesati, 1999.

"'Licet longinquis regionibus corpore separati': Letters as a Link in and to the Middle Ages." *Speculum* 76, no. 4 (2001): 877–95.

Epistolae: A Database of the Correspondence of Medieval Women. http://db.ccnmtl.columbia.edu/ferrante/index.html (11 February 2002).

"Is There a Medieval Tradition of Women's Writing?" In *Feminism and the Classics: Framing the Research Agenda,* edited by Judith Hallett and Janet Martin. Princeton, N.J.: Princeton University Press, forthcoming.

"Women and Letters, Literacy and Literature." In *The Roles of Women in the Middle Ages: A Reassessment,* edited by Rosmarie Thee Morewedge. International Medieval and Early Modern Studies. Binghamton, N.Y.: Center for Medieval and Renaissance Studies, forthcoming.

"Women in the Shadows of the Divine Comedy." In *Visions and Voices: Essays on Medieval Culture and Literature in Honor of Robert W. Hanning,* edited by Sandra Pierson Prior and Robert Stein. Notre Dame, Ind.: University of Notre Dame Press, forthcoming.

THE LEGACY OF GREECE
THE ORIGINS of GREEK THOUGHT
A HISTORY OF WOMEN

CHAPTER 71

Marcia L. Colish (1937–)
Intellectual Historian

E. ANN MATTER

AMONG MEDIEVAL INTELLECTUAL HISTORIANS, Marcia Colish is especially known for her incisive, focused, and exceptionally clear pursuit of ideas. Like a heat-seeking missile, she goes after the theoretical issues that have occupied her imagination over the course of her career: the intricate relationship (unnoticed or even denied by many) between scholastic logic and medieval literature, the shifting boundary between philosophy and theology in the medieval schools, the deep intellectual connections between historical periods that have often been studied in isolation from one another. Her prolific scholarship, especially her large studies of Peter Lombard and early cholasticism and the Stoic tradition in the Middle Ages, have earned her a special place among her peers.

One of the most remarkable aspects of this life of ideas is the extent to which it has been an ongoing quest. Colish gained the respect of historians of philosophy early in her career with her dissertation, a study of medieval sign theory that ranges from Augustine to Dante. This study was published by Yale University Press in 1968 as *The Mirror of Language: A Study in the Medieval Theory of Knowledge* and republished in a revised second edition by the University of Nebraska Press in 1983. Remarkably, Colish was not afraid to strike out in a new direction when, as a tenured full professor, she began the study of Greek in order to allow more sophisticated research into the Stoic tradition. The massive two-volume work that resulted from this new direction of research was *The Stoic Tradition from Antiquity to the Early Middle Ages* in two volumes: volume 1, *Stoicism in Classical Latin Literature,* and volume 2, *Stoicism in Latin Christian Thought through the Sixth Century.* Here, in typical Colish style, she took on the subject of the influence of Stoicism on Christian philosophy and theology and told the story in a far more thorough way than had ever been done before. Fearless launching into new areas of research, meticulous inquiry into tangled tales of intellectual history, and, above all, a clear vision of how the parts relate to become the whole—these are the Colish scholarly trademarks.

Marcia Colish was born in Brooklyn, New York, on 27 July 1937. In 1945 her family (consisting of parents and an older sister) moved to suburbia: Rockville Centre, Long Island. Colish attended public schools and South Side High School, from which she graduated in 1954. The Colishes were Jewish immigrants from somewhere in the Russian Empire (as Marcia Colish often explained, "Colish is an Ellis Island name") who valued education and professional careers. Colish's father was an orthodontist, and her only sibling, her sister Faith, became a corporate attorney in Manhattan. Colish comments, "[It was a] typical boring suburban upbringing. What was formative was that our parents encouraged us to do well in school, and to make use of the cultural opportunities of NYC which was thirty minutes away by train. There was never an issue of the appropriateness of higher, then still higher, education for my sister and me. I always liked school and when I got to my senior year in college and had to figure out 'what next?' realized that school was my natural habitat, so I went immediately to grad school without passing GO."[1]

Colish earned her B.A. at Smith College in 1958. Here she was particularly influenced by Sidney R. Packard, one of the last students of Charles Homer Haskins. Colish says: "It was he who got me excited about the Middle Ages and it was he who introduced me to medieval intellectual history (I had never heard of intellectual history before then). By the end of my sophomore year, I was hooked."[2] In Colish's memory Packard and almost all of the professors at Smith took their women students very seriously and imparted to them the confidence to go ahead in academic fields. The exception to this was the noted medievalist Eleanor Shipley Duckett, already retired, whom Colish met only once in her years at Smith. Duckett was, ironically, less than encouraging about graduate study for women! Colish found Smith to be the "natural habitat" she had expected: "I should add that, at the time, for Smithies there were a variety of ways to be OK—being social, being athletic, being creative, being a do-gooder, being political. Being a scholar was one of them. I got a lot of good vibes from classmates (although very few of them went directly on to graduate or professional school, and although the class before mine—1957—provided the database for Betty Friedan's *The Feminine Mystique*) as well as support from professors."[3]

This was a tumultuous period for medieval historians. Colish recalls the intellectual context:

> To put things into historical perspective, it is worth recalling that this was the 1950s, the high tide of the "revolt of the medievalists" when Renaissance scholars were being put on the defensive and medievalists thought they were fighting the good fight and proving that the Dark Ages was a myth. In that context as well I came to two conclusions, which time has only strengthened: first, that one has to be trained in an interdisciplinary

manner in order to do medieval anything, and second, that much of the garbage the medievalists and Renaissance scholars were flinging at each other's periods stemmed from their mutual ignorance: in order to do either period well one has to know both of them, which was what I determined to do even as an undergraduate. Mr. Packard possessed, and impressed on me, the ability to achieve a sympathetic understanding of positions and thinkers whether or not one agrees with them. I also noted that his name was always that of the first borrower on the library cards of the medieval books on the new book shelf in the library. In any event I ended up taking all his courses and doing my honors thesis with him and seeking his advice about graduate programs. I would have to put him way ahead of anyone else in terms of making me what I am today.[4]

From Smith, Colish went to Yale to study medieval and Renaissance history. Here she was one of a cohort of students who went on to distinguished careers, including Miriam Chrisman, Robert Walton, Richard Marius, John Headley, Francis Oakley, and Ann Weikel. From the same workshop, so to speak, but in a slightly later generation, were Diane Owen Hughes and Edward Peters. This group of intellectual comrades, perhaps even more than the professors, made Yale an intellectually formative time: "Grad school professors were supportive too. It was actually in grad school that I was happiest, up to that time, since I was hanging out with fellow-students who all had the same intellectual commitments and values that I did. These folks have proven to be my most enduring friends, cycling and recycling themselves into my life in unexpected and wonderful ways."[5]

It was also at Yale that Colish made the decision to further explore the spiritual side of her intellectual fascinations by being baptized and received into the Roman Catholic Church. Here, too, she encountered the single most important scholarly work she read as a student, M.-D. Chenu's "Grammaire et theologie au 12e siècle," a chapter in his *La Theologie au 12e siècle*. This really gave her the idea for her dissertation and inspired her even longer running interest in medieval semantic theory that informs her work in an ongoing way. Also, it could be said that, in terms of her academic career, this focus labeled her as a forerunner of the "linguistic turn" when it became fashionable and so, as Colish notes, "did me [her] no harm professionally."[6]

Colish received an M.A. at Yale in 1959 and began her doctoral work with Roland Bainton, the famous historian of Reformation thought. On a personal level Colish's first *Doktorvater*, Roland Bainton, made a strong impression. She says: "[Bainton influenced me] not particularly in the sense of subject matter or methodology. Rather in the way he had a truly universal sympathy, in the Rankean sense. He could truly suspend his own likes and dislikes and get into the head of thinkers in the past, grasping their ideas and viewpoints and expressing them sympathetically. On another level, he was a model to emulate for the clarity of his writing, however abstruse the subject, and his ability to pitch his style to his audience at whatever level, from scholarly peers to the annual show on the New Haven TV, Luther's Christmas sermon for children."[7]

When an illness in Bainton's family made working with him rather difficult, Colish switched advisers and finished her dissertation with the very young Jaroslav Pelikan. Pelikan proved to be a excellent academic mentor for Colish, a historian of ideas who, like her, ranges from the patristic period to the early modern period and gives close attention to the intersecting and overlapping currents of intellectual thought, as he showed in his five-volume history of Christian doctrine, published decades later. Colish says that she found herself in agreement with the treatment of tradition in Pelikan's oeuvre, but as she never took classes with him, his influence "was an ex post facto thing."[8] Marcia Colish received her Ph.D. from Yale in 1965.

Of course, the years of Colish's college and graduate education predated feminism in the academy. Nevertheless, she had a lot of positive support from her professors, especially from Packard, who, she says, was "a feminist avant la lettre.... [H]e thought the seven sisters were the only places where women could get a first-rate Ivy League education, and he thought they deserved it. Further, he kept trying to get students to write research papers on women's history, to my knowledge getting no takers during my college years."[9]

But when she went on the academic job market, Colish did meet some of the prevailing attitudes toward women. In her first year of interviews, at the American Historical Association in 1960, a senior professor at a large university (she says she disremembers which) remarked to her that his school did not hire women, on principle. In typical Colish style she understood this as more their problem than hers: "Deplorable as that was, I have to add that these were the days of the old boy network and folks at Yale of either sex were part of it; all my coevals got good jobs, one woman even at Yale."[10]

Colish also had no trouble finding an academic position. She taught at Skidmore College for one year (1962–63) and in 1963 went to Oberlin College as an instructor in history. When she finished her Ph.D. in 1965, she was promoted to a tenure-track assistant professor position. The majority of her teaching career was at Oberlin: she was promoted to associate professor with tenure in 1969, appointed a professor in 1975, and held the chair named for her distinguished predecessor, Frederick B. Artz, from 1985 until her retirement in 2001.

It is perhaps the greatest irony of Marcia Colish's academic career that she spent over thirty years teaching undergraduates at Oberlin College, so she never had the opportunity to develop her own school of doctoral students. During this time she did teach other people's graduate students, including serving on exam and dissertation committees and teaching graduate seminars at Yale, as she would again in 2003. In fact, as her academic fame grew, Colish had several offers from schools with graduate programs where she could have had her own doctoral students. But she always chose to stay at Oberlin. In this too she was emulating her mentor, Sidney Packard, who was a leading expert on Norman pipe rolls. Packard's work was significant, Colish says, because:

He added to what was known about the contents of the Normal pipe rolls and the operation of the Norman Exchecquer, specifically on the eve of the loss of Normandy to France. The main available documentation until them consisted of Thomas Stapleton's edition. The MSS Packard found, edited, and commented on bring to light a number of things: financial debts owed by a variety of Normans, some biggies some not, the itineraries of King John and William Marshal between April 1202 and June 1203. Even more important was the discovery that the Norman Exchecquer was dependent on the English Exchequer. This was the beginning of a major revisionist handling of the whole question of what the Normans brought to England in the Conquest. The reigning orthodoxy was that they had developed a precocious centralized ducal government as well as a highly coherent and regulated feudalism, and that these institutions were imposed on the conquered Anglo-Saxons. Nowadays, historians do not think that the Norman situation was as crystallized as all that but much more fluid. Rather, what the current consensus view sees as happening is that, given the situation of the Conquest, with William I able to decide what to keep of the Anglo-Saxon system, what to junk, what to import from Normandy and how to shape it up, William and his immediate successors were in a position to develop the precocious centralization and monetarization of government much faster than anyone else. And, given the need to raise funds from England with this new, efficient system in place, in order to deal with their continental problems, they continued to turn the crank in England leaving the governments of their continental lands more or less as they had been. As for Normandy, the eventual shaping up of its ducal institutions was a reimportation back from England of administrative methods already far ahead in England. Up to the point of the French conquest of Normandy in 1204, Norman financial administration had thus come to resemble England's more closely that was the case with any two other regimes. So I think we can say that Packard's findings constituted the beginning of the turn away from the orthodoxy of the day re Norman-to-English influence toward the more recent and current view that re fiscal administration, the flow was English-to-Norman.[11]

When Packard won an honorary degree from the University of Caen, he could have moved to a research university, but he decided to stay at Smith. The gratitude with which Colish tells this story of early influence by a truly first-rate scholar of the Middle Ages could be echoed by the many Oberlin students of the second half of the twentieth century who had the pleasure of knowing her, and of whom I am one. Even at a school that treasures and encourages excellent scholar-teachers, many of whom are famous for their rapport with a lively and unconventional student body, Colish stood out for her energy, intellectual acuity, sparkling wit, and surprisingly offbeat humor. Her sophisticated wisecracks about the most surprisingly arcane and erudite subjects, delivered with complete nonchalance and a marked New York accent, were famous in our generation. "Medieval dualism," Colish would say, "can be understood as taking place in two modes: the express train or the scenic route." Or, talking about the child of Heloise and Abelard, she said, "And they named him 'Astrolabe'... which is a bit like naming a child 'Nosecone' today." (I must confess that I have shamelessly stolen this one for my own teaching, bringing the name up to date from decade to decade: "Mainframe," "Quark," "Microchip.") And then, when our class elected her as the faculty member we wanted to hear give a collegewide lecture (for the required weekly chapel service, more like a culture requirement even then), she came up with an attack on the simplification of difficult ideas and titled it "Mental Slenderella," a term many of us immediately appropriated for our own working vocabulary.

Colish is a world-class lecturer, using language in such an interesting admixture of the elegant and the colloquial. The brisk pace with which her lectures unfolded also gave rise to student legends about the Colish boot camp of intellectual history: "Drop a pencil," I was solemnly warned, "and you lose a decade." But as another former student, Lynn Walterick, recalls:

> Though certainly she proceeded at headlong pace, she was incredibly careful, indeed thoughtful, with her locutions and her presentation; in no way did she simply motor-mouth undifferentiated facts in a dizzy and unmemorable way. Her lectures were the antithesis of unmemorable. I think Marcia is, in an abiding way, a performer. She knew when she got off a good one, she knew how to deploy her sentences and shape her pronouncements (and that they were!): she'd deliver a zinger, and then pause ever so briefly... and this incredible smile would absolutely transform her face... fast as lightning but warm as the sun... and then off she'd go, shaping the next part of the performance.[12]

Here, too, Colish took a leaf from her undergraduate mentor, Sidney Packard, about whom she says, "He was a consummate lecturer who had his material down cold and who constructed a lucid and elegant lecture every time, landing that baby at the exact moment before the end of the class period. His star turn was an illustrated lecture on the Bayeux tapestry, which he allowed me to sit in on in my junior and senior years. On doing so, although I had thought the lecture perfect when I first heard it as a sophomore, I realized that he constantly kept his lectures up to date."[13] This would be a familiar description to Oberlin students of "Miss Colish," as we called her. However much we enjoyed the zip and the humor of her classroom style, it was well known among Oberlin students that Colish was demanding of the highest levels of concentration and sophisticated thinking. She expected from her students the clarity and precision for which she is so justly famous.

Nothing shows the success of Marcia Colish's teaching at Oberlin more clearly than the list of students who passed through her classes and are now professional medievalists: just to name a few and in no particular order, Gillian Alghren, Ray Clemens, Barbara Newman, Christopher Baswell, Katherine Tachau, and myself. These are only some of the Oberlin students who, inspired by the combination of Colish in history, Grover Zinn in religion, and Robert Longsworth in English, went on to graduate study and academic careers. But many other Oberlin students were also deeply marked by their intellectual exchanges with Colish. For example, Lynn Walterick, now an independent literary editor, summarizes Colish's influence on her life:

> Over the years, anyone who has come to know me at all well has sooner or later (and it's usually been sooner) heard all about the remarkable Miss Colish. In her I saw, perhaps for the first time, how multifaceted the intellectual life can be: substance AND style, brilliance AND hilarity, intensity AND kindness. There's a phrase I've always remembered from the end of "A Midsummer Night's Dream," when Hippolyta is describing the story everyone has told of that topsey-turvey [sic] night in the forest: it makes "something of great constancy," she says. And that just about captures Marcia for me: her great—and unforgettable—constancy, which certainly made a difference in how I've looked at the world.[14]

The cult of Marcia Colish, then, was by no means limited to young medievalists.

Perhaps like all accomplished academics, Colish is a person of subtle contradictions: the consummate New Yorker who spent decades in northern Ohio or the elegant dresser among the fuzzy throng of Oberlin students. Walterick remembers a story Colish told us one year, probably about 1970, after she returned from a research trip to Rome:

> She was going to the Vatican Library to do research one summer day, and as usual she was all dolled up in some outfit, and up she zoomed to the gates, briefcase in hand, presenting herself for entrance as Scholar Colish. And the Swiss Guards gave her to understand that no ladies wearing miniskirts would be admitted to the Library. She was completely indignant but couldn't persuade them that she wasn't wearing a miniskirt. So off she zoomed to the nearest newsstand, and bought a copy of Vogue or some such, and zoomed back to the Guards, magazine open to an appropriate page of miniskirted models. "ECCO!" she says to them: "THIS [tapping the magazine] is a miniskirt. THIS [tapping her own hem] is not...." And in she went.[15]

Colish was as cosmopolitan in her personal life, even in Oberlin, as she was in her academic choices. For a number of years she served as the advisor to the Oberlin Catholic Student Association, attending our (sometimes strange but always aesthetically interesting) liturgies in Fairchild Chapel and serving as a model of a Catholic Christian adult amid the restless secularity of the Oberlin student world. In terms of sheer style, she made a big impression: She drove a Peugeot when almost no one in this country did. She cooked us undergraduates dishes we did not know, like saltimbocca alla Romana, and gave us Frascati to drink, observing that "it didn't travel very well from Italy, but . . ." Her students responded with typically inane undergraduate humor: one April Fools' issue of the *Oberlin Review* sent her up as "Marcia Cooldish," who sternly reuked a colleague for a sexist remark at a faculty meeting.[16] We were young, we were gauche, but we knew that Colish was cool, a model of an intellectual adult that we might aspire to emulate.

Much of Colish's scholarly life is enviable. With the support of fellowships from the National Endowment for the Humanities, the American Council of Learned Societies, the John Simon Guggenheim Memorial Foundation, and Oberlin College (which acknowledged their star medieval historian with ten travel grants), Colish traveled throughout Europe and the Mediterranean world, working in manuscript libraries and visiting the sites of her scholarship and teaching. These experiences were often brought back into the classroom; for example, she always delivered her famous lecture on the pilgrimage to Santiago de Compostela (easily as excellent and famous as Packard's lecture on the Bayeux tapestry) wearing the silver shell that she had earned as a pilgrim on the route.

Years of leave for research also took her far and wide, to almost every research institute and think tank available to humanists: the American Academy in Rome (1968–69); the Institute for Research in the Humanities at the University of Wisconsin (1974–75); the National Humanities Center (1981–82); Cambridge, Massachusetts, where she was a visiting scholar at Harvard University and the Weston School of Theology (1982); the Institute for Advanced Study at Princeton (1986–87); the Woodrow Wilson Center in Washington, D.C. (1994–95); and the Rockefeller Foundation's Villa Serbelloni in Bellagio, Italy (1995). To this list should be added the honors given to Colish by the Yale University Graduate School Alumni Association, which awarded her the Wilbur Cross Medal in 1993, and the Medieval Academy of America, which named her a fellow in 1988 and gave her the prestigious Haskins Medal in 1998 for her book *Peter Lombard*. Always an active participant in professional associations, Colish has served on several committees of the American Historical Association and was the president of the Medieval Academy of America in 1991–92.

But, of course, more than her students' fond stories or the many honors accorded her, it is Colish's five books that constitute her ultimate legacy. Each one of these is a tour de force of scholarship, marked by the precision, clarity, and synthesis that are her intellectual trademarks. After her first book, *The Mirror of Language,* Colish worked for nearly two decades on her study of Stoicism, a two-volume work of nearly eight hundred pages. *The Stoic Tradition from Antiquity to the Early Middle Ages* was published by Brill in 1985 in two volumes, *Stoicism in Classical Latin Literature* and *Stoicism in Latin Christian Thought through the Sixth Century.* Some might argue that this remarkable study is the magnum opus of Colish's career; although her book on Peter Lombard could also be considered a candidate for this honor. In the years between the first and second book, while studying Greek and extending her mastery of medieval philosophy, Colish also published twenty articles, some in the top journals in the field such as *Speculum, Renaissance Quarterly,* and *Traditio.*

In 1994 Colish published the other book that may be considered her magnum opus, the book that won her the Haskins Medal of the Medieval Academy, her two-volume study of the early scholastic thinker Peter Lombard. *Peter Lombard* (also published by

E. J. Brill) is an excellent example of Colish's academic interests, the result of many years of thinking about the importance of the *early* scholastics. Her intuition was that these figures were most important for the development of the scholastic method but had been largely ignored in favor of serious study of the towering figures of later Scholasticism such as Bonaventure and Thomas Aquinas. Through her work on the Lombard, Colish has become interested in the gloss on the *Sentences,* by Pseudo-Peter of Poitiers. She has collected all the microfilms of the various redactions of this text and hopes to find a collaborator, preferably one in Europe, with whom to work on a critical edition

Colish's most recent book, *Medieval Foundations of the Western Intellectual Tradition, 400–1400,* is the medieval volume of the Yale Intellectual History of the West. It has been very successful; it is already available in an Italian translation, and a Polish translation is forthcoming. This work could only have been written by someone who had spent decades thinking about medieval thought and culture and explaining it to others. For one who knew Colish as a teacher, it offers many familiar echoes. It is interesting to note that the historical contours of this book are similar to those of Colish's first book, *The Mirror of Language,* beginning with the so-called Patristic period and ending with the so-called Renaissance. What is different is the far broader cultural portrait Colish paints in this book: she includes portraits of Byzantium, Islamic and Jewish civilization, the world of courtly love literature, mysticism, devotion and heresy (including medieval women writers), and economic and political theory. It is very fitting that this book has been translated into Italian under the title *La cultura del medioevo (400–1400),* for it truly is a cultural history and perhaps best shows how Colish's conception of intellectual history has changed over the years. Like her undergraduate mentor, Sidney Packard, she never tells the story in quite the same way. One of the most interesting themes of this book is the demolition of the idea of a "medieval synthesis" ending in the so-called thirteenth, greatest of centuries, substituting alternative story lines.

In the course of almost four decades of scholarship and teaching, Marcia Colish has, of course, also had to deal with the normal woes of human existence: two bouts with cancer, both successfully resolved, and the death of both her parents in one year. But whatever difficulty she has faced, she has always done so with energy, optimism, and a deep religious faith, the Colish characteristics that made such an impression on her students. When she retired from Oberlin in 2001, the symposium organized in her honor featured Oberlin graduates from the 1960s to the late 1980s, all with Ph.D.s and academic positions, presenting a series of papers on as broad a range of topics as one could imagine, but all intellectually connected to their experience with Marcia Colish.

Colish now lives in Guilford, Connecticut, in a condominium overlooking the salt marshes that she bought years before her retirement. From here she has easy access to the libraries and academic community of Yale, where she has contact with faculty and students. She has been a visting fellow in the Yale history department and was a visiting professor in 2003, when she taught two graduate seminars. Naturally, she has a new research project, a book tentatively titled "Ambrose's Patriarchs," which explores the common themes linking four treatises by Ambrose, one on each of the patriarchs Abraham, Isaac, Jacob, and Joseph. Each of these works was intended for a different didactic purpose, but altogether, Colish believes, it is possible to see the outlines of Ambrose's main preoccupations: spiritual, ethical, and political. This is exactly the sort of study only someone like Colish would think of doing, putting together seemingly disparate treatises to make a coherent whole.

Other recent work, including, "Remapping Scholasticism," the Gilson Lecture at the Pontifical Institute of Medieval Studies at Toronto in 2000 and "Haskin's *Renaissance* Seventy Years Later: Beyond Anti-Burckhardtianism," forthcoming in the *Haskins Society Journal*, could be said to represent her latest ideas on the subject of the road map, the turning points and landmarks in it, and its eventual destination(s).[17] These pieces show how the debates about periodization that characterized the field Colish was attracted to forty years ago are still under discussion. Of course, Colish will be a part of that ongoing discussion. If it is true, as it is often said, that we just become more ourselves as we get older, then the Marcia Colish of her retirement years will be even more incisive, more interested in showing intellectual connections, more non-judgmental and even-handed in evaluating intellectual trends in medieval and early-modern Europe than her work has already shown her to be. And this will be, as Colish was wont to say way before Martha Stewart took over the expression, "a good thing."

NOTES

1. E-mail from Marcia L. Colish to E. Ann Matter, 10 July 2002.
2. Ibid.
3. Ibid.
4. E-mail from Marcia L. Colish to E. Ann Matter, 5 July 2002.
5. E-mail from Marcia L. Colish to E. Ann Matter, 10 July 2002.
6. E-mail from Marcia L. Colish to E. Ann Matter, 14 January 2002.
7. Ibid.
8. Ibid.
9. E-mail from Marcia L. Colish to E. Ann Matter, 5 July 2002.
10. Ibid.
11. E-mail from Marcia L. Colish to E. Ann Matter, 9 August 2002. See also *Miscellaneous Records of the Norman Exchecquer, 1119–1204,* ed. and commented by Sidney R. Packard, Smith College Studies in History, vol. 12, nos. 1–4 (Northampton, Mass.: Dept. of History of Smith College, 1926–27) and *Magni rotuli Scaccarii Normanniae sub regibus Angliae,* ed. Thomae Stapleton. (London: sumptibus Soc. antiq. londiniensis, 1840–44). For more recent scholarship that shows the impact of Packard's work, see David Charles Douglas, *William the Conqueror: The Norman Impact Upon England* (Berkeley: University of California Press, 1964), and David Bates, *Normandy before 1066* (London: Longman, 1982).
12. E-mail from Lynn K. Walterick to E. Ann Matter, 8 July 2002.
13. E-mail from Marcia L. Colish to E. Ann Matter, 5 July 2002.

14. E-mail from Lynn K. Walterick to E. Ann Matter, 9 July 2002.
15. E-mail from Lynn K. Walterick to E. Ann Matter, 8 July 2002.
16. Dennis Filter, "GF Committee to Study Grievance Procedure," *The Oberlin Review*, 99, no. 44, Tuesday, 13 April 1971, 1, 8.
17. Colish's Gilson lecture was published in 2000 as *Remapping Scholasticism*.

Select Bibliography of Works by Marcia L. Colish

"The Mime of God: Vives on the Nature of Man." *Journal of the History of Ideas* 23 (1962): 3–20. Reprinted in *Race, Gender, and Class: Early Modern Ideas of Humanity*, ed. Maryanne Cline Horowitz, 321–38. Rochester: University of Rochester Press, 1992.

The Mirror of Language: A Study in the Medieval Theory of Knowledge. New Haven: Yale University Press, 1968. 2nd. rev. ed., Lincoln: University of Nebraska Press, 1983.

"A Twelfth-Century Problem." *Apollo* 87, n.s., 77 (1968): 36–41.

"Eleventh-Century Grammar in the Thought of Saint Anselm." In *Arts libéraux et philosophie*, Actes du IVme congrès international de philosophie médiévale, Montréal, 27 août–2 septembre 1967, 785–95. Montréal: Institut d'Études Médiévales; Paris: J. Vrin, 1969.

"The Idea of Liberty in Machiavelli." *Journal of the History of Ideas* 23 (1971): 323–50. Reprinted in *Renaissance Essays* 2, ed. William J. Connell, Library of the History of Ideas, 10. 180–207. Rochester: University of Rochester Press, 1993; and in *Great Political Thinkers: Machiavelli*, ed. John Dunn and Ian Harris (Aldershot, Eng.: Edward Elgar Publishing, 1997), 2:559–86.

"Peter of Bruys, Henry of Lausanne, and the Façade of Saint-Gilles." *Traditio* 28 (1972): 451–60.

"The Roman Law of Persons and Roman History: A Case for an Interdisciplinary Approach." *American Journal of Jurisprudence* 19 (1974): 112–27.

"Avicenna's Theory of Efficient Causation and Its Influence on Saint Thomas Aquinas." In *Tommaso d'Aquino nel suo settimo centenario*, Atti del congresso internazionale, Roma-Napoli, 17–24 aprile 1974, vol. 1: *Tommaso d'Aquino nella storia del pensiero*, 296–306. Napoli: Edizioni Dominicane Italiane, 1975.

"Medieval Allegory: A Historiographical Consideration." *Clio* 4 (1975): 341–56.

"Saint Thomas Aquinas in Historical Perspective: The Modern Period." *Church History* 44 (1975): 433–49.

"Seneca's *Apocolocyntosis* as a Possible Source for Erasmus' *Julius Exclusus*." *Renaissance Quarterly* (1976): 361–68.

"Cicero's *De Officiis* and Machiavelli's *Prince*." *Sixteenth-Century Journal* 9 (1978): 81–93. Reprinted in *Great Political Thinkers: Machiavelli*, ed. John Dunn and Ian Harris, 2:205–17. Aldershot, Eng.: Edward Elgar Publishing, 1997.

"Saint Augustine's Rhetoric of Silence Revisited." *Augustinian Studies* 9 (1978): 15–24.

"Pauline Theology and Stoic Philosophy: An Historical Study." *Journal of the American Academy of Religion* 47, supplement (1979): B 1–21.

"The Stoic Hypothetical Syllogisms and Their Transmission in the Latin West in the Early Middle Ages." *Res Publica Litterarum* 2 (1979): 19–26.

"Historical Writing Then and Now: Against Exegesis." *Book Forum* 5 (1980): 270–78.

With Harold D. Woodman and Mildred Alpern. "Three Notes on the Relationship between Writing and Teaching History." *The History Teacher* 13 (1980): 543–60.

"Cosmetic Theology: The Transformation of a Stoic Theme." *Assays* 1 (1981): 3–14.

"John the Scot's Christology and Soteriology in Relation to His Greek Sources." *Downside Review* 100 (1982): 138–51.

"Saint Anslem's Philosophy of Language Reconsidered." In *Anselm Studies,* vol. 1, edited by Gillian R. Evans, 113–23. London: Kraus International, 1983.

"The Stoic Theory of Verbal Signification and the Problem of Lies and False Statements from Antiquity to Saint Anselm." In *Archéologie du signe,* edited by Lucie Brind'Amour and Eugene Vance, 17–43. Toronto: Pontifical Institute of Mediaeval Studies, 1983.

"Carolingian Debates over *Nihil* and *Tenebrae:* A Study in Theological Method." *Speculum* 59 (1984): 757–95.

"Teaching and Learning Theology in Medieval Paris." In *Schools of Thought in the Christian Tradition,* edited by Patrick Henry, 106–24. Philadelphia: Fortress Press, 1984.

The Stoic Tradition from Antiquity to the Early Middle Ages. Vol. 1: *Stoicism in Classical Latin Literature;* Vol. 2: *Stoicism in Latin Christian Thought through the Sixth Century.* Studies in the History of Christian Thought, 34. Leiden: E. J. Brill, 1985. Paperback reprint with addenda and corrigenda, Leiden: E. J. Brill, 1990.

"Another Look at the School of Laon." *Archives d'histoire doctrinale et littéraire du Moyen Âge* 53 (1986): 7–22.

"Gilbert, the Early Porretans, and Peter Lombard: Semantics and Theology." In *Gilbert de Poitiers et ses contemporaines: Aux origines de la logica modernorum,* edited by Jean Jolivet and Alain de Libera, 229–50. Napoli: Bibliopolis, 1987.

"Systematic Theology and Theological Renewal in the Twelfth Century." *Journal of Medieval and Renaissance Studies* 18 (1988): 135–56.

"Augustine's Use and Abuse of Tyconius." In *A Conflict of Christian Hermeneutics in Roman Africa: Tyconius and Augustine,* edited by Wilhelm Wuellner, 42–48. Berkeley, Calif.: Center for Hermeneutical Studies, 1989.

"Early Porretan Theology." *Recherches de théologie ancienne et médiévale* 46 (1989): 58–79.

"Cicero, Ambrose, and Stoic Ethics: Transmission or Transformation?" In *The Classics in the Middle Ages,* edited by Aldo S. Bernardo and Saul Levin, Medieval and Renaissance Texts and Studies 69, 95–112. Binghamton, N.Y.: Medieval and Renaissance Texts and Studies, 1990.

"Mathematics, the Monad, and John the Scot's Conception of *Nihil.*" In *Knowledge and the Sciences in Medieval Philosophy,* Proceedings of the Eighth International Congress of Medieval Philosophy, Helsinki, 24–29 August 1987, 2:455–67. Helsinki: Publications of the Luther-Agricola Society, 1990.

"From *sacra pagina* to *theologia:* Peter Lombard as an Exegete of Romans." *Medieval Perspectives* (1991): 1–19.

"The Neoplatonic Tradition: The Contribution of Marius Victorinus." In *The Neoplatonic Tradition: Jewish, Christian and islamic Themes,* edited by Arjo Vanderjagt and Detlev Pätzold, 57–74. Köln: Jürgen Dinter, 1991.

"*Quae hodie locum non habent:* Scholastic Theologians Reflect on Their Authorities." In *Proceedings of the PMR Conference* 15, edited by Phillip Pulsiano, 1–17. Villanova, Penn.: Augustinian Historical Institute, 1991.

"Die Neoplatoonse traditie: Die bijdrage van Marius Victorinus." In *Philosophen in actie,* edited by Theo A. F. Kuipers, translated by Lodi Nauta, 223–39. Delft, Neth.: Eburon, 1992.

"Peter Lombard and Abelard: The *Opinio Nominalium* and Divine Transcendence." *Vivarium* 30 (1992): 139–56.

"Peter Lombard as an Exegete of Saint Paul." In *Ad litteram: Authoritative Texts and Their Medieval Readers,* edited by Mark D. Jordan and Kent Emery Jr., 71–92. Notre Dame, Ind.: University of Notre Dame Press, 1992.

"*Psalterium Scholasticorum*: Peter Lombard and the Development of Scholastic Psalms Exegesis." *Speculum* 67 (1992): 531–48.

"Stoicism and the New Testament: An Essay in Historiography." In *Aufstieg und Niedergang der römischen Welt,* edited by Wolfgang Haase, 2:26:1, 334–79. Berlin: Walter de Gruyter, 1992.

"*Habitus* Revisited: A Reply to Cary Nederman." *Traditio* 48 (1993): 77–92.

"From the Sentence Collection to the *Sentence* Commentary and the *Summa*: Parisian Scholastic Theology, 1130–1215." In *Manuels, programmes de cours et techniques d'enseignement dans les universités médiévales,* edited by Jacqueline Hamesse, 9–29. Louvain-la-Neuve, Belg.: Institut d'Études Médiévales, 1994.

"Intellectual History." In *The Past and Future of Medieval Studies,* edited by John Van Engen, 190–203. Notre Dame, Ind.: University of Notre Dame Press, 1994.

Peter Lombard. 2 vols. Brill's Studies in Intellectual History, 41. Leiden: E. J. Brill, 1994.

"The Development of Lombardian Theology, 1160–1215." In *Centres of Learning and Location in Pre-Modern Europe and the Near East,* edited by Jan Willem Drijvers and Alasdair A. MacDonald, 207–16. Leiden: E. J. Brill, 1995.

"Early Scholastic Angelology." *Recherches de théologie ancienne et médiévale* 62 (1995): 80–109.

Section editor. "Medieval Europe: Church and Intellectual History." In *American Historical Association Guide to Historical Literature,* edited by Mary Beth Norton and Pamela Gerardi, 3d. ed., 1:621–24, 675–703. New York: Oxford University Press, 1995.

"Christological Nihilianism in the Second Half of the Twelfth Century." *Recherches de théologie ancienne et médiévale* 63 (1996): 136–45.

"The Virtuous Pagan: Dante and the Christian Tradition." In *The Unbounded Community: Papers in Christian Ecumenism in Honor of Jaroslav Pelikan,* edited by William Caferro and Duncan G. Fisher, 43–91. New York: Garland, 1996.

Medieval Foundations of the Western Intellectual Tradition, 400–1400. The Yale Intellectual History of the West. New Haven: Yale University Press, 1997. 2nd printing, 1998. Paperback edition, 1999. Translated into Italian under the title *La cultura del medioevo (400–1400),* trans. Elisabetta Gallo, Le vie della civiltà (Bologna: Società editrice il Mulino, 2001). Polish translation forthcoming.

"The Sentence Collection and the Education of Professional Theologians in the Twelfth Century." In *The Intellectual Climate of the Early University: Essays in Honor of Otto Gründler,* edited by Nancy van Deusen, Studies in Medieval Culture, 39, 1–26. Kalamazoo, Mich.: Medieval Institute Publications, 1997.

"Machiavelli's *Art of War*: A Reconsideration." *Renaissance Quarterly* 51 (1998): 1151–68.

"Peter Lombard." In *Routledge Dictionary of Philosophy,* edited by Edward Craig, 5:821–22. London: Routledge, 1998.

"Re-envisioning the Middle Ages: A View from Intellectual History." In *The Future of the Middle Ages and the Renaissance: Problems, Trends, and Opportunities for Research,* edited by Roger Dahood, Arizona Studies in the Middle Ages and Renaissance, 2, 19–26. Turnhout, Belg.: Brepols, 1998.

With Nancy van Deusen. "*Ex utroque et in utroque: Promissa mundo gaudia, Electrum* and the

Sequence." In *The Place of the Psalms in the Intellectual Culture of the Middle Ages,* edited by Nancy van Deusen, 105–38. Albany: State University of New York Press, 1999.

"Peter Lombard." In *Dictionary of Biblical Interpretation,* edited by John H. Hayes, 2:273–74. Nashville, Tenn.: Abingdon Press, 1999.

"Republicanism, Religion, and Machiavelli's Savonarolan Moment'" *Journal of the History of Ideas* 60 (1999): 597–616.

Introduction to *Medieval Scholarship: Biographical Studies on the Formation of a Discipline,* vol. 3, *Philosophy and the Arts,* edited by Helen Damico, 3–12. New York: Garland, 2000.

Remapping Scholasticism. Etienne Gilson Series, 21. Toronto: Pontifical Institute of Mediaeval Studies, 2000.

"Peter Lombard." In *The Medieval Theologians,* edited by G. R. Evans, 168–83. Oxford: Blackwell, 2001.

CHAPTER 72

My Life and Works (1941–)

CAROLINE WALKER BYNUM

I OFTEN THINK we might gauge cultural change best simply by asking how people at various points in the past would have answered the question: "Who are you?" For the answer—the wife of Livius, the man of Guillaume, a servant of God, an Englishman, a butcher, a sinner, an employee of General Motors, a woman—takes us deep into social structure, values, and culture. It matters then that my answer to this question—and not only for the purposes of this essay—can be: I am a historian of the religion and culture of western Europe in the period between the principate of Augustus and the Council of Trent.

But what does *that* mean as an answer? One elaboration might be: I am the author of a set of books on the European Middle Ages. For surely, taken together, the contents of these books reflect what I "do," although at first glance their range may seem less to provide a definition than to suggest an almost dilettantish curiosity. Nonetheless it is a place to start. What then have I done in my books? What do they suggest I am?

The first, *Docere Verbo et Exemplo: An Aspect of Twelfth-Century Spirituality,* dealt with ideas of edification in treatises of spiritual advice written by and for members of twelfth-century male religious orders. A doctoral dissertation that never quite grew up into a book, it nonetheless grappled with large issues of how self-conscious ideas about community relate to institutional structure, how ideals are passed on in socialization, how and whether one person can actually affect the fundamental values of another. In other words, what does it mean to teach? It attempted to devise a method of probing texts—their silences and slippages as well as their explicit agendas—to find places where groups with a shared heritage might reveal differences in basic assumptions. Then came *Jesus as Mother,* a series of essays, the most influential of which

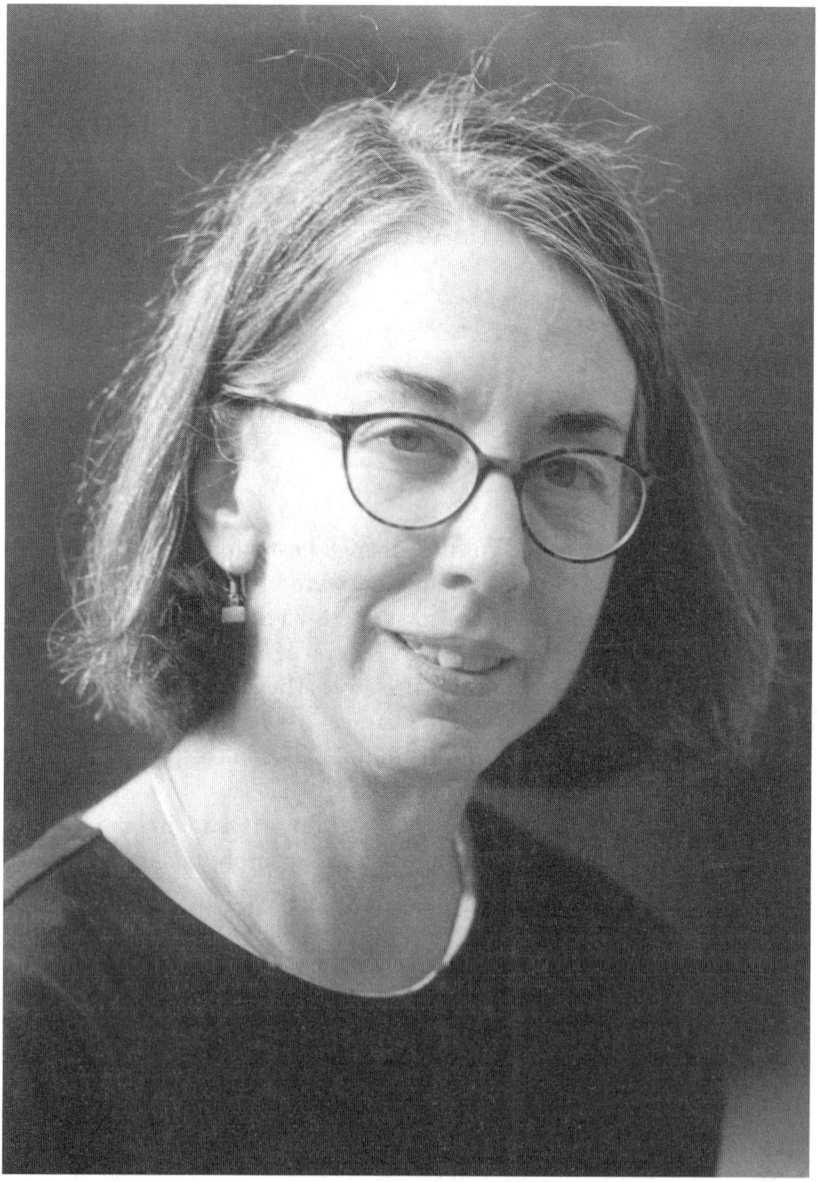

focused on the use of maternal and female images in the religious writing of the twelfth and thirteenth centuries done by both women and men. And then *Holy Feast and Holy Fast: The Religious Significance of Food to Medieval Women,* not—despite the title—so much about food as about women's religiosity. Rejecting both a long and misogynistic tradition of denigrating women's religious writing and a rather simplistic tendency, characteristic of the 1970s, to assume a "female" need for "female" images, it attempted a structural analysis of the characteristics of the surviving literature by and about women's piety, contrasting that structure to the structures of men's writing and practices and embedding female religiosity in the gender expectations and the religious practices of the society. Often paired with Rudolph Bell's *Holy Anorexia,* it was in fact an argument against isolating a single aspect of religious practice such as food abstention both from other food practices (such as the Eucharist, food multiplication miracles, food distribution, etc.) and from other forms of denial and celebration (such as extreme asceticism or mystical ecstasy).

Half a decade later *Fragmentation and Redemption,* another set of essays, explored the assumptions about body and person behind the female piety studied in *Holy Feast and Holy Fast.* And in 1995 *The Resurrection of the Body* tackled one of the basic assumptions of Western eschatology: the expectation (found in rabbinic Judaism and Islam as well as in Christianity) that the body returns at the end of time. Analyzing texts of mainstream (and very difficult) theologians from the patristic period to the early fourteenth century, I attempted to employ the same method of reading for slippage, silence, and metaphor I had used in *Docere Verbo et Exemplo;* then, not content with abstruse texts and offbeat readings, I also insisted that both explicit theology and implicit assumptions should be embedded in social practices concerning death, burial, and access to divine power. The result: a difficult book. But behind the complex method was a simple observation: if the body comes back—indeed must come back—then the person is not an immortal soul but a psychosomatic unity. Conventional condemnation of the Western tradition as dualist—a condemnation obsessively repeated in modern textbooks both conservative and poststructuralist—is hence fundamentally off-base. Not only were medieval attitudes—both folk and philosophical—not body-hating; they also lead pressingly, perhaps unavoidably, to current questions about personal identity, including questions about the basis and construction of gender.

Most recently another collection, *Metamorphosis and Identity* (published June 2001), explores twelfth- and thirteenth-century ideas of change itself. How can something change and remain the same thing? Why did medieval thinkers care so much about the answer? Concerned with stories and techniques of metamorphosis, these essays diagnose a resistance to change at the heart of exactly those new discourses (such as alchemy, werewolf tales, Ovid commentary, treatises on spiritual growth, eucharistic theology) that explore it.

Hence the topic of my most recent scholarly work is identity itself—the question that must be addressed by any autobiographer. Is there then any identity behind my own metamorphoses? A perduring self behind my history? One way of answering this would be to see whether any set of concerns ties the books together. And upon only a little reflection, I find it easy to tell the story of my scholarship this way.

The treatises I studied in *Docere Verbo et Exemplo* seemed to me to betray an acute anxiety about the exercise of authority in community, and to my surprise the male authors in question articulated their anxiety in complex female images. The title essay of the collection *Jesus as Mother* was simply a presentation of this surprised observation, but the essay raised further questions, for studying female images used by men led me quite naturally to ask whether and how cloistered women used such images. The comparison proved anything but simple, however; women did use the images differently, but the significance of the contrast was not easy to assess. Male and female roles do not provide equal access to power; hence women's differing use of gendered symbols and images reflects the whole sex-gender system—but how exactly does it reflect women's attitudes and assumptions? There seemed to be something wrong about assuming that gender was best explored through looking at gendered imagery or at explicit theories about gender. *Holy Feast and Holy Fast* arose then from the simpler and more basic question: What were the dominant images of religious writing by and about women? It was an empirical question. And the answer was also a simple one: food. But the ramifications of taking food practices seriously in all their manifestations and trying to embed them in their social context led me inexorably (or so it seemed) to the study of body—not only as concept or image but also as lived, for the birthing, lactating, fertile female body *was* food, as was, of course, the body of God. I came to see corporeality, lived bodiliness, as the heart of women's piety, not only (or primarily) because women were conceptualized by medical, theological, philosophical, and spiritual discourses as especially bodily but also because somatic phenomena (such as stigmata and other exudings, ecstatic states and encounters, miracles in which the Eucharist appeared as the human Christ, etc.) were central to what women were described as doing and what they said themselves. Body seemed, for the women I was reading, a means of access to God and glory as well as a venue for self-control. Far from a soul-body split, what I found was a complex understanding of psychosomatic person. Thus, the sense I discovered in medieval piety of women's corporeality led, in the essays of *Fragmentation and Redemption,* to a study of body itself. If body is crucial to person, if it is the locus of religious approach and a partner in moral failure, then the markers body carries—sex, race, beauty, and so on—must in some way be essential to self. Raising this question led me to engage with, and disagree with, certain feminist notions of body as trap and of Christianity as inherently dualist but also with certain other feminist notions of body as empowerment. But above all it led me to write the *Resurrection of the Body*—an exploration of the profound paradox that must rest at the heart of a religion in which body is central to person yet hope resides finally in the stability and permanence of *requies aeterna.* If self is psychosomatic and (because somatic) particular (that is, sexed, colored, aged, right- or left-handed, tall, etc.), how can it be eternal (that is, either perfected or unchanging)? If body is crucial to person, if indeed matter (the principle of potency that makes it possible for a thing to become another thing) is necessary in a world of existing substances, how can anything perdure through time? *The Resurrection of the Body* was a historical argument about changing conceptions of the body that returns, and I explored those changes through a close examination of images and texts—a method of the sort I had developed already in *Docere Verbo et Exemplo* and *Jesus as Mother*. But just as the food of *Holy Feast and Holy Fast* led to body, so the body of *Resurrection* led to the question of survival through change—the crucial ontological question itself. How can anything at all be? Hence, most recently *Metamorphosis and Identity*.

Both in method and in substance certain concerns link my graduate student days in the 1960s to the present moment in the new millennium: obsession with the question of individual identity (to which questions concerning body and gender are crucial), a conviction that binaries and dualisms fail fundamentally to capture the basic issues of the Western intellectual tradition, a stubborn commitment to beginning historical inquiry with the specific language (the arguments, analogies, images, borrowings, and silences) of texts rather than employing the popular pointillist approach of constructing a general picture of society illustrated by textual examples. But there are two obvious problems with the way I just told my own story. First, I—even the academic I—am not my books. Ever since as a rather bossy nine-year-old I organized my sister, the cat, and the eight-year-old twins from across the street into my "classroom," teaching has been my primary love and overriding commitment. From the things I have chosen to do with my life, I can see that some basic need to communicate and share what I was learning drove me from long before I was certain what that learning was. I worked with autistic children in the Massachusetts Children's Hospital when I was an undergraduate and tutored retarded teenagers while I was in graduate school. In an almost insanely naive belief that an Ivy League institution in the early seventies could be pushed to welcome women scholars, I organized the Women's Faculty Group at Harvard while I was an assistant professor there and subsequently, at considerable personal cost but with heady determination, led the Committee on the Status of Women—a committee that failed completely (in the short run) to effect reforms. I moved to Seattle in part because I had ascertained that I could adopt a child as a single parent there (something I did not think would be possible in the mid-1970s in Cambridge, Massachusetts). In 1993–94 I took on the job of Dean of General Studies at Columbia—a position that appealed to me exactly because "GS" is the college for nontraditional students (single mothers, adults who have made radical career changes, folks with—in some cases—the liability of academic failure behind them).

And there is a second problem with my opening story. It is internalist intellectual history. The limits of such an approach are today obvious. I can describe the course of my work over the past forty years as the story of one idea or methodological conundrum leading to another: the topic of the individual in community leads to that of male anxiety, which leads in turn to a need for female comparisons, which comparison leads on to body and identity; a concern with the metaphor of a seal in wax as an image of socialization leads to a concern with the metaphor of reassemblage of particles as an image of resurrection. But ideas do not grow inexorably from other ideas; approaches do not blindly drive curiosity. Even if I can find a perduring intellectual self through the changing ideas, that self had an inception in family and society and was pushed by social context at every twist and turn. The point seems almost too obvious to state. But a noninternalist story is far harder to tell. Aware of a flood of recent work on autobiography and memory as well as of postmodern suspicion of authorship, whether of texts or of lives, how can I say what was crucial about my own formation? Why did I become a medievalist—a historian of Europe's remote past? Why did questions of identity, gender, and community rather than questions of power, status, and the economy animate me? Why, in a graduate school environment where anthropology was the chic alternative and social history the rage, did I cling so to texts and language? When metaphysics (not to mention God) was dead and class conflict the fall-back explanation, why did ontology engage me? Why did paradox, not binary opposition, seem both my preferred mode of discourse and the key to much past thought as well? It is easy to see how the ways in which I did not fit my environment led to my troubles settling on an undergraduate major and later on a dissertation topic. (More than once as an undergraduate I found my papers marked with "A+ but this isn't history!!") But why didn't I fit my cohort? And in what ways did I, of course, fit perfectly well?

Even if I understood more than I do, I could not here tell my whole story. So I have chosen to focus on two points in the life cycle that perhaps explain some of the themes that tie together the intellectual biography I fashioned above: my childhood and the period of my early thirties.

I was born in Atlanta, Georgia, in 1941, six months before Pearl Harbor. Four aspects of my childhood in particular seem to me now to have shaped the course my intellectual life took. The first is World War II. My earliest memories—those somatic, atemporal memories of early childhood in which objects seem to exist outside time and space—are related to the war: my father's air-raid warden's helmet; the little American flag I was given to carry up and down the street outside my house, reciting, along with other neighborhood children, "The war is over, the war is over"; a ration card my mother clutched as she waited in line at the butcher's. My earliest exposure to adulation was my father's for FDR; the earliest example cited to me of evil was the Holocaust; my first uneasy awareness of the psychological phenomenon I came later to understand as rationalization was my parents' defense of Hiroshima.

Europe shadowed my early years. My mother's closest friend in graduate school had been English; we sent her food during the war (I can just remember helping to pack the boxes), and after it was over, she sent us cartons of wonderful British children's books to say "thank you." (Hence I grew up in a world where sweaters were "jumpers," car hoods "bonnets," and there was a real possibility one might suddenly discover one was descended from an earl or a baron.) High culture for my parents was European; the basic moral challenges were posed by European experiences. Although the Atlanta in which I grew up was preintegration, deep South, and like every middle-class white child, I was cared for in part by a black maid, the real issue of "otherness" in my childhood was Jewishness. I think I was almost adolescent before I was really aware of segregation. Anti-Semitism impinged much earlier. My first close friend was Jewish and told me seriously that one should take only tub baths because gas might come out of showerheads. It was not long before I began to feel in some obscure way ashamed of inconsistencies and nastinesses in the Christianity I learned in Sunday school. I remember feeling not only angry but in some way at fault when I was told by the other children in third grade that I couldn't have Michael Bass (I still recall his name) as a boyfriend because he was Jewish. References to the guilt of the Jews in the Maundy Thursday liturgy troubled me from the time I was old enough to attend, all the more so because I suspected (perhaps unfairly) that my parents might defend such references if I admitted that I noticed.

Even more than the distant shadow of Europe, Christianity loomed over my childhood. Themselves the children of devout and racist southern Protestants, my parents had flirted with atheism while doing graduate study in the north only to adopt the Episcopalianism of upwardly mobile southerners when they returned to Atlanta and their first child was born. To my mother then, trapped increasingly in the suburban housewife role of the late forties and fifties, Christianity took on a consuming importance, justifying what she perceived to be the necessary renunciation of much that she craved. She demanded a matching commitment to Christianity from her children.

Church was a requirement I experienced as both burden and liberation. Like any child raised in a liturgical tradition, I early acquired a sense of language as something almost tangible in its reliability; the rhythms of the *Book of Common Prayer* were something one could lean on, roll in, masticate as well as sing. But religion was a source of guilt as well; it required a purity of mind of which I was totally incapable and a conviction of one's own rectitude that I found untenable and uncharitable. At the same time, however, religion was a place where one could raise questions never permitted in school. Christ not only told his disciples to turn the other cheek; he also threw the moneychangers out of the temple. It was Job, with his insistence that there is no justice, who received an answer from God, even though that answer, adducing hippopotami and whales, left something to be desired in philosophical coherence. There seemed to be something in the very contradictions I encountered that went beyond either aesthetics or sanctimony. A bright but timid child, I was quiet and incurious during my first few years of school. In church I was somehow intellectually alive. I didn't exactly pray there, and I was certainly never "saved." But I think I sometimes philosophized.

Christianity and Europe. Two shaping forces. But there was also, of course, the South. For I was southern on both sides almost as far back (it wasn't far) as anyone could remember. Although my father came from a poor mining town in northern Alabama and his father had only an eighth-grade education, there was talk that my paternal grandmother was related somehow to Light-Horse Harry Lee. My mother's father was a country doctor in the Shenandoah Valley of Virginia, and her mother (whose father was only a conductor on the local railroad) had vast and stultifying social pretensions. Although it was never clear who exactly in her family had fought in the War between the States, she collected old cannon balls with fervor and took more pride in her membership in the United Daughters of the Confederacy than in her role as soloist in the Baptist choir. Southern clans are full of secrets; southerners talk with silences. "Yes, maybe" sometimes indicates a categorical "no"; a certain sort of smile means "I totally disagree." I was a teenager before I was fully aware that the issue of race lay like a gigantic fault line under family conversations and family gatherings. I was nearly adult before I had any idea how much it cost my parents to challenge inherited assumptions about race or understood the depth of meaning behind my father's repetition of what I thought was only a book title, "You can't go home again."

It is often said that medieval Europe has affinities with the antebellum South, and such affinity is sometimes adduced to explain the fact that there are rather a large number of American medievalists with southern roots. This may be so. But I attribute not so much my medievalism as my historicism to my southern past. In my childhood still the past lay heavy on the American South—the only region of the country to have lost a war, the only defeat in American history to have been "deserved" and "good." In such an environment the past is insistent, as fact and as moral challenge. How could one's own grandparents believe in such wrong? I do not think I was drawn to the Middle Ages by any felt analogies between Fulk Nera of Aquitaine and Simon Legree, or between Scarlett O'Hara and Eleanor of Aquitaine. The Atlanta of my childhood had no special affinity with that of *Gone with the Wind*. But I am certain I became a historian because of my southern roots and that I have always heard the emptinesses and slippages, and the assumptions, of texts so loudly because, as a quiet and observant child, I heard around me such complex, communicative, and ambivalent silences.

But if my childhood was framed by region, religion, and world-historical events, it was also, like all childhoods, shaped by family. As an English teacher, my father was exempt from the draft, and, when I was very small, he became the surrogate parent for an entire neighborhood of children whose fathers were off at war. My house hosted the neighborhood Christmas party; my father took the children of the entire block trick-or-treating at Halloween. Sometimes withdrawn and awkward with adults, because of a continuing depression that perhaps foreshadowed the early-onset Alzheimer's he would suffer in middle age, he was to children a magic parent—attentive, funny, and full of stories.

Nonetheless it was my tense, intellectual mother who was the weight in my heart, whose ambivalences and enthusiasms became my own. She had grown up as an only child in a small Virginia town, pushed by an unloving mother toward social ambitions she never shared. After undergraduate study at Hollins and an M.A. at the University of Virginia, she horrified her parents by becoming engaged to a tractor salesman. Her bargain then: she'd give up the engagement if her parents would pay for her to go to Harvard and get a Ph.D. instead. To my grandmother it was the lesser of two evils.

My mother received her degree in the bottom of the Depression, with a dissertation on the problem of nonbeing in Plato's *Parmenides,* written for Raphael Demos and Alfred North Whitehead; she married a fellow graduate student and returned to the South.

My father's salary as a teacher of English at Georgia Tech was not high. Academic salaries were meager in the forties. We lived in a lower-middle-class neighborhood on the edge of a far wealthier Jewish community. (Part of my early fascination with Judaism was clearly owing to the fact that the intellectuals and cosmopolitans I encountered as a child were for the most part Jewish.) It was a neighborhood of stay-at-home mothers; housework, even when supported by black maids, was still backbreaking labor. My mother made our clothes, ironed far into the night, cooked produce my father grew in the back garden. Her frustration was palpable. The slap of an iron on an ironing board still sounds to me angry. When her second child was born and she decided to give up her job at Georgia State College for Women to do what both she and my father felt was right—stay home with the children—she burned all her notes from graduate school in a fierce and self-punishing act of renunciation. I grew up with a sense, learned partly from my father, that high-achieving women were peculiar and threatening, that there was something shameful about my mother's academic past. I also grew up with a sense, learned from her, that to be female is to make acts of sacrifice and self-denigration. And yet she had inner resources beyond those I encountered anywhere else. I knew that, much as she loved me, she would never simply "let" me win an argument; even in trivial things, she held to truth. Much of my adolescence was devoted to trying to best her at something. If my father's rather commonsense curiosity about his region led me eventually toward history, my mother's skill at philosophical argument pointed me there also, but by a circuitous route. For the argument from historical context turned out to be my first successful weapon against her absolutism and analytical power. The one adolescent retort I could muster to which she had no answer (and I was a southern daughter, so retorts were always made somewhat obliquely) was simply: you think that because you grew up in Virginia in the 1910s, because you're a woman, because you went to Harvard, because you're a mother, and so on. History became my weapon of choice. But even then, the targets against which I brandished it were almost always philosophical.

As I said earlier, I cannot tell my whole life story: adulthood is a long time. I am sixty-three, and I have been many different selves. But if I search for a turning point in which the course was somehow set, I think I find it in the early 1970s, and so I have chosen that as the other long moment about which to speak.

I received my Ph.D. in 1969 from Harvard, submitting my dissertation on the very day students occupied University Hall to protest ROTC on campus. I became an assistant professor as much by accident as by recruitment. Like the other students with top records in the department, I had been offered an instructorship in history; when the university abolished the instructor rank, they had no choice except to fire us or promote us. They did a little of both, but I survived. With the university blowing up around me, I set out to teach, to mentor, and—noticing somewhat belatedly the absence of women—to organize pressure to increase their numbers. I am a little old to claim true sixties membership, but I too was propelled forward by a sixties sense of optimism and responsibility, of rebellion and relevance. I marched in the streets of Boston and sobbed my way through "We Shall Overcome." The night LBJ announced that he would not run again, I swarmed into Harvard Square with thousands of others, embracing and crying, certain we had changed the world.

By the mid-seventies things were different. In 1971 my first marriage ended in an acrimonious divorce. In the spring of 1973 I was not promoted by the Harvard history department. The following fall, my closest friend was murdered by a rapist. And the long shadow of my father's Alzheimer's (a new disease in those days, one that seemed shameful as well as horrible) fell across the entire half-decade. Despite successes in teaching, despite vigorous political work heading the Committee on the Status of Women, despite a position I was lucky enough to land at the Harvard Divinity School in which promotion might have come, I was lonely; my work had gone stale; I felt as mute as I had in kindergarten, when it seemed that talents totally different from mine were required. I mourned for my marriage; I mourned for my friend; I mourned for my father. The Committee on the Status of Women had written a magnificent report (the prose was mostly Michael Walzer's), but there were still hardly any women at Harvard. (Eleven out of six hundred faculty members in 1972 were female; all were in the untenured rank.) I was uncomfortable with the sexual politics at the Divinity School, where I was sexually harassed (I had no language with which to label the phenomenon in those days) by several colleagues. I knew I needed to leave, but leave-taking is hard. I had heard the news of Kennedy's assassination in the Smythe Classical Library while reading Bede's *Ecclesiastical History;* I had read *Piers Plowman* for the first time cuddled in a blanket on the banks of the Charles River in springtime; passionate discussions with undergraduates over Plotinus as well as over Marxism were forever associated in my mind with the Dunster House dining room. My past—who I *was*—seemed inscribed on the very bricks and mortar of Harvard buildings. Because the world of Cambridge was increasingly for me empty of people, it was hard to think of leaving place.

But in 1976 I left. I moved to the University of Washington in Seattle. That very summer, with unpacked boxes all around me, I wrote the article that became the title essay of *Jesus as Mother,* and I filed papers to adopt a child as a single parent. Immediately I knew the decision was right. The radical break—leaving Harvard, leaving the East, putting behind me the noise and ambition and sexism of an elite private university—gave me back myself.

Hence, if the roots of my historical sense and of my constant engagement with ontology lie in my childhood, my preoccupation with change and identity may have a more recent impetus. To move from one coast to another with only a cat for company is not really such a radical change, but to my thirty-five-year-old self it felt momentous; it took courage. My Harvard colleagues had after all advised against it. But in Seattle I was once again productive, energetic, intellectually curious.

The lessons of my new life were freeing ones and other than I had anticipated. One could change and remain the same. Some of my keen sense of the way objects and bodies carry self was honed by that move. It was in Seattle that I realized how a table and a kitten rooted me in a continuing self, kept me every day the same, far more than a stream of memories that pointed only backward. Just as the father I was losing to an insidious disease was in some way still present in the slant of an eyebrow, the quirk of a smile, although he no longer remembered his daughter, so I carried in my body who I was, although there was no one on the West Coast to provide the corroboration of a common past. Not only *Jesus as Mother* but also *The Resurrection of the Body* and *Metamorphosis and Identity* were born in that summer of unpacking, as I shed Harvard, took on the Pacific Northwest, and thought about change.

I have omitted much in even the moments I have touched on: the struggle to learn languages, the inspiration of teachers, the dawning of feminism in my consciousness and that of my generation, and above all the books that changed my life—Augustine when I was seventeen, M.-D. Chenu when I was twenty-four, Peter Brown and Mary Douglas a little later, Bernard of Clairvaux, Bernard Williams, and Ovid later still. And I have left the story since 1976 untold except insofar as my own academic work gives glimpses. But I have covered enough, I think, to suggest a pattern—an identity, so to speak, behind the metamorphoses.

I will not sum up. Lives, like history itself, have no summation. Bodies endure, I think, but their stories are neither linear nor simple. The story I have told about myself, my family, my generation, my region, could be told in another way. If it ends with a kind of happiness, that is only a matter of my choice of where to end it. In the introduction to *Fragmentation and Redemption* (1991), I spoke of the historian's stance as "the comic mode." Writing at the height of the "linguistic turn"—historians' postmodernism—I stressed the perspectival and the partial. But what I said a decade ago about history strikes me as still true today—and not only about history but about lives and life stories as well.

> [T]he comic is not necessarily the pleasant, or at least it is the pleasant snatched from the horrible by artifice and with acute self-consciousness and humility. In comedy, the happy ending is contrived. Thus, a comic stance toward doing history is aware of contrivance, of risk. It always admits that we may be wrong. A comic stance knows that there is, in actuality, no ending (happy or otherwise)—that doing history is, for the historian, telling a story that could be told in another way. For this reason, a comic stance welcomes voices hitherto left outside, not to absorb or mute them but to allow them to object and contradict. Its goal is the pluralistic, not the total. It embraces the partial as partial. And, in such historical writing as in the best comedy, the author is also a character. Authorial presence and authorial asides are therefore welcome; methodological musing . . . is a part of, not a substitute for, doing history.[1]

If I close by quoting myself, it is not arrogance, I hope, nor creative exhaustion, but rather a final assertion both that there is a perduring self behind all the changes of a life (I still think what I thought ten years ago!) and that that self is always seen from a particular place and moment. Ask me in ten years, and I'll tell you a different story. But it will still be one shaped by a southern girlhood, a stay-at-home mother, a European war, the including and excluding red brick walls of Harvard, sunsets over Puget Sound, and the ideas of medieval theologians.

Notes

A somewhat different version of this essay appeared as "Curriculum Vitae: An Authorial Aside," *Common Knowledge* 9.1 (winter, 2003): 1–12.

1. Bynum, *Fragmentation and Redemption*, 25.

Select Bibliography of Works by Caroline Walker Bynum

Docere Verbo et Exemplo: An Aspect of Twelfth-Century Spirituality. Harvard Theological Monographs. Missoula, Mont.: Scholar's Press, 1979.

Jesus as Mother: Studies in the Spirituality of the High Middle Ages. Berkeley: University of California Press, 1982.

Editor with Stevan Harrell and Paula Richman. *Gender and Religion: On the Complexity of Symbols.* Boston: Beacon Press, 1986.

Holy Feast and Holy Fast: The Religious Significance of Food to Medieval Women. Berkeley: University of California Press, 1987.

Fragmentation and Redemption: Essays on Gender and the Human Body in Medieval Religion. New York: Zone Books, 1991.

The Resurrection of the Body in Western Christianity, 200–1336. New York: Columbia University Press, 1995.

Editor with Paula Gerson. *Body-Part Reliquaries. Gesta* 36, no.1 (1997).

Editor with Paul Freedman. *Last Things: Death and the Apocalypse in the Middle Ages.* Philadelphia: University of Pennsylvania Press, 2000.

Metamorphosis and Identity. New York: Zone Books, 2001.

Works Cited

Bell, Rudolph. *Holy Anorexia.* Chicago: University of Chicago Press, 1985.

List of Contributors

Michael Adams is professor of English at Albright College. Like Margaret Ogden, he graduated from the University of Michigan, where he served as an assistant on the staff of the *Middle English Dictionary*. He is editor of *Dictionaries: Journal of the Dictionary Society of North America* and has been named the next editor of *American Speech*, beginning in 2006. He is the author of *Slayer Slang: A "Buffy the Vampire Slayer" Lexicon* (2003).

Levon Avdoyan received his doctorate from Columbia University in Ancient history and in Armenian Studies. He has served as the classics, Byzantine, and medieval studies specialist at the Library of Congress from 1982 until 1992, when he moved to his present position as that institution's Armenian and Georgian specialist.

Constance Hoffman Berman is professor of history at the University of Iowa–Iowa City. She is the author of three books—*Medieval Agriculture, the Southern French Countryside, and the Early Cistercians* (1986), *The Cistercian Evolution: The Invention of a Religious Order in Twelfth-Century Europe* (2000), and *Women and Monasticism in Medieval Europe: Sisters and Patrons of the Cistercian Order* (2002)—and numerous articles.

Elaine C. Block spent most of her academic career at Hunter College–City University of New York, where, among other projects, she developed courses in art and civilization offered jointly by Hunter College and the Metropolitan Museum of Art. As professor emerita she divides her time between Paris and New York, focusing on the study of medieval misericords. She has recently published *Corpus of Medieval*

Misericords in France (2003), coedited a bilingual book, *Les Stalles de la Cathedrale de Rouen: Histoire et iconographie* (2003), and coedited *Lexicon for Medieval Choir-Stalls* (2004).

Julia Boffey studied English at Cambridge before going on to graduate work at York and subsequently to teach at Queen Mary, University of London. Most of her published work is on Middle English verse and its manuscripts. She has recently collaborated on a revision of *The Index of Middle English Verse*.

Joyce Boro did her graduate work in English at Oxford University and she is now an Assistant Professor of Medieval and Early Modern English literature at Université de Montréal. She has published several articles on Lord Berners and early Tudor romance and her edition of Berners's *Castell of Love* will be published in 2005. She is currently writing a book on the reception of medieval Spanish romance in Early Modern England.

Marie Borroff retired in 1994, after teaching thirty-five years at Yale. She has written on language and style in *Sir Gawain and the Green Knight* and in the poetry of Frost, Stevens, and Moore. Her translations of *Gawain, Pearl,* and *Patience* were published in one volume in 2001. Since then, she has completed translations of *Cleanness* and *St. Erkenwald*. A collection of her essays, *Traditions and Renewals: Chaucer, the Gawain-Poet, and Beyond*, appeared in 2003. She spends her summers in Maine.

Christine Bromwich, née Shire, graduated from York University in 1967 with a degree in English, Allied literature (Russian, French, or Italian), and education. Her interest in countries emerging from colonial domination came from Helen Roe's talks about the long history of Anglo-Irish relations. Her teaching has included classes for refugees and teaching English as a second or other language in the United Kingdom as well as over twenty years of teaching English as a foreign language to adults, in Iraq, Nepal, Yemen, China, and Ireland.

Elizabeth A. R. Brown has taught at Harvard University, the City University of New York, L'École des hautes études en sciences sociales, New York University; and Yale University. She has served as president of the Fellows of the Medieval Academy of America (1997–99). Her most recent book is *Saint-Denis, la basilique* (2001).

Phyllis R. Brown, associate professor in English and the Program for the Study of Women and Gender and chair of her department at Santa Clara University, has published articles on Anglo-Saxon poetry, Hrotsvit of Gandersheim, Heloise, Guillaume de Machaut, and Louise Labé and coedited the three volumes of *Women Writing Latin: From Roman Antiquity to Early Modern Europe* and *Hrotsvit of Gandersheim: Contexts, Identities, Affinities, and Performances*.

Mitzi M. Brunsdale is professor of English at Mayville State University, Mayville, North Dakota. She has published over fifty scholarly essays and six books, among them, *Sigrid Undset: Chronicler of Norway* (1988), *Dorothy L. Sayers: Solving the Mystery of Wickedness* (1990), *James Joyce: The Short Fiction* (1993), *James Herriot* (1996), and *A Student Companion to George Orwell* (2000). She is currently at work on *A Biographical Dictionary of Fictional Detectives*.

Charles S. F. Burnett is professor of the history of Islamic influences in Europe at the Warburg Institute in London. Recent books include *The Introduction of Arabic Learning into England* (1997) and the coedited *Scientific Weather Forecasting in the Middle Ages: The Writings of Al-Kindi* and *Abū Ma'šar on Historical Astrology: The Book of Religions and Dynasties* (both 2000).

Caroline Walker Bynum is professor of European medieval history at the Institute for Advanced Study in Princeton and University Professor emerita at Columbia University in New York City, where she was the first woman University Professor. She is a specialist in religious and intellectual history of the later Middle Ages. Her books, from *Jesus as Mother* (1982) to *Metamorphosis and Identity* (2001), have dealt with women, gender and the history of the body.

Jane Chance is professor of English and the study of women and gender at Rice University and author or editor of nineteen other books, including *Woman as Hero in Old English Literature* (1986), *Medieval Mythography*, volumes 1 and 2 (1994, 2000), and *Gender and Text in the Later Middle Ages* (1996). She edits three series, the Boydell and Brewer Library of Medieval Women, the Greenwood Guides to Historic Events in the Medieval World, and the Praeger Series on the Middle Ages.

Marjorie McCallum Chibnall is a fellow of Clare Hall-Cambridge and an honorary fellow of Girton College, Cambridge. Her publications include *The Ecclesiastical History of Orderic Vitalis* (ed. and trans., 1969–80); *The Empress Matilda* (1991); *The Normans* (2000); and *Piety, Power, and History in Medieval England and Normandy* (2000).

Nicola Coldstream is an architectural historian of the thirteenth and fourteenth centuries. Educated at Cambridge University and the Courtauld Institute of Art, London, she taught medieval art history for many years before becoming deputy editor of the Grove Dictionary of Art (1996). Her books include *Masons and Sculptors* (1991), *The Decorated Style: Architecture and Ornament, 1240–1360* (1994), and *Medieval Architecture* (2002).

Carolyn P. Collette is professor of English language and literature on the Alumnae Foundation at Mount Holyoke College, where she holds the Alumnae Association Chair and also chairs medieval studies. Her recent publications include *Species,*

Phantasms, and Images: Vision and Medieval Psychology in the Canterbury Tales (2001) and "The Matter of Armenia in the Age of Chaucer" (in *Studies in the Age of Chaucer*, 2001).

Julie Crosby completed her Ph.D. at Columbia University in May 2002, under the guidance of Joan Ferrante. Her dissertation, "Divas of the Dark Ages: Women and Early Medieval Drama," is presently being prepared for publication.

David Day holds a J.D. degree from the University of Houston and a Ph.D. in English from Rice University. He has published several articles on legal issues in *Beowulf* and is currently lecturer in literature and communications in the School of Human Sciences and Humanities at the University of Houston–Clear Lake.

Anne Reiber DeWindt received her Ph.D. from the University of Toronto in 1972. Her research interests have focused on the social history of the medieval English village and small town. She has been a history instructor at Wayne County Community College in Detroit, Michigan, since 1970. Her book on the monastic town of Ramsey, coauthored with Edwin B. DeWindt, will be published soon.

Mary Dockray-Miller is an associate professor of English at Lesley University in Cambridge, Massachusetts. She is the author of *Motherhood and Mothering in Anglo-Saxon England* (2000) and coauthor of *Integrative Group Treatment for Bulimia Nervosa* (2002).

A. S. G. Edwards is professor of English at the University of Victoria. He is currently completing (with Julia Boffey) a *New Index of Middle English Verse*. He is coeditor of *English Manuscript Studies 1100–1700*, a member of the editorial boards of *Middle English Text* and *The Book Collector*, and on the council of the Scottish Text Society. He has been a Guggenheim fellow and a fellow of the Society of Antiquaries.

Deanna Delmar Evans, professor of English at Bemidji State University, has published in *Studies in Scottish Literature, Neophilologus, Medieval Feminist Newsletter*, and other journals. She has written biographical entries for the *Dictionary of Literary Biography, Catholic Women Writers*, and other reference volumes. Recently she edited "The Babees Book" for *Medieval Literature for Children* (2003).

Jennifer FitzGerald is an Honorary Senior Research Fellow of the School of English, Queen's University, Belfast, and currently Adjunct Faculty in the Department of Women's Studies, San Diego State University. Her most recent publications are on Toni Morrison and Helen Waddell. She is currently writing a critical monograph on the latter and editing the unpublished writings of Waddell and her friend Maude Clarke.

Ilene H. Forsyth is the Arthur F. Thurnau Professor of the History of Art, emerita, at the University of Michigan. She has also taught at the University of California–Berkeley,

Columbia University, Harvard University, and the University of Pittsburgh. She is author of *The Throne of Wisdom* (1972), *The Uses of Art: Medieval Metaphor in the Michigan Law Quadrangle* (1993) and numerous articles on such Romanesque sites as Moissac, Saulieu and Savigny.

Carmela Vircillo Franklin (classics department, Columbia University) specializes in medieval Latin texts and manuscripts. Most recently she wrote "Grammar and Exegesis: Bede's *Liber de schematibus et tropis*" (in *Latin Grammar and Rhetoric: Classical Theory and Medieval Practice*, ed., Carol D. Lanham, 2002); and *The Latin Dossier of Anastasius the Persian: Hagiographic Translations and Transformations* (2004).

Robyn Fréchet is an art historian in Paris, specializing in manuscript illustrations. Fréchet's book, in preparation, is titled "Lessons of Love according to Francesco da Barberino, Reading, Writing and Visualizing in Early Fourteenth century Northern Italy."

Rebecca L. R. Garber received her Ph.D. from the University of Michigan, taught at Wayne State University for three years, and authored *Feminine Figurae* (2003), an examination of representations of idealized female figures created by women religious. Currently she teaches at the Rudolf Steiner High School in Ann Arbor, maintains the German pages for the Online Reference Book for Medieval Studies, and is translating the sister-books for publication in the series Vox Mystica.

Ana M. Gómez-Bravo is an associate professor of Spanish at Purdue University. She has published on medieval rhetoric and poetics, late-medieval reading modes, and forms of authorship in fifteenth-century Iberia. Her first book was *Repertorio métrico de la poesía cancioneril castellana del siglo XV* (1998). She is currently working on a book on poetic practice and the interrelations of authorship, gender, and material and social culture.

Renate Haas is professor of English at the University of Kiel. She has published widely on English literature and the history of English studies. Together with Balz Engler (University of Basel), she has initiated the EHES project, which focuses on the history of English as a discipline in Europe.

Kevin J. Harty is professor and chair in the English department at La Salle University in Philadelphia. He is the author or editor of ten books, including *King Arthur on Film* (1999), *The Reel Middle Ages* (1999), and *Cinema Arthuriana* (2002). He studied paleography and Anglo-Norman at the University of Pennsylvania with Ruth J. Dean, who also served as a second reader for his dissertation, "The Apocalyptic Unity of the Chester Mystery Cycle" (1974).

John C. Hirsh is professor of English at Georgetown University. He works on Chaucer and late-medieval religion and literature and is the author of several books, including *Hope Emily Allen* (1988) and *The Boundaries of Faith: The Development and Transmission of Medieval Spirituality* (1996), which continues themes and studies begun by Hope Allen.

Shaun F. D. Hughes, associate professor of English at Purdue University, has published two previous articles on Elizabeth Elstob. His most recent work is "The Reemergence of Women's Voices in Icelandic Literature, 1500–1800," in *Cold Counsel: Women in Old Norse Literature and Mythology* (2002), and "Late Secular Poetry," in the *Blackwell Companion to Old Norse-Icelandic Literature and Culture* (forthcoming).

Penelope D. Johnson teaches medieval history at New York University. She is the author of *Prayer, Patronage, and Power: The Abbey of La Trinite, Vendome, 1032–1187; Equal in Monastic Profession: Religious Women in Medieval France;* and articles on women and monasticism. Currently she is working on issues of gender and language.

Irving A. Kelter is associate professor and chair of the history department at the University of Saint Thomas, Houston. He received his Ph.D. in history from the Graduate School of the City University of New York in 1989, where he served as Pearl Kibre's research assistant from 1976 until 1985. Among his published works are essays on early-modern cosmology and religion.

Elspeth Kennedy received her D.Phil. in modern languages from Oxford in 1951 and then taught French at the University of Manchester and served as a tutorial fellow at Saint Hilda's College, Oxford. She has published editions and monographs about the noncyclic prose romance of *Lancelot du Lac* and Geoffrey de Charny's *Book of Chivalry*. Now retired, she edited *Medium Aevum* from 1990–2002.

Deeana Copeland Klepper is assistant professor of religion at Boston University. Her work on Nicholas of Lyra and the Christian use of Hebrew and Jewish interpretative traditions in the later Middle Ages owes a great deal to Beryl Smalley's pioneering efforts.

Dickran Kouymjian holds the Haig and Isabel Berberian endowed professorship of Armenian Studies and is director of Armenian Studies, California State University, Fresno. He has taught at Columbia University and the University of California–Berkeley, and in Beirut, Cairo, Paris, and, on a Fulbright senior lecturership, Armenia. Among his dozen books is the coauthored *Album of Armenian Palaeography* (2002).

Henrietta Leyser, a fellow of Saint Peter's College, Oxford, came to Oxford in 1959 to read history at Saint Hilda's College, under the tutelage of Beryl Smalley. Her own work on medieval women and religion is deeply indebted to the imaginative vision and intellectual rigor of Beryl's training.

Meredith Parsons Lillich is professor of medieval art and architecture at Syracuse University. Her scholarly publications are on medieval stained glass, the arts of monasticism (particularly the Cistercians), and heraldry. Her most recent book is *Stained Glass before 1700 in the Collections of Upstate New York,* Corpus Vitrearum United States of America, part 2 (in press).

Kathryn L. Lynch is Katharine Lee Bates and Sophie Chantal Hart Professor of English at Wellesley College. She writes on the medieval dream vision, Chaucer, Shakespeare, and medieval cultural geography. Her most recent book is an edited collection of essays, *Chaucer's Cultural Geography* (2002).

Alfonso Maierù holds the chair in the history of medieval philosophy at the University of Rome "La Sapienza." He has published on medieval logic (*Terminologia logica della tarda scolastica,* 1972), on Dante, and on the universities and mendicant schools (*University Training in Medieval Europe,* 1994). He coedited *Studi sul XIV secolo in memoria di Anneliese Maier* (1981).

Janice Mann, associate professor of art history and assistant to the president at Bucknell University, researches Spanish Romanesque architecture and sculpture and the historiography of those fields. She is just completing *Frontiers and Identities: The History and Historiography of Romanesque Art in Eleventh-Century Christian Spain.*

E. Ann Matter is professor of religious studies at the University of Pennsylvania. She teaches and writes on the history of Christian culture in the medieval and early-modern periods. She has recently edited and translated the *Revelations* of Lucia Brocadelli, the court prophet of sixteenth-century Ferrara, and is at work on a study of Maria Domitilla Galluzzi, a seventeenth century Italian visionary.

Jo Ann McNamara is a historian, professor emerita from Hunter College and the Graduate Center of the City University of New York. She has published extensively on subjects related to medieval women, particularly religious women. Her most recent book is *Sisters in Arms: Catholic Nuns through Two Millennia* (1996).

Gerald Morgan (b. 1935) graduated from Cambridge University in English and from Oxford in Celtic Studies. After many years as a high school principal in Wales, he moved sideways into academia to teach Welsh history and culture at the University of Wales, Aberystwyth. He has written numerous books and articles, many in Welsh, including *A Welsh House and Its Family: The Vaughans of Trawsgoed* (1997), and edited *Nanteos: A Welsh House and Its Families* (2001).

Deborah Nelson-Campbell has taught in the Department of French Studies at Rice University since 1974. She is the author of two critical editions, *The Songs Attributed to Andrieu Contredit d'Arras* (1985) and *The Lyrics and Melodies of Adam de la Halle* (1990), as well as a critical bibliography of Charles d'Orléans (1992). Her most recent book is *The Journals of Tommie L. Hubbard: Life in Madison County, Kentucky, 1898–1900* (2003).

Rory O'Farrell graduated in mathematical science from University College, Dublin. He has worked as a photographer, a designer, and a builder of early microcomputers, specializing in graphics. Long involved in Irish antiquarian studies, he prepared an exhibition, *Monuments in Danger,* for the Royal Society of Antiquaries of Ireland. As an illustrator of antiquarian publications, including those of Helen Roe, he chairs the board of trustees of the Cambrian Archaeological Association.

Patricia R. Orr took her doctorate at Rice University in medieval history, specializing in English medieval legal history. She is a visiting professor at the University of Houston and Houston Baptist University. Her publications include works on women's activities in medieval English courts of justice.

Catherine Parsoneault is a program director in the Division of Universities and Health-Related Institutions of the Texas Higher Education Coordinating Board. She received her Ph.D. in musicology from the University of Texas at Austin in 2001, with a dissertation titled "The Montpellier Codex: Royal Influence and Musical Taste in Late Thirteenth-Century Paris." She is at work on a lengthier biography of Yvonne Rokseth.

Russell Poole is professor of English at the University of Western Ontario. His publications include *Viking Poems* (1991), *Skaldsagas* (edited volume, 2000), and numerous articles on medieval topics, along with studies on medievalism and on women's education as depicted in Victorian fiction.

Marjorie Ethel Reeves was born in 1905 in Wiltshire, England, and passed away in 2003, while this collection was in production. A medieval historian and a fellow and vice principal of Saint Anne's College, Oxford University, she had numerous publications to her credit, including two major works on Joachim of Fiore and a third coauthored with historian Warwick Gould. She was an elected fellow of the British Academy, and in 1996 she was appointed Commander of the British Empire for her service to history.

Christine M. Rose is professor of English at Portland State University. She is coeditor, with Elizabeth Robertson, of *Representing Rape in Medieval and Early Modern Literature* (Palgrave, 2001) and has published on Chaucer—especially "The Man of Law's Tale"—and medieval manuscripts. She is currently working on a book about medieval conduct manuals for women.

Michelle M. Sauer is assistant professor of English at Minot State University, Minot, North Dakota. Her edition of the *Wooing Group and A Discussion of the Love of God* is forthcoming. Her other publications cover the areas of anchoritism, mysticism, asceticism, Church history, and queer theory.

Elizabeth Scala is associate professor of English at the University of Texas at Austin. She is the author of *Absent Narratives, Manuscript Textuality, and Literary Structure in Late Medieval England* (2002). Her essay in this volume is part of a book in progress titled "Edith Rickert and the Community of Academic Women at the University of Chicago, 1896–1936."

Jana K. Schulman is associate professor in English at Western Michigan University. Her interests include Old English and Old Icelandic literature, language, and law. She has edited the *Rise of Medieval Europe, 500–1300 A.D.* (2002) and published "Hrotsvit and the Germanic Warrior Hero" (in *Germanic Notes and Reviews*, 2003), "Make Me a Match: Motifs of Betrothal in the Sagas of the Icelanders" (in *Scandinavian Studies*, 1997), and "Sutton Hoo: An Economic Assessment" (in *Voyage to the Other World*, 1992).

Elizabeth Shipley teaches English at Karlsruhe University of Education. Her current postdoctoral research is in a project on cultural-studies pedagogy with emphases on gender and intercultural communication, directed by Professor Renate Haas at the University of Kiel.

A student of Helaine Newstead's during her final years, Gale Sigal coedited a collection of essays in her honor, *Voices in Translation: The Authority of "Olde Bookes" in Medieval Literature* (1992). Sigal's book *Erotic Dawn-Songs of the Middle Ages: Voicing the Lyric Lady* was published in 1996. She teaches medieval and English literature at Wake Forest University, where she held the Zachary T. Smith Associate Professorship in the Humanities and now chairs the English department.

Liliana V. Simeonova is a full-time associate professor at and a deputy director of the Institute of Balkan Studies (Bulgarian Academy of Sciences). She is the author of numerous articles and papers on medieval history and cultural anthropology; her monograph is titled *Diplomacy of the Letter and the Cross: Photios, Bulgaria, and the Papacy, 860s–880s* (1998).

Harriet Spiegel is professor of English at California State University, Chico. Her research interests include explorations of the representation of gender in medieval beast literature. She has written on medieval fables, including an edition and translation of the twelfth-century Anglo-Norman *Fables* of Marie de France.

Anne Rudloff Stanton (Art History and Archaeology, University of Missouri–Columbia) studies Gothic illuminated manuscripts and their users. Her most recent publications include *The Queen Mary Psalter: A Study of Affect and Audience* (2001), "The Psalter of Isabelle of France, Queen of England: Isabelle as the Audience" (*Word and Image* 18, 2002), and "Isabelle of France and Her Manuscripts, 1308–1358," in Kathleen Parsons, ed. *Capetian Women* (2003).

Marilyn J. Stokstad is Judith Harris Murphy Distinguished Professor of Art History, emerita, at the University of Kansas. Among her books are *Santiago de Compostela in the Age of the Pilgrimages* (1978), *Art History* (1995; 3rd ed., 2004), and *Art: A Brief History* (2000; 2nd ed., 2004); she coauthored *The Scottish World* (1981), *Gardens of the Middle Ages* (1983), and *Medieval Art* (1986; 2nd ed., 2004). She has served as president of the College Art Association (1978–80) and of the International Center of Medieval Art (1993–96).

Debra L. Stoudt earned her Ph.D. in German from the University of North Carolina, Chapel Hill, and is professor of German at the University of Toledo. She has published on the lives and works of the medieval German mystics and the relationship between magic and medicine in the Middle Ages.

Sandra Ballif Straubhaar (Ph.D., Stanford, 1982) is a lecturer in Germanic studies at the University of Texas at Austin. She researches and teaches a number of topics including medieval Scandinavia, the heroic archetype, the Indo-European folk tale, women's poetry, and postmodern popular medievalism.

Susan Mosher Stuard is professor emerita of history at Haverford College. She received her bachelor's degree from Smith College and her Ph.D. from Yale University. She has written on women, gender, slavery, and economy and society in medieval Europe. Her most recent project is *Gilding the Market in Fourteenth-Century Italy* (2004).

Edith Sylla is a historian of late-medieval and early-modern science. She has worked recently on Margaret Cavendish and G. W. Leibniz in relation to the scientific revolution, on Jacob Bernoulli and mathematical probability theory, and on Walter Burley's natural philosophy. She is professor of history at North Carolina State University.

Vasilka Tapkova-Zaimova is an emerita professor of the Institute of Balkan Studies (BAS) and currently sits on the institute's academic council. She is the author of numerous studies on medieval history. Her main books are *Nashestvija i etnitcheski promeni na Balkanite prez VI–VII vek* (1966) and *Dolni Dunav—granichna zona na vizantijskija Zapad. Kum istorijata na severnite i severoiztotchnite bulgarski zemi, kraja na X–XII vek* (1976).

Euan Taylor received his Ph.D. in education from Darwin College, Cambridge, in 2000. His Ph.D. dissertation on the history of education was titled "Helen Cam: The

Academic Life and the Idea of Community"; both his M.A. and Ph.D. degrees were funded by the British government's Economic and Social Research Council. Currently he works for London Underground Limited (London's metropolitan transport system—"the Tube").

Marie-Hélène Tesnière has been an archivist-paleographer since 1977 and has served as curator of manuscripts—specialist in the medieval collection—in the manuscript department of the Bibliothèque nationale since 1979. She has also served as curator of the *Trésors de la Bibliothèque nationale* [Treasures of the National Library] exhibit at the Library of Congress in 1995. She has published many articles on French humanism of the fourteenth and fifteenth centuries, most especially in relation to the texts and illustrations of Livy and Boccaccio.

Cordelia Warr is lecturer in art history at University of Manchester. She has published on female patronage and the representation of women in fourteenth-century Italian art and is currently writing a book on physical and spiritual clothing in Italian art, 1215–1545.

Gina Weaver is a third-year graduate student at Rice University who intends to specialize in the American postmodern period. She has served as typist-qua-editor in the final stages of preparing this collection.

Angela Jane Weisl is associate professor of English at Seton Hall University. She is the author of *The Persistence of Medievalism: Narrative Adventures in Contemporary Culture* (2003) and *Conquering the Reign of Femeny: Gender and Genre in Chaucer's Romance* (1995) and the coeditor of the forthcoming MLA *Approaches to Teaching Chaucer's Troilus and Criseyde and the Shorter Poems* and *Constructions of Widowhood and Virginity in the Middle Ages* (1999).

Elspeth Whitney is associate professor of history at the University of Nevada, Las Vegas. She is the author of *Paradise Restored: The Mechanical Arts from Antiquity through the Thirteenth Century* (1990), *Medieval Science and Technology* (2004), and articles on medieval technology as well as on the European witch hunts.

Ulrike Wiethaus is professor of the humanities, interdisciplinary appointments, at Wake Forest University. She has published *Ecstatic Transformation* (1995), edited *Maps of Flesh and Light: The Religious Experience of Medieval Women Mystics* (1993), coedited *Dear Sister: Medieval Women and the Epistolary Genre* (1993), and translated *The Life and Revelations of Agnes Blannbekin* (2002).

Since retiring from a professorship at Ladycliff College (at the gates of West Point), Charity Cannon Willard has published *Christine de Pizan: Her Life and Works* (1985), *Le*

Livre des trois vertus de Christine de Pizan (1989), *A Medieval Woman's Mirror of Honor: The Treasury of the City of Ladies* (1989), and *The Writings of Christine de Pizan* (1995), and edited *The Book of Feats of Arms and of Chivalry* (translated by Sumner Willard, 1999).

Janet Hadley Williams is honorary visiting fellow in English, School of Humanities, the Australian National University, and on the council of the Scottish Text Society. She coedited and contributed to *A Day Estivall: Essays on the Music, Poetry and History of Scotland and England in Honour of Helena Mennie Shire* (1990) and edited and contributed to *Stewart Style 1513–1542: Essays on the Court of James V* (1996). Her latest book is *Sir David Lyndsay: Selected Poems* (2000).

Josette A. Wisman is associate professor of French studies at American University. She has edited epistles from and written numerous articles about Christine de Pizan. Her most recent published works are "D'une Cité à l'autre: Modernité de Christine de Pizan gynéphile" (*Romanische Forshungen,* 2000), and "The Resurrection according to Christine de Pizan" (*Religion and the Arts,* 2000).

Photograph and Citation Credits

Portrait of Elizabeth Elstob (1683–1756) courtesy of the Medieval Institute, Western Michigan University Special Collections.

Portrait of Anna Brownell Jameson (1794–1860) courtesy of the Picture Library, National Portrait Gallery, London, St. Martin's Place, London.

Photograph of Lina Eckenstein (1857–1931) from the Pearson Papers, Special Collections, and courtesy of University College, London, Library.

Photograph of Mary Bateson (1865–1906) courtesy of the Principal and Fellows, Newnham College, Cambridge.

Photograph of Elise Richter (1865–1943) reproduced by kind permission of Ernst Reinhardt Verlag, Munich and Basel, and taken from *Führende Frauen Europas: Elga Kerns Standardwerk von 1928/1930,* new and revised edition by Bettina Conrad and Ulrike Leuschner (Munich and Basel: Ernst Reinhardt, 1999), 49. Permission for Elizabeth Shipley to translate eight pages of the abridged self-portrait by Elise Richter also courtesy of Ernst Reinhardt Verlag, Munich and Basel, and likewise taken from the new edition of Elga Kern's collection of self-portraits of leading European women *Führende Frauen Europas: Elga Kerns Standardwerk von 1928/1930,* new and revised edition by Bettina Conrad and Ulrike Leuschner (Munich and Basel: Ernst Reinhardt, 1999), 53–61.

Photograph of Caroline F. E. Spurgeon (1869–1942) reproduced by kind permission of Ernst Reinhardt Verlag, Munich and Basel, and taken from *Führende Frauen Europas: Elga Kerns Standardwerk von 1928/1930,* new and revised edition by Bettina Conrad and Ulrike Leuschner (Munich and Basel: Ernst Reinhardt, 1999), 89.

Photograph of Georgiana Goddard King (1871–1939) courtesy of Bryn Mawr College Library.

Photograph of Edith Rickert (1871–1938) courtesy of University of Chicago Department of Special Collections.

Photograph of Mildred Pope (1872–1956) from the College Archives, courtesy of the Principal and Fellows of Somerville College, Oxford.

Photograph of Bertha Haven Putnam (1872–1960) and citations from the "Mount Holyoke in the Twentieth Century" interviews courtesy of the Mount Holyoke College Archives and Special Collections.

Photograph of Nellie Neilson (1873–1947) courtesy of the Mount Holyoke College Archives and Special Collections.

Photograph of Evelyn Underhill (1875–1941) from King's College, London, courtesy of the Evelyn Underhill Society homepage (http://www.evelynunderhill.org).

Photograph of Dame Bertha Surtees Phillpotts (1877–1932) courtesy of the Mistress and Fellows, Girton College, Cambridge.

Photograph of Eleanor Shipley Duckett (1880–1976) courtesy of Smith College Archives, Smith College, Northampton, Mass.

Photograph of Hope Emily Allen (1883–1960) courtesy of the Pallis Family.

Photograph of Laura Hibbard Loomis (1883–1960) by an unknown photographer, courtesy of the Wellesley College Archives.

Photograph of Helen Maud Cam (1885–1968) courtesy of the Mistress and Fellows, Girton College, Cambridge.

Photograph of Margaret Josephine Rickert (1888–1973) courtesy of Burling Library, Grinnell College.

Photograph of Charlotte D'Evelyn (1889–1977) courtesy of Mount Holyoke College Archives.

Photograph of Eileen Edna La Poer Power (1889–1940) courtesy of the Estate of Eileen Power and the Mistress and Fellows, Girton College, Cambridge.

Photograph of Helen Waddell (1889–1965) from the Audio-Visual Unit, Queen's University, Belfast, by permission of her niece, Mary Martin. Citation of Helen Waddell's letters by permission of Stanbrook Abbey, Worcester.

Photograph of Yvonne Rihouët Rokseth (1890–1948) from *Die Musikforschung* 3:2 (1950), copyright Bärenreiter-Verlage, Kassel.

Photograph of Elisabeth Busse-Wilson (1890–1974), courtesy of the Archiv Burg Ludwigstein.

Photograph of Nora Kershaw Chadwick, C.B.E. (1891–1972), from plate 32 accompanying the obituary notice by Kenneth Jackson published in *Proceedings of the British Academy* 57 (1972): 535. Photograph is by Elliott & Fry.

Photograph of Maude Violet Clarke (1892–1935) from the College Archives, courtesy of the Principal and Fellows of Somerville College, Oxford. Citation of Helen Waddell's letters by permission of Stanbrook Abbey, Worcester, and of Maude Clarke's papers by permission of the Principal and Fellows of Somerville College, Oxford. Citation of Maude Clarke's letters to Lucy Sutherland from the Lucy Stuart Sutherland Uncatalogued Papers by permission of Mary Clapinson, Keeper of Special Collections and Western Manuscripts, Bodleian Library, Oxford.

Photograph of Dame Joan Evans (1893–1977) by permission of the Society of Antiquaries of London, Burlington House, Piccadilly, London W1J 0BE.

Photograph of Dorothy L. Sayers (1893–1957) used by permission of the Marion E. Wade Center, Wheaton College, Wheaton, Illinois.

Photograph of Doris Mary Parsons Stenton (Lady Stenton) (1894–1971) from the Stenton Archives, courtesy of the Reading University Library.

Photograph and Citation Credits

Photograph of Helen M. Roe (1895–1988) courtesy of the Royal Society of Antiquaries of Ireland.

Photograph of Suzanne Solente (1895–1978) courtesy of the Bibliothèque nationale de France.

Photograph of Sirarpie Der Nersessian (1896–1989) courtesy of Dumbarton Oaks, Washington, D.C.

Photograph of Vera Ivanova-Mavrodinova (1896–1987) courtesy of her daughter, Professor Liliana N. Mavrodinova.

Photograph of Vasilka Tapkova-Zaimova (1924–) courtesy of Vasilka Tapkova-Zaimova. Permission to translate into English excerpts from the memoirs of Vasilka Tapkova-Zaimova originally published in *Istoritcheski pregled,* fasc. 1–2 (1998), 51–63, has been granted by Vasilka Tapkova-Zaimova.

Photograph of Margaret Schlauch (1898–1986) courtesy of the New York University Archives.

Photograph of Pearl Kibre (1900–1985) courtesy of Irving Kelter.

Photograph of Dorothy Whitelock (1901–1982) courtesy of the Principals and Fellows, Newnham College, Cambridge.

Photograph of Ruth J. Dean (1902–2003) courtesy of Kevin Harty.

Photograph of James Bruce Ross (1902–1995) in March 1960, courtesy of Mary Martin McLaughlin.

Photograph of Marie-Thérèse d'Alverny (1903–1991) courtesy of Charles Burnett.

Photograph of Christine Mohrmann (1903–1988) courtesy of A. A. R. Bastiaensen.

Photograph of Mary Dominica Legge (1905–1986), © The British Academy, 1989. Reproduced by permission from *The Proceedings of the British Academy,* vol. 74.

Photograph of Anneliese Maier (1905–1971) from *Edizioni di Storia e Letteratura, Studi sul secolo XIV in memoria di Anneliese Maier* (Rome, 1981).

Photograph of Marjorie Ethel Reeves (1905–2003) courtesy of Marjorie Ethel Reeves.

Photograph of Beryl Smalley (1905–1984) courtesy of Prudence Pinsent. Portions of Henrietta Leyser's essay, "Beryl Smalley (1905–1984)," published originally in *Medieval Scholarship: Biographical Studies in the Formation of a Discipline,* vol. 1, *History,* ed. Helen Damico and Joseph B. Zavadil (New York: Garland, 1995), 313–24, have been reproduced by permission of Routledge, Inc., part of the Taylor & Francis Group.

Photograph of Cora Elizabeth Lutz (1906–1985) courtesy of the C. Elizabeth Boyd '33 Archives, Wilson College.

Photograph of Helaine Newstead (1906–1981) courtesy of the Graduate Center, City University of New York.

Photograph of Margaret Ogden (1909–1988) courtesy of University of Michigan News and Information Services records, Bentley Historical Library, University of Michigan. Citations from the Middle English Dictionary Records courtesy of the Bentley Historical Library, University of Michigan.

Photograph of Régine Pernoud (1909–1998) courtesy of her nephew Jérôme Pernoud.

Photograph of María Rosa Lida de Malkiel (1910–1962) courtesy of *Romance Philology.*

Photograph of Helena Mennie Shire (1912–1991) courtesy of her daughter Alisoun Gardner-Medwin.

Photograph of Marjorie McCallum Chibnall (1914–) by Edward Leigh courtesy of Marjorie McCallum Chibnall.

Photograph of Charity Cannon Willard (1914–) courtesy of Charity Cannon Willard.

Photograph of Rachel Bromwich (1915–) courtesy of Gerald Morgan.

Photograph of Jane Hayward (1918–1994) by Peter Barnet, courtesy of the Metropolitan Museum of Art, the Cloisters Archive.
Photograph of Marie Borroff (1923–) courtesy of Marie Borroff.
Photograph of Nina G. Garsoïan (1923–) courtesy of Nina G. Garsoïan.
Photograph of Elizabeth Salter (1925–1980) courtesy of Queen Mary College, London.
Photograph of Rosemary Estelle Woolf (1925–1978) courtesy of Somerville College, Oxford, Archives.
Photograph of Ilene H. Forsyth (1928–) courtesy of University of Michigan Photo Services, Bob Kalmbach.
Photograph of the Morgan Madonna courtesy of the Metropolitan Museum, gift of J. Pierpont Morgan, 1916.
Photograph of the Samson Monolith courtesy of the Duke University Museum of Art.
Photograph of Elisabeth Gössmann (1928–) courtesy of Elisabeth Gössmann.
Photograph of Elaine C. Block (1929–) courtesy of Elaine C. Block.
Photograph of Rosemary Cramp (1929–) courtesy of Rosemary Cramp.
Photograph of Jo Ann McNamara (1931–) courtesy of Jo Ann McNamara.
Photograph of Elizabeth A. R. Brown (1932–) courtesy of Elizabeth A. R. Brown. "I May, I Might, I Must," copyright © 1959 by Marianne Moore, © renewed 1987 by Lawrence E. Brinn and Louise Crane, Executors of the Estate of Marianne Moore, from The Complete Poems of Marianne Moore by Marianne Moore. Used by permission of Viking Penguin, a division of Penguin Putnam Inc.
Photograph of Meredith Parsons Lillich (1932–) courtesy of the Syracuse University Photo and Imaging Center.
Photograph of Sister Benedicta Ward, S.L.G. (1933–), courtesy of Sister Benedicta Ward, S.L.G.
Photograph of Susan Mosher Stuard (1935–) courtesy of Haverford College.
Photograph of Joan M. Ferrante (1936–) courtesy of Margo Dobbertin, School of General Studies, Columbia University, Office of Alumni Affairs, from *The Owl: The Alumni Magazine of the School of General Studies* (fall/winter 2001), 18. Quotations from interviews with Professor Ferrante conducted by Julie Crosby and from her lecture "They Were There All the Time" used by permission of Joan M. Ferrante. Quotations from Julie Crosby's interview with Robert W. Hanning and from his remarks in honor of Professor Ferrante's sixty-fifth birthday celebration, held at Columbia University on 10 November 2001, used by permission of Professor Hanning.
Photograph of Marcia L. Colish (1937–) courtesy of Marcia L. Colish.
Photograph of Caroline Walker Bynum (1941–) courtesy of Elaine Barrasco / *Columbia College Today* (alumni magazine).

Index

AAUP (American Association of University Professors), 305
AAUW (American Association of University Women), 525, 527, 674, 794
Abba (Underhill), 191
Abelard, Peter: Ross's scholarship, 582; Waddell's scholarship, 323, 325, 326–28, 329, 330
ACLS (American Council of Learned Societies), 234, 235, 567
Adams, Michael: contributor's note, 1007; on Margaret Ogden, 697–707
Adams, Norma, 169, 170
Adams, Pauline, 390, 621, 833
Adventure, An (Jourdain), 402, 414–15
Advisory Board for Redundant Churches, 885
Ady, Cecilia, 647–48
Aitken, Jack, 740
Akrabova-Zhandova, Ivanka, 507
Akst, Daniel, 923
Alain de Lille, d'Alverny's scholarship, 587
Albertson, Mary, 917, 920
Albright, Patricia, 306
Alcuin, Friend of Charlemagne (Duckett), 218, 219, 223

Alderman, Pauline, 347, 348
Alexander, Lord Lindsay, 29
Alexander Montgomerie: A Selection from His Songs and Poems (Shire, editor), 737
Alfred the Great (Duckett), 218, 219, 221
Ælfric: Bateson's translation of, 70; Elstob's translation of, 3, 7, 14
Algazel, d'Alverny's scholarship, 589–90
Alghren, Gillian, 986
Alkindi, d'Alverny's scholarship, 589–90
Allen, Hope Emily: as agnostic, 232–33; *Ancrene Riwle* as focus of work, 229, 230, 231–32, 234, 236; awards and honors, 234; Cambridge and, 230; critical reception of works, 232, 234; D'Evelyn and, 304; education of, 228; employment as editor, 234; as etymologist, 700; family of, 227–29, 230; financial support of work, 227, 234; gender "appropriate" scholarship and, xxxii; Herbert as collaborator with, 233; manuscript study, 233; Margery Kempe and, 231, 235–37; as mentor, 700–701; mysticism as focus of work, 230–31, 235–36; Ogden and, 234, 699, 700–701; Oneida community and, 227–29, 231;

Allen, Hope Emily (*continued*)
pictured, 228; publication history of, 230, 231, 233; reputation as scholar, 231; Rolle as focus of work, 229, 230, 231, 232–34; scholarly circle of, xxxiv; scholarly legacy of, 233, 304
Allen, Philip Schuyler, 328–29
Alonso, Amado, 723
Alonso, Dámaso, 726
Ambrose, Colish's scholarship, 990
American Academy in Rome, 988
American Association of Teachers, 567
American Association of University Professors (AAUP), 305
American Association of University Women (AAUW), 525, 527, 674, 794
American Council of Learned Societies (ACLS), 234, 235, 567
American Historical Association, 167, 171, 174–76, 909, 984
American Philological Association, 674
Amos, Margaret, 770
Ancrene Riwle (*Ancrene Wisse*): Allen's scholarship, 229, 230, 231–32, 234, 236; D'Evelyn's scholarship, 295, 304
Ancrene Wisse. See *Ancrene Riwle* (*Ancrene Wisse*)
An der Grenze von Scholastik und Naturwissenschaft (Maier), 633
Anderson-Smith, Myrtle, 741
Andrew of Saint Victor, Smalley's scholarship, 661–62
Andrews, Charles, 169, 170, 171, 175, 176
Andrews, Verity, 453
Anglo-Norman in the Cloisters (Legge), 617
Anglo-Norman Lapidaries (Evans), 405
Anglo-Norman Letters and Petitions (Legge), 616, 617
Anglo-Norman literature: "Ancestral Romance" as genre, 618; biblical texts, 571; chanson de geste tradition and, 569; Dean's scholarship and, 569–72; devotional texts, 571–72; hagiographic texts, 571; homiletic texts, 571; Legge's scholarship and, 617–19; linguistic studies, 570; political verse, 569; proverbial texts, 569–70; romance tradition, 569; satire in, 569–70; scientific and technological texts, 570–71; songs, 569
Anglo-Norman Literature (Dean), 568–72
Anglo-Norman Literature and Its Background (Legge), 617–19
Anglo-Norman studies, 147, 150–54; Battle Conference on Anglo-Norman Studies, 757. See also Anglo-Norman literature
Anglo-Norman Text Society (A.N.T.S.), 148, 615
Anglo-Saxon and Norse Poems (Chadwick), 370
Anglo-Saxon England (F. M. Stenton), 451, 559
Anglo-Saxon Reader (Sweet, revised by Whitelock), 558
Anglo-Saxon Saints and Scholars (Duckett), 218, 223
Anglo-Saxon studies: Corpus of Anglo-Saxon Stone Sculpture, 888; Cramp's scholarship, 889–90; Duckett's scholarship, 218, 223; E. Elstob's scholarship, 3, 13–14; hagiographic texts, 571; literature, 889–90 (*see also specific works*); stone sculptures, 887–88, 893; Whitelock's scholarship, 451, 553–54, 557–58; wills and legal history, 451, 553–54
Anglo-Saxon Wills (Whitelock), 451, 554
Annales School, 960–61
Annual International Congress of Medieval Studies at Kalamazoo, 786, 848, 880
Anselm of Canterbury, Ward's scholarship, 947–48
Anselm of Canterbury (Ward), 948
Anthony of Sourohz, 947, 949
anthroposophy, 343
Antiquarian Society, 7
anti-Semitism: Jews as the Other, 1001; Nazism and, xxxiv, 82; Weston on causes of, 52 n. 72
A.N.T.S. (Anglo-Norman Text Society), 148, 615
Arab Emirates in Bagratid Armenia, The (Ghevondyan, Garsoïan, translator), 807
Arabic and Islamic studies: d'Alverny's scholarship, 587, 589–91, 592–93; Ferrante and, 973; at West Point, 765

Archaeological Data Service, 888
Archaeological Society, 892
archaeology: as academic discipline, 896; art history and, 401; Ivanova-Mavrodinova and Bulgarian archaeology, 496, 504, 505, 506–7; material archaeological evidence and documentary evidence, 890–91; Montelius and, 207; M. Rickert and, 287; Roe and Irish archaeology, xxxi, 462–63, 467; women and, xxv (*see also* Cramp, Rosemary; Evans, Joan)
architecture: Iberian architecture and G. G. King, 111–21; Ruskin on cathedrals, xxiv
Aretino, Spinello, 28
Armenia and the Byzantine Empire (Der Nersessian), 484
Armenia in Period of Justinian (Adontz, Garsoïan, translator), 807
Armenian studies: Der Nersessian's scholarship, 484. *See also* Garsoïan, Nina G.
Armor of Light, The (Lillich), 940
Arnim, Julianna, 547
art history: archaeology and, 401; Clarke's scholarship and the Wilton Diptych, 387; as discipline, 940; Forsyth on art history as career, 839–55; Jameson and iconography, 25–33; Lillich's scholarship, 935, 936–37, 938–41; L. H. Loomis and, 245; as major at Bryn Mawr, 113; misattribution of works, 27–28; misericords (*see* Block, Elaine C.); modernism, 120, 715–16; Pernoud and modern art, 715–16; Pernoud's scholarship, 715–16, 717; photography and, 940; primacy of the artist and, 31–32; private collection in England, 27; Rickert's scholarship, 286, 287–88, 289; sexism in education and career opportunities, 783. *See also* Evans, Joan; stained glass
Arthurian legend, xxviii; Borroff's scholarship, 793–94, 795; Celtic origins, 247, 686–87, 688–89; controversies regarding, 40; Grail legend and, 40, 45–46; popular culture and, 48, 49; Welsh connections to, 39–40, 771–72, 775. *See also* Newstead, Helaine; Weston, Jessie Laidlay

Arthur of the Welsh, The (Bromwich, Jarman, and Roberts editors), 776
Art in Medieval France (Evans), 409, 410–11
Arzt, Silvia, 867
Askew, Pamela, 582
Astell, Mary, 7
Atkinson, Richard, 892
Auchinleck manuscript, 245–46
Audience of Beowulf, The (Whitelock), 557
Augustine, xxvi, 10, 194
Ausgehendes Mittelalter (Maier), 625
Austin, David, 890
Austrian Federation of University Women, 82
autobiographical writing: E. C. Block on misericords, 873–83; Borroff on her career, 789–800; E. A. R. Brown on alterity and the grotesque, 915–25; of Busse-Wilson, 357; Bynum on her scholarship, 995–1006; Bynum on identity and, 997–99; M. C. Chibnall's memoir, 747–57; Evan's *Prelude and Fugue*, 404, 405, 407, 414, 415; Forsyth on art history as career, 839–55; gender and, xxviii; gender difference and, xxviii; Jelinek on women and, xxv–xxvi; Lillich's memoir, 933–41; McNamara on women's networking, 901–11; Reeves on Oxford, 647–55; Richter's "Education and Development," 82–88; self-representation in, xxviii; Stuard on feminism and women's history, 955–66; Tapkova-Zaimova's memoir, 509–17; Willard on career and being an army wife, 759–66
Avdoyan, Levon: contributor's note, 1007; on Nina G. Garsoïan, 803–10
Avicenna (Ibn Sīnā), d'Alverny's scholarship, 589–91
Ayloffe, Joseph, 448

Bailey, Richard, 893
Bainton, Roland, 983–84
Ball, Joanna, 561
Ballard, George, 15–16
Ballinger, Sir John, 138–39
Barber, C. L., 46

Barber, Leila, 120
Barbier, Patrick, 878
Barker, Ethel Ross, 186, 189
Bar-Lamb's Ballad Book, The (Underhill), 185
Barnard, George Grey, 783
Barnard College: Ferrante and, 970; Forsyth and, 843; Gildersleeve and, 106
Barnes, Viola, 175
Barolini, Teodolinda, 977
Bartlett, Robert, 316
BAS (Bulgarian Academy of Sciences). *See* Bulgarian Academy of Sciences (BAS)
Baswell, Christopher, 986
Bately, Janet, 558
Bates, David, 453
Bates, Katharine Lee, 241
Bateson, Anna, 69, 73
Bateson, Mary: Ælfric as focus of work, 70; audience for works, 73; awards and honors, 72; *Cambridge Medieval History* and, 70, 73; *Cambridge Modern History*, contributions to, 70; Creighton as mentor of, 69, 70, 71; death of, 72; *Dictionary of National Biography*, contributions to, 70; as editor, 72; education of, 67–69; encyclopedia and anthology contributions, 73; family of, 67–68, 73–74; Girton College and, 69; as linguist, 70; Maitland as mentor of, 71; Manchester University, 72; municipal history as focus of work, 71–73; Newnham College and, 69, 70, 71–72; personal life of, 69, 71; pictured, 68; publication history of, 70, 72; scholarly circle of, 69; scholarly legacy of, 73; as suffragist, 73–74; as teacher, 70–72; as translator, 70; *Victoria County History of Northampton*, contributions to, 70
Battle of Maldon (Byrhtnoth), 561
Baugh, Albert, 566
Bayet, A., 505
Beasts and Saints (Waddell, translation), 328
Beaujouan, Guy, 635–36
Beazley, John, 401
Becker, Carl, 921

Becket Conflict in the Schools, The (Smalley), 664, 665
Beckmann, Emmy, 359
Becoming Visible (Bridenthal et al.), 910, 959
Bede: archaeology at sites associated with, 888–89, 890; Elstob and Wheloc's edition of, 8, 10, 11; Ward's scholarship, 947, 951
Bedford College, Spurgeon and, 101
Bédier, Joseph, 40, 44–45, 115, 246, 427
Beeson, Charles H., 138
Begin Here (Sayers), 431
Beginnings of English Society, The (Whitelock), 557
Beljame, Alexandre, 101
Bengsch, Alfred, 863
Bennett, H. S., 172
Benson, Robert Hugh, 186–87
Bentham, Jeremy, 650
Bentinck, William Cavendish, 16
Benton, John F., 582, 917
Beowulf: R. Cramp's scholarship on, 889
Berenson, Bernard, 112, 114–15, 229, 401; M. Rickert and, 286
Berenson, Mary, 112, 229, 286
Berkshire Conference of Women Historians, 908–10, 966 n.2
Berman, Constance Hoffman, xxxiv; contributor's note, 1007; on James Bruce Ross, 575–82
Besevliev, Vesselin, 509, 510, 511, 517
Bethmont, Sylvie, 880
Béthune manuscripts, 474
Bethurum, Dorothy: on C. Brown, 308 n.32; on D'Evelyn's work, 304; education and career of, 250 n.12. *See also* Loomis, Dorothy Bethurum
Bezzola, Reto R., 618, 716
Bible for the Common Reader (Chase), 218
biblical texts: Anglo-Norman literature and, 571; historical contexts for reading of, 862; Smalley's Bible exegesis scholarship, 657, 660–62, 663, 664, 666
Bibliography for Teachers of History, A (Power), 313
Bickerman, Elias, 804

Bigongiari, Dino, 674–75
Biller, Natalie, 303
Billiet, Frédéric, 878, 880
Billings, Julia, 673
biographical writing: biographical essays and, xxix–xxx; D'Evelyn on, 295; Evans as family biographer, 401, 414; Kern's collected self-portraits of European women, 82, 99; Miller on narrative criticism and, xxviii; D. Stenton on F. M. Stenton, 451–52. *See also* autobiographical writing
Birkenmajer, Alexander, 589, 592
Birley, Eric, 893
Bischoff, Bernhard, 592
Biser, Eugen, 865–66
Bivoet-Williamson, Maya, xxvi
Bjarnadóttir, Anna, 207
Black, J. B., 754
Blackwell, Basil, 617
Blair, Claude, 416
Blair, Peter Hunter, 559
Bloch, Herbert, 919
Bloch, Marc, 92 n.26, 316, 921, 960–61
Block, Elaine C.: on art as primary source in elementary schools, 875; Billiet as collaborator with, 878, 880; children of, 875; contributor's note, 1007–8; Cornell University and, 873; education of, 873; on Fancelli family workshop, 881–82; films made by, 876, 877; financial support for work, 877; on Gaillon stalls, 878, 882–83; Hunter College and, 876; as independent scholar, xxxi, xxxii, xxxiii; marriage of, 875; Martinez as collaborator with, 876; McMunn and, 876; Metropolitan Museum and, 875–76; misericords as focus of work, xxxii, xxxiii, 876–83; Museum of Modern Art, New York and, 877; nomenclature and terminology used in misericord study, 880–81; Patrimony Day tours led by, 882; pictured, 874; as pioneer in field, xxxi; Project Muse and, 875; publication history of, 878, 880; on public's access to and knowledge of misericords, 883; C. Reno and, 876; Reynard Society and, 876–87; on Saint-Claude in the Jura restoration efforts, 881–82; scholarly circle of, 876–77, 878; Sorbonne and, 873; as teacher, 875; University of Wisconsin and, 875; Varty and, 876–77, 878, 879; Willard and, 876
Blöndal, Sigfús, 203, 204, 208
Blunt, Christopher, 558
Boardman, Elizabeth, 561
Boase, T. S. R., 408
Bock, Friedrich, 627–28, 629
Bodgener, Henry, 194
body, the: Bynum's scholarship, xxxii, 924, 997–99; division of the body during the Middle Ages, 924
Boffey, Julia: contributor's note, 1008; on Elizabeth Salter, 815–20
Bois-Reymond, Lucy de, 59
Book of Hugh and Nancy, The (Duckett and Milner-White), 222
Book of Margery Kempe: Allen and, 231, 235–37; Chambers and, 816
Boorman, John, 49
Borghese manuscript collection, Maier's cataloging of, 628–29
Boro, Joyce: contributor's note, 1008; on Rosemary Estelle Woolf, 825–33
Borough Customs (Bateson), 72
Borroff, Marie: administrative career of, 797–98; awards and honors, 791, 799; Chaucer as focus of work, 799; "Chicago School" of criticism and, 789–91; contributor's note, 1008; Crane and, 789, 793; Donaldson as mentor, 793, 795–97; education of, 789–91, 792; financial support of scholarship, 794; Frost, Moore, and Stevens as focus of work, 794, 797; Kökeritz and, 793, 795; Maclean and, 789, 791; as musician, 791, 792; *Norton Anthology of English Literature,* contributions to, 796; Olson and, 789, 791; philology as focus of work, 793–96; pictured, 790; as poet, 791; poets Frost, Moore, and Stevens as focus of work, 792–93; J. C. Pope and, 793, 795; publication history of, 796, 797; *Sir*

Borroff, Marie (*continued*)
  Gawain poet as focus of work, 793–94, 795, 796–97, 799–801; Smith College and, 789; on "sound symbolism," 797; as teacher, 789, 791–92, 794–96, 799; University of Chicago and, 789; verse translation as focus of work, 791, 796–97, 799–800; on writing style as distinctive, 792; Wycliffe as focus of work, 799; Yale University and, 793, 794–96, 797–99
Bott, G. Michael, 453, 561
Bowman, Claude Charleton, 136
Boyce, Gray C., 543
Boyle, Leonard, 922
Bracton's Note Book (Stenton), 446
"Bradford, Brother" (monk), 878
Bradley, John, 464–65, 466, 467
Bradley, S. A., 818
Brainerd, Mary Bowen, 248–49
Branner, Robert, 784, 936
Bran the Blessed in Arthurian Romance (Newstead), 686, 687
Braudel, Fernand, 960
Brearley School, Manhattan, 970
Bridenthal, Renate, 910, 959
Brief Account of the Military Orders in Spain (King), 114
Brightland, John, 13–14
Bristol and Gloucester Archaeological Society, 411
British Academy, 234, 329, 374, 589, 806
British Academy for the Sylloge of Coins in the British Isles, 558
British Federation of University Women, 102
British Museum, 885
Brittain, Vera, 384–85, 392 nn.27–28
Brockbank, Philip, 818
Bromwich, Brian, 778
Bromwich, Christine, 778; contributor's note, 1008; on Helen M. Roe, 459–67
Bromwich, John, 463, 772
Bromwich, Rachel Amos: Arthurian connections to Welsh literature and, 771–72; awards and honors, 773; Cambridge and, 773; N. Chadwick and, 774; children of, 772; Dafydd ap Gwilym as focus of work, 775–76; education of, 769–71, 772; Evans as collaborator, 776; family of, 769, 772; Foster and, 773, 776; Hoare as mentor, 770; Jackson and, 770, 772, 773; Jarman as collaborator, 776; as linguist, 770, 776; marriage to John Bromwich, 772; as mentor, 777; Newnham College and, 770; O'Brien and, 772; personal life of, 773, 777; pictured, 768; publication history of, 773, 776; Queen's University, Belfast, and, 772; religious life of, 769; Roberts as collaborator, 776; Roe and, 463; *Studies in Early British History*, contributions to, 773; University College of Wales, Aberystwyth, and, 773; University College of Wales, Bangor, and, 772; Welsh language and literature as focus of work, 771, 776, 777; Welsh triads as focus of work, 772–75; C. Williams and, 772, 773
Brooks, Cleanth, 48
Brown, Allen, 757
Brown, Beatrice, 305
Brown, C. S., 277
Brown, Carleton, 229, 528, 830; Bethurum on, 308 n.32; as D'Evelyn's mentor, 297–98, 304
Brown, Elizabeth A. R.: on alterity of Middle Ages, 918, 923–25; on Bynum, 923; on Cantor, 917, 921; as contributor, xxxi, 1008; d'Alverny and, 922; on documents as artifacts or "texts," 921; education of, 917, 919–22; family of, 917; on Freedman, 917–19; Goffart and, 922; on the grotesque, 918, 926 n.11; on Haskins's legacy, 919; mentors of, xxxiii; on objectivity in scholarship, 920–21; pictured, 915; G. Post and, 919; on scientific methodology, 920–21; on shifting world views, 922–23; on Spiegel, 917–19; on Strayer, 917, 921, 927 n.11; Swarthmore College and, 919; on taxation and Philip the Fair, 923–24; on C. H. Taylor, 919
Brown, Lucy, 828
Brown, Phyllis: contributor's note, 1008; on Rosemary Cramp, 885–97

Brown University, 137
Bruce, James Douglas, 40
Brugger, Ernst, 40
Brunsdale, Mitzi M.: contributor's note, 1009; on Dorothy Sayers, 423
Bryn Mawr College: Allen and, 229, 230; Cam and, 260; D'Evelyn and, 296–97, 300; Duckett and, 216; Frank and, 273–74, 275; Garsoïan and, 804; G. G. King and, 111–12, 116, 119–20; Neilson at, 167, 170, 172; Putnam and, 159; Spurgeon and, 102. *See also* Thomas, Martha Carey
Bücher, Karl, 359
Bühler, Curt, 766
Bulgarian Academy of Sciences (BAS), 496, 500, 506, 508; Tapkova-Zaimova's memoirs, 509–17; women at BAS, 513–14, 517
Bulgarian Women's Union (BWU), 498
Bureau, Pierre, 879
Burgess, John William, 543
Burgevin, Leslie, 302
Burmov, Alexander, 510, 513
Burnett, Charles S. F.: contributor's note, 1009; on Marie-Thérèse d'Alverny, 585–93
Burroughs, Louis B., 274
Bury, Richard de, 546–47
Busman's Honeymoon (Sayers), 428, 429–30
Busse-Wilson, Elisabeth: autobiographical writing of, 357; children of, 353; critical reception of works, 355, 360; Droste-Hülshoff as focus of work, 354; education of, 353, 356–57; family of, 353; feminism and scholarship of, 354–55, 356–57, 360, 361; German mysticism scholarship and, 358–61; Grundmann and, 360; Hesse and, 355; as independent scholar, 353, 356; Mann and, 355–56; marriage to Kurt Busse, 353; pictured, 352; political oppression and, xxxiii, xxxiv, 353–54, 356; psychological analysis used in work, 360–61; publishing history of, 353–54; reputation as scholar, 353; St. Elisabeth of Thuringia as focus of work, 353, 354–55, 361; as teacher, 353–54; University of Leipzig and, 357
Butler, Hubert, 462

Butler-Bowdon, William E. I., 235
Buzandaran Patmut'iwnk', Garsoïan scholarship, 807–8
BWU (Bulgarian Women's Union), 498
Bynum, Caroline Walker: the body and corporeality as focus of work, 924; E. A. R. Brown and, 923, 924, 925; children of, 1004; Columbia University and, 999; contributor's note, 1009; on divorce, 1004; education of, 1003–4; family of, 999, 1001–3, 1004; on feminism, 1005; gender as focus of work, 997–99; Harvard University and, 1003–4; on historian's stance, 1005; on identity, 999; as medievalist, 1000; as mentor, 1003–4; on "Otherness," 1001; personal life, 1004–6; pictured, 996; publication history of, 995–99, 1004–5; on race, 1002; religious life of, 1001; reputation as scholar, xxxii; as teacher, 999, 1003–4; University of Washington and, 1004; on Vietnam era, 1003–4; on women in academe, 1003; women's spirituality as focus of work, 997; on WWII, 1000–1001
Byrne, Muriel St. Claire, 433
Byzantine studies: Der Nersessian's scholarship, 484, 485; Forsyth's scholarship, 839–45, 847–48, 849, 850–52; Garsoïan's scholarship, 803, 805–8. *See also* Tapkova-Zaimova, Vasilka

Cahn, Walter, 848
Callcott, Lady Maria, 28
Calvert, Theodora, 312
Cam, Avice, 255
Cam, Edith, 255
Cam, Helen Maud: awards and honors, 260, 268; E. A. R. Brown and, 919; Cambridge and, 264–66, 267; Chibnall and, 752–53; critical reception of works, 265; education of, 257–59; family of, 255–57, 263; financial support of work, 263–64; Girton College and, xxx, 261, 264; Harvard and, 266–67; Hayes-Robinson as mentor, 260; International Commission for the History of Representative and Parliamentary

Cam, Helen Maud (*continued*)
Institutions and, 267; Jones and, 261; legal studies as focus of work, 267–68; London School of Economics and, 260, 263; Maitland's papers edited by, 267; Neilson and, 169, 172; papers of, xxx; pictured, 256; political activism of, 259, 264; publication history of, 265, 266; religious life of, 259; reputation as scholar, 265; scholarly circle of, 261–62, 265; sexism in university system, 264–66, 393 n.35; as socialist, 257, 259, 264; as teacher, 261, 262; travel, 266; Vinogradoff as collaborator, 261–62, 263; women's education and, 264, 266

Cam, Katherine "Kate," 255, 263

Cam, Norah, 255, 258, 260, 267

Cambridge Medieval History, 70; E. Power's contributions to, 316

Cambridge Ritualists, 40, 46

Cambridge University: Allen and, 230; Bromwich and, 773; Cam and, 264–66, 267; N. Chadwick and, 367, 370–71, 373; M. M. Chibnall, 754; Duckett and, 215, 222; gender bias at, 264–66; Kibre's scholarship and, 545; married women as faculty at, 755; M. K. Pope and, 149; Salter and, 817; sexism in hiring at, 755; Shire and, 735, 737; "titles to degrees" award to women, 755; Whitelock and, 557, 559–60; women's colleges first establish at, 69. *See also specific colleges of*

Cambridge Women's Suffrage Association (CWSA), 73–74

Campbell, Gladys, 789

Campbell, Marian, 416

Cankova-Petkova, Genoveva, 509

Cantor, Norman, xxvii, 45, 393 n.35, 917, 921

capital relief sculpture, Romanesque, pictured, 851

Carcavi manuscript, 474

Cargill, Oscar, 524

Carnot, Claude, 405

Carolingian Portraits (Duckett), 218, 221, 222

Carpenter, Nan Cooke, 280

Carter, Sebastian, 738

Cartulary and Terrier of the Priory of Bilsington (Neilson), 172–73

Carus-Wilson, Nora, 317, 318, 753

Carver, Martin, 893

Casella, Mario, 279

Cassidy, Frederic G., 700

Castro, Américo, 723

Catalogue of Incipits of Mediaeval Scientific Writing in Latin (Kibre and Thorndike), 544

Catholic Tales and Christian Songs (Sayers), 426

Cavadini, John, 672, 678

Caviness, Madeline, 940

CCWH (Coordinating Council for Women in History), xxvii–xxviii

CCWHP (Coordinating Committee for Women in the Historical Profession), xxvii–xxviii, 907–8, 909, 910

Celt and Saxon (Chadwick), 374

Celtic Britain (Chadwick), 374

Celtic Realms, The (Chadwick), 367

Celtic studies: Arthurian legend and, 247, 686–87, 688–89; N. Chadwick scholarship, 367, 373, 374–75; Newstead's scholarship, 686–87, 688–89; Weston and Grail scholarship, 47

Celts, The (Chadwick and Dillon), 367, 375

Cendrars, Blaise, 715

Centre de recherche d'histoire et de civilization de Byzance, 806

Centre national de la recherché scientifique (CNRS), 588

Chadwick, Carol, 176

Chadwick, Hector Munro: ASNAC department and, 770; marriage and collaboration with Nora Chadwick, 367, 371, 770; Phillpotts and, 202, 203; syllabus revision and, 553; Whitelock and, 553, 555

Chadwick, Nora Kershaw: academic reputation of, 374; on atheism, 375; audience for works, 369, 372, 374–75; awards and honors, 372, 374, 375; Cambridge and, 367, 370–71, 373 (*see also* Newnham College *under this heading*); Celtic studies as focus of work, 367, 373, 374–75; critical reception of works, 368, 372, 375;

Dillon and, 367; education of, 367; family of, 367, 368, 369–70, 372 (*see also* marriage under this heading); field research of, 371, 373–74; Girton College and, 373; Hector Munro Chadwick as mentor, 368; Irish language as focus of work, 371; marriage and collaboration with Hector Munro Chadwick, 367, 368, 369–70, 371, 372, 770; as mentor, 368, 373; Newnham College and, 367, 368, 370, 373, 374; Norse as focus of work, 367, 368–69, 370–71; organizational affiliations, 364; personal life of, 370 (*see also* family of *under this heading*); pictured, 367; popular culture and works of, 375; publication history of, 367, 368–69, 370–71; religious life of, 375; shamanism as focus of work, 372; Shire and, 735; *Studies in Early British History*, contributions to, 373; as teacher, 368; as translator, 369; University of Saint Andrews and, 368
Chambers, E. K., 46
Chambers, R. W., 232, 234, 816
Chance, Jane: contributor's note, 1009; editor's introduction, xxiii–xxxv
Chaplais, Pierre, 922
Charette, Arthur, 5
Charlesworth, Dorothy, 892
Chase, Mary Ellen, 216–18, 222, 223–24
Chaucer: A Biographical Manual (Hammond), 92–93
Chaucer, Geoffrey: Auchinleck manuscript linked to, 245–46; Borroff's scholarship, 799; D'Evelyn on teaching of works, 302–3; Frank's scholarship, 277; Hammond's scholarship, 92–93, 94–95; Loomis's scholarship, 245–46; E. Rickert's scholarship, 129, 135, 138–39; M. Rickert's scholarship, 286, 287, 288; Salter's scholarship, 817, 818, 820; Schlauch's scholarship, 523; Spurgeon's scholarship, 103–4, 105
Chaucer's Constance and Accused Queens (Schlauch), 523, 527
Chaucer's World (Rickert), 139, 288
Cheek, Mary Ashby, 301
Cheltenham Ladies' College, 261

Cheney, Christopher, 663
Chenu, Marie-Dominique, 592
Cheyette, Fredric, 919
Cheyney, E. P., 172
Chibnall, Marjorie McCallum: Aberdeen University and, 753–54; Black and, 754; Cam and, 752; Cambridge and, 754; Church and State issues as focus of work, 751–52, 757; Clare Hall College and, 757; as contributor, xx, 1009; as economic historian, 753, 757; education of, 747–49; Empress Matilda as focus of work, 757; family of, 747, 754; Galbraith and, 750, 754, 755–56; German study of, 750–51; Girton College and, 754; on history as agent for world peace, 749, 751; Jamison and, 749, 750, 751; on Legge, 619; marriage to Charles Chibnall, 754; mentorship of, xxxi; Newnham College and, 753; Oderic as focus of work, xxxiii, 755–56; on Oxford, 749–50; Paris study of, 752; pictured, 748; Postan and, 752–53; E. Power and, 311–20, 752–53, 757; Powicke and, 751, 753–54; scholarly circle of, xxxiv, 752–53, 757; as teacher, 753, 756, 757; University College, Southampton, and, 753; WWII work and experiences, 753
Chief Middle English Poets: Selected Poems, The (Weston), 38, 43
children: academic careers and motherhood, 582, 905, 906–7, 937, 938; as audience for works, 55, 59, 81, 222; Eckenstein and, 55, 58, 59, 60, 61; education of, 59, 60, 875; Ross on the history of childhood, 580–81; Stuard on work and, 965–66; as theologians, 857–59
Chotzen, T. M., 771, 776
Chrétien de Troyes: Newstead's scholarship, 686–87, 691; Richter's scholarship, 79; Weston's scholarship, 40
Chrisman, Miriam, 983
Christ, Karl, 276
Christian Latin: Mohrmann and Nijmegen school, 600–603, 605, 607; Mohrmann's scholarship, 599, 601–3, 605–6, 607

Christine de Pizan, xxxii, xxxiii; Solente's scholarship, 475–78; Willard's scholarship, 761–62, 763, 764
Christliche Mystik, Die (Görres), 358
Christ within Me (Ward), 952
Chronologische Phonetik des Französischen . . . (Richter), 79
chronology of women medievalists, xliii–xlvi
church and state issues, 9, 751–52, 757
Cipolla, Carlo, 747
City of Cambridge (Cam), 266
Civil Rights movement in U.S., 907, 920
Clagett, Marshall, 544, 634–35
Clapham, Sir Alfred, 401
Clapham, J. H., 319–20
Clapham, Margaret, 314
Clare Hall College, 757
Clark, Kenneth, 818
Clarke, Maude Violet: awards and honors, 390; Brittan and, 384–85, 392 nn.27–28; constitutional history as focus of work, 387–88; critical reception of works, 388; death of, 390; education, 381; family of, 381, 386; as fictionalized character, 384–85; Galbraith and, 387, 390; Legge and, 390, 616; manuscript studies of, 386–87; McKisack and, 390; Namier linked to, 384–85; as novelist, 324; *Oxford History of England* contributions, 388; pictured, 380; publication history of, 386; Queen's College Belfast and, 381, 385, 390; religious life of, 390; reputation as scholar, 387; scholarly circle of, xxxiv, 389–90; scholarly legacy of, 390; sexism in university system, xxxii, 381, 393 n.35; Somerville College, Oxford and, xxxii, 381–82, 385; Sutherland and, 385, 386, 390; as teacher, 381–82, 385; travel, 386; Waddell and, 324, 381, 382, 385, 388, 390; on Woolf's *To the Lighthouse*, 389
Clarke, Richard, 390
Clarke, Stewart "Chang," 386
Classical Association of the Atlantic States, 674
"classical women's history," period of, 358
Clayette miscellany, 475

Cleanness, Borroff's scholarship, 799
Clemens, Ray, 986
Clemoes, Peter, 559, 561
Clifford, Geraldine Jonçich, 137
Clingan, Edmund, 905
Cloud of Unknowing, The (Underhill translation), 190, 194
Clouds of Witness (Sayers), 428
Clough, Blanche Athena, 69
Clover, Mary, 204, 209
Cluniac Art of the Romanesque Period (Evans), 407
CNRS (Centre national de la recherché scientifique), 588
Cockerell, Sydney, 287, 289
codicological studies, 288, 474, 588, 764
Cohen, Gustave, 343
Cohen, Miriam, 582
Coldewey, John, 534
Coldstream, Nicola: contributor's note, 1009; on Joan Evans, 399–415
Coleman, William, 693
Colish, Marcia L.: awards and honors, 988; Bainton as mentor, 983–84; Duckett and, 982; education of, 983–84; family of, 982; financial support of, 988; Lombard as focus of work, 981, 988–89; as mentor, 986–87; Oberlin College and, 984, 987–88, 989–90; organizational affiliations, 988; Packard as mentor, 982, 984–85, 989; Pelikan as mentor, 983–84; personal life of, 982, 987–88, 989; pictured, 980; publication history of, 981, 988; religious life of, 983; on "revolt of the medievalists," 982–83; St. Ambrose as focus of work, 990; scholarly circle of, 983; semantic theory as focus of work, 983; Skidmore College and, 984; Smith College and, 982; Stoicism and Christian philosophy as focus of work, 981–82, 988; as teacher, 984, 985–87; Yale and, 983, 988, 989–90
Colker, Marvin, 676
Collette, Carolyn P.: on Charlotte D'Evelyn, 295–306; contributor's note, 1009–10
Collingwood, R. G., 749

Collins, Sarah Huff, 17 n.4
colonization and colonialism, 316, 374
Columbia University: Bynum and, 999; Ferrante and, 970–71, 973–74; Fisher and, 761; Forsyth and, 841–43; Garsoïan and, 805–6; Hayward and, 784; Kibre and, 541, 543; Lillich and, 936–37; Malkiel and, 725; McNamara and, 903–4; Newstead and, 686; Schlauch and, 527, 529; tenure, salary, and promotion discrimination at, 974
Companion to the Most Celebrated Private Galleries (Jameson), 27
Comparative Studies in Nursery Rhymes (Eckenstein), 58, 62
Conant, Kenneth John, 407
confession as genre, xxvi
Conflict of Love and Honor, The (Ferrante), 971
Connecticut Academy of Arts and Sciences, 674
Connecticut College for Women, 672
conservative school, xxiii
Constable, Giles, 583, 919
constitutional history, Nellie Neilson and, 169–76
Converse, Florence, 242
Conway, William Martin, 58, 414
Cook, Blanche Wiesen, 907–8
Cook, Walter, 112
Cooper, Sandi, 908
Coordinating Committee for Women in the Historical Profession (CCWHP), xxvii–xxviii, 907–8, 909, 910
Coordinating Council for Women in History (CCWH), xxvii–xxviii
Coppola, Francis Ford, 41, 49
Cordelier, John. *See* Underhill, Evelyn
Cornell University: E. C. Block and, 873; Lillich and, 935
Cornford, Francis M., 46, 202
Corpus of Anglo-Saxon Stone Sculpture, 885, 887
Corpus Vitrearum Medii Aevi committee, 781, 783, 784, 785, 940
Corrigan, Dame Felicitas, of Stanbrook Abbey, 332, 390

Cothren, Michael, 785
Coulton, G. G., 312, 313, 329
Council for British Archaeology, 885
Councils and Synods (Whitelock), 560
Cournos, John, 425
Courtauld Institute of Art, London, 401
Craigie, William A., 699
Cramp, Rosemary: Abbess Hild of Whitby compared with, 887, 893–94, 897; Anglo-Saxon literature as focus of work, 889–90; Anglo-Saxon stone sculpture as focus of work, 887–88, 893; as archaeologist, 885, 887, 888–91, 892; Atkinson as mentor, 892; on Austin's archaeological stance, 890; on documentary and material archaeological evidence, 890–91; as editor, 885, 887; education of, 891–92; field work of, 892–93; financial support of work, 887–88; Harden as mentor, 892; Hawkes as mentor, 892; as mentor, 893, 894–95, 896; Merovingian and Carolingian sculpture as focus of work, 895; methodology and scope of work, 890; Morris on, 893–94; organizational affiliations, 885, 896; pictured, 886; publication history of, 885, 887, 888; Saint Anne's College and, 892, 893; Saint Mary's College and, 894; scholarly circle of, 892, 893; scholarly legacy of, 885–87; on shoddy archaeology, 896; as teacher, 891–92, 893–94; University of Durham and, 893–96; Whitelock and, 892
Crane, R. S., 789, 793
Cranz, Edward, 677
creativity: Sayers and, 430, 431–32; scholarly-creative divide and, 329, 335 n.62
Creighton, Mandell, 69, 71
criticism: Borroff on "Chicago School," 789–91; feminist criticism and audience, xxix–xxx; narrative criticism, xxviii; postmodern criticism, xxiii. *See also* critical reception of work *under specific individuals*
Crittall, Elizabeth, 753
Cronne, H. A., 750
Cropper, Margaret, 191

Crosby, Julie: contributor's note, 1010; on Joan M. Ferrante, 969–77
Crosby, Sumner McKnight, 783
Crothers, David, 798
Crozet, René, 588, 618
Culhwch and Olwen (Bromwich), 776
Curtius, Ernst Robert, 726
Cuttino, George Peddie, 917
CWSA (Cambridge Women's Suffrage Association), 73–74
Cyrugie of Guy de Chauliac, The (Ogden), 705

Dafydd ap Gwilym: Bromwich's scholarship, 775–76; Chotzen scholarship, 771
d'Alverny, Marie Thérèse: Alain de Lille as focus of work, 587; Arabic and Islamic studies as focus of work, 587, 589–91, 592–93; as archivist, 585–87; awards and honors, 589, 593 n.1; Bibliothèque national de France and, xxxiii, 585–87; E. A. R. Brown and, 922; Centre d'études supérieures de civilisation médiévale at Poitiers, 588; Centre national de la recherche scientifique, 588; direction of *Archives d'histoire doctrinale . . .*, 588–89; École des chartes and, 585; education of, 585; family of, 585, 592; as feminist, 593 n.7; French history as focus of work, xxxiv; Hebrew and Judaic studies as focus of work, 587, 589; legacy of, 591; manuscript studies, 585–87; as mentor, 589; organizational affiliation, 589; personal life of, 591; philosophy as interest of, 587, 589; pictured, 586; as pioneer in field, xxxi; publication history of, 587, 590; religious life of, 592; reputation as scholar, 589; scholarly circle of, 589, 591–92; Smalley and, 589, 661; as teacher, 587, 589; translators as focus of work, 590–91, 592; Vajda and, 587
Damico, Helen, xxvii
Dana, Rosamond W., 547
Daniel, Glyn, 374, 375, 410
Dante Alighieri: Ferrante's scholarship, 973; Hammond's translation of, 93; Sayers's fiction and, 428; Sayers's scholarship and translation of works, xxxi, 425–26, 432–34

Dante Society of American, 975
Darby, Delphine Fitz, 114, 120
Dark Tide, The (Brittan), 384
Darlington, R. R., 558
Dart, Thurston, 736
Daunt, Marjorie, 816
Davidson, Hilda R. E., 375–76
Davies, Mary Llewellyn, 312
Davis, Glyn, 415
Day, David, xxxi; on Bertha Haven Putnam, 157–64; contributor's note, 1010
Day, Mabel, 816
Dean, Ruth J.: as Anglo-Norman scholar, 566–67, 568, 569–72; Anglo-Norman Text Society and, 615; awards and honors, 565, 567; as editor, 566, 567; Legge as friend and collaborator, 566, 615, 616–17; manuscript studies of, 567; as mentor, xxxi, 566; Mount Holyoke College and, 567; organizational affiliations, 567; Oxford University and, 566, 567; pictured, 564; M. K. Pope and, 147, 566, 567; publication history of, xxxiii, 566–67; Rosenberg and, 567; scholarly circle of, 566; scholarly legacy of, 572; as teacher, 567, 568; Trevet as focus of work, 566; University of Pennsylvania and, 565–66; Wellesley College and, 567
Death and Life in the Tenth Century (Duckett), 218, 221
Decaux, Abel, 341
de hOir, Siobhán, 464, 465, 467
Delaissé, L. M. J., 290, 764
Delany, Sheila, 533, 534, 535 n.11
Delbouille, Eugène Vinaver, 618
De Luca, Don Guiseppe, 629, 632–33
De Luca, Maddalena, 632
Demaitre, Luke, 542
Demus, Otto, 841
Der Nersessian, Arax, 483, 485, 486
Der Nersessian, Sirarpie: Armenian art as focus of work, 484, 485, 486–90; as art historian, 484; awards and honors, 485; Byzantine illumination as focus of work, 484, 485; collections cataloged, 485; death of, 486; Dumbarton Oaks (Harvard) and,

484, 485, 490; École des hautes études, 484; education of, 484, 485; family of, 483, 485, 486; as feminist, 484–85; Garsoïan and, 804; Ivanova-Mavrodinova and, 505; as linguist, 486; manuscript studies as focus of work, 484; as mentor, 490; pictured, 483; publication history, 484; scholarly circle of, xxxiv, 484; scholarly legacy of, 490; support of scholarship, 483–84; as teacher, 484, 490; T'oros Roslin as focus of work, 486, 489; Turkish genocide in Armenia and, 483; Wellesley College and, 484, 490; Yovsēp'ian and, 485, 490
Derrida, Jacques, xxix, 918, 922
Deschamps, Paul, 115
Desert Christians, The (Ward), 948–49
Desert Fathers, The (Waddell, translation), 328
detective fiction, Sayers's medieval scholarship and, 427–30
Detschew, Dimitar, 509
de Van, Guillaume, 347–48
de Van, Odile Ledieu, 342, 347–48
D'Evelyn, Charlotte: as administrator, 295; affiliation with organizations, 305; Allen and, 304; *Ancrene Riwle* scholarship, 295, 304; audience for works of, 298–99, 303–4; awards and honors, 298, 305–6; on biographical writing, 295; C. Brown as mentor, 297–98, 304; on changes in college community, 302–3; critical reception of works, 304; eccentricities of, 295, 302; education of, 295–97; on Eve in Paradise as explorer, 306; family of, 297, 298–99; financial support of work, 298; Idley as focus of work, 304–5, 306; literature as cultural study and, 302; Marks and, 302, 303, 305, 307 n.20; Mill and, 301; Mount Holyoke and, 297, 300–303, 305–6; on Oxford, 298–300; as pacifist, 298, 301; pictured, 296; *Pricke of Conscience* as focus of work, 298, 299; publication history of, 295, 300, 303–4; reputation as scholar, 302; scholarly circle of, 300–301; as teacher, 295, 302; as women's rights advocate, 301; on Woolley, 301; on WWI, 298

Devergramme, Gabrielle, 881
Devil to Pay, The (Sayers), 430
devotional texts, Anglo-Norman literature, 571–72
Dewar, Michael, 370
DeWindt, Anne Reiber: contributor's note, 1010; on Nellie Neilson, 167–76
DeWindt, Edwin, 176
Diary of an Ennuyée, The (Jameson), 31
Dickenson, J. C., 409
Dickins, Bruce, 555
Dictionary of American English, 699
Dictionary of National Biography, 699
Dictionary of the Middle Ages, 808
Dictionnaire de musique de Riemann, 343
Diehl, Charles, 484, 505
Dietrich, "Miss" [no first name identified], 301
Dieulacres Chronicle, 387
Dijksterhuis, E. J., 633–34
Dillon, Myles, 367
d'Indy, Vincent, 339, 341
"Discipline" (unpublished novel by Clarke and Waddell), 381, 385
Divine Comedy, The (Sayers translation), 425–26, 428, 432–34
Docere Verbo et Exemplo (Bynum), 995–98
Dockray-Miller, Mary: contributor's note, 1010; on Mary Bateson, 67–74
Documents in the Case, The (Sayers), 428
Dodwell, C. R., 289
Dolley, Michael, 558
"Domesday Monachorum, The," 173
Donaldson, E. Talbot, 793, 795–97
Döpfner, Julius, 864
Dorez, Léon, 473
"double dating" for manuscript bibliographies, 702
drama: Forsyth's liturgical drama scholarship, 848–49; Frank and medieval French drama, 275–78; Phillpotts's scholarship on Scandinavian drama, 207; Sayers as dramatist, 425, 430–31; Waddell's scholarship, 324; Woolf's mystery play scholarship, 831
Dress in Medieval France (Evans), 407
Dronke, Peter, 332

Droste-Hülshoff, Annette von, 354
Druids, The (Chadwick), 367, 374
Duckett, Eleanor Shipley: audience for works, 215, 217–18, 219; awards and honors, 213, 223; Bryn Mawr and, 216; Cambridge and, 215, 222; Chase and, 216–18, 222, 223–24; as classicist, 221; Colish and, 982; critical reception of works, 215–16, 219, 221–22; death of, 224; education of, 215; as feminist, 219–20; fiction for children by, 222; gender and authorial voice, 220–21; history as focus of work, 217–18; personal life of, xxxii–xxxiii; pictured, 214; publication history, 215, 218; queenship and, 220; religious life of, 218–19; reputation as scholar, 221–22; scholarly circle of, 222; Smith College and, 213, 215, 216, 224; as teacher, 213, 214, 216, 217; University of London and, 215; Western College for Women, Oxford, Ohio, 216
Duhem, Pierre, 630, 631–32
Dujcev, Ivan, 510, 511, 512, 513, 516, 517
Dumbarton Oaks (Harvard) and, 484, 485, 490
Duncan-Jones, Elsie, 372
Duncan-Jones, Katherine, 833
Dunchad: Glossae in Martianum (Lutz), 675
Dunlevy, Mairéad, 464
Dupuy, Claude, 473–74
Dupuy, Jacques, 473–74
Dupuy, Pierre, 473–74
Dürer, Albrecht, 57–58
Durham and Northumberland Architectural and Archaeological Society, 885
Dzwonczyk, Kristina, 50

Earliest Lincolnshire Assize Rolls, The (Stenton), 444–45, 446
Earliest Northamptonshire Assize Rolls, The (Stenton), 445–46
Early English Text Society (EETS), 235, 699
Early Irish Reader, An (Chadwick), 371
Early Scotland (Chadwick), 373
Early Treatises on the Practice of the Justices of the Peace . . . (Putnam), 161

Eastlake, Charles, 28
Eastlake, Elizabeth, 28, 29
eccentricity, as gender difference, xxv
Ecclesiastical History (Oderic Vitalis, Chibnall editor), 755–56
Eckenstein, Lina Dorina Johanna: audience for works, 55, 59; children and, 55, 58, 59, 60, 61; Conway as collaborator, 57–58; death of, 57; Dürer as focus of work, 57–58; education as concern of, 59, 60, 61; Egypt as focus of work, 57, 61; family of, 55, 57, 58; as independent scholar, 55–57; as linguist, 57–58; monasticism as focus of work, 59–61; nursery rhymes as focus of work, 58, 62; pictured, 56; scholarly circle of, 58, 59, 61; scholarly legacy of, 62; scope of work, 55; Sinai as focus of work, 61; as socialist, 59; as translator, 60; Women's Freedom movement and, 57; women's history and, 59; women's rights activism, 59
Eckenstein, Oscar, 55, 57, 58
École de Louvre, 505
École des chartes: d'Alverny and, 585; history of, 473; Pernoud and, 714; E. Power and, 312; Solente and, 471–73
École des hautes études, 484; Der Nersessian and, 484; Garsoïan and, 805, 806; Ivanova-Mavrodinova and, 504; Willard and, 765
economic history: E. A. R. Brown on taxation and Philip the Fair, 923–24; Cam and, 260; M. C. Chibnall and, 753, 757; Chibnall's scholarship, 753, 757; Economic History Society, 311, 315; Neilson and, 172, 173–74; E. Power and, 316–18; Shire and, 735–36. *See also* London School of Economics (LSE)
Economic History Review, 315
Economic History Society, 311, 315
Edda and Saga (Phillpotts), 210, 211
Eddas, 202, 205, 207, 210–11, 370–71
Edgeworth, Maria, 29
education: admissions and enrollment discrimination, 69, 81, 101, 105, 148, 861; Mary Astell and women's education, 7; Bateson's efforts on behalf of women's education, 74; Bulgarian educational

opportunities for women, 496–99; Busse-Wilson as advocate of girl's education, 361; Cam's efforts to provide education for working class women, 264; "certificates" instead of degrees awarded to women, 69, 72, 755; of children, 59, 60, 875; coeducational schools, 133–34, 542–43; degrees awarded to women, 69, 72, 101, 265–66, 382, 404–5, 426, 755, 864; Duckett's fictional comparison of British and U.S. school systems, 222; Eckenstein and, 59, 60, 61; Elstob on women and learning, xxv, 9–10; familial support and pursuit of, 130; financial support of research in the humanities, 303; French women's educational opportunities, 471–73; G.I. Bill of Rights and higher education, 901; German reforms, post-WWII, 861; government policy and access to, 909; graduate programs and women, 69; Hickes as proponent of women's education, 18 n.28; as human right in Bulgaria, 497–99; opportunities for women in the United States, 102–3, 130, 759; Pernoud on discrimination in education, 720 n.11; Project Muse, teaching reading through art in elementary school, 875; Richter's autobiographical essay on, 82–88; scholarly-creative divide and, 329, 335 n.62; sexual impropriety as a concern in women's education, 382–83; women's decision to pursue, 130; WWI and reforms in, 105, 206; WWII and changes in, 827–28, 901–3. *See also* women's colleges

"Education and Development" (Richter, autobiographical essay), 82–88

Edwards, A. S. G.: contributor's note, 1010; on Eleanor Prescott Hammond, 91–96

Edwards, Nancy, 893

Edwards, Philippa, 332, 390

EETS (Early English Text Society), 235, 699

Egyptology, 57, 61

Einerman, Betty, 547

Eisenmann, Linda, 137

Eisenstein, Elizabeth, 583

Elder Edda and Ancient Scandinavian Drama, The (Phillpotts), 207

Eliot, T. S., Weston and, 39, 41, 45, 48

Elisabeth of Thuringia, Busse-Wilson's scholarship, 353, 354–55, 361

Elliott, Kenneth, 736–37

Ellis, Ellen Deborah, 160, 302

Ellis, Havelock, 391–92 n.21

Ellison, Ruth, 818

Elstob, Charles, 3, 15

Elstob, Elizabeth, xxvii; Astell and, 7; audience awareness, 10; critical reception of works, 11–13; death of, 16; disposition of papers, 15–16; education of, 3–4, 6; family of, 3–6, 8, 16; as "Frances Smith," 15; as governess, 16; as grammarian, 3, 13–14; Hickes and, 9, 13, 14, 15; Oxford and, 6; patronage and financial support of, 12–13, 15; personal relationship with research, xxv, 11; pictured, 4; political content of work, 9, 12, 14–15; publication history of, 3, 14, 18 n.19; Queen Anne and, 9, 12, 14; Queen's College and, 5–6; religious role of women, 9, 12; St. Gregory as focus of work, 10–12; Saxon circle at Queen's College and, 5–6, 16; scholarly and social circles of, 6–8, 16; sources available to, 8, 13–14; as translator, 3, 6; William Elstob as mentor, 6, 8; on women's education, xxv, 9–10; works and publication history, 3, 6–7, 8–9, 12, 14

Elstob, Matilda, 5, 6, 7, 15

Elstob, William, 3, 5–6, 11, 14

Emperor Constantine, The (Sayers), 430, 431

employment: academic career opportunities for women, xxv, xxx–xxxiii, 67, 81–82, 101, 133–34, 137–38, 179 n.65; as administrators of Colleges, 208, 285, 560, 797–98, 805–6; Bulgarian academic career opportunities, 496–97, 499–500; children and women's careers, 582, 905, 906–7, 937, 938; corporate or private sector employment, 909; discrimination in, 605, 671–72, 906, 907; emerging fields of scholarship and opportunities for women, 604; hiring

employment (*continued*)
  discrimination, 755, 974, 984; as librarian or archivist, xxxii; marriage and, 137, 248–49, 251–52 n.51, 385, 605, 671–72, 755, 761, 906, 907, 965; nonacademic, xxxii, 16, 909; Pernoud as "unemployed intellectual," 714; in publishing, xxxii, 72; salary inequities, 138, 938, 974; support of independent scholarship and, xxxv. *See also under specific individuals*
Endless Web, The (Evans), 414
Enforcement of The Statutes of Laborers . . ., The (Putnam), 159–60
England before Elizabeth (Cam), 266
"England's Trust," xxiii–xxiv
English and International (Salter, Pearsall and Zeeman editors), 819
English Art 1307–1461 (Evans), 404, 408–9, 410
English Friars and Antiquity in the Early Fourteenth Century (Smalley), 664, 665
English Historical Documents (Whitelock), 557, 560
English Historical Review, 70, 72
English Jewellery from the Fifth Century A.D. *to 1800* (Evans), 405
English Justice between the Norman Conquest and the Great Charter, 1066–1215 (Stenton), 449–50
English Medieval Literature and Its Social Foundations (Schlauch), 532–33
English Mystery Plays, The (Woolf), 831–32
English Place-Name Society, 558
English Posies and Posy Rings (Evans), 405
English Religious Lyric in the Middle Ages, The (Woolf), 829–30
English-Saxon Homily on the Birth-Day of St. Gregory, An (Elstob), 3
English Society in the Early Middle Ages (Stenton), 448
English studies, 101, 103
English Taste in Landscape in the Seventeenth Century (Ogden and Ogden), 707
"English Transition," 94–95
English Verse between Chaucer and Surrey (Hammond), 93

English Woman in History, The (Stenton), 441–42, 449
English Writings of Richard Rolle, The (Allen), 234
Epistolae (Ferrante and Hanning, online database), 972–73
Erez, Ariela, 878
Erez, Menahen, 878
Erikson, Erik, 919
Essays on Manuscripts and Rare Books (Lutz), 677
Evans, Arthur, 399, 401, 411, 413, 414
Evans, D. Simon, 776
Evans, Deanna Delmar: contributor's note, 1010; on Cora Elizabeth Lutz, 671
Evans, Evan, 771
Evans, Joan: as archaeologist, 399–401, 402, 407–8; as art historian, 408–9; autobiographical writing (*Prelude and Fugue*), 404, 405, 407, 414, 415; awards and honors, xxxii, 412–13; Cluniac art as focus of work, 407–8, 411, 415; Courtauld Institute of Art, London, 401; critical reception of works, 404, 407, 409, 415; education of, 399, 404; as family biographer, 401, 414; family of, 399, 401–2, 411–12, 413, 414; as financially independent, 399, 412; France as focus of work, 405–6, 407, 409, 410–11, 415; C. Hancock ("Nannie") and, 402, 405; Horsfield and, 406, 414; as indexer, 401; jewels and jewelry as focus of work, 401, 404, 405; E. Jourdain and, 402–4, 405, 414–15; M. Jourdain and, 402–4, 405; as librarian, 403, 404; medieval culture as focus of work, 405–6; naturalism in design as focus of work, 411; Oxford and, 399–401, 404–5; *Oxford History of English Art*, contributions to, 408–9, 410; on patronage and the arts, 406, 407; as philanthropist, 413–14; pictured, 400; as poet, 404; publication history of, 402, 405, 407, 411; religious life of, 403; reputation as scholar, xxxii; Royal Archaeological Institute and, 411; Ruskin as focus of work, 411; scholarly circle of, 405, 408;

scholarly legacy of, 409, 415; Society of Antiquaries and, 413–14; as teacher and mentor, 412; as translator, 404, 406; travel, 401, 402–3, 405, 406; University College London, 401; Wheeler and, 411–12, 413, 414; WWII as context for work, 410–11

Evans, Sir John, 399

Ewert, A., 618

Eyre of London, The (Cam), 267–68

Faithfull, Lilian, 99

Fawtier, Robert, 920

Febvre, Lucien, 960

feminism: in Bulgaria, 498; Busse-Wilson's scholarship, 354–55, 356–57, 360, 361; Bynum on, 1005; d'Alverny and, 593 n.7; Der Nersessian and, 484–85; D'Evelyn as women's rights advocate, 301; Duckett and, 219–20; Eckenstein and women's rights, 57, 59; E. Elstob on women's education, xxv, 9–10; *Feminist Studies* (CCWHP journal), 910; Ferrante on women's rights, 973; Friedan's *The Feminine Mystique* and, 982; McNamara and, 901, 904, 905, 907; Richter on women's rights, 87; self-representation in autobiographical writing and, xxviii; Stuard on, 955–66; Waddell and, 323–24. *See also* suffrage; women's history

Feminist Studies (CCWHP journal), 910

Fergusson, Francis, 46

Fergusson, Peter, 416

Ferrante, Joan M.: audience for works, 973; Barnard College and, 970; Brearley School and, 970; Columbia University and, xxxii, 970–71, 973–74; education of, 970; family of, 969–70, 976 (*see also* marriage *under this heading*); football and, 969, 974; Hanning as collaborator and friend, 972, 974, 975; Heilbrun and, 972; Jackson as mentor, 971; as linguist, 969, 970–71; marriage to Carey McIntosh, xxxv, 975, 976–77; as musician, 975; oral tradition as focus of work, 971, 972; organizational affiliations, 975; personal life of, 969, 975–77; pictured, 968; publication history of, 971, 972; Radcliffe College and, 970; on religion and women's rights, 973; religious life of, 976; reputation as scholar, xxxii; scholarly circle of, 975; Serbo-Croatian epics as focus of work, 971; teaching and, 972; Tristan legend as focus of work, 971

Fight for Right Movement, 104

Fisher, Dorothy Canfield, 761

Fisiak, Jacek, xxxiii, 525, 526

Fitch, Marc, 413

FitzGerald, Jennifer: contributor's note, 1010; on Helen Waddell, 323–32; on Maude Violet Clarke, 381–90

Five Hundred Years of Chaucer Criticism and Allusion (Spurgeon), 99, 103, 105

Five Red Herrings (Sayers), 428

Flasdieck, H. M., 704

Fleming, Atherton "Mac," 427–28, 434

Fleming, John Anthony, 425, 436 n.19

Fleming, William, 937

Flower and the Leaf, The (Hammond), 94

Flowering of the Middle Ages, The (Evans), 415

Flügel, Ewald, 704

Focillon, Henri, 484, 505

Fontaine, Charles, 276

Fontes Graeci (Dujcev, translator), 510

Fontes historiae Bulgaricae (Bulgarian Academy of Sciences), 511

Fontes Latini historiae Bulgaricae (Bulgarian Academy of Sciences), 513

Ford, Richard, 119

Forsyth, George H. Jr., 845–46

Forsyth, Ilene H.: on art history, 854–55; audience for works, 854; awards and honors, 847–48; Barnard College and, 843; Byzantine art as focus of work, 839–45, 847–48, 849, 850–52; capital relief sculpture as focus of work, 842–43, 850–52; contributor's note, 1010–11; Demus and, 841; education of, 841–43; on fragmentation and permutation of form in Romanesque period, 852–53; Harvard and, 847; Hawkins and, 846; liturgical drama as focus of work, 848–49; Madonna and Child sculpture as

Forsyth, Ilene H. (*continued*)
focus of work, 843–45, 849; marriage and collaboration with George H. Forsyth Jr., 845–47; Megaw as mentor, 846; as memoirist, xxxiii; Michigan Law Quadrangle as focus of work, 853; mosaics as focus of work, 846, 847–48; pictured, 840; publication history of, 849, 852, 853; reliquaries as focus of work, 850; Romanesque sculpture as focus of work, 842–45, 850–53; Schapiro as mentor, 841–42, 845, 850; scholarly circle of, 848; Sinai fieldwork of, 846–47; Sinai icons as focus of work, 847; stone identification as focus of work, 853–54; as teacher, 842–43, 847; travel, 839; University of Michigan and, 839, 847–48; Van Nice as mentor, 846
Foster, Charles Wilmer, 442, 443, 445
Foster, Idris, 773, 776
Fotitch, Tatiana, 618
Foucault, Michel, 918, 922, 923
Foulet, Lucien, 279
Fourteenth-Century English Poetry (Salter), 819
Fowler, Dorothy Ganfield, 906
Fragmentation and Redemption (Bynum), 995–97, 998
Frank, Grace: awards and honors, 273; Bryn Mawr and, 273–74, 275; death of, 275; as editor, 274; family of, 273; French theater as focus of work, 275–78; *Jeu d'Adam* scholarship, 277, 281; marriage to Tenney Frank, 273; as mentor, 280; Miner as collaborator with, 276; as musician, 274–75; organizational affiliations, 274; poetry as focus of work, 276; proverbs as focus of work, 276–77; publication history of, 276, 277–78; as reviewer, 280; E. Rickert and, 279; scholarly legacy of, 275, 280; Spitzer and, 279–80; as teacher, 274; *Tristan et Iseut* scholarship, 279, 281; University of Chicago, 273; Villon's poetry as focus of work, 278–79; during WWI, 274
Franklin, Carmela Vircillo: on Christine A. E. Mohrmann, 599; contributor's note, 1011
Frank Merry Stenton (Stenton), 451

Frappier, Jean, 618
Fraser, Olive, 739–40
Frauenfrage im Mittelalter, Die (Bücher), 359
Frazer, James, 40, 41, 45, 46
Fréchet, Robyn: contributor's note, 1011; translation of Tesnière on Solente, 471–78
Freedman, Paul, 917–19
Freeman, Alice, 137
Freeman, Anne, 919
French language, Pope's study of Anglo-Norman and, 150–54
Frendmand, Alice, 971
Friedman, William F., 288–89
Fries, Maureen, xxviii
From Latin to Modern French (Pope), 148, 150–54
From Ritual to Romance (Weston), 39, 45
Frost, Robert, 794
Furnivall, Frederick James, 103–4

Gage, Matilda, 955
Galbert of Bruges, 579, 580
Galbraith, Vivian H., 387, 388, 390, 749, 750, 754
Gamer, Helena, 791
Gantcheva, Liuba T. (Yana Yazova), 502–3
Garber, Rebecca L.: contributor's note, 1011; on Elisabeth Gössmann, 857–67
Gardner, Alice, 70, 71
Gardner, Edmund, 649–50
Gardner, Helen, 236; Reeves and, 652; St. Hilda's College and, 554
Gardner-Medwin, Alisoun, 373, 741
Garmonsway, G. N., 816
Garrett, "American Miss," xxv, 505
Garrett, Mary, 102
Garsoïan, Nina G.: administrative career of, 805–6; Armenian and Byzantine studies focus of work, 803, 805–8; Armenian identity of, 804; audience for works, 806; awards and honors, 806; Bickerman as mentor, 804; Bryn Mawr and, 804; Columbia University and, 805; Der Nersessian as mentor, 804; *Dictionary of the Middle Ages*, contributions to, 808;

early Christianity as focus of work, 805, 808, 809, 810; École des hautes études and, 805, 806; education of, 804; family of, 803–4; Institut Catholique, Paris, and, 805; Iranian language studies of, 805; Lycée Français de New York and, 804; Mattingly as mentor, 804; as mentor, 806; organizational affiliations of, 806; Paulicianism as focus of work, 805, 808; personal life of, 803–4, 806; pictured, 802; political oppression of, xxxiv; publication history of, 807, 808–9; reputation as scholar, 807; scholarly legacy of, 807, 809; Smith College and, 805; Sorbonne and, 806; as teacher, 805, 806; as translator, 807, 809; travel and, 809; University of Rome-Las Sapienza and, 806

Gateway to the Middle Ages, The (Duckett), 215, 218, 219, 222, 223

Gaudy Night (Sayers), 428, 429, 577

Gazzard, Francis, 286

Geertz, Clifford, 918

gender: academic system as gendered, 135–37; academic titles and, 127–28, 135–36; authorial voice in Duckett's works and, 220–21; Bynum's scholarship on, 997–99; gender politics in academe, 674; Gössmann's religious scholarship and, 857–59, 862–63, 866, 867; grammar as an excuse for sexism, 13; historiography and, 955, 957; initials used to disguise, 140 n.2; mysticism and, 194–95, 358–61. *See also* sexism

gender difference: "appropriate" subjects of study and, xxxii, 72, 81, 128, 138, 194, 312, 358; autobiographical writing and, xxviii; eccentricity as, xxv; first person pronoun (I) and, xxviii–xxix; medieval women writers and, xxv–xxvi; Patterson's privileging of male perspective, xxiii–xxiv; the personal in women's scholarship, xxv, xxviii; Self / Other dichotomy and, xxvi–xxvii, xxviii; sumptuary laws and, 962; Wittig on gender and language, xxiii. *See also* sexism; sexuality

Geschichte der deutschen Mystic im Mittelalter (Preger), 358–60

Gesta Regis Henrici secundi Benedicti Abbatis (anonymous), 448–49

al-Ghazālī (Algazel), d'Alverny's scholarship, 589–90

Ghost of Versailles, The (Iremonger), 414–15

Gibson, Edward, 5

Gibson, Margaret, 952

Gift of Tongues, The (Schlauch), 530, 534

Gildersleeve, Virginia, 105, 106

Gildon, Charles, 13–14

Gillam, John, 893

Gilson, Étienne, 344, 585, 588, 592

Ginzberg, Eli, 937

Giotto, 27–28

GIRS (Group international de recherche sur les stalles), 880–81

Girton College: Bateson and, 69; Cam and, 263–64; Chibnall and, 754, 755, 756; Duckett and, 223; Phillpotts and, 202, 204, 208; E. Power and, 311; Salter and, 817

Gjuzelev, Vasil, 507

Glazer, Penina Migdal, 137–38

Gneuss, Helmut, 558

Goethe, Ottilie von, 29

Goffart, Walter, 922

Goldbrunner, Hermann, 638

Golden Bough, The (Frazer), 41, 45, 46

Golden Sequence, The (Underhill), 191

Gómez-Bravo, Ana M.: contributor's note, 1011; on María Rosa Lida de Malkiel, 723

Gorres, Joseph von, 358, 361

Gospels in the Schools, The (Smalley), 664–65

Gössmann, Elisabeth: Biser and, 865–66; children of, 863; discrimination in education, 861, 864; education of, 860–63, 864; family of, 857–59; gender and religion as focus of work, 857–59, 862–63, 866, 867; Grabmann Institute and, 862–63, 864; Hildegard of Bingen and, 862–63, 867; honors and awards, 867; Japanese religious practices as focus of work, 864–65; LMU-Munich and, 861, 863, 865–66; marriage to Wilhelm Gössmann, 863; mystics as focus of work,

Gössmann, Elisabeth (*continued*) 863; pictured, 858; political oppression, xxxiii, xxxiv; religious life of, 857–59; Schmaus and, 861, 864; Schmid and, 862; scholarly circle of, 863; Seishin University, Tokyo, 864–65; sexism and impact on career of, xxxi; Shmaus and, 861, 862; Sophia University in Tokyo and, 863–64; as teacher, 863, 865, 866–67; theology as focus of work, 861–62; Universität Münster and, 860–61; women medieval writers as focus of work, 862–63, 866
Gothic Manuscripts (Sandler), 290
Gowing, Christopher, 892
Grabar, Andre, 504
Grabmann Institute for Research in the Philosophy and Theology of the Middle Ages, 862–63, 864
Grafinger, Christine, 638
Graham, Rose, 618
Grail legend: in popular culture, 48, 49; Weston's research and theories, 47–48
Grammar of Anglo-Saxon Ornament (Cramp), 887
Gramsci, Antonio, 356
Les Grandes Époques de l'art en Occident (Pernoud), 715, 717
Gray, Douglas, 833
Grayson, Janet, 37, 41, 49
Green, Monica, 957
Greene, Dana, 184, 185, 187, 190, 193, 194, 195
Greene, R. L., 830
Gretsch, Mechthild, 20 n.54
Grey World, The (Underhill), 185–86
Grézes, Marie, 879
Gribelin, Simon, 8–9
Grieg, Edvard, 344
Grierson, Philip, 219
Grinnell College, M. Rickert and, 285, 286
Grinnell College, Rickert and, 286
Grodecki, Louis, 936, 937–38, 940
Groeneboom, P. C., 599
Grooms, Chris, 778
Group international de recherche sur les stalles (GIRS), 880–81

Growth of Literature, The (Chadwick and Chadwick), 367, 371–72, 374, 770
Gründler, Otto, 786
Grundmann, Herbert, 359–60
Guarnieri, Romana, 638
Gueorgiey, Vladimir, 511–12, 517
Guignebert, Charles, 343
Guillaume d'Orange (Ferrante), 972
Guingamor; Lanval; Tyolet; Le Bisclaveret (Weston, translation), 38
Gunn, Thom, 738
Guy de Chauliac, Ogden's scholarship, 697, 704, 705–6
Gwyer, Barbara, 649

Haas, Renate, 88; on Caroline F. E. Spurgeon, 99–107; contributor's note, 1011
hagiography: Anglo-Saxon hagiographic texts, 571; "Friends of Saints" group, 910; Ward on purpose of, 951. *See also* Busse-Wilson, Elisabeth; *specific saints*
Halcyon Club, 40
Hall, James, 25
Ham, Roswell, 301–2, 307 n.14
"Hamadryad, The" Evans, 404
Hamlin, Ann, 464
Hammond, Eleanor Prescott: Chaucer as focus of work, 92–93; critical reception of works, 95; Dante as focus of work, 93; death of, 95; education of, 91; on "the English Transition," 94–95; family of, 91; Lydgate as focus of work, 92, 94; personal life of, 91, 95; publication history, 92–93, 95; Rickert and, 132, 140 n.1; scholarly legacy of, 93; scope of interests, 95; Shakespeare as focus of work, 93; as teacher, 91; as translator, 93; University of Chicago and, 91–92; Wellesley College and, 91
Hamson, Jack, 740
Hancock, Caroline, 402, 405
Handbook to the Public Galleries of Art, A (Jameson), 28
Hangman's Holiday (Sayers), 428
Hanning, Robert, 972, 974, 975
Harbison, Peter, 467

Harden, Donald, 892
Harkness, Georgia, 195
Harlots of the Desert (Ward), 949
Harper, William Rainey, 134
Harrison, Jane, 40, 46
Hart, Sophie Chantal, 241
Hartnett, P. J., 462
Harty, Kevin J.: as contributor, xxxi, 1011; on Ruth J. Dean, 565
Harvard University: E. A. R. Brown and, 919; Bynum and, 1003–4; Cam and, 266–67; Der Nersessian and Dumbarton Oaks, 484, 485, 490; Forsyth and, 847; Kibre and, 543
Harvey, John, 410
Haskell, Francis, 28, 406
Haskins, Charles Homer, 174, 543, 917, 919, 982
Hastings, Margaret, 171, 175, 176
Hastings, Maurice, 410
Hatcher, Anna G., 280
Have His Carcase (Sayers), 428, 429
Haveley, N. R., 818
Haverfield, Francis John, 892
Haverford College, 959
Hawkes, Christopher, 892
Hawkins, Ernest, 846
Hayes-Robinson, Margaret, 260, 262
Hayward, Jane: American art as focus of work, 785; as art historian, 783; awards and honors, 781, 786; Branner and, 784; Columbia University and, 784; Corpus Vitrearum and, 784, 785; Crosby as mentor, 783; as draftsperson and illustrator, 783; education of, 781–83; exhibitions curated by, 781, 784–85; International Center of Medieval Art and, 786; Kalamazoo congress of medievalists and, 786; Lyman Allyn Museum and, 784; as mentor, 785; Metropolitan Museum of Art and, 781, 784–85, 787; organizational affiliations, 785–86; Pennsylvania Academy of Fine Arts and, 781–83; personal life of, 786; pictured, 782; publication history of, 784; scholarly circle of, 785–86; scholarly legacy of, 787; stained glass as focus of work, 781, 783; as teacher, 784; WWII experiences of, 781–83; Yale and, 783–84

Headley, John, 983
Healy, Patrick, 467
Hearne, Thomas, 11–12
Heart of Spain (King), 114, 116
Hebrew and Judaic studies: d'Alverny's scholarship, 587, 589; Smalley and, 666
Heilbrun, Carolyn, xxx, 972
Heitland, Margaret Bateson, 73
Hellman, C. Doris, 544
Heloise, Abbess of the Paraclete: reputation as scholar, 334 n.39; Ross's scholarship, 582; Waddell's scholarship, 327, 328
Henderson, Charles, 217
Henderson, Isabel, 375
Henneman, John, 919
Henry, François, 466
Herbert, J. A., 186, 233
Herford, C. H., 330
Hesse, Hermann, 355
Heusler, Andreas, 207
Hibbard, Laura, Rickert and, 140 n.1
Hickes, George, 5, 6, 9, 13, 14, 15, 18 n.28
Hicks, Ruth, 673
High King of Heaven (Ward), 952
Hild, Abbess of Whitby, 887, 893–94, 897
Hildburgh, W. L., 409
Hildegard of Bingen, 60, 359; Gössmann's scholarship, 862–63, 867
Hillcroft College for Working Women, 264
Hilton, Walter, 193, 194
Hippocrates Latinus (Kibre), 545
Hirsch-Reich, Beatrice, 651
Hirsh, John C.: contributor's note, 1012; on Hope Emily Allen, 227–37
Histoire de le bourgeoisie en France (Pernoud), 717
Histoire Littéraire de la France (Solente), 477
Historians in the Middle Ages (Smalley), 664
Historians on Trial (Mutaftchieva and Tchitchovska, editors), 512, 514
Historic Buildings and Monuments Commission of English Heritage, 885

History of Bulgaria (Bulgarian Academy of Sciences), 514
History of Childhood, The (Ross), 580–81
History of Our Lord, The (Jameson and Eastlake), 28–29
History of Sinai, A (Eckenstein), 61
History of the Society of Antiquaries (Evans), 414
Hoare, Dorothy, 770
Hoccleve, Thomas, 93–94
Hodder, Karen, 818
Hodgson, Phyllis, 816
Holcomb, Adele M., 25
Holdsworth, Mary, 895
Holtby, Winifred, 389
Holy Feast, Holy Fast (Bynum), 995–97, 998
Homily on the Nativity of St. Gregory (Ælfric, Elstob), 7, 8–12
homophobia, xxxii, xxxiii, 383–84, 391–92 n.21, 392 nn.27–28
Hopkins, John, 416
Hopkins, William, 10
Hopper, John, 693
Horsfield, Agnes, 406, 414
Horstman, Carl, 232
Hours of Catherine of Cleves, E. C. Block on folio, 92, 875
House of the Soul, The (Underhill), 191
Howard, Sir Esme, 205
Howell, Martha, 358
Hroswitha (Hrotsvit) of Gandersheim, 60, 359
Huch, Ricarda, 362 n.11
Hudson, John, 10–11
Hughes, Diane Owen, 983
Hughes, Kathleen, 559
Hughes, Shaun F. D., xxv; contributor's note, 1012; on Elizabeth Elstob, 3–16
Huizinga, J. M., 406
Hulbert, James R., 139, 699, 791
Hundred and the Hundred Rolls, The (Cam), 265
Hunt, John, 467
Hunt, Morton, 683, 687
Hunt, Richard, 592

Hunt, Roger, 663
Hunter, George, 828
Hunter College: E. C. Block and, 876; faculty as mentors, 905–6; Kibre and, 541; L. H. Loomis and, 244; Newstead and, 685, 686; women's history and, 909–10
Huntington, Archer, 113, 114
Hutton, Ronald, 375
Huyskens, Albert, 354

I (first person pronoun), xxviii–xxix
Ibn Sīnā (Avicenna), d'Alverny's scholarship, 589–91
Icelandic studies: Chadwick's scholarship, 368–69; Phillpotts and, 201–11; Schlauch's scholarship, 528, 529
iconography: Block on choir stall misericords, 876–80; Clarke's scholarship and, 387; Der Nersessian and Armenian iconography, 485, 487; Jameson's work and, 25–33; Roe and Irish iconography, 463, 466; Rokseth's work in music iconography, 345; Warburg and, 829
Idley, Peter, 295, 304–5
independent (nonacademic) scholarship: of Block, xxxi, xxxii, xxxiii; of Busse-Wilson, 353, 356; of Eckenstein, 55–57; of Phillpotts, 203–4; support of, xxxv; of Waddell, 325
Infeld, Helen Schlauch, 533, 536 n.23
Infeld, Leopold, 533
Influence of Saint Bernard, The (Ward), 952
Inge, William, 193
Institut Catholique, Paris, 805
Institute for Advanced Study at Princeton, 988
Institute for Research in History, 909
intellectual history. *See* Bynum, Caroline Walker; Colish, Marcia L.; d'Alverny, Marie Thérèse
Intellectual Life in the Middle Ages (Ward and Smith), 952
International Center of Medieval Art (ICMA), 786
International Commission for the History

of Representative and Parliamentary Institutions (ICHRP), 267
International Federation of University Women (IFUW), 82, 106–7
International Popular Tale and Early Welsh Tradition (Jackson), 690
International Society of Anglo-Saxonists, 890
Internet resources: Corpus of Anglo-Saxon Stone Sculpture, 888; *Epistolae* (Ferrante and Hanning, online database), 972–73; Network for the History of Women Religious, 911
Inventing the Middle Ages (Cantor), xxvii, 917
Iohannis Scotti: Annotationes in Marcianum (Lutz), 674–75
Ireland: N. Kershaw's Irish language scholarship, 371; political history of, 459–61; Roe and Irish archaeology, xxxi, 462–63, 467. *See also* Celtic studies; Trinity College, Dublin
Iremonger, Lucille, 414–15
Irish High Crosses with Figure Sculptures Explained (Roe), 463
Irving, Edward, 566
Ivanova-Mavrodinova, Vera: as archaeologist, 496, 504, 505, 506–7; cataloging as focus of work, 504–5; children of, 506; death of, 503; Der Nersessian and, 505; École de Louvre and, 504, 505; École des hautes études and, 504; education of, 495–96, 504, 505; family of, 503 (*see also* marriage *under this heading*); financial support of work, 505–6; Grabar and, 504; marriage to Nikola Mavrodinov, 496, 506; National Archaeological Museum and, 503, 504; pictured, 494; scholarly circle of, 505, 507; scholarly legacy of, 504–5; WWII events, 506

Jackson, Kenneth, 368–69, 370, 371–72, 375, 690–91, 770, 773
Jackson, William T. H., 971
Jacobstahl, Gustav, 346
Jacopone da Todi, 194
James, Henry, 229

James, M. R., 287, 663
James, William, 193
Jameson, Anna: audience for works, 28, 29; critical reception of works, 31; death of, 29; family of, 25–26; financial support of work, 27; iconography and, 25, 30, 32; influences on, 30–31; Lanzi and, 31; marriage to Robert Jameson, 26; National Gallery in London and, 28; pictured, 26; publication history of, 27, 28–29, 31; scholarly legacy of, 25; subject of art as focus of art criticism, 32; travel and, 31; Vasari and, 31–32
Jamison, Evelyn, 749, 750, 751
Jaufré Rudel, 279
Jelinek, Estelle, xxv–xxvi
Jenkins, Marianna, 120
Jesus as Mother (Bynum), xxxii, 995–97, 998, 1004
Jeu d'Adam, 277, 281
jewels: Evans's scholarship on, 401, 404, 405; stained glass as gems, 939
Jewett, Sophie, 241, 249 n.7
Jex-Blake, Katharine, 208
Jex-Blake family, 201, 208
Joachim of Fiore, 666; Reeves's scholarship, 649–50, 651, 652–54; Smalley on, 662
Joan of Arc, Pernoud's scholarship, 716–17
Johnson, C., 265
Johnson, Ellen, 934
Johnson, Penelope D.: contributor's note, 1012; on Lina Eckenstein, 55–62
Johnstone, Hilda, 164
Joly de Fleury collection, 474
Jones, Charles W., 675
Jones, Howard Mumford, 329, 700
Jones, Malcolm, 878
Jones, Mary Gwaldys, 261, 265
Jónsson, Finnur, 203
Jónsson, Runólfur, 5
Joslin, David, 755
Jourdain, Eleanor, 402–3, 405, 414–15, 417 n.27
Jourdain, Margaret, 402–4
Juan de Mena, Malkiel scholarship, 726–27, 728

Judaic studies. *See* Hebrew and Judaic studies
judicial history. *See* legal history
Juliana, Woolf scholarship, 828
Julian of Norwich, xxv–xxvi, xxviii; Margery Kempe and, 236–37; Ward's scholarship, 950–51, 952
Jullian, Philippe, 414
Justin, Gale, 693
Just Vengeance, The (Sayers), 430, 431

Kahn, David, 289
Kaiser-Wilhelm-Institute für Kunst- and Kulturwissenschaft, 628
Kalamazoo, Annual International Congress of Medieval Studies at, 786, 848, 880
Kane, George, 816
Kantorowicz, Ernst, 919
Keats's Shakespeare (Spurgeon), 105–6
Kelter, Irving A: contributor's note, 1012; on Pearl Kibre, 541–47
Kelter, Janice Gordon, 547
Kennedy, Elspeth: contributor's note, 1012; on Mildred K. Pope, 147–55
Kent Keepers of the Peace (Putnam), 161–62
Kenyon, Kathleen, 892
Kepler, Thomas, 193
Ker, Neil, 558, 663
Ker, W. P., 40, 203, 204, 207, 389
Kern, Elga, 82, 99
Kershaw, Nora. *See* Chadwick, Nora Kershaw
Keynes, Simon, 561
Kibre, Adele, 541
Kibre, Pearl: awards and honors, 546; Columbia University and, 541, 543; critical reception of works, 545; death of, 541; education of, 541, 542–43; family of, 541; financial support of work, 546; Harvard and, 543; Hunter College and, 541; manuscript studies as focus of work, 545–46; medical history as focus of work, 544; as mentor, 541, 905; organizational affiliations of, 546; Paetow and, 543, 545; pictured, 540; publication history of, 545–46; Roberts and, 542, 905; scholarly circle of, 542, 543, 544; scholarly legacy of, 546–47; scientific history as focus of work, 544; Siraisi and, 542; as teacher, 541; Thorndike as mentor and collaborator, 543–45; University of California and, 541–42, 542; women's history and, 545
Kidson, Peter, 415
al-Kindī (Alkindi), d'Alverny's scholarship, 589–90
Kindred and Clan in the Middle Ages (Phillpotts), 204–5
King, Donald, 412
King, Georgiana Goddard: awards and honors, 112; Berensons and, 112, 114–15; Bryn Mawr and, 111–12, 116, 119–20; critical reception of works, 118; education of, 112; family of, 112; financial support of research, 113; gender and scholarship of, 118–19; Lowber as collaborator with, 116; as mentor, 120; personal life of, 112, 118, 119–20, 121; pictured, 110; publication history, 113, 114; religious life of, 117; as reviewer, 120; Santiago pilgrimage and cultural exchange, 115–17; scholarly circle of, 116, 120; scholarly legacy of, 119–21; Stein and, 112, 120; G. E. Street and, 114; as teacher, 113, 119–20
King, Heather, 465–67, 467
King's College, University of London: Spurgeon and, 99, 104; Underhill and, 104
Kisselintchev, Assen, 510
Kitchin, G. W., 70
Klenke, Sister Amelia, 691
Klepper, Deeana Copeland: on Beryl Smalley, 657–67; as contributor, xxv, 1012
Knott, Thomas A., 699
Knowles, David, 222, 947
Köbling, Eugen, 245
Koch, Josef, 628
Kökeritz, Helge, 793, 795
Koledarov, Petar, 516
Kondo, Hisara, 878
Koonz, Claudia, 910, 959
Korean War, 762, 920
Kossov, Dimitar, 513
Kostova, Emilia, 517

Kottaner, Helenne, xxvi–xxvii
Kouymjian, Dickran: contributor's note, 1012; on Sirarpie Der Nersessian, 483–90
Kozma, Der Nersessian's scholarship, 488
Krapp, George P., 527
Krautheimer, Richard, 578
Krey, Philip, 666
Kristanov, Tzvetan, 511
Kristeller, Paul, 677
Kuhn, Sherman M., 706–7
Kuhn, Thomas, 923
Kurath, Hans, 701, 703, 706
Kury, Gloria, 577, 583
Kyllmann, Otto, 324–25, 330

Labande, Edmonde René, 588, 618
Labaudy, Jean, 714
Labowsky, Lotte, 829
Lacombe, Georges, 660–61
Lacy, Norris J., 38
Ladycliff College, 763–64
Lafond, Jean, 938
Laidlaw, James, 740
Lamar, Howard, 798
Lambert, Andrew, 561
Lamprecht, Karl, 357
Landscapes and Seasons of the Medieval World (Salter and Pearsall), 830
Langer, William L., 919
Langland, John: Salter's scholarship, 816, 818, 820; Woolf's scholarship, 829
Langlois, Charles, 312
Lapsley, Gaillard, 265
Lathbury, Martha, 401–2
Latin Writers of the Fifth Century (Duckett), 215, 223
Law Finders and Law Makers (Cam), 267
Lawrence, Marion, 120, 841
Leavis, F. R., 818
Leben der Heiligen Elisabeth von Thüringen, Das (Busse-Wilson), 354–56
Leech, Kenneth, 951
Lees-Milne, James, 412
legal history: Anglo-Saxon wills, 451, 553–54; Bateson's scholarship, 71–73; Cam's scholarship, 267–68; Chibnall's Church and State scholarship, 751–52, 757; Clarke's scholarship, 387–88; Irish constitutional history, 387–88; Legge's scholarship, 615–16; Neilson and, 174; Packard and, 984–85; pipe roll scholarship, 443–44, 447, 448–49, 984–85; Putnam's scholarship, 157, 159–60, 161–64; Stenton's scholarship, 441, 444–48, 449–50; Stuard's scholarship, 955–57. *See also* Selden Society
Legend of Lancelot, The (Weston), 49–50
Legend of Sir Perceval (Weston), 44
Legends of the Madonna (Jameson), 25, 28, 29
Legends of the Monastic Orders (Jameson), 28
Le Gentil, Pierre, 618
Legge, James, 324, 613
Legge, Mary Dominica: Anglo-Norman literature as focus of work, 617–19; Anglo-Norman Text Society and, 615; awards and honors, 619; Clarke and, 390, 616; critical reception of works, 616, 617–18; R. J. Dean as friend and collaborator, 566, 615, 616–17; education of, 615; family of, 613–15; gender-appropriate subjects and, xxxii; Holdsworth as collaborator, 615–16; legacy of, 619–20; as legal historian, 615–16; organizational affiliations, 619; Oxford and, 613; pictured, 614; M. K. Pope and, 615, 618; publication history of, 161, 615–16, 617, 618; religious life of, 615; Royal Holloway College and, 616–17; Schlauch and, 618; scholarly circle of, xxxiv, 618; Somerville College and, 621 n.27; as teacher, 161, 619; University College, Dundee and, 616; University of Edinburgh and, 616
L'Église arménienne et le grande schisme d'orient (Garsoïan), 810 n.1
Legouis, Emile, 101
Lejeune, Rita, 618
Leland, Virginia, 138
Lemay, Richard, 544
Lemé, Kristiane, 878
Lendinara, Patrizia, 757
Lerner, Robert E., 657, 666

lesbianism, xxxii, xxxiii, 383–84, 391–92 n.21, 392 nn.27–28
Letters of Heloise and Abelard, Waddell's scholarship, 323, 325, 326–28, 329, 330
Letter to the Monks of Eynsham (Ælfric, Bateson translation), 70
Levett, A. Elizabeth, 383, 392 n.23
Levin, Richard, 798
Levine, Philip, 676
Levy, Brian, 878
Lewent, Kurt, 971
Lewis, C. S., 329, 335 n.62, 690, 818
lexicography. *See* Ogden, Margaret
Leys, Agnes, 660
Leyser, Henrietta: on Beryl Smalley, xxv, 657–67; contributor's note, 1012–13
Liber de diversis medicinis (Ogden, editor), 697, 699
Liberties and Communities in Medieval England (Cam), 266
library and archival work, xxxii. *See also under specific individuals*
Life in Medieval France (Evans), 405–6
Life of Anthony (Athanasius), Mohrmann's scholarship, 602
Life of the Spirit and the Life of Today, The (Underhill), 189
Lightman, Marjorie, 909
Lillich, Meredith Parsons: as art historian, 935; Branner and mentor, 936; children of, 935, 937, 938; Columbia University and, 936–37; contributor's note, 1013; Cornell University and, 935; education of, 934–35; family of, 933–34 (*see also* children *under this heading;* marriage *under this heading*); financial support of work, 938; Grodecki and, 936, 937–38, 940; E. Johnson as mentor, 934; Lafond as mentor, 938; marriage to Richard Lillich, xxxi, 935, 937; on Medieval aesthetics, 938–39; Oberlin and, 933; pictured, 933; publication history of, 938, 940, 941; reputation as scholar, xxxi; stained glass as focus of work, 935, 936–37, 938–41; Stechow as mentor, 934; Syracuse University and, 937; as teacher,

937; travel, 934–35, 937; Université libre de Bruxelles, 934–35; on WWII, 933
Lillich, Richard, xxi, 935, 937
L'Illustration du "Roman de Barlaam et Joasaph" (Der Nersessian), 485
Lindsay, Jean, 266
Lipson, Ephraim, 315
Lishev, Strashimir, 511
Little, Charles, 848
liturgical drama, Woolf's scholarship, 831–32
Liturgical Movement and liturgical reform, Mohrmann and, 603–4
Livre de la Mutacion de Fortune (Christine de Pizan, Solente translator), 477, 766
Livre de la Paix (Christine de Pizan), 764
Livre de la Passion, Le (Frank, translation), 276
Livre des Fais et bonnes meurs de Charles V (Solente), 476–77
Livre des Faits d'armes et de chevalerie (Christine de Pizan, B. G. S. Willard translator, C. C. Willard editor), 765
Livre des trois vertus (Christine de Pizan), 761–62
Lloyd-Jones, Hugh, 167
Lodge, David, 41
Lods, Jeanne, 618
Loewe, Raphael, 667 n.9
Lombard, Peter, Colish's scholarship, 981, 988–89
London School of Economics (LSE): Cam and, 260, 263; E. Power and, 311, 312, 314, 315, 316; Shire and, 735–36
Longmans (publisher), 29
Longsworth, Robert, 986–87
Loomis, Dorothy Bethurum: on C. Brown, 308 n.32; on D'Evelyn's work, 304; education and career of, 250 n.12; Roger Sherman Loomis and, 242; scholarly circle of, xxxiv
Loomis, Laura Hibbard: art history and, 245; awards and honors, 241; Chaucer and Auchinleck manuscript as focus of work, 244–46; critical reception of works, 244; education of, 239, 241; family of, 239–41, 247 (*see also* marriage *under this heading*);

Hunter College and, 244; Jewett as mentor, 241; marriage and collaboration with Roger Sherman Loomis, 239, 241, 243, 246–47; pictured, 240; publication history of, 244, 246, 248; reputation as scholar, 247; E. Rickert and, 140 n.1, 249 n.7; Schoepperle and, 242; scholarly circle of, xxxiv, 239, 241, 242–43; as teacher, 240, 243–44; University of Chicago and, 241; Wellesley College and, 239, 241, 243–44, 248

Loomis, Roger Sherman, 40, 41, 47; marriage and collaboration with Laura Hibbard, 239, 241, 243, 246–47; marriage to Gertrude Schoepperle, 242; Newstead and, 685, 688; Schoepperle and, 242; Weston and, 40, 41, 47; wives as colleagues, 242

Lopez, Robert S., 955

Lot, Ferdinand, 474

Love, Nicholas, Salter's scholarship, 816, 817, 819–20

Loveluck, Christopher, 893

Low, Seth, 543

Lowber, Edith H., 116

Lowe, E. A., 138, 566, 922

Lowes, John Livingston, 330

Loyn, Henry, 558, 560

Lucas, George, 49

Ludwig-Maximilians-Universität-München (LMU-Munich), 861, 863, 865–66

Lumiansky, R. M., 566

Lumière du Moyen Âge (Pernoud), 715

Luthe, Hubert, 863

Luttrell, Claude, 821 n.5

Lutz, Cora Elizabeth: audience for works, 677–78; awards and honors, 672, 673, 674; Beinecke Library cataloging, 671, 673, 677, 678; Cavadini and, 672, 678; children and, 678; classical studies as focus of work, 676–77; Connecticut College for Women and, 672; Cranz and, 677; critical reception of work, xxxi–xxxii, 674–76; death of, 673, 679; education of, 672; family of, 671; Hicks and, 673; Judson College, Alabama, 673; Kristeller and, 677; legacy of, 678–79; Martianus Capella as focus of work, 674–75; E. A. Matter and, 673–74, 676; as mentor, 673–74; Mowatt and, 673; organizational affiliations, 674; personal life of, 671, 672; pictured, 670; publication history of, 674, 675, 676, 677; Remigius of Auxerre as focus of work, 675–76; reputation as scholar, 674; scholarly circle of, 673, 677; Shailor and, 672, 673, 677; Stiles as focus of work, 678; as teacher, 672–73; on teacher-scholars, 678–79; Wilson College and, 673, 676, 677; Wynne on, 677; Yale and, 671, 672 (*see also* Beinecke Library cataloging *under this heading*)

Lycée Français de New York, 804

Lyceum, 40

Lydgate, John, Prescott's study of, 92, 94

Lynch, Kathryn L., 140 n.1; contributor's note, 1013; on Laura Hibbard Loomis, 239–49

Lynn, Robert, 798

Lyon, Steward, 558

lyrics, 829–31

Lyrics from the Chinese (Waddell), 324

Mabinogion: Bromwich's scholarship, 770, 772, 773–75; Newstead's scholarship, 685–86, 687, 690

MacGregor, Arthur, 893

Mack, Maynard, 795

Maclean, Norman, 789, 791

MacQuarrie, John, 194–95

Madonna and Child, Romanesque sculpture pictured, 844

Magna Carta 17, Stenton's scholarship, 447

Magnus, Laury, 693

Magnússon, Eiríkr, 202, 203, 204

Magoun, F. P., 95

Maier, Anneliese: audience for works, 637; awards and honors, 637; beatific vision debate and, 625, 633; Beaujouan on, 635–36; Bock and, 627–28; Borghese manuscript collection, cataloging of, 628–29; Bradwardine's function and, 636; Clagget and, 634–35, 636–37; critical reception of works, 633–36; Crosby and, 636–37; death

Maier, Anneliese (*continued*)
of, 633; De Luca and, 629, 632–33; Dijksterhuis on, 633–34; Duhem and, 630, 631–32, 635; family of, 627, 629–30; father's work and, 627, 629–30; financial support of work, 627, 628; impetus theory as focus of work, 630–31, 634, 636; Kant as focus of work, 627, 629–30; Koch and, 628; legacy of, 637; library work and, xxxii; Max-Planck-Gesellschaft and, 628; A. Mercati and, 628; G. Mercati and, 628; Moody and, 636–37; Odier on, 629; Pelzer and, 629, 631–32; personal life of, 627, 629–30; pictured, 626; political oppression, xxxiii, xxxiv; publication history of, 630–33; religious life of, 628; reputation as scholar, 625, 633–38; as reviewer, 636–37; scholarly circle of, 628; scope of work, 625; as teacher, 628; University of Cologne and, 628; Vatican Library and, 627–29, 638

Maier, Heinrich, 627, 629–30

Maierù, Alfonso: on Anneliese Maier, 625–38; contributor's note, 1013

Maitland, Frederic W., 71, 157, 267

Mâle, Émile, 115, 484

Malkiel, María Rosa Lida de: Alexander legend as focus of work, 725; awards and honors, 723–25, 725; Columbia University and, xxxiv, 725; death of, 726; Dido in Spanish literature as focus of work, 726; as editor of journals, 725; education of, 723, 725; family of, 723, 725; Josephus as focus of work, 727; Juan de Mena as focus of work, 723, 726; Judaic studies as focus of work, 727, 728; Judaism and, 723, 727; as linguist, 725; marriage to Yakov Malkiel, 725; methodology used by, 725–26; personal influences on professional life, 726–27; pictured, 724; publication history of, 723, 727; religious life of, 723; reputation as scholar, 725; as reviewer, 726; scholarly circle of, 723, 726; scholarly legacy of, 728; as teacher, 723, 725; as translator, 723; University of Buenos Aires and, 723; University of California, Berkeley and, 725

Malkiel, Yakov, 79, 691, 725

Malraux, André, 717

Man Born to Be King, The (Sayers), 431

Manchester University: Bateson and, 72; M. K. Pope and, 148, 155; Ward and, 945

Manderfeld, Viola, 791

Manley, John Matthews, 128, 132, 135, 139–40

Manly, John, 241, 243, 288, 291

Mann, Sir James, 410

Mann, Janice: contributor's note, 1013; on Georgiana Goddard King, 111–21

Mann, Thomas, 355

Manners, Sir John, xxiii–xxiv

Manning, David, 693

Manuscripta (Duckett), 221

manuscript studies: Allen's scholarship, 233; Clarke's scholarship, 386–87; codicological studies, 288, 474, 588, 764; d'Alverny's scholarship, 585–87; R. J. Dean's scholarship, 567; Der Nersessian's scholarship, 484; Kibre's scholarship, 545–46; L. H. Loomis's scholarship, 244–46; Maier's scholarship, 628–29; postmodernism and, 992; Prescott and, 91–96; M. Rickert's scholarship, 286–90; Smalley's scholarship, 661; Solente's scholarship, 473–74; Willard's scholarship, 764, 765

Manuscrits arméniens illustrés (Der Nersessian), 485

Map, Walter, 691

Margarete Ebner, 360–61

Margery of Kempe, xxv–xxvi, xxviii, xxxii, 231, 235–37

Marie de France, 279

Marius, Richard, 983

Mark of Gender, The (Wittig), xxiii

Marks, Jeanette, 301, 302, 303, 305, 307 n.20

Marquet de Vasselot, Jean J., 405

marriage: academic careers and, 137, 248–49, 251–52 n.51, 385, 755, 761, 965; alternatives, 60–61, 314; Christine de Pizan on widowhood, 766; discrimination in employment and, 605, 671–72, 906, 907; L. H. Loomis on, 246; Lutz on, 672; Martha Carey Thomas on, 260–61;

monasticism as alternative to, 60–61; name dilemmas of married women scholars, 846, 905, 906; in Sayers's fiction, 429–30. *See also under specific individuals*
Marsh, George L., 95
Martianus Capella, Lutz's scholarship, 674–75
Martin, Mary, 332, 390
Martinez, Maurice, 876
Martin-Hawking, Heather, 827
Martiros, Der Nersessian's scholarship, 488
Martz, Louis, 795, 830
Marxism: Schlauch and defection to Poland, 523–25; Schlauch Marxist writings, 526, 531–32, 535 n.11; Smalley as Marxist, 662. *See also* Socialism
Matheson, A. A., 374
Mathissen, F. O., 48
Matisse, Henri, 715, 716
Matre, Rachel, 547
Matter, E. Ann: contributor's note, 1013; Lutz and, 672, 673–74, 676; on Marcia L. Colish, 981–90
Mattingly, Garrett, 804
Mavrodinov, Nikola, 515
Max-Planck-Gesellschaft and, 628
McArthur, Ellen A., 71, 74
McCarthyism, xxxiii, 523–24, 920
McIlwain, Charles Howard, 919
McIntosh, Carey, 975, 976–77
McIntosh, Millicent, 970
McKelvey, Richard L., 702–3
McKisack, May, 388, 390
McLaughlin, Mary Martin, xxxiii, 580, 581–82
McNamara, Jo Ann: Berkshire Conference of Women Historians and, xxxiv, 908–10; children of, 903, 905, 907; Columbia University and, 903–4; contributor's note, 1013; on Coordinating Committee for Women in the Historical Profession, 907–8, 909, 910; education of, 901–3; family of, 901 (*see also* children of *under this heading*; marriage of *under this heading*); on feminism, 901, 904, 905, 907; on financial support for historical research, 909; on Fowler, 906–7; marriage of, 903; monasticism as focus of work, 910–11; Mundy and, 904; pictured, 902; on support network during graduate school, 904–5; as translator, 911; University of Pennsylvania and, 901; women's history and, 909–10
McNamara, Lisa, 547
McVaugh, Michael R., 697, 706
Mead, G. R. S., 40
Mechanisierung des Weltbildes im 17. Jahrhundert, Die (Maier), 630–31
Mediaeval Romance in England (L. H. Loomis), 242, 243, 244, 247, 248
medical history: Kibre's scholarship, 544; Ogden's scholarship, 697, 704, 705–6; Solente's manuscript studies and, 474
Medieval Academy of America, 175, 305, 525, 546, 567, 589, 674, 806, 975
Medieval Agrarian Economy (Neilson), 172
Medieval City State, The (Clarke), 386
Medieval Club of New York, 683
Medieval English Nunneries (Power), 314
Medieval Feminist Forum, xxvii
Medieval Fonts of Meath, The (Roe), 467
Medieval Foundation of the Western Intellectual Tradition, 400–1440 (Colish), 989
Medieval French Drama, The (G. Frank), 278
Medieval Latin Lyrics (Waddell), 326
Medieval People (Power), 315
Medieval Portraits from the East and West (Duckett), 218
Medieval Representation and Consent (Clarke), 387–89
Medieval Scholarship (Damico), xxvii
Medieval Theory of Authorship, The (Minnis), 667
Medieval Vistas (L. H. Loomis), 245
Medieval Women (Power), 319
Meditations of the Life and Passion of Christ (D'Evelyn), 295, 300, 303–4
Meech, Sanford B., 699
Megaw, Peter, 846
Meillet, Antoine, 484
Melman, Billie, 358
Memoirs of the Early Italian Painters (Jameson), 28, 31–32

Menéndez Pidal, Ramón, 726
mentors and mentorship, xxxi, xxxiii, xxxiv–xxxv; in German academic system, 357; McNamara's autobiographical essay on women's networking in scholarship, 901–11. *See also under specific individuals*
Mercati, Angelo, 628
Mercati, Giovanni, 628
Metamorphosis and Identity (Bynum), 997
Meyer, Paul, 475
Meyer, W., 602
Meyer-Lübke, Wilhelm, 81, 84, 85
Meyvaert, Dom Paul, 558
Mézieres, Philippe de, 277
Middle Atlantic States Archive of Medieval Manuscripts on Microfilm, 565
Middle English Dictionary, 697, 699, 700, 701–5
Middle English Prose Style (Stone), xxviii
Middle English studies: Ogden's contributions to *The Middle English Dictionary,* 697, 699, 700, 701–5; Weston on biographical data of Middle English authors, 42; Weston's scholarship, 38, 42, 43. *See also specific literary works and authors*
Mijatev, Krustjo, 511
Mill, Anna Jean, 297, 301, 302
Millar, Eric, 287
Miller, Edward, 753
Miller, Nancy K., xxviii, xxix–xxx
Millet, Gabriel, 484, 505
Mills College, 297, 305
Milner-White, Eric, 222
Mind of The Maker, The (Sayers), 430, 431
Miner, Dorothy, 276
Minet, Susan, 414
Miniature Painting in the Armenian Kingdom of Cilicia (Der Nersessian), 486–90
Minnis, A. J., 667
Miracle de Théophile (Rutebeuf), 276
Miracles and the Medieval Mind (Ward), 947
Miracles of Our Lady, Saint Mary, The (Underhill), 186
Miroir des miséricordes, Le (proceedings of Toulouse conference), 879

Mirror of Language, The (Colish), 981, 988, 989
Miséricordes: Images Profanes des lieux sacrés (Billiet and Block), 880
Misericordia International, 878–79
misericords: Block as independent scholar of, xxxiii; Block as pioneer in field, xxxi, xxxii; Block's scholarship, xxxi, xxxii, xxxiii, 876–83; nomenclature and terminology used in misericord study, 880–81; public's access to and knowledge of misericords, 883
misogyny. *See* sexism
MLA (Modern Language Association), 237, 241, 274, 305, 525, 567, 683
Modern Humanities Research Association, 305, 567
Modern Language Association (MLA), 237, 241, 274, 305, 525, 567, 683
Modus Tenendi Parliamentum, 387–88
Moe, Henry Allen, 528, 529
Mohrmann, Christine A. E.: audience for works, 603; awards and honors, 606–7; Catholic University of Nijmegen and, 600, 606–7; Christian Latin as focus of work, 599, 601–3, 605–6, 607; death of, 599; education of, 599–600; family of, 599; Groeneboom and, 599; legacy of, 606–7; as linguist, 604; monastic linguistics as focus of work, 602; Nijmegen School and, 599, 600, 603, 605, 607; personal life of, 599, 605; pictured, 598; publication history of, 599, 603; religious life of, 599, 603–4; Roman Catholic liturgical renewal and, 603–4; Schrijnen as mentor, 599, 604–6, 607, 610 n.42, 611 nn.43–47; as teacher, 599, 603, 605; University of Amsterdam and, 606; University of Utrecht and, 600, 606
Monastic Architecture in France for the Renaissance to the Revolution (Evans), 415
monasticism: *Ancrene Wisse* (Ancrene Riwle), 231–32; Bateson's essays on, 73; Cramp's archaeological scholarship, 885, 888–89; Eckenstein's scholarship, 59–62; Evans's scholarship, 407–8; Garsoïan and Armenian monasticism, 810; McNamara's scholarship,

910–11; *Medieval English Nunneries* (Power), 314; Mohrmann's study of monastic linguistics, 602; monastic life as alternative to marriage, 60–61; Ward's scholarship, 947, 948–50

Monastic Life at Cluny (Evans), 407

Monkwearmouth and Jarrow (Cramp), 888–89

Montelius, Oscar, 203, 207

Monteverdi, Angelo, 618

Montpellier Codex, Rokseth's scholarship, 342, 345

Moore, Hubert Stuart, 184, 185, 187, 197 n.54

Moore, Marianne, 792, 794, 925

Moore, Samuel, 699

Morand, Kathleen, 412

More Latin Lyrics (Waddell), 332

More Than Lore (Talbot), 136

Morgan, Gerald: contributor's note, 1013; on Rachel Bromwich, 768

Morgan, Marjorie, 821 n.5

Morien (Weston, translator), 38

Morley, Edith, 101

Morris, Christopher, 755, 893

Morris, William, xxiv

Mory, Robert M., 707

Moser, Maria Katharina, 867

Mosher, Charles Hull, 963–64

Mosher, Doris Sherman, 963–64

Mount Holyoke College, 179 n.65; R. J. Dean and, 567; D'Evelyn and, 297, 300–303, 305–6; Ham as president of, 301–2, 307 n.14; Neilson at, 169–71; Putnam at, 160–61; women faculty at, 300–301

Mowatt, Marian H., 673

Mundy, John, 904

Murder Must Advertise (Sayers), 428

Murder of Charles the Good, The (Galbert of Bruges, Ross translator), 579, 580

Murdoch, John, 638

Murphy, Dennis, 25

Murray, Gilbert, 46, 210

Murray, Margaret, 61

Musial, Magdalena, 357

music history: Anglo-Norman songs, 569; Frank as musician, 274–75; Rokseth's scholarship, 339, 345; Scottish songs, Shire's scholarship, 735, 736, 737, 740

Music of Scotland, 1500–1700 (Shire and Elliot), 737, 740

Musonius Rufus: "The Roman Socrates" (Lutz), 676

Mussafia, Adolph, 81, 83, 86

Mutaftchieva, Vera, 512, 514, 517

Mynors, Roger, 663

Myrrour of the Blessed Lyf of Jesu Christ (Love), Salter's scholarship, 816, 819–20

mystery fiction, Sayers's medieval scholarship and, 427–30

Mystery of Sacrifice, The (Underhill), 191

mysticism: Allen and, 230–31; female body and, xxxii; gender and, 194–95; German scholarship on, 358–61; Gössmann's scholarship, 863; Jourdain and Moberly and apparitions at Versailles, 402–3, 414–15; Margery Kempe as mystic, 235–36; Rhineland spirituality and, 236; Spurgeon's scholarship, 104; Underhill's study of, 183, 185–86, 187–91, 192–95, 235–36

Mysticism (Underhill), 187–88, 190, 193

Mysticism in English Literature (Spurgeon), 104

Mystic Way, The (Underhill), 188

Namier, Lewis, 384

Nansen, Fridjof, 202

Nash-Williams, V. E., 893

National Humanities Center, 988

National Socialist Party of Germany, xxxiv; Chibnall and, 751; church's role in Nazi period, 861; Gössmann family and, 859, 860; Richter's death in Theresienstadt, 82; Schlauch's refutation of Nazi "Aryan" claims, 530–31; Weston's anti-Nazi pamphlets, 39, 48

National Union of Women's Suffrage Societies (NUWSS), 74

Nations in the Medieval Universities, The (Kibre), 545

Nature in Design (Evans), 411

Navarro, José de, 368, 371–72

Navarro, Michael de, 778

Nazis. *See* National Socialist Party of Germany
Negotiating the Past (Patterson), xxiii
Negrin, Francisco, 922–23
Neilson, Katharine, 120
Neilson, Nellie: American Historical Association and, 167, 171, 174–76; Andrews as mentor of, 169, 170, 171, 175, 176; audience for works of, 173; awards and honors, 174–75; Cam and, 261, 262; contributions to anthologies and collections, 173–74; critical reception of works, 172; D'Evelyn and, 300; discrimination in career, xxxii; economic history as focus of work, 172, 173–74; editorial work of, 175; England and, 167–69; family of, 169; legal history as focus of work, 173, 174; as mentor, 170, 176; Mount Holyoke College and, 169–71; organizational affiliations, 169–71; personal life, 167, 169, 176; pictured, 168; E. Power and, 173; publication history, 172–73; Putnam and, 160, 174; reputation as scholar, 175; scholarly circle of, 169; as teacher, 160, 169–71; University of London and, 175
Nelson, Janet, 558
Nelson-Campbell, Deborah: contributor's note, 1014; on Grace Frank, 273–81
Network for the History of Women Religious, 911
networking, xxxiv; institutional genealogy of women medievalists, xliii–xlvi; McNamara's autobiographical essay on, 901–11. *See also* scholarly circle *under specific individuals*
Newall, Hugh Frank, 210–11
Newhall, "Miss" [no first name identified], 301
Newman, Barbara, 986
Newnham College: Bateson and, 69, 70, 71–72; "certificates" instead of degrees awarded to women, 72; Chadwick and, 367, 368, 370, 373, 374; Chibnall and, 753; Salter and, 816, 817; Shire and, 735; Whitelock and, 553, 556, 560
Newstead, Helaine: audio recordings by, 691; awards and honors, 683, 686; Celtic influences in Arthurian romances as focus of work, 686–87, 688–89; Chrétien de Troyes as focus of work, 686–87, 691; Columbia University and, 686; education of, 685; family of, 685; Goldin on, 688; Hunter College and, 685, 686; on Jackson's work, 690; Klenke and, 691; on Lewis's work, 690; as linguist, 686; R. S. Loomis and, 685, 688; *Mabinogion* as focus of work, 685–86, 687, 690; Morgain le Feé as focus of work, 688–89; as musician, 685; *New Yorker* profile on, 683–84, 687, 692–93; Nicolson and, 693; organizational affiliations, 683; personality of, 692; personal life of, 692–93; pictured, 684; publication history of, 686, 687; reputation as scholar, 683, 687–88; as reviewer, 691; scholarly legacy of, 687; source study approach in work, 687–88, 689–90; as teacher, 685, 686; Tristan legend as focus of work, 683, 687, 689, 691; University of New York Graduate Center and, 692
Nichols, John, 910
Nicolson, Marjorie, 693
Niebur, Ettie, 878
Nijmegen School, 599, 600–603, 605, 607
Nikolaev, Vsevolod, 511, 512, 513, 516
Nine Tailors, The (Sayers), 428
Ní Ruaidh, Eibhlín. *See* Roe, Helen
Ní Shuilibhín, Nora, 463
Nitze, William A., 138
nonacademic scholarship. *See* independent (nonacademic) scholarship
Nordic studies: Chadwick's scholarship, 368–69; Phillpotts and, 201–11; Schlauch's scholarship, 528, 529
North, Helen, 917
Northrup, Clark, 704
Northumbria's Golden Age (Cramp), 891
Noyes, John Humphrey, 227
nursery rhymes, 58, 62
Nutt, Alfred, 38, 40

Oakley, Francis, 983
Oberlin College: Colish and, 984, 987–88, 989–90; Lillich and, 933

O'Brien, Michael, 772
occultism: Jourdain and Moberly and apparitions at Versailles, 402–3; Weston and, 40, 46, 48
Oderic Vitalis: Chibnall's scholarship, xxxiii, 755–56
Odier, Jeanne Bignami, 629
O'Farrell, Rory: contributor's note, 1014; on Helen M. Roe, 459–67
Officina di Studi Medievali, 757
O'Fíach, Thomas, 463
Ogden, H. V. S. "Harry," 700, 707
Ogden, John, 707
Ogden, Margaret: Allen as mentor and friend, 234, 699, 700–701; as bibliographer for MED, 697, 701–3; children of, 701, 707; Craigie and, 699; critical reception of works, 703–4, 705; *Dictionary of American English*, contributions to, 699; "double dating" technique for manuscript bibliographies and, 702; education of, 699; family of, 697–99, 701, 707 (*see also* marriage *under this heading*); financial support of work, 705; Guy de Chauliac as focus of work, 697, 704, 705–6; Knott and, 699, 700; Kuhn and, 706–7; Kurath and, 701, 703, 706; as lexicographer, 704–5; marriage to and collaboration with H. V. S. "Harry" Ogden, xxxv, 700, 707; McKelvey and, 702–3; McVaugh as collaborator, 697, 706; medical texts as focus of work, 697, 699, 704, 705–6; Meech and, 699; *Middle English Dictionary*, contributions to, 697, 699, 700, 701–5; Moore and, 699, 700; Palmer and, 702–3; pictured, 698; publication history of, 699, 705, 706, 707; scholarly circle of, xxxiv; University of Chicago and, 699; University of Michigan and, 699, 700; Wallner and, 705; Watson and, 699
Ohm, Thomas, 861
Ólafsson diaries, 204, 208
Old English, Elizabeth Elstob and, 3–16
Oldest Library Motto and Other Library Essays, The (Lutz), 677

Olieu, Pierre Jean. *See* Olivi, Pierre Jean (Fr. Petrus Johannis Olivi)
Olivi, Pierre Jean (Fr. Petrus Johannis Olivi), 585, 666
Ólsen, Björn Magnússon, 203
Olson, Elder, 789, 791
Oneida community, 227, 232
Des origines au Moyen Âge (Pernoud), 716
Ormanian, Maghakia, 483
Orr, John, 618
Orr, Patricia R.: contributor's note, 1014; on Doris Mary Stenton, 441–53
Osborn, Lucretia Perry, 106
Oschinsky, Dorothea, 753
Osieczkowska, C., 505
O'Sullivan, Deirdre, 893
Other and Otherness: Brown on the alterity of the Middle Ages, 915–25; gender difference and, xxvi–xxvii, xxviii; Jews as the Other, 1001. *See also* gender difference
Ouy, Gilbert, 765
Owen, Morfydd, 778
Oxford History of English Art, 408, 410
Oxford University: Chibnall on, 749–50; R. J. Dean and, 566, 567; degrees for women, 101, 382, 404–5, 426; D'Evelyn on, 298–300; E. Elstob and, 6; Evans and, 399–401, 404–5; Reeves and, 647–52; Reeves on, 647–55; sexism at, 16, 101, 382, 404–5, 426; Smalley and, 659, 663; syllabus revision at, 749–50; teaching methods at, 648, 750; Ward and, 945; Whitelock and, 555, 556; women admitted to, 148; women's life at, 825–27; R. E. Woolf and, 830; during WWII, 650–51, 825–27. *See also specific colleges of*

Pächt, Otto, 651
Packard, Sidney R., 982, 984–85, 989
Paetow, Louis John, 543, 545
Page, Raymond, 559
Painting in Britain (Rickert), 289–90
Pallis, Marietta, 230
Pallot, Eric, 881
Palmer, Alice Freeman, 133

Palmer, Charles E., 702–3
Panofsky, Erwin, 112, 919
Pantin, William, 663–64
Papanicolaou, Linda, 785
Paris, Gaston, 40, 44, 46
Park, Katharine, 924
Parker, Elizabeth, 848
Parry, Sir Thomas, 775
Parsoneault, Catherine: contributor's note, 1014; on Yvonne Rihouët Rokseth, 339–49
Paskaleva, Virginia, 513, 517
Passion d'Autun, La (Frank, translation), 276
Patch, Howard Rollins, 304
Path of Eternal Wisdom, The (Underhill as "Cordelier"), 187
Patience, Borroff's scholarship, 799
patronage, medieval: Evans on arts patronage, 406, 407; Legge on Anglo-Norman literature and, 618
Patrons and Painters (Haskell), 406
Pattern (Evans), 411
Patterson, Lee, xxiii
Pavlov, Todor, 511, 512, 515, 516
Pearl, The: Borroff's scholarship, 796–97; Jewett translation, 249 n.7; Weston on, 44
Pearsall, Derek, 815, 818, 820
Pearson, Maria Sharpe, 59
Pei, Mario A., 219
Pelican History of England, Stenton's contribution to series, 448
Pelikan, Jaroslav, 984
Pelzer, August, 629, 631–32
periodization: "revolt of the medievalists" and, 982–83, 990; Stuard on, 959–60; Victorian perceptions of the Middle Ages, 29–30
Pernoud, Régine: as *Archeologia*'s historical director, 717; Archives nationales and, 716, 717; as archivist, 714; as art historian, 715–16, 717; audience for works, 711, 715, 716; awards and honors, 715; Bezzola and, 716; bourgeoisie and, 713, 717; Cendrars and, 715; critical reception of works, 715–16; as curator, 716; death of, 719; distrust of University system, 716; École des chartes, 714; education of, 711–14, 716; family of, 711–13, 714–15, 716, 717; film collaborations, 717; Joan of Arc as focus of work, 716–17; Labaudy as collaborator, 714; Malraux and, 717; Matisse and, 715, 716; Museum of French History and, 716–17; pictured, 712; publication history of, 714, 715; religious life of, 713, 715; Rivière and, 716; as teacher, 713–14; travel, 714; as "unemployed intellectual," 714; University of Aix-en-Provence, 714; Vigne as collaborator, 717; women's history and, 716–17
Perry, Sir Cooper, 313
personal, the: autobiography and narrative criticism, xxviii; biographies of scholars and, 167; depersonalization in writing and, xxx; Evan's scholarship and personal interests, 406; first person, used in writing, xxviii–xxx; gender difference and, xxv, xxviii; Malkiel's scholarship and, 726–27; the Other as personal, xxvi–xxvii; in women's scholarship, xxv. *See also* autobiographical writing
Peter Abelard (Waddell), 326–28, 330
Peterborough Chronicle, The (Whitelock), 557
Peter Idley's Instruction to His Son (D'Evelyn), 295, 304–5
Peter Lombard, Colish's scholarship, 981, 988–89
Peter Lombard (Colish), 988–89
Peters, Edward, 983
Petrie, Hilda, 61
Petrie, Sir W. M. Flinders, 61
Pevsner, Nikolaus, 289, 407, 409
Pfister, Oskar, 360–61
Phelan, Edwin, 467
Philip the Fair, 923–24
Phillips, Margaret Mann, 154–55
Phillpotts, Bertha Surtees: awards and honors, 202, 204, 205; critical reception of works, 205, 207; death of, 211; Eddas as focus of work, 205, 207, 210–11; education of, 202; employment of, 203–4; encyclopedia contributions of, 203; family of, 201, 203, 204, 209, 210–11; field research of,

203–4; financial support of work, 202, 203, 204, 208–9; Girton College and, 202, 204, 208; Icelandic studies as focus of work, 202–5, 208; as independent scholar, 203–4; Magnússon as mentor, 202–3, 204; marriage to Newall, 210–11; as mentor, 209, 210; pictured, 200; *Poetic Edda* as focus of work, 202, 205, 207; publication history of, 202–3, 204–5, 207, 211; reputation as scholar, xxxi; scholarly circle of, 205; scholarly legacy of, 201, 208; in Sweden during WWI, 205–6; teaching and administrative career of, 203, 205, 206–7, 208, 210; as translator, 204, 208; typological sequence theory and, 207

Phillpotts, Brian, 203, 204

Phillpotts, Owen, 203

philology: American Philological Association, 674; Boroff on requirements at Yale, 793–96; Duckett and classical, 215, 216, 217, 218; Phillpotts's impatience with conventional, 203, 207; Richter's contributions to French phonetics and Romance philology, 79, 81; as subject pursued by Bulgarian women scholars, 500–501; transition to literature studies as academic emphasis, 103, 104

Philosophie der Wirklichkeit (F. Maier), 627

philosophy: Stoicism and Christian philosophy, 981–82, 988

philosophy, history of: Colish's scholarship, 981–82, 988; d'Alverny's interests, 587; Grabmann Institute for Research in the Philosophy and Theology of the Middle Ages, 862–63, 864; Society for the Study of Medieval Philosophy, 589

photography, art history as discipline and, 940

Pidsak, Sargis, 486

Piers Plowman (Langland), Salter's scholarship, 817, 820

Pilch, Herbert, 704

pilgrimages, Santiago pilgrimages and King's theories, 115–17

Pipe Roll Society, 443–44, 448

Pirckheimer, Charitas, Abbess, 60

Pirenne, Henri, 579

Pirro, André, 341–42, 343–44

Pitcairn, Raymond, 781, 783

Place in Legal History of Sir William Shareshull, The (Putnam), 163–64

Plamenac, Dragan, 341

Pleas before the King and Justice (Stenton), 447

Plucknett, Theodore, 157, 164

Plumb, Nelly, 375

Poetic Edda, 202, 205, 207

Poetry and Prophecy (Chadwick), 372

Pokorny, J., 529

Political Vision of the Divine Comedy, The (Ferrante), 973

politics: Anglo-Norman political verse, 569; Cam as political activist, 259, 264; E. Elstob and, 14–15; Garsoïan and political oppression, xxxiv; gender politics in academe, 674; German political oppression, 353–54 (*see also* National Socialist Party of Germany); Gössmann and political oppression, xxxiii, xxxiv; Irish politics, 459–61; Lafond and French political oppression, 938; Maier and political oppression, xxxiii; McCarthyism, xxxiii, 523–24; medieval academics and, xxiii; political oppression of women scholars, xxxiii, xxxiv, 82; E. Power's political activism, 313; religion linked to in Elstob's works, 9; Schlauch's defection from U.S., 523–24; Weston's political activism, 39, 48. *See also* Marxism; Socialism; suffrage

Pollack, Thomas C., 524

Polyphonies du XIIIe siècle (Rokseth), 339, 345–46

Pomata, Gianna, 390

Pomeroy, Sarah, 910

Poole, Russell, xxxi; on Bertha Surtees Phillpotts, 201–11; contributor's note, 1014

Pope, J. C., 793, 795

Pope, Mildred Katherine: Anglo-Norman and French as focus of work, 150–54; Anglo-Norman Text Society, 148; awards and honors, 148, 567; Cambridge University and, 149; R. J. Dean and, 147, 566, 567;

Pope, Mildred Katherine (*continued*)
education of, 147–48; employment of, 147; family of, 147; Legge and, 615, 618; as linguist, 147–48; Manchester University and, 148, 155; Oxford and, 567; Phillpotts and, 205; Reid as collaborator and, 149; *Romance of Horn* as focus of work, 149–50; Sayers and, 425, 426, 427; scholarly circle of, xxxiv, 147; scholarly legacy of, 147, 154–55; as teacher, 148; during WWII, 149

Popova-Matafova, Fani, 501–2

popular culture: Chadwick's scholarship and, 375; Grail legend, 48, 49; Weston's scholarship and, 41, 48

Portable Medieval Reader, The (Ross), 580

Portable Renaissance Reader, The (Ross), 580

Porter, Arthur Kingsley, 112, 115, 120, 408, 463

Post, Chandler, 112

Post, Gaines, 544, 919

Postan, M. M., 752; collaboration with E. Power, 316, 317, 318–19, 320; marriage to E. Power, 318–20; E. Power as mentor of, 317, 318, 320

Poulle, Emmanuel, 591

Pounder, Robert, 582–83

Powell, Margaret Joyce, 262

Power, Eileen Edna Le Poer: audience for works, 315; awards or honors, 263, 313; Carus-Wilson and, 318; Chibnall and, 752–53, 757; Clapham and, 314; "classical women's history" and, 358; colonization as interest of, 316; contributions to history series, 316; Coulton and, 312, 313; death of, 753; École des chartes, 312; as economic historian, 316–18; as editor, 315; education, 310; family of, 312; financial support of work, 312, 313; "gender-appropriate" subjects and, xxxii; Girton College and, 312; on history teaching, 313; on India and China, 313; London School of Economics, 311, 312, 314, 315, 316; as mentor, 317, 318–19, 320; Neilson and, 173; as pacifist, 312; pictured, 310; as pioneer in field, xxvii; political activism, 313; M. Postan, collaboration with and marriage to, 316, 317, 318–19, 320; publication history of, 313, 314, 315, 316, 319; radio broadcasts of, 311, 315; reputation as scholar, 311; scholarly circle of, xxxiv, 312, 316; scholarly legacy and, 318; sexism in university system and, 319; students' recollections of, 312; as suffragist, 312, 319; Tawney and, 315, 318; as teacher, 315, 317–18; as translator, 316; travel, 313; on Waddell's work, 331; women's history and, 319; wool trade as focus of work, 316–18; WWI and, 312; WWII and lectures of, 318

Powicke, F. Maurice, 324, 330, 452, 555; Chibnall and, 751, 753–54; revision of Oxford syllabus, 749; Smalley and, 660–61

Practical Mysticism (Underhill), 189

Pratt, Robert, 566

Prayers and Meditations of Saint Anselm, The (Ward), 947

Preface to Spenser, A (Shire), 739

Preger, Wilhelm, 358–59

Prelude and Fugue (Evans), 404, 405, 407, 414, 415

Preparatory to Anglo-Saxon England (Stenton), 451

Pre-Raphaelites, xxiii, 44

Price, Hereward T., 700

Pricke of Conscience (anonymous): Allen's scholarship, 230; D'Evelyn's scholarship, 298

Primov, Borislav, 514

Princeton University, 988; sexual discrimination in admissions policy, 841

Proceedings before the Justice of the Peace (Putnam), 162–63, 164

Procop, Marek, 591

Profane Arts / Arts profanes (Misericordia International), 879

Project Muse, 875

Protic, Andrej, 504, 515

Proverbes en rimes (Frank and Miner, translation), 276–77

proverbs: Anglo-Norman proverbial texts, 569–70; as focus of work, 276–77, 569–70

psychoanalysis: E. Brown on psychoanalytical

insights, 919; Busse-Wilson's use of psychological categories of analysis, 360–61

publishing: by Group international de recherche sur les stalles (GIRS), 881; Ninth of May publishing and Shire, 738; obstacles, as barrier to scholarship, 303; pseudonym use, 187; by Society for the Study of the Bible in the Middle Ages, 666; women and use of initials, 140 n.2; women's employment in, xxxii, 72, 132; women's history as marketable, 958; by York Medieval Texts, 818–19. *See also specific individuals for publishing histories*

Purkis, George, 433

Putnam, Bertha Haven: Bryn Mawr College and, 159; Cam and, 261; compilation and editing of records, 161; D'Evelyn and, 300; education of, 159; English legal history as focus of work, 157, 159–60, 161–64; family of, 157–59; Mount Holyoke College and, 160–61; Neilson and, 160, 174; pictured, 158; as pioneer in field, xxxi; publication history of, 161–63; reputation as scholar, 164; scholarly circle, 160; as teacher, 157

Quare, Deborah, 416
Quast, Matthias, 638
Queen Mary College, London, 735, 736
Queen's College, Waddell on sexism at, 332 n.8
queenship, 220
Queen's University, Belfast, 381, 390, 772
Quellenhefte zum Frauenleben in der Geschichte (Beckmann and Stoss), 359
Quest of the Holy Grail, The (Weston, translation), 38
Quest Society, 40, 41
Quirk, Randolph, 704, 821 n.5

Rabindranath Tagore, 189
Raby, F. J. E., 330
Radcliffe College: E. A. R. Brown and, 919; Ferrante and, 970; scholarly circle of, 919

Radding, Charles M., 917
"Radiance and Reflection" (Hayward, exhibition curator), 781, 785
Raftery, Joseph, 467
Rainbow like an Emerald (Lillich), 941
Raleigh, Walter, 103
Rand, E. K., 329, 330, 675
Randolph, Mary, 7
Rask, Rasmus, 14
Ratti, Achille, 275–76
Ravnopravie (Equality) (Bulgarian Women's Union), 498
Rawlinson, Christopher, 5
Raymond Pitcairn collection, 781, 785
Read, Jane, 453
Reconstructed Carmelite Missal, The (M. Rickert), 287–88, 289
Reeves, Marjorie Ethel: Ady as inspiration to, 647–48; audience for works, 654; contributor's note, 1014; education of, 647–48, 649–50; Gardner and, 649–50, 652; Gwyer and, 649; Hirsch-Reich and, 651; Joachim de Fiore as focus of work, 649–50, 651, 652–54; Oxford University and, 647–52; Pacht and, 651; publication history of, 651; Saint Anne's College and, 651–52; Saint Hugh's College, 647; scholarly circle of, xxxiv, 652–54; Smalley and, 652–53; as teacher, 648–49, 650–51; on truth in scholarship, 654; Westfield College, Hampstead, 649; Whitelock and, 652; WWII experiences, 650–51
Reid, T. B. W., 149
Reid Hall, Paris, 752
religion: church and state, 9, 751–52, 757; Elstob on, 9, 10; Ferrante on religion and women's rights, 973; Gössmann's scholarship on gender and, 857–59, 862–63, 866, 867; monasticism and women's religious experience, 59–61; women and Catholic hierarchy, xxvi; women and spirituality, 11, 236–37; women in hierarchy of church, xxvi, 194, 195 n.11, 197 n.73. *See also* religious life *under specific individuals*

Religiöse Bewegungen in Mittelalter (Grundmann), 359–60
Remigius of Auxerre, Lutz's scholarship, 675–76
Renaissance Society of America, 674
Reni, Guido, 30
Reno, Christine, 876
representativity, xxviii
Resurrection of the Body (Bynum), 998–99
Reviewing Committee of Export of Works of Art, 885
Reyes, Alfonso, 723
Reynard Society, 876–88
Reynolds, Barbara, 433, 434
Richard Brathwaits Comments . . . (Spurgeon edition), 103
Richards, I. A., 48
Richmond, Ian, 412
Richter, Elise: Austrian Federation of University Women and, 82; death of, 82; "Education and Development" (autobiographical essay), 82–88; education of, 81, 82–87; family of, 81; as linguist, 79; personal life of, 81, 82; philology as focus of work, 79, 81; pictured, 80; political oppression by Nazis, xxxiv, 82; publication history of, 79, 84, 85; reputation as scholar, 79; as teacher, 81–82, 84, 87; University of Vienna and, 81; on women's rights, 87
Richter, Helene, 82
Rickert, Edith: Chaucer as focus of work, 135, 138–39; as code-breaker, 134, 289; education of, xxxi, 129; employment of, 132; England and, 132, 135; family of, 129, 130, 131–32, 285–86; fiction authorship of, 134; financial support of, 132; Frank and, 279; "Ladies of the Round Table" and, 135; L. H. Loomis and, 140 n.1, 249 n.7; Manley as mentor and collaborator, 128, 132, 135, 139–40, 291; mentorship of women scholars, 135, 138; personal life of, 131–32; pictured, 126; as pioneer in field, xxvii; publication history, 140; on research and scholarship, 130–31; M. Rickert and, 286, 288, 291; scholarly circle of, xxxiv; as teacher, 128–29, 130, 131, 132, 135; University of Chicago and, 128–29, 131, 132, 133, 134, 135, 137; Vassar College and, 129, 131
Rickert, Ethel, 285–86
Rickert, Margaret: art history as focus of work, 286, 287–88, 289; audience for works, 290; Chaucer as focus of work, 288; as code breaker during WWII, 288–89; death of, 285; education of, 285, 286–87; family of, 285–86; Grinnell College and, 285, 286; library employment of, 286; manuscript studies, 286–90; *Pelican History of Art*, contributions to, 289; publication history of, 287, 288; reconstruction of Carmelite missal, 287–88; on retirement, 291; E. Rickert and, 286, 288, 291; Scheerre as focus of work, 288, 289; scholarly circle of, xxxiv, 286, 287, 289; scholarly legacy of, 285, 288, 289–90; as teacher, 286, 288, 290; University of Chicago and, 286–87
Ridgeway, William, 202
Rieu, E. V., 433, 434
Rihouët-Coroze, Simonne, 342–43
Rila Saint and His Dwelling, The (Dujcev), 513
Ritson, Joseph, 92
Rivière, Georges-Henri, 716
Robbins, Rossell Hope, 830
Roberts, Phyllis Barzillay, 542, 904–5
Roberts, William, 547
Robinson, Fred C., 797
Robinson, Margaret, 186
Robinson College, Cambridge, 737
Robson, C. A., 621
Roccaro, Cataldo, 757
Roe, Helen: as archaeologist, xxxii, 462–63, 467; as art historian, 467; audience for works, 464; awards and honors, 465, 466; "David Cycle" as focus of work, 463; death of, 467; eccentric work habits of, 464; education of, 461–62; employment of, xxxv, 465, 468; field research of, 463; financial support of work, 462; iconography and, 463, 466; as indexer, 465; Irish High

Crosses as focus of work, 463; Irish nationalism and Irish identity of, 461, 463–64, 467; Irish politics as context for work, 459–61; as lecturer, 465–66; as librarian, 465, 468; as mentor, 464–65, 466; Ní Shuilibhíin and, 463; pictured, 460; publication history of, 462, 463, 465, 466; reputation as scholar, 465; scholarly legacy of, 466–67; Trinity College, Dublin and, 461–62; WWI experiences of, 461

Roger of Howden, Stenton's scholarship, 448–49

Rogers, Samuel, art collection of, 27

Rokseth, Peter H., 342, 343, 344, 348

Rokseth, Yvonne Rihouët: anthroposophy and, 343; audience for works, 339, 348–49; awards and honors, 344; children of, 342, 343, 346, 347–48; as composer, 341, 344, 348; G. de Van and, 347–48; *Dictionnaire de musique de Riemann,* contributions to, 343; MS Dijon 517 as focus of work, 342; education of, 339, 341, 343–45; family of, 339 (*see also* children of *under this heading;* marriage *under this heading*); female musicians as focus of work, 346; Grieg as focus of work, 344; as librarian, 344–45; marriage to Peter H. Rokseth, 342, 343, 344; Montpellier Codex as focus of work, 342, 345–46; on music appreciation, 349; as organist, 341, 343; pictured, 340; Pirro as mentor, 341–42, 343–44; publication history of, 341, 343, 345, 346, 347; reputation as scholar, 341; scholarly legacy of, 339, 348–49; Schrade and, 339, 348; Sorbonne and, 339, 341; as teacher, 344, 346–47; Thibault and, 341–42, 343, 348; as translator, 341; WWII, as member of Resistance, 346–47, 348

Rolle, Richard: Allen's scholarship, 229, 230, 231, 232–34; Underhill's scholarship, 187, 193; Ward's scholarship, 952

Romance in Iceland (Schlauch), 530

Romance of Horn by Thomas (Pope), 148–50

Romanesque Architecture of the Order of Cluny (Evans), 407

Romanski, Stefan, 516

Roscoe, Celia, 60

Rose, Christine M.: contributor's note, 1014; on Margaret Schlauch, 523–34

Rose, H. E. G., 607

Rosen, Edward, 544

Rosenberg, Eleanor, 567

Rose-Tree of Hildesheim, and Other Poems, The (Weston), 39

Ross, James Bruce: audience for works, 580; awards and honors, 575; Carolingian studies as focus of work, 578–79; childhood as focus of work, 580–81; death of, 575; education of, 577–78; Krautheimer and, 578; Kury on, 577; legacy of, 580, 582; McLaughlin as collaborator, 580, 581–82; as medievalist, 577–78; pictured, 576; publication history of, 577–78, 579, 580–81; Renaissance humanism as focus of work, 577, 580–81; Rome as focus of work, 578; as teacher, 575–76, 580; J. W. Thompson and, 578; University of Chicago and, 577–78; Vassar and, 575–77, 579–80; Wellesley and, 575; women's history and, 578, 581–82

Rossetti, Christina, 44

Rossier, James, 566

Rostaing, Charles, 618

Roueché, Charlotte, 416

Round, J. H., 452

Rouse, Mary, 664

Rouse, Richard, 664

Roussel, Albert, 341

Rovighi, Sofia Vanni, 638

Rowse, A. L., 221

Royal Anthropological Institute, 374

Royal Archaeological Institute, 387, 411

Royal Commission on Ancient and Historical Monuments of Scotland, 885

Royal Historical Society, 174, 387, 558, 945

Royal Holloway College: Cam and, 258–59, 262; Salter and, 816

Royal Irish Academy, 465

Rubenstein, Annette, 526, 535 n.11

Rubinstein, Nicolai, 753

Rudiments of Grammar (Elstob), 13–14

Rule of Saint Benedict: Dean and Legge's scholarship, 566, 602, 616–17; Mohrmann's scholarship, 566, 602
Rule of Saint Benedict, The (Dean and Legge, editors), 566, 602
Rupert of Deutz, 666
Ruskin, John, xxiv, 411
Russian Primary Chronicle, The (Bulgarian Academy of Sciences), 510
Rutebeuf, 276
Ruysbroeck, 194
Rynne, Etienne, 466

Sacred and Legendary Art (Jameson), 25, 28, 30–31
Sacred and The Profane, The (Block, editor), xxxiii
Sadowski, Yun, 306
Sagas: N. Chadwick's scholarship, 368–69; Phillpotts's scholarship, 210–11; Schlauch's scholarship, 528, 529
Saint Anne's College, Oxford: Cramp and, 892, 893; Reeves and, 651–52; Ward and, 945
St. Augustine, xxvi, 10, 194
Saint Dunstan of Canterbury (Duckett), 218, 223
St. Elisabeth of Thuringia, Busse-Wilson's scholarship, 353, 354–55, 361
Saint-Gelais, Mellin de, 276
St. Gregory, 10
Saint Hilda's College, Oxford, 663; Smalley and, 659–60, 663; Whitelock and, 554, 556
Saint Hugh's College, Oxford, 647–48; Reeves and, 647–48; R. E. Woolf and, 825–28
Saint Mary's College, Durham, 894
Salet, Francis, 343
Salter, Elizabeth: Bedford College and, 816; Cambridge and, 817; Chaucer as focus of work, 817, 818, 820; children of, 817; death of, 815; education of, 815–16; *English and International,* contributions to, 819; family of, 815–16, 817; Girton College and, 817; Langland as focus of work, 816, 818, 820; N. Love as focus of work, 816, 817, 819–20; marriage to Christopher Zeeman, 817; marriage to David Salter, 817; Newnham College and, 816, 817; Pearsall and, 815, 818, 820; pictured, 814; publication history of, 815, 818, 819; scholarly circle of, 816, 818; scholarly legacy of, 815, 820; as teacher, 816–18, 819; University of London and, 816; University of York and, 817–19; visual arts as focus of work, 818, 820; York Medieval Texts publishing and, 818–19; C. Zeeman and, 817; N. Zeeman and, 815, 817
Saltire Society, 737
Sandler, Lucy Freeman, 290
Sardinian Painting (King), 116
Sato, Teruo, 618
Sauer, Michelle M., contributor's note, 1015
Saussure, Ferdinand de, 600
Savage, Henry L., 304
Saxon circle at Queen's College, Oxford, 5–6, 16
Sayers, Dorothy L.: audience for works, 430, 433; Bédier and, 427; children of, 425, 436 n.19; Cournos and, 425; critical reception of works, 426, 427; Dante as focus of work, xxxi, 425–26, 428, 432–34; as dramatist, 425, 430–31; education of, 423–25; family of, 423 (*see also* children of *under this heading;* marriage *under this heading*); financial support of, 425, 426; heroes and works of, 423, 425, 428, 430–31, 435; as linguist, 423; marriage to Atherton "Mac" Fleming, 427–28, 434; as mystery author, 425, 427–30; as perfectionist, 577; pictured, 423; as poet, 426; M. K. Pope and, 148, 425, 426, 427; publication history of, 425, 427; religious life and ideas, 425–26, 431, 434; Reynolds and, 433, 434; Scott-Giles and, 433; Somerville College, Oxford and, 425; as teacher, 425, 426; Thomas of Britain as focus of work, 425, 426–27; as translator, 425, 426, 432–35; Whelpton and, 425, 427, 435 n.15; Williams and, 432; WWII experiences of, 425, 432
Sayings of the Desert Fathers, The (Ward), 948–49

Scala, Elizabeth, xxxv; contributor's note, 1015; on Edith Rickert, 127–40
Scale of Perfection (Hilton, Underhill translation), 190, 194
Scandinavian studies, 209–10. *See also* Icelandic studies
Scarisbrick, Diana, 416
Schapiro, Meyer, 841–42, 845, 850
Scheerre, Herman, 288, 289
Schlauch, Margaret: American Association of University Women, 525; audience for works, 532–33; awards and honors, 534; C. Brown and, 528; Chaucer as focus of work, 523, 527, 528; Columbia University and, 527, 529; as Communist, 525; critical reception of works, 527; death of, 526; education of, 523, 526; family of, 526–27, 533; Fisiak and, 525, 526; folklore studies as focus of work, 527–28, 532; Guggenheim grant to support work, 527–29; Icelandic studies as focus of work, 528, 529, 530, 532; Krapp and, 527; Legge and, 618; as linguist, 527; as Marxist scholar, 526, 531–32; McCarthyism and persecution of, xxxiii, 523–24; as mentor, 525, 530; Nazi "Aryan" claims refuted by, 530–31; New York University and, 523, 524; organizational affiliations, 525; personal life of, 533–34; publication history of, 527, 530, 532; reputation as scholar, 525, 528, 530; scholarly legacy of, 527–28; scope of scholarship, 527; as teacher, 523, 524, 526–27, 530; University of Connecticut and, 525; Vassar College and, 525; Warsaw University and, 525, 533
Schmaus, Michael, 861, 862
Schmid, Josef, 861, 862
Schmidt, Bruno, 798
Schoepperle, Gertrude, 242
Schofield, William Henry, 40, 43, 230
Scholarly Privileges in the Middle Ages (Kibre), 545, 546
Schoolmasters of the Tenth Century (Lutz), 677–78
School of Charity, The (Underhill), 191

Schouwink, Wilfried, 878
Schrade, Leo, 339, 348
Schrijnen, Joseph, 600, 601–2, 604–6, 607, 610 n.42
Schulmann, Jana K.: contributor's note, 1015; on Dorothy Whitelock, 553–61
scientific and technological texts, 570–71. *See also* medical history
Scott, Kathleen, 288, 289
Scott-Giles, C. W., 433
Scottish Text Society, 737
Scudder, Vida Dutton, 95, 241
Seanchas Ardmhacha (Roe), 463
Segal, Robert A., 47
Seidel, Linda, 848
Seishin University, Tokyo, 864–65
Selden Society, 173, 447, 751; Legge and, 615–16; Stenton and, 446, 447
Setton, Kenneth, 221, 544
sexism: academic titles and, 81, 101; admissions and enrollment discrimination, xxiv–xxv, xxxi–xxxii, 16, 81, 101, 105, 542–43, 841; in art history education and career opportunities, 783; Cambridge University and, 264, 265–66, 270 n.37, 319, 755; Cantor on systemic prejudice in academe, 393 n.35; Columbia University and, 974; in critical reviews, 19, 40, 215, 243; in degree awards, 72, 101, 265–66, 382, 404–5, 426, 755, 864; Eckenstein on matriarchal "golden age," 59; employment discrimination, 605, 671–72, 755, 906, 907, 974, 984 (*see also* promotion and tenure *under this heading*); financial support of research done by women, 313; "gender-appropriate" subjects of study and, xxxii, 72, 81, 128, 138, 194, 312, 358; in German academic system, 81, 83, 86–87, 356–57, 358; graduate programs and, 102; grammar as an excuse for, 13; Harvard University and, 229; library access and, 270 n.37; marginalization of women in academe, 567; in Nazi Germany, 353–54; Oxford University and, 16, 101, 382, 404–5, 426–27; Pernoud on discrimination in education, 720 n.11;

sexism (*continued*)
  Princeton and, 841; in promotion and tenure decisions, 135, 138, 706–7, 938, 974, 1004; Queen's University and, 324, 332 n.8; salary inequities, xxxii, 138, 938, 974; sexual harassment, 1004; as subject of fiction, 324; at Syracuse University, 938; at University of Chicago, 706–7; Wilson College and, 673–74, 676
Sexton, Eric, 463
sexuality: Busse-Wilson and female sexuality, 361; homophobia, xxxii, xxxiii, 383–84, 391–92 n.21; monasticism and, 61–62; Weston and sexualization of Grail legend, 47
Shackford, Martha Hale, 241
Shailor, Barbara A., 672, 673, 677
Shakespeare, William: Hammond's scholarship, 93; Spurgeon's research on, 99, 105–6
Shakespeare's Imagery and What It Tells Us (Spurgeon), 99, 106
Shank, Sister Lillian Thomas, 910–11
Sharova, Krumka, 517
Sheehan, Donald, 965
Shepard, Geoffrey, 821 n.5
Shepard, Mary, 785
Shipley, Elizabeth: contributor's note, 1015; on Elise Richter, 79–89
Shire, Edward, 735, 739
Shire, Helena Mennie: audience for works, 736–37, 739; audio recording by, 740; awards and honors, 733, 737, 740; BBC programmes, 736; Cambridge University and, 735, 737; Carter and, 738; N. Chadwick and, 735; children of, 735, 736; as cultural historian, 737; Dart and, 736; education of, 733–35; Elliott as collaborator, 736–37; family of, 733, 735, 736, 739, 740; financial support of scholarship, 737; Fraser's poetry as focus of work, 739–40; Hamson as collaborator with, 740; Laidlaw and, 740; London School of Economics and, 735–36; marriage to Edward Shire, 735, 739; as mentor, 738, 739; music as focus of work, 735, 736, 737, 740; Newnham College and, 735; Ninth of May publishing and, 738; organizational affiliations, 737; pictured, 734; Poland and, 736; publication history of, 737, 739, 740–41; Queen Mary College, London and, 735, 736; radio broadcasts by, 736; as reviewer, 738–39; Robinson College, 737; Saltire Society, 737; scholarly circle of, 738; scholarly legacy of, 740–41; Scottish Text Society, 737; Stewart as collaborator with, 738; as teacher, 735–36, 738, 739; Workers Educational Association and, 735; WWII experiences, 735
Shirley, John, 92
Sidgwick, Eleanor Balfour, 71
Sidgwick, Rose, 105, 106
Sigal, Gale: contributor's note, 1015; on Helaine Newstead, 683–93
Signs and Wonders (Ward), 947, 951
Simeonova, Liliana V., xxv; on Bulgarian women's education and career opportunities, 495–503, 508; contributor's note, 1015; on Gantcheva, 502–3; on Popova-Matafova, 501–2; translation of Tapkova-Zaimova memoir, 509–17; on Vasilka Tapkova-Zaimova, 495; on Vera Ivanova-Mavrodinova, 495
Simpson, Amanda, 416
Sinnrech-Levi, Deborah, 693
Siraisi, Nancy G., 542
Sir Christopher Hatton's Book of Seals (Stenton), 447
"Sir Cleges" and "Sir Libeaus Desconus" (Weston, translation), 38
Sir Gawain and the Green Knight: Borroff's scholarship, 793–94, 795; Carey's scholarship, 102; Weston translation of, 43, 44
Sir Gawain at the Grail Castle (Weston, translation), 38
Sisam, Kenneth, 555, 558
Sizer, Lyde Cullen, 137
Skeat, Clara, 69
Skendi, Stavros, 971
Skidmore College, Colish and, 984
Skilliter, Susan, 738
Slade, Cecil, 443, 450

Slater, Miriam, 137–38
slavery, 10, 961–62
Sloane, Patricia, 48
Smail, "Otto," 755
Smalley, Beryl: Andrew of Saint Victor as focus of work, 661–62; audience for works, 664; Bible exegesis as focus of work, 657, 660–62, 663, 664, 666; Cheltenham Ladies' College and, 659; as Communist, 662–63, 667 n.14; d'Alverny and, 589, 661; as eccentric, 664; education of, 659, 660; family of, 657–59; Girton College, Cambridge and, xxv, 661; the gloss as focus of work, 661; impact of WWII, 662–63; of Joachim of Fiore, 662; Lacombe and, 660–61; Langton as focus of work, 660–61; Leys and, 660; Loewe and, 667 n.9; manuscript studies and, 661; as Marxist, 662; Minnis on, 667; Oxford and, 659, 663; in Paris, 660–61; personal life of, 659–60; pictured, 658; as pioneer in field, xxvii; Powicke and, 660–61; publication history of, 661, 663, 664; Reeves and, 652–53; religious life of, 659–60, 662; Royal Holloway College, 661; Saint Hilda's and, 663; scholarly circle of, xxxiv, 658, 663–64; scholarly legacy of, 657, 666–67; sexism in university system, 393 n.35; as teacher, 659, 660
Smalley, Suzanne, 659–60
Smart, Alastair, 828
Smith, Bonnie G., 386
Smith, Frances, identity assumed by Elizabeth Elstob, 15
Smith, George Gregory, 323–24
Smith, Jonathan, 561
Smith, Lesley, 666, 952
Smith, Mary Chase, xxxiii
Smith, Phyllis P. A., 306
Smith, R. A. L., 753
Smith, Robert, 959
Smith College: Borroff and, 789, 791–92, 794; Colish and, 982; Duckett and, 213, 215, 216, 224; Friedan's *The Feminine Mystique* and, 982; Garsoïan and, 805; Stuard and, 957, 965–66

Snegarov, Ivan, 509, 513
Snell, Ada, 160
Socialism: Cam and, 257, 259, 264; Eckenstein and, 59; Stuard and, 965; Union of Women Socialists, 498. *See also* Marxism
Society for Armenian Studies, 806
Society for Church Archaeology, 885
Society for Medieval Archaeology, 558
Society for the Study of Medieval Language and Literature at Oxford, 305
Society for the Study of Medieval Philosophy, 589
Society for the Study of the Bible in the Middle Ages (SSBMA), 666
Society of Antiquaries, 374, 387, 399, 410, 411, 413, 485, 885, 896
Society of the Advancement of Scandinavian Studies, 525
Sofia University, 496, 499, 500; Tapkova-Zaimova and, 509–17
Söhngen, Gottlieb, 861
Solente, Suzanne: awards and honors, 477, 478; Christine de Pizan as focus of work, 475–78; La Clayette miscellany and, 475; collection cataloging by, 475; death of, 478; Dupuy manuscript collection as focus of work, 473–74; education of, 471–73; French history as focus of work, xxxiv; "gender-appropriate" subjects of scholarship and, xxxii, xxxiii; as indexer of collections, 473–74; Joly de Fleury collection index, 474; Lot and, 474; manuscripts discovered by, 474; as paleographer, 474; pictured, 472; publication history of, 473, 474, 476, 477–78; scholarly legacy, 478
Solomon, Barbara, 130, 133
Some Account of Gothic Architecture in Spain (Street, King edition), 114
Some Aspects of Medieval Culture in Ireland (Roe), 467
Somers, Mary, 909
Somerville College: Clarke and, 381–82, 385; Legge and, 621 n.27; Sayers and, 425; Woolf and, 829; during WWI, 382–83
Somner, William, 13

Song, Dance and Poetry of the Court of Scotland under King James VI (Shire), 737
Song of Roland, The (Sayers translator), 425, 426, 434–35
Sophia University in Tokyo, Gössmann and, 863–64
Sorbonne: E. C. Block and, 873; Garsoïan and, 806; Rokseth and, 339, 341; Spurgeon and, 101
Soul of the Countess and Other Stories, The (Weston), 39
South English Legendary (D'Evelyn and Mill), 295, 301, 303, 304
Southern, Richard, 664, 947, 950
Spain, G. G. King and Iberian architecture, 111–21
Spell of Words, A (Eckenstein), 58, 60
Spens, Janet, Phillpotts and, 205
Spiegel, Gabrielle, 917–19, 958
Spiegel, Harriet: contributor's note, 1015; on Mary Dominica Legge, 613–20
Spinello Aretino, 28
Spitzer, Leo, 279–80
Spurgeon, Caroline Frances Eleanor: awards and honors, 102, 103; Bedford College and, 101, 106; Chaucer as focus of work, 103–4, 105; education of, 99; education reform and, 105–6; family of, 99; financial support for work, 102, 106; Furnivall and, 103–4; Gildersleeve and, 105; International Federation of University Women and, 106–7; King's College and, 99; mysticism as focus of work, 104; personal life of, 105; pictured, 100; political activism of, 104–5; publication history of, 103, 104, 106; reputation as scholar, 99; scholarly support of, 103–4; Shakespeare as focus of work, 105–6; Sorbonne and, xxxi, 101; as teacher, 101, 102, 105; Trinity College, Dublin, and, 101; University College, London, and, 99
Spurling, Hilary, 404
SSBMA (Society for the Study of the Bible in the Middle Ages), 666
stained glass: *Corpus Vitrearum Medii Aevi* committee, 781, 783, 784, 785, 940; Hayward's scholarship, 781, 783; Lillich's scholarship, 935, 936–37, 938–41; as medieval medium, 939
Stanbury, Sarah, xxvii
Stanhope, Mary, 13
Stanton, Anne Rudloff: contributor's note, 1015–16; on Margaret Rickert, 285–91
State University College at Brockport, 959
State University of New York, Stuard and, 959
Stechow, Wolfgang, 934
Steegman, John, 29, 32
Steffes, Johann Peter, 861
Stein, Gertrude, 113, 120
Steiner, Rudolf, 343
Stenton, Doris Mary: death of, 452; education of, 441–42; financial support of work, 442; Foster as mentor, 442, 443, 445; importance of integrity of primary sources, 445, 447; intimacy with English geography, 442, 448; legal history as focus of work, 441, 444–48, 449–50; Magna Carta 17 (1215) as focus of work, 447; marriage to Sir Frank Merry Stenton, xxxv, 441–43, 449, 450–51, 453; personal life of, 443, 450–51, 452; pictured, 440; pipe rolls as focus of work, 443–44, 447; Pipe Roll Society and, 448–49; publication history of, 442, 446, 447; reputation as scholar, 452; Roger of Howden as focus of work, 448–49; scholarly circle of, xxxiv; scholarly legacy of, 452–53; Selden Society and, 447; Slade on, 443; as social historian, 448; F. M. Stenton as mentor, xxxv, 442, 443; Whitelock and, 451, 555–56, 559; on women in academia, 556; women's history and, 444, 449
Stenton, Frank Merry, 441–43, 449, 554–55, 558, 559
Stephenson, C., 265
stereotyping. *See* sexism
Stern, L. C., 776
Steven, Vera, 375
Stevens, Wallace, 792, 794, 800
Stever, Sarah, 176
Stewart, Marion, 738

Stewart Style, 1513–1542 (Shire), 740
Stieglitz, Alfred, 120
Stoic Tradition from Antiquity to the Early Middle Ages (Colish), 981–82, 988
Stokes, Margaret, 466
Stokstad, Marilyn J.: contributor's note, 1016; on Jane Hayward, 781–87
Stone, Robert, xxviii
Stories and Ballads of the Far Past (Kershaw), 368
Stories from Holy Writ (Waddell), 331
Stoss, Irma, 359
Stoudt, Debra L.: on Benedicta Ward, 945–53; contributor's note, 1016
Stratford, Neil, 416
Stratigraphical Museum at Knossos, 413
Straubhaar, Sandra Ballif: contributor's note, 1016; on Nora Kershaw Chadwick, 367–76
Strayer, Joseph R., 917, 921, 927 n.22
Street, Fanny, 259–60, 262, 263
Street, George S., 114
Strong Poison (Sayers), 428–29
Strygowski, Josef, 487
Stuard, Susan Mosher: audience for works, 958; on balance of professional and personal life, 965; Bridenthal and Koonz as collaborators, 959; on children and work, 965–66; contributor's note, 1016; education of, 955–57, 963, 964; on Eleanor Shipley Duckett, 213–24; family of, 962–65; on feminism, 955; as file clerk, 964–65; financial support of work, 959; Haverford College and, 959; legal history as focus of work, 955–57; on methodology and women's history, 960–61; on periodization of history, 960; pictured, 956; publication history of, 957; religious life of, 963, 964; on "Silent Generation," 965–66; on slave trade and women as chattel, 961–62; Smith College and, 957, 965–66; as socialist, 965; State University College at Brockport and, 959; State University of New York and, 959; on sumptuary laws and fashion, 962; as teacher, 959; women's history as focus of work, 957–62; Yale and, 955, 965

Stubbs, William, 387, 749
Studien zur Naturphilosophie de Spätscholastik (Maier), 625
Studies in Anglo-Saxon Sculpture (Cramp), 887
Studies in Early British History, 373, 773
Studies in English Trade in the Fifteenth Century (Postan, editor), 316
Studies in Medieval Thought and Learning form Abelard to Wyclif (Smalley), 664
Studies in the Hundred Rolls (Vinogradoff and Cam), 263
Study of the Bible in the Middle Ages, The (Smalley), 661–62, 663, 664, 666
Style in Ornament (Evans), 411
Sudre, Léopold, 279
suffrage: Bateson and, 73–74; in Bulgaria, 497–98; Cambridge Women's Suffrage Association, 73; National Union of Women's Suffrage Societies, 74; E. Power as suffragist, 319
Sullivan, Richard, 219, 221
sumptuary laws, 962
Surette, Leon, 48–49
Susannah Shakespeare (Hammond), 93
Sutherland, Lucy, 385, 386; Clarke and, 390
Swan, Laura, 950
Swarthmore College, 920; E. A. R. Brown and, 919
Swift, Emerson, 841
Sylla, Edith: on Anneliese Maier, 625–38; contributor's note, 1016
Syracuse University: Lillich and, 937; treatment of women faculty, 938

Tachau, Katherine, 986
Talbot, Marion, 133, 136
Tapkova-Zaimova, Vasilka: Bulgarian Academy of Science and, 509–17; contributor's note, 1016; education of, 495–96, 509; marriage of, 496; memoir of, 509–17; Mutaftchieva and, 517; Paskaleva and, 513, 517; pictured, 494; political oppression of scholarship under Communism, 508, 510–17; reputation as scholar, 508; scholarly circle of, 517; scholarly legacy of, 508; Sofia University,

Tapkova-Zaimova, Vasilka (*continued*) 509–17; Todorova and, 513, 517; as translator, 510; on women at BAS, 513–14, 517
Taste and Temperament (Evans), 411
Tatler, The, 7
Tawney, R. H., 315, 318
Taylor, Charles Holt, 919
Taylor, Euan: contributor's note, 1016–17; on Helen Cam, 255–68
Taylor, Lily, 261
Taylor, M. B., 892
Tchangova, Yordanka, 507
Tchervenkov, Vulko, 512, 515
Teall, John, 917
Te Deum (Rokseth), 348
Temperley, Harold, 265
Tendencies (Sedgwick), xxviii
Tenney, Frank, 274
Teresa de Cartagena, xxv–xxvi
Terrier of Fleet (Neilson), 172–73
Tesnière, Marie-Hélene: contributor's note, 1017; on Suzanne Solente, 471–78
Then and There (Reeves), 654
Théry, Gérard, 588
Thibault, Geneviève, 341–42, 343, 348
Thomas, Martha Carey, 102, 112, 229, 260, 273–74, 275
Thomas of Britain, Sayers's scholarship, 425, 426–27
Thompson, A. Hamilton, 312
Thompson, James Westfall, 578
Thomson, Anne, 561
Thoresby, Ralph, 12
Thorndike, Lynn, 543–45
Thorne, Samuel E., 919
Thorpe, Benjamin, 3
Thorpe, Lewis, 436 n.19, 618
Throne of Wisdom (Forsyth), 850
Thwaites, Edward, 5, 6, 13
Time and Chance (Evans), 414
Todorov, Nikolay, 517
Todorova, Tzvetana, 513, 517
Tolhurst, Fiona, xxviii
Tolkien, J. R. R., 329, 335 n.62, 448, 555
T'oros Roslin, 486, 489
To the Glory of Her Sex (Ferrante), 972

To the Lighthouse (Woolf), 389
Tout, Thomas Frederick, 71–72
Toynebee, Paget, 147
Trade and Cities of Armenia in Relation to Ancient World Trade, The (Manandian, Garsoïan, translator), 807
translation: Waddell on translation of poetry, 326; Ward on "translator's charity," 950; Weston on translation of poetry, 44. *See also under specific individuals*
Traube, Ludwig, 602
Traver, Hope, 297
Treize Motets et un prélude (Rokseth), 343
Très Riches Heures du Duc Berry, The, Block on, 873–75
Trevet, Nicholas, 566
Trickett, Rachel, 413, 825–27
Trinity College, Dublin, 101, 202; Phillpotts and, 205; Roe and, 461–62; Spurgeon and, 101
Trinkhaus, Charles, 544
Trioedd Ynys Prydein (Bromwich), 772, 773–75, 777
Tristan in Brittany (Sayers), 426–27, 436 n.19
Tristan legend, 279; Ferrante's scholarship, 971; Newstead's scholarship, 683; Sayers's translation of, 426–27, 436 n.19; Weston's translation of *Tristan and Iseult,* 279
Trois Chansonniers français du XVe siècle (Rokseth), 343
Trotula of Salerno, 957
Tübingen Gospels, Der Nersessian's scholarship and, 487
Tudor-Craig, Pamela, 412, 413, 416
Tudor Economic Documents (Power and Tawney), 315
Tutin, Marguerite, 259–60
Tweedy, Rosamund, 330
Two Baptismal Fonts in County Laoighis (Roe), 466–67
Tzvetkova, Bistra, 508, 517

Unconquered Knight, The (Evans), 406–7
Underhill, Evelyn: Allen and, 235; audience for works, 188, 191, 193; *Book of Margery Kempe* and, 235–36; critical reception of

work, xxxi; as editor of the *Spectator*, 190–91; education of, 184, 185; family of, 183–84, 192, 195 n.2, 195 n.8, 196 n.49; King's College and, 104, 185; Moore and, 184, 185, 187, 197 n.54; mysticism as focus of work, 183, 185–86, 187–91, 192–95, 195 n.8; as novelist and poet, 185, 187; as pacifist, 192; pictured, 182; as pragmatic or practical, 184, 187, 189, 190; preservation and value of original texts and, 193–94; publication history of, 185, 186, 187, 191; on relationships with men, 197 n.54; religious life of, 183–85, 186–87, 188–89, 192–93; reputation as scholar, 191–92, 194–95; Rolle as focus of work, 187; scholarly legacy of, 193–94; as translator, 186, 189, 190, 194; travel and, 185; von Hügel and, 189–90, 193; Ward and, 191; on woman's role, 194, 195 n.11; WWI and, 192
Union of Women Socialists, 498
Université libre de Bruxelles, Lillich and, 934–35
University College, Hull, 828–29, 830
University College, London: Evans and, 401; Spurgeon and, 99
University College, Oxford, 5–6
University College, Southampton, 753
University College of Wales, 772, 773
University of Buenos Aires, 723
University of California, 541, 542–43; Forsyth and, 847; Malkiel and, 725
University of Chicago: Borroff and, 789–91; Frank and, 273; Hammond and, 91–92; L. H. Loomis and, 241; Ogden and, 699; E. Rickert and, 128–29, 131, 132, 133, 134, 135, 136, 137, 140 n.1, 141 n.6; M. Rickert and, 286–87; Ross and, 577–78; sexual discrimination at, 706–7
University of Cologne, 628
University of Durham, Cramp and, 893–96
University of Leipzig, 357
University of London: Neilson and, 175; Phillpotts and, 210
University of Massachusetts, 305
University of Pennsylvania: Dean and, 565–66; McNamara and, 901

University of Pittsburgh, Forsyth and, 847
University of Rome-Las Sapienza, Garsoïan and, 806
University of Toulouse, 879
University of Vienna, Richter and, 81
University of Wales, 39–40
University of Washington, Seattle, 1004
University of Wisconsin, Institute for Research in the Humanities, 988
University of York, Salter and, 817–19
Unnatural Death (Sayers), 428
Ure, Nan, 367
Ureña, Pedro Henríquez, 723
Uses of Art, The (Forsyth), 854

Vajda, Georges, 587
Van den Abeele, Baudouin, 878, 879
Vane, Harriet, 577
Van Nice, Robert, 846
Van Straten, Roelof, 25
Varty, Kenneth, 876–77, 878, 879
Vasari, Giorgio, 32
Vassar College: Rickert and, 129–30, 131; E. Rickert and, 131; Ross and, 575–77, 579–80; Schlauch and, 525
Vazharova, Zhivka, 507
Venerable Bede. *See* Bede
Victoria and Albert Museum, 413
Victorian era: perceptions of the Middle Ages during, 29–30; schools of medieval scholarship during, xxiii
Vie et mort de Jeanne d'Arc (Pernoud), 717
Vietnam War, 765, 1004
Vigne, Jean, 717
Vigneron, Robert, 791
Viking Club, 202
Viking Society, 205, 558
Villon, François, 278–79
Vinaver, Eugène, 147, 154
Vinogradoff, Paul, 157, 317; Cam and, 261–62, 263
Virgin imagery: Forsyth's scholarship, 843–45, 849; Jameson's scholarship, 25, 31
Vising, John, 567
Vlachov, Tousche, 514–15
Vojnov, Mikhail, 510–11, 516

Volk, Hermann, 862
Voltaire, François-Marie Arouet, 276
von Hügel, Baron Anatole, 204
von Hügel, Baron Friedrich, 189–90, 193
von Schurmann, Anna Maria, 9

Waddell, Helen, xxxiv; asceticism and, 325, 328; audience, 330; awards and honors, 330; Clarke and, 324, 381, 382, 388, 390; Coulton, 329; critical reception of works, 325, 328–30, 332; drama as focus of work, 324; education of, 323, 324; family of, 323; feminism and scholarship of, 323–24; financial support of scholarship, 324; as independent scholar, 325; Kyllmann and, 324–25, 330; *Letters of Heloise and Abelard* as focus of work, 323, 325, 326–28, 329, 330; love poetry as focus of work, 324; Lowes and, 330; as novelist, 324, 326–28; personal life of, 323, 329–30; pictured, 322; as poet, 324, 326; on poetry, 332; E. Power on, 331; publication history of, 324, 326, 331–32; on Raby, 330; reputation as scholar, 328–30; scholarly circle of, 330; sexism at Queens College and, 332 n.8; on translation of poetry, 326; as translator, 325–26, 329–30, 331; WWII's impact on, 331
Wagner, Anthony, 412
Wagner-Verein, 40
Waite, A. E., 41
Wallace, Patrick F., 464, 465
Wallace-Hadrill, Michael, 222
Waller, Ralph, 952
Wallner, Björn, 705
Walterick, Lynn, 986, 987
Walton, Robert, 983
Wandering Saints of the Early Middle Ages (Duckett), 218, 219
Wandering Scholars, The (Waddell), 324–25, 328–29
Waning of the Middle Ages, The (Huizinga), 406
Wanley, Humphrey, 5, 15
Warburg, Aby, 829
Warburg Institute, 937
Ward, Benedicta, S. L. G.: Anthony of Sourohz and, 947, 949; awards and honors, 951; Bede as focus of work, 947, 951; Christian spirituality as focus of work, 952–53; early Christian "desert fathers and mothers" as focus of work, 948–50; as editor, 952; education of, 945; gender "appropriate" subjects and, xxxii; Julian of Norwich as focus of work, 950–51, 952; Manchester and, 945; miracles as focus of work, 950–51, 952; mysticism as focus of work, 952; Oxford and, 945; pictured, 946; publication history of, 947, 948, 949, 950; religious life of, 945, 952–53; reputation as scholar, 950; Rolle as focus of work, 952; Royal Historical Society, 945; Saint Anne's College and, 945; St. Anslem as focus of work, 947–48; scholarly legacy of, 951; Smith as collaborator, 952; Southern as mentor, 947, 950; support of scholarship, 947, 952–53; as teacher, 945; as translator, 948–49, 950; Waller as collaborator, 952; Wolfson College and, 945; women in early Christianity as focus of work, 949–50
Ward, Reginald Somerset, 191
Warner, Marina, 25
Warr, Cordelia: on Anna Jameson, 25–33; contributor's note, 1017
Wathelet-Willem, Jeanne, 618
Watkins, E. I., 190
Watson, George, 699
Way of Saint James, The (King), 115–18
Weaver, Gina: contributor's note, 1017; on Helen Cam, 255–68
Weikel, Ann, 983
Weil, Simone, 195
Weisinger, Herbert, 46
Weisl, Angela Jane: contributor's note, 1017; on Jessie L. Weston, 37–50
Weitzmann, Kurt, 847
Wellesley College: R. J. Dean, 567; Der Nersessian and, 484, 490; faculty of, 241; Hammond and, 91; Hibbard and, 239, 241, 243–44, 248; L. H. Loomis and, 239, 241, 243–44, 248; marriage and employment at, 137

Welsford, Enid, 367, 369–70, 372–73, 735
Welter, Barbara, 909
Wemple, Suzanne, 904–5
Werckmeister, O. Karl, 848
West, R. H., 277
Westfield College, Hampstead: Phillpotts and, 206–7; Salter and, 816
Weston, Jessie Laidlay: as Arthurian scholar, 38, 42–43; audience, 38, 41, 44–45; awards and honors, 39; Bédier and, 40–41, 44; on biographical data of Middle English authors, 42; J. D. Bruce and, 40; *Cambridge History of English Literature,* contributions to, 38, 41; *Cambridge Medieval History,* contributions to, 38, 41; Cambridge Ritualists and, 40, 46; controversies and feuds, 40, 48–49; critical reception of works, xxxi, 38, 40, 42, 48–49; death of, 42; education, 37–38; Eliot's *The Waste Land* and, 39, 41, 45, 48; *Encyclopedia Britannica,* contributions to, 41; family of, 37, 41–42; financial support of work, 41–42; folklore societies and, 40; Frazer and, 40, 41, 45, 46; German culture and, 39, 40, 48; Grail legend as field of research, 47–48; Grayson on, 37, 38, 41, 49; W. P. Ker and, 40; R. S. Loomis and, 40, 41, 47; as mentor, 41; "nature cults" as field of research, 47; occultism and, 40, 46, 48; Paris as mentor of, 40, 44, 46; personal life of, 41–42; as poet and short-story author, 39; on poetry in translation, 44; political pamphlets of, 39, 48; popular culture and, 41, 48; publication history, 37, 38–39; reputation as scholar, 40, 47; Schofield and, 40, 43; scholarly circle and support for work, 40, 44–45, 46; scholarly legacy of, 46, 48; on scholarship, 49–50; Segal on, 47; support, 41–42; as translator, 38, 40, 43–44; WWII and, 39
Wetter, Friedrich, 863
Wheeler, Bonnie, xxviii
Wheeler, Mortimer, 411–12, 413, 414
Whelpton, Eric, 425, 427, 435 n.15
Whenes, Franz-Josef, 354
White, Beatrice, 816

Whitelock, Dorothy: Alfred the Great as focus of work, 557–58, 560; as Anglo-Saxon historian, 557–58; Anglo-Saxon wills as focus of work, 553–54; awards and honors, 553–54, 558, 560; Cambridge and, 557, 559–60; H. M. Chadwick and, 368; N. Chadwick and, 375; Cramp and, 892; death of, 560–61; education of, 553; family of, 533, 554–55; N. Ker and, 558; literature valued by, 556–57; as mentor, 556; Newnham College, Cambridge and, 553, 556, 560; organizational affiliations, 558; Oxford and, 555, 556; personal life of, 533, 554–55; pictured, 552; as pioneer in field, xxvii; publication history of, 556, 560; Reeves and, 652; St. Hilda's College, Oxford, 554, 556; scholarly circle of, xxxiv, 558, 559; scholarly legacy of, 559–60; sexism in university system, 393 n.35; as social historian, 556–57; D. Stenton and, 451, 555–56, 559; F. Stenton as mentor, 451, 554–55, 558, 559; as teacher, 554, 556; Wulfstan (archbishop of York) as focus of work, 556
Whitney, Elspeth: contributor's note, 1017; on Pearl Kibre, 541–47
Who Are the Aryans? (Schlauch), 530–31
Whose Body? (Sayers), 427
Wiethaus, Ulrike: contributor's note, 1017; on Elisabeth Busse-Wilson, 353–61
Willard, B. G. Sumner, 759, 761, 765–66
Willard, Charity Cannon: as army wife, 761, 762–64; Block and, 876; Christine de Pizan as focus of work, xxxiii, 759, 761–63, 766; contributor's note, 1017–18; École des hautes études and, 765; education of, 759, 765; family of, 759 (*see also* marriage *under this heading*); financial support of scholarship, 764; Ladycliff College and, 763–64; manuscript studies of, 764, 765; marriage and collaboration with B. G. Sumner Willard, xxxi–xxxii, xxxv, 759, 765–66 (*see also* army wife *under this heading*); pictured, 760; publication history of, 764; as teacher, 759–61, 762–63; Vietnam War

Willard, Charity Cannon (*continued*)
  demonstrations, 765; on Woolf's *A Room of One's Own,* 759; WWII experiences, 761
William of Sens, Sayers's dramatization of life of, 430–31
Williams, Charles, 432
Williams, Ifor, 772
Williams, Janet Hadley: contributor's note, 1018; on Helena Mennie Shire, 733–41
Williams, Mary, 39–40, 174, 175
Windswept (Chase), 218
Winton Diptych, 387, 411
Wisdom of the Desert Fathers, The (Ward), 948–49
Wiseman, Josette A.: contributor's note, 1018; on Régine Pernoud, 711–19
Wittig, Monique, xxiii, xxv
Wittkower, Rudolf, 937
Wixom, William, 781, 848
Wlodek, Sophie, 589
Wolff, Philippe, 753
Wolff, Robert Lee, 919
Wolfson, Harry, 919
Wolfson College, Ward and, 945
Woman as Image in Medieval Literature . . . (Ferrante), 972
Woman under Monasticism (Eckenstein), 59–60, 62
Women and Their Letters in the Early Middle Ages (Duckett), 218, 219
Women in Medieval Society (Stuard, editor), 957–58
women's colleges, xxiv–xxv, xxxiv; Cambridge first establishes, 69; *vs.* coeducation institutions, 132–33; elitism and vocationalism at, 130; as "home" for women scholars, 133–34, 390; status and privileges of, 554; teaching load at, 385; United States and, 102, 130; WWI and, 206. *See also specific schools*
women's history: "classical women's history," period of, 358; Eckenstein and, 59; Ferrante's scholarship, 972; Gage's efforts, 955; Gretsch on role of Elstob, 20 n.54; Hunter College and, 909–10; Kibre and, 545; McNamara on lack of, 905, 909–10; need for, 928 n.42; Packard and, 984; Pernoud and, 716–17; E. Power and, 319, 358; Ross and, 578, 581–82; Stenton and, 444, 449; Ward's scholarship on women in early Christianity, 949–50
women's rights: D'Evelyn as advocate of, 301; Eckenstein's activism, 59; Ferrante on, 973; religion and, 973; Richter and, 87. *See also* feminism; suffrage
Woodbridge, Benjamin, 79
Woolf, Rosemary Estelle: as critic, 829; critical reception of works, 828, 831; death of, 833; education of, 825; family of, 825; Langland as focus of work, 829; lyric as focus of work, 829–31; mystery plays as focus of work, 831; Oxford and, 830; personal life of, 833; pictured, 825; as pioneer in field, xxvii; publication history of, 828, 829; Saint Hugh's, Oxford and, 825–28; scholarly circle of, 828; Somerville College and, 829; as teacher, 828–29, 830; Trickett and, 825, 828; University College, Hull and, 828–29, 830
Woolf, Virginia, xxiv–xxv, xxxiv–xxxv; Clarke on *To the Lighthouse,* 389; Willard on *A Room of One's Own,* 759
Woolley, Mary Emma, 160, 169, 301
Workers Educational Association, 735
World War I: destruction of medieval stained glass during, 940; D'Evelyn on, 298; G. Frank during, 274; impact on women's lives and opportunities, 104, 462, 496; Phillpotts in Sweden during, 205; E. Power during, 312; E. Rickert's codebreaking efforts during, 134, 288–89; Roe's experiences during, 461; Somerville College during, 382–83; Underhill's writing during, 192
World War II: Bynum on, 1000–1001; Cam during, 262–63, 266; Chibnall's observations on Germany, 751; Chibnall's work during, 753; culture theft during, 347; Evans's work, war as context for, 410–11; Gössmann's experiences in Nazi Germany, 859–60; impacts on higher education,

827–28, 901–3; International Federation of University Women and, 106–7; Ireland and, 461; Ivanova-Mavrodinova's work during, 506; Neilson on, 169; Oxford during, 825–27; E. Power's lectures during, 318; reforms after, 265; M. Rickert's code breaking during, 288–89; Roe's experiences during, 462; Rokseth as member of Resistance, 346–47, 348; Sayers's experiences during, 425, 432; Smalley's experiences during, 662–63; Stenton's work during, 447; Waddell's activities during, 331; women's opportunities and, 827. *See also* National Socialist Party of Germany

Wormald, Francis, 287, 289, 592

Worship (Underhill), 191

Wrenn, C. L., 555, 828, 892

Wright, E. H., 529

Wright, Edith Armstrong, 275

Wright, Mary Clabaugh, 795

Writings Ascribed to Richard Rolle (Allen), 233

Wundt, Wilhelm, 360

Wyatt, Thomas, 94

Wycliffe, John: Borroff's scholarship, 799; Smalley's scholarship, 664, 665

Wynne, Marjorie G., 677

"Wynnere and Wastoure" (anonymous), 163, 820

Yale University: administration of, 797–98; Borroff and, 794–96; Colish and, 983–84, 988, 989–90; Hayward and, 783–84; Lutz and, 671, 672; Stuard and, 955, 965

Yardley, Herbert, 134

Yarrow, Sir Alfred, 208–9

Year Books of Edward II, Vols. 20 and 21 (Holdsworth and Legge), 615–16

Yorkshire Archaeological Society, 558

Yorkshire Sessions of the Peace (Putnam), 162

Younghusband, Sir Francis, 104

Yovsēpʻian, Catholicus Garegin, 485, 490

Zarnecki, George, 416

Zeal of Thy House, The (Sayers), 430

Zeeman, Christopher, 817

Zeeman, Nicolette, 815, 817

Zinn, Grover, 986–87

Zöega, Geir Tómasson, 203

Zwei Grundprobleme der scholastischen Naturphilosophie (Maier), 633

Zwei Untersuchungen zur nachscholastishchen Philosophie (Maier), 625